THE OXFORD ENCYCLOPEDIA OF
MARITIME HISTORY

# THE OXFORD ENCYCLOPEDIA
## OF
# MARITIME
# HISTORY

John B. Hattendorf

*Editor in Chief*

## VOLUME 1

ACTIUM, BATTLE OF—EX VOTO

OXFORD
UNIVERSITY PRESS
2007

# OXFORD

UNIVERSITY PRESS

Oxford University Press, Inc., publishes works that further
Oxford University's objective of excellence
in research, scholarship, and education.

Oxford   New York
Auckland   Cape Town   Dar es Salaam   Hong Kong   Karachi
Kuala Lumpur   Madrid   Melbourne   Mexico City   Nairobi
New Delhi   Shanghai   Taipei   Toronto
With offices in
Argentina   Austria   Brazil   Chile   Czech Republic   France   Greece
Guatemala   Hungary   Italy   Japan   Poland   Portugal   Singapore
South Korea   Switzerland   Thailand   Turkey   Ukraine   Vietnam

Copyright © 2007 by Oxford University Press, Inc.

Published by Oxford University Press, Inc.
198 Madison Avenue, New York, New York, 10016
http://www.oup-usa.org

Library of Congress Cataloging-in-Publication Data

The Oxford encyclopedia of maritime history / John B. Hattendorf, editor in chief.
p. cm.
Includes bibliographical references and index.
ISBN-13: 978-0-19-513075-1 (hbk. : alk. paper)
ISBN-10: 0-19-513075-8 (hbk. : alk. paper)
1. Navigation—History—Encyclopedias.
2. Naval history—Encyclopedias.
3. Naval art and science—History—Encyclopedias.
I. Hattendorf, John B.
VK15.O84 2007
623.803—dc22
2006100162

# EDITORIAL AND PRODUCTION STAFF

*Acquiring Editor*
Christopher Collins

*Development Editors*
Joe Clements   Martin Coleman   Mark Mones   Eric Stannard

*Managing Editor*
Georgia Shepherd Maas

*Associate Editor*
Timothy H. Sachs

*Assistant Editor*
Abigail Powers

*EDP Coordinator*
Nancy Tan

*Editorial Assistant*
Robert Repino

*Copyeditors*
Jonathan G. Aretakis   Dorothy Bauhoff   Heidi Bogardus   Sylvia Cannizzaro
Melissa Dobson   Kerry Doyle   Gretchen Gordon   Katherine H. Maas   Alan Thwaits

*Proofreaders*
Katharyn Dunham   Carol Holmes   Kaari Ward

*Index Prepared by*
Katharyn Dunham, ParaGraphs

*Compositor*
Apex Publishing

*Manufacturing Controller*
Richard Hollick

*Design*
Book Type

*Cover Design*
Joan Greenfield

*Art Research*
Shira Bistricer
Ben Keene
Tobi Zausner

*Director of Editorial Production and Development*
Timothy J. Dewerff

*Publisher*
Casper Grathwohl

# CONTENTS

THE OXFORD ENCYCLOPEDIA OF
## MARITIME HISTORY

# LIST OF ENTRIES

# INTRODUCTION

Maritime history has, in some respects, been an ignored dimension of global history. Indeed, we have become so used to thinking of our world as "earth" and as a "terrestrial orb" that we sometimes have completely forgotten that those words refer only to land and that they exclude the essence of things maritime. Maritime history is the field of historical study that encompasses humankind's relationships to the seas and oceans of the world. It is a multidimensional, humanistic study of human activities, experiences, interactions, and reactions to the vast water-covered regions that account for more than 70 percent of the globe. A student who pursues the maritime theme may approach it from a variety of vantage points, including science, technology, industry, economics, trade, politics, art, literature, sociology and social issues, religion, military and naval affairs, international relations, cartography, comparative studies in imperial and colonial affairs, institutional and organizational development, communications, migration, intercultural relations, natural resources, sports, and recreation.

The subject of maritime history is a broad theme in global history that cuts across the standard boundaries of academic disciplines. In many respects it is a broad new and developing interdisciplinary field of scholarly research and writing, although it has deep roots in much older scholarship in specific and highly focused parts of the field. The study of some areas within maritime history is a relatively recent activity. Perhaps the oldest subject area of maritime history within the English-language tradition is the history of maritime exploration. In this subject area one thinks immediately of Richard Hakluyt and the great compilation of early voyage accounts that he made in the Elizabethan age: *The Principal Navigations, Voyages, Traffiques, and Discoveries of the English Nation* (1598–1600), the work that a late-nineteenth-century Regius Professor of History at Oxford University, James Anthony Froude, called "the prose epic of the English nation." Hakluyt's collection was followed by others, as well as by the widely read firsthand accounts of the seamen of later centuries, such as George Anson and James Cook. The typical volumes in this genre were largely devoted to voyage narratives and to descriptions of distant parts of the world. Such works became so widely read that they were even parodied in the eighteenth century by writers such as Jonathan Swift in his satirical masterpiece *Gulliver's Travels* (1726).

To look at a different aspect of maritime history, Admiralty Secretary Josiah Burchett wrote the first general naval history to appear in the English language: *A Complete History of the Most Remarkable Transactions at Sea* (1720). Typical of early work on naval affairs, it was a record written by a professional whose interests in the subject were largely limited to professional matters. Equally typical, it was limited to naval operations and accounts of battles between warships, although it had the merit of using official reports as the basis for its final chapters. Studies of port cities, labor conditions, shipbuilding, fishing, and maritime business activities all came much later, as did studies of maritime art and literature. At first the focus was largely on national maritime events, and the scope only slowly widened to include a full appreciation of maritime accomplishments by other countries. Only in the late nineteenth century did historians such Sir John Knox Laughton, Alfred Thayer Mahan, and Sir Julian Corbett develop the foundation for a broader, analytical approach to naval history.

A quarter of a century ago maritime scholars in the English-speaking world were typically divided into small subspecialties. They rarely crossed from one subspecialty to another or made any attempt to see the whole range of the broad maritime field, with its complex interdependencies and interrelationships. Although this was not true of maritime history written in some other languages, historians in the English-speaking world tended to label themselves by their subspecialties rather than by the broad field, identifying themselves as naval historians, maritime economic historians, historians of maritime science and technology, or historians of exploration. In the 1980s historians of yachting and seaside recreation, maritime art and literature, or maritime labor and social history had only just begun to make a major impact in the field. At first they, too, remained isolated within small groups that shared a focus on their own subspecialty, sometimes fiercely defending the unique characteristics of their own special topic even against others in the maritime field. In addition many subspecialists tended to define themselves by national focus, often further restricting themselves to particular periods within one national history.

In the late 1980s and 1990s this situation began to change. Some individual historians began to take a much wider view and began to make links between subspecialties, opening up new approaches and new areas for investigation. By the 1990s it became clear that the overarching common connection behind all of these varied approaches was represented in the meaning of the adjective "maritime": human activities relating to or involving ships, shipping, navigation, mariners, and those people and activities bordering on, living in, or associated with activities connected to the seas and oceans.

Under the overarching label of maritime history, each of the subspecialties has a tie to a specific range of academic approaches.

The maritime economic historian has a fundamental tie to the academic fields of economic and business history; the naval historian has connections to the diplomatic, military, and international history fields; the historian of navigation has a fundamental tie to the history of science and technology; the student of maritime art or maritime literature has connections to the wider fields of art history or literature; and the historian of exploration has ties to the history of imperial expansion and global cultural interaction. Each of these connections to particular academic disciplines and specialized academic fields of interest helps to define those particular subspecialties, but they are all interconnected through having the maritime element in common. It is this common maritime element, with its cross connections and relationships across the various subspecialties, that becomes a revealing and important extension of broad aspects of national and international events ashore.

For example, in broad terms the study of maritime imperial and international rivalry requires a special focus that links the domestic politics of major powers to international politics and economics and includes comparative maritime technological skills and usages. Such a maritime interpretation of international relations is basic to the understanding of the interactions of the major powers in peace and in war from ancient times to the present. Even when viewed at its most basic level, a ship is built in a particular place and is a product of certain national, political, economic, social, technological, and industrial factors. When that ship puts to sea it enters a different realm, with an international and global dimension that may involve specific circumstances such as wars, cross-cultural relations, imperial competition, scientific research, the exchange of goods, the transmission of species and information, or the accumulation of capital through trade. At the same time, when that ship leaves the network of activities that created it and prepared it to cross seas and oceans, it remains a microcosm of the society that it left ashore. For much of human history sea passages were long and isolated experiences in a ship at sea, lasting for many weeks and even months out of sight of land. This created a social dimension within ships that became another determinant that affected the outcome of individual voyages and, on a larger scale, affected broad labor issues within maritime affairs.

When viewed in its full broad spectrum, maritime history has a distinct series of related themes that can be followed over long periods of world history. The conception behind *The Oxford Encyclopedia of Maritime History* is to present this range of historical themes and information in a readily accessible summary form, for use both by the general public and by scholars. This encyclopedia is addressed to users—whether general readers, college and high school students, or scholars—seeking information, definitions, ideas for research papers, an overview of recent scholarship, or an introduction to the many aspects of maritime history. Up until now this information could be gleaned only with difficulty from a wide-ranging professional library devoted to maritime affairs; there has been no single English-language scholarly reference for this field.

The first maritime encyclopedia was probably Père Georges Fournier's *Hydrographie* (Paris, 1643), but its purpose was to provide a reference for the technical and specialized aspects of maritime affairs in its own day and not to serve historical purposes—regardless of how valuable it has become for that use in more recent times. The only single works of comparable scope to this are the *Enciclopedia general del mar,* edited by José Ma. Martínez-Hidalgo y Terán, 8 volumes (Madrid, 1957–1958; second edition, 1968), which is a combination dictionary and encyclopedia that includes the scientific details from the physical and biological aspects of marine science as well as historical information, and the *Dictionnaire d'histoire maritime,* edited by Michel Vergé-Franceschi, 2 volumes (Paris, 2002), a wide-ranging dictionary of short entries on world maritime history. In English, there have also been some important reference works on specific aspects of maritime history, such as *The British Museum Encyclopedia of Underwater and Maritime Archaeology,* edited by James P. Delgado (1997); *Ships of the World: An Historical Encyclopedia,* edited by Lincoln P. Paine (1997); *Naval Warfare: An International Encyclopedia,* edited by Spencer C. Tucker, 3 volumes (2002); and *The Oxford Companion to Ships and the Sea,* edited by Peter Kemp and I. C. B. Dear (1976; second edition, 2005). None of these, however, has sought to be a reference work for the entire field of maritime history in the way that this encyclopedia has.

To compile a scholarly reference encyclopedia in the field of maritime history, which had become so fragmented into subspecialties and has only recently begun to coalesce into a larger whole, has required a wide-ranging effort in scholarly collaboration. In order to bridge the various subspecialties and to build the larger view that we all agreed was needed, we brought together a team of subject area editors and advisory editors who each represented a subspecialty, but who were at the same time willing and able to contribute to the wider perspective that we sought. In addition, we sought the advice of a wide range of advisory and consulting editors, all of whom contributed substantially to broadening the scope of the final product. Working in cooperation under the editor in chief, each individual subject-area editor had the primary responsibly of conceptualizing the scope for each of the articles in his or her area and reviewing the completed articles, passing on judgments for the editor in chief's further advice and final approval.

The area editors were, in the area of art, iconography, and seamen's arts, Dr. Boye Meyer-Friese, Altonaer Museum, Hamburg, Germany, and Dr. Joost C. A. Schokkenbroek, curator at the Nederlands Scheepvaartmuseum Amsterdam; in the area of ships, boats, yards, and docks, Professor Emeritus Jaap R. Bruijn, Rijks Universiteit Leiden, the Netherlands; in the area of maritime economic history, Professor Peter N. Davies, Department of Economic and Social History, University of Liverpool, as well as former president of the International

Commission on Maritime History, and Adrian Jarvis, Center for Port and Maritime History, University of Liverpool, and former secretary-general of the International Commission on Maritime History; in the area of naval history, Professor Andrew Lambert, War Studies Department, Kings College London; in the area of the history of navigation and marine sciences, Professor Karel Davids, Vrije Universiteit Amsterdam; in the area of social history, ports, and seamen, Professor Frank Broeze, University of Western Australia, and Associate Professor Malcolm Tull, Murdoch University Business School, Australia; in the area of maritime exploration, Professor Emeritus Glyndwyr Williams, Queen Mary University of London; in the area of maritime law, Professor David Attard, director of the IMO International Law Institute in Malta, and Judge David H. Anderson, member of the International Tribunal for the Law of the Sea at Hamburg, Germany; and in the area of maritime literature, Professor Robert D. Foulke, Skidmore College, Saratoga Springs, New York.

The encyclopedia had further valuable advice from the advisory editors: in the area of ancient history, from Professor Emeritus Lionel Casson, New York University; in the area of medieval history, from Professor Richard Unger, University of British Columbia; in the area of maritime studies in general, from Professor Sarah Palmer, Greenwich Maritime Institute, University of Greenwich, England; in the area of nineteenth-century economic history, from Professor Lewis R. Fischer, Memorial University of Newfoundland; in the area of twentieth-century naval history, from Associate Professor Malcolm H. Murfett, National University of Singapore; in the area of Asian history, from Professor Wang Gungwu, East Asian Institute, National University of Singapore; in the area of German naval history, from Captain Dr. Werner Rahn, former chief of the Militärgeschichtliches Forschungsamt, Potsdam, Germany; in the area of German shipping and shipbuilding, from Professor Dr. Lars U. Scholl, director of the Deutsches Schiffahrtsmuseum, Bremerhaven, Germany; in the area of French maritime history, from Professor Michel Vergé-Franceschi, Université de Tours; in the area of Spanish and Portuguese history, from Professor Carla Rahn Phillips, University of Minnesota; on Latin American history, from Dr. Jorge Ortiz Sotelo of the Asociación de Historia Marítima y Naval Iberoamericana at Lima, Peru; in the area of Arab maritime history, from Dr. John Carswell, former director, Islamic Department, Sotheby's London; in the area of Jewish and ancient history, from Dr. Nadav Kashtan, Department of Maritime Civilizations, University of Haifa; on the Indian Ocean, from Professor Michael N. Pearson, University of New South Wales, Australia; in the area of yachting history, from Mr. Revell Carr, former director of Mystic Seaport Museum, Connecticut, and Mr. John Rousmaniere; and in the area of fishing, sealing, and whaling, from Professor Briton C. Busch, Colgate University, Hamilton, New York, and Professor Poul Holm, Roskilde Universiteitscenter, Denmark. In addition

Professor Roger Knight, former deputy director of the National Maritime Museum, Greenwich, and now Professor of Naval History, Greenwich Maritime Institute, University of Greenwich, and Professor N. A. M. Rodger, University of Exeter, England, served as consulting editors and, whenever needed, provided general advice and encouragement throughout the eight-year project.

On some topics the goal of the encyclopedia in providing broadly based articles and analytical summaries of global themes in maritime history stretched above and beyond the present state of scholarship in maritime history. Some topics could be put together by getting different authors to write specific pieces to create a composite article on a theme. Others topics have just not been fully researched enough to produce such an article, and in such cases we had to report on the current state of knowledge. Despite these acknowledged limitations and frustrations, we present this encyclopedia as the pioneer effort in scholarship that it is. We look forward to others who can now use this first stepping-stone to build upon it and to widen and further develop a global understanding for the field of maritime history.

There are more than 900 articles in the *Oxford Encyclopedia of Maritime History,* arranged in alphabetical order. More than 400 contributors from 49 different countries have joined in this eight-year project to write broad articles that summarize, in clearly written English, the current state of historical understanding on this global topic. The encyclopedia includes more than 400 illustrations and more than 60 maps and nautical charts.

## How to Use the Encyclopedia

A typical article has three parts: the narrative, end references, and bibliography. To guide readers from one article to related discussions elsewhere in the encyclopedia, end references appear right after the narrative. In addition, there are cross-references within the body of a few articles. A selective bibliography at the end of an article directs the reader who wishes to pursue a topic in greater detail to the most important scholarly works in any language plus the most useful works in English. Within the encyclopedia's main alphabetical listing, blind entries direct the user from an alternate form of an entry term to the appropriate article. For example, the blind entry "Admiral's Cup" tells the reader to see "Yachting and Pleasure Sailing." This example underscores the point that an encyclopedia such as this is very different in conception from a dictionary. While a dictionary is a comprehensive collection of entries on specific topics, an encyclopedia entry subsumes broad areas of such specifics and attempts to provide a broad analytical that links them in a broad summary of current scholarly understanding.

At the end of the last volume there are a topical outline (which shows how articles relate to one another and to the overall design of the encyclopedia), the directory of contributors, and the index. Readers interested in finding all the articles on a broad particular theme (for instance, literary genres, art history, economic history, or naval affairs) may consult the topical outline. Also, the comprehensive index at the end of the last volume lists all the topics covered in the encyclopedia, including those that are not entry terms themselves.

## ACKNOWLEDGMENTS

There is a long list of hardworking and very talented individuals who deserve warm and heartfelt thanks for their contributions in bringing this project to fruition. The intellectual origins behind this encyclopedia lie with a number of different institutions and with many of the individual scholars who formed the editorial and advisory boards of this encyclopedia. The contributors have expressed their personal scholarly opinions, which are not the opinions or policies of myself, Oxford University Press, or any government.

My long association with the John Carter Brown Library at Brown University and its former director, Dr. Norman Fiering, led to a series of two National Endowment for the Humanities Summer Institutes on Maritime History in 1992 and 1993 that were designed to stimulate university teaching in early modern European maritime history and exploration at a time when it had virtually disappeared from American university campuses but remained a lively topic elsewhere. My association with Professor Paul M. Kennedy at Yale University led to a series of three conferences dealing with the state of world maritime history in 1993, with ways to improve the quality of naval history in 1994, and with naval policies and strategies in the Mediterranean in 1997. My close association that began in 1970 with Robert G. Albion and Benjamin W. Labaree at the Munson Institute of American Maritime History at Mystic Seaport Museum turned into annual participation in the summer course there and eventually led to two more National Endowment for the Humanities Summer Institutes on Maritime History at Mystic Seaport in 1995 and 2006.

These associations brought with them both broad insights into the field and the initial connections to many of the distinguished scholars whose names are listed on the editorial page of this encyclopedia and whose sound advice and devoted efforts have brought this work to its conclusion. From our one and only face-to-face editorial board meeting, which we held at Oxford in April 1999, to the final completion of the project, we have had extraordinarily good working relationships, with an open, constructive exchange of ideas. I am deeply grateful to each and every one of the editorial board members for their steadfast support and devotion to completing the task. I am very sorry to record that three key people involved with the project at its outset—Derek Howse, Frank Broeze, and Briton C. Busch—did not live to see it come to fruition.

At Oxford University Press, Senior Editor Christopher Collins conceived the encyclopedia and—acting on the recommendation of

Derek Howse, former head of the Navigation and Astronomy Department at the National Maritime Museum, Greenwich—persuasively inveigled me into taking on the job of editor in chief, despite my protests at having too many other commitments. Chris Collins's successor as editor responsible for the project, Timothy DeWerff, deftly helped us through a difficult period in mid-passage and very effectively put the project on its firm course toward completion. Under his direction a series of successive development editors served as the outside editors' direct points of contact with the Press and provided invaluable help on a day-to-day, article-by-article basis: Mark Mones, Martin Coleman, Joe Clements, and Eric Stannard. Their various assistants, including Abigail Powers and Tim Sachs, did heroic work in keeping track of contracts and the flow of manuscripts through the editorial chain of review, and in looking after the gathering mound of completed work. In the final stage of the project Managing Editor Georgia Maas effectively organized and facilitated the copyediting and proofreading effort, and Tim Sachs and Shira Bistricer worked together in their difficult assignment of trying to follow my suggestions to gather the 400 illustrations, while Ben Keene did a magnificent job in organizing and adjusting the cartographic program to meet our specialized maritime needs.

As an erstwhile neighbor and tenant of the Oxford University Press, having once rented and lived in one of the Press's early nineteenth-century workers' cottages in Great Clarendon Street at Oxford, I have an inkling that there are a huge number of people with whom an editor never has the opportunity to meet, but whose work for the Press is essential to a large, complicated production such as this. I thank them all warmly and am delighted to have this encyclopedia become a part of my own university's academic publishing tradition that extends over five centuries.

FEBRUARY 2007                                        JOHN B. HATTENDORF

THE OXFORD ENCYCLOPEDIA OF
MARITIME HISTORY

# A

**Actium, Battle of** The Battle of Actium, fought on September 2 in 31 B.C.E., is remembered for its famous commanders, for ending a complicated and expensive civil war, and for its enduring consequences to Rome. The campaign leading to the battle is a classic example of the influence of sea power worthy of, and indeed mentioned by, the American naval officer and historian Alfred Thayer Mahan (1840–1914). The battle itself illustrates the tactics in the long era of galley warfare that are well but inconsistently described in ancient sources.

## The Campaign

In the summer of 33 B.C.E. Mark Antony (Marcus Antonius) brought his substantial army of sixteen legions to Ephesus on the Aegean coast of Asia Minor, inviting Cleopatra, queen of Egypt, to join him with munitions, money, and her fleet. As his relations with Cleopatra waxed and those with Rome waned, he contemplated a descent on Italy and soon moved his forces to Greece. Rome, badly needing the wealth of the east, feared a break by Antony or even dominance by its eastern provinces centered in Cleopatra's Alexandria. A climax was coming. But during 32 B.C.E. neither of the opponents, Octavian (Gaius Julius Caesar Octavianus) nor Antony, was ready to move against the other. In Rome, Octavian had to lobby for support and the isolation of his former compatriot Antony. In Antony's army many of his best soldiers were Roman who did not want to fight Romans, and he needed to persuade them their destiny lay with him.

By the winter of 32–31 B.C.E., Antony was preparing to invade Italy and march to Rome. Accompanied by Cleopatra, he established a camp on the west coast of Greece. According to Plutarch, their forces numbered five hundred galleys and one hundred thousand soldiers plus cavalry. The army was spread along the coast, but most of the fleet was positioned well forward in the Gulf of Ambracia (Arta). During the winter, however, the fleet lost perhaps a third of its crews to disease. Meanwhile Octavian, now with the full yet reluctant backing of the

Roman Senate, assembled perhaps eighty thousand soldiers and 250 galleys in the heel of Italy. Early in March 31 B.C.E., his fleet, superbly trained by his military commander, Marcus Vipsanius Agrippa, began to attack and seize the bases Antony had established to safeguard his supplies from Asia Minor and Egypt. While Antony's attention was drawn southward to his line of communications, Octavian crossed from Italy and assembled his army north of the Gulf of Ambracia in the hope of destroying Antony's unready, unprotected fleet. Antony hastened up from Patras and, aided by some deception, arrived just in time to establish his army near Actium, a promontory on the south entrance to the gulf. Octavian soon arrived to establish his own army about eight kilometers (five miles) north of the narrow strait and instituted a siege by land and a blockade by sea.

Mark Antony, a superb general, tried to force a battle of armies, but Octavian and Agrippa were well entrenched and circumspectly avoided it. As spring stretched into summer, Antony and Cleopatra found they could break neither the siege nor the naval blockade. With the enemy fleet bottled up, Agrippa was free to further destroy Antony's sea communications. By attacking from Leucas to Patras to Corinth, he imposed on the eastern army an ever more tenuous land-line of supply. Meanwhile the low plain near Actium proved as unhealthy for the Antony's army in the summer as it had for the eastern fleet in the previous winter.

Mark Antony and Queen Cleopatra could withdraw their army eastward but not without exposing their fleet to destruction with dreadful consequences. Roman historians say Cleopatra urged a sea battle so that she might escape in the process, but this is too facile and Cleopatra too easy to blame. In fact a sea battle was probably Antony's only choice. Though undermanned, his vessels were larger and stronger than Octavian's and superbly built. They were, however, less maneuverable and barely ready for action, for Agrippa had designed Rome's ships well, trained the crews assiduously, and fine-tuned his fleet's skills in the course of tearing up Antony's line of supply.

**Bronze Prow from the Battle of Actium.** The figure wearing a helmet and with an aegis strapped under the arm and over the shoulder probably represents the goddess Athena. © THE TRUSTEES OF THE BRITISH MUSEUM

### The Battle

The historian William Rodgers, drawing from sources of the period, makes a detailed argument that the battle fleet of Antony and Cleopatra had been reduced from 500 to around 180 galleys to face Octavian's 250. We know that because he could not man all his ships, Antony had destroyed many of them in the harbor. Antony intended to bring his fleet out on August 29, but a storm delayed him until September 2. Octavian and Agrippa were well warned by a general who a few days earlier had brought his soldiers out and switched sides. Antony arrayed his fleet, bows out and close to the coastline, inviting the western fleet to attack where it could not exploit its maneuverability. Agrippa did not take the bait, however, and waited for the enemy to come to him. Sometime in midmorning Antony's left wing became impatient and moved forward. The Roman right pretended to retreat, and Antony's galleys moved away from the coast, whereupon the Roman fleet could use its maneuverability to concentrate two or three smaller galleys selectively on single enemy ships.

Nevertheless, historians say the battle was closely fought and undecided when, around two in the afternoon, Cleopatra's sixty galleys, purportedly held in tactical reserve, abruptly hoisted sail, charged through the western fleet, and stood out to sea. Almost at once Antony set off after her, accompanied by a modest number of his galleys that were able to dump their fighting towers and bend on sails. Roman legend says his was the irrational act of a lovesick man, but more likely it was according to a plan of escape that perhaps was prematurely forced on him by Cleopatra while victory was still possible. If that is so, his plan to take his fleet with him failed because most of it was too closely engaged to escape. Indeed, the eastern fleet seems not to have known until later what had happened. In late afternoon the survivors were able to row back past Actium and into the gulf.

But the matter was settled. Mark Antony knew it, for it is said that for three days he sat inconsolably and alone on the bow of Cleopatra's flagship. Although Antony got word to his army commander, one Canidius, to conduct a fighting retreat, that once-formidable eastern army disintegrated, some surrendering and others simply walking away. Most of the fleet was also lost—Plutarch says three hundred galleys, which might be true if one counts the ships Antony burned before the battle for lack of crews.

Roman historians gleefully blamed the defeat on Cleopatra for running away. A wiser conjecture of later historians is that Antony lost because he had alternative objectives, which of necessity he could reveal to only a few combatants. His fleet would fight to win, but when it appeared that they could not, then they would save themselves by sailing away together on the reliable afternoon breeze out of the north. In support of this opinion, we know the eastern galleys had not left their sails ashore, which was common practice in preparation for battle under oars. But an ambiguous combat objective is always a chancy thing, and in the event it took too much coordination to succeed.

## Consequences

The Battle of Actium brought an end to the confusion and civil war that had plagued the Roman world before and after the assassination of Julius Caesar in 44 B.C.E. After Cleopatra and Mark Antony fled the battle scene with their army and navy destroyed, Octavian first returned to Rome to consolidate his now unchallengeable power. A year later he pursued Antony and Cleopatra to Egypt, where, unable to negotiate honorable terms of survival, both committed suicide, Queen Cleopatra famously by the bite of an asp. Employing patience and skillful leadership, Octavian brought stability and prosperity to Rome. Eight years after

Actium, Octavian felt secure enough to declare himself Caesar Augustus, the first Roman emperor.

In a culture riddled with brutality and venality, Antony, Cleopatra, and Octavian each exhibited vast talent accompanied by overweening hubris. Antony and Octavian had been frequent collaborators, and one may imagine their fatal confrontation at Actium was not without personal regret. Antony had his well-deserved admirers, who shared his fear of autocratic rule by Octavian and the end of the Roman Republic. Cleopatra was the archetypal female leader whose charms, firmness, wealth, and administrative skills might have made Alexandria the center of Roman civilization. Octavian ended a civil war that threatened to bankrupt Rome and reduce the republic to chaos. As Caesar Augustus, he is esteemed for transforming an oligarchy into an empire that was efficiently managed and more beneficial to Roman citizens than were the last days of the republic. Still, one may point to Marcus Vipsanius Agrippa as the personality whose military prowess and loyalty were the example to emulate, though his memory is largely lost among the more extravagant heroes of those times.

[*See also* Ancient Navies, *subentry on* Rome; *and* Tactics.]

## Bibliography

Carter, John M. *The Battle of Actium: The Rise and Triumph of Augustus Caesar*. London: Hamilton, 1970.

Dio Cassius Cocceianus. *Dio's Roman History*. Translated by Earnest Cary. London: W. Heinemann; New York: Macmillan, 1914–1927.

Grant, Michael. *The Army of the Caesars*. New York: Scribners, 1974.

Merivale, Charles. *History of the Romans under the Empire*. 7 vols. London: Longman, Roberts, and Green, 1851–1862.

Mordal, Jacques. *Twenty-five Centuries of Sea Warfare*. Translated by Leo Ortzen. New York: Potter, 1965.

*Plutarch's Lives*. "Antony." Translated by John Dryden, with corrections and revisions by Arthur Hugh Clough. Harvard Classics, vol. 12. New York: Collier, 1909.

Rodgers, William M. *Greek and Roman Naval Warfare: A Study of Strategy, Tactics, and Ship Design from Salamis (480 B.C.) to Actium (31 B.C.)*. Annapolis, Md.: U.S. Naval Institute, 1937; reprinted 1980.

Syme, Ronald. *The Roman Revolution*. Oxford: Clarendon, 1939.

WAYNE P. HUGHES JR.

***Admiral Graf Spee,*** German pocket battleship of the *Deutschland* class.

Length/beam/draft: 186 m × 21.3 m × 7.25 m. Tons: 16,020 displacement. Hull: steel. Machinery: diesel, 52,050 shaft horsepower, 2 screws; 28 knots. Built: Marinewerft Wilhelmshaven, 1936.

Named after Admiral Graf von Spee who went down in SMS *Scharnhorst* at the battle of the Falklands in 1914, *Admiral Graf Spee*, often called *Graf Spee*, was one of three German pocket battleships—the other two being *Deutschland* (later renamed *Lützow*) and *Admiral Scheer*. Pocket battleships were at least superior to cruisers in gunnery and were superior to capital ships in terms of speed. Ships of this class were ideally suited for commerce raiding. Because the 1922 Washington Treaty restricted the construction of battleships, most other sea powers could not answer directly with similar or superior vessels.

*Graf Spee* was five times detached to Mediterranean waters from 1936 to 1938, during the Spanish Civil War. After a short career in World War II—during which she sank nine merchant vessels in the South Atlantic and in the Indian Ocean between September 25 and December 13, 1939—she met her fate in the Battle of the River Plate, the first major naval action of the war. She was sighted by the British cruisers *Exeter*, *Ajax*, and *Achilles*. After a heavy engagement, the *Exeter* had to withdraw because of severe damage. When the *Ajax* was likewise considerably damaged, Commodore Harry Harwood broke off the battle and retired under cover of a smokescreen. Instead of pursuing the cruisers, Captain Hans Langsdorff, whose ship had also suffered damage and who had used much of his ammunition, entered the neutral harbor of Montevideo on December 14, where he was allowed to stay for seventy-two hours. Since he believed that superior forces were waiting for him, Langsdorff regarded a breakout attempt as impossible. To remain in interment in the port was no option, either. So he decided—with the permission of naval headquarters in Berlin—to scuttle the vessel outside the three-mile limit on December 17, after having tried to destroy all valuable and secret equipment and after having landed most of his crew. Langsdorff shot himself the following day, paying with his life "for any possible discredit on the honour of the flag."

*Graf Spee*'s support ship, the tanker *Altmark* with 299 British prisoners on board, managed to reach Norwegian waters in February 1940. There *Altmark* was illegally—and in violation of Norwegian neutrality—entered by a strong boarding party from the destroyer HMS *Cossack*; all the British prisoners were liberated. The incident was in itself minor, causing jubilation in England, but it was used by Germany to legitimize its occupation of Denmark and Norway two months later.

[*See also* Battleship; Cruiser; *and* Warships, *subentry on* Modern Warships.]

## Bibliography

Gilbey, Joseph. *Langsdorff of the "Graf Spee": Prince of Honor.* Hillsburgh, Ontario: Gilbey, 1999.

Grove, Eric J. *The Price of Disobedience: The Battle of the River Plate Reconsidered.* Annapolis, Md.: Naval Institute Press, 2000.

Grove, Eric, ed. *German Capital Ships and Raiders in World War II.* Vol. 1, *From "Graf Spee" to "Bismarck," 1939–1941.* Naval Staff Histories. London: Frank Cass, 2002.

Rahn, Werner. "German Naval Strategy and Armament, 1919–1939." In *Technology and Naval Combat in the Twentieth Century and Beyond*, edited by Phillips Payson O'Brien, pp.109–127. London and Portland, Ore.: Frank Cass 2001.

LARS U. SCHOLL

**Admiral Popov**    This experimental circular ironclad, a remarkable type of warship, was the result of a quest for a gun platform of maximum stability. To obtain this goal, the Glasgow shipbuilder John Elder patented a "circular floating battery" in 1867, though it was never built. The Russian naval constructor Aleksandr Aleksandrovic Popoff (1821–1891) designed *Nowgorod* (2,500-ton displacement) and *Vitse-admiral Popoff* (3,600 tons) for the defense of the Dniestr estuary and the Straits of Kertch. These ships were launched from the New Admiralty Dockyard in Saint Petersburg in 1873 and 1875, respectively. They were, according to Fletcher, "circular only at the water-line," with projections at opposite sides, to facilitate steering and provide a bow. According to Hovgaard, the central feature of *Vitse-admiral Popoff* was a circular armored breastwork (18 inches thick, the same thickness as the armor belt at the waterline), 7 feet high, in which were mounted two 12-inch "disappearing" guns weighing 40 tons. There were 8 smaller guns, mounted in the unarmored superstructure surrounding the breastwork or barbette. Under the flat bottom were 12 external box girders or keels, about 12 inches square, parallel to the ship's longitudinal axis. Three sets of engines provided motive power for six screws, for a maximum speed of eight sea miles per hour (Hovgaard). In practice, the ships proved a failure, mainly because they were impossible to control when going downstream or trying to turn. Also, the engines proved unsatisfactory because they were complex and demanded excessive power to maintain even moderate speed. So the ships seem to have been soon relegated to harbor duties.

Nevertheless, the Russian navy continued to experiment with this type of ship. In 1879/1880, Elder built *Livadia*, ostensibly to provide Emperor Aleksandr II, who was prone to seasickness, with a comfortable means of conveyance. She had a displacement of about 4,500 tons and had an entirely flat bottom, the lower blades of the three screws protruding nine feet below the hull. On her trial run she easily exceeded the designed speed of fourteen sea miles per hour. So the model experiments conducted by the Netherlands naval constructor Dr. B. J. Tideman had proved their worth. During the voyage from Scotland to the Black Sea, she met very rough weather in the Bay of Biscay. Nevertheless, she remained "remarkably steady," rolling not more than four degrees. In 1883 *Livadia* was discarded as an imperial yacht and renamed *Opyt* (Experiment). Her end came as late as the Bolshevik period, when she was broken up after having served as a repair ship for the Black Sea Fleet.

[*See also* Navies, Great Powers, *subentry on* Russia and the Soviet Union, 1700 to the Present.]

### Bibliography

Dirkzwager, J. M. *Dr. B. J. Tideman, grondlegger van de moderne scheepsbouw in Nederland.* Leiden, Netherlands: Brill, 1970.
Fletcher, R. A. *Warships and Their Story.* London: Cassell, 1911.
Hovgaard, W. *Modern History of Warships.* London: Spon, 1920.

PHILIP M. BOSSCHER

**Admiral's Cup.** *See* Yachting and Pleasure Sailing.

**Admiralty Law.** *See* Law, *subentry on* Private Maritime Law.

**Advertising** Shipping is an international enterprise, and advertising has long played a crucial part in its commercial success. The promotion of cargo services through ships' agents is essential, but the most familiar forms of advertising have been for passenger services—whether the services were for immigrants, for the transport of government officials and armed forces to distant lands, or for holiday cruising. Posters, newspaper and magazine advertisements, and postcards have all played an important role in advertising shipping services.

Historically, governments have been supportive of their major shipping lines. Ships carried the mail, and shipping

**Advertising.** A Cunard White Star poster from the 1930s promotes the London & North East Railway's connection for passengers sailing to and from the United States and Canada. ART RESOURCE, NY

was also a matter of national pride. In an unprecedented event for Cunard in 1936, some seven hundred members of the British House of Commons and House of Lords, along with their guests, visited the British ocean liner *Queen Mary*; subsequently, King George V and Queen Mary, who had launched the ship in 1934, presented a signed photograph of themselves to be hung on board. Likewise, at a ceremony that took place in Southampton, England, in 2004, *Queen Mary*'s successor, the British-registered but American-owned *Queen Mary 2*, was named by Queen Elizabeth II, who had launched *Queen Elizabeth 2* in Scotland in 1967.

Shipping companies have also promoted themselves through the buildings they occupy, although few do so today. The buildings were designed to dominate their surroundings, with the name of the company prominently displayed as part of an effort to advertise the company's shipping services. Among surviving examples, albeit under other ownership and used for different purposes, are the Cunard buildings in Liverpool, England, and in New York. Indeed, parts of the interior of the Liverpool building were designed to look like the interior of ships operating from Liverpool after World War I.

But shipping companies have also advertised through ship models, sailing lists, promotional leaflets, house magazines, and calendars, as well as—for passengers already on board—through souvenirs, menus, and passenger lists. Considerable advertising was also done through postcards and posters. Postcards were often sold to immigrants for sending farewell messages to relatives. The traditional poster began to be used in the second half of the nineteenth century and flourished during the interwar period of the twentieth century. Marine artists were influenced by the art deco approach of Frank Pick (1878–1941), who was ultimately the managing director of the London Underground. For shipping companies, this approach led to exaggerated images of the ships, which dwarfed the other images around them. Such examples showing ships in New York can be seen in the work by Odin Rosenvinge (1880–1957) that features *Aquitania* for Cunard and the famous work by Adolphe Mouron (1901–1968), better known as Cassandre, that features the bow view of *Normandie* for the French Line.

Kenneth Shoesmith (1890–1939) felt that the ships he portrayed looked even more appealing when shown in the place they were sailing to rather than in the place they were sailing from, and he adopted this approach widely in advertising for cruises. Earlier, in 1890, an enduring set of images had been published by the artist W. W. Lloyd for the Peninsular and Oriental Steam Navigation Company (P&O). These were watercolors and pen-and-ink sketches depicting the kind of experiences that a passenger might have en route to India. The experiences are well observed and sometimes humorous, and the sketches were widely used by the company on menus well into the twentieth century.

A decision to travel with a particular company was often based on the size of its ships and on the ships' speed. Companies built ships with four funnels, even if one was a dummy, because passengers felt that such ships looked more impressive than vessels with three and offered a quicker passage and thus less chance to get seasick. Bonds forged with the captain and crew have also always been important in retaining passengers. To this end, companies often list the senior officers by ship in company brochures. Companies have also introduced loyalty schemes for repeat passengers, offering discounted fares and other benefits that are not available to first-time passengers.

To attract passengers, shipping companies have over the years tried to improve both accommodations and cuisine. When in 1921 the United States placed restrictions on immigration, third-class space—which was that traditionally used by immigrants—was significantly undersubscribed on many ships. This situation was dealt with to some extent by diverting ships to cruising. But on ships not so diverted, a tourist class of accommodation was introduced that, for approximately the same fare as third class, offered amenities normally associated with second and even first class. This led ultimately to tourist class becoming the equivalent of second class, which was abolished in the mid-1930s, and by 1936 cabin class had superseded first class.

Shipping companies also advertised by means of trade fairs and exhibitions where models of ships were displayed and passenger accommodation was re-created. An exhibition by Cunard included a model of its first *Mauretania* and marketed the ship as the eighth wonder of the world, comparing its size with that of the great Egyptian pyramid at Giza and with that of the Capitol in Washington, D.C. Prior to *Queen Mary*'s maiden voyage in 1936, Cunard gave a series of dinners for invited guests at the Trocadero in London; the restaurant was adapted to create the appearance and atmosphere of parts of the ship. The introductions of such vessels were national events, and some companies chose to mark the introductions by issuing medallions. Britain's royal mint produced three thousand bronze medals and five in gold to mark the maiden voyage of *Queen Mary*. One of the gold medals was presented to King George V and another to Queen Mary. Two others were presented to the president of the United States, Franklin Roosevelt, and to Mrs. Roosevelt, and the fifth went to the chairman of Cunard, Sir Percy Bates (1879–1946). Bates's medal can be seen at the Merseyside Maritime Museum in Liverpool. Medallions commemorating the introduction and service of *France*, owned by the French Line, were minted from 1962, and in 2004 medallions marked the introduction into service of *Queen Mary 2*.

The Blue Riband, the accolade for the fastest crossing of the North Atlantic, had its origins in the late nineteenth century. The contest caught the public's imagination and engendered national pride. From an advertising standpoint, the benefit to the nation with the Blue Riband holder was considerable. Countries able to distinguish themselves in this way were Britain, France, Germany, Italy, and the United States. The longest-serving holder was the first *Mauretania*, holder from 1907 until 1929, and the last holder was *United States* of United States Lines. Vessels arriving in New York after a record-breaking run, particularly if on a maiden voyage, were met with wild enthusiasm by the ships and crowds that had gathered to greet them.

Whereas the Blue Riband was an accolade with no official physical form, the Hales Trophy was a real loving cup. The award was conceived in 1934 by Harold K. Hales, who was the British member of Parliament for Hanley in Staffordshire. The award was to be presented to the Blue Riband holders on the North Atlantic. Winners included the Italian *Rex*, followed by the French Line's *Normandie* and Cunard's *Queen Mary*, although the trophy was refused by Cunard's chairman, Sir Percy Bates. After a long interval, the last ocean liner to win the award was *United States* of United States Lines.

A measure of the public's love of some ships can be gauged from the reaction to the withdrawal from service of the first *Mauretania*. As she sailed for the breaker's yard from Southampton, members of the public who had never sailed on her, as well as former passengers, gathered to pay their last tributes in various ways, and a piper played a lament on her arrival at the breaker's.

[*See also* Cruising; Passenger Trades; Portraits, *subentry on* Ships; *and* Ship Models.]

### Bibliography

Brinnin, John Malcolm. *The Sway of the Grand Saloon: A Social History of the North Atlantic.* New York: Delacorte Press, 1971.

Butel, Paul. *The Atlantic.* Translated by Iain Hamilton Grant. New York: Routledge, 1999.

Green, Edwin, and Michael Moss. *A Business of National Importance: The Royal Mail Shipping Group, 1902–1937.* London: Methuen, 1982.

Gregory, Alexis. *The Golden Age of Travel, 1880–1939.* London: Cassell, 1991.

Kludas, Arnold. *Record Breakers of the North Atlantic: Blue Riband Liners, 1838–1952.* London: Chatham, 2000.

Maxtone-Graham, John. *The Only Way to Cross.* New York: Macmillan, 1972.

Wall, Robert. *Ocean Liner Postcards in Maritime Art 1900–1945.* Woodbridge, U.K.: Antique Collectors' Club, 1998.

RICHARD BATEMAN

**Aegospotami.** *See* Ancient Navies.

**Agents and Managers** In principle, the profession of agent is as old as that of the foreign-trading merchant. After itinerant traders were replaced by resident burghers, who did not travel anymore with their merchandise, good and reliable contacts abroad became necessary. Such contacts were needed not only in the actual transactions of selling the exports and buying the imports, but also for information on trading prospects and, for maritime transport, in the increasingly complicated processes of clearing customs, paying port dues, and obtaining the necessary permissions and legal documents required by the local and state authorities.

Quite often, such a contact person was a member of the family or a compatriot temporarily or permanently staying abroad, but it could also be a foreign merchant with whom a more or less permanent business relationship had been established. In early modern times, a successful export or import business required a real network of such business friends, and the wider the scope of trade, the wider the network needed. Merchants within a network typically acted reciprocally as agents for each other. Accordingly, there was seldom any real division of labor between merchants and agents, at least not before the early nineteenth century. Very few merchants made agents' services their principal occupation, and still fewer specialized as shipping agents—clearing, chartering, and purchasing ships. This was only natural, because there was no real division of labor between foreign trading and shipping: most merchants were also shipowners, and even if that was not the case, a shipowner (or the manager of a ship-owning company) usually relied on the same mercantile networks as the merchant who charted the ship. The only division of labor was that different merchants specialized in trading with different countries (this was because reliable networks required time and effort to develop).

In practice, it was not the merchant or shipowner (or manager) who did the actual business with the agent. Rather, it was the master of the ship, who was also a kind of agent to the shipowner. Thus, for example, in the late eighteenth century, when a Scandinavian ship arrived in Marseille or Genoa, the master contacted the local business friend of his principal, who then not only acted as a customs and port agent and a selling agent for the cargo of timber or tar but also helped the master find a new freight or to buy a cargo of salt, if that was required. Moreover, the business friend drew bills of exchange to settle the accounts for sold or bought commodities or freight.

In some cases when normal merchant networks were difficult to maintain, special agent arrangements were established. One example of such special agents was the Far

East compradors, native traders who specialized in acting as middlemen between European and local merchants. As the word "comprador" suggests, this system dates back to the time of the Portuguese invasion of India and China. Another case was the consuls that the Dutch, British, and French governments sent in the sixteenth and seventeenth century to the Ottoman Empire to watch the mercantile interests of their citizens. Gradually these countries also established such consular services in other European countries, as did other governments as well. In spite of their diplomatic status, these consuls, at least the eighteenth-century Scandinavian consuls in the Mediterranean, often also acted as ordinary mercantile agents.

Early examples of specialized shipping agents can be found in Elsinore, Denmark, where The Sound toll was paid by ships entering or leaving the Baltic. As paying the toll involved either measuring the ship and/or estimating the volume or value of the cargo, and as there were different exemptions from time to time, it became increasingly common to hire a local agent to take care of the complicated process. Examples of such eighteenth-century agents were the houses of Holm and Glöerfelt, which cleared many Finnish and Swedish ships. The former, at least, was also a ship chandler—a most natural business combination, as many ships also replenished their stores in Elsinore. Indeed, it seems that in many undeveloped markets, ships chandlers also acted as chartering agents. As their premises typically included parlors or coffee rooms in which shipmasters used to meet (as vividly recorded for the Far East by Joseph Conrad in *Lord Jim*), they were able to collect and supply information on potential freight opportunities.

The growth of competitive freight markets was connected with the development of commodity exchanges. In the seventeenth century the most important institution of this sort was the Amsterdam Exchange, not the least because Dutch shipping at that time was so important, especially in the Baltic trade. This trade also formed the background of the Baltic Exchange in London, which claims that it began from commodity dealers' and shipowners' meetings in the Virginia and Baltic Coffee House from 1744 onwards; indeed, it seems that it became a real freight chartering exchange only in the beginning of the nineteenth century. Gradually it developed into the foremost hub of information for the shipping world and a central institution for chartering agents.

Ocean shipping started to grow rapidly in the second quarter of the nineteenth century, and with the gradual removal of the old mercantilist navigation acts and other restrictions, freight markets became more international than ever before. At the same time, the division of labor between shipping and foreign trade increased. Both developments greatly increased the demand for specialized shipping agents (in particular, for chartering agents). Indeed, this seems to be the period when this profession was actually born, or at least became visible. That first happened, of course, in big ports like London, Liverpool, Amsterdam, and Hamburg, but already in the late 1830s, specialized freight agents were also to be found in the Mediterranean ports of Marseille and Trieste. That the business took off during this period is also indicated by the fact that many well-known and important firms in this branch were established then. Thus John Good moved to Hull in 1833 and started a ship-chandler and ship-broking business; roughly at the same time August Bolten in Hamburg joined an agency firm started by William Miller, a Scot; Angier Brothers in London started its activities in the 1840s; and Clarksons of London date its history back to 1852.

The electric telegraph became a splendid tool for chartering agents: it not only made the collection of freight data go much more quickly than before, but in the beginning, when charges were high, it was a special asset for agents, who could distribute the costs between a good number of customers. The new communication technology also changed the connections between the main actors of shipping in one important respect: it enabled direct communication between chartering agent and shipowner or manager, thus reducing the role of the shipmaster in the decision making. Another development that widened the business of shipping agents was the beginning of regular shipping-line traffic: liner companies needed reliable, competent agents to represent them in all the ports their ships were visiting.

In modern shipping, the spectrum of agents was widened also by shipping newspapers and periodicals, as well as information and research firms, who remit to their customers data on, for example, recent chartering, new building, and shipping sales, plus analyses of the outlook for the shipping business. In a way, these players can be regarded as a superstratum of agents, because their customers, to a great degree, consist of ordinary shipping agents.

[*See also* Shipping Companies, *subentries on* Coastwise Cargo Companies, Ocean Cargo Companies, *and* Sea Passenger Companies; *and* Trade, *subentry on* Integration in Shipping Industries.]

## Bibliography

Very little systematic research on shipping agents exists to date. A remarkable example is Lewis R. Fischer and Helge Nordvik, "Economic Theory, Information, and Management in

Shipbroking: Fearnley and Eger as a Case Study, 1869–1972," in *Management, Finance, and Industrial Relations in Maritime Industries: Essays in International Maritime and Business History*, eds. Simon P. Ville and David M. Williams, Research in Maritime History, no. 6 (St. John's, Newfoundland: International Maritime Economic History Association, 1994). See also Hugh Barty-King, *The Baltic Exchange: The History of a Unique Market* (London: Hutchinson, 1977); Gordon Boyce, *Information, Mediation, and Institutional Development: The Rise of Large-Scale Enterprise in British Shipping, 1870–1919* (Manchester: Manchester University Press, 1995); and Yrjö Kaukiainen, "International Freight Markets in the 1830s and 1840s: The Experience of a Major Finnish Shipowner," in *Global Markets: The Internationalization of the Sea Transport Industries since 1850*, eds. Gelina Harlaftis and David J. Starkey, Research in Maritime History, no. 14 (St. John's, Newfoundland: International Maritime Economic History Association, 1998).

Studies on mercantile networks have proliferated in recent times. See, for example, Olaf U. Janzen, ed., *Merchant Organization and Maritime Trade in the North Atlantic, 1660–1815*, Research in Maritime History, no. 15 (St. John's, Newfoundland: International Maritime Economic History Association, 1998); Sanjay Subrahmayam, ed., *Merchant Networks in the Early Modern World* (Aldershot, U.K.: Variorum, 1996); Leos Muller, *The Merchant Houses of Stockholm, c. 1640–1800* (Uppsala, Sweden: S. Academiae Ubsaliensis, 1998); Jari Ojala, "Approaching Europe: The Merchant Networks between Finland and Europe during the Eighteenth and Nineteenth Centuries," *European Review of Economic History* 1 (1997): 323–352.

Articles on different countries' consular systems were published in *Business History* 23 (1981). Early histories of modern shipping-agent firms can often be found on their Web sites, for example, John Good (http://johngood.co.uk/history/), Clarksons (http://clarksons.co.uk/history.html), and August Bolten (http://augbolten.com/company/). For the background of Angier Brothers, see "Fifty Years' Freights," *Fairplay*, January 8, 1920, 225.

YRJÖ KAUKIAINEN

# Aircraft Carrier

The U.S. Navy carried out pioneer flights from ships in 1910, but the first attempt to use ship-launched aircraft operationally came with the British-improvised seaplane carrier *Hermes* in 1913, followed by a purpose-built ship, *Ark Royal*, in 1914–1915. Wartime developments were rapid and culminated in a strike in 1918 launched from HMS *Furious* against zeppelin sheds. The first ship with a full-length flight deck, the British *Argus*, was completed just before the end of World War I.

Royal Navy developments were stultified by politics, and the U.S. Navy took the lead with two very big carriers. The size of these two ships enabled them to launch large numbers of aircraft, suggesting that the carrier might replace the battleship. The number of aircraft involved led to the development of flight-deck machinery such as arrester wires, crash barriers, and catapults. The practices of the U.S. Navy and the Royal Navy began to diverge with the more powerful American aircraft normally parked on deck above an open hangar built on top of the hull. The flimsy British planes were kept in a closed hangar within the deep main hull of the ship, giving greater protection from both the weather and fire. A later variation in British ships was to armor the hangar up to cruiser standards.

The early years of World War II showed the value of including a carrier in a task force. The destruction of the U.S. battle line at Pearl Harbor in 1941 both showed the striking power of carrier air groups and forced the U.S. Navy to operate carrier battle groups without battleships. At Midway (1942), the Japanese carrier force lost four of its few carriers, together with many of its best air crews, a defeat from which it never recovered. As more and more of the big Essex-class carriers entered service, the U.S. Navy was able to win complete air supremacy over areas of the Pacific. Smaller carriers played an important role in the anti-submarine war.

After the war, the carrier world was dominated by the United States. Driven by the desire to contribute to the nuclear deterrent, designers built new ships very big—the first group of eight, the Forrestals, were of nearly 80,000 tons carrying 90 aircraft. The introduction of jet aircraft much reduced the fire risk, but the jets' high landing speed led to numerous accidents. The Royal Navy was operating much smaller, war-built ships, and suffered badly before coming up with three innovations that greatly reduced the number of accidents: the angled flight deck, the mirror landing sight, and the steam catapult.

In 1961, the American *Enterprise* was completed as the first nuclear-powered carrier. Nuclear power increased the endurance of the ship, and the machinery did not need the very large airways of earlier ships, airways that so obstructed the hangar. Then followed the nine ships of the Nimitz class: 90,000 tons and 90 powerful aircraft. These giants can dominate the airspace over large areas and can operate free of many political restraints.

Other countries cannot afford such ships, and several countries have built ships of only up to 20,000 tons. These are used primarily for anti-submarine warfare, using helicopters, but they have a strike capability using V/STOL (vertical or short takeoff and landing) fighters.

[*See also* Anti-Submarine Warfare; Warships, *subentry on* Modern Warships; *and* Wars, Maritime, *subentry on* World Wars.]

## Bibliography

Brown, David K. *The Grand Fleet: Warship Design and Development, 1906–1922.* London: Chatham, 1999.

Brown, David K. *Nelson to Vanguard: Warship Design and Development, 1923–1945.* London: Chatham, 2000.

Brown, David K., and George Moore. *Rebuilding the Royal Navy: Warship Design since 1945.* London: Chatham, 2003.

Brown, David K., ed. *The Design and Construction of British Warships 1939–1945.* Vol. 1, *Major Surface Vessels.* London: Conway Maritime Press, 1995.

Friedman, Norman. *British Carrier Aviation.* London: Conway Maritime Press, 1988. Friedman, Norman. *U.S. Aircraft Carriers.* Annapolis, Md.: U.S. Naval Institute, 1983.

Layman, R. D. *Naval Aviation in the First World War.* London: Chatham, 1996.

DAVID K. BROWN

# *Alabama*

(formerly *Enrica*), auxiliary bark (1 funnel, 3 masts). \Length/ beam/draft: 67.1 m × 9.7 m × 4.3 m (220′ × 31.75′ × 14′). Tonnage: 1,050 tons. Hull: wood. Complement: 148. Armament: 6 × 32-pounders, 1 × 110-pounder, 1 × 68-pounder. Machinery: direct-acting engine, 600 indicated horsepower, 1 screw; 13 knots. Built: Laird Bros., Birkenhead, England, 1862.

At the start of the American Civil War, the Confederate States faced an overwhelmingly superior U.S. Navy. With no prospect of building its own blue water force, the South ordered several commerce raiders from British yards with which to disrupt northern trade. The most successful of the raiders was CSS *Alabama*, under Captain Raphael Semmes. Between September 1862 and April 1864, she captured fifty-two merchant ships, valued at $4,613,914. Of her other encounters, ten were bonded, one was sold, another released, and yet another commissioned as a commerce raider. *Alabama* also sank USS *Hatteras* off Galveston, Texas.

*Alabama*'s career took her from the North Atlantic to the Caribbean and South Atlantic, and then east to South Africa and Singapore. Returning to Europe for a refit, Semmes anchored at Cherbourg, France, on June 11, 1864. Three days later the screw sloop USS *Kearsarge* arrived off the port, and on July 19 Semmes sailed out of Cherbourg to meet her. The raider was no match for the Union cruiser, which reduced her to a sinking condition in an hour. Semmes escaped on a British yacht. While the sinking of *Alabama* did not affect the outcome of the Civil War, her loss was a blow to Confederate morale.

The devastation caused by the Confederate raiders is often cited as a cause of the decline of U.S. international shipping in the late 1800s. During the war, insurance rates for U.S. flag ships rose 900 percent, and 900 ships transferred to foreign registry. Following the war, the United States insisted that in letting the Confederacy purchase commerce raiders from British yards, Britain had violated its own declared neutrality and was therefore liable for the destruction wrought by those ships. An international tribunal adjudicated the so-called *Alabama* claims and, under the Treaty of Washington (1871), found that the British government had not exercised "due diligence" and awarded the United States $15.5 million in damages.

In 1984, French divers discovered the ship's remains lying about 9.5 kilometers (about 6 miles) off Cherbourg. The site is under the protection of a joint French and American authority, and archaeological recovery is ongoing.

[*See also* Warships, *subentry on* Modern Warships.]

## Bibliography

Cook, Adrian. *The "Alabama" Claims: American Politics and Anglo-American Relations, 1865–1872.* Ithaca, N.Y.: Cornell University Press, 1975.

"CSS *Alabama* Association." http://www.css-alabama.com.

Hearn, Chester G. *Gray Raiders of the Sea: How Eight Confederate Warships Destroyed the Union's High Seas Commerce.* Camden, Maine: International Marine Publishing, 1992.

Robinson, Charles M., III. *Shark of the Confederacy: The Story of the CSS "Alabama."* Annapolis, Md.: Naval Institute Press, 1995.

Semmes, Raphael. *Memoirs of Service Afloat.* 1868. Reprint. Secaucus, N.J.: Blue and Grey Press, 1987.

LINCOLN P. PAINE

# Albuquerque, Afonso de

(c. 1462–1515), governor of Portuguese India whose vision and tireless energy helped shape the Portuguese seaborne empire in Asia. Albuquerque was around fifty when nominated by King Manuel I as governor of Portuguese India. Until his assumption of power in 1509, the Portuguese presence in Asia was little more a naval force based in Cochin and Cannanore, on the southwest Indian coast, under Francisco de Almeida, the first Portuguese viceroy. It is unclear why Dom Manuel went back on his apparent promise to allow Almeida an indefinite term. Nonetheless, the king chose to limit his term in office to three years, and in 1506 gave Albuquerque secret letters patent to succeed him in 1508, though as governor and without the title of viceroy.

Albuquerque, the second son of an important nobleman, served at court and in Morocco before sailing in two fleets

**Afonso de Albuquerque.** A portrait from a manuscript by Lizuarte de Abreu, c. 1558, depicting Portuguese viceroys and governors in India. The Pierpont Morgan Library, Ms. M. 525, f. 5 / Art Resource, NY

Portugal to be a land-based power in Asia and was content to be the guest of two Malabar rajas. Albuquerque, in contrast, reasoned that Indian potentates would not recognize Portugal as legitimate in Asia so long as it possessed no territory of its own. Accordingly, when he learned that, as a virtual island, Goa might make a defensible base and that its Hindu populace was restive under its new ruler, the Adil Shah of Bijapur, he stormed and captured it with difficulty in 1510. The following year he took his main force and sailed for Malacca, where Sequeira, when he visited, suffered from the treachery of its powerful sultan, losing his factor and some crewmembers. Albuquerque boldly assaulted the bridge, dividing the city into halves, and staved off the sultan's counterattacks, including a final one of war elephants. At this the sultan fled, leaving this vital transit point between the Indian Ocean and the China Seas in Portuguese hands.

Returning to Goa, Albuquerque found that the Adil Shah's forces had returned and occupied the northern part of the island, at Benasterim, where it was divided from the mainland by only a shallow channel. In a great bombardment rare for the age, he massed artillery on the flank of Bernasterim and introduced small vessels into the channel; then he pounded the Bijapuri forces into submission. His next objective was Aden, at the mouth of the Red Sea: its capture would allow Portugal to cut off all intercourse between the Middle East and the Indian Ocean. This time fortune was against him because the citadel was on high alert, fearing not the Portuguese, but an investment by the Ottoman Turks. He gathered twenty ships for his attack in 1513, but reefs impeded navigation, and Portuguese scaling ladders were too short for the city's high walls, so the attempt had to be abandoned. Albuquerque then sailed into the Red Sea in search of an alternate base to control passage of that sea, but his ships became becalmed on Kamaran Island, and many men died of fevers while waiting for a reversal of the monsoon winds that would allow passage back to Goa. No doubt Albuquerque planned to return one day and finish the project. As it was, reports of his failure strengthened his enemies and resulted in his recall two years later.

Albuquerque spent the rest of 1514 in Goa, creating a government for Portuguese Asia, but by the end of that year, Ormuz, the drawstring to the Persian Gulf, had attracted his attention. A boy sultan, Saifu-d-Din, had become its nominal ruler, and his powerful adviser, Reis Hamed, was scheming to make the city a Persian tributary. Albuquerque arrived there in March 1515 and arranged a meeting with both, who came heavily armed. A scuffle ensued, and the

dispatched from Portugal, the second in 1506. He had to struggle with Almeida over his nomination. Almeida put him under arrest, but he was rescued in 1509 when Fernando Coutinho, the Marshal of Portugal, arrived in India and installed him in office. Even the crown proved an initial obstacle because Dom Manuel and his council had ineptly divided Almeida's jurisdiction into three zones, of which Albuquerque was to command only the central one. As governor, Albuquerque realized this setup would hopelessly complicate Portuguese operations in Asia. But fortune played into his hands when one nominee, Jorge de Aguiar, drowned and the other, Diogo Lopes de Sequeira, returned to Portugal. He then assumed supreme command.

His first move was to create a permanent base for Portuguese power. Almeida had never felt it important for

Portuguese stabbed Reis Hamed to death, whereupon the youthful ruler accepted Portuguese hegemony and Albuquerque constructed a great fortress. On the way home, Albuquerque learned that Dom Manuel had dismissed him, but by then he was mortally sick with dysentery and died on the Mondovi River within sight of Goa. Albuquerque thus gave shape to the Portuguese empire, which endured for more than a century. Dom Manuel soon repented of his dismissal of Albuquerque and loaded Albuquerque's son with honors.

It is hypothetical whether Albuquerque was the real author of Portugal's aggressive comportment in Asia, or whether he merely acted at the behest of Dom Manuel and his council. Portuguese aggressiveness, whether carried out upon explicit order from Lisbon or on Albuquerque's own initiative, was apparent as early as Pedro Álvares Cabral's visit in 1501, and it was amplified the following year by Vasco da Gama's almost unprovoked bombardment of Calicut. Almeida, Albuquerque's immediate predecessor, had already been instructed in 1505 to capture Aden, near the mouth of the Red Sea. Albuquerque himself was an old fighter, hardened by service in a Morocco known for give-no-quarter combat. He later reminded his king that he had taken Goa on royal orders. The safest thing to say is that Albuquerque was admirably suited by background and talent to conquer Goa, Malacca, and Ormuz, which later became foundation stones of the Portuguese empire in Asia.

[*See also* Portuguese Indian Ocean Exploration Voyages, 1497–1515.]

## Bibliography

Albuquerque, Afonso de. *Albuquerque, Caesar of the East: Selected Texts by Afonso de Albuquerque and His Son.* Edited and translated by Thomas F. Earle and John Villiers. Warminster, U.K.: Aris and Phillips, 1990.

Albuquerque, Afonso de. *Cartas de Afonso de Albuquerque, seguidas dos documentos que as elucidam.* 7 vols. Lisbon: 1884–1935.

Albuquerque, Brás de. *Comentários do Grande Afonso de Albuquerque.* 2 vols. Coimbra: Imprensa da Universidade, 1923. After Afonso de Albuquerque's death, King Manuel required his natural son, Brás, to assume his father's name; thus early versions of texts such as this one might give the name Afonso, rather than Brás. Brás, Albuquerque's son, compiled the Comentários, which date from 1557, drawing on no longer extant sources about his father's exploits.

Diffie, Bailey Wallys, and George Davison Winius. *Foundations of the Portuguese Empire, 1415–1580.* Minneapolis: University of Minnesota Press, 1977.

GEORGE WINIUS

**Alecto.** *See Rattler.*

**Alexandria** The port of Alexandria is the principal port of Egypt and handles over three quarters of the country's foreign trade. It is located on the western extremity of the Nile River delta on the north coast of Egypt. Situated approximately 200 kilometers (124 miles) from Cairo, the port is separated into two harbors: the Eastern Port and the Western Port, which are divided by a T-shaped peninsula. Although fishing vessels may use both harbors, large commercial shipping is confined to the west harbor. The main goods exported from the port of Alexandria include cotton, oil products, fruits, and vegetables; grain and liquid bulk cargo form the main imports. The commercial significance of the harbor prompted major improvements and expansion in the first quarter of the twentieth century.

Alexandria was founded in 332 B.C.E. by the Macedonian king Alexander III (Alexander the Great, 356–323 B.C.E.), although that city's port, originally named Rakouda, dates to 1900 B.C.E. Alexander's successor, Ptolemy I (r. 323–285 B.C.E.), was determined to make the port city the intellectual, cultural, and commercial capital of the Mediterranean; and by the second century B.C.E., the famous library and the lighthouse of Alexandria marked the area as a place of importance in the ancient world. The port continued as a great nexus for trade until Muslim forces captured the city in 642. The decision to move the capital to what is known as present-day Cairo caused the port city of Alexandria to decline to little more than a fishing village.

The occupation of the region (1798–1801) by the forces of Napoléon Bonaparte (later Napoléon I, r. 1804–1814, 1815) signaled the beginning of a renewed era of importance for Alexandria. In the early nineteenth century Egypt's ruler Muhammad Ali Pasha dredged its harbor after selecting the location as a base for the Alexandria Maritime Arsenal. Ali then embarked on a shipbuilding program to provide battleships for his new naval fleet. In addition to constructing the largest dockyard in the country, Ali erected a lighthouse on the peninsula of Ras el-Tin. By the middle of the nineteenth century, the port of Alexandria had evolved into the major entrepôt of the eastern Mediterranean. Indeed, the facilities and position of the port even encouraged the Royal Navy to appoint it as headquarters of its Mediterranean squadron until the end of World War II.

The importance of the port in the nineteenth century grew with the advent of the American Civil War (1861–1865). This conflict proved a boon to Egypt's cotton producers, and profits from this crop prompted large-scale attempts

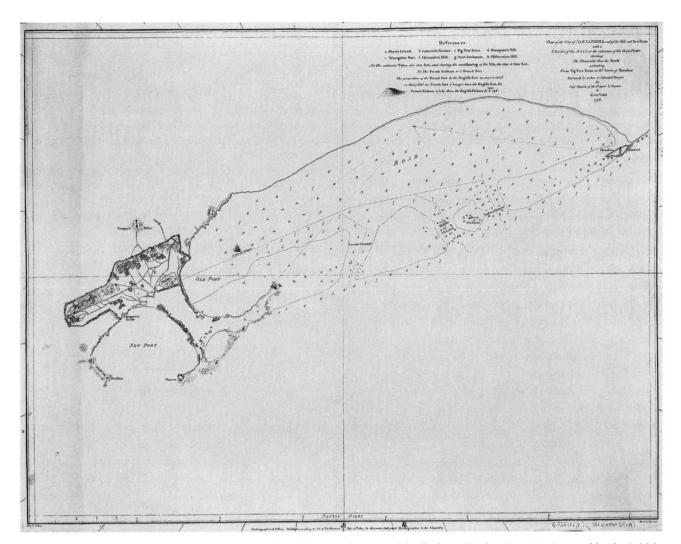

**Alexandria Harbor.** Captain Barre and Lieutenant Vidal of the French Navy originally drew this chart in 1798. Captured by the British, Alexander Dalrymple, the hydrographer of the Royal Navy, issued it as one of the first Admiralty charts in 1801. © NATIONAL MARITIME MUSEUM, LONDON

to improve the country's agriculture and manufacturing efforts. Buoyed by a reinvigorated economy, the Ottoman viceroy of Egypt, Said Pasha (r. 1854–1863), borrowed heavily from European sources in order to begin work on the Suez Canal. Unable to repay the debt, Egypt fell under the supervision of France and Great Britain; the latter's fleet would later bombard Alexandria in 1882, in a successful effort to crush a nationalist uprising that led to British occupation of the country.

Because of its high level of activity in the early twenty-first century, the port of Alexandria continues to experience chronic delays. The government of Egypt hopes that planned port improvements will alleviate many of the difficulties.

[*See also* Mediterranean Sea; Ports, *subentry on* Characteristics of Cities; *and* Suez Canal.]

### Bibliography

"Alexandria." In *Encyclopedia of the Modern Middle East and North Africa*, edited by Philip Mattar. 2d ed., Detroit, Mich.: Macmillan Reference, 2004. Provides a concise and useful history of the city of Alexandria.

"Egyptian Maritime Data Bank." http://www.embd.gov.eg/English_v/index_e.htm. The Egyptian Maritime Data Bank connects the headquarters of the Maritime Transport Ministry with Egyptian ports and provides useful data and background information.

Forster, E. M. *Alexandria: A History and a Guide*. Garden City, N.Y.: Anchor, 1961. First published 1922. Provides some useful background material on the history of the city.

CLAIRE PHELAN

**Altmark.** *See Admiral Graf Spee.*

**America** (later *Camilla, Memphis*), schooner (2 masts). Length/beam/draft: 29 m × 7 m × 3.4 m (95′ × 23′ × 11′). Tonnage: 170 tons, 50/95 displacement. Hull: wood. Complement: 25. Designer: George Steers. Built: William H. Brown, New York, 1851.

The vessel for which yachting's celebrated America's Cup is named, *America* was built specifically to challenge English supremacy in shipbuilding and yacht racing on the occasion of Great Britain's Great Exhibition of 1851. Abandoning the traditional hull form of a bluff bow (the beam widest about a third of the way aft, and a tapered stern), *America* had a fine bow, with the beam widest roughly amidships, and a subtle taper aft. "If she is right," exclaimed an English observer, "then all of us are wrong." The masts raked backward at a severe angle of about fourteen degrees, and she was rigged with a mainsail, a boomless foresail, and a single jib.

In July 1851 *America* anchored before the Royal Yacht Squadron on the Isle of Wight. Unfortunately for her owners, a syndicate of New York Yacht Club members who hoped to recoup the $20,000 that the schooner had cost with the winnings from match races, *America*'s mere appearance deterred prospective competitors. She lay unchallenged until syndicate head John C. Stevens decided to compete for the Royal Yacht Squadron's Hundred Guineas (£105) Cup, a 53-mile race around the Isle of Wight without time allowance, "open to yachts belonging to the clubs of all nations." *America* was the only non-English entrant in a fleet of seven schooners and eight cutters. Despite making a bad start and breaking a jibboom (acquired in England), she sailed to a commanding victory in a triumph admired in England and greeted with rapture in the United States.

*America* subsequently passed through a succession of owners. During the Civil War (1861–1865) she was owned by Confederate interests until captured by the Union Army in 1862. Ending the war as a U.S. Naval Academy school ship, she was laid up in 1866. In 1870 she competed in the first race for the cup named in her honor. Sold in 1873, she sailed and raced in private ownership until 1917. She was donated to the Naval Academy in 1921. In poor condition, she was destroyed in 1942 when snow collapsed the shed in which she was stored. The New York Yacht Club withstood 25 challenges over 132 years before the America's Cup was lost to *Australia II* in 1983. A replica of *America* was built in 1967, and another in 1995.

[*See also* America's Cup; Crusing Literature, *subentry on* Yacht Racing; *and* Yachting and Pleasure Sailing.]

### Bibliography

Boswell, Charles. *The "America": The Story of the World's Most Famous Yacht.* New York: David McKay, 1967.

Rousmaniere, John. *America's Cup Book, 1851–1983.* New York: Norton, 1986.

Rousmaniere, John. *The Low Black Schooner: Yacht "America" 1851–1945.* Mystic, Conn.: Mystic Seaport Museum Stores, 1985.

LINCOLN P. PAINE

## American Literature

This entry contains two subentries:

An Overview
Sea Fiction

---

## An Overview

American sea literature has roots in Greek, Roman, Irish, and Norse mythology, the Bible, and the English Renaissance, whenever humans have gazed on the sea or sailed across it. The sea has been a significant force within the body of American literature since colonial times, when men chronicled successes and catastrophes crossing the Atlantic. The genre of "sea-deliverance narratives" developed—tales written by survivors who experienced something terrifying or violent on the sea, have been transformed by it, and are compelled to tell their stories. This tradition began as a narrative of a voyage; in America it also incorporated a search for the New World and presumed a trust in God's providence. Early examples include the *Log of Christopher Columbus* (1492–1493), William Strachey's "True Reportory of the Wracke, and Redemption of Sir Thomas Gates" (1625), John Josselyn's *Account of Two Voyages* (1639), chapters of Increase Mather's *Essay for the Recording of Illustrious Providences* (1684), Cotton Mather's *Magnalia Christi Americana* (1702) and *Pietas in Patriam: The Life of His Excellency Sir William Phips* (1697, 1702), Richard Steere's *A Monumental Memorial of Marine Mercy* (1684), John Barnard's *Ashton's Memorial* (1725), and Henry Norwood's "A Voyage to Virginia" (1732).

By the eve of the American Revolution, the label "American" no longer identified an aboriginal, but indicated

**American Literature.** A page from one of Herman Melville's journals, written at Constantinople December 16, 1856. LIBRARY OF CONGRESS, PRINTS AND PHOTOGRAPHS DIVISION

stock from the old world transformed by the new. Voices and subjects became distinctly American. Briton Hammon, a black slave, recounted shipwreck, capture, and escape in his *Narrative* (1760). The displaced Frenchman J. Hector St. Jean de Crèvecoeur expressed a vibrant new maritime nationalism in "Nantucket" in *Letters from an American Farmer* (1782). Philip Freneau infused his maritime poetry with patriotism and Romanticism in, for example, "The British Prison Ship" (1780), "Argonaute" (1795), and "Hatteras" (1795). Washington Irving, born the last year of the American Revolution, made three round-trip voyages across the Atlantic Ocean and used nautical references in *The Sketch Book of Geoffrey Crayon, Gent.* (1819–1820), *Tales of a Traveller* (1824), two books on Columbus's voyages and companions (1828, 1831), and "The Haunted Ship: A True Story—As Far as It Goes" (1835).

When Ticknor, Reed, and Fields published *Thalatta: A Book for the Sea-Side* in Boston in 1853, they couldn't have known that they were making publishing history.

Edited by Samuel Longfellow (1819–1892), younger brother of Henry Wadsworth Longfellow (1807–1882), and by Thomas Wentworth Higginson (1823–1911), the unassuming volume seems designed as light reading for a summer day with friends at the beach, as the first poem, "Prelude," by Caroline Sheridan Norton, suggests. Yet this collection is remarkable in that it is the first anthology published in America entirely devoted to the theme of the sea. The title of the volume, Greek for "sea," is taken from Xenophon's *Expedition of Cyrus* and appears in the book's epigram: "As soon as the men . . . beheld the Sea, they gave a great shout, 'Thalatta! Thalatta!' " The volume's 127 poems represent a hundred poets, including some of the most highly regarded in America: Ralph Waldo Emerson (1803–1882), Henry David Thoreau (1817–1862), Oliver Wendell Holmes (1809–1894), James Russell Lowell (1819–1891), John Greenleaf Whittier (1807–1892), Richard Henry Dana Sr. (1787–1879), and Henry Wadsworth Longfellow (whose six poems exceed in number those of all other poets except "Anonymous"). Homer (ninth–eighth century B.C.E.), William Shakespeare (1564–1616), Scottish ballads, and translations from German and Spanish appear alongside the contemporary British poets John Keats (1795–1821), Robert Browning (1812–1889), Elizabeth Barrett Browning (1806–1861), William Wordsworth (1770–1850), Samuel Taylor Coleridge (1772–1834), Lord Byron (George Gordon Byron, 1788–1824), and Sir Walter Scott (1771–1832). The organization of the volume seems random, even haphazard, without attention to chronology, nationality, or thematic development. There are clusters of poems about storms at sea, but the overall tone of the collection is elegiac, pastoral, and nostalgic.

One of the first novels composed in America also had a nautical theme. *Mr. Penrose: The Journal of Penrose, Seaman* (1815) was written by the Englishman William Williams (1727–1791) during the thirty years that he lived in America. Born in Bristol, England, where he also died, Williams was sent to sea by his parents because he failed academically. After wandering the Caribbean, he settled in Philadelphia, where he dabbled in music and theater, painted landscapes and portraits, and did detail painting for the shipbuilders Thomas and James Penrose, whom he honored by using their surname for the main character in his only novel. The plot revolves around Llewellin Penrose, a Welsh sailor who is shipwrecked, imprisoned by Spaniards, and deserted on the Mosquito Coast (the east coast of present-day Nicaragua and Honduras). It chronicles twenty-seven years of the man's life, including his philosophy, marriage, fathering a daughter named "America," and various adventures and disasters. A posthumous, bowdlerized edition was followed by a pirated German translation. David Howard Dickason restored the manuscript to Williams's own style, wrote an introduction, and published the novel in 1969.

## James Fenimore Cooper

With *The Pilot: A Tale of the Sea* (1824), James Fenimore Cooper (1789–1851) published the first sea novel in English, a distinct genre he developed that uses seamen as principal characters and uses seas and ships as primary settings. The novel is set during the American Revolution off the northeastern coast of England. Sailors from two Continental ships go ashore to retrieve a mysterious Scottish pilot who turns out to be America's first naval hero, John Paul Jones (1747–1792). In a breathtaking scene, Jones rescues an American frigate from near disaster among shoals in a fierce storm. The other memorable character in the novel is the old salt and coxswain Long Tom Coffin, who melodramatically harpoons a right whale during one episode and pins a British officer to the mast of his own ship in another, who can navigate in any sea but gets lost on land, and who goes down as his beloved schooner *Ariel* breaks up in a storm—his body is never found. The novel is one of intrigue, combat, and adventure on the high seas.

Cooper himself had been a sailor, first as a passenger in sloops plying the Hudson River and then shipping before the mast at sixteen in a merchantman bound for England. On his eighteenth birthday he made landfall in Delaware. He served in the navy for two years before he married, and his interest in naval affairs was lifelong. His Leatherstocking Tales, set inland on the frontier wilderness, ensured Cooper an enduring popularity, but he also penned novels of social criticism and a dozen novels about the sea. Nine of his sea novels are most memorable. The first three—*The Pilot*, *The Red Rover* (1827), and *The Water-Witch* (1830)—are all romantic and exuberant, written at the height of Cooper's career. The middle three—*Mercedes of Castile* (1840), *The Two Admirals* (1842), and *The Wing-and-Wing* (1842)—depend more on history and documentation, from Christopher Columbus to the Napoleonic era. Finally, *Afloat and Ashore* (1844), *Jack Tier* (1845–1848), and *The Sea Lions* (1849) are somber and realistic, focusing more on hardship and the seamier side of maritime life. Cooper uses maritime themes and imagery only somewhat less importantly in *The Monikins* (1835), *Homeward Bound* (1838), *The Pathfinder* (1840), and *The Crater* (1847). His nonfiction maritime works include *The History of the Navy of the United States of America*

(1839), *Ned Myers* (1843), *The Battle of Lake Erie* (1843), and *Lives of Distinguished Naval Officers* (1846). From the time of publication of his naval history, Cooper was involved in disputes regarding the accuracy of his history and his integrity as a historian, particularly involving his account of Oliver Hazard Perry (1785–1819) and Jesse Duncan Elliott (1782–1845) on Lake Erie. His subsequent lawsuits largely determined the course of libel law in the United States, while his later historiography consistently exhibits his adversarial role with his literary nemesis, Alexander Slidell Mackenzie, whose court-martial for the *Somers* mutiny affair Cooper brilliantly analyzed in 1844. Cooper revised his naval history for publication in 1840, 1841, and 1846. Even posthumous editions of 1853 and 1856 included new material from Cooper's manuscripts, and his work was standard until the outbreak of the Civil War. Robert Montgomery Bird's *Adventures of Robin Day* (1839), a picaresque nautical adventure novel, is highly derivative of Cooper, and Herman Melville (1819–1891) and Joseph Conrad (1857–1924) both acknowledge Cooper's significant influence on their own work.

## Edgar Allan Poe and Richard Henry Dana

Edgar Allan Poe (1809–1849), whose poetry, essays, and short fictions of gothic horror eclipse his nautical writing, nevertheless infuses nautical detail into much of his work. He both had substantial experience at sea himself and relied heavily on source material describing voyaging and nautical disasters, particularly that of Jeremiah Reynolds (1799–1858) and Benjamin Morrell (1795–1839). Poe crossed the Atlantic twice as a child and traveled on coastal vessels both in and out of the army. Short fictions that contain notable nautical reference or inference or nautical characters include "The Gold Bug," "The Balloon Hoax," "Hans Pfall," "King Pest," and "The Murders in the Rue Morgue." Among poems set by the sea or using sea imagery are "Annabel Lee," "The City in the Sea," "To Helen," "The Valley of Unrest," and "To One in Paradise." Three of his most famous tales rely on the sea significantly: "A MS. Found in a Bottle" (1833), "A Descent into the Maelstrom" (1841), and *The Narrative of Arthur Gordon Pym* (1838), his only novel-length work. In the story, Pym experiences a year of terrifying adventures on a variety of vessels, including being stowed away, being shipwrecked, surviving cannibalism and sharks, and surviving the death of the rest of the crew. When he encounters a strange white shape near the South Pole, his journal abruptly ends.

Richard Henry Dana Jr. (1815–1882) left a privileged life at Harvard for work on board a merchant vessel and is credited with single-handedly moving American sea fiction away from the Romantic and toward the realistic. His "voice from the forecastle" first-person account is *Two Years before the Mast* (1840), which includes a compelling narrative of a flogging alongside a picture of the drudgery of the hide trade on the coast of California and an analysis of the dehumanizing effects of the isolation of life at sea. He also wrote a manual explaining nautical vocabulary and procedure, *The Seaman's Friend* (1841). As a Brahmin, a lawyer, and a sailor, during the *Somers* mutiny affair Dana was widely recognized as the major voice bridging life at sea and civilization ashore. Although a supporter of naval authority, he became an abolitionist and unflagging supporter of sailors' rights. He exerted a great deal of influence on Herman Melville, who called him his "sea-brother" in an 1849 letter.

## Herman Melville

The greatest American author of sea literature is Herman Melville (1819–1891), whose works are both inextricably linked with his own experiences at sea and infused with sources drawn from his vast reading. With his family in desperate financial straights, he went to sea in 1839 at age nineteen to help support them, signing on board a merchant vessel that traveled round-trip from New York to Liverpool. This voyage forms the basis for a novel about a greenhorn, which was published as his fourth book, *Redburn: His First Voyage* (1849), a potboiler about an adolescent ship's boy who becomes disillusioned with the harsh realities of life on board ship. A year after the Liverpool voyage, Melville traveled by canal boat and steamboat on U.S. inland waterways, experiences he drew on for sections of *Moby-Dick* (1851) and *The Confidence-Man* (1857).

In 1841, with no previous experience at whaling, Melville signed on board the whaleship *Acushnet* for her maiden voyage in the Pacific, which became the basis of fictional sailor Ishmael's adventures on board *Pequod* in *Moby-Dick*, Melville's most famous work. Dedicated to the American writer Nathaniel Hawthorne (1804–1864), *Moby-Dick* is multilayered and complex: part travelogue; part myth, adventure tale, spiritual quest, comedy, and philosophical speculation; part treasure trove of cetological lore. Ishmael becomes bosom buddies with the South Sea Pacific islander Queequeg, a crackerjack harpooner, and together they sign on board a whaler captained by Ahab, a man obsessed and full of vengeance toward the

**American Literature.** Jack London (1876–1916) as a young man. THE GRANGER COLLECTION, NEW YORK

white whale who tore off his leg. It soon becomes clear that what is driving the ship's mission is not filling the hold with whale oil but Ahab's revenge; First Mate Starbuck at one point considers mustering the crew to mutiny, but charismatic Ahab holds them all in such thrall that they are powerless to do anything against his will. The novel ends in a three-day pursuit of Moby Dick that culminates in Ahab becoming tethered to the body of the white whale in the lines of his harpoon. Moby Dick then staves *Pequod*; ship, whaleboats, and crew all vanish in a spinning black vortex. Ishmael alone survives by floating on Queequeg's wooden coffin for a day and a night, until he is spotted and rescued by another whaleship. *Moby-Dick* was both unpopular and misunderstood in Melville's day and was not reprinted during his lifetime.

Toward the end of 1841, *Acushnet* anchored off the Galápagos Islands, and Melville gathered material for a set of ten sketches about the islands and their strange currents, which he published as "The Encantadas" (1854). The following

July, Melville and his friend Toby Greene jumped ship on Nuku Hiva in the Marquesas Islands. Melville's time in the interior forms the basis for his first novel, *Typee* (1846). This Polynesian travel narrative was enormously popular, and Melville followed it a year later with another book in a similar vein: *Omoo* (1847), which incorporates his adventures on the whaleship *Lucy Ann* and imprisonment for mutiny on Tahiti. Late in 1842, Melville spent time on board the whaleship *Charles and Henry*, time that is reflected in his third book, *Mardi* (1849), an open-ended political-philosophical romance. At the end of 1843, Melville began duty on board the naval frigate *United States*; the mistreatment of the crew that he observed, including brutal and frequent floggings, is reflected in *White-Jacket* (1850) and a novella published posthumously, *Billy Budd, Sailor* (1924).

Although two volumes of Melville's poetry—*Battle Pieces* (1866) and *Timoleon* (1891)—are not along maritime themes, *John Marr and Other Sailors* (1888) relies heavily on Melville's lifelong interaction with the sea. The fictional John Marr is obviously modeled on Melville himself: an aging man misunderstood, lonely, and bereaved. After working nearly two decades as a customs inspector in New York City, Melville died in obscurity; three decades later, a renaissance of interest in his work was ignited with Raymond Weaver's *Herman Melville: Mariner and Mystic* (1921) and continues to the present.

A number of minor writers contemporary with Melville also went to sea and published accounts of their adventures. These accounts include *Narrative of Four Voyages to the South Seas and Pacific* (1832) by Benjamin Morrell, *Tales of the Ocean and Essays of the Forecastle* (1841) by John Sherburne Sleeper (under the pseudonym of "Hawser Martingale"), *Sailors' Life and Sailors' Yarns* (1847) by John Codman (under the pseudonym Captain Ringbolt), *Voyages and Travels* (1817) by Amasa Delano, and *Etchings of a Whaling Cruise* (1846) by John Ross Browne, a work that Melville not only praised but drew on for *Moby-Dick*.

### Sailor-Writers

By the end of the nineteenth century, an important group of sailor-writers emerged, encouraged by the success of Joshua Slocum's circumnavigation and publication of his *Sailing Alone around the World* (1900). These men went to sea as working seamen before the mast and then entered the literary world following the tradition of Cooper, Dana, and Melville, but with two major differences. Their perspective of the sea was, first, shaped by the scientific revolution expressed in Charles Darwin's *On the Origin of Species* (1859), which held that life originating in the sea evolved through natural selection. Second, the great, majestic sailing ships were gradually being replaced by steam, and an intense competition ensued. The fourteen books of Morgan Robertson (1861–1915), who traveled both by sail and by steam, establish his claim as one of the most memorable minor writers. Virtually unknown today, Thornton Jenkins Hains (1866–?), who used the pseudonym Captain Mayn Clew Garnett, published *The Strife of the Sea* (1903), *The Voyage of the Arrow* (1906), and *The Chief Mate's Yarns* (1912). James Brendan Connolly (1868–1957) was experienced on Gloucester fishing boats and collected his stories under the title *Out of Gloucester* (1902). The best sea fiction of Arthur Mason (1876–1955) is contained in *The Flying Bo'sun* (1920), a novel, and in *The Cook and the Captain Bold* (1924), short stories. Felix Riesenberg (1879–1939) went to sea at sixteen, made many Cape Horn passages, and was a cadet on an ocean liner. His novel *Mother Sea* (1933) followed two technical books, *The Men on Deck* (1918) and *Standard Seamanship for the Merchant Service* (1922). Bertram Marten "Bill" Adams (1879–?) cut short a sailing career because of ill health, but he wrote an autobiography, *Ships and Women* (1937), a collection of stories, *Fenceless Meadows* (1923), and a book of poetry, *Wind in the Topsails* (1931).

Jack London (John Griffith London; 1876–1916), mainly known for his Alaskan stories, had a broad and varied life of sea adventure that he drew on for his masterpiece, *The Sea-Wolf* (1904), a work also grounded in Nietzscheism and Spencerian Darwinism, and for other sea-based works, including the semiautobiographical *Martin Eden* (1909), *Adventure* (1911), *South Sea Tales* (1911), and *The Mutiny of the* Elsinore (1914). *The Cruise of the* Snark (1911), serially written while London attempted an ill-fated circumnavigation in a yacht that he had largely designed himself, developed a lasting following among yachtsmen second only to Slocum's—although the book itself is less nautical than accounts of the same voyage by his wife Charmian and young crewmate Martin Johnson.

William McFee (1881–1966), who more fully embraced the reality of steam than any of the sailor-writers, wrote *Casuals of the Sea: A Voyage of a Soul* (1918), *Derelicts* (1939), and *Swallowing the Anchor* (1925). Born on board a barque at sea off Cape Horn, Lincoln Ross Colcord (1883–1947) wrote a novel, *The Drifting Diamond* (1912), and two short story collections, *The Game of Life and Death* (1914) and *An Instrument of the Gods* (1922). His older sister Joanna Carver Colcord (1882–1960), also born at sea, published the first comprehensive collection of American sea songs, *Roll and Go: Songs of American Sailormen* (1924; revised 1938) and *Sea Language Comes Ashore* (1945). Richard Matthews Hallet (1887–1967) had a law degree from Harvard before entering commercial sailing and writing *The Lady Aft* (1915), *Trial by Fire* (1916), and *The Rolling World* (1938), his autobiography. Archie Binns (1899–1971) collaborated with Felix Riesenberg on *The Maiden Voyage* (1931) and wrote several novels based on the Pacific Northwest, the best of which is *Lightship* (1934).

Perhaps the main thrust of American literature of the sea in the twentieth century was nonfiction prose: from William Beebe's *Galapagos: World's End* (1924) and Robert Cushman Murphy's *Oceanic Birds of South America* (1936) through John Steinbeck's *Log from the Sea of Cortez* (1941; revised 1951), sea and science were melded to inform works as disparate (and as similar) as Murphy's own *Logbook for Grace* (1947), Ernest Hemingway's *The Old Man and the Sea* (1952), and Peter Matthiessen's *Far Tortuga* (1975).

[*See also* Cruising Literature; English Literature; Fiction, *subentry on* Naval Novel; Literature; Poetry; Whaling, *subentry on* Literature; *and biographical entries on figures mentioned in this article*.]

## Bibliography

Auden, W. H. *The Enchafèd Flood; or, The Romantic Iconography of the Sea*. New York: Random House, 1950. In three essays, Auden offers seminal commentary on the Romantic consciousness, explaining the differing perspectives between land and sea journeys and discussing the meaning of the sea journey from Romantic to modern literature. He shows how the opposing imagery of the sea and the desert govern artistic vision and expression.

Bender, Bert. *Sea-Brothers: The Tradition of American Sea Fiction from "Moby-Dick" to the Present*. Philadelphia: University of Pennsylvania Press, 1988. This fine analysis of the sea and its meaning in American literature covers motifs of the voyage, meditation, shipwreck, despair and isolation, and brotherhood, examining works of Hemingway, Melville, Crane, London, and Peter Matthiessen, as well as ten more minor sailor-writers.

Busch, Briton Cooper. *Whaling Will Never Do for Me: The American Whaleman in the Nineteenth Century*. Lexington: University Press of Kentucky, 1994. Busch explores the motivation that drove men to go on multiyear voyages in pursuit of the whale, and their options if they wished to cut their voyage short. He examines issues of race and status, work and desertion, religion, whalers' wives, and waterfront havens.

Carlson, Patricia Ann, ed. *Literature and Lore of the Sea*. Amsterdam: Rodopi, 1986. Carlson has collected twenty-three expanded essays on various aspects of the sea and seafaring that were originally presented at Popular Culture Association sessions on "Literature and Lore of the Sea." The three thematic sections are "Historical Analogues," on nautical tradition; "Literary Classics," on British and American authors; and "Timeless Appeal," on the sea in human imagination.

Foulke, Robert. *The Sea Voyage Narrative*. New York: Twayne 1997. This overview traces how human attitudes about the sea have shaped the sea voyage narrative, how archetypal patterns predominate in these narratives, how the sea affects human sensibility, and how nautical character types have evolved. Foulke offers new readings of Homer, Columbus, Cook, Melville, Hemingway, and Conrad.

Gidmark, Jill B., ed. *Encyclopedia of American Literature of the Sea and Great Lakes*. Westport, Conn.: Greenwood, 2001. With more than four hundred entries exploring literary works, authors, themes, ports, and places central to America's connection with the sea, the book is an indispensable reference tool and guide for scholars and general readers alike.

Huntress, Keith, ed. *Narratives of Shipwrecks and Disasters, 1586–1860*. Ames: Iowa State University Press, 1974. Twenty-four shipwreck narratives spanning nearly three hundred years are included in this collection, each prefaced by a brief introduction by Huntress. A chronological checklist of narratives of shipwrecks and disasters is provided.

Kemp, Peter, ed. *The Oxford Companion to Ships and the Sea*. London and New York: Oxford University Press, 1976.

Laing, Alexander. *The American Heritage History of Seafaring America*. Edited by Joseph J. Thorndike. New York: American Heritage, 1974. The book examines events that led to the evolution of the distinctive character of the American seafarer, among them the revolutionaries John Adams and John Hancock and the merchant-adventurers Amasa Delano, Nathaniel Brown Palmer, and Robert Bennet Forbes. The technology of sail is also examined, as well as steam, oil, and nuclear power.

Miller, Pamela A., comp. *And the Whale Is Ours: Creative Writing of American Whalemen*. Boston: David R. Godine; Sharon, Mass.: Kendall Whaling Museum, 1979.

Philbrick, Thomas. *James Fenimore Cooper and the Development of American Sea Fiction*. Cambridge, Mass.: Harvard University Press, 1961. The interest of America in the sea and its affairs during the first half of the nineteenth century is examined in depth, with a focus on how the works of James Fenimore Cooper and his contemporaries portray the ocean as a symbol for nature and the human condition.

Smith, Myron J., Jr., and Robert C. Weller. *Sea Fiction Guide*. Metuchen, N.J.: Scarecrow Press, 1976. This extensive bibliography of British and American maritime novels includes many annotated entries as well as indexes of pseudonyms and joint authors, of book titles, and of book topics.

Springer, Haskell, ed. *America and the Sea: A Literary History*. Athens: University of Georgia Press, 1995.

Stein, Roger B. *Seascape and the American Imagination*. New York: Potter, 1975.

Wharton, Donald P., ed. *In the Trough of the Sea: Selected American Sea-Deliverance Narratives, 1610–1766*. Westport, Conn.: Greenwood, 1979. This work collects for the first time fourteen sea-deliverance narratives of the colonial period, all except one in complete versions. They are good tales of historical merit—powerful accounts of storms, abduction, and piracy.

JILL BARNUM

# Sea Fiction

In 1806, as the United States was preparing to enter a golden age of maritime activity, James Fenimore Cooper sailed as a common seafarer on board the merchantman *Sterling*. He soon became a midshipman and served for three years before ending his sea career in 1811. In 1824 he published the first American sea novel, *The Pilot*. In subsequent years, a number of other young Americans such as Richard Henry Dana, Herman Melville, and Jack London followed Cooper's example by making literary careers from their own experiences before the mast. This was a natural pattern for several reasons. First, the national identity had been shaped in large part by America's development as a maritime power in war and commerce, an identity that produced naval heroes and folk heroes before the frontiersman or cowboy began to figure in American mythmaking. Second, stories of adventures at sea have always appealed to the human imagination—tales of exposure to terrific storms, suffering and deprivation, encounters with strange peoples and places or with the unknown. More important, from antiquity the voyage or journey narrative has appealed to the human psyche as a chief means by which all peoples have sought to understand their existence and shape cultural values. The greatest works of American sea fiction proceed in this way, as a series of sea voyage narratives, each in quest of meanings that could suffice in its own time—Cooper's *The Sea Lions* (1849), Melville's *Moby-Dick* (1851), London's *The Sea-Wolf* (1904), Ernest Hemingway's *The Old Man and the Sea* (1952), Peter Matthiessen's *Far Tortuga* (1975), or even the much shorter tale by Stephen Crane, "The Open Boat" (1897).

As the dates of these works indicate, notable American sea fiction is not limited to the age of sail, though this was once thought to be the case. This is not to suggest that American novelists welcomed the age of steam as Walt Whitman did in 1856, singing of "those splendid resistless black poems, the steam-ships of the sea-board states" (letter to Ralph Waldo Emerson). Indeed, many American sea novels in the twentieth century are set on sailing ships and often celebrate that simpler and disappearing kind of sea experience. Still, a sizable body of sea fiction centering on voyages by steam, gasoline, or diesel-powered vessels demonstrates that the sea has not lost its power to excite the imagination. The *Titanic* disaster shattered the myth of "unsinkable" ships, and the sea experience continues to offer fictional material for adventure or escape, for narratives of initiation, or for analyses of the social order on board ship.

Yet, while all of these are important reasons why American sea fiction thrived even after the age of sail, more important reasons are to be found in literary history and the history of ideas. First, American sea novels often follow the pattern set by Dana's *Two Years before the Mast* (1840), where he wrote from the common sailor's point of view, expressing the nation's democratic values. Second, and even more important in terms of the narrative's quest for knowledge, sea novelists writing after the publication of Charles Darwin's *On the Origin of Species* (1859) have contemplated the sea-origins of life on earth and the human being's place in it. Whereas novelists such as Cooper or Melville had evoked the mysterious sea of Genesis, with the spirit of God moving over the face of the waters, post-Darwinian novelists exploited the sea setting as the ultimate perspective from which to contemplate the struggle for existence, human nature, and *Man's Place in Nature* (the title of T. H. Huxley's book of 1863).

## National and Maritime History

Even scholars of American literature are often surprised to learn that Cooper published at least eleven sea novels, most of which are impressive in their depictions of ships, nautical crises, seascapes, and naval battles. Actually, as Thomas Philbrick showed in 1961, Cooper originated the sea novel and won the admiration of such later sea novelists as Herman Melville and Joseph Conrad. He began his career with a trilogy of Romantic and nationalistic sea novels, *The Pilot*, *The Red Rover* (1827), and *The Water-Witch* (1830). The trilogy concerned itself with the development of American independence, *The Pilot*, for example, including a character patterned on John Paul Jones and Cooper's first portrait of an heroic sailor who embodied the democratic ideal, Long Tom Coffin. Also in this early trilogy Cooper revealed his career-long interest in maritime history, a field in which his own significant contributions are *The History of the Navy of the United States of America* (2 vols., 1839), *Lives of Distinguished American Naval Officers* (1846), and a long piece on the trial of the *Somers* mutiny.

In the early 1840s Cooper continued to draw on maritime history, particularly in *Mercedes of Castile* (1840), a novel based on the first voyage of Christopher Columbus, spiced up with a fictional love story, and in *The Two Admirals* (1842), where he advocated that the navy be organized into separate fleets commanded by different admirals. But *The Two Admirals* also features one of Cooper's famous descriptions of sea battle and exemplifies a notable development in his sea fiction, a more pronounced interest in character studies, here in his impressive portraits of the two admirals. In his last sea novels Cooper moved well beyond the Byronic Romanticism of his earlier work toward more meditative works that conceived of the sea voyage as a journey toward enlightenment. In *Homeward Bound* (1838), for example, one character remarks that "Life is like a passage at sea"; and in Cooper's last (and many think his best) sea novel, *The Sea Lions* (1849), Captain Gardiner's ordeal in Antarctica leaves him awestruck with nature's sublimity and leads to his spiritual regeneration. Also in these later novels, there is an increased degree of realism in Cooper's presentation of life at sea. This development is attributed largely to his close reading of Dana's *Two Years before the Mast* (1840), but also to his renewed acquaintance with a sailor from his years' work on board *Sterling*. Cooper rewrote and edited his friend's account of thirty-six years at sea, *Ned Myers: A Life before the Mast* (1843).

During the 1830s and 1840s a number of minor writers, mostly in the short story, capitalized on America's absorption in maritime affairs. However, only Edgar Allan Poe's stories "A MS Found in a Bottle" and "A Descent into the Maelstrom" and his short novel *The Narrative of Arthur Gordon Pym* (1838) have made a lasting impression, more for their gothic nature, the imprint of his literary genius, and his interest in polar exploration than for their treatment of maritime life.

## The Mysterious Sea

Still, Poe's interest in polar exploration, like Cooper's, is related to developments in mid-nineteenth-century science that Cooper began to draw on in *The Sea Lions* and that Melville, above all, embraced as the underlying motive for his most ambitious sea voyage narratives in *Mardi; and A Voyage Thither* (1849) and *Moby-Dick* (1851). Cooper and, far more profoundly, Melville responded to the troubling rise of geological and evolutionary thought by embracing the pre-Darwinian view of biology known as natural theology. Undergoing his spiritual regeneration, Cooper's Captain Gardiner stands in awe of "the Almighty power" that lay behind all "natural objects, and their origin"; he contemplates not only the stars but the "wonderful mechanism" and "beauty" of the tiniest insect as "the least of [the Creator's] works." But as Ishmael explains at the outset of *Moby-Dick*, the ocean's most powerful attraction is life itself. Explaining that "meditation and water are wedded forever," Ishmael surmises that we are drawn to "rivers and oceans" because they reflect the image of ourselves, "the image of the ungraspable phantom of life; and this is the key to it all." Thus, by shaping his narrative as a meditation on life, biologically, Melville revolutionized the sea novel. But of course he develops his famous cetological materials (concerning whales) as natural theology, emphasizing that the whale is the creator's most magnificent animal, as in the biblical stories of Job and Jonah. For this reason his playful use of his zoological sources (for example, his plan to classify the whales by their size, as though they were books, or his decision to classify the whale as a fish, based on the superior authority of "holy Jonah") serves to support his thesis that mere science is powerless to grasp the mystery of God's greatest creature. Ishmael concludes, "dissect him how I may . . . I know him not, and never will." Although the defiant Ahab surely expresses much of Melville's own spiritual unrest (rather like Alfred, Lord Tennyson's restless meditation *In Memoriam* (1850) on the fossil record and Nature's bloody tooth and claw), Melville willed his faith by destroying Ahab and, sadly, by insisting that the great sperm whale is "immortal in his species" and could never be hunted to extinction.

Because of *Moby-Dick*'s metaphysical intensity, even an experienced seafarer of the next generation such as Joseph Conrad thought it unreadable. Paradoxically, the greatest of all sea novels is little concerned with the kind of nautical realism that readers often expect in reference to commanding, sailing, or navigating ships. But the novel's metaphysical grandeur is inseparably linked with another of Melville's achievements, his decision, following Dana and drawing on his own experience, to narrate this voyage through the voice of a common sailor. In this way he gave us an essentially American book, celebrating the Christian-democratic values that were also being tested by events leading to the Civil War (1861–1865). Challenging conventional Christian views by "marrying" Ishmael and the cannibal Queequeg, Melville envisioned nature and the nation unified and presided over by the "great democratic God!" In this way Melville's greatest work differs profoundly from the masterpieces of sea fiction from other cultures; that is, in his reverence for "that democratic dignity which, on all hands, radiates without end from God; Himself! . . . The Centre and circumference of all democracy!"

Of Melville's several other sea novels, *Typee* (1846), *Redburn* (1849), *White-Jacket* (1850), and *Billy Budd, Sailor* (completed in 1891, 1924), are the most important. The first three draw on Melville's own experience as whaler, merchantman, and midshipman. In the last, his second masterpiece, and in his great sea story "Benito Cereno" (1855), Melville develops intense psychological and moral analyses of the captains' efforts to deal justly with evil and the threat of mutiny. Melville's portrait of Captain Vere in *Billy Budd* is so subtle and ambiguous that critics have long debated his own judgment of both the captain and the innocent sailor whom he executes. *Billy Budd* is also notable for its stark departure from Melville's quest for and celebration of "the ungraspable phantom of life." Though his faith in a Christian reality was still relatively intact, Melville was embittered by the Darwinian analysis of life and the higher criticism that questioned biblical truth.

## Sea-Origins of Life

At the end of the nineteenth century and for the first decades of the twentieth, a younger generation of minor writers responded to the eclipse of sailing ships by following the example of Dana and Melville, some helping to create a new literature of steamships. The most notable of these were Morgan Robertson, Thornton Jenkins Hains, James Brendan Connolly, Arthur Mason, Felix Riesenberg, Bill Adams, William McFee, Lincoln Ross Colcord, Richard Matthews Hallet, and Archie Binns. Robertson is still remembered for his uncanny foretelling of the *Titanic* disaster in *Futility; or, The Wreck of the* Titan (1898), and Binns's *Lightship* (1934) continues to impress its few readers. Born after the Darwinian revolution, none of these writers attempts to revivify the mysterious sea of *Moby-Dick*, and some, especially Robertson, explore the new political Darwinism that Alfred T. Mahan had postulated in *The Interest of America in Sea Power, Present and Future* (1897).

A surprising number of sea stories are included among the most important works in American fiction from the 1890s to the present. The first of these is Stephen Crane's "The Open Boat" (1897), widely thought to be one of the greatest stories of all time. In this largely autobiographical story of shipwreck, Crane uses the sea voyage narrative to explore the human's insignificance in the universe and, consequently, to rediscover for himself the traditional values of compassion and brotherhood. In 1904 Jack London drew on his own experience as a sealer to produce *The Sea-Wolf*, giving us the unforgettable sea captain Wolf Larsen, while plotting a narrative that (quite unconvincingly) envisions evolutionary progress beyond that which is embodied in Wolf. Lacking only the most recent and highest evolutionary attribute that Darwin had theorized, the moral sense, Larsen fails to survive because of the laws of sexual selection, when the heroine selects the narrator, Humphrey Van Weyden.

Continuing to explore the evolutionary reality in proximity to the sea, but without London's youthful enthusiasm for evolutionary progress through sexual love, Ernest Hemingway gave us in *To Have and Have Not* (1937) Harry Morgan, an elemental man, whose most promising attribute is that he is actually engaged in the struggle for existence. Especially because of their sexual vitality (Hemingway compares Morgan's lovemaking to that of a sea turtle), Morgan and his wife are superior to the novel's impotent yachtsmen and neurotic women. In *The Old Man and the Sea* (1952), however, Hemingway produced a masterpiece of sea fiction by adhering more closely to the essential pattern of the traditional sea voyage narrative. During his voyage into the Gulf Stream, Santiago suffers, catches, and then loses the great marlin to voracious sharks; but, more importantly, he comes to terms with the economy of all life. Though "for a long time now eating had bored him," Santiago comes to realize that he too must kill and eat, distasteful as this is because he regards the fish as his brothers. Frequently witnessing the primal scene of nature's voraciousness, as when he watched the flying fish leap into the air in order to escape the ravenous dolphins, and exhibiting his own masterful skills as a fisherman, it is ironic that Santiago should withdraw from this necessity to eat. Yet this is the key to his strange, saintlike quality: he thinks that "the punishment of hunger . . . is everything." Eventually, and ritually, he forces himself to eat; he sees "the prisms [of sunlight] in the deep dark water," illuminating the reality of life on earth; and he is spellbound to see the majestic beauty of the leaping marlin. Thus, one hundred years after *Moby-Dick*, Hemingway submits to and celebrates the necessary violence of life that enraged Ahab. Immediately before he began *his* final chase, Ahab looked out to sea and exclaimed, "Look! see yon Albicore! Who put it into him to chase and fang that flying-fish? . . . Who's to doom, when the judge himself is dragged to the bar?"

Inevitably, the fictional exploration of a Darwinian ocean led to an ecological vision of life and endangered seas that Cooper, Melville, or Conrad could not foresee. The first and greatest sea novel in this vein is Peter Matthiessen's *Far Tortuga* (1975), and it is not by accident that Matthiessen is himself a distinguished naturalist and experienced seafarer. Set in the Caribbean, approximately in the 1960s, this sea voyage narrative begins by depicting the watery planet spinning within the solar system and by suggesting the precariousness of life on earth. It recounts a doomed voyage aboard the turtling schooner *Lillias Eden*, which embarks too late in the season for the depleted turtle banks. Repeatedly, Matthiessen pictures the polluted sea and dramatizes human conflicts ashore and aboard the vessel. *Eden*'s makeshift and incomplete conversion from sail to diesel power suggests humanity's blind, headlong assault on the ocean resource. For Matthiessen, the green turtles are as wonderful and mysterious as the whale was for Melville, but they face extinction. Yet, in detailing these bleak circumstances, Matthiessen is not without hope. He continues to draw from the sea voyage narrative the characteristic and perhaps necessary optimism that it has always conveyed. The promise here is not only in the novel's warning imagery of endangered seas, but in Matthiessen's portraits of Captain Raib Avers and an ordinary seaman named Speedy. Though Raib loses his vessel and his life, he knows the sea, reveres its mysteries, and wields the captain's authority with a degree of humility that is rare in sea fiction. Speedy not only seems well equipped to survive in life, but exhibits his own respect for life when, after the shipwreck, he releases a bound turtle that had been taken aboard the catboat for provisions. Closing the novel without a period, only the image of "a figure alongshore, and white birds towarding," Matthiessen suggests his hope for what he calls the "old morning sea."

[*See also* Cooper, James Fenimore; Dana, Richard Henry, Jr.; Fiction, *subentry on* Sea Fiction; Imaginary Voyages; London, Jack; Melville, Herman; Literature; *and* Whaling, *subentry on* Literature.]

### Bibliography

Auden, W. H. *The Enchafèd Flood; or, The Romantic Iconography of the Sea*. New York: Random House, 1950.

Bender, Bert. *Sea-Brothers: The Tradition of American Sea Fiction from "Moby-Dick" to the Present*. Drawings by Tony Angell. Philadelphia: University of Pennsylvania Press, 1988.

Foulke, Robert. *The Sea Voyage Narrative*. New York: Twayne, 1997.

Gidmark, Jill B., ed. *Encyclopedia of American Literature of the Sea and Great Lakes*. Westport, Conn.: Greenwood, 2001.

Lewis, Charles Lee. *Books of the Sea: An Introduction to Nautical Literature*. Annapolis, Md.: Naval Institute Press, 1943.

Philbrick, Thomas. *James Fenimore Cooper and the Development of American Sea Fiction*. Cambridge, Mass.: Harvard University Press, 1961.

Springer, Haskell, ed. *America and the Sea: A Literary History*. Athens: University of Georgia Press, 1995.

Sylvester, Bickford. "Hemingway's Extended Vision: *The Old Man and the Sea*." *PMLA* 81, no. 1 (1966): 130–138.

Wharton, Donald P., ed. *In the Trough of the Sea: Selected American Sea-Deliverance Narratives, 1610–1766*. Westport, Conn.: Greenwood, 1979.

BERT BENDER

# Americas

This entry contains four subentries:

---

## Exploration Voyages, 1492–1509

The heroic age of European forays westward into the Ocean Sea—the Atlantic Ocean—began in 1492, with Christopher Columbus's first historic voyage. Nonetheless, to begin the story there tends to highlight the uniqueness and legendary quality of that experience and to neglect its context. Columbus's four voyages, and the many others that followed until 1509, were the logical extension of efforts that stretched back to the late thirteenth century at least and gathered momentum from the early fifteenth century onward.

Many of the merchants, adventurers, kings, and princes who dared to dream of voyages out into the great Ocean Sea were inspired by the lure of spices, fabrics, and other exotic goods that filtered into Europe via trade routes from the Far East. The presence of powerful Muslim states in the eastern Mediterranean added a religious incentive, inspiring some travelers to seek allies in the area beyond Muslim control, including the legendary Kublai Khan of the Mongols whom Marco Polo had described in the late thirteenth century. Various overland missions in the thirteenth and early fourteenth centuries traveled to the Mongol court, bringing back tales that enhanced Polo's account. The Black Death that struck much of the known world in the mid-fourteenth century severed the commercial links between Europe and Asia, but the memories persisted.

By the early fifteenth century, Europe was recovering from the demographic and economic ravages of the Black Death, and adventuresome Europeans sought new opportunities for trade and profit. At the same time, the growing strength of the Muslim Ottomans made the Eastern Mediterranean less hospitable to Christian merchants. According to some ancient and modern geographers, a route around Africa to Asia seemed viable, and Portuguese mariners and merchants led the way in exploring that possibility and establishing fortified trading posts at several strategic points on the coast. The

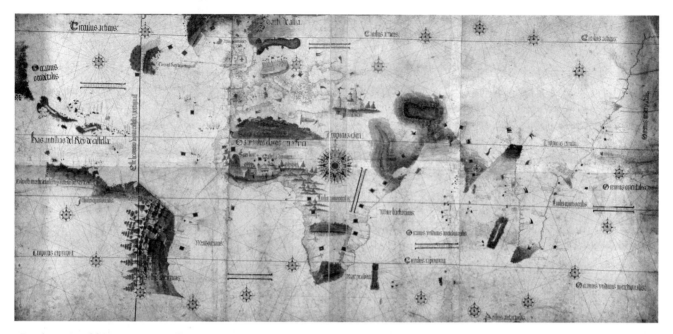

**Cantino's World Map.** In 1502 Albert Cantino, an agent of the Duke of Ferrera, secretly brought this map to Italy. It was the first map to show the papal line of demarcation from the 1494 Treaty of Tordesillas and the earliest to show a recognizable part of the Brazilian coast. Scala / Art Resource, NY

Portuguese crown also launched new initiatives westward into the Atlantic in search of islands described in ancient texts, claiming both the Azores and Madeira in the process. In both African and Atlantic exploration, merchants and mariners from the kingdom of Castile competed with the Portuguese. In the late 1470s Queen Isabella of Castile and her husband Ferdinand of Aragon launched the definitive conquest of the Canary Islands, following more than a century of sporadic efforts by others.

### Christopher Columbus

The advent of the printing press in the late fifteenth century found a growing audience of readers, including Columbus, who were inspired by the legendary tales of Asian wealth. Although very little is known about Columbus's early life, the available documentation leaves little doubt that he was Genoese, probably born in 1451 in or near the city of Genoa in northwestern Italy to a family of artisans and shopkeepers active in civic affairs but far from wealthy. His formal education was rudimentary at best; his knowledge of classical geography and cosmography seems to have been self-taught after he reached adulthood. Columbus went to sea at an early age, serving on commercial voyages in the Mediterranean and gaining valuable seafaring

experience. Sometime in the mid-1470s, he took up residence in Lisbon, where his brother Bartholomew already lived. With Lisbon as a base, he traveled down the African coast at least as far as Guinea, and into the Atlantic at least as far as the Canary Islands, the Azores, and Madeira. His later writing suggests that he also traveled into the North Atlantic as far as Bristol (England), Galway (Ireland), and probably Iceland. In 1478 or 1479 he married into a family of Italian origins that had been naturalized and ennobled in Portugal, with property on the island of Porto Santo, near Madeira. Columbus acquired maps and papers from his wife's family that presumably increased his knowledge of Atlantic seafaring.

During the seven or so years that he spent in Portugal, Columbus formulated his scheme to sail westward in search of a viable route to Asia and tried to gain support from the Portuguese crown. He failed, perhaps in part because geographers of the time generally thought the westward distance to Asia was much farther than Columbus calculated. Moreover, treaties signed in 1479 gave Castile the rights to exploration west of the Canaries, and gave Portugal the rights to exploration south and east of the Canaries around Africa, a route that showed increasing promise of finding a sea route to India. Westward exploration by Portugal bore the risk of renewed conflict with Castile without any guaranteed benefit.

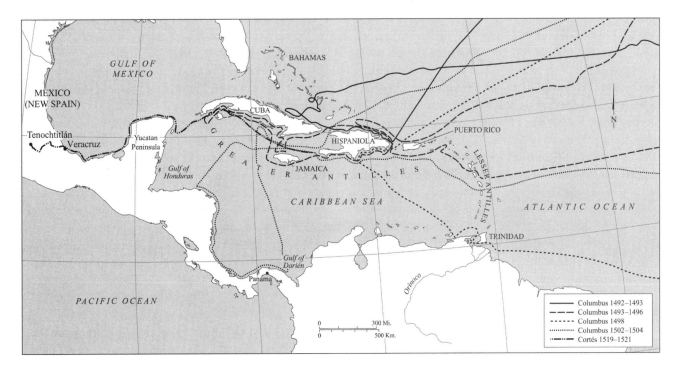

**Map of Americas Exploration, 1492–1521.** MAP BY BILL NELSON

Thwarted in Portugal, and newly widowed, Columbus moved to Spain in 1485 to plead his case. The crown was short of money because of a war against the Muslim kingdom of Granada, and Columbus's scheme seemed to hold more risks than benefits. Nonetheless, while experts at court studied his proposals, the monarchs supported Columbus with grants to discourage him from departing for France or England. At last, with the Granadan war won in 1492, and despite the misgivings of their experts, the monarchs backed his scheme, making two ships available for his use and putting up about one-eighth of the cost of the voyage. The rest of the money came from bankers and merchants in Cordoba and Seville, many of them Italians, and from royal courtiers who had been persuaded by Columbus's extraordinary skills as a self-promoter.

If his scheme succeeded, Columbus hoped to gain status and wealth from trade with Asia—the same goal that generations of mariners and merchants had sought from seaborne exploration and trade—and to discover and claim new lands along the way for his royal sponsors. He also hoped to bring the knowledge of Christianity to Asian peoples. That too had been a goal of prior explorers, and it held special interest for the Spanish monarchs. They had just taken over the last Muslim enclave in the peninsula and were in the process of forcing the Jewish community

to either convert to Christianity or leave Spain. If Asia could be given the Christian message, biblical prophesies regarding the second coming of Christ would move closer to realization. However alien such goals may sound to modern ears, they motivated a wide spectrum of fifteenth-century Europeans, including Columbus and Queen Isabella. The documentary evidence for Columbus's fervent Christianity leaves no doubt about his sincerity.

After securing royal support, Columbus went to southwest Spain and chartered a *nao* (merchant vessel) called *Santa María* that was owned by Juan de la Cosa. A royal warrant also gave him the use of two small caravels called *Pinta* and *Niña*, which would be captained, respectively, by Martín Alonso Pinzón and Vicente Yáñez Pinzón. With their help, Columbus assembled a crew of nearly a hundred men for the three ships. The region had produced generations of sailors who knew the waters off the coasts of Iberia and Africa, but they needed persuading before signing on with a foreign commander to sail into the unknown.

The three ships left from Palos de la Frontera on August 3, 1492, dropped down to the Canary Islands, then headed due west into the Ocean Sea on September 8. Columbus maintained his westward course for a month with minor variations, but sighted no land. In response to grumbling among the crew, he agreed to shift more toward the southwest on October 7. He seems to have thwarted a serious threat of mutiny on October 10, and the next night a crewman sighted land. The voyage from the Canaries had taken only thirty-three days of mostly clear sailing. On October 12, European assumptions about the vastness of the Ocean Sea disappeared with the first landfall. The identity of the island where he first landed remains as controversial as it is inconsequential. The important point was that Columbus's 1492 voyage encountered land where he expected to find Asia. For the rest of his life, Columbus continued to superimpose his mental map of Asia and its outlying islands on the physical reality of islands and mainlands in the Americas. He initially believed Cuba to be Cipango (Japan). He also believed that he was near the biblical Garden of Eden, and the lush vegetation on many Caribbean islands reinforced that belief.

After several months of exploration, the temporary desertion of Martín Alonso Pinzón and *Pinta*, and the grounding and wreck of *Santa María* on Hispaniola, Columbus decided to sail for Spain, leaving thirty-nine men behind. The return voyage was as difficult as the outbound voyage had been easy. Martín Alonso and the *Pinta* rejoined Columbus, but it took weeks to find the proper winds to carry them eastward, as supplies of food and water diminished. Then fierce winter storms separated the two caravels and threatened their survival. In early March, Columbus was forced to land in Lisbon before continuing on to southwestern Spain. Martín Alonso landed *Pinta* in Galicia in northwestern Spain and sailed into Palos on March 15, a few hours after Columbus arrived in *Niña*. Although none of them knew where they had been or what the voyage might mean, they had proven that land–presumably a part of Asia–lay just a few weeks away in the west. That extraordinary news, which rapidly spread through Europe, inspired nearly two dozen additional voyages by 1509.

Columbus himself was the first to return across the ocean, leading an expedition of seventeen ships and more than twelve hundred colonists in 1493. This time he sailed southwest from the Canaries and landed in the Lesser Antilles, working his way from there northwestward to Hispaniola. In the eleven months since he had sailed for home, the thirty-nine men he left behind had all died, either from disease or in conflicts with the local people, which did not bode well for the future. Moreover, Columbus's talents lay in seafaring, not in colonizing or administration. He chose a poor site on Hispaniola for the new colony, alienated many of the settlers, and left his brother in charge of the deteriorating situation while he explored the southern coast of Cuba and visited Jamaica. He believed that he was

near the Malay Peninsula and convinced himself that Cuba was part of the Asian mainland, which he required his men to attest to in writing. Returning to the colony, he further alienated the settlers, waged war against the now-hostile Indians, and captured hundreds to be sold into slavery, despite royal prohibitions.

When Columbus finally returned to Spain in 1496, he faced a far different reception than he had three years earlier. The monarchs had sorted out rival claims with the Portuguese by various papal bulls and the 1494 Treaty of Tordesillas and were beginning to assert much firmer royal control over the overseas enterprise. They were also losing confidence in Columbus and had given permission for others to explore the new lands in 1495, although Columbus persuaded them to reinstate his monopoly the following year.

## John Cabot

Explorers from elsewhere in western Europe were also venturing out in search of new lands and the Asian mainland. Medieval Norse voyages to the west had few lasting consequences, but by the fifteenth century fishermen from western England and Ireland knew the northern seas as their counterparts in Portugal and Spain knew the south. It is not surprising that Bristol would be a major staging area for English attempts to stake claims in the new western lands. Reports in the late 1490s mentioned several earlier attempts by Bristol seafarers to find legendary islands in the western oceans, but only the voyages in 1480 and 1481 are documented, and it is not clear where they went. After Columbus's first voyage, however, the Italian-born John Cabot moved to Bristol to pursue his dream of a northward passage across the Ocean Sea. He had failed to secure support from either Portugal or Spain for his scheme, but in 1496 he struck a deal with Henry VII of England to find new lands in the west to claim for the English crown and to rule in its name. Leaving Bristol in May 1497 in *Matthew*, he sailed west-southwest to Cape Breton Island, then east and northward along the east coast of Newfoundland through the great cod-fishing grounds later called the Grand Banks, to Cape Bauld. He returned to Bristol in August. Like Columbus he had found new lands only weeks away from Europe, and he also thought that he had reached the mainland of Asia, ruled by descendants of Kublai Khan, whom Marco Polo had visited two centuries before. Cabot led another expedition in May 1498, this time with five ships, but it is not clear what it accomplished. Only one damaged vessel made it back to Ireland; Cabot himself presumably died on the voyage.

## Columbus's Third Voyage

Farther south, Iberian explorers continued to probe the western lands. The Spanish monarchs backed Columbus on a third voyage in 1498, with precise instructions as to how he should run the settlements overseas, including the distribution of land to settlers to foment self-sufficiency. He left the Canaries in late June and dropped far south to the Cape Verde Islands before crossing the ocean. He made landfall at the island of Trinidad on August 1 and later explored the coast of Venezuela. The great volume of water flowing from the mouths of the Orinoco River led him to hope that he had reached the terrestrial paradise promised in the Bible at the end of the east. Even from that new landfall, Columbus sailed unerringly northwest to Hispaniola. The colony was in open rebellion against him and his brother, and colonists returning to Spain spread word of their maladministration. An examining magistrate sent by Ferdinand and Isabella in 1500 promptly arrested Columbus and his brother and sent them back to Spain in chains.

## Columbus's Successors

The monarchs had already ended Columbus's monopoly and issued several licenses to explore the new lands. In 1499, three former associates of Columbus—Alonso de Ojeda, Juan de la Cosa, and Amerigo Vespucci—explored the coast of South America east of the Orinoco to northern Brazil; along the way they named Venezuela (for Vespucci's Venice) and explored the Gulf of Maracaibo. Pero Alonso Niño, who had also sailed with Columbus, led another expedition on part of the same route in 1499. He was financed by the brothers Cristóbal and Luis Guerra, ship-biscuit purveyors in Seville who hoped to exploit the pearl fisheries near Trinidad.

On all these early voyages, finding and naming new lands was tied to the search for profitable opportunities to exploit. The Portuguese discovery of a sea route to India in 1497 opened the possibility of a lucrative Asian trade. Heading for India in 1500, Pedro Álvares Cabral sailed far out into the ocean for the westerlies that would carry him around the Cape of Good Hope—and discovered the eastern tip of Brazil. Other less famous landfalls were made in Brazil in 1499–1500 as explorers sought profit in the new lands. Vicente Yáñez Pinzón, the captain of *Niña* in 1492, explored the mouth of the Amazon River and Brazil's northern coast in 1499–1500, as Cabral made his landfall farther east. Vespucci explored the northwestern coast of Brazil for Portugal in 1499, with Diego de Lepe close behind him on a Spanish expedition. Vespucci sailed for Portugal again in 1501–1502 with Gonçalo Coelho, exploring down the eastern coast of South America perhaps as far as the Río de la Plata. Although Brazil lay on the Portuguese side of the line drawn by the Treaty of Tordesillas, the southwest trend of the coastline left the southern reaches of the new continent on the Spanish side.

Portugal sponsored several official voyages to the North Atlantic as well, testing the northern extension of the Tordesillas line. In 1500, Gaspar Corte-Real sailed from Terceira Island in the Azores northwest to Greenland, west to Labrador, then south to Newfoundland, before returning to Lisbon. With renewed royal support, he took two ships back to Labrador and Newfoundland in 1501 and may have gotten as far as Nova Scotia. Near the Grand Banks he captured several dozen Beothuk Indians, who were carried back to Lisbon in one of the ships to be sold as slaves, but Corte-Real's vessel and the other ship were presumably lost at sea. His brother Miguel led another Portuguese expedition in 1502. He, too, was lost at sea, but the Corte-Real brothers had staked Portugal's claims to the lucrative fishing grounds off Newfoundland, which Portuguese fishermen and entrepreneurs exploited for centuries thereafter. The extent of Portuguese coastal exploration in the North Atlantic appeared on the map by Juan de la Cosa (c. 1502), the so-called Cantino world map (1502), and Jorge Reinel's map of North America (1503).

Henry VII of England continued to be interested in overseas exploration, but he had no success encouraging merchants in Bristol to follow John Cabot's voyages. Instead, the next English efforts to explore across the ocean were led by Portuguese from Terceira Island in the Azores. João Fernandes, João Gonsales, and Francisco Fernandes arrived in Bristol in 1501 and led an expedition that year for England, but it is not clear whether they explored any new lands. João Fernandes evidently died on the voyage; his associates returned and joined forces with John Cabot's son Sebastian and two Englishmen who had previously worked with the Cabots: Hugh Eliot and Robert Thorne. Together they made annual voyages across the ocean from 1502 to 1505, exploring the extent of the cod fishery from Labrador to Cape Cod. The rich fisheries would take hard labor to exploit, and they seemed to border a truly new land, not the fabled mainland of Asia.

Sebastian Cabot determined to keep looking for a northwest passage to Asia and made the last of the early Bristol voyages in 1508–1509, although with financing from the Netherlands rather than England. He may have reached the

Hudson Strait before dangerous icebergs threatened to wreck his ships. Turning south, if his own account is to be trusted, he seems to have sailed past Labrador and Newfoundland and southwest down the coast of North America. He wintered over—perhaps in the Chesapeake region—and may have known that he could find the Gulf Stream from there to carry him back to England. Henry VII had died in the interim, and his immediate successors showed little interest in pursuing the search for a northwest passage to Asia. Cabot subsequently went to work for Spain, where he was even less likely to find royal sponsorship for northern voyages.

### Columbus's Final Voyage

The Spanish monarchs sponsored Columbus on a fourth and final voyage in 1502. Forbidden even to land in the colonies that he had once ruled, he spent a year exploring the coast of Central America from Honduras to the Gulf of Darién, and another year marooned on Jamaica. He returned to Spain in early November 1504, just a few weeks before the death of his patroness Queen Isabella. He spent the two remaining years of his life in a futile quest to recover the status and honors that he had forfeited. His former associate Juan de la Cosa attempted to found a colony at the Gulf of Urabá in 1504, as did the enterprising biscuit makers Cristóbal and Luis Guerra. Juan Díaz de Solís and Vicente Yáñez Pinzón sailed for the crown in late June 1508. By the time they returned to Spain in August 1509, they had probably explored the Honduran coast from Columbus's 1502 landfall around Yucatán and the Gulf of Campeche to Tampico.

### Attainments

By 1509—only seventeen years after Columbus's first voyage—expeditions sponsored by Spain or Portugal had mapped hundreds of islands in the Caribbean and the Atlantic coastlines of Central and South America from Tampico to Brazil. Similarly, in North America rival voyages sponsored by England and Portugal had defined the outlines of hundreds of miles of coastline and come upon one of the richest fishing grounds on earth. In the process European mariners sailing for one or more of the rival monarchies had learned most of the secrets of the Atlantic Ocean, although they were still unsure what lands they had explored on the other side.

[*See also* Cabot, Sebastian; Cartography, *subentry on* Speculative Cartography; *and* Columbus, Christopher.]

## Bibliography

Dunn, Oliver, and James E. Kelley Jr., eds. and trans. *The "Diario" of Christopher Columbus's First Voyage to America, 1492–1493*. Abstracted by Fray Bartolomé de las Casas. Norman: University of Oklahoma Press, 1989. The best translation available, with text in Spanish and English on facing pages.

Fernández-Armesto, Felipe. *Before Columbus: Exploration and Colonization from the Mediterranean to the Atlantic, 1229–1492*. Philadelphia: University of Pennsylvania Press, 1987.

Fernández-Armesto, Felipe, ed. *The Times Atlas of World Exploration*. London: Times Books, 1991.

Flint, Valerie I. J. *The Imaginative Landscape of Christopher Columbus*. Princeton, N.J.: Princeton University Press, 1992.

Guedes, Max Justo, and Gerald Lombardi, eds. *Portugal-Brazil: The Age of Atlantic Discoveries*. Lisbon, Portugal: Bertrand Editora, 1990. Beautifully illustrated exhibition catalog.

Harley, J. B. *Maps and the Columbian Encounter: An Interpretive Guide to the Travelling Exhibition*. Milwaukee, Wis.: Golda Meir Library, University of Wisconsin, 1990.

Lestringant, Frank. *Mapping the Renaissance World: The Geographical Imagination in the Age of Discovery*. Berkeley: University of California Press, 1994.

Parry, J. H. *The Age of Reconnaissance: Discovery, Exploration, and Settlement, 1450 to 1650*. New York: Praeger, 1969. Still the best general introduction; available in several subsequent editions.

Penrose, Boies. *Travel and Discovery in the Renaissance, 1420–1620*. Cambridge, Mass.: Harvard University Press, 1952.

Phillips, William D., Jr., and Carla Rahn Phillips. *The Worlds of Christopher Columbus*. Cambridge, U.K., and New York: Cambridge University Press, 1992.

Pope, Peter E. *The Many Landfalls of John Cabot*. Toronto and Buffalo, N.Y.: University of Toronto Press, 1997.

Quinn, David B. *England and the Discovery of America, 1481–1620, from the Bristol Voyages of the Fifteenth Century to the Pilgrim Settlement at Plymouth: The Exploration, Exploitation, and Trial-and-Error Colonization of North America by the English*. New York: Knopf, 1974.

Quinn, David B. *North America from Earliest Discovery to First Settlements: The Norse Voyages to 1612*. New York: Harper and Row, 1977.

Russell, Peter. *Prince Henry "The Navigator": A Life*. New Haven, Conn.: Yale University Press, 2000.

Russell-Wood, A. J. R. *A World on the Move: The Portuguese in Africa, Asia, and America, 1415–1808*. New York: St. Martin's Press, 1993.

Smith, Roger C. *Vanguard of Empire: Ships of Exploration in the Age of Columbus*. Oxford: Oxford University Press, 1993.

CARLA RAHN PHILLIPS

# Exploration Voyages, 1500–1620 (Eastern Coast)

At the opening of the sixteenth century the discoveries of Christopher Columbus in the south and those of John Cabot in the north were considered disconnected events occurring

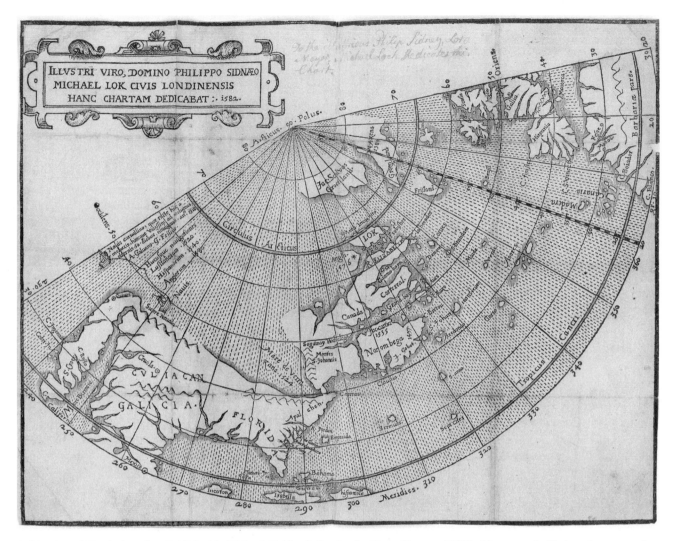

**Lok's Map of North America.** Published in Richard Hakluyt's first book, *Divers Voyages* (1582), this was probably based on a map by Girolamo de Verrazano, who had presented it to Henry VIII about 1525 and shows the western sea that Verrazzano imagined in the middle of the continent. As the first detailed representation of North America in an English publication, it had great influence on early English understanding. COURTESY OF THE JOHN CARTER BROWN LIBRARY, PROVIDENCE

somewhere along the fabled shores of China or India. The vaguely charted and largely unknown coast of eastern Asia had been their goal, but strange and heretofore unrecorded islands and coasts were encountered and understood to be barriers impeding the way to lusted-for Oriental riches. Under the sway of the Ptolemaic maps and worldview ruling the day, informed Europeans were convinced that Columbus and Cabot had reached Asia's fringing islands. However, the early sixteenth-century voyages of Juan Ponce de León and Giovanni da Verazzano suggested the existence of a separate North American continent stretching from Florida to Labrador. With this realization the page of discovery was turned from encounter to that of exploration.

Only slowly, through the determined probing of explorers such as Jacques Cartier, Samuel de Champlain, and Henry Hudson, did the existence and scope of a continent-size American landmass enter the minds of European leaders and decision makers. Well into the seventeenth century those seeking sponsorship of North American exploratory voyages by monarchs and investors continued to stress the proximity and ease of access to the fabled Orient.

### Juan Ponce de León: La Florida Encountered

Juan Ponce de León (1460–1521), a veteran of the reconquest of Spain from the Moors, volunteered to sail with

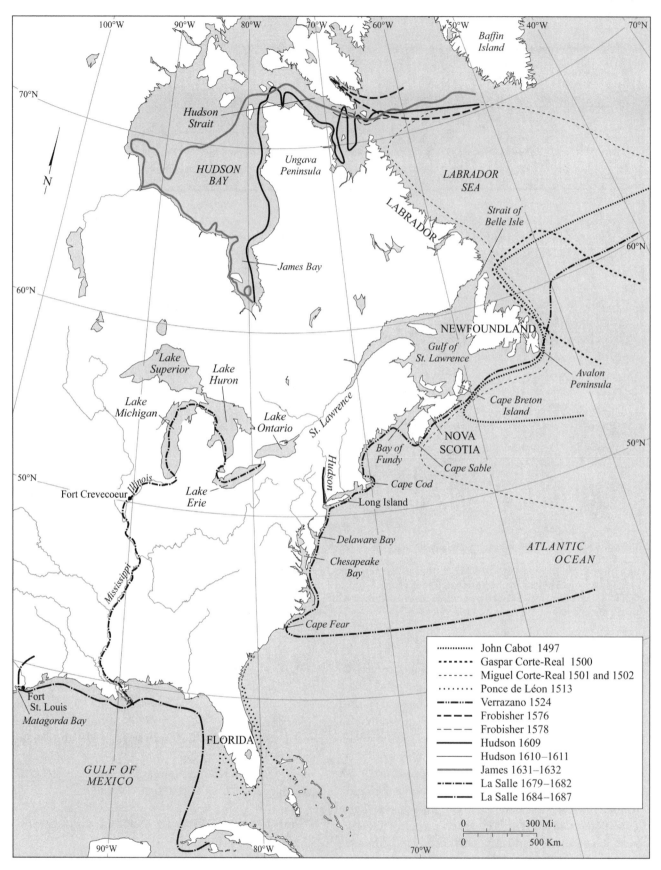

**Map of Americas Exploration, Eastern Coast.** MAP BY BILL NELSON

Map labels:

Baffin Island

Hudson Strait

HUDSON BAY

Ungava Peninsula

James Bay

LABRADOR SEA

LABRADOR

Strait of Belle Isle

NEWFOUNDLAND

Gulf of St. Lawrence

Avalon Peninsula

Lake Superior

Lake Huron

Lake Michigan

Lake Ontario

Lake Erie

St. Lawrence

Cape Breton Island

NOVA SCOTIA

Cape Sable

Bay of Fundy

Fort Crevecoeur

Illinois

Hudson

Cape Cod

Long Island

Delaware Bay

Chesapeake Bay

Mississippi

Cape Fear

ATLANTIC OCEAN

Fort St. Louis

Matagorda Bay

FLORIDA

GULF OF MEXICO

N

Legend:

............. John Cabot 1497
▄ ▄ ▄ Gaspar Corte-Real 1500
- - - - Miguel Corte-Real 1501 and 1502
∙∙∙∙∙∙ Ponce de Léon 1513
▬·▬·▬ Verrazano 1524
▬ ▬ ▬ Frobisher 1576
— — — Frobisher 1578
▬▬▬ Hudson 1609
──── Hudson 1610–1611
▬▬▬ James 1631–1632
▬·▬·▬ La Salle 1679–1682
▬··▬·· La Salle 1684–1687

0        300 Mi.
0        500 Km.

Columbus on the discoverer's second voyage to the New World. After distinguishing himself by vanquishing Indians and founding settlements on Hispaniola, Ponce de León requested permission in 1508 to lead an expedition to the island that the Indians called Buriquien (now Puerto Rico). Placer gold was found in the rivers, and he was appointed *adelantado*, or governor, of the settlement. The mining operations on Puerto Rico soon made Juan Ponce de León one of the richest men in the Indies.

In 1512 he sought and received King Ferdinand's permission to, at his own expense, "go and discover the Islands of Beniny," which were rumored to lie somewhere to the north. In 1535 the historian Gonzalo Fernández de Oviedo y Valdès wrote that it was from the Indians of those islands that we now know as the Bahamas that Ponce de León learned of "the fable of the fountain which rejuvenates or makes old men young." Rather than the fountain of youth, however, it is clear that his main motivation was the quest for Indian slaves and economic opportunity. Finding the Bahamas already nearly emptied of Indians by earlier slave raiders, he pushed his ships on to the northwest until, according to historian of the Indies, Antonio de Herrera y Tordesillas, in April 1513 they came to anchor near a shore they called La Florida, because "they discovered it in the time of the Feast of Flowers."

Landing to take formal possession and quiz the inhabitants of what they believed to be a large island, the Spaniards sailed south along the Florida coast south of Lake Worth Inlet. On April 21, Ponce de León's small fleet of three ships encountered the effects of the Gulf Stream. In an account that rings with authenticity we are told that the Spaniards "saw such a current that, although they had a strong wind, they could not go forward, but rather backward, and [although] it seemed that they were going on well . . . finally it was seen that the current was so great it was more powerful than the wind." The two vessels nearest the land anchored, but the current was so strong that the cables twisted and the third vessel, which was farther out to sea, could find no bottom. It was drawn away from land and out of sight even though the day was clear.

On shore Ponce de León's party was soon involved in a fight with the local Indians. According to Herrera two Spaniards were wounded by arrows and spears tipped with "sharpened bones and fish spines," but the Indians were unscathed. Capturing one to serve as a pilot and language informant, the Spaniards sailed round "the Cape of La Florida, which they named Cabo de Corrientes, because the water ran so swift there that it had more force than the wind, and would not allow the ships to go forward,

although they put out all sails." They named the rocks and islands making up the Florida Keys Los Martires because "the rocks as they rose to view appeared like men who were suffering."

Deciding to return home to Puerto Rico the Spaniards planned to search for islands that their Indian captives had described to them. Setting out from an island they named Matanca to commemorate the Indians that they had killed there, they sailed west into the Gulf of Mexico until they reached a group of rocky islets they called Las Tortugas, because on one they had captured "in one short time in the night . . . one hundred and sixty tortoise."

The Spaniards persisted in believing that Florida was an island. The Indians that they encountered tried to correct their misapprehension but to no avail. In concluding his review of the expedition Herrera noted, "The discovery by Juan Ponce of La Florida so ended, without knowledge that it was the mainland; nor for some years thereafter was that assurance obtained." Although his original landings and contacts on Florida's Indian-defended beaches failed to produce anything of exceptional value, Ponce de León decided to return in 1521 to attempt to found a colony. He may have been encouraged to undertake such an effort by the early reports of Hernán Cortés's discovery of the Aztecs and their fabulous supplies of gold and other portable wealth.

Using his own great personal wealth Ponce de León organized and equipped an expedition numbering about two hundred colonists with fifty horses as well as other animals and sailed for the southwest tip of Florida. Shortly after the Europeans landed a devastating Indian attack forced a hasty retreat, and Ponce de León received a mortal arrow wound. The wealthy discoverer and would-be conquistador of Florida died in Cuba shortly after the survivors arrived there.

## Giovanni da Verrazano: Linking North and South

News of North America's littoral north of Florida was first broadcast to the Europeans by Giovanni da Verrazano (c. 1485–c. 1528). A well-educated native of Florence, Verrazano persuaded Francis I of France to support a voyage to the west. Like most others at the time he firmly believed that somewhere between Ponce de León's La Florida and the codfish-rich coasts reported by Cabot there would be found a sea passage leading to Cathay and the Spice Islands. Accounts circulating from the survivors of

Magellan's circumnavigation helped Verrazano convince the French king to back such a venture.

With a single ship, *Dauphine*, Verrazano and a complement of fifty men with provisions for eight months departed from the Madeira Islands in early 1524. Employing the tried and true technique of latitude sailing, they sailed west across the Atlantic close to the 32nd parallel of north latitude. Land was sighted after covering, by Verrazano's reckoning, twelve hundred leagues (approximately thirty-six hundred miles). Sailing first to the south but fearing an encounter with the Spanish, he turned north toward the uncharted regions where he hoped to find his anticipated passage to the Orient. Large fires were sighted on shore as they approached the coast. To Verrazano this was proof that the land was inhabited. Farther north he described the land lying at what he reported to be latitude 34°N. Inland from the sandy shore he reported seeing "many beautiful fields and plains full of great forests, some sparse and some dense." Palms, laurels, cypress, and other aromatic tree varieties not common in northern Europe led him to the belief that "they belong to the Orient by virtue of the surroundings." The Indians also "resemble the Orientals," Verrazano wrote, "particularly from the farthest Sinarian regions."

As they continued north Verrazano and his men observed that the coast "veered to the east." Sailing in safe depths offshore in the vicinity of the Carolina Outer Banks they "found there an isthmus one mile wide and about two hundred miles long, in which we could see the eastern sea from the ship, halfway between west and north." To his Orient-seeking eye, the broad interior sounds lying behind the Carolina barrier islands could only be the sea "which goes around the tip of India, China, and Cathay." Verrazano continued sailing along this imagined narrow isthmus, "hoping all the time," he wrote, "to find some strait or promontory where the land might end to the north, and we could reach those blessed shores of Cathay."

This misconception of a narrow isthmus barring access to Asia was greatly reinforced by its inclusion in maps prepared by the explorer's brother, Girolamo da Verrazano, who accompanied him on the voyage. The belief that the continent of North America was pierced by a deep embayment of the Pacific Ocean persisted into the seventeenth century. Called the "Mare de Verrazano," it was copied by mapmakers, contributing mightily to hopes that a sea route to Asia could be easily won.

Encountering the flow of what he referred to as "a very great river," Verrazano entered the Hudson River estuary. He is honored there now by the impressive Verrazano Narrows suspension bridge. Likening New York's upper bay to "a very beautiful lake," the Frenchmen were impressed by the many canoe-borne Indians that they saw. Unfortunately a sudden shift in the wind made it necessary for them to return to the ship and sail onward. Verrazano wrote that he regretted their hasty departure from what later became New York harbor "on account of its favorable conditions and beauty" and the suspicion that the surrounding hills showed signs of mineral deposits.

Sailing eastward in sight of land they coasted the length of Long Island and "discovered a triangular-shaped island" that appeared to be similar in size to the Island of Rhodes. This island is now known as Block Island, but it is the nearby mainland state that acquired the name Rhode Island. Verrazano described the island as being "full of hills covered with trees, and highly populated to judge by the fires we saw burning continually along the shore."

Landing in Rhode Island's Narragansett Bay, Verrazano enjoyed his longest sojourn ashore and compiled an ethnographically rich account of the Indians living there. Ever seeking evidence of an Asian connection he noted that "both men and women have various trinkets hanging from their ears as the Orientals do." Calling the country he visited "Refugio," Verrazano reported it to be at the latitude of Rome. Significantly, Providence, Rhode Island, is located at nearly the same latitude as Rome.

Continuing along the coast for 150 leagues (approximately 450 miles) Verrazano found the land to be "somewhat higher, with several mountains which all showed signs of minerals." In what experts assume to have been Casco Bay a somewhat harsher climate was reflected in what was, to his eyes, a far less inviting landscape than he had experienced in Narragansett Bay and farther south. However, the Frenchmen were attracted by the Indians' "skins of bear, lynxes, seawolves and other animals" and attempted to barter for them. After sailing another 150 leagues they approached the land that Cabot had discovered in latitude 50°N. By now the expedition's stores and provisions were running out and they turned toward France.

In summarizing his voyage to the king of France, Verrazano told how he eventually came to the realization that he had not reached his goal—Asia—but rather had found an unexpected new land. A true son of the Renaissance, Verrazano was no slave to tradition or dogma. His report to the king resounds with the ring of dogma-shattering modernity:

> Nevertheless, land has been found by modern man which was unknown to the ancients, another world with respect to the one they knew, which appears to be larger than

our Europe, than Africa, and almost larger than Asia, if we estimate its size correctly. All this land or New World, which we have described above is joined together, but is not linked with Asia or Africa (we know this for certain), but could be joined to Europe by Norway or Russia.... Therefore the continent would lie between two seas, to the east and west.

Verrazano's hopes of persuading Francis I to support a follow-up voyage were never realized. The French king had led his country into a disastrous war in Italy and was taken prisoner there. With no hope of royal backing, Verrazano and his brother traveled to Portugal, where they became involved with enterprises on the African coast. Verrazano met his death in the New World in 1528, when he was killed by Indians while harvesting brazilwood on the coast of South America.

As far as the lands sighted by Verrazano in the southern part of his track were concerned, the only serious attempt to explore and settle them was made by the English in their first major colonizing effort. In 1585 more than a hundred settlers landed in Roanoke Island on the Outer Banks of (modern) North Carolina, but the demoralized colonists returned home the next year. A further attempt to settle the region, named Virginia in honor of the Virgin Queen, Elizabeth I, was made in 1587, again with more than a hundred settlers. They were led by John White, who had accompanied the earlier expedition as an artist. This time the venture included several families, but it ended in tragedy, for White was unable to organize a relief expedition, and by the time he returned to Roanoke in 1590 the settlers had disappeared. Among them was his own daughter, together with her husband and daughter Virginia (the first English baby to be born in North America). All that remained of the enterprise were accounts and charts of the Roanoke region, and the superb paintings by John White of the Algonkian people, whose role in the fate of the lost colonists is still uncertain. It was the first decade of the next century before the English established permanent colonies in North America.

## Jacques Cartier: France Returns to Canada

Usually credited as being the discoverer of Canada, Jacques Cartier (1491–1557) was reared in the small port of Saint-Malo, Brittany. Little is known concerning his youth, but it appears that he had achieved a reputation as an able navigator and seaman by 1534. In that year he received a royal commission to sail to China by way of the "Baye des Chasteaulx," as the Strait of Belle Isle, a long narrow arm of the sea separating Labrador and Newfoundland, was

then known. The "castles" in the name of the strait are doubtless a reference to the gleaming white icebergs that float south through its waters in the summer months. After an easy crossing the two-ship, sixty-one-man expedition set out to test Verazzano's theory of the northern land connection with Europe.

After making a landfall at Cape Bonavista, Cartier turned north to skirt the coast and entered the Strait of Belle Isle and then sailed south along the west coast of Newfoundland. He spent the summer exploring the Gulf of Saint Lawrence. From Cape Cormorant he crossed to the Magdalen Islands and on to Prince Edward Island, which he failed to realize was an island. It was in the Bay of Chaleur that Cartier encountered a source of wealth that eventually became the hallmark and treasure of New France: furs. As the Frenchmen rowed their longboat toward shore, Indians on the beach began signaling their desire to trade by holding furs aloft on sticks.

For Cartier the Bay of Chaleur itself proved to be a disappointment when he realized that it was merely a bay and not a strait leading to Asia. Backtracking out of the bay he turned north along the Gaspé Peninsula coast. At Gaspé Harbor, Cartier met a group of about three hundred Indians in forty canoes engaged in mackerel fishing. He recognized that these were very different people from those that he had traded with earlier. He learned that they had traveled far and that in their home country they grew what he termed "indian corn like pease, the same as in Brazil, which they eat in place of bread, and of this they had a large quantity with them." Cartier provided a wealth of ethnographic details concerning these interior Indians who had canoed down the Saint Lawrence to the coastal fishery.

As the expedition prepared to return to France, Cartier had a thirty-foot cross erected at the mouth of the harbor. Three fleurs-de-lis on a shield and an engraved board inscribed with gothic letters spelling out "Long Live the King of France" were fastened to it as the Frenchmen knelt and prayed in front of the fascinated Indians. Cartier wrote that the Indian chief complained that "all this region belonged to him, and that we ought not to have set up this cross without his permission." Eager to placate the Indians, Cartier "explained to them by signs that the cross had been set up to serve as a land-mark and guidepost on coming into the harbor, and that we would soon come back and would bring them iron wares and other goods." Taking advantage of the Indians' desire for gifts and trade, he then suggested that he be allowed to take two of the chief's sons to France and bring them safely home when he returned. With his two young Indian passengers on board, he sailed back north up the Strait of Belle Isle and home to Saint-Malo.

Although he had found no clear passage to the Orient, Cartier had every reason to be pleased with the results of his first voyage of exploration. In five months he had circuited the Gulf of Saint Lawrence and encountered large groups of Indians eager to trade rich stocks of prime furs for European goods of small value. In the month following Cartier's return to Saint-Malo the king granted him a second commission, ordering him to "conduct, lead and employ three ships equipped and victualed for fifteen months, for the perfection of the navigation of lands by you already begun." He chose as his flagship a three-masted vessel of the type used by fishermen on the Newfoundland banks and named her *La Grande Hermine*. It proved to be a very well-suited and reliable vessel.

As on his first voyage Cartier entered the Gulf of Saint Lawrence by way of the Strait of Belle Isle but without bothering to land at Newfoundland. On July 15, 1535, the flagship anchored where the two Indian boys had said farewell to their family and friends the year before. Now back in familiar surroundings they acted as guides for the expedition. They told Cartier that it was not far from their landing site to the place where "began the kingdom of Saguenay," which lay up the great river they called Hochelaga.

Cartier's interest was intensified when the Indians told him that the river was navigable by canoes for so great a distance that they had never heard of anyone ever having reached its end. Being further informed that the upper Saint Lawrence narrowed and its waters were fresh, Cartier postponed exploration of the river as he continued probing for a strait on the north side of the Gulf that would lead through the land to the western sea and a path to the Orient.

When no strait was found, Cartier sailed up the Saint Lawrence River. He received a welcome from the powerful Indian chief known as Donnacona, who dwelled with his people near the site of present-day Quebec City. Cartier wrote of being favorably impressed with the fine land and its productivity. He found the nearby Isle d'Orleans fertile and with such a profusion of grapevines that he named it Bacchus's Island. Leaving the main expedition, he and a small party pushed on up the Saint Lawrence River to the large fortified Indian town of Hochelaga, near the site of modern Montreal. He wrote of being met by "more than a thousand persons . . . who gave us as good a welcome as ever a father gave his son, making great signs of joy." Before taking leave of Hochelaga, Cartier assiduously

gleaned as much geographical intelligence as possible concerning the geography, natural wealth, and peoples of Canada's interior.

Returning downriver to his ships and main party, Cartier prepared for the onset of winter near the site of what is now Quebec City. The winter proved to be far more severe than the Frenchmen had anticipated. When relationships with Donnacona's people began to sour, Cartier was forced to strengthen the fortifications around his encampment. An illness that he called "the pestilence" broke out and proved fatal to more than fifty Indians. Fear of infection caused the French to further isolate themselves from the Indians and the fresh foods that they normally received in trade. It was not long before scurvy began to take a serious toll in the French camp. Cartier finally eased their isolation and called for one of the Indians that he had taken to France to come into the camp and tell him how to cure their illness. The Indians ground the leaves and bark of spruce trees and prepared a decoction that the French were at first reluctant to drink. Finally a few of the most desperate tried it and soon benefited from the ascorbic acid in the needle-and-bark mixture.

On July 16, 1536, Cartier arrived home in Saint-Malo accompanied by a dozen kidnapped Indians, who, it was hoped, would "relate to the king the marvels he had seen in the western lands." A scheme for the colonization of Canada was organized, and the king made Cartier its "captain general." In May 1537 five vessels with supplies for two years sailed with fifteen hundred passengers with the goal of establishing a permanent settlement in New France. A series of mishaps resulted in Cartier's being replaced as leader by Jean-François de Roberval. The unbridled ferocity of Canadian winters combined with escalating Indian hostilities ended the colonization efforts in 1543, when the survivors were repatriated in France.

Although Cartier's efforts to colonize the lands that he had discovered failed, the results of his explorations proved fruitful and provided data for a generation of geographers and mapmakers who made it increasingly clear that North America was a vast continent with no clear prospect of an easy seaway through it to Asia but nonetheless was worthy of exploitation in its own right.

### Samuel de Champlain: Founder of New France

Like Cartier, Samuel de Champlain (c. 1570–1635) was reared in a small port town on the Channel coast of northwestern France and, as he wrote, was "from a very young age interested in the art of navigation, along with a love of the high seas." While still in his teens, Champlain sailed from Honfleur to Spain and from there to the West Indies, Bermuda, and South America. Between 1603 and 1635 he traveled from France to Canada on a total of twelve voyages. In 1602, Champlain was appointed hydrographer royal, and in 1603 he joined a small expedition with the aim of exploring the Saint Lawrence River to the highest point reached by Cartier. Champlain's duty was to prepare a descriptive report with maps detailing what was discovered. In addition to what he was able to see himself, Champlain gained a great deal of geographical intelligence from the Indians he encountered, including knowledge of the existence of Lake George; the Hudson River; lakes Ontario, Erie, and Huron; and Niagara Falls. He was excited by the prospect that the linked Great Lakes might provide a passage to China. In his report he described the country as eminently well suited for settlement and, most important, the Indians as friendly and eager to trade their furs with the French.

A two-ship expedition with 120 colonists was mounted the next year, but, in spite of Champlain's recommendations, it was sent to Acadia rather than the Saint Lawrence to exert monopoly control over the casual and unregulated fur trade taking place in the area between latitudes 40° and 46°N. Champlain's duty was again to explore and report on the waterways and country found there. Sailing up the Bay of Fundy the expedition chose a small island in the Saint Croix River, which serves today as the boundary between Canada and the United States. After surviving an exceedingly hard winter on the island, Champlain was asked to find a more favorable site for settlement. On the other side of the bay he chose a protected site called Port Royal. Again the harsh Canadian winter proved fatal, with twelve of the forty-five settlers succumbing to scurvy. Throughout the period in Acadia, Champlain was busy either exploring in a small boat or interrogating Indians for geographical intelligence. He sailed and explored south along the coast of New England and prepared detailed charts of the inlets and harbors that he explored. Champlain reached the conclusion that Acadia offered little in the way of a large and lucrative fur trade and that settlement should be promoted in the Saint Lawrence valley, where a route to the Orient waited to be discovered.

In 1608 the nobleman holding the royal privilege to the trading monopoly with whom Champlain was allied decided to follow his advice and shift his interest from Acadia to the Saint Lawrence valley. A settlement was established where Cartier had encamped near what is now Quebec City. As with that earlier colonial venture, the harsh

Canadian winter once more proved devastating—fifteen of the twenty-eight would-be colonists died before it was over. Champlain's faith in the suitability of settling at Quebec was shaken but not lost as the group went on to build the permanent foundations of a New France at the site that is often called the Gibraltar of North America, where the Saint Lawrence narrows enough to be commanded by shore-mounted guns. While the settlement was being built Champlain ranged far in his explorations, reaching into present-day New York State to the lake that now bears his name and up the Saint Lawrence to learn more about potential routes to Asia. In an Indian conflict in which Champlain allied with local tribes, his French soldiers helped win a decisive battle against the Iroquois. France came to regret this victory when the New York–dwelling Iroquois were provided with guns by the Dutch and rose in power to exact a fierce toll on French fur traders and settlers alike.

Subsequent seasons saw Champlain extending his explorations beyond the Lachine Rapids on the Saint Lawrence and up the Ottawa River valley to Lake Nipissing and Georgian Bay on Lake Huron and south across a lake- and river-strewn route to link up with Lake Ontario. Wisely choosing to winter in France in 1609, 1610, and 1611, and to spend the whole of 1612 there, Champlain had ample time to present his discoveries in a series of detailed and colorful reports, many of which were published with his maps.

## Henry Hudson: Discovery and Mutiny

Most widely known as the discoverer of the North American river and bay that bear his name, Henry Hudson (c. 1550–c. 1611) was an English navigator who first gained recognition leading voyages in quest of a northeast passage. In 1607 he sailed as far as the northern end of Spitzbergen Island in the service of London's Muscovy Company. In the following year Hudson succeeded in making a landing even farther east, on Novaya Zemlya, but was forced to turn back by a frightened and near mutinous crew. More than a simple mariner, Hudson developed a convincing theory that the polar sea could be navigated all the way across the pole to establish a direct route from Europe to Asia. In addition, he was convinced through his correspondence with Captain John Smith that there was a passage to Asia somewhere just to the north of Virginia. He based this latter idea in part on the fact that the coast from 37° to 41°30′ had not been thoroughly explored since Verazzano had sailed along it in 1524.

When Hudson was called to Holland by the Dutch East India Company, its leaders listened to his theories but commissioned him to return to the quest for a northeast passage. In 1609 he sailed under the company's flag north along the Norwegian coast, where once again his crew threatened mutiny if he would not turn back. Rather than return to Holland, Hudson steered west across the Atlantic. After land was sighted off Newfoundland, he turned his ship—the famous *Half Moon*—south. Reaching the latitude of Cape Hatteras, Hudson turned north to begin a careful examination of the coast to find his theorized passage to Asia.

After an investigation of Delaware Bay, Hudson sailed on to present-day New York Harbor. On September 11, 1609, *Half Moon* began her exploratory cruise up the Hudson River until it began to narrow excessively near the site of Albany. Penetration farther upriver in a small boat confirmed that no strait leading to the west lay that way, and in Hudson's mind the expedition had ended in failure. Returning across the Atlantic he made a landfall at Dartmouth in England. He and other Englishmen in the crew were not allowed to leave their homeland when the ship was sailed home to Holland.

In 1610 a group of wealthy English adventurers who believed that a more direct route to Asia could still be found in the west provided Hudson with a crew and the ship *Discovery* to sail in search of a northwest passage. After making a landfall off the northern Labrador coast, Hudson sailed on through the water body now called Hudson Strait to enter the great gulf known as Hudson Bay. Believing that he was in the Pacific Ocean, Hudson sailed south into James Bay. When no outlet was found, the poorly equipped *Discovery* was forced to winter over. Biting cold, near starvation, and deep depression, coupled with the knowledge that Hudson was only awaiting the thaw so that he could renew his exploration westward, drove most of the crew to mutiny. Before sailing home to England, however, *Discovery*'s mutineers loaded Hudson, his son, and seven who remained loyal to him in a small open boat and cast them adrift. Needless to say, they were never seen again. Captained by Robert Bylot, *Discovery* proved to be a survivor and successfully returned to England with what remained of the crew.

[*See also* Atlantic Ocean, *subentry on* Exploration Voyages, 1330s–1480s; Cabot, Sebastian; Columbus, Christopher; Northwest Passage, *subentry on* Exploration Voyages, 1500–1800; Vikings, *subentry on* Norse Voyages of Exploration.]

## Bibliography

Aldrich, Robert. *Greater France: A History of French Overseas Expansion*. New York: St. Martin's Press, 1996.

Baker, Daniel B., ed. *Explorers and Discoverers of the World*. Detroit, Mich.: Gale Research, 1993.

Fuson, Robert Henderson. *Juan Ponce de León and the Spanish Discovery of Puerto Rico and Florida*. Blacksburg, Va.: McDonald and Woodward, 2000.

Goetzmann, William H., and Glyndwr Williams. *The Atlas of North American Exploration: From the Norse Voyages to the Race to the Pole*. New York: Prentice Hall General Reference, 1992.

Quinn, David B. *England and the Discovery of America, 1481–1620*. New York: Knopf, 1973.

Quinn, Frederick. *The French Overseas Empire*. Westport, Conn.: Praeger, 2000.

Winship, George Parker, ed. *Sailors Narratives of Voyages along the New England Coast, 1524–1624*. New York, B. Franklin, 1968.

LOUIS DE VORSEY

# Exploration Voyages, 1500–1616 (South America)

The first European explorers to see the coast of what is now northern Brazil and the mouth of the Amazon River were probably Vicente Yáñez Pinzón (c. 1461–c. 1524) and Amerigo Vespucci (1454–1512), both early in 1500. Pinzón had been the owner and captain of Christopher Columbus's caravel *Niña* in 1492 and became one of the most skilled Spanish seamen of his age. Armed with a royal license, Pinzón made a remarkably fast—twenty days—crossing of the Atlantic Ocean from the Cape Verde Islands to a point farther south than any previous explorer had reported reaching. His landfall in January 1500 may have been at either Mucuripe Point, near the city of Fortaleza (latitude 3°41′ S), or Cape São Roque, near Natal in the northeastern "bulge" of Brazil—although Pinzón himself later claimed that it was Cape Santo Agostinho, even farther south (latitude 8°20′ S), near Recife in Pernambuco. Pinzón then coasted westward, probably along the so-called east-west coast toward Pará and the mouth of the Amazon. He reported fresh and muddy water at the mouth of a huge river, which he called Marañón, sailed up for some distance, and seized thirty-six of its friendly natives. Pinzón then continued northwestward to the Caribbean and the Orinoco. Some authorities feel that Pinzón's Atlantic crossing was far too rapid for him to have reached Brazil. But he was a reliable navigator and was convinced that he had crossed the equator, so most scholars credit him with being the first to see the Brazilian coast and the Amazon River, even though he wrote very little about his findings.

**Francis Drake with Native South Americans.** Theodor de Bry published this view of Sir Francis Drake with native South Americans, during his 1595–1596 voyage. From *Americae*, part VIII (1599). BILDARCHIV PREUSSISCHER KULTURBESITZ / ART RESOURCE, NY

### Amerigo Vespucci and Pedro Álvares Cabral

Amerigo Vespucci was the agent in Seville of the Florentine Medici princes. He joined Alonso de Ojeda and Juan de la Cosa to obtain a royal license in 1499, but when they reached what is now French Guiana they parted company, and Vespucci took two caravels southeastward. He investigated the mouth of a great muddy river, possibly the Amazon, but its forested banks prevented a landing. Vespucci then claimed to have sailed southeast, perhaps to Cape São Roque, before being driven home by adverse currents.

There is no doubt about the next landfall in Brazil. It was made by a fleet of thirteen Portuguese ships bound for India and commanded by Pedro Álvares Cabral (c. 1467–1520). Driven westward in the South Atlantic, the flotilla followed land birds until it reached land. Cabral was aware that in the Treaty of Tordesillas of 1494, Pope Alexander VI had awarded Spain and Portugal each half the world to convert to Christianity. The dividing line between the spheres of influence was 360 leagues (1,145 nautical miles) west of the Cape Verde Islands; land to the east of this line thus fell to Cabral's king, Manoel I. The landing was

on April 22, 1500, near a round hill that the Portuguese named Monte Pascoal (Easter Mount, at some 18° S), near what later became Porto Seguro and midway between Rio de Janeiro and Salvador da Bahia.

Cabral's fleet spent only nine days in Brazil, during which it claimed the land for Portugal, built a cross and celebrated mass, and traded and fraternized with the indigenous people. Fortunately, Cabral sent one ship back to Portugal with a report to the king by his scribe Pero Vaz de Caminha. This letter gave a vivid and accurate account of the native Tupinambá (still thought to be Asian "Indians," a name that has stuck to this day), praising their friendliness, simple but effective way of life, aptitude for conversion to Christianity, beauty, and naked innocence. Vaz de Caminha drowned later in the voyage, during which eight ships sank, but the letter to King Manoel is hailed as the first anthropological document about Brazil.

The ships that survived from Cabral's fleet returned from India laden with valuable spices and silks. Pausing at the Cape Verdes in June 1501, they encountered three ships under Gonçalo Coelho that had been sent by the king of Portugal to investigate Cabral's discovery. Coelho's

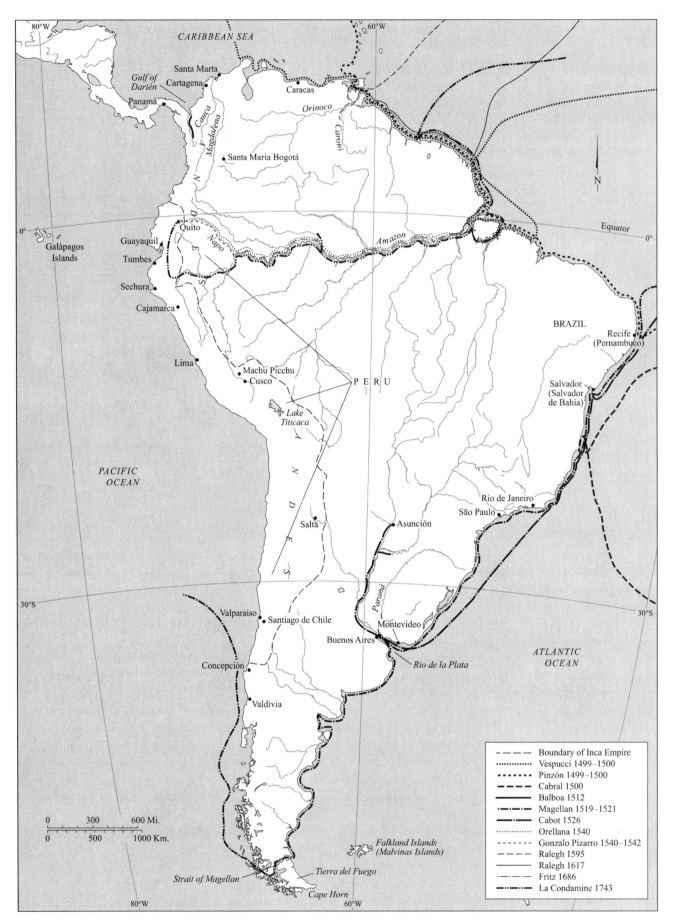

**Map of Americas Exploration, South America.** MAP BY BILL NELSON

**THE OXFORD ENCYCLOPEDIA OF MARITIME HISTORY**

ships contained Amerigo Vespucci, by now a self-styled cosmographer, and the Florentine sent a report to his Medici patron that scarcely mentioned that he was a mere passenger with the squadron. Vespucci's lively description of Brazilian Indians, flora, and fauna contained errors and exaggerations, and some of his navigational calculations were wildly inaccurate. The Portuguese colonial administrator Antonio Galvão said that Coelho reached thirty-five degrees south, which was the latitude of the Río de la Plata (River of Silver, known in English as the River Plate), but Vespucci claimed that they sailed to fifty degrees south—in bleak southern Patagonia, although he described only tropical vegetation. The conclusion of Duarte Leite, Samuel Eliot Morison, Francis Rogers, and some other modern scholars is that Vespucci was little more than an ambitious merchant with superficial scientific knowledge. What set him apart was the publication of his letter "Mundus novus" (New World) to Pier Francesco de' Medici. Spain and Portugal guarded reports from the New World as state secrets, but Vespucci's letter appeared in fifteen editions, in five languages, between 1503 and 1507. This best-selling description of amazing discoveries caused a sensation. The Burgundian cosmographer Martin Waldseemüller was so impressed that he put the name "America" on a map in 1507. As a result, the boastful Florentine has two continents named after him.

## Martim Afonso de Sousa and Juan Díaz de Solís

In the ensuing decades, Portuguese and Norman French merchantmen sailed to Brazil to barter for brazilwood (*Caesalpina echinata*, which contains a crimson dye), parrots, and, occasionally, slaves. The Atlantic seaboard of Brazil was mapped and charted by these seafarers. Then in 1530 the king of Portugal sent a five-ship flotilla under Martim Afonso de Sousa to complete the exploration and start planting colonists in Brazil, which the Portuguese regarded as theirs because—as they argued with some exaggeration—the coast between the mouths of the Amazon and Plate rivers apparently lay east of the Line of Tordesillas.

The Spanish were eager to find a southwest passage around the new landmass, because they desperately wanted to get to the wealth of India and China. The experienced pilot Juan Díaz de Solís (c. 1470–1516) investigated the mouth of the Plate but was killed by Charrúa Indians. Cristóbal de Haro, the wealthy agent of the German Fugger Bank, also explored southward, in 1513–1514. Haro then joined Cardinal Juan Rodríguez de Fonseca (the powerful

bishop of Burgos who had organized Columbus's second fleet and other voyages) to finance the Portuguese soldier and seaman Fernão de Magalhães (c. 1480–1521) in another attempt.

## Ferdinand Magellan

Magalhães, known to history as Ferdinand Magellan, became a Spanish subject, obtained a royal license from King (and Holy Roman Emperor) Carlos, and sailed in September 1519 with five ships and 270 men. The ships were well armed, with cannons, smaller guns, and especially swords, pikes, and armor for the men, and they carried plenty of trade goods to appeal to both simple and sophisticated natives. Magellan's flotilla moved via the Canaries, the west coast of Africa, the doldrums, Rio de Janeiro, and the River Plate, to the south of what is now Argentina. He named this treeless, semidesert prairie Patagonia (Land of Big Feet) because its tall people had their feet wrapped in the fur of cameloid guanacos. The sailors ate seals and penguins (which they called "flightless ducks"), which abound on this coast. They were pounded by frequent storms but carefully surveyed every bay and cape in the quest of the southwest passage.

Magellan's voyage, one of the greatest in the annals of exploration, had a fine chronicler in Antonio Pigafetta (c. 1491–c. 1534), a Lombard gentleman from Vicenza. But it was bedeviled by dissension, caused by hostility between Spaniards and the few Portuguese, by the presence of too many superfluous grandees, and by homesickness and the hardships of the Patagonian winter. At the desolate Puerto San Julián (latitude 49°20′ S) in April 1520, Magellan had to quell a full-scale mutiny, which he did with a combination of cunning, seamanship, and resolute action, as well as with fighting that resulted in some deaths. The flotilla then endured the bleak winter months, gathered food, and careened the ships, at San Julián and farther south at Santa Cruz.

Most of Magellan's men wanted to abandon the miserable enterprise, but the commander pressed on, determined to find a passage if one existed. On October 21 the ships rounded another treeless promontory that they named Cape of Virgins. For three weeks they endured storms, erratic winds, powerful currents, and "bays full of shoals and shingle, with very lofty cliffs" in "country that was rocky and also stark with eternal cold [glaciers]." They saw the fires of invisible inhabitants of the land to the south, which they named Tierra del Fuego (Land of Fire).

Magellan's flotilla investigated many inlets that proved to be blind alleys, for the strait is tortuous, complicated, and in some places quite narrow. But they noticed that the tidal flow was stronger than the ebb, which indicated another ocean ahead. So they persevered and eventually emerged onto a "vast and mighty sea," with the huge continent they had been exploring stretching northward in a straight line. Magellan boldly sailed west, with no idea of the magnitude of the southern Pacific Ocean. The great explorer was killed in a skirmish in what is now the Philippines. Two years later, in September 1522, the one surviving ship–*Victoria*, under Juan Sebastián de Elcano (c. 1476–1526)–limped back to Spain, having achieved the first circumnavigation of the world. The Spanish authorities were dismayed to learn that an immense ocean separated the new discoveries from the riches of India and China and that their part of this "New World" was the forbidding wasteland of Patagonia.

### The Pacific Coast

Six years after Vasco Núñez de Balboa (1475–1519) had crossed the Isthmus of Panama in 1513, the Spaniards founded on the Pacific shore a town that they called Panama. Ships were built on this "South Sea," and there were tentative explorations–northwestward along Central America, and southeastward to South America in 1522 by Pascual de Andagoya. The coast of what is now Colombia is a humid place of tropical forests, mudflats, and mangroves, but Andagoya learned from its indigenous people of trade with an advanced civilization farther south. They called that rich land Birú or Perú.

A leading citizen of Panama was Francisco Pizarro (c. 1475–1541) who, although illiterate and the illegitimate son of a military captain, had won prestige through twenty-two years of campaigning in these Indies. Pizarro had been with Balboa in 1513 and put his cross on the document claiming the South Sea for Spain. Now almost fifty, with an *encomienda* (commission) of Indian tribute payers, an interest in a horse stud, and appointment as an *alcalde* (mayor) of Panama, Pizarro should have contemplated well-earned retirement. Instead, he became obsessed with the quest for Peru–the tough professional soldier thus became a fanatical Don Quixote.

Pizarro and his partner Diego de Almagro (1475–1538) acquired one of Andagoya's ships and embarked in November 1524 with eighty men and four horses. The voyage down the dismal coast of Colombia was a disaster. Their various landfalls had such evocative names as "Port

of Hunger" and "Burned Village," and Almagro lost an eye in a skirmish with hostile natives. Back in Panama, with nothing to show for their hardships, they determined to try again. On March 10, 1526, Pizarro, Almagro, and a third partner agreed to commit all their fortunes to another attempt. Their second voyage involved two ships with 160 men and some horses. It lasted from December 1526 to early 1528. At a time when Pizarro was camped ashore, his pilot Bartolomé Ruiz sailed ahead and achieved the first breakthrough. He captured an oceangoing Inca raft, which had been sailing up the coast to trade for pink spondylus shells that were prized by the Incas. The raft was full of evidence of an advanced civilization: gold and silver ornaments, "including crowns and diadems, belts and bracelets, leg armour and breastplates," embroidered cloths, jewels, pots, and even a tiny scale for weighing gold or emeralds. Most of the raft's crew swam for the shore, but Ruiz captured two boys who were later trained to be interpreters between their Quechua language and Spanish.

For a period in 1527 the expedition camped on an island that they called Isla del Gallo (Cock Island–because it resembled a cock's comb), at two degrees north, near the Colombia-Ecuador border. Pizarro then moved his force north to a terrible uninhabited island they knew as Gorgona (3° N). Men were dying of disease and starvation, scavenging for crabs and edible seaweed. When Almagro sent a ship with reinforcements, the desperate men smuggled a message to the governor of Panama in which they begged to be rescued from a "crazed slaughterer." The governor ordered that any of the men might leave the clutches of their fanatical leader. Pizarro drew a famous line in the sand and challenged his men to cross it, to attempt the conquest of Peru, but only thirteen did so; the rest sailed delightedly back to Panama. The determined few now sailed down the coasts of Ecuador and Peru in a voyage of pure discovery. They saw coastal towns and were dazzled by the prosperity and sophistication of these outposts of the Inca Empire. Pizarro's men were not equipped for fighting, and they encountered nothing but hospitality.

Back in Panama, the partners decided that Pizarro must return to Spain to meet King Charles and obtain official permission to conquer the newly discovered land. He saw the king at Toledo in June 1528, showed him Inca objects, and he gained a *capitulación* (royal license) that greatly favored him over his partner Almagro. The third expedition, which sailed from Panama in December 1530, was better equipped with men and horses than the earlier voyages. This was a military venture, the goal being conquest rather than exploration. Pizarro made a strange decision: to land on the forested coast of Ecuador rather than the open desert shores of Peru. The conquistadores spent a year skirmishing and hacking down this coast, from roughly one degree north to three degrees south, before crossing from Puná Island in the Gulf of Guayaquil to the Peruvian mainland, on a flotilla of rafts, in May 1532.

Pizarro's extraordinary conquest of Peru followed this landing. He marched inland with only 162 men to meet the Inca Atahualpa in November 1532; he captured, ransomed, and executed him, and then moved through the Andes to take the Inca capital Cuzco. In January 1535, Pizarro founded a new capital, Lima, on the coast. During these years the northern Pacific seaboard of South America was well explored and charted by Spanish ships—even though between April and September it could take months for a vessel to battle south from Panama against coastal winds and the northerly Humboldt Current.

## Explorers of Chile

Pizarro's partner Diego de Almagro had been awarded the governorship of territory beyond Peru. In 1536, Almagro followed Inca roads to investigate what is now Chile, while his pilot Alonso Quintero sailed down to meet him at about thirty-two degrees south. This was the latitude of Santiago and its port, Valparaíso, towns founded in 1541 by Pedro de Valdivia (c. 1498–1553), the conqueror and settler of Chile.

In 1545 the Spaniards stumbled across the world's largest silver mine, at Potosí in the altiplano of what is now Bolivia. This treasure-house and the enormous mining town that grew around it could scarcely have been farther from Spain. It thus spurred exploration of southern Chile, to see whether that route might prove easier (and safer from pirates) than the complicated voyage via Panama and the Caribbean. The energetic Governor Valdivia encouraged exploration of the labyrinth of islands of Chile's southern coast, a region of temperate forests, stormy channels, rains, glaciers, and northerly winds and currents. He founded Chile's main ports—Valparaíso, Concepción, and Valdivia—and in 1553 sent two ships under Francisco de Ulloa to try to enter Magellan's strait from the west. They succeeded in doing this, with considerable hardship, after having mapped Chiloé Island and the sound between the Chonos islands. In 1557–1559 another exploration was sent, under Juan Fernández Ladrillero, a highly experienced seaman from Andalusia. After months of suffering, Ladrillero managed to pass through the strait and return. He left a report that contains a wealth of navigational information and practical advice, including a graphic warning about the thunderous calving of glaciers. But such dangers and hardships meant that the southern route was ignored for the next twenty years.

## Francis Drake and Willem Schouten

The Spanish authorities never expected danger from the strait, but in 1578 Queen Elizabeth's "sea dog" Francis Drake (c. 1540–1596) passed though, during what went on to be the second circumnavigation. *The World Encompassed*, by Drake's nephew John Drake, included excellent descriptions of the native Yahgans, of the "grisly sight of the cold and frozen mountains," of the risk of sudden violent winds now called williwaws, and of "birds which the Welch men name Pengwin." Once in the Pacific, Drake's ship *Golden Hind* was swept south and westward, into the apparently open sea south of the new continent. That part of the Southern Ocean is now called Drake Passage. Drake raided undefended ports of the Pacific coast as far north as California, and this prompted the Spaniards to try to catch him if he returned by the Strait of Magellan. The man they sent was Pedro Sarmiento de Gamboa (1532–?1592), an experienced soldier and navigator who had discovered the Galapagós Islands in 1567, who had campaigned against the last Inca, Tupac Amaru, and who wrote a competent *History of the Incas* in 1572. Sarmiento failed either to intercept "El Draco" or to plant a colony on the Strait of Magellan; but in 1579–1580 he made the most thorough and accurate survey of this passage until that of Captain Robert Fitzroy (and Charles Darwin) in HMS *Beagle* 250 years later.

All that remained to be explored was the southernmost tip of South America. This was done in 1616 by a Dutch flotilla commanded by Willem Corneliszoon Schouten (c. 1567–1625). After some daring seamanship, the flotilla came in sight of the southern cape, "all high hilly land covered over with snow, ending in a sharp point, which we called Cape Horn" at fifty-six degrees south. (This Horn was named after a town near Amsterdam, but Spaniards translated it as *Hornos*, meaning "ovens.") Schouten also named the strait to the southeast of Tierra del Fuego after his patron Le Maire, and named the islands east of it Staten, after the Dutch government. His discoveries established the route used by all subsequent sailors and completed the maritime exploration of South America.

[*See also* Atlantic Ocean, *subentry on* South Atlantic; Magellan, Ferdinand; *and* Pacific Ocean, *subentry on* South Pacific.]

## Bibliography

Caminha, Pero Vaz de. "Letter to King Manoel, Porto Seguro, Brazil, 1 May 1500." In *The Voyages of Pedro Álvares Cabral to Brazil and India*. Translated by William Brooks Greenlee. Hakluyt Society, 2d ser., vol. 81. London: Hakluyt Society, 1938.

Drake, John (probably). *The World Encompassed by Sir Francis Drake Carefully Collected out of the Notes of Master Francis Fletcher*. London: Nicholas Bourne, 1628. Edited by N. M. Penzer. London: Argonaut Press, 1926. Facsimile, edited by A. L. Rowse. Cleveland, Ohio: World Publishing, 1966.

Hemming, John. *The Conquest of the Incas*. London: Papermac, 1993.

Hemming, John. *Red Gold: The Conquest of the Brazilian Indians*. London: Papermac, 1995.

Jansz, Willem. "Journal ofte Beschryvinghe van de wonderlicke Reyse, ghedaen door Willem Cornelisz Schouten van Hoorn, inde Jaren 1615, 1616, en 1617." Translated by William Philip. In *Hakluytus Posthumus or Purchas His Pilgrimes*, by Samuel Purchas. London, 1619. Reprint. Glasgow, Scotland: James MacLehose, Hakluyt Society, 1906.

Magellan, Ferdinand. *The First Voyage round the World, by Magellan*. Translated and edited by Lord Stanley of Alderley. Hakluyt Society, 1st ser., vol. 52. London: Hakluyt Society, 1874. Translated from the accounts of Pigafetta.

Markham, Sir Clements R., ed. *Early Spanish Voyages to the Strait of Magellan*. Hakluyt Society, 2d ser., vol. 28. London: Hakluyt Society, 1911.

Morison, Samuel Eliot. *The European Discovery of America: The Southern Voyages, 1492–1616*. New York: Oxford University Press, 1974.

Parry, J. H. *The Discovery of South America*. London: Paul Elek, 1979.

Pigafetta, Antonio. *Il primo viaggio intorno al mondo* (1522). Edited by Camillo Manfroni. Milan: Istituto Editoriale Italiano, n.d. *Magellan's Voyage around the World by Antonio Pigafetta*. Translated by James A. Robertson. Cleveland, Ohio: Arthur H. Clark, 1906. *Magellan's Voyage: A Narrative Account of the First Circumnavigation*. Translated by R. A. Skelton. New Haven, Conn.: Yale University Press, 1969. *The Voyage of Magellan: The Journal of Antonio Pigafetta*. Translated by Paula Spurlin Paige. Englewood Cliffs, NJ: Prentice Hall, 1969.

Vespucci, Amerigo. "Mundus novus" (1503). Letter to Lorenzo di Pier Francesco de' Medici. In *Paesi nuouamente retrouati: Et Novo Mundo da Albergio Vesputio Florentino intitulato*, by Fracanzano da Montalboddo. Vicenza, Italy: Henrico Vicento, 1507. *The Letters of Amerigo Vespucci and Other Documents Illustrative of his Career*. Translated by Clements R. Markham. Hakluyt Society, 1st ser., vol. 90. London: Hakluyt Society, 1894. *The Vespucci Reprints*. Princeton, N.J.: Princeton University Press, 1916.

Xeres, Francisco de. *Verdadera relación de la conquista del Perú y provincia del Cuzco* (1534). *Reports on the Discovery of Peru*. Translated by Clements R. Markham. Hakluyt Society, 1st ser., vol. 47. London: Hakluyt Society, 1872.

JOHN HEMMING

# Exploration Voyages, 1539–1794 (Northwest Coast)

European efforts to gain knowledge of the northwest coast of America made slow and halting progress. The region's distance from Europe, contrary winds that hindered vessels sailing north from Spain's Mexican ports, and a disappointing hinterland all discouraged exploration. The first serious attempts were made in the decades after the Spanish conquest of Mexico, when Hernán Cortés sought to extend his control northward. In 1535 he reached La Paz near the southern tip of Baja California and decided to send ships along the coast to the north to search for the rumored sea passage to the Atlantic later known as the Strait of Anian. Under his instructions, Francisco de Ulloa entered the Gulf of California in 1539 and then sailed north along the Pacific shores of Baja California, at least as far north as Isla des Cedros in latitude 28° N. In the following year Hernando de Alarcón, too, reached the Gulf of California, carrying supplies for the inland expedition of Francisco Vásquez de Coronado. Alarcón entered the Colorado River and followed it by boat some ninety miles to its junction with the Gila, but failed to make contact with Coronado. In 1542 Juan Rodríguez Cabrillo commanded a more ambitious seaborne thrust to the north, reached the harbor of San Miguel (now San Diego, California), and became the first European to land in Alta California. He held his course farther north, but because of his distance off the coast failed to sight such significant harbors as Monterey and San Francisco. Despite Cabrillo's death on the voyage, the expedition explored nine hundred miles of unknown coastline as far as Cape Blanco in latitude 43° N, but it found neither riches nor any strait leading east. There was no further exploration north from New Spain until near the end of the century.

## Francis Drake

In the second half of the sixteenth century the waters of the North Pacific remained long undisturbed by European ships except for the annual galleon from Manila to Acapulco, which often sighted the northern Californian coast toward the end of its long voyage but rarely landed. It was the arrival of the English seaman Francis Drake that jolted Spanish officialdom out of its comfortable assumption that the Pacific was a Spanish lake. In the spring of 1579, after raiding settlements and ships along the Pacific shores of Spanish America, Drake's treasure-laden ship, *Golden Hind*, approached the northwest coast somewhere near the present California-Oregon border. Why Drake had sailed so far north is still not clear. He may have been searching for the entrance to the Strait of Anian (in English terminology, the Northwest Passage) by which to return home by a short route or for a favorable wind to take him across the Pacific or simply for a harbor where he could refit out of reach of the Spaniards. Exactly how far north Drake sailed is a subject of contention. One account says 42° N, another 48° N, and it has more recently been argued that he reached 53° N in Alaskan waters. Faced with what a crew member described as "extreme and nipping cold [and] most vile, thicke and stincking fogges," Drake turned back south and found a harbor where he stayed five weeks. The landing site is also far from certain, although Drake's Bay in California is the favored location. There relations with the local Indians (the coastal Miwok, if Drake was indeed in northern California) were good, and allegedly with their consent Drake took possession of the region and named it New Albion. On the maps, at least, New Albion was to have a long life—a standing challenge, if only on paper, to Spanish claims of dominion over the Pacific seaboard of the Americas. Two hundred years later the British were to revive their claim to New Albion as James Cook and his successors reached the northwest coast.

## Spanish Activity after Drake

Spanish reaction to Drake's irruption into the Pacific was leisurely, despite the arrival in the North Pacific in 1587 of another English raiding expedition, led by Thomas Cavendish, who captured the Manila galleon off Cape San Lucas (the southernmost extremity of Baja California). No Spanish ship reached the area of Drake's activities in Alta California until one of the Manila galleons did so in 1595; but the lumbering and heavily laden vessel was wrecked while investigating the coast. Seven years later Sebastián Vizcaíno, commanding a more purposeful expedition, sailed north from Acapulco and followed Cabrillo's track of sixty years earlier. At Monterey he found a sheltered harbor well supplied with wood and water that might serve as a port of call for the Manila galleon on the last leg of its long voyage to Acapulco. But beating against headwinds, and with the crews suffering from scurvy, it took Vizcaíno's ships nine months to reach Cape Mendocino just north of latitude forty degrees north. Vizcaíno turned back, but the smallest of his vessels, the pinnace *Tres Reyes*, managed to get north of Cape Blanco in latitude forty-three degrees north. There the boatswain, Esteban López, who took command of the vessel after the death of the captain and

pilot, reported that the coast turned northeast, apparently into the entrance of the Strait of Anian.

Despite this alluring prospect, the Spanish now abandoned their attempts to push north from their thinly held frontier province of New Mexico. They had not found what they had expected: the Strait of Anian, gold and silver mines, nor populous towns and cities. Apart from the pearl fisheries of the Gulf of California, the region seemed to hold little of immediate value. Moreover, the Spanish were becoming convinced that if there was a Strait of Anian somewhere to the north, perhaps it had better remain undiscovered. As one viceroy of New Spain remarked, with backward glances at the exploits of Drake and Cavendish, such a discovery could "awaken someone who was asleep." The best protection for New Spain's northern frontiers might well be their inaccessibility.

Throughout the seventeenth century the northwest coast of America remained among the least-known areas of the inhabited globe. Even so, apparently an elementary question as whether California was an island or a peninsula was not settled in favor of the latter until the journeys of the Jesuit father Eusebio Kino across the head of the Gulf of California in 1698–1702. By the end of the seventeenth century overland explorers coming from the east had not yet reached far beyond the line of Lake Superior and the Mississippi. On the Pacific coast the farthest pinprick marked on the Spanish charts remained Cape Blanco. Beyond that stretched the longest unexplored coastline in the world. The next known point of land was Asiatic Kamchatka, and what lay between was a matter of speculation and rumor, a void in which Jonathan Swift could place Gulliver's Brobdingnag—a land of giants—and geographers could place the Strait of Anian and imaginary islands. On the opposite brinks of this area stood the peninsulas of California and Kamchatka, five thousand miles apart, the one hot and arid, the other snow-covered and fogbound for much of the year. The physical contrast was indication enough of the immensity of the task attempted in the eighteenth century, which can best be seen as a giant, if hesitant, pincer movement. The Russians in the far north and the Spaniards from their bases in New Spain slowly groped their way toward each other, although the final crossing of the gap that still lay between them in the 1770s was made by the British explorer James Cook.

## The Russian Arrival

The first European approach by sea to the northwest coast of America was made by a Danish navigator, Vitus Bering, working in the service of the Russian government. In 1728 he sailed in the tiny *St. Gabriel* from Kamchatka north to the strait now known by his name. He had, it seemed, reached the eastern extremity of Asia, but haze hid the American shore and he failed to bring back definite information as to whether the continents were separated. In 1731 Bering was entrusted with a second, more ambitious expedition. After years of struggle along the overland route from Saint Petersburg across Siberia, he sailed with two vessels from Petropavlosk on the east coast of Kamchatka in 1741. His second in command, Alexei Chirikov, sighted the American coast in latitude 55°21′, but there lost both his ship's boats with their crews and was unable to land. Bering, meanwhile, had swung farther north toward the Alaskan coast, where he landed briefly at Kayak Island. On its return voyage his ship was wrecked near Kamchatka, and Bering and many of his crew died. The American landfalls of Bering's second expedition are among the defining moments in world geography, although this was clearer in retrospect than at the time, when the failure to publish reliable accounts and charts of the voyage led to much confusion about the significance of the Russian discoveries. For the moment the main impact of the expedition was commercial—the survivors reported that the area across the sea east of Kamchatka was rich in sea otters, fur seals, and foxes, and at least twenty trading ventures followed in their tracks in the middle decades of the century. In peculiar flimsy vessels often held together by leather thongs the *promyshlenniki* (Russian colonists) came near to exterminating the sea otter population and killed or enslaved many of the native Aleuts.

For a century and a half New Spain had made no sustained attempt to advance its northern frontiers, but by the 1760s alarmist reports about the Russian presence on the Alaskan coast prompted a change of policy as the Spaniards extended their military and missionary activity into Alta California. In 1769 a land party from La Paz reached San Diego and then Monterey (last seen by Europeans on the Vizcaíno expedition in 1603) and finally the great bay of San Francisco. In 1775, Juan de Ayala made the first recorded European entry through the Golden Gate and reported that the harbor was the best in the South Sea. Despite the establishment of missions and presidios at strategic points along the coast, the Spanish position in Alta California was still precarious because supply voyages from the Mexican ports could take three or four months against the headwinds, and it became a priority to find a land trail from Sonora to the Californian posts.

During these years of Spanish exploration the Russian threat from the north remained undefined but worrying, and in 1774 Juan Pérez sailed for the northwest coast in *Santiago* to latitude fifty-five degrees north, where the crew traded with the Haida Indians—the first contact between Europeans and the Indians of the northwest coast. The following year two vessels sailed north. *Santiago*, now commanded by Bruno de Hezeta, turned back because of sickness on board, and on its return voyage sighted a large opening in the coast. It was the entrance of one of North America's major rivers, the Columbia, but the vessel did not cross the bar. Seventeen years later the American trader Robert Gray entered the river and named it after his ship, *Columbia*. Meanwhile, Juan Francisco de la Bodega y Quadra, in the tiny *Sonora*, sailed far north and became the first Spaniard to reach Alaskan waters, but he saw no trace of the Russians. The fur traders were still confined to the Aleutians and nearby islands, and did not set up a permanent establishment in Alaska until 1784—and then at Kodiak, not on the mainland.

## James Cook

Spanish feelings of relief were short-lived, for during 1776 reports reached New Spain from Madrid warning that a British discovery expedition was heading for the northwest coast commanded by the most celebrated navigator of the century, Captain James Cook. After two voyages to the South Pacific, Cook was now bound to the north in search of the Pacific entrance of the Northwest Passage. His instructions were influenced by the fallacy that polar seas were ice-free, as well as by a fanciful map of the Russian discoveries drawn by Jacob von Stählin that showed a wide strait leading north between the "island" of Alaska and the American mainland. *Resolution* and *Discovery* arrived on the Oregon coast—"New Albion," as Cook was careful to call it—in March 1778. From its first landfall the ships sailed farther north and anchored at Nootka Sound, on the oceanic coast of Vancouver Island, where the local Indians displayed spectacular skills in handling their canoes and built wooden dwellings with intricate totemic carvings. In late April the ships left for Alaskan waters. The scenery was dramatic, with towering, snow-capped volcanic peaks. Hopes ran high of a strait that would take the ships north into an ice-free polar sea, but the coast turned inexorably west. The ships followed Prince William Sound until its shores closed in and traced Cook Inlet far inland. Once out to sea again, Cook edged along the tongue of the Alaskan peninsula until at last he was able to head north. Aleuts of Inuit stock now appeared in their kayaks, begging tobacco and repeating the word "Russ." In early August the ships finally reached a strait, but it was too far west to be the one shown on Stählin's map. Once they were through the opening, the reality of polar navigation was brought home to the crews when a mass of ice bore down on the ships. As the expedition retreated it was clear that it had rediscovered the strait reached by Bering fifty years earlier. Of Stählin's strait there was no sign, nor did the Russian traders encountered at Unalaska before Cook headed back to Hawaii (and to his death) have any knowledge of it.

In his final sustained feat of exploration Cook had achieved much. In a single season he had traced hundreds of miles of difficult coastline, charted the Alaskan peninsula, and precisely located Bering's strait. His explorations were preliminary surveys rather than the conclusive exercises that they had been in the South Pacific, for neither Cook nor his Russian and Spanish predecessors had determined whether the long stretches of coastline they sailed along were islands or mainland. The straits and gulfs marked on the maps of imaginative geographers might still exist, for the interior, sometimes even a few yards from the water's edge, was still unknown. But in outline, at least, the northwest coast of America was now firmly recorded on the world map.

When they returned home from the North Pacific, Cook's crews reported that they had traded sea otter skins worth a hundred dollars or more in Canton for a handful of beads. The quest for beaver had drawn men across North America almost to the Rockies, and the maritime traders in turn were quick to respond to this new lure. Expeditions were fitted out for the northwest coast, first by British merchants in China and India and then by others in Europe and the United States. By the early 1790s so many expeditions were trading along the coast—which until twenty years earlier had never seen the sails of a European vessel—that, as Washington Irving put it in his novel *Astoria*, it was as if a new gold coast had been discovered. As the traders reached the coast they realized that what Cook, sailing mostly offshore, had assumed to be mainland was a screen of islands, and that it was still possible that to the east a sea passage leading through the continent might yet be found. This now became the secondary quest of many of the maritime traders, and the primary objective of naval expeditions sent to the coast by France, Spain, and Britain.

## Cook's Successors

In 1786 the French navigator Jean François de Galaup, Comte de La Pérouse, examined Lituya Bay in Alaska for signs of a strait leading eastward, without success. In 1787, George Dixon, who had been on the coast with Cook, thought that Hecate Strait in the waters of (today's) northern British Columbia was the passage that Bartholomew de Fonte was thought to have discovered in 1640, and when William Barkley sighted a wide opening south of Nootka in latitude forty-nine degrees north, he was convinced that he had found "the long lost strait" that Juan de Fuca claimed to have sailed through in 1592. In 1790 Spain and Britain clashed over the possession of Nootka Sound and came close to war before the Nootka Sound Convention of October 1790 settled the issue—in favor of Britain more than of Spain. In the aftermath of the dispute both powers were determined to settle the rumors of a navigable northwest passage in the region. During the three summers of 1790–1792, Spanish vessels explored the intricate waterways lying inside the great mass of Vancouver Island. Farther north, Esteban José Martínez in 1788 and Salvador Fidalgo in 1790 reached Russian trading posts on the Alaska coast. In 1791 the prestigious "political-scientific" expedition of Alejandro Malaspina was diverted north from Acapulco to search Yakutat Bay in Alaska for yet another apocryphal strait, which purportedly had been discovered by Lorenzo Ferrer Maldonado in 1588.

By the time that George Vancouver's British naval expedition arrived in 1792, the Spaniards were satisfied that the straits described in the accounts of the voyages of Fuca, Fonte, and Ferrer Maldonado did not exist. Yet Vancouver followed to the letter his instructions to survey the northwest coast from thirty to sixty degrees north. After three summers of close survey work, often in torrential rain, Vancouver and his officers produced charts of meticulous accuracy, which, unlike those produced by the Spanish explorers, were published soon after the expedition's return to Europe. Among much else they showed that any transcontinental route would be not an open sea passage but a laborious series of rivers and lakes, portages and mountain passes. It was just such a journey that in 1793 brought the fur trader Alexander Mackenzie across the Rockies and to the Pacific coast, not far from where the boats of the Vancouver expedition were carrying out their surveys. The link between the land and sea exploration of northwestern America was complete.

[*See also* Cook, James, *and* Drake, Francis.]

## Bibliography

Bawlf, Samuel. *The Secret Voyage of Sir Francis Drake: 1577–1580*. Vancouver, B.C.: Douglas and McIntyre, 2003.

Cook, Warren L. *Flood Tide of Empire: Spain and the Pacific Northwest 1543–1819*. New Haven, Conn.: Yale University Press, 1973.

Frost, Orcutt. *Bering: The Russian Discovery of America*. New Haven, Conn.: Yale University Press, 2003.

Frost, Orcutt, ed. *Bering and Chirikov: The American Voyages and Their Impact*. Anchorage, Alaska: Alaska Historical Society, 1992.

Hayes, Derek. *Historical Atlas of the Pacific Northwest: Maps of Exploration of Discovery*. Seattle, Wash.: Sasquatch Books, 1999.

Mathes, W. Michael. "The Early Exploration of the Pacific Coast." In *North American Exploration*, edited by John Logan Allen, pp. 400–452. Vol. 1, *A New World Disclosed*. Lincoln and London: University of Nebraska Press, 1997.

Mathes, W. Michael. *Vizcaíno and Spanish Exploration in the Pacific Ocean 1580–1630*. San Francisco: California Historical Society, 1968.

Wagner, Henry R. *Spanish Voyages to the Northwest Coast of America in the Sixteenth Century*. San Francisco: California Historical Society, 1929. Reprint, 1966.

Williams, Glyn. *Voyages of Delusion: The Search for the Northwest Passage in the Age of Reason*. London: HarperCollins, 2002.

Wilson, Derek. *The World Encompassed: Drake's Great Voyage 1577–1580*. London: Hamilton, 1977. Reprint. London: Allison and Busby, 1998.

GLYNDWR WILLIAMS

# America's Cup

Sailing's most important competition, as well as the oldest continuously held event in international sport, the America's Cup is an international yachting competition that had thirty-one contests between 1870 and 2003. The event is named for its trophy, a silver ewer first awarded in 1851 by the Royal Yacht Squadron to the winner of a race around England's Isle of Wight. Originally called "the Squadron Cup" or (referring to its cost) "the £100 Cup" or "Hundred Guinea Cup," the trophy and event came to be known for the vessel that first won it, the New York schooner yacht *America*.

## The Rules

In 1857, *America*'s syndicate donated the trophy to the New York Yacht Club as "perpetually a Challenge Cup for friendly competition between foreign countries." The deed of gift (as amended) lays out the event's rules.

Races occur when the yacht club that last won the cup is challenged by a yacht club from another country to a match race. There are only two competitors, and they sail in waters of the defender's choice in large yachts with a maximum waterline length of 90 feet and a minimum of 44 feet (formerly 65 feet). A "mutual consent" provision encourages the defender and challenger to negotiate many conditions, such as the type of boat and the number of races to be sailed.

When the author of the deed of gift, George Schuyler, described the cup as a test of "the relative proficiency of the two countries in yachting," he summarized the three historic appeals of the America's Cup races: the spectacle of large yachts, the challenge of bow-to-bow competition between two boats, and national feeling. Even when the sailors were from other countries, the yachts' national identities have stimulated widespread interest among people who did not know a bow from a stern.

## Early Races, 1870–1937

In the first two matches, in 1870 and 1871, James Ashbury, an Englishman, was beaten before immense spectator fleets in New York Harbor. He did win one race in 1871 but lost the other four in the best-of-seven series. After two challenges from Canada, the British returned in 1885 and served as the sole challenger in the thirteen matches through 1958. In the event's low point, in 1895 the challenger, the Earl of Dunraven, charged the New York Yacht Club with cheating. Although the club was exonerated, bad feelings hung over the event until 1899, when a genial Scots-Irish merchant, Sir Thomas Lipton, issued the first of five challenges (the last was in 1930). An exemplar of the rule that grand events attract grandiose personalities, Lipton came close to winning in 1920 but never did take home what he called "the auld mug."

## Later Races, 1958–2000

Through 1937, most races were sailed in boats near the maximum length specified by the deed of gift, several of them longer than 130 feet on deck and with crews of as many as 70 professional sailors. After World War II, such boats were beyond the means of even wealthy sailors. The deed of gift was altered to permit boats of the International 12-metre class—boats of about 65 feet on deck and with mostly amateur crews of 11. After beating the Royal Yacht Squadron in 1958, the New York Yacht Club in 1962 came

*Alinghi* **winning the America's Cup.** The Swiss America's Cup-Class boat won the America's Cup at Auckland, New Zealand, with a crew of sixteen in 2003. Approximately 24 meters (80 feet) long, the boat is among the most technically advanced sailboats. © THIERRY MARTINEZ

in part because of an ingenious keel. For the second time in cup history (the first time was in 1920), the series came down to the final race. The Australians came from behind to win, ending the New York Yacht Club's 132-year winning streak.

In 1987, Conner, representing the San Diego Yacht Club of California, won the first America's Cup match held outside the United States, at Perth, Western Australia. Mutual consent quickly disintegrated. Surrounded by a cloud of law suits, in 1988 came a bizarre mismatch between a 120-foot keelboat from New Zealand and Conner's smaller but much faster catamaran, which won easily. The event recovered its bearings when challengers and defenders agreed on a new International America's Cup Class of 80-foot sloops, and the San Diego Yacht Club successfully defended the cup against Italy in 1992. Three years later, New Zealand, the world's most successful sailing nation, beat Conner in a dominating performance by Russell Coutts and his team. At Auckland in 2000, Coutts defended successfully against Italy.

The thirtieth match came at a turning point in the cup's long history. In six matches between 1983 and 2000, the trophy, which had previously changed hands only once, was won by three different challengers. As many as ten boats from half a dozen countries competed in elimination races for the right to sail in the cup match. With the stakes rising, the era of amateur sailors and part-time campaigns ended, and costs ran as high as $50 million per team, much of the funding provided by commercial sponsors attracted by worldwide television coverage. After the 2000 match, many top people on the superb 1995 and 2003 New Zealand boats were recruited by other campaigns. They included Coutts and his key people, who joined the *Alinghi* team of Switzerland and easily beat New Zealand in 2003.

With the thirty-second match scheduled for 2007 in Spain, the cup's first race in continental Europe, the America's Cup is expected to be more closely followed than ever in its long history of almost 160 years.

## Yachts, Captains, and Designers

America's Cup yachts of all types and sizes have usually been purebred, high-tech instruments built solely for day racing in moderate weather. Skittish to an extreme because of large sail areas, light construction, and small rudders, these boats require the most gifted of helmsmen. The short list of skippers who have been multiple winners includes some of the very best racing sailors in yachting history. The amateurs are the Americans Harold S. Vanderbilt (who

up against Australia, which in its first try won one race and came close to taking a second. Australians subsequently challenged regularly, often with very fast boats. The Americans kept winning because their campaigns were better organized, their boats were better sailed, and their crews were more familiar with Newport, Rhode Island, where the races were moved from New York in 1930.

Those advantages shrank beginning in 1970, when the New York Yacht Club permitted multiple challenges, which allowed two or more yacht clubs to undergo lengthy challenger eliminations. Even a losing team gained more experience at Newport than a winner had under the old regime. Well-financed challengers, meanwhile, worked hard on yacht design. In 1983, *Australia II*, owned by Allan Bond, was faster than defender Dennis Conner's *Liberty*,

won in 1930, 1934, and 1937) and Emil Mosbacher (1962, 1967). The professionals are the Americans Hank Haff (1887, 1895), Charlie Barr (1899, 1901, 1903), and Dennis Conner (1980, 1987, 1988), and the New Zealander Russell Coutts (1995, 2000, 2003).

The yachts' naval architects have included the elite of the world's yacht designers. The designers of the fastest boats include the Americans Edward Burgess, Nathanael G. Herreshoff, W. Starling Burgess, Olin J. Stephens II (designer or codesigner of the most winners, eight), and Douglas Peterson; the British designers George L. Watson, William Fife III, and Charles E. Nicholson; the Australians Alan Payne and Ben Lexcen; and the New Zealanders Laurie Davidson, Bruce Farr, and Tom Schnackenberg. Many of those names are enshrined in the America's Cup Hall of Fame at Bristol, Rhode Island.

[*See also America*; Farr, Bruce K.; Herreshoff, Nathanael; Stephens, Olin James; Watson, George Lennox; *and* Yachting and Pleasure Sailing.]

## Bibliography

Conner, Dennis, and Michael Levitt. *The America's Cup: The History of Sailing's Greatest Competition in the Twentieth Century*. New York: St. Martin's Press, 1998.

Dear, Ian. *Enterprise to Endeavour: The J-Class Yachts*. 4th ed. Dobbs Ferry, N.Y.: Sheridan House, 1999.

Knight, Lucia del Sol, and Daniel Bruce MacNaughton, eds. *The Encyclopedia of Yacht Designers*. New York: Norton, 2006.

Larsen, Paul C. *To the Third Power: The Inside Story of Bill Koch's Winning Strategies for the America's Cup*. Gardiner, Maine: Tilbury House, 1995.

Rousmaniere, John. *America's Cup Book, 1851–1983*. New York: Norton, 1983.

Rousmaniere, John. *The Low Black Schooner: Yacht America, 1851–1945*. Mystic, Conn.: Mystic Seaport Stores, 1986.

Stephens, Olin J., II. *All This and Sailing, Too: An Autobiography*. Mystic, Conn.: Mystic Seaport, 1999.

Stephens, William P. *Traditions and Memories of American Yachting*. 50th-Anniversary Edition. Brooklin, Maine: WoodenBoat Publications, 1989.

Thompson, Winfield M., and Thomas W. Lawson. *The Lawson History of the America's Cup*. Boston: Thomas W. Lawson, 1902.

JOHN ROUSMANIERE

**Amphibious Operations** War at sea has one overriding objective: to influence events on land. Until the advent of the submarine-launched ballistic missile, and later the cruise missile, the form of naval warfare that had the most direct and immediate impact on events ashore was the amphibious operation. Landing armies from the sea, whether designed for local raids or permanent occupation, has had a far quicker and more decisive effect on enemy societies than slow, silent economic strangulation by blockade.

### Early History

From the third millennium B.C.E., ships were mobilized to transport armies in the Mediterranean. The Egyptians, Greeks, Carthaginians, and Romans all used ships to project their power along the north-south axis and across to Asia Minor. The conquest of Britain by Julius Caesar in 55 B.C.E. and by Claudius in 43 C.E. relied on a sophisticated use of amphibious power. The vessel most suited for this type of warfare was the galley. Propelled by sail and oars, it could carry large numbers of fighting men over short distances. Navigation was seldom far from the sight of land, and the galley was essentially a coastal vessel, hugging coastlines and tied to ports for frequent watering and victualling. Its oars enabled it to navigate the difficult coastline of the Peloponnese and the Aegean, as well as the shallower southern shores of the Mediterranean. It could put in for shore when winds either failed or threatened. While the galley was the principal warship of the period, designed for fighting at sea, it could deliver substantial raiding parties and armies to most destinations. The galley remained in service as a mainstay of eastern Mediterranean seaborne empires, such as Venice and Ottoman Turkey, until the end of the sixteenth century. In the western Mediterranean, galleys from the Barbary states raided Christian states as far away as Ireland. France and Spain maintained their galley fleet until the middle of the eighteenth century. Similarly, in northern Europe, the Viking expansion in the eighth to tenth centuries depended on the sail-and-oared vessel. The shallow-draft Viking ship was well suited to the short sea crossings among Scandinavia, the southern Baltic coasts, Iceland, Britain, Ireland, Greenland, and beyond. The Viking ship could move easily up rivers, pushing the threat of attack and settlement to York and Novgorod. Duke William of Normandy's invasion of England in 1066 used similar vessels to land his army in Pevensey Bay.

Square-rigged sailing vessels, with their greater cargo capacity for victuals and water, could carry soldiers farther. They were used from the early Middle Ages to transport soldiers, and as these vessels developed aftercastles and forecastles, they evolved into warships to fight at sea. These

**Amphibious Operations.** The landing on Okinawa was the largest amphibious operation in the war against Japan. This view, taken on April 13, 1945, during an early phase of the three-month long operation that had begun 12 days before, shows battleships, cruisers, and destroyers in the distance with landing craft and troops on the beach. NATIONAL ARCHIVES AND RECORDS ADMINISTRATION

ships eventually became the line of battleships, with their broadside batteries, that dominated the seas between 1650 and about 1850. Their firepower and strength made them the key weapon for achieving a local superiority at sea. Eventually, they could cruise long distances to destroy commerce. They protected friendly amphibious forces and could engage enemy amphibious armadas, but they were not well suited themselves to the prosecution of amphibious war. In the two hundred years during which the wooden sailing battleship dominated naval warfare, a whole range of lesser-known vessels came into being to solve the problems created by amphibious operations. It is only toward the end of this period, in the 1790s, that the full range of vessels becomes apparent, but from the 1680s it is possible to see significant developments. Warships could be modified to transport soldiers, and merchant ships were easily converted into transports, but one of the key problems was to get the troops ashore quickly and in good order on open beaches. Ship's boats were initially used, but their relatively deep drafts meant that they grounded in deep water, leaving the soldiers to flounder with heavy personal equipment. Shallow-draft

bateaux were used in North America from the early eighteenth century, and by the 1750s specially designed landing boats were in use by the Royal Navy. The landing of heavy cannon was a particular problem that had to be overcome by cradles and boats that could be beached beam-on to the shore. Covering fire had to be provided. Small warships were initially used, but from the 1680s a new type of vessel—the bomb vessel, which carried one or two mortars—added significantly to the firepower of invading forces. By the 1790s, gunboats—ship's boats each armed with a single twenty-four-pound cannon—provided versatile inshore support. By the time of the Crimean War (1854–1856) steam paddle frigates were able to provide even more powerful mobile support inshore. The converted merchantman as transport evolved into the more specialized troopship, with its greater capacity for rapid disembarkation.

## British Supremacy

The growing domination of world trade by Great Britain during the second half of the eighteenth century owed as much to Brtain's ability to conduct effective amphibious operations as to the superiority of its battle fleet. British naval power was able to inflict significant disruption on French and Spanish colonial trade during the War of the Austrian Succession (1740–1748). This was largely achieved by the battle fleet in the Channel approaches (the Western Squadron) and by cruising squadrons based at Port Royal (Jamaica), English Harbour (Antigua), Gibraltar, and Port Mahon (Minorca). However, during the Seven Years' War (1756–1763), the British capacity to capture the colonial trade termini effectively destroyed enemy trade. It proved far more immediate and devastating than blockade and remained an essential part of British naval power into the nineteenth century.

This mid-eighteenth-century domination of amphibious warfare by Britain relied on a highly complex range of forces and logistics. It did not quickly spring into being, but owed much to developments that occurred during the first half of the century. Apart from the employment of frigate and bomb vessels for fire support, and the production of specialized landing boats, there were many other changes required, for which contemporary financial and organizational practice was ill prepared. Transports had to be hired, converted, and organized for employment all through the year. Victuals had to be provided for large numbers of soldiers. Landing procedures had to be developed, as did tactical deployment on landing. Cannon, ammunition, and all the accoutrements for siege actions had to be organized, landed, and serviced. For this last task, the employment of seamen ashore was a vital prerequisite. A large pool of manpower had to be found. The local resources of the colonies were an important source, so colonial societies had to be cajoled. Large sums of money were needed for a type of operation that was not, at the time, self-evidently decisive, so Parliament had to be carefully managed and persuaded. None of this was easily improvised at short notice, and while most other naval powers developed some capability, none developed infrastructure or practical experience to equal Britain's during the period 1750 to 1850.

From the mid-eighteenth century the results were spectacular. During the Seven Years' War, Britain captured Canada, Guadeloupe, Martinique, Dominica, Île de Gorée, Belle Île, Havana, and Manila. Amphibious operations contributed to success in India. The American Revolution (1775–1783) broke an important element in British amphibious power, in that it deprived Britain of vital American resources. Nevertheless, Britain was able to send substantial armies and all their supplies across the Atlantic for eight years. In 1776 the British mounted a major campaign against New York under the command of the brothers Admiral Richard Howe and General William Howe, which came close to destroying the rebellion. From that point on, British strategy was largely amphibious, using seaborne or river-borne forces to disrupt rebel-held territories and to support loyalist risings. Once France and Spain entered the war in 1778 and 1779, respectively, major amphibious campaigns were conducted in the Leeward Islands to protect British possessions.

Although the war was lost, British policy remained focused on maintaining its amphibious capability. During the French Revolutionary and Napoleonic Wars (1792–1815), the British followed an amphibious policy that secured a dominant position in world oceanic trade, frustrated French ambitions overseas, and supported military campaigns that drained French resources. This type of war provided the financial strength that eventually made it possible to fund European allies who finally defeated Napoleon on the battlefields of Germany and France in 1813–1814. Amphibious operations conducted in the colonies secured the West Indies and destroyed French colonial trade (1793–1798, 1809–1810). The Cape of Good Hope (1795), Ceylon (Sri Lanka), and posts in the East Indies (1796) fell to Britain. Armies were put ashore in Europe with varying degrees of success to divert French forces in Holland (1793–1794, 1799), North Germany (1805, 1807), Walcheren (1809), and Italy (1805–1806). Small operations on the French coast were aimed at disrupting invasion plans. Amphibious campaigns secured Egypt in 1801 and 1807. British naval superiority was reinforced by landings to secure local port facilities, such as Minorca in 1798 and Malta in 1799, or to destroy potential enemy warships, such as the attack on Copenhagen in 1807. Most significant of all was the operation that established a British army in Portugal in 1807. The Peninsular War (1808–1814) that followed was a major drain on Napoleonic France. The Duke of Wellington's army, which eventually drove its way across Spain to the Pyrenees, was maintained from the sea. All around the coast, the Royal Navy assisted Spanish resistance by conducting raids to divert French resources from the central front.

During the Napoleonic Wars, the reach, flexibility, and influence of British amphibious power were greater than ever before. From landing whole armies for occupation to small hit-and-run raids, the British army and the Royal Navy worked effectively together. This was only possible because of the overwhelming protection provided by the British battle fleet, which prevented any significant intervention against lumbering transports and dispersed forces. Amphibious capability under battle fleet protection remained the mainstay of British strategy for the next fifty years. British imperial expansion outside India was only made practicable by this amphibious capability (Burma, 1824, 1852, New Zealand, 1842 to 1845). The extensive land operations in the Crimea (1854–1855) depended on this capability. The amphibious assaults on Kerch and the coastal ports on the Sea of Azov up to Ternopol' during May and June 1855 did much to raise morale in the allied camp and seriously damaged the Russian supply system into Sevastopol.

Bombardment could be as powerful and persuasive as landing itself. The bombardment of Algiers in 1816 and of Acre in 1840 had demonstrated the power of naval gunfire. By mid-century, developments in propellants and explosives increased the destructive power of ships against land positions. The bombardment of the Russian dockyard and fortress of Sweaborg (Gulf of Finland) in 1855 presaged further destruction and was an important factor in the Russian decision to end the Crimean War. In the 1860s the Royal Navy built ships that were primarily designed for coastal bombardment to ensure that the French were in no doubt about the vulnerability of their ports. Landing was, however, still an important element of power projection, and while landings were not always successful—as the defeat at the batteries on the Peiho (Haihe) River on June 25, 1859, or the abortive Nile campaign of 1884 proved—amphibious capability remained an essential part of British imperial power.

## Modern Advances

Further technical changes during the second half of the nineteenth century had a significant impact on amphibious operations. The advent of steam power made landing a more precise activity, as steam pinnaces could tow in boats loaded with soldiers. Rifled artillery, chemical propellants, and explosives made covering fire more accurate and deadly. Steam vessels could support an army ashore, and steam made it possible to ensure that communications with the fleet would be secure in almost all weather. The successful bombardment and landings at Alexandria (July 11–12, 1882), the drive up the Nile to Khartoum in 1898, and the American operations in Cuba and the Philippines (1898) owed much to these technical changes. By the beginning of the twentieth century, the British army remained capable of an amphibious role, but its other role as imperial policeman, and the growing realization that it could be involved in a continental war, obscured its direc-

tion. The United States Army was little more than a frontier force, but the United States Marine Corps evolved into a dedicated amphibious army.

These technical changes, which significantly improved the prospects of amphibious warfare, had another effect that was more ambiguous. The British battle fleet no longer had unchallenged supremacy. France, Germany, and then the United States posed both quantitative and qualitative threats. The battle at sea became the focus of attention. Winning the battle at sea became the crucial factor in naval thought, and the critical question was how this could be done with the new steel and steam warships. Most navies and certainly most of the naval writers of the period from 1890 to 1939, including Captain Alfred Thayer Mahan (1840–1914) and Admiral Raoul Castex (1878–1968), hardly considered amphibious operations, or they thought them a distraction from the main purpose of the naval officer—to win the battle at sea. Similarly, soldiers' attention was turned to the great continental land battles. There were exceptions to this. The most important was Sir Julian Corbett (1853–1922), whose *Some Principles of Maritime Strategy* (1911) and two-volume history of the Seven Years' War (1907) placed amphibious operations within the context of the primary purpose of naval war—to have an impact on events ashore. According to Corbett, the Russo-Japanese War (1904–1905) demonstrated modern amphibious capability by the landing and maintenance of a Japanese field army in Korea, one capable of defeating a Russian field army at Mukden and successfully besieging the fortified port facility at Port Arthur.

With both naval and military attention deflected, it was hardly surprising, therefore, that during World War I (1914–1918) amphibious operations played a minor role. The first sea lord, Sir John Fisher (1841–1920), had ambitions to put an army on Germany's Baltic coast as late as 1915, but this came to nothing. The Gallipoli campaign (April to December 1915) was the largest amphibious operation of the war, but it was poorly planned and was executed against a background of inadequate intelligence and few improvements in technique or matériel. A plan to outflank the German right wing of the western front by landing a division in Flanders behind German lines during the third battle of Ypres (June to October 1917) was prepared but abandoned. Smaller operations had some success. The defense of Antwerp in August 1914 was a short-lived accomplishment for the Royal Marines. The attack upon Zeebrugge on April 1, 1918, was a far more dramatic example of the impact of seaborne forces.

Although the United States Marine Corps fought as a traditional infantry unit in France during the war, it had not lost its mission as an amphibious force. With the American position in the Pacific coming into potential conflict with Japanese ambitions after 1918, the Marine Corps and the U.S. Navy kept an eye on the potential operational needs of amphibious warfare. In Britain, meanwhile, the lessons of Gallipoli, where British troops had suffered heavy casualties, were not forgotten, nor did the horror of the experience blot out thinking about the future, but the purposes of amphibious operations were unclear. Defense of Hong Kong and Singapore, the possible need for an amphibious counterattack, the use of tanks in the first landing of a deployment, and the requirements for air cover all prompted development in aspects of amphibious operations such as landing craft, the concept of the mobile naval base, and changes in the *Manual on Combined Operations*. Nevertheless, given the changes in technology since the 1880s, Britain was, by 1939, unprepared for modern amphibious war both in theory and in dedicated matériel.

World War II (1939–1945) posed new challenges. One of the lessons from Gallipoli was the growing significance of the beachhead as the decisive area in the battle. In the eighteenth and nineteenth centuries, limited coastal defense-works and defending-force ground mobility usually gave an attacking force time and space to get ashore and organize before facing significant opposition. Failure to use this seaborne mobility could be disastrous. However, with the arrival of the machine gun and barbed wire, beach defenses became increasingly simple to improvise and made landings progressively more difficult. The casualties incurred by troops landing on V Beach at the Dardanelles on April 25, 1915, were largely caused by a few determined Turkish machine gunners. Getting ashore quickly and building up forces to protect the beachhead while additional forces are assembled for the breakout was clearly recognized. Accurate close-fire support was needed. That tanks had to be used in the first landing was understood, and that aircraft would be needed to defend the beachhead had been considered since 1921. However, against this, the power of the defense increased, particularly during the 1930s. Ground mobility was increased as motorized and armored units could move to the threatened zone with greater speed. Tactical air power was also a great threat to assembling invasion forces in narrow beachhead areas.

Between April and June 1940, Britain experienced all these features of modern amphibious warfare in Norway. Although landing in a nominally friendly country, British forces suffered from fast-moving German land forces,

German destroyers on their flank, and high-performance aircraft overhead. Once ejected from Europe, the only way back was through amphibious operations against increasingly powerful coastal fortifications, eventually known as Hitler's "Atlantic wall." In the meantime, successful small raids from the sea, such as at the Lofoten Islands (March 4, 1941), Vågø (December 27, 1941), and Saint-Nazaire (March 28, 1942), became an important element in British propaganda.

Likewise in the Pacific, the United States found itself involved in a predominantly amphibious war at the end of 1941. The Japanese had developed amphibious landing ships for use in China in 1937, but their rapid advance though the Pacific and Southeast Asia was largely owing to the lack of local defenses in the landing zones. The Americans faced a markedly different situation on the way back. After Guadalcanal (August 1942 to February 1943), neither the island-hopping campaign in the Pacific Ocean Area Command (under Admiral Chester Nimitz), nor the advance back to the Philippines from New Guinea by the South West Pacific Area Command (under General Douglas MacArthur), encountered massive defensive reinforcements. However, the Japanese created powerful beach defenses that had to be overcome. Getting ashore was the critical phase.

The importance of the beachhead led to major technical and operational innovations between 1942 and 1945. Early large-scale operations, such as Dakar (September 23, 1941) and Madagascar (May 5, 1942), exposed problems, often related to overoptimistic capability assessments. In particular, a disastrous landing at Dieppe (August 19, 1942) illustrated fundamental difficulties in analyzing information about a landing area, ranging from photographic reconnaissance to the geology of beaches. These experiences and the landings in North Africa (Operation Torch, November 1942) started to build up the knowledge required for offensive operations against defended areas. The same process was under way in the Pacific. The small step from Guadalcanal to the Russell Islands (February 1943) paved the way for the bigger leap to New Georgia (June 1943) and a campaign that culminated in the liberation of the Philippines in 1945. The heavy losses at Tarawa Atoll (November 1943) were a stepping-stone to improved doctrine and matériel that carried the U.S. Fifth Fleet to Okinawa in April 1945. From 1942, new ships for infantry, tanks, and rocket and gun support were being built and converted. Smaller vessels, different types of landing craft, and amphibious vehicles such as the DUKW ("duck") and the landing vehicle, tracked (LVT) series of amphibious tractors became vital to the diverse and flexible amphibious Allied armadas of 1943–1945.

The invasion of Sicily (July 10, 1943) marked the beginning of the Allied assault on fortified Europe. Some of the new vessels and vehicles were tested here. Airborne landings were coordinated with landings from the sea. Amphibious mobility assisted the campaign and was important in the rapid move to Italy (September 1943) and the attempt to outflank the German defensive positions south of Rome, known as the Gustav Line, by landing troops at Anzio (January to June 1944). It was here as well that the joint responsibilities of land, sea, and air commanders in such complex and large operations were tested. Throughout the Sicilian and Italian campaigns there were problems, but within a remarkably short period of time, lessons had been incorporated into the planning of the largest amphibious operation in history—Operation Overlord, the invasion of Normandy (June 6, 1944). The campaign in Europe retained an amphibious dimension until almost the end, as operations to clear the Scheldt estuary (November 1944) were vital to open up supply lines to the armies moving toward the Rhine. The Rhine crossings (March 1945) also demanded riverine capability.

In the Pacific, Admiral Nimitz and General MacArthur carried out the most sustained amphibious campaigns in history. They were in some respects less complicated than in Europe in that they did not involve delicate inter-Allied cooperation or interservice rivalries, but in other respects, particularly logistics, they required a massive maritime effort. The recapture of the Philippines (January to March 1945) and the capture of Okinawa (April to June 1945) sealed the fate of Japan.

## Postwar Strategy

Amphibious capability was an important element in settling the shape of the postwar world, particularly in the Far East. The landing at Inchon on the west coast of Korea on September 15, 1950, was a vital turning point in the Korean War. The air-mobile and sea-mobile capability of United Nations forces played a major part in the eventual outcome of the conflict. British defense policy east of Suez was based on a viable amphibious capability, while the attack on Suez on November 5–6, 1956, illustrated the limits of that capability in the new world order. For the next ten years Britain struggled to support its amphibious capabilities, but the government assessment of military capability and objectives, the Defence Review of February 1966, put an end to Britain's remaining global ambitions. For the United States, the Vietnam War (1965–1973) demonstrated the limitations of the world's largest and most sophisticated amphibious forces.

The dominating position of the European Central Front in the North Atlantic Treaty Organization (NATO) strategy and the relative costs and benefits of amphibious operations on a global scale did a great deal to push amphibious warfare into the background during the 1970s. United States amphibious operations remained important in local contexts such as Grenada and Lebanon in 1983, but the end of the Cold War in 1989 compelled planners to look at military operations as a complex series of global threats rather than as a bipolar contest between superpowers. This required highly variable levels of force intervention anywhere in the world. The shift in focus to projection of power by integrated military forces was apparent in United States planning documents such as the Department of the Navy publication . . . *From the Sea: Preparing the Naval Service for the Twenty-first Century* (1992) and the conceptual templates in the Joint Chiefs of Staff publications *Joint Vision 2010* and *Joint Vision 2020*. The key concept is a vision of conflict as a single battle space and the integration of land, sea, and air force operations to achieve maximum effect in any environment. The U.S. Navy intends to develop a sea-basing capability that will enable joint expeditionary forces to engage enemy land forces without substantial support from other forces. Though flexibility and responsiveness were not as effective as hoped in the early stages, Mogadishu (1990), the Gulf War (1991) and operations in the former Yugoslavia (1992–1999) and Afghanistan (2002) showed that both technology and doctrine were evolving toward effective flexible response.

Since the mid-1960s British amphibious capability had been focused on NATO's northern flank in conjunction with allied amphibious forces. However, the Falklands War (April to June 1982) did a great deal to revive the significance of amphibious warfare in Britain, in terms of both the military and naval lessons that it taught and its political profile. In 1996 the Permanent Joint Head Quarters was established, from which all joint operations would be planned and controlled, and the government review of defense priorities of July 1998, called the Strategic Defence Review (SDR), confirmed the shift to "expeditionary warfare," in which there would be a gradual merging of land, sea, and air operations to focus on a single battle space by 2015. These changes put amphibious operations back at the center of British strategic thinking, which was reflected in new platforms and weapons systems. In 2000 the Royal

Navy received HMS *Ocean*, its first new amphibious-warfare ship since 1965. Two new assault ships, HMS *Albion* and HMS *Bulwark*, joined the fleet in 2004. Two new large aircraft carriers were intended for 2015. The acquisition of submarine-launched Tomahawk cruise missiles in 1998 provided a capability for remote attacks on landlocked targets from the sea.

In the early twenty-first century amphibious operations were once again at the heart of American and British strategy. NATO, while expanding to include more land-orientated military forces, has accepted the importance of this expeditionary role. Missile and aviation technology has given bombardment from naval units, independent of landing operations, a much more significant role than ever before, but the ability to deploy land forces in enemy territories from the sea will remain a central element in naval warfare for the foreseeable future.

[*See also* Blockade; Galley; Strategy; Tactics; Wars, Maritime, *subentries on* Nineteenth-Century Wars, World Wars, *and* Wars after 1945; *and biographical entries on figures mentioned in this article.*]

## Bibliography

Aspinall-Oglander, C. F., comp. *Military Operations, Gallipoli.* 2 vols. London: Heinemann, 1929–1932.

Baer, George H. *One Hundred Years of Sea Power: The U.S. Navy, 1890–1990.* Stanford, Calif.: Stanford University Press, 1994.

Bartlett, Merrill L., ed. *Assault from the Sea: Essays on the History of Amphibious Warfare.* Annapolis, Md.: Naval Institute Press, 1983.

Castex, Raoul *Théories stratégiques.* 5 vols. Paris: Société d'Éditions Géographique, Maritimes et Coloniales, 1929–1935. Volume 5 is most relevant to amphibious operations.

Clifford, Kenneth J. *Amphibious Warfare Development in Britain and America from 1920 to 1940.* Laurens, N.Y.: Edgewood, 1983.

Corbett, Julian Stafford. *England in the Seven Years' War: A Study in Combined Strategy.* 2 vols. London: Longmans, Green, 1907.

Corbett, Julian Stafford. *Some Principles of Maritime Strategy.* London: Longmans, Green, 1911.

Coutau-Bégarie, Hervé. *La puissance maritime: Castex et la stratégie navale.* Paris: Fayard, 1985.

Evans, Michael. *Amphibious Operations: The Projection of Sea Power Ashore.* London: Brassey's, 1990.

*... From the Sea: Preparing the Naval Service for the Twenty-first Century.* Washington, D.C.: Department of the Navy, 1992.

Gardiner, Robert, ed. *The Age of the Galley: Mediterranean Oared Vessels since Pre-Classical Times.* London: Conway Maritime, 1995.

Guilmartin, John Francis, Jr. *Gunpowder and Galleys: Changing Technology and Mediterranean Warfare at Sea in the Sixteenth Century.* Cambridge, U.K.: Cambridge University Press, 1974.

Harding, Richard H. *Amphibious Warfare in the Eighteenth Century: The British Expedition to the West Indies, 1740–1742.* Suffolk, U.K.: Boydell, 1991.

Hore, Peter. *Seapower Ashore: 200 Years of Royal Navy Operations on Land.* London: Chatham, 2000.

Isely, Jeter A., and Philip A. Crowl. *The U.S. Marines and Amphibious War: Its Theory and Its Practice in the Pacific.* Princeton, N.J.: Princeton University Press, 1951.

*Joint Vision 2010.* Washington, D.C.: U.S. Joint Chiefs of Staff, 1996.

*Joint Vision 2020.* Washington, D.C.: U.S. Joint Chiefs of Staff, 2000.

Ladd, J. D. *Assault from the Sea, 1939–45: The Craft, the Landings, the Men.* Newton Abbot, U.K.: David and Charles, 1976.

Lambert, Andrew D. *The Crimean War: British Grand Strategy, 1853–56.* Manchester, U.K.: Manchester University Press, 1990.

Mahan, A. T. *The Influence of Sea Power upon History, 1660–1783.* Boston: Little, Brown, 1890. Reprint. Gretna, La.: Pelican, 2003.

Molyneux, Thomas More. *Conjunct Expeditions; or, Expeditions That Have Been Carried On Jointly by the Fleet and Army, with a Commentary on a Littoral War.* London: R. and J. Dodsley, 1759.

Pitt, Barrie. *Zeebrugge: St George's Day, 1918.* London: Cassell, 1958.

Pryor, John H. *Geography, Technology, and War: Studies in the Maritime History of the Mediterranean, 649–1571.* Cambridge, U.K.: Cambridge University Press, 1988.

Rogers, H. C. B. *Troopships and Their History.* London: Seely Service, 1963.

Speller, Ian, and Christopher Tuck. *Amphibious Warfare: Strategy and Tactics.* Staplehurst, U.K.: Spellmount, 2001.

Vagts, Alfred. *Landing Operations: Strategy, Psychology, Tactics, Politics, from Antiquity to 1945.* Harrisburg, Pa.: Military Service Publishing, 1946.

RICHARD HARDING

# Amsterdam

This entry contains two subentries:

Commercial Port
Naval Port

---

## Commercial Port

Unusually for a major port, the city of Amsterdam is not directly located on or near a seaboard. Instead, it borders the waterfront of the river IJssel at its junction with the river Amstel. The IJssel in turn was connected to the Zuider Zee and hence, more indirectly, with the North Sea. For many centuries, all trade and shipping coming from the North Sea had to be transferred near the island

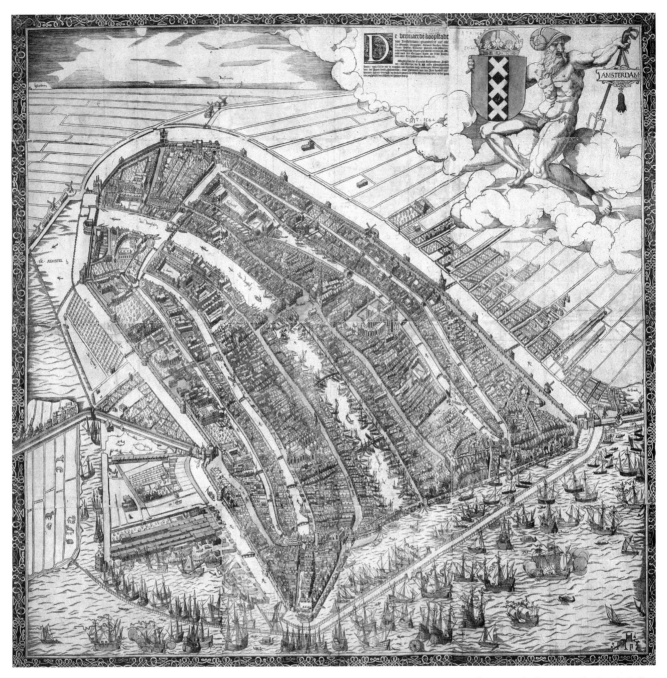

**Amsterdam.** Cornelis Anthonisz (c. 1505–1553) printed this 12-sheet wood block print in 1544. In the center is the Damrak, the city's first harbor, which was filled in during the nineteenth century. © British Library / Hip / Art Resource, NY

of Pampus into much smaller craft because of the shallowness of the waters. Large parts of the Zuider Zee were reclaimed in the twentieth century during the interwar years as part of a special employment program. By then, the port of Amsterdam had acquired a more direct route to the North Sea with the building of the North Sea Canal, which had opened in 1876.

Founded in the thirteenth century and granted special toll exemptions in 1275, Amsterdam became the largest trading city of the province of Holland during the fifteenth century, largely through its trade with the Baltic. In the second part of the sixteenth century, the outbreak of the Dutch Revolt (1568–1648) changed its scope and character dramatically. Although it was one of the last cities to join the rebel provinces (in 1578), it was without doubt the revolt's largest benefactor. The fall of Antwerp in 1585 and the closing of the Scheldt resulted in a mass exodus of migrants, ranging from skilled tradesmen and laborers to prominent wealthy merchants. Through their personal contacts and the founding of new businesses and institutions such as the Dutch East India Company (1602), the Wisselbank (1609), and the Exchange (1611), the city of Amsterdam took over Antwerp's previous role as the major trading entrepôt of Europe. Its claim to be the capital of the world was mirrored in the building of a magnificent new town hall begun in 1648.

In the first half of the seventeenth century, the city quadrupled in size, from around 50,000 people to just over 200,000. During the same period, the characteristic shape of the city with its system of canals was enlarged four times. Along its stretches great houses were erected, many of which still stand. The wealth and independence of Amsterdam's merchant elite ensured a sometimes fractious political scene, with only lukewarm support for the regime of the stadtholders. Small dockyards were located to the east of the city. The former storehouse and arsenal of the admiralty now houses the important maritime collections of the Nederlands Scheepvaartmuseum. The eighteenth century witnessed a relative decline, with London slowly taking over as the world's leading port, though Amsterdam remained the financial capital of Europe. In the first half of the nineteenth century an economic downturn set in: its population shrank and poverty was rife.

The period from 1870 to 1940 witnessed a short but impressive revival of Amsterdam's fortunes when its function as a port (instead of an entrepôt) finally came into its own. Improved accessibility by both water and rail, with the imposing Central Station built on the waterfront, and the introduction of the steam era in shipping resulted in extensive growth to the eastern and western side of the city. Burgeoning trade with Dutch colonial possessions in Indonesia and the growing transatlantic passenger trade provided further impetus.

However, after World War II, many of the quayside warehouses in the east fell derelict. This part of the city has been dramatically transformed in the early years of the twenty-first century through extensive urban redevelopment. With the building of a passenger terminal here, Amsterdam has also profited from the growing market for international cruises. The function of hub port is mainly concentrated to the west of the city with ongoing extensions (including the opening in 2002 of a unique terminal, which allows bulk handling on both sides of a ship) in order to compete with its main European rivals, Rotterdam and Antwerp.

[*See also* Antwerp; East India Companies, *subentry on* Dutch East India Company; Navies, Great Powers, *subentry on* Dutch Republic, 1577–1714; *and* Rotterdam.]

## Bibliography

Gelderblom, Oscar. *Zuid-Nederlandse kooplieden en de opkomst van de Amsterdamse stapelmarkt (1578–1630)*. Hilversum: Uitgeverij Verloren, 2000.

*Geschiedenis van Amsterdam*. 5 vols., Amsterdam: SUN, 2004–2006.

Israel, Jonathan I. *Dutch Primacy in World Trade, 1585–1740*. Oxford, U.K.: Oxford University Press, 1989.

Kuijpers, Erika. *Migrantenstad: Immigratie en sociale verhoudingen in 17e-eeuws Amsterdam*. Hilversum, Netherlands: Uitgeverij Verloren, 2005.

Riley, James C. *International Government Finance and the Amsterdam Capital Market, 1740–1815*. Cambridge, U.K.: Cambridge University Press, 1980.

Tielhoff, Milja van. *The "Mother of All Trades": The Baltic Grain Trade in Amsterdam from the Late Sixteenth to the Early Nineteenth Century*. Leiden, Netherlands: Brill, 2002.

Werkman, Evert, and Hylke van der Harst. *Amsterdam: Beeld van een haven 1870–1940*. Bussum, Netherlands: De Boer Maritiem, 1974.

OTTO VAN DER MEIJ

# Naval Port

Amsterdam was a major seaport for the Baltic grain trade since the late Middle Ages, yet even in the mid-sixteenth century it was still a small town with no more than about 30,000 inhabitants. After Spanish troops recaptured Antwerp in the Southern Netherlands in 1585, there was an influx of mainly Protestant refugees, and Amsterdam's intellectual, cultural, and commercial life began to flourish. Much of the trade formerly concentrated in Antwerp then moved to Amsterdam, and that contributed to growth in the shipbuilding industry. Merchant ships from Amsterdam sailed to all European destinations, the Mediterranean, Africa, the West Indies, and Asia. By the beginning of the seventeenth century the population of Amsterdam more than tripled.

A large city located like a half moon along the River IJ, Amsterdam became the hub of world trade. It had only one natural harbor, the Damrak, which was closed off from the River IJ by the Nieuwe Brug (New Bridge). On the roadway of this bridge was a movable board that could be lifted up when an inland vessel wanted to pass. The mast, after the rigging had been removed, could then go unhampered through the so-called ear hole, after which the gap was closed again for the passage of road traffic. Thus the entrance to the inner harbor of Amsterdam was in a sense no wider than 30 centimeters (12 inches). All seagoing vessels harbored in front of the city on the River IJ, which was protected by a row of wooden piles standing in the water with entrances open during daylight. From Amsterdam to the open sea (near the Isle of Texel, north of Holland), ships had to pass the numerous sandbars of the Zuider Zee.

The result was that the Dutch could not build ships with a draft capable of carrying a commercially viable amount of cargo. A method used to surmount this obstacle was the use, since around 1690, of ship's camels, a sort of floating dock that the ship entered in front of Pampus Island near Amsterdam. These camels were then pumped empty, and the ship was towed across the Zuider Zee. For vessels entering at Texel, lighters were available to take off a large part of the cargo or armament so that ships could pass the Zuider Zee and enter the IJ with less draft. Loading and unloading was generally done at anchor. Only smaller ships were able to find a place in the Damrak, where they could moor alongside the quays and unload straight into carts.

In the late sixteenth century the institution of the admiralty was imported into Amsterdam. Amsterdam was the most important of the five different admiralties forming the administration of the Dutch navy since the end of the sixteenth century. The other admiralties were based in Rotterdam, Hoorn/Enkhuizen, Dokkum (Harlingen since 1645) in the province of Friesland, and Middelburg in the province of Zeeland. Holland (at the time a province) provided most of the ships to the navy, and Amsterdam provided the largest ships, which could only be built on the Amsterdam naval yard.

Amsterdam's oldest naval harbor lay outside the city walls on the eastern side of the city. Early in the seventeenth century the harbor grew eastward. First the artificial islands of Uilenburg, Marken, and Rapenburg were formed. Later the artificial islands of Kattenburg, Oostenburg, and Wittenburg became the center of the Amsterdam shipbuilding industry. The booming sea trade secured a good income for the Amsterdam Admiralty. Its admiralty officials collected most of the common duties and thus enjoyed by far the greatest income of all the admiralties. Amsterdam outfitted more ships than the other admiralties, in the eighteenth century even more than all the others combined. The three less affluent admiralties built ships smaller than those of Amsterdam and Rotterdam. Because each admiralty was responsible for its own dockyards, recruitment, ship construction, and stores, there was little uniformity in ships or armaments, and local interests were strongly promoted.

Until the middle of the seventeenth century, ships were outfitted on the north side of the Rapenburg. The yard there lacked the opportunities to extend its premises. During the First Anglo-Dutch War of 1652–1654, larger men-of-war were built, and the shipbuilding industry moved to Kattenburg. The board of the admiralty and its administration stayed in the city's center. The city's government was the driving force for creating a standing navy. Such a navy required permanent accommodation for storing ships, provisions, and guns, and adequate facilities for repair work in the dockyard. All of these needs were met, since ample space was available in Kattenburg. A new dockyard, with a ropeyard, was constructed, along with a huge and well-designed storehouse, the so-called 's Lands Zeemagazijn, completed in 1656 by the architect Daniel Stalpaert (nowadays housing the huge Netherlands Maritime Museum). During the 1680s there were such large increases in the numbers of ships being launched that the area where ships could be safely harbored had to be extended. To increase the capacity of the harbor, more dredging was undertaken.

Until the beginning of the eighteenth century, many large men-of-war were built on Kattenburg, for instance, the *Gouden Leeuw* (Golden Lion), the flagship of Lieutenant-Admiral Cornelis Tromp. The end of the War of the Spanish Succession in 1714 also marked the end of Dutch naval activities on a wide scale. The only important events occurred in the Mediterranean, where privateers from the Barbary states were chased. Fleets were also sent to those states to negotiate peace treaties, but more often than not the peace was broken after a short time. Because of the lack of naval activity, many men-of-war lay in a deplorable state in the water near Kattenburg, sinking in the mud and rotting away.

Suddenly in 1780 war with England broke out, and new shipbuilding programs were scheduled. The Dutch navy was not successful in this war. After the peace treaty was signed, an ambitious shipbuilding program was mostly completed. The years 1785–1787 were full of political strife. Workers on Kattenburg were staunch supporters of the House of Orange. In 1787 they were attacked by their adversaries, the "patriots," and after heavy fighting Kattenburg was taken and plundered. Another disaster was a fire that destroyed 's Lands Zeemagazijn in 1791. The Zeemagazijn was soon rebuilt less expensively than originally. These unfortunate events marked the last years of the Dutch Republic. In the beginning of 1795, troops from revolutionary France invaded also the province of Holland. The Dutch navy in Den Helder surrendered, and for some time the shipbuilding industry in the Amsterdam port was laid to rest. Yet within a couple of years Kattenburg was again busy, since Amsterdam had become the center of shipbuilding under the new regime. Many large men-of-war were built to fight with the French against the British. In 1811 the French emperor Napoleon Bonaparte ordered augmenting the number of men working at the naval port from 997 to 2,800, a boost for the Dutch economy, but this augmentation was only partially realized.

In 1813 the French left the Netherlands, and soon thereafter the Dutch nation became a kingdom under William I, of the Orange family. Soon the building of the new Royal Dutch Navy began. A number of its ships were built on Kattenburg. The realization of the North Holland Canal, which was dug from Den Helder to Amsterdam from 1819 to 1825, gave the Dutch capital city a better port to the sea than it had ever had before. From the 1840s steamships began to replace the old wooden sailing warships. In 1867 the Amsterdam wharf was equipped to build the first iron ships. Its facilities for testing and towing models of new ships, installed by B. J. Tideman, made the wharf internationally famous. Around that time the North Sea Canal from IJmuiden to Amsterdam was dug. The new canal was opened in 1876 and at last gave Amsterdam an open waterway to the North Sea. In the 1880s plans were made to reorganize the state naval wharfs. The Amsterdam ropeyard was closed. Because of a lack of funds, the Amsterdam wharf itself remained unaltered. The last man-of-war, the *Zeven Provinciën* (Seven Provinces), was built in 1907. Eight years later, shortly after the beginning of World War I, the Amsterdam wharf was officially closed. The grounds remained in the possession of the Royal Dutch Navy under the name of Marine-Etablissement te Amsterdam (Naval Establishment at Amsterdam). At present the buildings are used for training new navy recruits. It is likely that in the near future the complex will be sold and navy services will move to Den Helder.

[*See also* Atlantic Ocean, *subentry on* North Atlantic Regional Navies; Navies, Great Powers, *subentry on* Dutch Republic, 1577–1714; North Sea, *subentry on* Regional Navies; Wars, Maritime, *subentries* Anglo-Dutch Wars *and* Portuguese-Dutch Wars; *and* Zeven Provinciën.]

## Bibliography

Barbour, Violet. *Capitalism in Amsterdam in the Seventeenth Century*. Baltimore: John Hopkins Press, 1950.

Boer, Michael Georg de. *De Haven van Amsterdam en haar verbinding met de zee*. Amsterdam: Gemeente Amsterdam, 1926.

Bosscher, P. M. "Amsterdam als marinebasis: Van 's lands werf tot Marine-Etablissement." *Marineblad* 75 (1965): 4–59.

Bruijn, Jaap R. *The Dutch Navy of the Seventeenth and Eighteenth Centuries*. Columbia: University of South Carolina Press, 1993.

Guicciardini, Lodovico. *The Description of the Low Countreys and of the Provinces Thereof*. Norwood, N.J.: W. J. Johnson, 1976. Reprint of the 2d edition of 1593.

Israel, Jonathan I. *Dutch Primacy in World Trade, 1585–1740*. Oxford: Oxford University Press, 1989.

Jones, J. R. *The Anglo-Dutch Wars of the Seventeenth Century*. London: Longman, 1996.

Kist, J. B., ed. *Van VOC tot werkspoor: Het Amsterdamse industrieterrein Oostenburg*. Utrecht, Netherlands: Matrijs, 1986.

Knap, G. H. *The Port of Amsterdam*. Amsterdam: De Bussy, 1970.

Meijer, G. Lutke. *De Amsterdamse haven door de Eeuwen Heen*. Amsterdam: De Bataafsche Leeuw, 1990.

Murray, John J. *Amsterdam in the Age of Rembrandt*. Norman: University of Oklahoma Press, 1967.

Sigmond, J. P. *De Nederlandse zeehavens tussen 1500 en 1800*. Amsterdam: De Bataafsche Leeuw, 1989.

Vries, J. de. *Amsterdam-Rotterdam: Rivaliteit in economisch-historisch perspectief*. Bussum, Netherlands: Van Dishoeck, 1965.

Wagenaar, Jan. *Amsterdam in zijne opkomst, aanwas, geschiedenissen*. 3 vols. Amsterdam: Buijten en Schipperheijn, 1971–1972. Reprint of the 1st edition of 1760–1767.

RONALD B. PRUD'HOMME VAN REINE

# Amundsen, Roald (1872–1928), Norwegian polar explorer. Roald Engelbregt Gravning Amundsen was born on July 16, 1872, at Borge, on the eastern shore of the Oslo Fjord. His father, a merchant-ship owner and master, died when he was only fourteen years old. Although Amundsen's mother persuaded him to embark on a medical career, his secret ambition was to be an Arctic explorer, for which he began to train during winter journeys in the mountains. When she died, he abandoned his studies and went to sea with the intention of gaining a master's certificate, so that he could lead expeditions as both explorer and ship's captain; the narratives of Arctic expeditions had taught him the disadvantages of dual command.

Amundsen's first experience of an exploring voyage (a Belgian one) was as second mate of *Belgica* from 1897 to 1899 under the command of Adrien de Gerlache. Beset in the ice of the Bellingshausen Sea after making a number of discoveries off the Antarctic Peninsula, *Belgica*'s complement of different nationalities spent an agonizing winter, which they survived mainly through the efforts of Dr. F. A. Cook.

**Roald Amundsen.** Oscar Edward Cesare (1885–1948) drew this pencil portrait in 1923. NATIONAL PORTRAIT GALLERY, SMITHSONIAN INSTITUTION / ART RESOURCE, NY

In the late nineteenth century, neither the North Pole nor the South Pole had been attained; nor had the Northwest Passage been navigated, although the maze of Arctic islands north of the American mainland had largely been charted by British expeditions earlier in the century. With six companions in *Gjøa*, a herring boat, Amundsen—in debt—slipped away from his creditors in 1903 and became the first to navigate the passage, wintering twice, first in Gjøahaven on King William Island and then on the north coast of the mainland at King Point, Yukon Territory. His expedition made magnetic observations on King William Island and made a sledge journey to the vicinity of the North Magnetic Pole. Amundsen not only studied his neighbors on King William Island, the Netsilik Eskimo, but also learned from them more techniques of polar travel. The 1903–1906 expedition made Amundsen famous, and after lecturing in the United States, he returned to Norway, but still lacked sufficient funds to pay off his creditors. The Norwegian government, newly independent from Sweden, cleared his outstanding debts in 1907. His narrative was translated into English and handsomely published in two volumes.

Amundsen next determined to reach the North Pole in Fridtjof Nansen's old ship, *Fram*. Forestalled in 1909 by Robert Peary, Amundsen made a dramatic switch the following year, aiming to be first to attain the South Pole. The British explorer Captain Robert Falcon Scott had already departed for the Ross Sea in *Terra Nova* with the same aim, but also as leader of a great scientific expedition. Amundsen, with eight companions and more than a hundred dogs, established winter quarters on the Ross Ice Shelf at the Bay of Whales, sixty miles nearer the pole than Scott's base on Ross Island. Amundsen's sole aim was to be first to reach the South Pole. Having departed again in debt, he had to succeed. Much thought was given to the sledges, tents, and other equipment during the winter, as well as to the marking of depots. The South Pole party consisted of Amundsen and four companions. The dogs pulled well, and the meat that the dogs provided kept the stronger ones going. The men, too, enjoyed their "dog cutlets." The party reached the South Pole on December 14, 1911, after ascending a previously undiscovered glacier, which Amundsen named the Axel Heiberg. The party was relieved to find no sign of the British there. The position of the pole was carefully determined, and a small tent was left containing a letter for the king of Norway, later found by Captain Scott. The party returned to base, where *Fram* awaited them after this brilliant dash to the South Pole—a success that Amundsen attributed to careful planning and the use of dogs. His achievement made world headlines, and his narrative was again translated and published in English. Yet the sole scientific results of this expedition of 1910–1912 appear to have been an appendix to his two-volume narrative concerning winter oceanographic observations from *Fram* in the South Atlantic.

During World War I, Amundsen was able to make enough money in shipping to build *Maud*, which he designed with an egg-shaped hull to enable her to rise from the grip of the sea ice. In June 1918 he left Norway to navigate the Northeast Passage (and be the second to do so), with the aim of drifting toward the North Pole after reaching Bering Strait. Owing to enforced winterings and the need for repairs, the years went by, and *Maud* never entered the northerly drift. She was impounded in Seattle in 1923 for unpaid debts. Amundsen, meanwhile, had bought an airplane, but he was unsuccessful in his attempt to fly across the Arctic. After losing the plane, he declared himself bankrupt, despite another grant from the Norwegian government. He regarded the expedition as a failure, the only result being a study made by Dr. H. U. Sverdrup of the Chukchi people from 1919 to 1920.

Occupying Amundsen's remaining years were two flights over the Arctic Ocean, financed and accompanied by Lincoln Ellsworth, a wealthy American. In the first, with two planes in spring 1925, they reached latitude 87°50′ N, where they crash-landed but managed to return in the N-25. Then in the airship *Norge*, under Amundsen's command, they made the first flight across the Arctic Ocean from Spitsbergen to Alaska in May 1926.

In June 1928, Amundsen flew in a French plane to rescue the Italian airship expedition led by General Umberto Nobile. The plane disappeared, and in the words of Roland Huntford, "Amundsen had vanished into the polar sea which was his only true home on earth" (*The Amundsen Photographs*, p. 198).

[*See also* Antarctica and the Southern Ocean; Arctic Ocean; Northeast Passage; North Pole; *and* Northwest Passage.]

### Bibliography

Amundsen, Roald. *My Life as an Explorer*. London: Heinemann, 1927.

Amundsen, Roald. *Roald Amundsen's "Belgica" Diary*. Edited by Hugo Decleir. Huntingdon, U.K.: Bluntisham Books, 1999.

Huntford, Roland. *Scott and Amundsen*. London: Hodder and Stoughton, 1979. Though biased against Captain Scott and taking no account of scientific work, this work is nonetheless well researched, the author having made use of Norwegian sources.

Huntford, Roland, ed. *The Amundsen Photographs*. London: Hodder and Stoughton, 1987. Lantern slides illustrating the Northwest Passage, the South Pole, and the *Maud* expeditions, with excellent introductions.

ANN SAVOURS

**Anchors**    The word "anchor" comes from the Greek *ágkura*, which is related to *agkúlos*, meaning angled or bent. Archaeologists have begun to develop a typology of eastern Mediterranean Bronze Age stone anchors, relating underwater discoveries with anchors found in temples in Lebanon, Syria, and Cyprus, correlating size, weight, shape, and type of stone used. They range in weight from 20 kilograms to half a ton or more. These anchors were simple

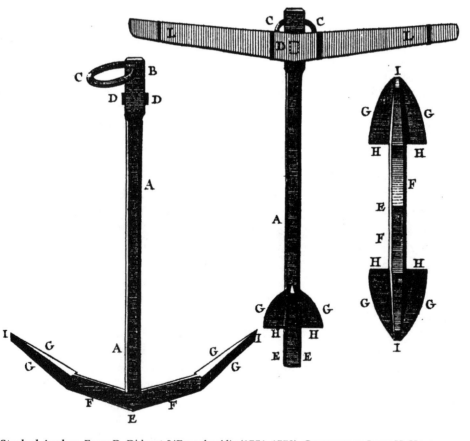

A Shank
B Hole for Ring
C Ring
D Nut
E Crown
F Arms
G Flukes
H Ears
I Bills
H Ears
L Hoops on Stock

**Stocked Anchor.** From D. Diderot *L'Encyclopédie* (1751–1772). COURTESY OF JOHN H. HARLAND

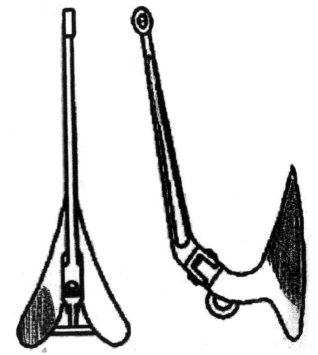

**Martin's Close-Stowing Anchor.** From Alston, *Seamanship* (1902). Courtesy of John H. Harland

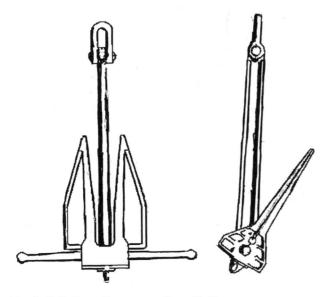

**Danforth Pattern.** Courtesy of John H. Harland

**CQR Pattern.** Courtesy of John H. Harland

**Forging an Anchor.** From D. Diderot, *L'Encyclopédie* (1751–1772). Courtesy of John H. Harland

**Cat Tackle.** From George Nares, *Seamanship* (1886). COURTESY OF JOHN H. HARLAND

**Stowed Anchor with Ring- and Shank-Painters.** From George Nares, *Seamanship* (1886). COURTESY OF JOHN H. HARLAND

perforated stones; their holding power depended on weight and friction alone. A stick inserted through holes in the anchor immensely improved the efficiency of the device, ensuring that one end dug into the seabed. An anchor made from a crooked tree root and a stone is attributed to the emperor Yü in China around 2205 B.C.E. Egyptian tomb furniture includes models with conical stakes and ropes for mooring from 2000 B.C.E., and tombs from 1600 B.C.E. show grooved or perforated stone anchors. A tomb from 1400 B.C.E. contained a T-shaped stone anchor.

In Britain the primitive anchor, or killick, was constructed of sticks, stones, and rope, and was designed to ensure that one stick would grab the bottom. Morton Nance has claimed that "killick" derives from a common

**Sheet-Anchor Stowed on Tumbler.** From George Nares, *Seamanship* (1886). Courtesy of John H. Harland

**Cable Hitched to Bitts.** From D. Lever, *Sheet-Anchor* (1819). Courtesy of John H. Harland

**Ship Moored with Two Anchors.** From J. H. Röding, *Allgemeines Wörterbuch der Marine* (1793–1798). Courtesy of John H. Harland

**Capstan, Cable, and Messenger.** From P. Le Compte, *Praktikale zeevaartkunde* (1842). COURTESY OF JOHN H. HARLAND

Celtic root meaning cock or male bird (Irish *coileac*). Such anchors, which were widely used by primitive seafarers, have been found in Europe, Asia, Africa, and the Americas. The Greek geographer Strabo credited Anacharsus with inventing the anchor with arms in about 600 B.C.E. Anchors made of metal and wood are depicted on Greek coins from the period 600 B.C.E.–400 B.C.E.

## Modern Developments

Stocked anchors similar to the type in use in the eighteenth and nineteenth centuries had been in use since Roman times, as shown by the anchor discovered in Lake Nemi, Italy, from 40 C.E. To the crown, or lower end of the shank, were attached the arms, terminating in flat palms or flukes. At the upper end of the shank was the ring, to which the cable was bent, and below this the stock sat at right angles to the arms in such a way that one of the anchor's arms dug into the bottom. Traditionally the stock was of wood, but later anchors were designed with an iron stock that could be folded flat against the shank when the device was not in use.

Apart from minor modifications such as the improved anchor of 1835, designed by Richard Pering, which had curved rather than straight arms, the anchor's general appearance remained basically unchanged until the first half of the nineteenth century. The stock ensured that one or the other arm would dig into the seabed, but it also caused the other arm to project upward and be in danger of being fouled by the hemp anchor cable. The problem was addressed first by using anchors with arms that pivoted on the shank, and ultimately by the development of the so-called stockless anchor. The unburied arm of William Porter's anchor, introduced in 1838, was able to swing around and lie almost flat against the shank. John Trotman improved on it in 1852 and won the Royal Navy's international anchor trials that year. An early stockless anchor had been invented by R. F. Hawkins in 1821, but it failed to gain acceptance. François Martin's close-stowing anchor, first manufactured in 1859, had flukes that pivoted on an axis parallel to the stock. It is considered the immediate ancestor of the modern stockless anchor.

British manufacturers such as Halls, Joseph Wright & Co, Noah Hingley & Sons, and Byers produced the most widely used types from 1886 on. After 1898 the American firm Baldt and after 1908 Canadian Steel Foundries produced anchors that competed with those of British manufacturers. From the 1920s firms in Italy produced anchors that were competitive with those produced in the United States and the United Kingdom.

Relatively light anchors with improved holding power were developed and used extensively on smaller vessels during and after World War II. Examples include the CQR plow anchor (1933), developed by Sir Geoffrey Ingram Taylor as an anchor for flying boats, and the Danforth anchor (1939), designed by Richard Danforth for the U.S. Navy.

Forging an anchor was technically demanding, time consuming, and expensive. In the late eighteenth century, for example, the component parts were brought to white heat and welded together by hammering. The anchor was swung out from the furnace, placed over the anvil, and struck repeatedly with a drop hammer.

The introduction of the stockless anchor in the 1880s allowed the shank of the anchor to be pulled up into a hawsepipe, vastly simplifying anchor stowage. In earlier days the stocked anchor had to be hauled up until the ring was clear of the water, allowing the cat tackle to be hooked and the anchor hauled up to the cathead. The fish tackle was then hooked to the crown of the anchor, the shank swung up to the horizontal and secured by ring and shank painters in such a way that it could be readily let go. A single tackle hanging from an anchor davit, hooked to a gravity band placed at the balancing point, was used to settle the Martin's close-stowing anchor on its sloping bed, and the stocked anchors of the last great sailing merchantmen were swung in and stowed on the forecastle in like fashion.

## Anchor Use and Management

The larger the vessel, the heavier its anchors. Brian Lavery has noted that after 1784 a Royal Navy warship carried four identically sized bower anchors (84 hundredweight, or 9,408 pounds, in the case of *Victory*). Two of these were carried at the catheads, designated "best bower" to port and "small bower" to starboard, and two abreast the forechannels, "sheet anchor" to starboard and "reserve anchor" to port. These were secured on tumblers so they could be released quickly. Before 1784 the bowers varied in weight. Traditionally the sheet would have been heavier than the best bower, which in turn was heavier than the small bower. Stowed in the forechannels were the stream anchor, substantially lighter than the bowers, and a series of progressively smaller kedge anchors. The working anchor was the best bower, and ordinarily this was dropped first. If conditions warranted, the second bower was let go, followed, if need be, by the sheet. This sequence—based on the tendency of storm winds in the Northern Hemisphere to shift clockwise—kept the three cables clear of one another. The stream might be used to anchor for a short period in calm weather, and the kedges were special-purpose anchors, taken out by a boat should it be necessary to "warp," or kedge, the vessel in a desired direction, hauling itself up to the anchor.

Management of the ship at anchor was an active rather than a passive process. Disaster could ensue if the cable became wrapped around the free arm, pulling the engaged arm out of the ground. Consequently the master of a vessel at anchor was much preoccupied with preventing the cable from getting afoul of the anchor. This was achieved by keeping the cable taut as the ship swung around the anchor so that the anchor turned steadily in the ground and the ring always pointed toward the ship, by heaving in or veering cable as required, by altering rudder angle, and by setting or taking in sail, according to the state of wind and tide. To facilitate such maneuvers, the anchor position was marked by a buoy.

Hemp cable was subject to damage by abrasion caused by dragging across the sea bottom. When chain cable came into use in the early 1800s the problem of abrasion was eliminated, and because the ship tended to ride to the heavy chain rather than the anchor itself, fouling of the free arm became less of a worry.

Hemp anchor cable was laid up left-handed, from three right-hand-laid ropes, and a common rule of thumb for determining its circumference was less than half an inch per foot (4 centimeters per meter) of maximum beam of vessel. Thus *Victory*, with a beam of 50 feet (15.24 meters), had cables 24 inches (61 centimeters) in circumference. Nominally the cable length was 100 fathoms (183 meters), but in practice cables were anywhere from 85 to 120 fathoms (155 to 220 meters) long, with two or more spliced together to form a "shot." The end of the cable was taken through the ring and clinched to itself with cable bends, forming a sort of running noose, rather than by being spliced. At anchor, the bitts around which the cable was hitched acted like a giant veering cleat, with the cable secured to the deck with stoppers.

Riding to one anchor, the vessel swung around as wind and tide dictated, the radius of the circle being determined by the scope of cable veered. However, when a large number of ships were involved, it was desirable to limit the swing. This was managed by mooring the vessel, placing her between two anchors so that she rode to one or other, depending on the direction of tidal current, but not changing position much. Care was then needed to avoid getting the two cables twisted in a "foul hawse."

In small vessels the anchor was recovered, or weighed, using a windlass; in larger vessels a capstan was used. If chain cable was being used, the links were securely gripped by specially shaped sprockets on the windlass. Because of their immense size and large bending radius, the hemp cables of larger vessels could not be handled directly by the capstan. Instead, three and a half turns of a smaller rope—a messenger—were taken around the capstan, and this in turn was clutched to the cable using lengths of sennit called nippers. These were applied at the manger and taken off before the cable disappeared belowdecks to be coiled in the cable tier.

All vessels are required to carry suitable anchors. However, because operational conditions vary, some vessels might never anchor in the course of a year while others use anchors constantly. The British Columbia ferries fall into the first category, as demonstrated in 2005 when *Queen of Oak Bay* lost power and caused considerable damage because the cable-releasing gear was so clogged with paint that the anchor failed to drop. In contrast, the captains of Greek ferries berthing in Aegean ports daily demonstrate their skill by executing the "Mediterranean moor," placing the stern of the ship against the jetty and using the anchor as a pivot.

[*See also* Ship's Equipment.]

## Bibliography

Curryer, Betty Nelson. *Anchors: An Illustrated History*. London: Chatham, 1999.

Harland, John H. *Capstans and Windlasses: An Illustrated History of Their Use at Sea*. Piermont, N.Y.: Pier Books, 2003.

Harland, John H. *Seamanship in the Age of Sail: An Account of the Shiphandling of the Sailing Man-of-War, 1600–1860, based on Contemporary Sources*. Annapolis, Md.: Naval Institute Press, 1984. See especially "Management of the Ship at Anchor."

Lavery, Brian. *The Arming and Fitting of English Ships of War, 1600–1815*. Annapolis, Md.: Naval Institute Press, 1987.

Nance, R. Morton. *A Glossary of Cornish Sea-Words*. Edited by P. A. S. Pool. Truro, U.K.: Federation of Old Cornwall Societies, 1963.

Tinniswood, J. T. "Anchors and Accessories: 1340–1640." *Mariner's Mirror* 31 (1945): 84–105.

JOHN H. HARLAND

# Ancient Navies

This entry contains eight subentries:

An Overview
Greece
Rome
Hellenistic States
Persia
Egypt
Carthage
Phoenicia

---

## An Overview

Because the Mediterranean Sea was a natural pathway for trade, communication, and competition, the ancient cultures that developed around its shores were all influenced to some degree by navies and the states possessing them. Although evidence exists of the use of naval power by numerous Mediterranean cultures as early as the second millennium B.C.E.—Egypt, Cyprus, Syrian Ugarit, Minoan Crete, and Mycenaean Greece—clear evidence for fleets of single-purpose warships, financed, built, and maintained by a ruler or state, does not appear much before the sixth century B.C.E. Prior to this time most navies were made up of privately owned multipurpose vessels, built for transporting goods and for fighting when necessary. Since the ships would have differed in performance, such fleets could not have relied excessively on swift, coordinated maneuvers.

Sometime during the mid-sixth century, however, a few states began to build and maintain single-purpose galleys—that is, vessels of moderate size, armed with a waterline ram and designed primarily for fighting under oars. This, in turn, allowed for the development of naval power in ways that had been previously impossible. For the next millennium, a number of interconnected factors influenced a state's decision and ability to build and maintain a navy: (1) the existence of strategic goals that can best be secured through the projection of power by sea, (2) steady sources of public revenue, (3) the will of a ruler or state to spend the required capital to build, maintain, and man single-purpose warships, and (4) access to the necessary natural and human resources like timber, forest products, metals, and human labor. The naval history of the period from c. 500 B.C.E. to c. 500 C.E. chronicles those states most influenced by these factors.

According to the historian Thucydides (c. 460–c. 400 B.C.E.), the first Greek city-state to build a navy according to the "modern"—that is, state-financed—way was Corinth. The decision involved a public commitment to making considerable expenditures on a regular basis and presumes a need (surely connected with its colonies) to justify the expense. The Corinthian example was followed soon thereafter by Samos and Phokaia (a Greek city on the western coast of Asia Minor), who each developed their own needs and steady sources of revenue. At this time, the fifty-oared galley, or pentekonter, was the preferred ship-of-the-line. Pictorial evidence reveals the craft as long and low to the water, with oars placed at both one and two levels. Built according to a single set of specifications, these galleys would have possessed similar performance characteristics, thus allowing for group offensive and defensive maneuvers—that is, for battle tactics.

The historian Herodotus (c. 484–c. 425 B.C.E.) records our earliest evidence for coordinated ramming strikes in a sea battle fought near Corsican Alalia around 535 B.C.E. He writes that sixty Phokaian vessels won a victory over twice as many Etruscan and Carthaginian ships. Despite their victory, Phokaian losses were considerable: forty ships were destroyed outright and twenty were rendered "useless" because their rams were somehow damaged (Herodotus says that the rams were "turned back" or "away"). Presumably, the Phokaian galleys were not yet engineered to take such a beating at the bows, which implies that maneuver-and-ram tactics were still a new feature of naval warfare. This state of affairs was about to change dramatically.

## Development of Trireme Navies

Although some scholars believe that triremes ("threes"), or galleys rowed from three levels, were invented before the sixth century, it seems clear that threes did not replace penteconters in popularity until the last quarter of the sixth century. The first to commission a large trireme navy was Cambyses, king of Persia from 530 to 522 B.C.E. In what must have been a massive program, he ordered the yards of Ionia, Cilicia, Cyprus, and Phoenicia to prepare his fleet, which was organized into ethnic squadrons. And though Herodotus implies that Egypt also possessed triremes at this time, Cambyses defeated the Egyptians and absorbed their forces. The Persians, therefore, must receive credit for establishing a new Mediterranean standard, that is, the trireme navy. Others, like Athens, Syracuse, and Carthage, followed their lead.

Of all the trireme powers, we know the most about Athens, which decided to build a fleet in the late 480s after the discovery of silver deposits made such a plan possible. Themistocles emerged as the plan's main proponent, convincing his fellow citizens to forgo a general distribution of profits and build two hundred triremes instead—an unprecedented number for such a small state. Three years later this new fleet helped to resist a Persian attempt to subjugate the city-states of Greece. In a pivotal sea battle fought near Athens in the Strait of Salamis, the Persians were soundly defeated, and without control of the seas the invasion of King Xerxes faltered. During the rest of the century (477–404 B.C.E.), Athens grew into a dominant naval power and the leader of the Delian League, an alliance that after mid-century more closely resembled an empire. Repeated conflict with Sparta and its allies, especially Corinth, led to a debilitating war that lasted twenty-seven years (431–404) and was chronicled by Thucydides in his famous history of the Peloponnesian War. Errors in judgment—especially a failed attempt to conquer Syracuse (415–413)—eventually cost Athens its democracy, its navy, and its empire. Although it reemerged during the fourth century at the head of a second, less powerful, naval alliance, it never regained its old power.

For almost two centuries Athens possessed a sizable navy, and because of its prosperity and its literate democracy, sufficient evidence still exists that reveals how the navy functioned. Athens built hundreds of triremes that were long, narrow, and low to the water and were manned by crews of 200, including 170 oarsmen, 10 marines, 4 archers, and others. The war fleet was built and repaired in naval yards at Athens's port city of Piraeus and was housed in covered slipways for protection from rot and teredo worms.

A board of ten "curators of the naval yards" kept meticulous records of both hulls and gear and carefully recorded those to whom they were given. Captains drawn from the propertied classes were required to shoulder some of the costs of fleet operations and were financially responsible for everything that they received. Although Athens, like most other naval powers, did not rely on professional admirals, it did reward skilled oar crews and took pride in the quality of its helmsmen, who were considered to be among the ranks of skilled professionals. During the fifth century and into the fourth century, Athenian citizens served as oarsmen and marines, along with free-born alien-residents (called *metoikoi*) who came from nearby states. Levels of pay were sufficient to allow sailors to support a family, and it seems likely that many lived in the suburb of Piraeus.

Authors like Thucydides (himself a naval commander) reveal that triremes were unseaworthy in choppy or rough water. Limited space inside the hull left no room for sleeping or food preparation, so fleets put ashore for meals and required a flotilla of merchantmen to carry camp gear and other supplies when the fleet was on an extended campaign. As a result, trireme fleets were ill-suited for lengthy sea voyages, were poor at enforcing blockades, and required coastal camps and the support of nearby settlements for food and water when not traveling in convoy with a supply fleet. Whenever possible, fleets hugged the coasts and preferred sheltered water for naval battles. In general, Athenian crews prided themselves on their ship-handling skills and practiced regularly to keep sharp. In battles Athenian commanders relied on these skills and, according to Thucydides, felt it a mark of inferior seamanship to resort to "infantry battles at sea"—those in which deck troops fought with one another on floating platforms. Fleets were made up of squadrons of varying sizes, which worked together in organized maneuvers and coordinated attacks. Contemporary accounts reveal that fleets were used to transport infantry forces, to provide logistical support to armies in the field, to convoy grain shipments, to carry communications and conduct reconnaissance, and to deny use of the sea to one's enemies for commercial and military purposes. We may reasonably assume that wherever trireme navies were built—Phoenicia, Cyprus, Carthage, Sicily, southern Italy—similar conditions prevailed.

## Development of Polyreme Navies

At the start of the fourth century B.C.E. (in 399, according to Diodorus), Dionysius of Syracuse introduced the *pentereis*, or "fives." Faced with a threat from Carthage, who may have first introduced "fours" (*tetrereis*), Dionysius seems to have made use of a tradition adopted from Corinth when Syracuse was under siege by Athens in 413. In order to defeat the Athenians, the Syracusans shortened and thickened their trireme bows and purposefully rammed the weaker bows of their enemies, who were unable to maneuver away in the constricted waters of the harbor. On this evidence it seems likely that fives and perhaps fours were designed to defeat threes in the frontal ramming attacks required to fight in constricted areas, like harbors and their entrances. Before long, these larger units—called "polyremes" by modern scholars to distinguish them from smaller vessels—were present in all the major navies, except at Athens, where they do not appear until the period 330–325. Despite the ambivalence of the Athenians (who felt no compulsion to abandon their old tactics), fives could carry more deck troops and proved superior to threes in frontal ramming contests. Later, in the third century, Roman fives (quinqueremes) carried up to 120 deck troops and 300 oarsmen.

## Philip and Alexander the Great

During the period of Philip II (r. 356–336 B.C.E.) of Macedon and his son Alexander III (Alexander the Great, r. 336–323), warfare on land and sea changed profoundly. The navy was always of secondary importance to the army, although its usefulness was demonstrated more than once in support of the army on coastal campaigns. A credible navy could transport troops, supplies, and weapons across and along bodies of water; it could also facilitate reconnaissance and improve the speed of sending and receiving messages. Additionally, under Alexander (and perhaps Philip as well), the navy became an enabling force when the objective included capturing and defending coastal cities. This was not because naval siege warfare was new: the Athenians had employed it vigorously at Syracuse in 415–413 during the Peloponnesian War. What changed with Alexander's successful siege of Tyre in 332 was the expectation that a siege could be shortened in direct proportion to the firepower that the attacker brought to bear on the city. The siege also revealed that harbors were a good place to focus one's attacks.

## Hellenistic Fleets

Following Alexander's death, the conflicts among his successors focused on the Mediterranean littoral and, as a result, fueled a furious naval arms race. Ship classes of larger and larger size were built in an effort to defeat rivals and gain access to their cities. The cost of a first-rate navy, which was always large, increased dramatically. Still, the money was spent and the ships were built. As a result the nature of naval power changed considerably during the late fourth and third centuries for those who had the money to spend. The navies that they produced were, like the armies, made up of a wide array of fighting forces and military hardware that allowed for maximum adaptability.

Large galleys, like "nines" and "tens," excelled at frontal ramming and at carrying siege machinery and marines. Smaller galleys, like threes, excelled at maneuver-and-ram warfare, and medium galleys, like fours and fives, fulfilled both purposes. Galleys smaller than threes, called *lemboi*, could be fitted with small catapults, used as messenger ships, or placed in gaps between the larger vessels in the battle line as support ships. Even the smallest open boats could be filled with combatants and incendiary materials and could be used for both defensive and offensive actions. Catapults—both stone and arrow-shooting varieties—were mounted on warships of varying sizes and were used to attack the marines and the troops assigned to protect the harbor fortifications. According to Philo, a third-century B.C.E. artilleryman who wrote a treatise on harbor attack and defense, special attention was focused on a city's harbor, for it was there that many cities had neglected their fortifications and were thus most vulnerable to attack.

## The Romans

The years of the third century B.C.E. also witnessed an increase in naval power among the Romans, who came into conflict with the Carthaginians and fought a series of wars, called the Punic Wars (264–241; 218–201), that left the Romans the dominant naval power in the western Mediterranean. The Romans chose to model their navy after the Carthaginians' and to build multipurpose fives whose decks they packed with marines for deck fighting. Although they made numerous mistakes and lost many ships during the course of their first war with Carthage, the Romans' superior stocks of manpower and shipbuilding timber helped them to prevail. By the end of the Second Punic War, the Roman navy was among the best, with maneuverable ships and disciplined marines. The Romans' capture of catapults from Syracuse in 212 also gave them the tools to wage effective naval siege warfare. Even so, the Romans never glorified their naval traditions and shunned developing a naval infrastructure commensurate with their imperial aspirations.

Following their victory over Carthage at the end of the third century B.C.E., the Romans preferred to let others, like the Rhodians, police the seas. Rhodes had a crack fleet built along Athenian lines that was skilled at maneuver-and-ram warfare with smaller units. But when the Rhodian state offended Rome during the Third Macedonian War (171–168), the Romans enacted a series of measures that cut Rhodian revenues, removed their independence, and degraded their ability to maintain a navy. The unintended result was an increase in piracy that progressively impacted Italian shipping during the second and first centuries until Pompey (Gnaeus Pompeius Magnus, 106–48 B.C.E.) was given a set of extraordinary powers to deal with the threat in 67 B.C.E. In a famous war lasting only three months, Pompey swept the sea clean of pirates and reestablished Rome's authority over the entire Mediterranean.

This authority, however, was fractured by a period of civil wars that witnessed armed strife between Roman generals whose armies and navies functioned like personal possessions. These struggles involved many generals, but the major rivals at sea were Pompey and Julius Caesar, then Pompey's son Sextus and Octavian, and finally Mark Antony and Octavian. Pompey's son Sextus was the only one of these men to stake his future solely on his navy. Based in Sicily, he attempted to cut the flow of grain to Rome and was eventually challenged and defeated by Octavian's admiral Agrippa off Sicilian Naulochus in 36 B.C.E. At roughly this same period Mark Antony based himself in Egypt with Cleopatra VII. In 32 B.C.E. he advanced on Italy with a large combined land and sea force that included sevens, eights, nines, and tens—warships that had not seen action for more than a century. One presumes that he was prepared to engage in naval siege warfare, but he never got the chance. Octavian crossed to Greece, intercepted Antony's advance, and fought a decisive battle with Antony and his forces off Actium in 31 B.C.E.

Thereafter, naval power receded in importance. Following his victory at Actium and the deaths of Antony and Cleopatra a year later, Octavian found himself in control of the Mediterranean basin. Faced with staggering empire-wide problems requiring massive expenditures, Octavian—now Augustus (emperor 27 B.C.E.–14 C.E.)—immediately reduced the size of his armed forces by more than 50 percent (from 60 or more legions to 28), decommissioned many of the ships in his possession, and assigned the rest to a few naval stations in Italy and southern Gaul.

The Romans continued this reliance on small fleet stations for some two centuries following Augustus, adding new stations as needed. River fleets of lighter warships were also placed at the mouth of the Nile (at Alexandria), on the Rhine, and at various places along the Danube. In 324 C.E., when Constantine the Great went to war with his coruler Licinius, neither could call on a standing fleet. At the end of the century, possession of a navy was so unimportant that Vegetius, the author of an influential military manual, *De re militari*, could write, "about the skills of naval warfare fewer things need to be said, since for some time now the sea has been peaceful and warfare is waged on land with barbarian nations." By the early sixth century, Byzantine emperors showed a renewed interest in naval warfare, but they relied on two-banked vessels called *dromones* (dromons) that were no longer fitted with waterline rams. With this fundamental change in warship design and the disappearance of ramming warfare, we pass from the ancient into the medieval period.

[*See also* Actium, Battle of; Mediterranean Sea; Minoan Seafaring; Salamis, Battle of; Technology and Weapons, *subentry* Ancient and Medieval to 1300; Wars, Maritime, *subentry on* Peloponnesian War; *and* Warships, *subentry on* Ancient Warships.]

## Bibliography

In general, see the specific bibliographies for the relevant sections on Greek, Hellenistic, Roman, Carthaginian, Phoenician, Persian, and Egyptian navies. Except for Vegetius, texts and translations of ancient authors can be conveniently found in the Loeb Classical Library (London and Cambridge, Mass.: Harvard University Press). For an English translation of Vegetius, see N. P. Milner, trans., *Vegetius: Epitome of Military Science* (Liverpool, U.K.: Liverpool University Press, 1993).

Basch, Lucien. *Le musée imaginaire de la marine antique.* Athens: Institut Hellénique pour la Préservation de la Tradition Nautique, 1987. Presents a wealth of iconographic evidence relevant to ancient navies.
Casson, Lionel. *The Ancient Mariners: Seafarers and Sea Fighters of the Mediterranean in Ancient Times.* 2d ed. Princeton, N.J.: Princeton University Press, 1991. General, accurate, and extremely readable treatment of ancient seafaring.
Casson, Lionel. *Ships and Seamanship in the Ancient World.* Rev. ed. Baltimore: Johns Hopkins University Press, 1995. The bible of ancient ships and seafaring, containing primary source quotations both in the original Greek and Latin and in translation.
Meijer, Fik. *A History of Seafaring in the Classical World.* New York: St. Martin's Press, 1986. Useful overview of ancient naval history that presents generally accepted views.
Morrison, John, and Robert Gardiner, eds. *The Age of the Galley: Mediterranean Oared Vessels since Pre-Classical Times.* London: Conway Maritime Press; Annapolis, Md.: Naval

Institute Press, 1995. An excellent, if slightly idiosyncratic, treatment of ancient galleys and galley warfare.

Rougé, Jean. *Ships and Fleets of the Ancient Mediterranean.* Translated by Susan Frazer. Middletown, Conn.: Wesleyan University Press, 1981. Translation of *La marine dans l'antiquité*, originally published in 1975. Solid, concise, and sensible, even if now slightly out of date.

Wallinga, Hermann T. *Ships and Sea-Power before the Great Persian War: The Ancestry of the Ancient Trireme.* Leiden, Netherlands: Brill, 1993. Detailed discussion of archaic-period Greek and Persian navies.

WILLIAM M. MURRAY

# Greece

If a navy is defined as one or more fleets of state-owned and/or state-operated warships that are used for the projection of military power in the pursuit of political objectives, it is doubtful that any Greek state can be said to have had a proper navy until the second half of the sixth century B.C.E. Although the Homeric poems and early Greek vase paintings show that ships were used for raiding and warfare in the eighth and seventh centuries B.C.E., these ships would have belonged to individuals, like the ship lent to Telemachus by Noemon in the *Odyssey* (book 2, lines 386–392).

### Triremes and the First Greek Navies

The earliest Greek ships specifically built for warfare and raiding seem to have been developed in the eighth century B.C.E. They were distinguished from other vessels by their high sides, by their elongated shape—allowing space for between thirty and one hundred oarsmen—and by the presence of a ram on the bow and a fighting deck for marines along most of the ship's length. Privately owned warships persisted in the Greek world until the last quarter of the fifth century B.C.E., but the establishment of the trireme as the principal warship type made the operation of such vessels prohibitively expensive.

The trireme was invented around 540 B.C.E., possibly at Carthage; within fifty years it had become the standard vessel for naval warfare. It was rowed by 150 or more oarsmen pulling oars of equal length and arranged in groups of three, sitting one above the other. Warships rowed by oarsmen on two levels had existed for some time, but the addition of the third tier of oarsmen, who usually rowed through an outrigger, allowed a substantial increase in the total number of oarsmen. This enabled the ships to move faster, which was a great advantage in ramming tactics, and also to accommodate more extensive fighting decks for

marines, which were desirable both for close exchanges of missiles and for boarding. The number of men needed to operate such ships effectively—two hundred for an Athenian trireme of the fifth century B.C.E.—was a major factor in their operating costs, as was the need for ship sheds, covered slipways to house the vessels when they were not in action. Consequently the running of an entire navy of triremes required a huge commitment of resources in terms of both money and manpower.

The first proper Greek navies were probably created by Corinth, Corcyra (Corfu), Aegina, Miletos, and Samos. Each of these city-states had strong maritime trading interests to promote and protect, as well as sufficient resources of manpower and money to build, maintain, and operate dozens of warships. Ancient historiographic tradition projected the origins of Greek navies further back into the past. In his discussion of ancient Greek sea power in Book 1 of his history of the Peloponnesian War, the fifth-century B.C.E. Athenian Thucydides refers to a tradition that the Cretan king Minos was the first to create a navy, in order to suppress piracy and increase his revenues. Thucydides dismisses this as mere legend, however, and claims that the first known sea battle was fought between Corinth and Corcyra around 664 B.C.E., that the Corinthians were the first to develop something like a proper navy, and that the first Greek-built triremes were made at Corinth.

Corinth was certainly growing in importance as a maritime trading port in the seventh century B.C.E., and increased rivalry with Corcyra, originally a Corinthian foundation, might well have led to conflict involving warships—but not necessarily on the scale familiar to Thucydides, who was used to fleets numbering more than a hundred ships. Seventh century B.C.E. painted pottery does occasionally depict fighting between ships, although never more than two at a time, and it is difficult to know what level of engagement would have constituted a sea battle in this period.

The islands of Aegina and Samos, and the Ionian city of Miletos, were also heavily dependent upon the sea for their prosperity, and they needed fleets both to defend their territory and to increase their influence in competition with other states. Under the rule of the tyrant Polycrates (c. 535–522 B.C.E.), Samos became a significant naval power in the eastern Mediterranean. By 525 B.C.E. Polycrates had a fleet of more than a hundred ships, forty of them triremes, with ship sheds to house them in, perhaps financed with aid from his ally Amasis, pharaoh of Egypt. Polycrates defeated the powerful city of Miletos at sea and captured several other cities and islands.

By this time, however, the recently created Persian Empire was overwhelming the peoples of the eastern Mediterranean, and places like Miletos and Samos were unable to resist the Persians. The citizens of one Ionian Greek city threatened with Persian domination, Phocaea, abandoned their homes and sailed to the western Mediterranean, where they had previously established a successful trading settlement at Massalia (Marseille). The Greek historian Herodotus records their victory around 535 B.C.E. against a combined Etruscan and Carthaginian fleet in a sea battle near Alalia (Aleria in Corsica) in which ramming tactics were used. By 500 B.C.E. many of the larger Ionian Greek city-states had fleets of triremes, but they were supplied and largely financed by the Persian king. In 499 B.C.E. the Ionians rebelled against Persian rule, but after initial success their combined navy of 353 triremes was defeated in 494 B.C.E. by a Persian fleet of some six hundred vessels from Phoenicia and Cilicia.

During King Xerxes' invasion of Greece in 480 B.C.E., more than a thousand Persian ships were deployed against around three hundred triremes assembled from the mainland Greek states, especially Athens and Corinth. Although many of its citizens were involved in maritime trade, Athens had developed its naval forces quite late by comparison with Corinth and the Ionians. The two hundred Athenian triremes that were vital to Greek victory at the Battle of Salamis in 480 B.C.E. were very recent constructions, having been commissioned at the instigation of Themistocles after the discovery of a rich vein of silver in the public mines in 483 B.C.E.

## Rise and Fall of Athens

The leading role played by the Athenian navy in the victory over the Persians in 480 B.C.E. brought tremendous prestige to the Athenians and an invitation from the Greek subjects of the Persian king to take charge in 478 B.C.E. of a maritime alliance that modern historians call the Delian League. The other league states quickly became subjects of Athens, which combined the states' human and financial resources with its own to create an extensive empire in the eastern Mediterranean. At the height of their wealth and power in the middle of the fifth century B.C.E., the Athenians, led by the statesman Pericles, controlled the largest naval force in the Greek world.

The Athenians established and maintained high skill levels among the crews of their triremes, making them initially far superior to the ships of Corinth and the other Greek states led by Sparta that challenged the Athenians in the Peloponnesian War (431–404 B.C.E.). The Athenians perfected trireme tactics that involved rowing through the opposing line and sailing around the enemy ships to ram at an acute angle from the side or rear. These two stages were called the *diekplous* and the *periplous*. The tactics required superior speed, maneuverability, and seamanship to be effective, which in turn required having well-maintained ships and well-trained, well-motivated oarsmen. An alternative was to use the ram or the projecting beams alongside a ship's prow to ram an enemy ship head-on, or at a slight angle; this tactic was favored by the Corinthians, whose ships tended to be slower.

Eventually, with the addition of experienced crews from Syracuse and with the backing of the Persian king's gold, Sparta and its allies won a decisive naval battle at Aigospotamoi in the Hellespont in 405 B.C.E., capturing or disabling most of the Athenian fleet and leaving the city of Athens vulnerable to attack from the sea, which forced the Athenians to surrender in 404 B.C.E. Although attempts were made by Athens's enemies to prevent a revival of its naval power, its dependence on maritime trade and the desire to re-create an overseas empire encouraged the Athenians to invest heavily in ships and harbor facilities in the fourth century B.C.E. But a series of conflicts with Sparta, Thebes, Persia, and Macedonia sapped Athenian resources and prevented a return to the full glory of the Periclean era.

Finally Athens was forced to submit to the Macedonians, first to King Philip II in 338 B.C.E. and then to his son Alexander the Great in 336 B.C.E. When Alexander died in 323 B.C.E., the Athenians made one last effort to assert their naval power, assembling a fleet to challenge the Macedonian regent Antipater, but the fleet was crushed in a naval battle off the island of Amorgos in 322 B.C.E. During the final years of the fourth century B.C.E. some very large Greek naval fleets were assembled, mostly consisting of ships much larger than triremes. This was partly a result of the greater availability of manpower—both rowers and marines—because the new rulers of Macedon, Egypt, and Asia could command huge resources from the remains of the empire of Alexander the Great. Their successors were not, however, able to match this level of naval power.

[*See also Odyssey, The*; Salamis, Battle of; Trireme; Wars, Maritime, *subentry* Peloponnesian War; *and* Warships, *subentry on* Ancient Warships.]

## Bibliography

De Souza, Philip. *The Peloponnesian War, 431–404 BC*. Oxford: Osprey, 2002. This fully illustrated history discusses all the major naval battles and includes a chapter on the career of a naval commander.

De Souza, Philip. "Towards Thalassocracy? Archaic Greek Naval Developments." In *Archaic Greece: New Approaches and New Evidence*, edited by Nick Fisher and Hans van Wees, pp. 271–293. London: Duckworth, 1998. A detailed discussion of the evidence for the development of Greek navies up to the fifth century B.C.E.

Gabrielsen, Vincent. *Financing the Athenian Fleet: Public Taxation and Social Relations*. Baltimore: Johns Hopkins University Press, 1994. A lively and detailed analysis of how the classical Athenian navy operated, focusing on its finances.

Gardiner, Robert, ed. *The Age of the Galley: Mediterranean Oared Vessels since Pre-Classical Times*. London: Conway Maritime Press; Annapolis, Md.: Naval Institute Press, 1995. This illustrated volume contains several essays by leading scholars on ancient Greek warships and navies.

Morrison, John S., John F. Coates, and N. Boris Rankov. *The Athenian Trireme: The History and Reconstruction of an Ancient Greek Warship*. 2d ed. Cambridge, U.K.: Cambridge University Press, 2000. This detailed account of the history of the trireme covers several important sea battles in detail and discusses all the evidence on which the reconstruction is based.

Morrison, John S., and R. T. Williams. *Greek Oared Ships 900–322 B.C.* Cambridge, U.K.: Cambridge University Press, 1968. A detailed study of the textual and iconographic evidence for ancient Greek warships of the archaic and classical periods.

Sabin, Philip, Hans van Wees, and Michael Whitby, eds. *The Cambridge History of Greek and Roman Warfare*, vol. 1. Cambridge, U.K.: Cambridge University Press, 2006. See B. S. Strauss, "Classical Naval Battles and Sieges," and Philip de Souza, "Hellenistic Naval and Siege Warfare."

Wees, Hans van. *Greek Warfare: Myths and Realities*. London: Duckworth, 2004. This fully referenced, authoritative study of ancient Greek warfare includes two chapters discussing naval warfare.

PHILIP DE SOUZA

# Rome

Although Rome never enthusiastically embraced a naval tradition, nor glorified in verse, song, or prose those who built, manned, and maintained its navy, it eventually so dominated the seas that Romans justifiably called the Mediterranean *mare nostrum* ("our sea"). Toward the end of the fourth century B.C.E. (in 311), we see the beginnings of a Roman fleet in the establishment of two officials, called *duumviri navales*, charged with overseeing two squadrons of ten vessels each. Most likely the Romans fitted out this fleet only as needed and relied heavily on crews, and perhaps ships, drawn from Rome's *socii navales* (naval allies) in southern Italy. One squadron appeared at Tarentum in 282, where it was attacked and defeated in an incident that led to war with Tarentum and King Pyrrhus, called in from

Greece for assistance. The famous "Pyrrhic victories" all occurred on land, however.

Between 264 and 241, Rome challenged Carthage, heretofore the dominant naval power in the western Mediterranean, for naval supremacy in the so-called First Punic War. A dispute in Sicily required Rome to have a fleet and, in 260, the Roman Senate authorized the building of a hundred quinqueremes ("fives," with five banks of oars) and twenty triremes (three banks) as well as the hiring and training of crews to man them. In a tour de force of ancient mobilization, the fleet put to sea only sixty days after the trees were cut. We know of one Carthaginian prototype that was used as a model, but surely shipwrights were hired who also worked from Greek designs, the quinquereme having been invented at Syracuse. To counter the superior ramming skills of their enemy, the Romans fitted to their foredecks a heavy boarding bridge called a *corvus*, which, when deployed, securely held an enemy vessel alongside. The *corvus* contributed to Roman victories at Mylae off Sicily's north coast in 260 and at Ecnomus off the island's south coast in 256.

## The Rise of Supremacy

The Romans eventually prevailed over their foes because of their superior reserves of timber and manpower, and their willingness to use them. The loss of ships and men on both sides was tremendous. Polybius, whose account chronicled the war, recorded losses of about five hundred quinqueremes for the Carthaginians and about seven hundred for the Romans. In 249 Rome possessed just twenty ships and temporarily lost the drive to reinitiate a naval war. Six years later, however, they decided to outfit another fleet, relying on loans from wealthy citizens for financing. Following the design of a particularly fast quinquereme that had been captured, they built two hundred copies and sent the fleet to blockade the harbors of Drepanum and Lilybaeum in western Sicily during the summer of 242. In March 241 this fleet engaged a relieving force sent by Carthage at the Aegates Islands and won a resounding victory. Peace was concluded soon thereafter. Among the terms of the peace agreement was the requirement that the Carthaginians pay more than 91 tons of silver (3,200 talents) in ten years' time—a sum used, perhaps, to defray the cost of fleet maintenance. This may help to explain why the Romans' fleet still numbered two hundred units in 229, when they used it to check Illyrian piracy in a war with Queen Teuta.

**Ancient Roman Navy.** Naumachia, a representation of a naval battle, from the Isis Temple in Pompeii, shows two Roman galleys in the first century C.E. that are probably larger than triremes, each with a full complement of marines embarked. ERICH LESSING / ART RESOURCE, NY

Because of Roman superiority at sea, there were no great sea battles during the Second Punic War (218–201). Rome's clear naval supremacy blocked the Carthaginians from ferrying their troops to Italy from Africa and forced Hannibal to make his dramatic march over the Alps. Accordingly, the Roman fleet was used to protect the coasts of Italy, intercept Carthaginian supply convoys, and plunder the African coast. In 214 the Romans laid siege to Syracuse with 130 ships. Lacking an ability to employ ship-mounted catapults, the Roman fleet suffered seriously when attacked with Archimedes' land-based catapults, scorpions, and grappling hooks. Using these devices the Syracusans frustrated their enemy's attempts to take their city from the sea, and when the Romans finally gained entry in 212, it was their land force that opened the breach.

Among the spoils of their victory, the Romans gained a large number of catapults and ballistae, and in 210 they used their new weaponry at the siege of a coastal Greek city called Anticyra. According to Livy, the siege was carried out simultaneously by sea and land, "the pressure from the sea being the heavier because it was the Romans who were applying it, and because they had siege artillery of all kinds on board their vessels." A few years later Publius Cornelius Scipio Africanus besieged Utica (near Carthage) and successfully resisted attempts to break the siege by using to perfection techniques described by Philo of Byzantium in a third-century Greek manual on siege craft called *Poliorketika*. Roman military men were famous for adopting useful techniques from their enemies.

In the following years the Romans extended their supremacy at sea by successfully concluding their war with Carthage (in 201) and then by waging brief wars with the Macedonian king Philip V (201–197) and the Syrian king Antiochus III (192–190). Initially concerned with ferrying troops and supplies to western Greece, Rome expanded its power into the eastern Mediterranean by working with the navies of Rhodes and Pergamum. A number of fleet actions off western Asia Minor—near Cissus in 191, Side in 190, and Myonessus, also in 190—put an end to Antiochus's naval aspirations and left Rome the master of the Mediterranean basin.

In spite of this supremacy, or more likely because of it, the Romans decommissioned their fleets and relied instead on Rhodes and Pergamum to police the eastern Mediterranean. A brief war with Macedon in 171 and another with Carthage in 146 did not spur the Romans to revert to major fleet-building operations. In mid-century the Romans established Delos as a free port, partly to demonstrate their displeasure at Rhodes's independent attitude. This act so reduced the income from harbor dues at Rhodes that Rome was no longer able to maintain its fleet, and as a result pirates on the nearby Cilician coast eventually brought chaos to every corner of the Mediterranean. By 67, the menace had become so serious and widespread that the Roman Senate entrusted Gnaeus Pompeius Magnus (Pompey) with extraordinary powers to address the problem. He first divided the Mediterranean into thirteen districts, each with its own commander and fleet. In an amazing campaign of three months, his district forces carried out simultaneous attacks, while he swept himself from west to east with a separate force and so eradicated the problem. The district squadrons that Pompey activated grew into the fleets that fought in Rome's civil wars and eventually evolved into the navy that turned the Mediterranean into a Roman lake.

## Augustus

In the mid-first century, rivalries between Julius Caesar and Pompey, between Augustus and Pompey's son Sextus Pompeius, and finally among Augustus, Marcus Antonius (Antony), and Cleopatra demonstrated once again the requirement of naval supremacy to those who would rule Rome and the Mediterranean. Although no great sea battles were fought between Caesar and Pompey, the latter amassed a fleet that was used by his son Sextus to cut off the grain supply to Rome. Forced to act, Augustus appointed Marcus Agrippa to coordinate the program required to neutralize Sextus. During the winter of 38 a massive mobilization effort produced a fleet of 370 ships, including units up to "sixes" in size. Agrippa also invented a new type of catapult-shot grapnel, called a *harpax*, that allowed an enemy vessel to be harpooned and then winched alongside for boarding. In 36 a decisive battle was fought off Sicily's northeastern tip near Naulochus. The casualty totals provide a broad picture of what happened: Sextus lost 183 of a total force of 300 warships—28 by ramming and 155 by capture and by fire. He never recovered.

The final conflict between Augustus and his rival Antony occurred five years later, off western Greece at Actium. In the years after Naulochus, Antony and Cleopatra had prepared a naval force reminiscent of third-century Ptolemaic fleets. In 32, they headed toward Italy with five hundred warships, including a number of larger units—"sevens," "eights," "nines," and "tens." The presence of these large warships, best suited for naval siege warfare, indicated that Antony was prepared to gain coastal cities by force, if necessary. Accordingly, Augustus crossed from Italy in the spring of 31 to keep the war from Italian shores. He met his rival at Cape Actium, south of Corfu on the western coast of Greece. By the end of summer, Augustus's admiral Agrippa had methodically cut Antony's supply lines and left him with few options other than retreat. In the final battle, fought on September 2, Antony and Cleopatra tried to escape with as much of their fleet as they could save. Although the battle accounts are laced with doubtful details, a war memorial built in the region soon after the event accords with the broad outlines of the tradition and implies that Antony lost about 140 units of a total force of 230 warships. This loss would include about 80 by ramming or capture and perhaps as many as 60 by fire.

After Actium, Augustus reduced the size of his armed forces by more than 50 percent (from sixty or more legions to twenty-eight). Since Rome now controlled the ports of the Mediterranean, Augustus thereafter relied on the navy for official communication, imperial missions, and pirate control. Because a large force was unnecessary for these purposes, he decommissioned many of the ships in his possession and assigned the rest to stations at Forum Iulii (on the southern coast of Gaul), Misenum (near Naples), and Ravenna (near the mouth of the Po on the Adriatic coast of Italy). The Romans continued this reliance on small fleet stations for some two centuries after Augustus. Inscriptions imply that the fleets at Misenum and Ravenna contained mostly "threes," although we know of one "six" at Misenum (probably the flagship), three "fives," and a limited number of "fours" and "liburnians," a class smaller than "threes."

## Other Fleets

Inscriptions and other sources dating from the first century C.E. and later refer to a number of provincial fleets, raised at different times and for different needs. In addition to those in Italy, fleets were reported in Syria (at Antioch), Britain, and the Black Sea and at Sicily and Rhodes. River fleets of lighter warships were also stationed at the mouth of the Nile (at Alexandria), on the Rhine, and at various places along the Danube. At Mainz remains of five oared river craft excavated in the 1980s reveal the nature of these warships. Long and narrow—one hull measured 21 meters by 2.7 meters (68.9 feet by 8.8 feet)—these vessels were built for speed and ease of rowing but lacked waterline rams. During the course of the fourth century these fleets were at best a piecemeal affair, and when Constantine went to war with Licinius neither could call on a standing fleet. The latest report of rammed warships (if that is what "trireme" implies) is from 324 C.E., when Constantine used much smaller ships to defeat the triremes of his rival Licinius in the approaches to the Hellespont. Not until the early sixth century was naval power used as a serious means of achieving political ends, but this occurred in the eastern Byzantine Empire, not the west. The navy of the Byzantine east, composed largely of two-banked vessels called *dromones*, no longer relied on attacks with a waterline ram and apparently was quite different from the force that had for centuries made the Mediterranean a Roman lake.

[*See also* Actium, Battle of, *and* Warships, *subentry on* Ancient Warships.]

## Bibliography

Briscoe, John. "The Second Punic War." In *The Cambridge Ancient History*. Vol. 8: *Rome and the Mediterranean to 133*

*B.C.*, edited by F. W. Walbank, A. E. Astin, M. W. Frederiksen, et al., pp. 44–80. 2d ed. Cambridge, U.K.: Cambridge University Press, 1989. Contains references to major primary sources; on the naval aspects of the war, see especially pp. 65–67.

Casson, Lionel. *The Ancient Mariners.* 2d ed. Princeton, N.J.: Princeton University Press, 1991. An accurate and extremely readable general treatment of ancient seafaring.

Casson, Lionel. *Ships and Seamanship in the Ancient World.* Rev. ed. Baltimore: Johns Hopkins University Press, 1995. The bible of ancient ships and seafaring, containing quotations from primary sources both in the original languages (Greek and Latin) and in translation.

Morrison, John. *Greek and Roman Oared Warships 399–30 B.C.* Oxford: Oxbow Books, 1996. Presents much useful evidence that is relevant to the classes of ancient warships, but its discussion and conclusions are uneven in quality; use with extreme caution.

Morrison, John. "Hellenistic Oared Warships 399–31 B.C." In *The Age of the Galley: Mediterranean Oared Vessels since Pre-Classical Times*, edited by John Morrison, pp. 66–77. Conway's History of the Ship, edited by Robert Gardiner. London: Conway Maritime Press, 1995. Idiosyncratic yet useful discussion of evidence for different classes of Hellenistic and Roman warships.

Murray, William M. "Reconsidering the Battle of Actium—Again." In *Oikistes: Studies in Constitutions, Colonies, and Military Power in the Ancient World Offered in Honor of A. J. Graham*, edited by Vanessa B. Gorman and Eric W. Robinson, pp. 339–360. Leiden, The Netherlands: Brill, 2002. An attempt to combine archaeological and literary evidence for the battle.

Rankov, Boris. "Fleets of the Early Roman Empire, 31 B.C.–A.D. 324." In *The Age of the Galley: Mediterranean Oared Vessels since Pre-Classical Times*, edited by John Morrison, pp. 78–85. Conway's History of the Ship, edited by Robert Gardiner. London: Conway Maritime Press, 1995. Adds important new information to Starr's fundamental treatment of the Roman imperial navy.

Scullard, H. H. "Carthage and Rome: III. The First Punic War." In *The Cambridge Ancient History.* Vol. 7, part 2: *The Rise of Rome to 220 B.C.*, edited by F. W. Walbank, A. E. Astin, M. W. Frederiksen, et al., pp. 537–569. Cambridge, U.K.: Cambridge University Press, 1989. Contains a comprehensive treatment of the war with references to primary sources.

Starr, Chester G. *The Roman Imperial Navy, 31 B.C.–A.D. 324.* 3d ed. Chicago: Ares, 1993. The standard treatment of the subject.

Thiel, J. H. *Studies on the History of Roman Sea-Power in Republican Times.* Amsterdam: North-Holland, 1946. Fundamental work on the Roman navy in Republican times.

WILLIAM M. MURRAY

# Hellenistic States

During the period from Alexander the Great, who began his reign in 336 B.C.E., to the Battle of Actium in 31 B.C.E., the strongest navies included warships that were more diverse in nature and in size than at any other time in antiquity.

## Alexander the Great

In order to understand how and why this came about, one must start with Alexander, antiquity's most successful military commander. Between 336 B.C.E. and 323 B.C.E. he destroyed the Persian Empire and conquered a vast territory stretching from Greece to the Indus River and from southern Russia to Egypt. He died unexpectedly in his thirty-third year, and without a strong successor, his generals fought over what Alexander had won and fragmented the empire into a number of kingdoms that they passed to their offspring. Although our understanding of these events is far from complete, the basic outlines are clear up to the third century, when the main historical narratives break off.

For Alexander, our evidence clearly shows that he understood the value of naval power but recognized its high cost. When he crossed into Asia from Greece, he resolved to avoid pitched sea battles and focused his attacks instead on the port cities of his enemy's fleet. During 334 and 333 he methodically captured the coastal cities of Asia Minor and Syria and then moved to the ports of Phoenicia. The strategy worked well until he reached Tyre, a well-defended city on a small island just off the mainland coast. Because capturing such a city required a naval blockade combined with attacks from all sides, Alexander constructed a causeway from the mainland to the island and began to gather a fleet of warships at nearby Sidon. Drawing on stocks of treasure that he had recently captured in Damascus, he spared no expense in preparing his forces. He gathered "threes" (triremes), "fours," and "fives" from Cyprus and Phoenicia, cut timber from the nearby mountains of Lebanon, and ordered his engineers to design and construct siege machinery of various kinds. He placed catapults, elevated towers, boarding bridges, and battering rams on the decks of his warships. He yoked pairs of ships together to create wider floating platforms, refit freighters to serve as workboats to remove underwater debris, and sent his heaviest vessels to ram the barriers placed at the harbor entrances. In the end, Alexander's forces simultaneously breached the walls and the harbor defenses and thereby took the city by storm. The outcome at Tyre, a city supposedly impregnable to attack, fostered a new expectation that a determined besieger could speed up the pace of a siege—always a tedious affair—if only he brought enough firepower to bear on the city. The siege took seven months in all.

Following Tyre, Alexander moved south to Gaza, which he captured in two months, and then he occupied Egypt without resistance, thereby completing his sweep of Persian naval bases. Once Egypt was secure, the campaign turned eastward, fighting was conducted largely on land, and the fleet played only a supporting role. Upon his death in 323, Alexander's crown passed to two weak successors: an infant son and a mentally deficient half brother. Not surprisingly, his generals prevented either one from unifying the kingdom, and by 310 both were dead. By 305 the strongest generals declared themselves kings over the regions that they ruled: Antigonus over Macedonia, Ptolemy over Egypt, Seleucus over Syria, and Lysimachus over Thrace. Except for Lysimachus, who was killed by a disinherited son of Ptolemy in 279, these dynasts and their progeny successfully established a balance of power that prevailed until Rome eclipsed them, one by one, during the second and first centuries B.C.E.

Because Alexander's successors focused their energies on controlling Mediterranean lands, the possession of an effective naval force—particularly a naval siege unit—emerged as a subject of intense competition. This need was demonstrated acutely to Antigonus in 315 when he found the Phoenician fleet in Ptolemy's possession and himself unable to capture Tyre as a result. To rectify the situation Antigonus embarked on a massive shipbuilding program, establishing shipyards at Tripolis, Byblos, and Sidon, a fourth at Cilicia, and a fifth at Rhodes. Eventually he gathered a navy sufficient to enforce a blockade and finally gained entrance to Tyre in 313. The lesson learned by Alexander in 332 was thus reaffirmed in 313, and Antigonus—along with his son Demetrius—emerged as the most aggressive naval power of all, driving a naval arms race with his rivals that produced bigger and bigger ships designed to attack and defend the coastal cities so important to everyone's aspirations.

## Bigger and Bigger Warships

These new "Hellenistic navies" required larger warships than were built before, and our sources imply that they were introduced in rapid succession. In 307, "sixes" and "sevens" are said to have helped Demetrius defeat Ptolemy off Cyprian Salamis; six years later Demetrius's fleet contained an "eleven" and a "thirteen," and by the time of his attack on Asia Minor in 288, his fleet included a "fifteen" and a "sixteen." By mid-century the fleet of Ptolemy II (285–246) included multiple numbers of fives to thirteens, and then one "twenty" and two "thirties."

The key to understanding these largest vessels might be found in Demetrius's siege of Rhodes (306–305 B.C.E.), when he attacked the harbor with giant floating siege towers. As a base for each tower he joined two freighters together with massive timbers. Once finished, the cumbersome constructions were successfully towed into place but then collapsed when bad weather caused the hulls to rock in opposite directions. Lysimachus may have figured a way to solve this problem when he built *Leontophoros*, a catamaran warship described by Memnon of Herakleia as a double-hulled "eight." One might guess that Ptolemy's twenty (a double "ten"?) and thirties (double "fifteens"?) were really scaled-up versions of Lysimachus's *Leontophoros*. We know that these monsters were catamarans from what we are told about the largest vessel from this age—a "forty," built during the reign of Ptolemy IV (221–203 B.C.E.). She was 128 meters long, was 17.4 meters wide, and stood more than 20 meters above the water at the bow and stern. She had two sterns, four steering oars, two helmsmen, two bows, and seven rams arranged on a V-shaped construction that joined the bows together. On her maiden voyage she carried 4,000 oarsmen, 2,850 marines, and 400 officers, enlisted men, and deckhands.

These behemoths are traditionally seen as examples of Hellenistic "gigantism"—an expression of regal megalomania that marks some public displays and building projects, particularly in Ptolemaic Egypt. The traditional view was that in battle these vessels were packed with marines and catapults and were used primarily for "bombard, grapple, and board" warfare. As the quality of available oar crews decreased, commanders began to rely less and less on ramming tactics and more on the skill of deck troops, particularly in boarding the enemy. Catapults were thought to play a role by disrupting the oar crews with deck-penetrating bolts. Since larger and larger warships were built to defeat smaller opponents by overwhelming them with superior firepower, most felt that the giant double-hulled vessels were built to accommodate batteries of catapults and masses of marines.

The little evidence we have for this period, however, does not support this traditional view. Though it is true that we lack a full record of major battles—we know, for example, little of mid-century sea battles between Antigonus and Ptolemy near Aegean Kos and Andros—we do possess collections of military "tricks," called stratagems (*strategemata*), that stem from other conflicts of the period. Surprisingly, those dealing with naval actions primarily concern coastal cities and attempts to capture them. Among the military tracts from this period we also possess a detailed set of directions on how to operate and defend against a naval siege unit. The directions were written during the mid-third century B.C.E. by Philo, an artillery engineer employed by a general named Ariston. In his work, called *Poliorketika* (Siege Tactics), Philo clearly describes how Ariston might use a mixed fleet of diverse warships to best advantage. Boarding attempts should be minimized, big ships should be used to break through harbor barriers and even ram sections of the wall whose foundations were placed in the sea, and commanders should employ deck troops skilled in fighting at sea, that is, troops who would follow orders and not rashly climb out onto enemy ships.

## Assessment

In the past, most discussions regarding Greek and Roman navies have been dominated by two basic models—one patterned after the Athenian navy, and the other patterned after the Roman navy. Resembling neither the Athenian nor the Roman examples, the navies of the major Hellenistic states require a third model, one that would include a range of vessels, from quite small to quite large, often fitted with siege machinery and artillery and often used to (among other things) attack the harbor installations of coastal cities. Three factors seem to have contributed to the development of such a navy: (1) the vast sums of Persian money liberated by Alexander's conquests, (2) advanced levels of technology applied to the solution of military problems, and (3) the frenzied struggle among Alexander's generals to carve out portions of empire for themselves at the expense of their rivals. These were unique conditions that did not apply to everyone, and for this reason other sea powers (like Rhodes, Carthage, and Rome) adopted models of naval power with different objectives. When these particular factors became less important or too expensive, as occurred during the second century B.C.E. when the stocks of Persian treasure had been spent, the unique kind of navy produced by the Hellenistic monarchs also disappeared—that is, until Mark Antony and Cleopatra VII made one brief, extravagant attempt to reestablish this kind of navy.

Traditionally, Octavian's defeat of Antony and Cleopatra at Actium (31 B.C.E.) was understood as the final triumph of small versus big, where victory turned on the excellence of Roman military virtue. In short, when manned by Roman and Italian soldiers, the smaller Roman fives proved superior to the Hellenistic eights, nines, and tens manned by troops of inferior skill and courage. Considering the Hel-

lenistic model of naval power described above, Antony and Cleopatra probably built their largest vessels to ensure entry into the ports of southern Italy, not to overwhelm their enemies in pitched battles at sea. That they never got to southern Italy demonstrates the strategic acumen of Octavian and Agrippa. During the winter of 32, Octavian moved a large force across the Adriatic to block Antony's advance. The final battle was fought far from the harbors of Italy, off the entrance to the Ambracian Gulf in a lightly populated region of western Greece. Thereafter, with no more rivals to fear at sea, Octavian mothballed Antony's largest warships and brought to a close the Hellenistic era of naval warfare.

[*See also* Actium, Battle of; Mediterranean Sea; Technology and Weapons, *subentry* Ancient and Medieval to 1300; *and* Warships, *subentry on* Ancient Warships.]

## Bibliography

Texts and translations of ancient authors can be conveniently found in the Loeb Classical Library (London and Cambridge, Mass.: Harvard University Press). See also Felix Jacoby, *Die Fragmente der Griechischen Historiker* (Leiden, Netherlands: Brill, 1954–1969).

Basch, Lucien. *Le musée imaginaire de la marine antique.* Athens: Institut Hellénique pour la Préservation de la Tradition Nautique, 1987. Presents a wealth of illustrative detail that supplements Morrison, *Greek and Roman Oared Warships;* evidence for the Hellenistic period appears on pp. 337–394.

Casson, Lionel. *The Ancient Mariners: Seafarers and Sea Fighters of the Mediterranean in Ancient Times.* 2d ed. Princeton, N.J.: Princeton University Press, 1991. General yet accurate treatment of Hellenistic naval developments can be found on pp. 127–142; influenced to a degree by Tarn, *Hellenistic Military and Naval Developments.*

Casson, Lionel. *Ships and Seamanship in the Ancient World.* Rev. ed. Baltimore: Johns Hopkins University Press, 1995. The bible of ancient ships and seafaring, containing primary source quotations both in the original Greek and Latin and in translation; a discussion of Hellenistic navies appears on pp. 97–140.

Foley, Vernard, and Werner Soedel. "Ancient Oared Warships." *Scientific American,* April 1981, pp. 148–163. Presents the argument that catapults made ramming obsolete.

Garlan, Yvon. *Recherches de poliorcétique grecque.* Athens: École Française d'Athènes, 1974. Scholarly study of Greek siegecraft, with the Greek text of Philo, a French translation, and commentary (pp. 281–404).

Morrison, J. S. *Greek and Roman Oared Warships.* Oxford: Oxbow Books, 1996. Presents literary and iconographic evidence for Hellenistic and Roman warships, but must be used with caution; see a review of the book by W. M. Murray in *International Journal of Nautical Archaeology* 27 (1998): 81–83.

Morrison, J. S. "Hellenistic Oared Warships, 399–31 BC." In *The Age of the Galley: Mediterranean Oared Vessels since Pre-Classical Times*, edited by J. S. Morrison and Robert Gardiner, pp. 66–77. London: Conway Maritime Press; Annapolis, Md.: Naval Institute Press, 1995. Convenient presentation of the basic evidence for various Hellenistic ship classes.

Tarn, W. W. *Hellenistic Military and Naval Developments*. Cambridge, U.K.: Cambridge University Press, 1930. Influential and generally accepted version of Hellenistic naval warfare on pp. 101–152; now requires substantial revision.

WILLIAM M. MURRAY

# Persia

All the information we have about the ancient Persian (Achaemenid) navy has been preserved by Greek historians, such as Herodotus, most of it in reports on Greco-Persian conflicts—with most by far, if not all, the reports going back to Greek informants. Independent Persian tradition is lost. There are no relevant primary documents, and no remains of ships or naval installations have been found or excavated. Therefore all modern interpretations that concern the development and organization of this navy and the long-term naval policies of the Achaemenid kings are at best plausible hypotheses.

## Genesis

The first action of Persian naval forces took place in 525 B.C.E. in connection with the conquest of Egypt—then a sea power—by Kambyses, the second Achaemenid king. It appears that Kambyses built his own ships, which were then manned by hired Phoenician rowers and sailors, just as, later, the expanded navy was manned by oar crews and sailors hired from among other subject peoples. Xerxes' armada is described in these terms by Diodorus. According to Herodotus, new subjects possessing a navy were deprived of it instead of being obliged to use it for the benefit of the Persians only. If Kambyses was the creator of the navy, its final organization and infrastructure, and especially its financial basis, were no doubt the work of the third Achaemenid king, Darius (522–486 B.C.E.).

## Strength and Organization

Kambyses' navy may be put at about three hundred triremes—the number needed to equal the navies of Egypt and its ally Polykrates of Samos, which threatened the Persian coastal possessions from the Hellespont to Palestine. This figure was clearly fundamental in the later develop-ment of the navy. The navy was eventually doubled and even quadrupled: fleets of six hundred are mentioned in 494 and 490, and Xerxes' fleet numbered twelve hundred. These enormous and generally suspected (and therefore emended) figures may be explained by assuming that these fleets, which operated far from their bases, included large numbers of reserve ships; that is, there were not enough full oar crews for all the ships.

After the debacle of Salamis in 480, the navy became much smaller—up to the end of the Peloponnesian war (431–404) it was denied its footing in the Aegean by the navy of the Athenian alliance (the Delian League), and this clearly reduced its potential by more than half. Even after the Delian League was dissolved in 404, the Persian navy never regained its old strength; four hundred is the largest figure referred to.

According to Herodotus and Strabo, the Persian navy had central bases in Cilicia (Aleion Pedion, east of modern Mersin, Turkey) and in Kyme-Phokaia (north-northwest of Izmir, Turkey), both isolated from the centers furnishing the crews. The Cilician base was evidently guarded by a strong garrison of troopers, paid out of the province's tribute. Of the other base, little is known. In 480 it had a high-born Persian governor (*hyparchos*) who commanded his own squadron of fifteen ships. Lost after 479, Kyme was again a Persian base by 386. Acco in southern Phoenicia may have been a third base. Conceivably, some small squadrons, such as the one in Kyme, were stationed in a few harbors (for instance, Halicarnassus and Sidon) to deal with emergencies, but these squadrons were too small to threaten the big bases in case of rebellion.

The command structure of the Persian navy is obscure. High commanders of fleets in action were, according to Herodotus, normally selected from the imperial (Iranian) aristocracy. Herodotus also reported that before the Ionian revolt in western Asia Minor (499–494) Greek subjects served as commanders of ships and larger units; after 404 even an Athenian and various non-Persians (Carians?) served as commanding officers of fleets. Nothing is known of the lower ranks. The ships of this navy were the rowed warships of the period, initially the trireme—which was probably a recent (not necessarily Greek) development in 525—and later the quinquereme.

## Record of Service

Two periods of the Persian navy's service may be distinguished. The first (525–479) is described in some detail by Herodotus and (for one episode) by the poet Aeschylus. The second (479–330) is reported in far less detail, by authors interested only marginally (Thucydides, Xenophon) or preserved indirectly (Ephorus, c. 405–330, whose work was abridged by Diodorus and quoted by, for one, Plutarch).

**The First Period: 525–479.** After Egypt had been subjected by Kambyses, Darius I employed the navy to strengthen Persian dominance over the coast of Asia Minor and the adjacent islands (for instance, the Persians occupied Samos c. 517), to conquer Thrace (for its gold and silver mines), and to launch the expedition against Scythia (c. 512). The revolt in western Asia Minor, which was possibly provoked in part by heavy conscription of oarsmen in 500 and started with the rebels' seizure of the mobilized fleet (200–300 triremes, expanded to 353), was crushed in the battle of Lade (494) by the eastern fleet, expanded to six hundred ships, followed by the overwhelming of Miletos, where the revolt had started.

Next, the fleet was employed in recovering and strengthening the Persian positions in the Aegean, specifically in Thrace (the disarming of Thasos occurred in 492). In 490 an amphibious expedition with six hundred triremes was ordered to subdue Naxos and other Cyclades and to punish Eretria and Athens for giving support to the Ionian rebels; the expedition was successful except for the attempt on Athens, which failed when the Persians lost the land battle of Marathon.

Persian policy was clearly defensive to a large extent; the chief aim was the elimination of potentially hostile navies (Thasos, Naxos). The Greek interpretation—that the policy was aimed at subjection of the European Greeks, if not of Europe—is based not on authentic information but on speculation, probably incited by the enormous scale of Xerxes' later attack (in 480).

Xerxes' attack, which the Greeks naturally saw as a manifestation of pure expansionism, was provoked—certainly in its magnitude—by the naval arms race that was started in Greece by Themistokles' navy law of 483, which followed similar building programs in the Greek west (as reported by both Herodotus and Thucydides). The complete annihilation of the newly built triremes, about 380 in number, was the primary objective of the Persian naval operations from the beginning, as Herodotus emphatically stated. Until it reached the Greek heartland the Persian navy's main task was to drive the Greek ships before it. The Persians lost many ships (well over two hundred) in a storm before they had contact with the enemy. The final attack on the Greek fleet, concentrated in the strait around the city of Salamis, was preceded by a reconnais-sance in force. This preparation revealed to Themistokles the Persian's battle plan, which he successfully disrupted with his celebrated message "that the Greeks were about to scatter in flight" (recorded by Aeschylus and Herodotus). Xerxes then closed the escape routes east and west of Salamis Island, using detachments taken from his striking forces. This caused lack of coordination between the vanguard and the second echelon and led to the crushing of the vanguard between the second echelon and the Greek defenders. The losses of the Persians probably amounted to half their effective strength, more than two hundred fully manned triremes with all hands. If, as is probable, these ships were mostly Phoenician, the loss in quality would have been even more disastrous. This defeat of the Persians left the Greeks masters of the Aegean.

In the operations of 479 the Persian commanders, having sent home the Phoenician ships after Salamis—presumably to prevent and resist possible Greek raids in the Levant—did not hazard confrontation with the Greek fleet of 110 triremes. At the end of the (land) battle of Mykale (southeast of Samos), the remnants of the Persian fleet were burnt by the victorious Greeks.

**The Second Period: 479–330.** After their disappearance from the Aegean, the Persian navy was much reduced in strength, although the recorded figures (mostly dubious) suggest that numerically it was still the equal—or more than that—of the fleets of the Athenian alliance that now controlled the Aegean. Athenian operations in the region of Cyprus culminated in two large-scale engagements. The first, the land and sea battle of Eurymedon, took place east of modern Antalya, Turkey, in about 468; according to Thucydides all two hundred Persian ships were lost. The second engagement (c. 450), also on land and sea, near modern Larnaka, Cyprus, was again a double defeat for the Persians. In both cases it is impossible, for want of detailed information (even on the Greek side), to determine the military and political objectives of both parties, but there is no reason to doubt that the Persians were on the defensive against Athenian attempts to extend the alliance. The Persians' defeats made them abandon, in the Peace of Kallias (c. 450), their position in the whole coastal region of western Asia Minor. Thucydides reported that it was only after the downfall of Athenian power after 412 and the rise of Spartan sea power in the Aegean that the Persian commander in that area announced the coming of 147 ships from Phoenicia—which, however, never arrived. Persian naval policy was, in fact, restricted to subsidizing the Spartans. This (unless it was a deliberate policy) suggests difficulties in finding sufficient crews in Phoenicia, a factor that might explain the apparent decline of the navy after Xerxes. The suggestion seems confirmed by the sequel: when, after the definitive elimination of the Athenian alliance, a Persian navy was mobilized against Sparta, it owed its victory in the battle of Knidos under the Athenian Konon (394) largely to Greek manpower and in particular to Athenian technical personnel. Also, when Artaxerxes III, sometime after 350, started preparing the reconquest of Egypt and called up his navy, Sidon initiated a revolt of the Phoenician cities. Phoenician reluctance to serve in the Persian king's navy may well have been the effect of the disastrous losses in the battles of Salamis and Eurymedon, which must have been particularly grievous for communities dependent on maritime trade. Such reluctance (not only on the part of the Phoenicians) might explain the curious contrast between the impressive numbers of the navy and its ineffectiveness, especially at the time of Alexander the Great's Persian expedition, when a fleet of four hundred ships is said to have held supremacy at sea but accomplished almost nothing. It certainly looks as though it was impossible in the long run to base the power politics of an empire on the capacities of the city-states within its domain.

[*See also* Athens; Salamis, Battle of; Strategy; *and* Tactics.]

## Bibliography

Briant, Pierre. *Histoire de l'empire perse de Cyrus à Alexandre*. 2 vols. Achaemenid History X. Leiden, The Netherlands: Nederlands Instituut voor het Nabije Oosten; Paris: Fayard, 1996.

Wallinga, H. T. *Ships and Sea-power before the Great Persian War: The Ancestry of the Ancient Trireme*. Leiden, The Netherlands; New York; and Cologne, Germany: Brill, 1993.

H. T. WALLINGA

# Egypt

Egyptian military activities in the Dynastic period (2950–525 B.C.E.) were focused on three main geographical areas. The first encompassed the kingdoms of Upper and Lower Egypt, stretching along the highly fertile and densely populated Nile Valley from the region of the First Cataract northward to the Delta. The second area lay south of the kingdom of Upper Egypt and encompassed the territories of Nubia and Cush, extending approximately from the First to the Fifth Cataracts of the Nile; the principal reason for Egyptian interest here was gold. The third area was the Levantine coastal region, which was important for maritime and overland trade, but which was also of great strategic significance because several states and empires bordering that region were major military threats.

## Ships and Shipbuilding

Egypt had ample resources of manpower but lacked wood for shipbuilding. The pharaohs of the Old Kingdom period (2575–2175 B.C.E.), who ruled a united Egypt, valued highly their seaborne trade with the Levant, which was a significant source of pinewood. Naval forces were used to establish and maintain Egyptian control in these regions, but the relative significance of the naval elements in pharaonic forces varied over time. The early pharaohs deployed naval vessels to transport by river and sea the soldiers who asserted the pharaohs' power, but they lacked permanent military forces. They also organized trading voyages down the coast of the Red Sea to the land of Punt (northern Ethiopia and Somalia), whence vital quantities of myrrh and frankincense were obtained, although not by force.

During the First Intermediate period (2125–1975 B.C.E.), the unity of Upper and Lower Egypt dissolved into political instability. The rulers of Upper Egypt, whose capital was Thebes, deployed naval flotillas along the Nile to reunify Egypt and project their power southward. Evidence from the end of the Middle Kingdom period (1975–1640 B.C.E.) has been used to argue that these naval elements formed the elite core of the first permanent Egyptian army. The Hyksos—Asian invaders who brought about the downfall of the Middle Kingdom and whose capital was at Avaris in the eastern part of the Nile Delta—were engaged in a protracted war by the Thebes-based pharaohs of the Seventeenth Dynasty, whose strategy depended on rapid movement along the Nile. An inscribed record of the campaign waged by Kamose (1541–1539 B.C.E.) in his third regnal year indicates that the pharaoh proceeded northward from Thebes, attacking some enemy cities and bypassing others. Many of Kamose's troops and most of his supplies must have been transported by ship. In the record Kamose boasts about the amount of precious wood used to construct his ships and is presented as commanding operations from a golden flagship.

It is clear that by the Second Intermediate period (1630–1539 B.C.E.) the royal flotillas comprised several ships commanded by aristocratic and princely officers whose status was higher than that of nonnaval officers and who reported directly to the pharaoh. The career of Ahmose son of Ebana, recorded in his tomb at El Kab, shows that

**Ancient Egyptian Navy.** This detail shows the Egyptians' enemies attacking at sea off the mouth of the Nile. It is from the relief on the main temple of Ramses III, Medinet Habu, Thebes, Egypt from about 1190 B.C.E. and is the only representation of an identifiable sea battle surviving from ancient times. ERICH LESSING / ART RESOURCE, NY

rapid promotion from the ranks to a series of naval commands was possible precisely because the ships were so vital. Ahmose fought against the Hyksos in the Delta, and he took part in the imperial expansion into Nubia, to the south of Egypt proper. Royal ships of this period were not genuine warships, having neither rams nor platforms for missile troops, but they could carry large numbers of soldiers. A reasonable estimate is that the maximum capacity of a seagoing ship was two hundred men, including all sailors, soldiers, and officers; Nile vessels might have had complements half as large again.

In the New Kingdom period (1539–1069 B.C.E.) the neglected Red Sea trading fleet was spectacularly revived by Queen Hatshepsut (1473–1458 B.C.E.), but as Egyptian forces increasingly campaigned away from the Nile and regularly encountered Asiatic armies with very substantial chariot elements, the military lost its amphibious structure and the relative status of the naval officers declined. The Egyptian military became land-focused, with professional chariot divisions as its core. Expeditions into Palestine and Syria both required and encouraged this transformation,

although troops carried in naval flotillas were deployed to considerable effect—for example, by Thutmose III (1479–1425 B.C.E.) against the port cities of the Lebanon.

In the reigns of Ramses II (1279–1213), Merneptah (1213–1204 B.C.E.), and Ramses III (1187–1156 B.C.E.) the incursions of the Libyans and of the northern confederations known as the Sea Peoples posed a major threat to Egypt. A raid by the latter into the eastern Nile Delta in the eighth year of Ramses III had to be partly met on water. A detailed epigraphic and pictorial record is preserved on the pharaoh's mortuary temple at Medinet Habu. It shows Egyptian land forces repelling the enemy, as well as a naval flotilla engaging them ship-to-ship, using vessels that seem to be designed for close combat on water. The vessels have what appear to be fighting platforms and raised gunwales to protect their oarsmen. They may have been modeled on contemporary Levantine vessels, or even on those of the Sea Peoples themselves, some of whom were employed as mercenaries by the Egyptians.

The next major naval development occurred when the Saite dynasty (664–525 B.C.E.) began to build up its military forces after the Assyrian invasions of Egypt in 671–667 B.C.E. The Saite pharaoh Necho (610–595 B.C.E.) created two fleets of oared galleys, possibly equipped with fighting decks and rams, one to protect Red Sea trading vessels and the other to supply and reinforce Egypt's Levantine allies. The Greek historian Herodotus claims that Necho's fleets consisted of triremes, but this may be an anachronism. Herodotus tells us that Necho started a canal linking the Red Sea with the Nile, but that he abandoned the project and instead commissioned Phoenician sailors to attempt a clockwise circumnavigation of Africa, looking for a sea route from the Red Sea to the Mediterranean. They may have succeeded, but discovered that the journey was too lengthy for regular voyages.

Egypt was conquered by the Achaemenid Persian king Cambyses in 525 B.C.E., and Egyptian-based warships played a major role in the campaigns of the Persian kings. Several hundred triremes crewed by Egyptians but under the command of Persian noblemen took part in the battles of Artemisium and Salamis in 480 B.C.E. Persian control over Egypt was often challenged and was never secure after a major revolt in 404 B.C.E. Consequently the Persian kings were unable to utilize their Egyptian naval contingents, which may well have been a factor in the failure of Darius III (336–330 B.C.E.) to resist Alexander the Great's invasion.

## Rule by Greeks and Romans

After Alexander's death in 323 B.C.E., Egypt came under the control of one of his generals, Ptolemy, whose Macedonian dynasty lasted nearly three hundred years. As before, the Red Sea and the Levantine coast were a major focus of Egyptian naval forces. However, the Ptolemaic kings' close involvement in the politics of the Greek world widened the scope of Egyptian naval endeavors, along the coastlines of the eastern Mediterranean and into the Aegean.

Egyptian warships of this period had rams and extensive fighting platforms and were powered by oarsmen seated on up to three levels. These vessels required thousands of rowers, and the ratings applied to such ships, varying from "threes" (usually called triremes) to "sixteens," refer not to the number of men pulling each oar, but to the total number of men in each vertical group of oarsmen. Hence a "five" would have oars at only three levels, but on the top two levels the oars were each pulled by two men, while the lowest level had one man to each oar. A few very large vessels were built by the Ptolemies, including a "twenty," two "thirties," and a "forty," but these were never used in naval combat, and if they were intended as anything other than display items, their function would have been as floating artillery platforms for attacks on coastal cities. The capture and defense of cities with major harbors was an essential element of Ptolemaic naval strategy in the Aegean and eastern Mediterranean. In the third and second centuries B.C.E. there were Ptolemaic naval bases at numerous cities on the southern coast of Anatolia, which was an excellent source of timber, and on several key islands from where experienced oarsmen could be recruited, including Samos, Thera, and Crete.

As the last surviving major independent kingdom in an eastern Mediterranean dominated by Rome, Egypt inevitably became entangled in the politics of the Roman aristocracy, whose leading figures looked to Egypt as a source of men, money, and ships. The final naval flourish of the Ptolemaic dynasty came in the reign of Queen Cleopatra VII (51–30 B.C.E.). While the Roman Republic disintegrated in a series of civil wars (49–31 B.C.E.), Cleopatra managed to charm first Gaius Julius Caesar and then Marcus Antonius (Mark Antony). Her alliance with Antonius ultimately brought Egypt into direct conflict with the forces of Gaius Octavius, Caesar's heir. The decisive confrontation occurred in 31 B.C.E. off the western coast of Greece. Octavius's forces managed to blockade the army and fleet of Antonius and Cleopatra at the Actium peninsula on the southern side of the Gulf of Ambracia. Antonius and Cleopatra escaped to Alexandria, where they committed suicide. Octavius took control of Egypt and became the first Roman emperor, naming himself Augustus.

[See also Actium, Battle of; Salamis, Battle of; Trireme; and Warships, subentry on Ancient Warships.]

## Bibliography

Berlev, Oleg. "The Egyptian Navy in the Middle Kingdom." *Palestinskij Sbornik* 80 (1967): 6–20. Written in Russian, Berlev's is a seminal article on the nature of the Egyptian military and the primacy of naval elements for the period 1975–1530 B.C.E.

Casson, Lionel. *The Ancient Mariners: Seafarers and Sea Fighters of the Mediterranean in Ancient Times.* 2d ed. Princeton, N.J.: Princeton University Press, 1991. Covers the main Egyptian developments as part of an authoritative survey of ancient seafaring.

Cifola, Barbara. "Ramses III and the Sea Peoples: A Structural Analysis of the Medinet Habu Inscriptions." *Orientalia* 57 (1988): 275–306. Discusses the strengths and weaknesses of the key inscriptions and images relating to the Sea Peoples and the wider context of Egyptian military and naval policies.

Fabre, David. *Seafaring in Ancient Egypt*. London: Periplus, 2005. Lavishly illustrated and thoroughly researched. Contains excellent sections on ports, ships, and personnel.

Landström, Björn. *Ships of the Pharaohs: 4,000 years of Egyptian Shipbuilding*. London: Allen and Unwin, 1970. Features detailed reconstruction drawings of Egyptian ships based on careful analysis of archaeological and iconographic evidence.

Lloyd, Alan B. "The Saite Navy." In *The Sea in Antiquity*, edited by Graham Oliver, Roger Brock, Tim Cornell, and Stephen Hodkinson, pp. 81–91. British Archaeological Reports International Series, no. 899. Oxford: J. and E. Hedges, Archaeopress, 2000. Discusses the major changes in technology and organization of Egyptian naval power at the end of the Pharaonic period.

Oren, Eliezer D., ed. *The Sea Peoples and Their World: A Reassessment*. Philadelphia: University Museum, University of Pennsylvania, 2000. Contains excellent chapters on aspects of the Sea Peoples and Egyptian naval and military activities in the Ramesside period.

Säve-Söderbergh, Torgny. *The Navy of the Eighteenth Egyptian Dynasty*. Uppsala, Sweden: Lundequistska Bokhandeln; Leipzig, Germany: Otto Harrassowitz, 1946. An old but still very useful analysis of the personnel and ships of the Egyptian navy in the Early New Kingdom period.

Spalinger, Anthony J. "Warfare in Ancient Egypt." In *A Companion to the Ancient Near East*, edited by Daniel C. Snell, pp. 229–241. Oxford: Blackwell, 2004. An excellent short introduction to ancient Egyptian warfare during the period c. 2650–1075 B.C.E.

Spalinger, Anthony J. *War in Ancient Egypt: The New Kingdom*. Oxford: Blackwell, 2005. Covers the period 1575–1100 B.C.E.

Van't Dack, Edmond, and Hans Hauben. "L'apport egyptien a l'armée navale lagide." In *Das Ptolemäische Ägypten*, edited by Herwig Maehler and Volker Michael Strocka, pp. 59–94. Mainz am Rhein, Germany: Philipp von Zabern, 1978. General survey of Ptolemaic naval affairs with detailed discussion of the Egyptian contributions.

Wallinga, Herman T. *Ships and Sea Power before the Great Persian War: The Ancestry of the Ancient Trireme*. Leiden, Netherlands: Brill, 1993. Presents a controversial hypothesis on the possible Egyptian origin of the ancient trireme, as well as analysis of the Egyptian contribution to the Persian navy.

PHILIP DE SOUZA

# Carthage

Carthage, a Phoenician colony of Tyre, was settled in the late ninth or early eighth century B.C.E. and thereafter pursued policies aimed at expanding its mercantile interests in the western Mediterranean. These policies required the simultaneous development of a fleet. By 700 Carthage had established a string of colonies in, among other places, Sardinia, western Sicily, and Malta and along the coast of Spain to facilitate the voyages of its merchant class. Carthage pursued this colonial policy by diplomacy and, if necessary, by force. In about 535 Carthage joined forces with Etruscans in one of the earliest naval battles recorded by Herodotus to drive off a group of Phocaean (Greek) colonists from Corsica. At roughly this same time, or perhaps a little later, the city sent out a commander named Hanno to found colonies along the Atlantic coast of Africa. His venture, chronicled in a short first-person account, included a naval force of sixty fifty-oared galleys called pentekonters. Treaties secured trading rights wherever possible. Polybius quoted from two early treaties made with Rome (in 509 and 348), and Aristotle referred to agreements made with Etruscans.

At the height of its power, from the sixth to the mid-third centuries B.C.E., the Carthaginian fleet was the undisputed master of the western Mediterranean. During the fifth century the colony relied largely on triremes ("threes"–ships with three banks of oars) built, presumably, according to a Phoenician tradition. According to Aristotle, the Carthaginians invented the quadrireme, or "four"; this must have followed soon after Dionysius introduced the first quinquereme ("five") at Syracuse around 399. By the third century the fleet consisted mainly of fours and fives, although threes and a "seven" were reported among thirty-one Carthaginian ships taken by the Romans off Mylae in 260. By the mid-second century the Carthaginians may have reverted to the less costly threes, to judge from the sizes of ship sheds excavated at Carthage. Remains of a small galley excavated near the Sicilian port of Marsala in the 1970s preserve evidence of this shipbuilding tradition.

The best known depictions of the Carthaginian fleet in action come from Polybius's account of the First Punic War (264–241). Although the Carthaginians eventually lost to Rome, they started the conflict with a superior fleet of lighter, faster, and more maneuverable warships. Despite these advantages they were less able to recover from their defeats than were the Romans, who showed a dogged perseverance in the face of adversity, an astonishing ability to learn from mistakes, and a policy of entering each battle with a superior number of vessels. By 242 Rome, having adopted a lighter and faster version of the quinquereme based on a Carthaginian example, brought the war to a close with a victory at the Aegates Islands, off the western tip of Sicily.

The Carthaginians never recovered their position of naval superiority. The Second Punic, or Hannibalic, War (218–201) was fought on land, the fleets serving mainly to ferry troops, supplies, and commanders from one theater to another. According to Polybius, the terms of peace included the surrender of Carthage's fleet to Rome, except for ten triremes. The Third Punic War (149–146) marked the last episode in the struggle with Rome. The war was decided by a siege of Carthage in which fleets again played a secondary role. Appian's account of the action preserves a clear description of Carthage's war harbor, which was circular with an island at the center. Ship sheds, built on the island as well as on the harbor's circumference, held a total of 220 ships. The area also contained shipyards where Appian said threes and fives were constructed from old timber during the final phase of the siege. Excavations conducted by the British in 1977–1978 have corroborated the main features of Appian's account: slipways were roughly the same width as those in Piraeus—that is, appropriate for threes—and might have numbered around 170. The entire complex, moreover, seems to have been built in the period between the Second and Third Punic Wars. Following the defeat by Rome in 146, the Carthaginian fleet was destroyed along with the city itself and the war harbor.

As for naval administration, little is known beyond the fact that admirals were often the same men who served as generals of the land armies. Captains were presumably chosen from the ruling class, but how they were selected remains unknown. Even less is known about the crews, who were likely drawn from local Punic populations, because we might expect some mention of recruitment difficulties in our literary sources had the crews been hired from abroad.

[See also Trireme and Warships, subentry on Ancient Warships.]

## Bibliography

Briscoe, John. "The Second Punic War." In *The Cambridge Ancient History*. 2d ed. Vol. 8: *Rome and the Mediterranean to 133 B.C.*, edited by F. W. Walbank, A. E. Astin, M. W. Frederiksen, et al., pp. 44–80. Cambridge, U.K.: Cambridge University Press, 1989. Contains references to major primary sources; on the naval aspects of the Second Punic War, see especially pp. 65–67.

Casson, Lionel. *The Ancient Mariners: Seafarers and Sea Fighters of the Mediterranean in Ancient Times*. 2d ed. Princeton, N.J.: Princeton University Press, 1991. An accurate and extremely readable general treatment of ancient seafaring; on the naval struggles between Rome and Carthage, see especially pp. 143–156.

Frost, Honor. "Marsala Punic Warship." In *The British Museum Encyclopedia of Underwater and Maritime Archaeology*, edited by James P. Delgado, pp. 260–262. London: British Museum Press, 1997.

Hurst, H. "Le port militaire de Carthage." *Les dossiers d' archéologie* 183 (1993): 42–51.

Hurst, H. "The War Harbour of Carthage." In *Atti del I Congresso internazionale di studi fenici e punici (Roma, 5–10 novembre 1979)*, pp. 603–610. Rome: Consiglio nazionale delle ricerche, 1983.

Scullard, H. H. "Carthage and Rome." In *The Cambridge Ancient History*. 2d ed. Vol. 7, part 2: *The Rise of Rome*, edited by F. W. Walbank, A. E. Astin, M. W. Frederiksen, et al., pp. 486–569. Cambridge, U.K.: Cambridge University Press, 1989. Contains references to major primary sources; on the naval aspects of the First Punic War, see especially pp. 545–566.

Wilson, Roger J. A., et al. "Carthage." In *The Oxford Classical Dictionary*, edited by Simon Hornblower and Anthony Spawforth, pp. 295–296. 3d ed. rev. Oxford: Oxford University Press, 2003.

WILLIAM M. MURRAY

# Phoenicia

Ancient Phoenicia—a region of the Levantine coast from modern Syria to northern Israel—was made up of city-states that were ruled by kings. Home to a powerful merchant class, each of the major cities developed a naval force to protect and foster its own particular interests. Clear evidence for these local navies can be detected in Egyptian and Assyrian documents dating to the late Bronze and early Iron ages (fifteenth to ninth centuries B.C.E.). The best-known period of Phoenician naval excellence was when the Persian king Kambyses (r. 530–522 B.C.E.) incorporated the naval resources from Phoenicia and other Mediterranean regions of his empire into the Persian navy. Ships from the Phoenician cities of Sidon, Tyre, Arados, and Byblos formed the backbone of this navy and continued to do so for centuries thereafter. The available evidence of this navy, limited mainly to Greek historical accounts by Herodotus and Thucydides, reveals the decisive role played by the Phoenician navy in the wars between Persia and Greece at the beginning of the fifth century. Of all the contingents, Sidon's was valued most highly by Xerxes, who selected a Sidonian vessel whenever he traveled by sea. Tyre ranked second in honor.

Despite their defeat by the Greeks at Salamis in 480 B.C.E. and the eventual failure of Xerxes' expedition a year later, the Phoenicians still held their place of honor throughout the fifth century and into the next. They fought with distinction against the Delian confederacy, and in 411 B.C.E. the threat of their arrival still caused fear among the Athenian fleet at Samos. In 396 B.C.E., after the defeat of Athens in the Peloponnesian War (404 B.C.E.), the Persians gathered a fleet for use against Sparta and placed it under the command of the satrap Pharnabazus and the Athenian general Conon. The fleet contained a Phoenician contingent of eighty triremes ("threes"—ships with three banks of oars) that served under the king of Sidon.

When Alexander the Great crossed to Asia in 334 B.C.E., Phoenicians opposed him at sea, but after Darius's defeat at Issus in 333 their allegiance wavered. First Arados, then Byblos, and finally Sidon surrendered to Alexander as he marched toward their homeland. The Tyrians, however, refused to capitulate, and forced a seven-month siege of their island city. Alexander eventually prevailed through a process of naval siege warfare that shifted the goals and objectives of naval warfare for centuries thereafter. From then on, the most powerful rulers knew that warships equipped to attack and defend coastal cities might be the difference between failure and success. This spurred a naval arms race that produced large, expensive ships and siege equipment that dominated naval warfare into the first century B.C.E. Throughout this period Phoenician contingents presumably continued to serve in the fleets of the Ptolemaic and Seleucid kings, depending on who controlled the Phoenician homeland. It is also assumed that Phoenicians served in the fleet of Antony and Cleopatra at Actium in 31 B.C.E. Following Octavian's victory at Actium, Phoenician naval units merged with the fleets of the Roman Empire.

The details of fleet command, organization, manning, and maintenance elude us except for generalities. Phoenician kings exercised supreme command over their navies and were accorded a high degree of independence by their Persian overlords. No local governors were installed, and the major fleet cities were allowed to mint their own coins. Not surprisingly, the cities of Sidon, Byblos, and Arados chose warships as identifying symbols on their coinage. Ship commanders, presumably, came from the elite classes, although we know nothing of the process by which they were selected. Crews were provided by the local populations, but again we do not know how. Herodotus reported that in the fleet of Xerxes in 480 B.C.E. Persians, Medes, and Sacae served as marines, although this must not always have been the case.

Phoenician naval excellence stemmed from a number of factors, including a long tradition of seafaring, access to ample supplies of timber and other shipbuilding materials, and a tradition of excellence in naval architecture and engineering. From the sixth century to the fourth century, Phoenicians relied primarily on the trireme as the main ship of the line; some believe that the Phoenician "threes" were built according to a different design and with a different type of ram than the Greek threes. By the mid-fourth century quinqueremes ("fives") appeared in the Sidonian fleet, and at Tyre in 332 they seemed indistinguishable from fives of Greek design. Phoenicians built ships in sections for Alexander's Arabian expedition at the end of his life; they constructed warships for Antigonos "One Eye" in shipyards located at Tripolis, Byblos, and Sidon in 315; and they contributed to the naval arms race attending the wars of Alexander's successors.

[*See also* Actium, Battle of; Salamis, Battle of; Trireme; *and* Warships, *subentry on* Ancient Warships.]

## Bibliography

Basch, Lucien. "La Phénicie." In *Le musée imaginaire de la marine antique*, pp. 303–336. Athens, Greece: Institut Hellénique pour la Préservation de la Tradition Nautique, 1987. Copious illustrative material.

Basch, Lucien. "Phoenician Oared Ships." *Mariner's Mirror* 55 (1969): 139–162 and 227–245. Presents evidence for differences in design between Phoenician and Greek oared warships.

Casson, Lionel. *Ships and Seamanship in the Ancient World*. Rev. ed. Baltimore: Johns Hopkins University Press, 1995. The bible of ancient ships and seafaring, containing quotations from primary sources in the original languages (Greek and Latin) and in translation.

Eph'al, I. "Syria-Palestine under Achaemenid Rule." In *The Cambridge Ancient History*. 2d ed. Vol. 4: *Persia, Greece, and the Western Mediterranean c. 525 to 479 B.C.*, edited by John Boardman, N. G. L. Hammond, D. M. Lewis, et al., pp. 139–164. Cambridge, U.K.: Cambridge University Press, 1988.

Maier, F. G. "Cyprus and Phoenicia." In *The Cambridge Ancient History*. 2d ed. Vol. 6, *The Fourth Century B.C.*, edited by D. M. Lewis, John Boardman, Simon Hornblower, et al., pp. 297–336. Cambridge, U.K.: Cambridge University Press, 1994.

Wallinga, H. T. *Ships and Sea-Power before the Great Persian War: The Ancestry of the Ancient Trireme*. Leiden, Netherlands: Brill, 1993. Detailed discussion of the formation of the Persian fleet under Kambyses.

WILLIAM M. MURRAY

**Ancient Navigation** Navigation in the ancient Mediterranean was accomplished largely without instruments. An abundant archaeological and literary record, especially after 800 B.C.E., reveals no trace of nautical charts, compasses, logs, optical instruments, celestial tables, chronometers, or barometers. Even so, sophisticated methods and techniques of navigation were developed, most of which took their cues from nature. This "environmental" navigation was similar in many ways to the navigation of the northern Europeans and Vikings of the early Middle Ages (fifth to tenth centuries), as well as the seafaring peoples of Oceania before and during the European Age of Discovery

**Ancient Navigation.** The Tower of the Winds in Athens is 12 meters (39.4 feet) tall and originally had a weather vane that pointed to the wind direction. Three of its eight sides are illustrated here with the west wind (*Zephyros*) on the left, the southwest wind (*Lips*) in the center, and the south wind (*Notos*) on the right. Its construction is attributed to the astronomer Andronicus of Cyrrhus, c. 50 B.C.E., but it may have earlier origins. PHOTOGRAPH BY DAN DAVIS

(fifteenth to seventeenth centuries). The configuration of the Mediterranean played the most significant role in shaping the development of ancient navigation. Although the relatively benign and tideless Mediterranean has been called a large lake and a seafaring nursery, its complex coastal morphology, weather systems, and open areas presented difficult challenges to the seafarers of antiquity. A number of techniques evolved to effect safe navigation: the interpretation of currents, sea swells, clouds, and winds; piloting by natural and manmade landmarks; using the sun and stars for seasonal benchmarks, orientation, proximate location, and course maintenance on the open sea; and constructing "mental maps" of well-traveled areas. Contrary to the popular notion that ancient seafarers always hugged the shoreline for safety, there are multiple mentions of voyages that occurred over the open sea and lasted several days and weeks. Indeed, Western literature begins with several descriptions of open-sea voyages (Homer's *Odyssey*, 3.165 and 14.252).

## Historical Overview and Sources

Deductive clues from archaeology provide nearly all evidence for the existence of navigational knowledge in the prehistory of the Mediterranean. The earliest traces of navigation date to the upper Paleolithic period (10,000–12,000 years ago), that is, before the development of agriculture. Obsidian (a hard volcanic stone) from the Aegean island of Melos has been found in Paleolithic levels in Franchthi Cave on mainland Greece, thus demonstrating the existence of seaworthy boats and nascent navigators at this early date. Similar clues indicating purposeful navigation are found in the presence of hunters on Cyprus at about the same time, and in the colonization of nearly all Mediterranean islands in the subsequent Mesolithic and Neolithic periods (8000–3000 B.C.E.). Many of these islands, then and now, lie far out of sight of land—for instance, the Maltese islands, which were settled by c. 5000 B.C.E. By the Early and Middle Bronze Ages (c. 3000–1700 B.C.E.), archaeology and textual sources signal a burgeoning of seaborne trade networks among Egypt, the cities of the Levantine littoral, Cyprus, and the Aegean. Galleys with wide, boom-footed sails appear in the Egyptian and Minoan iconography of seagoing ships from about 2300–2200 B.C.E. By the Late Bronze Age (1700–1100 B.C.E.), Syro-Canaanite, Cypriot, and Aegean ships ranged far afield, even as far as the western Mediterranean, for trade in exotic goods, metals, and other raw materials. Murals found at the Bronze Age site of Akrotiri on Thera (modern Santorini), a volcanic island north of Crete, provide the clearest depictions of galleys and sailing ships.

**Tenth through fourth centuries B.C.E.: Phoenicia, Carthage, and Greece.** By about 1000 B.C.E., the Phoenicians, ancestors of the Syro-Canaanites, dominated Mediterranean trade from the Levantine cities of Byblos, Sidon, and Tyre. They left very little writing themselves, and so our knowledge is dependent on the Hebrew Bible, Assyrian records, and later Greek authors. The Phoenicians established colonies and trading posts throughout the Mediterranean, founding Carthage (in modern Tunisia) in 814 B.C.E. (the traditional date) and venturing, over the next two centuries, beyond the Strait of Gibraltar to establish more colonies and trading posts along the Atlantic coasts of modern Spain, Portugal, and Morocco. By the sixth century B.C.E., the Carthaginians had become a significant military power and controlled most trade in the western Mediterranean. Phoenician seafaring and navigation prowess, especially outside of the Mediterranean, became proverbial even in their own day. The fifth-century B.C.E. Greek historian Herodotus (*Histories* 4.42) tells of Phoenicians commissioned by the Egyptian pharaoh Necho II (c. 610–595 B.C.E.) to circumnavigate Africa clockwise from the Red Sea.

The Greeks of the eighth through sixth centuries B.C.E. experienced their own seaborne colonization and trading movement. Like the Phoenicians, Greeks from various cities established colonies and trading stations in the central and western Mediterranean, and also in the Hellespont and Black Sea. Like the trading galleys of their Punic (Carthaginian) contemporaries, those of the Greeks ranged all over the Mediterranean, exploiting previously established trade routes and creating others anew. The Phoenician and Greek trading powers generally maintained a fragile equilibrium, although at times direct competition escalated into open warfare.

The seventh and sixth centuries B.C.E. would also define the two broad classes of vessel for the rest of antiquity. The first was the exclusively sail-driven merchant ship, whose cargoes of grain and wine and other bulk foodstuffs demanded larger, well-built hulls. In rare instances, two masts were employed. What oar systems these ships had were used for maneuvering in harbors or in calms. The second broad class of vessel was the ram-equipped war galley filled with rowers on multiple levels. The ram is attested as early as the eighth century B.C.E. on single-decked ships. But by about 700 B.C.E. the two-level galley (bireme) appears, originating either in Greece or in Phoe-

nicia. By the middle of the sixth century B.C.E., the trireme warship (with oars on three levels) made its debut with 170 rowers. The naval battles between Persia and Greece and between Athens and Sparta during the fifth century B.C.E. led to more refined tactics and increased navigational knowledge.

Navigational practices from the sixth to fourth centuries B.C.E. may be discerned in the numerous histories, geographies, and coast pilots. The coast pilot, called a *periplus* (literally "voyage around"), was essentially a travel account that traced the coastline by the sequence of headlands, prominent landmarks, harbors, beaches, watering areas, havens, peoples, and goods traded. Distances were usually measured in terms of a day's and/or night's sail. The earliest *periploi*, such as those of Scylax of Caryanda (mentioned in Herodotus 4.44) and of Hanno the Carthaginian (both c. 500 B.C.E.), already describe areas outside the Mediterranean. Although many of these and subsequent *periploi* contained tidbits of information regarding navigation and the state of knowledge of contemporary geography, there is virtually no evidence that they were employed at sea.

**Fourth through first centuries B.C.E.: The Hellenistic era.** With the death of Alexander the Great at Babylon in 323 B.C.E., the vast Hellenic empire that he had quickly built up disintegrated into three main powers, the Antigonids of Greece, the Seleucids of Asia Minor, the Levant, and Middle East, and the Ptolemies of Egypt. Over the course of the third, second, and first centuries B.C.E., the respective fleets of these powers fought each other for hegemony over the eastern Mediterranean. As ramming tactics gave way to large-scale boarding actions, warships and crew sizes grew ever larger, culminating with the invention of mammoth galleys known as "sixteens," "twenties," and "thirties," the numbers probably referring to the number of men per oar. There is textual evidence that Ptolemy IV (221–203 B.C.E.) even had a "forty" built (Athenaeus). This colossal catamaran, more a display piece than a functional warship, measured 128 meters (420 feet) in length, required 4,000 rowers to propel her, and carried 3,250 deckhands and marines.

The far-flung campaigns of Alexander and his successors produced a large corpus of travelogues and geographies. These were copied and studied by Greek intellectuals at Athens (a great center of learning since the fifth century B.C.E.) and Alexandria (where Ptolemy II had created an enduring intellectual climate in the Great Library). Regrettably, most of these accounts, such as Androsthenes' *periplus* of the Persian Gulf, or Timosthenes' *On Islands*,

*On Charts and Distances*, and *On Harbors*, are not extant. But many of them survived, such as Nearchus's travelogue of the Indus and Persian Gulf (in Arrian's *Indica*), the Red Sea *periplus* of Agatharcides of Cnidus (in Diodorus and Photius), and the accounts of the renowned explorer Eudoxus of Cyzicus, who attempted a circumnavigation of Africa (in Strabo 2.98–102). To these should be added Pytheas's remarkable voyages around Britain and the northern European coast (*On the Oceans*, partially extant in Strabo).

**Third century B.C.E. through fourth century C.E.: Carthage and Rome.** By the third century B.C.E., a powerful Carthage ruled the coasts of North Africa, western Sicily, Sardinia, Corsica, and southern Spain. Between 264 and 202 B.C.E., Punic interests in Sicily and Spain clashed with those of Rome, resulting in a series of conflicts known as the Punic wars. Rome became a naval power during these years, both winning and losing enormous sea battles. Roman perseverance led to the ultimate defeat of Carthage and the military, political, and economic ascension of her rival.

During the second and first centuries B.C.E., Roman seaborne trade in metals, oil, wine, and grain flourished in the western Mediterranean. From the early years of the Roman Empire beginning in the late first century B.C.E., Rome began maintaining a standing navy to protect the sea lanes from pirates and other enemies. The commercial ships that Rome's navy protected came in various sizes. The largest were grain ships and amphora carriers, which could be upward of 50 meters (164 feet) in length or longer, with a pair of quarter rudders on the stern and a pair of square sails—one on the main mast, the other (the *artemon*, the driving sail) hanging from a raking mast above the bow. Such ships transported an estimated 150,000 tons of grain annually to Rome from Alexandria during the first three centuries C.E. Two of the most detailed voyage narratives from the Roman era took place aboard such ships—Paul's voyage from Caesarea Maritima (modern Israel) to Rome (described in *Acts* 27), and the voyage from Egypt of the enormous grain ship *Isis*, described by Lucian (*Navigium*).

More extensive and complete geographies and *periploi* have survived from the Roman era and provide useful information on the nature and methods of navigation. These include Strabo's *Geographia* in seventeen books (late first century B.C.E.) and Pliny's *Naturalis Historia* in thirty-seven books (first century C.E.). The *Periplus Maris Erythraei* (Coast Pilot of the Erythraean [Red] Sea), ostensibly written by an Egyptian merchant dealing with Roman markets, dates to the middle of the first century C.E. It details the routes, distances, ports, and trade goods in the Red Sea, along the eastern coast of Africa, the Arabian coasts, and the west coast of India. But it also offers essential navigational information: proper departure times for different destinations, safe mooring areas, weather lore, currents, shoal waters to avoid, and valuable tide information. We are also given a description of the open sea voyages between ports on the Gulf of Aden and the west coast of India (between 1,100 and 1,300 nautical miles) using the monsoon (from Arabic *mausim*, meaning "season"), a wind system that reverses directions seasonally. The author credited an earlier Greek pilot named Hippalus as the first to use the southwest monsoon (June to October), after which the monsoon came to be called the Hippalus wind.

## The Mediterranean's Maritime Environment

The Mediterranean is a midlatitude, semiclosed, microtidal sea with a nearly isolated oceanic system. Its waters span some 3,800 kilometers (2,361 miles) end to end, average 400 kilometers (249 miles) in width, and include a surface area of about 2.96 million square kilometers (1.14 million square miles). It is divided into a western and an eastern basin by the peninsula of Italy and the island of Sicily. Passage between the two basins is accessible only by the Strait of Sicily and the Strait of Messina. Nearly the entire northern shore is mountainous and heavily indented by long peninsulas, gulfs, cul-de-sac seas, headlands, and natural harbors. By contrast, the shores of North Africa consist of long stretches of flat, sandy beaches with low hinterlands and few natural harbors, punctuated by the coastal plateau of Cyrene in modern Libya and the mountainous Maghreb coast of Morocco, Algeria, and Tunisia. Scattered mostly along the northern shores are over two thousand islets, isles, and islands. The larger of these, when combined with protruding land masses, help divide the Mediterranean into numerous smaller seas: the Ligurian Sea to the north of Corsica; the Tyrrhenian Sea amid Corsica, Sardinia, Sicily, and the Italic mainland; the Ionian Sea between Sicily and Greece; the Adriatic Sea between the Italic mainland and the Dalmatian coast; the Aegean Sea between the Greek mainland and Asia Minor. Other larger islands include Cyprus and the Aegean islands of Crete, Euboea, Lesbos, Samos, and Rhodes. Many islands and island groups cannot be sighted at sea level from mainland areas or other islands. In the west these include Ibiza and Formentera, the Balearic Islands of Majorca and Minorca, and Ustica off Sicily's northwest coast. Others are found in or near the Strait of Sicily, such as the Maltese Islands, the Pelagia ("High Seas") Islands, and Pantelleria. The length of shore of the entire Mediterranean amounts to some 22,000 kilometers (13,670 miles)—more than half the circumference of the earth.

The ubiquity of landmasses in the Mediterranean ensured that many maritime routes lay within sight of shore. However, there are three large areas of the Mediterranean that may be considered maritime deserts: the Algerian-Tyrrhenian Basin (176,000 square kilometers [68,000 square miles] of open water), the Ionian Basin (412,000 square kilometers [159,000 square miles]), and the Levantine Basin (272,000 square kilometers [105,000 square miles]). These areas are often enlarged because of common factors that limit visibility at sea, such as sea haze and windblown dust and sand from the Sahara (measured in the tens of millions of tons every year).

**Mediterranean currents.** The Mediterranean is deep, its basins reaching ocean depths: 2,700 meters (8,860 feet) on average, and 4,900 meters (16,000 feet) at its deepest, west of Greece. Its currents result from the fact that evaporation (80,000,000 tons/second) greatly exceeds the replenishment provided by its few major rivers. To maintain equilibrium, the Mediterranean receives its major inflow from the Atlantic via the Strait of Gibraltar. Here is where the general pattern of circulation is generated. The surface current maintains a steady eastward flow of about one knot as it flows through the Strait of Sicily and meanders along the Libyan coast toward Egypt's Nile Delta. Here, prior to the construction of the Aswan High Dam, Nile floods and general outflow boosted the Mediterranean's current to more than three knots. From Egypt the general stream flows northward toward Cyprus in a massive surface gyre, rotating in a counterclockwise direction along the Levantine coast and under Asia Minor. Upon reaching the north coast of Crete, the current splits in two. One branch continues on into the Ionian Sea past the Peloponnese, some of which turns south and back into the general flow heading eastward toward Egypt. The other flows into the southern Aegean where the general current is deflected by a profusion of islands and projecting headlands between Crete and Asia Minor. Here this branch encounters the Aegean current issuing southward from the Dardanelles, the result of the Black Sea's higher sea level. In most areas of the Mediterranean the current travels at the rate of between eight and twelve nautical miles per day. However, it is not rare to find faster-flowing currents in channels or straits aligned with the direction of prevailing winds, such as the Strait of Messina (where the current reaches up to seven knots), the narrows between Euboea and the Greek mainland (seven knots), and the channel between Samos and the Turkish mainland (three knots).

**Mediterranean winds and weather.** Mediterranean weather is dependent on larger, extra-regional climatic structures. In summer, the Azores High (a recurrent high-pressure system) flows steadily into the Indo-Persian Low over southwest Asia, resulting in northerly and northwesterly winds over the Mediterranean. This is compounded by an immense region of low pressure, caused by rising Saharan heat, in nearby North Africa; this draws in cool air over the European continent and intensifies the northerly winds. The intensity and constancy of these winds give them near trade wind status. In the eastern basin, ancient Greeks called their July and August northerlies the *etesians*, or "annual" winds (modern Greek *meltemi* or Turkish *meltem*). These are known to blow with gale force on occasion and to change to northwesterly and westerly by the time they reach the Levantine coast. In the western basin, winds are much more variable, with the Mistral (a northwesterly) and the Sirocco (southerly) slightly prevailing.

In autumn, the eastern basin sees northerly winds subside and give way to more variable and local winds. In the western basin, the Mistral picks up strength, and roving cyclonic depressions issue eastward intermittently out of the Gulf of Genoa and the southern Ionian Sea. Cool, continental highs spill wind into these roving lows, thus setting up recurrent patterns of rain and gale-force winds lasting several days. By winter, the Mongolian High and the North Atlantic Low produce cold, northerly winds and violent storms. Roving depressions bring blustery winds, confused seas, and swells that can climb to ten meters (thirty-three feet) or more. Sailing is, of course, a risky pursuit in these months. However, in early January, spells of mild weather occur periodically, particularly in the Adriatic and Aegean. To the ancient Greeks, these pauses were known as the *Meres Alkionides*, the "Halcyon Days." This window lasted a mere fortnight but offered a convenient—though still risky—opportunity to travel or trade by sea. In spring, the low over Italy draws in continental air and results in generally northerly winds (Bora) in the Adriatic and Aegean, though southerlies occur on occasion over much of the Mediterranean. By May, cyclonic depressions occur less regularly, and the weather structures of summer slowly begin to reassert themselves over the Mediterranean.

While seasonal winds set the general pattern of airstream circulation over the Mediterranean, they are complemented by other, more local wind effects that also operate at sea level. Diurnal breezes (caused by the uneven heating and cooling of land and sea), rising and falling winds near the coast, and those winds affected by their encounters with landforms are the products of more local processes determined for the most part by geography. As such, they round out the features of any one region's wind regime and lend a local character.

**The sailing season.** The rhythms of ancient seafaring life revolved around this weather cycle, with peak periods of maritime activity centered on the summer months, the period of longest days, clearest skies, and steadiest winds. Winter, in contrast, was a period of short days, generally decreased visibility for sighting land and landmarks, periodic stormy weather, variable winds, and increased cloud cover that blotted out the sun and stars. While religious festivals (such as the *Navigium Isidis*) inaugurated the opening of the sailing season in the spring, the usual practice was to rely on the rising and setting of certain stars and constellations (such as Arcturus, the Pleiades, and Orion) to signal the periods of safest navigation and *mare clausum* (when "the seas were closed").

Most modern scholars rely on two sources for specific dates of the sailing season. The first is the Greek epic poet Hesiod (c. 700 B.C.E.), who described the safest period of voyaging as the "fifty days after the summer solstice"—that is, July and August—although he alludes to a wider window of May to late September (*Works and Days* 663–677). The second is the Roman imperial administrator Vegetius (c. 400 C.E., more than a millennium later), who recommended less conservative dates of May 27 to September 14 as the safest time for voyaging, and May 15 to November 10 as the outside limits (*De re militari* 4.39).

Those voyages that took place from November to April are often thought to have been reserved for important governmental dispatches and military contingencies. But several lines of evidence strongly suggest that winter sailing was not exceptional. Close readings of both Greek and Roman historians reveal that naval fleets composed of galleys, i.e., the most susceptible to damage and disaster from winter seas, waged war, transported troops, collected tribute, raided commerce, and protected merchant ships during the depths of winter, albeit on a smaller scale. During and after the fifth century B.C.E., merchant ships appear to have operated nearly year-round. This is demonstrated, for example, by the *Ahiqar* scroll (475 B.C.E.)

from Elephantine, Egypt, which records the voyages of forty-two merchant ships (thirty-six from Ionian Greece, six from Sidon) that traded with Egypt from February to early December. The elder Pliny could describe a sailing season lasting from February 8 to November 11 (*Naturalis Historia* 2.47.122–125), though, as he stated, "not even the fury of the storms closes the sea." In the fifth century, government regulations were imposed on the sailing schedule. The *Codex Theodosianus* of 438 mandated a suspension of navigation between November and April for state-sponsored commerce. Henceforth, the Byzantine Empire and the various maritime republics of the central and western Mediterranean would pass edict after edict to limit the rhythms of commerce to the safest months.

## Systems, Instruments, and Methods of Navigation

Systems of navigation varied according to the type and purpose of the ships, the distance, and the destination. War galleys from the seventh and sixth centuries B.C.E. onward were designed specifically for speed and maneuverability on relatively calm seas, their bronze ram serving as the primary weapon. Because they were kept long, light, and shallow in draft, and because their sides were breached by a constellation of oar ports, some quite close to the water, they were exceptionally vulnerable in even moderate seas. And because they had little room for storing food and water with which to revitalize their large crews, they relied on accompanying merchant ships and made frequent stops on shore for supplies and rest. For these reasons, war galleys stuck to shore as much as possible, preferring routes that offered short crossings, convenient havens from storms, and safe anchorages for rest stops. While such crews likely had knowledge of open-sea navigational practices, their expertise was oriented primarily toward naval maneuvers and coastal navigation.

On the other hand, the hulls of merchant galleys and sail-driven merchant ships emphasized durability and seaworthiness over speed. High sides and relatively deep drafts shook off the swells, and a large square sail drove them and their heavy cargoes slowly along at fewer than five knots. As their seaworthiness could keep them at sea for extended periods, these ships were free for both short- and long-range navigation. Thus, whether their destinations took them down the same stretch of coast, to the next island over, or across the open sea, the crews of such ships were, by and large, competent in both coastal and open-sea navigational practices.

Any attempt to trace merchant routes must take into account archaeological evidence of point-to-point trade, literary evidence, the limitations of sail and hull technology, and factors of geography and meteorology. As replicas have shown, Late Bronze Age ships with boom-footed sails would have proven most efficient with following and quarter winds. With the presence of seasonal northerly and northwesterly winds in the eastern Mediterranean, such ships likely followed a counterclockwise circuit that included both open sea and coastal legs. Beginning in the Aegean, the open-sea route to Egypt (350 nautical miles) was made with following and quarter winds. From Egypt, the route led northward up the Levantine coast (a hazardous lee shore much of the year), westward under or over Cyprus and under the coast of Asia Minor (with helpful diurnal winds), and into the Aegean via Rhodes.

Although this route, with variations, would remain in effect in the eastern basin throughout antiquity, it is clear that the development of the brailed sail and deeper hulls of merchant ships in the first millennium B.C.E. opened up routes throughout the Mediterranean, routes that heretofore had been impossible. A replica of a fourth-century B.C.E. merchantman excavated off Kyrenia, Cyprus, has demonstrated that ancient ships with brailed sails and deep hulls could tack and sail as much as 50 degrees into the wind. Sailing close-hauled, however, takes severe tolls on ships and crews, and since speed is drastically reduced in such conditions (to as little as two knots), most crews waited patiently in port for more favorable winds.

**Navigation instruments.** The sounding lead is the only artifact from antiquity that may be labeled a navigation instrument. The lead, of conical or bell shape, was employed in antiquity to gauge depth by means of a knotted line. The base of the lead itself often contained a hollow cavity filled with tallow with which to retrieve a soil sample. Taken together, the information conveyed the depth and proximity to land, and helped specify the type or number of anchors required for good holding. Sounding leads first appear in Egyptian Nilotic scenes as early as the Middle Kingdom. Herodotus (2.5) and many later sources from the Roman era (such as *Acts* 27) describe their usage. Sounding leads are also a common find on excavated Roman wrecks.

Although the log, a device used to measure distance traveled at sea, saw widespread use from the late sixteenth century onward, the first-century B.C.E. Roman architect Vitruvius proposed a plan for a paddle wheel–driven geared

hodometer (*De architectura* 10.9.5–7). Had the invention (or some more efficient manifestation of it) been built and taken root, position estimation would have been much improved by means of more accurate deduced reckoning. As it was, pilots likely observed sea foam on the surface as a rough measure of speed and distance traveled.

Birds appear to have served some navigational function, however limited. Greek and Roman weather lore details the behavior of several species (cranes, herons, geese, petrels, ravens) on and over the sea before the onset of inclement weather. On the open sea, the known flight paths of migratory birds may have provided some directional clues. The practice of releasing birds (ravens, doves) to find land while upon the open sea is well known from mythology (for instance, Apollonius Rhodius, *Argonautica* 2.560–573), biblical accounts (Genesis 8:6–12), and Near Eastern literature (the Akkadian epic *Gilgamesh*). Birds even appear on ship lamps from the Nuragic culture of Sardinia. However, the use of birds for navigation appears to have been forsaken by the Roman era, provoking the elder Pliny to describe the alien practice among seafarers of Ceylon (Sri Lanka).

**Methods.** The configuration of the Mediterranean coastlines and the abundance of islands ensured that coastal navigation (coastal "piloting" in the modern conception of navigation) was a quite normal means of voyaging between landfalls. Such natural landmarks as headlands, offshore islets, river mouths, and conspicuous coastal cliffs and plains are easily recognizable and readily memorized. These were supplemented with such manmade coastal features as walled cities, watchtowers, promontory temples (for instance, the famed Temple of Poseidon atop Cape Sounion in Attica), and funeral mounds (Homer, *Odyssey* 4.655, 12.11, 24.80). Lighthouses became important civic structures during and after the third century B.C.E. The first lighthouse built on any scale was the Pharos lighthouse at Alexandria, one of the Seven Wonders of the Ancient World. At about 100 meters (328 feet) in height, with a fire burning continuously on top, it was visible from more than thirty nautical miles away. During the Roman era, dozens of smaller-scale lighthouses were erected at port cities in Italy, in northern Europe, and along the north African coast.

Navigation in the open areas of the Mediterranean called for a quite different set of skills. In the absence of coastal references, compasses, and nautical charts, ancient seafarers had to rely on a variety of natural clues for orientation, course maintenance, and position estimation. By day, aside from a rising and setting sun, steady winds and their resulting swells supplied one of nature's few orienting clues. Knowing the seasonal and local patterns of winds and how they played on the movement of the ship was crucial to maintaining an effective course. Such knowledge came from studying the "signature" of winds—that is, their strength, temperature, humidity, and orientation in relation to other clues such as the sun and the stars. Greek and Roman geographers and seafarers charted the winds using circular horizon diagrams, or wind roses. Although the number of wind names varied through the ages, ranging from Homer's four, to Aristotle's eleven (*Meteorologica*), to the elder Pliny's bilingual twelve (*Historia Naturalis*), the names of the cardinal winds in both the Greek and Latin traditions remained relatively unchanged into the early medieval period.

The most elaborate form of wind rose to survive antiquity is the Horologium of Andronicus in Athens, otherwise known as the Tower of the Winds. The small and elegant octagonal tower of Pentelic marble was built in the late first century B.C.E. as a monumental sundial and weather-vane. At the top of each external face were sculpted in relief the winged personifications of each wind, along with its name. The signature of each wind is made obvious by its attributes. Among the cardinal winds, *Boreas* (N) is heavily cloaked to indicate his cool temperature, strength, and dominance. *Apeliotes* (E) carries a sash of grains and fruits, the symbol of autumn. *Notos* (S) holds a water jar upside down, a reference to the oppressive (and evaporative) Sahara winds. *Zephyros* (W) bears flowers, an indicator of his gentle nature during springtime.

Navigating the open sea under the clear night sky of summer was perhaps easier than by day. Stars, constellations, and the haze of the Milky Way act as a sort of compass, rising, setting, and rotating in a steady, predictable pattern. The northern circumpolar stars and constellations (that is, those that orbit the north celestial pole and never rise or set) proved useful for orientation and course steering. The most famous of these (then and now) were the two bears, *Ursa Major* and *Ursa Minor*. Today, both constellations revolve around Polaris, a faint star within *Ursa Minor*. In antiquity, however, because of a phenomenon known as precession (first discovered by *Hipparchus* in the second century B.C.E.), *Ursa Major* and *Ursa Minor* revolved around the brightest star in *Ursa Minor*, Kochab. According to the third-century B.C.E. writer Aratus, Greek seafarers

take their mark by *Ursa Major*, whereas the Phoenicians cross the sea trusting in the other [*Ursa Minor*]. *Ursa Major*,

appearing clear at earliest night, is easily recognized; but the other is small, yet better for sailors; for all of her stars wheel in a smaller orbit; by her, then, the Sidonians sail their ships (Aratus, *Phaenomena* 37–44).

Circumpolar stars and constellations also provided a rough sense of geographic position. Because the earth is spherical, as one sails south, the north celestial pole sinks lower in the sky, and vice versa as one sails north. As a rule of thumb, the altitude of the polestar equals the latitude of the observer. In the Mediterranean, the difference in the pole star's altitude between the northernmost area (the head of the Adriatic) and the southernmost area (the Gulf of Sidra) is about 15 degrees, a difference easily visible to the naked eye. Those sailing the Atlantic coast, the Red Sea, and the Indian Ocean would have noticed even larger differences. This phenomenon was harnessed in antiquity to provide a means of roughly gauging one's northing and southing and for maintaining approximate east/west courses. This is best exemplified in the writings of the first-century C.E. court writer Lucan, who describes the voyage to Syria of the Roman general Pompey, in the autumn of 48 B.C.E., after his defeat at Pharsalus:

The never-setting pole star (Kochab), which does not sink beneath the waves, brightest of the twin Bears, guides the ships. When I see this one culminate and *Ursa Minor* stand above the lofty yards, then we are facing the Bosporus and the Black Sea that curves the shores of Scythia. Whenever Arctophylax (Boötes) descends from the mast-top and Cynosura [*Ursa Minor*] sinks nearer the horizon, the ship is proceeding toward the ports of Syria [south]. After that comes Canopus, a star content to wander about the southern sky, fearing the North. If you keep it on your left as you sail past Pharos, your ship will touch Syrtis [in the Gulf of Sidra] in mid-sea (Lucan, *Civil War* 8.174–85).

Those stars that rise in the east and set in the west were also of navigational significance, though precisely how is uncertain. The first reference to steering by the stars is found in Homer's *Odyssey*. While sailing from Calypso's isle, Odysseus watches "the Pleiades and late-setting Boötes, and the Bear . . . The beautiful goddess Calypso advised him to keep this one on his left as he sailed over the sea" (5.270–77). This and other references to sailing by the stars hint at the existence of some form of star-path sailing such as is found among the techniques of Polynesian navigators.

The environmental navigational methods of the Greco-Roman period continued in the subsequent eras of Mediterranean history. While significant milestones in noninstrumental navigation were made by early medieval explorers and adventurers of the North Atlantic (discovering North America in the tenth century), it was not until the rise of the maritime republics of Amalfi, Pisa, Venice, and Genoa in the twelfth and thirteenth centuries that revolutions in navigational instruments—the compass, the portolan chart, and eventually the log—and in navigational knowledge took place in the Mediterranean.

[*See also* Ancient Navies; Coastal Navigation; Hipparchus; Mediterranean Sea; Nautical Astronomy and Celestial Navigation; Navigational Instruments; Ptolemy; *and* Vikings, *subentry on* Norse Navigation.]

## Bibliography

### Primary Works
Allain, Michael L. "The Periplous of Skylax of Karyanda." PhD diss., Ohio State University, 1977.

Blomqvist, Jerker, ed. and trans. *The Date and Origin of the Greek Version of Hanno's "Periplus": With an Edition of the Text and a Translation.* Lund, Sweden: CWK Gleerup, 1979.

Casson, Lionel, ed. and trans. *"The Periplus Maris Erythraei": Text with Introduction, Translation, and Commentary.* Princeton, N.J.: Princeton University Press, 1989.

Diller, Aubrey. *The Tradition of the Minor Greek Geographers.* Lancaster, Pa.: American Philological Association, 1952.

Murphy, J. P., ed. and trans. *Ora Maritima; or, Description of the Seacoast from Brittany Round to Massilia, by Rufus Festus Avienus: Latin Text with Facing English Translation, Commentary, Notes, Indices, and Facsimile of the "Editio Princeps."* Chicago: Ares, 1977.

Oikonomides, Al N., ed. and trans. *Hanno, "Periplus; or, Circumnavigation of Africa": Greek Text with Facing English Translation, Commentary, Notes, and Facsimile of "Codex Palatinus Gr." 398.* 3d ed. Chicago: Ares, 1995.

Schoff, Wilfred H., ed. and trans. *Periplus of the Outer Sea, East and West, and of the Great Islands Therein by Marcian of Heraclea: A Translation from the Greek Text, with Commentary.* Philadelphia: Commercial Museum, 1927.

### Secondary Works
Casson, Lionel. *The Ancient Mariners: Seafarers and Sea Fighters of the Mediterranean in Ancient Times.* 2d ed. Princeton, N.J.: Princeton University Press, 1991.

Casson, Lionel. *Ships and Seamanship in the Ancient World.* 2nd ed. Baltimore and London: Johns Hopkins University Press, 1995.

Davis, Dan. "Navigation in the Ancient Eastern Mediterranean." MA thesis, Texas A&M University, 2000.

Dilke, O. A. W. *Greek and Roman Maps.* Baltimore and London: Johns Hopkins University Press, 1985.

Gardiner, Robert, ed. *The Age of the Galley: Mediterranean Oared Vessels Since Pre-Classical Times.* London: Conway Maritime Press, 1995.

Horden, Peregrine, and Nicholas Purcell. *The Corrupting Sea: A Study of Mediterranean History.* Oxford: Blackwell, 2000.

Hyde, Walter Woodburn. *Ancient Greek Mariners.* New York: Oxford University Press, 1947.

Morton, Jamie. *The Role of the Physical Environment in Ancient Greek Seafaring.* Leiden, Netherlands: Brill, 2001.

Taylor, E. G. R. *The Haven-Finding Art: A History of Navigation from Odysseus to Captain Cook.* New York: American Elsevier, 1971.

Wachsmann, Shelley. *Seagoing Ships and Seamanship in the Bronze Age Levant.* College Station: Texas A&M University Press, 1998.

DAN DAVIS

**Ancient Voyage Narratives** Sea voyages, whether real or imagined, formed the basis of many Greek literary texts as well as a few Roman ones, beginning with the archetypal sea voyage found in Homer's *Odyssey* (c. ninth century B.C.E.) and extending throughout antiquity and the early Middle Ages. The sequential, episodic structure of such voyage narratives, and the scope they offered both for feats of prowess and for exploration of foreign lands and peoples, made them an extremely rich resource for ancient poets and prose writers. Such voyage-based narratives often do not fit easily into modern genres—indeed it is sometimes hard to determine whether they should be classed as fiction or nonfiction—but they can be referred to here as *periploi* or "coastal tours," the term most often applied to them in antiquity. A *periplus* in Greek is a voyage extending along a stretch of coastline so as to permit regular stops at landing places along the way, and hence the word *periplus* came to refer also to the stage-by-stage written descriptions of such a voyage, just as the parallel term *periodos* could denote either a journey by land or a travelogue or even, in some cases, a map.

The Greek interest in *periploi* as a literary theme was already well advanced by the time that the *Odyssey* was written, as evidenced by the reference in Book 1 to "the homecoming of the Achaeans" as a popular story type. Such stories of returns from Troy to Greece involved sea voyages that sometimes took the heroes far beyond the Aegean, as seen in the case of Menelaus, whose wanderings to Egypt and elsewhere are retold in an inset narrative in Book 4 of the *Odyssey*. Menelaus's journey was doubtless retold at greater length in one of the cyclic epics known collectively as the *Nostoi* or *Return Journeys*, now almost entirely lost, along with the homeward voyages of other prominent Greek heroes. These archaic epic narratives were strongly influenced by the travel tales that the Greeks had heard from their own traders and colonists as well as from foreign peoples with whom they interacted, especially the Egyptians and the Phoenicians, who were already venturing far into the Atlantic by the fifth century B.C.E. Herodotus (fifth century B.C.E.), for example, gives evidence in the fourth book of his *Histories* that he was familiar with accounts of both Egyptian and Carthaginian attempts to circumnavigate Africa, and these could very well have been transmitted in the form of written voyage logs.

## Narratives of Actual Voyages

The earliest texts we know of that contain actual voyage narratives were Greek exploration logs of the sixth century B.C.E., now lost but known through fragments preserved by later writers. Scylax of Caryanda, an Ionian Greek commissioned by the Persian emperor Darius to explore the Indus river system, composed an account of his journey that described many weird and grotesque races of humans, including the Sciapods (Shadow-feet), whose legend endured well into early modern times. Herodotus describes Scylax's journey, evidently from firsthand knowledge of his book.

Beginning at the central Asian city of "Caspatyrus" (perhaps modern Kabul, Afghanistan), Scylax made his way down the Indus to the sea, then westward along the coast for thirty months before reaching Egypt (*Histories* 4.44). His assignment was probably to open up new trade routes between India and the Persian heartland on behalf of the Achaemenid Empire, but the information that he disseminated to his Greek audience had more to do with wonders, marvels, and exotica of the East than with geographic discoveries. Scylax's fame was such that a pretender in the fourth or third century B.C.E. assumed his name and published a more matter-of-fact *Periplus*, describing a circuit of the Mediterranean proceeding clockwise from the Pillars of Heracles (at the east end of the Strait of Gibraltar); this author is today designated "Pseudo-Scylax."

In the next century two Carthaginian explorers, the brothers Hanno and Himilco, both made coasting voyages in the Atlantic that were known to the Greeks through voyage logs. The *Periplus* of Hanno indeed can still be read in its entirety, thanks to the Greek translation of an originally Punic document that was said to have been set up as a dedication in a temple at Carthage. Hanno's *Periplus* describes a journey along the west African littoral that becomes progressively more ominous as it proceeds south, ending at a mountain called Chariot of the Gods, where Hanno turns back in fear of mysterious noises and nocturnal fires. What point of Africa Hanno reached is unclear, but his encounter with hairy wild men who he

says were called "gorillas" in the local language has given modern zoologists the name of the great apes. Himilco, for his part, went north from the Pillars where his brother went south, and after four months' sail came to a stretch of ocean so shallow and dense with seaweed that he claimed he could go no farther. Himilco's log did not have the good fortune to be preserved in Greek translation, as Hanno's was, but snippets of it survive in Avienus's *Ora maritima*. Modern opinion suggests that he reached the coast of Brittany.

The exploration of the East commenced by Alexander the Great resulted in one important *periplus*, written by Nearchus of Crete, now lost but recoverable from Arrian's *Indica*, a later adaptation of its contents. Nearchus was a boyhood friend of Alexander's who served as admiral of the great fleet built to sail down the Indus River and eastward along the coast of the Makran desert (325 B.C.E.). Nearchus found himself in difficulties from the start, his departure delayed by monsoon winds such that contact with Alexander's land army was lost; the army in any case had failed to locate food and water stocks so as to resupply the fleet. The *Indica* thus tells a rather grim tale in which Nearchus's men, dogged constantly by hunger and thirst, are forced to prey upon the primitive tribesmen of this remote region in order to eke out their survival. By the time his crews finally stumbled upon the Macedonian land forces in Carmania, Nearchus had been so ravaged by want and exposure that his old friend Alexander did not recognize him. The goal of Nearchus's voyage—to forge a sea link between western Asia and India—had been achieved, but after India ceased to be a part of the Macedonian Empire, this route was little used. Arrian retells the story of the voyage in his own words, as a corollary to his much longer tale of Alexander's Asian campaign; he doubtless omitted much of the navigational and geographic records that he found in the original and focused on the heroic elements of Nearchus's tale.

Sometime around 300 B.C.E., Himilco's path into the North Atlantic was retraced by Pytheas of Massilia, if we are to believe the fragmentary remains of the voyage log that bore the title *On the Ocean*. Exiting the Mediterranean through the Strait of Gibraltar, Pytheas went north as far as the British Isles and perhaps even glimpsed Iceland—if that was the land he called Thule, a name later much beloved by Roman poets. A true explorer and scientist, Pytheas made many important astronomical observations in northern latitudes, yet his credibility was questioned in antiquity, and some actually believed that he had made up the entire story of his journey. The *periplus* narrative, even in Hellenistic times, still suffered from the problem first posed by

Homer in his framing of Odysseus's wanderings. Because the narrative often dealt with phenomena seen only by its author, its audience was always unsure how much of its content could be regarded as true. Fiction writers, as we shall see, were quick to turn this uncertainty to their own advantage; indeed, one novelist seems to have quite deliberately spoofed Pytheas's log by situating extravagant inventions in the lands "beyond Thule."

The Hellenistic age, with its interest in practical science and its greatly enhanced navigational technology, produced many important exploration logs and *periploi*, though only fragments survive of most. Timosthenes of Rhodes, captain of the fleet organized by Ptolemy II (third century B.C.E.), wrote several accounts of his Mediterranean voyages, including *On Harbors* and *On Islands*. Agatharchides of Cnidus wrote a work titled *On the Erythraean Sea* in the second century B.C.E.—not strictly a voyage account but a compilation of much exotic ethnographic information; important passages are preserved by Diodorus Siculus, and an epitome of the whole is preserved in Photius's tenth-century *Bibliotheca*. Of Mnaseas of Patara (second century B.C.E.?), who wrote a *periplus* of the outer coasts of the *oikoumene* (inhabited world), and Menippus of Pergamum, who wrote a *periplus* of the Mediterranean Sea, very little is known. Arrian, mentioned above as author of an adaptation of Nearchus's voyage log, also published his own *Periplus of the Black Sea* in Hadrian's reign (117–138 C.E.), and this survives intact; it presents to Hadrian the keen observations made by Arrian in an exploratory circuit of this body of water. (Another work with the same title, by an anonymous author, preserves a more derivative and less interesting account of the Black Sea coasts.)

The best-known and best-preserved of these late Greek *periploi*, however, is the *Periplus of the Erythraean Sea*. Composed by an unknown author of the early empire, this text contains a detailed record of the harbors, sailing routes, and trade goods to be found along the Malabar Coast of India. Unlike most other *periploi*, which address themselves to a general audience, this one clearly is intended as a guide to navigation for western sea captains and traders plying the waters off India, waters that had in the first century C.E. become much more accessible to them thanks to a new understanding of the monsoon winds. From chapter 57 of this *periplus* we learn how Hippalus, evidently a Greek sea captain, discovered a seasonal pattern of these winds that allowed ships to go straight across the Indian Ocean from Arabia in midsummer and then back again in the winter; thereafter these monsoons were known to the Romans as the Hippalus winds.

Several very late Greek works of general geography also present themselves as *periploi*, though the distances they cover are greater than any single sea voyage could encompass. Marcianus of Heraclea wrote a *Periplus of the Outer Sea* describing the oceanic coasts of Europe, Africa, and Asia, and he also epitomized a *Periplus of the Inner Sea* (the Mediterranean) that he found among the writings of one Artemidorus of Ephesus. Similar in scope to the *Periplus of the Inner Sea* is the fragmentary *Stadiasmus* (or *List of Anchorages*) *of the Great Sea*, by an unknown author, a navigational manual designed for use in the Mediterranean Sea.

## Fictional Voyage Narratives

The fabulous wanderings reported in Homer's *Odyssey* can be regarded as the avatar not only of the *periploi* surveyed above but also of a long series of fictional or fantastic (or both fictional and fantastic) literary texts, again made up mostly of Greek rather than Roman works, which culminated in the great romance novels of the imperial age and Lucian's masterly satire, *True Histories*. As the title of Lucian's work suggests, these fictional *periploi* usually presented themselves to the reader as factual, though in some cases the conceit was so thin as to constitute a backhanded admission of fictionality. Nevertheless it is noteworthy that ancient writers, lacking a clearly defined genre framework into which pure fiction could be inserted, looked more to the *periplus* as a model than to any other literary tradition. As the *Odyssey* itself demonstrates, the audience of the voyage narrative felt relieved of the need to determine the narrative's truth status, and thus could enjoy the free inventions of myth and fantasy—a pleasure that the ancient world's strict ethical and philosophic codes otherwise denied them.

Already in the fourth century B.C.E. a Greek writer, Antiphanes of Berga, began framing fictional adventures in the guise of real voyage logs; his name later became attached to this pretense, such that Strabo and others attack as "Bergaeans" those whose *periploi* they mistrust. A near contemporary, Menippus of Gadara, composed literary flights of fantasy exploring not only distant lands but even the moon and sun; he, too, lent his name to the new breed of fiction that he created, "Menippean satire," though in modern usage this term has often shifted its meaning. Virtually nothing remains from the works of either writer, though Menippus's technique can partly be reconstructed from the satires of his late follower Lucian of Samosata. Indeed, Lucian often uses Menippus as a mouthpiece in his satires and sends him on celestial voyages into the sky or down under the earth, as though these two otherworldly realms were Menippus's natural domains.

With Alexander's opening up of India to Greek eyes in the late fourth century B.C.E. came a spate of fictions taking the Far East as their setting, including two important utopian novels, both of which present themselves as voyages into the Indian Ocean. Euhemerus of Messene's *Sacred Scriptures* describes a visit to a group of islands there, the largest of which was called Panchaea, and the discovery of a set of ancient inscriptions (for which the novel is named) recording a very early stage of political history. From these writings the author claims to have learned that Greek gods such as Uranus, Cronus, and Zeus were in fact only kings reigning in Panchaea, later deified by a grateful populace. The term "euhemerism" has subsequently been applied to the theory that the worship of gods arose as a way of honoring the dimly remembered leaders of long ago. A nearly contemporary novel by Iambulus described a different Indian Ocean island, the Island of the Sun—a communistic paradise with idealized social and political conventions. After landing there and living among the natives for seven years, Iambulus claims to have been expelled and forced to return home, as was his successor Hythlodaeus from Thomas More's *Utopia* (1516).

Iambulus's novel (along with Homer's *Odyssey* and other works) is invoked as a literary model by a second century C.E. Greek satirist, Lucian of Samosata, in his great reductio ad absurdum of the Greek *periplus* tradition, the two books of the *True Histories*. After an authorial prologue assuring the reader that nothing that follows is true, we are conducted on a bizarre tour of the western Atlantic, the moon and sun, and other locales beyond the reach of ancient navigation. A kaleidoscopic array of grotesque fantasies is paraded before our wondering eyes, until the narrator finally makes landfall and ends with a promise to relate in another volume his terrestrial adventures. Similar in spirit, though much longer and organized around an episodic love story, were the inventions of a lost novel, *Wonders beyond Thule*, known to us through an extensive Byzantine plot summary. Antonius Diogenes, the author of the second-century work, sent his hero and heroine on long journeys through northern Europe before finally reuniting them on Thule and sending them off even farther north.

No account of fictional Greek *periploi* would be complete without mention of the so-called Greek romances or erotic novels, of which there are six complete examples extant, all written between the first century B.C.E. and the fifth century C.E.; fragments of others can be dated to early Hellenistic times. All but one of the extant novels use travel by ship as a central narrative device, since their plots, which revolve around the separation and eventual reunion of idealized young lovers, require long strings of episodic perils and mishaps. As the hero and heroine wander from place to place, driven by sea storms and pirate attacks, they also have the opportunity to visit the many exotic ports of call (especially in the East) so beloved of Greek and Roman readers. This genre thus flourished in the same rich soil that produced the *periplus*, and satisfied a similar appetite in the ancient world for tales of voyages into distant seas.

[*See also* Imaginary Voyages *and* Literature, *subentry on* Voyage Narratives.]

## Bibliography

Agatharchides of Cnidus. *On the Erythraean Sea*. Translated and edited by Stanley M. Burstein. London: Hakluyt Society, 1989.

Casson, Lionel, ed. and trans. *"The Periplus Maris Erythraei": Text with Introduction, Translation, and Commentary*. Princeton, N.J.: Princeton University Press, 1989.

Herodotus. *The Histories*. Translated by Robin Waterfield. New York: Oxford University Press, 1998.

Lattimore, Richmond, trans. *The "Odyssey" of Homer*. New York: Harper and Row, 1967. Often reprinted.

Lucian of Samosata. *True History, and Lucius, or The Ass*. Translated by Paul Turner. Bloomington: Indiana University Press, 1958.

Oikonomides, Al N., ed. and trans. *Hanno, "Periplus; or, Circumnavigation of Africa": Greek Text with Facing English Translation, Commentary, Notes, and Facsimile of "Codex Palatinus Gr." 398*. 3d ed. Chicago: Ares, 1995.

Roseman, Christina Horst, trans. *Pytheas of Massalia, "On the Ocean."* Chicago: Ares, 1994.

Schoff, Wilfred H., ed. and trans. *"Periplus of the Outer Sea, East and West, and of the Great Islands Therein" by Marcian of Heraclea: A Translation from the Greek Text, with Commentary*. Philadelphia: Commercial Museum, 1927.

JAMES S. ROMM

## Ancient Voyages of Exploration

The archaeological remains of the Minoan civilization on Crete date back to 3000 B.C.E., indicating that its founders had made their way across the waters between the mainland and the island at least by then. Minoan objects found in other lands show that by at least 2000 B.C.E. the Minoans were conducting overseas trade with Egypt to the south and with Greece to the north. The Mediterranean farther westward was explored by the Phoenicians, that maritime people par excellence; setting out from their home ports in the Levant, by 800 B.C.E. the Phoenicians had planted the colonies of Utica and Carthage on the south shore of the sea and had even passed through the Strait of Gibraltar to found Cádiz beyond.

## The West Coast of Africa

The next advance of the Phoenicians was along the Atlantic coast of Africa. Archaeological remains prove the existence of a Phoenician colony in the seventh century B.C.E. at Mogador, close to three hundred nautical miles down the coast (31°34′ N) from the Strait of Gibraltar. Around 500 B.C.E. there was a dramatic move farther southward carried out by an expedition under the command of a certain Hanno, ruler of Carthage, whose report of the expedition is the one and only firsthand explorer's account to have survived from ancient times. It is not easy to follow his tracks, since the place-names he mentions are unfamiliar, the geographical descriptions offer little determining detail, and his reckoning of distances is not always trustworthy. The purpose of the enterprise was to plant colonies, so Hanno set sail with a large fleet filled with people; Hanno kept dropping the people off at various points as far as a place identified by most commentators as Cape Blanco (23°50′ N). From there he made an exploratory foray down the sub-Saharan coast that brought him to a "deep and wide river infested with crocodiles and hippotami"; this could well be the Senegal (c. 16° N). Farther on, Hanno came to a promontory that took two days to double; this could well be Cape Verde (14°52′ N). He then came to some islands where he saw "many fires being kindled" and heard the "din of tom-toms." He passed stretches of coast where the land was ablaze; at one point "a leaping flame . . . appeared to reach the stars. This was the highest mountain which we saw." Farther on he met with "wild people, the greatest number by far being women with hairy bodies; our interpreters called them 'gorillas.' " Hanno's men managed to capture three females. Their capture even of females would hardly have been possible had the creatures been what we call gorillas; they may have been chimpanzees or baboons. By this time supplies of food were running low, so the expedition headed home.

Hanno is the first to record the sort of things that later become commonplace in reports from Africa: tom-toms, the enormous grass fires the natives light to burn off stubble, bands of monkeys. There is much dispute about how far he got. Some commentators, identifying the tall fire-topped mountain as Mount Cameroon, hold that he rounded the bulge of Africa all the way to the Cameroons, but this involves squeezing into a voyage that seems to have taken less than two months the long passage through the Gulf of Guinea. Most commentators bring him no farther than Sierra Leone, eight degrees or so north of the equator. In any event, how far Hanno got is academic, for his voyage had scant effect on geographical knowledge and none on subsequent history. The Atlantic coast of Africa below the Canaries was to remain unknown until long after ancient times.

## The East Coast of Africa

Herodotus has an account of a circumnavigation of Africa that, if it actually took place, was a remarkable accomplishment. Pharaoh Necho (r. 610–594 B.C.E.), Herodotus reports, dispatched a fleet of Phoenician sailors to seek a route from the Red Sea around to the Mediterranean; presumably Necho, unaware of how far to the south Africa extended, imagined that the ships, after traveling the length of the Red Sea, would soon be able to turn right and sail westward along the continent's southern coast. Herodotus tells that the voyage took three years, including stops each autumn to sow and harvest crops for food. He notes one detail that to him was unbelievable but to us is quite the opposite: the sailors said that in going around Africa they had the sun to their right, that is, to the north; indeed they would have had it consistently so, once they were south of the Tropic of Capricorn. Herodotus's brief account has engendered endless controversy, running the gamut of opinion from dismissal of such a circumnavigation as an impossibility to demonstrations of how the circumnavigation could have been done just as Herodotus describes. The debate is academic: Necho's expedition had no effect on geographical knowledge.

The east coast of Africa up to the mouth of the Red Sea was well known by the second millennium B.C.E., for the Egyptians sent ships to bring back cargoes of frankincense and myrrh from there. Exploration farther along the African coast was carried on in the third century B.C.E. by Greek hunting parties that the Ptolemies, who had by then taken over the rule of Egypt, sent out to capture elephants for use in battle. The parties established camps along the eastern coast of the Red Sea and the northern coast of Somalia right up to Cape Guardafui, and these in time grew from hunting camps into trading posts. Then Greek traders, moving past Guardafui, founded posts farther south; by the mid-first century C.E. such settlements extended up to where Dar-es-Salaam (6°49′ S) now stands. A handful of Greek skippers sailed still farther, as far as a cape they called Prason. Prason marked the southernmost point of the world known to ancient geographers; commentators have suggested identifying it with Cape Delgado (10°30′ S).

## Northern Waters

For a long time the ancients were only dimly aware of the lands and waters in the north of Europe. The first clear light on this area was shed by Pytheas of Marseille as the result of a voyage he made there around 300 B.C.E. Little is known about Pytheas himself. We can take it for granted that he was a skilled navigator, but he was also an accomplished astronomer who was able to calculate the latitude of his hometown, getting it almost exactly right. His own writings have not survived; we know them only through random citations or paraphrases by later authors. That his account includes a description of the mining of tin in Cornwall may indicate that his voyage was backed by the merchants of Marseille to investigate access to the source of this vital import.

The first part of Pytheas's voyage is fairly certain. He passed through the Strait of Gibraltar, sailed around Spain and along the Breton coast, and crossed the English Channel to Cornwall. He then circumnavigated Britain, establishing that it was an island, that the island was triangular in shape, and that the shortest side faced the Continent. He gives figures for the length of each side; although their proportions are correct, they are almost double the true figures. When he was in northern Britain, Pytheas was told that, six days' sail north of Britain and a day's sail south of "the frozen sea," there was an "island of Thule." In this region there was an all-enveloping substance that Pytheas himself saw from a distance but can only describe in an obscure fashion: it was "neither sea nor air . . . but a mixture like the sea-lung [a form of shellfish or jellyfish] in which earth and air are suspended." Thule has been variously identified as the Shetlands or the Orkneys or Iceland or northern Norway; none of these places satisfies all the requirements. The mysterious substance has been identified as sea fog, icy slush, phosphorescence, and in other ways; the range of conjecture is wide. For the rest of Pytheas's voyage our information is hopelessly vague. He may have reached the mouth of the Elbe and returned home by following the coast of the Continent. Unlike Hanno's or Necho's, his voyage had a signal effect on geographical knowledge, filling in what hitherto had been a blank spot on the map.

## The Indian Ocean

Traders were using the seaways of the Indian Ocean from at least the beginning of the second millennium B.C.E.

Mesopotamian ships went from ports at the head of the Persian Gulf along the southern coast of what is today Iran and Pakistan to Indian ports at the mouth of the Indus; Indian ships did the journey in reverse. Arab seamen and perhaps others continued such voyaging for centuries. They undoubtedly learned to exploit the monsoons, the seasonal winds that—in the western Indian Ocean, Gulf of Aden, and Arabian Sea—blow from the southwest during the summer and from the northeast in the winter, thereby ensuring a favorable voyage both ways. The seamen who used the monsoons were able to keep this knowledge to themselves. When the Ptolemies took over the rule of Egypt at the beginning of the third century B.C.E., Greek seamen started taking part in the trade with Arabia and India, but they did so by sailing only as far as Aden and there exchanging their goods for goods brought to this point aboard Arab or Indian craft. Then a curious incident provided an opportunity to make the voyage all the way to India. Toward the end of the reign of Ptolemy VIII (r. 146–116 B.C.E.), an Indian was picked up from a stranded ship, the sole survivor, and brought to the court; the king had him taught Greek, and when he could communicate, he offered to pilot a group to India. The group included a certain Eudoxus, a leading citizen of the island of Cyzicus with a particular interest in geographical exploration, who exercised some form of command. The Indian surely did not offer to take a Greek expedition to India by following the coast; any seaman encountered on the docks at Aden could have done that—and had he done so, skippers who regularly plied these waters, or pirates who haunted them, would doubtless have kept the expedition from getting very far. He must have offered to pilot Eudoxus and his men over the open sea, and this must have involved divulging to them the phenomenon of the monsoon winds. The Greeks made the voyage without a hitch, no doubt sailing the eastward leg with the southwest monsoon and the return leg with the northeast monsoon. They brought back a valuable cargo of perfumes and precious stones; the king took over not only what the crown was entitled to but also what Eudoxus had loaded on board for his own account. A few years later, the king's successor sent Eudoxus on a second voyage to India; on the return leg he went too far south and, instead of making a landfall near Cape Guardafui, ended up somewhere on the African coast south of it. He then followed the coast north to Guardafui, where he was back in familiar waters. Again Eudoxus was bilked out of his cargo rights, and this led to two attempts to set out from Cádiz and sail around Africa to Egypt; neither of these got very far. When Augustus in 30 B.C.E. replaced the feeble rule of the later Ptolemies with efficient Roman administration, full advantage was taken of the opportunity Eudoxus had opened up: in Augustus's day more than a hundred vessels sailed to India annually, and some even ventured into the Bay of Bengal as far as ports at the mouth of the Ganges.

No formal voyages of exploration were taken eastward of India, but Greek geographers knew of certain areas there thanks to reports from traders. The Greek geographer Ptolemy (mid-second century C.E.) describes a "Golden Region" and a "Golden Peninsula," as well as lands beyond both. Most commentators agree that the "Golden Region" is Burma, while opinion is divided on whether the "Golden Peninsula" is Malay or Sumatra. Many days' sail beyond the "Golden Peninsula" lay the port of Cattigara, the point farthest east that Ptolemy was aware of. Its location is the object of much conjecture; the guesses range from Vietnam to the southern coast of China.

[*See also* Ancient Navies; Arab Seafaring; Exploration to 1500; *and* Ptolemy.]

### Bibliography

Cary, Max, and Eric H. Warmington. *The Ancient Explorers*. New York: Dodd, Mead, 1929.
Casson, Lionel, ed. and trans. *The "Periplus Maris Erythraei."* Princeton, N.J.: Princeton University Press, 1989. See pp. 45 and 235–236.
Desanges, Jehan. *Recherches sur l'activité des Méditerranéens aux confins de l'Afrique*. Rome: École Française de Rome, 1978. See pp. 392–397.
Roller, Duane W. *Through the Pillars of Herakles: Greco-Roman Exploration of the Atlantic*. New York and London: Routledge, 2006.
Thomson, J. Oliver. *History of Ancient Geography*. Cambridge, U.K.: Cambridge University Press, 1948. See pp. 71–72, 74–76, 143–150, and 313–316.

LIONEL CASSON

# Anian, Strait of

**Anian, Strait of** As the outlines of North America took shape on the maps of the sixteenth century, the question arose of the relationship of this new continent to Asia. With little in the way of exploration of the North Pacific to guide them, mapmakers speculated as to whether the Asian and American continents were joined by a land bridge or separated by water. Even after the Spanish conquest of Mexico, progress in exploring the Pacific coast to the north was slow, but sometime around 1561 the Venetian cartographer Giacomo Gastaldi issued a world map that not only showed Asia and America separated by a narrow channel but for the first time gave it a name: "Streto de Anian." Only a single copy of Gastaldi's map survives, but his depiction was soon adopted by other cartographers, including Gerardus Mercator and Abraham Ortelius, although none agreed on the exact width and location of the strait.

Throughout the second half of the sixteenth century the existence of the Strait of Anian remained a subject of speculation. When Francis Drake sailed north from Mexico in 1579 after his treasure-raiding exploits in the Pacific, it was rumored that he had returned home by way of the Strait of Anian. In the 1590s Juan de Fuca claimed to have passed through a strait between latitudes 48° N and 49° N on the northwest coast of America and from there into an inland sea. The final Spanish voyage to the north in this period was Sebastián Vizcaíno's in 1602–1603. One of his vessels sailed as far north as latitude 43° N in the region of Cape Blanco, where, it was reported, the coast turns to the northeast and the entrance to the Strait of Anian seems to begin. By now the Spanish authorities, with memories of raids by Drake and his successors still strong, had decided that if there was a strait to the north between the Pacific and Atlantic oceans then perhaps it had better remain undiscovered. This may explain why a voyage through the Strait of Anian claimed to have been made by Lorenzo Ferrer Maldonado in 1588 aroused no interest from the Spanish court when, in 1609, the navigator belatedly approached the court with an account of his supposed discovery.

The Strait of Anian was a key that might open different locks. For the English and other northern Europeans, who were searching for the Northwest Passage or Northeast Passage through Arctic waters, a strait that was roughly in the position marked on Gastaldi's map offered entry to the Pacific Ocean. The Spaniards, by contrast, had looked for the rumored strait farther south, near what was assumed to be the island of California. Little further light was thrown on the matter until 1728, when Vitus Bering sailed from Kamchatka to the easternmost tip of Asia in latitude 66° N. Four years later, another Russian expedition sighted land across the water to the east of Bering's landfall, which seemed to confirm that Asia and America were separated by a Gastaldi-type strait. Other maps, however, especially in France, continued to show a Strait of Anian entering the American continent well to the south, because this interpretation supported the French efforts of the first half of the eighteenth century to find an ice-free waterway to the Pacific from their bases in New France.

Although Bering's voyages were followed by additional Russian, and then Spanish, expeditions, not until James Cook's survey of 1778 was Bering Strait properly charted.

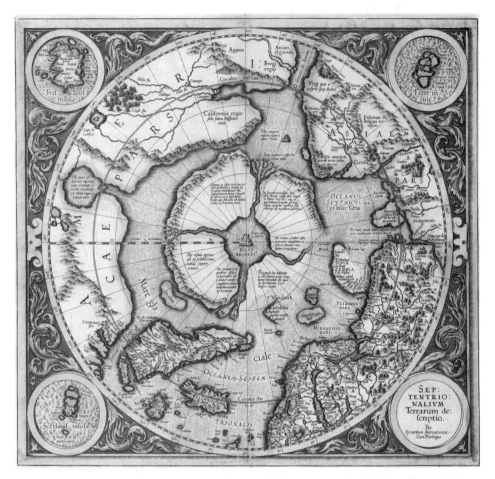

**Mercator's View of the Arctic.** The strait at the top of this 1595 map, leading from the Pacific into the Arctic, is labeled the Strait of Anian. No other map by Mercator proved to be so full of imaginary places, including the four islands surrounding the North Pole, marked by a towering rock, the four-foot tall pygmies that were identified as living in the Arctic north of Norway, and the island of Frisland in the upper left inset. © NATIONAL MARITIME MUSEUM, LONDON

It was accepted by many as the legendary Strait of Anian, but for others the enticing vision of an ice-free strait farther south lingered, and this vision was supported by the reports of voyages that had found great openings along the coast. The explorers and maritime fur traders who followed Cook to the coast filled in most of the gaps on the charts, but there was a final revival of interest in the Strait of Anian. In 1791 the Spanish government ordered Alejandro Malaspina's survey expedition north from Acapulco to Alaskan waters to check Ferrer Maldonado's account of his supposed discovery of 1588. The effort was fruitless, but the diversion of the prestigious Malaspina expedition was a reminder of the powerful impact that the Strait of Anian had on human imagination for more than two centuries.

[*See also* Cartography, *subentry* Speculative; Cook, James; Malaspina, Alejandro; Northeast Passage; *and* Northwest Passage.]

## Bibliography

Nunn, George E. *Origin of the Strait of Anian Concept*. Philadelphia: privately printed, 1929.

Polk, Dora Beale. *The Island of California: A History of the Myth*. Spokane, Wash.: Arthur H. Clark, 1991.

Wagner, Henry Raup. *The Cartography of the Northwest Coast of America to the Year 1800*. Berkeley: University of California Press, 1937.

Wagner, Henry Raup. *Spanish Voyages to the Northwest Coast of America in the Sixteenth Century*. San Francisco: California Historical Society, 1929.

GLYNDWR WILLIAMS

# Anschütz-Kaempfe, Hermann (1872–1931), German inventor of gyrocompasses. Born in Zweibrücken on October 3, 1872, Anschütz-Kaempfe was the son of Friedrich Wilhelm Anschütz, a teacher of mathematics in Zweibrücken and later in Neuburg an der Donau, and was the adopted son of Dr. Kaempfe, an Austrian art historian. Anschütz-Kaempfe studied medicine and then art history, after which he traveled in the Mediterranean and in the Arctic. After meeting the Austrian Julius von Payer (1842–1915), painter and explorer, he decided, about 1902, to undertake an expedition to the North Pole in a submarine equipped with a gyroscope. The Imperial Navy then still refused to acquire U-boats but was interested in instruments to replace the magnetic compass in armored warships. Anschütz-Kaempfe's first gyro instruments in 1904 were rejected by the German Navy and, in 1905, by the British Navy and aroused critics and competition by other Germany companies, such as Siemens. Only in 1908 did he and his company, Anschütz, in Kiel, succeed with a north-seeking gyrocompass, which was subsequently adopted by the German Navy and, from 1910, was also built under license by the British firm Elliott Brothers.

In the Anschütz gyrocompass, the spinning axis of the gyro was arranged in the horizontal plane floating in mercury, suspended slightly pendulous, thus harnessed by gravity so that its axis, by forces of precession, was brought in line with the north-south axis of the earth. Oscillations about this direction, due to gyroscopic inertia, were dampened by special devices. Max Schuler, a relative of Anschütz-Kaempfe, found that if the pendulous device had a period of eighty-four minutes—equal to a pendulum of the earth's radius—it also corrected for the disturbing influence of a ship's accelerations. This effect, called Schuler tuning, is fundamental to gyronavigational systems.

The competition of such inventors as Elmer Sperry led to priority claims. Albert Einstein, a former Swiss patent expert, in 1914 was asked for his opinion and found that Sperry had depended on Anschütz principles. Further improvements of the gyrocompass then gained from Anschütz-Kaempfe's growing friendship with such physicists as Einstein and Arnold Sommerfeld. He sought to mount the gyro system in a frictionless spherical case, and Einstein provided the solution for centering the floating sphere with a magnet coil. Attempts to combine the compass with an artificial horizon for artillery purposes were not completed in his lifetime.

In 1930 he transferred his controlling interest in his firm to the Carl-Zeiss Foundation. He died in Munich on May 6, 1931.

[*See also* Navigational Instruments, *subentry on* Measurement of Direction.]

## Bibliography

Broelmann, J. *Intuition und Wissenschaft in der Kreiseltechnik, 1750 bis 1930.* Munich: Deutsches Museum, 2002.

Fanning, Antony E. *Steady as She Goes: A History of the Compass Department of the Admiralty.* London: Her Majesty's Stationary Office, 1986.

Grant, G. A. A., and J. Klinert. *The Ship's Compass.* 2d ed. London: Routledge and Kegan Paul, 1970.

JOBST BROELMANN

# Anson, George (1697–1762), admiral of the Royal Navy and First Lord of the Admiralty. He was born April 23, 1697, in Staffordshire, England, to minor gentry, but his uncle was Thomas Parker, later first earl of Macclesfield and Lord Chancellor. Anson entered the navy in 1712 and had steady employment even after peace came in 1714. Promoted to captain in 1724, he spent a total of nine years as a frigate commander on the South Carolina station at Charleston. In 1737 he went to West Africa as captain of *Centurion* (60 guns). His fame and reputation rest on a daring voyage around the world lasting from 1740 to 1744, leadership as a seagoing admiral, and contributions to the navy as an institution.

Soon after Britain went to war with Spain in 1739, Anson was appointed commodore of a small squadron for a special mission to harass the Spaniards on the Pacific coast of South America. Tempestuous seas off Cape Horn prevented four of his seven warships from safely gaining the Pacific, and scurvy took a heavy toll. After recuperating on Juan Fernandez (now Isla Robinson Crusoe, Chile), Anson attempted to carry out his mission, but wound up crossing the Pacific to Canton. In 1743, near the entrance of San Bernardino Strait in the Philippines, he intercepted, fought, and captured a silver-laden galleon from Acapulco. In June 1744 *Centurion*, the only ship to complete the circumnavigation, arrived in England; of 1,700 men who set out, only 335 survived, and of these only 145 went around the world. Anson came home a hero and immensely wealthy.

Promoted to rear admiral in April 1745 and vice admiral in July 1746, Anson began an intense commitment to hard

**Anson in HMS *Centurion* capturing *Nostra Signora de Cabadonga*.** This event continued to be romanticized, as in this engraving from 1743, into the late nineteenth century. © Ann Ronan Picture Library / HIP / Art Resource, NY

service at sea. His name will always be connected with the Western Squadron, a strategic innovation that efficiently served to hamper French trade and expeditions. This squadron cruised off the French coast, its strength always superior to that of the French at Brest. Effectiveness depended on continual cruising despite harsh conditions and recurrent frustration. Anson set a strong example, which he later, as First Lord, expected to be followed. In April 1747, upon receiving intelligence of a departing French convoy, he raced southward and intercepted it just north of Cape Ortegal, Spain. In the battle, on May 3, his squadron captured nearly all the French warships. For this highly visible success King George II made him a peer.

Anson had been a member of the Admiralty Board since December 1744 and became First Lord in 1751. Familiar with the challenges of service at sea, he focused on improving the navy's fighting efficiency. Peacetime reductions in the naval budget put it out of his power to increase the size of the fleet, and when hostilities erupted again in 1755, the navy faced not only the endemic problem of manning ships but an inadequate number of ships in good repair. Still, in early 1756 two more ships could have been found for the squadron, which was ordered to the

Mediterranean under Admiral Byng to counter a French attack on Minorca. By giving too much priority to the Western Squadron at this moment, Anson made the next-to-worst mistake of his career, the worst being his approval of John Byng for the mission. That singularly unenterprising admiral used his lack of clear naval superiority to justify his ingrained defeatism, and failed to prevent the loss of Minorca. Byng was court-martialed, found guilty of negligence, and, notwithstanding the court's recommendation of clemency, executed. The mandatory death penalty had been instituted in 1749, with Anson's support, to bolster discipline. The government was also blamed, as was Anson, quite pointedly, and all those implicated were compelled to resign in November 1756.

In 1748 Lord Anson had married Elizabeth Yorke, daughter of the earl of Hardwicke, Lord Chancellor. There was an age difference of twenty-eight years, and their temperaments were opposite: she was vivacious and unguarded; he was outwardly taciturn and formal. Yet it was an affectionate marriage, and her death in 1760 was a severe blow.

In June 1757 Anson was restored to the office of First Lord—an appointment that Anson's highly placed father-in-law secured with an astute move to overcome William

Pitt's reluctance to appoint him. It helped that no one else was as well qualified, but the loss of Minorca had nearly ended Anson's career as First Lord. He was now able to follow through on reforms begun in the later 1740s: to bring the Marines permanently under the Admiralty and to improve British warship design, which he did by recognizing Thomas Slade's talent. In 1756 Anson began in earnest a program for building in private shipyards. Yet his three greatest contributions to eventual British naval success in the Seven Years' War were to ensure that none but reliable and enterprising flag officers commanded important squadrons, to persist with the strategy of the Western Squadron in spite of early disappointments, and to gear up the dockyard and victualing services at Plymouth to sustain it. Fresh greens and live cattle for fresh beef were sent and transferred at sea—an innovation that effectively warded off scurvy and made possible Admiral Sir Edward Hawke's great victory at Quiberon Bay, France, in November 1759.

Anson died in office on June 6, 1762. Though efficient in administration, he disliked administrative work and said that he was never happier than when commanding a squadron at sea. Deeply set in his character were the qualities necessary for the exercise of sea power: attention to training and discipline, professional acumen, courage, and, as a colleague noted, patience and perseverance.

[*See also* Corbett, Julian; Howe, Richard; Naval Administration; Naval Logistics, *subentry* To 1850; Navies, Great Powers, *subentry on* British Isles, 1500 to the Present; Shipboard Life, *subentry on* Naval Vessels; Strategy; *and* Wars, Maritime, *subentry on* Anglo-French Wars.]

### Bibliography

Pack, S. W. C. *Admiral Lord Anson*. London: Cassel, 1960.

Richmond, Herbert W. *The Navy in the War of 1739–48*. Vol. 3. Cambridge, U.K.: Cambridge University Press, 1920.

Rodger, N. A. M. "George, Lord Anson, 1697–1762." In *Precursors of Nelson: British Admirals of the Eighteenth Century*, edited by Peter LeFevre and Richard Harding, pp. 177–199. London: Chatham Publishing, 2000.

Williams, Glyn. *The Prize of All the Oceans: Commodore Anson's Daring Voyage and Triumphant Capture of the Spanish Treasure Galleon*. 1999. Reprint, Harmondsworth, U.K.: Penguin Books, 2001.

DANIEL A. BAUGH

# Antarctica and the Southern Ocean

Although today we know that the icebound land at the bottom of the world is the highest, driest, most windswept, and coldest of the seven continents, it was not until the late eighteenth century that its true nature was suspected. It was not until the early twentieth century that men departed from their winter quarters in ships or huts to make sledge journeys into Antarctica's interior, journeys that combined science with geographical exploration.

The continent is roughly snail-shaped, with its head, the Antarctic Peninsula, stretching north toward the tip of South America. A number of sub-Antarctic or peri-Antarctic islands surround it. Some of these islands, such as Macquarie Island, are smooth and green, while others, such as South Georgia, are jagged and clad in ice. The Southern Ocean is one of the stormiest seas in the world. To reach the continent, a mariner has to brave mountainous seas and then penetrate the belt of pack ice that guards its shores.

### Exploration by Sea

Three French expeditions preceded Captain James Cook's circumnavigation of Antarctica in 1776–1780. The first, in *Aigle* and *Marie* (1738–1739), was commanded by Jean-Baptiste Bouvet de Lozier, and the second, in 1771–1772, was commanded by Marc-Joseph Marion du Fresne, later succeeded by Julien Crozet, his second in command. All were officers of the Compagnie des Indes (French East India Company), which was interested in discovering islands in the South Indian Ocean where its ships and their crews could repair and rest. The third French voyage was commanded by Yves de Kerguelen, an officer in the Marine Royale who sailed with two vessels, *Fortune* and *Gros-Ventre*, in search of the so-called Southern Continent. The result of these eighteenth-century French voyages were the discoveries of the small, icy island now named Bouvetøya, the Prince Edward Islands, Îles Crozet, and Îles Kerguelen.

Then came the great second voyage of Captain James Cook in 1772–1775 commanding HMS *Resolution* and HMS *Adventure*, whose captain was Captain Tobias Furneaux. Cook circumnavigated Antarctica in the high southern latitudes, dispelling forever the myth of a fertile southern continent extending into temperate climes. This expedition discovered the South Sandwich Islands, and landed on South Georgia, taking possession of it for King George III, after whom the island was named. Captain Cook made the first crossings of the Antarctic Circle and sailed on longitude 106°54′ W to the high latitude of 71°10′ S off the present Walgreen Coast, in what is now known as the Amundsen Sea. This was on January 30, 1774, when

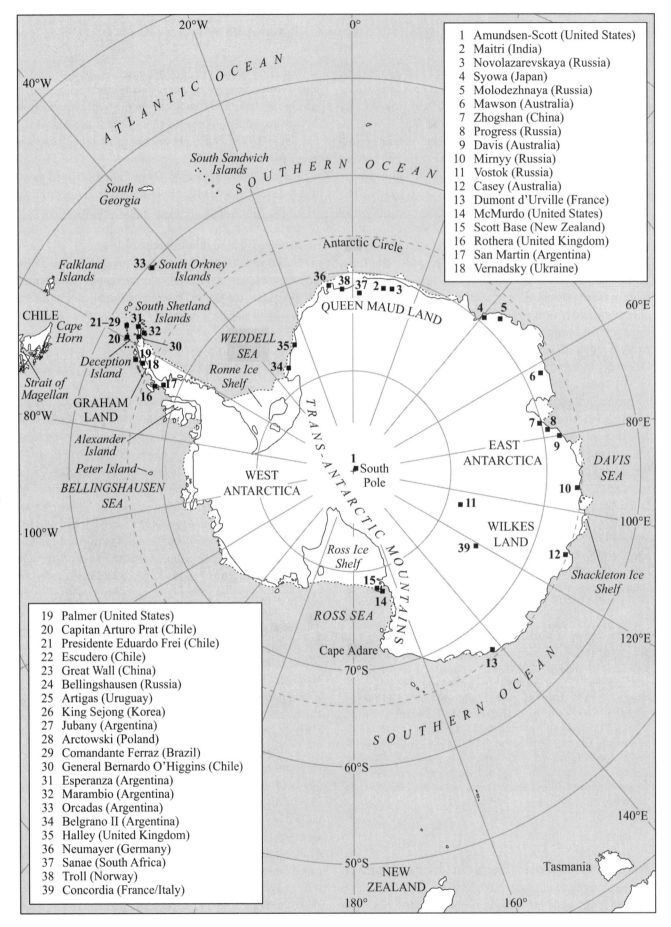

1 Amundsen-Scott (United States)
2 Maitri (India)
3 Novolazarevskaya (Russia)
4 Syowa (Japan)
5 Molodezhnaya (Russia)
6 Mawson (Australia)
7 Zhogshan (China)
8 Progress (Russia)
9 Davis (Australia)
10 Mirnyy (Russia)
11 Vostok (Russia)
12 Casey (Australia)
13 Dumont d'Urville (France)
14 McMurdo (United States)
15 Scott Base (New Zealand)
16 Rothera (United Kingdom)
17 San Martin (Argentina)
18 Vernadsky (Ukraine)

19 Palmer (United States)
20 Capitan Arturo Prat (Chile)
21 Presidente Eduardo Frei (Chile)
22 Escudero (Chile)
23 Great Wall (China)
24 Bellingshausen (Russia)
25 Artigas (Uruguay)
26 King Sejong (Korea)
27 Jubany (Argentina)
28 Arctowski (Poland)
29 Comandante Ferraz (Brazil)
30 General Bernardo O'Higgins (Chile)
31 Esperanza (Argentina)
32 Marambio (Argentina)
33 Orcadas (Argentina)
34 Belgrano II (Argentina)
35 Halley (United Kingdom)
36 Neumayer (Germany)
37 Sanae (South Africa)
38 Troll (Norway)
39 Concordia (France/Italy)

**Map of Expeditions to Antarctica.** Map by Bill Nelson

*Resolution*, by then separated from *Adventure*, encountered a vast field of ice that stretched to the southern horizon, where, in Cook's words, they "could not proceed one inch farther South" (*Journals*, edited by Beaglehole). In revising his journal, Cook expressed the opinion that "this Ice extended quite to the Pole or perhaps joins some land, to which it had been fixed from creation." A little more than a year later, on February 6, 1775, after discovering the South Sandwich Islands, Cook entered into his diary his conclusion that "this Southern Continent (supposing there is one) must lay within the Polar Circle, where the Sea is so pestered with ice that the land is thereby inaccessible." These lands would "never be explored," since navigation there was so dangerous. Its difficulty was "greatly heightened by the enexpressable horrid aspect of the Country, a Country doomed by Nature never once to feel the warmth of the Suns rays, but to lie for ever buried under everlasting snow and ice."

The next to circumnavigate Antarctica was Captain Thaddeus Bellingshausen of the Russian Imperial Navy in command of *Vostok* and *Mirnyy*, whose captain was Captain M. P. Lazarev. In 1819–1821, Bellingshausen went out of his way to complement Cook's voyage, sailing where Cook had not sailed. He certainly sighted—but did not recognize as land—two coastal areas of the present Dronning Maud Land, the first three days before Edward Bransfield's discovery of Trinity Land (part of the Antarctic Peninsula) on January 30, 1820. The sea to the west of the Antarctic Peninsula is now named after Bellingshausen. During this great voyage, *Vostok* and *Mirnyy* sailed over 42° of longitude within the Antarctic Circle (compared to Cook's 24°). Bellingshausen discovered the first land within the Antarctic Circle: a small island named after Peter the Great and a much larger area that Bellingshausen named Alexander Land, after the reigning tsar.

Between the voyages of Cook and Bellingshausen, a multitude of British and American sealers decimated the population of fur seals that Cook had reported at South Georgia, as well as those on other islands farther to the south. Information regarding new land discovered by these sealers became available only early in the nineteenth century, it being in the sealers' interests to keep the whereabouts of new sealing grounds to themselves.

During a trading voyage from Buenos Aires, Argentina, to Valparaíso, Chile, the brig *Williams*, whose master was William Smith, was blown off course while rounding Cape Horn in 1819. This led to the discovery of the South Shetland Islands and soon afterward of part of the coast of the Antarctic Peninsula. Smith confirmed his discovery in October of that year when he landed on King George Island. As a result, during the austral summer of 1819–1820, a surveying voyage was made on the orders of Captain W. H. Shireff, the senior British naval officer on the South America Station. To survey the South Shetlands, Captain Smith's brig *Williams* was chartered under the command of Edward Bransfield, master in the Royal Navy, with William Smith aboard. This expedition also discovered the northwestern coast of the Antarctic Peninsula, which Bransfield named Trinity Land on January 30, 1820. It, too, was surveyed, resulting in the first Admiralty chart to show a portion of the Antarctic mainland.

So numerous were the sealing voyages in the 1820s that mention can be made only of the more notable ones. In 1820–1821 an American sealing expedition from Stonington, Connecticut, consisting of five vessels, visited the South Shetlands. On November 16, 1820, one of these vessels, the shallop *Hero*, with shipmaster Nathaniel Brown Palmer, reported land that was later named Palmer's Land, part of the Antarctic Peninsula. The name now applies to the southern area of the peninsula. A British sealing expedition (1822–1824) in *Jane* and *Beaufoy*, with James Weddell as senior commander, charted the South Orkney and South Shetland Islands, as well as the Weddell Sea, into which Weddell penetrated to latitude 74°15′ S during a remarkably ice-free season.

The third circumnavigation of Antarctica was made in 1830–1833 by the brig *Tula*, whose master was John Biscoe, and the cutter *Lively*, whose master was George Avery. Sighting a range of *nunataks* (mountains) piercing the ice sheet, Biscoe made the first unequivocal discovery of land—which he called Enderby Land, after his employers—on the mainland of Antarctica. In the area of the Antarctic Peninsula, he discovered Adelaide Island and the Biscoe Islands, as well as part of the peninsula that he called Graham Land (the name now given to its northern section). On his return to England, Biscoe—who, with his crews, had endured great hardships and dangers—wrote to the hydrographer of the Navy, declaring his firm opinion "that this is a large continent, as I saw to an extent of 300 miles."

Three national expeditions next resulted in substantial discoveries, drawing back further the veil obscuring Antarctica and resulting in some notable publications and charts. The first expedition was French, in 1837–1840, commanded by J. S. C. Dumont d'Urville in *Astrolabe*, accompanied by C. H. Jacquinot in *Zélée*. Its most notable achievement was the discovery of the Antarctic land named Terre Adélie, after Madame d'Urville.

The next national expedition was American, in 1838–1842, with U.S. Navy lieutenant Charles Wilkes as senior commander of a squadron of five vessels. A series of land-falls and appearances of land were discovered and charted while sailing west off the coast of what was later called Wilkes Land, between longitudes 158° E and 94° E.

The third of these national expeditions, from 1839 to 1843, was led by that most experienced navigator in ice, Captain James Clark Ross of the Royal Navy. As a young midshipman and later with more senior rank, he had sailed and wintered during voyages searching for the Northwest Passage. In the well-strengthened and well-found bomb vessels HMS *Erebus* and HMS *Terror*, whose captain was F. R. M. Crozier, Ross went on a scientific voyage that had as one of its aims to reach the South Magnetic Pole, impor-tant to navigation. These ships were the first to force a way through the pack ice of the Ross Sea to discover South Vic-toria Land. Ross had already reached the North Magnetic Pole, in the Arctic, but his ambition to reach its southerly counterpart was frustrated when he found that icy moun-tains and glaciers barred the way. Some five hundred miles of this new land was roughly charted, but the most extraor-dinary discoveries were of the Great Ice Barrier (now the Ross Ice Shelf) and Mount Erebus, an active volcano not far away on Ross Island. The head of the Ross Sea was later named McMurdo Sound. The ships achieved a lati-tude of 78°10′ S—a record that stood for sixty years—during a second sweep to the south from the expedition's mag-netic headquarters in Hobart, Tasmania. (The Rossbank Magnetic Observatory was established at Hobart by Ross and the lieutenant governor of Van Diemen's Land [Tas-mania] on the way south. Here observations were taken regularly at very short intervals to compare with those taken during the voyage and those taken by other colonial observatories.) While completing their circumnavigation, *Erebus* and *Terror* made more discoveries to the east of the Antarctic Peninsula: the James Ross Island group.

Apart from numerous American sealing voyages to Îles Kerguelen, the South Shetlands, and Heard Island, few ships sailed the Southern Ocean during the later decades of the nineteenth century. The great oceanographic research voyage of HMS *Challenger*, the first steam vessel to cross the Antarctic Circle, took place in 1872–1876. Stones dredged from the continental shelf provided indications that Antarctica might indeed be a continent. In the last decade of the nineteenth century Sir John Murray, editor of the remarkable series of *Challenger* reports, together with Sir Clements Markham, president of the Royal Geo-graphical Society, campaigned for the dispatch of an offi-cial British expedition to the Antarctic. In addition, the International Geographical Congress of 1895, held in London, passed a motion saying that the exploration of the south polar regions was the greatest and most impor-tant task remaining.

## Exploring the Continent

The first to answer this call was the Belgian expedition in *Belgica* (1897–1899), commanded by Adrien de Gerlache. A number of discoveries were made west of the Antarctic Pen-insula. *Belgica* was trapped in the ice of the Bellingshausen Sea and drifted south for twelve months, but she eventu-ally escaped. She was the first exploring vessel to winter in the Antarctic. The next to do so was *Gauss*, carrying the German Antarctic expedition of 1901–1903, for which she was built along the lines of Fridtjof Nansen's *Fram*. Led by Professor Erich von Drygalski, this expedition discovered Kaiser Wilhelm II Land and climbed the extinct volcano Gaussberg. The scientific results ran to many volumes. The Swedish Antarctic expedition of 1901–1904, led by Otto Nordenskjöld in *Antarctic*, was less fortunate. The ship was crushed in pack ice on the eastern side of the Antarctic Peninsula, but shore parties and crew were rescued by *Uru-guay*, an Argentine vessel. Even so, the expedition managed to carry out a comprehensive scientific program.

In 1898 a private British expedition, led by Carsten E. Borchgrevink and financed by a newspaper magnate, departed in *Southern Cross* for the Ross Sea. The expedi-tion built a hut, which still stands, at Cape Adare, where members wintered. This was the first scientific party that intentionally wintered on the continent. Sir Clements Markham, though unable to get the British government to sponsor an Antarctic voyage along the lines of *Chal-lenger*, did raise funds from private donors and the gov-ernment sufficient to build the wooden auxiliary bark *Discovery* at Dundee, where she is now berthed. Markham was allowed a number of naval officers and men for the National Antarctic Expedition of 1901–1904. Its leader, Captain Robert Falcon Scott, was also in charge of the scientists and showed immense interest in their work. The expedition wintered twice in *Discovery*, which was delib-erately iced-in below Mount Erebus on McMurdo Sound. A hut was erected, partly in case of emergency and partly for storage and theatricals. It also stands, as do those of Ernest Shackleton (1907–1909) and Scott (1910–1913), whose ships, *Nimrod* and *Terra Nova*, did not winter.

Captain Scott led the first sledge parties to make exten-sive journeys on the Antarctic continent. These parties went first to within five hundred miles of the South Pole (to latitude 82°16′3″ S) and second up the Ferrar Glacier and onto the immense ice sheet that covers the continent. Thus began the so-called heroic age of Antarctic exploration. There followed an attempt on the South Pole by a party led by Sir Ernest Shackleton, who turned back within 97 miles of it. The pole itself was first reached by the Norwegian explorer Roald Amundsen on December 14, 1911, and a month later by Captain Scott on January 17, 1912. Scott and his four companions perished during the return journey, but he bequeathed a great scientific and literary legacy. The heroic age also included the Scottish National Expedition of 1902–1904, led by Dr. William S. Bruce in *Scotia*, two expeditions led by Commandant Jean-Baptiste Charcot (the first in *Français* and the second in *Pourquoi Pas?*), the German expedition led by Wilhelm Filchner in *Deutschland*, and Sir Douglas Mawson's Australasian Antarctic Expedition in *Aurora*. The heroic age ended with Sir Ernest Shackleton's *Endurance* expedition (1914–1916), of which the Ross Sea Party in *Aurora* (1914–1917) was a part. Shackleton's *Endurance* was beset by ice and sank in the Weddell Sea.

Other exploring vessels, whale catchers, whale factory ships, icebreakers, research ships, tourist vessels, and even yachts sailed the Southern Ocean during the rest of the twentieth century, and countless overland expeditions increasingly used motorized transport and aircraft. The Antarctic is so remote from other continents that ships have continued to be employed to carry personnel, materials, and supplies across the Southern Ocean. It is relatively easy to fly the six hundred miles or so from South America across Drake Passage, but flights of some two thousand or more miles are necessary from New Zealand and South Africa, and weather conditions on Antarctica can make landings hazardous. Hence the continent still has to be approached mainly by sea. Antarctica, sometimes called "a continent for science," is protected by the Antarctic Treaty of 1959 and other legislation.

[*See also* Amundsen, Roald; Cook, James; Expeditions, Scientific; North Pole; Pacific Ocean, *subentries on* Exploration Voyages, 1520–1700 *and* Exploration Voyages in the Eighteenth Century; Terra Australis Incognita; *and entries on ships mentioned in this article.*]

## Bibliography

Beaglehole, J. C. *The Life of Captain James Cook*. London: Hakluyt Society, 1974.

Bertrand, Kenneth J. *Americans in Antarctica, 1775–1948*. New York: American Geographical Society, 1971. A well-researched history.

Campbell, R. J. *The Discovery of the South Shetlands: The Voyages of the Brig "Williams" 1819–1820 as Recorded in Contemporary Documents and the Journal of Midshipman C. W. Poynter*. London: Hakluyt Society, 2000.

Cherry-Garrard, Apsley. *The Worst Journey in the World*. London: Chatto and Windus, 1922. A classic personal narrative mainly of Captain Scott's last expedition, 1910–1913.

Conrad, L. J. *Bibliography of Antarctica Exploration: Expedition Accounts from 1768 to 1960*. Washougal, Wash.: L. J. Conrad, 1999.

Cook, James. *The Journals of Captain James Cook on His Voyages of Discovery*. Edited by J. C. Beaglehole. 4 vols. Cambridge, U.K.: Cambridge University Press for the Hakluyt Society, 1955–1974.

Deacon, George. *The Antarctic Circumpolar Ocean*. Cambridge, U.K.: Cambridge University Press, 1984. A history of its exploration and oceanography for the layman.

Delépine, Gracie. *Les îles australes françaises*. Rennes, France: Ouest-France, 1995. A history and geography of the French sub-Antarctic islands.

Dunmore, John. *French Explorers in the Pacific*. Vol. 1, *The Eighteenth Century*. Oxford: Clarendon Press, 1965. A pioneering, well-researched study; includes Marion du Fresne and Kerguelen.

Fogg, G. E. *A History of Antarctic Science*. Cambridge, U.K.: Cambridge University Press, 1992. Covers several disciplines through three centuries.

Fogg, G. E., and David Smith. *The Explorations of Antarctica, the Last Unspoilt Continent*. London: Cassell, 1990. Beautifully illustrated by Smith; Fogg was a Fellow of the Royal Society.

Gurney, Alan. *Below the Convergence: Voyages towards Antarctica, 1699–1839*. New York: Norton, 1997.

Gurney, Alan. *Race to the White Continent: Voyages to Antarctica*. New York: Norton, 2000. The three national expeditions of the late 1830s and early 1840s.

Headland, Robert K. *Chronological List of Antarctic Expeditions and Related Historical Events*. Cambridge, U.K.: Cambridge University Press, 1989. A comprehensive annotated list, with entries dating from 700 B.C.E. to 1988, with references and bibliography.

Huntford, Roland. *Shackleton*. London: Hodder and Stoughton, 1985. A minutely researched, lengthy biography of Sir Ernest Shackleton (1874–1922).

Jones, A. G. E. *Antarctica Observed: Who Discovered the Antarctic Continent?* Whitby, U.K.: Caedmon of Whitby, 1982. An analysis of competing claims.

MacDonald, Edwin A. *Polar Operations*. Annapolis, Md.: U.S. Naval Institute, 1969. A manual of ice navigation containing historical background.

Rosove, Michael H. *Antarctica, 1772–1922: Freestanding Publications through 1999*. Santa Monica, Calif.: Adélie Books, 2001. A comprehensive bibliography.

Rosove, Michael H. *Let Heroes Speak: Antarctic Explorers, 1772–1922*. Annapolis, Md.: Naval Institute Press, 2000. Presents the perspectives of the explorers in their own words.

Savours, Ann. "John Biscoe, Master Mariner 1794–1843." *Polar Record* 21, no. 134 (1983): 485–491. A profile from original and published sources of the third circumnavigator of Antarctica.

Savours, Ann. *The Voyages of the "Discovery": The Illustrated History of Scott's Ship.* London: Virgin, 1992. In-depth research covering three Antarctic expeditions: Scott's first voyage (1901–1904), the oceanographic voyage of 1925–1927, and the British, Australian, and New Zealand Antarctic Research Expedition (BANZARE), led by Sir Douglas Mawson, of 1929–1931.

ANN SAVOURS

## Antioch

**Antioch**    Antioch on the Orontes River was founded c. 300 B.C.E. by King Seleucus I (surname Nicator, ruler of the Seleucid empire 306–281 B.C.E.) and was named after his father, Antiochus I (r. 280–261 B.C.E.). The site, part of Turkey since 1938, is now occupied by the modern city of Antakya. Seleucia Pieria (modern Magaracik) was founded simultaneously on an inlet eight kilometers (five miles) west of the Orontes mouth, twenty-six kilometers (sixteen miles) west of Antioch, to serve as the city's port. A canal connected the outer anchorage of the harbor with an inner basin. Both facilities were subject to siltation by the local stream and the Orontes. The emperor Vespasian (r. 69–79 C.E.) diverted the local stream with a dam and a rock-cut channel and tunnel system 1,300 meters (4,265 feet) long in an unsuccessful attempt to clear the harbor, which was a base for the eastern Roman fleet. The emperor Diocletian (r. 284–305 C.E.) dredged the harbor basins in the early fourth century, and in 346 the emperor Constantius II (r. 337–361) improved the facilities.

Since the prosperity of Antioch, a day's voyage up the Orontes, depended on Seleucia Pieria, several futile attempts were made by Roman and Byzantine emperors to dredge the mouth of the river sufficiently to allow entry to cargo ships. Despite the inland location and the hazards of frequent flooding and earthquakes, Antioch flourished as the capital of the vast Seleucid kingdom and later of the Roman province of Syria, and as an early and important center for the Christian church. The city linked trade routes originating in Mesopotamia and Arabia with the vast Mediterranean market. Literary sources record colonnaded streets, palaces, temples, churches, and luxurious villas. Occupation by Arab armies in 641 deprived Antioch and Seleucia of their administrative and economic importance, and the cities rapidly declined under Frankish, Mamluk, and Ottoman control. Because of siltation, earthquake damage, and constant occupation, few ancient structures remain visible, but a local museum displays Byzantine mosaics.

[*See also* Ancient Navies, *subentry on* Rome, *and* Wars, Maritime, *subentry on* Crusades.]

## Bibliography

Campbell, Sheila. *The Mosaics of Antioch.* Toronto: Pontifical Institute of Mediaeval Studies, 1988. An exhaustive study of the mosaics in their archaeological and art-historical context.

Downey, Glanville. *History of Antioch in Syria: From Seleucus to the Arab Conquest.* Princeton, N.J.: Princeton University Press, 1961. Exhaustive review of historical and archaeological data for Antioch for the period indicated, with some mention of Seleucia Pieria.

Elderkin, G. W., and Richard Stillwell, eds. *Antioch-on-the-Orontes.* Princeton, N.J.: Department of Art and Archaeology of Princeton University, 1934– . Presentation of the results of excavation at Antioch in the 1930s.

Grainger, John D. *The Cities of Seleukid, Syria.* Oxford and New York: Oxford University Press, 1990. Discussion of both cities in the Hellenistic period.

Liebeschuetz, J. H. W. G. *Antioch: City and Imperial Administration in the Later Roman Empire.* Oxford: Clarendon Press, 1972. Historical study of the later period.

JOHN PETER OLESON

## Anti-Submarine Warfare

**Anti-Submarine Warfare**    Anti-submarine warfare (ASW) has been defined as the art and science of depriving enemies of the effective use of their submarines, so any and all measures that contribute to this end might be considered ASW. Thus bombing, direct land attack on buildings and basing facilities, and attacks on submarine

**Anti-Submarine Warfare.** Invented in 1942, the hedgehog fired a barrage of twenty-four mortar rounds up to 183 meters (200 yards), each round weighing 34 kg (75 pounds) that landed in the water in an elliptical pattern designed to sink a submarine. This view, taken on November 28, 1945, on board HMS *Westcott*, shows a Mark 10/11 hedgehog launcher. BY PERMISSION OF THE TRUSTEES OF THE IMPERIAL WAR MUSEUM, LONDON, A 31000

communications are all, in different ways, ASW. However, this article will be largely about ASW as it is conducted at sea.

ASW dates from the end of the nineteenth century and the beginning of the twentieth; it began with the invention of the practical submarine, which by 1914 was crude but effective. The early boats were not true submarines: they spent most of their sea time on the surface, and were essentially submersible torpedo boats. The early submarines were slow, unreliable, and—quite often—as dangerous to themselves as they were to others. The range of visibility from the submarines' low towers was poor, but they did have two great advantages. The submarines could submerge to avoid detection, which was very important in the era before radar and sonar, and they had the very best and most deadly weapon until the advent of nuclear weapons in the mid-twentieth century: the torpedo.

World War I gave the submarine its first proper opportunity to demonstrate its potential, and not only did the submarine develop considerably, but it also sank several much larger surface warships. Germany also used submarines when it carried out several campaigns against merchant shipping. The German campaigns produced a huge problem for the Allies, probably bringing them as close to defeat as they ever came. What was to be done?

## Early Underwater Detection, Underwater Attack, and Tactics

To counter the submarine, there were three broad types of potential remedy: underwater detection, underwater attack, and tactics. Underwater detection posed an enormous scientific and technological challenge and engaged some of the best Allied minds. The physics of energy transmission in seawater were little known at the outset, but as is often the case, the exigencies of war pushed matters forward. As well as more exotic research, practical remedies were attempted, such as using towed wires and even training animals, such as sea lions and seagulls. In static locations, such as the Strait of Dover, nets and indicator buoys were deployed, but the real problem lay in the open seas.

It was soon discovered that the only realistic form of energy transmission through water lay with sound. Underwater detection using sound could take two forms: active or passive. Of these, passive was by far the simplest, both in itself and in terms of technical realization. Passive detection relied on the fact that a submerged submarine emitted noise, largely from its propulsion system, and this noise could be detected by a submerged microphone, known as a hydrophone. Usually the hydrophone was suspended below an escort ship, which had to be stopped. Early passive-detection systems were nondirectional and had originally been developed in 1906 as a means to detect icebergs. The French inventor Paul Langevin developed the first prototype submarine listening device in 1915, and further work was carried out by the British Board of Inventions in 1916, which handed the project on to the Anti-Submarine Division of the Admiralty. The committee developed a refined prototype in 1917 that was given the name "asdic." From 1918, devices were developed that could indicate the direction of the submarine, but no range. However, distant detection was rarely possible, so some general estimating of a submarine's position was practiced.

Active detection involved sending out a beam of pulsed sound into the water, which bounced off a submarine before returning to the transmitting ship. The direction of the beam gave target bearing. The speed of sound in water was known, so an estimate of range could be made, thus giving almost instantaneous target position. The effective distance that this type of active detection could be employed in was limited, but it was a useful tool. Both active and passive systems were known as "asdic" in British use up through 1948, when NATO standardized terminology and adopted the acronym that the U.S. Navy had used: "sonar," from the phrase "sound navigation and ranging."

Attacking a submarine underwater was difficult, largely because of the uncertainties about position. However, two factors worked to the advantage of a surface attacker, even if the target submarine's position was known only approximately. First, although of only a limited range, underwater explosions could be powerful. Second, early submarines were relatively fragile, and even a near miss could cause considerable damage to the submarine or its systems. Such damage might not lead to the submarine's loss, but it could well incapacitate the submarine for any immediate attack on shipping. After some experimentation, the depth charge became the weapon of choice. The depth charge was nothing more complicated than several hundred pounds of explosive in a case sufficient to stand immersion to the depth at which it would explode. The depth at which the charge would explode was determined by a hydrostatic pistol, which could be set prior to release. A number of these weapons could be released simultaneously, either by being rolled off the stern of the attacking ship or by being projected some distance from a ship's beam by means of cordite guns. The weapon and the means of firing it remained the staple of anti-submarine attacks until well into World War II.

But it is one thing to have, within fairly short range, the means of detecting a submerged submarine and then, within even shorter range, attacking it, and another thing to have and develop the tactics to deal with the submarine in general. As the U-boat was used in early 1917, these technical means were quite inadequate, because the majority of attacks by submarines were carried out on the surface against independent single ships. What was needed was a general means of anti-submarine defense.

This was to come in the spring of 1917, but not before Allied shipping losses had mounted to several hundreds of thousands of tons of ships every month. The expedient was a centuries-old technique, convoy. Merchant ships in convoy were grouped together for passage instead of sailing independently. Further, the merchant ships were provided with an escort of warships. Convoys concentrated warships at the point where submarines were likely to deliver an attack. Most important, in practice, submarines were deterred from attacking, and their successes dwindled markedly.

The other important innovation of the period, which continued to have important consequences in the future, was the employment of aircraft for ASW. The earliest aircraft, either lighter or heavier than air, were of limited range and speed, and they had limited ability to detect and attack submarines, either on the surface or submerged. Nevertheless, their presence often was enough to deter a submarine from pressing home an attack.

## New Technologies in World War II

The general view of the two decades between the world wars characterizes the Allies as complacent that sonar had solved the submarine problem, but recent research has indicated that this was far from the case. However, it would be true to say that the scale of the submarine's potential was probably underestimated.

The German submarine of 1939 was little different in its essential character from that of 1918, and there were relatively few of them, but from the outset of World War II the Germans began where they had left off and immediately began an attack on shipping. Initial results were relatively poor, but the German situation improved immeasurably with the fall of Norway, and then with the fall of France in the summer of 1940, which allowed much more convenient basing outside the North Sea and brought a consequent improvement in submarine effectiveness. Tactically, too, the expedient of group operations allowed searching for convoys before culminating in surface attacks at night. This caused a considerable problem for the British, and later for the Allies.

Technology provided many solutions. Submarines, which were active early in the war, had to make considerable use of the sea surface for speed, visual search, and radio communication, much of which was required by the German commander, Admiral Karl Dönitz. Submarines' use of the surface in the vicinity of convoys was progressively denied, first by the development and widespread fitting of shipborne radar and second by the development of direction-finding equipment for high-frequency radio signals on board ships.

It also became feasible to fit radar in aircraft, with great improvements being carried out both in radar performance and also in the aircraft themselves. At the beginning of the war, most aircraft were of limited range and endurance and could carry only a light load of weapons. By 1943, large, longer-range aircraft were in use, denying nearly the whole of the North Atlantic to submarines insofar as practical operations against convoys were concerned.

Submarines also had to be attacked, and the principal problem was how to attack underwater. Sonar had limited range and certainty of detection, but incremental improvements were made with it. The main weapon was the depth charge, which was incrementally improved throughout the war. However, the main difficulty was putting a lethal weapon close enough to the submarine. Most depth-charge attacks were carried out by overrunning the submarine and thus losing sonar contact. This difficulty was solved by means of ahead-thrown weapons such as Hedgehog and Mousetrap, which projected a pattern of contact-fused bombs into the water.

There were many other less obvious means by which Allied ASW improved during the war, such as intelligence (including code breaking known as Ultra), operational research, training, superior organization, and much greater shipbuilding capacity, especially in the United States.

Airborne ASW was a field that showed particular improvement, with not only the development of radar, but also the development of two additional sensors for the difficult target of the submerged submarine: sonobuoys and magnetic anomaly detection (MAD). Further, aircraft for most of the war were able to attack submarines on the surface only, with either depth charges (only really suitable against a surfaced submarine or one that had only just submerged) or rockets. German submarines, using the snorkel since its introduction in 1943—the snorkel was a prewar Dutch invention, called a *Schnorchel* in German—in order to stay submerged longer, were now less likely to be detected on the surface. A new weapon was called for, and the ASW homing torpedo was thus deployed in the latter part of the war, guided by the sound of the submarine itself. These torpedoes proved even more effective when used in conjunction with sonobuoys.

The Germans were acutely aware of the limitations of their submarines and, in particular, strove for improved underwater performance. Their main attempt, the Walther boat, was potentially excellent, but it used too radical a propulsion system and never attained operational service. Some features of the Walther boat, however, were incorporated in other submarines that began to be produced from 1944 onward, and these submarines were formidable, at least in their potential. In practice, few Walther boats put to sea, but their high underwater performance reemerged in the postwar years. In part, the proactive mining of their trials and exercise areas in the Baltic Sea was responsible for their nonappearance—yet another form of ASW.

The Allies fought a highly successful ASW campaign, and the Germans and Italians were competent, but the least accomplished of the major maritime participants in the war was undoubtedly the Japanese. The Japanese considered ASW as defensive and therefore not worthy of their martial tradition—for this they paid a huge price. The most successful antishipping campaign fought by submarines was that of the Americans against the Japanese. The majority of the Japanese merchant marine was lost during the war, mostly to submarines. There were two fundamental reasons for this: the quality of American submarines and their systems, and the Japanese neglect of ASW. The cost of this to Japan was high, hobbling its offensive operations, making defensive ones difficult to sustain, and strangling the flow of raw materials back to the Japanese home islands. This, as much as the atom bombs, was responsible for Japanese defeat.

### The Cold War and Beyond

The Cold War years saw much activity in ASW, even though there was little hot war action. Much of this came from the technical advances in submarines themselves and from the responses to these advances. The most important of these was the nuclear-powered submarine. Not only did the nuclear-powered submarine give virtually limitless endurance to submarines and give most of them a speed never before seen underwater, but also—and perhaps most important—it all but eliminated submarines' need to use the surface. Thus the nuclear-powered submarine removed what had been the submarine's greatest dependency (and thus vulnerability) in World War II, a dependency that in retrospect had made it only a submersible torpedo boat.

But ASW had not and did not continue to stand still. Some new devices that were deployed during the Cold War were direct developments of what had gone before. Aircraft were designed especially for maritime use, carrying improved radar, improved weapons, and—most important—sonobuoys. These were much more advanced than their wartime predecessors. Sonobuoys were now directional and active as well as passive. With improved guidance, both active and passive, and with greater speed, homing torpedoes, too, acquired a wider range of target types and conditions. Such torpedoes were also fitted to surface warships.

On surface ships, sonar was vastly improved. Its wartime performance had done little better than enable detection at only a few thousands yards, often less under realistic conditions. The development of lower frequency, omnidirectional sonars vastly increased both range and coverage. Several nations also developed variable-depth sonars, whose body could be lowered several hundred feet into the water, in an effort to overcome the limitations caused by the thermal structure of seawater.

Further, although the science of oceanography was much older than the Cold War, much of its expansion—especially in applied fields such as studying the behavior of sound in the sea—owed a great deal to the impetus of the Cold War. It is true to say that the efforts in understanding the sea, measuring it, and attempting to forecast its effect on naval operations comes from these decades. The Cold War was also the reason for the vast expansion in the development of specialist ships for oceanographic research.

Shipborne weapons systems, too, reflected improvements in submarines. Initially these took the form of relatively short-range rocket and mortar weapons, such as the British Mortar Mark X, which could project a pattern of explosive depth bombs up to 1,000 yards from the firing ship in any direction. Rocket weapons could either be unguided after firing, like the Russian RBU/MBU systems, or have a homing torpedo payload, like the American ASROC. Some weapons could carry a nuclear payload.

A further development was the use of helicopters in ASW. These could range from very light helicopters used solely to drop a lightweight homing torpedo on a submarine target, to much larger, medium helicopters, which were capable of autonomous searching using either active, dipping medium-range sonar or passive sonobuoys. The medium helicopters could also carry ASW weapons and were capable of integrating their information with that of an ASW task force. Such helicopters could be deployed either from aircraft-carrier-type ships or, latterly, even from larger frigates.

Also important were the long-range, fixed passive systems deployed by the United States, such as the Sound Surveillance System (SOSUS), later the Integrated Underwater Surveillance System (IUSS), which were capable of detecting nuclear submarines at great ranges, if with only limited accuracy. However, the limitation in accuracy was often offset by the ability of other units to locate and then track the submarines. These consisted of long-range maritime patrol aircraft, such as the P-3 Orion, in cooperation with vessels both above and below the surface.

The submarine came into its own in the Cold War period as an ASW ship, with the two main types of nonmissile submarines, nuclear and diesel-electric powered, having their own special characteristics. The diesel-electric-powered submarine was the stealthiest and quietest for optimum operation of passive sonar, but the nuclear submarine—with its combination of speed when needed, endurance, and large hull for a good sensor and weapon fit—was probably the best single ship for ASW in the whole armory. In the latter part of the Cold War, at least in the West, the surface ship became capable of playing a fuller part in ASW because of the advent of the towed passive sonar array, which was capable of reaching great depths and proved itself very effective in ASW operations, especially in conjunction with other units.

Since the end of the Cold War, probably from the early 1990s, it has been difficult to see what the future for ASW will be. One view is that ASW was a Cold War warfare specialty and one no longer likely to be needed. But there are still many nations in the world that own submarines, and so long as there are submarines, there will be a requirement for ASW. What may well be different are some of the technical challenges and responses. A western interest in expeditionary warfare implies littoral operations, and the main need there is for smaller, stealthier submarines. This may lead to interest in nonacoustic detection or different acoustic techniques. Similarly, weapons will have to adjust to operations in shallow water, and new tactics will have to be worked out to cover these circumstances.

[*See also* Atlantic, Battle of the; Convoy; Submarine; Tactics; Warships, *subentry on* Modern Warships; *and* Wars, Maritime, *subentries on* World Wars *and* Wars after 1945.]

### Bibliography

Baker, Richard. *The Terror of Tobermory: An Informal Biography of Vice-Admiral Sir Gilbert Stephenson, KBE, CB, CMG.* London: Allen, 1972.

Franklin, George. *Britain's Anti-Submarine Capability, 1919–1939.* London: Frank Cass, 2003.
Gardner, W. J. R. *Anti-Submarine Warfare.* London: Brassey's, 1996.
Gardner, W. J. R. *Decoding History: The Battle of the Atlantic and Ultra.* Annapolis, Md.: Naval Institute Press, 1999.
Hackmann, Willem Dirk. *Seek and Strike: Sonar, Anti-Submarine Warfare, and the Royal Navy, 1914–54.* London: HMSO, 1984.
Hartcup, Guy. *The Effect of Science on the Second World War.* New York: St. Martin's Press, 2000.
Hill, J. R. *Anti-Submarine Warfare.* Shepperton, U.K.: Ian Allan; Annapolis, Md.: Naval Institute Press, 1984.
Monsarrat, Nicholas. *The Cruel Sea.* New York: Knopf, 1951.
Waddington, C. H. *OR in World War 2: Operational Research against the U-boat.* London: Paul Elek Scientific Books, 1973.
Williams, Kathleen Broome. *Secret Weapon: U.S. High-frequency Direction Finding in the Battle of the Atlantic.* Annapolis, Md.: Naval Institute Press, 1996.

W. J. R. Gardner

**Antwerp**   The second-largest city in Belgium and the capital of the Flemish province of the same name, Antwerp is situated on both banks of the Scheldt River, about forty kilometers (twenty-five miles) north of Brussels and eighty-eight kilometers (fifty-five miles) from the North Sea. The area it occupies has been populated at least since the second century and was a major banking center by the middle of the fifteenth, establishing Europe's first stock exchange in 1460. The city's prominence was based on its port, the largest in Belgium and the most central to Europe's main centers of production. In the first half of the sixteenth century the port of Antwerp became the most important in Europe when that of Brugge lost its primacy as the Zwijn River, on which Brugge stands, began to silt up. By 1560 Antwerp was the second-largest European city north of the Alps. Its hospitality to foreign investment made it very cosmopolitan, and it became home to large Spanish, Portuguese, and Italian settlements as foreign trade shifted there. Jewish refugees expelled from Spain and Portugal formed a large community and created what remains Europe's major diamond cutting and trading center.

Antwerp began a long decline in the 1570s when Spain and the northern Netherlands entered into conflict. The city was sacked by the Spanish in 1576 and six thousand of its citizens were massacred in "the Spanish fury." In 1585 the city was captured by Parma and trade came to an end. When the Dutch gained control of the area, the merchants of Amsterdam caused the Scheldt to be closed to navigation, and Antwerp was cut off from commercial intercourse

**Antwerp.** This seventeenth-century painting from the Flemish school illustrates the port of Antwerp with fishermen selling fish on the quay alongside other merchants. ERICH LESSING / ART RESOURCE, NY

for the next two centuries. Its population, estimated at over one hundred thousand in 1575, sank to about forty-five thousand by 1800. Belgium was a part of the kingdom of the Netherlands from 1815, and Antwerp suffered greatly in the Belgian uprising that established the country's independence in 1830. It was not until 1863 that Belgium was able to reopen the Scheldt River to international commerce and restore the prosperity of its principal port. In both world wars of the twentieth century, Antwerp was occupied by the Germans after devastating battles, but it quickly recovered.

Long a flourishing center of artistic and intellectual life, Antwerp has been home to such noted baroque painters as Peter Paul Rubens, Anthony Van Dyck, and Frans Hals. It hosts an annual international book fair and supports important schools of medicine, engineering, business, architecture, and navigation. Its zoological garden, Gothic cathedral, and art museums are among Europe's most admired, and its National Museum of Shipping is considered the best on the Continent.

More than one quarter of Antwerp's workforce is dedicated to shipping and transportation, and most of the industry of the province, including petroleum refining, automobile assembly, metallurgy, and shipbuilding, is located in the port area of the city. The port of Antwerp is noted for its high volume; in the first half of 2006 a total of 7,547 seagoing vessels called at the port, with a gross register tonnage of 130,564,427 GRT.

[*See also* Shipping, *subentry on* The Netherlands.]

## Bibliography

Blom, J. C. H., and E. Lamberts, eds. *History of the Low Countries.* Translated by James C. Kennedy. New York: Berghahn Books, 1999.
Strubbe, Jan. *The Ports of Belgium: A Heritage for the Future.* Tielt, Belgium: Lannoo, 1987.

DENNIS WEPMAN

# Aquaculture, Social History of

Throughout history, people have managed aquatic environments to provide drinking water, fish, sea mammals, crustaceans, and various flora such as seaweed, water plants, and algae. Aquaculture is a form of aquatic management in which any plant or animal species that naturally lives in water is cultivated in order to ensure a stable or increased supply of it for domestic consumption, commercial sale, or recreational or public uses. There are many premodern and modern forms of aquaculture, including sea and ocean ranching, coastal lagoon farming, stocking and restocking in freshwater lakes and reservoirs, floodplain fisheries management, brush-park fisheries, pond culture, pen-and-cage culture, open-water culture, mollusk culture, and seaweed farming. Brush-park fisheries (called *samarah* in Cambodia, *katha* in Bangladesh, and *acadja* in Benin) are a form of fish-aggregation device in which tree branches are packed tightly in an inner circle and surrounded by a wooden structure or covered in aquatic vegetation. Fishers usually take nets and encircle the brush park, removing the branches and vegetation.

In the case of finfish and crustaceans, capture and harvesting techniques involve some control of aquatic environments through weirs, through pond stocking by means of natural passage of marine animals, through the fencing off of river sections and across rivers, through the controlling of water flows, through the storing of fish and crustaceans in baskets, and through active and passive stocking. The shift to greater control of fish supply occurred over time and was the result of growing demand for fish, shortages and unavailability of open-capture fish from other sources, growing populations, and expanded trade opportunities. In addition, local religious and political elites often bolstered their religious and political status through exclusive or redistributive control of farmed-fish supplies and the regulation of eating habits to meet religious and other objectives.

All premodern forms of aquaculture were linked symbiotically with the wider aquatic and terrestrial environments and had limited impact on the life history of species through transplanting or releasing of seed, fry, or fingerlings of diverse species into open waters. Local communities often held common property rights in water bodies, but the water bodies were also subject over time to increasing control by religious and political elites. This contrasts with many modern aquaculture practices, which exercise greater control over the life cycle of the managed and often single species to ensure certainty of supply and a greater commercialization of production, exchange, and distribution of the products.

Modern aquaculture is the product of a long history of aquatic management that dates back several millennia.

China is often mentioned as the birthplace of aquaculture, but it is more likely that aquaculture had multiple origins in many parts of the world, with some rudimentary forms of fish farming in Australia dated back as far as 8,000 years ago. In China, freshwater aquaculture began more than 3,500 years ago: inscriptions on "oracle bones" dating from this period mention the best times for planting or harvesting fish. Cultural, demographic, and environmental explanations for this development include pressures from the Chinese emperor for a regular supply of fish, fishers' practice of storing fish in baskets in water or trapping fish and keeping them in ponds near rivers, and a combination of more intensive exploitation of wetlands through irrigated rice cultivation and growing population pressure. China's rice-fish culture system is said to derive from pond culture during the Han dynasty (206 B.C.E.–220 C.E.), when farmers began placing carp fry from ponds into rice fields and then into lakes. Carp farming in China became popular around 1000 B.C.E., and in 500 B.C.E. Fan Li, a Chinese administrator, wrote an important treatise on fish culture in which he describes the best methods to raise fish. Carp monoculture was the most common form of fish cultivation at that time, and it was not until the seventh century C.E. that carp polyculture began. ("Monoculture" refers to the production of one species only, while "polyculture" refers to the production of more than one species.)

In Europe and North Africa, fish farming was practiced in Egyptian, Roman, Greek, and Etruscan times. In Ancient Rome, tanks, dams, and channels were used for fish farming on the Mediterranean coast. For example, in 100 B.C.E. the city of Cosa, to the north of Rome, had fish-farm tanks in the city's lagoon. Farmed and caught fish were dried, pickled, or salted and were traded and consumed locally. With the collapse of the Roman Empire, fish farming declined, but it revived in the eighth century C.E.

Early Roman and Etruscan lagoon fishing was the basis for valliculture, a form of aquaculture used for fattening and developed by the upper Adriatic populations by capturing and enclosing seasonally migratory fish species from the sea into the lagoon and delta areas. The French biologist Victor Coste observed valliculture in the Italian Comacchio lagoon in 1851, and valliculture is still practiced today.

In medieval England, fish farming was an important food source for the upper classes and as a religiously sanctioned food within the Christian calendar. Some of the fish produced were dried and salted for the winter and for sale.

In Latin America, pre-Columbian peoples were known to farm fish through complex weir systems, and under the chinampa agricultural system in Aztec Mexico, fish were caught in canals supporting the chinampa "islands." In the Pacific, Hawaiian society had several types of extensive fish ponds as part of a complex agricultural system dominated by a ruling aristocracy that monopolized the best fish for itself and also distributed fish to pond workers and others. In South Asia, freshwater fish farming has been practiced since ancient times, being partly indigenous in origin with some borrowing from China in the twelfth century C.E. In India, Kautilya's *Arthasastra* (a work on kingship written between 321 and 300 B.C.E.) includes references to fish ponds. Freshwater fish were raised in reservoirs that were often irrigation tanks. During the emperor Ashoka's time (268–233 B.C.E.), there are references to tank fishing in the Pillar Edicts. Along coastal India, several systems of fish and crustacean culture have existed for centuries. They include the *pokkali* fields and *chemmeen kettu* of Kerala, *bheris* of West Bengal, *gazani* farms of Karnataka, and *khazan* lands of Goa. In Southeast Asia, brackish-water aquaculture postdates freshwater production; brackish-water aquaculture is thought to have originated in Indonesia c. 1400 C.E. with the cultivation of milkfish under the *tambak* system.

While important historically, these early forms of culture fisheries can be described as "proto-aquacultural" or as a form of stock enhancement with limited intervention in faunal life cycles. It was not until the second half of the twentieth century that aquaculture developed on a large commercial scale.

Modern methods of aquaculture have been traced back to the fifteenth century with the artificial propagation of trout in France. The methods were further developed in Germany in the mid-1700s when a German soldier successfully fertilized trout eggs through pressing male and female bodies together, and then raised the hatched fish in tanks or ponds. Later scientific developments during the nineteenth and early twentieth centuries led to improved methods of cultivation, but before 1950 aquaculture production was of minor importance in the global supply of fish and crustaceans. Since then worldwide aquaculture production, mostly in developing countries in tropical and subtropical Asia, particularly China, has grown tremendously and in 2000 accounted for 32.2 percent of total fisheries landings by weight; 54.9 percent of the total came from marine or brackish water sources and 45.1 percent came from freshwater sources. Finfish accounted for more than half of annual production, followed by mollusks,

aquatic plants, crustaceans, and amphibians and reptiles. Of total global food-fish supply, more than 36 percent is now supplied from farmed sources, and of these more than 80 percent comes from inland freshwater sources.

Modern aquaculture is highly diverse and ranges from small-scale, village-based extensive pond culture serving local needs to industrialized, sometimes corporately owned intensive and semi-intensive production systems serving global markets. Industrial aquaculture is promoted by governments, business, and international development agencies as a new export sector for developing countries to increase food supplies, earn foreign exchange, provide local employment, reduce poverty, and contribute to national economic growth and sustainable livelihood strategies. Aquaculture is part of a global agri-food system within which aquatic commodities are distributed along global value chains to consumers in all parts of the world, particularly those in the wealthy countries of the north. Trade is controlled by private trading, wholesaling, and retailing companies in consumer countries.

This new industry consists of several interconnected subsectors that are hierarchically organized and spatially dispersed and that include not only fish and crustacean cultivation but also brood stock fishing, artificial hatchery production, wild seed collection, the processing and value-adding of products, and a variety of ancillary services such as trading, transport, and package manufacture. These subsectors are located in both rural and urban areas and have generated new forms of work and income, including small-scale aquaculture contract farming, corporately owned farming, hatchery and processing-plant employment, hunting-and-gathering-type wild seed collecting, terrestrial and air transportation, local trading networks and ancillary work in packaging, feed production and processing, and equipment manufacturing.

Much policy and academic debate has focused on the ways in which more industrialized export-oriented fish and crustacean farming, particularly of shrimp and salmon, has transformed the lives of rural communities, especially in coastal areas, and on the environmental, social, and economic costs and benefits associated with that transformation. Most marine and brackish-water aquaculture takes place along sensitive coastal environments that are already subject to a range of pressures such as artisanal and industrial fishing, natural and migration-induced population growth, tourism, and minerals exploitation. Key issues faced by the aquaculture industry are nutrient pollution, the use of wild fish products in aquaculture feeds, the introduction of exotic species, habitat—particularly mangrove—destruction, diminished biodiversity, changing land-use patterns, and the decline of traditional rural livelihoods. In the case of shrimp in Thailand, Vietnam, Honduras, India, Bangladesh, and other countries, shrimp farming has reduced the land available for agriculture and subsistence, destroyed arable land through salinization and farm effluents, destroyed mangroves, reduced drinking-water supplies, disrupted traditional landholding and land-use patterns, exacerbated rural income and landholding inequalities, and reduced access to common property resources.

Many of the negative impacts of aquaculture are partly the result of the relatively unregulated expansion of cultivation in the sector's early years, which led to protests from local farmers, the landless, and local and international NGOs. The demands made by opposition groups included protection of mangrove forests, restrictions on the expansion of aquaculture into farming land, and the dismantling of export-oriented industrialized forms of production and their replacement by modified traditional forms of aquaculture for serving local needs.

Since the 1980s, consumer countries and regional trading blocs such as the European Union and the United States have begun to introduce global aquaculture standards related to product and process quality, labor, and environmental and human rights. Increasingly there has been a shift away from the poor planning of the past toward a more integrated ecosystem approach. The new focus on integrated coastal management strategies aims to serve both social and environmental objectives by protecting local ecosystems and the many communities that depend upon them.

In those parts of Asia with large freshwater aquaculture sectors, food enhancement and security programs are being pursued to increase the access of small-scale farmers and the rural landless to cultured fish sources. In the more industrialized forms of aquaculture, voluntary codes of conduct for sustainable export-oriented aquaculture have been developed by the Food and Agricultural Organisation of the United Nations and by private business bodies such as the Global Aquaculture Alliance. Proposals to mitigate aquaculture's negative effects include land zoning, increased hatchery production to reduce dependence on wild seed, improved techniques of production within the improved extensive system, the promotion of mixed rice-shrimp farming and smallholder production, experiments with semi-intensive production methods, regulation of child labor, land taxes and effluent charges, reservation of land for other purposes, and the promotion of new income-earning opportunities for those displaced by fish

and shrimp farming and by the impact of new policies to promote more environmentally sustainable aquaculture practices.

Some local communities are beginning to promote what is variously referred to as "ecological aquaculture" and "sustainable aquaculture," which attempts to protect natural ecosystems through polyculture of species, replanting of local vegetation, rotation of aquaculture, and farming and nutrient recycling. This sustainable rural livelihoods approach focuses on smaller-scale aquaculture projects linked into agricultural cycles, relies more on local knowledge derived from community experience, and favors a comanagement or participatory approach in the organization of production, distribution, and marketing.

As open-capture fishing stocks plateau or decline, aquaculture will expand as a complement to and substitute for such stocks. A main challenge for local communities is to ensure that they are able to meet their environmental, social, and economic needs in the face of growing global demand for cheap sources of protein and the other products of a more commercialized aquaculture sector.

[*See also* Communities *and* Fishing.]

## Bibliography

Aston, Michael, ed. *Medieval Fish, Fisheries, and Fishponds in England*. British series 182, vols. 1 and 2. Oxford: BAR (British Archaeological Reports), 1988. Excellent compilation of articles on fish farming in medieval England, including descriptions of royal, monastic, and other fish ponds across the country.

Bailey, Conner, Svein Jentoft, and Peter Sinclair, eds. *Aquacultural Development: Social Dimensions of an Emerging Industry*. Boulder, Colo.: Westview Press, 1996. Focuses on the environmental and social impact of aquaculture in developed and developing countries.

Baluyut, Elvira A. *Aquaculture Systems and Practices: A Selected Review*. Rome: United Nations Development Programme, Food and Agriculture Organization of the United Nations, 1989. Useful descriptive overview of the wide range of aquaculture practices and systems throughout the world.

Black, Kenneth D., ed. *Environmental Impacts of Aquaculture*. Sheffield, U.K.: Sheffield Academic Press, 2001. Has a narrowly environmental approach to the impact of marine and freshwater fish cage culture, shellfish cultivation, and shrimp and fish farming in freshwater and coastal regions.

Coimbra, João, ed. *Modern Aquaculture in the Coastal Zone: Lessons and Opportunities*. NATO Science series: Life Sciences, vol. 314. Amsterdam: IOS Press, 2001. Addresses the technological, biological, and managerial challenges of coastal aquaculture, from Norway to Brazil.

Costa-Pierce, Barry A., ed. *Ecological Aquaculture: The Evolution of the Blue Revolution*. Oxford: Blackwell Science, 2002. Argues for a more ecologically based aquaculture and contains chapters on premodern aquaculture, methods of ecological aquaculture, and the contexts in which such production takes place. Essential reading for those interested in aquaculture's future directions.

De la Torre, Isabel, and David Barnhizer, eds. *The Blues of a Revolution: The Damaging Impacts of Shrimp Farming.* Tacoma, Wash.: Industrial Shrimp Action Network, 2003. Provides a sustained and sometimes polemical critique of large-scale industrial shrimp farming.

De Silva, Sena S., ed. *Tropical Mariculture.* San Diego, Calif.: Academic Press, 1998. Fourteen chapters dealing with the biological, social, economic, environmental, and historical aspects of coastal and marine aquaculture in Asia, Australia, and Latin America.

Edwards, P., D. C. Little, and H. Demaine, eds. *Rural Aquaculture.* Wallingford, U.K.: CABI, 2002. Based on a 1998 conference on fisheries and food security, the book has twenty three chapters written by fisheries and aquaculture experts.

Inland Water Resources and Aquaculture Service. *Review of the State of World Aquaculture.* FAO Fisheries Circular no. 886, rev. 2. Rome: Food and Agriculture Organization of the United Nations, 2003. Essential source of statistical information on global aquaculture.

Kirk, Robert. *A History of Marine Fish Culture in Europe and North America.* Farnham, U.K.: Fishing News Books, 1987. Easy-to-read review of aquaculture developments largely in Europe from Roman times to the mid-twentieth century.

Ling, Shao-Wen. *Aquaculture in Southeast Asia: A Historical Overview.* Seattle: University of Washington Press, 1977. Provides a brief history of aquaculture in Southeast Asia and an overview of current (1977) aquaculture activities in the region.

MacKay, Kenneth T., ed. *Rice-Fish Culture in China.* Ottawa, Ontario: International Development Research Centre, 1995. The result of a 1988 symposium held in China, the book provides a comprehensive introduction to the environmental, historical, social, and economic aspects of rice-fish farming in China. The book is available online free of charge at http://web.idrc.ca/.

Subasinghe, Rohana P., Pedro Bueno, M. J. Phillips, et al., eds. *Aquaculture in the Third Millennium: Technical Proceedings of the Conference on Aquaculture in the Third Millennium, Bangkok, Thailand, 20–25 February 2000.* Bangkok: NACA; Rome: FAO, 2000. A valuable source for both experts and general readers on official mainstream views of the current status and future prospects of aquaculture.

Svennevig, Niels, Helge Reinertsen, and Michael New, eds. *Sustainable Aquaculture: Food for the Future?* Rotterdam, Netherlands: A. A. Balkema, 1999. Contains regional case studies on a number of topics.

BOB POKRANT

**Arab Seafaring** From 632, the year of the Prophet Muhammad's death, until the victory at Talas (Kyrgyzstan) over the Chinese army, around 750, the conquests made in the name of Islam led to the creation of an immense empire reaching from the Chinese border in the east to the Pyrenees in the west, and from the Slavic lands in the north to sub-Saharan Africa in the south.

The maritime area of this new economic and geopolitical space included the Indian Ocean, the Mediterranean, the Red Sea, the Atlantic Ocean, the Caspian Sea, and the Aral Sea. Thus, from the beginning of the eighth century, the Muslim empire had within its sway thousands of kilometers of coasts, which would allow for the creation or the development of numerous activities connected with the sea: the exploitation of marine resources, the design of new boats, the creation of shipyards to build and repair war fleets, the construction or enlargement of ports, the opening of new trade routes and the revitalization of existing ones, the invention or perfection of navigation instruments, and so forth.

The first eight centuries of the Muslim empire (the seventh to the fourteenth centuries) comprise three large phases: the emergence of a new maritime power, close by the old ones and competing with them; the period of military and commercial monopoly; and the weakening and decline of Muslim power over the oceans and seas whose strategic points they had once controlled.

### The First Maritime Initiatives

Encircled by the Mediterranean, the Red Sea, and the Indian Ocean, the cradle of the new religion (Arabia and the Fertile Crescent) was not known as "the Arab Isle" for nothing. From time immemorial, this region had seen maritime activities such as fishing, coral harvesting, coastal trade, and long-distance trade with the nearby African shores as well as with ports as far away as India.

More specifically, it is known that for centuries before, the Yemeni ports had welcomed ships from Eritrea hauling wood and slaves. It is also known that the coastal regions of Bahrain, Oman, and Yemen were already trading with India, and that some merchants specialized in the importation of camphor, aloe resin, senna, and especially spices (pepper and cloves).

These activities presuppose a well-established tradition of shipbuilding, repair, and navigation, as well as a solid knowledge of sea routes and weather. This would explain why the Muslim conquest was carried out partly by sea; several years after Muhammad's death, military expeditions were organized out of certain ports in Oman, heading for the coasts of Persia and even India.

**Arab Seafaring.** This astrolabe was made by Mahmud ibn Shawka al-Baghdadi about 1294. © National Maritime Museum, London

With the accession of the third caliph, 'Uthman ibn 'Affan (d. 656), a state maritime policy began to emerge. The main reason for this was military necessity. To protect the newly acquired territories that bordered on the sea, means of defense against attack from abroad were required. For the same reason, and to head off any danger from the eastern Mediterranean, the Muslim powers, both Umayyad and Abbasid, decided it was wiser to neutralize the nearby islands by conquering them. Besides these two purely military concerns, there were also commercial needs, which arose more slowly but proved stronger. In fact, the conquests of the seventh and eighth centuries created a new economic space, sustained by the products of every region of the empire and by the communication network and the consumer demands of the new social classes that formed and developed in the Muslim urban centers. This soon necessitated revitalizing the traditional sea routes of the Red Sea, the African coasts, and the Indian Ocean, and controlling and securing the Mediterranean routes.

## Maritime Warfare in the Eastern Mediterranean

The Umayyad dynasty (661–750) inaugurated the Muslim empire's first maritime policy. Umayyah, the founder of the dynasty, was the creator of the policy. While he was governor of Syria, he assembled the first elements of the fleet that would attack the island possessions of the Byzantine Empire, such as Cyprus (648), Arwad (649), Kos, Rhodes, and Crete (653). During this period the shipyards at Alexandria, Tyre, and Acre were created or revived. The first, spectacular result of this new Mediterranean policy was the naval victory of the Muslims over the Byzantine armada in the famous Battle of the Masts in 655. A few years later, in 663, Byzantium was once again threatened by the region's new naval force. The swiftness with which the Muslims adapted to naval warfare is symbolized by their first admiral, Buir ibn Abi Arta' (d. 705), a companion of Muhammad, who until the age of forty seems to have had no naval experience whatsoever.

Succeeding the Umayyads, the Abbasids inherited all the maritime successes of their predecessors, and went on to consolidate and complete them. During their time, the port of Tyre was developed and the ports of Beirut and Laodicea were brought back into use. But the most important shipyard on the eastern coast was Tarsus, which had the advantage of being set back some distance from the sea and was thus better protected from the fleets that anchored there. In Egypt, besides the shipyards of Qulzum, taken over from the Byzantines, and Rawa, built by the Tulunids (868–905), the Abbasids added three new emplacements: Rosetta, Damietta, and Tinnis. There was even a naval base at Khandaq on the Cretan coast in the ninth and tenth centuries.

Among the caliphs who understood the usefulness of a functioning naval force was the Caliph al-Mutawakkil (r. 847–861), who seems to have become aware of this fact after the Byzantine raid on Damietta in 853. He decided to move the Tyre shipyard toward the port of Acre and to reorganize the Rawa shipyard on the Nile. He also ordered the fortification of the home ports and shipyards, equipping the latter with closed gates to keep enemy ships from penetrating.

Thanks to these projects, the Abbasids were able to pursue their policy of conquest of the Mediterranean islands and harassment of the Byzantine borderlands launched by their predecessors. In this way, Crete was conquered in 827, followed by Messina, Syracuse, and Salonika (Thessaloníki) in 904. In the same year, Constantinople was unsuccessfully besieged.

The second role played by the naval fleet was to protect the newly acquired Muslim territories. This resulted in the establishment of ports or naval bases on the most vulnerable coasts, such as those in the eastern Mediterranean and on the newly conquered islands. Their third role was to battle against the local powers who had notions of independence, like the Tulunids of Egypt early in the tenth century. A final role for the Abbasid fleet was policing the seas to protect the merchant ships from the pirates who ravaged the coasts of the Indian Ocean. One such intervention took place in 825, in Bahraini waters.

The Fatimids, coming to power in the tenth century, reinforced the Muslim fleets in the Mediterranean and in the Red Sea. Since this new power came into being in the Maghreb (northwest coast of Africa), its naval hegemony was first exercised in the western part of the empire. The instruments of this policy were the shipyards of al-Mahdiya (Mahdia) and Sousse, which allowed them to dispute the leadership with their adversaries in Andalusia, who likewise had pretensions to the Islamic caliphate. Later, these same shipyards helped to effect the conquest of Egypt.

Once they had taken political and military control of this strategic zone, yet another ambition led them to develop further their fighting fleet. In fact, the central Maghreb, Ifriqya, and finally Egypt were merely stages in their strategy to conquer the seat of power in Baghdad. With this in view, they first built a shipyard at Maqs, then another on the island of Rawa, in the Nile, which was later moved to al-Fustat (Cairo). They also resurrected the shipyards of Alexandria and Damietta, which specialized in building certain kinds of small craft, such as troop transports and ships specially designed to board other ships. Some of these constructions (such as the ones known as "grapplers") required as many as 140 oarsmen at a time. Merchant ships were also built there.

In the Red Sea, the Fatimids also assembled a fleet whose home port was Aydhab and whose job was to protect the merchant ships from pirate attacks. This gives the definite impression that the commercial traffic between Egypt and India was important and lucrative not only for the merchants, but for the state as well.

## The Ayyubid and Mamluk Navy

When Salah ad-Din al-Ayyubi (1138–1193) led the resistance against the Crusades in the Mediterranean, he undertook the job of forming a new fleet capable of protecting the Syrian and Egyptian coasts. To this end, he founded a ministry of the fleet, directed by his own brother, and had ships built of iron and wood imported from various regions of the Muslim empire, particularly the Maghreb, or purchased from the merchants of Pisa.

At the time that the Mamluks took power in Egypt, the situation in the Mediterranean had changed profoundly in favor of the military and merchant fleets of Christian Europe. This supremacy only increased during this dynasty's long reign. One consequence was that the raw materials for shipbuilding became rare and expensive, especially wood and iron. At this time, there were still a few wooded areas in Syria and Anatolia that supplied the shipyards, but their production was plainly insufficient. The iron situation was even worse. For a long time, this chronic shortage was offset by imports from sources on the northern coast of the Mediterranean. However, from this point on, the Italian merchants held the monopoly on these products.

A second factor, admittedly less important, had troublesome consequences for defense policy in the eastern Mediterranean, as the power of the Crusaders and their control of the eastern Mediterranean increased. To protect themselves better from their coastal incursions, the Ayyubid and Mamluk powers undertook a new policy which, from 1250 to 1322, consisted in systematically destroying Mediterranean ports so as not to let them fall to the Crusader navies. They likewise systematically destroyed all their fortresses to prevent the Crusaders from gaining a foothold and organizing a defense.

Besides these objective difficulties, there was also a considerable sociocultural element that perhaps prevented the Ayyubids and Mamluks from maintaining a naval policy as effective as that of the Fatimids in the east or of the Almohads in the Muslim west. The Mamluks came from a military society that had always favored land power, structured around cavalry.

In spite of all this, it quickly became apparent to the Egyptian authorities that, even if only for defensive purposes, they would need to maintain a fleet that would discourage dreams of conquest on the part of the new Mediterranean powers. The Sultan Baybars I (r. 1260–1277) was the initiator of this naval policy. In his day, there were three war ports in Egypt: Damietta, Alexandria, and Rosetta.

At the purely military level, the weakness of the Mamluk navy was apparent on several occasions, beginning in the second half of the thirteenth century. In 1270, there was the unfortunate expedition of Baybars to Cyprus. In 1426

and again in 1443, the fleet of Sultan Ashraf Barsbay (r. 1422–1438) met a similar defeat opposite Rhodes. In 1507 and in 1515, fleets sent out against the Portuguese ran afoul of a naval force whose superiority was due chiefly to firearms, which thereafter were used regularly on warships.

## Warships in the Western Mediterranean

Before the arrival of Islam, the seaboards of the Maghreb and Spain had a long tradition of trade between their own ports and those of the western Mediterranean. After the Phoenician and then the Roman hegemony, there followed a long period of varying trade patterns. One of the consequences of the rise of Muslim power was the reinsertion of the Maghreb and of Spain into the new world economy facilitated by the appearance of this new economic space and driven, at first, by the needs of the empire's new social classes. Hence, old ports were reactivated and new ones were built in new locations.

Military ports and installations arose later but lasted longer than those in the east. In the eighth century, economic and strategic motives prompted the Aghlabids of Ifriqya to define and implement a naval policy of their own. The first shipyard in the region was built at Tunis in 694. It seems that Coptic carpenters specializing in large-ship construction were recruited to carry out this project. Later, other shipyards were built at al-Mahdiya, Bejaïa, and Sousse. After acquiring control of Sicily, the Aghlabids made anchorages for their fleets at Palermo and Messina. After Sicily, the Aghlabids' next conquests were Malta and Sardinia. To consolidate control of their new possessions, they built shipyards at Palermo, San Marco in Lamis, Messina, and Malta.

This maritime policy, continued by the Umayyads of Spain and by the Fatimids, allowed the Muslim powers as a group to take complete control of the western Mediterranean between the end of the eight century and the beginning of the eleventh.

The Maghreb war fleets were of sufficient importance in the successive power strategies of the region that their command was one of the "dignities and functions of the state," as the historian Ibn Khaldin (d. 1406) writes.

In the tenth century, the ideological and political antagonism between the Umayyad caliphate in Spain and the Fatimid caliphate in the Maghreb was exacerbated by the threats that the Normans were beginning to pose on the Andalusian and Maghreb coasts. This led to an arms race and the rapid development of two competing naval forces, each one comprising about two hundred ships. To build and maintain these ships, the Umayyads customized a few specific ports, such as Tortosa, Denia, Málaga, Gibraltar, and possibly Cádiz. However, the most important shipyard was Almería.

The decline of the Umayyad caliphate in Andalusia and the crumbling of its power during the time of the Taifa principalities does not appear to have brought on a decline in Andalusian naval power, even if this "strike force" was no longer centralized in the hands of a single power. On the contrary, it seems that the departure of the Fatimids for Egypt resulted in serious weakening of the defense of the Maghreb coast. This development worked in favor of Christian attacks, often successful, against Muslim-controlled territory. It also corresponded to the revival of the Christian states, which proceeded to launch a double offensive. The first one, the Crusades, had as its aim the recovery of cities and lands that had been under Christian control before Islam. The second, carried out by the Italian merchant cities like Genoa and Venice, sought to break up the Muslim commercial monopoly.

In this lengthy confrontation, the Maghreb saw a respite during the Almoravid and Almohad dynasties. They managed to reestablish powerful and, more importantly, unified fleets with a view to protecting the Maghreb and Andalusian coasts, rather than an attack force like those of the ninth through the eleventh centuries.

## Navigation and Commerce in Islamic Lands

After the inevitable disruptions in international maritime commerce brought on by the Islamic conquests and the reactions of the attacked countries, economic activity gradually returned, along with a revival, on a larger scale, of commercial exchange, beginning in the ninth century.

The political unity of the empire, reinforced after a while by linguistic unity, probably worked in favor of this phenomenon, by increasing the circulation of persons and goods. This unity had the further, indirect effect of permitting a sort of cross-pollination of three great international trade networks: the Asian land route, the Mediterranean, and the Indian Ocean.

In contrast to naval military activity, which was almost unknown to the inhabitants of Arabia prior to the Muslim conquest, this type of economic activity was deeply rooted in the region's history. Mecca was already a commercial crossroads that took in both local products and those that arrived by ship from the ports of Bahrain, Oman, and Yemen. These latter products came from as far away as India and the Pacific islands.

The political and social transformations that took place, particularly when the Umayyad dynasty came to power,

thus fostered the growth of the long-distance trade that had previously existed on a smaller scale. It began with the increasingly distant incursions of Muslim merchants seeking new products or new ways to replenish the markets in the center of the empire, especially the two principal cities of Baghdad and Samarra, many of whose inhabitants were eager consumers of luxury and exotic goods.

From the mid-eighth century there is evidence of the presence of Arab and Persian merchants in Chinese ports, Guangzhou (Canton) in particular. Their success seems to have encouraged their coreligionists to follow their example and set up shop in other Asian ports.

In the ninth century, the shipping routes between the Persian Gulf and Asia were well mapped and marked with buoys, thanks to the mass of information gathered during the preceding decades by sailors and merchants. Vessels sailed from Basra, al-Obolla, and Siraf. Depending on the conditions, they followed either the coastal route, which was always navigable despite the danger of pirates, or the direct route on the high seas at times when they could take advantage of the monsoon winds. They reached the southern point of India, whence some ships would continue toward the Maldives, Malaysia, and Ceylon (Sri Lanka), much visited for the luxury items they could offer, especially spices, aloe, and precious stones. From there, some merchants continued even to China, following the Indochinese coast. In the ports where they landed, such as Guangzhou and Hangzhou, they sold manufactured products (textiles, rugs, wrought metals), and bought the local products so greatly prized by the elites of the Muslim empire (spices, silk, camphor, musk, and so forth). Arab accounts mention trade relationships even with Korean ports. Taking into account the meteorological factors on which long-distance navigation depended, particularly the annual monsoons, it has been estimated, based on the reports of Arab merchants and sailors, that a vessel based in Basra or Siraf took about twenty months to reach China and return to its home port.

The sea route along the eastern coast of Africa seems to have been in use to some extent well before Islam. Within the new empire, trade with these coasts increased and the trade zone was extended. Ships left the ports of the Persian Gulf and Yemen headed for Zanzibar, the Comoros, and the northern coast of Madagascar, dropping anchor in a few other ports scattered between Mogadishu in Eritrea (now capital of Somalia) and Sofala in Mozambique. Slaves were the largest African import for Muslim merchants. There were also ivory, tortoiseshell, amber, and the skins of wild animals.

In the Fatimid era, the vitality of maritime commerce is illustrated by the Geniza documents, and particularly by documents concerning families such as the Awkal and Mahrus, whose continuous activity in this realm provides information on more than a century of trade relations (980–1134) along the sea routes of the Red Sea and the Indian Ocean. It can also be seen that luxury products, like perfumes, which were sold in large quantities during the Abbasid period, were gradually replaced by more broadly consumed products such as cooking condiments, ingredients for sweets and pastries, dyes, and cosmetics. This reorientation of long-distance trade had two significant effects. First, the increase in the number of consumers of these products resulted in considerable growth in the amounts transported, which led in turn to the use of larger ships. Apparently it was also this growth that allowed the monopolies of a small number of families to give way to greater participation by a larger number of smaller merchants.

It can also be noted that the initiatives of the Fatimid powers in Egypt, both military and commercial, effectively led to a reorientation of large-scale trade, to the benefit of the city of Cairo, which became the principal crossroads for trade with Asia and the Mediterranean seaboard. Finally, there is one other change to be noted in comparison to the previous period, also revealed by the Geniza documents, concerning the disappearance of a second monopoly. In the Fatimid period, contrary to what was seen before the tenth century, Jewish merchants took part in international commerce more and more, on an equal footing with Muslims. They even signed contracts with the state to assure the protection of their ships and caravans.

## Techniques and Instruments of Navigation

A large portion of the knowledge and skills of the Arab navigators came from direct experience and training with older sailors. This knowledge included measurement techniques, observation of the sky, interpretation of weather phenomena, and all other events that can be observed at sea.

To measure angles and distances, navigators used traditional units. The *asbuc* (finger or digit) corresponds to approximately 1°48'. The *dubban* equals four fingers. The *zam* is one-eighth of the distance traveled by the ship between two apparent positions of a star at a distance of one finger. The *rhumb* is the angle between two of the thirty-two points of the compass, which is to say, 11°15'. The *tirfa* is the distance to be traveled in each *rhumb* in order to see a star's apparent position move by one finger.

To obtain their measurements, the navigators could ignore all of these units and use instead the gradations of an astrolabe and a sextant. However, from the Arab sailing instructions that have come down to us, it would seem that the most frequently used instrument was much simpler. It consisted of a set of three solid boards of increasing size, marked off in fingers.

The ship's position was estimated with reference to the elevation of certain stars. At some unknown time, navigators in the Indian Ocean did use maps. This fact is confirmed, at the end of the fifteenth century, by the accounts of Portuguese navigators who had direct contact with their Muslim colleagues, whom they met when they first began crossing the ocean.

Since neither the geographers nor the authors of nautical instructions mention the existence or the use of maps, they might well have been crude ones containing the approximate outlines of the coastlines along which the ships would sail, and also mentioning the ports, the principal harbors and natural obstacles, and the direction of the prevailing winds.

Whatever the case, and despite the rudimentary character of their instruments, experienced navigators succeeded in keeping on course on the high seas, sometimes within three degrees. This, at least, is what the precise data furnished by the great sailor Ahmad Ibn Majid (15th c.) would suggest.

## The Compass

The principle of the compass seems to have been known to Arab astronomers by the thirteenth century at the latest. In any event, its first use on land dates from this period. It was used at first to determine the *qibla* (the direction in which to face Mecca for prayer). Evidence for this use is found in late-thirteenth-century documents from Egypt, Yemen, and Central Asia.

The oldest known compass was called a *dasa* (bowl). It is a cup-shaped container, wider than it is high, filled with water, on top of which floats a magnetized needle. The first known description of it is by the sultan of Yemen and astronomer al-Malik al-Ashraf (d. 1296). This rudimentary instrument continued in use until the sixteenth century. However, the "dry" compass seems to have appeared quite early, for it was described in the thirteenth century. Ibn Majid reports that Muslim sailors in the Mediterranean used a needle fastened on an axis held up by a support, the whole assembly held in a housing.

Those who described and used this compass called it by several different names: *ibra* (needle), *bayt al-ibra* (needle box), *huqqa* (point), *samaka* (fish). This variety of terms suggests that the use of the compass spread independently in different regions of the empire.

## Conclusion

As in others realms of activity in the Muslim empire where practical skill was more important than theoretical knowledge, the maritime professions are known to us only by the rare written records that have come down to us. By their very nature, the military techniques of naval forces were kept secret, and we may never know in detail the history of their innovations, their refinements, and their circulation. The same is true of the techniques of shipbuilding, the assembling and training of forces, and the daily lives of the oarsmen and soldiers.

The history of the merchant marine is no better known, for we possess only a few documents, often late in date, and concerned only with navigation in the Indian Ocean. Thus, despite several centuries of commercial monopoly and military dominance, we know but little about the history of the fleets of the Maghreb and Andalusia or the history of the trade among the different ports of the Mediterranean.

Even the most important innovations, such as the triangular sail, the compass, and the stern-rudder, which became more widely used during the Muslim phase of the history of the Mediterranean and the Indian Ocean, remain shrouded in mystery and still incite speculation.

In this brief study, we have mentioned only the most important points to remember in the long history of the sea in Muslim territory. Further research will one day confirm our current impressions or replace them with answers from new sources, as was the case with the discovery of the Geniza documents.

[*See also* Communities *subentry on* Arab Communities; India; Indian Ocean; Mediterranean Sea; *and* Persian Gulf.]

## Bibliography

Brunschvig, R. "Ports et chantiers navals dans le monde méditerranéen musulman jusqu'aux Croisades." *N.M.A.M.* 1 (1978): 299–313.

Courtois, C. "Remarques sur le commerce maritime en Afrique au XIe siècle." In *Mélanges d'histoire et d'archéologie de l'Occident musulman II. Hommage à Georges Marçais*, pp. 51–59. Alger, 1957.

Dufourcq, Charles-Emmanuel. *Commerce du Maghreb médiéval avec l'Europe chrétienne et marine musulmane.* Actes du 1e Congrès d'histoire et de civilisation du Maghreb, I. Tunis, 1979.

In *L'Ibérie chrétienne et le Maghreb, XIIe-XVe siècles*, Aldershot, U. K. : Variorum, 1990.

Ehrenkreutz, A. S. "Bahriyya: La marine arabe jusqu'en 647/1250." *E.I.* 2, suppl. 1–2, (1980): 102–120.

Ehrenkreutz, A. S. "The Place of Saladin in the Naval History of the Mediterranean Sea in the Middle Ages." *Journal of the American Oriental Society* 75 (1955): 100–116.

Fahmy, Aly Mohamed. *Muslim Naval Organisation in the Eastern Mediterranean from the 7th to the 10th Century A.D.* 2d ed. Cairo: National Publication and Print House, 1966.

Fahmy, Aly Mohamed. *Muslim Sea-Power in the Eastern Mediterranean from the Seventh to the Tenth Century A.D.* Cairo: National Publication and Print House, 1966.

Grosset-Granger, H. "Une carte nautique arabe du moyen âge." *Navigation* 80, no. 7 (1974): 328–343. Republished in *Acta Geographica* 27 (1976): 33–46.

Grosset-Granger, H. "La navigation arabe." *Navigation* 47 (1964): 265–285.

Hamblin, W. "The Fatimid Navy during the Early Crusades, 1099–1124." *American Neptune* 46 (1986): 77–83.

Hassan, Ahmad Y. al-, and Donald R. Hill. *Sciences et techniques en Islam: Une histoire illustrée.* Translated from the English by Hachem El-Husseini. Paris: EDIFRA-UNESCO, 1991.

Hourani, George F. *Arab Seafaring: In the Indian Ocean in Ancient and Early Medieval Times.* 2d ed. Revised and expanded by John Carswell. Princeton, N.J.: Princeton University Press, 1995.

Ibn Khurdadhbah. *Livre des routes et des royaumes.* Edited and Translated by M. J. De Goeje. Leiden, Netherlands: Brill, 1889.

King, David A. "Astronomy for Landlubbers and Navigators: The Case of the Islamic Middle Ages." *Revista da Universidade de Coimbra* 32 (1985): 211–223.

Kunitzsch, Paul. "Zur Stellung der Nautikertexte innerhalb der Sternnomenklatur der Araber." *Der Islam* 43 (1967): 53–74.

Lev, Y. "The Fatimid Navy, Byzantium, and the Mediterranean Sea, 903–1036."*Byzantion* 54 (1984): 220–252.

Lewis, Archibald Ross. *Naval Power and Trade in the Mediterranean, A.D. 500–1100.* Princeton, N.J.: Princeton University Press, 1951.

Lombard, M. "Arsenaux et bois de marine dans la Méditerranée musulmane, VIIe–XIe siècles." In *Espaces et réseaux dans le haut moyen âge.* Paris: La Haye, 1972.

Mâhir, S. *La marine dans l'Egypte islamique et ce qui reste de ses vestiges* [in Arabic]. Cairo: Dar al-ma'arif, 1967.

Picard, Christophe. *La mer et les musulmans d'occident au moyen âge: VIIIe–XIIIe siècle.* Paris: Presses Universitaires de France, 1997.

Planhol, Xavier de. *L'islam et la mer: La mosquée et le matelot, VIIe–XXe siècle.* Paris: Librairie Académique Perrin, 2000.

Prinsep, James. "Note on the Nautical Instruments of the Arabs." *Journal of the Asiatic Society of Bengal* 2 (1836). In *Introduction à l'astronomie nautique arabe*, by Gabriel Ferrand, pp. 1–24. Paris: Libr. orientaliste Paul Geuthner, 1928.

Sirafi, Abû Saïd ibn Abd Allah al. *Relation de la Chine et de l'Inde: Rédigée en 851.* Translated by Jean Sauvaget. Paris: Belles Lettres, 1948.

Tibbetts, G. R. "Arab Navigation in the Red Sea." *Geographical Journal* 127 (1961): 322–334.

Zayyat, H. "Répertoire des noms de vaisseaux et embarcations en Islam, *Al-Machriq.*" *Revue Catholique Orientale* 43(1949): 321–364.

AHMED DJEBBAR
*Translated From the French by Johanna M. Baboukis*

# Archaeology

**Archaeology** Archaeology is the systematic study of past human life, behaviors, activities, and cultures using material remains (including sites, structures, and artifacts) and the relationships among them.

## Maritime and Underwater Archaeology

Archaeological sites can include the underwater remains of watercraft (ships, boats, and other vessels) and aircraft, as well as cultural artifacts accidentally dropped, lost overboard, or deliberately deposited into a body of water. They can also include the remains of structures originally built wholly or partly underwater (such as fish traps, crannogs, bridges, piers, jetties, and wharves). In addition, archaeology may examine the remains of human activity that originally took place on dry or marshy land subsequently inundated or submerged, either by rising water levels or by marine or fluvial erosion. Maritime archaeology is a subdiscipline of archaeology associated with seafaring and human interactions with the sea. Maritime archaeology can also include shore-based maritime industries (such as whaling and sealing) and sites and artifacts that, though not underwater, are related to maritime activities (such as lighthouses and harbor constructions). In his now classic book *Maritime Archaeology*, the late Keith Muckelroy argued that maritime archaeology is concerned with maritime culture in general, "not just technical matters, but also social economic, political, religious and a host of other aspects" (p. 4).

Contemporary definitions of maritime archaeology overlap with the definitions of a few related terms:

*Underwater archaeology*, which simply refers to the environment in which archaeology is practiced. It is any site where evidence is found underwater or in a submerged environment. Such evidence may exist beneath fresh (or inland) waters or beneath salt (or marine) waters. It may be visible on the bed of the water body or buried beneath sediment.

*Marine archaeology*, which is the archaeological study of human material remains submerged in a marine (or saltwater) environment. Included are shipwrecks, submerged aircraft, and other cultural sites and artifacts.

*Nautical archaeology*, which is the archaeological study of ships and shipbuilding. Like maritime archaeology, it can include sites that, though not underwater, are related to ships and shipbuilding, including ship burials, shipwreck remains located on land, and shipbuilding yards.

## Evolving Methods and Techniques

Because scuba diving using compressed air allows archaeologists to enter the underwater environment, the development of scuba tanks and their expanded use after World War II led to the emergence of maritime archaeology as a subdiscipline of archaeology. By the 1950s scholars were beginning to recognize the archaeological potential of such underwater sites as shipwrecks. The 1960s saw the development of many of the now standard methods and techniques used for underwater archaeological work—methods and techniques developed by researchers such as George F. Bass and his colleagues working on classical-period shipwreck sites in the Mediterranean. Underwater site survey, recording, and photography methods have become widely adopted and are used by maritime archaeologists around the world.

Scuba diving has its limits. For one, it is usually restricted to water depths of less than about forty meters. The development over the last twenty years of mixed gases using different mixtures of nitrogen, oxygen, and helium (for example, such gases as Nitrox and Trimix) has allowed maritime archaeologists to dive to greater depths and spend more time at underwater sites. Nevertheless, water temperatures and water depths beyond ten meters still severely restrict the time that can be spent at an underwater site to a fraction of the time that terrestrial archaeologists can spend at a comparable land site.

Alternatives to physically placing people using diving technology at an underwater archaeological site involve the use of manned submersibles or unmanned remotely operated vehicles (ROVs) and autonomous underwater vehicles (AUVs). Also used are other types of remote-sensing equipment and underwater geophysical equipment, such as side-scan sonars, magnetometers, metal detectors, subbottom profilers, and CHIRP systems (systems that use compressed high-intensity radar pulses). George F. Bass pioneered the use of manned submersibles on underwater archaeological sites with *Asherah*, launched in 1964. *Asherah* was used to survey and inspect shipwrecks, to allow the mapping of shipwrecks using stereo photogrammetry, and to extend the bottom time of the archaeological director during underwater excavations. ROVs are robotic devices that carry still

**Archaeology.** The excavation of Cavalier de La Salle's ship *Belle* in Matagorda Bay, Texas, shows an early stage in the construction of a cofferdam to excavate the vessel that was lost in 1686. © Texas Historical Commission

or video cameras and that are tethered by means of an umbilical cable to a support ship on the surface. They can also carry manipulating devices for excavation or recovery of materials ranging from geological samples to artifacts. AUVs are untethered underwater vehicles carrying similar but much smaller payloads and are therefore much less expensive than submersibles and ROVs.

### From Prehistory through the Classical Period to the Modern Era

In addition to shipwrecks, a wide range of other archaeological material can be found underwater. Archaeological sites that were once on land can be submerged or inundated by a number of natural processes and human activities. A rising sea level caused by melting glaciers at the end of the last ice age is simply one of these natural processes. Sites like Warm Mineral Springs and Little Salt Spring, both in Florida, have revealed information from Paleo-Indian burials dating back more than 10,000 years.

Indirect archaeological evidence suggests that watercraft date back at least 50,000 years, as the Australian Aboriginal people must have used watercraft to reach Australia at or before this date because travel from Asia to Australia has always required a sea crossing of at least eighty

kilometers. In the Mediterranean, evidence of a trade in obsidian (a dark natural glass formed from lava) from the island of Melos indicates that seafaring was taking place by the ninth millennium B.C.E. Direct archaeological evidence in the form of ship and boat finds from the earliest periods of seafaring have not yet been located.

Classical archaeology is the study of ancient civilizations around the Mediterranean, primarily, but not exclusively, the Greek, Roman, and Near Eastern civilizations. Direct archaeological evidence of boat- and shipbuilding (such as models, reliefs, and other depictions) date back to at least the fourth millennium B.C.E. The oldest complete vessels yet located are two Khufu ships, dating back to about 2500 B.C.E., that were found dismantled and buried next to the Great Pyramid of Khufu (Cheops) in Egypt.

In the early 1960s George F. Bass pioneered the underwater excavation of classical-period shipwreck sites in the Mediterranean with his groundbreaking excavations at Cape Gelidonya on the Coast of Turkey. The Cape Gelidonya site was a twelfth century B.C.E. (Bronze Age) shipwreck that was the first to be fully recorded and totally excavated underwater. Bass took standard terrestrial archaeological techniques for maximizing the amount of information retrieved from a site and applied them to underwater archaeology, thus establishing the basic

**Oseberg Burial Ship.** The excavation of the ship at Oslo was done in 1904. FOTO MARBURG / ART RESOURCE, NY

methodological principles still used on underwater archaeological sites. Bass went on to establish the Institute of Nautical Archaeology (INA) in 1972, and INA archaeologists subsequently excavated a number of classical-period shipwrecks at places including Kyrenia, Serçe Limani, Yassi Ada, and Uluburun, providing valuable information about early shipbuilding and trade in the Mediterranean.

In Europe our understanding of Viking Age shipbuilding, for example, has been considerably advanced through the study of a range of archaeological sites, such as the five eleventh-century ships found near Roskilde in Denmark (the Skuldelev ships), and of ship burials, such as the Gokstad, Tune, and Oseberg ships. Representing the classic clinker-built rowed long ship, these vessels have also revealed information about the beamier sailing cargo vessels known as knar, which were the seagoing cargo carrier of the eleventh through thirteenth centuries.

The hull timbers of a number of shipwrecks dating from the last five centuries or so have been raised from the seabed and placed on public exhibit in museums around the world. These include *Mary Rose* (1545) in Britain, *Vasa* (1628) in Sweden, *Batavia* (1629) in Western Australia, and *La Belle* (1686) in Texas. These ambitious, costly archaeological projects have in most cases proved to

be extremely popular with the general public. For example, the *Vasa* Museum in Stockholm is one of the most visited museums in Scandinavia.

As well as shipwreck sites, there have been a number of long-term, large-scale underwater archaeological investigations of harbor sites, such as Caesarea Maritima on the coast of Israel, and sunken cities, such as Port Royal in Jamaica. The seventeenth-century city of Port Royal was submerged as a result of an earthquake on June 7, 1692. Hundreds of thousands of artifacts have been excavated from the buildings and shipwrecks that now lie in shallow water. Animal bones provide evidence about diet, and other artifacts give direct evidence about the types of pewter, silver, ceramics, glassware, and clay tobacco pipes used by people of different classes at the time.

In addition to underwater sites, maritime archaeologists also investigate land sites associated with maritime industries and activities, such as fishing, sealing, and whaling. A good example is the integrated archaeological investigation of sixteenth-century Basque whaling-station sites and shipwrecks, which were conducted both on land and underwater at Red Bay on the coast of Labrador in Canada.

Archaeology can also provide insights into sites and structures dating from relatively recent periods, such as the nineteenth and twentieth centuries. Submarines, for example, have been the subject of archaeological excavations and investigations, including CSS *Hunley* in South Carolina, *Resurgam* in Britain, and the Australian submarine *AE2*, lost in the Sea of Marmara, Turkey. Archaeological work on *Hunley*, for example, has revealed previously unknown aspects about submarine technology used late in the American Civil War period, as well as the stories of the individual men who manned this dangerous piece of equipment.

## Legislation, Conventions, and Guidelines

The most common mechanism for protecting maritime and underwater artifacts and archaeological sites throughout the world is cultural-heritage legislation. In 1982 the United Nations Convention of the Law of the Sea (UNCLOS) provided that "states have the duty to protect objects of an archaeological and historical nature found at sea and shall cooperate for this purpose." National and provincial governments have the right to enact and enforce legislation and regulations to protect and preserve maritime archaeological heritage located on land or lying in their internal waters, territorial seas, and exclusive economic zones (EEZ). In addition, many national governments retain title to (or ownership of) ship and aircraft wrecks that once formed a part of that nation's military forces (army, navy, or air force). These property rights are not lost to that government because of the passage of time, and they apply whether the vessel or aircraft was lost in national, foreign, or international waters.

Archaeological activity should conform to all of the legislative and administrative requirements of the nation and province within whose lands, internal waters, territorial seas, or exclusive economic zones the work is being conducted. Many countries around the world have introduced legislation to protect all or part of their underwater cultural heritage, examples being the Protection of Wrecks Act (1973) in Britain, the Historic Shipwrecks Act (1976) in Australia, and the Abandoned Shipwreck Act (1987) in the United States. Some countries have realized the deficiencies of focusing solely on the shipwreck component of underwater heritage and are beginning to move to more generic protection measures.

Archaeologists and others involved with underwater heritage should also take into consideration international conventions and guidelines for the protection and management of the underwater cultural heritage, including the United Nations Convention on the Law of the Sea (UNCLOS) and the Convention on the Protection of Underwater Cultural Heritage (2001) of the United Nations Educational,

Scientific, and Cultural Organization (UNESCO). The UNESCO convention provides minimum standards for the protection of underwater cultural heritage and is being ratified by an increasing number of countries around the world. Even when a country has not ratified the convention, it is adopting the Annex to the Convention as a guideline for the practice of archaeology and the preservation of the underwater cultural heritage.

Archaeologists also need to follow various codes of practice and codes of ethics, such as the Code of Professional Ethics of the International Council of Museums (ICOM) and the Code of Ethics of the Australian Institute for Maritime Archaeology (AIMA). The ICOM code, as well as the recommendations made by the Advisory Council on Underwater Archaeology (ACUA), were adopted by the International Congress of Maritime Museums (ICMM) in 1993. These should be seen as the minimum standards for the responsible acquisition and curation of material from underwater archaeological sites.

## *Titanic*, Treasure Hunting, and Other Controversies

The sinking of the White Star passenger liner *Titanic* in 1912 was the most famous maritime disaster of the twentieth century and, as a result of recent feature films and activities on the site, is probably the most famous shipwreck of any century. In 1985 a joint expedition from the Woods Hole Oceanographic Institute in Massachusetts and the Institut Français de Recherches pour l'Exploitation in France, directed by Dr. Bob Ballard and Jean-Louis Michell, located the wreck in the very deep, international waters of the north Atlantic. Some people, including Dr. Ballard and many maritime archaeologists, take the view that *Titanic* should be considered as a gravesite and suggest that no artifacts should be raised from the wreck. Others, including RMS *Titanic* Inc., believe that it is acceptable to raise material from the wreck site. Over the last two decades a number of expeditions have brought up a significant number of artifacts from the site, some of which are on display at the National Maritime Museum in Greenwich outside of London.

Treasure hunting has been defined as the search for intrinsically valuable objects from archaeological sites for personal profit or private gain. Treasure hunting and tomb robbing on land have largely been made illegal on archaeological sites in most countries, but the trade in illegal antiquities, including items stolen from archaeological sites, remains one the world's largest and most lucrative illegal activities. In the popular imagination, shipwrecks are associated with treasure. Treasure hunters, or salvors as many of them prefer to be called, have long been active in searching for shipwrecks and recovering precious metals, jewelry, porcelain, and other objects of monetary value, which are then sold, usually at auction. Unfortunately, treasure hunting in the underwater environment has not been treated as it has on land, and it continues today, sometimes with the approval and support of national governments.

## Organizations

The Advisory Council on Underwater Archaeology (ACUA) and the Society for Historical Archaeology (SHA) are the primarily North American–based organizations concerned with the archaeology of the modern world (1400–present). The society and council jointly host the annual Conference on Historical and Underwater Archaeology, usually in a North American location, and selected maritime archaeology papers are published in the journal *Historical Archaeology*.

The Australasian Institute for Maritime Archaeology (AIMA), established in 1982, is a nonprofit organization dedicated to the promotion of maritime archaeology. While based primarily in Australia and New Zealand, it has supported maritime archaeological work in Australasia, Asia, and the Pacific. The institute hosts an annual conference in a different Australian city each year, sometimes in cooperation with other organizations, such as the Australasian Society for Historical Archaeology (ASHA). It publishes the annual *Bulletin of the Australasian Institute for Maritime Archaeology*, as well as a quarterly newsletter.

The Institute of Nautical Archaeology (INA), established in 1972, is an international nonprofit scientific and educational organization. It has been affiliated with the Nautical Archaeology Program at Texas A&M University since 1976. INA has supported underwater archaeological fieldwork primarily in the Mediterranean (particularly in Turkey), as well as in North America, Central America, and the Caribbean. It publishes the *INA Quarterly*.

The Nautical Archaeology Society (NAS) is an international voluntary organization established in 1981 to promote interest in, and to provide education, training, and information about, nautical archaeology. NAS conducts training through its internationally recognized four-part training courses. In addition, it publishes the quarterly *International Journal of Nautical Archaeology* (*IJNA*), as well as a quarterly newsletter.

[*See also Olympic, Titanic, and Britannic*; Salvage, *subentry on* Laws; *and* Shipwrecks.]

## Bibliography

"Advisory Council on Underwater Archaeology." http://www.acuaonline.org/.

"Australasian Institute for Maritime Archaeology." http://www.aima.iinet.net.au/.

Babits, Larry E., and Hans Van Tilburg, eds. *Maritime Archaeology: A Reader of Substantive and Theoretical Contributions*. Plenum Series in Underwater Archaeology. New York: Plenum Press, 1998. A reader covering a range of topics and issues in maritime archaeology, including definitions, ethics, research design, theory, methods, assessments of site significance, conservation, interpretation, and exhibition.

Bass, George F., ed. *A History of Seafaring Based on Underwater Archaeology*. New York: Walker, 1974. Extensively illustrated with many large maps and color photographs.

"CSS *Hunley* Project." http://www.hunley.org.

Dean, Martin, Ben Ferrari, Ian Oxley, et al., eds. *Archaeology Underwater: The NAS Guide to Principles and Practice*. London: Archetype Publications, 1992. Many black-and-white photographs and excellent line drawings.

Delgado, James, ed. *British Museum Encyclopaedia of Underwater and Maritime Archaeology*. London: British Museum Press, 1997. The best available single-volume introduction to underwater and maritime archaeology for both the expert and the nonexpert alike.

Gould, Richard A. *Archaeology and the Social History of Ships*. Cambridge: Cambridge University Press, 2000. An explicitly theoretically informed work that ranges across diverse subject areas, including the transition from sail to steam in maritime commerce, new technologies and naval warfare, and the archaeology of maritime infrastructure.

Gould, Richard A., ed. *Shipwreck Anthropology*. Albuquerque: University of New Mexico Press, 1983. Represents a wide range of approaches, and has papers by a number of the leading figures in maritime archaeology.

Green, Jeremy N. *Maritime Archaeology: A Technical Handbook*. 2d ed. Sydney, Australia: Elsevier Academic Press, 2004.

"Institute of Nautical Archaeology." http://ina.tamu.edu/.

"*Mary Rose* Trust." http://www.maryrose.org.

McErlean, Thomas, Rosemary McConkey, and Wes Forsythe. *Strangford Loch: An Archaeological Survey of the Maritime Cultural Landscape*. Belfast, U.K.: Blackstaff Press, 2002. A comprehensive work on the maritime cultural landscape of a Northern Irish loch, covering the submerged cultural landscape, intertidal archaeology, and a wide range of topics in maritime archaeology (such as fish traps, tidal mills, vernacular boats, and the kelp industry).

"MoSS Project." http://www.nba.fi/internat/MoSS/eng/index.html.

Muckelroy, Keith. *Archaeology under Water: An Atlas of the World's Submerged Sites*. New York: McGraw-Hill, 1980.

Muckelroy, Keith. *Maritime Archaeology*. Cambridge, U.K.: Cambridge University Press, 1978. This now classic work on maritime archaeology was informed by the "new" or "processual" archaeology pioneered by David Clarke, Keith Muckelroy's mentor at Cambridge University.

"Nautical Archaeology Society." http://www.nasportsmouth.org.uk.

"Port Royal Project." http://nautarch.tamu.edu/portroyal/.

Ruppé, Carol V., and Janet F. Barstad. *International Handbook of Underwater Archaeology*. Plenum Series in Underwater Archaeology. New York: Plenum Publishers, 2002. This 800-page work provides uneven coverage of the current situation in certain countries and some U.S. states, as well as of issues in underwater archaeology, such as legislation, technology, and government-agency involvement.

Staniforth, Mark, and Michael Hyde, eds. *Maritime Archaeology in Australia: A Reader*. Blackwood, Australia: Southern Archaeology, 2001.

"UNESCO 2001: Convention for the Protection of the Underwater Cultural Heritage." http://www.unesco.org/culture/laws/underwater/html_eng/convention.shtml.

"*Vasa* Museum." http://www.vasamuseet.se/vasamuseet/om.aspx.

MARK STANIFORTH

# Archives

Although maritime history is a subject that transcends national boundaries and stretches around the globe, many aspects of it are bound to the particular national origins of ships and the sailors that manned them. This is particularly true of archives and historical manuscript collections. Surviving records of governmental agencies are normally, but not always, found in national archives. In some cases, records that predate national archives or that were private records maintained by an individual were not considered official documents to be preserved by the state and have survived in private collections of personal papers. Some have subsequently been transferred to local, regional, library, museum, or university collections; others have even migrated from their country of origin to another through the work of collectors and scholars. The pattern of archival collection varies from country to country and is intimately tied to the quite separate ways in which each country's efforts at collection and maintaining historical records have developed.

Archival materials for maritime history may be found in a wide variety of collections, as suggested by the following summaries, which list some of the best-known collections of maritime manuscript material. In most countries, materials for maritime history are typically scattered through the full range of institutions that make archival materials available to scholars for research, ranging from national governmental archives and national libraries to local collections.

## Australia

The National Archives of Australia holds the Naval Board Minute Books, detailed drawings of ships of the Royal Australian Navy (ships' drawings and specifications, 1870–1957; drawings, plans, and specifications, 1910–1950), and naval record books giving the performance and engineering details of particular naval vessels. It also holds naval photographic collections, records of naval intelligence and naval disasters, and other naval records (e.g., ship's logs). Information on the Women's Royal Australian Naval Service (1942–1984) is available from the Australian Women's Archives Project (http://www.womenaustralia.info/).

## Canada

The Archives and Collections Society, in Ontario, holds maritime documents, photographs, plans and drawings, and over 1,500 charts. The John Burgess Library and Archives at the Naval Museum of Alberta holds documentary records relating to Canadian maritime history. The Historical Collections of the Great Lakes, at Bowling Green State University in the United States, holds historical materials documenting the Great Lakes region and connecting waterways. Its collections include materials related to commercial shipping, shipbuilding, navigation, maritime law, commercial fishing, shipwrecks, yachting, labor history, popular literature, freshwater ecology, recreation, and the history of Great Lakes ports on both sides of the Canadian–U.S. border.

The Maritime History Archive, on the campus of the Memorial University of Newfoundland in Saint John's, collects and preserves original documents and copies of documents relating to the history of sea-based activities in the North Atlantic region. The collection includes shipping records; business and photographic collections; maps, plans, and charts; and the Keith Matthews Collection on early fisheries and the settlement of Newfoundland.

## Denmark

The Manuscript Department of the Royal Danish Library, in Copenhagen, serves as Denmark's national manuscript collection and archive for the humanities. The library also has maps, posters, pictures, and photographs. Danish ancestors may be traced at the Danish National Archives, also in Copenhagen.

## France

The Archives Nationales (http://www.archivesnationales.culture.gouv.fr/) is decentralized, the Web site giving full details of where records are held. The Centre Historique des Archives Nationales, in Paris, holds documents from before 1958. The Centre des Archives Contemporaines, in Fontainebleau, holds documents from after 1958. The

Centre des Archives d'Outre Mer, in Aix-en-Provence, has records on former French possessions overseas. The Centre des Archives du Monde du Travail, in Roubaix, holds records of companies, unions, and so on. The Centre National du Microfilm, in Saint-Gilles-du-Gard, holds original microforms of documents preserved in other national or territorial centers. The Service Historique de la Marine has branches at Brest, Cherbourg, Lorient, Rochefort, and Toulon. The French Lines Association (a private organization, http://www.frenchlines.com/) gives access to maritime and port-related archival material.

## Germany

German national archives and military archives are held at the Militärarchiv, Bundesarchiv Deutschland, in Freiburg (http://*www.bundesarchiv.de/*). The naval archives at the Bibliothek für Zeitgeschichte (Library of Contemporary History), in Stuttgart, holds extensive documentary and photographic collections on German naval wars since the end of the nineteenth century. The library at the Bundesamt für Seeschiffahrt und Hydrographie (Federal Maritime and Hydrographic Agency), in Hamburg and Rostock, is the central maritime library in Germany. Its Web site (http://www.bsh.de/), in English and German, is linked to the archives of maps and charts.

## Italy

The prime starting point for Italy is the Sistema archivistico nazionale (National Archive) of the Ministero per i beni e le attivita' culturali. The home page of its Web site (http://archivi.beniculturali.it/) contains an overview of Italian national archives as well as basic contact information for all state archives.

## The Netherlands

Records relating to the Dutch East India Company (Vereenigde Oostindische Compaguie or VOC) and to early modern maritime history are held in the Dutch State Archives in The Hague (www.en.nationaal.archief.nl).

## New Zealand

Auckland Central City Library (http://www.aucklandcity-libraries.com/) holds the records of the Port of Auckland, boat plans by renowned designers, and large photographic collections of commercial ships.

## Poland

The State Archives (http://www.archiwa.gov.pl/) has its central archive of historical records in Warsaw. Online catalogs, with search guidelines in English, are in preparation. Published guides are available for sale at the Edition Department of the Head Office of State Archives (Wydzial Wydawnictw NDAP, Swietojerska 24, 00-202 Warszawa; e-mail: editions@archiwa.gov.pl). The Polish Institute and Sikorski Museum (20 Princes Gate, London SW7) contains archives documenting the role of the Polish Navy in World War II.

## Russia

The Russian State Naval Archive, in Saint Petersburg, houses the complete records of the Russian navy from 1696, when Peter I created the regular navy, to 1940. These include details of central administrative institutions, commands of fleets and flotillas, naval educational establishments and scientific and research institutions, naval ports, shipbuilding and other navy yards, hydrographic and scientific expeditions, and personal papers of eminent navigators and naval commanders.

## Spain

The prime resource for Spain is the Archivo Histórico Nacional (Spanish National Archives), located at Serrano, 115 28006 Madrid. Users can consult the online catalog of the Biblioteca del Centro de Información Documental de Archivos (http://www.mcu.es/jsp/plantilla_wai.jsp?id=1 5&area=archivos). This offers over 34,000 records from Spanish and Latin American archives.

## Sweden

The Swedish National Archives (http://www.ra.se/) are housed in two buildings, in Marieberg and Arninge. For the archives in Marieberg, the postal address is P.O. Box 125 41, SE-102 29 Stockholm, and the visiting address is Fyrverkarbacken 13-17. For the archives in Arninge, the visiting and postal address is Mätslingan 17, SE-187 66 Täby. The military archives (http://www.ra.se/kra/english.html) has records dating from the sixteenth century to the present, including listings of military personnel, personal files, drawings and descriptions of military equipment and buildings, and maps from all over the world.

The Statens Sjöhistoriska Museet (National Maritime Museum of Sweden), Djurgårdsbrunnsvägen 24, Box 27131, SE-102 52 Stockholm, has a photographic archive of more than 100,000 photographs illustrating sailing and steamships, freight and naval ships, and pleasure craft. Its archive contains 250 shelf-meters of documents and 50,000 plans detailing the development of the navy, shipping, shipbuilding, and pleasure boating in Sweden.

## United Kingdom

The National Archives at Kew (http://www.nationalarchives.gov.uk/) hold admiralty records and individual Royal Naval ships' records, including logs, paybooks, and ships' musters. It holds the Royal Navy's ratings service records between 1667 and 1923 (ADM 188 series) and microfilmed service records of naval officers (ADM 196 series). It also holds service records of the Royal Naval Division, the Royal Naval Reserve, the Royal Naval Volunteer Reserve, the Royal Naval Air Service, and Merchant Navy seamen employed in wartime. Records of seamen who entered the navy after 1923 are held by the Ministry of Defence at Hayes in Middlesex. Records of service after 1938 are held at HMS *Centurion*, Gosport, Hampshire. The National Archives' Web site offers helpful information leaflets.

The National Maritime Museum (http://www.nmm.ac.uk), at Greenwich, holds official records, including papers of the Board of Admiralty, Royal Navy Boards, Royal Dockyards, and related bodies of the seventeenth to nineteenth centuries. It also holds the personal papers of serving officers, including admirals David Beatty (1871–1936), Edward Hawke (1705–1781), Alexander Hood, 1st Viscount Bridport (1726–1814), and Horatio Nelson (1758–1805). It has several large collections of naval manuscripts, comprising letters, papers, journals, logs, and order books. It has some papers of the Royal Naval Air Service and business records of shipbuilding firms, including Vickers-Armstrong Ltd. It also has a film collection and large collections of historic photographs, ship plans, and charts.

The Imperial War Museum, in London, has personal diaries and letters of over 5,000 servicemen and records of senior naval commanders from both world wars.

There are important collections outside London. The Admiralty Library, Portsmouth, has papers of Admiral John Fisher (1841–1920). At Cambridge University, the Churchill Archives Centre holds private papers covering the history of the Churchill period, including those relating to sailors and the navy. The Royal Marines Museum, in Southsea, holds the archives of the corps (including material transferred from the Ministry of Defence), comprising divisional order books from 1664, personal correspondence, papers, diaries, and log books, all of serving officers. The Royal Naval Museum Library, in Portsmouth, holds papers and photographs relating particularly to the social history of the Royal Navy from the seventeenth century to the present. Its collection includes 200 logs and journals, hundreds of personal records of service, and the official collection of the Women's Royal Naval Service. The Liverpool Maritime Archives and Library at Merseyside Maritime Museum holds records relating to the history of the Port of Liverpool in its widest sense. The Plymouth Naval Studies Collection at the City of Plymouth Library contains ship logs, personal diaries, and historical and current admiralty charts for the area. It also houses an extensive collection of photographs of naval vessels.

## United States

The National Archives and Records Administration, in Washington, D.C., holds textual and microfilm records on naval and maritime-related matters, including service records, ship's muster rolls, cartographic holdings, historic films, and photographs. It also holds records of the Imperial Japanese Navy.

The Naval Historical Center (http://www.history.navy.mil/index.html), also in Washington, D.C., holds U.S. Navy records on operations, policy, and strategy from around 1939 to the present; selected personal papers; and ship's histories from 1959 to the present. It is the principal source of naval photographs prior to 1920.

The Department of Defense Visual Information Center, in California, has official photographs of the U.S. Navy and Marine Corps from 1982 to the present. The U.S. Naval Institute Photo Archive (http://www.usni.org), at Annapolis, Maryland, holds more than 450,000 images, many dating from the earliest days of the U.S. Navy.

The Naval War College Library (http://www.nwc.navy.mil/library/), in Newport, Rhode Island, has archives documenting the administrative and curricular history of the institution since its founding in 1884. It holds World War II Battle Evaluation Group records, and intelligence and technical source materials pertaining to technological developments and strategic and tactical problems of interest to the navy. In addition, it has more than 212 manuscript collections containing the personal and official papers of the college's presidents, professors, and naval officers who served on the staff or were affiliated with the institution. There are also more than 500 single manuscript items, including letters, journals, certificates, commissions, and signatures.

There are several key museum collections. The Historic Ship Nautilus and Submarine Force Museum, in Connecticut, contains documents and photographs relevant to the history of U.S. submarines. The Kendall Institute of the New Bedford Whaling Museum, in Massachusetts, has 2,300 logbooks and journals, and more than 100,000 documents relating to the American and international whaling industry. It also houses the Melville Society Archive. The Phillips Library at the Peabody Essex Museum in Salem, Massachusetts, has maritime archives, including family papers, institutional and business records, account books, and diaries. The Penobscot Marine Museum in Searsport, Maine, has manuscript and archive materials, 15,000 photographs, and 3,000 nautical charts. The Mariners' Museum Library, in Newport News, Virginia, contains more than one million manuscript items. Important collections include the plans and hull records of Chris-Craft Industries, the vessel plans of Harlan and Hollingsworth Corp. of Wilmington, Delaware, and the papers of the Hampton Roads Maritime Association. The Smithsonian Institution, in Washington, D.C., has a collection of ship plans resulting mostly from field documentation. Mystic Seaport Museum (http://schooner.mysticseaport.org), in Mystic, Connecticut, as half a million personal and commercial papers.

The J. Porter Shaw Library, in San Francisco, has an oral-history collection of over 975 interviews, as well as a large ephemeral collection. It has a chart collection covering the Pacific Basin and trade routes that touch it. Its collections of historical documents focus on commercial sailing and steam vessels dating from the gold rush to after World War II. Manuscript collections include logbooks; papers and drawings relating to ferry boats, lumber schooners, and freighters; and business records from c. 1878 to 1966. The Huntington Library, in San Marino, California, holds several groups of military and naval papers of the Revolutionary and Napoleonic periods. The Manuscripts Division of the William L. Clements Library (http://www.clements.umich.edu/manuscripts.html) at the University of Michigan also has important collections for naval history.

[*See also* International Commission for Maritime History *and* Libraries, *subentry on* Maritime Collections.]

## Bibliography

Brogan, Martha L. *Research Guide to Libraries and Archives in the Low Countries*. New York: Greenwood Press, 1991.

"Historical Manuscripts Commission UK, National Register of Archives." http://www.hmc.gov.uk.

Knight, R. J. B. *Guide to Manuscripts in the National Maritime Museum*. Vol. 1, *The Personal Collections*, and vol. 2, *Public Records, Business Records, and Artificial Collections*. London: Mansell Information Publishing, 1977 and 1980.

Latham, Robert, ed. *Catalogue of the Pepys Library at Magdalene College, Cambridge*. Cambridge, U.K.: D. S. Brewer, 1981.

Malevinskaia, M. E., ed. *Rossiiskii gosudarstvennyi arkhiv VMF: Spravochnik pofondam (1917–1940)*. 2 vols. Saint Petersburg, Russia: Blitz, 1996. This describes the holdings of the Russian State Naval Archives in Saint Petersburg for the years 1917 to 1940.

Maresquier, Erik Le. *Archives de la Marine: Guide du lecteur*. Paris: Imprimerie de la Marine, 1979.

Mathias, Peter, and A. W. H. Pearsall. *Shipping: A Survey of Historical Records*. Newton Abbot, U.K.: David and Charles, 1971.

Mayer, S. L., and W. J. Koenig. *The Two World Wars: A Guide to Manuscript Collections in the United Kingdom*. London: Bowker, 1976.

Mazur, T. P. *Annotironvannyi reestr opisei, Rossiiskii gosudarstvennyi arkhiv VMF (1696–1917)*. Saint Petersburg: Blitz, 1996. This is the annotated register to the Russian State Naval Archives for the pre-Revolutionary period.

Morriss, Roger. *Guide to British Naval Papers in North America*. London: Mansell, 1994.

"The National Archives, Kew, London." http://www.archives.gov/research_room/arc/index.html.

"National Maritime Museum, London." http://www.nmm.ac.uk/site/navId/005002.

"The Naval and Maritime Libraries and Archives Group." http://www.hants.gov.uk/record-office/collections.html

"The Naval Historical Center." http://www.history.navy.mil/sources/index.htm. Lists sources for U.S. naval history throughout the United States.

"Portsmouth Records Office, UK." *http://www.portsmouthrecordsoffice.co.uk*. Lists naval archives.

"The RLG Union Catalogue AMC file." http://lcweb.loc.gov/coll/nucmc/rlinsearch.html. Service provided by the U.S. Library of Congress.

Robertson, M., Bruce Henry, and Dorothy Popp. *Guide to British Historical Manuscripts in the Huntington Library*. San Marino, Calif.: Huntington Library, 1979.

Robertson, M., and Jean F. Preston, eds. *Guide to American Historical Manuscripts in the Huntington Library*. San Marino, Calif.: Huntington Library, 1979.

Rodger, N. A. M. *Naval Records for Genealogists*. London: Her Majesty's Stationery Office, 1988. This is a guide to the official records of the Royal Navy now in the National Archives.

Shy, Arlene, ed. *Guide to the Manuscript Collections in the William L. Clements Library*. Boston: G. K. Hall, 1978.

"The Smithsonian Institute, Washington, D.C." http://americanhistory.si.edu/csr/shipplan.htm. Lists the collections of ship plans.

"The Spanish History Index." http://vlib.iue.it/hist-spain/archives. html. Provides Internet resources on the history of Spain.

Taillemite, Etienne. *Les archives de la Marine conservées aux archives nationals*. Vincennes, France: Service Historique de la Marine, 1980.

"The UNESCO Archives Portal." http://www.unesco.org/web-world/portal_archives/.

Watts, Christopher T., and Michael J. Watts. *My Ancestor Was a Merchant Seaman: How Can I Find Out More about Him?* London: Society of Genealogists, 1986.

MARGARETTE LINCOLN

# Arctic Convoys

When Hitler invaded the Soviet Union in June 1941, Winston Churchill was quick to send British aid to the Russians, via the north Russian port of Murmansk. For the rest of the war these convoys—almost entirely British-escorted, although increasingly composed of American merchant ships carrying American supplies—were sustained with occasional suspensions as a vital confidence-building measure between the Western Allies and the Soviets. In grand strategy the cohesion between allies has always been the weakest point; consequently these almost impossible missions were imposed on the Royal Navy to cement the link with the Soviet Union. In addition they served to hold German capital ships out of the Atlantic, a threat that the British took very seriously until the middle of 1943, and then assumed an offensive role, as the chief killing ground of the U-boat war. The convoys also provided slightly more than four million tons of stores, approximately one-quarter of all Allied supplies to Russia, the remainder passing through Vladivostok and Iran, routes that were far safer but more costly in shipping tonnage and time. The convoys delivered 5,000 tanks, 7,000 aircraft, machine tools, trucks, food, and other essential supplies. In all there were 77 escorted convoys, treating each passage as a separate operation, and of 811 merchant-ship sailings, 720 arrived safely. The British lost 2 cruisers, 17 destroyers, and 13 other warships; the Germans lost the battleship *Scharnhorst*, 2 destroyers, 31 U-boats, and 2 other warships. The Luftwaffe's losses were also high.

The Arctic convoys were the most difficult and dangerous escort missions ever conducted. The route took the convoys close to the German air and naval bases in northern Norway, which could be quickly reinforced from Germany. In summer at such high latitudes daylight is effectively permanent, whereas in the dark winter months the edge of the ice sheet comes south, compressing the route. Evasion, a very effective tool in the Atlantic, was almost impossible. Extreme weather meant that survival time for men in the water was measured in seconds, and the British had to develop systems to heat and insulate their ships. Weapons often malfunctioned—HMS *Trinidad* torpedoed herself when the gyro in one of her own torpedoes froze. The sonar conditions were equally difficult, with a strong thermal layering effect that limited the range and accuracy of readings, especially in the Murmansk inlet. This had a significant impact on tactics. Heavy seas inflicted severe structural damage on warships, especially lightly built destroyers, and the formation of ice on the upper decks posed a serious risk of capsizing. Yet all these problems were overcome.

These operations were part of the Battle of the Atlantic. They were possible only while the Atlantic convoys were running successfully. Because of the heightened threat, the Arctic convoys were escorted by more powerful forces than those in the Atlantic, typically fleet destroyers and sloops with distant cover provided by cruisers, battleships, and carriers of the Royal Navy's Home Fleet. The primary task of the Home Fleet was to keep German heavy ships out of the Atlantic; the Arctic convoys kept them tied to Norway and tempted the Germans to risk them in action.

## Phases

The convoys can be divided into phases. In 1941 they arrived with little loss, opening links with the Soviets and meeting their immediate security needs with fighter planes and tanks. In 1942–1943 the key goal was the destruction of the German capital ships, especially the *Tirpitz*. Her arrival in the Atlantic threatened to disrupt the convoy system, with what would have been disastrous consequences. Instead Hitler kept the *Tirpitz* in Norway and, against the advice of Admiral Karl Dönitz, diverted U-boats out of the Atlantic to attack the Arctic route. This three-dimensional threat reached a peak with convoy PQ17 in June and July 1942. First Sea Lord Admiral Sir Dudley Pound decided that, despite the lack of clear intelligence, *Tirpitz* was about to attack the convoy and ordered it to be scattered. In fact, she was not out, and the dispersed ships were almost annihilated by air and U-boat attack. A reinforced escort fought through PQ18 in September 1942, largely for political reasons. The failure of a German attack by two heavy cruisers and six destroyers in December 1942 led Hitler to dismiss Grand Admiral Erich Raeder and order the heavy ships to be paid off. Dönitz kept the ships in service, but they achieved no more under his control. In spring and summer 1943 the British suspended the convoys to release forces

**Arctic Convoy.** Sailors clearing snow from the flight deck of the aircraft carrier HMS *Victorious* in March 1942, with a *King George V*-class battleship astern. By permission of The Trustees of the Imperial War Museum, London, A 8149

for the invasion of Italy and the Battle of the Atlantic, keeping the Home Fleet and an American task force ready in case the German heavy ships entered the main theater. After accepting defeat in the Atlantic, Dönitz tried to keep his U-boats active until the new Type XXI boat entered service. When serious reverses on the Russian front emphasized the need to stop the Arctic convoys, he ordered the last effective battleship, *Scharnhorst*, to attack. She was sunk in a well-prepared Home Fleet ambush in December 1943, made possible by intelligence gathered through Britain's Ultra project. Thereafter the Arctic was the only area where U-boat pack attacks continued. In December 1943 and January 1944, Dönitz moved twenty Atlantic U-boats to Norway, raising the number on station to thirty-three. He considered the Arctic suitable for pack operations with old boats, largely because air reconnaissance was available to locate convoys in time to form patrol lines. The Norway flotilla was not accorded priority for new equipment, notably the *Schnorchel* (snorkel—an apparatus that enabled U-boats to run off their diesel engines to avoid being detected by radar). The first boat equipped at Bergen did not reach the Arctic until mid-September 1944.

With *Tirpitz* crippled and finally sunk, the British ran convoys for the last eighteen months of the war with

powerful anti-submarine and antiair escorts, with the express purpose of drawing the U-boats into large-scale battles. These battles inflicted heavy losses on a U-boat arm already demoralized by defeat in the Atlantic, maintaining the Allies' ascendancy over this dangerous enemy. The combination of Home Fleet and Western Approaches forces, with escort carriers and good intelligence, made the Arctic the chief killing ground for U-boats during this period. In mid-1944 the convoys were suspended to release forces for Operation Overlord. By early 1945 the British were deploying groundbreaking anti-submarine weapons systems, including the sonar-controlled ahead-thrown Squid mortar, which offered a fifty percent kill ratio with a double salvo of only six projectiles against standard U-boats.

## Significance

The Arctic convoys were the most severe test that naval forces faced in World War II. In addition to the weather and enemy forces, air reconnaissance made evasion difficult. Consequently the escort forces were large—by 1945 there were as many escorts as merchant ships, and most of the escorts were large, modern units. Although the Arctic convoys have been widely studied, few historians have considered them as part of the Atlantic campaign that dominated the U-boat war. Roskill (vol. 3, pt. 2, pp. 261–262) believed that the turning point in the Arctic came with PQ18 in September 1942, basing his argument on the low level of mercantile casualties sustained thereafter. This analysis, using "safe and timely arrival" as the critical indicator, is not relevant to the Arctic convoys. Unlike the Atlantic convoys, they were sustained by political objectives and could be suspended in periods of acute danger or greater need elsewhere, as with the Atlantic crisis of mid-1943 and Operation Overlord. The Arctic must be seen as a subtheater of the Atlantic. Until the Battle of the Atlantic was won, the Arctic was a luxury. When the Arctic convoys resumed in late 1943, the commander in chief of the Western Approaches, Admiral Max Horton, secured the initiative and used it to break the will of the enemy by sinking U-boats. He knew that the U-boats would attack only heavily escorted convoys in the Arctic, so after February 1944 the critical factor in the Arctic was the ability of convoy escorts to inflict casualties on the enemy. The U-boat arm was defeated not by the Allies' ability to evade and beat off attacks, but because it suffered insupportable losses whenever it attacked.

The Arctic was an effective battleground because the Germans considered the convoys critical to the Eastern Front. German attacks persisted until the end of the war, because they were the only way in which U-boats could support land operations. As a result the Arctic convoys became, as Admiral Peter Gretton observed, "essentially offensive for it forced the enemy to give battle if he was to achieve his object" (Gretton, p. 156). Superior resources and sound strategy allowed the Royal Navy to set up a battle of attrition in the Arctic that the Germans could not win. The Arctic convoys also demonstrated the futility of a submarine-based *guerre de course*. Although the Germans effectively stopped the Arctic convoys in 1943 with air, surface, and submarine forces, the removal of the surface threat meant that they were simply unable to match the sheer weight of Allied resources deployed in 1944–1945. Consequently their efforts led only to a further erosion of the strength and morale of the U-boat arm. The Artic convoys were among the finest achievements of sea power.

[See also Atlantic, Battle of the, and Atlantic Ocean, subentry on North Atlantic.]

### Bibliography

Gretton, Peter. *Maritime Strategy: A Study of British Defence Problems*. London: Cassell, 1965.

Hessler, G. *The U-boat War in the Atlantic 1939-1945*. London: Her Majesty's Stationery Office, 1989.

Hinsley, F. H., ed. *British Intelligence in the Second World War: Its Influence on Strategy and Operations*. Vols. 2 and 3. London: Her Majesty's Stationery Office, 1979 and 1990.

Lambert, A. D. "Seizing the Initiative: The Arctic Convoys 1944–45." In *Naval Power in the Twentieth Century*, edited by N. A. M. Rodger. London: Macmillan, 1996.

Roskill, Stephen W. *The War at Sea, 1939-1945*. 3 vols. London: Her Majesty's Stationery Office, 1954–1961.

Ruegg, Bob, and Arnold Hague. *Convoys to Russia 1941-1945*. Kendal, U.K.: World Ship Society, 1992.

ANDREW LAMBERT

**Arctic Exploration.** *See* North Pole; Northwest Passage.

**Arctic Ocean** The Arctic Ocean is Earth's smallest ocean, and yet its area—14 million square kilometers (5.4 million square miles)—is five times larger than that of the Mediterranean Sea. Covered with perennial and seasonal sea ice, it is a relatively isolated, remote marine environment nearly enclosed by the Eurasian, Greenlandic, and North American land masses, and it has a single, deep connection to the Atlantic Ocean between Greenland and Svalbard. A second, narrow passage of modest depth, Nares Strait, between Greenland and Ellesmere Island in the Canadian Arctic Archipelago, has yet to be fully transited by an icebreaking ship (thereby preventing a true surface-ship circumnavigation of Greenland). All other passages around the Arctic Ocean perimeter are shallow and seasonally ice-clogged, including Bering Strait, the major (but narrow) connection between the Pacific and Arctic oceans. The confining nature of the Arctic's geography restricts the movement of sea ice, deep water, and heat into and out of the entire ocean. Such a physical setting exposes the marine waters and ice cover to significant influences of very cold air masses from the surrounding continental land areas.

The Arctic Ocean is characterized by broad continental shelves that have depths of 100 meters or less (331 feet or less) and have important sovereignty and jurisdictional implications for the five Arctic coastal states—Canada, Denmark/Greenland, Norway, Russia, and the United States. The continental shelves to the north of Eurasia and along the length of the Northeast Passage are the widest and largest in the global ocean. In addition, major waterways, such as the Lena, Ob, and Yenisey rivers in Siberia and the

TABLE 1. *Notable Arctic Voyages, 1878–1996*

| YEAR | SHIP (COUNTRY) | SIGNIFICANCE |
|------|----------------|--------------|
| 1878–1879 | *Vega* (Sweden) | First ship transit of the Northeast Passage, led by A. Nordenskiöld. |
| 1879–1881 | *Jeanette* (United States) | Ill-fated steamship voyage into the Chukchi Sea, led by G. De Long. |
| 1893–1896 | *Fram* (Norway) | F. Nansen's drift in the central Arctic Ocean to nearly 86° N. |
| 1898–1902 | *Fram* (Norway) | O. Sverdrup's mapping of the northeast Canadian Arctic Archipelago. |
| 1899 | *Yermak* (Russia) | Maiden polar icebreaker voyage operates to 81°28′ N off Spitsbergen. |
| 1903–1906 | *Gjøa* (Norway) | First ship transit of the Northwest Passage, led by R. Amundsen. |
| 1910–1915 | *Taymyr* and *Vaygach* (Russia) | Arctic Ocean Hydrographic Expedition by two icebreaking survey ships; discovered Severnaya Zemlya. |
| 1918–1925 | *Maud* (Norway) | Drift voyages in coastal Russian Arctic waters led by R. Amundsen and O. Wisting. |
| 1931 | *Nautilus* (United States) | First under-ice submarine operations off Spitsbergen, led by H. Wilkins. |
| 1932 | *Sibiryakov* (Soviet Union) | First ship transit of the Northeast Passage in a single navigation season. |
| 1937–1938 | Drift Station, SP-1 (Soviet Union) | First Soviet drift station near the North Pole, led by I. Papanin. |
| 1940 | *Komet* (Germany) | West to east transit of the Northern Sea Route by German navy raider. |
| 1940–1942 | *St. Roch* (Canada) | First west to east transit of the Northwest Passage, led by H. Larsen. |
| 1944 | *St. Roch* (Canada) | First Northwest Passage transit in a single navigation season, led by H. Larsen. |
| 1954 | *Labrador* (Canada) | First icebreaker and warship transit of the Northwest Passage, led by O. Robertson. |
| 1958 | *Nautilus* (United States) | First ship (nuclear submarine) Arctic Ocean crossing; first ship at the North Pole (August 3). |
| 1959 | *Skate* (United States) | First submarine Arctic winter voyage and first North Pole surfacing (March 17). |
| 1960 | *Seadragon* (United States) | First submarine transit of the Northwest Passage (August 18–21). |
| 1960 | *Lenin* (Soviet Union) | First nuclear surface ship (icebreaker) operates on the Northern Sea Route. |
| 1962 | *Leninski Komsomolets* (Soviet Union) | First Soviet nuclear submarine at the North Pole. |
| 1969–1970 | *Manhattan* (United States) | Experimental tanker voyages along the Northwest Passage and in Baffin Bay. |
| 1971 | *Dreadnought* (UK) | First British nuclear submarine at the North Pole. |
| 1977 | *Arktika* (Soviet Union) | First surface ship (nuclear icebreaker) at the North Pole (August 18). |
| 1984 | *Lindblad Explorer* (Sweden) | First passenger/tourist ship transit of the Northwest Passage. |
| 1990 | *Rossiya* (Soviet Union) | First tourist voyage by nuclear icebreaker to the North Pole (August 8). |
| 1991 | *Oden* (Sweden) *Polarstern* (Germany) | International Arctic Ocean Expedition: first nonnuclear ships (icebreakers) at the North Pole (September 7). |
| 1994 | *Polar Sea* (United States) *Louis S. St-Laurent* (Canada) | Arctic Ocean Section Expedition: first scientific crossing of the Arctic Ocean from Bering Strait to the North Pole (August 22) to Svalbard. |
| 1994 | *Polar Sea* (United States) *Louis S. St-Laurent* (Canada) *Yamal* (Russia) | Three-icebreaker rendezvous near the North Pole (August 23). |
| 1996 | *Yamal* (Russia) | First surface ship (nuclear icebreaker) at the Pole of Inaccessibility. |

Mackenzie River in western Canada, flow northward into the "frozen ocean."

This unique combination of a complex physical geography and high-latitude climatology—narrow straits and shallow coastal seas, large archipelagoes, north-flowing rivers, and extremely cold temperatures with the presence of thick, perennial sea ice—has shaped every aspect of the Arctic's rich maritime history. Undaunted by an

**Arctic Ocean.** *The Icebergs* by Frederic Church (1826–1900), 1861. Fascinated with the Arctic after the loss of the Franklin expedition in 1847, the American Hudson River School artist chartered a schooner in the summer of 1859 to sketch the icebergs in the waters off Newfoundland and Labrador as the inspiration for this large canvas. ART RESOURCE, NY

uncommonly severe climate and a host of navigational challenges, mariners have nevertheless for centuries searched the Arctic Ocean for shipping routes between the Pacific and the Atlantic, and sought riches from the Arctic's abundant living and nonliving natural resources. Despite many remarkable voyages and increasing marine activity in the region, especially during the past 120 years, early in the twenty-first century the Arctic Ocean remains the least explored and fully understood of our oceans.

Table 1 includes notable Arctic voyages spanning the 1878 "first ship transit" of the Northeast Passage (across the north of Eurasia by the Swedish explorer Nils Adolf Erik Nordenskiöld, in the whaler *Vega*) to the Russian nuclear icebreaker *Yamal*'s trans-Arctic voyage with tourists during the summer of 1996 with a stop on August 1 at the North Pole of (Relative) Inaccessibility (in theory the most difficult position to reach in the Arctic Ocean). This later voyage confirms the historic attainment of summer access to all regions of the Arctic Ocean by highly capable surface ships. The ships included in Table 1 also illustrate unique and diverse applications of marine technological developments to the Arctic: small, specially built wooden ships for polar exploration (for example, *Fram* and *Maud*); large steel icebreakers (the first large Russian icebreaker *Yermak* built in England in 1898 served for more than six

decades); nuclear submarines that can surface through sea ice and nuclear icebreakers (the first nuclear ship was the Soviet icebreaker *Lenin* completed in Leningrad in 1959); and the experimental tanker *Manhattan*, which operated in the Canadian Arctic in 1969–1970. The successful application of advanced ship designs to the challenges of effective and efficient icebreaking is another notable achievement in the maritime histories of the Arctic Ocean, Baltic Sea, and North American Great Lakes.

### Science and the Early Northern Sea Route

In the late nineteenth century opportunities and challenges remained for serious Arctic Ocean exploration. The Norwegian Fridtjof Nansen conducted an Arctic Ocean drift aboard the ship *Fram* (1893–1896), confirming his theory of transpolar ocean circulation. Also aboard *Fram*, Otto Sverdrup during the 1898–1902 period explored and mapped the eastern areas of the Canadian Arctic Archipelago. It was not until Roald Amundsen's voyage of the fishing vessel *Gjoa* during the 1903–1906 period that the fabled Northwest Passage was successfully transited by ship. However, Amundsen's effort in a small vessel hardly inspired confidence that the Northwest Passage could be a viable commercial route

**Map of the Arctic Ocean.** MAP BY MAPPING SPECIALISTS LIMITED

between the Atlantic and Pacific oceans. And it was not until 1932 that a ship completed a single-season transit of the Northeast Passage, that of the Soviet icebreaking steamer *Sibiryakov* (the voyage was not a total success in that the ship lost its propeller near Bering Strait and had to use improvised sails to reach open water prior to a long tow to Japan).

The tsars and the Soviet state understood that the north of Eurasia could be developed into a key Arctic marine transportation artery. The Russian navy organized the Arctic Ocean Hydrographic Expedition of 1910–1915, which was the first major charting effort along the Northeast Passage. Tsar Nicholas II established Murmansk in 1916 as a western terminus of the northern routes; the

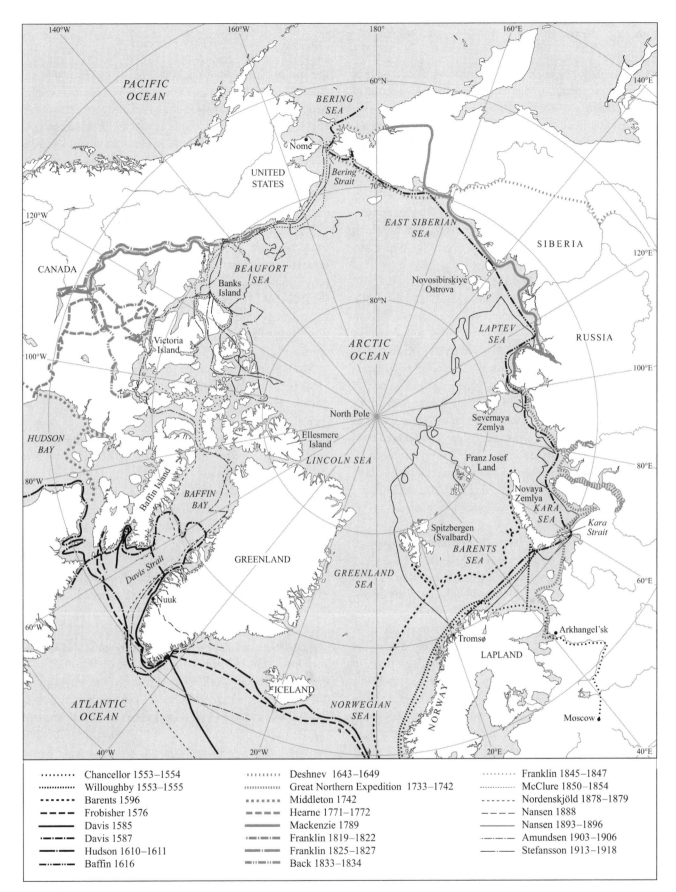

| | | | |
|---|---|---|
| ........ | Chancellor 1553–1554 | |
| ............ | Willoughby 1553–1555 | |
| - - - - | Barents 1596 | |
| – – – | Frobisher 1576 | |
| —— | Davis 1585 | |
| —·—·— | Davis 1587 | |
| —··—·· | Hudson 1610–1611 | |
| —···—··· | Baffin 1616 | |

| ........ | Deshnev 1643–1649 |
|---|---|
| ........... | Great Northern Expedition 1733–1742 |
| ▪▪▪▪▪▪ | Middleton 1742 |
| ▬ ▬ ▬ | Hearne 1771–1772 |
| ▬▬▬ | Mackenzie 1789 |
| ▪▪▪▪▪ | Franklin 1819–1822 |
| ▬▪▬▪ | Franklin 1825–1827 |
| ▪▬▪▬ | Back 1833–1834 |

| ........ | Franklin 1845–1847 |
|---|---|
| .......... | McClure 1850–1854 |
| - - - - | Nordenskjöld 1878–1879 |
| – – – | Nansen 1888 |
| —— | Nansen 1893–1896 |
| —·—·— | Amundsen 1903–1906 |
| —··—·· | Stefansson 1913–1918 |

**Map of Exploration Voyages in the Arctic Ocean.** MAP BY BILL NELSON

city remains today as the largest Arctic port and one that is ice-free year-round, ideal for shipments in and out of the Arctic by non-icegoing ships. The Soviet state also believed that the industrialization of the Arctic and associated main routes would reassert Soviet domination in the region. A Northern Sea Route Commission was formed in 1920, an Arctic Institute was established in 1925, and the Chief Administration of the Northern Sea Route (Glavsemorput) was created in December 1932. Glavsemorput's goal was the full economic development (including fishing and timber) of the Arctic region between the White Sea and Bering Strait.

World War II curtailed the Soviet Union's efforts to develop the Northern Sea Route. Naval action in the Arctic Ocean during the war focused primarily on Greenland, Svalbard, and the key shipping routes to Murmansk on the Kola Peninsula. The Barents Sea was a major operational area for German aircraft and naval units (U-boats and surface combatants) to attack Allied shipping bound for Murmansk. The German *Admiral Scheer* sailed into the Kara Sea in August 1942 north of the tip of Novaya Zemlya and sunk the icebreaking ship *Sibiryakov*. However, such Arctic surface actions and the operation of U-boats in the Kara Sea were limited since German naval commanders recognized that sailing in Arctic waters, even those partially ice-covered, was hazardous business.

## Cold War Geopolitics and Nuclear Ships

Three major developments define Arctic maritime history from the end of World War II to the dissolution of the USSR. Foremost, the Arctic Ocean played a key role as a buffer zone and strategic theater between the two superpowers. To that end, the Soviet and American navies waged a complex and undersea strategic match, both employing offensive and defensive systems in northern waters. Second, perhaps less heralded, was the unprecedented and successful operation of nuclear-powered ships above and below the Arctic sea ice cover. Third was the major investment, buildup, and operation of the Soviet Arctic marine transportation system along the Northern Sea Route. During this era it is important to note that nearly half the Arctic was a closed region, one where marine and terrestrial access was very tightly controlled by the Soviet Union.

During the Cold War the Arctic Ocean was the shortest distance between the adversaries for potential use of their bombers and later their intercontinental ballistic missiles. The Distant Early Warning (DEW) line and the Ballistic Missile Early Warning System (BMEWS) sites stretched across the top of North America from Alaska to the Canadian Arctic Archipelago and to northern Greenland. The construction and maintenance of these sites required summer convoys of logistics ships and supporting icebreakers that had not previously used these Arctic waterways so extensively. The indigenous people of the region, the Inuit, surely had never observed such large-scale marine activity. In 1950 the Soviet Union resumed its series of North Pole drift stations in the Arctic Ocean (the first established in 1937, but suspended during World War II) to provide year-round meteorological and oceanographic conditions in the central Arctic. Stations NP-1 through NP-31 (1937–1991) provided environmental data important to USSR national security and to operations along the Northern Sea Route. After a hiatus because of a lack of funding, new drift stations were established on April 25, 2003 (NP-32), and September 9, 2004 (NP-33).

The operation of nuclear submarines and nuclear icebreakers in the Arctic Ocean from the late 1950s until now must be considered one of the significant marine technological advances of modern maritime history. The nuclear submarine evolved into a formidable naval combatant that could operate under the Arctic sea ice cover with great stealth. The world's first nuclear ship, USS *Nautilus*, proved this concept during a historic Arctic Ocean crossing in the summer of 1958 (reaching the North Pole on August 3) while running submerged under the sea ice from Bering Strait to the Atlantic. USS *Skate* surfaced at the North Pole on March 17, 1959, and many more nuclear submarines from the United States, the Soviet Union, and the United Kingdom have followed during nearly five decades of naval under-ice operations. The large nuclear icebreakers developed by the USSR from the 1950s to the 1970s had the key attributes of high power and nearly unlimited endurance for sustained icebreaking along the remote regions of the Soviet Arctic. The icebreaker *Lenin*, the world's first nuclear ship, completed in 1959, had significant power (32,000 kilowatts, 44,000 horsepower) provided to three shafts. Larger icebreakers of the *Arktika* class (55,200 kilowatts, 75,000 horsepower) were built from 1975 to the early 1990s. Two large, shallow-draft nuclear icebreakers (*Taymyr* and *Vaygach*) were designed for operations in the Siberian rivers and estuaries; both were built in Helsinki, but the Russian reactors were installed in Saint Petersburg. A single nuclear commercial cargo ship, the *Sevmorput*, was also operational along the Northern Sea Route by 1986. In a demonstration of superior icebreaking capability *Arktika* became the first surface ship to reach the North Pole on August 17, 1977.

No history of the Arctic Ocean would be complete without mention of the extraordinary Arctic fleet and extensive polar operations conducted in the Soviet Arctic during the last decades of the USSR. More than one hundred specialized icebreaking ships were designed and employed along the Northern Sea Route and on the Siberian rivers. While Soviet engineers focused their efforts on nuclear power for icebreaking ships, the Finnish shipbuilder Wartsila developed a fleet of Arctic ships for the USSR from the mid-1950s to 1990. One of the most successful was a fleet of nineteen icebreaking cargo ships of the *Noril'sk* or SA-15 class (length 174 meters, 570 feet). Year-round navigation from Murmansk to the Yenisey River was attained during the 1978–1979 season. Peak traffic along the Northern Sea Route was reached in 1987: 1,306 voyages of freighters carrying 6.6 million tons of cargo. On October 1, 1987, the Soviet secretary general Mikhail Gorbachev gave a speech in Murmansk where he mentioned the possibility of inviting international shipping to use the Northern Sea Route. The International Northern Sea Route Programme (INSROP), organized by Norwegian, Japanese, and Russian interests from 1993 to 1999, documented all aspects of this Soviet Arctic experience and identified potential challenges facing future use of Russia's Northern Sea Route.

## Law of the Sea Challenges

A pattern of creeping national jurisdiction and sovereignty over Arctic marine areas, and most global marine areas as well, evolved during the later half of the twentieth century. The actions of the Arctic coastal states to assert rights in adjacent seas have been controversial and remain a key factor in the future of Arctic shipping and offshore development. Canada and Russia have been particularly active in establishing claims. A prime example was Canada's response to the celebrated voyage of the 155,000-ton tanker *Manhattan* along the Northwest Passage in 1969, which caused great concern by Canadians for sovereignty and environmental protection reasons. On April 1, 1970, Canada quickly adopted the Arctic Waters Pollution Prevention Act, which was applied to all waters of the Canadian Arctic Archipelago north of the 60th parallel as well to waters one hundred nautical miles beyond the archipelago. The entire region was divided into sixteen shipping safety control zones, each requiring a specific class of ship for entry depending on the time of year; all ships had to meet stringent pollution prevention, manning, and equipment requirements.

A long process to create an international legal regime for the oceans came to fruition in 1982 with adoption of the United Nations Convention on the Law of the Sea (UNCLOS). UNCLOS had immediate and profound implications for the maritime Arctic as well as setting the stage for further enclosure of the Arctic Ocean by the five Arctic coastal states. At the onset, the cornerstone concept of UNCLOS, the Exclusive Economic Zone (EEZ), allowed Arctic coastal states to declare their two-hundred-nautical-mile EEZ where they maintain sovereign rights over living and nonliving resources and national jurisdiction over marine activities (fisheries management and enforcement, for example). The basic freedoms of the high seas are preserved within each EEZ. The EEZs now cover large areas of the Arctic Ocean especially beyond the Canadian Arctic Archipelago and the Russian Arctic (for example, there is an EEZ around Franz Josef Land reaching into the central Arctic Ocean). Article 234 of the convention is a key provision influencing the Arctic in that it provides a right of the coastal state to implement special measures for the protection of the marine environment in ice-covered seas. Article 76 also will potentially influence the future Arctic Ocean in that it allows the coastal states to extend their boundaries beyond the EEZ in special circumstances and upon the approval of an UNCLOS commission reviewing Arctic state claims. This process has initiated extensive surveys of the Arctic Ocean seabed beyond the established EEZs to support the Arctic states' eventual claims.

On January 15, 1985, the Soviet Union established straight baselines in the Soviet Arctic across several major straits: Kara Gate (linking the Barents and Kara seas), Vilkitskii Strait (a major waterway between the Kara and Laptev seas), and Sannikov and Omitny Laptev straits (through the New Siberian Islands). The USSR considered the landward side of these baselines to be internal waters; the territorial sea of twelve nautical miles extended outward from these baselines. On January 1, 1986, Canada established straight baselines around the perimeter of the Canadian Arctic Archipelago, essentially extending full sovereignty over these waters considered by Canadian law to be internal waters. The United States has consistently opposed these claims by Canada and Russia, arguing that these are international straits and waterways in which all ships are entitled to passage and transit rights without limitations. Other maritime nations such as the United Kingdom have protested these claims that have expanded the Arctic internal waters of the states.

Several important Arctic maritime boundaries remain in dispute and unresolved. Russia and Norway disagree on their border in the Barents Sea, which has key implications for fisheries management and potential offshore oil and gas. Likewise, the United States and Canada have not resolved their marine boundary north of Alaska in the Beaufort Sea. Key Arctic boundaries between Canada and Denmark in Baffin Bay and between the United States and Russia in the Bering and Chukchi seas are not completely resolved. Each boundary dispute has important implications for international Arctic shipping and Arctic offshore seabed leasing.

## Multiple Uses and Arctic Climate Change

Early in the twenty-first century summer ship operations have been conducted throughout most of the Arctic Ocean. Large numbers of cruise ships have been observed in summer along the Greenland and Svalbard coasts. Year-round navigation on the western end of the Northern Sea Route has continued to the Yenisey River in the Kara Sea by commercial ore carriers operating between the Kola Peninsula and Dudinka, port city for the mining industrial complex at Noril'sk. However, in recent years there have been few full transits (trans-Arctic voyages) of the Northern Sea Route or Northwest Passage. No commercial ships have taken advantage of these full Arctic routes in summer, except for several icebreakers carrying tourists.

During the 1977–2005 period, sixty-five transits were made to the North Pole by polar icebreakers of Russia (fifty-three), Sweden (five), United States (three), Germany (two), Canada (one), and Norway (one). A remarkable twenty-one of these voyages were during the summers of 2004, 2005, and 2006 alone. Tourism and scientific research are the primary motivations to sail to the North Pole by icebreaker; forty-eight of the sixty-five North Pole voyages were for tourist passengers, and the remaining seventeen voyages were in support of scientific operations. Of significance to navigation, only a single voyage of the sixty-five did not occur during summer, and that was the Soviet nuclear icebreaker *Sibir*'s expedition (during nearly maximum Arctic sea ice conditions in early spring) that supported polar research from May 8 to June 10, 1987. *Sibir* reached the North Pole on May 25, 1987, operating in sea ice thicknesses of three meters (ten feet) and greater.

During the decade of the 1990s five historic trans-Arctic icebreaker voyages were made: a transit across the central Arctic Ocean by the nuclear icebreaker *Sovetskiy Soyuz* (Russia) with tourists in August 1991; transits by the *Louis S. St-Laurent* (Canada) and *Polar Sea* (United States) during July and August 1994 from Bering Strait

to the North Pole and to the Atlantic (the first scientific transect of the Arctic Ocean conducted by surface ship); and two 1996 Arctic Ocean crossings by the nuclear icebreaker *Yamal* with tourists. During late summer 2004 a small armada consisting of the nuclear icebreaker *Sovetskiy Soyuz*, the icebreaker *Oden* (Sweden), and the icebreaking ship *Vidar Viking* (Norway) outfitted for drilling conducted a unique scientific drilling voyage in the most remote region of the Arctic Ocean. In summer 2005 a sixth surface-ship crossing of the central Arctic Ocean was completed by the icebreakers *Oden* (Sweden) and *Healy* (United States) while conducting a scientific transect. These pioneering voyages provide a substantial record confirming that summer marine access to most areas of the Arctic Ocean has been achieved. In addition, early in the 1990s dedicated U.S. Navy nuclear submarines were used for science (the SCICEX program) on pioneering research expeditions that sampled much of the surface water masses of the central Arctic Ocean.

During the past five decades the observed extent of Arctic sea ice declined in all seasons. Arctic sea ice research, primarily using advanced satellite remote sensors that can monitor ice without the influences of weather or polar darkness, has shown that the perennial sea ice is shrinking in extent. Arctic sea ice thicknesses have also been observed to be significantly reduced. All of these changes are documented in a historic Arctic study, the Arctic Climate Impact Assessment (ACIA), released in November 2004 by the Arctic Council and the International Arctic Science Committee. ACIA reported that the Arctic is extremely vulnerable to observed and projected climate change and its impacts, and that the Arctic is now experiencing some of the most rapid and severe climate change on earth. Noted in ACIA is that potentially accelerating Arctic sea ice retreat improves marine access throughout the Arctic Ocean and sets the stage for longer seasons of navigation in all Arctic regional seas. One Arctic sea ice model simulation for the twenty-first century indicated the extraordinary possibility of the Arctic Ocean being ice-free for a short summer period by 2050. In practical terms for Arctic navigation this would mean the disappearance of perennial ice, the most difficult ice to break and transverse. These potential changes in Arctic marine access caused the Arctic Council to initiate a comprehensive Arctic Marine Shipping Assessment (AMSA) to be led by Canada, Finland, and the United States. AMSA will assess the current and future (to 2020 and 2050) social, economic, and environmental impacts of marine activities in all regions of the Arctic Ocean. Indigenous and traditional marine use of the Arctic's waterways will also be fully considered. AMSA when completed in 2008 should provide a set of plausible futures for marine use of the Arctic Ocean—futures of increased access and expanded shipping much different than for any other period in polar maritime history.

[*See also* Amundsen, Roald; *Nautilus*; North Pole; Northeast Passage; Northwest Passage, *subentry on* Exploration Voyages, 1815 to the Present; Ocean Governance, *subentry on* Exclusive Economic Zone; Skate; *and* United Nations Conferences on the Law of the Sea.]

### Bibliography

ACIA. *Impacts of a Warming Arctic: Arctic Climate Impact Assessment.* Cambridge, U.K., and New York: Cambridge University Press, 2004. A milestone and comprehensive assessment of the Arctic Council that includes as a key finding the improvement of marine access in the Arctic Ocean in an era of extraordinary climate change, and documents the rapidly decreasing Arctic sea ice cover.

Anderson, William R., with Clay Blair Jr. *Nautilus 90 North.* Cleveland, Ohio: World Publishing, 1959. Reprint. Blue Ridge Summit, Pa.: Tab Books, 1989. The captain of the U.S. Navy's nuclear submarine *Nautilus*, the world's first nuclear ship, describes the historic summer 1958 voyage under the Arctic sea ice from Bering Strait to the North Pole and into the Atlantic Ocean.

Armstrong, Terence. *The Northern Sea Route: Soviet Exploitation of the North East Passage.* Cambridge, U.K.: Cambridge University Press, 1952.

Armstrong, Terence. *The Russians in the Arctic: Aspects of Soviet Exploration and Exploitation of the Far North, 1937–57.* Fairlawn, N.J.: Essential Books, 1958.

Brigham, Lawson W. "Modern Icebreaking Ships." In *The Shipping Revolution: The Modern Merchant Ship*, edited by Robert Gardiner, pp. 154–158. London: Conway Maritime Press, 1992.

Brigham, Lawson W., ed. *The Soviet Maritime Arctic.* London: Belhaven Press; Annapolis, Md.: Naval Institute Press, 1991.

Brubaker, R. Douglas. *The Russian Arctic Straits.* Leiden, Netherlands, and Boston: Nijhoff, 2005.

Griffiths, Franklyn, ed. *Politics of the Northwest Passage.* Montreal and Kingston, Ontario: McGill-Queen's University Press, 1987.

Hayes, Derek. *Historical Atlas of the Arctic.* Seattle: University of Washington Press, 2003.

Nansen, Fridtjof. *Farthest North: Being the Record of a Voyage of Exploration of the Ship Fram 1893–96.* London: Constable, 1897. Reprint. New York: Modern Library, 1999.

Østreng, Willy, ed. *The Natural and Societal Challenges of the Northern Sea Route: A Reference Work.* Dordrecht, Netherlands: Kluwer Academic, 1999.

Pharand, Donat. *Canada's Arctic Waters in International Law.* Cambridge, U.K.: Cambridge University Press, 1988.

Smith, William D. *Northwest Passage: The Historic Voyage of the S.S. Manhattan.* New York: American Heritage Press, 1970.

Vaugh, Richard. *The Arctic: A History.* Phoenix Mill, U.K., and Dover, N.H.: Alan Sutton, 1994.

LAWSON W. BRIGHAM

## Arginusae. *See* Ancient Navies.

## Argo

*Argo* This legendary Greek ship is featured in one of the oldest Greek legends, that of the story of Jason and the Argonauts. Jason, a young prince, was the victim of his uncle Pelias, who had deprived Jason's father of the throne in Iolcus in Thessaly. When Jason reclaimed the throne, Pelias wanted to get rid of his rival. So Pelias induced Jason to fetch the Golden Fleece from Colchis on the Black Sea. Jason collected the noblest heroes in Greece and, with the help of the goddess Athena, built a ship. The ship was called *Argo* after her naval architect Argos and because of her speed (*argos* meant "swift" in classical Greek). She is the earliest known instance of a Greek ship being named. Sailing through the Dardanelles, the Bosporus, and the Black Sea, the Argonauts reached Colchis, where King Aeetes was reluctant to surrender the fleece and gave Jason a number of difficult tasks to complete. With the help of Medea, the king's daughter, Jason succeeded. Together with Medea, the Argonauts returned home with the fleece, but they lost their way and traveled all across Europe. They reached the North Sea and sailed back around Spain, through the Strait of Gibraltar, and along the coast of Libya. After protracted hardships they returned to Iolcus and dedicated *Argo* to Poseidon on the Isthmus of Corinth.

The legend of an expedition to the Black Sea precedes the Greek expansion, which in the eighth century B.C.E. led to a change in the name for the Black Sea from *axeinos* (unfriendly) to *euxeinos* (friendly). The legend may be based on a real expedition to the Black Sea before 1000 B.C.E., when the Black Sea area was as yet unknown to the Greeks. Unlike other heroes, Jason was not a raider who attacked cities for plunder, but an early Greek explorer who wanted to open up uncharted waters. He made his potentially profitable voyage of discovery in a galley, probably a *triaconter* or a *penteconter*, vessels manned by thirty or fifty oarsmen. *Argo* was already famous in Homer's time for her strength and speed. In addition, *Argo* was so light that the rowers could carry her on their shoulders. Descriptions by classical authors and representations on vases and reliefs from the sixth century B.C.E., however, give a different picture. *Argo* is presented as a larger ship, rowed from two or three levels and having all the characteristics of the ships from that century.

In 1984, Tim Severin attempted to retrace the legendary voyage in a galley designed by Colin Mudie, on the basis of pictorial and other evidence of a vessel from c. 1200 B.C.E. The 54-foot replica was constructed by Vasilius Delimitros at Spetses, Greece. After the voyage, the replica was placed at the Exeter Maritime Museum in England.

[*See also Argonautica, The*; Galley; *and* Warships, *subentry on* Ancient Warships.]

### Bibliography

Apollonius Rhodius. *The Argonautica*. Translated by R. C. Seaton. Cambridge, Mass.: Harvard University Press, 1967.

Casson, Lionel. *The Ancient Mariners: Seafarers and Sea Fighters of the Mediterranean in Ancient Times*. 2d ed. Princeton, N.J.: Princeton University Press, 1991.

Morrison, J. S., and R. T. Williams. *Greek Oared Ships 900–322 BC*. Cambridge, U.K.: Cambridge University Press, 1968.

Severin, Tim. *The Jason Voyage: The Quest for the Golden Fleece*. New York: Simon and Schuster, 1985.

FIK MEIJER

**Argonautica, The**   The story of the voyage of *Argo* to the Black Sea port of Colchis, and the quest for the Golden Fleece, was already "a concern to all" in earliest Greek times, according to Homer, but the story was first given full literary scope by the Alexandrian scholar and poet Apollonius of Rhodes in the third century B.C.E. His epic poem *The Argonautica* confines the story of *Argo's* journey to four books, following the preference of his age for narrative poems of only a fraction of the length of the monumental Homeric models. The *Argonautica* had a wide reception in antiquity, including at Rome, where it profoundly influenced Catullus, Virgil, and Seneca. Modern film adaptations of the story of *Argo's* voyage take their inspiration principally from Apollonius's poem.

According to the mythic accounts that Apollonius followed, *Argo* was the first vessel ever developed that was capable of crossing the open ocean; its design came straight from the goddess Athena, and its very planks were imbued with supernatural qualities, including one central beam that possessed the power of speech. Apollonius's poem begins at the moment that this construction is complete, and it ends, rather without warning, when the ship returns to the home port of Iolcus after completing its mission to fetch the Golden Fleece. Thus Apollonius defined his story as that of the ship itself, rather than that of the coming of age of his young hero, Jason; indeed, Apollonius declined to narrate the climactic events of Jason's life that either precede or follow the voyage of *Argo*. The entire epic thus consists of a journey, one that begins in Greek waters, crosses the Aegean and Black Sea to Colchis, and then returns to Greece by way of a circuitous and geographically impossible route through central Europe, northern Africa, and Crete. In this Apollonius followed the structural models of Homer's so-called Alcinoan tales and the story of Odysseus's maritime adventures in *The Odyssey*, as well as the model of the *periplus* texts popular in his own day, with their stage-by-stage descriptions of sea voyages in exotic parts of the globe.

*Argo* is imagined as an open-decked ship of the Homeric type, rowed by banks of pairs of oarsmen sitting abreast and with a central mast that could be inserted or removed as wind conditions required. A single helmsman, Tiphys, wielded the stern rudder that steered the ship; the stars and the sun were his only navigational guides. Such a primitive vessel lay very much at the mercy of waves and foul weather, and Apollonius explores in books 1, 2, and 4 of his poem a huge array of navigational perils both real and fantastic. Time and again the ship is saved from destruction: by the heroic fortitude of its oarsmen, by the cleverness of its navigator, or, when all human agency fails, by the intervention of the goddesses Hera and Athena, who watch protectively over Jason's journey. (Book 3, by contrast, takes place on land, in the realm of the Colchians, where Jason strives to win his fabled prize.) Apollonius plays close attention throughout to the technical aspects of sailing, keeping far closer track than Homer or other Greek narrative poets did of wind and tide conditions, nautical maneuvers, and the realities of life on shipboard.

Under Jason's command serves a crew made up of mythic heroes from all corners of the Greek world, each wielding a different superhuman or divinely inspired power. Chief among these are Heracles, with his enormous strength, resolve, and fearlessness; Orpheus, with his magical gift of song; and Zetes and Calaïs, sons of the North Wind, who can fly through the air using wings on their ankles. Despite his position as leader, Jason, alone among the Argonauts, has no special power or divine parentage—a paradox explored by Apollonius over and over throughout the poem. Time and again, Jason is characterized by the peculiar heroic epithet "resourceless" (Homer's Odysseus is constantly called "resourceful") and is portrayed, on numerous occasions, as a vacillating commander uncertain of what orders to give or what action to take. The irresolution of this hero, unique among the gallery of types found in classical epic, forms a pointed contrast to the bullheadedness of Heracles, Jason's principal foil in the poem. Indeed, Apollonius sets up an uncomfortable contrast between the two character types at the outset of the journey, when the Argonauts, asked to elect their own leader, unanimously choose Heracles rather than Jason; the younger and less capable man becomes captain only after Heracles declines the post.

Heracles is later left behind on a desolate coast after *Argo*'s helmsman, rushing to catch a favorable wind, leaves without him. This prompts one of Jason's worst moments in the poem: as his crew disputes the merits of going back to fetch Heracles, Jason sits in silent indecision, causing one of the men to accuse him of having connived at the stranding for his own selfish purposes. Finally, a divine apparition reveals that the fates had never intended Heracles to accompany the expedition, but the loss of face that Jason incurs, in his inability either to make a tough choice or to stand up to a challenge, reveals in high relief his defining traits of helplessness and passivity. One disaffected modern critic has remarked that Jason is "uninteresting when he is not repellent." A more favorable approach is to regard his character as part of an experiment in literary dissonance, similar to that attempted in modern times by James Joyce in *Ulysses*. By placing a human being of ordinary dimensions upon a mythic stage, Apollonius deliberately defeated the expectations of his readers and achieved a level of psychological realism unprecedented in ancient epic. Violating Aristotle's dictum that audiences need a hero to be better than themselves, Apollonius gave his main character the same doubts, frailties, and vulnerabilities that his readers would presumably experience, were they put in charge of *Argo*.

The psychological complexity of the *Argonautica* becomes most apparent in books 3 and 4, where Apollonius explores rather convincingly the ill-fated love affair that Jason enters into with Medea, princess of Colchis. Medea here in no way resembles the awesome figure portrayed by the tragic poets; she is merely a frightened teenager torn between her loyalty to her family and her coquettish affection for the handsome, boyish Jason. As we watch the intimacy of the two lovers deepen, we are, of course, in mind of the jealous rage that ultimately, long after the events of this poem, brings Medea to strike at Jason by murdering their children. But Apollonius, again, plays for dissonance by stressing the naïveté, charm, and erotic appeal of this younger Medea. Her support of Jason

in defiance of her father Aeetes seems motivated by a perfectly plausible adolescent rebelliousness, and the overenthusiastic embrace that Jason offers her arises out of the insecurities of his own situation. The affair has thus always carried great conviction among readers of the *Argonautica*, as demonstrated by Virgil's extensive adaptation of it in the Dido episode of his *Aeneid*.

Apollonius was a scholar as well as a poet—for a time he headed the compendious library at Alexandria—and his epic reflects the passions of his learned literary milieu. Many episodes contain answers, either implicit or explicit, to recondite questions of genealogy, geography, or mythic history. A Herodotean interest in the anthropology of the barbarian world pervades much of the fourth book, in which *Argo* wanders through the great rivers of central Europe—the Danube, Po, Rhine, and Rhone—driven by Zeus's wrath at the crew for the murder of Apsyrtus, Medea's half-brother. This inland route, contrived by Apollonius without regard to either previous versions of the story or the lack of connection among the rivers involved, seems to have been chosen so that *Argo* might explore the primitive world of the Celtic and Ligurian tribesmen, as well as pay visits to various characters from Homer's *Odyssey* thought to reside in the seas around Italy. A final diversion takes the ship, improbably enough, into northern Africa, where she becomes trapped for a time in Lake Tritonis before a god points the way back to open water.

Apollonius's style, like other aspects of his work, rings modern changes on time-honored epic conventions. Words unearthed from Homer are juxtaposed with words from wholly different poetic traditions, or with bizarre neologisms. The stately but rigid dactylic rhythms of the *Iliad* and the *Odyssey* are adapted to syntactic constructions of much greater suppleness and complexity. This tendency to distort archaic forms using modern technique is the hallmark of Apollonius's *Argonautica*, a daring experiment in literary adaptation practiced on the most ancient of Hellenic sea stories.

[*See also* Ancient Voyage Narratives; *Argo; and Odyssey, The.*]

## Bibliography

Beye, Charles R. *Epic and Romance in the "Argonautica" of Apollonius: Literary Structures.* With a foreword by J. Gardner. Carbondale: University of Illinois Press, 1982.

Campbell, Malcolm. *Echoes and Imitations of Early Epic in Apollonius Rhodius.* Mnemosyne Supplement 72. Leiden, Netherlands: Brill, 1981.

Clauss, James J. *The Best of the Argonauts: The Redefinition of the Epic Hero in Book One of Apollonius' "Argonautica."* Berkeley: University of California Press, 1993.

Goldhill, Simon. "The Paradigms of Epic: Apollonius Rhodius and the Example of the Past." In *The Poet's Voice: Essays on Poetics and Greek Literature*, pp. 184–233. Cambridge, U.K.: Cambridge University Press, 1991.

Green, Peter M., ed. and trans. *The "Argonautika" by Apollonios Rhodios*. Berkeley: University of California Press, 1997.

Hunter, Richard L., ed. *Apollonius of Rhodes: "Argonautica" Book III*. Cambridge, U.K.: Cambridge University Press, 1989.

Hunter, Richard L. *The "Argonautica" of Apollonius: Literary Studies*. Cambridge, U.K.: Cambridge University Press, 1993.

Papanghelis, Theodore, and Antonios Rengakos, eds. *A Companion to Apollonius Rhodius. Mnemosyne* Supplement 217. Leiden, Netherlands: Brill, 2001.

JAMES ROMM

## Ark Royal, British aircraft carrier.

Length/beam/draft: 24.3.8 m × 28.9 m × 6.9 m (800′ × 94.8′ × 22.8′). Tonnage: 27,000 displacement. Hull: steel. Complement: 1,600. Armament: 60 aircraft, 16 × 4.5″ guns. Armor: 4.5″ belt, 3.5″ deck. Machinery: steam turbine, 31 knots. Built: Cammell Laird, Birkenhead, England, 1938.

HMS *Ark Royal* was launched April 13, 1937, and completed November 16, 1938. Following Royal Navy tradition, it carried a name made famous by earlier ships. The name was first given, in 1587, to an English flagship that served in the Armada campaign of 1588 and was renamed in 1608. The name was reused for a World War I seaplane carrier (1914–1934). The third, and most famous, *Ark Royal* was the first modern aircraft carrier designed and built in Britain. She displaced 27,000 tons and could

**HMS *Ark Royal.*** The damaged aircraft carrier after *U-81* had torpedoed her off Gibraltar on November 13, 1941. BY PERMISSION OF THE TRUSTEES OF THE IMPERIAL WAR MUSEUM, LONDON, A 6334

carry up to sixty aircraft in two hangars. The ship had a high profile during the first two years of World War II. Sent into the western approaches to cover incoming merchant shipping in September 1939, she was attacked by a U-boat. A few days later, while operating in the North Sea with the Home Fleet, she was attacked by the Luftwaffe, which erroneously reported her sunk. German propaganda broadcasts asked, "Where is the *Ark Royal*?" After pursuing *Admiral Graf Spee*, she was heavily involved in the Norwegian campaign before forming the nucleus of Force H at Gibraltar, with the battlecruiser *Renown* and the radar-equipped cruiser *Sheffield*. This force opened the war against Italy with strikes around Genoa and, after the French surrender, attacked their fleet at Mers-el-Kebir on July 3, 1940. In a follow-up attack three days later, *Ark Royal*'s aircraft seriously damaged the battlecruiser *Dunkerque*. The finest hour of Force H came May 26, 1941, when *Ark Royal*'s Swordfish aircraft hit and crippled the German battleship *Bismarck*, leaving her to be sunk by the Home Fleet the next morning. Force H also escorted vital convoys into the Mediterranean and exercised effective control over the western basin of that sea in addition to dominating the mid-Atlantic. Returning from a Mediterranean sortie on November 15, 1941, *Ark Royal* was hit by a single deep-running torpedo from *U-81* and sank thirty miles off Gibraltar after slow flooding overwhelmed the pumps. This remarkable, well-publicized war record was compiled by a ship that never had a full complement of aircraft or pilots and had few, if any, modern fighters. The wreck was discovered in thirty-five hundred feet of water in December 2002.

After her loss the British ordered a new, much larger ship in 1943; it was completed in 1955. This *Ark*, which displaced 54,000 tons, remained in service until 1979. As the last Royal Navy conventional aircraft carrier, and the star of a 1976 BBC television series *Sailor*, her passing was greatly regretted. A fifth *Ark*, laid down in 1978 by Swan Hunter Shipbuilders in Wallsend, launched in 1981, and accepted into service on July 1, 1985, is a carrier for 20,000-ton helicopters and short-takeoff jets.

## Bibliography

Friedman, Norman. *British Carrier Aviation: The Evolution of the Ships and Their Aircraft*. London: Conway Maritime, 1988.

Roskill, Stephen W. *The War at Sea, 1939–1945*. Vols. 1 and 2. London: Her Majesty's Stationery Office, 1954–1956.

ANDREW LAMBERT

**Arnold, John** (1736–1799), British watchmaker who made significant contributions to the development of the chronometer. One of the most significant figures in the history of precision timekeeping, John Arnold can be said to have contributed more to the developed marine chronometer than any other maker. After apprenticeship to his father, the clockmaker John Arnold (1702–1776) of Bodmin in Cornwall, John spent two years in the Netherlands, returning to England and working for about five years as an itinerant mechanic. With money from a benefactor, William McGuire of St. Albans, he set himself up in business at Devereux Court. London, in May 1762. Ambitious and determined, Arnold prospered from the outset and in 1764 was introduced at court, presenting George III with a miniature watch set in a ring, for which he received £500, the first of a number of royal commissions.

Inspired by the work of John Harrison, in 1767 Arnold took up the manufacture of marine timekeepers, a business on which he would concentrate for the rest of his life. Although three timekeepers that he supplied for James Cook's second voyage of discovery to the Pacific in 1772 did not perform well, he soon introduced significant improvements in his designs, making them accurate and reliable yet simple and inexpensive. In 1769 Arnold and his wife, Margaret (1744–1789), produced their only son, John Roger Arnold (1769–1843), and the family moved to St. James Street that same year. In 1771 they moved shop again, to 2 Adam Street, and in 1779 set up a manufactory at Arnold's new home, Well Hall, at Eltham in Kent. A new shop was opened at 102 Cornhill, in the City of London, in 1783, and Arnold became a member of the Clockmakers' Company the same year. He was admitted to the livery of that company in 1796.

In 1775 Arnold patented the compensation balance and helical balance spring for chronometers, followed in 1782 by the invention of terminal curves for the spring. In 1779 his celebrated watch No. 36 was tested with great success at the Royal Observatory in Greenwich, and Arnold's supporter Alexander Dalrymple, a hydrographer, stated in a published account of the watch's trial that it should be termed a "chronometer," the first modern use of the term. From about 1783 Arnold took his son as an apprentice and then into partnership, trading as John Arnold & Son. After his retirement in 1796, his son continued the business at the Cornhill shop. Arnold died at Well Hall, Eltham, on August 25, 1799.

[*See also* Navigational Instruments, *subentry on* Measurement of Time.]

## Bibliography

Betts, Jonathan. "Arnold and Earnshaw: The Practicable Solution." In *The Quest for Longitude: The Proceedings of the Longitude Symposium, Harvard University, Cambridge, Massachusetts, November 4–6, 1993*, edited by William J. H. Andrewes, pp. 311–328. Cambridge, Mass.: Harvard University, 1996.

Mercer, V. *John Arnold & Son, Chronometer Makers, 1762–1843.* London: Antiquarian Horological Society, 1972.

Staeger, Hans. *100 Jahre Präzisionsuhren von John Arnold bis Arnold & Frodsham, 1763–1862. 100 Years of Precision Time-keepers from John Arnold to Arnold & Frodsham, 1763–1862.* Filderstadt, Germany: Eigenverlag, 1997.

JONATHAN BETTS

# Art

This entry contains two subentries:

An Overview
Historiography

---

## An Overview

Until the end of the sixteenth century, maritime art as a specific genre, involving specialized artists, did not exist. It is generally acknowledged that the "invention" of maritime art took place in the Netherlands. Nevertheless, works of art with a maritime character have been made in almost every society in which ships and the sea have played a significant role. In Mesopotamia and around the Mediterranean, navigation was an important element of daily life, resulting in countless painted murals, sculptures, pottery, and mosaics with images of ships and ports.

Throughout the Middle Ages, ships were depicted in books, on tapestries, or in paintings portraying biblical, classical, and contemporary historical events. The wanderings of mythical seafarers such as Ulysses were a popular theme. Artists illustrated biblical stories, including Noah's ark and the miraculous catch of fish, as well as events from the lives of saints who traveled by ship, such as Saint Paul and Saint Nicholas. The best-known rendering of a medieval maritime event is the Bayeux Tapestry, the pictorial report of William the Conqueror's fleet invading England in 1066.

A typical ship-related theme of the Middle Ages is the "Ship of Fools," a vessel filled with human foolishness. Hieronymus Bosch (c. 1450–1516), who lived in the duchy of Brabant in the Netherlands, was one of many artists to paint this symbolic ship. Present-day painters and draftsmen have continued to use the ship as a metaphor in their comments on society, the "ship of state," an image already used by Plato in his *Republic* (c. 360 B.C.E.), being the most common form. Political cartoonists who compare their country or its government to a ship—sometimes rudderless or running aground—can be found all over the world.

In the later Middle Ages maritime enterprises were increasingly depicted as the background of altarpieces or portraits. This was especially the case in the prosperous coastal regions of Europe: the Hanseatic towns and Flanders in the north and in the seaports of Italy. Hans Memling (c. 1433–1494) and Vittore Carpaccio (c. 1455–1526) both painted the ships of their hometowns, Bruges and Venice, respectively. They both did so on altarpieces illustrating the Legend of Saint Ursula, who traveled by ship in the company of eleven thousand virgins before dying a martyr's death.

### The Rise of Marine Painting in the Netherlands

The Flemish artist Pieter Brueghel the Elder (c. 1525–1569) is a key figure in the development of maritime art as a separate genre. In his broad oeuvre there is a specific group of works that show more than a passing interest in ships. Several subspecialties of marine painting in later eras are already present in his work: the ship portrait, the port view, and the storm at sea. Brueghel found patrons for these subjects in the coastal towns of Flanders. Antwerp had become one of the busiest ports in the world and an important center of print- and mapmaking, two disciplines that influenced the first generation of specialized marine painters.

Around 1600 the economic center had moved north, to the recently formed Dutch Republic. The affluent burghers and the local government bodies formed an excellent market for shipping scenes. Hendrick Cornelisz Vroom (c. 1566–1640) is the most important figure of a group of Dutch painters who portrayed, using a bright palette, the source of their patrons' affluence—proud merchantmen in the roadstead of Amsterdam—as well as naval battles and other events at sea. For the first time in history, marine painting had become a separate trade, practiced by scores of masters. In Vroom's wake, marine painting developed in different directions. Some marine painters can be classified as landscape painters, such as Jan van Goyen (1596–1656), who painted inland shipping in the watery Dutch landscape. Others specialized in storms and shipwrecks or beach scenes. Willem van de Velde the Younger

(1633–1707) created a wide range of works, depicting ships in harbor as well as dramatic naval battles. Whereas the Dutch painted mainly realistic marines, Italy was the land of the idealized, classical port scene. Claude Lorrain (1600–1682), who was French by birth but lived in Rome most of his life, painted seaports surrounded by imaginary antique buildings and colonnades under a brilliant Mediterranean sky.

## Art and Empire

Maritime art in Holland and similar countries—and at a later date in England—flourished in times that their maritime economies prospered. By the end of the seventeenth century England had become the leading maritime power in the world; during the same period the country also took the lead in maritime art. Two Dutchmen played an important role in this development: the Van de Veldes, the draftsman and painter Willem van de Velde the Elder (c. 1611–1693) and his son, the painter Willem van de Velde the Younger. In 1672, ironically during the third Anglo-Dutch War, they had crossed the North Sea to live in Greenwich, working there as the first (although unofficial) maritime court painters. Their influence is visible in the works of many eighteenth-century masters, including Peter Monamy (c. 1670–1749), Samuel Scott (1701/1703–1772), and Charles Brooking (c. 1723–1749). The "Dutch school" in England was characterized by its accurate depiction of ships, harmoniously arranged, with naturalistic effects of wind and light at sea. Marine painters glorified England's mighty ports, its navy, and its East India Company.

Apart from Claude Lorrain, who worked in Italy, French artists of the seventeenth century never had the same interest in the sea as their colleagues from rivaling seafaring nations. Neither did they receive much encouragement from the court or other authorities. Under Louis XV this changed. Claude-Joseph Vernet (1714–1789) even received a royal commission to paint the seaports of France. The thirteen paintings of the resulting series (now in the Musée de la Marine in Paris) show the influence of Lorrain.

In Russia the interest in marine art followed the country's rise as a maritime power. In 1771 Catherine the Great commissioned the German artist Jacob Philipp Hackert (1737–1807), court painter in Naples, to paint the Russian victory over the Turkish fleet in the battle of Chesmé (1770). She sent a squadron to Leghorn to show him her warships, and even had one of these ships blown up, in order to provide the artist with the best possible study material.

By far the most famous of the eighteenth-century maritime painters on the European Continent is the Italian Giovanni Antonio Canal, called Canaletto (1697–1768). Although his elegant *vedute* paintings of Venice are crowded with gondolas and other watercraft, ships in Canaletto's work primarily serve to accompany the architecture of the embankments.

## Romantic Seascapes

In the age of Romanticism, maritime themes became fashionable among a much larger group of artists than the specialists. The sea, symbolizing the unfathomable depths of the human soul, was the perfect medium to convey a range of human emotion. Romantic seascapes are often full of drama. One of the most striking examples is *The Raft of the Medusa* (1819; Musée du Louvre, Paris), by Théodore Géricault (1791–1824). This blood-curdling painting is one of the best-known maritime works of art ever made (and one of the largest, measuring 491 by 717 centimeters (16 × 23.5 feet).

Despite a growing interest in sea painting on the European Continent, England remained the center of maritime art. The first indication of a radical change in approach was already visible in the exotic and very personal views of the unknown world of the Pacific by William Hodges (1744–1797) and in the dramatic sea battles of Philippe-Jacques de Loutherbourg (1740–1812). The most radical innovator was Joseph Mallord William Turner (1775–1851). His seascapes, for example, *The Fighting Téméraire Tugged to Her Last Berth* (1839; National Gallery, London), represent a distinct break with the past. They have become almost abstract, brilliant renderings of light in sparkling colors. In his bold handling of paint Turner may be said to have painted as an Impressionist before the term existed.

Some American painters of the Romantic period excelled in telling stories on canvas. *Brook Watson and the Shark*, painted by John Singleton Copley (1738–1815) to commemorate an attack by a shark in Havana harbor (1778; Museum of Fine Arts, Boston), is a good example. The same wish to involve the spectator in an important event is expressed in *The Death of Nelson* (1808; National Maritime Museum, Greenwich, England), by Copley's countryman Benjamin West (1738–1820), who, like Copley, lived in Europe most of his life.

Romantic sea painting had many faces. A sharp contrast with Géricault's thrilling drama and Turner's striking colors are the silent seascapes, filled with doom, by the German painter Caspar David Friedrich (1774–1840). His painting *The Arctic Sea* (1823–1824; Kunsthalle, Hamburg, Germany) is a fine example.

During most of the nineteenth century marine painters were among the leading artists of their time. In Victorian England Clarkson Stanfield (1793–1867), Edward William Cooke (1811–1880), and others were extremely popular. In France Théodore Gudin (1802–1880) and Eugène Isabey (1803–1886) and in the Netherlands Johannes Christiaan Schotel (1787–1838) had a similar standing.

### Ship Portraits and Souvenirs

In the heyday of the sailing ship, the ship portrait was a typical phenomenon of marine painting. Painters of such portraits were usually skilled tradesmen rather than inspired artists. Their studio was a shop, and they sold pictures in watercolor and sometimes in oil paint to sea captains, shipowners, and passengers. In Catholic countries the ship portrait was connected to the old tradition of votive pictures. Most harbor towns had one or more of these "pier head artists," for example, the Roux family in Marseilles, Nicolas Cammillieri (1772/3–1860) in Malta, and Jacob Spin (1806–1875) in Amsterdam. Hoboken, New Jersey, was the base of Antonio Nicolo Gasparo Jacobsen (1850–1921), an American painter of Italian and Danish descent. He was one of the few painters who survived the rise of both the steamship and photography.

On the coasts of China the manufacture and sale of souvenir views of Canton and other harbor towns, with European sailing ships in the anchorages, became a flourishing industry.

### Impressionism

New movements in art gave rise to different visions of the sea. After 1850 painters in France and elsewhere left their studios to make oil paintings *en plein air* (in the open air), unlike those in earlier generations who never took more than their drawing utensils with them. The seacoasts of Europe became popular among artists of the new Impressionist movement, such as Paul Signac and Georges Seurat. In Normandy and Brittany, and on the coasts of Holland, Germany, and Denmark, artists searched for picturesque inspiration, be it among fishermen and their ships or the light of the seacoast.

The painting that gave the Impressionist movement its name was in fact a marine painting: *Impression, Sunrise* (Musée Marmottan, Paris), by Claude Monet (1840–1926), painted in Le Havre in 1872. Similar themes may be found in the works of Winslow Homer (1836–1910) and James Abbott McNeill Whistler (1834–1903), two American painters who broke away from the documentary style of sea painting of the Victorian period. Homer's marine paintings often focus on human activity at sea. Whistler is hard to place as a marine painter, as he was constantly experimenting with the effects of light and water. He was one of the first maritime artists to be influenced by Japanese art. His painting *Nocturne: Blue and Gold: Old Battersea Bridge, 1872–1873* (Tate Gallery, London) is derived partly from a woodcut by Hiroshige.

### Marine Art in the Twentieth and Twenty-First Centuries

The arms race of the European powers, which began in the last decades of the nineteenth century, is reflected in the maritime art of the twentieth century. Hans Bohrdt (1857–1945), Claus Bergen (1885–1964), and other painters illustrated and glorified the actions of the German war fleet during World War I as well as in the years of the Third Reich. Britain has an even stronger and far longer tradition of war artists, starting with the Van de Veldes in the seventeenth century. Norman Wilkinson (1878–1971) was the most outstanding British marine painter of the interwar years. The Royal Navy has continued into the twenty-first century its unique tradition of employing war artists to document its actions at sea.

Interest in maritime pictures has declined since the sailing ship was replaced by the steamship and eventually by the motor vessel. One group of artists considered this change a new challenge: the designers of posters for shipping companies. The most influential artist in this respect is Adolphe Mouron (1901–1968), better known as Cassandre, who created the ultimate evocation of a ship's hull on his impressive poster of the French liner *Normandie* (1935).

Impressionism was in fact the last avant-garde movement in art to produce works that can be labeled marine art. Maritime art in the sense of a more or less faithful account of the reality of the maritime world has become in the twenty-first century a niche industry, producing a commodity for which there is a steady demand in certain circles of ship lovers, collectors, and those with a professional interest in shipping.

[*See also* Artists; Bergen, Claus; Homer, Winslow; Painting; Tapestry; Turner, J. M. W.; Velde, Willem van de, Elder; Velde, Willem van de, Younger; Vroom, Hendrick Cornelisz; *and* Wilkinson, Norman.]

## Bibliography

Archibald, E. H. H. *The Dictionary of Sea Painters in Europe and America.* Woodbridge, U.K.: Antique Collectors Club, 2000.

Bellec, F., P. H. Bosscher, A. Erftemeijer, and Patrick Duval. *Sillages Neerlandais: La vie maritime dans l'art des Pays-Bas; Kunst in het kielzog: Het maritieme leven in de Nederlandse kunst.* Zutphen, The Netherlands: De Walburg Pers, 1989. Text in French and Dutch.

Bol, Laurens J. *Die holländische Marinemalerei des 17. Jahrhunderts.* Braunschweig, Germany: Klinkhardt and Biermann, 1973.

Buchholz, Karsten. *Ship Portrait Artists.* Hamburg, Germany: Buchholz Art Information Systems, 1997.

Cordingly, David. *Marine Painting in England, 1700–1900.* London: Studio Vista, 1974.

Cordingly, David. *Ships and Seascapes: An Introduction to Maritime Prints, Drawings, and Watercolors.* London: Philip Wilson, 1997.

Gaunt, William. *Maritime Painting: An Historical Survey.* London: Secker and Warburg; Amsterdam: De Arbeiderspers, 1975.

Hansen, Hans Jürgen. *Deutsche Marinemalerei. Schiffsdarstellungen, maritime Genrebilder, Meeres- und Küstenlandschaften.* Oldenburg, Germany: Gerhard Stalling, 1977.

Johnston, Paul Forsythe. "The Origins of Marine Art." In *Schatkamer: Veertien opstellen over maritiem-historische onderwerpen aangeboden aan Leo M. Akveld,* edited by S. de Meer et al., pp. 115–127. Franeker, Netherlands: Van Wijnen, 2002.

Scholl, Lars U. *Deutsche Marinemalerei, 1830–2000.* Helgoland, Germany: Maren Knauss, 2002.

Taylor, James. *Marine Painting: Images of Sail, Sea, and Shore.* London: Studio Editions, 1995.

REMMELT DAALDER

# Historiography

It is generally accepted that maritime art was first introduced in the Netherlands at the beginning of the seventeenth century. Though Portugal's maritime history predates that of the Netherlands, Portuguese maritime art never developed along the same lines. In Britain, which became the dominant maritime power at the end of the seventeenth century, maritime art developed from the winter of 1672–1673, when Willem van de Velde settled in Greenwich.

## Dutch Maritime Art

Because of the long history of Dutch maritime painting, its historiography provides a valuable case study for the overall historiography concerning maritime art and seascapes. According to Wolfgang Stechow, in his book *Dutch Landscape Painting of the Seventeenth Century* (1966), the basic criterion in formally defining a seascape has not so much been the expanse of water (although this is important) as the prominence of sailing boats in the composition of the work. A decisive element, in addition to a strong emphasis on the calm or agitated surface of the water, will be the relationship between the sailing boats (as the only commanding vertical or diagonal objects), the water, and the sky. It is apparent that this relationship is likely to parallel in many ways the relationship between land, sky, and trees or buildings in a landscape. Yet the fundamental idea that a seascape shows water and shipping—and thereby distinguishes itself from a landscape—is not sufficient for a complete definition. Beaches, coastal views, and river and lake scenes are considered maritime paintings as well. Often it is not quite clear whether a painting depicts a seascape, river view, or lake scene. Additionally, maritime art includes "pure" seascapes without ships, ship portraits, and portraits of naval heroes (with backgrounds depicting the sea and ships). Finally, there are allegorical marine paintings.

In the literature on the subject, art historians have written of "marine painting" as an independent genre only from the beginning of the twentieth century. Prior to that era, marine painting was considered a subcategory of landscape painting, as was the cityscape. The first general view of the subject was given by Fred C. Willis in his book *Die niederländische Marinemalerei* (Dutch Marine Painting; 1911). Willis divided marine painting into three periods. During the first period, which he called "Das Marine-Historienbild" (The Maritime History Picture), marine painting was mostly documentary; the Dutch artists Hendrick Cornelisz. Vroom (1566–1640), Cornelis Claesz van Wieringen (1580–1633), Adam Willarts (1577–1664), and Andries van Eertvelt (1590–1652) were prominent. These early marine artists painted for the most part recognizable historical subjects, like sea battles and triumphal processions. The focus was the ship's portrait, an accurate depiction of a specific ship, with less emphasis on the natural surroundings and the water. Because of the exacting nature of the paintings and the artists' long search for data on the subjects (which had sometimes taken place many years before), the process was long and laborious. These paintings were therefore very expensive and were completed almost entirely on commission.

Willis defined the second period as "Der graue Ton und die Stimmungsmalerei" (The Gray Tone and Atmospheric

**Art Historiography.** *An Engagement between the Spanish and the Dutch* by Cornelisz Verbeecq (c. 1590–1637), c. 1630. Verbeecq's bold brushwork in depicting the sea and sky placed him ahead of his contemporaries. © NATIONAL MARITIME MUSEUM, LONDON

Painting), Jan Porcellis (c. 1580–1632), his son Julius Porcellis (1610–1654), and Simon de Vlieger (1601–1653) were practitioners of this style. Their paintings depict everyday, nonspecific maritime scenes, often including unknown inland vessels. Paintings in this "tonal" style are characterized by earthy colors, such as brown, green, and gray. Paint was applied swiftly and in thin layers; the paintings were less expensive to produce and were therefore accessible to many.

In the third and final period, entitled "Die Erneuerung des Kolorismus. Effektstück und Vedute" (The Renewal of the Coloration, Effect Piece, and Vedute), a synthesis in marine painting was achieved. The coloration of the first period was combined with the atmospheric painting of the second period. At the end of the seventeenth century, artists like Lieve Verschuier (1630–1686) and Ludolf Backhuysen (c. 1631–1708) painted recognizable subjects again, in a colorful and attractive style. Somewhat surprisingly,

Willis had placed the paintings of Willem van de Velde the Younger (1633–1707) in the second period. Willis saw him as a representative of transition and his work as a synthesis of the historical and graphic traditions; for many art historians, Van de Velde the Younger's choice of subjects and his manner of painting in his later works place him more accurately in the third period.

In the surveys that appeared after Willis, there is harmony in the cyclic thought on the evolution of marine painting. The classification set up by Willis was adopted in broad outlines by later authors. The ideas on rise-prosperity-decline were formulated strongly by the art historian Wilhelm von Bode. In the chapter "Das Seebild bei den Holländer" (Dutch Marine Painting) in his book *Die Meister der holländischen und vlämischen Malerschulen* (Masters of the Dutch and Flemish Schools of Painting, 1917) he writes that the "tonal" phase shaped the flourishing period in marine painting of the seventeenth century. According to von Bode, tonal painting was "kün-stlerisch womöglich noch höher" (even more appreci-ated artistically) than the work of Jan van de Cappelle (c. 1624–1679), Jacob Cuyp (1594–c. 1651), and van de Velde. Bode spoke about the marine painters at the end of the seventeenth century in a negative manner. The final line is significant: "In diesem trauerigen Abschluss nahert sich die Seemalerei der Bakhuyzen und genossen wieder den Anfangen unter einem Vroom und van Antum" (In this sad termination, marine painting of Bakhuyzen and con-temporaries draws near to the beginning of, among others, Vroom and Van Antum).

The next author who treated Dutch marine painting was Admiral Lionel Preston. In his book *Sea and River Painters of the Netherlands in the Seventeenth Century* (1937) he refined the categories within the classification of Willis. Preston divided marine painting in the seventeenth century into four periods, beginning with the "Panoramists." These artists, working in the period 1597–1625, focused mainly on panoramas with an aim of simplifying the composition. By utilizing a high point of view, the painters achieved a composition in which all elements were distinguishable. By 1614 the phase of "Transition" had developed within the group of Panoramists. Several artists tried to paint the sea in a more naturalistic style and searched for inspiration in contemporary Italian painting. Preston called the following period that of the "Early Realists"; this era lasted from 1625 until 1645. The marine painters in this phase focused on rendering the natural landscape and emphasized waves, air, and weather conditions. The presence of ships was of secondary importance. Preston thought that the work of artists such as Jan and Julius Porcellis and Esaias van de Velde (1591–1630) reflected an exact reality. The phase of the "Mature Realists" began in 1645 and lasted until 1675. The progress in this period, compared to the Early Real-ists, is remarkable. Preston thought that the atmospheric perspective was portrayed more accurately, that the palette of colors was broader, and that a greater transparency was achieved. Above all, the beautiful atmosphere and wide vista attracted attention. Finally, there was the period of decline, the "Decadence," running from 1675 until 1700. Preston considered the return to the dramatic style and strong individual colors, for example in the works of Abraham Storck (1644–1708) and Ludolf Backhuysen, as a negative development. According to Preston, technique as well as the painting of atmosphere deteriorated at the end of the seventeenth century.

Exhibitions often represent the current interest in par-ticular subjects, and the catalogues offer a representative view of the research on these subjects. Moreover, they present a portrait of an era. Shortly after World War II, two exhibitions were held in which marine art was intro-duced as an independent subject. Both exhibitions were organized in Rotterdam; the first took place in the winter of 1945–1946 in Museum Boymans and was entitled *Het Nederlandse zee- en riviergezicht in de XVIIe eeuw* (The Dutch Seascape and River Paintings during the Seventeenth Century). The second, in the Maritiem Museum Prins Hen-drik, was entitled *Van Vroom tot Van de Velde. 17e eeuwse Nederlandse zeeschilderijen uit Engels bezit* (From Vroom to van de Velde: Seventeenth-Century Dutch Seascapes in British Possession). The introduction to the catalogue that accompanied the exhibition in Museum Boymans must be viewed in light of the freedom regained after World War II. Director J. C. Ebbinge Wubben wrote that at the end of the sixteenth and beginning of the seventeenth centuries, close and daily contact with the sea and rivers, through voyages of discovery, merchant travels, and battles at sea, had contributed significantly to the economic flourishing of the Dutch Republic. Subsequently, the representation of these events in the form of sea and river paintings was connected indissolubly with the history of the country. The exhibition showed how the representation of the water was intertwined with the history of the Dutch people. Shortly after the war, at a time when the Netherlands had to be rebuilt, Ebbinge Wubben expressed the desire that the Netherlands, and Rotterdam in particular, would experi-ence a new period of flowering and prosperity, just as it had in the seventeenth century.

The exhibition at the Museum Boymans showed sev-enty-eight paintings of thirty-one different artists. The second and third phases within the evolution of marine painting received the most attention. Apparently there was little appreciation for the early phase. The standard was the atmospheric depiction of reality; the works of the earlier "documentary" artists were exhibited merely as predeces-sors of paintings from the flourishing period. Although the reflection of Bode's ideas is still present, after 1950 a change is notable in the consideration of marine painting and seascapes.

The exhibition in the Maritiem Museum Prins Hendrik in 1950 contained paintings from British public and private collections. In total, seventy paintings by thirty-seven dif-ferent artists were exhibited, and all three periods received equal attention. In the accompanying catalog, the early phase was treated in a more positive way than in the exhi-bition in Museum Boymans five years earlier. This change in approach was obvious and probably cohered with the fact that these works of art were produced with great attention to detail. Paintings in the exhibition served a maritime historical purpose, more than an art historical one.

A third exhibition, focusing on seventeenth-century marine painting, was put on display in 1964 in the Dordrechts Museum. Under the title *Zee-, rivier- en oevergezichten. Nederlandse schilderijen uit de zeventiende eeuw* (Sea, River and Coastal Views: Dutch Paintings from the Seventeenth Century), 111 paintings by 65 artists were shown. In the exhibition catalog, director L. J. Bol divided marine painting into four parts: the early marinists, the tonal generation, the period of the silvery light, and the era of the van de Veldes. It is true that Bol arranged the periods in almost the same way as Willis, but he also thought of Willis's classification as too rigid and fixed. He thought that the artists could not be classified in certain phases; he also maintained that some of them painted in a tonal manner while occasionally producing a ship's portrait as well. Bol's starting point was not a certain order. He strongly advocated the early marine painters, writing that their underestimation was connected with the popularity of the Impressionist aesthetic concerning synthesis, tonality, atmosphere, space, and light.

The viewing of the national art of painting from the end of the sixteenth until the twentieth centuries was determined by the art of the nineteenth century, that is, the art characterized as Realism and Impressionism. In this context, the early marine painters were disparaged, for they "only" painted ship's portraits. Bol argued that the early marine artists for that very reason painted ships with carved sterns, picturesque rope work, white, gray, and brown sails, and colorful flags. The sky served as a background against which the rigging and sails stood out triumphantly. The water was an element of service: it carried the ships. The high waves appeared as a feared enemy, and large fish and monsters emphasized the dangers of the sea. According to Bol, the demands of atmosphere, tonality, and other Impressionist characteristics were actually compatible with this view. Here, in the early evolution of marine painting, other capacities played an important role: strong and bold colors, a tight design, and a festive, decorative style. The artists who belonged to this phase chose a high horizon in order to show a multitude of elements. This can be compared with the artists of still-life art who painted a high back edge of a set table. In both situations, all elements received equal attention from the artist; the composition concerned a "display" in which all objects would be equally visible.

A few years after the exhibition in Dordrecht, Bol published a survey on Dutch seventeenth-century marine painting, *Die holländische Marinemalerei des 17. Jahrhunderts* (Dutch Marine Painting of the 17th Century, 1973). In this study he classified the subject into three parts. First there was "Die farbige dokumentarische Marinemalerei" (The colorful documentary marine painting), then "Die tonalische Marinemalerei" (The tonal marine painting), and then "Von neuer, gezügelter Farbigkeit bis zur Buntheit" (From new, restrained colorfulness to piedness). Bol limited himself to the northern Netherlands. In his account he left out artists who worked in pen and ink because he regarded them as draftsmen. In his book, Bol incorporated many of the remarks he had made in his 1964 catalog. In his introduction he wrote "nicht diejenigen, die berühmt sind, bedürfen der Fürsprache, sondern jene, die unverdient geschmälert und vergessen wurden" (not the ones who are renowned need intercession, but those who are narrowed and undeservedly forgotten). In short Bol pleaded for a renewed judgment and rehabilitation of the early sea painters. Here, Bol refers to his own attempt to avoid value judgments: "auch wer sein Urteil frei und unabhängig wähnt, entgeht nicht der Bindung an das, was die eigene Zeit diktiert oder jedenfalls vorzieht" (even one who fancies one's judgment to be free and independent does not escape the tie to the dictates, or at least preferences, of one's own time). Bol acknowledged that his view on marine painting perhaps could be dictated by later artistic developments.

Two more recent exhibitions that presented a survey on Dutch marine painting were *Mirror of Empire: Dutch Marine Art of the Seventeenth Century,* shown in three U.S. museums in 1990–1991 (the Minneapolis Institute of Arts, the Toledo Museum of Art, and the Los Angeles County Museum of Art) and *Lof der Zeevaart: de Hollandse zeeschilders van de 17de eeuw* (Praise of Ships and the Sea: The Dutch Marine Painters of the Seventeenth Century), held in 1996–1997 in Museum Boijmans Van Beuningen in Rotterdam and the Staatliche Museum in Berlin.

*Mirror of Empire* focused on the historical aspects of Dutch marine art. The exhibition showed not only paintings but also drawings, prints, and cartographic material (maps, pilots, and globes) as well. A catalog was compiled by George Keyes. In his introduction he wrote that marine painting is the stepchild of the Dutch Golden Age, as not many studies and exhibitions have been devoted to the subject. Keyes wrote "until now it has never been the subject of a major exhibition surveying the full scope of the theme." According to Keyes, only a few monographs and partial studies preceded his catalog; he thus disregarded the influence of the surveys of Willis, Preston, and (especially) Bol, mentioning their studies only in a note.

Keyes's intention was to "encompass the range, quality, and importance of Dutch marine art and the way it mirrored the prosperity, aspirations, and values of seventeenth-century Holland." Among the 142 items exhibited were 55 paintings by 24 different artists. The choice to limit the number of paintings in order to have the works representative of outstanding marine painters was a deliberate one. Most of them were represented with one, two, or three paintings. Exceptions were made for Hendrik Cornelisz Vroom and his son Cornelis Vroom (1591–1661), represented by five works each, and for Ludolf Backhuysen, represented by six paintings; there were nine paintings by the van de Veldes.

Keyes divided the subject into seven different phases, resembling the arrangements made by Willis, Preston, and Bol. The first phase was that of the sixteenth-century origins, followed by the second phase, Hendrik Vroom and the beginnings of Dutch marine art. The third phase presented Jan Porcellis and the emerging tonal phase of Dutch marine painting. Then came the fourth period, Simon de Vlieger and his transformation of the legacy of Porcellis. This led to the fifth period, the era of Willem van de Velde the Elder and the return to the history piece. The overlap with landscape, circa 1650–1670, was treated by Keyes as the sixth. He ended his introduction with the seventh period, the final years of the seventeenth century, with Reinier Nooms, Ludolf Backhuysen, and other contemporaries of Willem van de Velde the Younger.

In addition to Keyes's introduction, the catalog contained other interesting articles as well. James Welu wrote about seascapes that are discernible in Dutch genre paintings. These paintings show that in Dutch interiors these works of art could be found in almost every type of setting. A study of these "paintings within paintings" indicates that maritime imagery had numerous meanings for the seventeenth-century viewer. Dirk de Vries contributed an article on Dutch marine cartography in the seventeenth century.

The repertoire of maritime subjects developed by the Dutch traditionally consisted of three categories: biblical, mythological, and moralizing subjects; historical events; and ship's portraits. After a period in which marine painting emerged for the first time as part of biblical and mythological subjects, around 1600 an independent genre originated with the Haarlem artist Hendrik Cornelisz Vroom as its most important representative. Vroom's main merits were his interest in historical events and his preference for exact description and details. Vroom, his fellow citizen Cornelis Claesz van Wieringen, and Adam Willarts from Utrecht dominated marine painting at the beginning of the

seventeenth century. For the further course of seventeenth-century marine painting, Keyes explicitly connected the developments with this triumvirate. In this way Jan Porcellis, the founder and most important representative of the monochrome, tonal phase in marine painting, was presented as a possible pupil of Vroom. Furthermore, Keyes points out that later marine painters continuously built on themes developed by Vroom and his contemporaries at an earlier stage. Simon de Vlieger, for example, showed a keen interest in the theme of the parade, though earlier sea painters had already depicted this subject. Willem van de Velde the Elder specialized in large-scale ship's portraits, returning to Vroom's tradition as well. Keyes wrote that with Willem van de Velde the Younger, who also produced large-scale historical seascapes, Dutch marine painting had come full circle.

In *Lof der Zeevaart*, Dutch marine paintings were presented as a coherent group. A total of 110 paintings by 49 different artists was presented. Here the aim was exclusively to study Dutch marine painting and its stylistic development. The organizers tried to isolate the paintings from their maritime context by diminishing the role of ship's types and historical events. By transferring the exhibition to two art museums, the artistic aspect of the paintings was emphasized. *Lof der Zeevaart* had some resemblance to *Mirror of Empire*, but there were also many differences. In Rotterdam and Berlin all the important history pieces that had played a key role in the development of the genre were gathered. The importance of marine painting was also underscored by the fact that many large paintings were on display. The exhibition also presented works of art of several lesser known yet important masters. An additional section was devoted to the renowned "pen paintings" by Willem van de Velde the Elder and others. In his essay "What One Can Do with a Pen: Pen Paintings and Maritime Scenes," Friso Lammertse discussed the history and technique of pen paintings, a specialty practiced exclusively in the northern Netherlands, and there confined to the subject of marine painting. In his essay "Maritime History in Paintings: Seascapes as Historical Sources," Remmelt Daalder explored the question of why many maritime history paintings date from long after the event they portray.

The same classifications of seventeenth-century marine painting are used over and over by art historians. With the classifications, as distinguished by Willis and others, one must take into consideration that the gradual development of marine painting in the seventeenth century is a construction of art historians. Bol was the first scholar who warned against the danger of classifying. He argued that all marine painters contributed in their own way to the development of the genre and should not be judged categorically, but rather according to their own merits.

## United Kingdom

British maritime painting really began with the arrival of Willem van de Velde the Elder and his son Willem van de Velde the Younger in England in the winter of 1672–1673. Their sudden departure from the Netherlands at a time of war might appear strange, but there were a number of reasons for their apparently unpatriotic behavior. David Cordingly mentions several in the exhibition catalog, *The Art of the Van de Veldes: Paintings and Drawings by the Great Dutch Marine Artists and Their English Followers* (1982). One of the most pressing was the invasion of the Netherlands by the French. It seems probable that domestic pressures also encouraged the van de Veldes to move. The elder van de Velde had a turbulent marriage, while that of his son was noted for its brevity. There were also maritime reasons for the van de Veldes to choose England as their new home. England was a major maritime nation: since the sea and shipping played almost as great a part in the life of this country as they did in Holland, there was obviously plenty of work for marine artists. This was encouraged by a declaration issued by King Charles II in June 1672 in which he invited Dutch people to settle in England. This offer was soon taken up by a number of artists, engravers, mapmakers, and craftsmen.

Attention has been paid to the Dutch and English period of the van de Veldes and their studio assistants and English followers such as Peter Monamy, Samuel Scott, and Charles Brooking. On these and other early marine painters, monographs have been written since the exhibition catalog of 1982. F. B. Cockett concentrates on the first marine painters in England in his book *Early Sea Painters 1660–1730: The Group Who Worked in England under the Shadow of the Van de Veldes* (1995). Cockett writes that in the time of the van de Veldes, other artists were active as marine painters, not only as their assistants or pupils. His book contains biographies of artists like Isaac Sailmaker, Jacob Knyff, L. D. Man, and Lorenzo A. Castro. Cockett also discusses the late van de Velde studio (1690–1707) and the two chief studio assistants, Johan C. van der Hagen and Cornelis van de Velde. The final chapter is devoted to several artists who occasionally painted marines but whose work is rare and seldom seen.

An interesting publication with respect to British marine painting in the eighteenth century is Eleanor Sian Hughes's dissertation "Vessels of Empire: Eighteenth-Century British Marine Painting" (2001). She argues that eighteenth-century marine painting was not a minor genre appealing to nautical specialists but rather a practice at the center of a newly formalized art establishment, a genre comprehensible for and of interest to the public at large, and a narrative vehicle through which eighteenth-century Britons told themselves about heroic action and national virtue. It is Hughes's perception that, while British marine painters certainly collected works by the van de Veldes and in some cases copied them, marine painting in eighteenth-century Britain was a separate tradition in its own right. British marine painting responded to an entirely different set of historical events, as well as to the exigencies of public display, which were not an issue in seventeenth-century Holland. Paintings of recent naval engagements were in demand from naval patrons and served a very different purpose from that of Dutch seascapes. British marine paintings of the eighteenth century, precisely those that depict battles and military and naval strategies, were a vital part of the way the empire was imagined.

Denys Brook-Hart's publications about nineteenth century marine painting (1974) and British twentieth-century marine painting (1981) are written for collectors of British marine paintings and provide guidelines for buying a painting. However, they also provide useful information on themes in marine art, some undervalued or little-known artists, and landscape painters who painted seascapes as well.

## United States

The history of maritime art in the United States began roughly at the end of the eighteenth century, during the British colonial period. In his book *A History of American Marine Painting* (1968), John Wilmerding states that, generally speaking, interpreters of American art have tended to break down the category of landscape painting into the pure landscape of the mountains and open spaces (for example, the Rocky Mountain School and the artists of the American West), paintings of rivers and inland waterways (the Hudson River School and painters of Niagara Falls or other natural wonders), and views of shorelines, harbors, or the open sea. Wilmerding concludes that marine painting as such, by comparison to other areas of American art, has been neglected. Rather than subordinate marine painting under the general heading of landscape,

Wilmerding chooses to place the genre on an equal level of related, coherent interest. Marine painting in America was freer from contemporary precedent than landscape painting, which frequently felt the alternative pressures of idealization, illustration, or literary motifs. Because marine painting was less bound to precedent than other genres—for example, portraiture—in terms of subject or style, it often permitted experimental and fresh expressions.

Marine painting in America stands in close relationship to both the maritime economy and social conditions of the country, as shipping, trade, and the War of 1812 illustrate.

Wilmerding's study of marine painting addresses itself foremost to the Atlantic coast, especially New England, and extends from the period of colonization up to the age of steam. The sources of American marine painting as a special genre may be found primarily in English painting of the seventeenth and eighteenth centuries, and later in the great tradition of Dutch marine painting and, to a lesser degree, French Romantic painting of the eighteenth and nineteenth centuries. The story begins in portraiture, in the less noticed yet telling vignettes in the backgrounds. It moves steadily from the colonial sidelines onto the broad arena of a republican nation, as likenesses of people yield to likenesses of places. The early nineteenth century signals the coming of age of American painting. By then, the artists' successive concerns for topography, narrative, and documentary illustration, as well as the materials or methods of painting for their own sake, are of major interest.

[*See also* Artists; Backhuysen, Ludolf; Painting; Velde, Willem van de, Elder; Velde, Willem van de, Younger; *and* Vroom, Hendrick Cornelisz.]

### Bibliography

Archibald, E. H. H. *The Dictionary of Sea Painters of Europe and America*. 3d ed. Woodbridge, U.K.: Antique Collectors' Club, 2000.

Beer, Gerlinde de. *Ludolf Backhuysen: Sein Leben und Werk (1630–1708)*. Zwolle, Netherlands: Waanders, 2002.

Bellec, F., Ph. Bosscher, and A. Erftemeijer. *Sillages neerlandais: La vie maritime dans l'art des Pays-Bas ; Kunst in het kielzog: het maritieme leven in de Nederlandse kunst*. Zutphen, Netherlands: Walburg Pers, 1989.

Bode, Wilhelm von. *Die Meister der holländischen und vlämischen Malerschulen*. Leipzig, Germany: Seemann, 1917.

Bol, L. J. *Die holländische Marinemalerei des 17. Jahrhunderts*. Braunschweig, Germany: Klinkhardt and Biermann, 1973.

Cockett, F. B. *Early Sea Painters 1660–1730: The Group Who Worked in England under the Shadow of the Van de Veldes*. Woodbridge, U.K.: Antique Collectors' Club, 1995.

*Concise Catalogue of Oil Paintings in the National Maritime Museum*. Woodbridge, U.K.: Antique Collectors' Club, 1988.

Cordingly, David. *The Art of the Van de Veldes: Paintings and Drawings by the Great Dutch Marine Artists and Their English Followers*. London: National Maritime Museum, 1982.

Cordingly, David. *Marine Painting in England, 1700–1900*. London: Studio Vista, 1974.

Goedde, Lawrence Otto. *Tempest and Shipwreck in Dutch and Flemish Art: Convention, Rhetoric, and Interpretation*. University Park: Pennsylvania State University Press, 1989.

Hughes, Eleanor Sian. "Vessels of Empire: Eighteenth-Century British Marine Painting." Ph.D. diss., University of California, Berkeley, 2001.

Mertens, Sabine. *Seesturm und Schiffbruch: ein motivgeschichtliche Geschichte*. Hamburg: Ernst Kabel Verlag, 1987.

Middendorf, Ulrike. *Hendrik Jacobsz. Dubbels (1621–1707): Gemälde und Zeichnungen mit kritischem Oeuvrekatalog*. Freren, Germany: Luca Verlag, 1989.

Preston, Lionel. *Sea and River Painters of the Netherlands in the Seventeenth Century*. New York: Oxford University Press, 1937.

Preston, Rupert. *Seventeenth Century Marine Painting of the Netherlands*. Leigh-on-Sea, U.K.: F. Lewis, 1974.

Robinson, M. S. *Van de Velde: A Catalogue of the Paintings of the Elder and Younger Willem van de Velde*. 2 vols. Greenwich, U.K.: National Maritime Museum, 1990.

Russell, Margarita. *Jan van de Cappelle, 1624/6–1679*. Leigh-on-Sea, U.K.: F. Lewis, 1975.

Russell, Margarita. "Seascape into Landscape." In *Dutch Landscape: The Early Years: Haarlem and Amsterdam, 1590–1650*, edited by Christopher Brown, pp. 63–71. London: National Gallery, 1986.

Russell, Margarita. *Visions of the Sea: Hendrick C. Vroom and the Origins of Dutch Marine Painting*. Leiden, Netherlands: E. J. Brill, 1983.

Stechow, Wolfgang. *Dutch Landscape Painting of the Seventeenth Century*. New York: Phaidon, 1966.

Willis, Fred. C. *Die niederländische Marinemalerei*. Leipzig, Germany: Klinkhardt & Biermann, 1911.

Wilmerding, John. *A History of American Marine Painting*. Salem, Mass.: Peabody Museum, 1968.

RON J. W. M. BRAND

# Artists

This entry contains fifteen subentries:

American
Argentine
Belgian
Brazilian
British
Chilean
Danish
Dutch

French
German
Japanese
Portuguese
Russian
Spanish
Swedish

---

# American

Though very few American marine paintings predate the Revolution, the maritime nature of the colonial American economy was reflected in seventeenth- and eighteenth-century portraiture through occupational references. Sitters often appeared before windows that looked out upon ships at sea, often rendered in considerable detail. Few painters, however, expanded these small marine views into full-fledged seascapes, with the notable exception of John Singleton Copley's *Watson and the Shark* (1778).

By the early 1800s, the end of the war and the rise of an independent merchant marine had fostered a demand for maritime painting in America. Nonspecialist native artists had begun incorporating marine scenes into domestic wall murals, but the demand for documentary ship portraiture was met in two ways: at first by importing works executed by painters in foreign ports (primarily watercolors), and then by the immigration of European artists. Michele Felice Cornè (1752–1845) left Naples on Elias Hasket Derby's ship *Mount Vernon*, arriving in Salem, Massachusetts, in 1800. Working in gouache or oil, he became the town's most prominent painter, executing portraits, landscapes and seascapes, history paintings, and many images of local ships. His composition of two frigates in close action was widely copied, eventually becoming an iconic American image. He inspired younger native-born New Englanders to begin painting in the Mediterranean style; the best known of these New England artists is George Ropes (1788–1819), the deaf-mute son of a sea captain. Cornè eventually moved to Boston and then Newport, Rhode Island, as other opportunities arose, but he was soon joined by other immigrants who introduced strains of the British and Dutch academic traditions to the American scene.

Thomas Birch (1779–1851) emigrated from England as a boy in 1793. He began painting marine scenes, particularly dual frigate engagements, in earnest by the War of 1812, and he produced ambitious coastal views during the 1820s and 1830s. Through observation of his father's painting collection, which included works by Jacob van Ruisdael and Jan van Goyen, he adapted the tight draftsmanship and strong depth perspective of the Dutch tradition to American scenery. Robert Salmon (1775–1845), on the other hand, arrived from Scotland and England as a mature artist steeped in conventions of the British marine school. In Boston from 1828, he developed an increasingly controlled use of light to exhibit precise detailing and differentiation of massed figures. His use of chromatic glazes to build up depth and atmosphere was heartily embraced by the following generation. These two artists created a large corpus of detailed and accurate American coastal scenes that inspired many followers among younger artists.

The following generation of marine artists built upon the American interest in topography, narrative, and documentary illustration in one of two ways, each of which evolved into a distinct stylistic approach. The popularity and diversity of ship portraiture increased in parallel with America's maritime commerce, and specialist painters, commercially oriented and often self-taught, flourished. Perhaps the best known was James Buttersworth (1817–1894), who emigrated from England to arrive in New York in the heyday of the clipper ship, about 1845. Quickly establishing a relationship with the lithographers Currier & Ives, Buttersworth's vibrant and dynamic images of these famous vessels were widely disseminated. With little interest in atmosphere or the optical effects of light and air, he was most concerned with the technical presentation of these grand vessels in their full complexity. He highlighted their hallmarks of speed and elegance, from hull form to rigging. When the clipper era passed, Buttersworth transferred his attention to sleek racing yachts rather than to more mundane working craft. Other ship portrait painters developed equally distinctive specialties, whether focused regionally, like the smooth and muddy Mississippi River waters of James Guy Evans (active 1840–1859) and Edward Arnold (1816–1866), or industrially, like the river steamboats of James Bard (1815–1897) or the ocean liners of Antonio Jacobsen (1850–1921).

By the mid-nineteenth century, academically trained artists who aspired to more than ship portraiture developed strains of Romantic idealism from classical history painting. They embraced the grandeur of subjects like bustling harbors with palpable atmosphere to capture national expansionist sentiment. Fitz Henry Lane (1804–1865), William Bradford (1823–1892), and Martin Johnson Heade (1819–1904) excelled at creating vast expanses of nature replete with shipwrecks, impending storms, and towering icebergs that were simultaneously topographic and symbolic, resonating with Americans far beyond those working in maritime industries.

As ship portraiture declined in demand and quality late in the century, seascapes reached their apogee of creativity and public appeal. Moving away from the imperative to document specific locations, artists like Winslow Homer (1836–1910) and Albert Pinkham Ryder (1847–1917) created bold interpretations of the physical presence of the sea, while Thomas Eakins (1844–1916) reflected the era's interest in science, presenting small boats and rowers with optical precision that approximated the emotional proximity of a photograph.

[*See also* Art; Painting; Portraits; *and biographical entries on figures mentioned in this article.*]

### Bibliography

Brewington, M. V., and Dorothy Brewington. *The Marine Paintings and Drawings in the Peabody Museum.* 2d ed. Salem, Mass.: Peabody Museum of Salem, 1981. The most extensive resource for images of American marine paintings.

Stein, Roger. *Seascape and the American Imagination.* New York: Clarkson N. Potter, 1975. Catalog of an exhibition that offered a creative interpretation of the subject.

Wilmerding, John. *A History of American Marine Painting.* Boston: Little, Brown, 2000. Reprint of a book originally published in 1968. Although the interpretation is becoming dated, it remains the only comprehensive reference on the subject.

DANIEL FINAMORE

# Argentine

The coastline of Argentina has drawn mariners for hundreds, perhaps thousands of years. Archaeological evidence points to fishing activities on inland rivers and along the coasts. European exploration along the Argentine coast was evident by the late fifteenth century. Despite Argentina's long relationship with the sea, the history of maritime art in Argentina has not been constant, a reflection of the political and social influences on this South American treasure.

The earliest maritime images of Argentina came from the journals and logs of European explorers. Theodor de Bry chronicled Magellan's visit to Patagonia, producing images of Patagonia and of Magellan's ships along the Argentine coast. The diary of Ulrich Schmidel, published by Levinus Hulsius at Nuremberg in 1599, had some of the earliest-known views of the settlement at Nuestra Senora Santa Maria del Buen Aire (today's Buenos Aires), including images of the port being attacked by Querendi Indians in 1536 and a view of Buen Aire from the sea. Schmidel included images of the town, but he also drew the local fishing boats and trade ships that dotted the harbor. Other art from this period includes an anonymous engraving from 1610 depicting Sir Francis Drake on the Río de la Plata and a 1628 painting by the Dutch artist Johannes Vingboons of the second incarnation of Buenos Aires. By including key landmarks in the profile of the new Buenos Aires, Vingboons's painting provides a chronological marker for change along the South American coast.

Images of trade ships in the port of Buenos Aires are rarely seen, because for nearly two hundred years much of Spain's transatlantic trade was controlled by northern ports. Some black market trade did continue, and local shipping was allowed, but the ports in Peru and Panama captured the majority of the shipping until 1778. Images of Argentina's maritime history came from other sources. Between 1708 and 1713, the engineer José Bermúdez de Castro captured the changing face of Buenos Aires via a series of maps, each of which included drawings of the ships that found refuge in the Río de la Plata. Ferdinand Brambila Ferrari (1763–1834) is credited with paintings of Buenos Aires and Montevideo around 1794, when he visited the area with the Malaspina expedition.

By the mid-1800s, a change in the political environment brought about a new vision of Argentina, with an emphasis on nativist, traditional values. As the country looked inward, maritime art took a back seat, though artists such as César Hipólito Bacle (1790/94–1838) captured images of local fishermen and merchant ships off the shore of Buenos Aires (c. 1840), and Agosto Ballerini (1857–1897) honored the Argentine navy in a mid-nineteenth-century painting.

Changes in immigration and increased trade introduced a change in the social and political dynamic by the end of the 1800s. An era of progressive thought brought economic and cultural growth, and by 1900 Buenos Aires had grown into a thriving cultural center with more than 129,000 inhabitants. Art schools were developed, and state-sponsored scholarships enabled students to travel to Europe to study art. The Academia de la Sociedad Estimulo de Bellas Artes was nationalized in 1905 and served as the cornerstone for artistic study in Argentina. Whereas the nineteenth century had focused on the old image of Argentina, the twentieth century brought with it a new sense of identity, which was decidedly more international and middle class.

Maritime artists in the twentieth century were divided in their approach. Many tended toward a traditional style and content. Artists such as Benito Quinquela Martin

(1890–1977), Victor Cunsolo (1898–1937), and Fortunato LaCamera (1887–1951) painted the views from their studios on the Riochuela River in styles reminiscent of the French Impressionists. They chose vivid colors, exaggerated shadow effects, and had colloquial subjects: brightly colored fishing boats, steel-gray docks, hard-working tugboats, or the dingy sails of the junks. Many of the artists lived or worked in an area of Buenos Aires known as La Boca, which was located, as the name implies, at the mouth of the Riochuela. They formed a community known as Grupo de la Boca, which produced some of Argentina's most lasting images of the river.

Some experimental artists also captured the essence of Argentina's relationship with the sea. In *Juanito en la laguna* (1973; Colección Lily Berni, Buenos Aires), Antonio Berni used found objects to create images of a small boy in a lagoon. Xul Solar (1887–1963) created a whimsical view of an Argentinean port with a floating city and stylized mountains in his work *Vuel Villa* (1936; Museo Xul Solar, Buenos Aires). Later artists ranged from the realistic paintings of Maria Emilia Trogrlic and Gustavo Salvador Peses to the complete abstraction of *Juncos en el Agua* by Celia Basavilbaso. In the twenty-first century, art photographers have joined the community of artists who are documenting the maritime community from an artistic perspective.

Although the modern era witnessed an expansion of maritime art, images of Argentina's coast and inland waterways have been in existence for hundreds of years. The earliest artists were explorers, historians, and engineers, documenting a new world. Present-day Argentine maritime artists are capturing the images of a new Argentina, which is culturally diverse, forward-looking, and artistically alive.

[*See also* Buenos Aires *and* Painting, *subentries on* Historical Themes *and* Political Themes.]

## Bibliography

"Artelista." http://www.aretlista.com/. Artelista displays some of the most promising Argentine artists of the twentieth and twenty-first centuries, ranging from the traditional to the abstract.

Bayon, Damian, and Murillo Marx. *History of South American Colonial Art and Architecture: Spanish South America and Brazil.* New York: Rizzoli, 1989.

Buschiazzo, Mario José. *Argentina, monumentos históricos y arqueológicos: Fotografías del autor.* México, D.F.: Instituto Panamericano de Geografía e Historia, Comisión de Historia, 1959.

Crassweller, Robert D. *Perón and the Enigmas of Argentina.* New York: Norton, 1987.

*Historia general del arte en la Argentina.* Series. Buenos Aires: Academia Nacional de Bellas Artes, 1994–2005.

Levene, Ricardo. *A History of Argentina.* Translated and edited by William Spence Robertson. Chapel Hill: University of North Carolina Press, 1937. Reprint. New York: Russell and Russell, 1963. This classic history of Argentina contains paintings and engravings that are some of Argentina's earliest maritime images, including works by Vingboons, Ryland, and Schmidel.

"100 Masterpieces by 100 Argentine Artists." Visual Arts, Konex Foundation. http://www.fundacionkonex.com.ar/ingles/bienales_del_arte/index.asp/. Fundacion Konex has collected some of Argentina's finest works, with special focus on twentieth-century art. The online collections include this exhibit of one hundred masterpieces, many of which have a maritime theme.

Rock, David. *Argentina, 1516–1987: From Spanish Colonization to Alfonsín.* Berkeley: University of California Press, 1987.

Scobie, James R. *Buenos Aires: Plaza to Suburb, 1870–1910.* New York: Oxford University Press, 1974.

Sullivan, Edward J. *Latin American Art in the Twentieth Century.* London: Phaidon Press, 1996.

LISA HUDGINS

# Belgian

From time immemorial, the sea has fascinated artists. The sea represented a privileged means of communication through which commercial exchanges with distant lands were made possible. Even in ancient civilizations, the sea and sailing vessels were full of symbolic meaning. In around the sixteenth century in the West, marine painting began to free itself from religious constraints and tended toward essentially historical and narrative painting. These works of art had an essentially documentary character, and the detail was therefore generally extremely accurate. A second category consisted of seascapes, which manifested a greater artistic freedom. It was only in the nineteenth century, however, that seascape painting succeeded in freeing itself from all external constraints, and artists were finally able to depict the beauty of the sea in its own right.

At the dawn of Belgian independence in 1839, commerce in the Atlantic took on a new impetus, and nautical life experienced an energetic resurgence of activity. Artists were drawn toward picturesque scenes of ports and commercial sailing vessels. These works are remarkable for their detail, the smooth texture of the paint, and their warm colors. These seascapes were painted in the peace and quiet of the artist's studio, using as references pencil and watercolor sketches made from life. Exponents of this style included Louis-Charles Verboeckhoven (1802–1889), Jacob Jacobs (1812–1879), Paul Jean Clays (1819–1900), François Musin (1820–1888), Egide Linnig (1821–1860), and Hendrik Schaefels (1827–1904).

Alongside these exponents of the Romantic tradition, some artists, particularly in the 1850s, oriented marine painting in a new direction; many new painting associations were founded at this time. Until then, the sea had merely been a background for narrative or descriptive painting. Now, however, artists were to rid it of its accessories, seeking inspiration above all from the instantaneous spectacle of the sea and rivers. The sole subject of the painting became the sea in its solitary grandeur, and a great many beautiful studies of the North Sea along its desolate barren coasts were produced. A large number of painters, Romantic at the debut of their artistic careers, later evolved toward a more realistic style. Others immediately took up this new form from the outset: Louis Artan (1837–1890), Léon Spilliaert (1881–1946), Robert Mols (1848–1903), and Henri Permeke (1849–1912). Many painters chose to settle along the Belgian coast to paint, including James Ensor (1860–1949), who had settled in Ostend and whose work was prodigious. In Belgian marine painting, just as in other areas of painting, Neoclassicism, Romanticism, Realism, and Impressionism all coexisted during the late nineteenth and early twentieth centuries. It is this wealth of novelty and contradiction that lends such charm and fascination to Belgian marine painting.

[*See also* Art; Painting; *and biographical entries on figures mentioned in this article.*]

## Bibliography

Berko, Patrick, and Viviane Berko. *Seascapes of Belgian Painters Born between 1750 and 1875.* Brussels: Knokke, 1984.

PATRICK BERKO *and* VIVIANE BERKO

# Brazilian

The history of maritime art in Brazil reflects the history of trade and empire in the South Atlantic. Brazil's strategic position along the southern trade routes made it the port of choice for mariners and the target of land battles for over three hundred years. First claimed by Portugal in 1500, Brazil was colonized by the Dutch from 1637 to 1654; it was then fought over by Holland, Spain, and France until it was reclaimed by Portugal. In 1889 it became the Estados Unidos do Brazil, a modern federation of twenty-one states.

The artistic identity of Brazil includes the influences of its indigenous peoples and each of the successive cultures that laid claim to the land, and thus its maritime art reveals a rich blend of native and European styles.

## Colonial Period

Much of Brazil's early maritime art came from the artists and draftsmen who traveled to Brazil, seeking to document the newly discovered territories. Images of the exotic Brazilian coast were sketched into personal journals and ship's logs. Maps and drawings allowed mariners to navigate the extensive Brazilian coast. There are few works by known artists, however, from the colonial period. Seventeenth-century engravings of Todos os Santos Bay, published in London, were some of Europe's first views of the Brazilian harbor. Dutch painter Frans Post (1612–1680) painted Brazilian coastal scenes in 1637. In the eighteenth century, Portuguese draftsmen Jose Joachim Freire (published in the *Viagem filosofia*) and Joachim Jose Codina (through the Gabinete de historia natural) created images that captured the period both culturally and historically.

Art in colonial Brazil is often associated with public structures, including churches and public plazas. Religious art and architecture are prevalent, but extant examples of maritime motifs are rare. Some examples include the eighteenth-century Hospice of Bôa Viagem, whose tiles depict Portuguese ships, and the Great Hall at Santa Casa da Misericórdia, which also has glazed tiles featuring a martime motif.

Six panels created for the pavilion at the Passeio Público in Rio also contain maritime scenes. Painted in the eighteenth century by painter and stage designer Leandro Joachim (c. 1738–1798), these works are considered some of the finest examples of eighteenth-century Rio artwork. These panels include a naval scene, a pilgrimage by sea, whaling motifs, and a view of Boqueirào Lagoon.

## Nineteenth-Century Brazil

In the nineteenth century, Brazilian art continued to exhibit many of the characteristics of its European counterparts. Numbers of European artists were beginning to travel or emigrate to Brazil, bringing their particular style of art with them. When Maria Leopoldina, Archduchess of Austria, traveled to Rio de Janeiro in 1817, her arrival was captured by Viennese artist Franz Frühbeck, who accompanied her (the works are now in the collection of the Hispanic Society of America). In a later expedition with Baron von Langsdorff, German draftsman and painter Johann-Moritz

Rugendas sketched views of Bahia and Rio de Janeiro, which were published after his return to Germany in 1825.

The nineteenth century also saw an increase in native Brazilian artists. After 1822, King Pedro II of Portugal established an academy of art in Brazil with a focus on teaching the European style. This early Brazilian art closely followed the tenets of neoclassicism and eclecticism, mirroring the changes in French, German, and Iberian schools. It was not until Brazil became officially independent that the style and content of its art began to change.

## Modern Period

When Brazil was proclaimed a republic in 1889, a freshness of artistic spirit seemed to capture the new country. The "Belle Epoche," as it was called, began in 1889 and lasted until well into the twentieth century, as Brazilians began to redefine their artistic canvas. The Semana de Arte Moderna (Week of Modern Art Festival) was established in São Paulo. Artists began to experiment with colors and media that were counter to the classical standards of the nineteenth century, and maritime art became expressive, modern, and uniquely Brazilian. *Porto de Gräo, Valencia, Espanha, 1927*, by Antonio Garcia Bento (1897–1929), depicts a port with swirling sky and brilliantly colored fishing boats (Museu Nacional de Belas Artes, Rio de Janeiro). In 1923 the artist Tarsila do Amaral (1886–1973) traveled to Paris and was exposed to the Cubist movement. As a result, her later images contain some elements of the geometric, blocky style, including *Port, 1953*, which was reminiscent of her cubist *Pau-brasil* phase, characterized by geometric shapes and a blue-rose landscape.

Maritime themes became more visible in the twentieth century as artists experimented with more distinctly Brazilian cultural and social themes. Osvaldo Goeldi's woodcuts (1895–1961) are filled with fishing motifs, while Alberto de Veiga Guignard's work (1892–1962) includes images of the Minas docks. Jose Pancetti (1902–1958) began painting seascapes in 1925 as a naval officer and continued his work even after he left the navy in 1946. His seascapes are his best-known works, demonstrating his love for the sea, as well as his experience as a sailor. Tomas Santa Rosa Jr. painted *Pescadores* (1943; Museu Nacional de Belas Artes, Rio de Janeiro), showing men in traditional garb with fishing pots and casting nets, standing on the dunes and staring out to sea. Santa Rosa revisited this theme repeatedly, creating a series of paintings by the same title—each one capturing a different aspect of the vibrant maritime community.

Artists like Tomas Santa Rosa, Jose Pancetti, Tarsila do Amaral, and their contemporaries have continued the tradition of documenting Brazilian maritime life, which began with the first explorer to Brazil's coast. They are contributing to the timeline of maritime art in a country whose culture and economy has been determined by the sea.

[*See also* Art; Painting; *and* Rio de Janeiro.]

## Bibliography

Falcão, Edgard de Cerqueira. *Reliquias da Bahia*. São Paulo, Brazil: Nas oficinas de "Graphicars," Romiti & Lanzara, 1940.

Gullar, Ferreira. "An Overview of Brazilian Art." *Diogenes* 191 (2000): 109–114.

Lemos, Carlos, Jose Roberto Teixeira Leite, and Pedro Manual Gismonte. *The Art of Brazil*. New York: Harper and Row, 1983.

Lemos de Oliviera, Celso. "Brazilian Literature and Art." *Hispania* 75 (1992): 988–999.

Martins, Luciana de Lima. "Navigating in Tropical Waters: British Maritime Views of Rio de Janeiro." *Imago Mundi* 50 (1998): 141–155.

LISA R. HUDGINS

# British

Since the seventeenth century, marine artists have specialized in the depiction of ships and the sea, generally in response to the patronage of the navy, sea officers, shipowners, or shipbuilders—or sometimes simply art collectors. From the seventeenth century through the nineteenth century, marine painters flourished in times of international conflict at sea, as well as by contact with those involved in international trade. From the rise of Romantic art in the late eighteenth century, the term "marine artist" also described artists such as J. M. W. Turner, for whom the sea itself provided inspiration.

## Origins in the Netherlands and England

Although depictions of ships occur in a variety of forms throughout antiquity, and notable isolated examples are found in Italian and north European Renaissance painting, it was in the late sixteenth century in the Low Countries that marine painting originated. Paintings by Pieter Brueghel the Elder (c. 1525–1569) and engravings of ship types after his drawings of about 1560 anticipate the kinds of images that were to be made at the end of the century by Hendrick Vroom (1566–1640), who pioneered the

**British Art.** This drypoint etching by W. L. Wyllie (1851–1931) captures a scene of lightermen on the Thames River in 1884. © NATIONAL MARITIME MUSEUM, LONDON

painting of naval battles, harbor views, storms, and beach scenes in which shipping predominates, and who was the first marine painter to work for an English patron. Vroom established a pattern for marine painting that lasted for the next two hundred years. During the seventeenth century, Dutch artists developed increasing interest in naturalistic depiction of the sea, but the government still needed a record of their own and the enemy fleets, a function fulfilled by the draftsman Willem van de Velde the Elder (1611–1693), who sometimes made drawings from a small boat, sometimes in the heat of battle.

In 1672/73, during the second Anglo-Dutch War, van de Velde moved to England with his son Willem the Younger (1633–1707), a painter, to work for Charles II. Through them the influence of Dutch marine painting passed to English marine painters, such as Peter Monamy (1681–1749).

### Eighteenth Century

By the mid-eighteenth century, marine artists were able to paint the actions of the colonial wars fought against Spain, France, and the American colonies. Samuel Scott

(1701/02–1772), also a topographical artist, painted pictures for the Anson family about actions against the Spanish that occurred during Lord Anson's circumnavigation (1739–1744); for Lord Sandwich, first lord of the Admiralty, Scott painted actions of the Seven Years' War. At this time, John Cleveley (c. 1712–1777) was painting a series of launches of newly built ships in the Royal Dockyard at Deptford, with which he was closely associated.

Charles Brooking (1723–1759), the most promising marine artist of his generation, painted well-observed coastal shipping subjects rather than naval actions. By the time of Brooking's early death, the French artist Dominic Serres (1719–1793) was becoming established in England; he became the leading marine painter of the actions of the Seven Years' War and the American Revolution. As a founding member of the Royal Academy and marine painter to King George III, he thus elevated the status of marine painting in England.

### Napoleonic Wars

Serres's successors recorded the major and minor actions of the wars with France, 1793–1801 and 1803–1815. Nicholas

Pocock (1740–1821), a Bristol sea captain, became a professional artist in the 1780s when he painted and exhibited pictures of battles of the American Revolution. He is thought to have been present—making drawings—at the battle of the First of June, 1794. From 1799 he made illustrations for the *Naval Chronicle*, and in 1804 he was a founding member of the Old Watercolour Society. Thomas Whitcombe (c. 1752–1824), Robert Dodd (1748–1815), Thomas Luny (1759–1837), and the Scottish-born artist William Anderson (1757–1837) were among the many artists who produced images of the war, often for the officers who took part in its actions. The print publishing trade was an important tool in their dissemination since its expansion in the second half of the eighteenth century. Naval officers were taught to draw by marine artists such as John Christian Schetky (1778–1874) from Edinburgh.

### Nineteenth Century

Although the end of the war in 1815 and the deaths of this generation of marine artists marked a decline in their form of naval marine painting, many examples were to be included in the Naval Gallery established at Greenwich Hospital in 1823 with the support of King George IV. His gifts included two important examples of Romantic art: Philippe-Jacques de Loutherbourg's *Battle of the Glorious First of June 1794* (1795) and J. M. W. Turner's *Battle of Trafalgar* (1824). In the first half of the nineteenth century, marine painting was increasingly influenced by the Romanic movement and became more closely allied to landscape. The works of artists such as Clarkson Stanfield (1793–1867), a curator of the Naval Gallery at Greenwich, and John Wilson Carmichael (1800–1868), both from the northeast of England, as well as Edward William Cooke (1811–1880), are evidence of this influence. George Chambers (1803–1840), from humble origins in Whitby, carried out commissions for naval officers as well as for Greenwich Hospital, but his watercolors are indebted to Richard Parkes Bonington (1802–1828).

### Ship Portraits

The painting of ship portraits was a specialized form of marine painting carried out by artists usually based in ports in Britain, as well as on the Continent, in America, and in China. Of varying talent, these artists provided accurate depictions or "portraits" of ships for their captains or owners. Among the most talented were William John Huggins (1781–1845), who worked in London and painted many East India Company ships, and Samuel Walters (1811–1882), who spent most of his life in Liverpool painting ships that visited the thriving port.

### Late Nineteenth and Early Twentieth Centuries

Around the middle of the century, opportunities arose for artists to produce illustrations for the new illustrated magazines, notably *The Illustrated London News*, and later *The Graphic*, for which both William Lionel Wyllie (1851–1931) and Charles Dixon (1872–1934) worked. Wyllie became the most versatile marine artist of the late Victorian period, with a deep interest in all aspects of the sea, producing oil paintings, watercolors, and etchings. During this period he was influenced by Turner and by James A. McNeill Whistler, as well as by the French Impressionists. Wyllie's subjects included the coast of northern France, the river Thames, yachting, and the navy, and toward the end of his life, incidents during World War I (which were also painted by Dixon).

During World War II, the artists commissioned by the War Artists Advisory Committee to depict naval subjects were not necessarily marine artists. However, Richard Eurich (1903–1992), Charles Pears (1873–1958), and Norman Wilkinson (1878–1971) all painted many naval subjects, the latter two also being illustrators. In late twentieth century, a number of "mainstream" artists, rather than specialists, painted aspects of Britain and the sea, while more traditional forms of marine painting were practiced by artists and societies across the world—encouraged in Britain by the Royal Society of Marine Artists.

[*See also* Art; Painting; Portraits; *and biographical entries on figures mentioned in this article.*]

### Bibliography

Archibald, E. H. H. *A Dictionary of Sea Painters*. 3d ed. Woodbridge, U.K.: Antique Collectors' Club, 2000.

Cordingly, David. *Marine Painting in England, 1700–1900*. London: Studio Vista, 1974.

Giltaij, Jeroen, and Jan Kelch. *Praise of Ships and the Sea: The Dutch Marine Painters of the Seventeenth Century*. Rotterdam, Netherlands: Museum Boijmans Van Beuningen, 1996.

Russett, Alan. *Dominic Serres, R.A., 1719–1793: War Artist to the Navy*. Woodbridge, U.K.: Antique Collectors' Club, 2001.

Wilmerding, John. *A History of American Marine Painting*. Salem, Mass.: Peabody Museum, 1968.

ROGER QUARM

# Chilean

In a country with more than 4,000 kilometers (2,485 miles) of coastline, one might expect the sea to be an axis of great significance in that country's cultural construction. In Chile, however, this is not the case. The culture of the country, perhaps because of its geography, which comprises an extensive central valley between two mountain ranges, has a rather inland character. Its culture is tied more closely to the land than to the sea, more closely to the interior than to the shore, and more closely to agriculture than to shipping. This situation has defined a thematic repertoire in the history of Chilean visual arts.

In spite of this inland sensibility, it is nevertheless possible to identify Chilean marine art. There are several painters and many works that have dealt with this theme, from those works painted from the edge of the sea to those produced from an oceanic perspective on the high seas. Marine art in Chile, especially in the nineteenth century, dealt with naval episodes connected to national history. Its first exponents were principally English artists and sailors who passed through the country. Among them are several English painters: Charles Wood Taylor, John Searle, and Thomas Somerscales.

Around 1819 the English painter and sailor Charles Wood Taylor (1791–1856), who is considered one of the precursors of Chilean republican painting, arrived in Chile. Born in Liverpool, he had immigrated to the United States in 1817. In Boston he began his work as a landscape painter. In 1820 the U.S. government contracted him as a draftsman on the scientific expedition of the frigate *Macedonian*, which carried him to the coasts of Mexico, Ecuador, Peru, and Chile. He designed the first Chilean national shield, adopted by the government in 1834. He lived in Chile for almost forty years, serving in artistic, military, and academic roles. He taught a drawing class at the Instituto Nacional, the first institution for instruction in formal and academic drawing in republican Chile. Employed by the Chilean navy, he participated in the expedition to liberate Peru, serving as a lieutenant of artillery in the battalion of engineers. As an artist, Wood developed a prolific opus, painting oils and watercolors with marine themes—ships, naval battles, ports—as well as landscapes and portraits. Some of his best-known works include *Captura de* La Esmeralda *por Lord Cochrane* (Capture of the *Esmeralda* by Lord Cochrane [private collection]) and *El desembarco de la* Escuadra *en la ensenada de Paracas* (The Unloading of the *Escuadra* in the Cove of Paracas [1920; Museo Histórico Nacionala, Chile]). His most important and best-known work, produced in Chile, was *El naufragio del* Aretusa (The Wreck of the *Aretusa* [1826; Museo Nacional de Bellas Artes, Chile]), which narrates the wreck of that vessel in the bay of Valparaíso after a storm and shows the ship with its hull collapsed under the fury of the natural elements. The work has been compared in Chile to *Raft of the Medusa* by Théodore Géricault. It has been credited, by some local writers, with inspiring pictorial Romanticism in the country.

Around 1830 another English sailor, John Searle (1783–1837), established himself in the country. Less information is available about the work of this artist, who was also in the Chilean navy. It is known that he had a narrow artistic connection with his compatriot Charles Wood Taylor and that he cultivated maritime themes prolifically.

During the second half of the nineteenth century, Thomas Jacques Somerscales (1842–1927), another English artist and sailor, arrived in Chile. Somerscales is considered the foremost exponent of marine art in Chile. He visited Valparaíso for the first time in 1864, staying three months. Then, during a long journey through the tropics, he contracted malaria and abandoned his naval career, settling in Valparaíso to improve his health. He lived in Chile first between 1869 and 1892, then between 1907 and 1918. His work, which dealt with various themes related to the national landscape, culminated in the naval episodes he painted, especially those connected to the War of the Pacific. This event, which pitted Chile against Peru in 1879, established this artist as a painter of the naval glories of the country. The impact of this historical event lent vigor to his work, leading him to perfect not only his capacity for capturing the movement of the waters with his colors and shapes, but also the dramatization of human emotions. His works *Combate naval de Iquique* (Naval Battle of Iquique [1879; Museo Nacional de Bellas Artes, Chile]), *Combate de Punta Gruesa* (Battle of Punta Gruesa [private collection]), and *Combate de Angamos* (Battle of Angamos [1897; Museo Nacional de Bellas Artes, Chile]) are prominent examples. The first two naval events occurred on May 21, 1879; the Battle of Angamos was fought on October 8 of the same year. He also painted several episodes connected to the Primera Escuadra Nacional (first national squadron), recording ships and battles. The value of his work goes beyond documentary testimony; his paintings unite historical fervor with aesthetic values of a high order.

Somerscales's legacy can be seen in an interesting group of Chilean artists, among whom Álvaro Casanova Zenteno (1857–1939) stands out as Somerscales's most faithful and best-known follower, as well as his friend and student. (He also rose to become subsecretary of the Chilean navy, serving between 1906 and 1913.) Casanova Zenteno painted histories of celebrated mariners and of Chilean naval glories, such as the battles of Iquique, Casma, and Angamos, as well as landscapes and fishing scenes. His sons Juan Casanova Vicuña (1895–1976) and Manuel Casanova Vicuña (1898–1975) followed the path traced by their father, producing an opus of minor acclaim. In addition, Juan de Dios Vargas Iñiguez (1855–1906), Guillermo Grossmacht (1896–1964), and Florentino Previts (1900–1966) also stand out among Somerscales's disciples.

Together, Wood, Searle, Somerscales, and Casanova Zenteno constitute the gestational nucleus of nineteenth-century Chilean marine painting. During the twentieth century, other important artists gave expression to the maritime geography of Chile, including Grossmacht, Horacio García (a disciple of Casanova Zenteno who produced important works relating to marine subjects and Chilean naval history), Benito Ramos Catalán, and Benito Rebolledo Correa, among others. All of these artists, with the exception of Grossmacht and García, distanced themselves from a literal approach in order to treat the subject matter from an aesthetic perspective, bearing witness to the coastal geography of the country and to the customs and traditions associated with the sea. Marine art in Chile has thus exhibited both aesthetic importance and historical significance. It constitutes a relevant chapter, albeit brief, in the history of Chilean visual arts.

[*See also* Art *and* Painting.]

## Bibliography

Bindis, Ricardo. *Pintura chilena 200 años: despertar, maestros, vanguardia.* Santiago de Chile: Ediciones Origo, 2006.

Cruz de Amanáber, Isabel. *Historia de la pintura y la escultura chilena, desde la Colonia al siglo XX.* Santiago de Chile: Editorial Antártica, 1984.

Ivelic, Milan y Gaspar Galaz. *Historia de la pintura chilena; desde la Colonia hasta 1981.* Valparaíso, Chile: Ediciones Universidad Católica, 1981.

Romera, Antonio. *Historia de la pintura chilena.* Santiago de Chile: Editorial Andrés Bello, 1976.

PEDRO EMILIO ZAMORANO PÉREZ
*Translated from the Spanish by Matthew Miller*

# Danish

Although the Dutchman Willem van de Velde the Elder (c. 1611–1693) made drawings in Danish waters in the 1640s and 1650s, the fifteen paintings by Bernhard Grodtschilling (1697–1776) that were sold to the king of Denmark in 1728 seem to be the first Danish ship paintings. In 1778 the academic Peter Brünniche (1739–1814) was appointed official painter of the Danish navy. Jes Bundsen (1766–1829) and Caspar David Friedrich (1774–1840) were among his pupils. Drawing was an important part of the education of naval officers, and many of them developed their artistic talents while in naval service. Toward the end of the eighteenth century, the naval carpenter T. E. Lønning (1762–1823) was admitted to the Danish Royal Academy of Fine Arts, and he became a painter while working as a shipbuilder. Lønning was greatly admired for his paintings of fleet maneuvers and of contemporary and historic episodes at sea, and particularly for his renderings of individual vessels. Jens Juel (1745–1802) was one of the first to depict a coastal scene, a crossing of the waters of the Lillebælt by moonlight, in 1787. As Danish landscape painting emerged as a genre, marine art came into being as well. With an extremely long coastal line and numerous islands, ever-changing weather, and a long tradition of shipping, Denmark certainly had the potential to develop marine art of great variety.

The principal figure in Danish marine art is C. W. Eckersberg (1783–1853), who was at first inspired by Lønning. One of Eckersberg's technical advisers was Jacob Petersen (1774–1855), who was active in Flensburg, Copenhagen, and London, portraying ships. Eckersberg's numerous marine paintings are highly accurate renderings of vessels in various situations, in different weather and waters, and they established standards for the subsequent generations of Danish marine art.

Marine painting was not part of academic teaching, but it could be studied at Eckersberg's private school. Of Eckersberg's numerous pupils, the following are his heirs in style and technique: Emil Normann (1798–1881), a naval officer who specialized in depicting various types of vessels and their maneuvers, Vilhelm Petersen (1820–1859), the shipbuilder J. Prömmel (1812–1870) from Hamburg, and Carl Dahl (1812–1865). Carl Bille (1815–1898), a sailor and sailmaker, briefly a pupil of Dahl's, continued the tradition in his early works. Bille's later works, coastal views of the rocky island of Bornholm and dramatic scenes at sea, reveal the influence of Norwegian and German marine art. Other followers of Eckersberg were Carl Emil Baagøe (1829–1902) and C. Eckardt (1832–1914).

From the 1830s, painters were frequently invited to cruise with Danish men-of-war, experiencing foreign waters, climates, and countries. These travels gave Danish

**Danish Art.** In 1846 the Danish Navy granted Carl F. Sorensen (1818–1879) permission to sail in a frigate to obtain firsthand experience of ships at sea. FINE ART PHOTOGRAPHIC LIBRARY, LONDON / ART RESOURCE, NY

marine artists a more comprehensive knowledge of the arts abroad than students of the Danish Academy could normally acquire. The academy, reflecting the intense nationalism of the period, espoused Danish motifs, encouraging its students to reject foreign influence and to follow the example of Eckersberg. Dutch seventeenth-century art in the Danish public collections was the appointed ideal.

Some Danish artists, including Anton Melbye (1818–1875), aspired to more dramatic pictorial effects; they were influenced by Romanticism and no doubt by J. C. Dahl's (1788–1857) paintings, which were frequently shown at Academy exhibitions. Strongly criticized as "European," Melbye left Denmark and found an audience abroad, as did his brothers Fritz (1826–1869) and Vilhelm (1824–1882), and Viggo Faurholdt (1832–1883). Others adopted a more moderate style, including Emanuel Larsen (1823–1859) and Carl Neumann (1833–1891), who eventually found a niche painting contemporary marine battle scenes.

Education in marine art continued to be a private matter. The next teacher of importance was C. F. Sørensen (1818–1879), renowned for fresh seascapes that disregarded details in favor of the broad brush. His work captured a moment in nature, the movement of the waves and the beauty of unexpected color and light. Sørensen's pupils included Christian Blache (1838–1920); Holger Drachmann (1846–1908), best known as a poet and later as a painter; and Carl Locher (1851–1915), who learned from French plein air painting. In the late nineteenth century and into the twentieth, marine artists such as Holger Lübbers (1850–1931), Christian Mølsted (1862–1930), Vilhelm Arnesen (1865–1948), Benjamin Olsen (1873–1935), Victor Quistorff (1882–1953), and Søren Brunoe (b. 1916) continued the tradition of Danish marine art.

[*See also* Art; Painting; Portraits; *and biographical entries on figures mentioned in this article.*]

## Bibliography

Bramsen, Henrik. *Danish Marine Painters*. Copenhagen: Burmeister and Wain, 1962.

Christensen, Mona, and Jan Faye. *Marinemaleren C. F. Sørensen*. Helsingør, Denmark: Helsingør Kommunes Museer, 1991.

Kvorning, Jytte. "Dansk marinemaleri i det 19. århundrede." PhD diss., University of Copenhagen, 1951. MS in the Det Kongelige Bibliotek, Copenhagen.

Magnussen, Rikard. *Vilhelm Arnesen.* Copenhagen: Foreningen for National Kunst, 1945.

Olsen, Claus, ed. *Holger Drachmann på Bornholm og Skagen.* Skagen, Denmark: Bornholms Kunstmuseum og Skagens Museum, 1996.

Poulsen, Hanne. *Danske skibsportrætter.* Copenhagen: Palle Fogtdal, 1985.

ELISABETH FABRITIUS

# Dutch

The Netherlands lost its leading position in the field of marine painting after the death of two of its most prominent painters: Willem van de Velde the Younger, who died in Westminster in 1707, and Ludolf Backhuysen, who died in Amsterdam in 1708. Van de Velde lived on as a source of inspiration for the emerging English school of sea painters, and Backhuysen continued to have a strong influence in the Netherlands throughout the eighteenth century.

Backhuysen's pupil Jan Claesz Rietschoof (1652–1719) and his son Hendrick (1687–1746), both from the town of Hoorn on the Zuider Zee, remained true to Backhuysen's style and themes. Hendrick's paintings of stormy roadsteads under the ominous light of an oncoming thunderstorm have often been taken for Backhuysen paintings. The Frisian painter Wigerus Vitringa (1657–1725) probably spent some time in Backhuysen's studio. He had the same predilection as Backhuysen for shipping scenes with richly decorated states' yachts. Even as late as 1775, the talented artist Hendrik Kobell (1751–1779) still worked in the manner of the great master who lived almost a century before him.

In the course of his long life Adam Silo (1674–1766) was active in many fields of the maritime sector. Before becoming a painter he was a shipwright at the Amsterdam East India shipyard, where he met Peter the Great in 1697. The Russian tsar later bought some of Silo's paintings for his private collection. Silo's work resembles that of his teacher Abraham Storck (c. 1635–1710). In spite of this master's thorough knowledge of ship construction, his pictures of merchant vessels at sea or whalers in the Arctic all have a certain stiffness.

Both Silo and Kobell also made etchings. There were several graphic artists, practicing mostly in Amsterdam and Rotterdam, who had a predominantly maritime oeuvre of high quality. Adolf van der Laan (c. 1690–1742) and Carel Frederik Bendorp (1736–1814) are two of the many engravers who published print series with maritime subjects like the herring fishery or Dutch warships in distress. Drawings by Kobell and Dirk de Jong (fl. 1779–1805) were reproduced as engravings by Matthias de Sallieth (1749–1791), for example a series of the ports in the Dutch Republic. After De Sallieth's death these prints were published as a book under the title *Atlas van alle de zeehavens der Bataafsche Republiek* (1802).

One of the few exciting events in Holland's late-eighteenth-century maritime history was the Battle of the Dogger Bank in the North Sea (August 15, 1781) between a Dutch and an English squadron escorting merchant ships. The brief battle produced no distinct winner, but the Dutch claimed the outcome as a major victory. This led to an outburst of patriotic fervor, accompanied by an overwhelming production of occasional poetry, prints depicting the battle, and portraits of Admiral Johan Zoutman and other "Dogger Bank Heroes." Engel Hoogerheyden (1740–1807) made a number of prints of the successive stages of the combat, which were copied over and over by lesser artists. Hoogerheyden, a citizen of Middelburg, was quite successful as a painter of maritime subjects, mostly of ships and shipping in his native province of Zeeland. His paintings are very precise, though often rather unemotional recordings of ships and roadsteads. One of his best works is the *Secrete macht in Vlissingen* (1805; Nederlands Scheepvaartmuseum Amsterdam), showing the large "secret" force of small Dutch warships in the harbor of Flushing, ready to join Napoléon's intended invasion of England.

By the end of the eighteenth century, Hoogerheyden was not the only new talent in maritime art. A colleague in Middelburg was David Kleyne (1754–1805), who made charming recordings of the inland and coastal shipping of his time, in oil and watercolor. Rotterdam, after Amsterdam the second port in the country, was the home of Gerrit Groenewegen (1754–1826), a former ship's carpenter, who began a new career after losing part of his right leg in an accident. Groenewegen's numerous etchings of ships and barges are a worthy continuation of Reinier Nooms's work more than a century earlier. Groenewegen's elegant drawings and watercolors of shipping and coastal waters were very popular in his time.

## Maritime Romanticism

Around 1800 the first Romanticists emerged, with the old harbor town of Dordrecht as their focal point, and the Golden Age of Dutch painting as their source of inspiration. For Dordrecht painters like Jacob van Strij (1756–1815), seventeenth-century masters such as Aelbert Cuyp, also a native of Dordrecht, were the great examples. Being

**Dutch Art.** *A Calm* by Hermanus Koekkoek (1815–1862). © GUILDHALL ART GALLERY /HIP/ ART RESOURCE, NY

a landscape painter in Dordrecht, a town surrounded by water, naturally led to maritime themes and subjects in Van Strij's oeuvre. His younger fellow townsman Martinus Schouman (1770–1848) was a specialist in this field. The most influential and famous sea painter of the Romantic period, however, was Schouman's pupil Johannes Christiaan Schotel (1787–1838). In order to experience the beauty and the power of the natural elements he made boat trips on the rivers around his native town and visited the French seacoasts. Schotel greatly admired Backhuysen and Willem van de Velde the Younger, and he made a number of prints based on paintings by the latter. In particular, Backhuysen's dramatic stormy seas inspired Schotel to make paintings in which the main message is the insignificance of man—symbolized by a ship—when confronted with the forces of nature. Another protagonist of the Romantic sea piece is the founder of the Koekkoek dynasty, Johannes Hermanus Koekkoek (1778–1851). Several members of this family specialized in marine painting, for which there was a growing market both at home and abroad. Hermanus Koekkoek (1815–1882), one of Johannes's sons, sold well in England. His scenes of ships and barges near the coast, often with a jetty or a beach in the foreground, are typical products of the rather calm course most of the Dutch Romantics followed.

During a short period in the 1840s, maritime art enjoyed royal patronage. Prince Hendrik of Orange-Nassau, brother of King Willem II, made a career in the navy. Every year a squadron of warships made a training trip to the Mediterranean; several times the prince was present, eventually as the commanding officer, and he invited young artists to join him on his frigate *Rijn*. Among the artists in residence were Albertus van Beest (1820–1860), Jan Hendrik Louis ("Louis") Meyer (1809–1866), and Petrus Johannes Schotel (1808–1865), son of Johannes Christiaan Schotel. The younger Schotel, art-master at the naval training school at Medemblik, generally worked in the same style as his father. Van Beest's sketchbooks, completed during his voyage with the prince in 1843, are proof of his talents as a draftsman. He emigrated to the United States in 1845, where he continued his career as a sea painter. Meyer was a technically skilled painter; his rendering of the waves of the sea was unequaled among his Dutch contemporaries. His paintings are often filled with a drama and pathos that is far more daring than the quiet pictures of hay barges and fishing vessels in which many of the *petits maîtres* of his generation excelled. The ominous canvas *Man Overboard* (1847; Nederlands Scheepvaartmuseum Amsterdam), based on an accident he witnessed on Prince Hendrik's ship, is a good example of his talent.

## Nationalistic Impulses

History painting, often bearing a maritime character, became popular in the nineteenth century. A famous figure in this field was Nicolaas Pieneman (1809–1860), whose *Death of Admiral De Ruyter in 1676* (1834; House of Orange-Nassau Historic Collections Trust, The Hague) shows that he was familiar with Benjamin West's famous and widely reproduced canvas *The Death of Nelson* (1808). Both pictures show a dying admiral on deck, surrounded by his officers. Whereas seventeenth-century artists painted battle scenes from a certain distance, the Romanticists loved to zoom in on the event, creating a more emotional impact. It was no coincidence that Pieneman chose de Ruyter, the popular Dutch naval hero of the Anglo-Dutch Wars, as his subject. Four years earlier the nation's pride had received a heavy blow when the united kingdom of Holland and Belgium, created after the Napoleonic Wars, broke apart. As a result of Belgian independence, the Netherlands's territory was reduced to its eighteenth-century size, and national self-esteem suffered in equal measure. Marine artists of the period, perhaps offering a balm for wounded national pride, often recalled the exploits of seventeenth-century Dutch naval heroes.

The need for hero worship sometimes bordered on the hysterical, as in the case of Jan van Speijk's suicidal action. In 1831 this navy officer deliberately blew up his gunboat in the port of Antwerp to prevent it from falling in the hands of the Belgian insurgents. Schouman, Johannes Schotel, Meyer, and Dominicus du Bois (1800–1840) were among the many artists who recorded this event in paintings and prints.

The majority of nineteenth-century painter-narrators found their inspiration in a more distant history, extolling the glorious deeds of the Age of Exploration and the wars against Spain and England. Charles Rochussen (1814–1894) did not restrict himself to maritime history but depicted a vast array of historical events. Well into the twentieth century, lithographed plates after his paintings and watercolors could be found in thousands of classrooms in the Netherlands and its colonies overseas.

The revival of marine painting during the nineteenth century went hand in hand with the partial recovery of Holland's position as a maritime nation. Around 1850 the Dutch seagoing fleet was ranked fourth in tonnage in the world. There was a great demand for simple ship portraits. Dirk Antoon Teupken (1801–1845) and Jacob Spin (1806–1875), both working in Amsterdam, sold watercolor ship portraits to captains, shipowners, and passengers. Behind the frigate, galliot, or *kof*, they painted the Dutch coast, but Spin was willing to exchange this background for the white cliffs of Dover or the roads of Batavia.

## Impressionism

A prominent but rather isolated position in Dutch marine painting is occupied by Johan Bartold Jongkind (1819–1891). With his spontaneously painted harbor views, he was a precursor of the Impressionists. As he worked most of his life in France, Jongkind had few followers in his native country. However, in the later decades of the nineteenth century, documentary and realistic Romanticism in Holland made way for a freer and more spontaneous style of painting as artists followed the French *plein air* painters of the Barbizon School. Many members of the so-called Hague School left their studios for the coast and the polders of Holland. Hendrik Willem Mesdag (1831–1915) created a vast oeuvre of paintings and watercolors of the sea and the beach at Scheveningen with the characteristic, almost square-rumped *bomschuiten* and the local fisherfolk. He even obtained a commission to paint a circular panorama painting, measuring 14 by 120 meters (46 by 394 feet), of the village and coast of Scheveningen, which remains one of the cultural attractions of The Hague. Another representative of the Hague School was Jozef Israels (1824–1911). His narrative paintings of the hard life of fishermen and their families are still highly romantic in content, and not always free of sentimentality. They were widely acclaimed at exhibitions, both in Holland and abroad. Louis Apol (1850–1936) was nicknamed the "winter painter" because of the continuous stream of snow landscapes he produced. In the summer of 1880 he joined a Dutch scientific expedition to the Arctic. The watercolors he made on board the schooner *Willem Barents* inspired him to produce a number of fascinating paintings of an almost unknown part of the world, including a large panorama painting of *Nova Zembla* (1896) similar to Mesdag's panorama at The Hague. Unfortunately, this enormous canvas was destroyed by fire during World War II.

The coasts of Holland held a great attraction for painters. They were fascinated by the traditional life of the fishermen, untouched—they thought—by the modernity of the city. Like Mesdag in Scheveningen, Jan Toorop (1858–1928) and Piet Mondrian (1872–1944) spent their summers in Domburg on the Zeeland coast, as Willy Sluiter (1873–1949) did in Katwijk (near Leiden). These coastal villages, with their inhabitants in traditional dress, also attracted painters from other countries, including Claude

Monet, who spent some time in Volendam near the Zuider Zee, and Max Liebermann.

## Twentieth-Century Marine Artists

In the twentieth century, the rise of modern and abstract art pushed marine painting away from the central position it still occupied in Mesdag's days. No marine painter rose to a position comparable to that of Johannes Schotel or Mesdag, and although modernists often included maritime motifs in their art, none can be labeled a sea painter. Still, numerous artists continued to specialize in the field of marine painting. Rotterdam's bustling port activities attracted dozens of artists often referred to as the "Rotterdam port painters." Most of them were faithful followers of the Impressionist Hague School, like Johan Hendrik van Mastenbroek (1875–1945) and Evert Moll (1878–1955). Oscar Mendlik (1871–1963), Hungarian by birth, settled in Holland in 1904. His specialty was the unfurnished sea piece: just the waves and the sky. Jan van der Zee (1898–1988) was a member of the Expressionist group "De Ploeg" in Groningen. Shipping on canals and lakes is often a theme in his colorful paintings.

In 1951 the Nederlandse Vereniging van Zeeschilders (Netherlands Association of Marine Painters) was founded. Its members, about thirty men and women, organize group exhibitions of maritime art, ranging from semi-abstract paintings to sculpture. Thus, the tradition that started in Holland around 1600 has continued into the twenty-first century.

Dutch marine paintings of the eighteenth to twentieth centuries can hardly be found in museums outside the Netherlands, with a few exceptions: the National Maritime Museum in Greenwich, U.K., with works by Adam Silo, Jan and Hendrick Rietschoof, and major art museums in Britain, France, and the United States (Jongkind, Hague School, especially Jozef Israels and Mesdag). In the Netherlands the two leading maritime museums, the Nederlands Scheepvaartmuseum Amsterdam and the Maritiem Museum Rotterdam, have the most comprehensive collections. The largest collection of Dutch art of the period before 1900, including marine painting, can be found in the Rijksmuseum, Amsterdam. The Haags Gemeentemuseum in The Hague has an extensive collection of painters of the Hague School.

[*See also* Painting, *subentry on* Seventeenth-Century Dutch Marine Painting, *and biographical entries on figures mentioned in this article.*]

## Bibliography

Bellec, F., P. H. J. Bosscher, A. Erftemeijer, and P. Duvall. *Sillages Néerlandais. La vie maritime dans l'art des Pays Bas / Kunst in het kielzog: het maritieme leven in de Nederlandse kunst.* Zutphen, Netherlands: De Walberg Pers, 1989. Text in French and Dutch.

De Groot, Irene, and Robert Vorstman. *Maritime Prints by the Dutch Masters.* Translated by Michael Hoyle. London: Gordon Fraser, 1980.

Marius, G. H. *Dutch Painters of the Nineteenth Century.* 1908. Reprint, edited by Geraldine Norman and translated by Alexander T. de Mattos. Woodbridge, U.K.: Antique Collectors' Club, 1973.

Wright, Christopher. *Paintings in Dutch Museums: An Index of Oil Paintings in Public Collections in the Netherlands by Artists Born before 1870.* London: Sotheby Parke Bernet, 1980.

REMMELT DAALDER

# French

Up to the French Revolution, the Académie enforced the primacy of religion and ancient history as the most valuable subjects—the so-called *grand genre*—for paintings. Landscapes and marine paintings were still considered marginal subjects, ranked far behind portraits, anecdotal *petit genre*, and still life. While British and Dutch traders were quarreling as to which of them should have the biggest share of the Portuguese Empire in India, the French court was content to enjoy the bronze gods of mythology that decorated the Grand Canal at Versailles. Far from any of France's four bordering seas, the royal palace was informed about maritime affairs largely through paintings and ship models.

Jean-Baptiste Colbert (1619–1683), Louis XIV's naval minister, encouraged a brilliant school of artists who created a visual record of French seamanship and of the organization of the distant royal naval dockyards. Among the artists were Pierre Puget (1620–1694), Louis Nicolas Van Blarenberghe (1716–1794), and the brothers Nicolas (1728–1811) and Pierre (1737–1813) Ozanne. The most famous marine artist of the period before the French Revolution was Claude-Joseph Vernet (1714–1789), marine painter to the king, who was entrusted with a series of twenty-four views of the French harbors. His brilliant disciple and pupil, Jean-François Hue (1751–1823), completed the unfinished series.

Despite the work of these talented artists, France had few painters who could record naval engagements when, in 1778, Louis XVI concluded a treaty of alliance and trade with the insurgents in colonial America. Though the French navy played a decisive role in the American

**French Art.** *Naval Combat off Grenada, 1779* by Jean François Hue (1751–1823) depicts the battle between the French fleet under the comte d'Estaing and Vice-Admiral John Byron, Royal Navy, July 6, 1779. RÉUNION DES MUSÉES NATIONAUX / ART RESOURCE, NY

Revolution (1775–1783), no major artist was capable of immortalizing the victories of the French fleets involved in the American conflict. Auguste-Louis de Rossel de Cercy (1736–c. 1791), an average naval officer and a mediocre painter, was entrusted with the job.

The French navy was ruined by the leveling policy of the Revolution, but the Napoleonic Wars (1803–1815) prolonged its further demise. In 1817, during Restoration, Louis Garnerey (1783–1857) was commissioned as marine painter to the great admiral of France. Ten years later the victory of the allied French, British, and Russian fleet over the Turkish fleet off Navarin aroused a tremendous infatuation with the navy in France, in contrast to the gloomy decades of the Napoleonic Wars. Three years later, Théodore Gudin (1802–1880) and Louis-Philippe Crépin (1772–1851) were commissioned for the first time as *peintres officiels de la marine* (official painters to the navy). At the moment when steam was transforming seascapes, these three artists were the founders of the French corps of marine painters to the navy. Because of competition and intrigues, some major artists, such as Eugène Isabey (1804–1886), Auguste Mayer (1805–1890), Henri Durand-Brager (1814–1879), and Eugène Boudin (1824–1898), did not enter the corps, but others, such as, Antoine Morel-Fatio (1810–1871), did.

Aside from the official interest in marine painting, a dynasty of self-made artists worked at Marseille portraying warships and merchantmen. From 1785 to 1882,

Antoine Roux and his sons Antoine, Frédéric, and François-Geoffroy were famous in the maritime world. Antoine Roux was born in Marseille in 1765. His father Joseph was established as hydrographer on the Quai du Port, and Antoine learned from him the art of making sea charts. Numerous British ships called at Marseille, and some officers who visited the small shop to purchase maps noticed the artistic proclivities of the young hydrographer. They engaged him to paint ship portraits, which enjoyed a great popularity at the time. Roux was the first artist to introduce the ship portrait in France. A prolific artist, he also painted numerous ex-voto works, visual offerings to the Virgin Mary by seamen in expiation of vows. Antoine died in 1835 during a pandemic of cholera.

His elder son, Antoine Roux the Younger (1799–1872), continued the family tradition as hydrographer and painter, though he was not as talented as his two brothers Frédéric and François-Geoffroy. Frédéric Roux was born in 1805 and entered the family tradition as a painter. During a visit to Marseille, two well-known artists, Carle and Horace Vernet (the son and the grandson of Claude-Joseph Vernet), noticed Frédéric's talent and persuaded his father to send him to Paris under their protection and teaching. By 1830, having become an acknowledged artist, Frédéric settled at Le Havre, where he became recognized as the painter of ship portraits for all the American captains calling there. He died at Le Havre in 1870.

François-Geoffroy Roux was born in 1811 in Marseille, where he remained, taking over his father's shop. An experienced watercolorist, he maintained the family tradition of hydrography and ship portraiture, attaining incomparable skill through painting a valuable series of warships launched between 1810 and 1880. He was nominated in 1876 as marine painter to the navy; he died at Marseille in 1882. Among other acknowledged ship painters of the period were Adolphe-Hippolyte Couvelay (1802–1867) and Edouard-Marie Adam (1847–1929).

By 1860–1865, Impressionism had jostled the French academics, and marine artists followed, more or less, the new movement. Four major artists of that period entered the corps of marine artists to the navy: Felix Ziem (1821–1911), Paul Signac (1863–1935), Eugène-Louis Gillot (1867–1925), and Albert Marquet (1875–1947). In addition, though he did not usually paint marine subjects, Edouard Manet (1832–1893) painted the naval engagement during the U.S. Civil War between USS *Kearsage* and CSS *Alabama* off Cherbourg in 1864 (John G. Johnson Collection, Philadelphia).

The corps of marine artists to the navy continued into the twenty-first century, progressing through different artistic trends and offering a diverse French artistic interpretation of marine art. The major representatives of the Neoimpressionist school were Charles Fouqueray (1869–1956), Jean-Louis Paguenaud (1876–1952), Georges Taboureau (1879–1960), Charles Millot (1880–1959), Léon Haffner (1881–1972), Maturin Meheut (1882–1958), Jacques Boullaire (1893–1976), François Desnoyers (1894–1972), Gustave Hervigo (1896–1993), Lucien-Victor Delpy (1898–1967), Albert Decaris (an engraver; 1901–1988), Pierre Péron (1905–1988), André Hambourg (1909–1999), Jean Even (1910–1986), Luc-Marie Bayle (1914–2000), and Jean Delpech (1916–1988). Three artists were considered the most prominent late twentieth-century French representatives of the tradition of marine painting: Marin-Marie (1901–1987), Roger Chapelet (1903–1995), and Albert Brenet (1903–2005).

[See also Art; Painting; Portraits; and biographical entries on figures mentioned in this article.]

## Bibliography

Bellec, François. *Carnets de voyages des peintres de la marine.* Rennes, France: Ouest-France Edilarge, 2002.

*Les peintres de la marine: une invitation au voyage.* Exhibition catalog, Château de Sédières. Corrèze, France: Conseil Général de la Corrèze, 2006.

Roux, Antoine. *Ships and Shipping.* Translated by Alfred Johnson. Salem, Mass.: Marine Research Society, 1925.

FRANÇOIS BELLEC

# German

The development of marine art in Germany is closely connected with political and economic changes during the nineteenth century. With rising emigration from Germany in the decades after the Napoleonic wars and increasing seaborne trade, artists began to show an interest in ships and the sea. Yet it was only after German unification in 1871 and growing industrialization that the ocean became an important conduit for the import of raw materials and the export of finished goods. These phenomena increased the market for images of ships.

In the 1830s German and Scandinavian painters teaching at academies of art sent their students to the seashore in the Netherlands, Belgium, Great Britain, Italy, or to resorts along the North and Baltic seas. Although there are earlier examples of seascapes, Andreas Achenbach (1815–1910) is generally regarded as one of the most seminal proponents of marine art in Germany. Though he never taught at the academy in Düsseldorf, he had a large following of pupils whom he interested in painting the sea. By mid-century, marine art tentatively began to diverge from landscape art. Dutch, Danish, Norwegian, and British influences are clearly discernable in those formative years as there was hardly a German tradition to lean on, since shipping was of limited importance to the German states. In 1888, when Kaiser Wilhelm II ascended to the throne, this situation changed dramatically. A naval enthusiast, he encouraged many autodidacts and academically trained artists to paint the warships of his Imperial Navy so that the public could understand Germany's drive for sea power. Moreover, expanding shipping companies like the North German Lloyd (NDL) and the Hamburg-America Line (HAL) wanted to show their new passenger steamers that were challenging British maritime hegemony. In short, many pre-1914 paintings unmistakably contained considerable elements of propaganda.

During World War I, military action was the dominant motif for the works of Claus Bergen (1885–1964), Hans Bohrdt (1857–1945), Carl Saltzmann (1847–1923), and Willy Stöwer (1864–1931), all of whom (apart from Bergen) were close friends of the Kaiser. Bohrdt's painting *Der letzte Mann* (The Last Man, 1915), of a German seaman standing on his sinking ship while waving the imperial flag in the face of the enemy after the Battle at the Falklands in 1914, is the best-known painting of the war at sea; it shaped the image of war for generations. When the war was lost and the Kaiser had fled to the Netherlands, marine artists lost their imperial patronage. The demand for marine art was significantly diminished by the loss of the merchant fleet and the dismantling of the Imperial Navy following the Versailles Treaty in 1919. Those painters who continued to focus on the sea survived mainly by producing images of a glorious past. Only after the recovery in the late 1920s, which included the launch of the famous passenger liners *Bremen* and *Europa*, which won the Blue Riband for the fastest East-West passage, did a new interest in marine art emerge. The NDL even invited painters like Bergen and Felix Schwormstädt (1870–1938) to sail on *Columbus*'s maiden voyage. Other artists like Walter Zeeden (1891–1961) benefited from the new interest in merchant, and later naval, shipping before and during World War II.

The market for marine paintings collapsed after the total defeat of the German army and fleet in 1945. The small group of marine artists who found a niche for their work concentrated primarily on the past. Moreover, photography began to replace images on canvas. In the postwar era, however, some young artists (such as Friedel Anderson, Ronald Franke, or H. D. Tylle) with no maritime background turned their attention to ships and the sea. Their work is generally characterized by a high degree of accuracy, while some have combined authenticity with an artistic bent that forgoes more realistic, sterilized conceptions of ships.

Marine art in Germany has never gained the same reputation as in Britain, France, or the Netherlands, and its quality has seldom reached the highest western European standards. As a result, German art museums have generally ignored this genre. Instead, marine art is found mainly in maritime museums, in the offices of shipping companies, and in middle-class homes, not least because the paintings are less expensive than marine art in Britain or North America.

[*See also biographical entries on persons mentioned in this article.*]

## Bibliography

Faas, Martin, ed. *Seestücke: Von Caspar David Friedrich bis Emil Nolde*. Munich: Prestel, 2005.

Hansen, Hans-Jürgen. *Deutsche Marinemalerei*. Oldenburg, Germany: Stalling Verlag, 1977.

Meyer-Friese, Boye. *Marinemalerei in Deutschland im 19. Jahrhundert*. Oldenburg, Germany: Stalling Verlag, 1981.

Scholl, Lars U. *Deutsche Marinemalerei 1830–2000*. Helgoland, Germany: Maren Knauß, 2002.

Scholl, Lars U. "Marinemalerei am Deutschen Schiffahrtsmuseum. Ein Überblick über 30 Jahre Forschung." *Deutsches Schiffahrtsarchiv* 25 (2002): 363–382.

LARS U. SCHOLL

# Japanese

In Japan there are few painters who paint the sea or marine phenomena. As a result there is little awareness in Japan of marine painting as a genre. Japanese culture, including the field of painting, has been strongly influenced by that of China, and Chinese scenic painting has focused on the land and mountains rather than on the sea. In addition, Japanese in their daily lives have feared the sea and have not actively pursued seafaring navigation. One can discern such fear in the Japanese saying "Under the deck is hell." Finally, during the Tokugawa period (1603–1867), shipbuilders were prohibited from making large ships, and as a result the Japanese were placed at an even greater remove from the sea. Nonetheless, there are renowned Japanese artists who have depicted the sea, including Hokusai Katsushika and Hiroshige (Utagawa) Ando.

Hokusai Katsushika (1760–1849), whose most representative work is the woodblock print series *Fugaku sanjurokkei* (*Thirty-six Views of Mount Fuji*), blended realism and traditional forms. In his prints he perfected depictions of prominent waves. Two of his most outstanding prints in this regard are *Kanagawa oki nami ura* (*The Great Wave off Kanagawa*), from the series *Thirty-six Views of Mount Fuji*, and *Kaijo no Fuji* (*Fuji of the Waves*), from the series *Fugaku hyakkei* (*A Hundred Views of Mount Fuji*). His other seascapes are depictions of scenery and shore waves that are better described as imaginative sketches of rough seas than as seascapes.

Hiroshige Ando (1797–1858) was a woodblock print artist who gained fame around the same time as Hokusai, and, like Hokusai, he created many masterful scenic images. Among these masterpieces, *Awa naruto no fukei* (*Naruto Strait*) is notable for its faithful depiction of the eddies of the sea at Naruto. Hiroshige also produced the print series *Nihon minatozukushi* (*The Harbors of Japan*). In this series, harbors are his main subjects, and the sea is usually placed in the background.

After the fall of the Tokugawa shogunate and the start of the Meiji period in 1868, Japan embarked on a program of

**Japanese Art.** *Shinagawa Sunrise* by Hiroshige Ando (1797–1858). The artist made this print as part of his "Fifty-three views of Tokaido" in 1834–1835. GIRAUDON / ART RESOURCE, NY

importing European culture, including European painting. No seascape artists of note appeared at this time. At the beginning of nineteenth century, Japan began strengthening its navy for defense purposes. To increase popular interest in the sea, the navy began supporting seascape artists. During the Sino-Japanese War of 1894–1895, there appeared many prints with naval themes, partly to inform about the war effort. Navy Lieutenant Wakabayashi Kin (1868–1941) published documentary prints of the Battle of the Yellow Sea. Because Wakabayashi, a naval officer, was very knowledgeable about ships and the sea, his prints were highly accurate. After the Russo-Japanese War of 1904–1905, the Ministry of the Navy commissioned Tojo Seitaro (1868–1929) to produce documentary prints of the Battle of the Sea of Japan. Tojo participated in actual fleet training exercises, observed fleet movements, and produced many prints.

Later, seascapes failed to thrive. Though oil painters such as Aoki Shigeru (1882–1911) painted Japanese fishermen along the shore, the sea in these paintings was but part of the general landscape. Such paintings were not intended as seascapes, and the artists were not considered marine artists.

In the 1930s, under the influence of public-relations efforts by the Imperial Japanese Navy, magazines for the young carried many illustrations of the sea and sea vessels, which became popular. Among these illustrators, Kabashima Katsuichi (1888–1965) and Iizuka Reija (1904–2004) are especially famous. In addition, Yamataka Goro (1886–1981), a shipbuilding engineer, used his technical knowledge to produce many high-quality documentary paintings of sea vessels.

[*See also* Hokusai Katsushika.]

## Bibliography

Hillier, Jack. *Hokusai: Paintings, Drawings, and Woodcuts*. New York: Phaidon, 1978.

Kobayasi, Tadashi, ed. *Ukiyo-e no rekishi* (A History of Ukiyo-e). Tokyo: Bijutsu-shuppan-sha, 2001.

Lane, Richard. *Hokusai: Life and Work*. London: Barrie and Jenkins, 1989.

Nagata, Seiji. *Hokusai: Genius of the Japanese Ukiyo-e*. Translated by John Bester. Tokyo and New York: Kodansha, 1995.

Nakada, Katsunosuke, ed. *Ukiyo-e ruikou* (Biographies of Ukiyo-e Artists). Tokyo: Iwanami shoten, 1991.

Yamataka, Goro. *Hinomaru sentai shiwa* (Modern History of Japanese Marchant Ships). Tokyo: Shisei-do, 1981.

KAZUSHIGE TODAKA
*Translated from the Japanese by Alan Thwaits*

# Portuguese

One may argue that the representation of maritime subjects in Portuguese painting began in the so-called Manueline period in the first half of the sixteenth century, coinciding with a moment of great economic growth following Portuguese maritime discoveries. That awareness of maritime power shows up as a consistent background feature in tableaus on altarpieces, in which evocations of the sea or rivers are frequent, as in the tableau of *São João em Patmos* (Santa Casa da Misericórdia, Lourinha) by the so-called Maestro de Lourinha, which has a broad and beautiful landscape background reminiscent of Joachim de Patinir, depicting a wide river crowded with vessels, including a caravel. This awareness is also evident in the anonymous *Retábulo de Santa Auta* (Altarpiece of Santa Auta; Museu de Arte Antiga, Lisbon), the central panel of which depicts the "martyrdom of the eleven thousand virgins," with a beautiful seascape background filled with ships adorned with the flag of Portugal; or in the likewise anonymous panel of the *Naves Manuelinas* (Manueline Ships; Greenwich Museum, London), from around 1520.

**Portuguese Art.** Beginning as an expressionist painter, Adriano de Sousa Lopes (1879–1944) became an official war artist during World War I and later went on to paint historical scenes from the age of maritime discoveries. His painting of *Henry the Navigator among His Men* was done in 1940. BILDARCHIV PREUSSISCHER KULTURBESITZ / ART RESOURCE, NY / STAATLICHE MUSEEN ZU BERLIN

Believed to depict the arrival of the infanta Lady Beatriz in Saboya, the panel is considered a foundational work of Portuguese painting; it also may be regarded as a precursor of the great nautical paintings of the seventeenth century. Around the end of the Manueline period, these Portuguese seascapes ceased being conventional and became more realistic and painterly, to the extent that one can assert that only the Dutch masters of the seventeenth century gave to the sea and to naval architecture the importance granted them in Portugal from the beginning of the sixteenth century.

Seventeenth-century Portuguese artists included André Reinoso, creator of a series of paintings on the life of San Francisco Javier (Church of San Roque, Lisbon), some of which depict nautical subjects in relation to the travels of the saint, such as *Naufrágio de S. Francisco Xavier na viagem a China* (Shipwreck of Saint Francis Xavier on the Trip to China), with a view of the ship carrying the saint in the midst of the storm, or *Sao Francisco Javier socorrendo a armada portuguesa em Malaca na cruzada contra os Achens* (Saint Francis Xavier Aiding the Portuguese Armada in Malacca in the crusade against the Achinese), showing in the background a wide perspective of the sea with the galleons of the Portuguese armada. The paintings reveal an inventive personality and a colorist who was equally at ease in the art of chiaroscuro. Also prominent were Bento Coelho (1620–1708) and Josefa de Ayala (1630–1684), whose painting *O Mês de Março* (The Month of March; Sao Martinho, Augusto Siqueiras collection) depicts a lovely seascape background with a port city in an inlet with galleons, galleys, and fishing boats.

Francisco de Rocha (1747–1792), also known as Francisco de Setúbal, active in Lisbon in 1777, painted ceilings with figures and seascapes in tempera, as well as easel paintings of landscapes and seascapes to decorate the salons of the principal families of Lisbon, including the palace of Juan Ferreira. The works of Francisco Vieira Portuense (1765–1805) suggest a classicism with pre-Romantic overtones from the influence of Angelica Kauffmann, with whom he worked in London. His well-known painting *Doña Filipa de Vilhena armando caballeros a sus hijos* (Doña Filipa de Vilhena Knighting her Sons), whose background depicts a seascape, also reflects the influence of British landscape painting (possibly from the Norwich school). His historical painting *Vasco da Gama desembarcando en la India* (Vasco da Gama Disembarking in India) was created for the palace of Ajuda and was transferred to Brazil in 1807 for the royal family. He also planned to illus-

trate an edition of *Os Lusiadas* (The Lusiads), but he never completed it; all that remains of the plan are the sketches (in the collection of the Duke of Palmela, Lisbon), which reveal a nautical character.

Domingo Antonio de Sequeira (1768–1837) bridges the eighteenth and nineteenth centuries, but he must, like his contemporary Goya, be considered an artist of the eighteenth century. His maritime painting *Alegoría de la vuelta de D. Juan VI del Brasil* (Allegory of the Return of D. Juan VI from Brazil), also in the collection of the Duke of Palmela (Lisbon), mirrors the composition of Goya's *La familia de Carlos IV* (The Family of Carlos IV; Prado Museum, Madrid), although with less sense of caricature. The sea is present throughout Sequeira's painting; the Portuguese royal family is highlighted at the center, transported above the waves by marine deities, while in the right background, ships appear with sails unfurled.

Relatively few seascape painters emerged from the landscape painting of Portuguese Romanticism, among them João Pedroso (1825–1890) and Luis Tomasini (1823–1902), quite mediocre artists, whose painting remained almost at the level of amateurs. From the Realist period, Miguel Angelo Lupi (1826–1883), an academic painter influenced by Parisian Realism, created a historical nautical work, the *Partida de Vasco da Gama* (The Departure of Vasco da Gama). The celebrated painter Silva Porto (1850–1893) was influenced by Charles-François Daubigny, with whom he studied in Paris, producing several sea-related landscape paintings. The seascapes of Marques de Oliveira (1853–1927) reveal a lyrical sensibility and a greater openness to light and atmosphere, as shown in the maritime landscape *Póvoa de Varzim* (National Museum of Contemporary Art, Lisbon). The principal *marinista* of the Naturalist period was João Vaz (1859–1931), who painted sensitive seascapes, although only irregularly within his extensive opus. He is usually considered the best seascape painter of his generation; his works demonstrate vibrations and transparencies not achieved by any other Portuguese painter of his time (*As piteiras*; National Museum of Contemporary Art, Lisbon). King Don Carlos de Braganza (1863–1908), the most notable landscapist of his generation, also produced seascapes of great sensitivity.

Sousa Lopes (1879–1944) was one of the most prominent artists of his time. He was an exceptional colorist, and his works reveal unusual harmonies, iridescence, and tonality. He was considered the most brilliant Portuguese painter of the sea and sky in the twentieth century. The Symbolist painter Antonio Carneiro (1872–1930) transferred to the landscape an aesthetic current, as in his seascapes of northern beaches, with unnatural coloring, pink and purple; the works approach Expressionism in certain examples from 1916, a rarity in Portuguese painting. Constantino Fernandes (1878–1920) painted a triptych of clearly Symbolist flavor, *O marinheiro* (The Mariner). José Malhoa (1855–1933) also painted several seascapes and used the sea as background in other compositions, with themes tied to middle-class life, ladies strolling or flirting on the shore of a luminous sea, *A orilla del mar* (National Museum of Contemporary Art, Lisbon). But he also tackled historical paintings relating to Portuguese naval history, with works such as the *Partida de Vasco da Gama* (The Departure of Vasco da Gama), as well as the works he created in 1907 for the Lisbon Military Museum to illustrate *Os Lusiadas* (The Lusiads).

The celebrated painter and literary figure Almada Negreiros (1893–1970) painted frescoes for the Estación Marítima de Alcántara (maritime station of Alcántara) in Lisbon between 1943 and 1945. Showing three views of the capital from the estuary of the Tajo River, with scenes of the daily life of the port—boats, fishermen, and women unloading coal on the wharves—the works demonstrate a pleasing modernism. After the success of this work, he obtained a commission to paint frescoes for Lisbon's second maritime station as well, the Estación Marítima da Rocha do Conde de Obidos, which he completed between 1946 and 1949; the work consisted of two facing triptychs with images of the maritime life of Lisbon, but this time including a content of striking social commentary. The technique in this work was more daring than that of the first, with a clearly Cubist affiliation, Almada Negreiros thus adopting the aesthetic of his generation, although belatedly.

[*See also* Art, *subentry on* Historiography, *and* Portraits, *subentry on* Celebrities.]

## Bibliography

França, José-Augusto. *A arte em Portugal no século XIX* . 2 vols. Lisbon: Livaria Bertrand, 1966.

França, José-Augusto, José Luis Morales y Marín, and Wifredo Rincón García. *Arte Portugués*. Vol. 30 of *Summa artis. Historia general del arte*. Madrid: Editorial Espasa Calpe, 1986.

Moura Sobral, L. de, ed. *Bento Coelho (1620–1708) e a cultura do seu tempo*. Exhibition catalogue. Lisbon: Ministério da Cultura, 1998.

Pereira, Paulo, ed. *História da Arte Portuguesa*. 3 vols. Barcelona and Lisbon: Temas e Debates, 1995.

Santos, Reynaldo dos. *Historia del arte Portugués*. Barcelona: Editorial Labor, 1960.

Santos, Reynaldo dos. *Oito séculos de arte portuguesa : História e espíritu*, vol. 1. Lisbon: Empresa Nacional de Publicidade, 1970.

ENRIQUE ARIAS ANGLES
*Translated from the Spanish by Matthew Miller*

# Russian

In 1696, Tsar Peter I (Peter the Great; r. 1682–1725) founded the Russian Navy. Shortly afterward marine art in Russia developed into an independent discipline. One of the first Russian representatives of a school of marine artists living and working in St. Petersburg was T. A. Wassiljew (1783–1838). Numerous romantic panoramas of the city and colorful paintings of heroic historical events by his hand have survived. In later years, especially during the nineteenth century, larger numbers of accomplished artists found inspiration for their work in the ships and their officers. The influence of foreign marine artists like the British painter J. M. W. Turner (1775–1851) and Fitz Henry Lane (1804–1865) in the United States on the most prominent Russian marine artists is unambiguous. The works of men like A. I. Ladjurner (1789–1855) and M. N. Worobjev (1787–1855) and his three most talented pupils, A. P. Bogoljubow (1824–1896), A. K. Beggrow (1841–1914), and Iwan Konstantinowitsch Aiwasowskij (1817–1900), are heavily influenced—or at least greatly inspired—by the Illuminists. Low horizons give ample room to atmospheric light of sun or moon, while ships are portrayed moored off important harbor cities.

The influence of European and American painting is most noticeable in the works by Aiwasowskij. During the 1840s Aiwasowskij, like Bogoljubow and Beggrow, employed by the navy staff, spent time in Italy, in part living on a stipend from the Saint Petersburg Academy of Art. Furthermore, he visited Germany, France, Spain, and the Netherlands, and became a member of the most famous European art academies. Throughout his prolific career—the artist left more than six thousand paintings—Aiwasowskij maintained close contacts with his colleagues abroad. Western influences can clearly be discerned in his *A View of Constantinople in Moonlight* (1846: State Russian Museum, Saint Petersburg) or in his *View of Odessa in a Moonlit Night* (1846; same repository). His keen eye for the most minute detail—be it the ship's rigging or the seafarers' clothing—is extraordinary. In more recent times, Leon Felixowitsch Lagorio (1827–1905) and M. A. Ananjew (1925– ) are prominent representatives of the new school in marine art. Often patriotic in nature, the coloration of their works is less brilliant than that of their predecessors. Finally, Evgeny Chuprun (1927–2003), Nadezhda Pavlovna Shteinmiller (1915–1991), and Alexander Tatarenko (1925–2000), with their colorful pictures of shipyards, ships portraits, and harbor scenes, were the most talented Russian marine artists during the last decades of the twentieth century.

[*See also* Art *and* Painting.]

### Bibliography

Bles, Harry de, and Graddy Boven, eds. *Een maritieme droom: Tsaar Peter de Grote en de Russische marine.* Amsterdam, Netherlands: De Bataafsche Leeuw, 1997. Also published in German under the title, *Ein maritimer Traum: Zar Peter der Grosse und die Russische Kriegsmarine.*

Bown, Matthew Cullerne. *A Dictionary of Twentieth Century Russian and Soviet Painters, 1900–1980s.* London: Izomar, 1998.

Nikolov, Russalka, ed. *Schiffahrt und Kunst aus Russland.* Hamburg, Germany: Schiffahrts-Verl. Hansa, 1995.

Swanson, Vern G. *Soviet Impressionism.* Woodbridge, U.K.: Antique Collectors' Club, 2001.

JOOST C. A. SCHOKKENBROEK

## Spanish

The first maritime representations in Spanish painting appeared, during the fifteenth century, in certain paintings of church altarpieces, such as the central tableau of the *Retablo de San Jorge* (Museo Diocesano, Palma de Mallorca) by Pedro Nisart, with a panoramic background of a cove with port and boats, or several tableaus with boats in the *Retablo de Santa Úrsula* (Museo de Barcelona) by Juan Rexach (c. 1411–c. 1485). In the sixteenth century, an interesting painting by Alejo Fernández (c. 1470–1543) depicts the *Virgen de los Navegantes* (Virgin of the Mariners; Archive of the Indies, Seville) sheltering Columbus and other Spanish explorers beneath her cloak, with a view below of the port of Seville with numerous boats at anchor. In the seventeenth century a number of painters appeared who cultivated sea themes with greater assiduity, such as Juan de la Corte (1597–1660), *El rapto de Helena* (The Rape of Helen; Prado Museum, Madrid) and Juan de Toledo (c. 1610–1665), whose paintings of maritime battles are also housed in the Prado, as well as the painter known as Enrique "de las Marinas" (1620–1680), whose sobriquet may be attributable to his being an excellent *marinista* (seascape artist) in the judgment of Acislo Antonio Palomino de Castro y Velasco (1655–1725), the Spanish historical painter and writer on art.

The eighteenth century saw an increase in interest in painting on marine matters. Several painters stand out: Luis Paret y Alcázar (1746–1799) painted *El muelle del arenal de Bilbao* (The Pier at Bilbao Beach; National Gallery, London) in 1784, and in 1786 Carlos III ordered him to paint views of the ports in the Bay of Biscay, a lovely series inspired by *Vistas de los puertos de Francia* (Views of the Ports of France) by Claude-Joseph Vernet. Mariano Sánchez (1740–1822) produced a collection of 120 paintings of ports, navy yards, and Spanish bays (Patrimonio Nacional) commissioned by Carlos IV. Manuel de la Cruz (1750–1792) also rendered views of Spanish ports. Fernando Brambilla (1763–1834) produced drawings and gouaches of vistas taken from the scientific-political expedition of Alejandro Malaspina through the Americas and the Pacific in the corvettes *Descubierta* and *Atrevida*; his style, a pre-Romantic classicism, separated him from the rococo of earlier artists. Bartolomé Montalvo (1769–1846) also painted pre-Romantic seascapes.

In the Romantic period, around 1830, with the awakening of Naturalist sentiment, Antonio de Brugada (1804–1863) was a prominent figure. Trained in Paris by the celebrated French marine artist Théodore Gudin (1802–1880), Brugada also was influenced by British Romantic painting and seventeenth-century Dutch painting (for example, Brugada's *Combate del Cabo de San Vicente* [Battle of the Cape of San Vicente]; Naval Museum, Madrid). Vicente Camarón (1803–1864) also produced seascapes that were clearly influenced by seventeenth-century Dutch painting. Other painters also occasionally pursued the painting of seascapes during the Romantic era, including Jenaro Pérez Villaamil and his brother Juan, Eugenio Lucas Velázquez, José Brugada (brother of *marinista* Antonio), and Luis Rigalt.

The great development achieved in landscape painting during the Realist period in the second half of the nineteenth century gave a boost to the painting of seascapes, which were also produced by the originators of Realism in Spain, Carlos de Haes (1826–1898) and Ramón Martí Alsina (1826–1894), masters and promoters of an entire generation of landscape and seascape painters. The students of Haes and Martí Alsina, and those who continued their work, almost all moved toward Realism, especially in the seascapes painted by a great number of them. Tomás Campuzano (1857–1934) and Rafael Monleón (1843–1900) were both students of Haes, the first from Santander, the second from Valencia. Campuzano was a frank and simple seascape painter, while Monleón was more flamboyant in his pursuit of the themes of nautical

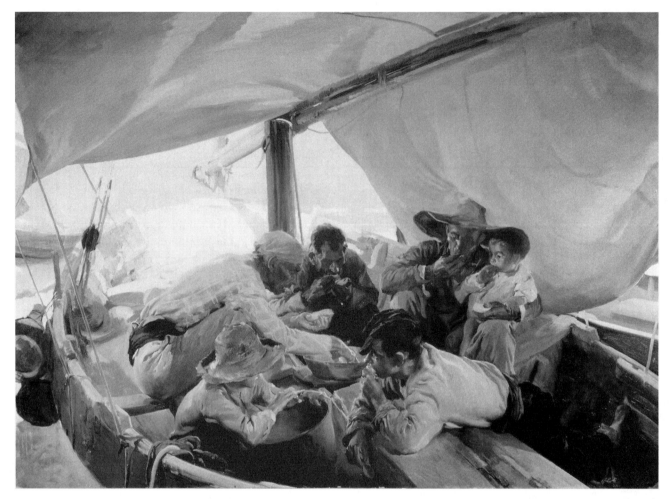

**Spanish Art.** *Eating in the Boat* by Joaquin Sorolla y Bastida (1863–1923). The Valencian artist was responsible for reviving seascapes in Spain by using a familiar perspective of life around the sea. SCALA / ART RESOURCE, NY / REAL ACADEMIA DE BELLAS ARTES DE SAN FERNANDO, MADRID

archaeology and history. A sailor by profession, Monleón, in his travels, became acquainted with Theodore Weber (1838–1907) in Britain, and he was a student of Paul Jean Clays (1817–1900) in Bruges. Restorer and promoter for the Naval Museum of Madrid, Monleón painted many canvases on historical and naval themes now held by that museum and by the Palacio Real in Madrid, as well as many other works on subjects including boats, ports, lighthouses, breakwaters, and beaches, some of which are now held by the Museo de Bellas Artes in Valencia.

Salvador Abril (1862–1924) and Javier Juste (1856–1898) were natives of Valencia. Juste, whose short and bitter life ended in madness, could have been the greatest seascape painter of his generation; his painting evolved from joyful coloring toward cold, sad tones and from placid themes, *Regatas en el Puerto de Valencia* ([Regattas in the Port of

Valencia]; Diputación Provincial, Valencia) toward more tragic and violent subjects, in keeping with the course of his mental decline. Salvador Abril was a successful and popular artist whose seascapes were greatly appreciated, as much in Germany and America as in Spain; his work, with a brilliant palette and great rigor in drawing, is technically sound and of consistently exemplary quality, as seen in *En alta mar* (On the High Seas; Museum of Valencia). Other seascape painters from Valencia included Ramón Lleonart, Enrique Saborit, and Pedro Ferrer Calatayud (1860–1944), trained at the Escuela de Bellas Artes of San Carlos de Valencia, whose technique was loose, synthetic, and Impressionist in style, *Sin rumbo* (Without Course; Museum of Valencia). Another outstanding seascape painter was Enrique Martínez-Cubells from Madrid (1874–1947), closely linked to Valencia by pictorial aesthetic and by family ties, *La vuelta de la pesca* (The Return of the Fish; Museum of Málaga). But it was Joaquín Sorolla y Bastida (1863–1923), the exceptional Valencian artist, who revived the traditional subject of seascapes, thematically abandoning traditionally Romantic subjects and offering a more quotidian and familiar perspective on life around the sea, *La vuelta de la pesca* (The Return of the Fish; Musée d'Orsay, Paris); technically, through his exuberant color and the vibration of his light, he achieved a courageous brevity and creative range, *Sol de tarde* (Afternoon Sun; Hispanic Society of America, New York).

The artists surrounding the painter Casto Plasencia in the so-called artists' colony of Muros (Asturias) also cultivated the genre of seascapes. Among them the Asturian painters Tomás García Sampedro, Felix González-Nuevo, and Ricardo Bolado stand out, along with the painters focused around Gijón, including Pío Escalera, Arturo Truán, Fermín Laviada, Nemesio Lavilla, and the brothers Ramón and Buenaventura Álvarez Sala. Juan Martínez Abades (1862–1920) was the most notable of these, being considered by critics the painter par excellence of the Bay of Biscay. Around 1890 his palette became more brilliant and luminous, with a serene atmosphere of calm in his composition and a great refinement in his drawing, *Los carboneros* (The Colliers; Museo Casa-Natal Jovellanos, Gijón). Inland schools also cultivated the painting of seascapes, as in Valladolid, where Mariano de la Fuente Cortijo did decorative painting at the same time that he was working on seascapes, most of which were of the Bay of Biscay.

The Andalusian school also had outstanding seascape artists, magnificently represented by the Cádiz painter Justo Ruiz Luna, *Combate naval de Trafalgar* (Naval Battle of Trafalgar; Ayuntamiento de Cádiz) and by Málaga painters José Gaertner, Guillermo Gómez Gil, Ricardo Verdugo Landi, José Fernández, and Emilio Ocón, the last two being the most influential over the seascape painters of the Málaga school. Emilio Ocón (1845–1906), head of the Escuela de Bellas Artes de Málaga, may be considered the finest *marinista* of the Mediterranean; he used simple forms with a vigorous style and bold brushwork, and he was an outstanding colorist. José Fernández Alvarado (1871–1935) was also a notable seascape artist; he achieved great success, distinguishing himself through the rigor of his process, his ambience, and his palette. Guillermo Mómez Gil, as well as José Gaertner and Ricardo Verdugo Landi, continued, after a fashion, in the footsteps of Ocón and Fernández Alvarado. A disciple of Ocón, José Gaertner (1866–1911) produced seascapes of marked assurance

from a early age, his career cut short by death when he was at the height of his career, *La Invencible* (The Invincible; Museo de Málaga). The renowned Ricardo Verdugo Landi (1871–1930) was also a disciple of Ocón, from whom he learned respect for nature and an admirable technique. His seascapes were well-known and highly regarded, leading one critic to describe him as the "poet of the sea." He was also an illustrator, working for the foremost weekly magazines of the time, always focusing on marine subjects.

Finally, there was a further multitude of painters who, with varying levels of dedication, developed the theme of the sea. Those in the Realist tradition included Ángel Cortellini, *Captura de la fragata inglesa Stanhope por D. Blas de Lezo* (Capture of the English Frigate *Stanhope* by D. Blas de Lezo; Museo Naval, Madrid), Francisco Pradilla, Jaime Morera y Galicia, Serfín Avendaño, Emilio Sánchez Perrier, Lorenzo Cerdá Bisbal, Antonio Ribas Oliver, Ignacio Pinazo, Eliseo Meifrén, Alejandro de Cabanyes, and Augusto Comas y Blanco. Those in the Impressionist tradition included Aureliano de Beruete, *Naufragio del vapor "Cabo Mayor" en el Cantábrico* (Wreck of the Steamship *Cabo Mayor* in the Bay of Biscay; private collection), Darío de Regoyos, Gonzalo Bilbao, and Adolfo Guiard. Those in the Symbolist tradition included Antonio Muñoz Degrain, *El Coloso de Rodas* (The Colossus of Rhodes; Real Academia de San Fernando, Madrid), Joaquín Mir, and Anglada Camarasa. Guillermo G. de Aledo, Javier Álvarez Prieto, and Antonio Molins Ristori are prominent marine painters active in the early twenty-first century.

[*See also* Painting, *subentries on* Historical Themes *and* Political Themes, *and* Portraits, *subentry on* Celebrities.]

## Bibliography

Arias Angles, Enrique. *Antonio de Brugada, pintor romántico y liberal* (Antonio de Brugada, Romantic and Liberal Painter). Madrid: Ayuntamiento de Madrid, Editorial Avapiés, 1989.

Arias Angles, Enrique. "Marinas españoles del siglo XIX." *Antiquaria* 42 (1987): 26–31.

Arias Angles, Enrique. "Veleros y vapores en la pintura española." In *IV Jornadas de Historia Marítima: La España marítima del siglo XIX (II): Cuadernos Monográficos del Instituto de Historia y Cultura Naval* 5, pp. 109–128. Madrid: Instituto de Historia y Cultura Naval, 1989.

Arias Angles, Juan Enrique. "Antonio Brugada pintor de la mar. Sus obras en el Patrimonio Nacional y en el Museo Naval." *Reales Sitios* 61 (1979): 40–52.

Arias Angles, J. E. "Aportación al catálogo de la obra de Antonio de Brugada: sus 23 cuadros de la Fundación Santamarca." *Villa de Madrid* 69 (1980, vol. 4): 14–18 and 78–83.

Garín Ortiz de Taranco, Felipe Ma. *Pintores del mar: Una escuela española de marinistas*. Valencia, Spain: Diputación Provincial, 1950.

Quesada, Luis, ed. *Imágenes de un coloso: El mar en la pintura española*. Exhibition catalogue. Madrid: Ministerio de Cultura, 1993.

ENRIQUE ARIAS ANGLES
*Translated from the Spanish by Matthew Miller*

# Swedish

With its extremely long coastal line and many bays and lakes, Sweden invites an artistic documentation of its maritime life. Since the beginning of the sixteenth century, the country has had an impressive navy, represented in paintings and drawings by foreign artists. During the seventeenth century the Dutch artist Willem van de Velde the Elder (1611–1693) made drawings of Swedish warships taking part in sea battles against the combined Danish and Dutch fleet along the Swedish coast. Swedish marine painting as an artistic discipline began only in the late eighteenth century. Swedish-born Elias Martin (1739–1818), who had received his artistic training in England, made pen drawings and paintings of Swedish maritime motifs. Jean-Louis Desprez (1743–1804) moved from France to Sweden in 1785 and became a painter of historical subjects and stage backdrops. He was commissioned by the king of Sweden to create large panorama-like paintings depicting sea battles of the Swedish-Russian war in the Finnish Gulf (1788–1790). The Swedish naval officer Johan Tietrich Schoultz (c. 1754–1807) made a fair number of smaller but very detailed oil paintings of naval battles and various episodes from the war. In his somewhat naïve works, the sea and the sky take up a great part of the pictorial space.

Another marine artist, exemplifying how a man with a military background could develop his artistic talents and become an excellent painter, is the army officer Johan Christian Berger (1803–1871). He studied at the Swedish Royal Academy of Art and in England and was influenced by Dutch seventeenth-century marine art, late eighteenth-century British watercolors, and the works of J. M. W. Turner. In 1841, Berger became court painter to the king. His marine paintings reveal his mastery of the depiction of sunlight, gleaming water, and the humid haze. Close to Berger, though less renowned, is Per Wilhelm Cedergren (1823–1896), another academic with a military background. He studied in France and from 1872 held the position of official artist of the Royal Swedish Navy.

As Romantic landscape painting gained prominence in the decades around 1850, marine painting also became an important genre, even though the Swedish Academy of Art made no distinction between landscape painting and marine painting. The most typical artist of the period is Marcus Larsson (1825–1864), whose sea pictures, characterized by a brilliant chiaroscuro, have eloquent titles, such as *Kronborgs slot i månsken* (Kronborg Castle by Moonlight) and *Brinnande ångbåt* (Burning Steamer). Since Marcus Larsson had no naval training, he was assisted by Cedergren, who painted the ships in Larsson's works.

Illustrative examples of the naval officer-artist are Rear Admiral Jacob Hägg (1839–1931) and Commander Herman af Sillén (1857–1908). As an artist, Hägg was an autodidact, while Sillén had studied in Paris and Berlin. Their paintings depict historical sailing warships and events of naval history, as well as contemporary steamers and massive armored cruisers. Sillén was more of a Romantic, an excellent colorist whose depictions of silvery gleaming water reveal the influence of the impressionists.

Other marine painters who used motifs similar to those of Hägg and Sillén include Ludvig Richarde (1862–1929), Arvid Johansson (1862–1923; mostly active in France), and Adolf Nordling (1840–1888). Nordling studied at the Swedish Academy of Art but was educated as a marine artist in Copenhagen by C. F. Sørensen. He was influenced by the impressionists, and his works have a fresh and expressive quality. His water is painted in a very animated and vivid manner, and his ships are sketchy and vague.

The breakthrough of open-air painting in Sweden in the 1880s coincided with a growing interest among artists in maritime life on and about the Swedish archipelago. Many painters found their motifs in the natural elements of the seaward skerries and among the people living there. Axel Sjöberg (1866–1950) belonged to the group of opponents who criticized the Swedish Academy for its antiquated attitude; he became an affectionate chronicler of the lives of the poor fishermen of the archipelago. Other marine painters, who used motifs from the east and west coast of Sweden, include Harald Lindberg (1901–1976), Gordon Macfie (1910–1971), and Roland Svensson (1910–2003). Artists such as Einar Palme (1901–1993) and Gösta Kaudern (1915–1992), who painted contemporary Swedish warships, continued the marine art traditions of the eighteenth and nineteenth centuries.

[*See also* Art; Painting; *and* Portraits.]

## Bibliography

Cnattingius, Bengt. *Johan Christian Berger*. Linköping, Sweden: Östergötlands och Linköpings Stads Museum, 1956.

Gauffin, Axel. *Marcus Larsson.* Stockholm: Wahlström and Widstrand, 1949.

Hägg, Christer. *Marinmålaren Jacob Hägg.* Stockholm: M. Ullman, 2003.

Hoppe, Ragnar. *Målaren Elias Martin.* Stockholm: Norstedt, 1933.

Jägerskiöld, Stig. *Svensksund.* Helsingborg, Sweden: Schildt, 1990.

Marten, Björn. "Hyllning till havet: Herman af Sillén—ett konstnärsporträtt." *Forum Navale: Skrifter utgivna av Sjöhistoriska Samfundet* 62 (2006): 15–36.

Strömberg, Martin. *Juniskäret: En bok om Harald Lindberg.* Stockholm: L. Hökerberg, 1963.

HANS SOOP

**Assizes of Jerusalem.** *See* Law, *subentry on* Classical and Medieval Law.

## Astronomers and Cosmographers

**Astronomers and Cosmographers** In the Renaissance and the early modern periods of European history, "astronomy" and "cosmography" were two overlapping terms for areas of science that contributed directly

**Astronomers and Cosmographers.** The Reverend Nevil Maskelyne (1732–1811) was Astronomer Royal from 1765 to 1811. Maskelyne produced the first *Nautical Almanac* in 1767. A graduate of Trinity College, Cambridge, and ordained in the Church of England, he never served in the church but instead became an assistant to Dr. James Bradley, the Astronomer Royal from 1742 to 1762. © NATIONAL MARITIME MUSEUM, LONDON

to the development of practical navigation in Europe. In these periods the definitions of the different scientific disciplines were only gradually developing, and they were only beginning to acquire their specific modern areas of interest. An understanding of the planets and stars was often linked to astrology, with astronomy as a science developing alongside it. As astronomy developed as a science, it became closely associated with and influenced by aspects of optics, geography, geometry, and plane and spherical trigonometry. At the same time cosmography as a broader field was the study of the entire visible universe and included the sciences that we now call geography and astronomy.

### Influence of Classical Learning

An important aspect of the origins of practical celestial navigation at sea is the recovery of learning from the classical world and the contribution of that learning to the major intellectual and theoretical developments in European history from the medieval period onward. As a result of the recovery of classical learning, the key works of Ptolemy (Claudius Ptolemaeus; c. 100–c. 170), the last known major astronomer of the ancient world, came to dominate thinking in astronomy and cosmography up to the mid-sixteenth century, particularly through the circulation and critique of Ptolemy's *Geography* and *Almagest*.

Ptolemy's astronomical studies in the *Almagest*, building on the now lost works of the ancient astronomer Hipparchus of Nicea (fl. second century B.C.E.), were known much earlier in western Europe than was his *Geography*. As early as the ninth century the *Almagest* was translated into Arabic, and consequently the most important Arabian astronomer, al-Battani (or Albategnius; c. 858–929), began the process of correcting Ptolemy's astronomical observations with observations of his own. This process resulted in the development of revised tables for predicting the time and position of celestial bodies (ephemerides), such as the tables that al-Zarqâlî (or Arzachel; 1028–1087) produced in Toledo.

Arab mathematicians and astronomers also made contributions to trigonometry by replacing the Greek chord with the Indian concept of the sine as a measurement of arc, along with other functions of the sine. The Mongol ruler Hulagu il Khan (1217–1265), a grandson of Genghis Khan and the first Ilkhan ruler of Persia, established an astronomical observatory at Maragha, appointing as its head Nasir al-din Tusi (1201–1274). The work done there over a twelve-year period ending in 1272 resulted in the more advanced Ilkhanic astronomical tables. At this time Arabic and Persian knowledge of astronomy and mathematics was far more sophisticated than that of western Europe, yet it was not transmitted to Europe until much later.

In 1175, Gerard of Cremona (c. 1114–1187) was working in the multicultural city of Toledo, the former capital of Moorish Cordoba that was then under the rule of Castile. There Gerard translated Arabic texts into Latin at the translation school established by Archbishop Raimondo of Toledo in the second quarter of the twelfth century. Among the works that Gerard translated from Arabic was Ptolemy's *Almagest*, then completely unknown in its original Greek text.

The translation school in Toledo was later supported by King Alfonso X "the Wise" of Castile (r. 1252–1284), who also opened other such schools. In 1252, Alfonso X ordered the preparation of revisions and corrections to the Tables of Toledo. Completed about 1272, the results of this work became known as the Alphonsine Tables. After they were first printed at Venice in 1483, they became widely used in western Europe.

In the development of European navigation the work of an Englishman working at the University of Paris, John of Holywood (or Johannes de Sacrobasco; c. 1200–1256), was highly influential. In his book *Tractatus de sphaera* he wrote an easily understandable summary of the *Almagest* based on Gerard of Cremona's translation. This very simplified version of Ptolemy was circulated widely in manuscript form and was published in more than forty printed editions between 1472 and 1647, finding its way into many navigation manuals as a simple explanation for the fundamentals of nautical astronomy. Through the printing of his thirteenth-century work in the fifteenth century, Holywood became the author who affirmed for many educated people—including Christopher Columbus, who owned a copy of the work—that the world was round, as the ancients had well understood.

### Calculation of the Calendar

A matter of particular importance to both astronomers and cosmographers was the accurate calculation of the calendar. A key figure in this development, as well as in the publication of ephemerides, was a Spanish Jew, Abraham Zacuto (c. 1450–1515), who compiled his *Almanach perpetuum* about 1474. Zacuto was a key figure among the Jewish and Muslim scientists, who provided the basis for modern nautical science through their knowledge of Arabic and Hebrew science, their training programs, and the manuals they compiled. Most important for navigation were Zacuto's tables for the declination of the sun at noon, given in degrees and minutes at any point on the ecliptic defined in whole degrees. Compiling these tables in Sala-

manca before the expulsion of the Jews from Spain, Zacuto sought refuge between 1492 and 1497 in Portugal, where he is believed to have served as royal astronomer under Kings João II (r. 1481–1495) and Manuel I (r. 1495–1521). Zacuto's tables circulated in manuscript for twenty years, and this was the form in which Columbus consulted them. Translated from Hebrew into Latin and Spanish by José Vizinho, the Jewish astrologer and physician to João II, Zacuto's tables were first printed at Leiria in 1496 and then four times at Venice between 1502 and 1528.

A German named Petrus Apianus (or Peter Apian; 1495–1552) was a very influential figure in the broad development of astronomy and cosmography. At Landshut, Bavaria, he published his *Cosmographicus liber* (1524), a highly influential book that was reprinted numerous times and translated into many languages. Apianus went to the University of Ingolstadt as professor of mathematics, and soon Emperor Charles V appointed him court mathematician. Among the significant books that Apianus wrote, several provided the intellectual background for practical developments in navigation, including his volumes on instruments, *Quadrans Apiani astronomicus* (Ingolstadt, 1532) and *Instrument Buch* (Ingolstadt, 1533), as well as his magnificently illustrated *Astronomicum Caesareum* (Ingolstadt, 1540), dedicated to the emperor, which included complicated movable volvelles to explain astronomy. One of the many contributions to knowledge in this work is Apianus's description of the theory of lunar distances as a means to find longitude.

A contemporary of Apianus's, Regnier Gemma Frisius (1508–1555), who was a professor at the University of Louvain, published in 1529 a corrected version of Apianus's 1524 book *Cosmographicus liber*. Then Frisius published his own work, *De principiis astronomiae et cosmographiae* (1530), in which he explained the theory of using a chronometer to compare local apparent time with the time at a point of departure in order to determine the difference in longitude between the two places.

### Navigation as Applied Cosmography

In the mid-sixteenth century a small number of Portuguese and Spanish cosmographers became increasingly interested in the subject of navigation as an applied form of their theoretical science. The greatest of the Portuguese mathematicians, Pedro Nunes (1502–1578), was a professor at the University of Coimbra and, from 1547, was Portugal's chief cosmographer. His book *Tratado da sphera com a theorica do sol e da lua* (1537) was a key contribution to the art of navigation. The first part of the book is an application of the works of others, including the anonymous Portuguese work *Regimento do estrolabio*; the *Tratado del esphera* (1535) by Francisco Falerio (fl. 1518–1535) of the Casa de Contratación in Seville, which included a translation of Johannes de Sacrobasco's summary of Ptolemy's *Almagest*; and the translation of the first book of Ptolemy's *Geography* by Georg von Peurbach (1423–1461). In his second part Nunes discarded Zacuto's widely used tables and replaced them with the ephemerides calculated by the German astronomer Regimontanus (Johannes Müller; 1436–1476). Nunes's *Tratado* described the loxodromic curve and explained the sailing of the shortest distance on the open ocean by using a great circle route. His book was the first navigational manual to mention the use of the cross-staff at sea. The most comprehensive Portuguese manual published up to that time, Nunes's *Tratado* quickly became the foundation for others that followed.

In December 1538 a Spanish cosmographer, Pedro de Medina (c. 1493–c.1567), joined the staff of the Casa de Contratación in Seville to make and sell charts and to sit on the examining board for licensing pilots. Like several other cosmographers, he promoted the idea that the practically oriented pilots should be thoroughly educated in astronomy and mathematics; Medina thus worked to change—over the objections of pilots—the licensing examinations so that pilots were required to know navigational theory. Medina's book *Arte de navegar* (1545) was the first in a series of navigational handbooks published by the cosmography teachers at Seville in their effort to encourage the practical application at sea of knowledge of astronomy, complementing the pilots' traditional and complete reliance on dead reckoning. Medina's book illustrates Spanish knowledge about celestial navigation in the mid-sixteenth century, and it shows that he was apparently unaware of the book that Nicolaus Copernicus (1473–1543) had published two years earlier, *De revolutionibus orbium coelestium* (1543), which completely changed the understanding of astronomy that Medina's book reflected. Despite this, Medina's book was translated into several languages and appeared in more than twenty editions up to 1663. Among the translators were such prominent officials such as Nicolas de Nicolai du Dauphiné (1517–1583), the royal geographer of France in the reign of King Henri II.

In the second half of the sixteenth century, *Breve compendio de la sphere y de la arte de navegar* by Martin Cortés (fl. 1551) was the most comprehensive of the nautical manuals and became the standard navigational text at the Casa de Contratación in Seville. This work marked the apogee of Spanish influence in the theory of navigation.

Containing the first detailed instructions for constructing a cross-staff and an astrolabe, it also had tables that showed the number of miles in each degree of latitude. In addition, it contained the first printed reference in Spanish to the fact that there is a difference between the geographical poles of the earth and the poles created by geomagnetism.

At this point no books on cosmography or manuals on navigation had been published in England. In a book noted for its elegant design, fine illustrations, and use of italic type, William Cuningham (b. 1531) published the first book on cosmography in English: *The Cosmographical Glasse, Conteinying the Pleasant Principles of Cosmographie, Geographie, Hydrographie, or Navigation* (1559). Cuningham argued for the usefulness of cosmography in the military and maritime defense of England. Among the points he made was a very early reference to Gemma Frisius's idea of using a chronometer to determine longitude.

Cuningham's book succeeded in stimulating an interest in geography and astronomy among educated Englishmen and set the stage for developments that followed among men concerned with overseas navigation. In 1558, while Philip II of Spain was married to Queen Mary I of England, William Borough, the chief pilot of the English Muscovy Company, had visited the Casa de Contratación in Seville and obtained a copy of Cortés's *Breve compendio*. Borough brought Cortés's book back to London, where Richard Eden (c. 1521–1576) translated and published it with the express purpose of promoting English overseas commerce. In the years between 1561 and 1630, Eden's translation was reprinted ten times and became the most widely used manual on navigation in the era that saw the first English overseas maritime ventures and the establishment of England's first successful overseas colonies. In 1581, John Frampton published the *Arte of Navigation*, a translation of Pedro de Medina's *Arte de navegar*. Although Medina's book had become more influential among European navigators, Cortés's book remained far more influential among English navigators.

Among the last of the cosmographers who made major contributions to practical navigation were the father and son royal cosmographers in Portugal, Luis Serrão Pimental (1613–1679) and Manuel Pimental (1650–1719). The father, Luis, originally wrote the textbook on navigation that is often considered the culmination of the classic Portuguese books on practical navigation and on the use of navigational instruments. Still in manuscript form at the time of his death, his book was edited and published by his son Manuel under the title *Arte practica de navegar e regimento de pilots* (1681). Eighteen years later Manuel published a similar book under his own name but clearly based on this father's work, entitled *Arte de navegar, emque se ensinam as regras practices* (1699), which was reprinted in four more editions, the last in 1762.

The position of Astronomer or Cosmographer Royal did not exist in the Dutch Republic. However, a transmission of knowledge from astronomy to seafaring was effected by astronomers and cosmographers associated with the East India Company, notably Petrus Plancius (1552–1622) and Willem Jansz. Blaeu (1571–1638).

## Accurate Astronomical Tables

Meanwhile the work of Johannes Kepler (1571–1639), Galileo Galilei (1564–1642), and Sir Isaac Newton (1642–1727) had led to the practical possibility of creating accurate astronomical tables that could use the positions of stars as well as planetary and lunar movements to determine accurate positions at sea. At the Paris Observatory established in 1667, Jean-Dominique Cassini (1625–1712) and the three successive members of his family that succeeded him concentrated on determining longitude by using eclipses of the satellites of Jupiter. In 1672 the Jesuits established a hydrographic school at Nantes to teach the theory and practice of celestial navigation. The need to create such accurate tables led Sir Jonas Moore (1617–1679) and Sir Christopher Wren (1632–1723) to recommend that King Charles II (r. 1660–1685) establish a Royal Observatory at Greenwich expressly for the purpose of improving navigation. The observatory was commissioned in 1675, and John Flamsteed (1646–1719) became Britain's first Astronomer Royal.

The first significant work of the Royal Observatory was Flamsteed's observations and catalog of three thousand stars, *Historia coelestis Britannica*. Published in a preliminary edition without Flamsteed's approval in 1712, it appeared in its final form in 1725. Flamsteed's successor, Edmond Halley (1656–1742), devoted much of his time as Astronomer Royal to making an eighteen-year series of observations of the moon in an effort to try to perfect tables for the lunar distance method of finding longitude. Halley's successor as Astronomer Royal, James Bradley (1693–1762), was the first at Greenwich to test the calculations of Johannes Tobias Mayer (1723–1762), professor of mathematics at the University of Göttingen, an institution founded in 1734 by King George II (r. 1727–1760) in his capacity as elector of Hanover. In calculating his tables Mayer had used a theorem created by the Swiss mathematician Leonard Euler (1707–1783), who was working

at the Berlin Academy under the patronage of King Fredrick the Great of Prussia from 1741 to 1766. Mayer submitted his tables to Great Britain's Board of Longitude in 1755 in a bid to win the prize to solve the problem of finding longitude at sea. Bradley reported to the Admiralty in 1765 that he was convinced of the accuracy of Mayer's tables, having compared them to 230 lunar observations of his own.

Building on these developments, the Reverend Dr. Nevil Maskelyne (1732–1811) published *The British Mariner's Guide* in 1763, in which he suggested that in order to have a practical solution to finding longitude at sea, tables of lunar distances should be calculated in advance and published in a form that mariners could readily use. This suggestion earned Maskelyne his appointment as fifth Astronomer Royal in 1765, and he proceeded to put his suggestion into effect by publishing the first *Nautical Almanac* in 1766, which had tables calculated for 1767, along with another publication in 1781 to explain the use of the lunar methods, *Tables Requisite to Be Used with the Nautical Ephemeris for Finding the Latitude and Longitude at Sea*. As Astronomer Royal, Maskelyne maintained and edited the *Nautical Almanac* for forty-four years as his principal contribution to practical navigation, while also making wider contributions to the science of astronomy.

In the two centuries following Maskelyne, a number of governments continued to employ astronomers. For example, in France the French navy established an additional observatory in Paris in 1748, led by Joseph-Nicolas Delisle (1688–1768) and Charles Messier (1730–1817). With the suppression of the Jesuits in 1763, Guillaume Saint Jacques de Silvabelle (1722–1801) carried on the astronomical work that had been done at the French navy's former observatory at Marseille by Père Esprit Pezenas (1692–1776). After 1825, a new observatory connected to the hydrographical school at Nantes dealt with correction of chronometers. In the United States, Congress supported astronomy and geographical science over other sciences. Astronomy was valued because it was seen as the pacesetter of the sciences, and also because the precise information that astronomers gathered made a practical contribution to navigation at sea—through compiling and maintaining tables and nautical almanacs, determining the precise time, surveying, and establishing exact geographical positions.

[*See also* Ancient Navigation; Halley, Edmond; Longitude Finding; Medina, Pedro de; Nautical Astronomy and Celestial Navigation; Nunes, Pedro; Observatories; Western Navigation; *and* Zacuto, Abraham.]

## Bibliography

Albuquerque, Luís M. de. *Navegação astronómica*. Lisbon, Portugal: Comissão Nacional para as Comemorações dos Descobrimentos Portugueses, 1988.

Albuquerque, Luís M. de, ed. *O livro de marinharia de André Pires*. Lisbon, Portugal: Junta de Investigações do Ultramar, 1963.

Boistel, Guy, ed. *Observatoires et patrimoine astronomique français*. Cahiers d'histoire et de philosophie des sciences, vol. 54, Lyon: ENS éd., 2005.

Chabás, José, and Bernard R. Goldstein. *Astronomy in the Iberian Peninsula: Abraham Zacut and the Transition from Manuscript to Print*. Transactions of the American Philosophical Society, vol. 90, part 2. Philadelphia: American Philosophical Society, 2000.

Cook, Alan. *Edmond Halley: Charting the Heavens and the Seas*. Oxford: Clarendon Press, 1998.

Cotter, Charles H. *A History of Nautical Astronomy*. London: Hollis and Carter, 1968.

Evans, James. *The History and Practice of Ancient Astronomy*. New York: Oxford University Press, 1998.

Davids, C. A. "Introduction." In *De principiis astronomiae et cosmographiae* (1553), by Gemma Frisius. Delmar, N.Y.: Scholars' Facsimiles and Reprints for the John Carter Brown Library, 1992.

Dick, Steven J. *Sky and Ocean Joined: The U.S. Naval Observatory, 1830–2000*. Cambridge, U.K.: Cambridge University Press, 2003.

Howse, Derek. *Nevil Maskelyne: The Seaman's Astronomer*. Cambridge, U.K.: Cambridge University Press, 1989.

Pedersen, Olaf. "In Quest of Sacrobosco." *Journal for the History of Astronomy* 16 (1985): 175–221.

Phillips, Carla Rahn. "Introduction." In *L'art de naviguer* (1554), by Pedro de Medina. Delmar, N.Y.: Scholars' Facsimiles and Reprints for the John Carter Brown Library, 1992.

Röttel, Karl, ed. *Peter Apian: Astronomie, Kosmographie, und Mathematik am Beginn der Neuzeit*. Buxheim, Germany: Polygon-Verlag, 1995.

Sandman, Alison Deborah. "Cosmographers vs. Pilots: Navigation, Cosmography, and the State in Early Modern Spain." PhD diss., University of Wisconsin-Madison, 2001.

Sanz, Carlos. *La "Geographia" de Ptolomeo, ampliada con los primeros mapas impresos de América, desde 1507*. Madrid, Spain: Librería General V. Suárez, 1959.

Taylor, E. G. R. *The Haven-Finding Art: A History of Navigation from Odysseus to Captain Cook*. London: Hollis and Carter, 1958. Reprint. New York: American Elsevier, 1971.

Waters, David W. *The Art of Navigation in England in Elizabethan and Early Stuart Times*. London: Hollis and Carter, 1958.

Waters, David W. "Introduction." In *Arte of Navigation* (1561), by Martin Cortés. Delmar, N.Y.: Scholars' Facsimiles and Reprints for the John Carter Brown Library, 1992.

Willmoth, Frances, ed. *Flamsteed's Stars: New Perspectives on the Life and Work of the First Astronomer Royal, 1646–1719*. Woodbridge, U.K., and Rochester, N.Y.: Boydell Press, 1997.

JOHN B. HATTENDORF

**Astronomy.** *See* Nautical Astronomy and Celestial Navigation.

# Athens

This entry contains two subentries:

> Commercial Port
> Naval Port

---

## Commercial Port

The port of Piraeus is located eight kilometers (about five miles) south of the modern city of Athens in the periphery of Attica, Greece. Piraeus owes its establishment in 493 B.C.E. to the Athenian "strategos" Themistocles, who advised the citizens of Athens to abandon the shallow Phaleron harbor and develop the deepwater harbor of Piraeus. The harbor of Piraeus soon became the principal commercial port of classical Hellenism, where, in the words of Thucydides, "From all the lands, everything enters."

The Athenian defeat in the Peloponnesian War (431–404 B.C.E.) and the development of the rival ports of Rhodes, Delos, Thessalonica, and Alexandria during the Hellenistic period (323–30 B.C.E.) weakened Piraeus's importance for maritime commerce in the eastern Mediterranean. The sack of Piraeus by the troops of Sylla in 85 B.C.E. and the invasion by the Goths under Alaric in 395 C.E. completed the destruction of the city. During the Byzantine and Ottoman periods the port of Piraeus was rarely used.

The proclamation of Athens as the capital of the modern Greek state in 1832, Athens's lack of agricultural resources, and the absence of a road network connecting Athens with the rest of the country all necessitated the reestablishment of the port of Piraeus. The strategic utility of switching the financial and commercial wealth of the nation from the island of Syros to the mainland port of Piraeus was another important consideration that led to its establishment. Modern Piraeus was established in 1835, and its first inhabitants came from the maritime islands of Hydra and Chios.

Before 1860 the port of Piraeus had seen little in the way of infrastructure development. Expenditure in harbor works increased, however, between the abdication of King Otto of Greece in 1862 and the outbreak of World War I in 1914. This expenditure largely reflected the increased maritime importance of Piraeus, resulting from the opening of the Suez Canal in 1869, the opening of the Corinth Canal in 1893, and the establishment of railway connections among Piraeus, the rest of the country (1869–1907), and Europe (1916).

By 1900, Piraeus had developed into the third-busiest port in the Mediterranean; its cargo traffic consisted largely of imports rather than exports. The growth of the port of Piraeus fostered the industrial and population growth of the city of Piraeus, which in turn reinforced that of the port, largely through its consumption of imported seaborne goods and raw materials. Notwithstanding the growth of the port of Piraeus, the port faced a number of pressing problems, such as inadequate storage facilities, delays in loading and discharging of cargoes, and instances of theft and destruction of recently discharged goods.

Administrative reform was implemented with a view to eliminating these problems, since the problems had pushed up the insurance fees and freight rates for cargoes to and from this port. Thus the Piraeus Port Committee was established in 1911 and assumed the management of the port from a number of bodies whose responsibilities had been frequently overlapping. This first experiment in administrative centralization and managerial autonomy of the port of Piraeus proved successful in developing the infrastructure of the port. Extensive construction works of quay ways, storage sheds, and other facilities did take place during the 1920s.

However, the Piraeus Port Committee had little success in increasing the efficiency of loading and discharging operations in Piraeus, thus prompting the Venizelos ministry to replace the committee with the Piraeus Port Authority in 1930. The Piraeus Port Authority took over the loading and discharging operations, using its own means and labor force, and also took over the scheduling and supervision of all port operations. It also enjoyed the right to charge vessels, cargoes, and passengers for the services and facilities offered. The administrative reform of the port of Piraeus was completed with the establishment of a free zone within it in 1932.

The Piraeus Port Authority, its free zone, and the large-scale port works of the 1930s held much promise for the future of Piraeus. However, the heavy bombing of Piraeus by German and Allied aircraft during World War II and the blowing up of port installations by the Germans in the course of their withdrawal from Greece in October 1944 resulted in the destruction of most of the port. The latter half of the 1940s saw the repair of war damage, and between 1955 and 1982 important modernizing projects were implemented following the expert advice of Demosthenes Pippas, professor of port and harbor engineering at the National Technical University of Athens. Since 1982 new plans have been drawn that combine the latest developments of sea transportation and cargo handling with the environmental, social, and other needs of the inhabitants of greater Piraeus.

In addition to the development of the port, Piraeus's other maritime infrastructure, such as telecommunications, financing, chartering, and official buildings, was also updated. This was partly a result of the maritime policy of the military dictatorship that ruled Greece between 1967 and 1974. The policy aimed at transforming Piraeus into an international shipping center, a center that would attract expatriate Greek shipowners whose total fleet strength topped the world list. Though few of the shipowners transferred their main decision centers to Piraeus, many expatriate Greek shipowners opened offices there; the offices carried out most of the activities of their firms, including technical and accounting functions and crewing. Moreover, the dictators' policy provided an opportunity for new shipowners, known as the "Piraeus Greeks," to enter the industry, even though most of them had no previous experience in shipping. Their emergence largely explains the persistently strong showing of the Greek-owned merchant fleet in world shipping.

At the beginning of the twenty-first century the port of Piraeus remained home to hundreds of Greek-owned shipping firms, and its excellent connections with all mainland and island destinations of the country makes Piraeus the principal terminus for Greek import trade. On the other hand, the fairly recent construction of dynamic new ports all around the eastern Mediterranean and the diversion of part of the foreign trade of Greece from sea routes to land routes—owing to Greece's accession to the European Economic Community (EEC)—may limit the development of the port in the foreseeable future. It remains to be seen whether the port of Piraeus will answer successfully the challenges of the modern globalized economy or will retreat to the insignificance of its medieval and early modern periods.

[*See also* Ports *and* Shipping, *subentry on* Greece.]

## Bibliography

Hadjimanolakis, Yannis E. "The Port of Piraeus through the Ages." http://www.greece.org/poseidon/work/sea-ports/piraeus.html.

Harlaftis, Gelina. *Greek Shipowners and Greece 1945–1975: From Separate Development to Mutual Interdependence.* London: Athlone Press, 1993.

Κοτέα, Μαειάνθη (Marianthi Kotea). Η Βιομηχανική Ζώνη του Πειραιά, *1860–1900* (*He Viomichaninike Zone tou Peirea, 1860–1900*). Athens, Greece: Panteion University Press, 1997.

Παρδάλη-Λαϊνού, Αγγελική (Angeliki Pardali-Lainou). "Η εξέλιξη του Λιμανιού του Πειραιά και η επίδρασή του στην οικονομική ανάπτυξη της ευρυτερης περιοχής του Πειραιά από το 1835 έως το 1985" ("He Ekselikse tou Limaniou tou Peirea kai he epidrase tou sten hecomike anaptikse tes evriteres perioches tou Pirea apo to 1835 eos to 1985"). PhD diss., Panteion University, Athens, Greece, 1990.

Τσοκόπουλος Βάσιας (Vasias Tsokopoulos). Πειραιάς, *1835–1870: εισαγωγή στην ιστορία του Ελληνικού Μάντσεστερ* (*Peiraias, 1835–1870: Eisagoge sten historia tou Hellenikou Manchester*). Athens, Greece: Kastaniotis, 1984.

ZISIS FOTAKIS

# Naval Port

Prior to the fifth century B.C.E., the Athenians did not have a proper naval or commercial harbor. Ships anchored or beached in the wide bay of Phaleron, southwest of the city. The Athenians began to fortify Piraeus, a rocky peninsula on the north side of the bay, roughly seven kilometers (four and a half miles) from the city of Athens, in 493 B.C.E., at the instigation of Themistocles, who held the office of eponymous archon in that year. The project was unfinished in 490 B.C.E., and Phaleron remained the naval station, although the Athenians had few warships at this time.

In 482, again at Themistocles' suggestion, the Athenians decided to use an unexpected surplus of revenues from their silver mines to finance the construction of a fleet of one hundred trireme warships. According to the Athenian historian Thucydides, Themistocles had a vision of an Athens "attached to the sea" and projecting its power by means of a navy. A large fleet operating out of a strong base at Piraeus was essential to this vision, because it would enable the Athenians to defy the armies of their Greek neighbors and also the Persian king. In 1987 the historian Robert Garland suggested that Themistocles' strategic vision logically implied moving the Athenian metropolis to Piraeus, although such a wholesale abandonment by the classical Athenians of their homes, sanctuaries, and cemeteries would have been unthinkable to them.

The principal advantage of Piraeus over Phaleron was that the peninsula encompassed three natural harbors. The largest, called Kantharos, lay on the northern side, with two smaller ones, Zea and Mounichia, on the southern side. In order to link the city to the port, construction of fortification walls, known as the Long Walls, began in 459 B.C.E., shortly after the Athenians had provided similar fortifications for Megara, a city to the west of Athens that also stood some distance from its seaport of Nisaia. Once completed in 457, the northern Long Wall, roughly six kilometers (about four miles) in length, ran from the southwestern quadrant of the city walls to the northeastern circuit of the Piraeus walls; a slightly shorter wall ran from the southern city walls to the settlement at Phaleron, effectively closing off landward access to the whole of Phaleron Bay, but still leaving the shores of the bay exposed to potential invaders. In 446 B.C.E. an additional "middle" wall was constructed, parallel to the north wall and only a short distance south of it, creating a narrow corridor between Piraeus and the city. The land within these walls was used for farming and residence during periods when the countryside around Athens was vulnerable to enemy raids.

The main naval harbors were ringed by ship sheds, which were long, roofed slipways, designed to shelter the warships from the weather while their hulls were dried out, cleaned, repaired, and sealed up with paint and pitch to prevent rotting and keep out the *Teredo navalis* shipworm. Some facilities must have been built in the 480s B.C.E., but the main construction program dates to the era of Pericles, specifically to circa 460–430 B.C.E. Excavation and architectural research has shown that some of the ship sheds were long enough to accommodate two trireme-size warships end to end, perhaps as the result of extensions in the mid-fifth century B.C.E. or reconstruction in the fourth century B.C.E.

In the mid-fourth century B.C.E., 196 ships could be housed at Zea, 84 at Mounichia, and 94 at Kantharos. By this time warships significantly wider than triremes were constructed at Athens, so some larger ship sheds must also have been built. In addition to its ship sheds, Piraeus had construction yards for new vessels and arsenal buildings to store naval equipment, all within a walled naval zone to which access must have been controlled, although thousands of people might have had business there on a daily basis. Of these buildings only a few ship sheds and the fourth century B.C.E. "Arsenal of Philon," a storehouse for rigging, rope, and sails on the northern side of Zea harbor, have been partially excavated. The arsenal was a magnificent two-story building constructed of local limestone and faced with marble. The Roman author Pliny the Elder thought that it bore comparison with the magnificent Temple of Artemis at Ephesus, one of the seven wonders of the world.

The Athenians recognized that the Periclean ship sheds, reputed to have cost the enormous sum of one thousand talents, were a superb architectural achievement. Modern estimates indicate that the resources required to build the ship sheds were probably greater than those needed for the more famous Periclean building program on the Athenian acropolis. Themistocles' original vision for Athens and Piraeus may have been largely defensive in nature, but it was swiftly transformed into an imperialist manifesto by Pericles and his followers.

The envy and fear that Athens's fifth-century maritime empire aroused among the Greeks, especially Sparta and its allies, led to the Peloponnesian War (431–404 B.C.E.). By this time Piraeus was also the busiest commercial port in the Aegean. Indeed, one of the immediate causes of that war was the decision of the Athenians to exclude their Megarian neighbors from access to the harbors and markets of Athens, which must have had a serious effect on Megarian trade. Athens used its naval power to dominate the Aegean both politically and economically, and to maintain extensive maritime trading links with the Black Sea and the eastern Mediterranean. Storehouses, offices for merchants and bankers, brothels, and many other businesses quickly grew up around the commercial harbor at Kantharos, with thousands of people, Athenian and non-Athenian, free and slave, living in the bustling town.

The potential vulnerability of the harbors at Piraeus to seaborne attack was demonstrated by a surprise Spartan raid led by Knemon in 429 B.C.E. Using forty Megarian ships based at Nisaia, Knemon sailed as far as Salamis, but he lost his nerve and did not directly attack Piraeus. Nevertheless, the Athenians were so alarmed that they narrowed the harbor entrances, built archery platforms along their lengths, and closed them off with movable chains. In 387 B.C.E. another surprise Spartan raiding party under Teleutias penetrated Kantharos harbor, and merchants and their wares were seized from the quayside. Nothing could protect the Athenians when a deadly plague swept across the Aegean in 430 B.C.E. It was brought to Athens by ships docking at Piraeus and carried from there to the city; Pericles was one of its victims.

Without a large fleet of warships, Piraeus was effectively defenseless, so when the bulk of the Athenian fleet was lost in 405 B.C.E., which caused the end of the Peloponnesian War, the city was forced to submit to the Spartans under Lysander, who entered the harbors and destroyed portions of the Long Walls to the sound of flutes and proclamations of freedom for the Greeks. Athens had also surrendered all but twelve of its triremes, but the Athenians quickly revived their naval ambitions, and the Long Walls were rebuilt with Persian aid by the Athenian admiral Conon in 393 B.C.E.

The fortifications of Piraeus could on occasion be held against those who controlled the city of Athens. Following the end of the Peloponnesian War in 404, a pro-Spartan oligarchy was installed in Athens. Democratic leaders opposing this regime occupied Piraeus and successfully resisted attempts to dislodge them, eventually forcing the oligarchs into exile. By this time, however, most of the Periclean ship sheds had been destroyed by the oligarchs, whose aim was to prevent the Athenians from re-creating the navy that had been so vital to the maintenance of democratic power. By about 375 B.C.E., however, there were enough ship sheds for one hundred triremes, and this capacity had more than tripled by 350 B.C.E. as successive politicians urged the Athenians to re-create the naval empire of the Periclean era. They struggled to outfit and crew these vessels, however, and their political influence waned as that of the kings of Macedon, Philip II and his son Alexander the Great, grew.

Piraeus continued to be an important port after Alexander's death in 323 B.C.E., although Athens never again had a substantial independent fleet, and its commercial dominance lessened. The surviving naval facilities made it an attractive base for the fleets of the various Hellenistic rulers who vied for control of the eastern Mediterranean. Following the defeat and destruction of the last significant Athenian naval force in 322 B.C.E., Piraeus was occupied by Macedonian garrisons to keep a check on the political ambitions of the Athenians. The last of these was bribed away in 228 B.C.E., but soon after, the ships of the Roman Republic and its allies were gathering in the harbors. The last great battle for the Piraeus occurred during a war between Rome and Mithradates VI Eupator, King of Pontus (120–63 B.C.E.). The Athenians sided with Mithridates, and the Roman general Lucius Cornelius Sulla was forced to lay siege to Athens and then Piraeus in 86 B.C.E. Sulla's destruction of Piraeus was so extensive that only the ruins of a few ship sheds and other facilities could still be seen around the harbors by the travel writer Pausanias in the second century C.E.

[See also Ancient Navies, *subentries on* Greece, Rome, Hellenistic States, *and* Persia; Wars, Maritime, *subentry on* Peloponnesian War; *and* Warships, *subentry on* Ancient Warships.]

## Bibliography

Blackman, David. "The Shipsheds." In *Greek Oared Ships, 900–322 BC*, by J. S. Morrison and R. T. Williams, pp. 181–192. Cambridge, U.K.: Cambridge University Press, 1968. An authoritative study of the archaeological evidence for ancient Greek ship sheds.

Eickstedt, Klaus-Valtin von. *Beiträge zur Topographie des antiken Piräus*. Athens, Greece: He en Athenais Archaiologikes Hetaireia, 1991. This scholarly study includes discussion of archaeological finds.

Gabrielsen, Vincent. *Financing the Athenian Fleet: Public Taxation and Social Relations*. Baltimore: Johns Hopkins University Press, 1994. A lively and detailed analysis of how the classical Athenian navy operated, both at sea and in port.

Garland, Robert. *The Piraeus: From the Fifth to the First Century BC*. London: Duckworth; Ithaca, N.Y.: Cornell University Press, 1987. An excellent and highly detailed study of the history, archaeology, and topography of the ancient port and town; includes illustrations, extensive notes, and a full bibliography.

Wycherley, R. E. *The Stones of Athens*. Princeton, N.J.: Princeton University Press, 1978. In this detailed study of the archaeology of Athens is a chapter on Piraeus as both harbor and town (pp. 261–266).

PHILIP DE SOUZA

# Atlantic, Battle of the

The Battle of the Atlantic was a six-year (1939–1945) struggle to secure the ocean routes vital to Allied victory against Nazi Germany during World War II. It was therefore not a battle in the traditional sense but rather a series of distinct campaigns in response to German initiatives. Allied objectives in the Atlantic—blockade of Axis Europe, securing Allied sea movements, and projection of military power—could be met without direct attack on Germany's maritime interests. Prior to 1939 the British took sensible precautions to organize and protect shipping through the Naval Control of Shipping and naval intelligence networks, including provision for the establishment of mercantile convoys and concentration on the maintenance of the battle fleet. Solid organization, excellent intelligence, and a powerful fleet formed the foundation of Allied defense of the North Atlantic throughout the war.

## German Objectives

The initiative in the Atlantic fell to the Kriegsmarine, a service woefully unprepared for a major naval war. Not surprisingly, German naval strategy during the "phony war" of 1939–1940 was simply to harass and contain Allied naval forces through a war on shipping conducted largely by surface ships, including disguised raiders. The importance of the U-boats remained to be demonstrated during the phony war, and torpedo failures marred their contribution to the Norway campaign in April 1940.

The Atlantic war began in earnest after the fall of western Europe in 1940, when the occupation of France and Norway gave Germany operational bases on the Atlantic and provided Germany with a clear and simple strategic objective: defeat of Britain by severing its maritime communications. It was this campaign that Winston Churchill dubbed the Battle of the Atlantic in early 1941.

The German assault consisted of a comprehensive attack on British shipping and port facilities by naval and air forces. It was estimated that if some 750,000 tons of shipping per month were destroyed for a year, Britain would sue for peace. The figure was an educated guess, because even the British were uncertain about their shipping needs. It seemed that they needed 47 millions tons of imports per year, but by 1942 the British managed on about half that.

## German Strategy

To attack this amorphous target the Germans applied all their resources over the winter of 1940–1941, but they were unequal to the task. Surface raiders caused the Allies anxiety, especially in February and March 1941, when the battle cruisers *Scharnhorst* and *Gneisenau* and the heavy cruiser *Hipper*, supported by very-long-range aircraft and submarines, roamed the Atlantic at will. They caused serious but brief disruption to shipping, accounting for only 6.1 percent of shipping destroyed by Germany during the war. By comparison, mines sank 6.5 percent, aircraft 13.4 percent, and unknown causes 4.8 percent. By May 1941, with longer days, fairer weather, and an increasing number of radar-equipped aircraft, German raider operations in the North Atlantic were no longer possible. The last raider to try, *Bismarck*, was sunk on May 26.

Instead, Germany came to rely on its U-boat fleet, which accounted for roughly 70 percent of Allied merchant ship losses. Admiral Karl Dönitz, until 1943 the head of the U-boat fleet, had wanted three hundred U-boats for a war against Britain, but in August 1940 he had twenty-seven and by February 1941 only twenty-one. Moreover, only a third of them were on station at a time: thirteen in August 1940 and only eight in January 1941. The number of U-boats increased dramatically in the spring of 1941, but by then Dönitz's chance had passed.

U-boat tactics by late 1940 were nonetheless innovative, producing their first "happy time" and catching the Royal Navy by surprise. The British believed that submarines would operate submerged and inshore, and so anti-submarine escort extended initially only to twelve degrees west and focused on defense against submerged attack. Once

**Battle of the Atlantic.** A large convoy of merchant ships is escorted by a Royal Navy battleship in April 1941. BY PERMISSION OF THE TRUSTEES OF THE IMPERIAL WAR MUSEUM, LONDON, A 3801

beyond the U-boat danger zone, U.K.-bound convoys were protected by cruisers and battleships, while westbound convoys were dispersed. It was understood that submarines could operate in the broad ocean, but finding and attacking escorted convoys there would be difficult.

However, Dönitz developed a solution to the problems of both search and attack on the high seas. Patrol lines of U-boats perpendicular to the convoy route, controlled by a shore-based plot through high-frequency radio communications, resolved the search problem. The "wolf pack" was then directed onto the target by headquarters, while the "shadower" transmitted a medium-frequency homing signal to help. The convoy was attacked at night, using the submarines as motor-torpedo boats, slipping inside the escort screen—and the convoy itself—on high-speed surface runs, escaping astern of the convoy or with a quick dive.

### The British Response

The Royal Navy was unprepared for this type of warfare, and losses to some convoys were alarming. At the end of October 1940 convoy SC7 lost twenty-one of its thirty ships, and HX79 lost twelve of forty-nine. The British responded by extending the escort system and, over time, denying tactical and strategic surface maneuverability to the U-boats. Over the winter of 1940–1941 the range of naval

and air anti-submarine escort expanded, and in March the British killed two of Germany's leading U-boat aces—Schepke and Prien—and captured the third, Kretschmer. In the following month they established bases in Iceland and opened Western Approaches Command in Liverpool to oversee anti-submarine defense of convoys. Permanent escort groups and new weapons and tactics were developed. In May 1941 the Royal Canadian Navy closed the gap in anti-submarine escort between British forces and those from Canada. The gap in air escort between the limits of Iceland- and Newfoundland-based aircraft remained for another two years and profoundly affected development of the battle.

Fairer weather and longer days curtailed German submarine success in the spring of 1941, and the German attempt to knock Britain out of the war faltered. Merchant shipping losses during 1941 amounted to 3.6 million gross registered tons, of which 2.1 million fell to U-boats: an average of about 250,000 tons per month, well short of Dönitz's objective. Meanwhile, British savings from rationing imports and reduced port congestion in 1941 amounted to some 3 million tons, while some 1.2 million tons of new shipping was launched. Moreover, in 1941 over 7 million tons of new shipping was on order in U.S. yards. Only for brief periods in 1942 and 1944 did Britain draw on its reserves of key commodities; in all other years imports outpaced consumption. The U-boat war in 1941 was therefore dramatic but not decisive. From the summer of 1941 until the spring of 1943, then, German strategy aimed to embarrass Allied plans and forestall the development of the second front. In this they failed as well.

What weighed heavily against Germany in the Atlantic by mid-1941 were several new elements. In June the British broke the German cipher system for U-boats in the Atlantic, and by August they were reading traffic with regularity and timeliness. This intelligence, gathered through the Ultra project, allowed convoys to be routed well clear of danger for much of the period, and it has been suggested that it saved three hundred Allied ships in late 1941. The German attack on Russia, Operation Barbarossa, begun on June 21, also eased much of the pressure in the Atlantic, and so did U.S. involvement in defense of Atlantic shipping following Churchill's meeting with Franklin D. Roosevelt in August. America took control of the western Atlantic, where by mid-September the U.S. Navy began to escort convoys between the Grand Banks and Iceland. The U.S. Navy was drawn into battles and suffered its first losses of the war—even before Pearl Harbor. German withdrawals to the Mediterranean and Norway eased the crisis around the trans-Atlantic convoys by November. Meanwhile, British forces escorting oceanic convoys in the eastern Atlantic inflicted a tactical defeat on the U-boats and their supporting long-range aircraft by employing new ten-centimeter-band radar, support groups, and an auxiliary aircraft carrier.

### The Aftermath of Pearl Harbor

The Atlantic war entered a new phase following the Japanese attack on Pearl Harbor on December 7, 1941. American industry and manpower gave the Allies promise of victory but in the meantime opened vast new theaters for Axis attack. By the spring of 1942, U-boats were enjoying their second "happy time." In May and June alone they sank over a million tons in U.S. waters—half their total score for 1941 in just two months. Allied merchant shipping losses peaked in 1942: some 8.3 million tons, of which 6.1 million fell to U-boats. It could not be sustained. New ship construction surged past losses in the fall of 1942, as American industry gained momentum. Moreover, the U-boats' success in the western Atlantic was the result of a monumental American strategic blunder.

In early 1942 the Americans trusted in "offensive" patrols by surface and air forces, protected lanes, and independently routed coastal shipping to defeat the U-boat menace. The results were catastrophic. Only the progressive extension of a convoy system within a wide and effectively patrolled air corridor reduced the threat from lone submariners. The Canadians started the first convoys in the American zone in March, and the U.S. Navy followed in May. As this system extended, it reduced tonnage sunk per U-boat day at sea and forced U-boats to move on. Much of 1942 was then about the further progressive denial of operating areas for U-boats dependent on surface maneuverability for both tactical and strategic success. By late 1942 expansion of the convoy system forced most U-boats back into the mid-ocean air gap, the only theater left where they could operate on the surface with impunity and hope to achieve decisive results. By August 1942 there were enough U-boats there to operate two large packs. The number of packs and their size increased dramatically over the next eight months, as the mid-Atlantic filled with U-boats.

The winter of 1942–1943 was the decisive and most complex period of the Atlantic war. In the preparation for the Allied landings in North Africa, oceanic convoys in the eastern Atlantic were stopped and all trans-Atlantic shipping was routed through the Western Hemisphere. This extended sailing times and reduced carrying capacity, and it made Britain utterly dependent on the main trans-Atlantic convoys just as the Germans were driven to attack them in force. The situation was further aggravated by the fact that the bulk of new merchant shipping was American while the vast majority of losses were British and by the unexpected high demand on British supplies by the landings in North Africa in November. Britain was therefore pushed into its gravest import crisis of the war just as the battle in the mid-ocean built to a climax.

The naval and air tactics, doctrine, and equipment necessary to deal with wolf packs improved markedly by 1942. Air patrols synchronized their efforts more effectively with convoy movements, while the introduction of white camouflage, higher patrol altitudes, and more effective fuses for depth charges contributed to increasingly successful air support. In August a few very-long-range Liberator aircraft operated in the mid-ocean—a development noted with concern by the Germans. Naval escorts now enjoyed the benefits of eighteen months of steady operational and tactical leadership, the development of sound and workable tactics and doctrine. New equipment on British escorts included ten-centimeter-band radar, which permitted effective barriers around the convoy at night in good weather, and shipborne high-frequency direction-finding sets that revealed the position of U-boats sending contact and shadowing reports. The only elements missing from the naval escort in 1942 were small escort aircraft carriers, which like so many other resources had been drawn off to the North African landings and the Russian convoys.

In the fall of 1942, British escort groups defended their convoys—usually the fast ones—effectively in the mid-ocean air gap. However, Canadian and American escorts, who made up about half of those operating in the air gap, lacked modern equipment, and their convoys—the bulk of them slow—were easy marks for German submariners: 80 percent of mid-Atlantic losses from July to December 1942 were suffered by Canadian-escorted convoys. When the British appointed a tough submariner, Rear Admiral Sir Max Horton, as commander in chief of the Western Approaches in November to tackle the mid-ocean problem, he immediately arranged to have the Canadian groups removed from the mid-ocean for refit and retraining. The only bright spot for the Allies in the mid-Atlantic at the very end of the year was the repenetration of the Atlantic U-boat cipher, which they had stopped reading in February. As the mid-ocean filled with U-boats in late 1942, precise intelligence became increasingly crucial. Through the winter of 1943 the number of operational U-boats ranged from 403 to 435, with an average of over 100 at sea each month, most in the Atlantic. Dönitz, who became head of the Kriegsmarine in January 1943, had his magic number and a free hand.

## The Turning Point

The Battle of the Atlantic climaxed in early 1943, spurred by bad winter weather, the rising numbers of U-boats, and another gap in special intelligence in the first three weeks of March. Every North Atlantic convoy was located by the Germans; half were attacked, and some 22 percent of the ships in those convoys were sunk. However, by then the seeds of the German defeat had been sown. In January 1943, Churchill and Roosevelt finally gave the Atlantic first priority. More aircraft, destroyers, and escort carriers were assigned to the North Atlantic. By late March, "support groups," one of them with a carrier, were reinforcing convoy escorts during their transit of the air gap. The Allied offensive—predominantly British—in the air gap was aided immeasurably by moderating weather in April, which gave freer rein to the escort's radars and destroyer sweeps guided by high-frequency direction-finding equipment.

The repenetration of the main U-boat cipher in the third week of March allowed these resources to be applied with devastating results. Reinforced convoys were used to draw U-boats into a battle of attrition they could not win. Lib-

erators closed the air gap in May, as more escort carriers arrived to join the battle. Nearly a hundred U-boats were sunk in the Atlantic during the first five months of 1943, forty-seven in May alone. At the end of May, Dönitz withdrew his battered packs; as far as the course of the war was concerned, the Battle of the Atlantic was decided by the spring of 1943.

Over the summer the punishing offensive continued, spearheaded by American "hunter-killer" groups built around escort carriers. Airpower, directed by Ultra, also devastated the U-boat fleet when it attempted to renew the offensive in the fall of 1943 with acoustic homing torpedoes. Allied shipping losses, which from January to May 1943 averaged 450,000 tons per month, dropped to approximately 200,000 during the last half of 1943, with only about 40,000 to 60,000 tons accounted for by submarines. Meanwhile the Mediterranean was opened to shipping in the summer, saving tonnage on the far eastern routes, and an enormous volume of new construction flowed from Allied shipyards—14 million tons in 1943—outstripping losses by about 11.5 million tons.

U-boats adopted a device called a *Schnorkel (snorkel)* in 1944 to permit continuous underwater travel, and plans for radically new types of U-boats were pushed forward. These developments gave rise to modern concepts of anti-submarine warfare, but the U-boat never seriously menaced Allied shipping or plans after 1943.

[See also Arctic Convoys; *Bismarck*; *U-9*; and *U-47*.]

## Bibliography

Assman, Kurt. "Why U-boat Warfare Failed." *Foreign Affairs* 28 (1950): 659–670.

Gardner, W. J. R. *Decoding History: The Battle of the Atlantic and Ultra*. Annapolis, Md.: Naval Institute Press, 1999.

Howarth, Stephen, and Derek Law, eds. *The Battle of the Atlantic 1939–1945: The 50th Anniversary International Naval Conference*. Annapolis, Md.: Naval Institute Press, 1994

Ireland, Bernard. *Battle of the Atlantic*. Annapolis, Md.: Naval Institute Press, 2003.

Milner, Marc. *Battle of the Atlantic*. Stroud, U.K.: Tempus; St. Catherines, Ontario: Vanwell, 2003.

Rahn, Wener. "The Atlantic in the Strategic Perspective of Hitler and Roosevelt, 1940–1941." In *To Die Gallantly, The Battle of the Atlantic*, edited by Timothy J. Runyan and Jan M. Copes, pp. 3–21. Boulder, Colo.: Westview Press, 1994

Salewski, Michael. *Die deutsche Seekreigsleitung 1935–1945*. 3 vols. Frankfurt am Main: Bernard and Graefe, 1970–1975.

Syrett, David. *The Defeat of the German U-Boats: The Battle of the Atlantic*. Columbia: University of South Carolina Press, 1994.

Westwood, David. *The U-boat War: The German Submarine Service and the Battle of the Atlantic, 1935–1945.* London: Conway Maritime, 2005.

White, David Fairbank. *Bitter Ocean: The Battle of the Atlantic, 1939–1945.* New York: Simon and Schuster, 2006.

MARC MILNER

# Atlantic Ocean

This entry contains five subentries:

---

## North Atlantic

The Atlantic Ocean as a whole is the second largest of the world's oceans. The division between the North Atlantic and the South Atlantic is often roughly made at the Equator, but a more precise division is created by the two Atlantic basins with their separate patterns of currents and wind systems. The divide between these two systems is made by the North Equatorial Counter Current, a current that shows a great deal of seasonal variability and occurs in the Atlantic between three and ten degrees north latitude.

### Origins of the Name

The traditional origins ascribed to the name "Atlantic" have many inconsistencies. In classical Greek and Roman myth, the name "Oceanus" was applied to the river that surrounded the inhabitable world. First applied as a name to all the known seas (that is, the Mediterranean and the Atlantic), it later came to be applied to the more distant and mysterious ocean in the west. In Greek myth, the name was personified by the figure of Oceanus, who was one of the twelve titans, the six sons and six daughters of Uranus (Heaven) and Gaea (Earth). In turn, Oceanus's sister and wife was the sea goddess Tethys, who together produced the thousand sea nymphs, known collectively as the "Oceanids," which became the patron goddesses of various seas, streams, and rivers. One of the Oceanids, Clymene, married a Titan, Lapetos. One of their children was Atlas. In myth, Zeus condemned Atlas to hold up the heavens on his shoulders. In turn, Mount Atlas in present-day Libya and the Atlas mountain range of Libya, Algeria, Morocco, and Tunis are associated with him, as places that hold up the heavens, through the Greek name for them, "Atlantikos." The name was also applied to the sea on the western African coast, and later the entire ocean. Plato, in his philosophical dialogues *Timeas* and *Criteas*, written about 360 B.C.E., described a huge mountainous island 700 kilometers (435 miles) wide in the ocean that was lost in an earthquake. In Latin, the name became "Atlanticum" or "Oceanus Atlanticus."

The first recorded use of the name "Atlantic" for the ocean is found in the *Histories* by Herodotus of Halicarnassus (c. 484–c. 430/420 B.C.E.), when he mentions in passing, "The sea frequented by the Greeks, that beyond the Pillars of Hercules, which is called the Atlantic" (book 1, 203). In English, seafarers commonly called it the "Western Ocean," although the word "Atlantic" is first recorded in the 1387 Higden Rolls as "Athlant," deriving from the French "Atlante." Philemon Holland's English translation of *The History of the World* (1601) by the Roman scholar Pliny the Elder (23–79 C.E.) records, "This river [Guadiana]…falleth into the Spanish Atlantick Ocean" (book 1, 51), while Henry Cockerham's *English Dictionarie, or Interpreter of Hard English Words* (1623; 2d ed., 1626) reports incorrectly that the "*Athlanticke Sea*, is the Mediterranean, or a part thereof." A century later, in 1732, Thomas Lediard's translation of the *Life of Sethos* reflected what had become the common understanding that "The Phoenicians…pass'd…into the Hesperian [Western] or Atlantick ocean" (vol. 2, p. 4).

The history of the cartography of this ocean area shows that the term "Atlantic" began to be applied in the late sixteenth century and the early seventeenth century. In earlier Spanish usage it was termed "Mare del Norte." In the general map of the world in Sebastian Münster's *Cosmographia Universalis* (Basel, 1544), the term "Oceanus Occidentalus" is used for the North Atlantic, while the South Atlantic is termed "Oceanus Aethiopicus." Abraham Ortelius used the term "Mare Atlanticum" in the world map in the first modern atlas, *Theatrum Orbis Terrarum* (1570). At the same time, Gerardus Mercator (Gerhard Kremer; 1512–1594) used the term "Oceanus Occidentalus" in his *Atlas of Europe* (c. 1570), but replaced it with "Oceanus Atlanticus" on his world map (1587). The Dutch geographer Bernhardus Varenius (1622–1650), in his *Geographica Generalis* (1650; edition improved by Sir Isaac Newton, 1672, p. 82), was the first to try to regularize the terminology by stating that the Atlantic, often called Mare del Norte, is the sea enclosed between the western shores of the old world and the eastern shore of new world.

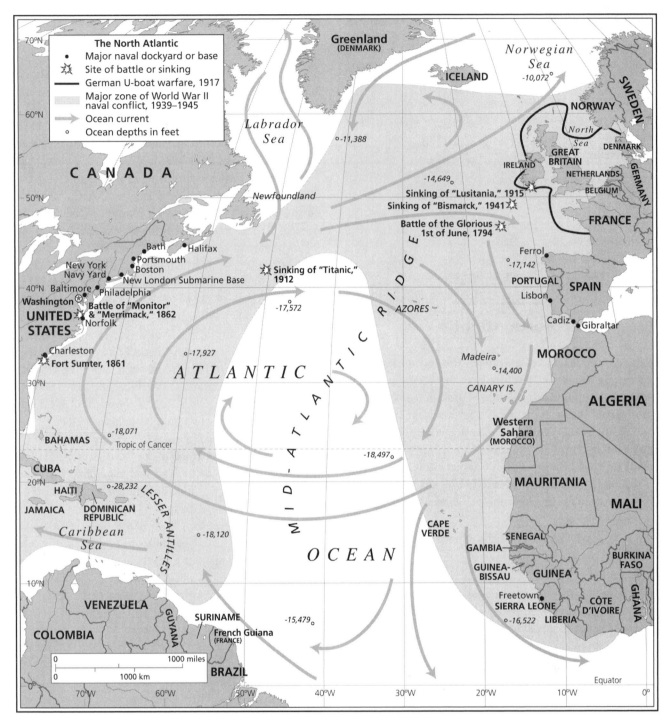

**Map of the North Atlantic.** MAP BY MAPPING SPECIALISTS LIMITED

## Prevailing Winds and Ocean Currents

As European seafarers moved beyond the initial phase of exploration in the North Atlantic region, they began to find by trial and error the prevailing winds and ocean currents that determined their routes. Christopher Columbus established the classic westward passage to America with his intuitive—or serendipitous—decision to make his transatlantic departure from the Canary Islands rather than from the Azores, thereby placing himself within a favorable part of the Atlantic wind and current system. From the Canaries, Columbus used the northeast trade winds, crossing below the region of the subtropical high pressure area that creates the calm or highly variable light winds in the hot region called the "Horse Latitudes" or "Calms of Capricorn" between thirty and thirty-five degrees north, and above the low pressure area of calm winds in the Equatorial or Intertropical Convergence Zone, which early seafarers named the "Doldrums," along the Equator.

Undocumented legend ascribes the naming of the Horse Latitudes to early Spanish seafarers who killed the horses they were transporting to the Americas—because of the calms that lengthened their voyage, they had used up their food supplies and drinking water. Part of this same area is the region of calm winds and little current that contains the Sargasso Sea, an area between twenty and thirty degrees north latitude and thirty to seventy degrees west longitude, which typically contains an elliptically shaped area with drifts of floating brown seaweed sometimes called Gulfweed, most of which is a brown algae, or Phaeophyta, which is usually *Sargassum natans* and somewhat less commonly *Sargassum fluitans*.

Columbus reported the Sargasso Sea, and it had also possibly been seen earlier by the fifth century B.C.E. Carthaginian, Himilco the Navigator, who according to the Roman writer Rufus Festus Avenius (fourth century C.E.), reported that "Many seaweeds grow in the troughs between the waves, which slow the ship like bushes.... Here the beasts of the sea move slowly hither and thither, and great monsters swim languidly among the sluggishly creeping ships" (*Ora Maritima*). The name reputedly originated with fifteenth-century Portuguese seafarers, who saw this type of algae's distinctive air bladders that allow it to float and thought that they resembled the *Sarga* grape, naming it *sargaço*.

With the Sargasso Sea as part of the ocean center, the North Atlantic Ocean current system rotates clockwise around it on its periphery. The current on the south of this is the Atlantic North Equatorial Current, which runs from the North African coast in the east toward the west between the Equator and about ten degrees north latitude. As it approaches the South American coast, it divides into two forks. One, the Caribbean Current, follows the coast of South America and moves clockwise around the Gulf of Mexico, while the other, the Antilles Current, runs northwestward mainly along the northern side of the West Indian islands. Both currents eventually merge into the most distinctive current of the North Atlantic, the northeasterly running Gulf Stream. Typical of the western side

of such large ocean-current patterns, the Gulf Stream is the strongest in the North Atlantic because of the western intensification created by the Coriolis effect and the variation of that force with latitude, while it is further driven by the prevailing winds. The warm water of the Gulf Stream arises in the Gulf of Mexico, passes through the Straits of Florida and follows the North American coastline from Florida past Newfoundland. At about 30°W longitude and 40°N latitude, the Gulf Stream splits into two branches. The southern branch moves toward Spain, Portugal, and the West African coast, joining the Canary Current to reticulate across the North Atlantic. The northern branch becomes the North Atlantic Drift, which contrasts with the wind-driven Gulf Stream, and moves forward by the thermohaline circulation effect caused by its relatively higher temperature and salinity. The North Atlantic Drift provides the fundamental variation to the weather in Iceland, the British Isles, and northern Europe, making it warmer than it otherwise would be. The North Atlantic Drift is the factor that makes an average relative difference of 30 degrees Celsius between locations on opposite sides of the Atlantic at the same latitude in Canada and in Norway.

Juan Ponce de León (1460–1521) first reported the Gulf Stream, when he sailed through the Strait of Florida and explored the coast of Florida. Ponce de León's log for April 22, 1513, recorded, as reported by Antonio de Herrera y Tordesillas in his *Historia general de los hechos de los Castellanos en las islas y tierra firme del Mar Oceano* (1601–1615), "A current such that, although they had great wind, they could not proceed forward, but backward and it seems that they were proceeding well." Although the Gulf Stream was known and used by navigators, Benjamin Franklin (1706–1790), with the assistance of his cousin the Nantucket whaler Timothy Folger (1732–1814), published the first attempt to chart it in 1769–1770 as a means to improve the speed of communication between North America and Europe (published 1786). A posthumously published map by Herman Moll (fl. 1678–1732), *A View of the General Trade-Winds, Monsoons, or Shifting-Winds* (1736), gave a generally correct view of the world's trade winds, but it was Matthew Fontaine Maury (1806–1873) who made the first systematic attempt to chart the currents and prevailing winds of the North Atlantic through his work in compiling standardized weather information from ships for his *Wind and Current Chart of the North Atlantic*, published in editions from the 1850s.

While Philippe Buache (1700–1773) produced the first thematic atlas of physical geography, suggesting the contours of the ocean floor based on some actual soundings in his *Cartes et tables de la géographie physique ou naturelle* (1779), the first true bathymetric chart of the Atlantic appeared in Maury's *Sailing Directions* (5th edition, 1853), and, as a result of the use of John M. Brooke's sounding device, this chart was quickly improved with three times the number of soundings in the 1855 edition of the same work. The deepest part of the Atlantic is the Puerto Rico Trench, along the boundary between the Atlantic and the Caribbean Sea. The trench is 800 kilometers (500 miles) long and reaches a maximum depth in a section called the Milwaukee Trench, first reported by the cruiser USS *Milwaukee* (CL-5) on February 14, 1939, at 9,219 meters (30,246 feet).

Edmond Halley (1656–1742) examined another physical property of the North Atlantic that was of immediate use to navigators in his expedition of 1698–1700 in HMS *Paramore* (or *Paramour*), the results of which were published in his *General Chart of the Variation of the Compass* (1701), the first chart to use isogonic lines to indicate points of equal variation on the globe.

## Trade Routes

The characteristic winds and currents on the surface of the North Atlantic were the key determining factors for trade routes that gradually developed. Several variations developed on the route between Europe and North America, and they can be characterized by the trade of the vessels involved, such as the sugar route, the tobacco route, and the fishing route to the Newfoundland banks. An interesting index of the time involved in transatlantic passage can be seen in the gradual shortening of the time taken to transmit news. The season of the year, as well as the optimum route for the season, made a difference in time of passage. In 1705 the average time for London news to be reported in the newspapers of Boston, Massachusetts, was 163 days. By 1745 this had declined to 85 days. Admiral Horatio Nelson's chase of the French fleet under Admiral Pierre Villeneuve (1763–1806) across the Atlantic from Cape Saint Vincent to Barbados covered 3,227 nautical miles in 24 days, while the same fleets took 38 days to cover the 3,459 nautical miles on the return passage. Several months later, the news of the battle of Trafalgar reached New England in 37 days. This was the same average time that it took after 1818, when the regularly scheduled sailing packets were established between New York and Liverpool. By 1857, however, the average had declined to 34 days. Between 1818 and 1832, the fastest packet crossed in 21 days sailing east (2,996 nautical miles in winter, 3,148 nautical miles

in spring) from New York to Liverpool, while the slowest took 29 days. On the westward passage from Liverpool to New York (3,540 nautical miles in winter, 3,723 nautical miles in summer), the fastest packet crossing took 34 days and the longest took 46 days.

During the sailing-ship era, the principal routes were not only those that took Europeans to the western shore of the Atlantic and back, but also those that carried Europeans back and forth to the Indian and the Pacific Oceans. The route across the North Atlantic to the Indian Ocean was first established in the voyage of Vasco da Gama (c. 1460–1524), who used both the North Atlantic and the South Atlantic wind and current systems to reach India in 1497–1498. This route went from European ports southwest to the Canary Islands, then on to the Cape Verde Islands and crossing the narrowest part of the North Atlantic to reach the northeast edge of South America, then following the Brazilian coast south to about latitude 20°S before heading in an easterly direction to the Cape of Good Hope. Similarly, the first voyage of circumnavigation under Ferdinand Magellan (c. 1480–1521) and Juan Sebastián Elcano (c. 1476–1526) in 1519–1522 stopped at the Canary and Cape Verde Islands before sailing toward Cape Saint Augustine, Brazil, and following the South American coast southward to enter the Pacific.

As Atlantic traffic patterns developed during the coming centuries for sailing vessels, Dutch, German, and Scandinavian navigators discovered that they could save weeks by sailing north around the British Isles to avoid sailing into the teeth of southwest winds. In sailing through the Atlantic bound for the Indian Ocean, the mid-Atlantic proved a particular problem. A navigator had to judge his position well, as the ideal routes were either along the Brazilian coast or in the middle of the Atlantic between Brazil and Africa. If a navigator approaching these areas sailed too far to the west, the South Equatorial Current and Caribbean Current could force a vessel into the Caribbean Sea. If one sailed too close to the African coast, the Guinea Current could force a vessel into the Gulf of Guinea, where there was little wind.

The western portion of the North Atlantic shares, along with the North Pacific, the South Pacific, and the Indian Ocean, characteristic tropical cyclonic storms. They very rarely occur in the South Atlantic Ocean; the first positively identified one occurred in 2004. All such storms have similar characteristics, but they have different names in different ocean areas. In the North Atlantic they are called hurricanes; in other regions they may be called hurricanes, typhoons, or cyclones. They occur during the summer and autumn months and only in the western part of the oceans, usually in the West Indies and Gulf of Mexico, but they can reach the New England and Canadian coasts. Christopher Columbus made the first documented report of a North Atlantic hurricane in June 1495. The first recorded hurricane to reach New England occurred in 1635. In 1775 a hurricane reached Newfoundland, killing a total of more than four thousand people. In August 1778 a hurricane off Newport, Rhode Island, interrupted an impending naval battle between French forces under Comte Jean-Baptiste d'Estaing and a British squadron under Admiral Richard Howe. The Great Hurricane of 1780 killed an estimated twenty-two thousand people in the deadliest hurricane on record. The Great September Gale of 1815 reached New England.

In 1898 the U.S. president William McKinley directed the U.S. Weather Bureau to establish a hurricane warning system. This work was eventually centered in the Miami, Florida, office, which in 1967 was designated the National Hurricane Center. In 1969 the civil engineer Herbert S. Saffir (b. 1917) developed a standard scale to measure hurricane strength. Modified in the early 1970s by Robert Simpson, director of the U.S. National Hurricane Center from 1967 to 1973, it became the Saffir-Simpson Hurricane Scale, which rates hurricanes from category one, the least powerful, through category five, the most powerful, in order of increasing intensity. Each intensity category specifies the range of barometric pressure, wind speed, storm surge, and damage potential.

Shipping in the northern portions of the North Atlantic crossing on a great circle route between Europe and Canada or the United States frequently encounters icebergs or extensive fields of ice. These are most commonly found in April, May, and June each year near the Great Bank of Newfoundland. Icebergs adrift in the Arctic find their way south on the Labrador Current. Most of the North Atlantic icebergs originate from the west coast of Greenland, with a few coming from Greenland's east coast and from Hudson Bay. Between 1904 and 1913, for example, icebergs were sighted as far south as 37°50′ N and as far east as 38° W. Field ice, formed in the Arctic or the shores of Newfoundland, also drifts southward with the Labrador Current.

A typical feature of the North Atlantic, floating ice has led to numerous accidents, disasters, and dramatic rescues in the area off Newfoundland and the Grand Banks. In 1833, *Lady of the Lake* sank with the loss of seventy people. In October 1871, Captain George Tyson and a group of nineteen others from the U.S. survey ship *Polaris* were separated from their ship and trapped on an ice flow

south of Littleton Island, between latitudes 77° and 78′N. Unable to return to their ship, they drifted for six months and covered over 2,400 kilometers (1,500 miles) before the sealing steamer *Tigress* rescued them on April 30, 1872, near Strait of Belle Isle in latitude 53°35′ N. Between 1882 and 1890, fourteen vessels were lost and forty seriously damaged by ice. Then, in one of the worst sea disasters in maritime history, RMS *Titanic* hit an iceberg and sank on the night of April 14–15, 1912, with the loss of fifteen hundred lives. Her wreck was found in 1985 at 41°43′55″ N, 49°56′55″ W, some 24 kilometers (13 nautical miles) from where she was originally thought to have sunk. Because of the annual variability of ice formation, no detailed examination of ice movement in the North Atlantic had been developed up to that time.

After *Titanic*'s sinking in 1912, the U.S. Navy assigned USS *Chester* and USS *Birmingham* to an ice patrol, but from 1913, U.S. Revenue Marine cutters undertook this duty. As a direct result of the *Titanic*'s sinking, the first International Convention for the Safety of Life at Sea met in London, opening on November 12, 1913. On January 30, 1914, a treaty was signed to establish and fund the International Ice Patrol from 1915. The signatories to the treaty agreed to share the costs, and the necessary surveillance and patrol duties were assigned to be carried out on behalf of the signatories by the U.S. Coast Guard, established in 1915 as the successor to the U.S. Revenue Marine. The U.S. Coast Guard has continued to carry out these functions since that time. From 1946 aircraft replaced Coast Guard cutters in doing the surveillance, and from 1979 computer modeling has been used to predict the limits of oceanographic drift of ice and rate of ice deterioration. In 1983 side-looking airborne radar, and in 1993 forward-looking airborne radar, began to be used to search for and track icebergs. Seventeen nations, including Belgium, Canada, Denmark, Finland, France, Germany, Greece, Italy, Japan, the Netherlands, Norway, Panama, Poland, Spain, Sweden, the United Kingdom, and the United States, contribute to the Ice Patrol.

## Records for Crossings

Eventually, crossing the Atlantic became a routine matter, and the length of time taken for a passage became an object of interest as well as of profit and even sport. As dictated by the winds and current pattern, the passage from Europe to America generally took longer than the passage from America to Europe. The average times for delivery slowly improved over the years.

The first steamship to cross the Atlantic was *Savannah*, Captain Moses Rogers, crossing from Savannah, Georgia, to Liverpool between May 22 and June 20, 1819. Popular interest in transatlantic speed records began in April 1838, when the steamship *Sirius* crossed from Cork to Sandy Hook in eighteen days, fourteen hours, and twenty-two minutes with an average speed of 8.03 knots. The following day, *Great Western* arrived in New York from Avonmouth in fifteen days, twelve hours, at an average speed of 8.66 knots. By the 1860s, rival shipping companies began to compete for what became known as the Atlantic "Blue Riband" as a means of publicizing the fastest passage, with separate awards for eastbound and westbound passages. Shipping company owners agreed that the winner could fly a blue pennant from its masthead to mark this distinction. In 1934, Sir Harold Hales (1868–1942), a member of parliament and an owner of the Hales Brothers Shipping Company, donated the Hales Trophy to the ship that crossed the Atlantic with the highest average speed. Many famous liners won the award, including Nord Deutsche Lloyd's *Kaiser Wilhelm der Große* in 1898 with a speed of 22.29 knots for the westbound passage; Cunard's *Lusitania* in 1909 with 25.65 knots; the Italia Line's *Rex* in 1933 with 28.92 knots; the Compagnie Générale Transatlantique's *Normandie* in 1937 with 30.58 knots westbound and 31.20 eastbound; Cunard-White Star Line's *Queen Mary* in 1938 with 30.99 knots westbound and 31.69 knots eastbound; and the United States Line's *United States* in 1952 with 34.51 knots westbound and 35.59 eastbound.

From such commercial interests, yachting and sporting interests in crossing the Atlantic also developed. In 1866 the first transatlantic yacht race left Sandy Hook, New Jersey, and sailed eastward to the Isle of Wight. The race was won by the New York newspaper publisher James Gordon Bennet Jr. in *Henrietta*, taking thirteen days, twenty-one hours, and fourteen minutes. The Anglo-American artist James E. Buttersworth (1817–1894) painted a view of the start.

In 1876, Alfred "Centennial" Johnson of Gloucester, Massachusetts, made the first west-to-east, single-handed crossing of the North Atlantic, in a 20-foot, gaff-rigged fishing dory, reaching Albertcastle, England, in ninety-six days. With his example in mind, fellow townsman and local schooner fisherman Howard Blackburn (1852–1932), a disabled seafarer who had lost his fingers and toes in a winter storm in 1883, followed Johnson's example in a 30-foot sloop *Great Western* in 1899, sailing to Gloucester, England, in sixty-two days.

Single-handed transatlantic yacht racing began in 1891 with a race between William Albert Andrews's 15-foot *Mermaid* and Josiah W. Lawlor's 15-foot *Sea Serpent*. Sailing from Boston, Massachusetts, Andrews capsized several times, and he was rescued six hundred miles from his destination. Although Lawlor capsized several times, he reached Lizard Point, England, in forty-five days.

In 1956, Francis Chichester (1901–1972) and Herbert Haslar (1914–1987) had the initial idea of a westward yacht race across the North Atlantic, against the prevailing winds. The British newspaper *Observer* agreed to sponsor such a race supervised by the Royal Western Yacht Club of Plymouth, England. A regular series, the Observer Single Handed Trans-Atlantic Race (OSTAR), was first raced in 1960 from Plymouth, England, to Newport, Rhode Island. This was the first single-handed ocean yacht race to be sailed. Subsequent transatlantic races have been held every four years, although the names have changed to reflect new sponsors: CSTAR, Europe 1 STAR, Transat, and so forth. A biennial race has been sailed from Newport, Rhode Island, to Bermuda since 1906.

The first modern sailors to row across the Atlantic were George Harbro and Gerard Samuelson in 1896. More recently, ocean rowing has become a sport. In 1992 a record was established for the fastest east-to-west passage in 35 days, with an 11-man rowing crew in a French boat, *La Mondial*, under Gerard Seibel. The first solo west-to-east transatlantic passage was completed in May–July 1969 by the British oarsman Tom McClean in the ocean rowboat *Super Silver* in 70 days, 18 hours, and 35 minutes, a record he beat himself in 1987 with a 55 day passage in *Skoll 1080*. An east-to-west solo record was first established the same year by John Fairfax in 180 days. In 2004, Emmanuel Coindre set a record as the first person to make a solo passage both ways across the Atlantic with a west-to-east passage of 62 days, 19 hours, and 42 minutes and an east-to-west passage of 42 days, 14 hours, 32 minutes in *Lady Bird*.

Records were also established for other types of Atlantic crossings. The first commercial submarine to carry cargo across the Atlantic was *Deutschland*, Captain Paul König, operated by Deutsche Ozean Rhederei, making two trips from Bremen to the United States in 1916. In May 1919 the U.S. Navy's flying boat, *NC-4*, with a six-man crew, made the first crossing of the Atlantic in a fixed-wing aircraft, flying between New York and Lisbon, stopping in Newfoundland and the Azores en route. A month later, in June 1919, Sir John William Alcock (1892–1919) and Sir Arthur Whitten Brown (1886–1948) were the first to fly nonstop across the Atlantic, in 16 hours, 27 minutes, flying from Saint John's, Newfoundland, to Clifton, County

Galway, Ireland, on June 15, 1919. On May 20–21, 1927, Charles Augustus Lindbergh made the first solo crossing of the Atlantic in 33.5 hours, flying from Roosevelt Field, Long Island, New York, over Ireland and England to Le Bourget Field, near Paris.

## Scientific Expeditions

The principal scientific expeditions in the Atlantic have included work from the 1840s of the U.S. Coast Survey under Alexander Dallas Bache and reports collected and published for the U.S. Navy by Matthew Fontaine Maury; the preparatory surveys for laying the Atlantic telegraph cable undertaken by HMS *Bulldog* in 1860 with observations by G. C. Wallich; the work of Achille Ernest Oscar Joseph Delesse, published in 1871, on the lithology of the ocean bottom; a number of expeditions by Louis Agassiz; and the 1869–1870 cruises of HMS *Porcupine* and HMS *Lightning*. These last cruises led to the 1872–1876 HMS *Challenger* expedition, commanded successively by captains George S. Nares and Frank Thompson, and under the scientific direction of C. Wyville Thomson of the University of Edinburgh. This expedition made an extensive study of the Atlantic in the first portion of its voyage around the globe and made additional observations on its return voyage, including botany, zoology, and oceanography. Other expeditions were the Norwegian North Atlantic Expedition in *Vöringen* during 1876–1878; the deep-sea sounding taken in the Atlantic by USS *Gettysburg* in 1876 and in the Caribbean, Gulf of Mexico, and coast of Florida in USS *Blake* by Alexander Agassiz in 1877–1880; French expeditions in *Travailleur* and *Talisman* in the Bay of Biscay and south to the Cape Verde Islands in 1880–1883; Prince Albert I (r. 1889–1922) of Monaco's observations of currents in the North Atlantic with his yachts *Hirondelle* and *Princess Alice* from 1885; USS *Albatross* for the United States Commission of Fish and Fisheries in 1883–1886; the 1889 Plankton Expedition undertaken by German scientists; and the German Atlantic Expedition in MS *Meteor* in 1925–1927. In 1969–1970, in a very different type of scientific expedition, Thor Heyerdahl (1914–2002) crossed the Atlantic from Morocco in his reed and papyrus raft *Ra* to prove that ancient Egyptians could have reached the Americas in such craft.

## Lighthouses

Lighthouses as aids to navigation have been a typical feature of the Atlantic. In Europe one of the first was established at Torre de Hércules, La Coruña, Spain (c. 200 C.E.). Others include the Caepio Light at Chipiona, Spain (20 B.C.E.); Boulogne, France, and Dover, England (c. 40 C.E.); and Hook Head, County Wexford, Ireland (c. 1220). In the Americas, the first light was established at Forte de Santo Antônio da Barra, near Salvador, Bahia, Brazil, in 1698. The first light to be established in North America was the light at Little Brewster Island, Massachusetts (1716). This was followed by Louisbourg, Cape Breton Island, Nova Scotia (1734); Beavertail, Conanicut Island, Rhode Island (1749); Sambro Island, Halifax, Nova Scotia (1760); Cape Henlopen, Delaware; Portland Head, Maine (1790); and Paradise (formerly Hog) Island, Nassau, Bahamas (1817). The first use of concentric prisms for a light, an invention of Augustin-Jean Fresnel (1788–1827), occurred in 1827 at Chassiron on the Ile d'Oléron, France, on the Bay of Biscay, while the first electrified light came into use at Dungeness, on the southern coast of England, in 1862.

## Historiography

In the decades immediately following World War II, professional historians in Europe and in America, including Charles Verlinden (1907–1996), Jacques Godechot (1907–1989), R. R. Palmer (1909–2002), Pierre Chaunu (b. 1923), and Bernard Bailyn (b. 1922), among others, developed the initial concepts of what came to be called "Atlantic history," focusing on the shared civilization of the nations bordering the Atlantic Ocean. They initially focused particularly on its origins and development in the early modern period, from the first explorations of the Atlantic through the revolutionary era, to create a distinctive Atlantic regional cultural identity linking maritime affairs to a broader cultural understanding that shows the mutual contributions of European, African, and American peoples; the westward migrations of peoples; the development of pan-Atlantic commercial, racial, and ethnic relations; and the spread of Enlightenment thought.

[*See also* Boston; Cádiz; Caribbean Sea; Lisbon; Liverpool; Mail Services; Maury, Matthew Fontaine; Newport; New York; Passenger Trades; Seaside Resorts; Slave Trade; Trade Routes; *and* Yachting and Pleasure Sailing.]

## Bibliography

Albion, Robert G. *Square Riggers on Schedule: The New York Sailing Packets to England, France, and the Cotton Ports.* Princeton, N.J.: Princeton University Press, 1938.

Bailyn, Bernard. *Atlantic History: Concepts and Contours*. Cambridge, Mass.: Harvard University Press, 2005.

Butel, Paul. *The Atlantic*. Translated by Iain Hamilton Grant. New York: Routledge, 1999.

Chaunu, Pierre, and Huguette Chaunu. *Séville et l'Atlantique: 1504–1650*. 8 vols. Paris: Colin, 1955–.

Eltis, David, Stephen Behrendt, David Richardson, and Herbert S. Klein, eds. *The Trans-Atlantic Slave Trade: A Data Base on CD-ROM*. Cambridge, U.K.: Cambridge University Press, 1999. See also the special issue of *The William and Mary Quarterly*, 3d series, vol. 58 (January 2001), devoted to this database.

Steele, Ian K. *The English Atlantic, 1675–1740: An Exploration of Communication and Community*. New York: Oxford University Press, 1986.

JOHN B. HATTENDORF

# North Atlantic Regional Navies

The North Atlantic has often been the ocean of dominant great power navies. In broad successive roles, Portugal, Spain, the Dutch Republic, Britain, and the United States have held the dominant naval roles in the North Atlantic, while France, Germany, and the Soviet Union have played key roles as competitor naval powers. Below the level of national great power navies, there has also been a series of small local and regional navies. In some cases, such as that of Portugal and Spain, the regional navies were former national great power navies, while others such as the United States were small navies on the way to becoming national great power navies.

## Late Eighteenth Century and Nineteenth Century

The first of the new navies to appear in the modern era was the group of fledgling naval forces that appeared from 1775, the separate state navies and the Continental Navy. In 1794 these became the United States Navy, which in the twentieth century grew into a great power navy.

While this new naval force was just beginning in the period of the French Revolution and Empire, those wars temporarily ended North Atlantic navies in the Netherlands, Spain, and Portugal. The Dutch navy was re-created in 1813–1814. Acquiring former French assets, it was momentarily the fourth-largest battle fleet in Europe, but it quickly reduced its size to a force that could protect trade. From the point of this initial reduction the Dutch fleet gradually grew, introducing steam-powered warships from the 1820s for use in local defense and colonial operations overseas.

The Spanish navy was effectively destroyed at the Battle of Trafalgar in 1805, and a number of the former officers and men from the Spanish navy eventually found new naval employment in the independent navies that emerged in South and Central America between 1810 and 1824. An effective new Spanish navy, using modernized ship design, was begun from the time of the administration of the Marqués de Molina in 1847–1851. During the 1850s and 1860s, Spanish naval expeditions went to Morocco and Cochin China, fought a war against three Latin American republics, and joined in a combined expedition with France to Mexico. By the 1870s and 1880s, plans for a modernized steam navy were repeatedly attempted and were successful from 1887, but the result of this effort was largely destroyed in 1898 during the war with the United States that resulted in the loss of Spain's overseas empire, including Cuba, Puerto Rico, and the Philippines.

With the French invasion of Portugal in 1807, the surviving vessels of the Portuguese navy moved to Brazil and engaged in operations in South America. With Brazilian independence in 1822, a nucleus of ships returned to Portugal, and construction began in 1823–1834 to form a new Portuguese navy. The naval ministries of Marquês Sá da Bandeira (1858–1859) and José da Silva Mendes Leal (1862–1864) began a period of modernized naval growth, with further development under João de Andrade Corvo in 1871–1879. From this period, the Portuguese navy was involved in operations in Angola and Mozambique, and also in Guinea and São Tomé (1890), Timor (1889, 1893, 1895), Macao (1880, 1884), and Rio de Janeiro (1893).

## Twentieth Century

The expenses and manpower strain that Britain had experienced in the South African War (Second Boer War) in 1899–1902 and the rise of naval competition in Germany and elsewhere from the 1890s led the British government to try to diversify imperial defense by encouraging the overseas British Dominions to support and develop their own naval forces. In the North Atlantic region, this led to the establishment of the Royal Canadian Navy in 1910. The process of its formation created a major political debate within Canada, but the service slowly developed throughout the following century, playing significant roles in the two world wars—roles that helped to define its strengths and distinctive identity in relation to both the Royal Navy, from which it derived, and its near neighbor, the U.S. Navy.

In one way or another, the world wars of 1914–1919 and 1939–1945 involved nearly all the naval forces in the

North Atlantic as either active participants or neutrals protecting their own shores and shipping. Beyond those major wars, Spain's navy was involved in the Spanish Civil War (1936–1939). While many of the officers joined or were killed attempting to join the Nationalist cause, the men remained largely loyal to the Republicans, and the warships were often anchored at Cartagena. The war involved a variety of foreign ad hoc multilateral naval operations that ranged from supporting one side or the other, evacuation of civilians, blockade, interdiction patrols, and antisubmarine operations. The navies of Argentina, France, Germany, Great Britain, Italy, Mexico, Netherlands, Norway, Portugal, the Soviet Union, Yugoslavia, and the United States were all involved in such operations.

Also in the interwar period, the Icelandic Coast Guard was formally established in 1926. Although Danish forces had been patrolling Icelandic waters since about 1859, the first ship built purposely for this duty came in 1906, and by 1929 the first coast-defense ship became part of the fleet.

Following World War II, there were two major naval developments in the North Atlantic. With the Cold War, one series of developments involved the navies of western Europe, Canada, and the United States in the context of the North Atlantic Treaty Organization (NATO). The other development saw the proliferation of navies among smaller and newly independent states, reflecting the trend in which the number of navies in the world tripled in the fifty years following 1945.

The first of the new navies in the North Atlantic was the Irish Naval Service. Although the Irish Free State had been established in 1922 (known as Eire from 1937 to 1949 and as the Republic of Ireland since 1949), it was only through the impetus of World War II that Ireland acquired two motor torpedo boats and established the Marine and Coastwatching Service in 1939 to protect its neutrality. The coast-watching function was disbanded in 1945, but the Marine was incorporated into the Irish Defence Forces in 1946 as the Irish Naval Service. Since 1971 the service has grown to eight offshore patrol vessels.

The largest proliferation of navies in the North Atlantic has appeared on the northwestern and western coasts of Africa, where fourteen new navies appeared between 1956 and 1978. Liberia was founded in 1842 but had no maritime tradition until it established a volunteer coast guard in about 1956. This was formally renamed the Ghana Navy in 1987. Nigeria began planning a navy in 1956 and established it in 1960. With assistance from the United Kingdom, Netherlands, Germany, and France,

the Ghana Navy expanded from 1978 through the mid-1980s. Guinea established a navy in 1958 that was supplied up until the 1980s by the Soviet Union. Its naval port, Conakry, became the most visited port of call in the Atlantic for the Soviet navy during the 1970s. In 1959, Ghana established its navy for coast guard and fishery-protection purposes. The Royal Moroccan Navy was established with French ships and equipment in 1960, and later participated in the Moroccan-Spanish naval action of 1973. Gabon established a volunteer navy in 1961, Senegal acquired patrol boats, and Côte d'Ivoire (Ivory Coast) established a coastal and river patrol force. Mauritania established its Islamic navy in 1966. In 1973, Sierra Leone established a small naval force, and Cameroon, which had patrolled its 402-kilometer (250-mile) coast with French assistance until 1973, created its own navy. Africa's smallest state, Equatorial Guinea, acquired its first armed patrol boats from the Soviet Union in 1974. Togo began to patrol its 56-kilometer (35-mile) coastline under the command of a French naval officer in 1976, while Benin created a navy in 1978 to patrol its 121-kilometer (75-mile) coastline.

The North Atlantic Treaty, signed on April 4, 1949, created the North Atlantic Treaty Organization (NATO) to create a collective security organization for the Atlantic area north of the Tropic of Cancer (latitude 23.45° N) against a possible attack from the Soviet Union and, from 1955, the Warsaw Pact. NATO's military and naval organization was an outgrowth and adaptation of the joint and combined command-and-control system that the western Allied powers had originally used during World War II. NATO had two coequal supreme allied commanders, one for military affairs—the Supreme Allied Commander, Europe—and one for naval affairs, the Supreme Allied Commander, Atlantic. The naval organization was established in April 1952 and based at Norfolk, Virginia, typically with NATO commanders serving simultaneously as national commanders. During the Cold War, the central role of the Supreme Allied Commander, Atlantic, was to ensure the use of the Atlantic Ocean for the support of allied military operations in Europe and to deny its use to the Soviet Union and the Warsaw Pact countries. With the reorganization of NATO's command structure, this command was disestablished on January 1, 2003, and its functions were transferred to the Allied Operations Command at Mons, Belgium.

The first officer to be the Supreme Allied Commander, Atlantic, was Admiral Lynde McCormick, U.S. Navy. From the outset, he had a British deputy. The first Deputy

Supreme Allied Commander was Vice Admiral Sir William Andrews, Royal Navy. From 1960, the Supreme Allied Commander, Atlantic, had two subordinate commanders in charge of geographical regions of the North Atlantic: the Western Atlantic (Westland) and the Eastern Atlantic (Eastland). Each of these two commands was further subdivided.

An American admiral commanded the Western Atlantic with two subareas: the Canadian Atlantic, under a Canadian admiral, and the Atlantic Ocean, under the Commander of the Western Atlantic himself. The Western Atlantic also had three island commands: Bermuda, under a British admiral; Greenland, under a Danish admiral; and the Azores, under a Portuguese admiral.

The Commander of the Eastern Atlantic was a British admiral, who simultaneously held the NATO position of Commander in Chief, Channel. As Commander, Western Atlantic, he had two subareas under his command, each commanded by a British vice admiral: the Northern Atlantic and the Central Atlantic. In addition, the Eastern Atlantic Command had two island commands: Iceland, under an American rear admiral, and the Faeroes, under a Danish naval captain. In 1965, a third region was established, the Iberian Atlantic, under the command of a Portuguese vice admiral. The Iberian Atlantic had one island command, Madeira, commanded by a Portuguese general. In addition, the Supreme Allied Commander had two functional commands under him: the Striking Fleet, Atlantic, and the Submarine Command, Atlantic, both commanded by American vice admirals.

On January 13, 1968, NATO established the Standing Naval Force, Atlantic. It was the first permanent international naval squadron ever established and initially consisted of five to nine destroyer-type ships, each vessel contributed by a different country, with the overall command of the force rotating annually from one country to another. This innovative arrangement allowed regional navies to operate on an equal footing with national great power navies, creating a wider range of naval cooperation and interoperability than had heretofore been available. On January 1, 2005, the Standing Naval Force, Atlantic, was renamed the Standing NATO Response Force Maritime Group One and placed under the command of Allied Command Operations in Belgium.

On May 11, 1973, NATO established the Standing Naval Force, Channel, a permanent naval force of minesweepers and mine hunters. Belgium, Britain, Denmark, the Netherlands, and Germany contributed vessels, and the command rotated annually among them. In 1998, the Standing Naval Force, Channel, was renamed Mine Countermeasure Force (North); on January 1, 2005, it was renamed Standing NATO Response Force Mine countermeasures Group One and placed under Allied Command Operations.

[*See also* Navies, Great Powers; North Sea, *subentry on* Regional Navies; *and* Wars, Maritime, *subentry on* World Wars.]

## Bibliography

[Brunicardi, Daire.] *A History of the Irish Naval Service.* Haulbowline, Ireland: Naval Base, 1989. See also the Web site of the Irish Defence Forces, http://www.military.ie/naval/history.htm.

Cable, James. *The Royal Navy and the Siege of Bilbao.* Cambridge, U.K.: Cambridge University Press, 1979.

Coverdale, John F. *Italian Intervention in the Spanish Civil War.* Princeton, N.J.: Princeton University Press, 1975.

Glete, Jan. *Navies and Nations: Warships, Navies, and State Building in Europe and America, 1500–1860.* 2 vols. Stockholm, Sweden: Almqvist and Wilsell International, 1993.

Hadley, Michael L., Robert N. Huebert, and Fred W. Crickard, eds. *A Nation's Navy: In Quest of Canadian Naval Identity.* Montreal and Kingston, Ontario: McGill-Queens University Press, 1996.

Hadley, Michael L., and Roger F. Sarty. *Tin-Pots and Pirate Ships: Canadian Naval Forces and German Sea Raiders, 1880–1918.* Montreal and Kingston, Ontario: McGill-Queens University Press, 1993.

Hattendorf, John B. "International Naval Cooperation and Admiral Richard G. Colbert: The Intertwining of a Career with an Idea" and "NATO's Policeman on the Beat: The First Twenty Years of the Standing Naval Force, Atlantic, 1968–1988." In *Naval History and Maritime Strategy: Collected Essays*, pp. 161–200. Malabar, Fla.: Krieger Publishing, 2000.

Hattendorf, John B., ed. *Ubi Sumus? The State of Maritime and Naval History.* Newport, R.I.: Naval War College Press, 1994. Chapters on naval historiography about Britain, Canada, France, Ireland, Spain, and Portugal.

Hobson, Rolf, and Tom Kristiansen, eds. *Navies in Northern Waters, 1721–2000.* London: Frank Cass, 2004.

*Jane's Sentinel Security Assessment.* Vol. 11, *West Africa*, 2006. This periodical includes a summary of naval activity in this region, with brief historical information on each West African navy.

Jordan, Robert S. *Alliance Strategy and Navies: The Evolution and Scope of NATO's Maritime Dimension.* London: Pinter Publishers; New York: St. Martin's Press, 1990.

Maloney, Sean M. *Securing Command of the Sea: NATO Naval Planning, 1948–1954.* Annapolis, Md.: Naval Institute Press, 1995.

Siegel, Adam B. "International Naval Cooperation during the Spanish Civil War." *Joint Forces Quarterly* (Autumn–Winter 2001–2002): 82–92.

JOHN B. HATTENDORF

# South Atlantic

The South Atlantic lies below the Equator, from the South American coast to the African coast and down to Antarctica. The western limit is the meridian of Cape Horn (longitude 67°17′ W) and the eastern limit is the meridian of Cape Agulhas (longitude 20°01′ E). South of Cape Horn lies the Drake Passage, connecting the Atlantic and Pacific oceans, between South America and the Antarctic Peninsula. Another interesting feature of the South Atlantic is the so-called Atlantic Narrows, where the northeastern tip of Brazil lies in the South Atlantic, 1,800 nautical miles from a point on the west coast of Africa and north of the Equator.

At the southern end of the South Atlantic lies Antarctica, the fourth largest continent. Its shape is somewhat circular, with a significant projection toward South America: the Antarctic Peninsula. Southwest of Tierra del Fuego lies the Scotia Sea. It is enclosed on its eastern side by an arc of islands running from Tierra del Fuego through South Georgia and the South Sandwich, South Orkney, and South Shetland islands. The western boundary of the Scotia Sea is at about longitude fifty-five degrees west, where it merges with the Drake Passage. South of the Scotia Sea is the Weddell Sea, a large sea penetration in continental Antarctica. A significant feature in this region is the so called Antarctic Convergence, a boundary area 20 miles wide, extending between 48° S and 60° S. This boundary area results from the meeting of colder, less saline waters surrounding the Antarctic continent with warmer, saltier waters coming south from the large oceans. The Antarctic Convergence forms a biological barrier that makes the waters south of it a special, closed ecosystem.

## Ports

On the South American side of the Atlantic, the main ports in Brazil are Recife, Salvador, Rio de Janeiro, Santos, and Porto Alegre. On the Río de la Plata, there are Montevideo in Uruguay and Buenos Aires and La Plata in Argentina. Moving south, Bahía Blanca is another important Argentinean harbor. On the northern side of the Strait of Magellan—not directly on the Atlantic but with a close relationship to it—is Punta Arenas. South of Tierra del Fuego, on the northern side of the Beagle Channel, lies Ushuaia—again, not on the South Atlantic (since it is west of the longitude of Cape Horn) but with a close relation to the Atlantic, the Drake Passage, and the Antarctic Peninsula.

Major ports on the African coast are Pointe Noire in the Republic of Congo (the former French Congo), Matadi in the Democratic Republic of Congo (the former Belgian Congo), Luanda and Lobito in Angola, Walvis Bay in Namibia, and Cape Town in South Africa.

## Discoveries and Western European Settlements

The South Atlantic was little known to Europeans until the age of discoveries. Portuguese navigators started venturing into the North Atlantic in the first half of the fifteenth century. They discovered the Azores, Madeira, and the Cape Verde islands, and then sailed south around the west coast of Africa. In 1471 they reached Annobón Island and in 1482 the mouth of the River Congo. Later, in 1487, they circumnavigated the southern tip of Africa. These Portuguese expeditions culminated in 1497–1498 with the discovery by Vasco da Gama of the sea route to India. Portuguese explorers also discovered Ascension Island (1501), Saint Helena (1502), and Tristan da Cunha (1506).

Christopher Columbus's first voyage (1492) added a new dimension to exploration and expansion by the Iberian powers. The Treaty of Tordesillas (1494) divided the world into Spanish and Portuguese areas. Portugal would rule east of the Tordesillas Line, which included the eastern tip of Brazil—discovered by the Portuguese in 1500—and the whole of Africa. West of the line, most of South America would be under Spain.

The significant efforts made in the early sixteenth century to find a passage to the west of South America—that is, the Pacific Ocean—led to the discovery of the Río de la Plata in 1516. A later Spanish expedition, led by Ferdinand Magellan in 1521, found a passage that was given his name. Magellan died during the voyage (1519–1522), but one of his ships achieved the first circumnavigation of the world.

Portuguese settlements in Brazil gave way to the cities of Recife (1535), Salvador (1549), São Paulo (1554), and Rio de Janeiro (1565). In the Spanish-ruled region, Buenos Aires was founded for the first time in 1536 but was attacked and eventually destroyed by the Indians. A second, successful attempt was made in 1580, and Buenos Aires grew to become the center of the Spanish presence in the area, displacing the previously founded Asunción (1537), located far up the rivers Paraná and Paraguay. Other European powers, including France and the Netherlands, attempted to settle in Brazil, but they did not succeed in the long run. In particular, the French settled in Rio de Janeiro from 1555 to 1559, and the Dutch took and settled in Recife from 1630 to 1654.

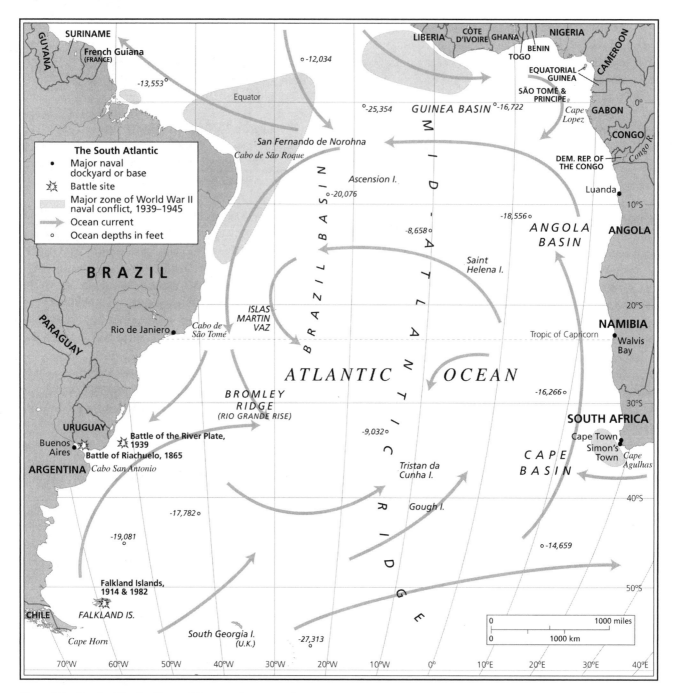

**Map of the South Atlantic.** Map by Mapping Specialists Limited

Cape Horn, the southernmost tip of South America, was discovered by the Dutch in 1616. At the time, the African side of the South Atlantic was receiving limited attention from the European powers, whose main interests were in the slave trade and in securing convenient stations for maritime routes to India. The Portuguese founded Luanda in 1576 and Benguela in 1617. Luanda became a center for slave trade; it was conquered by the Dutch in 1640, who remained there until 1648, when they were expelled by the Portuguese. In 1633 the Dutch annexed Saint Helena, which in turn was taken by the English East India Company in 1659. In addition, the Dutch settled in Cape of Good Hope in 1652, and Huguenots joined them in the late 1680s.

Despite the weakening of Portugal and Spain vis-à-vis Britain and France, mainly from the mid-eighteenth century on, their possessions in South America did not suffer significant disturbances until the Napoleonic Wars (1803–1815), aside from clashes between the Iberian powers looking to expand their South American holdings.

The eighteenth century also witnessed Commodore George Anson's voyage around the world, looking for suitable support stations for ocean routes. It was Anson who recommended the Falkland Islands (Islas Malvinas) as a convenient station for the route to the southeast Pacific.

Captain James Cook's second voyage (1772–1775) included, on January 17, 1773, the first crossing of the Antarctic Circle; he sailed around Antarctica but did not get within sight of the continent. Still, Cook concluded that there was a southern continent because pieces of rock could be seen on the icebergs. He also explored South Georgia and discovered the South Sandwich Islands on this voyage, in 1775.

Contention over possession of the Falkland Islands (Malvinas) started in the second half of the eighteenth century, and it involved not only Britain and Spain but also France, which was looking for new horizons after the loss of Canada. Spain was trying to keep outsiders away from its empire in the South Atlantic, while Britain was looking for a convenient station near Cape Horn. In 1764 the French settled in Port Louis on East Falkland (Isla Soledad). The British came to Port Egmont, West Falkland (Gran Malvina), in 1765–1766. The Spaniards complained about the French intrusion, and the French agreed to leave. The Spaniards replaced the French in Port Louis, which was renamed Puerto Soledad. The next move was the expulsion of the British by force from Port Egmont in 1770, but British pressure led to the restitution of their former possession in 1771. There were references to a secret agreement between Britain and Spain—never found in writing—suggesting that Spanish restitution was only symbolic, and that the British would leave shortly after their repossession. As a matter of fact, either because of the agreement or because they had other priorities, the British left Port Egmont in 1774, leaving a lead plaque with an inscription asserting their rights; the Spaniards were then the only permanent settlers remaining in the islands. Pressed by insurrection in South America, the Spaniards withdrew from Puerto Soledad in 1811.

In the mid-eighteenth century, Portuguese families from the Azores settled in the Ihlas Martin Vaz, 1,140 kilometers (708 miles) east of Brazil. Portugal moved the Brazilian capital in 1763 from Salvador to Rio de Janeiro, a location closer to the Río de la Plata. Previously, in 1726, Spain had tried to stop Portuguese southward expansion by creating a new settlement in Montevideo, on the eastern bank of the Río de la Plata. In 1776 another Spanish move to enhance its rule was the establishment of the viceroyalty of the Río de la Plata, which had its capital in Buenos Aires. The newly created viceroyalty comprised the approximate territories of what later became Argentina, Bolivia, Paraguay, and Uruguay. Montevideo was the seat of the main Spanish naval station in South Atlantic, and Puerto Soledad in the Falkland Islands (Malvinas) was under the authority of Montevideo. In 1778, Portugal ceded the islands of Fernando Póo and Annobón to Spain, which occupied them as a way to improve its strategic position in the South Atlantic.

The wars of the French Revolution and the French Empire led to a destabilization of Portuguese and Spanish rule in South America beginning in the 1790s. Among the contributing causes was the French invasion of Spain and Portugal, which severely weakened Spain's position and led to the settlement of the Portuguese court in Rio de Janeiro. Also contributing were the so-called "English invasions," launched from the Cape of Good Hope, an attempt to establish British settlement in the Río de la Plata area in 1806 and 1807. In spite of the eventual failure of the invasions, they gave the local populations a sense of self-determination that led to serious questionings of colonial rule. Another key factor was the British support of the rebellions in Spanish South America, which put an end to Spanish rule in the whole subcontinent in 1824.

Two naval episodes of the wars of independence in the South Atlantic should be highlighted. The first was the defeat of Spanish naval forces off Montevideo by an Argentinean squadron in 1814. This success was instrumental in the capture of Montevideo by the patriots, leaving the Spaniards without a suitable base in the southwest Atlantic from which to threaten rebellious Buenos Aires. The second episode was related to the proclamation of Brazilian independence in 1822: Admiral Thomas Cochrane, then serving the Brazilian government, led his squadron to the north of Brazil in 1823 and defeated Portuguese loyalist forces in the area, a major step toward securing the recently asserted independence.

A significant result of the Napoleonic Wars was the final acquisition of the Cape of Good Hope by the British in 1814, which gave the United Kingdom a key maritime position.

## Coastal Fortifications

During colonial times, coastal fortifications were built in every moderate-size coastal town on the western side of the South Atlantic. They were numerous on the Brazilian coast: Maranhão, Fortaleza, Ilha Fernando de Noronha, Natal, Recife, Salvador (Bahía), Rio de Janeiro, Angra dos Reis, Santos, Florianópolis, and others.

Of Spain's possessions in the South Atlantic, Montevideo, a key position at the mouth of the Río de la Plata, had its own defensive works. On the African side of the South Atlantic, Cape Peninsula in South Africa had significant fortifications.

## The Pax Britannica

Napoleon's fate was linked to the South Atlantic: after his defeat at Waterloo he was confined to Saint Helena, where he died in 1821. He remained buried there until 1840, when his body was returned to France.

Britain's position as a leading world power in the post-Napoleon era enhanced its trading status on both sides of the South Atlantic. Protection for this trade was given by the Royal Navy, which kept stations at Rio de Janeiro, the Río de la Plata, and the Cape of Good Hope. Britain also acquired Ascension Island in 1814 and Tristan da Cunha in 1816.

Brazil and Argentina had opposing claims over Uruguay, and they went to war in 1825–1828. The Brazilian navy had a clear superiority over the Argentine one, and it made a blockade of Buenos Aires that had a serious negative impact on trade. Argentine naval forces could only resort to hit-and-run tactics and raider warfare. However, attrition and political unrest on both sides and pressure from the great powers—essentially Britain—put an end to the conflict with a treaty that established Uruguay as an independent state.

Coming back to the Falkland Islands (Malvinas) in 1820, navy colonel David Jewett, an American serving the government of Buenos Aires, arrived in the islands in command of the frigate *Heroína*, hoisted the Argentinean flag, and took possession of the archipelago in the name of the Provincias Unidas, as Argentina was then known. In 1829 the government of Buenos Aires created the office of political and military commander of the islands and appointed an official, who effectively took his office in Puerto Soledad. Friction between the Argentinean governor and American seal hunters led to the intervention of USS *Lexington* in late December 1831, which resulted in the destruction of the Argentinean settlement and the imprisonment of some of the governor's collaborators. After the U.S. intervention, the government of Buenos Aires tried to restore its settlement in Puerto Soledad, but American action had triggered a British response in order to secure its interests in the

South Atlantic. The British eviction of the Argentineans from the Falkland Islands (Malvinas) took place in early 1833—and started a dispute that continued in the early twenty-first century.

In the first half of the nineteenth century the European presence on the African South Atlantic coast remained of little significance. An exception to this was South Africa, in which British immigrants after 1820 began to replace the Boer population in the coastal areas and impelled the Boers to move farther north in the 1860s. A second exception was the beginning of French occupation of the Congo area in the 1840s.

The opening of the Suez Canal in 1869 created a shorter route to India and the Far East, which lessened the importance of Saint Helena, Ascension Island, Cape Town, and the African South Atlantic harbors. Still, for many years a great proportion of merchant shipping was made of sailing vessels that were not suited to transit the Suez Canal and had to use the Cape route.

In 1884 the European powers reached an agreement regarding the borders of their colonial territories in Africa. On Africa's South Atlantic coast, the bordering possessions were the French territories of Gabon and Middle Congo (which later became part of French Equatorial Africa), the Portuguese enclave of Cabinda (north of the mouth of the River Congo), the Belgian Congo, the Portuguese colony of Angola, German South-West Africa (now Namibia), and the British Cape colony. (Natal, the other British possession in South Africa, was located on the Indian Ocean.)

The Boer War (1898–1902) ended with a total but costly British victory. British sea power was instrumental in deploying and supporting a large army. During the war the British held Boer prisoners of war on Saint Helena Island. After conquering the Boer republics, the British created the South African Union in 1910, amalgamating the Cape of Good Hope and Natal with Orange and Transvaal. This was the genesis of the current Republic of South Africa.

In the 1890s Argentina was involved in an arms race with Chile, over conflicting territorial claims in Patagonia. This arms race ended in 1902 when a settlement that included a naval arms-control agreement was reached.

In the early twentieth century a new naval arms race took place, between Brazil and Argentina. Brazil launched a significant naval expansion program in 1904–1906. The core of this buildup was two dreadnoughts to be built in Britain. After a heated debate, Argentina answered by ordering two larger battleships in 1909. The arms race was stopped by a combination of factors: an improved relationship between the rivals, a difficult financial situation in

Brazil, and the outbreak of World War I. Chile had joined the contest in 1910 by ordering two superdreadnoughts from British yards.

The opening of the Panama Canal in 1914 had a significant impact on the western South Atlantic basin. Sea traffic from the Atlantic to the Pacific was markedly reduced, and the southern passages—the Strait of Magellan and the Drake Passage—lost most of their importance.

## Hydrographic Surveys and Charting after the Discoveries

Surveying and charting of the South Atlantic had an early start when Spain sent the Malaspina expedition, which departed from Cádiz in 1789 and performed a major effort in the Río de la Plata area, as well as in Patagonia.

After the end of the Napoleonic Wars, the Pax Britannica—a period of relative peace attributed to British naval supremacy—witnessed an increase in ocean trade, which required better charting and more aids to navigation. Starting in the late 1810s, the French and the British pioneered surveys in the South Atlantic. As a result of these efforts, the first French charts of the South Atlantic coast of Brazil were published in the early 1820s; the first nautical publication about the east coast of South America was the French *Pilote du Brésil* (1820). The British followed suit in the 1830s, and published the *South America Pilot, Part I* in 1864. More charts of South American coasts came out in the first half of the nineteenth century, but the major steady flow came in the second half of the nineteenth century and in the early twentieth century. The establishment of hydrographic services in Brazil and Argentina in the second half of the nineteenth century facilitated additional surveying efforts and publication of charts.

On the African side of the South Atlantic, the first French charts were published in the 1820s and 1830s, followed by the British in the 1840s. Nautical publications of the African coast were started by the French *Manuel de navigation à la côte occidentale d'Afrique* in 1851–1852. The British followed suit with the *Africa Pilot, Part II* in 1868. Many more charts were produced beginning in the late nineteenth century. The first British charts of the Antarctic were published in 1901, and in 1917 Argentina issued one of the South Orkney Islands.

## World War I

The only significant naval action in the South Atlantic in World War I was the Falkland Islands battle, on December 8, 1914, when a German cruiser squadron under command of Admiral Maximilian von Spee attempted to raid Port Stanley. Spee was thoroughly defeated by a superior British force led by Admiral Sir Doveton Sturdee, which had arrived at the islands the day before to chase Spee's squadron.

Along the African South Atlantic coast, Allied naval superiority resulted in the conquest and occupation of German South-West Africa, completed in July 1915. Other Allied—mainly British—efforts in the South Atlantic were directed toward securing the flow of imperial and colonial troops, as well as of food and raw materials to Europe, and keeping German surface raiders at bay. South American Atlantic countries initially remained neutral, but Brazil joined the Allies in 1917.

## The Interwar Years

There were few significant episodes in the South Atlantic during the interwar years. On the African side, European colonies remained in the same condition, and the former German South-West Africa became a South African mandate, while South Africa remained inside the British Commonwealth.

Along the South American coast, an American naval mission was established in Brazil. Argentina, Brazil, and Chile were involved in arms-limitation talks at an inter-American conference held in Santiago, Chile, in 1923. Because of diverging positions between Brazil and Argentina, no significant agreement was reached. This, along with noncompletion of Argentinean and Chilean naval programs as a consequence of World War I, led to Argentine and Chilean naval buildups in the 1920s.

## World War II

During World War II the main maritime war efforts of the warring powers were located in the North Sea, the Mediterranean, the North Atlantic, and the Pacific Ocean. The Allies' naval superiority was a significant factor in keeping open the sea-lanes that, as in World War I, enabled the flow of troops, food, and raw materials from the South Atlantic countries and other overseas territories.

German surface raiders—both warships, such as *Graf Spee* and *Scheer*, and disguised merchant raiders—were active in the South Atlantic until 1942. The hunt for *Graf Spee* led to the Battle of the River Plate on December 13, 1939, in which the German raider was engaged by three British cruisers. The action was tactically indecisive. A few days after the fight, *Graf Spee*, which had taken refuge in Montevideo, was destroyed by her own crew a few miles off the port.

In addition to surface raiders, German U-boats were active in the South Atlantic until 1943. Ascension Island was used by the United States during World War II as a refueling and staging station for aircraft traveling from America to Africa. In the African area, the Cape of Good Hope route was widely used by the British to supply their forces in the Middle East, as an alternative to the Mediterranean route.

The outbreak of hostilities between Japan and the United States gave rise to strong U.S. pressure on the Western Hemisphere states to join the Allied cause. In 1942, Brazil declared war on the Axis powers and Uruguay severed diplomatic relations with them. Beginning in 1942, Brazil made a remarkable contribution to the Allied war effort. From autumn 1943 to autumn 1944 a small Norwegian garrison was stationed on South Georgia to defend it from the Japanese.

## Coastal Defenses in the Twentieth Century

Tensions in the area in the late nineteenth and early twentieth centuries led to the construction of significant—for those days—coastal fortifications in key positions along the South American coast. Brazilian defenses were located around Rio de Janeiro, Angra dos Reis, and Santos. The Argentinean fortifications were built in the late 1890s, close to the approaches of Argentina's main naval base, Puerto Belgrano, about five hundred miles south of Buenos Aires.

The Falkland Islands (Malvinas) obtained six-inch guns from HMS *Lancaster* in 1916, during World War I. Defenses were kept to a minimum between the wars and were strengthened again during World War II. Perceived threats from the sea in South Africa and South-West Africa (renamed from German Southwest Africa after the Treaty of Versailles) during World War II led to the installation of the so-called "heavy batteries" in Table Bay, Simonstown, and Walvis Bay.

## The Cold War

In the Cold War context, the United States pushed for the Inter-American Treaty of Reciprocal Assistance (the Rio Treaty) in 1947, which was conceived as an alliance against possible aggression by the Soviet bloc in the Western Hemisphere. The influence on Latin America by the United States, because of its preeminence in world affairs, grew significantly.

On the African side of the South Atlantic, the French colonies—Gabon and Middle Congo—obtained their independence in the early 1960s. The Belgian Congo did as well, but its intense internal conflict led to a United Nations peacekeeping operation.

Portugal tried to retain its overseas empire, in spite of aggressive guerrilla activities in most of its possessions. Eventually attrition from costly colonial warfare led to a change of government in Portugal and to the independence of its colonies, including Angola in 1975. But independence in 1975 did not bring peace to Angola, where a pro-Communist government with Soviet support was challenged by UNITA, an opposing guerrilla movement that had South African support. Thereafter, a Soviet and Soviet-sponsored military presence was prominent in Angola until the end of the Cold War. This Soviet effort was instrumental to the Soviet naval display in the South Atlantic, which remained a significant factor from the mid-1970s to the late 1980s. On the other hand, South African support of UNITA was linked to the need to deny a sanctuary in south Angola to SWAPO—South West Africa People's Organization—a guerrilla group struggling for Namibian independence.

South African administration of South-West Africa (now Namibia) was another conflicting issue. In spite of several United Nations resolutions asking for Namibian independence, South Africa kept its hold on the country until 1990, when Namibia became an independent state.

The Middle East conflict caused the closure of the Suez Canal in 1967 for eight years. Most of the oil for industrial countries came from the Persian Gulf and, with the canal closed, ships needed to go around Africa by way of the Cape of Good Hope, giving the route a renewed significance. The reopening of the Suez Canal in 1975 did not diminish this importance because in the meantime very large tankers had been built that could not pass through the canal. In addition to the oil route, the African side of the South Atlantic remained a significant sea-lane for African exports of minerals to the Northern Hemisphere.

On the South American side of the Atlantic, 1977 witnessed a serious deterioration of relations between Chile and Argentina because of a sovereignty issue over a group of islands south of Isla Grande de Tierra del Fuego. Both countries had agreed on arbitration, but when the results largely favored Chile, the Argentinean government declared the arbitration invalid. In an effort to reach an agreement, negotiations started in mid-1977 and continued to late 1978, with no compromise in sight. Crisis appeared imminent.

Fortunately, at the end of the year Pope John Paul II offered to mediate, an effort that was successful and resulted in the signing in 1984 of a Peace and Friendship Treaty.

At almost the same time the sovereignty dispute between Britain and Argentina over the Falkland Islands (Malvinas) escalated into real war in April 1982. The issue had remained confined to diplomatic channels since the British occupation in 1833. In 1965 a United Nations resolution invited both parties to negotiate the sovereignty issue. In March 1982 the landing of Argentinean scrap workers on South Georgia led to strained relations and the outbreak of a crisis, which seriously escalated when Argentinean forces landed in the Falklands on April 2, 1982, and on South Georgia on April 3. British reaction was swift: the United Nations Security Council passed a resolution asking for the withdrawal of Argentinean forces, and the British government broke off diplomatic relations with Argentina and ordered a task force to the South Atlantic. Mediation was attempted by the U.S. secretary of state, General Alexander Haig, with no results. Making use of the airbase on Ascension Island as an advanced logistics base, British forces recaptured South Georgia on April 25, 1982, and started harassing Argentinean positions in the Falklands (Malvinas) on May 1, 1982. The cruiser ARA *General Belgrano* was sunk by HMS *Conqueror* off Isla de los Estados on May 2, 1982, in what was the first combat engagement of a nuclear-powered submarine. A few days later the destroyer HMS *Sheffield* was crippled and eventually sunk by an aircraft-launched antiship missile—the first success in real action of such a missile. Further Argentinean air attacks sank and damaged British ships, but British carrier-borne aircraft and antiaircraft defenses took a heavy toll on the Argentineans. British forces landed on the western side of East Falkland (Isla Soledad) on May 21, 1982, and advanced toward Port Stanley (Puerto Argentino), which was eventually captured on June 14, 1982, putting an end to the war.

After the war, relations between Britain and Argentina remained strained for several years, with both parties refusing to declare a cease of hostilities and mend diplomatic relations. A détente process started in 1989 led to a set of agreements finalized in Madrid in February 1990. These agreements included a freeze of sovereignty issues, restoration of diplomatic relations, and a series of confidence-building measures that have been quite successful.

## The Antarctic Treaty

The Antarctic Treaty is an international agreement focused on preserving Antarctica for peaceful purposes, mainly for scientific research. The geographical area of application is south of sixty degrees south. It was signed in Washington, D.C., on December 1, 1959, and came into force in June 1961. The treaty halted existing territorial claims and forbids future claims. The claims of Argentina, Britain, and Chile significantly overlap, but no major controversies have arisen since the treaty went into force. Moreover, all three countries have the common interest of being claimants.

## After the Cold War

In the South American Atlantic basin during the twentieth century, Brazil and Argentina faced each other in what might be referred to as a friendly rivalry, with some peaks of strained relations. A détente process begun in 1979 led to increased cooperation, one outcome of which was the creation in 1991 of a common market, Mercosur, that included Brazil, Argentina, Paraguay, and Uruguay.

The end of the Cold War and the weakening of the Soviet Union—and its eventual dissolution in 1991—eliminated the Soviet presence in the South Atlantic and prompted the withdrawal of Cuban troops from Angola. However, political violence in Angola continued until the end of the civil war in 2002. Another significant event was the end of apartheid in South Africa, where the first majority government was elected in 1994.

The former Belgian Congo (now the Democratic Republic of the Congo) became independent in 1960, in the midst of political turmoil. In 1961 a reasonable degree of stability and order was achieved under General Sese Seko Mobutu as head of state. However, the social and economic backwardness of the country led to armed insurrection, and Mobutu was overthrown in 1997. In July 2003 a transitional government was established, but most issues remained unsolved as of the early twenty-first century.

## Fishing Industries

Off Patagonia lies a wide continental shelf that hosts large fisheries. A great number of fishing vessels are active in this area. Some are locally based, but many come from abroad, and most operate just outside of Argentina's 200-mile exclusive economic zone (EEZ). A suitable and effective means of preventing excessive catch in this area near the EEZ is still a serious pending issue

In the southeast Atlantic region, however, an agreement has been reached to control fisheries off the African coast. In April 2001 the South East Atlantic Fisheries

Organisation (SEAFO) Convention was signed by Angola, Namibia, South Africa, the United Kingdom (on behalf of Saint Helena and its dependencies of Tristan da Cunha and Ascension Islands), the European Community, Iceland, Norway, the Republic of Korea, and the United States. The convention covers a sizable part of the high seas of the southeast Atlantic. The convention's objective is "to ensure the long term conservation and sustainable resources in the convention area." It came in force in April 2003, and an executive secretary was appointed in March 2005.

## Assessment

It may be said that the South Atlantic is not a key ocean area, compared with the North Atlantic or the North Pacific. In the early twenty-first century, no sources of tension appear to be in sight in the South Atlantic, except for the sovereignty issue between Britain and Argentina over the Falklands (Malvinas—including South Georgia and the South Sandwich Islands).

The African side will retain its importance, mainly because of the oil route around the Cape of Good Hope—by which is conveyed about 30 percent of the oil imports of the industrial powers—and the export traffic to the industrial countries of minerals from Africa, including chromium, cobalt, manganese, and platinum and platinoids.

Likewise, the southwest Atlantic will maintain its relative significance because the southern passages (the Strait of Magellan and the Drake Passage) are an alternative route to the Panama Canal—and are the only route for ships exceeding the canal's capabilities. In addition, the southwest Atlantic and the southeast Pacific should continue to be the standard access routes to the Antarctic Peninsula, the most accessible part of Antarctica.

[See also *Admiral Graf Spee;* Americas, Exploration Voyages in, *subentry on* 1500–1616 (South America); Buenos Aires; Cape Town; Since Navies, Great Powers; Panama Canal; Rio de Janeiro; *and* Suez Canal.]

## Bibliography

Admiralty. *Africa Pilot*. Part 2. 8th ed. London: Hydrographic Department, 1930.

Admiralty. *The Antarctic Pilot*. 3d ed. London: Hydrographic Department, 1961.

Admiralty. *Catalogue of Admiralty Charts*. London: Hydrographic Department, 1950.

Admiralty. *South America Pilot*. Part 1. 8th ed. London: Hydrographic Department, 1932.

Admiralty. *South America Pilot*. Part 2. 13th ed. London: Hydrographic Department, 1942.

Breyer, Siegfried. *Battleships and Battle Cruisers, 1905–1970*. Garden City, N.Y.: Doubleday, 1973.

Gough, Barry. *The Falkland Islands/Malvinas: The Contest for Empire in the South Atlantic*. London: Athlone Press, 1992.

Kemp, Peter. *The History of Ships*. New York: Galahad Books, 1979.

Klotz, Frank G. *America on the Ice: Antarctic Policy Issues*. Washington, D.C.: National Defense University Press, 1990.

Johnston, T. R. *The Merchant Shipper's and Ocean Traveller's Atlas*. London: George Philip and Son, n.d. [1886].

Ratto, Héctor R. *La expedición Malaspina*. Buenos Aires: Centro Naval, 1936.

Roskill, Stephen W. *The War at Sea, 1939–1945*. 4 vols. London: Her Majesty's Stationery Office, 1954–1961.

Scheina, Robert L. *Latin America: A Naval History 1810–1987*. Annapolis, Md.: Naval Institute Press, 1987.

South East Atlantic Fisheries Organisation. http://www.seafo.org.

United States Hydrographic Office. *South America Pilot*. Vol. 2. 3d ed. Washington, D.C.: U.S. Government Printing Office, 1930.

GUILLERMO J. MONTENEGRO

# South Atlantic Regional Navies

The major South American Atlantic navies, the Brazilian and Argentinean navies, were founded in the early nineteenth century, in the midst of each country's struggle for independence, and their subsequent development was affected by events in the region. Brazil and Argentina went to war in the 1820s for the possession of what is now Uruguay; the war resulted in Uruguay's independence. The relationship between Brazil and Argentina during the nineteenth century and up to the early 1980s could be labeled as one of mutual distrust, which was reflected in their military and naval establishments. Another significant influence upon the development and sizing of Argentinean military and naval power was a long-standing rivalry with Chile, mainly over border issues, which lasted from the mid-nineteenth century up to the last quarter of the twentieth century.

## Naval Power and South American Independence

Naval power was instrumental in securing the successful conclusion of the wars of South American independence.

**Argentina.** When the first uprisings against Spanish rule began in 1810, Buenos Aires was the revolutionaries' key

**ARA** *General Belgrano.* During the Falklands War (known as the Malvinas War in Argentina), HM Submarine *Conqueror* (S48) sank the Argentine cruiser *General Belgrano* (C4) [ex-USS *Phoenix* (CL-46)] on May 2, 1982. Argentine and Chilean ships rescued 770 survivors, but there were 323 casualties. HO OLD / REUTERS

position in the Río de la Plata area. Montevideo, where the main Spanish naval station was located, remained on the Royalist side, and its locally based squadron harassed Buenos Aires, as well as the coasts and rivers controlled by the revolutionaries. Though it was besieged by land, Montevideo resisted successfully because it had its sea lines of communication open.

In 1811 the rebels in Buenos Aires created a small squadron to face the Spaniards, but the Spaniards utterly defeated the revolutionaries on the Paraná River. In 1814 a second attempt succeeded in capturing Martín García Island, a key position for the control of the Paraná and Uruguay rivers, and the squadron defeated the Spaniards off Montevideo in May 1814. Besieged by land and blockaded by sea, Montevideo surrendered in June 1814, leaving Spain with no suitable base in the South Atlantic to attempt to recover its possessions. Perhaps for this reason, Buenos Aires was never recaptured by the Royalists, as most of the Spanish American revolutionary cities were.

After the seizure of Montevideo, Argentinean naval efforts were dedicated mainly to raider warfare. A significant number of privateers served the government of Buenos Aires and caused serious disturbances to Spanish trade. In 1824 the Royalist armies were defeated at the Battle of Ayacucho (Peru). Though the last Spanish stronghold of Callao (Peru) did not surrender until early 1826, Spanish rule in South America had come to an end.

**Brazil.** Brazilian independence followed a different path from that of Spanish America. The Portuguese court settled in Rio de Janeiro in 1808 as a result of Napoléon's invasion of Portugal, leading to the arrival of a number of Portuguese warships, as well as the Portuguese Naval College, the origin of its Brazilian counterpart. Also among the new arrivals was the Brigada Real da Marinha (Royal Marine Brigade), which became the immediate ancestor of the current Brazilian Fuzileiros Navais (Marines). In 1808 several significant naval institutions were created, among them a naval ministry. At the end of the Napoleonic Wars in 1815, the king returned to Portugal, leaving his son Prince Pedro as Brazil's regent. Strained relations between Portugal and Brazil led to Brazil's proclamation of independence in 1822 by Prince Pedro, who took the title of emperor of Brazil.

The Brazilian navy had a decisive influence in defeating Portuguese Loyalist resistance at both ends of the country: in Uruguay to the south, which had been occupied by the Portuguese in 1816–1817, and in Salvador to the north.

## National South American Navies

New national navies were formed in the newly independent South American countries.

**Argentina.** Argentina's institutions took a long time to be established and accepted by the entire country. Various degrees of dissent and civil wars ravaged the country up to the early 1860s. In the early 1820s, the navy was almost nonexistent. When tensions with Brazil concerning the possession of the Banda Oriental of the Río de la Plata (present-day Uruguay) led to war, some degree of naval power had to be created almost from scratch. The Brazilian navy had a clear superiority over the Argentinean. Based in Montevideo, the Brazilians blockaded Buenos Aires, which had a significant impact on Argentinean trade. Argentinean naval forces resorted to hit-and-run tactics and raider warfare. War attrition and political dissent in both countries, as well as pressure from European world powers, led to a compromise by which the disputed territory became an independent state, Uruguay.

In the 1840s civil wars in Argentina also involved Uruguay. Opposition to Buenos Aires—both from Uruguayan nationals and Argentinean exiles—was centered in Montevideo. Buenos Aires naval forces imposed some degree of blockade on Montevideo, which resisted with its own naval forces. Several actions took place, and Britain and France intervened to protect their interests.

The governor of the province of Buenos Aires, Juan Manuel de Rosas, who had been Argentina's de facto head of state during the 1830s and 1840s, was overthrown in 1852 by a national uprising supported by Brazil. A national constitution was proclaimed, but diverging views between the province of Buenos Aires and the other provinces led to renewed internal struggles, in which both parties resorted to naval forces to support their overall military effort. Hostilities ended in 1861.

A dispute between Brazil and Paraguay led to war in 1864. Armed Paraguayan intrusions into Argentinean territory led to the signing of the Triple Alliance—Argentina, Brazil, and Uruguay—against Paraguay. Argentina's contribution to the war was made essentially of land forces. The allied naval forces, which were almost entirely Brazilian, performed a significant contribution to ground operations by securing control of the Paraná and Paraguay rivers.

In the late 1870s border issues with Chile, as well as Chilean settlements on the Patagonian Atlantic coast, led to the dispatch of a naval expedition to the troubled spots, which succeeded in reaffirming Argentinean rights. In 1881 a treaty was signed between Chile and Argentina to resolve the issue, but diverging interpretations generated an arms race in the 1890s in which naval weapons played a significant part. This arms race ended in 1902 with an agreement that included naval arms control.

In the early twentieth century, in response to the Brazilian naval program of 1904–1906, the Argentinean navy ordered two dreadnought-type battleships from U.S. yards. This episode began a sustained cooperative relationship between the U.S. and Argentine navies, which continued throughout the twentieth century, despite the ups and downs of bilateral political relations.

Argentina remained neutral during World War I, in spite of some merchant ships being sunk by German submarines. Following the failure of arms-limitation attempts at the 1923 Inter-American Conference, the Argentinean navy modernized its dreadnoughts in U.S. yards. In 1926 the Argentinean congress authorized a significant naval acquisition program, which included two cruisers, five destroyers, and three submarines. In the 1930s the remaining funds allowed the purchase of seven more destroyers. Another act of the Argentinean congress led to the ordering of a light cruiser from British yards by the mid-1930s. In this same period, indigenous naval construction received a significant impulse: nine minelayers or minesweepers were built in both navy and private yards.

Argentina remained neutral during most of World War II, declaring war on the Axis powers in early 1945. There was thus limited military cooperation from the Allies. The Argentinean navy purchased some frigate-type war surplus vessels in the late 1940s and endeavored to get some of the new equipment developed during the war, such as radar and sonar. The end of World War II gave way to an era of U.S. preeminence in the Western Hemisphere, which strongly influenced local military and naval establishments.

The U.S. Navy transferred two *Brooklyn*-class cruisers to Argentina in the early 1950s. Their commissioning was a significant step in acquiring ships updated with newly developed equipment. At the same time, however, the United States also transferred two such ships to Brazil and two to Chile, ending Argentina's absolute superiority in post–World War I cruisers in the Southern Cone—before these transfers, the Argentinean navy had three cruisers commissioned in the 1930s, and its neighbors had none. A major step forward for the Argentinean navy was the 1958 acquisition of the aircraft carrier HMS *Warrior*, which was renamed *Independencia*. She became the first operational carrier of the South Atlantic regional navies. Another major

Argentinean acquisition was the purchase in 1969 of the Dutch carrier HMNS *Karel Doorman* (the former HMS *Venerable*), which was commissioned in the Argentinean navy as *25 de Mayo*, replacing ARA *Independencia*.

In the early 1960s the Argentinean navy joined the U.S.-sponsored "Unitas" operations, in which the Brazilian and Uruguayan navies also took part. Along the same line, in the 1960s and 1970s bilateral regional training operations were begun with Brazil, Uruguay, and Paraguay. In the early 1960s a major cooperative step by South American navies was the establishment of a combined naval control of shipping organization, the Coordinador del Area Marítima del Atlántico Sur (South Atlantic Maritime Area Coordinator). The chair is rotated every two years among flag officers from Argentina, Brazil, and Uruguay. Paraguay is also a member of this organization.

In 1977 relations between Argentina and Chile became strained because of a sovereignty issue over a group of islands at the eastern end of the Beagle Channel. Tension increased seriously up to late 1978, when it was perceived that the crisis might escalate. Military forces of both sides were put on alert. However, mediation by Pope John Paul II averted further escalation, and the issue was resolved by treaty in 1984.

The Falklands (Malvinas) War of 1982 had a significant impact on the Argentinean navy. In March 1982 this conflict between Britain and Argentina was precipitated by the landing of a group of Argentinean scrap workers on the island of South Georgia. The crisis and subsequent war took the Argentinean navy by surprise. Argentina's most modern ships in commission were two British-built type-42 destroyers. One of them had been in Britain during most of 1981 conducting extensive trials. In addition, four destroyers being built in Germany were being fitted with British-made gas turbines because of a special Argentinean request to have common logistics with type-42 destroyers.

Escalation of the crisis led to Argentinean seizure of the Falkland Islands (Malvinas) on April 2 and of South Georgia on April 3. The British government ordered a task force to the South Atlantic to recapture the islands by force if necessary. Several attempts to mediate the conflict ended in failure, and on April 25, 1982, British forces recaptured South Georgia.

The major events of the war were a frustrated naval air action on May 2, the sinking of the cruiser ARA *General Belgrano* by HMS *Conqueror* in the late afternoon of the same day, and the crippling of HMS *Sheffield*, which eventually sank, by an air-launched Exocet missile on May 4.

British forces landed on the western side of East Falkland (Isla Soledad) on May 21, 1982. Aircraft of the Argentinean air force and naval aviation scored several successes against British ships, but British carrier aircraft and antiaircraft defenses caused major Argentinean losses. British ground forces advanced eastward through East Falkland and eventually captured Port Stanley (Puerto Argentino) on June 14, 1982, which brought the war to an end.

Changes in Argentinean domestic policy, as well as a more cooperative approach to relations with Brazil and Chile, resulted in reduced defense budgets, which restricted new acquisitions and modernizations. The carrier ARA *25 de Mayo* was decommissioned in the late 1990s because a major refit could not be funded.

The late 1980s and early 1990s showed a significant departure from Argentina's traditional noninvolvement in international affairs; military forces were detached to several peace operations. The most significant participation was in Desert Shield and Desert Storm (1990–1991), in which Argentinean warships were active in the operations area.

**Brazil.** After its participation in securing Brazil's independence, the Brazilian navy was actively involved in 1825–1828 in a war against Argentina. As mentioned, the disputed possession of present-day Uruguay led to the outbreak of hostilities. The Brazilian fleet was decidedly superior and blockaded Buenos Aires, and the Argentineans resorted to hit-and-run tactics and privateering. On land the Argentineans were a little more successful, but the exhaustion of both parties and pressure from European powers led to a peace settlement that granted Uruguayan independence.

The Brazilian navy was active in the 1830s and 1840s in successfully quenching some regional rebellions that threatened the unity of the empire. In the early 1850s the Brazilian navy was part of an overall military effort to support Argentinean revolutionaries who sought to overthrow Juan Manual de Rosas, the governor of Buenos Aires. Brazilian cooperation significantly contributed to the revolutionaries' success, and Rosas went into exile in Britain.

Strained relations between Paraguay and Brazil led to war in 1864, in which Argentina and Uruguay sided with Brazil in what was called the Triple Alliance. Though this was predominantly a land war, control of the Paraná River was essential for supporting the allied armies. The Brazilian navy made the major contribution to allied riverine power and succeeded in defeating the Paraguayan naval forces.

A Republican revolt overthrew the Brazilian monarchy in 1889, which led to a period of political instability in the 1890s. Most of the Brazilian navy revolted against the national government in 1893, and some naval actions took place, including the sinking of the rebel ironclad *Aquidaban* by the torpedo gunboat *Gustavo Sampaio*. Eventually the government party won the upper hand.

In the early 1900s, Brazilian leadership decided to regain South American naval supremacy, which Brazil had maintained during most of the nineteenth century. A significant naval buildup began in 1904–1906; at its core were two dreadnought-type battleships built in Britain. Argentina responded with a similar program in 1908, and Chile followed suit in 1910. The Brazilian Submarine Service became the first in the South Atlantic in 1913, when three Italian-built submarines were commissioned.

During World War I, Brazil sided with the Allies and declared war. Brazilian naval forces were sent to operate off northwestern Africa. They remained on station for three months until the war ended. In accord with subsequent relations between Brazil and the United States, strong ties were developed between their navies. Both Brazilian dreadnoughts were refitted in the United States, and an American naval mission was established in 1918.

Brazil and Argentina faced each other in the diplomatic arena at an International American Conference that took place in Santiago, Chile, in 1923. In the wake of the Washington Naval Treaty, one of the subjects to be dealt with at the conference was arms limitation. No progress was made on land armaments, and agreement on naval matters was precluded by diverging positions between Brazil and Argentina regarding capital ship tonnage limits.

Political instability and financial troubles hindered Brazilian naval acquisitions in the interwar years. One submarine was commissioned in the 1920s and three more in the 1930s. In 1937 the United States offered to lease six destroyers to the Brazilian navy, but reactions from Argentina (on the grounds of arms balance between the two nations) and Britain (because the lease threatened a traditional British arms market) resulted in the cancellation of the proposed transfer.

In late 1930s, Brazil ordered six destroyers from British yards, but these were taken over by the Royal Navy at the outbreak of World War II. Local naval construction did start at this time: three destroyers were laid down in 1937, and six more in the early 1940s. They were eventually commissioned between 1943 and 1951, a significant achievement for indigenous naval industry.

Brazil declared war on the Axis powers in 1942, and the navy's primary duty was as convoy escort in South Atlantic. In addition, Allied planes patrolled the South Atlantic from Brazilian airfields, twenty-five thousand Brazilian troops fought in Italy, and the Brazilian air force also took its share in the same theater. As a result of its participation in the war, the Brazilian navy acquired its long-desired parity with Argentina. Starting in 1944 the United States started transferring destroyer escorts to Brazil. Eventually, eight were delivered, which was a significant upgrade to Brazilian naval power.

In early 1950s two U.S. *Brooklyn*-class cruisers were transferred to the Brazilian navy; a major acquisition in 1956 was the purchase of the aircraft carrier HMS *Vengeance*, which was commissioned in the Brazilian navy as *Minas Gerais*. A dispute between the navy and the air force for the control of the carrier's air group delayed for years its full operational readiness.

Brazil participated in the "Unitas" program, the combined naval training operations begun by the U.S. Navy in the early 1960s, along with Argentina and Uruguay. Along the same lines, since the late 1960s, bilateral combined exercises were conducted with the naval forces of Argentina, Paraguay, and Uruguay. The establishment of a combined naval control of shipping organization with Argentina and Uruguay led to improved cooperation among South American navies.

The last decades of the twentieth century witnessed a significant update of the Brazilian navy thanks to U.S. transfers, acquisitions from foreign yards, and local naval construction. The culmination of this process was the purchase of the French aircraft carrier *Foch*, which was commissioned in the Brazilian navy as *São Paulo*. This achievement, together with the decommissioning of the Argentinean carrier *25 de Mayo*, left the Brazilian navy as the single regional navy operating carriers in South Atlantic.

**Uruguay.** Because it was located between two powerful neighbors, Uruguay needed some degree of naval power to assert its rights, and this has remained true despite limited resources. The origins of the Uruguayan navy may be traced back to late 1817, when José Gervasio Artigas, the leader of Uruguay's independence movement, issued the first letter of marque. In addition, Artigas's forces operated a riverine flotilla.

After Uruguayan independence in 1828, riverine forces were active in the 1830s and 1840s in the civil wars that took place in the area of the Río de la Plata, in which the parties involved had frequent support from neighboring countries. Uruguayan ships participated in the War of the Triple Alliance against Paraguay (1864–1870), mainly in logistical duties.

In the early 1960s, Uruguay joined the U.S.-sponsored "Unitas" training operations, and became a member, along with Argentina and Brazil, of a combined naval control of shipping organization. Regional combined training was also held on a regular basis with the Argentinean and Brazilian navies.

## African Navies

The first steps toward a South African naval service go back to 1885, when a unit of naval volunteers was established in Durban for harbor defense. After the creation of the Union of South Africa, a division of the Royal Naval Volunteer Reserve was formed in 1912. The South African Naval Services were established in 1922, but their significance was reduced during the interwar years because of financial limitations. The coming of World War II gave a new impetus to the service, which became the South African Seaward Defence Force in 1940. At the war's end, naval expansion also came to a halt. The nucleus of the postwar service, now named the South African Naval Force, consisted of three British-built frigates.

In 1951 the naval service was renamed the South African Navy, and it went through a period of expansion until the 1960s. Apartheid policies led to South African withdrawal from the Commonwealth and a search for alternative sources of naval equipment, which had been predominantly British.

In 1970 the South African Submarine Service began with the arrival of the first of three French-built submarines. In addition to the interruption of British equipment, in 1977 a United Nations arms embargo against South Africa further complicated weapons procurement. Main military weapons supplies were fulfilled by Israel and domestic industry. Border conflict and counterinsurgency operations weighed heavily in South African defense budgets, which affected resource availability for the navy. Since the early 1990s, however, the South African Navy did manage to conduct combined training operations with the South American navies. The end of apartheid in 1994 led to improved international relations. Despite limited navy budgets, a naval rebuilding program was undertaken in the early twenty-first century.

In West Africa in the second half of the twentieth century, independence from the European powers witnessed the birth of national armed forces in the former African colonies. However, in most cases limited resources precluded the development of significant naval forces; most of the West African naval services are, essentially, coastal patrol forces. The only exception is Nigeria, whose resources have allowed a reasonably sized navy.

## Access to Antarctica

Argentina is one of the twelve original signatories of the Antarctic Treaty, and it has a long-established tradition in the Antarctic region. In 1903, after the Swedish ship *Antarctic* was trapped in ice and eventually lost, an Argentinean vessel, ARA *Uruguay*, was sent to rescue Nils Adolf Erik Nordenskiöld's Antarctic expedition.

Argentina's uninterrupted presence in Antarctica began in 1904 when a scientific station was settled in the South Orkneys. The Argentinean navy pioneered national Antarctic activities, joined by the army and the air force in the 1950s. The Dirección Nacional del Antártico (National Antarctic Board) was created, but the navy carries the bulk of logistical support for the Argentinean bases, most of which are on the Antarctic Peninsula, with two more on the Weddell Sea coast. The proximity of Ushuaia, on the southernmost tip of Argentina, to the Antarctic Peninsula, with adequate harbor and airport facilities, makes this town an advantageous gateway to Antarctica.

South Africa was another of the twelve original signatories of the Antarctic Treaty, and it has been involved in Antarctic research since the International Geophysical Year (1957–1958). South African Antarctic activities are under the authority of the South African National Antarctic Program, under the auspices of the Department of Environmental Affairs and Tourism. In the early twenty-first century South Africa's active base is SANAE IV, in Queen Maud Land.

Brazil joined the Antarctic Treaty in 1975 and became a consultative party in 1983. The Brazilian Antarctic base on the Antarctic Peninsula is named Ferraz. The Brazilian Antarctic Program (PROANTAR) is under the Secretaria da Comissão Interministerial para os Recursos do Mar (Secretary of the Interdepartment Commission on Sea Resources), in which the Brazilian navy has played a significant role.

Uruguay became an acceding party to the Antarctic Treaty in 1980, acquiring consultative party status in 1985, and operates the Artigas base on the Antarctic Peninsula. The Instituto Antártico Uruguayo (Uruguayan Antarctic Institute), part of the defense ministry, is in charge of

Antarctic logistics. Thus all three South American navies have a significant share in the Antarctic activities of their respective countries.

[*See also* Antarctica and the Southern Ocean.]

### Bibliography

Breyer, Siegfried. *Battleships and Battlecruisers, 1905–1970.* Garden City, N.Y.: Doubleday, 1973.

Breyer, Siegfried. *Grosskampfschiffe Bd. 3: Mittelmeeranlieger, Russland/Sowjetunion, Niederlände, und ABC Staaten Südamerikas.* Munich: Bernard and Graefe Verlag, 1979.

Caillet-Bois, Teodoro. *Historia Naval Argentina.* Buenos Aires, Argentina: Emecé Editories, 1944.

Gardiner, Robert, ed. *Conway's All the World's Fighting Ships, 1860–1905.* London: Conway Maritime Press, 1979.

Gardiner, Robert, ed. *Conway's All the World's Fighting Ships, 1906–1921.* Annapolis, Md.: Naval Institute Press, 1985.

Gardiner, Robert, ed. *Conway's All the World's Fighting Ships, 1922–1945.* London: Conway Maritime Press, 1980.

Gardiner, Robert, ed. *Conway's All the World's Fighting Ships, 1947–1982.* Part 2, *The Warsaw Pact and Non-Aligned Nations.* Annapolis, Md.: Naval Institute Press, 1985.

Heitman, Helmoed-Römer. *South African Armed Forces.* Cape Town, South Africa: Buffalo Publications, 1990.

Heitman, Helmoed-Römer. *South African Arms and Armour.* Cape Town, South Africa: Struik Publishers, 1988.

Lorch, Carlos, ed. *The Brazilian Navy: Naval Power.* Rio de Janeiro, Brazil: Action Editora, 1997.

Meirelles da Silva, Theotonio. *Historia naval Brazileira.* Rio de Janeiro, Brazil: B. L. Garnier, 1884.

Montenegro, Guillermo J. "The Character and Extent of Mahan's Influence in Latin America." In *The Influence of History on Mahan*, edited by John B. Hattendorf, pp. 87–98. Newport, R.I.: Naval War College Press, 1991.

Scheina, Robert L. *Latin America: A Naval History, 1810–1987.* Annapolis, Md.: Naval Institute Press, 1987.

Vale, Brian. *A War betwixt Englishmen: Brazil against Argentina on the River Plate, 1825–1830.* London: Tauris, 2000.

Vidigal, Armando Amorim Ferreira. *A evolução do pensamento estratégico naval Brasileiro.* 3d ed. Rio de Janeiro, Brazil: Biblioteca do Exército, 1985.

GUILLERMO J. MONTENEGRO

# Exploration Voyages, 1330s–1480s

The rhetoric of discovery often employed to describe the remarkable series of voyages of exploration undertaken by the Portuguese in the Atlantic in the fifteenth century has sometimes clouded the fact that there was a great deal of continuity between these ventures and earlier voyages organized by the trading nations of the western Mediterranean. Not only did the Portuguese rely on navigational, cartographic, and colonial techniques of Mediterranean origins in order to pursue some well-established commercial agendas; they also benefited from fourteenth-century oceanic voyages, mostly by the Genoese and by Catalans from the island of Majorca in the Mediterranean. From at least the thirteenth century, Genoese and Catalan traders were particularly active in north African ports like Tunis, Bougie, and Ceuta, and had learned that the sources of gold were beyond the Sahara. They also undertook trading expeditions to Flanders and England, the Genoese using the Andalusian ports of Seville and Cádiz as bases.

## The Canaries

The permanent achievement of these Latin sailors as Atlantic explorers was the definitive mapping and early commercial exploitation of the Canary Islands, including some interesting attempts at colonization and even (in the case of Majorcans) missionary work. All this entailed regular navigation from Spain along the western coast of Africa and then south down to about 27°50′ N latitude. Yet these Mediterranean sailors rarely ventured much further south than Cape Juby (then taken to be Cape Bojador), at latitude 27°57′ N, although a few occasional attempts are well attested. They also failed to locate accurately the Atlantic archipelagoes of Madeira and the Azores, let alone to colonize them, notwithstanding the probability that the islands had at least been sighted on return voyages.

The evidence for these expeditions must be reconstructed from a limited number of documents and requires the support of cartography, but the overall picture that emerges is fairly clear. The first expedition to the Canaries—quickly identified with the "Fortunate Islands" of antiquity—was in 1336 by the Genoese Lanzarotto Malocello (possibly with Portuguese sailors) and led to the discovery of the island of Lanzarote, which today still bears his name. It—together with nearby Fuerteventura—was already represented in Angelino Dulcert's 1339 portolan chart, bearing the arms of Genoa (Dulcert himself was a Majorcan but probably of Genoese origin). News of this expedition led to many others, of which a number are well documented. Giovanni Bocaccio, for example, wrote in some detail about the Canary Islands on the basis of reports brought back by a 1341 expedition that was sponsored by the king of Portugal but was led by Genoese and Florentine captains and included a remarkably multinational crew of Spaniards and Italians. Thus Lisbon, Seville, Genoa, Florence, Palma de Mallorca (on Majorca), and probably Barcelona all received the news.

The rulers of Castile and Portugal were soon engaged in rival claims to the rights to conquer the islands. When, in 1344, the Avignon Pope Clement VI offered the title of Prince of Fortune to an independent Castilian adventurer, Luis de la Cerda, the kings of both Portugal and Castile reacted by claiming a previous right. Yet it was the Catalans who made the more sustained effort to colonize the islands, first under the authority of King James III of Majorca and after 1343 (when the island was reincorporated into the Kingdom of Aragon) under the authority of King Peter IV of Aragon. These expeditions (some of which are recorded for the years 1342, 1346, 1352, 1360, 1369, and 1386) varied in nature from conquest and commerce (mainly involving raiding for slaves) to missionary work. The documents relating to the 1351 voyage to Gran Canaria, for example, mention twelve native converts who spoke Catalan and were to be taken back to assist a mission (Ramon Llull's apologetic ideas remained influential in Majorca and at the Aragonese court). It is clear that Peter of Aragon, like his Majorcan predecessor, had imperialistic aims, since in 1366 he ordered a captain to patrol the waters of the African archipelago to exclude foreign (that is, Castilian and Portuguese) interlopers. However, the conquest of the Canaries was also part of a general crusading idea that involved encircling Morocco. In fact, the intense efforts of the 1340s coincide with a period of struggle against Moorish corsairs.

While these various fourteenth-century efforts led to a remarkably accurate mapping of the islands—as represented by, for example, the famous Catalan Atlas by Cresques Abraham of around 1375—Peter of Aragon could never devote sufficient attention to the project to sustain a permanent settlement, for he had other political priorities: the conquest of Sardinia and wars against Genoa and Castile. Peter's successors became further occupied with Sicily and in effect abandoned the Canaries.

In the first half of the fifteenth century, therefore, as the crown of Aragon under the new Trastamara dynasty revived its Mediterranean policy, the rulers of Castile and Portugal competed increasingly fiercely for the Atlantic islands. King Henry III of Castile, backed by a number of Seville entrepreneurs active since the 1390s, took the lead by forcing his sponsorship upon two French adventurers, Jean de Béthencourt and Gadifer de la Salle, who from 1402, and despite falling out, managed to colonize (or in Lanzarote, perhaps recolonize) the islands of Lanzarote, Fuerteventura, and Hierro. It was the availability of manpower from Andalusia (in southern Castile) that made this originally French (and predominantly Norman) venture a Castilian success, although the colonies remained economically precarious and reliant on continued slave raiding.

Prince Henry the Navigator of Portugal, that most consistent patron of Atlantic ventures in the first half of the fifteenth century, was determined to reassert the Portuguese claim and put up a determined if rather fruitless struggle that involved attacks on the great unconquered islands of Canaria (1424) and Tenerife (1434), appeals to a misinformed pope (1436), attacks on the smaller islands already settled and Christianized under Castilian jurisdiction (1448–1452), and various attempts to buy off the rivals. John II and then Henry IV of Castile failed to protect Andalusian interests with much vigor. Nonetheless, a number of military disasters (especially against native resistance) and diplomatic miscalculations (through dynastic marriages) frustrated Portuguese efforts in the Canaries. Eventually, the Treaty of Alcáçovas (1479), which placed Isabella on the Castilian throne at the expense of Juana, the wife (and niece) of Afonso V of Portugal, also awarded the islands to Castile. In exchange, Portugal retained a hard-won monopoly on South Atlantic exploration along the African coasts, occasionally questioned by Castile, at a time when the sources of African gold were finally found in the Gulf of Guinea.

The story of the Canaries reveals that while the early initiatives at exploration were often multinational, throughout the fifteenth century political patronage determined which nations colonies accrued to. In this role the Portuguese, led first by Prince Henry and later by John II, excelled. Prince Henry's activities were indeed extremely varied. For a long time his patronage of African exploration beyond "Cape Bojador" (really probably Cape Juby) was secondary to his interests in a crusade against Morocco and in the colonization of Atlantic islands, mainly to create new sources of revenue. While the Moroccan enterprise was a strategic fiasco, the colonization of Madeira and the Azores reasonably compensated for failure in the Canaries. What mattered here was the determination and consistency with which Prince Henry pursued these ventures, rather than a "pure" experience of discovery.

## Madeira Island and the Azores

Fourteenth-century cartography suggests that the island of Madeira and perhaps also the Azores were already known. Although coastal sailing to the Canaries was probably the norm, it is quite possible that on the way back to Europe the round ships (cogs) used, for example, by the Majorcans first sailed north (as one needed to do to reach the latitude of the Azores to catch the westerlies) and then east. The issue is difficult to settle because existing maps of this period offer a combination of real and imaginary islands in inexact locations, often mixing mythical names with new ones. The Madeira archipelago is unambiguously represented in Cresques Abraham's Catalan atlas of circa 1375, in Guillem Soler's portolan chart of 1385, and in other maps in the same tradition, with equivalents of the modern Portuguese names given in a kind of Genoese lingua franca (hence "insula de Legname" instead of "Madeira"). More controversially, they also show a group of eight islands that might represent the Azores, despite such fanciful names as "Brazil" and "Corvi Marini": the latitude is correct for the Azores, but the longitude is too easterly and the size is exaggerated. Whether this identification is correct or not, it was only in 1427 that the Portuguese rediscovered the Azores and began to travel there regularly with the aim of colonizing them, and it was therefore only after this period that cartographic representation, as in Gabriel de Vallseca's chart of 1439, became reasonably accurate.

Prince Henry successfully colonized these two uninhabited archipelagoes—Madeira and the Azores—through a system of feudal grants, seigniorial monopolies, and temporary fiscal privileges, all inspired by well-tried medieval techniques of colonization in the Iberian Peninsula. Madeira, rediscovered in the early 1420s, was colonized quickly. Since it was very fertile, the settlers soon developed a successful economy based on timber, wheat, wine, and (from the 1450s) sugar. The Azores were colonized after 1439, but slowly over a number of decades and with a significant contribution of Flemish settlers. The Azores also produced wheat and sugar, but on a lesser scale.

## Traditions, Myths, and Technology

Early European exploration of the Atlantic relied largely on the sophisticated navigational skills developed in the Mediterranean from the twelfth to the fourteenth centuries. The Canaries could be reached by the traditional methods of coastal navigation, and were incorporated into the cartography of the portolans (navigational charts) and *mappae mundi* (world maps). These maps relied on detailed coastal observation and a system of rhumbs that, through the use of the compass, allowed a pilot to determine direction and estimate distance with some accuracy. The predominantly Jewish (and after the 1391 massacres, new Christian) mapmakers of Majorca, who were also specialists in compass making, seem to have produced two kinds of charts: the simpler ones, to be taken on board, were similar to the Italian models and showed only the coast in great detail, while the more elaborate versions—which are also those that have been preserved in greater numbers—were richly illustrated and incorporated political and ethnographic information. The scope of these more elaborate maps was usually extended beyond the areas of Mediterranean navigation, to include all the known parts of Africa and Asia. In effect they were conceived as beautiful *mappae mundi*, presents worthy of princes. Whether made for navigational use or for aristocratic owners, these charts did not rely on a Ptolemaic projection with parallels and meridians.

The lack of a significant magnetic variation in the Mediterranean made it possible to calculate direction and to estimate distance without recourse to latitude or longitude. The challenge was how to navigate the unknown open and uncharted waters of the Atlantic, where reliance on dead reckoning was not suitable. The astrolabe and quadrant were known for the purposes of astronomical observations but were rarely used on board, the movements of the ship making it extremely difficult to observe accurately the relative position of stars or the Sun. For navigation in northern waters, latitude was often determined, roughly but quite correctly, with naked-eye observations of celestial bodies like the polestar. Longitude was more intractable, although Italians and Catalans used navigational tables (traverse tables) from at least 1300. These made it possible to calculate the course and distance covered on a chart through simple trigonometric calculations, provided the pilot correctly estimated the ship's speed. Yet again, this was difficult to do in open waters. In effect, although the Atlantic wind system was relatively stable, the winds and currents made it difficult to sail farther south than Cape Juby with these Mediterranean methods, and to return safely. The great achievement of the Portuguese in the fifteenth century was to learn the wind and current system of the South Atlantic by practical experience. Under Prince Henry, Portuguese navigators did not use nautical astronomy. It was only after 1460, after they reached Sierra Leone, that the quadrant is recorded to have been used by Diogo Gomes, and then only to correct the distances entered in a portolan chart, rather than to calculate absolute latitudes.

The Portuguese rounding of "Cape Bojador" in 1434 was thus thanks more to determination and political will than to any technological breakthrough. The idea was far from novel. As early as 1291 two Genoese brothers, Ugolino and Vadino Vivaldi, had attempted to sail around Africa in a galley to reach India in the East. Theirs was not a great choice of a vessel, and they were never heard of again. In 1346 the Majorcan Jaume Ferrer sailed south of "Cape Bojador" hoping to find the *riu d'or* (river of gold), possibly referring to the Senegal River. This aim continued to inspire Europeans up to the time of Prince Henry. Although the term *riu d'or* derived from classical geography, knowledge obtained in North African ports of the trans-Saharan gold trade was remarkably detailed in the Catalan atlas of Cresques Abraham, which also recorded (and illustrated) Ferrer's voyage. Conceivably, the Majorcan Jews who dominated Catalan cartography—some of them originally from North Africa—could still use local connections at the caravan terminals to obtain knowledge about the interior of West Africa up to "the land of the negroes from Guinea" and the kingdom of Mali, with remarkably few concessions to classical mythology. However, Ferrer's *uxer* (apparently a small galley, depicted with a Latin sail and oars by Cresques) also probably failed to return. Lack of knowledge of the powerful currents in that latitude and of the best ships to navigate the prevailing winds made it difficult to succeed in a single attempt.

The failed sailings were not forgotten, and they contributed to the mythology of the difficulty of navigating beyond "Cape Bojador." Hence the late-fourteenth century *Libro del conoçimiento de todos los reynos* (Book of Knowledge of All Kingdoms), an imaginary journey written in Castilian that obviously followed a map in the Catalan tradition, was inspired to complete (however fictionally) a journey south like Ferrer's in order to find the Guinea kingdoms and the gold described by the likes of Cresques Abraham. The journey included subsequently sailing east along a hypothetical gulf to reach the Nile and the Christian kingdom of Prester John. The book was taken seriously as a geographical resource by Jean de Béthencourt and Gadifer de la Salle, whose own narrative of conquest in the Canaries in turn inspired Prince Henry to seek the *riu d'or*.

It seems obvious that in *Crónica dos feitos notáveis que se passaram na conquista da Guiné por mandado do infante D. Henrique* (Chronicle of the Deeds of Arms in the Capture of Guinea by the Command of Prince Henry, c. 1461), Gomes Eanes de Zurara, the chronicler of Prince Henry's African ventures, rhetorically elaborated the mythology of "Cape Bojador" to serve his chivalric panegyric. While the practical difficulties of navigation were real enough, most cosmographers familiar with the largely empirical Italian and Catalan cartography would have rejected the idea that the lands beyond "Cape Bojador" were uninhabited (an idea that Zurara attributed to the reluctant sailors). Prince Henry's virtue was that he insisted on new attempts—as many as fifteen are mentioned by Zurara, although some

of those voyages may have been only piratical raids against Fez, well north of the cape—until eventually navigation around "Cape Bojador" was accomplished under the direction of Gil Eanes. Significantly, Gil Eanes was himself a squire of Prince Henry's household—a political agent, not a pilot. It eventually became clear that it was possible to continue sailing farther south. The *riu d'or* turned out to be farther south than expected, but the Atlantic was progressively opened up along the west African coast. By 1441, Nuno Tristão had reached Cape Blanco, and Cape Verde was reached three years later. The exploration of the Senegal and Gambia rivers soon followed, and when Prince Henry died in 1460, Portuguese sailors (or Italians under Portuguese patronage) were about to reach Sierra Leone and the Cape Verde Islands.

The difficulty of distinguishing the mythical islands of the medieval cartographic tradition from those actually found and colonized (after all, were not the Canaries the Fortunate Islands of antiquity?) explains the persistence of efforts to find further islands in the North Atlantic, with documented commissions from the 1460s to the 1490s. Along with numerous Portuguese efforts to sail west from the Azores to find "Antilia" or the "Seven Cities," which came to nothing because of the prevailing westerly winds, there were a number of voyages departing from Bristol in the 1480s, and perhaps the 1490s, in search of "Brasil." While cartographic fantasy inspired these fruitless attempts, the idea of reaching Asia by sailing westward was gaining currency at that time: the Florentine armchair cosmographer Paolo Toscanelli proposed it in the 1470s, and the Genoese sailor-entrepreneur Christopher Columbus did the same in the 1480s. Columbus's genius or luck was that by starting from the Canary Islands, he had the correct winds for the crossing. Hence one of the most notable unintended consequences of Castilian success in the Canary Islands was that the Catholic kings were ideally placed to become the successful patrons of any such voyage.

Though European traders, navigators, and chart makers overwhelming used empirical methods, the exploration of the North Atlantic was never primarily a scientific exercise. The main motivations for the early exploration of the North Atlantic combined economic, strategic, and ideological factors. Fishing, slaves, and the search for sources of gold were central to the exploration of the west African coast, and for the princes who patronized the voyages, these activities were also part of a crusade against Islam. Similarly, while the Atlantic archipelagoes were settled by Europeans in order to produce a variety of goods for export, they were also seen as having a strategic value for further exploration. The "gentile" peoples encountered in the Canary Islands and in Africa were soon subject to an ideology of evangelization and potential conquest, and also the more immediate possibility of slavery through violent raids or through purchase. In sum, the seeds of all the key ingredients of the later Portuguese and Spanish empires in the Atlantic were present in the earlier expeditions of the fourteenth and early fifteenth centuries.

[*See also* Cartography, *subentry* Speculative Cartography; Henry the Navigator; Portuguese African Exploration Voyages; Portuguese Literature, *subentry on* Chroniclers of Exploration; *and* Spanish Literature, *subentry on* Chroniclers of Exploration.]

## Bibliography

Abraham, Cresques. *L'atlas català de Cresques Abraham.* Barcelona, Spain: Diàfora, 1975. A modern edition of the most magnificent and information-rich fourteenth-century *mappae mundi* based on the tradition of portolan charts.

Abulafia, David. *A Mediterranean Emporium: The Catalan Kingdom of Majorca.* Cambridge, U.K.: Cambridge University Press, 1994.

Campbell, Tony. "Portolan Charts from the Late Thirteenth Century to 1500." In *The History of Cartography.* Vol. 1, *Cartography in Prehistoric, Ancient, and Medieval Europe and the Mediterranean,* edited by J. B. Harley and David Woodward, pp. 371–463. Chicago: University of Chicago Press, 1987. A reliable and innovative introduction to a technically complex subject.

Diffie, Bailey W., and George D. Winius. *Foundations of the Portuguese Empire, 1415–1580.* Minneapolis: University of Minnesota Press, 1977. Offers a good general account in English of the early Portuguese exploration.

Fernández-Armesto, Felipe. *Before Columbus: Exploration and Colonisation from the Mediterranean to the Atlantic, 1229–1492.* London: Macmillan Education, 1987. This is the most stimulating starting point on the subject written in English.

Jiménez de la Espada, Marcos. *Libro del conosçimiento de todos los reinos e tierras e señoríos que son por el mundo* (1877). Barcelona, Spain: Ediciones El Albir, 1980. A fascinating yet little-understood fourteenth-century source. There exists an English version by C. Markham, *Book of the Knowledge of All the Kingdoms, Lands, and Lordships That There Are in the World* (London: Hakluyt Society, 1912). More recently see also *The Book of Knowledge of all Kingdoms,* translated by Nancy F. Marino (Tempe: Arizona Center for Medieval and Renaissance Studies, 1999).

Mauny, Raymond. *Les navigations médiévales sur les côtes sahariennes antérieures à la découverte Portugaies (1434).* Lisbon, Portugal: Centro de Estudios Históricos Ultramarinos, 1960. A systematic discussion especially good on the Arabic geographical background.

Parry, J. H. *The Age of Reconnaissance: Discovery, Exploration, and Settlement, 1450 to 1650.* 2d ed. Berkeley: University of California Press, 1981. Includes an excellent discussion of navigation, ships, and charts.

Peres, Damião. *História dos descobrimentos portugueses.* 4th ed. Porto, Portugal: Vertente, 1992. First published in 1943.

Relaño, Francesc. *The Shaping of Africa: Cosmographic Discourse and Cartographic Science in Late Medieval and Early Modern Europe.* Aldershot, U.K.: Ashgate, 2002.

Randles, William G. L. *Geography, Cartography, and Nautical Science in the Renaissance.* Aldershot, U.K.: Ashgate/Variorum, 2000.

Rey Pastor, Julio, and Ernesto García Camarero. *La cartografía mallorquina.* Madrid, Spain: Departamento de Historia y Filosofía de la Ciencia, "Instituto Luis Vives," Consejo Superior de Investigaciones Científicas, 1960.

Rumeu de Armas, Antonio. *El obispado de telde: Misionarios mallorquines y catalane en el Atlántico.* Las Palmas, Spain: Biblioteca Atlántica, 1960. The remarkable but still little known story of fourteenth-century missions to the Canary Islands.

Russell, Peter. *Prince Henry "the Navigator": A Life.* New Haven, Conn.: Yale University Press, 2000. A comprehensive and revisionist account.

Sevillano Colom, Francisco. "Los viajes medievales desde Mallorca a Canarias." *Anuario de Estudios Atlánticos* 23 (1978): 27–57.

Zurara, Gomes Eanes de. *Crónica dos feitos notáveis que se passaram na conquista de Guiné por mandado do Infante D. Henrique.* 2 vols. Edited by Torquatro de Sousa Soares. Lisbon, Portugal: Academia Portuguesa da História, 1978–1981. A crucial narrative source. There exists an English version edited and translated by Charles Raymond Beazley and Edgar Prestage, *The Discovery and Conquest of Guinea,* 2 vols. (London: Hakluyt Society, 1896–1897).

JOAN-PAU RUBIÉS

**Atmosphere.** *See* Meteorology.

# Aubin, Georges

(1889–1981), French maritime writer. Georges Aubin was a sailor in the merchant navy, harking back to the era of tall ships and Cape Horners' adventures. Born in 1889 in Trentemoult, a village on the banks of the Loire across from the harbor of Nantes and home to many long-haul sailors, Aubin became a ship's boy at age fourteen. He first made a twenty-eight-month voyage on a three-master from Nantes. An officer in the merchant navy by 1908, he then became lieutenant on a sailing ship under the command of the illustrious captain Gilbert Lacroix, who himself left an important legacy of reference works on sailing-ship history at the time of its apogee, at the beginning of the twentieth century. Aubin was appointed to numerous commands, and distinguished himself during World War I in the fight against submarines. He came ashore for good in 1924, and from then on shared his vast experience with a number of shipbuilding companies.

Aubin's writings are all devoted to the glory of those rough and courageous sailors who contended with the oceans on board tall ships, described as cathedrals of steel and cloth. Aubin's works introduce us uncompromisingly but often tenderly to a long-lost world that continues to inspire great nostalgia in sea lovers.

In *L'empreinte de la voile* (The Mark of the Sail, 1955), Aubin captured the striking nature of daily life aboard those ships. *Nous, les cap-horniers* (We, the Cape Horners, 1957) brings together authentic accounts of dramas or extraordinary adventures that always take place against the background of the extreme conditions encountered around Cape Horn. *Les hommes en suroît* (The Men in the Southwester, 1963) is a novel whose dedication could be used as a summary of Georges Aubin's entire work:

> To the memory of my parents, friends, and comrades, sailors from Trentemoult, my small home, lost with their ships or taken alive by the mighty waves of the high seas, or simply dead in their beds, these raw memories of a harsh past that will never return.

Aubin died on January 1, 1981.

[*See also* Fiction, *subentry on* Sea Fiction; French Literature; *and* Literature, *subentry on* Voyage Narratives.]

JEAN-PIERRE BEAUVOIS

**Auckland** Auckland is situated on a narrow isthmus two-thirds of the way up the North Island of New Zealand. On the west coast at Onehunga on the Manukau Harbour, trade is limited by insufficient deep water. On the east coast, early British settlers identified the Waitemata Harbour, with its protected deep waters, as an ideal location for trading and they established a capital city there in 1840. Although the capital was transferred to Wellington in 1865, the port of Auckland has thrived; together with Wellington's, its business soon surpassed the southern ports of Dunedin and Lyttelton. Its principal exports have been drawn from the rich resources of its hinterland—dairy, wool, frozen meat, timber, kauri gum, and gold—and its imports are mainly of manufactured goods, oil, grain, sugar, and fruit. Its main trading partner has been the United Kingdom, along with the United States, Canada, Japan, Belgium, Germany, and Malaysia. Much of its traffic, however, has been the supply of mail and provisions to the many small islands within the Hauraki Gulf, transported in flat-hulled scows able to run up onto beaches. In addition to cargo trades, passengers

have been received from across the harbor at Devonport (particularly before the construction of the road bridge in 1959) and from as far afield as Britain. The accelerated postwar stream of European migrants gave rise to an overseas passenger terminal at Princes Wharf in 1961. Auckland has also developed as a major center of recreational sailing and as the home to a naval dockyard at Devonport.

Governance was vested in the Auckland Harbour Board in 1871, providing the impetus for land reclamation plans, dredging programs, and regular extensions to the list of deepwater wharves, culminating in the completion of a container terminal in 1971. Many renowned shipping companies have regularly deployed their vessels to Auckland, including P & O, Mitsui OSK, Port Line, Union Steamship, Shaw Savill Albion, New Zealand Shipping Company, and James Craig.

[*See also* Sydney *and* Unions, *subentry on* Australia and New Zealand.]

### Bibliography

Barr, John. *The Ports of Auckland, New Zealand: The Story of the Discovery and Development of the Waitemata and Manukau Harbours*. Auckland, New Zealand: Unity Press, 1926.

Rose, John. *Akarana: The Ports of Auckland*. Auckland, New Zealand: Auckland Harbour Board, 1971.

SIMON VILLE

# Autobiographies, Journals, and Diaries

This entry contains two subentries:

An Overview
Sailors' Journals and Diaries

---

## An Overview

Journals, autobiographies, and diaries are written to record events as seen through the eyes of the writer. Although often kept for the writer's personal reflection, at sea they are also in many circumstances an expansion of the logbook, the official record of a ship's voyage required by an official position. Motivations for these records include chronicling new lands or occupations, defending one's actions, communicating with loved ones far away, expressing one's emotions, instituting reform, or a combination of several of these.

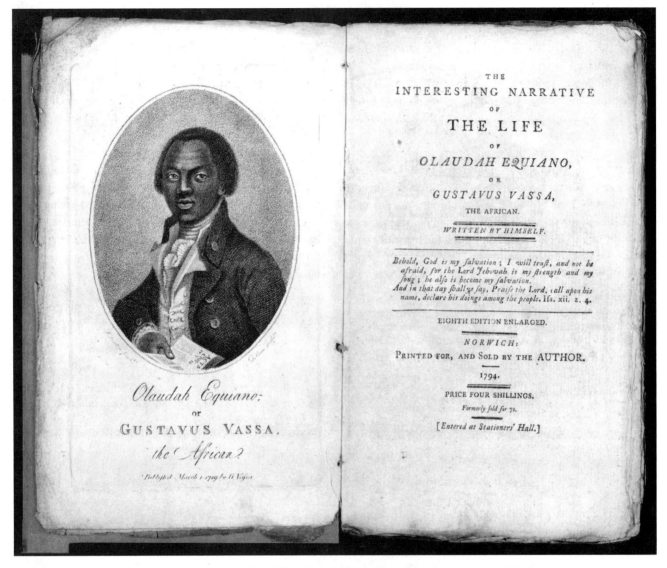

**Equiano's Autobiography.** Olaudah Equiano (1745–1797) published his autobiographical narrative in 1794. He recounts experiences of the Middle Passage from Africa to the American colonies and his life as a servant to a British naval officer and then as a merchant seaman. LIBRARY OF CONGRESS, PRINTS AND PHOTOGRAPHS DIVISION

How does one assess the literary value of such an account? The historical stature of the author and the degree of influence on contemporaries and subsequent generations form important considerations. The journals of Christopher Columbus (1451–1506) and James Cook (1728–1779) provide insight into the minds and actions of major historical figures. The autobiographies of the ordinary seamen Ned Myers and Israel Potter would be minor works if it were not for the fact that James Fenimore Cooper and Herman Melville rewrote them (1843, 1855). Cook's journal was a central source for Samuel Taylor Coleridge's "The Rime of the Ancient Mariner" (1798), as well as for later voyagers in the South Pacific. Despite his mocking of the English clergyman, scientist, and explorer William Scoresby as "Dr. Snodhead . . . in the college of Santa Claus and St. Pott's" (chapter 101), Melville borrowed extensively from Scoresby's journal for *Moby-Dick* (1851). Charles Darwin's *Journal of Researches . . . during the Voyage of the H.M.S.* Beagle *round the World* (1839) had a great impact on scientific thought before *On the Origin of Species* (1859). Lastly, works such as *Narrative of the Life of Frederick Douglass* (1845) or Richard Henry Dana's *Two Years before the Mast* (1840) have literary value for their own merits. Yet, even the most practical and unadorned entries can be remarkably poignant. The log-keeper aboard the whaleship *Columbus* wrote of rounding Cape Horn, "Strong double Reef Breezes from W squally weather head wind for EVER . . . " (entry for September 17, 1840).

## Exploration

Many journals of sailor-explorers offer a first glimpse of a world hitherto unknown to Europeans. These journals are often more descriptive than other types of sailors' journals. Christopher Columbus, James Cook, Joseph Banks (1743–1820), and Charles Wilkes (1798–1877) filled their journals with observations about the geography, people, language, and customs of newly discovered lands.

Though Christopher Columbus was not the first European to set foot on North American soil, Cecil Jane, editor and translator of the *Journal of Christopher Columbus* (1960), argues that he was the first to open the Atlantic Ocean. Columbus's original journal is now lost; however, a Dominican historian named Bartolomé de las Casas abstracted a copy of it around 1559. The first Spanish edition appeared in 1825, the first English in 1827. Since the only extant copy of Columbus's journal is an abstraction, many details were cut, and the reader is presented solely with what Bartolomé de las Casas thought important. A revised translation by Oliver Dunn and James E. Kelly, *The Diario of Christopher Columbus* (1989) has been complemented by David Henige's *In Search of Columbus: The Sources for the First Voyage* (1991), an elaborate critique and reconstruction of the text.

If Columbus's journal helped open the Atlantic Ocean, Captain Woodes Rogers's *A Cruising Voyage round the World* (1712) helped open the door to the Pacific Ocean. Rogers, accompanied by William Dampier, sailed throughout the Pacific from 1708 until 1711. Rogers's visit to the island of Juan Fernández and his recovery of the marooned Alexander Selkirk inspired Daniel Defoe and provided him with the details necessary for *Robinson Crusoe* (1719). Aside from influencing Defoe, Woodes Rogers's *Cruising Voyage* was widely read throughout Europe and became standard reading for navigators venturing to the Pacific Ocean.

In 1768 Captain James Cook ventured into the Pacific Ocean. The journal of his first voyage was published anonymously in 1771, with an official second edition, edited by John Hawkesworth, in 1773; the journal of his second voyage was published in 1777, and that of his third voyage in 1784. Because of Cook's fine work as a navigator, his

journals helped correct the way maps and charts were drawn. Furthermore, scientists and artists accompanied him on all of his voyages and meticulously collected specimens throughout the South Pacific, contributing greatly to the knowledge of the natural sciences.

Among the scientists that sailed with Cook on his first voyage (1768–1771) was Joseph Banks. Banks's journal, noteworthy because it is complementary to Cook's, was edited by Joseph Hooker and published in 1896. J. C. Beaglehole, the journal's next editor, said of Hooker's editing, "These volumes are not a journal, they are a scene of carnage" (p. 144). Beaglehole's *The Endeavour Journal of Joseph Banks* appeared in 1962. Banks, considerably more educated than Cook, was a keen observer, excellent at describing flora and fauna, native people's languages, and customs such as tattooing.

In 1838, the U.S. government commissioned Charles Wilkes to explore and survey the South Pacific, effectively continuing the work begun by Cook. Wilkes, like Cook, was accompanied by scientists and was ordered to pay special attention to geography and hydrography. Wilkes recorded his experiences in *Narrative of the United States Exploring Expedition during the Years 1838–1842* (1844). In the process, Wilkes discovered a portion of the Antarctic continent, now known as Wilkes Land.

## Shipwreck

As Donald P. Wharton notes in "The Colonial Era" (in Springer), the intensity and upheaval of shipwreck often drove people to write down their experiences. Shipwreck narratives were published for many reasons, including the attempt to make sense of the trauma, justification of the author's actions, disagreement with other published accounts, and profit.

The belief in divine providence was also a very important element in early shipwreck narrative. For seventeenth-century American writers, crossing the Atlantic was the trial by which one began a new life and a metaphor for the transition into a life of grace. Those who read sea-deliverance narratives were called on to bear witness to God's providence.

Shipwreck narratives vary according to author; often competing accounts of the same disaster exist. *Nottingham Galley* was wrecked on Boone Island off the coast of Maine in 1710. The captain, John Dean, published *A Narrative of the Sufferings, Preservation, and Deliverance of Capt. John Dean and Company* in 1711. Christopher Langman, the first mate, disagreed strongly with the captain's account.

His *A True Account of the Voyage of the* Nottingham-Galley was published the same year. Langman accuses the captain of deliberately trying to put the vessel ashore for the insurance. The captain, according to Langman, was a "Brute," certainly not the hero that he was in his own account. Langman's *Account* appeared only once, but Dean's *Narrative* continued in print and was the source for Kenneth Roberts's *Boon Island* (1956).

The trauma of shipwreck on unknown or unfriendly coasts could be followed by other harrowing experiences. In *A Narrative of the Uncommon Sufferings and Surprizing Deliverance of Briton Hammon, a Negro Man* (1760), Hammon, a black man, recounts the wreck of his vessel on the Florida capes, his captivity among the Indians, his four-year confinement in a Spanish dungeon, and his return to Boston, Massachusetts, after thirteen years. In 1815 the brig *Commerce* was lost on the African coast and the crew enslaved. Captain James Riley published *An Authentic Narrative of the Loss of the American Brig* Commerce . . . *with an Account of the Sufferings of her Surviving Officers and Crew who were Enslaved by the Wandering Arabs* in 1817. His "aim," writes Riley, "has been merely to record, in plain and unvarnished language, scenes in which I was a principal actor, of real and heart-appalling distresses" (p. iii). The popularity of Riley's *Narrative* led his first mate, Archibald Robbins, to publish his own story, *A Journal, Comprising an Account of the Loss of the Brig* Commerce (1817). Robbins's journal was ghostwritten, a common practice in the early publication of works by sailors. The mate disagrees with the captain as to why the *Commerce* was wrecked. This is a subject that Dean King explores in *Skeletons on the Zahara* (2004). Accounts of shipwreck on the African coast sprang into print. Some were true, such as Judah Paddock's *A Narrative of the Shipwreck of the Ship* Oswego . . . *and of the Sufferings of Master and the Crew while in Bondage among the Arabs* (1818), a source for James Fenimore Cooper's *Homeward Bound* (1838), and some were spurious, such as *An Authentic Narrative of the Shipwreck and Sufferings of Mrs. Eliza Bradley* (1820).

One of the most remarkable shipwreck narratives came from the pen of Owen Chase, first mate of the whaleship *Essex*. He published his account of the 1820 sinking of that ill-fated whaleship by an enraged sperm whale in 1821, only nine months after the crew was rescued. Part of his motivation was to present a positive view of his own actions. In contrast, Thomas Nickerson, fourteen at the time of the event, wrote an account of the shipwreck and rescue when he was seventy-one that remained unpublished for over one hundred years. Which is closer to the truth? Chase's account, contemporary to the event and based on a rough journal kept during the ordeal, but driven by Chase's desire for exoneration? Or Nickerson's written only as a record fifty-five years later? Nathaniel Philbrick's *In the Heart of the Son* (2002) reconsiders these events.

## Naval Personnel

A great number of sailors' journals were written by men who served in the navy. Many officers—men who came from wealthy or noble backgrounds and had been afforded an education—kept journals in order to protect themselves in case of court martial or other unfortunate circumstances. It was not until the late eighteenth century that the voice of the foremast hand was heard. Journals of foremast hands often provide insight into daily life in both the Royal and U.S. navies.

William Spavens served in the Royal Navy, British East India Company, and other merchant services during the mid-eighteenth century. He offers the unique perspective of a disabled foremast hand in *The Narrative of William Spavens, a Chatham Pensioner* (1796).

The years of the American Revolution and the Napoleonic wars produced numerous accounts of service afloat. Admiral Sir Thomas Pasley's *Private Sea Journals, 1778–1782* (1931) provide a British officer's perspective on the American Revolution. Pasley's diary stands in contrast to Thomas Dring's *Recollections of the* Jersey *Prison Ship* (1829). Dring was an American sailor captured by the British and held for five months in the prison ship *Jersey*. Dring's recollection is filled with details of the horrible conditions faced by prisoners of war. In addition, Jacob Nagle's *The Nagle Journal* (1988) and Christopher Prince's *The Autobiography of a Yankee Mariner* (2002) provide firsthand accounts of the turbulent years of the American Revolution from the perspective of forecastlemen. Nagle also gives fascinating details on the British settlement of Australia and the Napoleonic Wars at sea.

Thomas Cochrane's *The Autobiography of a Seaman* (1890) provides details about the life of an officer during the Napoleonic Wars and recounts his fantastic exploits. Patrick O'Brian based Jack Aubrey's fictional cruise in *Sophie* in *Master and Commander* (1970) on Cochrane's cruise in *Speedy*.

During the American Civil War, more sailors' journals appeared, including Raphael Semmes's *Service Afloat* (1887). Semmes's account not only offers a view of the war from a Confederate perspective, but also details the careers of two of the Confederacy's most successful commerce raiders, *Sumter* and *Alabama*.

## Slaves

Slave narratives presented the lives of enslaved peoples to those who would otherwise know nothing of them. Life at sea allowed slaves greater freedom and often the chance to escape or to earn enough money to buy their freedom. *The Interesting Narrative of the Life of Olaudah Equiano . . . Written by Himself* appeared in 1789. The fact that the narrative was written by Equiano and so titled adds power and credence to the work. Kidnapped into slavery at the age of eleven, Equiano was eventually sold to a British sea captain. Although a slave, he worked as a seaman on various vessels. In 1766, with the encouragement of his captain, Equiano was able to purchase his manumission from his master, but he continued at sea for many years. The greatest of the slave narratives remains the *Narrative of the Life of Frederick Douglass . . . Written by Himself* (1845). Douglass's apostrophe to the vessels on Chesapeake Bay—"You are loosed from your moorings, and are free; I am fast in my chains, and am a slave" (chapter 10)—is not the only maritime element of his narrative: he also worked as caulker in shipyards and eventually escaped to freedom using borrowed seaman's papers.

## Whaling

For centuries humans have hunted whales, first for the valuable oil rendered from whale blubber and later for baleen. Whalemen found their prey in all oceans, thus spending years at sea and traveling to exotic locales such as the Galápagos, the Hawaiian Islands, Australia, and the Arctic. From these men comes a body of writing that captures a unique profession. "For God's sake, be economical with your lamps and candles! not a gallon you burn, but at least one drop of blood was spilled for it" (chapter 45), Herman Melville admonishes in *Moby-Dick* (1851).

The British whaling captain William Scoresby made over seventeen voyages to the Arctic and published *Journal of a Voyage to the Northern Whale-Fishery* (1823). Though ostensibly a whaling captain, Scoresby was also a scientist; his scientific interests included surveying magnetics, hydrography, zoology, and cetology. Scoresby's journals provide one of the most complete descriptions of arctic life at the turn of the nineteenth century and they can now be followed in detail through the Hakluyt Society editions (2003 and after).

The same year Scoresby published his work, George Attwater was serving aboard the New Haven whaleship *Henry*. Attwater's experiences on that voyage are preserved in *The Journal of George Attwater* (2002). Besides including descriptions of life on board a whaler, Attwater's text contains references to the sinking of *Essex* (April 8, 1821) and reports of a white whale: "They said they saw a white whale & darst not fasten" (August 25, 1821). Furthermore, Attwater's journal contains the first known use of the word "scrimshaw" (May 30, 1823).

Nelson Cole Haley's *Whale Hunt* (1948) is the detailed narrative of an 1849–1853 whaling voyage written by an experienced whaleman. From the sighting of the whale to the rendering of the blubber, Haley's *Whale Hunt* gives one of the most inclusive accounts of the mid-nineteenth century American whaling industry, while Frank Bullen's *Cruise of the* Cachalot (1899) was widely read at the end of the century.

## Reform

For many mariners of Anglo-American extraction, serving in either the merchant service or navy, flogging was a routine part of shipboard life. Beginning with the publication of Richard Henry Dana's *Two Years before the Mast* (1840), a reform movement gathered momentum. Dana's account not only detailed life before the mast on a merchantman, but also raised objections to the practice of flogging.

Others followed closely in Dana's wake, including Samuel Leech's *Thirty Years from Home; or, A Voice from the Main Deck* (1843). Leech served for thirty years in both the British Royal Navy and the U.S. Navy; he records the treatment of the men by officers and the horrors of flogging. Leech's account served as a major source for Herman Melville's *White-Jacket* (1850), which is permeated with Melville's hatred of flogging.

## Observation

As fewer men were required to man ships, and as whaling and other trades declined, nonsailors went to sea for adventure, for health reasons, and to record a dying industry. Eric Newby signed on the four-masted barque *Moshulu* for what would be the final voyage of the Australian grain trade (*The Last Grain Race*, 1956). William Henry Tripp sailed on the last whaling voyage out of New Bedford, the 1925 cruise of the schooner *John R. Manta* ("*There Goes Flukes*," 1938). Probably the best account is the journal Robert Cushman Murphy kept for his wife Grace during his 1912 voyage on the whaleship *Daisy*, which he reworked into *Logbook for Grace* (1947).

## Women

Women went to sea first as passengers, servants, or slaves. Later, they traveled with their husbands, sharing the captain's cabin, particularly on board whaleships but also on board merchant vessels. These women often wrote journals, but rarely for publication. Only in the second half of the twentieth century has a strong interest in women at sea emerged.

One of the most horrific accounts is the *Narrative of the Shipwreck and Sufferings of Miss Ann Saunders…Written by Herself* (1827). Saunders was traveling with her fiancé on board *Francis Mary* when it was disabled. Those on board eventually resorted to cannibalism. Saunders withstood the harrowing circumstances better; therefore, she constantly carried a knife with which she cut off bits of flesh to serve the others. When her fiancé died, she thought it only right "to plead my claim to the greater portion of his precious blood, as it oozed half congealed from the wound inflicted upon his lifeless body!!!" (p. 15).

Whaling wives are the most fully documented of any group of women that went to sea. Journals not only passed the time during interminable whaling voyages but also served as a connection to friends and family at home and could be read as long letters. Annie Ricketson's journal of the 1871–1874 voyage on *A. R. Tucker*, published as *The Journal of Annie Holmes Ricketson* (1958), is lively and fun—and heartbreaking. She writes of the death of her baby one and a half days after it is born in the Azores.

Mary Chipman Lawrence kept a journal of her time on the whaleship *Addison* in 1856–1860. The journal became the basis for a religious tract, *A Good Catch; or, Mrs. Emerson's Whaling-Cruise*, by Helen E. Brown (1884). It was later reedited by Stanton Garner and published as *The Captain's Best Mate: The Journal of Mary Chipman Lawrence* (1966). The journal is deeply pious in its portrayal of what Garner calls the "pervasively religious atmosphere of the women's quarters" (p. xix).

Personal journals were different from logbooks. Charlotte Church, the captain's wife, kept the logbook for the 1909–1913 voyage of the whaleship *Charles W. Morgan* and referred to herself in the third person. Church was listed in the crew register as "navigator," thus giving her an official position rarely held by women at sea.

Women's narratives do not end with the decline of whaling. Now, however, women are no longer restricted in their roles. Leslie Leyland Fields's *The Entangling Net: Alaska's Commercial Fishing Women Tell Their Lives* (1997) is a collection from women fishermen on the Alaskan coast, and Linda Greenlaw's *The Hungry Ocean* (1999) recounts her time as a swordboat captain. Tania Aebi sailed around the world alone at the age of eighteen, as recorded in her *Maiden Voyage* (1989), written with the help of Bernadette Brennan.

[*See also* Cruising Literature; Logs and Ship's Journals; *and* Whaling, *subentry on* Literature.]

## Bibliography

Beaglehole, J. C., ed. *The* Endeavour *Journal of Joseph Banks, 1768–1771*. 2 vols. Sydney, Australia: Trustees of the Public Library of New South Wales in Association with Angus and Robertson Ltd., 1962.

Beaglehole, J. C., ed. *The Journals of Captain James Cook on His Voyages of Discovery*. 4 vols. Cambridge, U.K.: Hakluyt Society at the University Press at Cambridge, 1955–1974.

Gates, Henry Louis, ed. *The Classic Slave Narratives*. New York: Penguin, 1987.

Pope, Dudley. *Life in Nelson's Navy*. Annapolis, Md.: Naval Institute Press, 1981.

Sherman, Stuart, et al. *Whaling Logbooks and Journals, 1613–1927: An Inventory of Manuscript Records in Public Collections*. Revised and edited by Judith M. Downey and Virginia M. Adams, with the assistance of Howard Pasternack. New York: Garland, 1986.

Springer, Haskell, ed. *America and the Sea: A Literary History*. Athens: University of Georgia Press, 1995. Especially Donald P. Wharton, "The Colonial Era," pp. 32–45, and John Samson, "Personal Narratives, Journals, and Diaries," pp. 83–98.

Wharton, Donald P. *In the Trough of the Sea: Selected American Sea-Deliverance Narratives, 1610–1766*. Westport, Conn.: Greenwood Press, 1979.

MARY K. BERCAW EDWARDS *and* MATTHEW GEEZA

# Sailors' Journals and Diaries

There are several reasons why a mariner keeps a chronological account of a voyage. Such an account can serve as a legal record in case of incident or accident; document a claim of new territory; provide data that can be incorporated into nautical charts and tables of winds and currents; and record information to guide subsequent voyages in exploration, commerce, war, and the harvesting of marine resources. A shipboard diary can also be a place where physical and emotional hardships and exaltations of rapture are scribbled secretly, intended to be shared with no one else.

The terms "logbook" and "journal" are often used interchangeably, but the logbook is technically a legal document, recording daily details of weather, wind direction, position, soundings, and course traveled, and surrendered

**Journal of Captain James Cook**. A page from Cook's journal in HMS *Resolution* during his second voyage shows the entry for the period July 29 to August 2, 1772. Cook mentions that he has just taken on board a supply of water and wine at Madeira. On the same page, he mentions two of the chronometers he carried, Harrison's H4 and Kendall's K1. © NATIONAL MARITIME MUSEUM, LONDON

to the vessel's owner at the conclusion of the voyage. Logs were traditionally kept by the chief mate or the sailing master, though by the end of the nineteenth century they were more commonly maintained several times a day by watch officers. A journal is a personal account, kept by any member of a ship's company for his or her own private motives. Both kinds of documents can include descriptions of ports-of-call and of people encountered on a voyage, incidents of trade, and accounts of disciplinary actions and other aspects of shipboard life, as well as the standard nautical entries. A journal might also include private thoughts and observations, poems, song texts, and scientific data.

The tradition of keeping of an account of a voyage is an ancient one. The *periplus* of the Carthaginian admiral Hanno, describing a voyage down the west coast of Africa, survives from the fifth century B.C.E. and Aristotle is thought to have collected accounts of foreign travel for his library at Alexandria two centuries later. The dramatic potential of a voyage has also been explored since ancient times, with Odysseus and Sinbad being only two among many fictional captains whose exploits have been celebrated in folk literature from the shores of several continents. A sea voyage provided the perfect opportunity for an author to test his hero not only against the known dangers of enemies and the elements but also against the unknown world beyond, where fantastic and exotic adventures waited. The persistent popularity of fictional voyages led, inevitably, to a public interest in factual ones as well, but the widespread availability of nonfiction accounts of voyages waited until the Age of Exploration.

## Sources of Information

By the early sixteenth century it had become apparent to Europeans that the logbooks and journals of explorers could not only bolster colonial claims but also contained a wealth of information on the people, resources, and geography of the New World. The tradition of publishing shipboard accounts began with a compilation of Spanish voyages, which appeared as *De Orbe Novo* in 1516. The author, Pietro Martire d'Anghiera, not only had full access to shipboard sources and official Spanish documents but also knew many of the participants whose voyages were detailed in his volume, including Christopher Columbus, Ferdinand Magellan, Vasco Núñez de Balboa, and Hernán Cortés. Antonio de Herrera y Tordesillas compiled another monumental collection of Spanish voyage accounts, published in eight volumes in Madrid between 1601 and 1615.

In 1576, Richard Eden published an English translation of the collection of Pietro Martire d'Anghiera (known to the English-speaking world as Peter Martyr). The British geographer Richard Hakluyt published another compilation of voyages in English in 1582 as *Divers Voyages Touching the Discovery of America*. In 1589 he delivered the first version of what would became, a decade later, the three-volume *Principal Navigations, Voyages, and Discoveries of the English Nation* (1599–1600).

Hakluyt mined an extraordinary variety of sources for this important collection, and under his direction came the first published accounts of the voyages of John Cabot (c. 1451–1498), Francis Drake (1540/43–1596), Walter

Ralegh (1554–1618), Humphrey Gilbert (c. 1539–1583), Martin Frobisher (c. 1535–1594), and the first account in English translation of Hernando de Soto (1496, 1499, or 1500–1542) and others. Hakluyt's work served as a basis for the subsequent publications of Samuel Purchas (c. 1577–1626), who inherited Hakluyt's collection upon his death. Purchas published a first collection of voyage accounts in 1613 entitled *Purchas His Pilgrimage*, and followed it with the four-volume *Hakluytus Posthumous . . .* in 1625 and 1626. In total, Hakluyt and Purchas published almost twelve hundred accounts of voyages and influenced generations of mariners, editors, and publishers to follow.

It was not common until the turn of the eighteenth century for mariners to produce their own shipboard accounts for public consumption (though Antonio Pigafetta, who traveled on Magellan's expedition around the world, published his own account of the voyage around 1525, and Francis Drake prepared a narrative, *The World Encompassed*, in 1628). The English buccaneers William Dampier, William Hack, Woodes Rogers, and Edward Cooke all published swashbuckling accounts between 1697 and 1712 and were influential in inspiring Daniel Defoe and Jonathan Swift to create, respectively, the fictional *Robinson Crusoe* (1719) and *Gulliver's Travels* (1726), and to claim in both cases that the books were actual shipboard accounts.

## Fact and Fiction

As the line blurred between fact and fiction, so did the distinction between shipboard accounts written simultaneously with the events they described and more detailed narratives crafted later—either by the mariner who wrote the original account or by an editor on shore. The romantic expectations of the fictional narrative could not help but influence both sailors and their editors as they strove to create an account that would appeal to a land-based audience, and the role of memory, imagination, and the influence of genre began to make a mark on the published journals. In *Robinson Crusoe*, Defoe's hero makes this point very specifically when he tells his reader that it was better for them that he began to keep his journal after settling on his island rather than at the moment of his shipwreck, as then he was "in too much discomposure of mind; and my journal would have been full of many dull things." In the examples that he gives of comparative versions, the first is straightforward action and emotion, while the second is pompous, religious, and self-important.

In the second half of the eighteenth century, the publication of shipboard chronicles became especially important in establishing European colonial claims to newly discovered lands in the Pacific, and public interest in the exotic people and locations was extraordinarily intense. The official narrative of George Anson's Pacific expedition of 1741–1744 was one of the most popular books of its time. The French commander Louis-Antoine de Bougainville's journal of 1771 was important for establishing a romantic notion of Polynesians. His lush and idealized descriptions of Tahiti inspired not only subsequent travelers in the development of their own voyage narratives, but also the French philosophers Jean-Jacques Rousseau (1712–1778) and Denis Diderot (1713–1784), who articulated the concept of the "noble savage" and took Europeans to task for their treatment of native people. (Diderot would later complain that the frequency with which voyages were subsequently undertaken, and the profusion of Pacific voyage narratives "familiarized even the grossest minds with a spirit of indifference for the objects which would once have startled their imagination.")

The British Admiralty paid John Hawkesworth an astonishing £6,000 to prepare the accounts of four British voyages for publication in 1773–an indication of the importance not only of the expeditions themselves, but also of the perceived national interest in their representation in print. These voyages by John Byron, Samuel Wallis, Philip Carteret, and James Cook covered a remarkable amount of previously unexplored territory, dramatically increasing European knowledge of the Pacific. In his introduction to the volume, Hawkesworth particularly distinguished these accounts from those of the previous generations of explorers. The earlier voyages, he wrote, had "seldom any other motive for attempting the discovery of new countries than to conquer them," while the expeditions documented in his volume were for "more liberal motive . . . not with a view to the acquisition of treasure, or the extent of domain, but the improvement of commerce and the increase and diffusion of knowledge."

The most important text in Hawkesworth's collection described the first of the three voyages to the Pacific made under the command of Captain James Cook between 1768 and 1780. The voyages of Cook and Bougainville opened up a new era of voyaging; the emerging science of natural history was redefining the way the world was understood, and their shipboard accounts were seen as important observations of new regions, new cultures, and new species of animals and plants. On these voyages traveled naturalists and artists as well as mariners, and their journals were incorporated into the official account, which was then published under the name of the commander of the expedition.

(Samuel Purchas felt obliged to apologize to his readers in 1613 that some of his sources were common sailors, as opposed to aristocratic captains: "I mention Authors sometimes, of meane qualitie," he wrote, "for the meanest have sense to observe that which themselves see, more certainly then the contemplations and Theory of the more learned.") It was difficult to dislodge the bias that what captains had to say about a voyage was more interesting and important than the observations of men down the chain of command, but the enormous public interest in every possible account of the voyages of Anson, Cook, and others, led several of the men on board to publish their own accounts.

Narratives of American captains followed quickly after the first Yankee ventures into the Pacific and around the world. David Porter's *Journal of a Cruise . . .* was prepared for publication by Porter himself and published in 1822. *The Narrative of the United States Exploring Expedition during the Years 1838, 1839, 1840, 1841, 1842* was similarly prepared by the captain of the expedition, Charles Wilkes, who, like others before him, demanded all personal accounts be turned over to him to prevent the appearance of conflicting accounts and to guard against literary pirates who were ready to make a profit for themselves. Wilkes also demanded all the collections of natural history specimens and ethnographic artifacts (which would eventually become the core collection of the Smithsonian Institution). There were accounts of commercial voyages by master mariners, and accounts of shipwreck and captivity by common sailors, but American shipboard journals took a pronounced literary departure from British antecedents when the account of Richard Henry Dana Jr. was published in 1840 as *Two Years before the Mast*. Dana's perspective was not only American, but was purposefully from the forecastle rather than the quarterdeck.

## Changing Viewpoints

Though Dana was not from humble origins, he opened a door that made a broad reading audience interested in the accounts of common working sailors, not only for the observations over the rail but also for the philosophies shared within the ship. Dana's book influenced a number of American authors working in the maritime genre, including Herman Melville (1819–1891), James Fenimore Cooper (1789–1851), and Edgar Allan Poe (1809–1849). Following quickly in Dana's wake were not only fictional accounts of working tars but also autobiographical narratives from the likes of Samuel Leech and Nicholas Isaacs, who bested Dana with *Thirty Years from Home . . .* (1843)

and *Twenty Years before the Mast* (1845), respectively. Melville, Jack London (1876–1916), and Joseph Conrad (1857–1924) went further, drawing from their personal experiences at sea to develop richly textured descriptions of seafaring life.

There was some dialogue among readers and reviewers about whether the plethora of nautical journals available in the nineteenth century were hard-bitten realistic accounts, which would keep any reasonable young man from following in the sea boots of the authors, or whether they made the experience romantic enough to inspire lads to run away to sea. Some were specifically pointed in one direction or the other, with a fair number of nineteenth-century seafaring accounts introducing religious motifs that made the maritime adventure a metaphor for the voyage of life. An example is *A Good Catch; or, Mrs. Emerson's Whaling Cruise* (1884), which is based on the shipboard journal of Mary Chipman Lawrence, the wife of a Cape Cod whaling captain. As edited by Helen E. Brown, it expands a number of shipboard incidents into moral examples, making Mary and her husband, Captain Samuel Lawrence, the pillars of a rambunctious community of sailors.

Women's journals had been published before; Mary Ann Parker's account of a voyage from England to Australia on HMS *Gorgon* was first published in 1795, but it was unusual to find a female point of view until well into the twentieth century. Mary Chipman Lawrence's journal was published from the original manuscript in 1966 as *The Captain's Best Mate*, part of a wave of publications that brought shipboard logbooks and journals from the eighteenth and nineteenth century into print for the first time. Scholars and the public began to realize the valuable information contained in the unedited eyewitness accounts, as well as the varying points of view that different ranks (forty-four) and different genders might bring to the same experience. Unlike the narratives of officers (seven) or the account of Dana, these personal journals were not, for the most part, intended for a wide audience. Some are so poignant and personal that they cannot have been meant to be read by anyone other than the author; others address an audience of family members back home, providing an insight into the experience of a son, husband, daughter or sister, separated by a long sea voyage.

The vast majority of shipboard logs and journals remain unpublished. They are kept in repositories around the globe, and in them is a storehouse of information for historians, anthropologists, climatologists, biologists, and genealogists. Most of them show the repetitive nature of the work on shipboard, punctuated only occasionally by storms, disasters, exotic landfalls, and romantic descriptions. They contain a wealth of information unavailable elsewhere, however, and scholars are currently mining them for data to understand a number of scientific questions, including how the global climate has changed, what the impact of human predation has been on marine mammal and fish populations, and the impact of natural disasters like volcanoes and earthquakes in centuries past. Twenty-first-century researchers follow in an interesting intellectual wake: Benjamin Franklin (1706–1790) used unpublished whaling logs to develop the first map of the Gulf Stream, and the American naval officer and oceanographer Matthew Fontaine Maury (1806–1873) drew on similar sources for the creation of the first global representation of ocean currents.

Shipboard documents have also proven valuable in understanding the human dynamic of the encounter between Euro-Americans and indigenous people around the globe. The transfer of technology, along with diseases and other biota, led to enormous, often devastating social and cultural changes in the wake of European arrivals in the Americas, Asia, Africa, and the Pacific. In an ironic historical twist, the very same journals and logs that were used to document European claims to distant colonial lands two hundred and more years ago, are being used today by indigenous people to claim them back.

Mariners continue to keep regular logbooks as they travel the waters of the world. National and international regulations influence the format, and hourly reports are still compiled to contribute to regional and global weather maps, current charts, and pilot guides. The keeping of a personal journal or diary is also still an important part of the sea experience, and the reading public continues to be interested in the chronological accounts of sailors. Electronic communications systems make it possible now to follow a voyage in real time on a computer screen, but the curiosity of the reader and the importance of the data ensures that logbooks and journals will continue to be kept into the foreseeable future.

[*See also* Logs and Ship's Journals *and* Shipboard Life.]

## Bibliography

Asher, Adolf (originally Abraham). *Bibliographical Essay on the Collection of Voyages and Travels Edited and Published by Levinus Hulsius and His Successors, at Nuremberg and Francfort from Anno 1598 to 1660*. London and Berlin: A. Asher, 1839.

Davids, Karel. "Sources of Knowledge: Journals, Logs, and Travel Accounts." In *Maritime History*, vol. 2: *The Eighteenth Century and the Classic Age of Sail*, edited by John B. Hattendorf, pp. 79–85. Malabar, Fla.: Krieger, 1997.

Elliott, Danial. *Maritime History: A Hand-List of the Collection in the John Carter Brown Library (1474 to ca. 1860)*. Providence, R.I.: The John Carter Brown Library, 2005. The collection of the John Carter Brown Library is very complete for journals and narratives of early voyages between Europe and the Americas.

The Hakluyt Society. http://www.hakluyt.com/. Since its founding in 1847, the Hakluyt Society has continued the tradition of the publisher for whom it is named, publishing accounts of voyages of exploration and of cultural encounters. The Web site includes a complete bibliography of the Society's publications.

Knight, R. J. B., ed. *Guide to the Manuscripts in the National Maritime Museum*. 2 vols. London: Mansell, 1977–1980. Logs, journals and diaries are found throughout the collection both as part of personal papers listed in volume one, and in volume 2, section 1, Public Records, entry 5, Navy Board: Lieutenants' Logs; and in sections 5 and 6, Artificial Collections, entry 109, Foreign Navies: Logs and Journals; entry 112, Journals and Diaries; entry 117, Merchant Shipping: Logs; entry 130, Royal Navy: Logs.

National Maritime Museum (Great Britain). *Catalogue of the Library*, vol. 1: *Voyages and Travel*. London: H.M.S.O., 1968.

Naval Historical Center. http://www.history.navy.mil/faqs/faq73-1.htm. Contains a description of the information required by the Office of the Chief of Naval Operations for logbooks of U.S. Navy ships, and a guide to locating both modern and historical examples.

Public Record Office. http://www.nationalarchives.gov.uk/default.htm. The Public Record Office in London holds 5,000 logbooks of British Royal Navy Sailing Masters for the period from 1672 to 1871, and deck logs or other shipboard volumes for more than 175,000 vessels from 1799–1972. The Web site is a good entry point for accessing the logs, and has an excellent overview of the different types of shipboard records required by the Royal Navy.

Sherman, Stuart C. *Whaling Logbooks and Journals, 1613–1927: An Inventory of Manuscript Records in Public Collections*. Revised and edited for publication by Judith M. Downey and Virginia M. Adams, with the assistance of Howard Pasternack. New York: Garland, 1986.

Silveira de Braganza, Ronald Louis, and Charlotte Oakes, eds. *The Hill Collection of Pacific Voyages*. 3 vols. Annotations by Jonathan A. Hill. San Diego: University of California, 1974–1983. The standard reference work for published accounts of European and American voyages to the Pacific Ocean.

Tiele, Pieter Anton, ed. *Mémoire bibliographique sur les journaux des navigateurs néerlandais réimprimés dans les collections de de Bry et de Hulsius, et dans les collections hollandaises du XVII siècle, et sur les anciennes éditions hollandaises des journaux de navigateurs étrangers; la plupart en la possession de Frederik Muller. Rédigé par P. A. Tiele. Avec tables des voyages, des éditions et des matières*. Amsterdam: F. Muller, 1867.

United States. National Archives and Records Service. *List of Logbooks of U.S. Navy Ships, Stations, and Miscellaneous Units, 1801–1947*. Washington, D.C.: National Archives and Records Service, 1978.

MARY MALLOY

# Aviation

This entry contains two subentries:

Commercial Aviation
Naval Aviation

## Commercial Aviation

Scheduled transportation of passengers and goods by air was one of the developments that emerged from World War I. Although attempts to use airships and aircraft for transportation predated the war, technological constraints had precluded their development beyond high-profile demonstrations of what the future might hold.

### Creating Empire Links

In technological terms World War I had been of overriding importance to aeronautical development, with state intervention pushing aircraft and airship production from handicraft to industry. Government intervention had not, however, created a viable market for air transportation. In Europe, circumstances after 1918 did not favor the development of a new means of transport. Money was lacking because the costs of the war had put prolonged constraints on national budgets. Only in the United States was the economic situation any different—but given the technology of 1918–1919, the vast distances between the major population centers precluded the emergence of any air service other than that of the U.S. Post Office, carrying mail.

Nonetheless, aviation in itself provided such an appealing vista that the illogical beckoned. Aeronautically inclined entrepreneurs on both sides of the Atlantic realized that state subsidies would be needed for air transportation. To entice a government under financial constraints to invest in a new, unproven transportation technology required an appeal to sentiments at the political level. In Europe, recovering from the war, this meant appealing to national prestige. In the United States, aviation planners appealed to a different kind of prestige: that of the Post Office as a federal instrument for the creation of a national network for rapid airmail services.

In France—but soon thereafter also in the smaller countries of northwestern Europe and in the Soviet Union—the development of air transportation pivoted on prestige-driven government funding. Even in Germany, where aviation had been curtailed by the Allied powers, public funds were poured into air transportation, in defiance of the former enemy. After several years of hesitation Britain followed suit with subsidies in 1921. European air transport remained an unprofitable business into the 1940s, dependent on subsidies. The few routes on which any money was made were those across water, because the time savings were greater.

In the United States, civil air transportation did not make a significant start until 1925, when the federal government decided to privatize airmail carriage, creating the preconditions for the development of commercial air transportation through legislation. Although the American airlines did slightly better than their European counterparts did, they, too, could exist only because of public money, in the form of highly remunerative airmail contracts.

For the leading countries in western Europe, one of the prime incentives for governmental support for air transport was the potential development of national service to imperial possessions. Hence financial support for British air services, when it came, was geared toward the establishment of British service to India and various African colonies. Similarly, French money was directed toward the development of a service to the French colonial possessions in Southeast Asia and to colonial North Africa, as well as to Argentina and Chile, where France held substantial commercial interests. The Dutch focused on a national air service to the Netherlands East Indies, while Belgian funds went into an air service to the Belgian Congo. Services became operational from the late 1920s.

In the United States the pattern was not altogether different. The federal government supported the development of international air services in its own hemisphere from the second half of the 1920s, and in the mid-1930s across the Pacific to the Philippines, through its chosen instrument, Pan American Airways.

Like the shorter continental routes, such imperial services hardly made economic sense. Few ever approached the breakeven point. The prime customers—and vital operational sponsors—were governments and national postal services, valuing improved imperial communications.

Although imperial air services were potentially disruptive to the national shipping lines, the load capacity of the aircraft of the day was very limited, and the inroads that the fledgling airlines made into the monopolies of shipping

**Commercial Aviation**. A Pan American Airways seaplane in flight, c. 1940. LIBRARY OF CONGRESS, PRINTS AND PHOTOGRAPHS DIVISION

services to the overseas possessions were negligible. Moreover, some shipping companies protected their long-term interests by investing in air carriers, thus becoming part owners with their own representatives on the airline boards.

## From Imperial Commerce to Commercial Empires

At the end of World War II the new military, political, and economic ties between the United States and western Europe created a new situation. Demand for rapid passage across the North Atlantic skyrocketed. Trial services across the ocean had started late in 1937, and scheduled flights followed in June 1939.

In 1945 American air carriers took the lead in developing the route. They were the only ones that had long-range aircraft available, although their European counterparts were not far behind in recognizing the potential of this new market. The North Atlantic route turned out to be so profitable that it developed into the number one moneymaker for the international airline industry. The decolonizations in Asia in the late 1940s and 1950s and in Africa in the 1960s added to this process, shifting the focus in world air transportation to the Atlantic area.

Air travel across the North Atlantic increased annually throughout the 1950s. This process was boosted by fare cuts, which were the principal economic effects of changes in aircraft technology (bigger aircraft and jet propulsion, which halved journey time). The market expanded from the affluent and those in a rush to the ordinary citizen. As air transport became cheaper, new types of passengers appeared. Whereas a typical sea traveler embarked—often with one-way passage—on a transatlantic journey that would take five to seven days, the speed of aircraft lured new types of traveler: the businessman on a short trip and the tourist with just a few days to spend. In 1952, Pan American Airways initiated large-scale leisure travel across the Atlantic, offering tourist-class services to Paris. Competing airlines followed. Over twenty years—from 1950 to 1970—American tourist visits to France increased by more than 500 percent, to 1.35 million. In 1958 transatlantic air passenger numbers passed the one million mark. That same year a new, even cheaper air ticket was introduced: economy class. Prices for these tickets were another 20 percent below those for tourist class, bringing the total fare cuts since 1946 to about 50 percent. In October 1958 transatlantic jet services were also introduced; as a result, air transport became the dominant long-distance travel mode. Before the next decade was out, aircraft had replaced ocean liners as the prime means of passenger transportation. The market share of the shipping lines dropped from 43 percent in 1958 to 6 percent in 1968, before seaborne passenger services were abandoned.

Freight transportation presented a different picture. Although air shipment of piece goods also increased annually, the introduction of the standardized sea container in the early 1960s enabled such cost savings in shipping that the airlines did not capture a discernible share of the transatlantic market until after the introduction of wide-body jets in the 1970s, which offered enough cargo volume to be more cost-effective.

Services across the Pacific also came into their own after 1945, although flights had started a full decade before, in November 1935. That year Pan American won the U.S. Post Office transpacific airmail contract and was granted a twenty-five-year authorization for mail and passenger services to Manila. Scheduled services through to Hong Kong began in April 1937, two months before the first trial flights across the North Atlantic. As for other long-distance routes, time savings over the Pacific were considerable: early services took six to seven days to cross, whereas ships needed three weeks on average.

American transpacific routes were further developed in the course of the war effort. Postwar commercial services were initiated in July 1947 between Chicago, Seattle, and Tokyo, with flights continuing to Shanghai, Hong Kong, and Manila. Thereafter operations expanded as a result of the Korean War. In the first seventy-five days of the fighting, American air carriers supplied most of the transpacific airlift. In the course of the conflict, U.S. airlines under contract from the Pentagon flew more than 100,000 military personnel and a substantial share of the army supplies and equipment bound for Korea.

International competition was relatively slow to develop. It was not until 1954 that Australian and Japanese airlines gained landing rights on the American west coast. As on the transatlantic routes, aircraft won out against passenger shipping. But unlike the situation on the North Atlantic, political circumstances rather than economic development had the overriding impact on developments. The Korean and Vietnam conflicts acted as crucial incentives for the growth of air-traffic volume. Under military contracts resulting from the Vietnam War, U.S. airlines led the way in developing air transport across the Pacific to South Vietnam and neighboring American allies. However, Pacific air transportation's inroads into the market for shipboard carriage were less evident than on the Atlantic, since Pacific shipping was traditionally geared more toward freight than toward passengers. On the transpacific routes, airlines developed a market that had not been there before. Nonetheless, the outcome was comparable: by the end of the 1960s aircraft had largely replaced ships in all but cargo transportation.

[*See also* Mail Services; Passenger Trades; *and* Shipping Companies.]

## Bibliography

Besse G., and G. Desmas. *"Conjoncture" of Air Transport: The General Interaction between Air Transport and General Technical, Economic, and Social Trends.* Paris: Institut du Transport Aérien, 1966.

Courtwright, David T. *Sky as Frontier: Adventure, Aviation, and Empire.* College Station: Texas A&M University Press, 2005.

Davies, R. E. G. *A History of the World's Airlines.* London: Oxford University Press, 1964.

Dienel, Hans-Liudger, and Peter Lyth, eds. *Flying the Flag: European Commercial Air Transport since 1945.* London: Macmillan, 1998.

Dierikx, Marc, and Bram Bouwens. *Building Castles of the Air: Schiphol Amsterdam and the Development of Airport Infrastructure in Europe, 1916–1996.* The Hague, Netherlands: SDU Publishers, 1997.

Endy, Christopher. *Cold War Holidays: American Tourism in France.* Chapel Hill: University of North Carolina Press, 2004.

Fennes, René J. *International Air Cargo Transport Services: Economic Regulation and Policy* Leiden, Netherlands: private printing, 1997.

Staniland, Martin. *Government Birds: Air Transport and the State in Western Europe.* Lanham, Md.: Rowman and Littlefield, 2003.

MARC DIERIKX

# Naval Aviation

The potential of aviation in maritime warfare, especially for reconnaissance, was clear from the start of aerial navigation, and navies were soon experimenting with the new technologies of flight. The rigid airship offered the most practical solution for a long-range maritime platform. The Royal Navy ordered one in May 1909, but construction difficulties delayed completion and the project failed. Only Germany could produce such aircraft, and the German navy received its first zeppelin in 1912. Zeppelin airships were key reconnaissance assets for the German navy during World War I, playing a core role in fleet operations.

**Naval Aviation.** Commissioned on March 15, 1917, *L 43* was the first naval airship capable of operating at altitudes over 5,500 meters (18,000 feet). She was shot down off the Dutch coast on May 23, 1917. By Permission of The Trustees of the Imperial War Museum, London, Q 58464

### Early Stages

Early airplanes, both land planes and seaplanes, had too short a range and were too unreliable to be very effective in naval work. In 1910–1911 the U.S. Navy experimented with takeoffs and a landing with static cruisers (and used aircraft from ships at anchor to reconnoiter inland during operations in Mexico in 1914). However, Britain, frustrated in its lighter-than-air developments, soon took the lead, forming a naval air service in 1912 and experimenting with takeoffs from battleships, both at anchor and under way. In 1913, in that year's fleet exercises, the Royal Navy fitted out the cruiser *Hermes* as the first operational seaplane carrier to simulate a zeppelin. But there remained serious operational difficulties in operating aircraft that had difficulties taking off and that could not land on a ship's deck. When war broke out, therefore, the Royal Naval Air Service was primarily a shore-based force engaged in operations of both a maritime and a more general nature. Both it and the German navy pioneered the strategic bombing of land targets.

British seaplane carriers converted from merchantmen were used both to attack zeppelin sheds and to support fleet and amphibious operations, but it took the whole duration of the war to develop a fully satisfactory aircraft carrier from which aircraft could take off and on which they could land. An experimental landing under way was carried out in 1917 on board the large cruiser *Furious*, which had been completed as a partial carrier. This feat

could not be satisfactorily repeated, however, even when the ship was fitted with a flying-on deck aft of her central superstructure. The first satisfactory carrier with an unobstructed deck, HMS *Argus*, a converted liner, joined the Grand Fleet (the name used during World War I for the Home Fleet) only in October 1918, although by then all capital ships were equipped with airplanes to be launched in action from the tops of turrets, to gain and exploit air superiority, and to ditch in the sea when their fuel ran out. By 1918 the Grand Fleet was deploying over 130 aircraft.

During World War I aircraft played an increasingly important part in naval actions in many theaters. During a sweep into German waters by the Harwich Force in 1918, aircraft—both flying boats and fighters—were towed on lighters by destroyers. One, a Sopwith Camel, shot down a patrolling zeppelin, but German naval seaplanes sank all six British coastal motorboats, which it had been hoped would sink German ships in the Ems River. Earlier, in the Black Sea, the Russians had extended the reach of their fleet with innovative seaplane carrier operations. Austrian, Italian, and British aircraft contributed to the Adriatic maritime campaign. An Austrian aircraft sank a French submarine in September 1916, the first such success by any country.

Allied flying boats, seaplanes, land planes, and nonrigid airships all took part in anti-U-boat operations, first flying patrols and then, more successfully, in support of convoys. Ships in convoy with air escort were almost completely safe. Only one or two U-boats were sunk by aircraft, but the threat of being spotted and attacked by the aircraft or by surface ships operating with them was a potent deterrent that forced submarines down and interfered with their mobility.

## Between the Wars

After World War I all three major navies made aircraft carriers an important part of their fleets. The Washington Naval Treaty of 1922 encouraged this by, instead of scrapping them, allowing the conversion of incomplete capital ships into carriers. The U.S. battle cruisers *Lexington* and *Saratoga* were completed as carriers in 1927, as were the Japanese battle cruiser *Akagi* and, a year later, the battleship *Kaga*. Both navies had converted auxiliaries into carriers in 1922 to begin training a seaborne air arm. The British completed ships laid down or taken over for conversion during the war, including the former Chilean battleship *Eagle* and a new *Hermes*, the first ship to be laid down as a carrier. *Furious* was converted into a proper through-deck carrier, and similar conversions were carried out on her two half-sister ships *Glorious* and *Courageous*. More new carriers of further improved design were commissioned and laid down in the 1930s.

Britain was soon overtaken, however, by the United States and Japan in the size and quality of its naval air arm. The fundamental reason was that the strategic air warfare pioneered by naval aviators during the war had come to be seen as potentially the dominant form of war. Britain, facing a serious air threat from mainland Europe, put its main aviation effort into the development of the independent, land-based Royal Air Force (RAF) for deterrence and defense. Naval aviation was a part of the RAF (albeit as an autonomous "Fleet Air Arm" after 1924); this complicated policy making until 1939, when the Navy took over complete control but the land-based priority remained. It was fortunate for the U.S. Navy that the staged 1921 experiments in which aircraft sank defenseless static hulks were seen for the meaningless stunts they were, and it retained control over what was effectively half of America's air force; the situation was similar in Japan. By 1939–1940, although the doctrines of all three major navies emphasized the support of the surface fleet, the Japanese and Americans were on the verge of demonstrating that carriers equipped with large numbers of modern aircraft were emerging as the new capital ships.

The interwar period saw virtually all large surface warships equipped with catapults and floatplanes for reconnaissance and gunnery spotting. Land-based maritime aircraft also acquired extra reach. The U.S. Navy, which needed to deal with Pacific distances, persevered with large airships until a series of accidents and the development of flying boats with a competitive range forced a change of policy in the mid-1930s; the pioneer carrier *Langley* was converted into a mobile tender to give these aircraft more strategic mobility. Japan, concerned about inadequate numbers of traditional surface platforms, took the lead in the development of long-range, land-based maritime air striking forces using fast, twin-engined torpedo bombers.

## World War II

The Germans and Italians were wedded to the independent air force for political as well as strategic reasons, but the Luftwaffe had trained personnel and suitable aircraft for maritime operations. Its bombers were thus able to neutralize the British Home Fleet during the 1940 Norwegian campaign. Britain lacked the fighters, fighter control systems, and effective antiaircraft gun defenses to put up effective resistance. Nevertheless, land-based British Fleet Air Arm dive-bombers were able to sink the German cruiser *Königsberg* alongside at Bergen. She was the first major naval unit to succumb to air attack.

British investment in strategic air defenses was vindicated by the RAF's defeat of the German attempt in the summer of 1940 to neutralize British sea power and bomb the country into submission. The capability of the Fleet Air Arm was dramatically demonstrated at the end of the same year, when the attack that had been planned against the German fleet at anchor in 1918 by Sopwith Cuckoos from HMS *Argus*—an operation obviated by the Armistice—was executed in November 1940 by Swordfish torpedo bombers from HMS *Illustrious* against the Italian fleet at Taranto. Three Italian battleships were sunk, one permanently, and Italian sea power was crippled. Only German air power was able to turn the tables, but not completely.

The Japanese learned lessons from Taranto and started their offensive in December 1941 with a much more formidable carrier attack on the American fleet at Pearl Harbor. In addition, Japanese land-based torpedo bombers sank the British capital ships *Prince of Wales* and *Repulse* at sea, the first such achievement. Their traditional battle fleet crippled, the Americans were lucky that their carriers were away on aircraft transport missions. Carrier task forces thus formed the basis of the U.S. fleet that first mounted counterstrikes, including one with Army medium bombers on Tokyo. This was followed by the engagement in the Coral Sea, the first fleet action in which the forces did not sight each other, and then the climactic battle of Midway in June 1942, when four Japanese carriers were sunk by three American carriers, one of which was also lost. The remaining Japanese gun-armed battle fleet withdrew from the remaining American carriers, a decisive moment in naval history.

In the Atlantic, as predicted by prewar Royal Navy doctrine, British carrier-based torpedo bombers had crippled the battleship *Bismarck* in May 1941, leading to its sinking by two battleships. Land-based bomber attacks forced the battleships *Scharnhorst* and *Gneisenau* out of Brest, France, in 1942, and air-delivered mines damaged them during their transit back to Germany. *Gneisenau* never went to sea again after incurring bomb damage in dock, *Bismarck*'s sister *Tirpitz* was neutralized and eventually sunk by a mix of carrier-based and land-based bombers, and few surviving German ships escaped the bombing holocaust of 1945.

From late 1942 the U-boat war was dominated by air power as German submarines were concentrated in the mid-Atlantic gap, where Allied air power could not operate. Conflicting priorities delayed an adequate response, but eventually small escort carriers and very-long-range, land-based aircraft decisively turned the tide and won the Battle of the Atlantic in 1943.

In the Mediterranean the advent of radar and associated fighter control techniques solved the conundrum of antiair warfare. Similar methods were used in the Pacific. After the destruction of the cream of the Japanese naval air arm in the attritional fighting around the Solomon Islands in 1942–1943, the untrained Japanese carrier replacements were shot out of the sky in the greatest carrier fleet action of the war, in the Philippine Sea in June 1944. Its main fleet assets destroyed, Japanese surface forces were all too vulnerable to air attack, which accounted for the two largest battleships ever built, *Musashi* and *Yamato*, in 1944–1945.

## Naval Aviation since World War II

The end of World War II with two nuclear strikes on Japan put U.S. land-based bombers and aircraft carriers in competition for delivery of the apparently decisive new weapon. Although carriers acquired nuclear capabilities and retained them until the 1990s, the role that sustained them in the American and other Western navies was as mobile bases for the projection of conventional air power in more limited contingencies. Korea, Suez, and Vietnam were three notable examples. Improvements in carrier design—angled decks, steam catapults, and mirror landing aids—allowed the operation of high-performance jet aircraft. Only the United States was able to afford fully capable super carriers. Even Britain seemed to fall by the wayside with its decision to abandon large carriers in 1966, but the development of vectored-thrust short-takeoff/vertical-landing aircraft allowed smaller ships of cruiser size to provide some fixed-wing organic air capability. These were used by the British with decisive effect in the Falkland Islands war of 1982. The Soviets also developed air-capable cruisers that were developed into proper carriers just as the Cold War ended.

Both the British and Soviet ships had their origins in ships designed to operate helicopters. The helicopter revolutionized both anti-submarine and amphibious warfare in the 1950s. The first operational helicopter landing was carried out by the British from two converted small carriers at Suez in 1956. The helicopter also offered a means of hovering and dipping sonar to find submarines. In succeeding decades, as well as being carried in specialist ships, helicopters became the standard equipment of frigates and destroyers for anti-submarine weapons delivery and anti-surface-unit warfare surveillance and strike.

Land-based aircraft also proved their value in Cold War maritime warfare: in the West with predominantly anti-submarine maritime patrol aircraft using sonobuoys as sensors, and in the Soviet Union with long-range antiship target acquisition and aircraft and missile firers. Working in synergy with other units, surface and subsurface, these were valuable platforms. The final years of the Cold War threatened climactic fleet actions between U.S. carriers and Soviet land-based naval aircraft.

Since the Cold War, in an era of expeditionary warfare, carriers are making a renaissance, not least in the British Royal Navy, which plans to build two 65,000-ton ships to provide the RAF with mobile bases. Most major warships are air-capable. Air power and sea power are, more clearly than ever, two sides of the same coin.

[*See also* Aircraft Carrier *and* Atlantic, Battle of the.]

## Bibliography

Friedman, Norman. *British Carrier Aviation: The Evolution of the Ships and Their Aircraft*. Annapolis, Md.: Naval Institute Press, 1988.

Friedman, Norman. *U.S. Aircraft Carriers: An Illustrated Design History*. Annapolis, Md.: Naval Institute Press, 1983.

Hezlet, Sir Arthur. *Aircraft and Sea Power*. London, Peter Davies, 1970.

Hone, Thomas C., Norman Friedman, and Mark D. Mendeles. *American and British Aircraft Carrier Development, 1919–1941*. Annapolis, Md.: Naval Institute Press, 1999.

Layman, R. D. *Before the Aircraft Carrier: The Development of Aviation Vessels, 1849–1922*. Annapolis, Md.: Naval Institute Press, 1989.

Layman, R. D. *Naval Aviation in the First World War: Its Impact and Influence*. Annapolis, Md.: Naval Institute Press, 1996.

Melhorn, Charles M. *Two-Block Fox: The Rise of the Aircraft Carrier 1911–1929*. Annapolis, Md.: Naval Institute Press, 1974.

Polmar, Norman. *Aircraft Carriers: A Graphic History of Carrier Aviation and Its Influence on World Events*. Garden City, N.Y.: Doubleday, 1969.

Reynolds, Clark G. *The Fast Carriers: The Forging of an Air Navy*. Huntington, N.Y.: R. E. Krieger, 1978.

ERIC J. GROVE

# B

**Backhuysen, Ludolf** (1630–1708), Dutch painter. Backhuysen was born on December 28, 1630, in Emden, East Frisia, the son of a notary who had immigrated to Emden from Westphalia. Backhuysen's self-portraits, his calligraphy samples in Latin, and his friendships with a number of poets all indicate that he attended Emden's Latin school, as appropriate to his social class. In a self-portrait from 1699 (now at the Amsterdams Historisch Museum), the artist displays his knowledge of calligraphy, astronomy, and naval sciences. He probably owed this knowledge to Herman Friesenburg, who taught these subjects in Emden from 1605 to 1656.

Around 1649, Backhuysen moved to Amsterdam. There he worked as an office scribe for the Huguenot merchant Bartolotti, who was also from Emden; Backhuysen presumably got this position through his father. He lived in Bartolotti's elegant house at Herengracht 170–172. In 1656, Backhuysen is mentioned for the first time—and three times—in the city archives of Amsterdam, and all three mentions are connected with trading in glass. Between 1657 and 1680, he married four times. A daughter survived from the third marriage, a son from the fourth. There is a notarized contract signed May 10, 1660, between Backhuysen and Onno Onnensz. from Delfzijl regarding an apprenticeship, stating that Backhuysen will teach his pupil "drawing, ship-painting, and everything that the master's craft demands, instructing, stimulating, encouraging, and helping him, as it befits an honest master." His master's fee was the same as Rembrandt's.

Between 1662 and 1663 we find mention of Backhuysen in Hoorn, where he rented a house, probably in search both of clients and of subjects for paintings. A document dated November 1663 (Rijksprentenkabinet, Amsterdam) attests to his admission to the Saint Lukas Guild in Amsterdam. Backhuysen's first and most important commission of a maritime historical painting (*View of Amsterdam*, Louvre, Paris) dates from 1665. A fee list from 1680 shows that Backhuysen enjoyed a comfortable lifestyle. Among his possessions were thirty-two paintings, many among them landscapes by Dutch contemporaries like Hendrick Cornelisz Vroom and Jan van Huchtenburgh. Until at least 1685, Backhuysen was also teaching calligraphy. There is an entry in the Amsterdam archives dated December 6–12, 1689, in which the maritime painter Aernout Smit admits to having copied two years previously a square painting by Ludolf Backhuysen for Hendrik Grel.

In 1699, Backhuysen was appointed first director of the Municipal Art Collection in Amsterdam's Town Hall (today the Royal Palace) together with Mischiel Musscher. Among his tasks were lecturing, curating sales exhibitions, and probably also giving drawing classes. Numerous notarized documents from the 1690s indicate that Backhuysen was a busy artist. He granted various powers of attorney for his business affairs. In the year 1700 he proved his academic attitude by signing a petition that sought to bar the glassmakers and "coarse painters" (sign painters and so on) from the Saint Lukas Guild. On October 22, 1701, he was granted the patent to publish his series of etchings *D'Y Stroom en Zeegezichten*.

On November 7, 1708, at one o'clock in the morning, Backhuysen died after a prolonged illness. On November 12, he was buried in the Westerkerk in Amsterdam. In accordance with the funeral ceremony that he devised himself, fellow artists—whose names are known for posterity—carried his coffin.

According to Backhuysen's biographer, Arnold Houbraken, Backhuysen began his artistic career as a draftsman shortly after his arrival in Amsterdam. The chalk drawing of a figure seen from the back punting wood (Rijksprentenkabinet, Amsterdam) is inscribed on the verso by his son Joannis with the words, "This is the first drawing my father made from nature." Stylistically, the sheet can be dated to about 1650. The earliest known dating, 1656, is found on a grisaille (auctioned in London by Bonhams on December 8, 2004, lot 20, and now in an American private collection). Three further grisailles by Backhuysen, in various small and large formats, can also be attributed to the 1650s by their style (Rijskmuseum, Koninklijk College Zeemanshoop, Nederlands Scheepvaartmuseum, all in Amsterdam). The similarities in design between these

**Ludolf Backhuysen.** The harbor at Amsterdam seen from the Ijssel bay. Erich Lessing / Art Resource, NY

grisailles and the grisailles by the contemporary master of this genre, Willem van de Velde the Elder, is obvious. But from the beginning, it is clear that Backhuysen's objective was not to document the maritime subject, but to render it artistically. This was the goal that he regarded as his main challenge throughout his career, and it remains the basic prerequisite for understanding his entire maritime oeuvre.

Thus even in his early grisailles, real circumstances, such as ships or places, are secondary to the artistic composition. Another consequence is that nonchalant idlers appear next to the expert mariners in Backhuysen's pictures. *Ships with Storm Approaching* (Museum der bildenden Künste, Leipzig) must be assumed to be Backhuysen's earliest known oil painting (1656, no longer legible). The subject of the painting goes back to Simon de Vlieger. The intermediary was probably Hendrik Dubbels, who worked in the studio of de Vlieger and is supposed to have taught Backhuysen oil painting. The painting is a mature and fine example of the atmospherical, gray-blue maritime painting style of the mid-century. Backhuysen's talent for the interplay of stormy elements is already obvious here. The stormy waters of Allaert van Everdingen, reputed to have been his first teacher, may have given him the inspiration. But

soon it became obvious that the stormy sea—down to hurricanes—was Backhuysen's element. During his own lifetime and in the following period, he was known as the master of stormy seas. The Leipzig painting, together with the previous grisailles, represents a further step on Backhuysen's way to a new style of maritime painting: the air is no longer hazy, but clear. Subjects appear refined to the viewer. Representing light and shadow, the whites and grays are less nuanced, have more contrast, and appear fresher.

Backhuysen enjoyed rapid success. As early as 1658 he cooperated for the first time with the highly sought-after portrait painter Bartholomäus van der Helst, supplying maritime backgrounds for a number of portraits. Later Backhuysen cooperated with Abraham van den Tempel, Isaac de Moucheron, and Johannes Lingelbach. During the early 1660s he developed his style more fully and experimented with picture composition, and he expanded subjects that he adapted from Simon de Vlieger, Jan Theunisz. Blanckerhoff, and Hendrik Dubbels. Backhuysen rapidly outstripped Dubbels in particular, his former teacher, in the skill of composition and the natural and vibrant rendition of clouds, water, and the ships between them. Backhuysen soon added local accents of color to the gray-blue color palette, making the contrasts between light and dark and the varying prominence of the subjects more marked. This tendency was heightened by using diagonal points of reference to combine the entire group of subjects in the paintings.

Finally, in 1664, Backhuysen's *Light Seas* (Gemäldegalerie, Berlin) was the first of his seascapes painted according to these Baroque precepts. In 1665 he was commissioned to paint a view of Amsterdam for the French foreign minister in Louis XIV's cabinet, Hugues de Lionne. Backhuysen created a political maritime history that demonstrates—in its opulent Baroque array—the Dutch naval powers, their Swedish ally, and the power of the Dutch Protestant citizenry. The new colors and the almost informal diagonal dynamic movements in the painting were the ideal vehicle for an optimistic mood, which the Dutch needed in the face of the English and French menace. With *Light Seas*, Backhuysen became the leading painter of maritime histories in the country. The optimistic atmosphere and the patriotic content always take precedence over documentary exactness. This is also true in the other subjects painted by Backhuysen, such as storms, shipwrecks, and portraits.

During the 1660s and 1670s, Backhuysen developed and then mainly painted variations on new themes, such as yachts, or boats in a tempestuous surf (for example, the painting at Cannon Hall Museum, Barnsley, U.K.). He also painted large-format tempests and shipwrecks—frequently off a foreign coast (such as those at the Washington Museum, U.S., and the Brussels Museum), which certainly helped to give rise to his reputation as a painter of storms. The poetic appeal of these paintings suggests that Backhuysen studied contemporary literature and the traditional political allegory of the state as a ship. At the same time he created numerous drawings, both as sketches and as stand-alone works of art meant for sale. Many of his paintings (such as *Ships in the Roads at Enkhuizen*, Schwerin, Germany) were copied by less talented hands. It must be assumed that even early on, Backhuysen had a studio with numerous coworkers, including Jan Claesz. and Hendrik Rietschoof, Abraham Storck, Hendrik Dubbels, Wigerus Vitringa, Gerrit Pompe, and Michiel Maddersteg. Starting in the 1680s, Backhuysen created numerous artistically acceptable portraits and self-portraits.

Always progressive, Backhuysen adapted classicistic landscape elements by Nicolas Poussin in 1682 in *Rising Storm* (Museum Schwerin). The pure seascape, however, remained his main focus. Soon after Willem III became regent in 1672 (king of England as William III, r. 1689–1702), his naval activities began to be represented in the maritime painting of Backhuysen (such as the painting at the Rijksmuseum, Amsterdam). The large-scale maritime histories of Backhuysen's later period flatter their royal subject with representative, ceremonious, and official imagery, all in brilliant colors. Even though the renditions are more sedate, the tenor remains optimistic. With the series of ten etchings *D'Y Stroom en Zeegezichten*, Backhuysen proclaimed his authorship of ten of his most successful subjects to protect them from pirating.

Backhuysen continued to have influence after his death. He was a role model for the Romantics, such as Caspar David Friedrich. Also in the eighteenth century, Backhuysen was copied by such artists as Cornelis Ploos van Amstel. The English maritime painter William Anderson was one of his many copiers in the nineteenth century.

[*See also* Artists, *subentry* Dutch; Painting; *and* Portraits.]

## Bibliography

Beer, Gerlinde de. *Ludolf Backhuysen (1630–1708): Sein Leben und Werk*. Zwolle, Netherlands: Waanders Uitgevers, 2002.

Beer, Gerlinde de, Eymert-Jan Goossens, and Bert van de Roemer. *Backhuysen aant het roer! Backhuysen at the Helm!* Amsterdam, Netherlands: Stichting Koninklijk Paleis, 2004. Catalog of an exhibition at the Royal Palace, Amsterdam; in both Dutch and English.

Hofstede de Groot, Cornelis. *Beschreibendes und kritisches Verzeichnis der Werke der hervorragendsten holländischen Maler des XVII. Jahrhunderts*. 10 vols. Esslingen, Germany: Neff, 1907–1928. See volume 7 (1918).

Houbraken, Arnold. *De Groote Schouburgh der Nederlantsche Konstschilders en Schilderessen* (1718–1721). 3 vols. Maastricht, Netherlands: Leiter-Nypels, 1943. See volume 2.

GERLINDE DE BEER
*Translated from the German by Alexa Nieschlag*

# Ballads and Chanteys

Song on shipboard was used to coordinate working rhythms, enliven the spirit in leisure hours, and give voice to the joys, pleasures, frustrations, and resentments for which the common seaman had few alternative means of expression. Music could greatly enhance the quality of life and leisure on board. The seaman William H. Chappell expressed this idea viscerally in his journal aboard the whaleboat *Saratoga* of New Bedford, Massachusetts, in 1852: "It is said that music hath the power to sooth the savage breast and it is eaven so … my ears is charmed with music at this time and it is with great difficulty that I can keep my thoughts upon writing. I never was so lucky as to get on board a ship before that had any musician ... but now the Capt[ain] plays the fiddle and the 2nd mate plays an accordion which is much better than a fiddle. It all helps to pass away the time ..." (Nicholson Collection, Providence Public Library). As for chanteys— shipboard work songs—Richard Henry Dana Jr. writes in *Two Years before the Mast*, "A song is as necessary to sailors as the drum and fife to a soldier. They can't pull in time, or pull with a will, without it. Many a time, when a thing goes heavy, with one fellow, yo-ho-ing, a lively song ... has put strength in every arm."

## Ballads

The defining characteristics of what constitutes a proper ballad—and the specific conditions of authorship, provenance, and transmission required for a true "folk ballad"—have long been disputed. However, in general terms a ballad is a narrative song that tells a story, often rooted in history, myth, legend, popular culture, or current events; the story is often epic in scope, often conveys a moral mandate, and characteristically involves love, danger, death, or other classic forms of high drama. Folk ballads are said to have arisen anonymously among the common people, who cherished and transformed the ballads as they passed from singer to singer and from place to place through the generations. Scholarly descriptions of how this process works have occasionally approached the mystical. For the purposes of the nautical manifestations at issue here, suffice it to say that among the so-called common folk who transmitted and transformed such ballads and songs, sailors have figured prominently since the Middle Ages, and even more prominently as the naval and merchant services grew in importance and influence during the Enlightenment in the eighteenth century and during the Industrial Revolution in the nineteenth.

Ballads of various sorts have long been resident in western culture. In the broadest sense, Homer's *Iliad* and *Odyssey* were originally epic ballads—poetic narratives intended to be sung and transmitted orally (rather than through written or printed texts), containing all the elements of dramatic tension and intrigue that typify lesser ballads of later vintage. Even a narrower definition would include the ancient bardic traditions of Ireland, the courtly troubadour chansons of medieval France, and the songs of the analogously peripatetic minstrel singers who flourished throughout Renaissance Europe. Ballad scholarship in the nineteenth century, which sought to anthologize and analyze Anglo-Scots-Irish ballads, revealed many cogent affinities among ballads in English and coeval manifestations in German, Scandinavian, Slavic, and Celtic traditions.

**Black-letter ballads.** However liberal or restrictive the term "ballad" needs to be when it is applied to early precursors, the earliest ballads that survive in English are relics of a tradition with origins in the Middle Ages, a tradition that in Tudor times evolved into parallel oral and printed repertoires. Accordingly, in the sixteenth century, when England's and Scotland's urban populace had become sufficiently literate to sustain a market for inexpensive printed texts hawked on street corners, folk ballads that had hitherto been transmitted orally were now codified in print, and new ballads were created wholesale, specifically tailored for street-corner sale. Known as "black-letter ballads" for the typefaces used in their printing, they were cheaply produced and cheaply sold, commonly with crude woodcut ornaments of varying relevance to the texts they accompanied, but without musical notation. Not only was the public generally unable to read music, but the melodies used for ballads were presumed to be universally familiar. Printed ballads often specified the air to which the ballad was to be sung; the melodies were transmitted orally even after the texts were committed to print. Ballad airs were only lightly regarded and, like the hymn tunes of later vintage, were largely interchangeable, the pivotal feature being the meter. Thus some ballads were customarily sung to only one particular tune, while others had no specific melody of their own and were sung to whatever air seemed to fit the words and spirit of the text. The tunes were in any case subject to constant extemporaneous revision. Unlike formal composed music, there were no strict rules and no inviolate guidelines.

Throughout the sixteenth and seventeenth centuries, black-letter ballad texts were customarily registered at the Registry Office in London—at the time, the closest equivalent to copyright, and it is through Registry Office lists that many of the titles and dates (of registry, if not of original authorship) are preserved. The survival today of a large inventory of ballads is largely thanks to the collecting impulses of Samuel Pepys—a man more famous, but not more significant, as the London diarist and Admiralty administrator. An avid collector of ship models and nautical mementos, Pepys was also the first and foremost grand-scale accumulator of printed and manuscript ballads. His gleanings, now preserved at Magdalene College, Cambridge University, constitute the richest trove, but the Roxburghe Ballads at the British Library, the Euing Collection at Glasgow, and ballad holdings at Harvard and Oxford Universities are all likewise massive, together offering as complete a representation of the genre as could reasonably be wished. Happily, since the mid-nineteenth century, most of these ballads have been anthologized in various "complete" and "selected" editions, sometimes in facsimile, more often in typeset transcriptions. Such editions provided the basis for Francis James Child's straightforward anthology *English and Scottish Ballads* (4 vols., Boston, 1857) and for his monumental annotated compendium, *The English and Scottish Popular Ballads* (5 vols., Boston, 1882–1898). The latter established a canon that spawned a century's worth of topical, thematic, and regional collections, leading to B. H. Bronson's landmark opus, *Traditional Tunes of the Child Ballads* (4 vols., Princeton, N.J., 1959–1972), in which, at last, many of the airs and variants of the original canon are gathered, complete with musical notation and musicological concordances.

Unfortunately, for reasons not entirely clear, Child's anthology (and hence the canon religiously adhered to by Child's followers) contains only 305 ballads, and it unaccountably omits at least as many (perhaps twice as many) others equally worthy of inclusion. Thus to obtain a comprehensive view across the entire span of the ballad literature, the conscientious scholar must scour the remaining anthologies and collections to discover the many treasures that Child deliberately or inadvertently excluded.

Also unfortunately, Child's most visible flaws include unfamiliarity with nautical terminology, naval warfare, and maritime history, and a decidedly naive, pro-English (which is to say, non-Scottish and non-Irish) bias. These flaws occasionally put him at a considerable disadvantage and place a controversial, often inappropriate spin on sociopolitical aspects of some ballads, leading Child into unsupportable misinterpretations of which the political historian and maritime aficionado need beware.

Indeed, Child's flaws are not inconsequential, as the nautical content of Child's canonical ballads is substantial. Simultaneous with the rise of literacy that supported a market for printed ballads, the Tudor era gave rise to Britain's naval and mercantile prowess, which persisted and increased over the ensuing four centuries. Ships, shipping, the navy, and the sailors who peopled the burgeoning maritime trades were increasingly significant and increasingly visible in common culture. Accordingly, mariners— including buccaneers like Walter Ralegh and Francis Drake and the outright naval heroes of England and Scotland, as well as lesser naval figures and the common seamen themselves—figure prominently in the ballads.

**Broadside ballads.** This emphasis on sailors and sailing was even more the case in a later genre of ballads, the so-called broadside ballads of Industrial Revolution vintage. So named because they were characteristically printed on the broadside of a single sheet—similar to the black-letter ballads, but in modern typefaces—these ballads were also sold cheaply on street corners to an ever-expanding market of increasingly literate and semiliterate consumers. As literacy extended downward into the middle and working classes, coeval with urbanization and industrialization, broadside ballads became, if anything, even more vernacular and grassroots in content and appeal than their black-letter precursors: devoted less to legendary and mythological subjects, and less to the rarefied activities of generals, princes, and kings, broadside ballads were more often concerned with the ordinary affairs of common folk—middle-class, even working-class people, such as farmers, merchants, tradesmen, publicans, soldiers, and, most of all, sailors. While the most frequently encountered subject of the black-letter ballads is Robin Hood, the typical protagonists of the latter-day broadside ballads are sailors.

Broadside ballads were widely disseminated. They were printed and sold not only in London, but in various seaports and some inland backwaters, and likewise in the colonies and former colonies—Newcastle, Liverpool, Bristol, Birmingham, and Manchester; Edinburgh, Glasgow, and Dublin; New York, Boston, Philadelphia, and Sydney. Most of the surviving specimens are competently classified by G. Malcolm Laws in *American Balladry from British Broadsides* (Philadelphia, 1957) and *Native American Balladry* (Philadelphia, 1950), both of which also contain rudimentary lists of British and American ballad printers. Many broadside ballads entered oral tradition, surviving there into the twentieth century, when they were collected by folklorists and printed in anthologies; there is accordingly a large literature of folksongs in which authentic broadside ballads figure prominently. Others must have fallen out of favor, or were never popular at all, and have been irretrievably lost; however, a few and hitherto unknown broadside ballads have been discovered in whalers' shipboard journals, suggesting that these ballads must have found some favor in nautical circles, however briefly.

All this being said, distinctions must be drawn among ballads that feature sailors as generic protagonists or use seafaring as a mere plot device; the much smaller number of ballads that were actually adopted by sailors, who sung them at sea or in taverns and coffeehouses ashore; and the still smaller number of ballads that were created by sailors themselves, which may contain technical terms and insights indigenous to the seafaring trades and are presumed to reflect first-hand the true spirit and sentiments of working mariners. For example, "The Sailor's Onely

Delight, Shewing the brave Fight between the *George-Aloe*, the *Sweepstake*, and certain Frenchmen at Sea" (Child no. 285) is not sailors' work. It has a probable historical basis in the issuance of official letters of marque to an English privateer named *Sweepstake* in 1596, in which year the ballad may have first appeared; the ballad was not officially registered, however, until 1611, and it is featured in *The Two Noble Kinsmen*, a play published in 1634 that is attributed to William Shakespeare and John Fletcher. However, in sailors' hands over the next century and a half, "The Sailor's Onely Delight" evolved into the straightforward narrative of a battle between the Royal Navy and common pirates, preserving the original structure and meter, and perhaps the same tune; but the new incarnation reflected the more timely, very real concerns of actual sailors, and it remained popular on shipboard well into the twentieth century as "High Barbary" or "The Coast of Barbary" (Laws no. K-33).

Not only were many broadside ballads taken to sea, but it is clear from their nautical allusions and technical lingo that a few of them, at least, must have been made by sailors themselves, and (from transcriptions in shipboard journals and copybooks) that many were preserved and cherished at sea long after their popularity ashore had waned. One of several ballads entitled "The Jolly Sailor" is a sailor's fantasy in which a rich and beautiful lady falls in love with a common sailor and convinces him to marry her and leave the sea for a life of leisure. The ballad's author, exact age, and origin are unknown, and, like most broadside ballads, it is simple hackwork of middling quality and dates from the early nineteenth century, when it appeared as "The Jolly Sailor, or The Lady of Greenwich." A Yankee whaler transcribed a version into his journal in the 1840s, it was carried to the California Gold Rush in the barque *Perseverance* of Providence in 1849, and it was reprinted in New York in the 1860s, presumably based on the printer's expectation that, even at that late date, he could sell a few copies—quite an extraordinarily long run for a fairly inconsequential pop-culture piece. A ballad commonly known as "Boston" from the fairly late text collected by Captain W. B. Whall around 1870—though versions excavated from whalers' journals of the 1850s and 1860s show it actually to have nothing intrinsically to do with Boston—is a powerful deepwater narration of sea storms and sailors' vituperation that could have been written only by a sailor. Concerning "Unmooring," a ballad of roughly the same vintage, Captain Whall writes (in 1910) that it "is an example of the purely professional song, dear to the old-time sailor, and full of seamanship. It was a favorite

with the prime old shellback, and was all the more successful in that it had a chorus about the girls." A real deepwater shellback would scorn the transparently inept poetic efforts of a mere landlubber. Rugged original ballads of the whaling trade, "graven by the fishermen themselves" (in Herman Melville's words), are legion. There were more poets than harpooners in many Yankee whaleboats, and there was ample leisure time on the whaling grounds to explore poetry and ballad making, as well as scrimshandering and journal keeping.

Sailors, like the members of any other occupational group, harvested most of their amusements and diversions from the general culture. But more so than most other groups, in ways akin to the analogous circumstances of soldiers and cowboys, the sailor's prolonged separation from hearth and home, his perpetual isolation at sea, and his customary, enforced exclusion from polite society ashore, occasioned an entire body of ballads and songs—and a host of other, occupationally rooted traditions and pastimes—unique and exclusive to seafarers. These can provide some of the most intimate insights into the mores and character of seafaring in the age of sail.

## Chanteys

Chanteys (also "chanties," "shanteys," or "shanties") are work songs informally used to coordinate shipboard working rhythms when hoisting sail, weighing anchor, loading cargo, and, occasionally, furling sail, hauling nets, and rowing. Theories about the origin and orthography of the term "chantey" abound, but its true etymology is obscure. Ironically and unaccountably, it seems to derive from the French *chanter* ("to sing"), though the practice on British and American ships certainly predates any appearance of chanteying among the French. Whatever the spelling, "chantey" is always properly pronounced "shanty" (in the French manner of "chandelier," "chevron," and "chardonnay") and refers as much to chanteys' specific occupational use as to the songs themselves.

Chanteying descends directly from West African work songs and was primarily a phenomenon of the American and British merchant services commencing just after the Napoleonic Wars. Earlier example are known, such as the sea ballad "John Dory," with roots in the fourteenth century, "Haul on the Bowline," said to derive from the reign of Henry VIII, and other call-and-response sea songs of later vintage; all of these may have been intended to be sung at sea labor. The great English whaler William Scoresby, as a young boatsteerer out of Whitby, records his whaleboat's crew singing at the oars while towing a whale carcass in the Arctic in 1785. But as a generalized practice, chanteying came into use when, in the resurgent North Atlantic trade after the War of 1812, American and British mariners emulated the practice of the African-descended longshoremen whom they encountered singing at their work, loading cargo in the southern American cotton ports. Not only is singing at work inherently infectious, but on shipboard it proved effective in allaying boredom, increasing efficiency, and elevating crew morale in an era when merchant ships tended to be chronically undermanned. Meanwhile, slaves and free blacks were serving in the crews of merchant vessels and whalers in increasing numbers, bringing their songs and age-old African singing traditions with them. These became intermingled with folk genres and popular songs from the general culture, resulting in a distinctive occupational type, a polyglot soup of African, Anglo-Scots-Irish, American, and miscellaneous foreign influences, peppered with technical lingo and salty exuberance. Chanteying in Scandinavian, French, German, and other European vessels derived from the Anglo-American example in a characteristically international shipboard labor pool; many Continental European chanteys are merely adaptations of British and American chanteys; a few others are indigenous.

Typically, chanteys were sung by whatever portion of a ship's crew might be at work on a given task, led by a so-called "chanteyman" ("shantyman"), who was formally or informally selected from the crew, and unaccompanied by musical instruments. For ostensible reasons of discipline, chanteying was frowned upon or prohibited outright in the naval services. According to the poet John Masefield, "The chantey is the invention of the merchant service. In the navy they have what is called the silent routine, and the men fall back upon their ropes in silence, 'like a lot of soldiers,' when the boatswain pipes…. In the merchant service, where the ships are invariably undermanned, one sings whenever a rope is cast off the pin." Melville's stint in the navy, the basis for *White-Jacket* (1850), led him to express regrets—similar to those voiced by Dana—about "non-musical" ships: "When I listened to these jolly Africans, thus making gleeful their toil by their cheerful songs, I could not help murmuring against the immortal rule of men-of-war, which forbids the sailors to sing out, as in merchant vessels, when pulling ropes, or occupied at any ship's duty."

Respecting their origin, chanteys can be identified as belonging to four groups: (1) songs and chants adopted directly from the African American stevedores, of which few survive in their original forms; (2) chanteys indigenous to the merchant service—the characteristic body of songs made up by sailors themselves for the performance of specific shipboard tasks; (3) songs imported intact from general culture and turned to the purpose of shipboard labor; and (4) various kinds of hybrids, mostly adaptations and derivations from popular culture. Like any folk process of oral tradition, chanteys, as they were passed from ship to ship and hand to hand, were expanded and improvised upon until they became inextricably intermixed and their distinctions obscure.

Respecting function, chanteys are classified into three main types—hauling chanteys, heaving chanteys, and special-occasion chanteys—distinguished primarily by the task for which each was intended, but also, therefore, by rhythm and structure.

**Hauling chanteys.** Hauling chanteys are of four species: long-drag chanteys, short-drag chanteys, furling-sail chanteys, and sweating-up and hand-over-hand chanteys.

(1) "Long-drag" or "long-haul" halyard chanteys were used for hoisting topsails, the largest and heaviest sail aboard a square rigger, as well as for other types of heavy hauling, and occasionally (though not customarily) for rowing and other rhythmic chores of long duration. These chanteys are typified by a call-and-response format, with a single line sung as a solo, followed by a one-line chorus joined by all hands; the crew would haul on the accentuated downbeats of the chorus (the words in capital letters):

SOLO:      As I was a-walking down Paradise Street
CHORUS:    To me WAY, aye, blow the man DOWN!
SOLO:      A pretty young damsel I chanced for to meet
CHORUS:    GIVE me some time to BLOW the man down!

(2) "Short-drag" or "short-haul" chanteys were for working topgallants, royals, and the other smaller sails higher aloft, and for working sheets, clew lines, buntlines, and braces to position square sails:

SOLO:      Boney was a warrior
CHORUS:    Away ay-YAH!!
SOLO:      A harrier and a terrier
CHORUS:    John Fran-SWAH!

(3) A small family of chanteys were intended for furling sail aloft, which requires a unified haul among several hands to gather, fold, and tuck the bunt. The structure of these chanteys is unique, the important feature being a recognizable burden

(sung as a solo or in unison) leading up to final syllable that was the signal to haul:

To me way, hey, yah! We'll pay Paddy Doyle for his BOOTS!
To me way, hey, yah! We'll all throw much at the COOK!

Or:

SOLO:        Oh do, my Johnny Boker, come rock and roll
               me over;
CHORUS:    Do, my Johnny Boker, DO!

(4) Technically, furling-sail chanteys are short-haul types intended for a special purpose, as are "sweating-up" and "hand-over-hand" chanteys, which are used for setting jibs, staysails, and the smaller square sails high aloft. While almost any halyard chantey might do, one that was particularly associated with hand-over-hand work is nowadays probably the most famous chantey of all:

SOLO:        What shall we do with a drunken sailor?
CHORUS:    What shall we do with a drunken sailor?
               What shall we do with a drunken sailor?
               Early in the morning.

**Heaving chanteys.** Heaving chanteys are the types used for working the capstan, brake windlass, and pumps—thus for weighing anchor, cutting-in whales, loading cargo, and pumping ship. These may be generally (but not rigidly) subdivided by rhythm and structure. "Capstan" chanteys are suited to walking around the capstan in waltz or march time. They are often structured like halyard chanteys, the distinction being more one of customary usage than of rhythm or format:

SOLO:        Oh the times are hard and the wages low.
CHORUS:    Amelia, where you bound to?
SOLO:        The Rocky Mountains is my home.
CHORUS:    Across the Western Ocean.

However, they frequently have a longer solo of followed by a chorus of two or more lines; and, because of the long duration of the tasks for which they are intended (weighing anchor, loading cargo, cutting-in, and pumping ship could take hours), the lyrics are often balladlike narratives:

SOLO:        From the West Indies docks I bid adieu
               To lovely Sal, and charming Sue;
               Our ship's unmoored, our sails unfurled,
               We are bound to plough the watery world.
CHORUS:    For we are outward bound;
               Hurrah! we are outward bound!

The stroke required to work the seesawlike "jiggity-jig" brake windlass has a more staccato rhythm than capstan work. Many of the same chanteys were also used to operate the bilge pumps, which entailed a similar up-down motion. The extent to which chanteys were interchangeable among capstan, windlass, and pumps was evidently a matter of individual preference among chanteymen and crews. Halyard and capstan chanteys were converted for "walkaway," a method of hoisting sails by walking along the deck with the halyard rather than by hauling it in place. Similarly, halyard chanteys were sometimes recruited for use at the windlass and pumps. Often shore songs were employed; others were hybridized, such as "Banks of the Sacramento," a ubiquitous derivative of Stephen Foster's "Camptown Races."

**Special-occasion chanteys.** A few ceremonial and occasional chanteys were reserved for special occasions. The "Salt Horse Chantey" or "Poor Old Man," though unrelated to practical heaving and hauling, had ritual significance as an ironic tribute to the sailors' having paid off, after a month or two at sea, wages received in advance. "Homeward bound" songs for the capstan and windlass are specific chanteys (or variants of chanteys) purported to have been sung only on the last leg of a voyage, when the bowsprit was pointed home. One, "Leave Her, Johnny, Leave Her"—which is actually a variant of "Across the Western Ocean," quoted above—was sung only when warping the ship into the dock at the very end of a voyage.

As occupational work songs, chanteys were seldom if ever sung on shipboard for any purpose not connected with working the ship. As early as the 1870s they were being popularized and romanticized in arrangements for the parlor, glee clubs, and schools. Meanwhile, as steam propulsion gradually supplanted commercial sail, chanteying aboard ship descended into increasing obsolescence and by 1930 had become extinct. In his play *Moon of the Caribbees*, written around the time of the World War I, and later in *The Hairy Ape* (1921) and *Mourning Becomes Electra* (1930), Eugene O'Neill employs chanteys as a point of pride, symbolic of "real" deepwater sailors, as distinguished from the newer breed of steamship men who—like the Hairy Ape—work inside a machine and therefore never have any practical use for chanteys.

[*See also* Music.]

## Bibliography

Colcord, Joanna C. *Songs of American Sailormen*. New York: Norton, 1938. Revised and expanded edition of *Roll and Go: Songs of American Sailormen*. Indianapolis: Bobbs-Merrill, 1924.

Doerflinger, William Main. *Songs of the Sailor and Lumberman.* New York: Macmillan, 1972. Revised and expanded edition of *Shantymen and Shantyboys: Songs of the Sailor and Lumberman.* New York: Macmillan, 1951.

Firth, Charles H., ed. *Naval Songs and Ballads.* Publication of the Navy Records Society, vol. 33. London: Navy Records Society, 1907.

Frank, Stuart M. "Ballads and Songs of the Whale-Hunters, 1825–1895: From Manuscripts in the Kendall Whaling Museum." 2 vols. PhD diss., Brown University, 1985.

Frank, Stuart M. *The Book of Pirate Songs.* Sharon, Mass.: Kendall Whaling Museum, 1998.

Harlow, Frederick Pease. *Chanteying aboard American Ships.* Barre, Mass.: Barre Gazette, 1962.

Hugill, Stan. *Shanties from the Seven Seas.* London: Routledge and Kegan Paul; New York: Dutton, 1961. Abridged reprint with an introduction by Stuart M. Frank. Mystic, Conn.: Mystic Seaport Museum, 1994.

Luce, Rear-Admiral Stephen B. *Naval Songs.* New York: W. A. Pond, 1883.

Mead, John Halstead. "Sea Shanties and Fo'c'sle Songs, 1768–1906, in the G. W. Blunt White Library at Mystic Seaport." PhD diss., University of Kentucky, 1973.

Shay, Frank, ed. *American Sea Songs and Chanteys from the Days of Iron Men and Wooden Ships.* New York: Norton, 1948. Revised and expanded from *Iron Men and Wooden Ships.* New York: Doubleday, Page, 1924.

Walser, Robert Young. "The Shantyman's Canon." MA thesis, University of Wisconsin, Madison, 1995.

STUART M. FRANK

**Ballast** "Ballast is any solid or liquid placed in a ship to increase the draft, to change the trim, to regulate the stability, or to maintain stress loads within acceptable limits" (National Research Council, p. 23). As such, the need to ballast a vessel has been one of the most fundamental aspects of the history of shipping. Permanent or fixed ballast, consisting of iron, lead, concrete, or other material, and usually installed at the time of vessel construction, is of interest to nautical architectural history, but the use of movable ballast has an enduring maritime history. Nonpermanent ballast consisted of dry or solid ballast for millennia, and was replaced by water ballast only in the nineteenth century. Many vessels sailed on a ballast leg or ballast voyage, when trade patterns necessitated carrying cargo in only one direction (and such remains the case on many modern routes as well). Vessels on such voyages are said to be in ballast or in ballast trim.

### Solid Ballast

Solid ballast consisted of a staggering variety of materials whose desirable qualities included weight (and preferably

**Ballast.** Carried in water ballast, probably in a single ship from a European port to the Great Lakes c. 1985–1986, zebra mussels have dramatically invaded the fresh water environment and altered the ecology of the Great Lakes. GREAT LAKES ENVIRONMENTAL RESEARCH LAB / NOAA

substances of high density, to reduce volume), inexpense, ease of availability, and the ability to be safely secured in the hold (even if such were not always the case). Earth, rocks, stone, gravel, sand, and kentledge (pig iron), were the predominant forms of solid ballast for hundreds to thousands of years. Of these, wet sand ballast often caused problems in terms of spoiling cargo, choking pumps, or shifting if improperly secured. Absent these materials, military surplus (cannons and shot), building materials (including rubble and ruins), coral, oyster shells, and cowry shells, among many other resources, were used. Red roof tiles were carried as ballast by Basque whalers in the 1500s from southern Europe to Labrador (for example, to Red Bay). In the nineteenth century Swedish sailors reduced "Red Rock" in San Francisco Bay to half its size by carrying the rock back as ballast and then selling it for paint pigments upon returning.

Solid ballast was carried and discharged along coastlines, across oceans, and between oceans. Testimonials to the scale of this activity remain in geographic names around the world, such as Ballast Point, Ballast Lane, Ballast Island, Ballast Cove, Ballast Quay or Key, Ballast Reef, Ballast Ground, Ballast Hill, Ballast Cove, and Ballast Grounds. Some of these were sites where ballast was both obtained and discharged; most such sites today bear no resemblance to their original use but retain their names.

Solid ballast was dumped anywhere it was most convenient when no longer needed (a practice known as ballast shooting), if port authorities (including the ballast master, a position that existed from at least the 1600s to the 1800s) were not in sight to make sure ballast was offloaded to designated shore sites. Prohibitions against dumping ballast in the fairway and in other navigable channels date to at least sixteenth-century England. Richard Henry Dana Jr. (chap. 29) writes of dumping ballast in California in the harbor channel "when the coast was clear." The discharge of ballast (both legal and illegal) resulted in a permanent layer of ballast litter coating the world's shores, leading to a rich history of foreign ballast being recognized by coastal geologists and marine and urban archaeologists. Many coastal cities claim that certain of their streets, as well as many older government, church, and other buildings, were constructed of ballast stones. Ballast piles are frequently used by marine archaeologists to site shipwrecks (such as HMS *Bounty*, most of whose ballast stones remain in place on Pitcairn Island), and, in turn, the origin of the rocks can at times be used to reconstruct trade routes.

Trinity House of London oversaw ballast operations and "ballastage" (a duty paid for taking up ballast) in the Thames River starting in the sixteenth century. From at least the 1700s on (and likely earlier) the ballast industry in the Thames was divided into three groups of laborers: the ballast-getters (the men who gathered the gravel from the river bed), the ballast-lighters (those who carried the gravel to the ships) and the ballast-heavers (those who loaded the gravel onto the ships); evidently these men lived in certain districts in London. A London song, "The Ballast Heaver," circa 1780, exists from this era. Concerns over labor conditions were rife by the nineteenth century, leading to the formation of a "Ballast Heavers' Office" (opened in 1853) and the Ballast-Heavers' Brotherhood of London (founded in 1854)—ironically just as the use of ballast water was coming into play. "Thames ballast" (shingle rock) and "London ballast" (city refuse) were known around the world. The use of workers dedicated to supplying ballast has ancient roots: the *corpus saburrariorum* was the guild of sand ballast heavers in the port of ancient Rome.

Solid ballast was used well into the twentieth century: "a great portion of the Franklin Delano Roosevelt [FDR] Drive in Manhattan (also known as East River Drive) is built on fill obtained from the debris from the blitz of England during World War II which was loaded on ships and deposited in New York City" (Rose), continuing a centuries-old tradition of filling in the margins of the city with ballast from around the world. The "Bristol Basin Plaque" in New York City, first erected in 1942, may be the only monument in the world celebrating ballast history. Beach sand from Europe was also brought back by Liberty ships during World War II to areas such as Staten Island, to be used for shoreline fill. Martin Lee speaks of taking on sand ballast as late as 1948, and such incidences doubtless continued on occasion for some years.

## Water Ballast

Water ballast systems were introduced in the nineteenth century, facilitated in large part by the transition from wooden sailing ships to iron steamships. Experiments with built-in water-ballast tanks date from the mid-1840s, but the use of water as ballast commenced more regularly in the 1850s in colliers trading between the Tyne and London, in order to reduce the time and expense in moving dry ballast. Curiously, this had an economic impact on ships' masters, for whom it is said it was an accepted practice to order and pay for solid ballast, but which was then delivered short, with both the master and ballast supplier pocketing the extra money (shorting ballast resulted in many unstable vessels, now corrected in part with the advent of water ballast). Over the next thirty to forty years, water ballast tanks were widely adopted, and the ancient gathering, loading, and discharging of rock, sand, and other materials began to fade away. Commencing in 1880 (but not before), *Lloyd's Register* began recording the types and capacities of water ballast tanks on various vessels.

The movement of both dry and water ballast has been implicated in the global dispersal and introduction of many nonnative species. The appearance of many species of exotic plants (known as ballast waifs), littoral amphipods, insects, seashells, corals, and other organisms on distant shores around the world has long been linked to the dumping of soil, rocks, and beach sand, a phenomenon extensively explored by botanists and entomologists. Tungiasis is a parasitic human skin disease caused by the sand flea (jigger) *Tunga penetrans*, which typically burrows into feet; the flea is native to Central and South America and the Caribbean, but was introduced in 1872 to Africa in ballast sands; it now occurs in almost every sub-Saharan African country. Seawater ballast is held to have dispersed hundreds if not thousands of species around the world since the nineteenth century.

[See also Shipbuilding Materials, *subentry on* An Overview; Ship Construction; *and* Ship's Equipment.]

## Bibliography

"Bristol Basin Plaque." http://brisray.com/bristol/blitz2.htm.

Carlton, James T. "Transoceanic and Interoceanic Dispersal of Coastal Marine Organisms: The Biology of Ballast Water." *Oceanography and Marine Biology Annual Review* 23 (1985): 313–371.

Dana, Richard Henry, Jr. *Two Years before the Mast: A Personal Narrative of Life at Sea.* New York : Harper, 1840.

Emery, K. O. "Ballast Overboard!" *Science* 162 (1968): 308–309.

Emery, K. O., C. A. Kaye, D. H. Loring, and D. J. G. Nota. "European Cretaceous Flints on the Coast of North America." *Science* 160 (1968): 1225–1228.

Frear, H. P. "Use of Water Ballast for Colliers in the Pacific Coast Trade." *Transactions of the Society of Naval Architects and Marine Engineers* 5 (1897): 151–174.

Lee, Martin. "The Ballasting of the Twentieth-Century Deep Water Square Rigger." *Mariners Mirror* 86 (2000): 186–196.

Lindroth, Carl Hildebrand. *The Faunal Connections between Europe and North America.* New York: Wiley, 1957. The classic analysis of the history of the movement of ballast from Europe to North America, as revealed by the geography of coast-dwelling beetles.

Mayhew, H. "Labour and the Poor: Concerning the Earnings and Conditions of the Ballast Heavers and Lumpers of the Metropolis." Extracts from the *Morning Chronicle* of January 1, 4, 8, and 11 (1850). London: Printed by William Ostell. A detailed history of the culture and economics of Thames River ballast industry in the mid-nineteenth century.

National Research Council. *Stemming the Tide: Controlling Introductions of Nonindigenous Species by Ships' Ballast Water.* Committee on Ships' Ballast Operations, Marine Board, Commission on Engineering and Technical Systems, National Research Council. Washington, D.C.: National Academy Press, 1996.

Rose, F. Peter. "A Flint Ballast Station in New Rochelle, New York." *American Antiquity* 33, no. 2 (1968): 240–243.

Stevens, Robert W. *On the Stowage of Ships and Their Cargoes: With Information Regarding Freights, Charter-Parties, &c.* 6th ed. London: Longmans, Green, Reader, and Dyer, 1873.

JAMES T. CARLTON

# Ballin, Albert

**Ballin, Albert** (1857–1918), German director of the Hamburg-America shipping line. In 1885, Albert Ballin was the head of Morris & Company, a small firm of emigration agents in Hamburg. Morris & Company had an interest in the Carr Line, which joined with the Sloman Line in 1886 to form the Union Line. Ballin did not come from a wealthy family, and there is little to indicate that at this time in his life he had the powerful connections that might be thought necessary to his future rise, if not quite from rags certainly to riches.

In 1886 he became passenger manager of the Hamburg-America Line, which, presumably at his instigation, first pooled sailings with and then purchased the fleets of the Carr and Union lines, ten vessels in all. Despite his youth and lack of directly relevant experience, within two years Ballin was elected to the board, and in 1899 he became director general. While this position did not give him complete power, it certainly made him by far the most important individual within a very large company that by now owned more than 500,000 gross registered tons (GRT) of shipping. Despite the uncertain trading conditions of the period, within the next fifteen years the fleet grew to more than 1.3 million GRT, making Hamburg-America by far the largest shipping company in the world in terms of tonnage. Its capitalization was equally impressive at some 260 million deutschmarks, and it was paying consistently substantial dividends. Hamburg-America traded successfully on virtually every major route except to Australia. While it would be simplistic to attribute all this to Ballin alone, he was by now the most powerful man in world shipping and played at least the leading part.

Some of the secrets of his success remain obscure, others do not. Compare the sense of timing that ensured that Cunard's new pair of express liners *Lusitania* and *Mauretania* arrived in service in 1907 just as a recession was beginning, while Hamburg-America's *Imperator* appeared in 1913, with quasi-sisters *Bismarck* and *Vaterland* close behind. For most trades and most countries, 1913 was the best trading year in all history. Ballin could have been bolder, but had war (to which he was strongly opposed) not interposed it is reasonable to assume that the company would have consolidated its dominance.

Making good guesses about the trade cycle and planning investment on the basis of those guesses is important, but top-class entrepreneurs are also marked by an ability to play the game by different rules from those of their competitors, and so it was with Ballin. He evinced enthusiasm for joining conferences but saw them not so much as a tool for putting an end to competition but rather as a different framework within which he could continue to seek complete hegemony for his firm, sometimes ruthlessly at the expense of his newfound "allies." This was perhaps not as unscrupulous as it sounds, for the conferences tended to benefit their weaker members more than their stronger, but the result was the same: a continuing centralization of power in Ballin's hands. In this sense his influence extended far beyond Germany, for it was the need to compete with Hamburg-America that led to the consolidation of medium-to-large shipping companies around the world into huge groups like the International Mercantile Marine Company (IMM) or Ellerman Lines.

The speed and effectiveness of the reconstruction of the German merchant marine after the ruinous terms of the Treaty of Versailles were remarkable: what might have been achieved had Ballin not died suddenly in 1918 at the relatively early age of sixty-one remains a matter for speculation.

[*See also* Shipping, *subentries on* Germany *and* State-owned Shipping; *and* Shipping Companies, *subentries on* Ocean Cargo Companies *and* Ocean Passenger Companies; Shipping Conferences and Cartels.]

### Bibliography

Most published work on Ballin has appeared only in specialist journals, often in German. There is a short account of the development of the company in N. R. P. Bonsor, *North Atlantic Seaway: An Illustrated History of the Passenger Services Linking the Old World with the New*, Vol. 1 (Prescot, U.K.: Stephenson, 1955). The best work in English is Frank Broeze, "Albert Ballin: The Hamburg-Bremen Rivalry and the Dynamics of the Conference System," *International Journal of Maritime History* 3, no. 1 (June 1991): 1–32. German readers may refer to *Neue Deutsche Biographie* (Berlin: Duncker and Humblot, 1953– ), Vol. 1, p. 562.

ADRIAN JARVIS

# Baltic Sea

This entry contains two subentries:

An Overview
Regional Navies

## An Overview

The Baltic Sea, including the Gulfs of Bothnia, Finland, and Riga but excluding The Sound and the Danish straits, has an area of around 380,000 square kilometers (236,000 square miles) and an average depth of 60 meters (196 feet). It is essentially a large lake, with only narrow outlets to the oceans. Several major rivers flow to the Baltic, and most of Europe's largest lakes—including Ladoga, Onega, Peipus, Vättern, and Mälaren—have their outlets in it. The salinity is low, tidewater is almost nonexistent, and most of the coasts are archipelagic and dominated by wide river estuaries or covered with long sandbanks. This has made the coastal areas suitable for transport with local craft, for naval and amphibious operations with small and oared vessels, and, in modern times, for maritime leisure activities.

Early on, the coastal population did develop the necessary skills to navigate and make use of water for transportation. Several Baltic regions are known recruiting sites for seamen—not only for Baltic shipping but also for western Europe. The southern part of the sea, in particular, has favorable conditions for fish. Coastal fishing with small boats has been important, both as a source of food for the local population and as a large-scale activity for the market. Although the climate is unusually warm for a region so far to the north, the northern Baltic is covered by ice almost every winter. During severe winters most of the sea is icebound for a few months, but modern icebreakers can normally keep it open for shipping. Before the advent of steam, the cold weather, short days, and frequent gales made Baltic seafaring dangerous from December to March even with the most advanced types of sailing ships.

From economic, cultural, political, and strategic points of view, the Baltic Sea connects eastern, northern, and central Europe with one another and with western Europe. Trade among the Baltic regions and between them and western Europe has long been primarily seaborne. Inland waterways have also been important for trade and military logistics, and most major cities in the Baltic were founded close to river estuaries. The large rivers flowing from the plains of eastern and central Europe—the Oder, the Vistula, the Niemen, the Dvina, the Narva, and the Neva-Volchov—are navigable far into the continent, and Lake Mälaren provides access for shipping to inland ports in central Sweden. Most rivers in Sweden, which is more mountainous, have waterfalls and are less navigable, but they have been valuable for floating timber from the forests. Consequently, the Baltic is the center of a maritime network of transportation far beyond its coast, and the inland waterways have also been key to political control by seaborne armed forces. The right to collect custom duties on trade on rivers and narrow parts of the sea was important for local power groups and state-formation activities. Several ports served as centers for political, economic, military, and naval activities, often stemming from ambitions to control the sea and the littoral territories.

Geostrategically, the Baltic provides advantages to those who are able to control the sea or deny its use to enemies. The ability to use these advantages has shifted with technological and political development. The many changes to political borders that have taken place around the sea since state formation began are closely related to changes in economic and strategic power relations between sea and land power. Warfare in the Baltic has also often been amphibious, rather than strictly continental or maritime, as important lines of operations cross both land and sea.

Until the late Middle Ages, technology gave advantages not only to transport by sea over that on land but also to short-range and coastal transports over long-distance trade. Sea power and amphibious capability depended on local bases and was intertwined with regional trade and regional political power. Beginning in the fifteenth and sixteenth centuries, advances in maritime technology enhanced the

**Map of the Baltic Sea.** MAP BY MAPPING SPECIALISTS LIMITED

economic advantages of long-distance transport and naval operations. Foreign shipping came to dominate the Baltic, but the early growth of strong regional states with navies made it difficult for foreigners to gain political influence in the region by naval power. Permanent navies, separated from the mercantile and local interests, also increased the power of territorial rulers in a region where land could be controlled from the sea.

From the mid-seventeenth century, the rapid rise of large navies in western Europe opened the Baltic for interventions and political influence from outside, as control of the sea meant control of both trade and military lines of operations. By the early nineteenth century the Baltic had become an arena for great power contests in which western European sea power might confront the naval and military power of Russia. From the late nineteenth century technological development increasingly restricted naval operations in this inland sea as torpedo craft, mines, long-range coastal artillery, and air power posed threats to surface forces. During this period the Baltic was also the base area for the naval powers of Germany and Russia, both of which periodically developed world-power ambitions. It was easy to defend but also easy to blockade, and the Scandinavian peninsula became a tempting base for these land-locked sea powers.

## The Prehistoric and Medieval Baltic Sea

As far as is known, the littoral territories around the Baltic went unmentioned in written history until the beginning of the second millennium A.D. However, archaeological evidence, as well as many stone carvings of sea vessels, confirm that seaborne communications have been important for thousands of years. Where land was rugged or practically impenetrable, with large forests and few open plains, most inhabitants lived near the sea or inland waterways, where even primitive craft could provide useful means of transportation. The importance of the sea raised technological and organizational challenges to the Baltic peoples—the development of shipbuilding for the open sea and distant ventures was connected to economic and political power. Scandinavians first appear in western and eastern Europe as late–Iron Age seafarers (called Vikings from the ninth to the eleventh centuries) who, with sailing and oared vessels of fairly advanced design, went as far as North America and along Russian rivers to the Black Sea. Within the Baltic, western Slavs (the Wends), Balts, and Estonians used similar vessels, at least in the eleventh to the thirteenth centuries. Ships were essential for efficient

plunder, profitable trade, defense of coasts, and transport of settlers within or outside the Baltic area. They also became objects of prestige for powerful men and chieftains with ambitions to become rulers over larger territories.

In a maritime district, state formation and trade tend to interact. The Baltic region is a good example, although little is known of Baltic political history and maritime networks of trade before the eleventh century. Historically, political power over wider territories correlated with success at raiding for plunder, which in the Baltic was usually a seaborne activity. The next stage was the raising of tributes instead of plunder, a process that continued into early state formation when the tribute raisers undertook to protect those who regularly paid for that service. In the Baltic protection usually meant defense of coasts and seaborne trade with naval forces, and protection was often paid for through taxes on maritime activities: shipping, trade, and fishing. Better protection of shipping meant lower costs of transportation and more opportunities for long-distance exchange of goods.

The geography of the early Baltic states shows that state formation was usually influenced by the ability to use the sea and protect coastal communities. Denmark was formed around the seas and straits that connect the Baltic with the ocean, and Swedish state power developed along the eastern coast of the Scandinavian peninsula and in the fertile areas around its great lakes. The two Scandinavian countries were divided by deep forests. By the twelfth century both countries, as well as Norway, had developed maritime defense organizations—the *leding* (Danish), *ledung* (Swedish), or *leidang* (Norwegian)—to which the coastal population paid taxes by building, manning, and provisioning vessels of the traditional Nordic type: an open boat with sail and oars. These might be used for defense of the coast against raids and of trade against piracy as well as for offensive operations with fleets carrying armies across the sea. In the east, early Russian state formation was shaped by rivers and lakes, resulting in a mercantile state centered in Novgorod. The practically independent island of Gotland and its only town, Visby, was, until the thirteenth century, a hub in Baltic trade because it was situated halfway between the German and Russian centers of trade and the Gotlanders had a strong tradition of seaborne long-distance trade.

The people on the southern and eastern coasts of the Baltic were tribal, pagan, and increasingly proficient at raiding the Scandinavian coasts from the sea in search of plunder and slaves. During the twelfth and thirteenth centuries the political map of the Baltic was reshaped by Scandinavian and, increasingly, German expansionist activities. Danish kings and bishops organized seaborne crusades against the Wends in the southern Baltic and the Estonians, and these areas were brought under Danish control. Sweden similarly took control over southern Finland in the thirteenth and early fourteenth centuries in competition with Novgorod, which extended its rule to the Neva estuary.

In around 1200 a powerful Danish maritime empire existed, supported by a large naval force. It was the largest political entity in the Baltic at the time, but it was gradually overtaken by a three-pronged German expansion that began in the twelfth century. German merchants took control of trade, partly with the use of cogs (flat-bottomed, high-sided ships) with much larger cargo capacity than the Nordic vessels. For protection and political cooperation they formed the Hansa, an alliance of trading cities; this cooperation may have been key to their success. The Hansa cities could also use their ships for naval purposes, and until the early sixteenth century they remained the leading sea power in the Baltic. Trade was based on privileges negotiated with territorial rulers and on a network of German merchants that settled in important ports in the Baltic. German knights undertook crusades against Livonia, Prussia, and Estonia, offensives that began with seaborne expeditions and, to a large extent, continued on rivers and in coastal waters. The local population usually had sizable forces of ships and often defended themselves at sea, but in the end the Germans gained control over the eastern Baltic. Finally, German and Germanized princes took control over the southern Baltic coast and made it a part of the German empire. The leaders of Mecklenburg and Pomerania, as well as the Polish and Lithuanian rulers and the German emperors, showed little interest in the Baltic Sea, an attitude that remained largely unchanged until the nineteenth century.

During the thirteenth century German merchants rose to preeminence in distant trade within the Baltic and between the Baltic and the rest of Europe. The Hansa was organized primarily around trade along the Novgorod-Reval-Lübeck-Hamburg-Brugge-London axis, but trade with Scandinavia and southern Germany was also important. As the central entrepôt between eastern, western, and northern Europe, Lübeck grew to be the major mercantile and shipping city in the Baltic. When the route around Jutland was regarded as too dangerous, trade passed across the Jutland isthmus on rivers or on land and goods had to be loaded and unloaded at Lübeck. Several Hansa ports—Wismar, Rostock, Stralsund, Greifswald, Stettin (Szczecin), Elbing (Elblag), and Gdánsk (Danzig)—grew along the south Baltic coast in a continuation of earlier Wendish and Prussian urbanization activities. Of these, Gdánsk became the most important in the long run, as it handled the growing Polish grain trade with western Europe. In the eastern Baltic, Riga, Reval (Tallinn), and Narva were founded as fortified settlements for trade with eastern Europe. Stockholm was founded as the main port for the Lake Mälaren valley and the iron and copper districts in central Sweden. The port also controlled trade in the Gulf of Bothnia. Köbenhavn (Copenhagen) grew as a result of its central position in Denmark and at The Sound. Stockholm and Köbenhavn became the largest cities and political capitals of their states.

A medieval maritime enterprise of great significance was the Scania fishery, with centers at Skanör and Falsterbo, which flourished from the thirteenth to the fifteenth centuries and provided income to Danish kings and archbishops. Enormous quantities of herring migrated south through The Sound every spring and the catch was sold on the continent by German traders, who also provided salt from Lüneburg for preservation. In the early fifteenth century the herring all but disappeared, and Baltic fishing activities have never since been able to compete with the Atlantic or North Sea fisheries in economic importance. Fishing remained important for the coastal population, however.

## The Early Modern and Modern Baltic Sea

In early modern times, maritime technology, trade, and political power continued to interact and change the Baltic region. Beginning in the fifteenth century improved sailing ships made it economical to use the route around Jutland, at least for bulk cargo. It was used by ships from western Europe, primarily the Netherlands, which sailed to the Baltic Sea. Lübeck still dominated trade in rich cargo, but its position as the leading entrepôt of the Baltic was increasingly threatened. The city attempted to mobilize the Hansa against the Dutch and for interventions in the power struggles within Scandinavia. In 1429 the Danish kings began to collect tolls on the growing trade through The Sound. Foreign traders were required to pay tolls for protection when they used the Baltic Sea. From around 1500 increasingly specialized warships armed with heavy guns were used by the Scandinavian rulers. This made it much easier to break the German maritime control of the Baltic. During the sixteenth century Denmark-Norway and Sweden developed permanent navies as instruments of royal policy. They both increased the rulers' control of their territories and made it possible to control the Baltic Sea, over which they even began to claim a *dominium*, a monopoly on violence and armed protection. Both navies quickly adopted the maritime and naval technology that from the mid-sixteenth century had been rapidly developing in western Europe.

When temporarily armed merchantmen lost much of their naval potential, the political power of Lübeck and the Hansa in northern Europe and the Baltic evaporated. Long-distance trade in the Baltic became increasingly safe from piracy and armed intervention from regional competitors, conditions that favored shipping from western Europe. Sweden used its new control of the sea and the fragmented political structure around the Baltic to create an empire, with conquests along the eastern and southern coasts of the Baltic. The Danish navy, the only potential adversary at sea, interfered only occasionally with this expansion, as Denmark did not seriously compete in Baltic empire building. By 1660 most of the Baltic Sea was politically a Swedish lake, although Prussia and the economically important river estuaries of Vistula and Niemen remained outside Swedish control. Denmark retained a strategic hold on the straits to the ocean. Economically, it was primarily a Dutch lake and a major source of income for the Dutch maritime and mercantile society. The period 1656 to 1678 saw conflicts and even naval wars between Sweden and the Dutch Republic over control of the Baltic.

The great expansion of maritime trade and permanent navies in western Europe made the Baltic region a center for essential naval supplies, timber, masts and spars, hemp, flax, tar, guns, and high-quality iron for hull fastenings. This stimulated economic growth and increased the income from custom duties to those who controlled the trade routes. The Swedish, Danish, and, later, Russian navies began to make systematic surveys of coastal waters and produce charts, which during the seventeenth and eighteenth century gradually made navigation less dependent on local knowledge and traditional descriptive manuals about coastal routes. From the mid-seventeenth century on, the expansion of western European navies made it possible for the Dutch, English, and French to intervene in the Baltic, usually in the interest of balance of power and always with the aim of protecting their trading interests.

In 1700 Russia, in shifting alliances with other powers, commenced a determined effort to gain a Baltic coast and create a Baltic navy. Most of the Swedish empire was destroyed in that process. In the eighteenth century Denmark-Norway, Sweden, and Russia were the three

Baltic naval powers, and the British replaced the Dutch as the leading foreign shipping and trade power in the sea. Nordic and German maritime activities were also important, however, and Baltic shipping and merchant interests became increasingly involved in trade around the world. Eighteenth-century warfare in the Baltic was highly maritime and amphibious, and Russia and Sweden created the last large oared naval forces in the world in order to control strategically valuable shallow waters in the region. København; Karlskrona (founded in 1680); Sveaborg (founded in 1747), outside Helsinki; and St. Petersburg–Kronstadt (founded in 1703) became some of Europe's largest naval bases. Russia's continued expansion to the west also affected the Baltic, and by 1815 this empire was fully established as the dominant power in the region.

The remarkable changes in maritime technology during the nineteenth century eliminated the need for Baltic naval stores. It also made sea transportation faster and less expensive, which favored seaborne trade and stimulated economic transformation and growth in the region. Small steamers became important along the coasts and on internal waterways, but sailing ships remained valuable for long-distance trade, partly because wages for seamen until the twentieth century were lower than in western Europe. Germany and the Scandinavian countries developed as major shipping and shipbuilding nations, thus making the Baltic an important factor in the world's maritime economy. In 1857 Denmark acquiesced to international demands to abolish the anachronistic Sound toll and an international convention declared The Sound an international seaway. In 1887–1895 Germany built the Kiel Canal between the North Sea and the Baltic Sea, partly to facilitate strategic movements of the new German navy. It also became one of the world's most frequented routes for shipping.

Technological preconditions for naval operations in the Baltic changed drastically. The nineteenth century—especially during the Napoleonic Wars and the war between Russia, Britain, and France of 1854–1856—saw the culmination of foreign naval interventions in the region. The British navy demonstrated its ability to dominate the Baltic even without local bases, a notable geostrategic fact for the Baltic states. In contrast, the two world wars saw hardly any foreign warships in the Baltic Sea, and naval operations between Germany and Russia were dominated by the use of naval mines, strong coastal defenses, submarines, and light surface forces. The two battle fleets never met. Germany was able to control the entrance to the Baltic in both wars. Only the period of German and Russian naval weakness between the wars made western interventions possible, and a British force operated against revolutionary Russia in 1919.

Russia had regarded the Gulf of Finland as a defense perimeter for St. Petersburg since the eighteenth century, and new technology facilitated such a strategy. Before 1914 Russia had developed an extensive coastal artillery in Finland and Estonia. Its determination to re-create a defense perimeter in the Baltic explains Russia's aggressive policy against Finland and the Baltic states in 1939–1940 and its attempts to make the Baltic a closed sea after World War II. In recent decades the dissolution of the Soviet Union and the Warsaw Pact and the expansion of the North Atlantic Treaty Organization alliance and the European Union have made the Baltic, for the first time in several centuries, into a region where naval operations by the great powers seem unlikely.

Since the late twentieth century most of the transoceanic shipping routes have ended outside the Baltic, in Antwerpen, Rotterdam, Hamburg, and Göteborg. Regional shipping remains important, however, and has been transformed by a network of ferry lines. The construction of bridges and tunnels across the Great Belt and The Sound has changed this only marginally.

The Baltic has also been a fruitful area for underwater archaeology. It hosts numerous shipwrecks, many in shallow and protected waters and well preserved because of the absence of marine organisms that destroy wooden hulls in other waters. Together with the many ports, naval bases, and coastal fortifications from various eras, the wrecks give the region an unusually rich maritime heritage.

[*See also* Danish Sound Dues; Hanseatic League; Kiel Canal; Medieval Navies, *subentry on* Northern Europe and Scandinavia; Scandinavian Literature; Svensksund, Battle of; Vikings; *and* Viking Ship.]

## Bibliography

Anderson, R. C. *Naval Wars in the Baltic, 1522–1850.* 2d ed. London: Francis Edwards, 1969. Originally published in 1910. Broad survey of naval operations, with emphasis on chronological and quantitative facts rather than strategic analysis. More reliable about facts than later surveys of Baltic naval warfare in English.

Attman, Artur. *The Russian and Polish Markets in International Trade, 1500–1650.* Gothenburg, Sweden: Institute of Economic History of Gothenburg University, 1973. This and the following book bring together Attman's studies of markets and trade routes in eastern Europe and the power struggle in the Baltic over control of trade between eastern and western Europe.

Attman, Artur. *The Struggle for Baltic Markets: Powers in Conflict, 1558–1618.* Gothenburg, Sweden: Kungl. Vetenskaps- och Vitterhets-Samhället, 1979.

Bogucka, Maria. *Baltic Commerce and Urban Society, 1500–1700: Gdansk/Danzig and Its Polish Context.* Aldershot, U.K.: Ashgate, 2003. A collection of important articles about a great trading city in the Baltic by a leading historian on Polish mercantile history.

Cederlund, Carl Olof. *The Old Wrecks of the Baltic Sea: Archaeological Recording of the Wrecks of Carvel-Built Ships.* Oxford: British Archaeological Reports, 1983. A standard reference on its subject, including a detailed catalog of wrecks.

Christensen, Aksel E. *Dutch Trade to the Baltic about 1600: Studies in the Sound Toll Register and Dutch Shipping Records.* Copenhagen, Denmark: Einar Munksgaard, 1941. A pioneering quantitative study of Baltic trade based on the rich but difficult Sound toll registers and Dutch notarial archives.

Christiansen, Eric. *The Northern Crusades: The Baltic and the Catholic Frontier, 1100–1525.* London: Macmillan, 1980. 2d ed. London: Penguin, 1997. A broad and systematic survey of all Baltic countries and the German military expansion in the southern and eastern Baltic.

Dollinger, Phillipe. *The German Hansa.* Translated and edited by D. S. Ault and S. H. Steinberg. London: Macmillan 1970. 2d ed. London: Routledge, 1999. The most comprehensive standard work on its vast subject.

Ellmers, Detlev. *Frühmittelalterliche Handelsschiffart in Mittel- und Nordeuropa.* Neumünster, Germany: Wachholtz, 1972. An important study of shipping and trade in northern and central Europe from 700 to 1200 based on an interpretative synthesis of archaeological, historical, and linguistic empirical research.

Gemzell, Carl-Axel. *Raeder, Hitler und Skandinavien: Der Kampf für einen maritimen Operationsplan.* Lund, Sweden: Bibliotheca Historica Lundensis, 1965. A study of how the German quest for Atlantic naval bases brought Scandinavia into World War II.

Hattendorf, John B., and Richard W. Unger, eds. *War at Sea in the Middle Ages and Renaissance.* Woodbridge, U.K.: Boydell, 2003. Contains chapters by Niels Lund, Jan Bill, and Jan Glete about Scandinavian naval development from the Viking era to the sixteenth century.

Heeres, W. G., ed. *From Dunkirk to Danzig: Shipping and Trade in the North Sea and the Baltic, 1350–1850: Essays in Honour of J. A. Faber.* Hilversum, The Netherlands: Verloren, 1988. Includes articles in English about Dutch, Swedish, and German trade.

Israel, Jonathan I. *Dutch Primacy in World Trade, 1585–1740.* Oxford: Clarendon Press, 1989. A systematic survey of the Dutch position as entrepôt and shipping center for Europe and the world, including a reinterpretation of Dutch trade with the Baltic.

Jeannin, Pierre. *Marchands du Nord: Espaces et trafics à l'époque moderne.* Edited by Philippe Braunstein and Jochen Hoock. Paris: Presses de l'École Normale Supérieure, 1996. A collection of articles about early modern Baltic trade, including important studies of merchants as entrepreneurs and The Sound's toll registers as a source for statistics.

Kirby, David, and Merja-Liisa Hinkkanen. *The Baltic and the North Seas*. London: Routledge, 2000. A synthesis of recent research on maritime geography, technology, trade, power struggles, and seafarers.

Lindblad, J. Thomas. *Sweden's Trade with the Dutch Republic, 1738–1795: A Quantitative Analysis of the Relationship between Economic Growth and International Trade in the Eighteenth Century*. Assen, The Netherlands: Van Gorcum, 1982. An econometric study of the changing relationship between Sweden and the declining Dutch economy.

Rystad, Göran, Klaus-R. Böhme, and Wilhelm M. Carlgren, eds. *In Quest of Trade and Security: The Baltic in Power Politics, 1500–1990*. 2 vols. Lund, Sweden: Lund University Press, 1994–1995. Articles about the long-term development of the Nordic navies, strategies, and defense policies as well as about international politics in the Baltic, by authors from Denmark, Sweden, Britain, and the Netherlands.

Troebst, Stefan. "Debating the Mercantile Background to Early Modern Swedish Empire-Building: Michael Roberts versus Artur Attman." *European History Quarterly* 24 (1994): 485–509. A historiographical study about different interpretations of Swedish empire building.

Varenius, Björn. *Det nordiska skeppet: Teknologi och samhällsstrategi i vikingatid och medeltid*. Stockholm, Sweden: AWI, 1992. A reinterpretation of archaeological and iconographic sources about Iron Age and medieval Nordic ships.

JAN GLETE

# Regional Navies

The Baltic Sea is a crossroads of western, eastern, and northern Europe. During the late medieval period the region was where German economic, political, and cultural influences became important. In the early modern era strong territorial states and empires within the region interacted with strong western European mercantile and naval powers. From a maritime point of view the area was important for its suppliers of naval stores. Beginning in the eighteenth century it was increasingly dominated by Russian and Prussian-German state– and empire–building. Periodically, until the late twentieth century, the Baltic Sea—together with the North Sea and the Arctic Ocean—was the base area for the navies of states with superpower ambitions that went far beyond this region.

The Baltic, an inland sea surrounded by strategically important cities and territories, has been the site of closely interconnected naval and military operations. Many of the border zones between land and sea have shallow waters, narrow passages, small islands, and large river estuaries—the setting for amphibious, coastal, and archipelagic combat and mine warfare. In the early modern period, control of the air has been strategically important, but control of the sea with naval power gave an army considerable leverage and operational freedom. It could be sent across the sea or it could be concentrated and maintained in a tactical area with better maritime than land communication and released from defensive tasks along the coasts. In modern warfare, light surface forces, submarines, and mine-warfare forces have good opportunities to delay or prevent offensive operations by superior forces. These factors, together with the rise of air power, have made it increasingly difficult for foreign navies to operate in the Baltic Sea.

## 1500–1700

In the late Middle Ages political power in the Baltic was closely connected with trade. The leading sea power was the German Hanse and its informal capital, Lübeck. The power of the territorial states was small in comparison to the resources of their societies. The Nordic and Polish-Lithuanian kings, the German princes, and the German Order that controlled the eastern Baltic had limited ability to mobilize these resources. With large merchantmen and concentrated financial resources, mercantile cities could exercise much political influence in an area where maritime lines of communication were crucial for trade and power projection.

In around 1500 two territorial states broke the connection between trade and sea power and developed a new combination of centralized territorial and naval power. The rulers of Denmark-Norway and Sweden acquired gun-armed warships as instruments in their struggle for complete control of their own territories. The permanent Nordic navies and royal control of the sea lines of communication were early and important parts of the centralization of political power from local society to the kings. The two navies were also the result of the division of the old Nordic Union, a complicated process that entailed both a conflict between a Danish and a Swedish center of power and several conflicts within the three Nordic kingdoms. The result—two territorial states—were ruled from Copenhagen and Stockholm, which were also strategically convenient centers for naval power in the southern and northern Baltic, respectively.

No competitor for supremacy in the Baltic appeared until the eighteenth century. Lübeck made a final effort as a junior naval partner in alliance with Denmark against Sweden during the war of 1563 to 1570. Sigismund Vasa, the exiled king of Sweden (who was also king of Poland), developed a small navy in the 1620s. This was coordinated with Habsburg efforts to create a Baltic navy, but the Polish-Habsburg warships were taken by Sweden in 1632. In the seventeenth century the Duke of Courland and the Elector of Brandenburg also had small navies, but these were partly mercantile enterprises that only marginally influenced the Baltic. Lack of other competition stimulated claims from rivals Denmark and Sweden that they had a *dominium* over the Baltic Sea and that they had the right to collect custom duties from shipping as payment for protection. The Danish Sound toll was the most important example of that.

Conflicts between the two Nordic states were not inevitable, and for long periods their territorial ambitions were directed to the east and the south. Their navies could also be used for blockades and displays of power against Continental enemies. The Swedish navy was extensively used for such purposes, whereas Denmark had more limited ambitions. Each of the two ruling dynasties—the Oldenburgs in Denmark-Norway and the Vasas and their successors in Sweden—was well aware, however, that it must be able to defend its sea lines of communication against the other Baltic naval power. The size of each navy was therefore determined by the ambition to at least equal the other. Seven wars from 1563 to 1700 showed that naval power was essential for the defense of the Danish isles and the Swedish empire that was created from 1561 to 1660 in the eastern Baltic and northern Germany. If control of the sea were lost, both powers would lose the ability to prevent amphibious attacks and transfer military resources to threatened parts of their territories. From the mid-seventeenth century the Dutch and British navies also began to intervene in Baltic warfare in alliance with one of the two Nordic naval powers. This made it necessary for them to further expand their navies, and they took part in the western European naval competition.

## 1700–1780

Nordic naval power, which had been the result of innovative government activities, was not closely connected with strong maritime interest groups. The role of the ruler was even more pronounced in the development of the Russian navy: it was part of the modernization and westernization project of Tsar Peter I. These ambitions were a driving force behind the Great Northern War (1700–1721), in which Russia became the successor to Sweden as the great power in the Baltic. The later part of that conflict (1709–1721) was a maritime war in which control of the sea determined nearly all military operations. Russia's naval ambitions were far from natural in a century when major

continental powers such as Austria and Prussia had ports and mercantile marines but practically no navies.

The transfer of the Russian capital from Moscow to Saint Petersburg made the navy essential for defense of the Gulf of Finland. This remained a crucial task until the twenty-first century. But Russia's ability to launch offensive operations in the Baltic also depended on its naval capability. The oared flotilla could support army offensives in Finland and against the coasts of Poland and Brandenburg-Prussia. Until the 1780s the sailing navy was not strong enough for offensive operations against the other two Baltic navies, but it could decide the balance of power between them.

Denmark-Norway and Sweden fought their last major naval war from 1709 to 1720. After that Denmark ceased to fight for reconquest of territories lost to Sweden and opted for a defensive and increasingly neutral position in European politics; a strong battle fleet was an important part of this policy. Sweden continued to wage wars in order to regain something of its great power position, and, as the wars had to be fought in the Baltic, the navy had a key role in military planning. The oared flotilla, manned mainly by the army, became increasingly important for combined operations, but up to the 1780s much effort was also made to maintain the battle fleet at a level equal to that of the Russian or Danish navy. The alliance value of the navy was regarded as important in Swedish foreign policy, and France frequently subsidized Swedish naval preparations. Although peace was much more common than war in the Baltic after 1721, there were long periods of tension and preparation for war and the Baltic powers were closely connected to the fluid European alliance system.

## 1780–1870

During the Russo-Turkish War of 1768–1774, Russia deployed battle fleets from the Baltic to the Mediterranean. After 1780 the Russian Baltic fleet was greatly enlarged and a second battle fleet was formed in the Black Sea. This was a part of Catherine II's expansionist Balkan policy, and in the early 1800s Russia replaced Spain as the third-largest naval power.

During the 1780s and 1790s Denmark-Norway and Sweden still had ambitions to be major naval powers, but the increasing cost of warships made this difficult to achieve. The Revolutionary and Napoleonic Wars (1792–1815) caused a dramatic realignment of borders and power structures in the Baltic. Denmark-Norway became involved in conflicts with Great Britain, which saw the

Danish-Norwegian navy as a threat to the European balance of naval power. It was captured by the British at Copenhagen in 1807. Sweden lost Finland to Russia in 1809 and attempted to compensate with a conquest of Norway from Denmark in 1814. The result was a loose Swedish-Norwegian union without any administrative coordination of the armed forces; it lasted until 1905.

By 1815 the Baltic Sea had become an area of contest or cooperation between the two superpowers Great Britain and Russia. The smaller Baltic powers, now far from dominant, had to use the sea as a barrier against invasions from the great powers in the east, west, and south. Future British, or possibly French, naval interventions were more or less taken for granted—and became a fact in 1854–1855, during the Crimean War. The days when Sweden and Denmark could use their battle fleets as elements of the European balance of power and instruments of offensive warfare were gone, but up to the 1860s small battle fleets as well as oared flotillas were maintained. The role of the navy in Swedish defense policy was questioned, but the premise of the policy was that it might at least make a seaborne invasion from Russia more difficult and create time for help to arrive.

The political upheavals in Germany in 1848–1850 started a process in which a new German navy was regarded as a symbol of national unification and maritime self-confidence. After a brief liberal attempt during those years to assemble a German navy from the maritime cities, Prussia took over and developed a navy. It was a regional force, and in the German-Danish wars in 1848–1850 and 1864 Denmark was still superior at sea to the German-Prussian forces.

## 1870–1945

After the unification of Germany in 1871 the new Imperial Navy was expanded to become one of Europe's large naval forces. From the late 1870s it was more powerful than the Russian Baltic fleet, which created a new situation for the two smaller states in the region. To Sweden, Germany was a potential ally against Russia whereas it was the only probable enemy for Denmark. Both developed coastal-defense navies with armored ships of limited size but with a few heavy guns, surface torpedo vessels, and (after 1900) submarines. This combination of ships remained unchanged in both navies until the 1940s, but their doctrines for using their ships differed.

The rise of German sea power made it likely that Germany would attempt to control the Danish straits in a future war. This might lead to interventions from other sea powers. Danish defense policy became increasingly dominated by defeatist attitudes, and the navy was reduced in the early twentieth century. Copenhagen was fortified as a last redoubt against an invader and the navy's assignment was to support its defense. Mines, coastal artillery, and torpedoes provided new ways to guard the straits and preserve Danish neutrality, and the navy received the task of laying and defending minefields. This neutrality policy of a secondary role for the navy was followed in 1914–1918 and gave an advantage to the Germans. In 1940, during World War II, the Germans occupied Denmark to seal off the Baltic. When the Germans attempted to seize the Danish navy in 1943, the Danes scuttled many of their own warships.

Swedish defense policy had been tailored since 1809 to address a Russian invasion, which was expected to come from the sea and be aimed at central Sweden. This would be a large-scale amphibious operation, involving 50,000 to 100,000 soldiers. The Swedish navy was given the task of delaying the transportation of Russian soldiers, equipment, and stores to enable the home army to defeat a weakened invader. Nineteenth-century technological changes created new opportunities for coastal defense, and the Swedish armored ships and torpedo craft were intended to form a striking force against the invader's transport fleet. The attack on an amphibious transport fleet remained the core of Swedish naval doctrine until the end of the twentieth century. The navy, which was strengthened from around 1900 to 1920, unexpectedly became a major force in the Baltic in the 1920s, when Germany and the Soviet Union were weak. It was expanded again during World War II. Compared with most other regional navies, the Swedish navy had an unusually strong industrial base with domestic manufacturers and exporters of weapons, warships, and marine engines.

After World War I five navies belonging to new independent states appeared in the Baltic. A chief goal of their defense policies was the delay of invasion from the Soviet Union or (in the 1930s) Germany, until help from the West arrived by the sea. The idea was that their navies would limit the enemy's freedom of operation, which explains the emphasis on submarines. Finland inherited a strong Russian coastal artillery and built two armored coast-defense ships as well as submarines and motor torpedo boats. Poland built destroyers and submarines and developed the port of Gdynia as a base that might also be used by its ally France. Estonia and Latvia each built two submarines, but Lithuania had only a coast guard. During World War II the Finnish navy fought in two wars against the Soviet Union, while the Polish navy operated as an exile force in Britain.

The three other states were occupied by the Soviet Union and lost their independence.

## 1945–2000

The Cold War divided the Baltic navies into three groups. It was a region in which the Warsaw Pact countries were supposed to take to the offensive on land while the North Atlantic Treaty Organization (NATO) might or might not have enough forces to keep control of the entrance to the Baltic Sea. The Polish and East German navies were developed as regional forces for protection of the Warsaw Pact armies' northern flank and for amphibious operations. They retained an individuality, however. Poland continued to use a small number of destroyers, frigates, and submarines as it had before 1945, and the East German navy was a revival of the light surface forces of the former German navy. It consisted of numerous coastal antisubmarine vessels, fast attack craft, minesweepers, and amphibious craft, and it grew into a considerable force in the 1970s and 1980s.

The regional NATO navies were those of West Germany and Denmark, which were intended for defense of the straits and for strikes against seaborne Warsaw Pact logistical support to the advancing armies. Consequently, both navies had a combination of warships with sea control and short-range strike capability. The Danish navy was reconstructed with German motor torpedo boats and minesweepers and British submarines and escorts, and it gradually replaced them with new vessels. The West German navy was formed in 1955 with destroyers, frigates, small submarines, fast attack craft, minesweepers, and a strong force of navy-controlled aircraft. It also had many depot and supply ships because the peacetime bases were likely to be unusable in wartime.

Although Sweden had one of Europe's largest regional navies in 1945, postwar defense policy limited its role in relation to the strong air force. The navy, including the coast artillery, retained the task of providing anti-invasion defense of the east coast while the ability to protect shipping was reduced. All major surface warships were phased out by the 1980s, but the submarine, fast attack craft, and mine-warfare forces were kept modern. Sweden remained nonaligned although the Soviet Union retained its traditional role as the only probable enemy. If Sweden had been attacked by the Soviet Union, the Swedish archipelagos would have been a probable base area for the German navy with its large shipborne logistical force.

The peace treaty of 1947 forbade Finland's navy to have torpedo-armed vessels. By the 1970s it was allowed to acquire missile-armed vessels, which markedly increased its capability. Finland's defense policy had to be molded to suit Soviet interests, and the main task of the navy was to guard Finnish waters against infringements from NATO so that the Soviet Union would not have an excuse for deploying its forces on Finnish territory.

The end of the Cold War in 1989–1991 caused reductions of the Baltic naval forces. The East German navy disappeared, and its warships were sold after the unification of Germany. The three navies of Estonia, Latvia, and Lithuania reappeared as small sea-control forces. The Danish and Swedish navies began to adapt to a status that might entail deployment on long-distance operations as parts of European Union or United Nations forces.

[*See also* Copenhagen, Bombardment of; Danish Sound Dues; Medieval Navies, *subentry on* Northern Europe and Scandinavia; *and* Svensksund, Battle of.]

## Bibliography

Anderson, R. C. *Naval Wars in the Baltic, 1522–1850.* 2d ed. London: Francis Edwards, 1969. Broad survey of naval operations, with emphasis on chronological and quantitative facts rather than strategic analysis. More reliable about facts than later surveys of Baltic naval warfare in English.

Åselius, Gunnar. *The Rise and Fall of the Soviet Navy in the Baltic, 1921–1941.* London: Frank Cass, 2005. A study of Soviet naval planning and capabilities in the Baltic.

Barfod, Jørgen H. *Niels Juel: A Danish Admiral of the 17th Century.* Copenhagen, Denmark: Marinehistorisk Selskab, 1977. A biography of the most successful Danish naval commander in the early modern period.

Berge, Anders. "The Swedish Navy in the Inter-War Period: Strategic Thinking at the Crossroads." *Militärhistorisk Tidskrift* (1983): 101–114. The strategic debate in the Swedish navy in a period of political and technical uncertainty.

Beskrovny, Ljubomir G. *The Russian Army and Fleet in the Nineteenth Century: Handbook of Armaments, Personnel, and Policy.* Edited and translated by Gordon E. Smith. Gulf Breeze, Fla.: Academic International Press, 1996. Originally published in 1973. A general history of the Russian armed forces in the nineteenth century.

Beskrovny, Ljubomir G. *Russkaja armija i flot v XVIII veke (ocherki).* Moscow, Russia: Voendizat, 1958. A general history of the Russian armed forces in the eighteenth century.

Feldbaek, Ole. *Denmark and the Armed Neutrality, 1800–1801: Small Power Policy in a World War.* Copenhagen, Denmark: Akademisk Forlag, 1980. A study of Denmark's foreign and maritime policy as a background to the British naval attack on Copenhagen in 1801.

Frantzen, Ole L. *Truslen fra øst: Dansk-norsk flådepolitik, 1769–1807.* Copenhagen, Denmark: Marinehistorisk Selskab, 1980. Danish naval policy from the period when a regional Swedish-Danish war was still the most likely conflict to the time when Denmark became involved in a superpower confrontation.

Gemzell, Carl-Axel. *Organization, Conflict, and Innovation: A Study of German Naval Strategic Planning, 1888–1940.* Lund, Sweden: Esselte, 1973. A study of German naval planning that also provides information about the strategic situation in the Baltic.

Glete, Jan. "Coastal Defence and Technological Change: Technology, Doctrine and Organization within Sweden's Coastal Defence." In *The Swedish Armed Forces and Foreign Influences, 1870–1945,* edited by Göran Rystad, pp. 57–76. Stockholm, Sweden: Militärhistoriska Förlaget, 1992. The development of the Swedish navy from a sailing battle fleet and oared flotilla in 1850 to a coastal defense fleet in the 1880s.

Glete, Jan. "Naval Power and Control of the Seas in the Baltic in the 16th Century." In *War at Sea in the Middle Ages and Renaissance,* edited by John B. Hattendorf and Richard W. Unger, pp. 217–232. Woodbridge, U.K.: Boydell and Brewer, 2003. The rise of the Danish and Swedish navies as a part of the early modern state-formation process.

Glete, Jan. "Sails and Oars: Warships and Navies in the Baltic During the Eighteenth Century (1700–1815)." In *Les marines de guerre européennes, XVII–XVIIIe siècles,* edited by Martine Acerra, José Merino, and Jean Meyer, pp. 369–401. Paris: Presses de l'Université de Paris-Sorbonne, 1985. A survey of the Danish, Swedish, and Russian navies.

Hobson, Rolf, and Tom Kristiansen, eds. *Navies in Northern Waters, 1721-2000.* London: Frank Cass, 2004. Articles about the Baltic navies and Baltic naval policy, including a survey of the Danish, Swedish, and Russian navies from 1721 to 1814.

Lisberg Jensen, Ole. *I skyggen af Tyskland: Den danske flådes historie, 1864-1920.* Copenhagen, Denmark: Marinehistorisk Selskab, 2005. The Danish navy in the period when it adapted to a position as a guardian of the neutrality of the Danish straits.

Probst, Niels M. *Christian 4.s flåde: Den danske flådes historie, 1588-1660.* Copenhagen, Denmark: Marinehistorisk Selskab, 1996. A study of Danish-Norwegian naval technology and policy, administration, shipbuilding, and operations.

Rystad, Göran, Klaus-R. Böhme, and Wilhelm M. Carlgren, eds. *In Quest of Trade and Security: The Baltic in Power Politics, 1500–1990.* 2 vols. Lund, Sweden: Lund University Press, 1994–1995. Articles about the long-term development of the Nordic navies, strategies, and defense policies as well as about international politics in the Baltic, by authors from Denmark, Sweden, Britain, and the Netherlands.

Saul, Norman E. "The Russian Navy 1682–1854: Some Suggestions for Future Study." In *New Aspects of Naval History: Selected Papers Presented at the Fourth Naval History Symposium, United States Naval Academy, 25–26 October 1979,* edited by Craig L. Symonds, pp. 131–139. Annapolis, Md.: U.S. Naval Institute Press, 1981. An introduction to the historiography of the Russian navy.

Steensen, R. Steen, ed. *Flåden gennem 475 år.* 2 vols. Copenhagen, Denmark: Martin, 1974. A major history of the Danish navy from 1500 to the 1970s.

Svensson, A. Artur, and Otto Lybeck, eds. *Svenska flottans historia, 1521-1945.* 3 vols. Malmö, Sweden: Allhem, 1942-1945. A leading history of the Swedish navy, written mainly by sea officers and naval architects. Richly illustrated.

JAN GLETE

**Baltic Straits.** *See* Straits, *subentry on* An Overview.

# Banking and Credit

This entry contains two subentries:

Early
Late

## Early

European banking, as a principal agency for supplying commercial credit, has twin roots, one for each of its two historic branches: deposit and transfer banking, dating from ancient Greece (fifth century B.C.E.), and bills of exchange banking, dating from late thirteenth-century Italy. Not only in ancient Greece, but everywhere else in the western world, deposit banking arose from money changing. Since most gold and silver coins were legal tender only within the jurisdiction of the issuer, governments licensed private money changers (*trapezites, argyropatês, argentarii*) to exchange foreign for domestic coins. In so doing, money changers necessarily had to safeguard their coin inventories, and thus merchants and wealthy citizens solicited money changers'

***The Money Changer and his Wife.*** Quentin Metsys (c. 1466–1530) painted this portrait in 1514. SCALA / ART RESOURCE, NY / LOUVRE, PARIS

services to provide secure repositories for their own coins and precious metals. In becoming deposit bankers, most money changers found that they needed to maintain a cash reserve of only about one-third of deposit liabilities, which enabled them to lend the remaining two-thirds.

To economize on the use of coin and to offer clients a considerable convenience, these money-changer bankers permitted depositors to make payments by book-account transfers, on oral or written instructions (documented in Athens by 254 B.C.E.). Though such banking also flourished in Hellenistic Egypt and in the Roman Empire, it evidently did not survive the latter's decline, and in western Europe it was resuscitated in northern Italy only from the 1180s. Subsequently such banking spread to Catalonia, France, the Low Countries, and Germany. It did not spread to England before the seventeenth century, however, because the English government had decreed (from at least 1222) that all foreign coins be exchanged exclusively at the offices of the crown's Royal Exchanger (to be surrendered as bullion to the Tower Mint), and the government strictly enforced a ban on private money changing and commerce in precious metals–a ban that endured until the Civil War–era of the 1640s. Thereafter, with the removal of such constraints, deposit and transfer banking, with fractional-reserve lending, rapidly developed in England, almost entirely within the London guild of goldsmiths–who had earlier served, albeit illegally, as money changers and bullion dealers, and who were also the first systematically to combine deposit and foreign-exchange banking.

## Foreign-Exchange Banking

Arguably, foreign-exchange banking, also known as bills of exchange or acceptance banking, was the much more important form of banking, especially for maritime commerce. It was uniquely the creation of later medieval Italian merchants, and its origin lay in the earlier *instrumentum ex causa cambii* or *lettre de foire*, which had come to be widely used in transacting commerce at the Champagne Fairs from the later twelfth century. In this form, it was a formal notarized bond by which one merchant acknowledged receiving a loan, generally in some Italian currency, and agreed to make repayment to the lender's agent at one of the Champagne Fairs, in the local French currency, at a stipulated rate of exchange. By the late thirteenth century, an alternative financial instrument had emerged in the bill of exchange (*cambium, lettera di cambio, lettre de paiement*), which was not a loan contract but rather an informal

(holograph) letter of payment that involved two principals in one city and two agents abroad. For example, in Florence, merchant A, known as the *datore* or giver, supplied another merchant, B, known as the *prenditore* or taker, with investment funds in, say, gold florins, by buying a *cambium* or bill of exchange from B. In drawing his bill on his financial agent C in Bruges (possibly another merchant-banking firm), merchant B instructed C, known as the *pagatore*–the payer or acceptor–to make payment, usually in three months' usance (maturity), to merchant A's financial agent in Bruges, known as the *beneficiario* or payee, at a stipulated rate of exchange, that is, at so many pence Flemish *groot* per gold florin. Only after agent C had agreed to accept the bill did it become valid. Florentine merchant B would thus use these funds to purchase, for example, spices and silks and to lease space on a ship bound for Bruges, where his *fattore* or agent would arrange the sale of these goods and then deposit the proceeds with financial agent C; this enabled merchant B to redeem the bill, when financial agent D presented it for payment on the maturity date. This agent D would then arrange to remit these funds to his principal in Florence by acting in turn as a *datore*, buying a *recambium*–that is, by investing the funds in the maritime trade of some other Bruges-based Italian merchant and receiving in return a copy of the latter's bill of exchange, drawn on a Florentine merchant-banking firm, that designated merchant A (the original *datore*) as the payee (*beneficiario*).

As both an investment and a transfer instrument, the bill of exchange or acceptance bill was the most important European contribution to the development of commercial-financial capitalism in that it served three vitally important functions. First, because it was not a loan contract, but in effect a purchase of foreign financial assets, the bill of exchange offered merchants an effective mechanism to avoid (or evade) the universal usury prohibition on any interest exacted above the principal of the loan. For the investor, the gain lay in the difference in the exchange rates of the original *cambium* and the *recambium*, which typically offered the *datore* a profit of about 10 percent. De Roover and many other historians consider that gain to be instead "loan interest disguised within the exchange rates." Second, the bill of exchange became by far the most important mechanism for financing trade in general, but especially for financing maritime commerce. Third, in financing such commerce or in simply remitting funds abroad, such bills obviated the increasingly serious risks of physically transporting coin and bullion between ports or cities, since all financial transactions were undertaken in the local currencies of the principal's and agent's towns.

The rapid diffusion of the bill of exchange, almost entirely—if not entirely—undertaken by Italian merchants, coincides with both the height of the revivified ecclesiastical campaign against usury and, from the 1290s, the increasingly widespread disruptions of traditional overland Continental trading routes in war-torn Europe. Such disruptions soon led to the decline of the land-based Champagne Fairs and the establishment of direct maritime trading routes from Italy to northern towns (Southampton, London, and Bruges, by the 1320s), where Italian merchants retained permanent resident *fattori* agents who could transact both trade and financial remittances on their behalf with such bills. From the later fourteenth century, English merchants, in conducting cross-Channel trade with the Low Countries, also came to use bills of exchange; subsequently, in 1436, the English were responsible for establishing the first legal guarantees for payments of bearer bills, in a judicial decision of London's law-merchant mayor's court. But many, if not most, English merchants, in conducting itinerant trade with the new or reviving fairs of the Low Countries, preferred to use the three-party bill obligatory, which—though it was not notarized—indeed resembled the earlier *instrumentum ex causa cambii* of the Champagne Fairs.

### The *Commenda* and the *Compagnia*

Much earlier, with the so-called commercial revolution of the eleventh and twelfth centuries, the Italians had used a much different commercial or investment contract to finance their maritime Mediterranean trade: the *commenda*, which was borrowed directly from the much older Arabic *qirad* contract. Valid for one maritime venture only, but often renewable, its most striking feature was the limitation of liability for both the investor and the active maritime merchant. In its pure form, the investor supplying the capital received 75 percent of any profits—but no interest, since this was not a loan. Indeed, if the venture failed, the active seafaring merchant was not obligated to make any repayment, while the investor was not liable for any other commercial obligations assumed by the seafaring merchant. In the bilateral version, the seafaring merchant himself put up one-third of the capital, and any profits were split fifty-fifty (which division in fact still meant a 75 percent return on capital and 25 percent payment for labor and enterprise). But in the later Middle Ages, the *commenda* evidently gave way to bills of exchange, at least in port towns permitting principal-agent relationships.

For land-based commerce and industry, the Italians—and western Europeans in general—used what was the virtually unchanged descendent of the Roman partnership contract, known as the *compagnia*. The *compagnia* was a much more permanent contract, valid for the duration of the partnership, in which the partners shared profits and losses according to their capital investments, but with the stipulation that all partners bore unlimited liability for all debts and obligations of the firm.

### The Joint Stock Company

By the fifteenth or sixteenth century—in England, verifiably from 1553—some partnerships, specifically devised to finance long-distance maritime trade, had evolved into the joint stock company, with negotiable shares (that is, transferable by sale), a feature not possible with traditional partnerships. In a new age of European overseas expansion, this financial organization was employed to create and maintain many large-scale maritime enterprises with long-term ventures, which required very large capitals: enterprises such as the Muscovy Company (1553), the Turkey Company (1581; reorganized as the Levant Company in 1591), the East India Company (1600)—and also the Dutch East India company, the Vereenigde Oostindische Compagnie (VOC, 1602)—the Hudson's Bay Company (1670), and the Royal African Company (1672). Most of these companies protected investors with charters of incorporation, but in England, joint stock companies without such charters remained subject to unlimited liability until the Joint Stock Companies Act of 1856–1857. In contrast, it was much earlier, from the 1670s, that the French government had accorded limited liability (that is, liability limited to the amount of the capital investment) to silent or nonactive investors. In this era, too, most of the French joint stock companies were also based on long-distance maritime trade, rather than being industrial ventures of financial enterprises, which became predominant only from the mid-nineteenth century.

[*See also* Chartered Companies; East India Companies; Joint Stock Companies; Shipping Companies; Trade; *and* Trade Routes.]

### Bibliography

Blomquist, Thomas. "The Early History of European Banking: Merchants, Bankers, and Lombards of XIIIth-Century Lucca in the County of Champagne." *Journal of European Economic History* 14 (Winter 1985): 521–536.

Bogaert, Raymond. "Banking in the Ancient World." In *A History of European Banking*, edited by Herman Van der Wee and Ginette Kurgan-Van Hentenryk, 2d ed., pp. 13–70. Antwerp,

Belgium: European Investment Bank, Mercatorfonds, 2000. An English translation of *De bank in Europa* (Antwerp, Belgium: Mercatorfonds, 1991).

De Roover, Raymond. *L'evolution de la lettre de change, XIVe–XVIIIe siècles*. Paris: S.E.V.P.E.N., 1953.

De Roover, Raymond. *Money, Banking, and Credit in Mediaeval Bruges: Italian Merchant-Bankers, Lombards, and Money Changers*. Cambridge, Mass.: Harvard University Press, 1948.

De Roover, Raymond. *The Rise and Decline of the Medici Bank, 1397–1494*. Cambridge, Mass.: Harvard University Press, 1963.

Goldthwaite, Richard. "Local Banking in Renaissance Florence." *Journal of European Economic History* 14, no. 1 (spring 1985): 5–55.

Goldthwaite, Richard. "The Medici Bank and the World of Florentine Capitalism." *Past and Present* 114 (February 1987): 3–31.

Kerridge, Eric. *Trade and Banking in Early Modern England*. Manchester, U.K.: Manchester University Press, 1988.

Le Goff, Jacques. *Marchands et banquiers du moyen âge*. Paris: Presses Universitaires de France, 1956.

Lopez, Robert. "The Dawn of Medieval Banking." In *The Dawn of Modern Banking*, edited by the Center for Medieval and Renaissance Studies, University of California, Los Angeles, pp. 1–23. New Haven, Conn., and London: Yale University Press, 1979.

Mueller, Reinhold. *Money and Banking in Medieval and Renaissance Venice*. Vol. 2, *The Venetian Money Market: Banks, Panics, and the Public Debt, 1200–1500*. Baltimore and London: Johns Hopkins University Press, 1997.

Munro, John H. "Bullionism and the Bill of Exchange in England, 1272–1663: A Study in Monetary Management and Popular Prejudice." In *The Dawn of Modern Banking*, edited by the Center for Medieval and Renaissance Studies, University of California, Los Angeles, pp. 169–240. New Haven, Conn., and London, Yale University Press, 1979.

Munro, John H. "The 'New Institutional Economics' and the Changing Fortunes of Fairs in Medieval and Early Modern Europe: The Textile Trades, Warfare, and Transaction Costs." *Vierteljahrschrift für Sozial- und Wirtschaftsgeschichte* 88, no. 1 (2001): 1–47.

Parker, Geoffrey. "The Emergence of Modern Finance in Europe, 1500–1750." In *The Fontana Economic History of Europe*, edited by Carlo Cipolla. 6 vols. London: Collins, 1972–1976. Vol. 2, *The Sixteenth and Seventeenth Centuries* (1974), pp. 527–594.

Postan, Michael. "Private Financial Instruments in Medieval England." *Vierteljahrschrift für Sozial- und Wirtschaftsgeschichte* 22 (1930). Reprinted in Michael Postan, *Medieval Trade and Finance* (Cambridge, U.K.: Cambridge University Press, 1973), pp. 28–64.

Scott, William Robert. *The Constitution and Finance of English, Scottish, and Irish Joint Stock Companies to 1720*. 3 vols. Cambridge, U.K.: Cambridge University Press, 1912. Reprint. Gloucester, Mass.: Peter Smith, 1968.

Usher, Abbott Payson. *The Early History of Deposit Banking in Mediterranean Europe*. Vol. 1, *The Structure and Functions of the Early Credit System: Banking in Catalonia, 1240–1723.*

Harvard Economic Studies, vol. 75. Cambridge, Mass: Harvard University Press, 1943. Reprint. New York: Russell and Russell, 1967.

Van der Wee, Herman. "Anvers et les innovations de la technique financière aux XVIe et XVIIe siècles." *Annales Économies, Sociétés, Civilisations* 22 (1967): 1067–1089. Reprinted as "Antwerp and the New Financial Methods of the 16th and 17th Centuries." In *The Low Countries in the Early Modern World*, by Herman Van der Wee, translated by Lizabeth Fackelman, pp. 145–166. Aldershot, U.K.: Variorum; Cambridge, U.K.: Cambridge University Press, 1993.

Van der Wee, Herman. "European Banking in the Middle Ages and Early Modern Period (476–1789)." In *A History of European Banking*, edited by Herman Van der Wee and Ginette Kurgan-Van Hentenryk, 2d ed., pp. 152–180. Antwerp: European Investment Bank, Mercatorfonds, 2000. An English translation of *De bank in Europa* (Antwerp: Mercatorfonds, 1991).

JOHN MUNRO

## Late

Before the introduction of steam vessels in the mid-nineteenth century and the later availability of limited liability, shipping involved sailing vessels of a few hundred tons and ownership based on partnerships, a mode of finance widely used in Europe. In Britain such partnerships usually consisted of twenty or so people, but the business of managing a vessel rested with one or two. In line with established practice, divisors of four were used—that is, shares in a vessel were expressed as one-eighth, one-sixteenth, one-thirty-second, and sometimes one-sixty-fourth—but with the Merchant Shipping Act of 1855 the one-sixty-fourth fraction became the norm. Smaller ships usually had single owners, but ships over 250 tons were financed by distributing shares among the manager's friends and commercial acquaintances. Every ship was a capital entity with a unique list of shareholders. For the manager this was an alternative to a mortgage, while investors could reduce risk by spreading their investment over several ships. The shares effectively possessed limited liability since the investment was in property and investors had an opportunity for profit sharing. Shares could usually be sold through the local press. Even though the risks of investment were considerable, given the variability of freight rates and the vagaries of the weather, investors tolerated low returns in the hope of an occasional bonanza.

While the sixty-four-share system provided long-term capital, working capital in the early nineteenth century came from country banks. Bank credit was available in two forms. Three-month bills of exchange were widely used by factors and commission houses to finance the movement of goods, and the bills were discounted by local banks. The country banks also made advances to local shipowners, the credit being available for several years. For example, in the early nineteenth century the Liverpool bank of Leyland & Bullins made advances to some seventeen ships. Many country banks failed during the various financial crises that occurred from 1793 to 1815, but this had more to do with speculative imports and general commercial difficulties than with specific bad debts on the part of shipping concerns. Extensive use of bill finance and cheap bank credit also featured in the building up of the Dutch commercial fleets in late eighteenth and early nineteenth centuries.

From the 1860s onward the possibility of forming joint-stock companies with limited liability provided shipping with a source of long-term capital. Shipowners were tardy, however, in making the conversion from the sixty-four-share system. For example, the Liverpool-based Booth Steamship Company was not converted until 1881, and Bibby Son & Company was not converted until 1891. Few shipping companies sought capital from the stock market. In the absence of a developed capital market Greek shipping companies, for instance, had no such alternative means of finance; they continued to rely on a limited circle of investors—a system that was the basis of the large family-owned Greek shipping fleets into modern times.

Steam vessels had considerable advantages over sail, yet the switch to steam from sail was gradual. The cost of steam vessels with iron hulls was considerable, but many merchants stayed with sail because they believed that sail was the only economical way to transport bulk cargoes over long distances. Capital for conversion and management of new vessels came from several sources. Most shipping lines built up internal funds in good trading times, while others resorted to mortgages from shipbuilders, which were paid off later from earnings. Arrangements whereby shipbuilders provided finance for shipowners were common in northeast England. An alternative was the lending by local banks against mortgages on ships, the loan being covered by the value of the steamers. Certainly in the years before World War I shipping was financed largely by internal funds supplemented by borrowing, mainly from nonmarket sources. There was little assistance from the government.

Government assistance for shipping was first introduced in the 1880s. It involved encouraging shipping lines to join conference arrangements, preferential mail contracts, and favorable railway rates for goods shipped in national vessels. British shipping interests were critical of such assistance. World War I brought handsome profits to British shipowners, but rather than retain the profits for fleet replacement the shipowners increased dividends and surplus funds were used to buy ships at inflated prices. When prices collapsed after World War I, many companies found themselves overcapitalized in relation to postwar valuations, while hasty amalgamations left some shipping lines with unwieldy capital structures.

Disdain for state support in Britain changed in the uncertain economic conditions in the years after World War I. The most prominent example of government assistance involved the construction of two passenger liners for the Cunard Line, which was eager to counter competition on the Atlantic crossing. In the immediate postwar years Cunard had used the bill market to finance new construction, paying off short-term bills in annual installments from depreciation allowances. Construction of *Queen Mary* was begun in 1930 but had to be suspended three months before the scheduled completion date because the fall in earnings prevented the company from setting aside sufficient depreciation allowances to cover maturing bills. The government refused assistance, and work was stopped for two years. Eventually the government relented and advanced £3 million to enable the ship to be launched. A further £5 million was promised for the sister ship, *Queen Elizabeth*. World trading conditions and Continental rivalry overcame government reluctance. Still, Cunard's rivals from France and Germany on the Atlantic run were able to draw heavily on bank credit, in line with traditional Continental practices, and had greater government support.

After 1945 British shipping lines earned profits sufficient to justify going to the market to finance ship replacement, but they continued to rely on self-finance. Between 1945 and 1960 none of the liner companies listed in the London market raised new equity capital. They also had a marked reluctance, unlike many of their Continental rivals, to borrow money, even though the interest cost could have been set against tax liabilities. As with other forms of investment in the 1950s and 1960s, initial allowances were available to stimulate shipbuilding, and this may have ameliorated the decline of the British fleet. Unfortunately, in 1984 the government took away the attractive inducement of 100 percent first-year investment allowances. It was not until 2000, following the continued reduction in the size of the British merchant fleet, that the government introduced a tonnage tax. Under the new scheme shipping companies are subject to low-level taxation based on the size of the fleet rather than on profits earned. This placed some sixty British shipping groups on an equal footing with their international competitors.

[*See also* Joint Stock Companies; Shipping, *subentry on* State-owned Shipping; *and* Shipping Companies.]

## Bibliography

Davis, Ralph. *The Rise of the English Shipping Industry in the Seventeenth and Eighteenth Centuries.* London: Macmillan, 1962.

Fayle, C. Ernest. *A Short History of the World's Shipping Industry.* London: Allen and Unwin, 1933.

Kirkaldy, Adam W. *British Shipping: Its History, Organisation, and Importance.* London: Kegan Paul, Trench, Trübner, 1914.

Mance, Harry Osborne. *International Sea Transport.* Oxford: Oxford University Press, 1945.

Sturmey, S. G. *British Shipping and World Competition.* London: Athlone Press, 1962.

Thornton, R. H. *British Shipping.* 2d ed. Cambridge, U.K.: Cambridge University Press, 1959.

W. A. THOMAS

## Banks, Joseph

**Banks, Joseph** (1743–1820), English naturalist. A member of the Lincolnshire gentry, Joseph Banks was educated at Harrow, Eton, and Christ Church, Oxford. There he received little formal scientific education but was given sufficient freedom to develop his youthful interest in natural history.

Soon after he left Oxford in 1764 he demonstrated the enthusiasm for combining scientific inquiry with maritime exploration that was to be a continuing feature of his life. In 1766 he joined an expedition to Newfoundland and Labrador as a botanist and, soon afterward, achieved Europe-wide fame as a naturalist when he became a member of James Cook's great *Endeavour* voyage from 1768 to 1771. This was the last of Banks's major voyages apart from a trip to Iceland in 1772 and a five-week trip to the Dutch Republic in 1773.

Though Banks was thereafter confined to England he continued to promote expeditions that could serve Britain's scientific and imperial interests. He was able to further such goals because of his standing as president of the Royal Society from 1778 until his death in 1820—a post that led to Banks becoming the de facto adviser to the government on innumerable scientific and imperial matters.

His determination to use his botanical knowledge to assist British interests in the West Indies led to the ill-fated *Bounty* expedition of 1787 to 1789, commanded by Banks's client William Bligh. As virtual superintendent of Australian affairs—a role that followed from his key role in the colony's foundation—Banks was anxious to promote the exploration of that largely unknown continent: hence his active role in the organization of the voyage of *Investigator* under Matthew Flinders, which circumnavigated Australia from 1801 to 1803.

Banks, then, did much to forge the close association between naval exploration and the promotion of science that continued to bear rich fruit in nineteenth-century Britain with voyages such as those of *Beagle*, *Blossom*, and *Challenger*.

[*See also* Cook, James.]

## Bibliography

Beaglehole, J. C., ed. *The* Endeavour *Journal of Joseph Banks, 1768–1771.* Sydney, Australia: Trustees of the Public Library of New South Wales, in association with Angus and Robertson, 1962.

Carter, Harold B. *Sir Joseph Banks (1743–1820): A Guide to Biographical and Bibliographical Sources.* Winchester, U.K.: St Paul's Bibliographies in association with British Museum (Natural History), 1987.

Gascoigne, John. *Joseph Banks and the English Enlightenment: Useful Knowledge and Polite Culture.* Cambridge, U.K.: Cambridge University Press, 1994.

Gascoigne, John. *Science in the Service of Empire: Joseph Banks, the British State, and the Uses of Science in the Age of Revolution.* Cambridge, U.K.: Cambridge University Press, 1998.

Lysaght, A. M. *Joseph Banks in Newfoundland and Labrador, 1766: His Diary, Manuscripts, and Collections.* Berkeley: University of California Press, 1971.

JOHN GASCOIGNE

## Barbarossa

**Barbarossa** (c. 1466/1475–1546), Ottoman admiral and pirate. The man known to Western history as Barbarossa was born Khidr (or Khizr), the son of a Turkish soldier, on the Greek island of Lesbos. The youngest of four brothers, he began his career inauspiciously as a potter but soon joined his oldest brother, Aruj, a mercenary and occasional pirate, attacking Christian shipping in the Mediterranean. The two brothers successfully raided European ships off the coast of Spain and North African towns in Tunis and Algiers. When in 1492 the Spanish expelled the Moors and thousands of homeless Muslims poured across the strait to Africa, Aruj and Khidr seized the opportunity to recruit the exiled Moors for their raids against the Spanish.

In 1516 the brothers captured Algiers, of which Aruj declared himself monarch. Needing the protection of the Ottoman Empire, Aruj surrendered the title in return for aid and was named its governor. When Aruj was killed in a battle with the Spanish in 1518, his younger brother took charge of the pirate band. The nickname Barbarossa, used only by Christians, originally applied to the red-bearded Aruj but passed to Khidr with the command. At this time Khidr also took the name Khair ad Din ("Defender of the Faith"), by which he was known for the rest of his life to fellow Muslims. As fierce a warrior as his brother, Khair ad Din was a shrewder politician and submitted his holdings in North Africa to the Ottoman Empire by accepting Turkish rule in North Africa. He was appointed deputy to the sultan, Selim I (r. 1512–1520), and received the title *beylerbey* (commander general). In 1519 he successfully defended Algiers from the Spanish and resoundingly defeated them again in 1529. In 1534 he captured Tunisia, and made his base in Tunis, its capital.

Although the galleon, a large sailing craft, was becoming the fighting vessel of choice in the Mediterranean because of its power and its capacity to hold heavy armament, Khair ad Din preferred the man-powered galley, with its single bank of oarsmen, or the swifter oared galleot. For his purposes—capturing rather than sinking his enemy—these more maneuverable vessels proved far more efficient. His brilliant seamanship in defending the Turkish domain in North Africa and the percentage of his plunder that he paid the sultan earned him high rank and influence. In 1533 Selim's successor, Süleyman I (r. 1520–1566), named him admiral in chief. Two years later Charles V—the Holy Roman emperor (r. 1519–1556) and king of Spain as Charles I (r. 1516–1556)—succeeded in retaking Tunis (1535), but at the Battle of Préveza in 1538 Khair ad Din defeated Charles's fleet led by its admiral Andrea Doria. This victory is credited with initiating more than three centuries of Turkish domination of the eastern Mediterranean. As late as 1544, Khair ad Din led a Turkish fleet that smashed the Spanish and helped France recapture Naples.

Beginning as a despised pirate, Barbarossa Khair ad Din Pasha, by daring and consummate skill, made himself the master of the Barbary Coast. Known as the founder of the kingdom of Algiers and of the Turkish navy, he died richly honored in his palace in Constantinople (Istanbul), a national hero in Turkey.

[*See also* Doria, Andrea, *and* Wars, Maritime, *subentry on* Christian-Turkish Wars.]

## Bibliography

Bradford, Ernle. *The Sultan's Admiral: The Life of Barbarossa.* New York: Harcourt, Brace, 1968.

Fisher, Godfrey. *Barbary Legend: War, Trade, and Piracy in North Africa, 1415–1830.* Oxford, U.K.: Clarendon, 1957.

Heers, Jacques. *The Barbary Corsairs: Warfare in the Mediterranean, 1480–1580.* Translated by Jonathan North. London, Greenhill, 2003.

Wolf, John B. *The Barbary Coast: Algiers under the Turks, 1500–1830.* New York: Norton, 1979.

DENNIS WEPMAN

**Barque**  "Barque" or "bark" appears to have been a generic term for a small sailing vessel as early as the fifteenth century. By the eighteenth century a "barque" was a three-masted cargo ship with a boxlike capacious hull, bluff bows, no upper works, and no ornaments at the bow or stern. The deck was full, the transom square, the floors flat, and the bilges hard. The sides were almost vertical. There could be two or even three decks. Capacity could rise to more than 1,000 tons. Typically there were square sails on the fore- and mainmasts, and the mizzen carried a gaffsail and, on larger versions, a gaff-topsail. The simple rig kept crew size low and thus costs down. By the late eighteenth century, the barque was a popular cargo ship for moving bulk goods like wood and coal in northern Europe.

In southern Europe, the "barque" or "barca" was by the Renaissance a small coastal vessel carrying a single sail. By the eighteenth century it had become a cargo- or warship that carried a lateen sail on the mizzenmast and possibly even a small sail on a fourth pole above the stern. The fore- and mainmasts sometimes had three square sails each, but in the Provençal and many other versions, the foremast carried a single huge lateen sail in place of the square ones. The vessel had a low and broad hull and was almost double-ended, with the greatest width rather far forward.

In the nineteenth century, the barque was a seagoing four-masted ship with four or five square sails on each of the three masts forward. The mast at the stern carried a gaff sail. Also typical for a nineteenth-century barque is the lack of any square sail on the mizzenmast. Barques could reach 3,000 tons or even, in extreme cases, 5,000 tons. By around 1900, interchangeable and generally simplified sails and yards made it possible to handle the rig largely from the deck with steam winches. Large barques with mixed rigs were effective in long-distance trades and thus were among the last commercially viable sailing ships, some still in use in the mid-twentieth century.

[See also Trading Vessels, *subentries on* Early Modern Vessels *and* Modern Vessels.]

## Bibliography

Gardiner, Robert, ed. *Sail's Last Century: The Merchant Sailing Ship 1830-1930.* London: Conway Maritime Press, 1993.

Harland, John. *Ships and Seamanship: The Maritime Prints of J. J. Baugean.* London: Chatham, 2000.

MacGregor, David. *Merchant Sailing Ships 1775-1815: Their Design and Construction.* Watford, U.K.: Model and Allied Publications, 1980.

Villiers, Alan. *The War with Cape Horn.* New York: Scribners, 1971.

RICHARD W. UNGER

**Barrow, John** (1764–1848), second secretary of the British Admiralty and promoter of exploration. John Barrow was born at Dragley Beck near Ulverston, England, on June 19, 1764, the son of a smallholder. As a result of hard work, patronage, and an element of luck, he rose to become second secretary of the Admiralty, and he was an unstinting promoter of exploration. The influence of a series of patrons took Barrow to Beijing with the British diplomat George Macartney, 1st Earl Macartney, as comptroller of his household and interpreter on his somewhat humiliating visit to China as Britain's first ambassador in 1792; to Cape Town as private secretary to Macartney when Macartney was appointed governor-general of Cape of Good Hope in 1796; and finally to the Admiralty as second secretary appointed by the first lord of the Admiralty, Henry Dundas, 1st Viscount Melville, in 1804.

Barrow was second secretary—which meant handling the daily administration of the Admiralty, with the vast correspondence that this involved—for forty years (with the exception of one year, 1806–1807), until he retired in 1845. In this position he was able to pursue his chief interest: the exploration of unknown parts of the globe, particularly the polar regions and Africa. In the Arctic his particular focus was the Northwest Passage, where he repeatedly used the argument that it would be intolerably embarrassing if some other nation (specifically Russia) were to gain the prize first.

Between 1818 and his retirement in 1845, Barrow was instrumental in dispatching twelve expeditions to the polar regions. These included, in 1818, John Ross's expedition to Baffin Bay in *Isabella* and *Alexander*, and David Buchan's expedition to attempt a crossing of the Arctic Basin in *Dorothea* and *Trent*; in 1819–1820, William Edward Parry's expedition in *Hecla* and *Griper*, which penetrated right through Parry Channel to within sight of Banks Island, and John Franklin's first overland expedition, which surveyed the coast by canoe from the mouth of the Coppermine to Kent Peninsula; in 1821, Parry's expedition to Foxe Basin in *Fury* and *Hecla*, when he was blocked by ice in Fury and Hecla Strait; in 1823, George Francis Lyon's unsuccessful attempt in *Griper* to reach Repulse Bay, when Lyon aimed to explore the coast west from Melville Peninsula; and in 1824, Parry's abortive try at penetrating south from Lancaster Sound into Prince Regent Inlet in *Fury* and *Hecla*.

In 1825, Barrow dispatched Franklin on a second coastwise boating expedition, which successfully explored the Arctic coast from Return Reef (near Prudhoe Bay) in the west to the mouth of the Coppermine in the east. Then in 1827, Parry (in *Hecla*) made an attempt at the North Pole from Svalbard, using boats mounted on runners; the attempt was defeated by the ice drift. In 1836, George Back was sent to Hudson Bay in *Terror* to explore the Arctic coast west from Repulse Bay, but with no greater success than George Lyon had. Then in 1839, James Clark Ross (John Ross's nephew) was sent south in *Erebus* and *Terror*. In two seasons in a row he penetrated into the Ross Sea, discovering the Ross Ice Shelf and Mount Erebus.

Finally, during the last few months prior to his retirement in 1845, Barrow was planning Sir John Franklin's last expedition, in search of the Northwest Passage, in *Erebus* and *Terror*. When the two ships had not been heard from for several years, a massive series of search expeditions was mounted, some by the Royal Navy, but others by the Hudson's Bay Company, the U.S. Navy, and private individuals. Though largely ineffectual in determining the fate of Franklin's expedition, these search expeditions had the beneficial spin-off of exploring and mapping most of the rest of what is now the Canadian Arctic Archipelago.

As regards Barrow's other area of primary focus, North Africa, he dispatched a total of six expeditions, mainly aimed at tracing the course of the Niger; with only one exception, they were naval expeditions only to the extent that the expeditions reached their starting points by sea. Three of these expeditions—those of James Ritchie, accompanied by Lieutenant George Lyon (1818), of Dr. Walter Oudney and Lieutenant Hugh Clapperton (1821–1825), and of Major Gordon Laing (1825–1826)—started from Tripoli (now Tarabalus), Libya. Only the last two expeditions penetrated right across the Sahara, and only Laing's expedition reached the Niger, at Timbuctoo (now Tombouctou).

**John Barrow.** Barrow drew this view of a Chinese walled city and boats in 1793 while serving as comptroller in Lord Macartney's household during his diplomatic mission to Peking. © BRITISH LIBRARY / HIP / ART RESOURCE, NY

But Laing's expedition did not throw any new light on the Niger's farther course. Of the expeditions coming from the south, that of Lieutenant Hugh Clapperton, starting from Badagri, in the extreme southwest corner of present-day Nigeria, reached and crossed the Niger at Bussa, but it failed to recognize the Niger under its local name of the Quorra. The details of the course of the Niger were finally revealed by Richard Lemon Lander in 1830–1831.

Barrow's impact on the exploration and mapping of the Arctic, the Antarctic, and North Africa was immense. While he was made a baronet by William IV (r. 1830–1837) in 1835, more recently he has not been accorded due recognition.

[*See also* Franklin, John, *and* Northwest Passage.]

## Bibliography

### Primary Works

Barrow, John. *An Auto-Biographical Memoir of Sir John Barrow, Bart., Late of the Admiralty, Including Reflections, Observations, and Reminiscences at Home and Abroad, from Early Life to Advanced Age.* London: Murray, 1847.

Barrow, John. *A Chronological History of Voyages into the Arctic Regions.* London: Murray, 1818.

### Secondary Works

Fleming, Fergus. *Barrow's Boys.* London: Granta Books, 1998.

Lloyd, Christopher. *Mr. Barrow of the Admiralty: A Life of Sir John Barrow, 1764–1848.* London: Collins, 1970.

WILLIAM BARR

**Basilika.** *See* Law, *subentry on* Classical and Medieval Law.

**Battleship** The first modern battleship was arguably the French *Gloire* (1859), a wooden-hulled ship with iron armor and a broadside of numerous guns. She was countered at once by the British *Warrior*, whose iron hull enabled her to be much bigger and faster. Initially, guns got bigger and hence fewer in number while armor got thicker over a smaller part of the hull. For nearly a century, the battleship was the most expensive and technically advanced artifact in national armories.

From 1870 a few very big guns were mounted on turntables. Shortly afterward, the compound engine was introduced, the greatly improved fuel economy of which enabled sails to be dispensed with and hence crew numbers reduced. France led the way in steel hull construction (as opposed to iron) in *Redoutable* (1878). Steel was also used for engines, guns, and armor. Developments in explosives led to the need for longer gun barrels and hence breech loading. The next development came in the use of steel armor with a hardened face, nearly three times as effective as iron.

Until the introduction of the torpedo, the battleship was invulnerable to the weapons of other ships. By 1905 the torpedo had a range of about 9,100 meters (10,000 yards). This placed the emphasis on the big gun, and the British battleship *Dreadnought* was the first "all big gun ship." She triggered another race that led to much bigger ships with 15-inch guns. Battleship actions in World War I were few and inconclusive.

The major navies were ready for another race after the war, but the Washington Treaty (1922) imposed a moratorium and a size limit. When battleship building resumed in 1937, the emphasis was on protection against torpedoes and bombs, still within a 35,000-ton limit—though several navies cheated. By the end of World War II, the battleship's role was as an escort to the aircraft carrier. This was the end. The battleship died, not because it was vulnerable but because of its limited ability to hurt the enemy.

[*See also* Aircraft Carrier; *Dreadnought*; *and* Wars, Maritime, *subentry on* World Wars; and Warships, *subentry on* Modern Warships.]

**Bibliography**

Beeler, John. *Birth of the Battleship.* London: Chatham, 2001.
Brown, David K. *Before the Ironclad: Development of Ship Design, Propulsion, and Armament in the Royal Navy, 1815–1860.* London: Conway Maritime Press, 1990.
Brown, David K. *The Grand Fleet: Warship Design and Development, 1906–1922.* London: Chatham, 1999.
Brown, David K. *Nelson to Vanguard: Warship Design and Development, 1923–1945.* London: Chatham, 2000.
Brown, David K. *Warrior to Dreadnought: Warship Development, 1860–1905.* London: Chatham, 1997.
Friedman, Norman. *U.S. Battleships: An Illustrated Design History.* Annapolis, Md.: U.S. Naval Institute, 1985.
Lambert, Andrew. *Battleships in Transition.* London: Conway Maritime Press, 1984.
Raven, Alan, and John Roberts. *British Battleships of World War Two.* London: Arms and Armour Press, 1976.

DAVID K. BROWN

**Bazán, Álvaro de, Marqués de Santa Cruz** (1526–1588), admiral considered to be imperial Spain's greatest. Son of Álvaro de Bazán the elder, who commanded both Atlantic squadrons and Mediterranean galleys, Álvaro de Bazán was born at Granada on December 12, 1526. He served alongside his father and in 1543 fought the French at Muros Bay. In 1554 he sailed in the armada that took Philip of Spain to wed Mary Tudor of England. When his father died in 1555, he became commander of his father's Atlantic squadron. After war with France ended, Bazán turned to the war against Barbary corsairs and assembled in 1562 a galley squadron at Gibraltar. He blocked with cement and rock the corsair lair at Tetuan, and he participated in the capture of another corsair lair, that of Peñón Vélez de la Gomera. In 1565 he planned the relief of Malta, which was being besieged by the Turks. King Philip II promoted Bazán to command the thirty galleys of Naples, and in 1569 made him Marquis of Santa Cruz. Murals of Bazán's naval triumphs decorate his palace at Viso del Marqués in La Mancha.

In 1571, Bazán commanded the Holy League's rearguard at Lepanto, smashing an attempted Turkish rally to ensure the league's victory. In 1572 he captured a big Turkish galley, an episode related in *Don Quixote* by Lepanto veteran Miguel de Cervantes.

Like his father, Bazán was interested in warship construction, and he designed galleasses. In 1578 he took command of Spain's galley squadron, and he saved Tangier and Ceuta after the defeat of King Sebastian of Portugal in Morocco. For Philip's annexation of Portugal in 1580, Bazán assembled an armada at Cádiz and planned with the Duke of Alba, Philip's army commander, a combined operation for the capture of Lisbon. Alba invaded Portugal and met the armada at Setúbal. Alba's soldiers embarked, and Bazán ferried them to Cascais, downriver from Lisbon. Taken by surprise, Lisbon's defenders under Dom António, Philip's rival for the throne, hurried from prepared positions upriver and were routed by Alba, supported by Bazán's galleys. Bazán then corralled the Portuguese navy.

Dom António's supporters, aided by France and England, seized the Azores except for São Miguel. In July 1582 off São Miguel, Bazán—armed with twenty-five large ships, including two Portuguese galleons—encountered a French-Portuguese fleet of thirty large and more than thirty small vessels. On July 26 he fought the Atlantic's first major blue-water battle, combining gunfire and boarding tactics to win decisively. In 1583 he conquered the remaining Azores and then suggested to Philip that he invade England, backer of Philip's enemies. Philip shelved the suggestion and let the armada dwindle, but he made Bazán a grandee and Captain General of the Ocean Sea.

In 1585, war with England became open. Francis Drake attacked Vigo in Spain, then raided the Caribbean. Philip ordered Bazán to form a new armada to pursue Drake, and Philip asked Bazán to plan the attack of England. Bazán proposed an armada of 150 galleons and armed great ships, 6 galleasses, 40 galleys, and more than 300 transports and small craft. It would embark 55,000 infantry, 1,600 cavalry, and artillery and supplies to invade Ireland or England. Philip had another proposal from the duke of Parma, commander of the 35,000-strong army of Flanders. Poring over the plans, Philip reduced the size of the armada and debated whether it should land troops in Ireland or Wales, or should instead reinforce Parma's army and cover its crossing to Kent.

In April 1587, Drake struck Cádiz, disrupting Spanish preparations. Bazán sailed in pursuit too late. He covered the return of the treasure fleets, but autumn storms damaged his armada. In Lisbon he found orders to sail forthwith with 6,000 reinforcements to join Parma and cover Parma's invasion of England, rather than, as Bazán thought had been agreed, to make his own landings in Ireland or Wales. Bazán argued that damage repair, shortages, and wintry weather prevented his sailing. Many at court claimed that Bazán opposed the revised orders because he did not want to serve under Parma. Though investigation proved him right about the condition of the armada, Bazán's heath was failing, and he died in Lisbon on February 9, 1588. An aggressive and innovative commander, many believe that he might have succeeded with the armada that he had created.

[*See also* Cádiz; Lepanto, Battle of; Navies, Great Powers, *subentry on* Spain, 1500–1805; *and* Wars, Maritime, *subentry on* Anglo-Spanish Wars.]

### Bibliography

Altolaguirre y Duvale, Angel de. *Don Álvaro de Bazán, primer marqués de Santa Cruz de Mudela.* Madrid, Spain: Tip. de los Huérfanos, 1888.

Herrera Oria, Enrique. *Felipe II y el marqués de Santa Cruz en la empresa de Inglaterra.* Madrid, Spain: Instituto Histórico de Marina, 1946.

Pierson, Peter. "Thunderbolt of War." *MHQ: Quarterly Journal of Military History* 13, no. 4 (summer 2001): 54–63.

PETER PIERSON

## Beachy Head, Battle of

In November 1688, William (r. 1689–1702), Prince of Orange and statholder of the Dutch Republic, landed in England at the invitation of seven leading English politicians. King James II (r. 1685–1688) fled from England, first to France and then to Ireland. William of Orange, now William III, having accepted the English crown with his wife Mary (r. 1689–1694), James's daughter, declared war against France. The first sea battle of the War of the English Succession between the English and French fleets at Bantry Bay in May 1689 was a French victory.

In March 1690 the French had landed six thousand troops as reinforcements for James. With matters getting worse in Ireland, William decided to go to Ireland to take charge of the war, leaving Mary in London with a small council to assist and guide her. Admiral Arthur Herbert, Earl of Torrington (1648–1716), commanded the allied Anglo-Dutch fleet of fifty-eight ships, made up of thirty-six English ships and twenty-two Dutch ships commanded by Admiral Cornelius Evertsen (1642–1706). The French fleet of seventy ships, made up from the Brest and Toulon fleets, was commanded by Admiral Anne-Hilarion de Contentin, Comte de Tourville (1642–1701). Tourville's orders, drawn up by Jean-Baptiste Colbert, Marquis de Seignelay, the French naval minister, were to seek out and destroy the

**Beachy Head Commemorative Medal.** King Louis XIV issued this commemorative silver medal, sculpted by H. Roussel, in 1690. The reverse of the medal, shown here, shows a large trophy of sterns of stranded ships carrying Dutch and English flags and a standing winged Victory holding a wreath and a palm branch in her hands. © NATIONAL MARITIME MUSEUM, LONDON

allied fleet. This would leave the channel open for France to land troops in England and regain the throne for James.

## The Preparations

When the allied fleet saw the French fleet off the Isle of Wight on June 25, it was apparent that the French were stronger. Torrington's fleet was not at full strength; both the admiral and rear admiral of the blue squadron (Torrington's rear squadron) and thirty-nine ships were missing. Edward Russell (1652–1727), who had originally been appointed admiral of the blue squadron, had refused the appointment allegedly on grounds of ill health. Consequently, Henry Killigrew (1648–1712) had been appointed the admiral designate of the blue, but he was returning from the Mediterranean where his fourteen ships had been damaged by a storm. The rear admiral designate of the blue, Sir Cloudesley Shovell (1650–1707), who had twenty-five ships with him, had been delayed sailing from Ireland where he had escorted William III.

Torrington held a council of war of both the English and the Dutch flag officers on June 25, at which it was

decided not to fight, since the French were too strong, but to retire to the Gunfleet and to wait for Shovell and Killigrew to reinforce them. Torrington informed Queen Mary and her council of the council of war's decision. The allied fleet continued to shadow the French. On June 27, Queen Mary told Torrington that "you should upon any advantage of the wind give battle to the enemy," but also left it to his discretion to avoid the French fleet if he did not fight, and to sail westward toward Plymouth to await reinforcements. When Torrington received the queen's order on June 29, he called another council of war of the English and the Dutch admirals to discuss the queen's orders; a five-hour debate ensued, during which Admiral Evertsen made it clear that in his view the allies were not strong enough to fight the French. The council of war's decision was to obey Mary's orders and fight.

## The Engagement

June 30 was a fine day with a calm sea and a light northeasterly breeze. The Anglo-Dutch fleet formed into line of battle, with the Dutch as the white or vanguard squadron; the center was the red squadron, under Torrington and his vice admiral Sir John Ashby (1646–1693), as well as the rear admiral of the red, Sir George Rooke (c. 1650–1709). The rear was formed of the thirteen ships of the blue squadron under Rear Admiral Sir Ralph Delavall (1645–1707). The allied fleet sailed toward the French, who were drawn up in line of battle on the starboard tack. At 8:00 A.M. the two fleets were only three miles apart, and Torrington hoisted the red flag, which was the signal to engage. Because it was spread across the sea, the French center sagged in the middle of the line in the shape of a bow. With his longer line, Tourville probably intended to overlap the allies, but he was prevented by Torrington and his squadron sailing south toward the French rear, which was the weathermost and could have weathered the allied center and rear if left unengaged.

The Dutch under Evertsen continued toward the head of the French vanguard on the same course and at about 9:00 A.M. began their action. However, by steering for the head of the French vanguard, the Dutch opened up a gap between themselves and Torrington's fleet. The Dutch vanguard, commanded by Admiral Gerard Callenburg (1642–1722), anchored eight or nine ships short of the head of the French vanguard, commanded by Philippe de Villette-Mursay (1632–1707), which stretched ahead unengaged until it had enough room to double on the Dutch. Torrington's vice admiral of the red, Sir John Ashby, noticed the gap that the Dutch had created and sailed in an attempt to close the gap. Unfortunately, Ashby by this action opened up another gap between his squadron and the allied center.

Delavall led his thirteen ships making up Torrington's blue squadron under the fire of the French rear and began to fight at about 9.30 A.M. when he was within pistol shot, about 270 meters (300 yards). Delavall and his ships were very hotly engaged and managed to drive the French ships *Fleuron*, *Modeste*, and *Terrible* out of the French rear. Torrington and his squadron did not engage until nearly 10:00 A.M. but found it difficult to come to close quarters because of the sag in the French center. Instead, they opened fire at long range and continued to fight at long range. Nevertheless, the center under Torrington experienced heavy fighting, and most of his ships suffered casualties. Torrington's flagship *Royal Sovereign* had nine killed and thirty-three injured.

By 1:00 P.M. the Dutch were completely surrounded by the French and were suffering under heavy fire. At about the same time, Delavall and his ships of the blue squadron found themselves heavily engaged with the French center. At about 2:00 P.M., Torrington, seeing the Dutch in disorder and overpowered by the French, decided to try to support them, but the breeze died away. Torrington worked his way down to the Dutch, using his boats for a tow. At 4:00 P.M., with the tide on the ebb, Torrington signaled the Dutch to anchor, and they did so. The French were caught unawares and drifted away out of range. Then Torrington towed his ships between the heavily damaged Dutch and the French, who had anchored.

Over the next few days the allied fleet, pursued by the French, made its way up channel. The Dutch lost thirteen out of twenty-two ships. *Friezeland*, a Dutch 68-gun, had her decks covered with dead and wounded; only 120 of the original crew of 350 survived. Her timbers were so badly shattered that when she drifted into the French fleet they removed the survivors and burned the ship. The English lost only a third-rate, *Anne*, which was run aground near Hastings and was burned by her captain to avoid her being taken by the French.

## The Aftermath

This English-Dutch defeat meant that the French fleet under Tourville had control of the English Channel and could have either invaded England or cut William and his forces off from England. However, because of sickness in his fleet and a shortage of provisions, Tourville did not take advantage of his control of the Channel; neither did he have the troops necessary to invade. Instead, the French landed near Teignmouth in Devon, burned the town, and then returned to France, where Tourville was criticized for his actions.

The next day, July 1, 1690, William's decisive victory over the French at the Battle of the Boyne offset the allied naval defeat. The damaged allied ships were quickly repaired, and by August 1690 the allied fleet was back in control of the Channel by sheer numbers. In September 1690 a naval expedition captured the important ports of Cork and Kinsale. Torrington became a scapegoat for the Dutch; he was tried by a naval court-martial in December 1690 and was acquitted. The defeat at Beachy Head was avenged two years later in May 1692 when Edward Russell, commanding a vastly superior force (ninety-nine allied ships to the forty-four ships of the French fleet, again commanded by Tourville), defeated and burned the French ships at the battle of Cape Barfleur on the northeast tip of the Cherbourg Peninsula. Torrington's "a fleet in being"—a fleet kept virtually intact that by its very presence would prevent an enemy fleet from invading—became a key concept in naval thought.

[*See also* Chatham; Evertsen Family; Intelligence; Navies, Great Powers, *subentries on* British Isles, 1500 to the Present, Dutch Republic, 1577–1714, *and* France, 1660 to the Present; Tourville, Anne-Hilarion de Cotentin de; *and* Wars, Maritime, *subentry on* Anglo-French Wars.]

## Bibliography

Black, Jeremy. *Britain as a Military Power, 1688–1815*. London: UCL Press, 2000.

Bruijn, Jaap R. *The Dutch Navy of the Seventeenth and Eighteenth Centuries*. Columbia: University of South Carolina Press, 1993.

Ehrman, John. *The Navy in the War of William III, 1689–97: Its State and Direction*. Cambridge, U.K.: Cambridge University Press, 1953. Though it needs replacing because of later research, it is still the best account of naval administration for William's reign.

Harding, Richard. *Seapower and Naval Warfare, 1650–1830*. Annapolis, Md.: Naval Institute Press, 1999. Excellent account of the development and use of the battle fleet.

Lee, C. D. "The Battle of Beachy Head: Lord Torrington's Conduct." *Mariner's Mirror* 80 (1994): 270–289. Presents a different view of Beachy Head.

Le Fevre, Peter. "Arthur Herbert, Earl of Torrington, 1648–1716: 'A Fine Man … Both in Courage and Conduct.' " In *Precursors of Nelson: British Admirals of the Eighteenth Century*, edited by Peter Le Fevre and Richard Harding, pp. 19–41. London: Chatham, 2000. An important reappraisal of a major naval figure of William III's reign.

Le Fevre, Peter. " 'Meer Laziness' or Incompetence: The Earl of Torrington and the Battle of Beachy Head." *Mariner's Mirror* 80 (1994): 290–298. Challenges the view in Lee and argues that circumstances were responsible.

Peter, Jean. *Le duel entre Tourville et Seignelay: Beveziers et Plymouth* (1690). Paris: Economica, 2001.

Symcox, Geoffrey. *The Crisis of French Sea Power, 1688–1697: From the Guerre d'Escadre to the Guerre de Course.* The Hague: Martinus Nijhoff, 1974. The orthodox view of French naval strategy.

Tunstall, Brian, and Tracy Nicholas, eds. *Naval Warfare in the Age of Sail: The Evolution of Fighting Tactics, 1650–1815.* Annapolis, Md.: Naval Institute Press, 1990. Good account of the development of sailing and fighting instructions.

PETER LE FEVRE

## *Beagle*, barque, three masts.

Length/beam/draft: 27.5 m × 7.5 m × 3.8 m (90.3′ × 24.5′ × 12.5′). Tonnage: 235 builder's measurement. Hull: wood. Complement: 75. Armament: 5 × 6-pounders, 2 × 9-pounders. Designer: Sir Henry Peake. Built: Woolwich Dockyard, England, 1820.

*Beagle* was the Royal Navy hydrographic survey ship in which Charles Darwin (1809–1882) embarked on a circumnavigation of the world from 1831 to 1836. It was on this voyage that Darwin made those observations that laid the foundation for his theories of evolution and natural selection—theories that helped redirect the course of modern scientific thought. Darwin's presence on this voyage of *Beagle* was fortuitous. It was customary for such expeditions to include naturalists, and the twenty-one-year-old botany student was recommended with faint praise. He was not, according to his teacher, a "finished naturalist, but … amply qualified for collecting, observing, and noting, anything new to be noted in Natural History." Darwin did not publish *On the Origin of Species* until 1859, but he commented that "The voyage in the *Beagle* has been by far the most important event in my life and has determined the whole of my existence."

The voyage with Darwin was *Beagle*'s second. Her first (1826–1830), to the waters around Patagonia, was so stressful that her commander killed himself and command fell to Robert FitzRoy, under whom Darwin also sailed. While the ship was engaged in coastal surveys of Brazil and Argentina, including the Beagle Channel south of Tierra del Fuego, Darwin worked ashore. His study of fossils in Argentina first suggested to him a relationship between living and extinct species, and it was during a one-month stay in the Galápagos Islands 600 miles west of Ecuador that Darwin encountered the thirteen species of finches whose distinctive beaks pointed the way toward a theory of natural selection. Departing the Galápagos, *Beagle* conducted additional surveys across the Pacific to New Zealand and Australia, and then surveys in the Indian Ocean en route back to England. *Beagle*'s last voyage (1837–1843) took her back to Australia, where her commander, John Lort Stokes, named the Fitzroy River and the settlement of Darwin. In so honoring his former shipmates, Stokes observed that "monuments may crumble, but a name endures as long as the world."

In 1845, *Beagle* became the stationary *Beagle Watch Vessel* of the Preventive Service, a forerunner of Britain's Maritime and Coastguard Agency. She was broken up in about 1870.

[*See also* Barque.]

### Bibliography

Barlow, Nora, ed. *Diary of the Voyage of H.M.S. "Beagle."* Works of Charles Darwin, Vol. 1. New York: New York University Press, 1988.

Basalla, George. "The Voyage of the *Beagle* without Darwin." *Mariner's Mirror* 43 (1962): 42–48.

Darling, Lois. "HMS *Beagle*: Further Research or Twenty Years A-Beagling." *Mariner's Mirror* 64 (1978): 315–325.

FitzRoy, R., and P. P. King. *Narrative of the Surveying Voyages of His Majesty's Ships "Adventure" and "Beagle" between the Years 1826 and 1836, Describing Their Examination of the Southern Shores of South America and the "Beagle"'s Circumnavigation of the Globe.* 3 vols. London: Henry Colburn, 1839.

Thomson, Keith S. *HMS "Beagle": The Story of Darwin's Ship.* New York: Norton, 1995.

LINCOLN P. PAINE

## Beaufort, Francis

(1774–1857), British rear admiral and hydrographer. Francis Beaufort was born on May 27, 1774, in Navan, County Meath, Ireland. His father, Daniel Augustus Beaufort, was the rector of Navan. Beaufort's formal education may have been limited to three years as a day pupil at Master Bates Military and Marine Academy in Dublin and five months at Trinity College, Dublin, where he studied astronomy. His seagoing career began in 1789 in the East Indiaman *Vansittart*, in which he assisted in his first survey work, of the Gaspar Strait (present-day Kelasa Strait, Indonesia) for the East India Company. Service in several Royal Navy frigates followed his appointment as a midshipman in 1790. In 1805, Beaufort developed his system of standardized descriptions for recording the wind and weather; the first records in his code are in his log for January 13, 1806.

Promoted to captain in 1810, Beaufort surveyed the southern coast of Asia Minor in 1810–1812. This survey was brought to an abrupt close when he was severely wounded by armed Turks. Ashore, he published the results of this survey in *Karamania* in 1817. Nominated by Richard Edgeworth and supported by Sir Joseph Banks, Beaufort was elected a fellow of the Royal Society in July 1814; Beaufort was also a fellow of the Royal Astronomical Society from 1829, the year of the society's founding.

Beaufort became Hydrographer of the Navy in 1829. He issued precise instructions for surveys and minutely scrutinized the results before authorizing them for publication. He standardized the design of the Admiralty Chart, and he nurtured the connection between navy and civilian scientists. Both the naturalist Charles Darwin (1809–1882) and the biologist Thomas Huxley (1825–1895) began their careers under Beaufort's auspices. He published the first corrections to charts in the *Admiralty Notices to Mariners*.

Now Beaufort could order reporting that used his wind scale and weather notes, first by his own ships, and then in 1835 by all the ships of the fleet. Although the Meteorological Office was set up only later under the Board of Trade, these reports started the data bank on which all weather forecasting is based.

In his long reign, Beaufort became a national and international authority on an ever-widening range of marine and scientific subjects. He was involved with the mounting of the disastrous expedition of Sir John Franklin to the Arctic (1845–1847) and, when it disappeared, the attempts to discover the expedition's fate.

Placed on the retired list and promoted to rear admiral on October 1, 1846, Beaufort became Knight Commander of the Bath (KCB) on April 28, 1848. When the Crimean War broke out in 1854, Beaufort was worn out, having served as hydrographer for twenty-five years. He submitted his resignation, but he was persuaded to continue in office for a last year, finally retiring in January 1855. He died on December 17, 1857, at Brighton and was buried at Saint John-at-Hackney Church, London.

[*See also* Hydrographical Departments *and* Meteorology.]

## Bibliography

Courtney, Nicholas. *Gale Force 10: The Life and Legacy of Admiral Beaufort, 1774–1857*. London: Review, 2002.

Friendly, Alfred. *Beaufort of the Admiralty: The Life of Sir Francis Beaufort 1774–1857*. New York: Random House, 1977.

Ritchie, George Stephen. *The Admiralty Chart: British Naval Hydrography in the Nineteenth Century*. New ed. Edinburgh, U.K.: Pentland Press, 1995.

ROGER O. MORRIS

# Beautemps-Beaupré, Charles-François

(1766–1854), French hydrographer. Charles-François Beautemps-Beaupré was born in La Neuville-au-Pont, a small town in Champagne, on August 6, 1766. His father was a hatter and his mother belonged to a family of farmers, yet Beautemps-Beaupré's cousin, Jean-Nicolas Buache (1741–1825), held the position of first geographer of the king. Beautemps-Beaupré began studying cartography around 1780 in Paris and Versailles. Under the direction of Buache and Charles-Pierre Claret de Fleurieu (1738–1810), deputy inspector of the Dépôt des Cartes et Plans de la Marine, Beautemps-Beaupré drew charts for Jean François de Galaup, Comte de La Pérouse (1741–1788) for his exploratory voyage to the Pacific (1785–1788).

Appointed surveyor to the Dépôt in 1785, Beautemps-Beaupré prepared charts for Antoine-Raymond-Joseph Bruni d'Entrecasteaux (1737–1793), whose voyage (1791–1793) was in search of the missing La Pérouse. Beautemps-Beaupré served as hydrographer during d'Entrecasteaux's voyage and did the surveying for many charts, mainly in New Holland (Australia) and Van Diemen's Land (Tasmania). He used a new method, derived from the reflecting circle of Jean-Charles de Borda (1733–1799). Making more than one astronomical observation at the same time gave very accurate latitude and longitude. The method, and astronomical bearings made by calculating angular distances between the sun and landmarks, were used for the first time during a voyage with great reliability. Graphically and in real time, the geodesy and the astronomy were checked and the charts drawn up quickly.

Intercepted by the British navy off Saint Helena on June 10, 1795, Beautemps-Beaupré's charts inspired the Admiralty to send Matthew Flinders for the first voyage around Van Diemen's Land (1798–1799). When Beautemps-Beaupré returned to Europe he became Napoleon Bonaparte's hydrographer. Then emperor, Napoleon sent Beautemps-Beaupré to survey the coasts of France's empire where projects of naval dockyards were in progress: the eastern coast of the North Sea in Antwerp and on the Schelde River, the eastern coast of the Adriatic, and the southern coast of the Baltic. There he did the surveying for secret charts

(1799–1814) for Napoleon—large-scale manuscripts with many colors, details, and formats. These charts were given to the nations that participated in the Congress of Vienna (1815), and the charts were engraved and published several years later both in France and in other countries.

Beautemps-Beaupré taught practical surveying to engineers and naval officers, and he published a manual of hydrography, *Exposé des méthodes employées pour lever et construire les cartes et plans* (1808), which was translated by Captain Richard Copeland of the British navy and published under the title *An Introduction to the Practice of Nautical Surveying, and the Construction of Sea-Charts* (1823). Elected to the Institut de France on September 24, 1810, Beautemps-Beaupré was appointed deputy hydrographer on June 6, 1814. From 1816 to 1843 he surveyed the west coast of France, completing twenty surveys in twenty-three years and covering 4,020 kilometers (about 2,500 miles). The resulting charts, published in the *Pilote français* (1823–1843, 6 volumes, 146 charts), were among the most elegant and sophisticated ever made, using advanced position and sounding devices. Beautemps-Beaupré was appointed hydrographer to the Dépôt Général de la Marine on January 14, 1826. Even during his lifetime he was considered the father of modern hydrography because of his new methods, explained in the *Exposé des travaux relatifs à la reconnaissance hydrographique des côtes occidentales de France* (1829). Beautemps-Beaupré died on March 16, 1854, in Paris.

[*See also* Hydrographical Departments; Marine Science Instruments; *and* Navigational Instruments.]

## Bibliography

Chapuis, Olivier. *À la mer comme au ciel: Beautemps-Beaupré et la naissance de l'hydrographie moderne, ou l'Émergence de la précision en navigation et dans la cartographie marine (1700–1850)*. Paris: Presses de l'Université de Paris-Sorbonne, 1999.

OLIVIER CHAPUIS

# Behaim, Martin  (1459–1507), German cartographer.
Behaim descended from a family of merchants established in Nuremberg, Germany, since the fourteenth century. About 1484 he went to Lisbon on a trade mission, where he became known as Martinho of Bohemia. There he married Joana de Macedo, daughter of Jobst von Hürter, a Fleming, captain-donatary (or grant-holder) in the Azorean islands of Pico and Faial.

Little is known of Behaim's activities in Portugal, but he was probably a commercial correspondent. The chronicler João de Barros stated in his work *Décadas da Ásia* (Decades of Asia, 1552) that Behaim was a counselor to King João II, and that he had been a disciple of John Regiomontanus. Nineteenth-century historians ascribed major contributions to Behaim, but Ernest Ravenstein, who wrote the most complete biography, *Martin Behaim: His Life and His Globe* (1908), raised serious doubts about the veracity of these accounts and also about the claim that Behaim had introduced the astrolabe (an instrument used to observe and calculate the position of celestial bodies) to navigation. Indeed, from *De rebus gestis Joannis II*, by Manuel Telles da Silva, Marquis of Alegrete, it can be deduced that this instrument was already in use in 1481, before Behaim reached Portugal. Also questionable is whether Behaim participated in any of the voyages in which Diogo Cão reached the mouth of the Congo River in 1482–1488—a doubt suggested by Hartmann Schedel in *Chronicle of the World* (1493).

What is certain is that Behaim collected and transcribed *Da prima Inventione Guinee*, recording the oral memories of the Portuguese pilot Diogo Gomes of the discoveries along the coast of Africa in the mid-fifteenth century. These writings were included in *The Manuscript of Valentim Fernandes*, a German printer established in Portugal.

In 1490 Behaim returned to Nuremberg, where he became involved in the construction of a globe, paid for by the town council. For this purpose he used knowledge of the geography of Africa from the time of Ptolemy (c. 90–c. 168) up to the time of Bartolomeu Dias (c. 1450–1500). Behaim's elongated representation of the African continent has some similarities to that drawn in 1489 by Henricus Martelus, but there are differences suggesting a contemporary Portuguese understanding of African geography. The globe has a diameter of 508 millimeters (20 inches) and is located at the German National Museum in Nuremberg. It is a highly important visual record of the European image of the world just before Christopher Columbus's voyages. Behaim left Nuremberg in 1496 to return to Lisbon, where he died in 1507.

[*See also* Cartography.]

## Bibliography

Alegrete, Manuel Telles da Silva, marquez de. *De rebus gestis Joannis II*. Lisbon, 1689.
Baião, António, ed. *O Manuscrito Valentim Fernandes*. Lisbon: Editorial Atica, 1940.

Barros, João de. *Décadas da Ásia*. Lisbon, 1552.

Morris, John Gottlieb. *Martin Behaim: The German Astronomer and Cosmographer*. Baltimore: Maryland Historical Society, 1955.

Ravenstein, Ernest George. *Martin Behaim: His Life and His Globe*. London: Philip, 1908.

Schedel, Hartmann. *Chronicle of the World*. Originally published in 1493. New York: Taschen, 2001.

A. Estácio dos Reis

# *Belgica* (1884–1940), three-rigged barque.

Length: 34.6 m. Molded breadth: 7.158 m. Extreme breadth: 7.540 m. Depth: 4.090 m. Mean draft on ballast: 2.743 m. Full-load draft: 3.962 m. Light displacement: 338 m3. Loaded displacement: 598 m3. Registered tonnage: 172 tons. Auxiliary engine: 35 nominal horsepower. Speed: 7 knots.

*Belgica* was used for the Belgian Antarctic expedition of 1897–1899 led by Adrien Victor Joseph de Gerlache de Gomery (1866–1934). Trapped in the pack ice of the Bellingshausen Sea, *Belgica* was the first ship to winter successfully in the Antarctic. Formerly the Norwegian *Patria*, *Belgica* was built at Selvig near Drammen, Norway, by Christian Jacobsen, and was first used as a sealer or whaler. For the Antarctic expedition, the ship's hull was covered by a lining of greenheart that protected her from ice floes. The construction of the bow made *Belgica* able to climb onto the ice and break it with her weight. The stem was reinforced and protected by hoops of cast iron. The vessel was equipped with an auxiliary engine manufactured at Nylands Værksted in Oslo and was barque rigged. She had two decks, of which the first was a full deck. When Gerlache bought the *Patria* for his Antarctic expedition, he renamed her *Belgica*, and from 1896 she flew the Belgian colors. Because she had been purchased for a specific scientific expedition in polar seas, she underwent a lifting in Sandefjord, Norway, at Christensen's shipyard, to offer housing not only to the crew, but also to a scientific team able to live and work on board during an expedition expected to last a couple of years.

Gerlache, a junior naval officer, took the initiative for the expedition, which he planned himself and of which he was commander. Second in command was George Lecointe (1869–1929), a lieutenant of artillery in the Belgian army, who was also appointed as the expedition's hydrographer. The second mate was the Norwegian Roald Amundsen (1872–1928), who later became a famous polar explorer in his own right. The third mate was Jules Melaerts (1876–?), while Henri Somers (1863–?) and Max van Rysselberghe (1878–?) were chief engineer and second engineer, respectively. All of them, except the Norwegian Amundsen, were Belgian citizens. The scientific team was more international. Henryk Arctowski (1871–1958) was a Polish geologist, oceanographer, and meteorologist. The American Frederick Albert Cook (1865–1940) was both the expedition's surgeon and its photographer. A Belgian lieutenant of artillery, Emile Danco (1869–1898), was in charge of geophysical research, but he died during the expedition. The Polish Antoine Dubrowolski (1872–1954) was assistant meteorologist, while the Romanian Emile-Georges Racovitza (1868–1947) was the expedition's zoologist and botanist. Of the rest of the initial crew—only eight hands—three were Belgians, while the other five were Norwegians.

The expedition started from Antwerp on August 16, 1897, and was supported by the Belgian Royal Society of Geography. After exploring the northwest coast of the Antarctic Peninsula, *Belgica* was beset in the ice from March 4, 1898, and the crew was forced to winter on board. A year later, on March 14, 1899, *Belgica* finally got free and set course to Antwerp, where she arrived on November 5, 1899. The results of this successful expedition were published in ten volumes that dealt with hydrography, astronomy, magnetical observations, meteorology, oceanography, geology, zoology and botany, physiology, and anthropology. The expedition was the beginning of Belgium's interest in exploring Antarctica, a tradition that continues today.

Philippe, Duke of Orleans, bought *Belgica* in 1905 for hunting polar bears near Greenland. Still flying the Belgian colors and still commanded by Gerlache, *Belgica* was used for several expeditions to the North Pole (1905), to the Barents and Kara Sea (1907), and to Greenland, Spitsbergen, and Franz Josef Land (1909).

In 1915 the Norwegian firm Kristian Holst at Harstad bought *Belgica*. Renamed *Isfjord*, she was used to supply mineworkers on Spitsbergen and to transport fish and coal. In 1930, *Isfjord* was used as a barge at the Lofoten Islands. In 1940, the British expeditionary corps in Norway claimed the ship, using her for the storage of highly explosive shells. But the same year, bombed by the Luftwaffe, *Isfjord* sank at Harstad. *Isfjord*'s wreck was localized by archaeologists in 2006.

[*See also* Antarctica and the Southern Ocean.]

## Bibliography

Cook, Frederick A. *Through the First Antarctic Night, 1898–1899: Centennial Edition with Selected Photos from the Original*

*Edition and Recent Color Photos from Antarctica*. Pittsburgh, Pa.: Polar Publishing, 1998.

Gerlache de Gomery, Adrien de. *Voyage of the "Belgica": Fifteen Months in the Antarctic*. Translated by Maurice Raraty. Banham, U.K.: Erskine Press; Bluntisham, U.K.: Bluntisham Books, 1998.

Decleir, Hugo, and Claude De Broyer, eds. *The "Belgica" Expedition Centennial: Perspectives on Antarctic Science and History, Proceedings of the "Belgica" Centennial Symposium, 14–16 May 1998*. Brussels: VUB Brussels University Press, 2001.

CHRISTIAN KONINCKX

**Bergen** A populated area situated on the west coast of Norway, Bergen was given town status by King Olaf III Haraldsson (Olaf Kyrre) in 1070. The reason for this royal interest was Bergen's role in the growing foreign trade, especially in fishing products. As early as the Viking age, Bergen was a center of trade across the North Sea. From the eleventh century Europe's population grew, and the fasting rules of the church created a market for dried fish, Norway's first large-scale export product. Bergen's geographical location—conveniently linking the sailing route to the northern fishing ground with the British Isles and northern continental Europe—made the town a busy emporium for the new trade. In 1217, King Håkon IV Håkonsson signed a trade agreement with England, giving the merchants of both countries the right to carry on trade and sea transport between the two kingdoms. Bergen trade and shipping flourished, and in 1248 the English monk Matthew Paris reported that two hundred or more ships could be seen together at one time in its safe and spacious harbor.

In the beginning, Bergen's maritime trade was dominated by Norwegian and English merchants. Bergen's English counterpart was the town of King's Lynn in Norfolk because of its ability to meet the Norwegian demand for grain and malt. From the middle of the thirteenth century, Bergen's export of fish to the German Baltic cities, especially Lübeck, grew in importance, and Baltic rye gradually replaced English wheat in Bergen's import trade. By prohibiting all foreigners from trading north of Bergen (c. 1310), the king strengthened the town's hegemony in Norwegian foreign trade. However, German merchants ignored the royal decree, started to settle permanently in Bergen, and took over by force more and more of the town's commerce and trade, especially after the onset of the Black Death in 1349. The self-governing German colony was situated at the waterfront in the oldest part of town, in the Middle Ages known as Bryggen ("the Wharf"; now designated a World Heritage site by the United Nations). Sometime before 1360, a German Kontor (office) was opened in Bergen under the protection of the Hanseatic League, controlled by the Hanseatic town of Lübeck. The Germans dominated Bergen's trade and commerce through their control of the import of grain and salt. They also controlled the export of stockfish and had a monopoly of trade with northern Norway. However, the Germans faced constant competition from English, Scottish, and Dutch merchants.

In the fifteenth century the power of the Germans in Bergen reached its peak. Bergen's position as a northern European seafaring and trading center was, however, in no way reduced. By means of Hanseatic trade and shipping, Bergen grew to a seafaring town of European dimensions. A considerable fleet of German ships carried Norwegian stockfish to steadily expanding markets.

The power of the Hansa began to weaken in the sixteenth century, and independent Bergen citizens began to challenge Hanseatic domination in trade and commerce. The basic cargo in this renewal of Bergen activity was primarily herring. The herring fisheries expanded vigorously and, for this commodity, the Hanse could claim no privileged rights.

The voyages of exploration led to the establishment of new markets for shipping and trade, and the tide of wealth from the New World had an impact on Bergen's trade. In 1616 the Danish East India Company was founded, and Bergen citizens had powerful interests in the company. During this period, the whaling expeditions to the Artic were also equipped from Bergen, and trade and shipping prospered. In 1638 the Danish-Norwegian king Christian IV deemed the traffic of Bergen to be at times greater than that of Copenhagen.

In the sixteenth and seventeenth century, in order to strengthen its own economic position the royal power favored the establishment and growth of a new Norwegian citizenry that could compete with the Hanseatic merchants. These citizens were not only of Norwegian origin but also included people from Denmark, Holland, England, and Scotland who had immigrated to Bergen, which was considered a town of commercial opportunity. By restricting the trading privileges of the German Kontor and other foreigners, the king made it possible for the new citizenry to prosper. Thus from the middle of the sixteenth century the German Kontor gradually lost its power; the Germans either returned to their homeland or integrated with the town's collective economic life. The Bergen Hanseatic Kontor lived on and became the longest surviving of all the Hanseatic Kontors. In 1754 it was replaced by a Norwegian Kontor, which existed until 1898.

The English Navigation Laws of 1651 had a favorable effect on Bergen's shipping, since trade between Norway and the British Isles had to be carried out by British or Norwegian ships; their most important competitors—the Dutch—were thus excluded. Bergen's merchants began to regard ships as a good investment. During and after the War of Spanish Succession (1701–1714) and the Great Nordic War (1700–1721), Bergen's trade and shipping went through a period of great fluctuations with many setbacks. The Seven Years' War (1756–1763) had a similar effect upon the Bergen fleet: domestic shipping increased and foreign shipping declined.

All this changed as a result of the American Revolution and the Napoleonic Wars. From 1777 to 1807, when Denmark and Norway became involved in warfare, Bergen's shipping experienced a new, marked period of prosperity. By 1806, Bergen had become Norway's largest seafaring town, with 306 ships that handled 10,600 commercial loads. But the war years of 1807 to 1815 and the postwar depression almost halved Bergen's shipping.

The great turning point and breakthrough for Bergen shipping came in the 1850s, when Norwegian shipping began to be employed to a greater degree in transport between foreign ports. The demand for tonnage increased because of the new mass-production industries in Europe, the abolition of the Navigation Laws, and the Crimean War. Norway became one of the major carriers of the world. In the country's transition from sail to steam, Bergen took the lead. Shipping had been a sideline to trading in Bergen during the days of the sailing ships; now ship owning became a profession. At the same time, the city's maritime business diversified with the establishment of several shipbuilding enterprises.

Prior to World War I, shipping in Bergen differed from Norwegian shipping in general. As early as 1883, Bergen had more steamship than sail-ship tonnage; for Norway as a whole this was not the case until the beginning of the twentieth century. From 1870 to 1900, Bergen enjoyed the financial resources and technical expertise that were essential for a changeover from sail to steam, a process that accelerated after the opening of the Suez Canal. England had shown the way, and Bergen—traditionally looking westward—soon followed suit. The transition to steam did not, however, lead to major change in the traditional structure of the Bergen fleet; the tramp trade continued to be the main activity of the fleet, and part-ownership and single-ship companies were the rule.

The Bergen fleet was reduced by more than one-fourth during World War I. The rebuilding of the Norwegian shipping industry after the war was marked by a new transition: the changeover from steam to motor liners and tankers. In this case, Bergen lagged behind and was replaced by Oslo as the growth center of Norwegian shipping. Bergen's slow progress is explained by its lack of large multiship companies able to afford large capital investment. Ships registered in Bergen were for the most part steamers sailing in tramp trades. Because liners and tankers were less vulnerable to fluctuations on the world market than tramp freighters were, the Bergen fleet was harder hit by the two major crises of the interwar period than the remainder of the Norwegian merchant fleet was. The weakness of Bergen's shipping was, then, both organizational (single-ship ownership) and structural (tramp ship).

Bergen's shipping suffered heavy losses during World War II. The restoration of the Norwegian merchant fleet in general and that of Bergen in particular led to the final break with the old form of organization within the shipping industry. In order to raise the capital to rebuild, limited liability joint-stock companies became the natural economic form of organization, and greater continuity and better use of capital was achieved through the formation of multiship companies. Consequently, joint ownership and single-ship ownership gradually disappeared. Following the war Bergen had to cater to increasingly larger and more specialized ships. In the early twenty-first century Bergen was a leading shipper of chemicals and liquid gas.

[See also Hanseatic League.]

### Bibliography

Volumes 1–5 of *Bergen og sjøfarten* (Bergen, Norway: Bergens Sjøfartsmuseum): Bernt Lorentzen, *Fra Olav Kyrres tid til året 1814* (1959); Johs. B. Thue, *Skipsfart og kjøpmannskap, 1800–1860* (1980); Lauritz Pettersen, *Fra kjøpmannsrederi til selvstendig næring, 1860–1914* (1981); Atle Thowsen, *Vekst og strukturendringer i krisetider, 1914–1939* (1983); and Tore Nilsen, *Mot nye utfordringer, 1939–1973* (2001).

ATLE THOWSEN

# Bergen, Claus

**Bergen, Claus** (1885–1964), German marine artist. The son of the illustrator Fritz Bergen (1857–1941), he was born in Stuttgart on April 18, 1885. After a private education he was accepted at the Munich Royal Academy, where the American-German landscape artist Carl von Marr (1858–1936) and the marine artist Hans von Bartels (1856–1913) were among his most influential teachers.

Bergen started his career as an illustrator of Karl May's travel books. From 1908 to 1913 he traveled to Cornwall five times to paint the fishing village of Polperro.

During World War I he was able to avoid military service and instead painted naval actions in the North Sea and the Atlantic. When the High Sea Fleet returned from the Battle of Jutland (May 31–June 1, 1916), he was in Wilhelmshaven and used officers' accounts as sources for his paintings, but he was never officially appointed as a war artist. In January 1917 thirty-seven of his works were displayed in Wilhelmshaven. The same year he was allowed to join Lieutenant Commander Hans Rose of *U-53* on one of his patrols. In 1924, Bergen was invited by the North German Lloyd shipping company to sail on the maiden voyage of *Columbus*, and in 1926 he received a commission from the Deutsches Museum in Munich to paint twelve large canvases depicting the *Die Entdeckung der Erde* (The Discovery of the Globe). That same year he sailed on the battleship *Hessen* to the Mediterranean and went aboard the yacht *Amida* on her voyage to New York, where he presented his paintings at the Gainsborough Galleries, and then he also exhibited his work in Chicago.

Bergen's fame as an excellent war painter helped him to get many commissions during the Third Reich (he joined the Nazi Party in 1922–1923 and again in 1932). He illustrated books about the navy in World War II and was invited by Admiral Karl Dönitz to his headquarters in France. Between 1937 and 1944 thirteen of his paintings were exhibited at the Nazi propaganda show at the Haus der Deutschen Kunst in Munich. Although Hitler liked Bergen's work and bought some of his paintings for the Reich's Chancellery, he rejected requests by Admiral Erich Raeder and Admiral Dönitz to give Bergen the title of professor. Bergen's appointment as professor by the Bavarian king in 1918 remained invalid because of the turmoil following the armistice.

His propaganda canvases (such as the large painting *Gegen Engelland*), which were intended to decorate a commemorative hall dedicated to submarine warfare, were confiscated by U.S. occupation forces in 1945 because they were considered to glorify war, and for a short period he was not allowed to paint in his studio. Other paintings, like *Skagerrak*, originally displayed in the naval school at Flensburg-Mürwik, were confiscated by British occupation forces and are now part of the collection of the National Maritime Museum in Greenwich. Bergen's *U-Boat on a Mission* hung in the war room of the Headquarters of the Commander, Submarine Force, Atlantic Fleet, in Norfolk,

Virginia, until 1978, when the Americans returned war art to Germany. In 1963, Bergen presented his painting *Atlantic* to President John F. Kennedy.

After 1945, Bergen concentrated at first on nonmilitary motifs–quite a number of scenes from his sketchbook from Polperro were turned into paintings–but before his death he returned to naval topics. He died of blood poisoning in Garmisch, Bavaria, on October 4, 1964. Bergen undoubtedly was one of the most eminent German marine artists of the twentieth century. Although his fame was based mainly on his war art, his nonmilitary output is also impressive. The German Maritime Museum in Bremerhaven staged the first comprehensive exhibition of his work in 1982. The museum and the Bavarian community of Lenggries, where the artist's estate is deposited, hold the largest collection of his paintings in public ownership.

[*See also* Art, *subentry on* An Overview, *and* Artists, *subentry* German.]

## Bibliography

Herzog, Bodo. *Claus Bergen: Leben und Werk.* Gräfelfing, Germany: Urbes, 1987.

Hormann, Jörg M., and Eberhard Kliem. *Claus Bergen: Marinemaler über vier Epochen.* Hamburg, Germany: Koehler, 2002.

Meyer-Friese, Boye. *Marinemalerei in Deutschland im 19. Jahrhundert.* Oldenburg, Germany: Stalling, 1981.

Scholl, Lars U. *Claus Bergen, 1885–1964: Marinemalerei im 20. Jahrhundert.* Bremerhaven, Germany: Oltmanns and Burfeind, 1982.

LARS U. SCHOLL

# Berthoud, Ferdinand

**Berthoud, Ferdinand** (1727–1807), Swiss clock maker who developed a superior marine chronometer. Ferdinand Berthoud was born on March 19, 1727, at Plancemont in Switzerland. In 1741, he was apprenticed to his brother, Jean-Henri, a clock maker. Four years later he moved to Paris and tried to make marine chronometers, because that was the most difficult–and most lucrative–challenge in clock making in the mid-eighteenth century. He wrote *Essai sur l'horlogerie* (1763) for the French navy, because the government saw a need for the training of new clock makers and he was recognized as an excellent instructor. Berthoud was not satisfied with his early chronometers, but, under the direction of François-Louis de Goimpy and Jean Chappe d'Auteroche, his third clock was tested at sea in 1764 in the corvette *Hirondelle*, during the first French voyage to test chronometers. The test was unsuccessful, but Berthoud corrected his work and delivered an improved clock to Chappe d'Auteroche for his voyage to California in 1768.

In 1766 Berthoud was given the exclusive commission to furnish the French navy with chronometers (his eighth design) for an important voyage under the command of Charles-Pierre Claret de Fleurieu and Alexandre-Gui Pingré in the frigate *Isis* (1768–1769). Again the clock's performance was disappointing. Still, Berthoud was successful in marketing it, thanks to effective advertising and the protection of the very powerful Fleurieu. With the financial resources provided by the navy's commission, Berthoud was able to produce more chronometers than even his main rival, Pierre Le Roy (1717–1785), the inventor of the free escapement chronometer and the real father of modern French clock making. This success was important in an era when England led the production and technology of marine timekeeping instruments. Neither Berthoud nor any other French clock maker could develop a chronometer that was simpler and cheaper than the British models.

At the end of the eighteenth century the main problem for the French was that their chronometers were too fragile. The government therefore wanted new clock makers to be trained in the up-to-date British techniques. Berthoud became involved in that task by publishing several books (although he did not reveal all his secrets of clock making). In his *Traité des horloges marines* (1773)—as Fleurieu did at the same time in his *Voyage fait par ordre du roi en 1768 et 1769, à différentes parties du monde, pour éprouver en mer les horloges marines inventées par Monsieur Ferdinand Berthoud* (1773)—Berthoud wrote of the importance of marine chronometers, not only for finding longitude at sea but also for surveying new charts with more accuracy. Fleurieu had previously written about the topic in his *Nouvelle carte réduite de l'océan Atlantique ou Occidental* (1772), in which he recorded longitudinal distances with remarkable accuracy. Berthoud's reputation as a theorist of navigational timekeeping grew with the publication of *Les longitudes par la mesure du temps* (1775), directly inspired by Fleurieu's book.

Although the exportation of chronometers was restricted to friendly nations, the French government promoted free circulation of the technical knowledge as a way to recruit apprentice clock makers. After a long period of secret research, clock making became a public affair when John Harrison received money from the British Board of Longitude in 1773. Louis XVI had sent Berthoud four times to offer money to Harrison for his expertise, but the British clock maker refused to accept the offers and the French government remained ignorant of Harrison's clock-making principles until they were published in England in 1763 and translated into French in 1767.

Within France the competition was as strong as it was in the international theater. Berthoud and Le Roy claimed credit for the technical discoveries. Fleurieu and Berthoud were the leaders of the "timekeeper school"—*l'école chronométrique*—and the astronomer Pierre-Charles Lemonnier (1715–1799), specialist in lunar distances, led the "lunar school." (To solve the problem of longitude at sea, the timekeeper school promoted clock making. The drawback was the high cost of chronometers, which was a greater obstacle in France than in England. The few available marine clocks were reserved for some French officers involved in scientific endeavors. The lunar school promoted calculating distances between the moon and stars, a method that was less expensive but too complicated for most sailors.) Around 1770 Lemonnier and the prominent Cassini family of French and Italian astronomers and cartographers, recognizing the value of the chronometers, supported Leroy. Their selection arose from feelings in the French scientific community and the navy against Fleurieu and Berthoud, whose leadership in the field—almost monopolistic—was resented by the other clock makers, who were not funded as well by the French government. In his monumental *Histoire de la mesure du temps*, published in 1802, Berthoud at last recognized that Le Roy had played a great part in French clock making and eventually used Le Roy's methods. In addition to serving as the official clock maker to the navy, Berthoud was appointed to the French Institut and the Royal Society of London, but from a technological point of view Le Roy was the primary innovator in French clock making, owing to his invention of the detached escapement.

Berthoud died on June 20, 1807, at his home in Groslay, near Montmorency. Because of his numerous books, his influence was widespread in Continental Europe. His nephew, Pierre-Louis Berthoud (1754–1813), succeeded him in his business.

[*See also* Harrison, John; Longitude Finding; Nautical Astronomy and Celestial Navigation; Navigational Instruments, *subentry on* Measurement of Time; *and* Rewards and Prizes.]

## Bibliography

Cardinal, Catherine, ed. *Ferdinand Berthoud (1727–1807)*. La Chaux-de-Fonds, Switzerland: Musée International de l'Horlogerie, 1984.

Chapuis, Olivier. *À la mer comme au ciel: Beautemps-Beaupré et la naissance de l'hydrographie moderne, ou l'Émergence de la précision en navigation et dans la cartographie marine (1700–1850)*. Paris: Presses de l'Université de Paris-Sorbonne, 1999.

Cotter, Charles H. *A History of Nautical Astronomy*. London: Hollis and Carter, 1968.

Gould, Rupert T. *The Marine Chronometer: Its History and Development*. Woodbridge, U.K.: Antique Collector's Club, 1989.

Howse, Derek. *Greenwich Time and the Discovery of the Longitude*. Oxford: Oxford University Press, 1980.

Sabrier, Jean-Claude, and Jean Le Bot. "Ferdinand Berthoud, horloger mécanicien du roi et collaborateur de l'Encyclopédie." In *La mer au siècle des encyclopédies*, edited by Jean Balcou, pp. 323–331. Paris: Champion; Geneva, Switzerland: Slatkine, 1987.

OLIVIER CHAPUIS

# Bibby, James

(1812–1897), British shipowner. During his lengthy career, James Jenkinson Bibby was involved in some of the most important developments in the Victorian shipping industry, including the transitions from sail to steam and from wood to iron, the creation of steamship liner fleets, and the shift from family firms toward corporate business structures.

Bibby took over from his father, John, on the latter's death in 1840 and expanded an already considerable sailing fleet working in Liverpool's Mediterranean trades. From 1850 he began to invest in steamships and successfully managed the transition to a much more capital-intensive era. By the late 1860s Bibby had the largest steam fleet in Liverpool, with more than 40,000 gross tons registered with the Liverpool Steamship Owners Association; only the various firms linked to the Cunard line could claim a larger total tonnage.

Like many successful steamship owners, Bibby had close ties to shipbuilders. He gave a string of orders to Harland & Wolff in Belfast, facilitated by family connections between Wolff and Bibby's partner, Gustav Christian Schwabe. Bibby/Harland ships were pioneering (and in their day controversial) for being much longer in relation to their width than had previously been considered safe.

Bibby's shipowning remained rooted in the "64ths system" of extended partnerships and by the 1860s his fleet was part of a collaborative network of Mediterranean operators. He was well placed to benefit from carrying Egyptian cotton to Liverpool in the early 1860s, when transatlantic supplies were curtailed by the U.S. Civil War. By the late 1860s, however, Bibby was faced with another set of choices, with strong pressure to diversify the company's routes and to take advantage of the new limited-liability company structures. Changes in Mediterranean trade after the opening of the Suez Canal also threatened the firm's activities, and Bibby had no immediate family able to succeed him when he retired. In 1873 the Bibby fleet was ceded to his junior partner, Frederick Leyland.

Bibby was the first chair of the Liverpool Steamship Owners Association (founded in 1858), and he lobbied the new Mersey Docks & Harbour Board on behalf of the steam trades. He refused, however, to stand for election to the board itself. This was a common dilemma: Victorian shipowners sought a considerable say in the management of their ports but were often reluctant or unable to give their time to office-holding.

Unusually, Bibby returned to the shipping industry more than a decade after his "retirement," by starting his nephew in business. Their first vessels were also built by Harland & Wolff, and operated to Burma from 1889. By the time of Bibby's death in 1897, the new company was earning government contracts as an approved carrier of colonial officials. Bibby's career, with its mixture of continuity and transition, and of pragmatic response to new business opportunities, is a useful illustration of the flexibility demanded of the Victorian shipowner.

[*See also* Shipping Companies, *subentries on* An Overview *and* Ocean Passenger Companies, *and* Shipping Industry, *subentry on* Entrepreneurs and Financiers.]

## Bibliography

Cottrell, P. L. "Liverpool Shipowners, the Mediterranean and the Transition from Sail to Steam during the Mid-nineteenth Century." In *From Wheelhouse to Counting House: Essays in Maritime Economic History in Honour of Professor Peter Neville Davies*, edited by L. R. Fischer, pp. 153–202. Saint John's, Newfoundland: IMEHA, 1992. An analysis of the activities of the port's major Mediterranean traders, including Bibby.

Haws, Duncan. *The Burma Boats: Henderson and Bibby*. Uckfield, U.K.: TCL, 1995. A chronological survey of the firm's history and a fleet list with vessel specifications.

Milne, Graeme J. *Trade and Traders in Mid-Victorian Liverpool: Mercantile Business and the Making of a World Port*. Liverpool: Liverpool University Press, 2000. Chapter 6 includes an analysis of Bibby's shipowning network in the 1850s and 1860s.

Moss, Michael, and John R. Hume. *Shipbuilder to the World: 125 Years of Harland and Wolff, Belfast, 1861–1986*. Belfast: Blackstaff, 1986. History of Bibby's main shipbuilding collaborator.

Watson, Nigel. *The Bibby Line, 1807–1990*. Liverpool: Bibby, 1990. An illustrated company history.

GRAEME J. MILNE

# Biblical Archetypes

**Biblical Archetypes** That the sea and ships can symbolize or convey spiritual meaning is well known. A recent example is a log entry made by the young English single-handed sailor Ellen MacArthur while racing across the Atlantic in a 21-foot sloop in 1997. "I now feel so wonderfully in tune with the boat and the sea that I know I shall really miss this once the race is over. At night I watch the sun go down and in the morning the sky is there above me, a wonderful feeling of space and timelessness." Artless and wholehearted, her declaration of confidence in the sea might not have been possible were it not for revolutions in weather forecasting, communications, and boatbuilding, or for the radical new vision of the sea as a playground that appeared in the late nineteenth century and further evolved into the sport of yachting.

Until relatively recently, however, the sea was perceived with suspicion, if not contempt. Typical is Joseph Conrad's declaration in *The Mirror of the Sea* (1906): "I looked upon the true sea—the sea that plays with men until their hearts are broken, and wears stout ships to death. Nothing can touch the brooding bitterness of its soul." The fathomless deep was long identified as the home of cruel primeval chaos in the form of sea monsters, sudden storms, and rogue seas. The sea, sailors, ships, and seamanship itself have been understood as distinctive archetypes, all playing roles in great seafaring moral and spiritual dramas called "sea deliverance narratives."

## Superstition and Ships

The idea of the sea as a perennial setting of chaos is as old as seafaring, and is based on certain indisputable facts, for example, that fishing villages have suffered mortality rates comparable to those of infantry regiments in combat. The record of calamity has been acknowledged often and in various ways. Many heartrending ballads have been sung of wives and children vainly awaiting the return of their husbands' and fathers' dories. In 1892, in an address honoring the 250th anniversary of the founding of the Massachusetts seaport of Gloucester, a clergyman produced a brief jeremiad acknowledging the darker side of the town's commercial success: "The shadow of this picture of enterprise is that cast by the weeds of the widow, and the picture

**Biblical Archetypes.** This early Christian mosaic of a sea monster and Jonah is from the fourth century C.E. and is in the Basilica at Aquileia, Italy. SCALA / ART RESOURCE, NY

itself is marred by the tears of the fatherless . . . The ocean is our mausoleum, and few are the hearts here which look upon its floods without a shudder."

Out of such concerns have sprung many versions of the aphorism, "He who will learn to pray, let him go to sea." The Hebrew word for "despair" is derived from the word for "deep sea," as in the penitential Psalm 130: "Out of the depths I cry to thee O Lord." Mariners, therefore, are famous for their piety. It was written in the Talmud (the compilation of Jewish oral laws and commentaries), many centuries ago, "Most ass-drivers are wicked, while most camel-drivers are worthy men; and most sailors are pious" (Almbladh). While a real sailor knows that "piety is no substitute for seamanship" (to quote Donald Wharton), many mariners have faith in higher forces. Belief takes two forms: superstition and conventional religious faith, each of which turns the usual shoreside, secular beliefs on their head.

Seafarers have believed, for example, that a black cat is good luck aboard a ship, that white is a symbol of evil, and that a reliable omen of a fatal voyage is the appearance of a rabbit on the path while sailors are making their way to the wharf, at which point all smart seamen will turn on their heel and run back home. In addition, there are certain objects that, if taken on board, will cause catastrophe. One is a banana, and another is an umbrella. On the list, too, are a solitary bird, a citizen of Finland, an ordained minister, and a red-haired virgin, any one of which can and will sink a ship. Presumably that virgin was a woman; in many traditional cultures, women were thought to bring bad luck. These beliefs are founded on the assumption that the sea is a topsy-turvy world where truth runs contrary to usual land-bound expectations. The subtext is that the sea's contrary nature must be recognized before a sailor becomes a qualified seaman.

This complexity is seen in the ship itself. As a symbol, it is both masculine as it thrusts forward and feminine with its womb-like hold keeping out the wild, chaotic deeps (this is why ships are called "vessels"). The medieval Jewish commentator Rashi described a good vessel as a "dancing ship" that, lilting across the water, is inherently safe. That is not enough comfort for most sailors. They seek special protection by giving their ships and boats the names of gods, goddesses, or beloved human beings.

As is well known, many ships' names have been female, and ships and boats have been referred to as "she" (except in the case of warships, which may be called "it"). As Don H. Kennedy points out in his study of ships' names, in many languages the words for "ship" and "boat" are in the feminine case. Another reason for the choice of female names is that the vast majority of merchant seamen have been men; when a lonely sailor thinks of home, he automatically thinks of women, and so he brings a little bit of home with him when he chooses a female name for the ship or boat.

Naming ships for people in general and women in particular has an extremely long history running from ancient Greece and Rome until the present day. In a study of American commercial ships' names, Kennedy found that a majority were personal names about equally divided between female and male. Sometimes, however, the balance disappears. Between 1789 and 1795, in the port of Boston, 41 percent of commercial ships' names were female and only 13 percent were male.

Besides personal qualities, ships' names have often been associated with values. Warships tend to be mighty (*Invincible*, *Intrepid*) and passenger ships large (*Great Eastern*, *Titanic*). Of the sixty-three yachts that raced for the America's Cup—a competition between nations—through 2003, forty-four (70 percent) carried patriotic names such as *Columbia* (a nickname for "United States"), *Southern Cross* (from Australia), and the straightforward *New Zealand*. Only seven America's Cup yachts were named for women.

The tradition of female names slipped in the late twentieth century. Most commercial ship names were little more than corporate identifications devoid of any trace of romance and personality. That could be said to some degree of the names of yachts. Of the 880 boats registered in a national yacht club in the United States in 2006, only seventy-two (8 percent) were feminine.

## Noah's Ship

The vulnerability of seafarers, their reputation for unusual piety, and the special caring of the gods for ships are illustrated in the Bible's three great sea stories. These are the accounts of Noah's ark, Jonah's flight, and the apostle Paul's shipwreck. Dreadful as these stormy tales are, all have happy endings and positive consequences because of a healthy tension between religious belief and seamanship, faith and naval architecture.

The Noachian story concerns the ship that saved humanity and animals in a great chaotic flood (Genesis 6–9). The outlines of Noah's flood can be seen in several other accounts of Mesopotamian deluges. His story probably was influenced by the Gilgamesh Epic, which comes down from ancient Babylonia (now Iraq) and was a version of the Epic of Atrahasis and other flood tales dating back to well before 2000 B.C.E. These stories very likely were inspired by an actual flood whose location, timing, and extent have inspired intense controversy among archaeologists. According to one theory, in approximately 5600 B.C.E. the Mediterranean Sea rose precipitously, overran the Bosporus Strait, and, as it transformed a vast freshwater lake into the Black Sea, drove away many people, who might have included Noah in his ark.

As Raphael Patai points out in *The Children of Noah: Jewish Seafaring in Ancient Times*, the account of Noah's flood is unlike most of the others in that the vessel of salvation is a true, seaworthy ship with a sharp bow. Real ships allow sailors the freedom to take their fate in their own hands and choose their own course. Besides specifically instructing Noah to build the ship of the familiar shipbuilding material cedar (known as gopher wood) and telling him exactly how to caulk and waterproof it, God lays down the vessel's shape. The dimensions are to be 300 cubits in length and 50 in width. Just what a cubit was is the subject of scholarly debate, but the important point is not the ship's length but its proportions. With a length-to-beam ratio of six to one, this is no boxy container to be blown about passively but a slim, easily driven, potentially fast vessel. Noah is to seek his own safety. Seamanship is one of the factors of free will that counts in salvation. The mariner, then, stands for self-sufficiency.

Less clear than the vessel's proportions are the divine specification to provide health-giving light for the passengers and crew through a window. In the Talmud, the rabbis interpreted this to mean not a mere skylight but a divine, illuminated pearl that (in Patai's translation) "shone for all the creatures that were in it like a candle that shines in the house, and like the sun shining at noontide." With this magical light, the ship is as habitable as any sailor could wish.

Noah's ship is a success. After forty days—which in the Bible means "a long time"—Noah, in his well-lit and sturdy ship, senses that land is near and sends out birds to find it. His faith has protected him, as have his ship and his seamanship.

## Jonah's Awakening

In the irony-intensive Old Testament book of Jonah, the ship is the home of heathens who, with the help of a storm, correct a misguided believer. The Jewish prophet Jonah cravenly takes ship to sail to the ends of the earth (Tarshish, probably Gibraltar) with the aim of avoiding a divine but unwelcome call to convert the Jews' worst enemies, who dwell in the imperial city of Nineveh. God sends a storm to alert Jonah to the fact that he will never escape his failings, but the prophet is so apathetic that he lies sleeping in the ship's hold, ignoring not only the storm but also the needs of the vessel. To the sailors, Jonah is their worst nightmare—a bad shipmate.

The Old Testament scholar Phyllis Trible observes that the Hebrew words describing Jonah's state are not those commonly used in the context of ordinary healthy sleep. Rather, they indicate a trance-like state typical near death. The Talmud explains that Jonah suffers "because of the anguish of his soul." Trible has observed, "Lying down to sleep in the innards of the ship, he is close to becoming an inanimate object, a replacement for the wares that the sailors have hurled overboard." Jonah, then, is helpless and pulling away from life itself.

The prophet's passivity contrasts sharply with the dutifulness of the heathen seamen. The ship's captain, outraged by his passenger's behavior, awakens Jonah, drags him on deck, and orders him to pray to his own god if he wants to be saved. When the suspicion arises that he is the cause of the ship's troubles, he finally shows a spark of life and offers to throw himself into the sea as propitiation. Decent people that they are, the sailors refuse and instead pray to Jonah's God. Finally acceding to Jonah's demands, they throw him into the sea. At that, the storm ceases, the ship is saved, and a "great fish" appears to rescue Jonah by swallowing him whole.

Finally awakened to his calling, Jonah addresses God by offering a thanksgiving for his rescue from "the heart of the seas," and the fish hurls him out onto the shore. Thanks to the pious seamen, he is reborn and goes on to convert the Ninevites.

## Paul's Miraculous Voyage

The New Testament's great sea story makes subtle alterations to the themes we have been following. This is the account of the gale survived by the apostle Paul that is laid out in the early history of the church titled the Acts of the Apostles (chapters 27–28). Here, seamanship and faith again triumph hand in hand, but, unlike the Jonah story, the passenger is no "inanimate object" but an unusually knowledgeable seaman. Some biblical scholars believe that this story may be modeled on a standard classical storm-at-sea story of the sort inspired by the *Odyssey*, with the addition of dramatic and sometimes miraculous behavior.

In about 60 C.E., the early Christian apostle Paul is taken as a prisoner aboard a grain ship bound for Rome, where he will be tried as a Roman citizen on charges of fomenting rebellion. The reader knows that Paul is a veteran of many voyages and a tentmaker, a trade that included making sails, and expects that he knows a little of seamanship. His skill goes unacknowledged by his Roman captors, who ignore his prediction of a northeast gale and his advice to anchor in a harbor of refuge. As the gale hits, they can only reef the sails, reinforce the weak hull by wrapping it with ropes, and run before the storm, meanwhile lightening ship by jettisoning cargo, improving stability by cutting down some of the spars, and easing the ship's motion by deploying a drogue or sea anchor. There is enough detail here to provide a seamanship lesson in storm management, but the author chooses to turn the storm into a sermon on the subject of Paul's powers and authority in both God's and the temporal realms, in other words, as a faithful man and as a mariner.

As conditions worsen and the crew despairs, Paul steps forward decisively to report that an angel has come to him and promised that they all will survive. After many days of misery and terror, the sailors sense, as good seamen always do from the changing shape of the waves, that they are nearing shore. All but assuming command, Paul distributes bread, saying words like those in the Christian formula at Holy Communion. Doubly fortified, the sailors ingeniously cut the anchors' cables and sail the ship onto a shoal. As Paul promised, everybody survives.

As in the Noah and Jonah stories, able seamanship and deep faith work together to tame the malicious place of chaos that Conrad called "the true sea" and deliver humans from the heart of the sea.

[*See also* Motifs, *subentry on* Religious Motifs; Religion, *subentry on* Seafarers' Religion; *and* Ship Names and Naming.]

### Bibliography

Almbladh, Karin. *Studies in the Book of Jonah*. Upsala, Sweden: Acta Universitatis Upsaliensis, 1986.

Beck, Horace. *Folklore and the Sea*. Mystic, Conn.: Mystic Seaport Museum, 1973.

Clifford, Richard J., and Roland E. Murphy. "Genesis." In *The New Jerome Biblical Commentary*, edited by Raymond E. Brown, Joseph A. Fitzmyer, and Roland E. Murphy. Englewood Cliffs, N.J.: Prentice-Hall, 1990.

Foulke, Robert. *The Sea Voyage Narrative*. New York: Routledge, 2002.

Kennedy, Don H. *Ship Names: Origins and Usages during 45 Centuries*. Newport News, Va.: The Mariners Museum, 1974.

Limburg, James. *Jonah: A Commentary*. Louisville, Ky.: Westminster/John Knox, 1993.

MacArthur, Ellen. *Taking on the World*. Camden, Maine.: International Marine, 2003.

Morison, Samuel Eliot. "Captain Codman on the Mutiny in Dorchester Church, and the Seamanship of Saint Paul." *American Neptune* 2 (April 1942): 99–106.

Patai, Raphael. *The Children of Noah: Jewish Seafaring in Ancient Times*. Princeton, N.J.: Princeton University Press, 1998.

Rad, Gerhard von. *Genesis: A Commentary*. Translated by John H. Marks. Rev. ed. Philadelphia: Westminster, 1972.

Rousmaniere, John. *After the Storm*. New York: McGraw-Hill/International Marine, 2002.

Rousmaniere, John. *The Luxury Yachts*. The Seafarers. Alexandria, Va.: Time-Life Books, 1981.

Ryan, William, and Walter Pitman. *Noah's Flood: The New Scientific Discoveries about the Event that Changed History*. New York: Simon and Schuster, 1998.

Trask, Rev. J. L. R. "The Gloucester of Yesterday and the Gloucester of Tomorrow." *Memorial of the Celebration of the 250th Anniversary of the Incorporation of the Town of Gloucester, Mass., August 1892*. Boston: Mudge, 1901.

Trible, Phyllis. "The Book of Jonah: Introduction, Commentary, and Reflections." In *The New Interpreter's Bible*. Vol. 7. Nashville, Tenn.: Abingdon, 1994–2004.

Wharton, Donald, ed. *In the Trough of the Sea: Selected American Sea-Deliverance Narratives, 1610–1766*. Westport, Conn.: Greenwood, 1979.

White, Jefferson. *Evidence and Paul's Journeys: An Historical Investigation into the Travels of the Apostle Paul*. Hilliard, Oh.: Parsagard, 2001.

Wilson, A. N. *Paul: The Mind of the Apostle*. New York: Norton, 1997.

JOHN ROUSMANIERE

## Bilbao

Founded in 1300 on the coast in northern Spain, the city of Bilbao became, during the fourteenth and fifteenth centuries, the center of a dynamic trade between Spain and England and the Low Countries, exporting Castilian wool and Basque iron and importing Flemish cloth and foodstuffs. From the beginning of the sixteenth century on, Bilbao merchants and mariners expanded toward other types of trade, such as trade with Newfoundland fisheries and trade with Spanish colonies in America—activities that promoted the shipbuilding industry across the river. After the economic crisis of the seventeenth century, Bilbao, during the eighteenth century and the first half of the nineteenth century, reinforced its dominance over the other ports of northern Spain by means of its good communications with the Spanish mainland.

From 1870s on, this commercial city transformed into an industrial and financial center. Bilbao exported increasing amounts of iron ore to England and Germany and imported British coal to feed its iron and steel mills. Imports also included the raw materials and industrial goods demanded by the mechanical and chemical industries and the modern shipyards set up in the province of Biscay during those years. The great increase in maritime traffic made necessary to improve the access and navigation conditions across the Nervión estuary and to build up an external port (1902), which gradually captured the majority of traffic.

At the beginning of the twentieth century, Bilbao was not only Spain's main port but also the center of heavy industry and of shipping in Spain and, along with Madrid, shared the status of being a major financial center. Throughout the twentieth century, the successive enlargement of the external port, the establishment of an oil refinery, and the improvement of highway and railway connections with the Spanish mainland allowed Bilbao to maintain itself among the top five Spanish ports.

The severe economic crisis of the late 1970s and the process of industrial restructuring during the 1980s have transformed Bilbao into a city that is less industrial and more services-oriented. One of the most evident symbols of this change is the opening of the Guggenheim Museum in 1997. Nevertheless, Bilbao retains its nature and vocation as a maritime city. Evidence of this includes, first, the big enlargement of its port and the striking improvement of its regular maritime connections, carried out in the 1990s, and, second, the 2003 establishment of a great Maritime Museum, located on the lands of a former shipyard.

[*See also* Cartagena, Spain, *and* Unions, *subentry on Cofradías* in Spain and Latin America.]

## Bibliography

Cámara de Comercio, Industria y Navegación de Bilbao. Servicio de Estudios. *El puerto de Bilbao y su zona de influencia*. Bilbao: Cámara de Comercio, Industria y Navegación de Bilbao, 1970.

De la Puerta, Natividad. *El puerto de Bilbao como reflejo del desarrollo industrial de Vizcaya, 1857–1914*. Bilbao: Autoridad Portuaria, 1994.

Fernández de Pinedo, Emiliano. "El desarrollo de Bilbao y sus actividades, 1300–1936." In *Exposición Centenario 1886–1986*, pp. 18–46. Bilbao: Cámara de Comercio, Industria y Navegación, 1986.

Guiard, Teófilo. *Historia del Consulado y Casa de Contratación de Bilbao y del comercio de la Villa*. Bilbao: Imprenta y Librería de José de Astuy, 1913.

JESÚS M. VALDALISO

**Bireme.** *See* Warships, *subentry on* Ancient Warships.

## *Bismarck,* German battleship.

Length/beam/draft: 251 m × 36 m × 10.55 m. Tonnage: 41,200 tons; full load, 50,500 tons. Hull: steel. Complement: 2,200. Machinery: 3-shaft Curtis steam turbines for 150,170 shaft horsepower, 3 screws; 30 knots. Armament: 8 × 38-cm guns, 12 × 15-cm guns. Armor: main belt up to 36 cm; deck, 12.4 cm.

In World War II, only four German capital ships saw action. *Bismarck* and her sister ship *Tirpitz* (both about 42,000 tons Washington standard) were deployed in the Atlantic from 1941 on. But *Bismarck* was sunk during her first mission under the code name Operation Rheinübung. The chase and eventual demise of this superbattleship stirred emotions on both the British and the German sides and established *Bismarck*'s lasting fame in both countries.

Launched on February 14, 1939, in Hitler's presence at the Blohm & Voss shipyard in Hamburg, *Bismarck* entered service on August 24, 1940. With fleet commander Admiral Günther Lütjens aboard, she sailed in the company of the heavy cruiser *Prinz Eugen* from Gotenhafen (now Polish Gdynia) on May 18, 1941, for operations against British convoys in the North Atlantic. The two other battleships, *Gneisenau* and *Scharnhorst*, were—contrary to the original plans to use all large surface units in a joint attack—ordered to remain in Brest for repairs. *Bismarck* and *Prinz Eugen* were detected by a Swedish cruiser on their passage through the Kattegat and were spotted by air reconnaissance while they were fueling in Bergen, Norway. The ships were sighted again by the patrolling cruisers *Suffolk* and *Norfolk* in the Denmark Strait between Iceland and Greenland, and they made contact with the old British battle cruiser *Hood* and the newly commissioned battleship *Prince of Wales*, a task force that was much stronger. In a brief action on May 24, *Hood*'s main magazines exploded, and she sank within four minutes, while *Prince of Wales* was damaged and forced to turn away. *Bismarck* was hit three times, and her forward fuel tank was damaged, which impaired her speed and range of action.

Instead of having the damage repaired and refueling in Norway, Lütjens headed for Saint-Nazaire in France, while *Prinz Eugen* slipped away to operate independently in the mid-Atlantic. After a few ineffectual exchanges with British spotter vessels, *Bismarck* managed to lose them in a burst of speed in the early hours of May 25. For thirty-six hours the British lost contact with her, and it was only after desperate—and somewhat chaotic—attempts to locate her that *Bismarck* was sighted by a Coastal Command Catalina flying boat 700 miles west of Brest at 10:30 A.M. on May 26. In the evening hours, an aircraft from the carrier *Ark Royal*

**Battleship *Bismarck*.** This photograph from astern was taken in 1940–1941, showing the stern anchor in its recessed well, folding propeller guards, and armor belt. COURTESY OF THE U.S. NAVAL HISTORICAL CENTER

hit *Bismarck* with a torpedo that put her steering gear out of action and immobilized her rudders. Unable to steer and reduced in speed, she was systematically battered by HMS *Rodney*, *King George V*, *Norfolk*, and *Dorsetshire*.

*Bismarck* ended her maiden voyage at 10:36 A.M. on May 27, 1941. More than 2,100 of her crew died; 110 survivors were rescued by HMS *Dorsetshire* and *Maori*, and five were picked up later by German vessels. Scuttled by her own crew, she received the coup de grâce from torpedoes launched from HMS *Dorsetshire*. The fate of *Bismarck* ended the deployment of German battleships in worldwide actions, while it boosted the morale of the Allies after many setbacks in the opening stages of World War II.

[*See also Ark Royal*; Navies, Great Powers, *subentries on* British Isles, 1500 to the Present *and* Germany, 1848–1945; Warships, *subentry on* Modern Warships; *and* Wars, Maritime, *subentry on* World Wars.]

### Bibliography

Bercuson, David J., and Holger H. Herwig. *The Destruction of the "Bismarck"*. New York: Overlook Press, 2001.

Elfrath, Ulrich, and Bodo Herzog. *The Battleship "Bismarck": A Documentary in Words and Pictures*. West Chester., Pa.: Schifer, 1989.

Grove, Eric, ed. *German Capital Ships and Raiders in World War II*. Vol. 1, *From "Graf Spee" to "Bismarck," 1939–1941*. Naval Staff Histories. London: Frank Cass, 2002.

Kennedy, Ludovic. *Pursuit: The Chase and Sinking of the Bismarck*. London: Collins, 1974.

Koop, Gerhard, and Klaus-Peter Schmolke. *Battleships of the Bismarck Class: "Bismarck" and "Tirpitz," Culmination and Finale of German Battleship Construction*. Translated by Geoffrey Brooks. London: Greenhill Books; Annapolis, Md.: Naval Institute Press, 1998.

Müllenheim-Rechberg, Burkard, Freiherr von. *Battleship "Bismarck": A Survivor's Story*. Translated by Jack Sweetman. Rev. ed. Annapolis, Md.: Naval Institute Press, 1990.

Rhys-Jones, Graham. *The Loss of the "Bismarck": An Avoidable Disaster*. London: Cassell, 1999.

Winklareth, Robert J. *The "Bismarck Chase": New Light on a Famous Engagement*. London: Chatham, 1998.

LARS U. SCHOLL

# Blackbeard  (?–1718), pirate. Blackbeard—whose real name was Edward Teach and who was probably

English—became a symbol of the final stages of the great era of buccaneering.

A large man with a huge beard, Blackbeard went into battle with a gunner's match woven into his beard so that he faced his enemies with smoke dancing around his head, armed with multiple swords, pistols, and daggers. A notoriously cruel man, he was not above maiming his victims on a whim. Sometime after 1713 he entered the crew of Benjamin Hornigold. By 1716, Blackbeard commanded a vessel in company with Hornigold, and they terrorized the Caribbean. At the height of his career Hornigold accepted an offer of amnesty, but his protégé continued his ventures in *Queen Anne's Revenge*. Shortly thereafter Blackbeard came into contact with Stede Bonnet and *Revenge*; he deposed Bonnet as captain and kept him imprisoned on his own ship.

In the spring of 1718, in command of four vessels, Blackbeard sailed to North America seeking new prey. This venture climaxed in May 1718 in a weeklong blockade of Charles Town (South Carolina). He then sailed away, only to lose his ship and another of his flotilla in the treacherous sandbanks off the coast. Shortly thereafter he marooned twenty-five of his men and made off with all the booty. He sailed to North Carolina, where Governor Charles Eden gave him a pardon. That did not placate Governor Alexander Spottswood of Virginia, who sent two sloops to pursue Blackbeard at sea. Blackbeard was finally cornered at Ocracoke Inlet on November 22, 1718, where he died from multiple shot and sword wounds. During his career he had captured at least forty-five ships.

[*See also* Buccaneers and Buccaneering *and* Piracy.]

### Bibliography

Hughson, Shirley Carter. *The Carolina Pirates and Colonial Commerce, 1670–1740*. Baltimore: Johns Hopkins University Press, 1894.

Johnson, Captain Charles. *A General History of the Robberies and Murders of the Most Notorious Pyrates and Also Their Policies, Discipline, and Government from Their First Rise and Settlement in the Island of Providence in 1717 to the Present Year 1724, with the Remarkable Actions and Adventures of the Two Female Pyrates, Mary Read and Anne Bonny, to Which Is Prefix'd an Account of the Famous Captain Avery and His Companions, with the Manner of his Death in England*, edited by Manuel Schornhorn. London: Dent, 1972.

ROBERT C. RITCHIE

## *Black Book of the Admiralty.* See Law, *subentry on* Classical and Medieval Law.

## Black Sea

**Black Sea** The Black Sea, known to the ancients as *Pontus Euxinus* (hospitable sea), is fed by major European and Eurasian rivers—the Danube, Dnestr, Dnepr, and Don—and its waters are therefore far less salty than those of the Mediterranean. It has no habitable offshore islands and, except for the shallow Sea of Azov, no clear geographical subunits. Its diminutive size makes it a compact entity. The distance from the Bulgarian port of Burgas in the west to the Georgian port of Batumi in the east is just under 1,200 kilometers (750 miles), and the distance from the tip of Crimea in the north to the Turkish port of Inebolu in the south is only about 260 kilometers (160 miles). (Ancient sailors claimed that at the midpoint of the north–south crossing, they could see both coasts at the same time.) It is connected to the oceans only at the Bosporus and Dardanelles straits, which link up with the intervening Sea of Marmara. Water is constantly exchanged with the Mediterranean through the straits, a fresher upper current flowing out of the Black Sea and a saltier lower current flowing into it.

### Origins and Early Explorers

Some seven to ten millennia ago, the sea was a low-lying freshwater lake about two-thirds of its present size. At some point during this period, perhaps around 7,500 years ago, the lake was invaded by the waters of the Mediterranean, which hollowed out the straits and formed the sea as it is today. The denser salt water sank to the bottom of the lake and set up a strong density gradient. The decay of organic matter in the salty depths depleted the oxygen supply, while new freshwater was continually delivered into the top layer by the major rivers of the north and west. Today, below about 200 meters (660 feet), the sea is anoxic (that is, lacking in oxygen) and devoid of nearly all life forms. The stratification in the sea itself—brackish, oxygenated water on top, salty hydrogen-sulfide-infused water in the depths, which reach below 2,000 meters (6,600 feet)—has remained in place since the formation of the sea.

There have been attempts to link the emergence of the Black Sea to the apocalypse myths of the ancient Near East, such as the biblical flood or the epic of Gilgamesh. But there is as yet little scientific consensus about such a rapid transformation of the ancient lake into a sea. One result of the sea's strange origins—the large anoxic zone—does make it a propitious venue for underwater archaeology. The absence of destructive microorganisms means that wood-hulled ships on the seabed should be much better preserved than in other locales. Initial research in the early 2000s uncovered the remarkable remains of

**Black Sea Warships.** Ottoman warships *Malataya* and *Kadikoy* at the Imperial Naval Arsenal in Constantinople, c. 1880–1893. LIBRARY OF CONGRESS, PRINTS AND PHOTOGRAPHS DIVISION

Hellenistic- and Byzantine-era ships off the coasts of Bulgaria and Turkey.

The earliest known explorers on the sea were Greeks, probably from Asia Minor. They rowed and sailed through the straits already in the first half of the first millennium B.C.E. Tradition has them searching for precious metals (a story encapsulated in the legend of Jason and the golden fleece), but commerce quickly became their primary vocation. Greek cities in the Mediterranean, especially the powerful Miletus in Asia Minor, set up permanent outposts to trade with indigenous peoples along the coasts and farther inland. Some Greeks may even have made their way up the northern rivers and into the Eurasian steppe. In time these outposts grew into major cities in their own right, some having the title of *polis* (city-state) and boasting temples and other public buildings. Inhabitants produced dried fish for shipment to the Mediterranean and served as middlemen in the grain trade between the non-Greeks of the interior and the Aegean world. Among the most famous of the Black Sea cities were Sinope (modern Sinop, Turkey), perched on a peninsula that juts out from the southern coast, and Chersonesus (near modern Sevastopol, Ukraine), on the southwestern edge of Crimea.

Ancient sources from Herodotus (fifth century B.C.E.) to Strabo (63/64 B.C.E.–after 23 C.E.) speak of the wealth of the Black Sea ports and note the strong interactions between Greek colonists and indigenous peoples of the hinterlands. Already by the fourth century B.C.E., however, connections with the Mediterranean had begun to decline. Grain from Egypt undercut the need for Black Sea supplies, while independent local rulers emerged from the cultural mixing of Greeks with Thracians, Scythians, and other peoples along the coasts. The famous Bosporan kingdom, situated on the Kerch strait at the entrance to the Sea of Azov, developed a powerful navy in the Hellenistic period and eventually became a prized ally of the Romans.

In the second and first centuries B.C.E., Rome expanded into the Black Sea world, sometimes through outright conquest, at other times by striking deals with Hellenistic monarchs and indigenous rulers. Yet much of the coastline

**Map of the Black Sea.** MAP BY MAPPING SPECIALISTS LIMITED

remained largely foreign, controlled by a shifting array of "barbarian" peoples. Ovid, exiled to the western coastal city of Tomis (modern Constanta, Romania) in the first century C.E., wrote of the "trousered" barbarians who would sweep down on the city's inhabitants. Another description of the seacoasts from the second century C.E., written by a Roman governor in the service of the emperor Hadrian, contains the same mix of reportage and fantasy as the *Histories* of Herodotus, written some six centuries earlier.

## Byzantine Centuries

When the Roman capital was moved to Constantinople in 330 C.E., the new capital sat squarely within the Black Sea world. Connections across the sea were strong in the early Byzantine centuries. Successive groups of northerners, from the Goths to the "Northmen" to the Slavs, cooperated with Byzantines or made war against them, according to the circumstances. Byzantine emperors were often concerned with how to appease powerful political and economic powers north and west of the sea while ensuring that they continued to provide the hides, wax, amber, slaves, and other products to the imperial capital.

For much of the later Byzantine centuries, Italians were the drivers of economic life around the sea. From the middle of the thirteenth century, Italian merchants, particularly the Genoese, were given trading privileges around the coastline. In short order they established powerful ports that took advantage of the growing trade routes to India and China, many of them built atop earlier Greek foundations. Italian administrators in Caffa (modern Feodosiia, Ukraine, in Crimea), looked out for Genoese interests. The Venetian port of Tana (on the lower Don River) was the major jumping-off point for the overland journey to central Asia and the Far East. By striking bargains with the Tatar-Mongol khans, who now controlled the Eurasian steppe, Italians and other Europeans could ensure safe passage overland and then offload their goods to ships waiting for the cross-sea journey to the Mediterranean.

From the mid-thirteenth century through much of the fifteenth century, the Black Sea lay at the center of a global commercial network stretching from Europe to China. That network was intimately familiar to European merchants—so familiar, in fact, that Marco Polo barely mentions his sail across the Black Sea on his return journey from the east; writing about it in detail, he said, would have been superfluous. Europeans' knowledge of the Black Sea world can also be seen in the array of medieval sailing charts, or *portolans*, drawn mainly by Italian and Catalan map-makers. The shape of the sea is broadly correct, relative distances are accurate, and harbors and inlets are shown with surprising detail.

### The Ottomans

Europe's close connections with the sea ended with the rise of the Ottoman empire. The Ottoman conquest of Constantinople in 1453 and of the important port city of Trebizond (modern Trabzon, Turkey) in 1461 set the stage for the absorption of the entire littoral into the Ottoman domain. Italian hegemony was ended and trade redirected to supply the growing Ottoman capital. The major powers beyond the coastline—the principality of Moldova in the northwest, the Crimean Tatars in the north, and the princes of Georgia and the Caucasus in the east—were increasingly drawn into the Ottoman sphere of influence.

Historians often speak of the Black Sea during the centuries of Ottoman control as a "Turkish lake." It is certainly true that the Ottomans impeded naval access through the straits and imposed severe restrictions on most commercial vessels coming from the Mediterranean. (The effective ending of the Tatar-Mongol empire and the overland route to China, the reorientation of European trade to the New World, and the opening of direct sea routes to the Far East had already undercut the importance of the Black Sea even before the Ottoman conquest.) Still, powerful cross-sea connections remained. Trade in animal products from the northern steppe and in slaves from the north and east continued apace. So significant was the movement of people, in fact, that the Black Sea economy in the two centuries or so after the Ottoman conquest was driven in large part by the slave trade.

The Black Sea represented a major strategic asset to the Ottomans. Piracy was minimal, and there were no significant maritime powers around the sea. The combination of a peaceful sea and the wild steppe to the north—a natural buffer inhabited by nomads and traversed by raiding parties of Crimean Tatars—also kept at bay the growing powers of Poland and Muscovy. Yet in the late sixteenth century, a new force challenged Ottoman hegemony. The Cossacks, born of a cultural mix of steppe peoples, renegade peasants, and local Slavs, began to develop as a military force along the northern rivers. Over the next several decades they were able to launch raids on Ottoman fortresses (the most famous being their 1637 siege of the fortress at Azov, on

the lower Don River) and eventually to challenge Ottoman galleys on the open sea. Their sleek open-decked boats, sitting low in the water and outfitted with small cannon, could quickly be upon a lumbering galley or merchant ship. In the seventeenth century Cossack boats were also engaged in attacks on the southern coast.

### Russia and the Soviet Union

Increased Ottoman patrols eventually countered the Cossack threat, but the rise of Russia presented a new challenge to the Ottomans on the sea. Until the late seventeenth century, Russia had little connection to the Black Sea world, since it was physically separated from the coast by the inhospitable steppe. However, through a combination of conquest, peace treaties, and active colonization, Russia gradually opened routes to both the Caspian and the Black Sea via the Volga and Don rivers. Under Peter the Great (r. 1682–1725), the expanding empire launched its first major naval experiment in the south: the construction of a flotilla that could be dispatched down the Don River and engage Ottoman troops garrisoned at the fortress of Azov. In 1696, Peter's flotilla successfully captured the fortress, but in 1711, Russia was forced to return Azov to Ottoman control.

Peter's experiment failed, but it did mark the beginning of the gradual opening of the sea to Russian and other naval and commercial vessels, usually as a result of Ottoman losses in major wars. Under the treaty of Belgrade in 1739, Russia was once again given the Azov fortress and was granted limited trading rights on the sea. In 1774, under the treaty of Küçük Kaynarca, the Ottomans agreed to allow merchant vessels flying Russian flags to sail unimpeded. Over the next several decades, that concession was extended to other foreign merchantmen as well. Under Catherine the Great, Crimea was taken out of Ottoman hands and fully absorbed into the Russian empire. Under the treaties of Adrianople (1829) and Hünkâr Iskelesi (1839), the Ottomans recognized full Russian naval rights on the sea and guaranteed free passage through the straits.

These treaties not only marked a monumental change in the international status of the sea, but also provided a political context allowing the commercial takeoff of the new ports that sprang up along the Russian coast from the late eighteenth century forward. Odessa emerged as the major export center of southern Russia, a quintessential imperial seaport. Farther to the east, Kherson and Nikolaev became outposts of the new Russian naval industry. And in Crimea,

Sevastopol—boasting the finest natural harbor on the entire sea—grew as the main naval station of the Russian Black Sea fleet.

During the Crimean War (1854–1856), the Black Sea region became the center of major land and naval battles, the most spectacular being the stunning annihilation of the Ottoman fleet at Sinop (November 1853) and the long siege of Russian forces at Sevastopol by the allied forces of the United Kingdom, the Second French Empire, the Kingdom of Sardinia, and the Ottoman Empire. The treaty of Paris, which ended the war in 1856, made the sea fully neutral and international: neither Russians nor Ottomans were to keep anything larger than patrol boats on the water, coastal defenses were to be demolished, and the sea was to remain open to all commercial traffic.

The second half of the nineteenth century saw the further development of Russia's ports, fueled first by the burgeoning export trade in grain and later by the export of petroleum from the Caucasus. Older cities such as Odessa grew in population and wealth, while the newer ports of Novorossiisk, Batumi, and Rostov (on the Don River) took advantage of their positions as purveyors of the new raw materials of industry, such as coal, manganese, and oil. The advent of steam transport meant that most of the major port cities were now connected by direct and circular routes run by Russian, Austrian, and other companies, and also linked with the Mediterranean and European cities upriver on the Danube. Yet the Russian government remained concerned about the restrictive military provisions of the Paris treaty and, in 1870, unilaterally abrogated the neutrality clause.

A new naval arms race, now involving the production and acquisition of armored, screw-driven ships, began between the two Black Sea empires. Nevertheless, during the Russo-Turkish war of 1877–1878, most of the Russian navy remained concentrated in the Baltic Sea, while the Ottoman naval presence in the Black Sea theater amounted to a squadron on the Danube and at Istanbul. The rest of the Ottoman fleet sat out the war in the Mediterranean and Red seas. Where possible, the navies tended to avoid direct contact, preferring instead to shell the coastline. In World War I, the only significant battle was a fog-bound encounter off the coast of Crimea involving the former German dreadnought *Goeben* (under the Ottoman flag), a battle that ended with no more than a dozen casualties. Conditions in both fleets were often dire. The famous mutiny aboard the Russian cruiser *Potemkin* in 1905 highlighted the inhuman conditions faced by many seamen.

Following the collapse of both the Ottoman and Russian empires, a major concern of the great powers was to create an international legal regime to govern the status of the sea and the straits. The Lausanne treaty (1923), signed by the new Turkish government, affirmed full freedom of navigation through the straits in times of peace, but it set limits on the passage of naval vessels. The straits themselves were to be demilitarized. The new Turkish Republic frequently called for a revision of the Lausanne provisions, and in 1936 the Montreux convention returned sovereignty of the straits to the Turkish state while reaffirming the principle of free passage in peacetime. With the exception of new safety regulations introduced unilaterally by Turkey in the 1990s, the Montreux convention has governed access to the sea into the twenty-first century.

Naval engagements during World War II were limited because of Turkey's neutrality and the Axis forces' swift conquest of the northern littoral following the German invasion of the Soviet Union. Yet from such lesser ports as Poti and Batumi, the Soviet navy was able to run interference operations, forcing German ships to spend much of the war in Romanian and Bulgarian ports. Jews and other refugees flocked to the Black Sea ports in hopes of securing passage abroad, but the journeys sometimes ended in tragedy. In 1942 the passenger ship *Struma* was sunk off the entrance to the Bosphorus, probably by a Soviet submarine, with the result that some 800 Jewish refugees en route from Constanta to Palestine were killed.

From the late 1940s, most of the littoral remained under the control of the Soviet Union itself or one of its new satellites, Romania and Bulgaria. Turkey, a member of the North Atlantic Treaty Organisation (NATO), became the vanguard of the West against the Soviet threat. The Soviet Union repeatedly attempted to revise the terms of the Montreux convention and to restrict naval access to the fleets of littoral states—a change that would have placed the sea nearly totally within Communist control. The United States regularly sent military missions through the straits to demonstrate that the Montreux principles remained valid.

In the second half of the twentieth century, the development policies of both Turkey and the Communist states of the north contributed to a severe environmental crisis. Intensive agriculture increased runoff and pollution from fertilizers, unregulated industrialization allowed chemicals to drain into the sea, and large-scale fishing led to the rapid decline of several commercial fish species in the sea. Waste from even farther afield—from western and central Europe via the Danube—added to the degradation of an already fragile marine environment. These changes had profound effects on coastal communities: fishing fleets were laid up and fish processing centers were closed down, tourism declined, and immigration from the coast to inland cities increased.

There was some effort in the 1990s to address these issues through the establishment of the Black Sea Economic Cooperation Organization. But continued interstate rivalries and a lack of funds blocked the growth of a genuinely cooperative Black Sea region. Yet there were some environmental improvements, owing largely to the collapse of state-supported agriculture in the former Communist countries and greater monitoring of industrial pollution. The discovery of significant petroleum deposits in the post-Soviet countries of the Caspian basin raised the question of export routes via the straits. The Turkish government remained adamant that tanker traffic via Istanbul should be restricted to ward off a major catastrophe in the tight shipping channel. These issues were resolved with the construction of a new pipeline running from Baku on the Caspian, via Tbilisi, Georgia, to the Turkish port of Ceyhan on the Mediterranean.

[*See also* Constanța; *Goeben*; Istanbul; Navies, Great Powers, *subentry on* Russia and the Soviet Union, 1700 to the Present; Odessa; *and* Straits, *subentry on* Laws Governing Straits.]

## Bibliography

Ascherson, Neil. *Black Sea*. London: Jonathan Cape, 1995. An engaging portrait of the Black Sea world by an experienced journalist.

Ballard, Robert D., et al. "Deepwater Archaeology of the Black Sea: The 2000 Season at Sinop, Turkey." *American Journal of Archaeology* 105, no. 4 (October 2001): 607–623. Underwater research aimed at discovering sunken ships and settlements on the ancient seacoast.

*Black Sea Pilot*. London: Hydrographic Office, Admiralty, in multiple editions from the mid-nineteenth century forward. The major source for detailed information on geography and oceanography,

Bratianu, Gheorghe Ioan. *La mer Noire, des origines à la conquête ottomane*. Munich: Romanian Academy Society, 1969. A classic synthesis by a major Romanian historian.

Braund, David. *Georgia in Antiquity: A History of Colchis and Transcaucasian Iberia, 550 BC–AD 562*. Oxford: Clarendon Press, 1994.

Bryer, Anthony, and David Winfield. *The Byzantine Monuments and Topography of the Pontos*. 2 vols. Washington: Dumbarton Oaks Research Library and Collection, 1985. A splendid survey of geography, architecture, and history along the southern coast.

Frantz, Douglas, and Catherine Collins. *Death on the Black Sea: The Untold Story of the* Struma *and World War II's Holocaust at Sea*. New York: Ecco, 2003.

Herlihy, Patricia. *Odessa: A History, 1794–1914*. Cambridge, Mass.: Harvard Ukrainian Research Institute, 1986.

King, Charles. *The Black Sea: A History*. Oxford: Oxford University Press, 2004. A comprehensive survey from ancient times to the twenty-first century.

Nekrasov, George. *North of Gallipoli: The Black Sea Fleet at War, 1914–1917*. Boulder, Colo.: East European Monographs, 1992.

Ostapchuk, Victor. "The Human Landscape of the Ottoman Black Sea in the Face of the Cossack Naval Raids." *Oriente Moderno* 20, no. 1 (2001): 23–95.

Ovcharov, Nikolai. *Ships and Shipping in the Black Sea: XIV–XIX Centuries*. Translated by Elena Vatashka. Sofia, Bulgaria: Saint Kliment Ohridski University Press, 1993. A good survey of ship types, based on graffiti carvings in Bulgarian churches.

Phillips, Edward J. *The Founding of Russia's Navy: Peter the Great and the Azov Fleet, 1688–1714*. Westport, Conn.: Greenwood Press, 1995.

Ryan, William, and Walter Pitman. *Noah's Flood: New Scientific Discoveries about the Event That Changed History*. New York: Simon and Schuster, 1998. A popular account of the controversial "flood thesis."

Tsetskhladze, Gocha R., ed. *The Greek Colonisation of the Black Sea Area: Historical Interpretation of Archaeology*. Stuttgart, Germany: Franz Steiner, 1998.

Zaitsev, Yu., and V. Mamaev. *Marine Biological Diversity in the Black Sea: A Study of Change and Decline*. New York: United Nations Publications, 1997. A good overview of the sea's physical peculiarities and fauna.

CHARLES KING

## Blaeu, Willem Janszoon (1571–1638),

Dutch publisher, cartographer, and astronomer. Willem Janszoon Blaeu (also known as Willem Jansz. Blaeu) was born Willem Janszoon on December 9, 1571, in or near the city of Alkmaar, Holland, the son of a fishmonger. After receiving his first schooling in Alkmaar, he moved to Amsterdam to be trained in the same trade as his father. From an early date, however, Willem Janszoon also showed a keen interest in the mathematical arts. In the winter and spring of 1595–1596 he studied astronomy at Tycho Brahe's observatory on Hven, Denmark. Having returned to Amsterdam in May 1596, Willem Janszoon produced his first celestial and terrestrial globes and soon thereafter began to sell maps, charts, and navigational instruments as well. In the early 1600s he entered the book trade and rapidly extended his business into one of the leading publishing houses of the Dutch Republic.

In order to distinguish himself from his competitor Jan Janszoon, Willem Janszoon in 1621 adopted the surname "Blaeu" (or Latinized "Caesius"). Over the years the Blaeu firm published a substantial number of atlases, maps, navigational manuals, astronomical tables, and instructions for the use of cartographic aids. Although born a

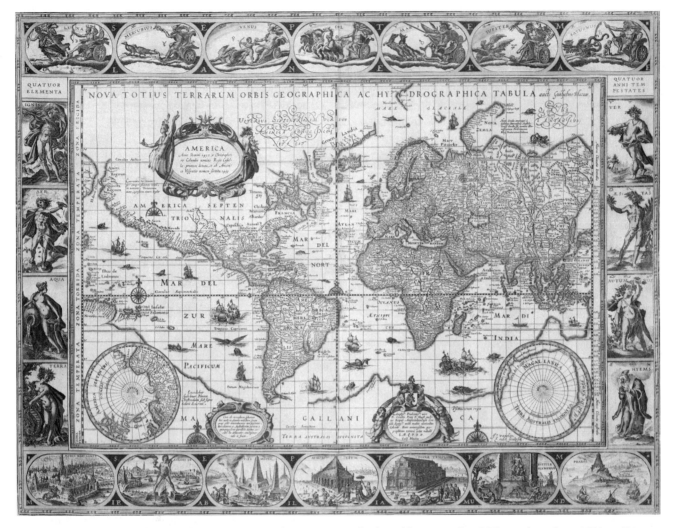

**Willem Blaeu's Chart of the World, 1630.** Drawn on the Mercator projection, this map prefaced Blaeu atlases from 1630 until it was superseded by a two-hemisphere map in 1662. THE NEW YORK PUBLIC LIBRARY / ART RESOURCE, NY

Mennonite himself, Willem Janszoon Blaeu published a large quantity of Catholic devotional works. In 1633, Blaeu was appointed mapmaker and examiner of pilots of the Chamber Amsterdam of the Dutch East India Company (VOC). The driving force behind this appointment was his friend, VOC director Laurens Reael, who was as eager a student of mathematics and geography as Willem Janszoon himself was. After his death in Amsterdam on October 21, 1638, the firm of Blaeu was continued by Willem's son Joan and his grandchildren Willem, Pieter, and Joan until the beginning of the eighteenth century.

The publisher's list of Willem Janszoon Blaeu in the fields of navigation, astronomy, and cartography was a mixture of books composed by himself and books written by other authors, such as astronomical cum navigational manuals of the Franeker professor of mathematics Adriaan

Metius. The most important books authored by Blaeu himself were sea atlases first published in 1608 and 1623, *Het licht der zee-vaert* and the *Zeespiegel*. These sea atlases, which contain charts of all the seas around Europe and of parts of the Atlantic as well as coastal elevations, sailing instructions, and a brief instruction in the art of navigation, went through many reprints and also appeared in English translation in 1612 and 1625, respectively, as *The Light of Navigation* and *The Sea Mirrour*. Furthermore, Blaeu in 1634 published a treatise on the use of celestial and terrestrial globes and also composed a table to aid seamen to find the variation of the compass by a single amplitude observation of the sun. The *Zeespiegel* and these other books later formed part of the standard set of equipment issued to ships of the VOC. The printed cartographic output of the Blaeu firm included, among other things, a plane chart of the seas around Europe (published in 1605) and a chart of the Atlantic on Mercator's projection (published in 1608). Like other publishers in Amsterdam, Blaeu subcontracted part of his production to suppliers in the nearby town of Edam, which already had a reputation in mapmaking before the rise of Amsterdam as a leading center of cartography. The charts produced under Blaeu's supervision as hydrographer of the East India Company circulated only in manuscript.

Blaeu always kept abreast of the latest developments in astronomy, geography, and the art of navigation and made several contributions in these areas himself as well. He described in *Het licht der zee-vaert* a new method of observing the sun with a cross-staff backward and introduced in the *Zeespiegel* an improved version of the backstaff (called the *hoekboog*). In the 1620s he measured quite accurately the length of the nautical mile. Blaeu was an early advocate of the Copernican system. His new map of the world of 1619 depicted the universe as a heliocentric system, and a tellurion (Latin *tellurium*) completed in 1634 showed the earth moving around the sun. In his treatise on the use of globes (first published in 1634 and reprinted nine times in Latin, five times in Dutch, three times in French, and once, partially, in Japanese), Blaeu explained how these devices could be used both "according to the opinion of Ptolemy with a fixed earth" and "after the natural proposition of Nicolaus Copernicus with a moving earth." However, the idea of finding longitude at sea by observing magnetic declination, which in the early seventeenth century still enjoyed considerable support among scholars and seafarers, never found any favor with Blaeu. Several times Blaeu acted as an expert adviser to the States-General on new proposals for solving the problem of determining longitude at sea. Shortly before his death he served jointly with Laurens Reael and the professors of astronomy and mathematics Martinus Hortensius and Jacob Golius on a committee appointed by the States-General to examine a proposal submitted by Galileo Galilei.

[*See also* East India Companies, *subentry on* Dutch East India Company.]

### Bibliography

Davids, C. A. *Zeewezen en wetenschap: De wetenschap en de ontwikkeling van de navigatietechniek in Nederland tussen 1585 en 1815*. Amsterdam: De Bataafsche Leeuw, 1986.

Keuning, Johannes. *Willem Jansz. Blaeu: A Biography and History of His Work as a Cartographer and Publisher*. Revised and edited by Marijke Donkersloot-De Vrij. Amsterdam: Theatrum Orbis Terrarum, 1973.

Koeman, Cornelis, and Peter van der Krogt. *Koeman's "Atlantes Neerlandici."* Vol. 2, *The Folio Atlases Published by Willem Jansz. Blaeu and Joan Blaeu*. 't-Goy-Houten, Netherlands: HES-De Graaf, 2000.

Krogt, Peter van der. *Globi Neerlandici: The Production of Globes in the Low Countries*. Utrecht, Netherlands: HES, 1993.

Vermij, Rienk. *The Calvinist Copernicans: The Reception of the New Astronomy in the Dutch Republic, 1575–1750*. Amsterdam: Koninklijke Akademie van Wetenschappen, 2002.

Waters, David W. *The Art of Navigation in England in Elizabethan and Early Stuart Times*. London: Hollis and Carter, 1958. 2d ed. with revisions. Greenwich: National Maritime Museum, 1978.

Zandvliet, Kees. *Mapping for Money: Plans and Topographic Paintings and Their Role in Dutch Overseas Expansion during the 16th and 17th Centuries*. Amsterdam: Batavian Lion International, 1998.

KAREL DAVIDS

# Blake, Robert

**Blake, Robert** (1598–1657), British admiral. The son of a Bridgwater, Somerset, merchant, Blake was educated at Oxford. Other aspects of his early life are obscure, although it is probable that he served for some time in merchant ships. He served as a member of Parliament for Bridgwater in the "Short Parliament" of 1640, and from 1646 onward. At the outbreak of the civil war, he became an officer in the regiment of Edward Popham, also from Somerset, and was promoted to lieutenant-colonel after distinguishing himself at Bristol in 1643.

Blake's defense of two besieged garrisons—Lyme in 1644 and Taunton in 1644–1645—gave him a national reputation, and in February 1649 he was one of three "generals-at-sea" appointed by the republican government to command the fleet. Arguably the most junior of the three, Blake, like the others, was given the command to cement the loyalty of a fleet that had rebelled against Parliament in 1648, and to impose on the navy the sort of discipline that had become the norm in the New Model Army. In practice Blake was the most active of the generals. In 1649 he blockaded Prince Rupert's squadron in Kinsale, pursuing him to Portugal in the following year. Blake's depredations against Portuguese shipping forced King João IV to abandon his support of Rupert, and Blake then pursued the prince into the Mediterranean. Following his return to England, Blake oversaw the recapture of the Scilly Islands and Jersey (1651).

In May 1652 Blake's fleet encountered the Dutch under Maarten Harpertszoon Tromp off Dover, and the first battle of the first Anglo-Dutch War began. Blake, now sole general-at-sea, had the better of this engagement, as well as another off the Kentish Knock in October, but in December he attacked a greatly superior Dutch fleet off Dungeness and saw his fleet badly mauled. He offered to resign but was kept on in a new joint command, and he also oversaw major reforms in the fleet, including increases in seamen's pay and the introduction of a new tactic, the "line of battle," which emphasized the concentration of broadside fire. He fought in two of the great English victories of 1653, Portland and the Gabbard, but was subsequently too ill to go to sea.

In 1654 Blake was sent to the Mediterranean to impose terms on the dey of Tunis, whose ships had been attacking English merchantmen, and in April 1655 he destroyed the dey's galleys in Porto Farina. By then England was at war with Spain, and in 1656 Blake was sent with a fleet to intercept the returning Spanish bullion fleet from the Americas. He learned in April 1657 that the fleet had moored at Santa Cruz, on Tenerife, and despite the formidable defenses of the harbor, he launched a brilliantly successful attack that destroyed all the Spanish ships—although the bullion was safe ashore.

Blake's health worsened on the voyage home, and he died on August 7, 1657, as his flagship entered Plymouth Sound. He was given a state funeral befitting a hero of the republic and buried at Westminster Abbey. Blake's letters give ample testimony of his firm Puritan faith, but his boldness as a commander and organizational skills provided an example that inspired many subsequent sea officers, including Horatio Nelson.

[See also Wars, Maritime, *subentry on* Anglo-Dutch Wars.]

### Bibliography

Baumber, Michael. *General-at-Sea: Robert Blake and the Seventeenth-Century Revolution in Naval Warfare*. London: John Murray, 1989. The fullest modern biography, albeit ultimately unconvincing in its advocacy of Blake as the instigator of line-of-battle tactics.

Capp, Bernard S. *Cromwell's Navy: The Fleet and the English Revolution, 1648–60*. Oxford: Oxford University Press, 1989. A thorough and impressive survey, setting Blake in the context of the navy and the state that he served.

Cogar, William B. "Robert Blake; The State's Admiral (1599–1657)." In *The Great Admirals: Command at Sea, 1587–1945*, edited by Jack Sweetman, pp. 58–81. Annapolis, Md.: Naval Institute Press, 1997. A good short survey of Blake's career.

J. D. DAVIES

**Blockade**　The word "blockade" refers to a type of naval operation used to prevent ships from having access to or being able to leave an enemy's coast or home waters. There are two versions of blockade—military and commercial—although they often operate together. Military blockade, the containment of an enemy's warships, is part of command of the sea and sea control. It might be the result of a successful battle or campaign or of the deterrent effect of a general preponderance of force. Commercial blockade is the denial of an enemy's ability to use the seas for merchant shipping for import and export. This denial undermines the war-making ability and the general economy of the enemy state or states.

Rules governing blockade have developed over the years; under international maritime law, properly declared blockades must be observed by neutral nations. Merchant ships suspected of breaking a declared blockade can be legally stopped and searched, and if their cargoes are considered to be "contraband of war" they can be seized by the belligerent concerned after condemnation in a formal hearing at a prize court. Blockades can be carried out only by a power that is in command of the sea. Although attacks intended to sink or capture merchant ships or to seize their cargoes may be called "blockades," such attacks are more properly called "commerce raiding" or *guerres de course*. A specialized form of defensive blockade may be implemented against a particular commodity, for example, drugs, slaves, or even illegal immigrants.

Blockade can be either close, exerted by ships operating near an enemy's coast, or distant, exerted by ships operating on the other side of an enemy's sea communications, some distance away. Distant blockade was often used in the age of sail—Julian Corbett called it "open blockade"—and it became the norm once more in the twentieth century because of the increasing effectiveness in the littoral of sea-denial assets, notably underwater weapons.

The concept of blockade began when navies were able to patrol consistently off an enemy's coast. One of the first examples occurred in the first Anglo-Dutch War after the English victory of the battle of Gabbard in 1653. Their ships lay for a time off the Dutch coast, which prevented the movement of enemy vessels and had a great economic cost for the Netherlands.

Close blockade was a demanding strategy, and more than a century passed before it began to be developed systematically. Only the British had a sufficiently strong combination of well-placed bases, numbers of ships both large and small, and skilled seamen to maintain a presence off the French Atlantic coast. The 1759 blockade prevented coastal shipping from servicing the French Atlantic dockyards and ruined many individual merchants who were

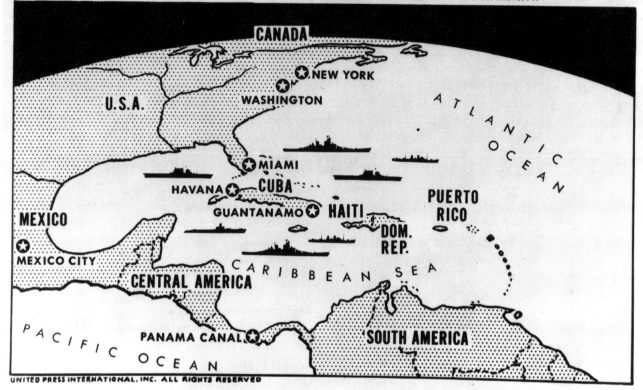

NXP1352660-10/23/62-WASHINGTON: This pictorial newsmap indicates the extent of the US blockade of Cuba, which may be tested at any time 10/23 since ships of both Soviet Russia and its satellites were reported churning through the North Atlantic toward Cuba. The Defense Department said late 10/22 it was prepared to sink any Soviet ship carrying missiles or other offensive weapons toward Cuba if the vessel refused orders to turn away. Pres. Kennedy declared 10/22 that Soviet missiles and other offensive weapons had turned Cuba into an armed camp capable of hruling destruction at the heart of the U.S. as well as neighboring Central and South American nations. UPI TELEPHOTOrb

**Blockade.** The U.S. naval blockade during the Cuban Missile Crisis. This map was published in the *New York World-Telegram*, October 23, 1962. LIBRARY OF CONGRESS, PRINTS AND PHOTOGRAPHS DIVISION

vital to the maintenance of the French sea power. The reduction of shipping also reduced the numbers of available French seamen.

### The Nineteenth Century

Because of inadequate strength, a more open blockade was reverted to in the War of American Independence and the early days of the French Revolutionary War, but close blockade was revived in 1800 and was maintained into the Napoleonic Wars. It was the successful blockade of the French fleet—more than the British victory at Trafalgar—that prevented Napoleon from executing his planned invasion of Britain in 1804–1805.

The strategic standoff that resulted forced Napoleon in 1806 to use his dominance of the continent to try to ban British ships from continental ports. All cargoes required a certificate of origin, and goods of British ownership or origin were subject to seizure. This "Continental System" was countered by a tightening of the British maritime blockade. The Orders in Council of 1807 authorized the seizure of all ships trading directly with Napoleonic Europe that did not go through British ports. Napoleon countered with orders to seize any ships doing as the British required. The British got the best of the confrontation as the French economy suffered and Napoleon was forced into overextending himself to plug loopholes in his system.

The emphasis on economic warfare in the Napoleonic period led to an increase in blockade declarations, many of which could not be imposed in an orderly fashion because of naval weakness. In 1826–1827, therefore, Britain and the United States, the owners of the two leading merchant marines, agreed that for a blockade to be legally binding it had to be effective—that is, had to be maintained by a force sufficient to deny access to the enemy coast or at least to create evident danger to ships coming from or going to the blockaded ports.

This agreement was written into the Declaration of Paris of 1856, signed at the end of the Russian War. The declaration reflected the operations of Russia's enemies during the war. Privateering, or commerce raiding by commissioned merchantmen, was formally abolished. It was held that the neutral flag covered enemy goods, except for specified "contraband of war." Neutral goods other than contraband were not liable to capture even under an enemy flag. Before, all enemy goods had been considered contraband, so the Declaration did, at least superficially, put a significant limit on traditional British blockade rights. However, the British government considered this concession to be worth the abolition of privateers, the major threat to British trade. If privateering began again, then the British could revert to their old blockading ways.

When the American Civil War broke out in 1861, President Lincoln immediately declared a blockade of the Southern states. Although the United States was not a party to the Declaration of Paris, Lincoln announced that the blockade was to be carried out in accordance with "the Law of Nations." A "competent force" was to be posted to prevent the entrance and exit of vessels from Southern ports. Ships were to be warned and turned back; if they tried again, they were to be captured and sent to "the nearest convenient port" for proceedings against both the ship and its cargo.

At first the federal blockade was imposed successfully with relatively few ships, but, as an illicit trade in contraband grew with the construction of specialist blockade-running steamers, much greater effort had to be put into stationing relatively small warships as close as possible to the entrances to Confederate ports. This blockade confirmed that the advent of steam greatly increased the effectiveness of blockade operations. To support the relatively short range of steam blockaders, bases were seized along the Southern coast. The result is considered by some to have been one of the most effective blockades in naval history. There is debate as to whether the Union blockade was a severe handicap for the Confederacy in its dependence on seaborne trade for its supply of manufactured products; whether the prevention of the export of cotton, the South's main source of income, was an even more serious blow; and whether the blockade shortened the war significantly.

## The Twentieth Century

During the Russo-Japanese War (1904–1905) the Russian Far Eastern fleet was effectively blockaded by the Japanese in Port Arthur, where it was destroyed after a long siege. After that conflict more international effort went into codifying the laws of commercial blockade. Germany proposed the International Court of Appeal to which the decisions of national prize courts could be taken, but this proposal was defeated in the British Parliament. In 1908 a conference was nevertheless convened in London to redefine the rules of commercial blockade, and it resulted in 1909 in the Declaration of London. This declaration created two lists: "absolute contraband," which included military equipment such as guns and explosives, and "conditional contraband," which covered food, fuel, and clothing if it was "shown to be destined for the use of armed forces or of a government department of the enemy state." Conditional contraband could not be seized except when found on board a vessel bound for enemy territory. There was also a "free list" containing a large number of raw materials. Such was the international legal situation when war was declared in 1914.

There had been much debate in early-twentieth-century Britain over the type of blockade to be adopted in the case of a future war with a major continental power. As late as 1911 the First Sea Lord, Sir Arthur Wilson, had expressed enthusiasm for close blockade, but Admiral Sir George Callaghan, the commander in chief of the Home Fleet, reacted strongly against this idea, and in April 1912 close blockade was officially abandoned. At the end of the year new plans were sent to Callaghan based on the idea of a distant blockade that would close the entrances to the North Sea and make sweeps and patrols to the south as appropriate. Such a deployment might tempt out the German Fleet to fight at a disadvantage. Distant blockade was retained despite its failure to prevent an "enemy landing" in the Humber by Sir John Jellicoe's "enemy" fleet in the 1913 exercises. Hopes were placed in minefields, air patrols, and a reorganized surface and submarine flotilla to guard the southern North Sea. When war broke out in 1914 Sir John Jellicoe's Grand Fleet deployed to northern Scottish ports, from which it exercised its distant blockade for the next four years. German movement into the Atlantic was successfully prevented, and a successful commercial blockade of European ports was imposed.

Although the United Kingdom never ratified the London Declaration, when war broke out in August 1914 it published an Order in Council that reflected the declaration's provisions. The order defined two types of contraband goods: those whose import into enemy countries was absolutely prohibited (such as weapons, warships, aircraft, animals suitable for warlike use, and "implements and apparatus designed exclusively for the manufacture of ammunition") and those that were on a conditional list, including food, fuel, bullion, vehicles, and similar items that were contraband only if destined for an enemy government. In the succeeding months more Orders in Council were issued to prevent the movement of conditional contraband through neutral countries. Both the "absolute" and "conditional" lists were also extended. Food was included on the absolute contraband list when the German government took control over all foodstuffs.

In the early stages of the war the commercial blockade was imposed by intercepting all neutral shipping proceeding to Dutch and Scandinavian ports. The Strait of Dover was largely blocked by a minefield, which allowed all shipping passing by that route to be easily intercepted in the Downs. A greater challenge faced the Northern Patrol that had to guard the 610 miles of the Greenland–Iceland–U.K. gap. The patrol was provided by the Tenth Cruiser Squadron of old armed merchant cruisers, and it was supplemented by armed trawlers capable of coping with the heavy seas encountered in these waters.

By the time the Northern Patrol was fully operational in March 1915, a new Order in Council had been issued. This banned any merchant vessel that had sailed after the beginning of the month from reaching any German port. Similarly, any merchant vessel that had sailed from a German port would not be allowed to proceed with her voyage. All merchant ships that were carrying cargoes to or from the enemy might be required to discharge their cargoes in an allied port.

This order was officially a reprisal for the German declaration in February of a counterblockade in the form of unrestricted submarine warfare. Instead of the elaborate British system of diversion, examination, and condemnation, the Germans simply sank allied and neutral ships found in the war zone around Britain, sometimes even torpedoing them without warning. The Germans justified this measure as countering the extension of British measures into a "starvation blockade." The United States disliked both forms of blockade, but its reaction to the German style was more rigorous than to the British. Following the sinking of the liner *Arabic* in August 1915, the Germans called off their offensive.

The British used their control of steam coal to make agreements with neutral countries and gain their assistance in the application of the blockade. A system of "letters of assurance," or "Navicerts," was introduced. These letters, issued by the Contraband Committee in London, were given to merchant captains after careful investigation at the port where the ship was loaded; the letter showed that the cargoes were as stated, that they were going to acceptable destinations, and that they were within the limits of the goods allowed for each neutral country. Neutral countries were allocated a certain "ration" of items, sufficient for domestic demands but not for reexport to Germany. The Navicerts reduced delays in British or Allied ports to the time necessary to examine the passengers and verify the cargo.

Very few ships were able to approach Europe without being subject to British blockade. In the second half of 1916 only three ships of any importance reached Scandinavia without being examined. German attempts in 1916 to restore the unrestricted U-boat campaign foundered on American opposition, although a more restricted campaign began again later in the year. At the beginning of 1917 the Germans decided to restore the unrestricted campaign. The campaign allowed control of shipping to be maintained by preventing ships from calling for examination in the United Kingdom but enforcing examination calls at foreign ports by means of bunker regulations.

The unrestricted U-boat campaign soon brought America into the war. This greatly simplified the commercial blockade because the United States had been the main loophole in the blockade. Almost all cargoes could be controlled at their source. The units of the Northern Patrol were diverted to escort the convoys that eventually neutralized the U-boat offensive.

From the autumn of 1914 until the end of January 1918—the period during which the Northern Patrol was on station—12,979 vessels (including 4,520 fishing craft) were intercepted and boarded and 2,039 vessels called at British ports voluntarily. Only 742 vessels were not intercepted. The blockade had the effect of cutting Germany's imports of food and raw materials from outside Europe by over half. The direct effects on German industry and military potential were not as great as the British had hoped, but by 1916 food shortages were beginning to be felt in Germany, and these became worse as the war continued. The situation had more to do with inefficiencies in the food-distribution system than with absolute shortages, but the blockade put that system under pressure that it could not sustain. Many people in the cities suffered in the "starvation blockade," and this suffering had some effect in creating the disillusion and discontent that fostered the revolution that took hold following the defeat of Germany's armies in the field. The blockade was continued after the Armistice as a way of pressuring the Germans into accepting Allied peace terms.

The declared effects of the British World War I blockade were exaggerated, and great hopes were put in economic blockade as the key to defeating Germany in the strategy of the Neville Chamberlain government in 1939. The Northern Patrol of old cruisers and armed merchant cruisers supported by the main fleet at Scapa was restored in a naval deployment that mirrored that of 1914. A global contraband control was set up from the Orkneys to Aden. In the first six weeks of World War II almost 345,000 tonnes of cargo was seized, and German merchant shipping almost disappeared.

Adolf Hitler's conquest of Europe prevented the blockade from having much offensive potential. Occupation of the mainland coast also assisted blockade running, which became more important when the invasion of the Soviet Union prevented the use of the overland route for imports of rubber and edible oils from the Far East. Between April 1941 and May 1942, 75 percent of the cargoes dispatched from Japan to Germany got through, and six ships carried valuable machinery in the other direction. In late 1942 this passage became more difficult. Between August 1942 and May 1943, eighteen of the thirty-two blockade runners on the Far East–Europe route were either sunk or turned back.

Blockade running ceased with the occupation of the French coast in 1944. In all, nineteen blockade runners were lost, of which fifteen were sunk or captured by surface ships or scuttled themselves when intercepted, two were sunk by aircraft, and two were sunk in error by U-boats. Of twenty-one ships that left France for the Far East with 69,300 tons of cargo, fifteen with 57,000 tons arrived safely. Of the thirty-five that started from the East with 250,700 tons of cargo, only sixteen with 111,490 tons arrived. Once the Allies had exerted sea control in the central and South Atlantic, with air bases on the South African and American coast and in the Azores and on Ascension Island, it was difficult for the blockade runners to succeed.

As in World War I, Germany was denied assured access to the world ocean. Its surface warships could operate only as fugitive raiders. Again the main German effort at retaliation was with a submarine *guerre de course*. It soon became unrestricted once more, but it was eventually defeated, as before, by the convoy system. In the Pacific the Americans also resorted to unrestricted submarine warfare that, together with aerial mining, effectively subjected the sea-dependent Japan to an all-too-effective blockade by 1945. The success reflected both American sea control and Japanese failures to develop an effective defensive system.

In the postwar era the application of blockades has been constrained by the fact that a blockade is, in international law terms, an act of war. War in a legal sense was outlawed in the United Nations charter. Nevertheless, just as force has been used within the terms of the charter, so interdiction of maritime communications has been used as an instrument of policy. During the Korean War of 1950–1953, U.N. naval forces successfully blockaded the coast of the areas of the peninsula occupied by Communist forces. In the 1962 Cuba crisis the United States declared a carefully defined maritime "quarantine" of Cuba to prevent the import of more ballistic missiles from the Soviet Union and to exert pressure on the Soviet Union to withdraw those that had already been deployed.

After the end of the Cold War, United Nations–authorized maritime embargoes were imposed by combined naval forces on both Iraq and the former Yugoslavia. These embargoes involved the stopping and searching of ships suspected of carrying embargoed material, but legally they were not officially blockades. The advent of the helicopter as standard equipment of modern surface combatants has greatly assisted the effectiveness of boarding. Following the U.S.-led operations in Afghanistan, a major international maritime interdiction effort was deployed against Al-Qaeda personnel trying to escape by the sea.

[See also Atlantic, Battle of the; Brest, Blockade of; Downs, Battle of the; Privateering; Prizes; Strategy; Tactics; *and* Wars, Maritime, *subentry on* World Wars.]

## Bibliography

Anderson, Bern. *By Sea and by River: The Naval History of the Civil War*. New York: Da Capo, 1989.

Bell, Archibald C. *A History of the Blockade of Germany and the Countries Associated with Her in the Great War*. London: Her Majesty's Stationery Office, 1961.

Consett, M. W. W. P. *The Triumph of Unarmed Forces*. London: Williams and Norgate, 1923.

Corbett, Julian S. *Some Principles of Maritime Strategy*. Annapolis, Md.: Naval Institute Press, 1988.

Elleman, Bruce, and S. C. M. Paine, eds. *Naval Blockades and Seapower: Strategies and Counter-Strategies, 1805–2005*. London: Frank Cass, 2005.

Gardiner, Robert. *Fleet Battle and Blockade: The French Revolutionary War 1793–1814*. London: Chatham, 1996.

Grainger, John D., ed. *The Maritime Blockade of Germany in the Great War*. Aldershot, U.K.: Ashgate, for the Navy Records Society, 2003.

Jones, Virgil C. *The Civil War at Sea*. 3 vols. New York: Holt, Rinehart and Winston, 1960–1962.

Leyland, John, ed. *Papers Relating to the Blockade of Brest 1803–1805*. Vols. 14 and 21. London: Navy Records Society, 1899 and 1902.

Medlicott, William N. *The Economic Blockade*. The History of the Second World War, Civil Series, vol. 1. London: Her Majesty's Stationery Office, 1952.

Morriss, Roger, ed. *The Channel Fleet and the Blockade of Brest, 1793–1801*. Aldershot, U.K.: Ashgate, for the Navy Records Society, 2001.

Offer, Avner. *The First World War: An Agrarian Interpretation*. Oxford: Oxford University Press, 1989.

Roskill, Stephen W. *The War at Sea*. 3 vols. London: His Majesty's Stationery Office, 1954–1961.

Wise, Stephen R. *Lifeline of the Confederacy: Blockade Running during the Civil War*. Columbia: University of South Carolina Press, 1988.

Woodman, Richard. *The Victory of Sea Power: Winning the Napoleonic Wars 1806–1814*. London: Chatham, 1998.

ERIC J. GROVE

# Bodega y Quadra, Juan Francisco de la

(1744–1794), Spanish naval captain and explorer. Born in Lima, Juan Francisco de la Bodega y Quadra was the son of Tomás de la Bodega y Quadra, a Bizcayan merchant, and a Peruvian aristocratic mother, Francisca de Mollinedo. He enlisted in the Spanish navy in 1762, serving in several ships before being sent in 1774 to the naval department of San Blas, Nayarit, on the Pacific coast of Mexico.

In 1775, Bodega y Quadra commanded the tiny sloop *Sonora* in a voyage north to search for signs of Russian establishments and a strait leading to the east, and he reached latitude 58°30′ N. He was the first Spaniard to reach Alaska and the first to land on the northwest coast (though not the mainland). In 1779, after news of Cook's arrival on the coast the previous year, he sailed north again, this time in *Nuestra Señora de los Remedios* (alias *Favorita*), in company with his senior officer Ignacio de Arteaga, who was in *Nuestra Señora del Rosario* (alias *Princesa*). At their farthest north at Hinchinbrook Island (near Prince William Sound), the two officers claimed the region for Spain. At latitude 60° N, it was the most northerly of all Spanish acts of possession in America, and the expedition's failure to come across any signs of British or Russian activity either there or farther south at Bucareli Sound gave a misleading sense of security to the Spanish authorities in Mexico.

Upon his return and after a short stay at Lima, Bodega y Quadra sailed to Cuba and then on to Spain. In 1789 he returned to San Blas, but now promoted to captain and to commander in chief of the naval department. While in this role, he led the Spanish border commission of 1792 that was responsible for returning to Great Britain the facilities and territories captured by the Spanish at Nootka Sound three years before, a requirement of the Treaty of San Lorenzo de El Escorial. The negotiations at Nootka on behalf of Britain were conducted by Captain George Vancouver. Bodega y Quadra gained Vancouver's respect and friendship, and they agreed to name the main island of the area under dispute Quadra and Vancouver (later known simply as Vancouver). But many issues remained unresolved.

Bodega y Quadra collected important ethnographic and natural specimens, and he produced detailed and accurate charts of the northwest coast, assisted in the 1792 expedition by a team of Spanish scientists.

[See also Americas, *subentry on* Exploration Voyages, 1539–1794 (Northwest Coast), *and* Pacific Ocean, *subentries on* East Asia Seas *and* Eastern Pacific.]

## Bibliography

Bodega y Quadra, Juan Francisco de la. *El descubrimiento del fin del mundo (1775–1792)*. Madrid, Spain: Alianza Editorial, 1990.

Palau, Mercedes, Freeman Tovell, Pamela Sprätz, and Robin Inglis, eds. *Nutka 1792: Viaje a la costa noroeste de la América Septentrional por Juan Francisco de la Bodega y Quadra*. Madrid, Spain: Ministerio de Asuntos Exteriores de España, 1998.

Soler, Emilio. "Bodega y Quadra … Bibliografía" (1999). http://www.sge.org/sge07/04/noroeste_americano.asp

JORGE ORTIZ SOTELO

# Boeier.

*See* Trading Vessels, *subentry on* Early Modern Vessels.

# Bohrdt, Hans

(1857–1945), German marine artist. Hans (Johannes) Bohrdt was born on February 11, 1857, into a family of civil servants: his father was a clerk at the Supreme Court of Justice in Berlin. Little is known about his youth, which he lived in hardship from the age of twelve, when his father died. When he was fifteen his eldest brother, Paul, a ship's surgeon, invited him to Hamburg to join him on a voyage on board the sailing vessel *Palmerston* of the Rob. Sloman Neptun Schiffahrts shipping company. Bohrdt was so overwhelmed by the activity in the port and by the cruise that he decided to become a marine painter. He traveled to Africa, the Americas, the Pacific, India, and England, thinking that a genuine marine artist could paint ships and the sea only by viewing them through the eyes of a seaman. Bohrdt also believed that Impressionist painters were wrong in neglecting objective realism. He settled permanently in Berlin in 1886, married Anna, daughter of the painter Carl Koch, in 1889, and became a member of the Verein Berliner Künstler (Association of Artists in Berlin). From 1881 he displayed his paintings at the yearly exhibitions of the Royal Academy of Arts in Berlin.

His first contacts with the German royal court go back to 1888, when Kaiser Wilhelm II (r. 1888–1918) ascended the throne following the deaths of his grandfather and father within a span of only a few months. To mark the death of the two emperors and the ascension of the third, a Festschrift was published that included six illustrations by Bohrdt. From the late 1880s Bohrdt began to present his paintings regularly in Berlin. William II was impressed and bought several for the Prussian state and for himself. Bohrdt chose his motifs from public events, such as the emperor's visit to Spithead in 1889, the opening of the Kiel Canal (1895), or the emperor's sailing yacht *Meteor*. The prominent art critic Hans Rosenberg published a flattering assessment of Bohrdt's work in one of the leading art journals, and Bohrdt received yet another royal blessing when thirteen of his paintings were displayed at the Royal Academy in 1892. Two years later Bohrdt was invited to join the emperor on his yearly voyages on board the yacht *Hohenzollern*. They became friends. Although Bohrdt gave the emperor some drawing lessons, he persuaded him to reign and to leave the arts to himself and fellow marine artists like Willy Stöwer and Carl Saltzmann, who also sailed frequently on board the vessel.

Besides glorifying the rise of the German merchant marine and the Prussian and German maritime past, Bohrdt devoted much of his artistic work to the imperial navy in peace and at war. His best-known painting, *Der letzte Mann* (The Last Man), depicts a German sailor standing on a sinking cruiser after the Battle of the Falkland Islands in 1914, waving the imperial flag defiantly at the British victors. Although he recorded naval actions during World War I, he was not a war artist cum reporter. After 1918, with the emperor living in exile in the Netherlands, Bohrdt lost all imperial patronage. When the Versailles Treaty (1919) mandated handing over the merchant marine and the navy to the Allies, there were few contemporary subjects for painters like Bohrdt, and the public seemed uninterested in his art. Only gradually did he begin to receive commissions from shipping companies like the Norddeutscher Lloyd (North German Lloyd) to record the maiden voyages of their postwar passenger liners *Columbus*, *Bremen*, and *Europa*. Apart from occasional exhibitions, Bohrdt's art was no longer prized in the 1930s. After his home was destroyed in the last days of World War II, Bohrdt lived on the grounds of the Hindenburg Hospital, where he died on December 19, 1945.

Though Bohrdt had no pupils and founded no school, he had a strong influence on German marine art during William II's reign. He painted the sea and the ships that sailed on it, was deeply impressed by the maritime activities in ports such as Hamburg, and was interested in shipbuilding and trade. He was an active yachtsman and liked the races at Cowes (Isle of Wight) and Kiel. Yet portraying the hard work of seamen and shipbuilders, for example, was beyond his ability or interest. In 1995 the Deutsches Schiffahrtsmuseum (German Maritime Museum) presented the first retrospective exhibition of the artist's oeuvre.

[*See also* Art; Artists, *subentry* German; *and* Painting.]

## Bibliography

Meyer-Friese, Boye. *Marinemalerei in Deutschland im 19. Jahrhundert*. Oldenburg, Germany: Stalling, 1981.

Scholl, Lars U. *Deutsche Marinemalerei, 1830–2000*. Helgoland, Germany: Maren Knauß, 2002.

Scholl, Lars U. *Hans Bohrdt: Marinemaler des Kaisers*. Hamburg, Germany: Koehler, 1995.

LARS U. SCHOLL

**Bombay.** *See* Mumbai.

**Bomb Vessel.** *See* Warships, *subentry on* Early Modern Warships.

**Bonington, Richard Parkes** (1802–1828), English painter. Born on October 25, 1802, at Arnold, near Nottingham, Richard Parkes Bonington was the only child of, and a pupil of, Richard Bonington, a former keeper of Nottingham jail as well as a painter, drawing master, and supplier of art materials. In late 1817 the family moved to Calais, where Bonington senior and two Nottingham partners started a lace-making concern and where his son had some tuition in marine watercolors from the French painter Louis Francia. Early in 1819 the Boningtons moved to Paris to open a lace outlet, and the boy began copying Dutch and Flemish paintings in the Louvre. He also became one of the pupils of the historical painter Baron Antoine-Jean Gros and met many young French artists. However, though attracted by the historical Romanticism of the Scottish writer Sir Walter Scott (1771–1832) and the German writer Johann Wolfgang von Goethe (1749–1832), Bonington soon left Gros to concentrate on naturalistic landscape painting.

The first of Bonington's several tours in Normandy, in late 1821, resulted in watercolors shown at the Paris Salon of 1822 and elsewhere, rapidly winning him patrons and admirers, including the young painter Jean-Baptiste-Camille Corot. Bonington was soon busy making drawings for several topographical and historical publications, including those for Ostervald's *Excursion sur les côtes et dans les ports de Normandie* (1823–1825) and for his own *Restes et fragments d'architecture du moyen age* (1824)—the results of a new tour in Normandy and Belgium in 1823.

In February 1824, with Alexandre Colin (1798–1875), Bonington went for a short visit to Dunkerque but stayed for nearly a year, focusing on marine oil paintings and showing four at the Paris Salon that August. This was the first Salon at which British artists were invited to exhibit. Bonington won a gold medal for his *Fish Market near Boulogne* (1824; now at the Yale Center for British Art), and he and John Constable (1776–1837) were hailed as exemplars for the French Romantic landscape school.

In the summer of 1825, Bonington visited London, where he received introductions to notable private collections, sketched with Eugène Delacroix (1798–1863), and began to do plein air oil landscape studies. He also discovered the work of J. M. W. Turner (1775–1851), although Bonington's sea pieces, unlike Turner's, were mainly calm coastal views, with ships rarely shown in more than a stiff breeze. After returning to sketch with the French painter L. G. Eugène Isabey in Normandy, Bonington briefly shared Delacroix's Paris studio and, under his influence, began painting historical subjects in oil.

Bonington's talent burst unexpectedly on London in two fine oils of the French coast shown at the British Institution in February 1826. He subsequently took his own studio in Paris and, with a friend and pupil, Charles Rivet, made a summer tour through northern Italy and Switzerland, which provided subjects for exhibited works in his last two years. These consolidated Bonington's fame in France and England for his brilliance in both oil and watercolor, not least in marine and Venetian views. His rendering of historical subjects favored by French contemporaries became increasingly popular as well.

Bonington revisited London and first exhibited at the Royal Academy in 1827. He returned in January 1828, just before showing two Venetian pictures at the British Institution. His last entries to the Paris Salon and the Royal Academy in February and May 1828 included historical, Venetian, and marine subjects, but in late May he collapsed, reportedly from sunstroke while sketching on the Seine; tuberculosis was the real problem. In September his parents brought him to London for treatment, but he died there on September 23, 1828.

Many leading British artists attended Bonington's funeral, and his father sold much of his residual work in London in 1829. A great deal went to collectors; the rest was dispersed in three London sales of 1834, 1836, and 1838, the last two on the deaths of Bonington's parents. In a career of barely ten years, Bonington's precocity as a draftsman developed into fluent and brilliant mastery of color, both oil based and water based, and with lasting effects on both French and British art. The Wallace Collection, London, and the Yale Center for British Art, New Haven, Connecticut, have exceptional holdings of Bonington's work, and there are other important public collections in London, Nottingham, and Paris.

[*See also* Artists, *subentry* British, *and* Painting.]

## Bibliography

Noon, Patrick. *Richard Parkes Bonington: On the Pleasure of Painting*. New Haven, Conn.: Yale Center for British Art, Yale University Press, 1991. Exhibition catalog.

Pointon, Marcia. *Bonington, Francia, and Wyld*. London: Batsford in association with the Victoria and Albert Museum, 1985.

PIETER VAN DER MERWE

# Borda, Jean-Charles de (1733–1799),

French mathematician and naval captain. Born into a noble family at Dax, France, on May 4, 1733, the tenth of sixteen children, Borda was nephew to the naturalist J. F. de Borda (1718–1804). After completing his education at the Jesuit College at La Flèche, he enrolled in the Chevaux-légers, in which company he taught mathematics. René Réaumur's *correspondant* in the Académie Royale des Sciences from May 1753, his paper "Sur le jet des bombes," read to the Académie in 1756, led to his election as *adjoint géomètre* on June 27, 1756. Active at the Battle of Hastenbeck (1757), Borda soon after transferred to the engineering corps to have more opportunity for scientific work. With a view to joining the marine, he studied at the École du Génie at Mézière in 1758 and 1759. Papers on the resistance of air and fluids and on aspects of naval architecture followed, and his attachment to the French navy was confirmed in November 1767. Promoted to *associé géomètre* (June 30, 1768) in the Académie des Sciences, he represented this body, with Jean René Antoine, marquis de Verdun de la Crenne (1741–1805) and Alexandre Guy Pingré (1711–1796), on the voyage of *La Flore* (1771–1772) to Africa and America to test new methods and instruments for latitude and longitude.

The three academicians were all also members of the Académie de la Marine. Their report was Borda's first extended publication on practical navigation. It strongly endorsed both timepiece and lunar distance methods of finding longitude and the value of octants and sextants. The latter, however, could be improved, "c'est ce qu'un de nous a essayé de faire en lui substituant un cercle entier" (*Voyage*, 1728, p. 10).

Borda's thoughts fructified three years later when he commissioned, probably from Étienne Lenoir (1744–1832), his improved form of the reflecting circle invented in 1752 by the Göttingen astronomer Tobias Mayer (1723–1762). This instrument could measure angles wider than can a sextant (needed sometimes for lunar distance observations) and, since the same measurement can be repeated, reduces the error arising from scale graduation and observation, when the results are averaged. Borda's circle came slowly into use during the following decade, accelerating after Borda published a *Description* of it in 1787. In the third chapter of this work, Borda described his method of calculating lunar distances to find longitude. Recognized for several decades as one of the best of numerous proposals, this "cleared the distance" from the effects of parallax and refraction in order to ascertain the angle at the earth's center subtended between the directions from the center of the moon and the center of the other celestial body used in the calculation.

In 1773, promoted to lieutenant and named Chevalier in the Order of Saint Vincent, Borda was sent in the ship *Boussole* to map the Canary Islands, where he met James Cook. Seeing active service as a captain in North America during the American Revolution, he was captured by the English in 1782 after the battle of Dominica but was released on parole. In 1783 he replaced Henri-Louis

Duhamel du Monceau as Inspector-General of the Navy, creating a range of standardized ships-of-the-line with his protégé Jacques-Noël Sané. In 1784 he was appointed Inspecteur des Constructions Navales et Directeur de l'École des Ingénieurs. After the French Revolution, as chairman of the Commission des Poids et Mesures, he was preoccupied with the metric system and the introduction of the new standards that it required. The methods and instruments used by Pierre-Françoise-André Mechain and Jean-Baptiste-Joseph Delambre for measuring an arc of the meridian between Dunkerque and Barcelona were largely devised by Borda. A major contribution was Borda's calculation of decimal trigonometrical tables (1804), as part of his proposal for a right angle of 100 degrees. President of the first class (mathematics) of the Institut de France (1796–1797), Borda was also a member of the Bureau des Longitudes. He died in Paris on February 14, 1799.

[*See also* Mayer, Tobias.]

## Bibliography

Borda, Jean-Charles de. *Description et usage du cercle de reflexion; avec différentes methods pour calculer les observations nautiques.* Paris: Didot, 1787, with further editions in 1802, 1810, and 1816.

Mascart, Jean. *La vie et les travaux du Chevalier Jean-Charles de Borda (1733–1799): Episodes de la vie scientifique au XVIIIe siècle.* Lyon and Paris: A. Picard, 1919.

Verdun de la Crenne, Jean René Antoine, marquis de, Jean-Charles Borda, and Alexandre Pingré. *Voyage fait par ordre du Roi en 1771 et 1772, en diverse parties de l'Europe, de l'Afrique et de l'Amérique; pour vérifier l'utilité de plusieurs méthodes et instrumens, servant à déterminer la latitude et la longitude, tant du vaisseau que des côtes, isles et écueils qu'on reconnoît: suivi de recherches pour vérifier les cartes hydrographiques.* Paris: Imprimerie Royale, 1778.

ANTHONY TURNER

**Boston**    Boston, the capital of Massachusetts, was once one of America's most important seaports. Settled in 1630 by English Puritans and named Boston after a city in Lincolnshire, England, the port was an important trading center in the Atlantic world of the seventeenth and eighteenth centuries. Boston ships carried on an extensive trade within the British Empire, particularly with the West Indies, where fish were exchanged for sugar and molasses. After independence in 1783, Boston extended its trade to all parts of the world, including China, India, and South America. Boston's mercantile activities gave rise to the establishment of banks and insurance companies in the town (Boston became a city in 1822). Wealth derived from these enterprises helped to underwrite the founding of several educational, cultural, and medical institutions, including Harvard College (in nearby Cambridge), the Massachusetts Historical Society, and Massachusetts General Hospital.

Although Boston remained an important port in the nineteenth century, its relative position declined. Because Boston lacked good rail and water access to the expanding American West, Boston's international trade shifted toward New York and other ports to the south. Port activities saw a resurgence during World War I and World War II, but the advent of containerization harmed on the port. Lacking sufficient space in the old section of the port, container facilities moved to the edge of the city. Lack of good rail and road access to these terminals, coupled with the navigational limits of the harbor, made their full utilization difficult. Only a few major shipping lines serve the port.

Despite the commercial limitations of the port, Boston's modern waterfront has become a vibrant and exciting venue. Government and private investment, including the construction of a cruise ship terminal, support maritime activity, and Boston continues to be New England's principal port. The harbor has also become a major recreational asset for the region. The Boston harbor islands have been developed into parkland, and environmental cleanup projects have greatly improved water quality.

[*See also* Shipping, *subentry on* United States, *and* Ports.]

## Bibliography

Baker, William A. *The History of the Boston Marine Society, 1742-1967*. Boston: Boston Marine Society, 1968.

Federal Writers' Project. *Boston Looks Seaward*. Rev. ed. Boston: Northeastern University Press, 1985.

Morison, Samuel Eliot. *The Maritime History of Massachusetts, 1783-1860*. Boston: Houghton Mifflin, 1921.

WILLIAM FOWLER

# Boudin, Eugène (1824–1898),

French painter, pastelist, and etcher. Eugène Boudin was born in Honfleur, Normandy, into a modest family of seafarers. His father was a pilot from Le Havre, and his mother was employed as a maid on board the pilot ship. After having spent some years as a ship's boy and having had some petty jobs, Boudin understood that his talent for drawing could offer a better way to earn a living.

A self-taught artist, Boudin learned to paint by studying painters and their masterpieces; in particular, the Flemish and Dutch masters whom he studied in Belgium lastingly inspired him and influenced his style. Boudin was encouraged to work in Paris artists' studios to improve his technique, but he quickly deserted the city, which he hated, and returned to his beloved Normandy. At that time, this maritime province was the holy land of the Impressionists. Some of these inventive painters were living among a friendly and talented community, hosted by a small guesthouse: the Auberge Saint-Siméon near Honfleur. Extremely shy and modest about his works, Boudin was encouraged to pursue a career in painting by masters who admired his talent, such as Eugène Isabey (1804–1886) and Gustave Courbet (1819–1877), but chiefly by Claude Monet (1840–1926) and the Dutch-born Johan Barthold Jongkind (1819–1891), who were both pioneers of the new Impressionist school. The poet Charles Baudelaire (1821–1867) was also enthusiastic about Boudin's painting and urged him to show his work to art dealers.

When his technique attained maturity after 1860, Boudin agreed to enter the seething Paris art market, and he participated in 1874 in the first exhibition of the Impressionists. He then visited Rotterdam, Antwerp, and the northern coasts of France. When he came back, Paul Durand-Ruel (1831–1922), a brilliant Parisian collector and art dealer who introduced the Impressionists in France and in the United States, staged an exhibition of Boudin's works in Paris in 1883. Boudin died at Deauville, Normandy, seventy-four years old, leaving more than 3,800 oil paintings and numerous pastels.

Boudin painted some still-life pictures at the beginning of his career because he had clients for these subjects, but his unique inspiration was seascape, and more precisely, shores, harbors, and fashionable beaches of Normandy. His style and precepts were characteristic of the Impressionist school, which deserted studios for painting landscapes from life. Boudin wrote in his diary, "Three strokes of a brush from life are better than two days facing an easel in a studio." His palette was delicate, coherent with "the gray painting" style, and he was chiefly anxious to catch the ever-changing tonal and atmospheric effects of the fleeting light through slightly cloudy skies. Courbet said that Boudin was the "king of the sky." In fact, the vast pearly skies of the seashores of Normandy, Picardy, and Flanders attracted every painter of the Impressionist school. Moreover, Impressionism was named after the seascape *Impression, soleil levant* (Impression at Sunrise), painted in the harbor of Le Havre by Claude Monet and exhibited in 1874.

[*See also* Artists, *subentry* French; Painting; *and* Art.]

### Bibliography

Bergeret-Gourbin, Anne-Marie, et al. *Eugène Boudin, 1824–1898.* Honfleur, France: Association Eugène Boudin, 1992. Exhibition catalog.

Ducros, Jean. *Art et marine: Trois millénaires d'art et de marine.* Paris: Marine Nationale et Ville de Paris, 1965.

FRANÇOIS BELLEC

# Bouguer, Pierre

**Bouguer, Pierre** (1698–1758), French scientist and author of books on naval architecture and navigation. Pierre Bouguer, best known as the father of naval architecture, was born on February 10, 1698, in Le Croisic, France, to Jean Bouguer and Marie Françoise Josseau. Jean Bouguer had been a sailor wounded in the battle of Bantry Bay in 1689 in Ireland, before moving to Le Croisic as the first professor at the newly formed School of Hydrography to teach navigation and piloting to merchant ship officers. In 1698, Jean Bouguer published *Traité complet de la navigation*, one of the first comprehensive treatises on the subject.

**Pierre Bouguer.** Jean Baptiste Perronneau (1715–1763) painted this portrait in pastels in 1753. RÉUNION DES MUSÉES NATIONAUX / ART RESOURCE, NY

From an early age, Pierre Bouguer was surrounded by students learning mathematics and navigation, and he demonstrated a remarkable genius in those subjects—although his best friend was a future poet, Paul des Forges Maillard. In May 1714, Jean Bouguer died, and the sixteen-year-old Pierre successfully applied to fill his post, teaching navigation to students often twice his age. In 1722 he began his long association with the Paris Académie Royale des Sciences, assisting with an official study on the dimensions of ships. A few years later he wrote a treatise that mathematically analyzed the masting of ships, eventually gaining him a prize from the Académie and widespread recognition. Bouguer's further research into ship theory—the use of science and mathematics to predict a ship's characteristics and performance, as part of ship design—was encouraged and supported by the minister of the navy, Jean-Frédéric Phélypeaux, Count of Maurepas, who assigned Bouguer to the school of hydrography in Le Havre, leaving Pierre's younger brother Jean to teach in Le Croisic. Pierre Bouguer never married.

In 1735, Maurepas assigned Bouguer to participate in the geodesic mission of the Académie des Sciences to Peru to measure three degrees of arc of the earth's latitude at the equator, in order to determine the true figure of the earth. During his nine-year stay in Peru, not only did Bouguer carry out these measurements as well as experiments in physics and gravitation (including the examination of gravitational anomalies that now bear his name), but he also wrote the first definitive synthesis of naval architecture, *Traité du navire*, published in 1746 after his return to France. In this book he developed every one of the major ship theories that were later used by naval architects for the next fifty years, including the important concept of the metacenter as a measure of stability—a concept used by naval architects to this day. Bouguer's *Traité du navire* formed the basis of instruction for the French navy's first school for engineer constructors, established by the French naval administrator Henri Louis Duhamel du Monceau and a model that was emulated throughout Europe.

Bouguer continued his researches into astronomy and navigation as well as ship theory, publishing *Nouveau traité de navigation* in 1753 and *De la manœuvre des vaisseaux* in 1757. His reputation as a prolific and respected scientist became diminished, however, by a long and public conflict with Charles-Marie de la Condamine, one of his companions on the geodesic mission, over the scientific findings of that expedition. In 1758, during his final sickness—probably as a result of an aembic liver infection—Bouguer completed his *Traité d'optique sur la gradation de la lumière,* the first work on photometry, which was published post-humously. Pierre Bouguer died at his home in Paris on August 15, 1758.

[*See also* Duhamel du Monceau, Henri-Louis; Juan y Santacilia, Jorge; *and* Naval Architecture.]

## Bibliography

Bouguer, Pierre. *Optical Treatise on the Gradation of Light.* Translated by W. E. Knowles Middleton. Toronto: University of Toronto Press, 1961.

Fauque, Danielle. "Du bon usage de l'éloge: Cas de celui de Pierre Bouguer." *Revue d'histoire des sciences* 54 (2001): 351–382.

Ferreiro, Larrie D. *Ships and Science: The Birth of Naval Architecture in the Scientific Revolution, 1600–1800.* Cambridge, Mass.: MIT Press, 2007.

Lamontagne, Roland. *La vie et l'oeuvre de Pierre Bouguer.* Montreal: Presses de l'Université de Montréal, 1964.

Nowacki, Horst, and Larrie Ferreiro. "Historical Roots of the Theory of Hydrostatic Stability of Ships." Preprint 237. Berlin: Max Planck Institute for the History of Science, 2003.

LARRIE D. FERREIRO

**Bounty.** *See* Mutiny.

**Boyle, Robert** (1627–1691), British scientist and one of the key figures in the great flowering of natural philosophy (often referred to as the Scientific Revolution) that took place in the second half of the seventeenth century. He wrote extensively on science, philosophy, and religion, and through his own work and that of the Royal Society, founded in 1660, sought to put knowledge of natural phenomena on a sound experimental and observational footing. Boyle is principally known for his discoveries in chemistry and physics, but his scientific interests were wide ranging, and he used extensive contacts with engineers, travelers, and seafarers to gather information on the natural world, including the ocean. For Boyle, marine research had a twofold potential: it promised practical benefits, through improvements in navigation, and it led to advances in earth science.

Born on January 25, 1627, at Lismore Castle, Munster, Ireland, Boyle was the youngest son of the first Earl of Cork. His adolescence was shaped by the events of the English Civil War. After a brief spell at Eton, he was educated abroad, mainly in Geneva, and when he returned to England, he lived chiefly on his estate at Stalbridge, Dorset, where he devoted himself to literary pursuits. By the late 1640s he had taken up scientific research, and about 1655 he moved to Oxford, where a group of followers of the experimental method was based. He never married, and after moving to London in 1668, he shared the house of his favorite sister, Lady Ranelagh.

Through the development of apparatus and the dissemination of pamphlets, such as the *Directions for Seamen*, Boyle was aware of the efforts being made by the Royal Society to obtain information about natural phenomena at sea. His list of "Other Inquiries concerning the Sea," published in the *Philosophical Transactions* in 1666, included queries about sea water: Did the proportion of salt vary, and what were its medicinal and other properties? He also sought information about the depth and nature of the sea floor, the configuration of individual seas and oceans and their relationship to one another, and water movements. About this time Boyle was a member of various official bodies concerned with English overseas trade and colonies and used his contacts to collect information about the sea from individuals ranging from divers to diplomats, sometimes having observations made especially for him. As a chemist, Boyle was principally interested in the nature of the sea's salinity, and he supplemented reports from his informants with his own laboratory investigations. The scope of Boyle's published work on the depth, temperature, and salinity of the sea was necessarily restricted by the limited data and the rudimentary nature of the equipment available to him, as well as by his adherence to the experimental method, which forbade reliance on speculations unsupported by evidence. Though these essays formed only a minor part of his output, they established new ways of looking at the sea and paved the way for later, more detailed investigations. Boyle continued to be interested in seafaring and was later involved with attempts to develop a reliable shipboard desalination process. He died on December 30, 1691, in London.

[*See also* Marine Science Instruments; Meteorology.]

## Bibliography

Deacon, Margaret. *Scientists and the Sea, 1650–1900: A Study of Marine Science.* London and New York: Academic Press, 1971. Reprinted, Aldershot, U.K.: Ashgate, 1997. See especially chapter 6, "Marine Science in the Works of Robert Boyle," pp. 117–131, and appendix 3, "Other Inquiries concerning the Sea," p. 410.

Hunter, Michael. "Robert Boyle." In *Oxford Dictionary of National Biography.* Oxford: Oxford University Press, 2004.

Hunter, Michael, and Edward B. Davis, eds. *The Works of Robert Boyle*. London: Pickering and Chatto, 1999. The definitive edition of Boyle's works. See especially "Of the Temperature of the Submarine Regions," vol. 6, pp. 343–354; "Relations about the Bottom of the Sea," vol. 6, pp. 355–364; "Observations and Experiments about the Saltness of the Sea," vol. 7, pp. 389–412; and "The Fourth Section Belonging to the Tract formerly Publish'd under the Title, Relations about the Bottom of the Sea," vol. 7, pp. 413–417.

Maddison, R. E. W. "Studies in the Life of Robert Boyle, F.R.S. Part II: Salt Water Freshened." *Notes and Records of the Royal Society of London* 9 (1951–1952): 196–216.

McConnell, Anita. *No Sea Too Deep: The History of Oceanographic Instruments.* See pp. 5–11. Bristol: Adam Hilger, 1982.

MARGARET DEACON

## Breakbulk Cargoes

Breakbulk cargoes are cargoes consisting of a mixture of goods. A relatively recent term in the shipping industry, "breakbulk" denotes mixed cargoes that are not "unitized"–that is, not consolidated into standard-size containers. Breakbulk, or "general cargo" as it was formerly termed, was carried from the very earliest days of sea trade and continued to be carried in sailing ships through the first six decades of the nineteenth century.

Global cargo flow has been based largely on exports of manufactures and luxury goods from Europe from about 1800, from the United States from the late nineteenth century, and from the Far East from the mid-twentieth century. Most cargo was carried in breakbulk form until the development of container services. Such goods have been exchanged for raw materials, fuel, and foodstuffs. For example, the American wooden three-masted ship *Charles Cooper* (cargo capacity about 1,500 tons) sailed from New York in 1857 bound for Antwerp loaded with 223 bales of cotton, 854 barrels of flour, 106 cases of pearl ash, 1,500 cases of rosin, 50 tons of logwood, 49 hogsheads of tobacco, 267 tierces (barrels) of rice, 204 bags of pimentos, 284,651 pounds of bacon, 7,467 bags of coffee, 9,316 pounds of lard, and 2,722 pounds of beeswax, with smaller amounts of salt cod, provisions, and barrel staves. The return cargo was mainly manufactures such as glassware and window glass, nails, or part-processed materials such as refined tin, lead, and zinc, plus many cases of unspecified manufactured goods. In 1957 the Harrison Line's steel-hulled diesel cargo liners (cargo capacity about 10,000 tons) were sailing from Liverpool for East African ports such as Mombasa, Beira, and Durban loaded with motor cars, railway materials, machine tools, electrical equipment, textiles, whiskey, and British brands of food. In return, they carried canned foods, tobacco, copper, chrome and vanadium ores, coffee, timber, hides, sisal, rayon pulp, and other types of raw materials.

Such general cargoes came in an assortment of packages and sizes, and the stowage problem that this variety caused was the most critical for any vessel whether sail, steam, or motor. By its nature, general cargo had a high value and so it had to be loaded carefully to ensure that it was not damaged or stolen. This brought additional costs in terms of time and stevedoring labor and in materials such as wooden or matting dunnage to protect the cargo from the sides of the ship and ensure that it did not topple over on the voyage. At the same time, cargoes had to be loaded in such a way that they did not jeopardize the stability of the ship. The heaviest consignments such as railway rails and the strongest containers (often barrels) had to be placed in the bottom of the hold, with lighter goods on top. The problem of loading was compounded by the fact that most of this type of cargo was carried by cargo liners–ships sailing to a timetable. This meant that the shipowner needed a network of contacts (shipbrokers) to sell space in his ship's holds to ensure full cargoes for every sailing. To complicate matters still further, some cargoes were seasonal. The tea crop from China and India is a good example. Finally, the shipowner had to provide a number of calls at different ports en route to provide the service his shippers demanded. This not only added to the expense of the voyage but also, again, had implications for the stowage of cargo. Cargo had to be loaded in the order of a delivery without compromising the stability of the ship or the integrity of fragile items. A good example was Nedlloyd's service from London in 1967, calling at Marseille, Genoa, Port Said, Jidda, Djibouti, Sabah, Honiara, and Tarawa.

Safe loading of breakbulk cargoes depended on experience and various commonsense rules such as placing dry goods toward the stern. It brought into being a working diagram–the cargo plan–and by the late twentieth century the use of manual calculators (loadicators) and later computers. Powered ships also had water ballast tanks that could be used to assist the trim of the ship. By the late nineteenth century most vessels also had divided holds; the upper hold or between decks could be used for lighter goods and also for passengers in dormitory accommodation. The addition of lighter shelter decks of various configurations also added more cargo, cattle, and passenger space. Specialized storage space developed from the 1880s, such as refrigerated holds for fruit or meat and deep tanks for liquids such as latex or palm oil.

Discharging breakbulk cargo brought another set of problems. Most European and North American ports had dockside cranes for cargo handling, while many discharge ports were no more than anchorages with lighters. Cargo-handling equipment was essential for keeping to a time-table. In a sailing ship this amounted to simply a hand winch and a pulley block in the rigging. Steamers were fitted with derricks, single spars pivoted at the bottom of a mast that could be raised and swung with a load of cargo hoisted by a steam winch. The number of derricks and winches multiplied with the increasing size of a ship. For example, the Danish cargo liner *Nora Maersk* of 1934 (trading on a round-the-world service based in New York with a 9,300-ton cargo capacity) had five sets of holds and between decks served by twenty-three derricks. Most could only lift a maximum of five tons, with one for the number-two hold with a forty-five-ton lift. This could be used for heavy indivisible items such as electrical transformers. In the 1950s the invention of the Stulcken derrick and the development of steel mechanized (McGregor) hatch covers made it possible for much heavier loads to be carried. Increasing the electrical-generating capacity on a ship made it possible to fit faster electric or hydraulic winches and latterly cranes, although all these innovations came with increased first costs and higher maintenance than the old steam winch. Ship designers also tried to eliminate internal pillars within the holds, and this made it possible to deploy forklift trucks and pallets when moving cargo. The last cargo liners of "combo" ships were equipped to carry both breakbulk and containers. A good example is the *Maron*-class ships of about 15,000 tons cargo capacity built between 1980 and 1985 mainly for trade to West Africa, with Velle derricks at all five hatches capable of lifting containers or breakbulk consignments.

The United Kingdom was preeminent in the development of the breakbulk cargo liner. There were pioneer ventures to Brazil and the Mediterranean from the 1840s. But the full potential for long-distance trades was realized by Alfred Holt's Blue Funnel compound-engine steamers plying out to the Far East from 1865. The design of such ships distilled into a "three-island" profile, with raised forecastle and two holds; the central structure with bridge, accommodation, and engines and a third hold; followed by two more holds and a raised poop to accommodate ratings and stokers. Size grew and stabilized around the 5,000- to 10,000-gross-ton range until the 1960s. This decade also saw new vessels with their engines three-quarters of the way aft or right aft, which made for better use of the main body of the hull and more efficient cargo handling.

Beginning in the 1880s, propulsion changed from compound to triple-expansion steam engines, and there were continuing detailed improvements in steam power. The most significant were the use of heavy oil instead of coal in the boilers and the adoption of turbines. Diesel engines offered further economies of space and fuel economy at the cost of mechanical complexity. The first diesel cargo liner was the Danish East Asiatic Line's *Selandia* of 1912. British and American owners tended to stick to steam and used turbines in preference to diesel engines until after World War II; the latter were rapidly adopted by the competing Scandinavian companies.

Competition in the breakbulk trades was often fierce. Apart from joining cartels (conferences) to maintain freight rates, owners would attempt to fit out their vessels to gain an advantage. This might be in the provision of extra speed—the Ben Line of Leith was a notable exponent of this ploy in the 1950s and 1960s. It could also be in providing faster turnaround times through additional cargo gear and improved shoreside cargo-receiving facilities. Breakbulk cargo is still carried but not on the main trade routes, which have gone over entirely to container or Ro-Ro (roll-on, roll-off) ships since 1970.

[*See also* Bulk Cargoes; Container Ship; Shipping; Shipping Companies; Shipping Industry; *and* Shipping Revolution.]

## Bibliography

Corlett, Ewan. *The Revolution in Merchant Shipping, 1950–1980*. London: Her Majesty's Stationery Office, 1981.

Craig, Robin. *Steam Tramps and Cargo Liners, 1850–1950*. London: Her Majesty's Stationery Office, 1980.

House, D. J. *Seamanship Techniques*. 2 vols. Oxford: Heinemann Newnes, 1989–1990.

Kummermann, Henri, and Robert Jacquinet, eds. *Ships' Cargo, Cargo Ships*. Hounslow, U.K.: MacGregor Publications, 1979.

Stevens, Robert White. *On the Stowage of Ships and Their Cargoes, with Information regarding Freights, Charter Parties, &c., &c.* 7th ed. London and New York: Longmans, Green, Reader, and Dyer, 1894.

Strachan, Michael. *The Ben Line, 1825–1982: An Anecdotal History*. Wilby, U.K.: Michael Russell Publishing, 1992.

Thomas, R. E., revised by O. O. Thomas. *Stowage: The Properties and Stowage of Cargoes*. 5th rev. ed. Glasgow: Brown, Son, and Ferguson, 1963.

Woodman, Richard. *Voyage East*. 3d ed. Bebington, U.K.: Avid Publications, 2002. Also titled *The Antigone*, this is a fictional but nevertheless accurate account of working the last generation of breakbulk cargo liners of the Blue Funnel Line.

MICHAEL STAMMERS

# Brest, Blockade of

**Brest, Blockade of** Throughout the wars of the French Revolution and Empire (1793–1814), the strategic center of gravity in the Anglo-French conflict lay just off the western coast of Brittany. So long as the British could keep the French Atlantic fleet under control, Britain's command of the sea would remain unchallenged. Such command was critical because the French fleet, based at Brest, was ideally placed to convoy an invasion force to Britain or Ireland, sortie to the West Indies, or attack British sea-going commerce. By closely blockading the French fleet in harbor the British could secure their command of the wider ocean, facilitating offensive operations in other theaters, from the West Indies to South America, while denying the French the naval stores and sea time they needed to become seaworthy and efficient. Ships and men left in harbor decayed.

The main British fleet throughout the eighteenth century was the Channel, or Grand, Fleet, which had the primary task of keeping control of the French force at Brest. The fleet included almost all the first-rate and second-rate three-decked battleships, those imposing centers of fighting power that guaranteed British control of the sea. Fighting power, not speed, was the ultimate desideratum. That this fleet fought only one fleet and two squadron actions in twenty-two years demonstrates how successful it was in preventing the French from using their fleet.

The need for the Royal Navy to find some means to deal with France's premier Atlantic naval base at Brest was apparent from the time of the Nine Years' War in the 1690s, but the idea to do this through the use of a powerful western squadron was not widely recognized until the war of 1739–1748. During the Seven Years' War (1756–1763), the British had developed afloat logistics and seamanship to sustain a fleet off Brest for long periods. However, this strategy depended on a significant superiority of force and was not used in the American War of Independence. Nor was it used in the early years of the new conflict that begin in 1793; both Lord Howe and Lord Bridport preferred an open blockade, keeping the fleet secure in British anchorages.

In 1793 the collapse of the French naval officer corps—occasioned both by the Revolution and by France's having only half as many battleships as Britain—led the key decision makers to rely on using convoys for trade and military shipping, for occasional sorties, and for reports from cruisers. Consequently the only major fleet action between the two primary fleets, the so-called Glorious First of June 1794, was fought so far out to sea that it could not be named for a prominent landmark, and it was brought on by British attempts to intercept a major French convoy. In late 1794 the French fleet put to sea without opposition, capturing merchant ships and a battleship, and sending reinforcements to the Mediterranean. This enraged the British ministers, and in July 1795 they demanded a close blockade, which was established to cover the landing of troops and supplies for royalist rebels in Quiberon Bay. Gradually the close blockade ran down, and in December 1796 a French expedition reached Ireland unchallenged, though it was dispersed by severe weather. In March 1797 the British Admiralty ordered a strict, systematic blockade, but Lord Bridport proved reluctant to act on these orders. Further French sorties in 1799 persuaded the Admiralty to relieve him and achieve greater control over the fleet by appointing as his successor an arch proponent of the close blockade, Admiral Earl St. Vincent from the Mediterranean command. By early 1800 a close and continuous blockade of Brest had been imposed. To render the blockade effective, St. Vincent needed more ships, tighter discipline, and above all the very best officers, men like Cuthbert Collingwood and James Saumarez. St. Vincent took risks to keep his ships stationed off Cape Ushant. In the dark days of the war, enforcing the close blockade was critical to British survival and ultimately critical to its ability to secure a drawn peace with France in 1801. The British intelligence network operating from the Channel Islands into Brittany provided generally reliable insights into the state of the dockyard and the ships. Similarly excellent logistics, especially the improved ration of lemon juice—which finally defeated scurvy in 1800—new charts, and local knowledge all played a part in the success. The Channel Fleet was also responsible for blockading the subordinate French Atlantic ports of L'Orient and Rochefort. Although a French squadron escaped from Brest in early 1801, the policy was sustained when St. Vincent became first lord of the admiralty in February 1801. By then he had been able to detach key ships and officers to create a new Northern Fleet, under Hyde Parker and Horatio Nelson, to meet the emergency of the armed neutrality. The policy of detaching squadrons for specific operations became a feature of the next conflict. It was greatly facilitated by the completion of a telegraph system among the Admiralty, Portsmouth, and Plymouth. The new commander in chief, Admiral the Honorable William Cornwallis, continued St. Vincent's system—without quite the same ferocity—all the way until the Peace of Amiens. By 1801 the Channel Fleet held station through all weathers and rarely saw an

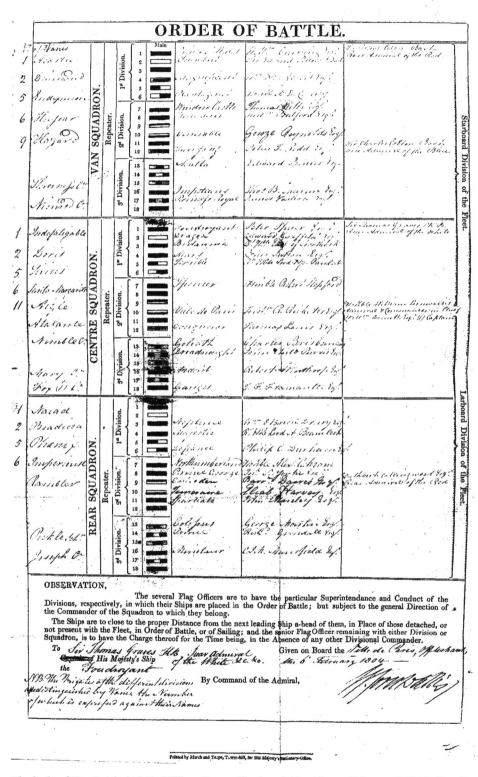

**Blockade of Brest.** Admiral Sir William Cornwallis signed this order on February 6, 1804, directing how the fleet would form in case of a major engagement with the French fleet. © NATIONAL MARITIME MUSEUM, LONDON

English harbor. This service bred outstanding seamen and combat-ready ships. By contrast, the French moldered in port, unable to keep their ships fit for sea for want of both supplies and seagoing training.

The success of the close blockade was so obvious that when the peace of Amiens collapsed in May 1803, Cornwallis was already at sea, and for the next eighteen months he and his deputy, Lord Gardner, sustained the effort through the crisis of the naval war. Cornwallis's Channel Fleet was the certain shield of British strategy, a force that was not defeated, decoyed, or disturbed by any of Napoleon's complex combinations. The fleet allowed Nelson to act as the swift sword, chasing and later annihilating any enemy forces that were able to put to sea. The crisis of the Trafalgar campaign occurred in the approaches to Brest, on August 22, 1805, when Admiral Ganteaume attempted to put to sea as Napoleon ordered, and Cornwallis, much as he wished to let the Frenchmen out and then annihilate them, did his duty by driving them back into harbor, whence they did not emerge again until after Trafalgar. Still, a powerful squadron under Robert Calder was detached to meet and defeat Admiral Pierre Charles Silvestre de Villeneuve on his return from the West Indies on July 22. Nor were the British content to rest on the defensive: on at least three occasions, significant offensive plans were developed for large-scale amphibious attacks or fire-ship raids to destroy the French fleet, but none of the plans came to fruition.

After Trafalgar the French largely abandoned the concept of having a main fleet in favor of detaching squadrons to cruise against British commerce. While these were a nuisance to the British, they were also, as Mahan recognized, a confession of failure. One such sortie in 1809 left the French exposed in the Aix Roads, where Thomas Cochrane famously subjected them to a stunning attack with rockets and explosion vessels. Lord Gambier's failure to follow up the opportunity led to a court-martial and much bad blood. However, the French were mightily relieved to escape annihilation.

The blockade of Brest was a costly exercise: it tied up the best ships and men in the Royal Navy for close to twenty years, and ships of all classes were lost in the difficult and imperfectly charted approaches to the French harbor. Indeed, the need to improve the charts of this operational area was one motivating factor for the development of British hydrography and the creation of a new department at the Admiralty. Similarly, the logistics demands placed on the base at Plymouth and the anchorage at Torbay led to piecemeal upgrades of the large-scale purpose-built postwar victualing complex at the Royal William Yard, Devonport. Sustaining the blockade over such a long period was the greatest feat of seamanship in wartime in the age of sail. As A. T. Mahan wrote in his 1892 study *The Influence of Sea Power upon the French Revolution and Empire*, "Those storm-beaten ships, upon which the soldiers of the *grande armée* never looked, stood between them and the dominion of the world." Yet it was his near contemporary Sir Julian Corbett who produced, with *The Campaign of Trafalgar* (1910), the finest study of how the strategy of which the blockade was the lynchpin functioned in the ultimate test. Corbett's case study of British grand strategy was developed to teach the naval officers of his own generation, the men who conducted the blockade of Imperial Germany between 1914 and 1918.

It was fitting that when Napoleon surrendered in 1815 it was to a British battleship, one that had fought at the battles of the Glorious First of June, the Nile, and Trafalgar; it was then blockading the French Atlantic coast as part of the Channel Fleet.

[*See also* Blockade; Nile, Battle of the; Strategy; Tactics; *and* Trafalgar, Battle of.]

## Bibliography

Leyland, John, ed. *Dispatches and Letters Relating to the Blockade of Brest, 1803–1805*. London: Navy Records Society, 1898 and 1901.

Morriss, Roger. *The Channel Fleet and the Blockade of Brest, 1793–1801*. Aldershot, U.K.: Ashgate, for the Navy Records Society, 2001.

Ryan, A. N. "The Royal Navy and the Blockade of Brest, 1689–1815: Theory and Practice." In *Les marines de guerre européennes, XVII–XVIIIe siècles*, edited by Martine Acerra, José Merino, and Jean Meyer, pp. 175–193. Paris: Presses de l'Université de Paris-Sorbonne, 1987.

Ryan, A. N. "William III and the Brest Fleet in the Nine Years' War." In *William III and Louis XIV: Essays (1680–1720) by and for Mark A. Thomson*, edited by Ragnhild Hatton and John Bromley, pp. 49–67. Liverpool: Liverpool University Press, 1968.

ANDREW LAMBERT

**Bridges, Harry** (1901–1990), labor leader. The fiery head of the West Coast Longshoremen and the International Longshoremen's and Warehousemen's Union (ILWU), Harry Bridges led the American dockworkers' unions for forty years. He was born Alfred Renton Bridges in Melbourne, Australia, on July 28, 1901. He attended

Catholic schools until he was sixteen and worked in his father's real estate business and as a clerk at a stationery store before following his heart to sea.

A dispute aboard the ship *Ysabelin* in 1920 convinced Bridges to leave the ship when she landed in San Francisco. He paid his $8 head tax and started sailing on American ships. In 1921, when he entered New Orleans during a maritime strike, he volunteered for picket duty and within a short time was in charge of the pickets. In 1922, Bridges took a job as a longshoreman in San Francisco, having had enough of the itinerant life of the sea.

Conditions and pay were as bad as the work. The work was controlled by a company union ("blue book union") called the Longshoremen's Association of San Francisco. To maintain control of the docks, the employers used an elaborate system of spies to weed out the more troublesome workers. Workers complained to the American Federation of Labor (AFL), but little happened. In 1932 conditions worsened, and Bridges led a new unionization effort. The workers published *The Waterfront Worker* to spread the word.

On March 23, 1934, rank-and-file workers were on strike. Bridges was branded as a Communist, but the workers stayed loyal. Communists played a key role in the strike, and Bridges probably was a member of the Communist Party. The party advised and provided publicity and organizational tools, but it did not direct the union, Bridges, or the strike. On July 5 ("Bloody Thursday"), the police stormed the pickets in an effort to open the port; over a hundred were wounded, and two strikers were killed. That night the National Guard mobilized and occupied the port. In response to the violence, unions called a general strike for the entire city. Bridges and his band of radicals organized the West Coast workers into the International Longshoremen's Association (ILA)—and by 1936, Bridges was the West Coast leader of the union.

Bridges also led the Maritime Federation, a collection of maritime unions. His hold on the rank and file was so strong that he led them right out of the AFL into the newly formed ILWU and the Congress of Industrial Organizations (CIO)—and then back out of the CIO. Business leaders tried unsuccessfully to get Bridges deported, charging that he was a Communist and had lied on his naturalization papers.

In the 1950s Bridges watched as his industry was in turmoil. He was convinced that mechanization, speedup, and quicker port turnaround times were inevitable. In 1960 he helped negotiate the Mechanization and Modernization Agreement (M & M), a revolutionary labor contract that still informs the industry. The M & M embraced the con-

tainerization revolution. Through a tax on containers, the agreement paid a "guaranteed wage" to workers displaced by technology and guaranteed that all newly created jobs would be unionized jobs.

Bridges served as leader until 1977. That year he gave his blessing as the independent ILWU reaffiliated with the AFL-CIO. Bridges died on March 30, 1990.

[*See also* Unions, *subentries on* An Overview *and* United States.]

## Bibliography

Cherny, Robert. "The Making of a Labor Radical: Harry Bridges, 1901–1934." *Pacific Historical Review* 70, no. 4 (2001): 571–599.

Larrowe, Charles. *Harry Bridges: The Rise and Fall of Radical Labor in the United States.* New York: L. Hill, 1972.

Schwartz, Harvey. "Harry Bridges and the Scholars: Looking at History's Verdict." *California History* 59, no. 1 (1980): 66–79.

RICHARD GREENWALD

**Brig.** *See* Trading Vessels, *subentry on* Early Modern Vessels; Warships.

**Brigantine.** *See* Trading Vessels, *subentry on* Early Modern Vessels.

**Briscoe, Arthur** (1873–1943), British marine artist. Arthur John Trevor Briscoe was born in Birkenhead, England, on February 25, 1873. He was raised in a wealthy family, where small fortunes were made in both the cotton trade and the publishing business. After having attended Shrewsbury School, where he developed a particular interest in painting and drawing, Briscoe joined his father in his travels through America and Japan. Upon his return, he studied art at the Slade School of Fine Art in London. Professors Henry Tonks and Frederick Brown were his teachers. Thereafter Briscoe crossed the Channel to study in Paris at Julian's Atelier for eighteen months. Back in England he moved to Maldon. Here with others he established the Blackwater Sailing Club. In 1899, at the age of twenty-six, he bought a small cutter, *Doris*, and sailed this vessel around the Essex coast. In 1901, Briscoe got married. That same year he acquired a larger vessel, *Vera* (eight tons). A little later, a son was born. With his family he cruised the waters between Cornwall, Normandy, and

Zeeland (in the Netherlands). In 1904 Briscoe was invited to write a volume in the series "The Country Hand-books." He wrote *A Handbook on Sailing* under the pen name of Clove Hitch. The illustrations, however, were made under his proper name. Two years later, in 1906, Briscoe had his first one-man show at the Modern Gallery in Bond Street, London. Though a vivid painter by that time, his show included thirty-five watercolors. His star rose rapidly when Briscoe started to create illustrations for the widely read *Illustrated London News*.

A rigorous sailor, Briscoe grasped every opportunity to get on board large vessels and document the sailor's life in oil or ink. In 1925, Briscoe was invited to embark on the Polish sail-training ship *Lwow*, and join the crew in their voyage from Rotherhithe to Genoa. The well-educated artist taught the Polish cadets English sailing terms, while at the same time prolifically producing one etching or sketch after the other of life on board this vessel. Back in England, Briscoe produced a large series of etchings of life at sea. With the help of London-based publisher Harold Dickins the artist printed a run of seventy-five of his etchings. Initially, they sold for between £2 and £6 per edition. Briscoe's name became internationally renowned once his work was sold to the American market. New York collectors of maritime art contributed immensely to his fame—and prosperity. During the late 1920s, the prices commanded by his etchings had multiplied many times over. Collectors were prepared to pay no less than £40 to £60 per set—the equivalent of the monthly wage of a captain on a merchantman. By the 1930s, his work had become very popular and valuable. As a result of the economic recession shortly before and immediately after World War II, the popularity of Briscoe's work—as reflected in sales—decreased. Thanks to publicist and sailor Alex Hurst, Briscoe's work experienced a revival. Many collectors—amateurs as well as professionals—came to realize once more that Briscoe's oeuvre was unique. Although many contemporary artists depicted ships in oil or ink, hardly anyone had such a keen eye for the harsh and horrid circumstances under which the sailors conducted their tasks and duties. And finally, nobody could render the very nature of life at sea in such meticulous manner as Briscoe. As such, his strong compositions document the workings of the last great commercial sailing ships.

Over the years, Briscoe's work has been acquired by many of the major museums in the world. The artist's maritime oeuvre can be seen in the National Maritime Museum at Greenwich, in his home country. Other maritime institutions, like the two important Dutch maritime museums—the Nederlands Scheepvaartmuseum in Amsterdam and the Maritiem Museum Rotterdam—hold dozens of his etchings. Furthermore, Briscoe's work is represented in the collections of many renowned fine art museums scattered all over the world. The Scottish Arts Council, the Fine Arts Museum in San Francisco, the Museum of Fine Arts in Boston, the New York Public Library, but also the Israel Museum in Jerusalem all hold Briscoe's works in their collections.

[See also Artists, *subentry* British; *and* Painting, *subentry on* Historical Themes.]

## Bibliography

"Arthur Trevor Briscoe RI, RE (1873–1943)." http://www.art-gallery.co.uk/sell_artists/arthur_briscoe.html

Hurst, Alexander A. *Arthur Briscoe, Marine Artist: His Life and Work*. Brighton, U.K.: Teredo Books, 1974.

*Modern Masters of Etching. Arthur Briscoe*. Introduction by Malcolm C. Salaman. London: the Studio Limited; New York: William Edwin Rudge, 1930.

Taylor, James, in association with the National Maritime Museum Greenwich. *Marine Painting: Images of Sail, Sea and Shore*. London: Studio Editions Limited, 1995.

Wilson, Arnold. *A Dictionary of British Marine Painters*. Reprint, Brighton, U.K.: Dolphin Press, 1974.

JOOST C. A. SCHOKKENBROEK

## Brooking, Charles

**Brooking, Charles** (1723–1759), marine painter. Born in Deptford, England, in 1723, Brooking was the son of Charles Brooking (1677–1738), who had an artist's colorman and a commercial paint-making and painting business near Plymouth, but who, when bankrupted by the Admiralty's decision not to decorate its ships so finely, moved to Ireland. There he made the first detailed map of Dublin, and published it in 1728. He drew ships well, as can be seen in his topography, and almost certainly he tutored his son in drawing. The boy's first oils were painted in 1740, when he was seventeen and living in East Greenwich, London. Though primitive, they showed great promise. After his father's death, Brooking was living in the Leicester Square area of central London, where he attended the church of Saint Martin's in the Fields. He and his wife Mary had three children. Two of his sons are known to have gone to sea.

Brooking painted attractive sea scenes with naval vessels for nautically minded people, but he fell into the hands of an unscrupulous dealer, who, on receipt of Brooking's oil paintings, expunged the signature. Taylor White, a circuit judge and secretary of the Foundling Hospital in London, endeavored to track this unknown painter down. In 1753, at White's second attempt with an advertisement in a London broadsheet, Brooking responded and thus was discovered. He became successful, painting a huge marine for the Foundling Hospital in sixteen days. But he became ill and was treated for a perpetual headache caused by the intensity of his work. Later he is believed to have caught tuberculosis. He died on March 25, 1759, and was buried in the churchyard of Saint Martin's, which has now become Trafalgar Square.

Brooking's works can be seen in the National Maritime Museum at Greenwich, in the Tate Britain Gallery at London, in the Center for British Art at Yale University, and in many other collections. His lyrical marine paintings were unequalled in the eighteenth century, the finest days of sail. Some consider him the greatest English marine painter of all time. There were no great naval battles in his short period of production, and Brooking's twelve battle scenes show duels fought by the Royal Family Privateers. He was more interested in the beauty and composition of his paintings than in staid portraits of ships. He improved upon the compositions of Willem van de Velde the Younger (1611–1693) and Peter Monamy (1681–1749). Monamy may have worked in the van de Velde studio in Greenwich and would have been known to Brooking. Extant in 2006 are about 240 of Brooking's oils—of which about half are properly signed—30 drawings, and 28 engravings. His oil paintings, mainly small, rarely come to auction. The drawings are very scarce, but fine engravings by Boydell, Ravenet, Canot, and Godfrey may be found in antique print shops in London.

[*See also* Artists, *subentry* British; Monamy, Peter; Portraits, *subentry on* Ships; *and* Velde, Willem van de, Younger.]

## Bibliography

Joel, David. *Charles Brooking (1723–1759) and the 18th Century British Marine Painters*. Woodbridge, U.K.: Antique Collectors' Club, 2000. Most of Brooking's paintings and drawings and all of his engravings are illustrated, and the book includes a catalog raisonné of Brooking's work.

Robinson, Michael S. *Van de Velde: Catalogue of Paintings*. Greenwich, U.K: National Maritime Museum, 1990.

DAVID JOEL

# Brown, Guillermo (1777–1857), commander

of Argentinean naval forces. An Irishman by birth, Brown came into the service of the government of Buenos Aires in the early 1800s and led the Argentinean naval forces for three decades. Argentinean naval historians have asserted that Admiral Brown had the "Nelson touch" because of his inspired leadership, courage, audacity, initiative, and devotion to duty.

William Brown was born in Foxford, near Castlebar, County Mayo, on June 22, 1777. In 1786, Brown traveled with his father to Philadelphia. After his father's death, he went into the merchant marine as a cabin boy. His nautical experience and knowledge led him to get his certificate of qualification as a ship's master by the age of nineteen. In 1796 he was impressed into the Royal Navy, and he served in the Caribbean, acquiring valuable warship experience. Captured by the French in 1798, Brown was imprisoned in Metz, from where he escaped but was recaptured. Thereafter he was imprisoned in Verdun, escaped again, and succeeded in reaching England.

On July 29, 1809, Brown married Elizabeth Chitty in London, and then traveled to South America. He settled in Buenos Aires in April 1810. On May 25, 1810, the Spanish viceroy, Baltasar Hidalgo de Cisneros, was overthrown in Buenos Aires, which was the first step toward Argentinean independence. Montevideo remained on the loyalist side, and its ships blockaded Buenos Aires. The first squadron armed by the government of Buenos Aires was utterly defeated by the Spaniards based in Montevideo in March 1811.

In early 1814 there was another attempt to build up an Argentinean navy in order to gain control of the Río de la Plata. Brown accepted command of this new squadron. In mid-March 1814, Brown captured Martín García Island, which was the key to the rivers Paraná and Paraguay. His next objective was to defeat the Spanish squadron at Montevideo, which was besieged by Buenos Aires's ground forces without success, because the city still had sea communications open. The Spanish squadron was defeated off Montevideo on May 17, 1814. With its supplies cut off by both land and sea, Montevideo surrendered on June 23, 1814, leaving Spain with no base on the western side of the South Atlantic.

In 1815 and 1816, Brown led a privateering expedition to the Pacific—off the Chilean and Peruvian coasts—with remarkable success, harassing Spanish-held coastal towns. Thereafter, Brown returned to the Atlantic, and at the end of this venture he was imprisoned by British authorities in Barbados. In 1817 he joined his family in England, but he returned to Buenos Aries in 1818.

A dispute between Brazil and Argentina over territory on the left bank of the Río de la Plata—which later became

Uruguay—started a war in late 1825. Superior Brazilian naval power, based in Montevideo, allowed the Brazilians to blockade Buenos Aires. Brown successfully challenged this superiority with hit-and-run tactics, defensive actions, and raider warfare. He even managed to bottle a detached Brazilian squadron in the Uruguay River, defeating it on February 9, 1827. The war ended in August 1828. Brazil and Argentina compromised, agreeing that Uruguay, the disputed province, should become an independent state.

Brown continued to serve his adopted country, holding the position of governor of Buenos Aires in 1828 and 1829. In the mid-1830s he returned to naval service during a period when Argentina was harried by civil wars, as well as by French and British interventions. He retired in 1845 at the age of sixty-eight. On March 3, 1857, Guillermo Brown died in Buenos Aires, and he was buried with full honors. His grave is a conspicuous memorial in a traditional cemetery.

[See also Atlantic Ocean, subentry on South Atlantic Regional Navies; Buenos Aires; and Privateering.]

## Bibliography

Aguinis, Marcos. *Brown.* Buenos Aires: Ediciones DAIA, 1977.

Arguindeguy, Pablo, and Horacio Rodríguez. *Guillermo Brown: Apostillas de su vida.* Buenos Aires: Instituto Browniano, 1994.

Comisión Nacional de Homenaje al Almirante Guillermo Brown. *Despachos del Minsitro Estadounidense en Buenos Aires, Coronel John M. Forbes a su Gobierno, sobre la actuación del Almirante Brown al Mando de la Escuadra Argentina, 1826–1828.* Buenos Aires: Academia Nacional de la Historia, 1957.

Comisión Nacional de Homenaje al Almirante Guillermo Brown. *Documentos del Almirante Brown.* 2 vols. Buenos Aires: Academia Nacional de la Historia, 1958–1959.

Comisión Nacional de Homenaje al Almirante Guillermo Brown. *Memorias del Almirante Brown.* Buenos Aires: Academia Nacional de la Historia, 1957.

Hudson, Thomas N. *Admiral William Brown: Master of the River Plate.* Buenos Aires: Libris, 2004.

Ratto, Héctor R. *Historia de Brown.* 2 vols. Buenos Aires: La Facultad, 1939.

Vale, Brian. *A War betwixt Englishmen: Brazil against Argentina on the River Plate, 1825–1830.* London: Tauris, 2000.

GUILLERMO J. MONTENEGRO

**Bruges.** *See* Brugge.

**Brugge**    Before the small community of Brugge (Bruges), in Belgium, developed into an international center of trade in the twelfth century, its impact did not extend beyond the city borders. Its transformation began in 1134, when, as the result of a storm tide, the nearby town of Damme became connected to the sea by an estuary called the Zwin. Philip of Alsace (c. 1142–1191) decided to link Brugge to Damme with a canal. Now that it was directly connected to the sea, Brugge would become the meeting point for trade to and from the low countries, with cloth as the most important export. Brugge became the gateway to the sea for the County of Flanders, as well as its administrative capital. Regular commercial relations were established with England, the Atlantic coast of France, and northern Europe. It became the focus of the economic worlds of the North, Eastern, and Mediterranean seas and the Atlantic coast.

The city's importance attracted foreign traders, who started settling in Brugge on a permanent basis. Italian merchants introduced Asian and Arabic products in the low countries and made use of sophisticated financial techniques such as the bill of exchange. Brugge would become the busiest money market in Europe, with the exception of Italy. The presence of merchants from northern Germany led to a privileged bond with the German Hansa. Brugge also had an important cultural impact with the production of hydrographic maps and charts and the construction of architectural treasures such as Italian merchant houses and consulates. At the end of the fourteenth century, however, its status as a center of international trade was threatened by political and military events and natural forces.

Since its enormous growth beginning in the middle of the twelfth century, the city had had to contend with the sea. Land reclamation and the construction of dikes helped to prevent flooding of the inner city and the surrounding areas. But because of those interventions the Zwin began to silt up. The city lost its direct gateway to the open sea and thus its most important economic advantage. From around 1575 through the 1650s Brugge was increasingly dealt blows by international political and military events such as the Treaty of Münster, which ended the Dutch Revolt (1568–1648). As a result of this treaty the Zwin and the river Schelde were officially closed for navigation, and Antwerp took Brugge's place as the region's leading port and trade city. By the seventeenth century Brugge was little more than a center for local trade and of limited importance. It would take until the mid-twentieth century for the city—or, more accurately, region—to resurface as a port city. In Zeebrugge, about fifteen kilometers (nine miles) from the old city center, the old fishery port was transformed into a modern seaport. Since the 1960s, with substantial financial support from the Belgian government, facilities have been built for passenger service to the United Kingdom on Ro-Ro (roll on, roll off) ships, transport of liquid bulk cargo, and the handling of containers.

[*See also* Hanseatic League *and* Ports, *subentry on* Characteristics of Cities.]

## Bibliography

De Witte, Hubert. "The Maritime Topography of Medieval Bruges." In *Maritime Topography and the Medieval Town*, edited by Jan Bill and Birthe L. Clausen, pp. 137–144. Copenhagen, Denmark: National Museum, 1999.

Vandewalle, André, ed. *Hanzekooplui en Medicibankiers: Brugge, wisselmarkt van Europese culturen.* Brugge, Belgium: Stichting Kunstboek, 2002.

Vermeersch, Valentin, ed. *Bruges and Europe.* Antwerp, Belgium: Mercatorfonds, 1992.

Vermeersch, Valentin, ed. *Bruges and the Sea: From Bryggia to Zeebrugge.* Antwerp, Belgium: Mercatorfonds, 1982.

Vermeersch, Valentin, and Jeroen Cornilly, eds. *Bruges.* Antwerp, Belgium: Mercatorfonds, 2002.

STEPHAN VANFRAECHEM

# Brunel, Isambard Kingdom (1806–1859),

British engineer. He was born at Portsmouth, England, on April 9, 1806, the son of Marc Brunel, who was at that time installing his epochal block-making mills in the Portsmouth dockyard. The elder Brunel later worked on steam sawmills, bridges, steamships, and the Thames tunnel. He also provided his son with a bilingual scientific, technical, and engineering education, including advanced mathematics and study with Abraham-Louis Breguet (d. 1823), the French chronometer maker. Isambard also served as an apprentice in the workshops of Henry Maudslay, the leading British marine engineer. Marc Brunel also introduced his son to Charles Babbage, the inventor of an "analytic engine" now considered the forerunner of the modern computer. While Babbage's advanced understanding of mathematics, science, and engineering was beyond the comprehension of most engineers, Brunel regularly sought his advice. Brunel's peculiar genius lay in straddling the then largely separate worlds of science and engineering. When Dionsysus Lardner claimed that ships could not steam across the Atlantic, Babbage and Brunel destroyed his argument with a devastating combination of theory and practice.

Brunel's dominant ambition was to be recognized by his peers as the engineer of his era. He did not seek honors or titles, and he left little money. For Brunel the advance of engineering, in due subordination to his God, was the ultimate reward. However, Brunel was not the selfless hero portrayed by Victorian hagiographers; he was a complex, flawed human being. Driven by an obsessive-compulsive personality, he took refuge in endless work, chain-smoking cigars during the ceaseless motion of days that began early and rarely ended in a night's sleep. Cursed with insomnia, he simply used the extra time to work. He was also reckless with his own life, and not always careful with those of his friends. Brunel cannot have been an easy man to work for, demanding the same total commitment and perfection from his subordinates that he required of himself. Yet he could also be a good friend, notably to Francis Pettit Smith, the screw propeller patentee. While Brunel built bridges (notably the Albert Bridge at Saltash), docks, and other maritime structures, as well as railways and buildings, his major role in the field lay in the engineering of the modern ship.

Brunel's career took off when he won a competition to build the Clifton Suspension Bridge in Bristol, England, in 1831. He then won the competition to engineer the Great Western Railway, running between London and Bristol. In 1835, in a moment of genius, he proposed extending the line to New York with a steamship. The big paddle-wheel liner *Great Western* of 1838, the first successful transatlantic steamship, employed the diagonal framing developed by Robert Seppings. Brunel took no fee for this work, and he invested his own money in the company. For Brunel the development of the steamship was an engineering legacy from his father, and an opportunity to test his vast range of engineering skill. In 1840, Brunel, who had by then gained wide recognition, adopted the screw propeller for his second liner, the *Great Britain*, which he had decided to build in iron. This ship was completed in 1845, and although her career on the North Atlantic was short, she revolutionized ship design and engineering to such an extent that she is rightly considered the first modern ship. She is preserved at Bristol in her original building dock. In 1841, Brunel was retained by the Admiralty to engineer the pioneer screw warship HMS *Rattler*, which provided key data for the development of screw propulsion.

Brunel's final ship project, the astonishing 22,000-ton *Great Eastern* of 1858, designed to steam to Australia and back without refueling, was conceived and executed in five years, despite being more than twice as big as any other vessel afloat. This time his vision outran the materials technology of the age, and although the ship worked well, it was considered financially impractical. A titanic battle of wills with the builder, John Scott Russell, and a series of setbacks during the launch and early trials undermined Brunel's health. On board *Great Eastern*, supervising preparations for sea trials on September 5, 1859, he had a stroke. He lingered just long enough to hear of a tragic explosion on board before he died on September 15.

Although he lived only to the age of fifty-three, Brunel had taken ship design to a scale and power that dwarfed the imagination of his contemporaries, earning himself a colossal reputation and undying fame. An engineer of astounding range, Brunel had also created tunnels, bridges, railways, docks, and open-span and prefabricated buildings. Nowhere was his ability more obvious than in his work with ship design. In less than twenty years he had completely transformed the materials, powering, scale, and structure of the ship.

[*See also* Naval Architecture.]

## Bibliography

Griffiths, Denis, Andrew Lambert, and Fred Walker. *Brunel's Ships*. London: Chatham Publishing, 1999.

Pugsley, Alfred, ed. *The Works of Isambard Kingdom Brunel*. Cambridge, U.K., and New York: Cambridge University Press, 1976.

Rolt, L. T. C. *Isambard Kingdom Brunel*. London and New York: Longmans, 1957.

ANDREW LAMBERT

**Buache, Philippe** (1700–1773), French geographer and cartographer. Philippe Buache was a preeminent figure in the field of French cartography in the eighteenth century. He was the son-in-law of the equally celebrated cartographer Guillaume Delisle (1675–1726). His vast body of work encompassed all kinds of cartographic works, often very novel concepts like a map of the earth's tremors, a chart of the length of the pendulum, cross-sections of Paris during the floods, a diagram of the rivers in the Seine basin, and so forth. Here, only his cutting-edge innovations in the field of maritime cartography shall be considered.

From 1737 onward, he designed the first isobaths, linking the data collected by various marine devices measuring water depth in the Channel and producing his *Carte et coupe du canal de la Manche ... qui présentent ... la pente du fond de ces deux Mers* (Map and Section of the Channel ... which Represent ... the Incline of the Sea Bed of These Two Seas). The importance of this innovation went unrecognized at the time, and nobody took any interest in it until the end of the century. At the same time, he drew up a map where America and Africa appeared linked by the small island of Noronha, suggesting a submarine link of the two continents.

In 1739, in the wake of the French East India Company's sea voyages to the Southern hemisphere commanded by Jean Baptiste Charles Bouvet de Lozier (1705–1786), Buache threw himself into a polar-projection design of his *Carte des Terres australes ... où se voyent les nouvelles découvertes faites en 1739 au Sud du Cap de Bonne Espérance* (Map of the Southern Territories ... Showing the New Discoveries Made in 1739 to the South of the Cape of Good Hope), in which he indicated "floating ice." In 1744, he followed this with a *Carte physique de la Grande Mer ... avec la représentation de ce que l'on conjecture sur la Mer Glaciale antarctique* (Physical Map of the Great Ocean ... Incorporating Assumptions about the Antarctic Glacial Sea). To this map, he added two accounts in which he clearly distinguished the southern continent (Australia) from an antarctic sea that mirrored the Arctic Ocean; he added a *Carte des Terres australes* (Map of the Southern Territories) in 1754. In order to justify the presence of floating icebergs, which, according to contemporary theory, should have been composed of freshwater, he imagined mountainous terrains under the ice cap–a hypothesis that was confirmed for the southernmost part of the American continent only nowadays.

All these different studies soon enabled him to present a general theory of the globe, according to which oceans and lands are linked by submerged mountains or mountains emerging from the waters in the form of islands or continental mountains (1744, 1752). On November 15, 1752, Buache presented his paper "Essai de géographie physique ... sur l'espèce de charpente du globe composée des chaines de montagnes qui traversent les mers comme les terres" (A Structure of the Globe Composed of Mountain Chains Traversing Both Seas and Lands) to the Académie des Sciences. His theory, which received recognition by posterity much later on, gave rise to abundant systematization.

The hope of finding a route to China via America was never far from the minds of Buache's contemporaries. In Canada, the Jesuit missionaries were influenced by the native Indian tales of lakes of foul water, and Claude Dablon finally invented a Western Sea in 1669. The great French cartographer Delisle argued for the existence of this sea in various manuscripts, documents that he never published. However, in 1708 an apocryphal letter, *Relation* (Account), from Admiral Bartholomew de Fonte, admiral of New Spain and Peru, was published in London that proclaimed the possibility of reaching the Davis Strait and Hudson Bay via the Pacific Ocean. This letter, an obvious fallacy, ended up alerting the English and from 1735 onwards it gave rise to English expeditions to these regions from Hudson's Bay.

In France, Joseph-Nicolas Delisle, the brother of Guillaume Delisle, presented this letter to the Académie des Sciences in Paris in 1750, relying on his brother's manuscripts as well. He published, in 1751, *Explication de la carte des nouvelles découvertes au Nord de la Mer du Sud* and, after that, a *Map*. Buache availed himself immediately of this hypothesis, and presented a summary of de Fonte's discoveries to the same Académie in 1752.

Between 1753 and 1755, he published numerous studies, accompanied by eleven maps, under the same title *Considérations géographiques et physiques sur les nouvelles découvertes au Nord de la Grande Mer* (Geographical and Physical Reflections on the New Discoveries North of the Great Ocean). He considered all possible arguments: comparisons of different texts of the *Relation*, discussions of latitudes, the width of the Northern Strait, discussions of English maps, tides and currents, ancient seafaring, and so forth. On many of his maps, he extended the Western Sea by a great gulf to the north of San Francisco, oriented toward the Hudson Bay. He drafted the outline of Alaska and of the Aleutian Islands and was able to place the Northern (Bering) Strait accordingly.

In 1768, Robert Sayer and Thomas Jefferys published, in London, *Great Probability of a North-West Passage*. Some enlightened minds, such as Benjamin Franklin (1706–1790) and Dalrymple, were convinced. Undaunted, the English pressed James Cook (1728–1779) to explore the length of the western coast of Canada, without success. George Vancouver (1757–1798) was the one to deliver final proof in 1794 that there is no sea passage to the East.

The measure of the audacity of Buache's thinking lies in the order he imposed on the globe, using original concepts that would subsequently open up new avenues. He can be considered a distant precursor of the German geophysicist Alfred Lothar Wegener (1880–1930) and the theory of tectonic plates.

[*See also* Cartography, *subentry on* Speculative Cartography, *and* Northwest Passage.]

## Bibliography

Lagarde, Lucie. "Le Passage du Nord-Ouest et la Mer de l'Ouest dans la cartographie française du XVIIIème siècle, contribution á l'étude de l'oeuvre de Deslisle et Buache." *Imago Mundi* 41 (1989): 19–43.

LUCIE LAGARDE
*Translated from the French by Alexa Nieschlag*

## Buccaneers and Buccaneering

The buccaneers were adventurers who preyed on Spanish ships and settlements in the Caribbean and along the Pacific littoral of South America during the latter half of the seventeenth century. Although some buccaneers were also pirates, seaborne criminals, most were landsmen who only embarked in ships to prosecute amphibious operations. The buccaneers' antecedents were English, French, and Dutch interlopers, illicit traders who infiltrated Spain's trade with its American colonies from the beginning of the sixteenth

**Buccaneer Bartolomew "el Portugués."** This image appeared in Alexander Exquemelin's *Buccaneers of America* (London, 1684–1685). © BRITISH LIBRARY / HIP / ART RESOURCE, NY

century. They gravitated to the islands of Hispaniola and Tortuga, where their practice of smoking or roasting meat on grills, in the manner of Amerindians, inspired the English word "buckaneer" from the French *boucan,* meaning "smoke," and *boucaner,* "to cure or smoke flesh."

Tapping Spain's silver lifeline to the New World aligned the interests of the buccaneers with England's unofficial foreign policy. From 1654 the buccaneers mounted a systematic campaign of terror against Spanish settlements, which received tacit approval in London. In 1655 the buccaneers ensconced themselves in the embryonic English colony in Port Royal, Jamaica, which became their most important base in the Caribbean. Successive governors of the island legitimized the activities of the buccaneers by granting privateer commissions against Spain. These operations were the island's best defense and almost its only livelihood.

Despite the settlement of differences between England and Spain by the Treaty of Madrid in 1670, the buccaneers' most spectacular successes were achieved under the leadership of Henry Morgan (1635–1688), himself lieutenant-governor of Jamaica from 1674. His feats are recorded in Alexander O. Exquemelin's *De Americaeneche Zee-Roovers* published in Amsterdam in 1678, and printed in English as *Bucaniers of America* in 1684. Morgan undertook a series of preemptive strikes on Spanish towns throughout the region. After they assaulted Panama in 1671 the buccaneers split booty amounting to £30,000 and Morgan barely managed to restrain his men from invading Peru. Exquemelin's ostensibly eyewitness account is replete with sensational tales of daring against an exotic backdrop; it constitutes a festive historical romance whose influence and appeal is unsurpassed by any other source.

In April 1680 another party of buccaneers crossed Darién to sack Panama. After failing to secure the city they hijacked vessels anchored in the bay and burst loose into the Pacific. For the next eighteen months, mainly under the leadership of Captain Bartholomew Sharpe, they scoured the coast in search of prizes. When Sharpe finally headed for home a great storm blew him far to the south of the Strait of Magellan so that he became, perforce, the first English captain to round Cape Horn in an easterly direction. Sharpe's exploits aroused intense interest at court when it became known that he had seized a secret book of charts and pilot instructions from a prize on the coast of modern Ecuador. The charts covered the entire Pacific coastline from California to Cape Horn and their value, in English hands, was inestimable. King Charles II (r. 1660–1685), prompted by Christopher Monck, Duke of

Albemarle, had the charts illicitly copied under the very nose of the Spanish ambassador to whom they had been returned.

Sharpe's narrative was first printed in Captain William Hacke's *A Collection of Original Voyages* (1699). The provenance of the manuscripts reveals that senior members of the Royal Society, including its president, Samuel Pepys (1633–1703), scrutinized the voyage. The drive by scientists to obtain disciplined, truthful voyage narratives had begun as early as 1666 when the Society published "Directions for Sea-men, Bound for Far Voyages" in *Philosophical Transactions.* The "Directions" guided mariners in the composition of their journals so that they might be rendered "pertinent and suitable for [the Society's] purpose." Sharpe's narrative was crucial because in his passage round Cape Horn he had sailed farther south than any other mariner. His claim that the great southern continent, *Terra Australis Incognita,* was a fiction was omitted from the published copy of his journal.

Besides Sharpe, six other crew members also left narratives of the voyage. The navigator and cartographer Basil Ringrose left a reliable account published in an expanded edition of *Bucaniers of America* (1685). William Dampier also recorded the expedition, his brief coverage being incorporated in *A New Voyage Round the World* (1697). The bias in Dampier's account is evidence of meticulous editorial process designed to divorce the author from his buccaneering past. The editor, possibly Hans Sloane, secretary and later president of the Royal Society, refashioned Dampier's narrative to reflect information of scientific interest. A similar process is observable in Lionel Wafer's *A New Voyage and Description of the Isthmus of America* (1699). Wafer had abandoned the expedition in April 1681, with Dampier and about forty others, intending to return overland to the Atlantic coast. During the march a quantity of gunpowder was ignited, accidentally injuring Wafer's knee so badly that he was left behind at mercy of *"wild* Indians." Wafer's narrative of life among the Kuna intermingles with a natural history of Darien designed to downplay buccaneering while emphasizing contemporary scientific preoccupations.

In March 1684 *Batchelor's Delight,* commanded by Captain John Cook, joined *Nicholas,* commanded by Captain John Eaton, off Valdivia (in modern-day Chile). Together they sailed to Juan Fernández, where they recovered a Moskito Indian whom Sharpe had marooned accidentally three years earlier. Dampier, who was on board *Batchelor's Delight,* describes how the castaway survived his island solitude in a passage in *New Voyage.* After leaving

Juan Fernández, Cook and Eaton sailed for the Galápagos where Cook's pilot, William Ambrose Cowley, compiled the first English map of the archipelago. Cowley's map and a narrative he kept of his voyage were also published in Hack's *Collection*.

On May 28, 1685, in one of the last significant actions undertaken by the buccaneers, a force of ten ships and almost a thousand men assembled to blockade the Bay of Panama. Under Captain Edward Davis the buccaneers prepared to intercept the Spanish treasure fleet from Lima. Dampier, Ringrose, and Wafer were among those present. Fourteen heavily armed Spanish vessels duly arrived, forewarned, empty of treasure and resolved to fight. Although the battle was inconclusive it was enough to fracture the buccaneers' alliance. Dampier's rueful observations on this occasion coincide with the start of a terminal decline in the buccaneers' fortunes: "Thus ended this days Work, and with it all that we had been projecting for 5 or 6 Months; when instead of making ourselves Masters of the Spanish Fleet and Treasure, we were glad to escape them" (*New Voyage*).

In 1685 hostilities broke out between France and Spain, and in 1689 England joined the Spanish side. Almost the last action of the buccaneers was the attack on Cartagena in 1697, led by the governor of French possessions in Hispaniola. After the fall of Cartagena the buccaneers, a third of the attacking force, were denied their due share of the booty. In retaliation they besieged the city until dispersed by a combined English and Dutch squadron. The buccaneers' fortunes were finally eclipsed by the Treaty of Ryswick in 1697, which ended the Nine Years' War. The majority of the buccaneers were rehabilitated, entering the service of their respective countries. Others settled as planters, but many reverted to piracy, infesting the coasts of North America until their suppression in the nineteenth century.

[*See also* Americas, *subentry on* Exploration Voyages, 1500–1616 (South America); Blackbeard; Caribbean Sea; Dampier, William; Pacific Ocean, *subentry on* Exploration Voyages, 1520–1700; Piracy; Privateering; Prizes; *and* Wars, Maritime, *subentry on* Anglo-Spanish Wars.]

## Bibliography

### Primary Works

Dampier, William. *A New Voyage Round the World*. Edited by Sir Albert Gray, with a new introduction by Percy G. Adams. New York: Dover, 1968.

Esquemeling, John. *The Buccaneers of America*. Edited by Henry Powell. London: Swan Sonnenschein, 1893.

Hacke, William. *A Collection of Original Voyages*. Introduction by Glyndwr Williams. New York: Scholars' Facsimiles, 1993. See Cowley's Voyage, pp. 1–45; Sharpe's Voyage, pp. 1–55, sigs. A2–2C4.

Wafer, Lionel. *A New Voyage and Description of the Isthmus of America*. Edited by L. E. Elliott Joyce. Oxford: Printed for the Hakluyt Society, 1934.

### Secondary Works

Bradley, Peter T. *The Lure of Peru: Maritime Intrusion into the South Sea, 1598–1701*. Houndmills, Basingstoke, Hampshire: Macmillan, 1989.

Lynham, Edward. "William Hack and the South Sea Buccaneers." In *The Mapmaker's Art: Essays on the History of Maps*, pp. 101–116. London: Batchworth, 1953.

Ringrose, Basil. *A Buccaneer's Atlas: Basil Ringrose's South Sea Waggoner; A Sea Atlas and Sailing Directions of the Pacific Coast of the Americas, 1682*. Edited by Derek Howse and Norman J. W. Thrower, with special contributions by Tony A. Cimolina, and a foreword by David B. Quinn. Berkeley: University of California Press, 1992.

Williams, Glyndwr. *The Great South Sea: English Voyages and Encounters, 1570–1750*. New Haven, Conn.: Yale University Press, 1997.

JAMES KELLY

# Buenos Aires

**Buenos Aires** The Río de la Plata (Silver River) in southeastern South America was first explored by Europeans in 1516 by the navigator Juan Díaz de Solís, traveling under the orders of the king of Spain. Later, in order to avoid the advances of the Portuguese in this region, the Spaniard Don Pedro de Mendoza signed a capitulation agreement on May 21, 1534, and organized a great expedition that arrived at the mouth of the Río de la Plata (in Argentina) in January 1536, establishing a port settlement on the southern coast that he called "Nuestra Señora de los Buenos Ayres" (Our Lady of Fair Winds) next to a river he called "Riachuelo de los Navios" (Ships Brook), probably on February 3, 1536, Saint Blasius Day.

After numerous difficulties and disease, Mendoza left the port in 1537 to head back to Spain, but he died on the high seas on June 23 of that year. Four years later, in June 1541, the Buenos Ayres governor Domingo Martínez de Irala moved the inhabitants of the settlement upriver to the city of Asunción (Paraguay), which had been founded in August 1537 and quickly constituted itself as a nucleus intended to head the neighboring regions. The protests following the depopulation were massive and vehement. A port at the mouth of the Río de la Plata was imperative to Paraguay and Tucumán for the export of their products; it enabled the arrival of seagoing vessels and allowed the smaller trade ships to reach the interior of the continent.

On April 9, 1579, Juan de Garay was given power as lieutenant governor to "populate a city in the Port of Buenos Ayres," and he departed from Asunción with sixty-six people, some by land with animals and others in the caravel *San Cristóbal de la Buenaventura* and in the brigantines *San Miguel*, *Santiago*, and *Todos los Santos*. On June 11, 1580, he founded the city of Trinidad and the nearby port called "Puerto Nuestra Señora Santa María de Buen Ayre."

Such was the importance of the port of Buenos Aires that scarcely had it been founded when pirates made their presence known in front of it, suggesting its strategic location and the important role it could play to offer access from the sea to the land—access that was a boon for settlers of the villages in the interior but was a threat to the commerce of Lima, Peru. The Río de la Plata route saved many miles on the road, or the difficulties of an alternative trip across the Isthmus of Panama, to reach the distant silver mines of Potosí, Bolivia, a difficult trip that took almost two years, by which time the price of the merchandise had doubled. Through the port of Buenos Aires, one had only to make a trip by sea from Spain and another by land to reach Potosí across wide plains.

Trade restrictions that had been in place in the region since 1556 were lifted after the fusion of the Spanish and Portuguese crowns in 1580, and commercial traffic grew exponentially in the years after the first export from Buenos Aires to Brazil in 1587. In the face of this, trade protests from Lima increased, and in 1594 commerce was prohibited through the port of Buenos Aires. One exception was the lottery system, inaugurated by the crown in 1595, that authorized the sale of six hundred black slaves in the port city every year.

Prohibited by decree, commerce through the port of Buenos Aires could only be done with a special license from the king. The seventeenth century found Buenos Aires in a full fight to gain freedom of trade, but this port city did not have a safe port for its boats. Numerous proposals were presented to the colonial authorities, while contraband flourished in the city. In 1755, Juan Echeverría proposed putting up a stone pier in the northern zone of the city, and during 1771 the engineering firm Rodríguez y Cardozo carried out another project. Similar proposals came from the engineer Pedro Antonio Cerviño in 1796 and the Italian native Eustaguio Giannini in 1805. But up until almost the end of the nineteenth century, disembarking at the port of Buenos Aires involved serious problems for passengers and merchandise. On arriving at the banks of the Río de la Plata near the city of Buenos Aires, travelers endured an ungainly process in which they were picked up by small barges and transferred to enormous horse-drawn carts while still meters from the coast; on the carts they were carried to solid ground and finally deposited.

As of 1770 there had been more than sixty port and embankment projects proposed. The first homeland governor took firm charge of the port projects. In a port rebirth in 1855, the so-called Passengers Dock was built in front of the harbormaster's office; the customs house, called the New Customs House, was built by the English engineer Eduardo Taylor behind the actual governor's house; and a wharf was added at Barracas–La Boca by the Argentine engineer Luis Augusto Huergo.

On December 22, 1884, the Argentine president Julio Argentino Roca, along with the former presidents Bartolomé Mitre, Domingo Faustino Sarmiento, and Nicolás Avellaneda as witnesses, signed a contract to build the Port of the City of Buenos Aires. In April 1886, the plans and complementary documents for the work on the port were approved. Construction started on March 27, 1887, and ended in 1897. But the port's official inauguration was not until the first ship docked on January 28, 1889, in a ceremony aboard the battleship *Admiral Brown*.

In view of the extensive growth in port traffic, a law was passed in 1908 authorizing an expansion of the port, a project that was inaugurated in 1919 by President Hipolito Yrigoyen. In 1991 renovations began to transform the deactivated 1889 port into a promenade preserving the great wharfs, and in 1997 this public area opened as the Madero Port Zone of the Autonomous City of Buenos Aires.

[*See also* Americas, *subentry on* Exploration Voyages, 1500–1616 (South America), *and* Ports.]

## Bibliography

Lewis, Colin M. *Argentina: A Short History*. Oxford: Oneworld Publications, 2002.

EDGARDO JOSÉ ROCCA

# Bulk Cargoes

The term "bulk cargo" indicates unpackaged cargo that can be poured, tipped, or pumped into the holds or tanks of a ship, although in the nineteenth century the term was used to indicate a cargo exclusively, or almost exclusively, of one commodity. At the turn of the twenty-first century, iron ore, coal, and grain accounted for some 65 percent of seaborne movements of dry bulk cargo. Other important bulk cargoes are bauxite, sugar, wood,

wood pulp, wood chips, and fertilizers. (Full cargoes such as cars and packaged lumber are sometimes referred to as "neobulks.") These bulk cargoes, usually shipped in full shiploads, form the basis of the chartering tramp market. There are also a number of bulk cargoes that use specifically designed vessels between dedicated terminals. Examples are cement carriers (introduced in 1900), wine tankers (1946), fruit-juice carriers (1985), and molten-sulfur carriers (1960s). One of the earliest specialist vessels was the molasses tanker, which can be traced back to 1912, and in the late 1920s the British Athel Line was building at least two substantial molasses tankers. Such specialist ships are often part of a vertically integrated logistics operation—that is, an operation in which the production, distribution, and perhaps the retail outlets of a commodity are in the control of one organization, as is true with many oil products.

Bulk cargo carried on a general-purpose cargo ship can present certain dangers. In 1873 a witness before the Royal Commission on Unseaworthy Ships testified that grain was the most dangerous of all bulk cargoes. In 1880 there was an effort to reduce the problem of grain shifting. The Merchant Shipping Acts of 1894 set the standard from then until 1914. The International Maritime Organization now has in place a code for the safe carriage of bulk cargoes. The major problems in carrying bulk cargoes are improper weight distribution, which results in structural damage, reduction of stability during a voyage as a result of cargo shifting, and spontaneous heating. In addition, a ship operator must consider the damage done as the bulk cargo is dropped or poured into the hold. For instance, some cargoes of scrap iron include such items as large car engines, which may be dropped fifty or sixty feet. Many cargoes may also bring with them an all-pervading cloud of penetrating dust.

The dry bulk carrier is a large single-deck ship that carries unpackaged cargo. Statistics concerning bulk carriers may not always be consistent, because different authors at different times have arbitrarily determined at what size a single-deck vessel will be classed as a bulk carrier. Although for centuries there have been ships carrying bulk coal and grain, the modern concept of bulk cargoes being loaded and discharged quickly into single-deck "open hatch" dry cargo ships from modern terminals equipped for handling bulk cargoes dates only from the mid-1950s.

Shipping textbooks written before the 1950s refer to bulk cargoes but not to bulk carriers. The Liberty ship was a popular vessel for the carriage of bulk cargoes, and some were "jumbo-ized" for this trade. There were a few large bulkers (around 18,000 deadweight tons [dwt]) before

World War II, but these were on the Great Lakes as part of a vertically integrated operation. Like container ships, bulk carriers were born of economic necessity. In the period after the Korean War, tramp freight rates were depressed even though demand was increasing, so a less expensive means of carrying tramp cargoes had to be found. Before this time it was not technically possible to build open-hatch ships.

Large bulk carriers usually trade between special terminals and therefore seldom have any derricks or lifting gear. Since smaller bulk carriers must be prepared to discharge anywhere, they typically have their own gear. Technology to improve the handling of bulk cargoes was introduced as early as the end of the nineteenth century. For instance, in 1888 grabs were mentioned for discharging grain in London as an alternative to grain elevators, and in 1899, George Hulett developed a clamshell bucket that held fifteen tons of iron ore for loading Great Lakes ships. By 1935 there was an ore-discharging plant in Rotterdam.

The popular sizes of large bulk carrier are:

*Handysize* (10,000–25,000 dwt). These carriers can trade to most ports in the world, though 20,000 dwt is about the largest size that can use the Saint Lawrence Seaway. There were some 77.4 million dwt in this class in 2000.
*Handymax* (35,000–50,000 dwt). There were some 45.5 million dwt in this class in 2000.
*Panamax* (about 65,000 dwt). This class of carrier is the largest that can use the Panama Canal, since the canal's limiting lock width is just over 32 meters (105 feet), with a maximum length overall of 290 meters (950 feet). The Panamax class is important because much of the ore trade is through the Panama Canal. There were some 70.5 million dwt in this class in 2000.
*Capesize* bulkers (100,000–180,000 dwt). These are used mainly for ore and coal on specific routes between well-equipped terminals. There were some 86.6 million dwt in this class in 2000.
*Very large bulk carriers* (VLBC; 180,000+ dwt). Most VLBCs trade between Australia and Japan.

In 1972 dry bulk carriers made up 17 percent of world gross tonnage, and in 1995 bulk carriers made up 32 percent of world gross tonnage. There were about 4,600 bulk carriers in 1995, with a total deadweight tonnage of more than 200 million. Liberia and Panama were the main countries of registry. By 1980, the total deadweight tonnage of bulk carriers was increasing faster than the number of carriers, indicating an increase in their average size.

Experiments with dry-and-wet bulk carriers began in the 1920s, but it was not until the 1950s that combination types were built in any numbers and that universal bulk carriers

(UBCs) were developed; still, by the 1980s this type of carrier had largely disappeared. They were superseded in the early 1950s by ore/oil (O/O) carriers and in 1965 by ore, bulk, oil (OBO) carriers. Around 1970 the Conbulker was introduced, fitted for carrying containers, packaged timber, and bulk cargo, or a combination of these.

[See also Bulk Carrier; Container Ship; International Maritime Organization; and Oil and Petroleum Products.]

### Bibliography

Alderton, Patrick M. Sea Transport: Operation and Economics. 4th ed. London: Thomas Reed, 1995.

Alderton, Patrick M., and S. Cross. "Specialised Cargo Ships." In The Shipping Revolution: The Modern Merchant Ship, edited by Robert Gardiner, pp. 119–136. London: Conway Maritime Press, 1992.

Fleming, D. K. "Modern Tramp Ships, Bulk Carriers, and Combination Carriers." In The Shipping Revolution: The Modern Merchant Ship, edited by Robert Gardiner, pp. 12–31. London: Conway Maritime Press, 1992.

Nossum, Birger. The Evolution of Dry Bulk Shipping. Oslo, Norway: Gan Grafisk, 1996.

United Nations Conference on Trade and Development. Secretariat. Review of Maritime Transport. New York: United Nations, published annually.

PATRICK M. ALDERTON

# Bulk Carrier

The bulk carrier was designed to transport free-flowing liquid, gaseous, or dry cargo. Because of the low value of the cargo, transportation costs were more important than speed. Before World War II, tramp steamers transported most bulk cargo, with the exception of oil. The postwar economic boom in Europe, America, and Asia resulted in a major growth in the demand for ores, coal, grain, and mineral oil. Bulk carriers bridged the geographical distance between mines and markets.

The typical postwar bulk carrier was the mass-produced Liberty type of 10,000 gross tons, built in the United States between 1942 and 1946. In the 1950s some Liberty ships were lengthened and adapted for the better carriage of bulk cargo. Economies of scale—the larger the ship, the lower the transportation costs—led to the construction of much larger bulk carriers in the 1960s. A typical Japanese-built bulk carrier of the mid-1970s was 100,000 tons. This was too large for the Panama Canal, although suitable for the Suez Canal.

Some newly built ships were single-purpose bulk carriers with scheduled routes traveled at regular intervals

(for example, entering service in 1986, Berge Stahl of over 360,000 tons carried Swedish ore to Continental Europe). These ships are compartmented and have beams to strengthen the ship's structure. They depend entirely on specialized shore-based cranes at dedicated terminals for loading and unloading. In the 1980s very large bulk carriers fell out of favor. Shipowners settled for smaller ships that could enter almost all deep-sea ports.

The trade in bulk is characterized by regional imbalances resulting in a lack of return cargo. Multipurpose bulk carriers, capable of carrying different types of cargo (for example, oil and ores), solved this problem. This led to the construction of oil-bulk-ore carrier (OBO) in the early 1960s. OBOs are more expensive to build and operate than single-purpose bulk carriers, and they are usually smaller in size (200,000 tons).

[See also Bulk Cargoes.]

### Bibliography

Gardiner, Robert, ed. The Shipping Revolution: The Modern Merchant Ship. London: Conway Maritime Press, 1992.

FERRY DE GOEY

# Bullen, Frank.

See Literature, subentry on Sea Essays; Whaling, subentry on Literature.

# Burke, Arleigh

(1901–1996), American World War II combat commander and Cold War chief of naval operations. Arleigh Albert Burke remains best remembered for commanding destroyers in the Solomon Islands in 1943, where he received the nickname "31 Knot Burke" for his preferred tactical speed when driving his squadron into combat.

The grandson of a Swedish immigrant, Anders Bjorkegren, Burke was born on a farm three miles east of Boulder, Colorado. He never completed high school but won appointment to the U.S. Naval Academy. Graduating in 1923, he pursued gunnery as a specialty, combining sea duty with the acquisition of a master's degree in chemical engineering and critical experience in the development and procurement of weaponry. As a result, despite a record-breaking destroyer command in 1939–1940, he found himself stuck in Washington, D.C., as an inspector of gun mounts through early 1943. A year in the

South Pacific, particularly his five months commanding Destroyer Squadron 23 in the Bougainville campaign, distinguished him as one of the navy's most successful tactical innovators. His longest wartime tour, however, was in naval aviation, as chief of staff to Vice Admiral Marc Mitscher in the fast-carrier task forces during the Marianas, Leyte, Iwo Jima, and Okinawa campaigns. Burke was subsequently chosen for critical postwar assignments at the forefront of the service's political battles over the shape of the military establishment and the navy's role in national defense and in developing Cold War strategy. He played a key role in building the navy's headquarters staff in Japan during the Korean War and spent six months attempting to negotiate a truce with the Communists. His experience and reputation led President Dwight Eisenhower to choose then Rear Admiral Burke over ninety-two senior admirals as chief of naval operations in 1955.

As the last chief of naval operations to command operational fleets directly, Burke was a committed Cold War warrior who was instrumental in commanding forces and advising U.S. leaders in Cold War crises in Suez, Lebanon, Indonesia, Taiwan, Berlin, and Cuba. He also fought, with little success, numerous battles against increased unification in defense of the navy's inherent flexibility and independence of command. He believed above all in the integrity and talents of U.S. naval officers and sailors and in "loyalty up and down" to seniors and subordinates. His philosophy of command encouraged individual responsibility and initiative to meet the uncertainties of combat.

Burke's tour as chief of naval operations laid the foundation for U.S. naval superiority through the end of the Cold War and beyond. His legacies include the creation of the Polaris missile program; the decision to build only nuclear-powered submarines; increased navy capability to fly and fight at night and in all weather; and the construction of the first classes of guided-missile destroyers, large-deck amphibious helicopter assault ships, and a new class of fast fleet logistic support ships; the introduction of computers in seagoing command and control; the launching of the United States' first electronic reconnaissance satellite; and a deep and continuing emphasis by the navy on cooperation with allied and friendly navies. In 1982, in recognition of his lasting achievements, a class of more than sixty new guided-missile destroyers was named in his honor. Burke died in Bethesda, Maryland, on January 1, 1996.

[*See also* Naval Administration *and* Navies, Great Powers, *subentry on* United States, 1775 to the Present.]

## Bibliography

Potter, E. B. *Admiral Arleigh Burke: A Biography.* New York: Random House, 1990.
Rosenberg, David Alan. "Arleigh Albert Burke." In *The Chiefs of Naval Operations,* edited by Robert William Love Jr., pp. 262–319. Annapolis, Md.: Naval Institute Press, 1980.
Rosenberg, David Alan. "Arleigh Albert Burke." In *Men of War: Great Naval Leaders of World War II,* edited by Stephen Howarth, pp. 506–527. New York: St. Martin's Press, 1993.
Rosenberg, David Alan. "Arleigh Burke: The Last CNO." In *Quarterdeck and Bridge: Two Centuries of American Naval Leadership,* edited by James C. Bradford, pp. 360–393. Annapolis, Md.: Naval Institute Press, 1996.

David Alan Rosenberg

***Buys***    A Dutch vessel of late-medieval origin, built until around 1850, the *buys* was associated primarily with herring fisheries but was occasionally also used for transport. The *buys* was a keel vessel of 15 to 18 meters (49 to 59 feet) from stem to stern, with three low, square-rigged masts. It was typically manned by twelve men and two boys. Its bulwark had an opening for drift nets on both sides. The fore- and mainmasts were lowered during fishing to let the ship and nets drift with the current. Most ships held about twenty to thirty lasts (approximately fifty to eighty tons), with fourteen barrels of herring weighing one last. The *buys* was the backbone of the Dutch Republic's herring fishery, with up to six hundred vessels being built in the shipyards of herring cities such as Enkhuizen, Vlaardingen, and Maassluis.

The construction of *buys* changed little in the sixteenth and seventeenth centuries, but the flat stern, "platte spiegel," was gradually abandoned for the round stern, "rond achterschip." After 1700 the *buys* were equipped with only two masts. The change quite likely reflects a preference for easy handling over speed, and thus indicates the decline of piracy in the North Sea.

The *buys* herring fishery season was summer and autumn. Around 1750 the *hoekerbuis* was introduced to allow for all-year operations, combining the strengths of the *buis* and the *hoeker* (a stronger two-masted vessel of late-medieval origin built for cod fishing in the North Atlantic). The *hoekerbuis* used drift nets to catch herring in the North Sea in the summer and autumn and was refitted for long-lining for cod off Iceland in winter and spring.

[*See also* Fishing Vessels.]

## Bibliography

Kranenburg, H. A. H. *De zeevisscherij van Holland in den tijd der Republiek*. Amsterdam, Netherlands: H. J. Paris, 1946.

Ploeg, J. "Speurtocht naar Haringbuizen." *Mededelingen van de Nederlandse Vereniging voor Zeegeschiedenis* 25 (1972): 25–31.

Vliet, Adri P. van. *Vissers in oorlogstijd: De Zeeuwse zeevisserij in de jaren 1568–1648*. Middelburg, Netherlands: Koninklijk Zeeuwsch Genootschap der Wetenschapen, 2003.

POUL HOLM

**Byzantium.** *See* Istanbul.

# Cabot, Sebastian

**Cabot, Sebastian** (c. 1481/82–1557), Venetian-born explorer and cartographer in English and Spanish service. One of the more controversial figures in the history of early modern exploration, Sebastian Cabot was one of three sons of John Cabot, for whose accomplishments he apparently assumed undue credit. Probably born in Venice about 1481 or 1482, he immigrated to England with his family shortly thereafter. Sebastian's name is first recorded in Henry VII's 1496 patent to John Cabot. In 1515 he told the historian Peter Martyr that he had commanded two ships to the northwest, but the documentary record is blank until 1505, when Henry VII granted him an annuity for what he "hath doon unto us in and aboute the fyndynge of the newe founde landes." This may have been for his work as a navigator or pilot with the Bristol-based Company of Adventurers into the New Found Lands, which launched several expeditions between 1503 and 1505. The clearest evidence for Cabot's own transatlantic voyaging dates from 1509, when Henry VIII confirmed his annuity "for his good and gracious discovery of the New Land." Where this voyage led is unclear. Peter Martyr (1534) writes that Cabot reached latitude 55°N, while Giovanni Battista Ramusio (1556) says he attained 67½°N—the latitude of Hudson Strait and a way "towards eastern Cathay." These accounts may refer to separate voyages, one from before 1505 and the other in 1508–1509.

In 1512, Cabot joined Henry VIII as a cartographer on an Anglo-Spanish campaign against France. The same year, Ferdinand of Aragon recruited him for Spain's Casa de la Contratación; by 1518 he was *piloto mayor*, responsible for examining pilots, distributing navigational instruments, producing charts, and keeping up-to-date the *padrón real* upon which such charts were based.

Cabot led an expedition bound for the Moluccas in 1526. On the coast of Brazil, he heard rumors of a silver-producing realm accessible via the Río de la Plata. The loss of his flagship on a reef apparently convinced him that a transpacific voyage was too risky, and after marooning several of his recalcitrant officers, Cabot sailed up the Plata to the Paraná and Paraguay rivers, reaching as far as Asunción. Upon his return to Spain in 1530 he was tried and convicted of disobedience and murder (for the death of two of the marooned men), but after paying a fine he resumed his duties as *piloto mayor*.

In 1544, Cabot published a world map, one copy of which survives in Paris. To help pilots compensate for compass variation, which was poorly understood, Cabot employed one scale for latitude and another for longitude. Previously, some cartographers had used different latitude scales for the eastern and western halves of their maps. In a 1544–1545 lawsuit featuring Cabot, the cosmographer major, and their respective protégés, two-scale maps were prohibited altogether. The captions of the Paris map were poorly written, but scholars have particularly challenged one which claims that Cabot and his father reached Newfoundland in 1494, three years before John Cabot's first attested voyage.

Cabot returned to England in 1548 and embarked on the least controversial stage of his career. Whatever his failings, he was an accomplished navigator with a combination of talents not readily available in Edward VI's England, where there was renewed interest in overseas navigation. Granted an annuity of 250 marks, Cabot was "one of the vectors through which expertise in the new celestial navigation reached England" (Pope, p. 54). As governor of what became known as the Muscovy Company, he drafted the instructions for Sir Hugh Willoughby and Richard Chancellor's 1553 expedition around Norway in search of markets for English wool and a northeast passage to China. Although this voyage had mixed results in the short term, it proved a nursery for English explorers.

At a banquet before his own departure to Russia in 1556, Stephen Borough (a veteran of the 1553 expedition) described how Cabot "for very joy that he had to see the towardnes of our intended discovery, he entred into the dance himselfe, amongst the rest of the young and lusty company." This is one of the few surviving descriptions of Cabot, a year from death but a venerable survivor of the

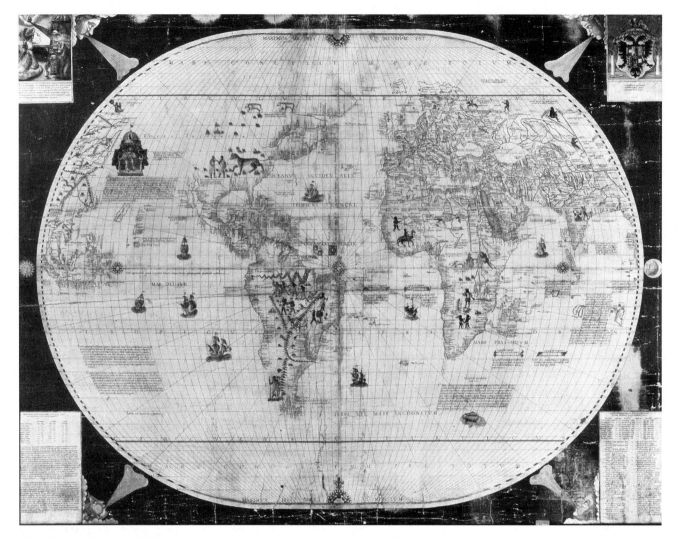

**Cabot's Map of the World.** Sebastian Cabot designed this engraved map in 1544. THE BRIDGEMAN ART LIBRARY / BIBLIOTHÈQUE NATIONALE DE FRANCE, PARIS

first generation of transatlantic explorers and still a vigorous promoter of a northern route to the Orient.

[*See also* Americas.]

## Bibliography

Andrews, Kenneth R. *Trade Plunder and Settlement: Maritime Enterprise and the Genesis of the British Empire, 1480–1630.* Cambridge, U.K., and New York: Cambridge University Press, 1984.

Hakluyt, Richard. *The Principal Navigations, Voyages, Traffiques, and Discoveries of the English Nation.* 1600. Reprint. London: J. M. Dent, 1927. Includes documents on the Muscovy Company.

Kelsey, Harry. "The Planispheres of Sebastian Cabot and Sancho Gutiérrez." *Terrae Icognitae* 19 (1987): 41–58.

Lamb, Ursula. "Science by Litigation: A Cosmographic Feud." *Terrae Icognitae* 1 (1969): 40–58.

Medina, José Toribio. *El Veniciano Sebastian Caboto al servicio de España.* 2 vols. Santiago, Chile, 1908. Covers Cabot's Spanish service.

Parry, J. H. *The Discovery of South America.* New York: Taplinger, 1979.

Pope, Peter E. *The Many Landfalls of John Cabot.* Toronto: University of Toronto Press, 1997.

Quinn, David B. *New American World: A Documentary History of North America to 1612.* 5 vols. New York: Arno Press, 1979.

Skelton, R. A. "Cabot, Sebastian." In *Dictionary of Canadian Biography*, vol. 1, 1000–1700. Reprinted with corrections. Toronto: Toronto University Press, 1979.

Williamson, James A. *The Cabot Voyages and Bristol Discovery under Henry VII.* Cambridge, U.K.: Hakluyt Society, 1962.

LINCOLN P. PAINE

# Cádiz

This entry contains two subentries:

Commercial Port
Naval Port

---

## Commercial Port

Cádiz is a harbor city in which it is difficult to distinguish where the city begins and where the harbor ends; the border between city and harbor was even more ambiguous in ancient times. The lack of space not only caused a blurring of city and harbor but also has made Cádiz a densely populated area.

### From Its Origins to Its Decline in the Middle Ages

Some scholars believe that Cádiz was founded as "Gadr" by Phoenician merchants from Tyre sometime between 1100 and 700 B.C.E.; most scholars believe that Cádiz is at least three thousand years old. The city became an important seaport from which tin, copper, and other Tartessian-Turdetanian goods were exported. Named "Gadeira" by the Greeks and "Gades" by the Romans, it was a well-known worship center of the Melqart-Heracles temple. An ally of Carthage during the Punic Wars, Cádiz acknowledged the supremacy of Rome in 205 B.C.E. In 49 B.C.E., "Gades" was bestowed Roman citizenship by Julius Caesar, putting it legally on a level with the rest of the Roman Empire. The historian Strabo considered Gades one of the most important cities of the empire. Indeed, Rome's socioeconomic success was highly indebted to an important family from Gades, the Balbus, who had much influence in Roman politics at the end of the Roman Republic.

Around the fourth century C.E., Gades began a difficult period that nearly consigned it into oblivion; it was invaded by Vandals, Byzantines, and Visigoths. The demolition of the temple of Heracles started the Moorish Qadis decline. But Cádiz harbor enjoyed renewed prosperity in the late Middle Ages when King Henry IV of Castile gave the city economic and defensive infrastructures. In 1492 twenty-five ships containing eight thousand expelled Spanish Jews sailed from Cádiz to North Africa.

### Cádiz's Commercial Splendor

Cádiz was the departure harbor for Columbus's second voyage as well as for other minor expeditions. It became the headquarters of the Casa de Contratación (House of Trade), a government institution for controlling all trade with the New World, from 1495 until 1503, when the headquarters was moved to Seville. From 1509 onward Cádiz served as register of ships arriving from the Spanish American colonies, avoiding Seville's control. Cádiz endured several raids during the sixteenth century, mainly from Barbary corsairs but also from Sir Francis Drake in 1587; especially cruel was the Anglo-Dutch raid of 1596, during which the city was sacked for fifteen days. Reinforcement of its defensive structures made the city nearly impregnable; nevertheless, it was blockaded and its population subjected to epidemics. Cádiz survived an assault by an Anglo-Dutch force of 14,000 during the War of Succession (1700–1714).

The publication of the book *Emporio del orbe, Cádiz ilustrada*, by Fray Jerónimo de la Concepción, in Amsterdam in 1690 helped to highlight the leading role of Cádiz in the trade with the Spanish American colonies. This role was reinforced after the establishment of the Bourbon and the transfer of the Casa de la Contratación back to Cádiz in 1717, making the Cádiz harbor head of the Spanish shipping monopoly with its American Colonies. The consulate and the Comandancia General del Departamento Marítimo became crucial organs of trading control and of defense of the coastal space near the harbor. The presence of La Carraca dockyard turned Cádiz bay into a strategic site for defense of the commercial routes with African, American, and Asian colonies.

### Decline and Fall, and Present and Future Plans

From 1796 the bay of Cádiz was subjected to a strong blockade by the British Royal Navy, a blockade that continued until 1808 except for a brief interruption encouraged by the Treaty of Amiens in 1802. In 1805 the city became a harbor from which France's Spanish battle fleet sailed to be defeated by Horatio Nelson's squadron on October 21 near Cape Trafalgar.

Cádiz lost its relevance again because of the Tratado de Libre Comercio of 1778, and the Peninsular War (1808–1814), and the independence of the American colonies were the final blows to the harbor's supremacy. Furthermore, competition from Gibraltar became a key element in its decline. As a response, the harbor merchants applied for the franchise of the harbor sea room, which was obtained in 1829 without any revitalization in return. The lack of adequate infrastructures began to be tackled in the late nineteenth century and early twentieth century.

The shallow draft of the bay, the attraction of Algeciras harbor with its better natural conditions, and the development of an important group of chemical industries related to Cepsa's oil refinery, all pushed Cádiz harbor into the background. Eastern European competition led to a decline in the naval industry and in the number of shipyards. Today the harbor is one more stopover for tourist cruises sailing from the Mediterranean to the Atlantic. The Dragados Offshore factory, plans for new transport infrastructures (including a new bridge over the bay), and projects associated with the bicentennial of the Cortes de Cádiz (2012) may help revive the fortunes of Cádiz harbor.

[*See also* Mediterranean Sea *and* Ports.]

### Bibliography

Alemany Llovera, J. *Los puertos españoles en el siglo XIX*. Madrid, Spain: MOPT, 1991.

Aubet, María Eugenia. *The Phoenicians and the West: Politics, Colonies, and Trade*. Translated by Mary Turton. Cambridge, U.K.: Cambridge University Press, 1993. Originally published as *Tiro y las colonias fenicias de Occidente* (Barcelona, Spain: Crítica, 1994).

Bustos Rodríguez, Manuel. *Cádiz en el sistema atlántico: La ciudad, sus comerciantes y la actividad mercantil (1650–1830)*. Madrid, Spain: Sílex, 2005.

Fierro Cubiella, Juan A. *Historia de la ciudad de Cádiz*. Cádiz, Spain, 1993.

Gámez Duarte, Feliciano. *Luchar contra el mar, edificar en el viento: La compañía gaditana Viniegra, 1797–1829*. Cádiz, Spain: Ministerio de Educación, Cultura y Deportes, 2000.

Pérez Galdós, Benito. *Cádiz*. Madrid, Spain: Cátedra, 2003.

Ramos Santana, Alberto. *Cádiz en el siglo XIX: De ciudad soberana a capital de provincia*. Madrid, Spain: Sílex, 1993.

Ringrose, David R. *España, 1700–1900: El mito del fracaso*. Madrid, Spain: Alianza, 1996.

Solís, Ramón. *El Cádiz de las Cortes: La vida en la ciudad en los años 1810–1813*. Madrid, Spain: Alianza, 1969.

FELICIANO GÁMEZ DUARTE

## Naval Port

Cádiz is a city permanently tied to its port. The founding of old Gades by Phoenician mariners and merchants—the date, though undocumented, has traditionally been set at around 1100 B.C.E.—can be explained by its location at the confluence of the Mediterranean Sea and the Atlantic Ocean. However, its expansion into a great port center dates only from the sixteenth century, when the small nucleus of population founded in the thirteenth century moved down from the highlands toward the shores of the sea.

These days Cádiz takes advantage of its excellent geographical conditions. The natural port sits at the entrance to the bay of the same name, and its docks can provide shelter for numerous deep-draft ships. The bay gives way to an even more protected inlet called Puntal (or Puntales), a true second bay, which was the preferred mooring for ships of the Spanish colonial fleet. Moreover, the port functions as the center of an extensive naval complex dedicated to the construction and maintenance of ships, which ultimately benefits other maritime activities like fishing and salt production.

During the course of the sixteenth century, the city took on its current physical form, with the plaza of the Corredera (today called Plaza de San Juan de Dios) as administrative center and Calle Nueva as the hub of expansion and heart of the commercial activity generated by the port's traffic. However, in the final years of that century, the city suffered the attack of Francis Drake in 1587 and the sacking and burning by Robert Devereux, Earl of Essex, in 1596, forcing the city to take defensive measures that continued for two centuries. The city, which has only three exits to the outside world (Puerta del Mar and Puerta de Sevilla in the port and Puerta de Tierra facing the rural interior), became a veritable fortress protected by a complete wall constructed in various phases (the bay, the area of La Caleta, and, finally, Campo del Sur) and dotted with imposing bastions (San Felipe, Santa Catalina, La Candelaria)—to the extent that in 1726 an eyewitness could consider Cádiz an authentic, unconquerable bastion that was "fearsome to its enemies and the envy of foreign nations."

With its fortunes essentially linked to those of maritime commerce, Cádiz has grown without cease since the latter half of the seventeenth century, when colonial boat traffic began to think of the city as an alternative to the complicated navigation of the official route that ran to Seville via the Guadalquivir River. This tendency was reinforced in 1679 when Cádiz was conceded the *tercio de buque*, the privilege of loading in its port a third of the cargo on vessels bound for America. But the definitive triumph for Cádiz came in the eighteenth century, when the authorities decided in its favor the long-running dispute with Seville and decreed the transfer to Cádiz of the organizations that regulated overseas commerce—the Casa de la Contratación (House of Trade) and the Consulado or Universidad de Cargadores a Indias—making the city the new center of the so-called Carrera de Indias (the route of the Indies, or the colonial convoy system; 1717).

Also in the eighteenth century, Cádiz, seat of the Intendencia General de la Marina de España (general administration of Spanish shipping), established in 1717, became

**Cádiz.** *The Defense of Cádiz against the English* by Francisco de Zurbarán (1598–1664), 1625. Don Fernando Girón gives orders to his generals while the naval battle is in progress behind them. ERICH LESSING / ART RESOURCE, NY / MUSEO DEL PRADO, MADRID

a great military port. The first training center for naval officers, the Academia de Guardias Marinas, was also established in 1717, and the Armada's first Colegio de Cirugía (surgical college) was established in 1748, setting the city up as the head of one of the Iberian Peninsula's three maritime departments. At the same time, a naval shipyard, La Carraca (1729), was built in the area, specifically for the construction of warships.

This city, mercantile and military, rich and orderly, dynamic and cosmopolitan, middle class and well educated, experienced its most illustrious years between 1717 and 1797, overcoming even the crisis of 1778, when the Decreto de Libre Comercio (free-market decree) took away its status as the exclusive port for colonial traffic and forced it to compete with twelve other metropolitan ports. This was the period that produced the city's great urban expansion and that gave it its now familiar features, such

as its emblematic buildings (including a new customhouse made necessary by the increased traffic), its merchant houses, and its *torres-miradores* (view towers), including the famous Torre de Vigía and the Torre Tavira, which gave constancy to the movement of the port, the arrivals and departures of ships that beat out the rhythmic pulse of the city.

Nevertheless, the closing years of that century marked the beginning of the city's decline, the major milestones of which were the abolition of the Casa de la Contratación in 1790, the commercial crisis brought on by the prolonged English blockade that began in 1797, the yellow fever epidemic of 1800 (which took between seven thousand and eleven thousand lives, followed by a second outbreak in 1804 that killed about five thousand more), the Peninsular War of 1808–1814 (although in 1810 the famous Cortes de Cádiz [court of Cádiz] opened to uphold the no less famous constitution of 1812), and finally the emancipation of the American provinces, which was the coup de grâce that deprived the city of its principal source of wealth (1824).

Cádiz never regained its former splendor, despite restoration efforts during the nineteenth century, when it obtained the temporary concession of status as a free port (1829–1831) and continued to maintain a steady exchange of goods and passengers with Cuba, Puerto Rico, the Philippines, and the Latin American republics. At the beginning of the twenty-first century, Cádiz has renewed and diversified its maritime activities with the creation of the Zona Franca (duty-free zone), the reinvigoration of the fishing industry and the shipyards, and the construction of docks for container ships and of a new shipping office. But the city's zenith is a thing of the past.

[*See also* Navies, Great Powers, *subentry on* Spain, 1500–1805; Ports; *and* Wars, Maritime, *subentry on* Anglo-Spanish Wars.]

## Bibliography

Bustos Rodríguez, Manuel. *Cádiz en el sistema atlántico: La ciudad, sus comerciantes y la actividad mercantil (1650–1830)*. Cádiz, Spain: Sílex and Universidad de Cádiz, 2005.

Bustos Rodríguez, Manuel. *Los siglos decisivos* (The Decisive Centuries). Vol. 2 of *Historia de Cádiz*. Madrid, Spain: Sílex, 1990.

García-Baquero González, Antonio. *Cádiz y el Atlántico (1717–1778): El comercio colonial español bajo el monopolio gaditano*. 2d ed. Cádiz, Spain: Diputación Provincial, 1988.

García-Baquero González, Antonio. *Comercio colonial y guerras revolucionarias: La decadencia económica de Cádiz a raíz de la emancipación americana*. Seville, Spain: Escuela de Estudios Hispano-Americanos, 1972.

MARINA ALFONSO MOLA and CARLOS MARTÍNEZ-SHAW
*Translated from the Spanish by Matthew Miller*

## Calcutta. *See Kolkata.*

## Callao
The important and strategically located Peruvian port of Callao is situated in a wide bay opposite the island of San Lorenzo, which protects the city from the prevailing southerly winds. Because of its proximity to Lima, the former capital of the Peruvian viceroyalty, Callao became the leading west coast port for the Americas. It was the final destination for merchandise shipped from Seville, which was sent to the Pacific via the Isthmus of Panama. It was also the main base for the Armada del Mar del Sur, a naval institution established in 1580 in Callao to protect the silver trade routes, which originated at Potosí, in upper Peru (now Bolivia), and went to Spain by way of Arica.

Defensive walls were built in the seventeenth century following attacks headed by Francis Drake (1580), Joris van Spilbergen (1615), and Jacques L'Hermite (1624). The city was totally destroyed by a tsunami in 1746 but recovered its importance within a few years. Between 1747 and 1774 new fortifications were built, including the Fortress of Real Felipe, which became the most important structure in the port and remains in use as the Peruvian Army Museum. The Spanish navy, based at Callao by the late eighteenth century, provided maritime defense to Central and South America. Its facilities were subsequently used by the Peruvian navy, and the Peruvian Naval Museum is housed at the former headquarters of the Spanish navy.

During the wars leading up to Peruvian independence, Admiral Thomas Lord Cochrane, then in command of a Chilean squadron, captured the Spanish navy frigate *Esmeralda* (1820) in a daring night raid on the port. Callao changed hands between patriots and loyalists several times, until January 1826, when it was incorporated into the newly formed Peruvian republic. In the following decades the port competed with Valparaíso for control of the sea routes along the west coast of South America. This struggle eventually led to war between Peru and Chile, in 1836–1839, and again in 1879–1883.

Toward the middle of the nineteenth century, largely because of guano exports to Europe and the United States, Callao recovered its lead in exports and trade in the region. As a result of this economic growth, the first floating dock on the west coast of South America was built in 1866 by the Pacific Steam Navigation Company.

On May 2, 1866, the port came under attack from a Spanish squadron under the command of brigadier Casto Méndez Núñez. The Chilean fleet also blockaded the port for several months in 1880, with a number of minor skirmishes taking place in the bay.

The piers dating to colonial times were redeveloped and enlarged during the nineteenth century. In the 1920s and 1950s substantial expansions included the addition of shipbuilding and repair facilities. The latter were dedicated mainly to supporting and maintaining one of the world's most important and successful fishing fleets, but they were diversified in 1958 when the navy shipyard began to construct oceangoing vessels.

Beginning in the 1940s, urban expansion was both significant and uncontrolled, and Callao merged with Lima. The city has nonetheless maintained its cultural identity through its music, food, local press, and sports. The Fortress of Real Felipe, the Naval Museum, and a number of nineteenth-century houses, as well as the former pier and BAP *Abtao*, a submarine museum, form the core of its tourist attractions.

[*See also* Pacific Ocean, *subentry on* Eastern Pacific, *and* Ports.]

### Bibliography

Arrús, H. Darío. *El Callao en la época del coloniaje, antes y después de la catástrofe de 1746*. Callao, Peru: Imprenta de El Callao, 1905.

Dextre, Nello Marcos Sánchez. *Historia del Callao*. 2 vols. Callao, Peru: Centro de Investigaciones Históricas del Callao, 1989.

Melo, Rosendo. *El Callao, monografía histórico-geográfica*. 3 vols. Lima, Peru, 1899–1901.

JORGE ORTIZ SOTELO

## Camouflage. *See* Dazzle Painting.

## Canadian Literature
As with much of Canadian literature, its works about the sea can be divided geographically and historically, as well as by literary form. The three major geographic categories are the Maritimes/ Atlantic, the Arctic/Northwest Territories, and the Pacific. To begin with nonfiction and histories, there are stories of explorers, which some see as legends. These go back to the sixth-century visit supposedly made by Saint Brendan and, later, Leifr Eiríksson and his Vikings.

### Early Literature

The first important writing about the region that became Canada came from two French explorers. These explorers claimed the colony of New France, most of which is now the province of Quebec. Jacques Cartier, who explored the Saint Lawrence River in the 1530s, is often credited with writing the first important piece of Canadian literature. His journal, *Premiere voyage de Jacques Cartier au Canada*, though, had an odd publishing history, supposedly being a translation from French into Italian, then English, then back to French. Giovanni Ramusio's Italian translation appeared in 1556 and John Florio's translation of Ramusio's version into English was printed in 1580. Because of the multiple layers of authorship, many scholars doubt this book's authenticity. There is great confidence, though, in the *Voyages* (1603) volumes from Samuel de Champlain, which detail his explorations. An edited version of his hundreds of pages of reports, *Oeuvres de Champlain*, was published in 1870.

Many of the most compelling stories came from members of the religious orders and their fellow explorers of the river and lake systems. *The Jesuit Relations and Allied Documents: Travels and Explorations of the Jesuit Missionaries in New France* were written by members of the order and collected annually by their Superior in New France, then shipped back to the Provincial in Paris from 1611 to 1791. The *Relations* exist today both in microfiche and in a 73-volume collection (1959). These annual reports are filled with stories ranging from first sightings of streams to accountings of local crops to interactions with the indigenous peoples. In addition, the collection contains letters and diaries of the members. Father Louis Hennepin of the Recollet order, as described in his *Nouvelle decouverte d'un tres grand pays situé dans l'Amerique* (1697; *A New Discovery of a Vast Country in America, 1698*), traveled with Robert Cavelier, Sieur de La Salle, to reach the mouth of the Mississippi River in 1682. Collectively, the reports of the missionaries and the *voyageurs*, with their fur trapping exploits, fueled much of the fever to explore.

The British explorers also left records of their adventures. John Cabot, part of the very first wave of European explorers of the New World, came to Newfoundland in 1497. He was followed by a more organized program of exploration and establishment of commercial outposts by people like Martin Frobisher, who started searching for the legendary Northwest Passage in 1576, and Henry Hudson in 1610. Thanks to their work, the Hudson Bay Company, which controlled massive amounts of territory and enterprise, was established in 1670. Captain James Cook, who later gained fame for his quest into the Pacific, carefully mapped the Gulf of Saint Lawrence and coastline in 1759.

Among the major influences are the exploits of Arctic explorers from the 1770s to the 1820s, like Samuel Hearne, Sir Alexander Mackenzie, and Captain John Franklin. Hearne's book, *Journey from Prince of Wales Fort in Hudson Bay to the Northern Ocean*, came out in 1795. Six years later was MacKenzie's *On the River St. Lawrence: Through the Continent of North America* (1801). Franklin's *Narrative of a Journey to the Polar Sea* (1823) is not, though, about his most famous Arctic voyage, when he and his crew were lost in 1847. In the 1950s through 1970s, Farley Mowat reedited many of the explorers' journals, including Hearne's, into new collections. He followed them with a study of the easternmost province, *New Founde Land* (1989).

Literature of the last major region begins with Captain Cook's journal of his short visit in 1788 to what became the British Columbia coast. George Vancouver, who was on that voyage with Cook, returned as a captain and wrote about it in *Voyage of Discovery to the North Pacific Ocean and Round the World in the Years 1790-1795* (1798). There are also stories handed down by the indigenous—or First Nations'—peoples about the coast and Vancouver Island. These include the stories and poems of E. Pauline Johnson (1861-1913), who took the name Tekahionwake in 1886.

## Literature of the Maritimes

The Maritimes are, of course, the oldest of the European settlements, and speak in the most diverse, creative voices. The first storytellers are the people of the First Nations. New France was also known as Acadia and is the initial setting for Henry Wadsworth Longfellow's *Evangeline* (1847). The stories of the struggle of the earlier inhabitants to survive the English, including colonists from New England, have been made into recent historical fiction, like novelist and historian Victor J. H. Suthren's *The Black Cockade: Paul Gallant's Louisbourg Command* (1977) about the attacks on the French settlement in Nova Scotia during the 1740s. Many contemporary Francophone writers of Acadian literature, like poet Ronald Despres (*Paysages en contrebande*, 1979) and fiction writer Louis Hache (*Toubes jersiaises*, 1980), have continued to explore the relation of Acadians to the sea. A different style, focusing on the everyday people of the islands, belongs to Norman Duncan and his stories of life around Newfoundland and Labrador, like *The Way of the Sea* (1903). He also wrote a series of stories, led by *Doctor Luke of the Labrador* (1904), based on the life of missionary doctor Sir Wilfred Grenfell (1865-1940), who also wrote his own books on the region.

Suthren's famous swashbuckling hero, Edward Mainwaring, has fought many of the naval battles of the eighteenth century in numerous books like *Captain Monsoon* (1993). With the military victory by the British over the French in 1760, the region was settled by a heavy influx of immigrants from England and Scotland. A colorful name for one of their descendants, especially from Nova Scotia, is a "bluenose," and the schooner *Bluenose* (1921) was one of Canada's most legendary sailing ships (a full-size replica of the ship is now anchored in Halifax harbor). The cities of Halifax and Saint John quickly became centers for colonial publishing and writers. Then, the American Revolution brought many Tory loyalists to Canada. This war and the sea ties from Halifax to Liverpool have been celebrated for almost two centuries in popular fiction such as Thomas Raddall's *His Majesty's Yankees* (1942) and *Pride's Fancy* (1946), which also takes place in the West Indies.

## Later Works: Poetry and Drama

Much of the great Canadian literature of the sea comes from poet E. J. Pratt. In 1923 he published his first collection, *Newfoundland Verse*, which established his prowess in narrative verse. He followed with other books, including *The Roosevelt and the Antinoe* (1930) about the heroic rescue of a ship's crew in the mid-Atlantic. In 1935 Pratt created his epic poem *The Titanic*, very often called a classic of Canadian literature, on the tragic pride that people had in believing they could conquer the sea.

Sir Charles Roberts (1860-1943) also took up the power of the sea late in his career with *The Iceberg and Other Poems* (1934). Following Pratt's example of the epic, historically based narrative poem is Frederick Watt's sixty-page documentary poem *Who Dare to Live* (1943), on the North Atlantic convoys of World War II. William Howard Pugsley's novel *Saints, Devils, and Ordinary Seamen* (1945) is another contemporaneous tale of the convoys. Many of them, like many luxury liners before the war, used Halifax as a main port. Nova Scotia native Hugh MacLennan wove many great stories about the Maritimes. His novel *Barometer Rising* (1941) is built around the tragic explosion of a munitions ship in the massive Halifax harbor during World War I.

Continuing the tradition of poetry that uses the sea as both subject and image are the Fiddlehead poets. They take their name from an influential literary magazine, the decoration on a ship's bow, and a local plant. Centered in New Brunswick, especially at the university in Fredericton, poets like Fred Gogswell (1917– ), Alden Nowlan (1933– ), and Robert Gibbs (1930– ) explore life in an environment dominated by the sea, as in Gibbs's poems "The *Manes P.* Aground off Fort Dufferin" (1971) and "Travels: Eastbound/Westbound" (1985).

The first play produced in North America is said to have been performed on a flotilla of French ships at anchor. "Le Theatre de Neptune en la Novelle-France," a 1606 spectacular of mythical gods and rhymed couplets, was written by Marc Lescarbot. Drama has grown steadily in Canada, as exemplified by Michael Cook and his Newfoundland plays during the late twentieth century. Bringing much of the province's sound and texture to the stage, his works include *Quiller* (1975), about a provincial outpost, and *On the Rim of the Curve* (1977), showing the demise of the Beothuk, Newfoundland's aboriginal people. *The Gayden Chronicles*, which tells the story of a Royal Navy rebel hanged in 1812, was produced in 1979. A different theme, of Newfoundland's conflict over accepting confederation into the rest of Canada from the late nineteenth into the middle of the twentieth century, is in Tom Cahill's *As Loved Our Fathers* (1974).

## Novels

The Saint Lawrence River, and its modern incarnation as the Saint Lawrence Seaway, which connects the Great Lakes to the Atlantic, has always been important in politics, society, and economics. A popular novel of its time, *Altham: A Tale of the Sea* (1848), was published in London but follows the main character, paralleling the life of author John Swete Cummins, from Great Britain to the ocean to the Gulf of Saint Lawrence. These waterways are the focus in Charles Sangster's collection *The St. Lawrence and the Saguenay and Other Poems* (1856), especially the title piece. Sangster is sometimes called the poet laureate of colonial Canada. The Gulf of Saint Lawrence is the setting for the popular novel of a later time, *The Sacrifice of the Shannon* (1903) by Albert Hickman, about an ice breaker and her crew. The period of the War of 1812, much of which was fought along the Saint Lawrence and the Great Lakes, is discussed by award-winning political and social commentator Pierre Berton in works like *The Invasion of Canada* (1980) and *Flames across the Border* (1981).

The Arctic and the upper reaches of the Northwest Territories were Canada's own great frontier, one they did not share with the United States. Recently, much of the Arctic area was renamed the Nunavut Province. It is home to the Inuit; their language and stories are now part of official school curricula. Many Inuit poems were collected and recorded by ethnologists in the first quarter of the twentieth century. The region's tradition for narrative adventure, established by the explorers a century before, became the basis for some of what we now call science fiction. In Robert Watson's *High Hazard: A Romance of the Far Arctic* (1929), the hero finds a lost, prehistoric northern world. These fairy-tale-like works are part of Canada's own sea mythology. An extreme is E. J. Pratt's humorous fantasy *The Witch's Brew* (1925), about a drunken fish and other creatures of the deep, which also served as a satire on Prohibition. Others come from children's literature, such as George H. Griffin's *At the Court of King Neptune: A Romance of Canada's Fisheries* (1932) and *Legends*

*of the Evergreen Coast* (1934). There was even a comic book series staring Nelvana, "Queen of the Crystal World" during World War II. *The Boatman* (1957; revised 1968) by Jay Macpherson is a collection of poetic re-creations of classic and religious parables that are often compared to the work of William Blake.

Because of the many epic, real-life adventures along the Pacific Coast, many writers use it as a metaphoric location representing ideas such as perseverance or salvation. George Bowering focuses on a historical hero in the book-length poem *George Vancouver* (1970); his novel *Burning Water* (1980) is a fictionalized story of Vancouver's search for the Northwest Passage. Jack Hodgins's *Spit Delaney's Island* (1977), though, is a book of parables, many ending in redemption, set on Vancouver Island. This setting continues in his novels about the Barclay family, particularly *The Resurrection of Joseph Bourne* (1980), in which a tidal wave brings both a lost ship and a magical woman to the island. More recent works of fiction set along the Pacific shore include Malcolm Lowry's allegoric *October Ferry to Gabriola* (1970), Audrey Thomas's *Intertidal Life: A Novel* (1984), and William Gaston's *Deep Cove Stories* (1989).

Moving in different thematic directions is Sharon Pollock's play *The Komagata Maru Incident* (1978), based on a 1914 clash when Sikh immigrants were not allowed to disembark in Vancouver. Also, there are the highly imaginative, gothic poems in Susan Musgrave's *Songs of the Sea-witch* (1970) and *The Impstone* (1976).

In addition to maritime literature by Canadians, there are relevant writings by others about Canadian waters, such as Rockwell Kent's *N by E* (1930), about a romantic voyage to Labrador that ends disastrously, and Jonathan Raban's brilliant *Passage to Juneau* (1999), which links an autobiographical voyage through the inside passage in British Columbia with Vancouver's explorations.

[*See also* American Literature; Americas; Atlantic Ocean, *subentry on* Exploration Voyages, 1330–1480s; English Literature; French Literature; Literature; Northwest Passage; Pacific Ocean, *subentries on* Exploration Voyages; *and* Vikings, *subentry on* Norse Voyages of Exploration.]

## Bibliography

Gair, Reavley, ed. *A Literary and Linguistic History of New Brunswick.* Fredericton, New Brunswick: Fiddlehead Poetry Books and Goose Lane Publishing, 1985.

Maitland, Alan, ed. *Favourite Sea Stories from Seaside Al.* Toronto: Viking, 1996.

New, Wiliam H. *A History of Canadian Literature.* Basingstoke, U.K.: Macmillan Education, 1989.

Suthren, Victor, ed. *Canadian Stories of the Sea.* Toronto: Oxford University Press, 1993.

Toye, William, ed. *The Oxford Companion to Canadian Literature.* Toronto: Oxford University Press, 1983.

MICHAEL W. YOUNG

# Canals. *See* Rivers, Canals, and Inland Waterways.

# Canton. *See* Guangzhou.

# Cape Town

Cape Town was established by the Dutch East India Company in 1652 as a refreshment station for ships trading between Europe and Asia. Its site at Table Bay was chosen because of available fresh water and meat obtained by barter with local Khoikhoi pastoralists. During the period of Dutch rule (to 1795), a sizable settler farming colony developed in Cape Town's hinterland that was crucially dependent on imports through its harbor, including rice and slaves from Madagascar, India, and Southeast Asia as well as militia and company employees from northern Europe. As a result, Cape Town had a small (approximately sixteen thousand) but highly transient and ethnically diversified population by 1800.

In 1806 Cape Town became the administrative headquarters of the British Cape Colony. Its trading activities grew as British imperial interests in the South Atlantic and Indian Oceans expanded in the mid-nineteenth century, although there was some rivalry with Port Elizabeth as the colony expanded eastward. However, the discovery of diamonds at Kimberley (1867), connected by rail to Cape Town, boosted the city's economy. A new harbor was built, and the city was transformed by trading houses, banks, and a new imperial parliament. During the South African (or Anglo-Boer) War (1899–1902) Cape Town was the major port for troop landings, as well as the recipient of refugees from the war-torn interior.

In the first half of the twentieth century, Cape Town lost its fiscal hegemony to Johannesburg, on the goldfields of the Witwatersrand, while sharing the status of political capital of the Union of South Africa (formed in 1910) with Pretoria. Clothing and textile manufacture provided its largest economic sector, but suffered from slumps and uncertain markets during the Depression years of the 1930s. Urban poverty was a growing issue during this time, although the increase in shipping because of troop movements during World War II (1939–1945) partially disguised the scale of the problem. In the aftermath of the war, a new deep harbor basin was constructed and land was reclaimed from the shoreline in the expectation of future growth.

This was not to be. Not only did air transport, centered on Johannesburg, come to rival sea routes, but also the implementation of apartheid from the 1950s destroyed the city's infrastructures. Capetonians classified as "non-white" were forcibly removed from the city center into poorly built townships on its periphery. The mixed-race area of District Six, alongside the docks, was demolished in the 1960s. Meanwhile many black South Africans who were prevented from owning property established huge squatter settlements on the outskirts of Cape Town, which lacked any basic facilities. It was here that resistance to apartheid in the 1980s was most marked.

The advent of democracy in South Africa (1994) has not ended these huge social and economic disparities among Cape Town's population of some 3 million, the majority of whom still live in "informal settlements" where unemployment rates reach 60 percent. By contrast, central Cape Town has become a major international tourism venue. Its waterfront, which had fallen into decline in the 1970s and 1980s, has been revamped as a major heritage and retail site that mirrors key dockside redevelopments elsewhere in the world and has restored the city's links with its maritime past. Cape Town's split personality is also evident in its contrasting cultural icons—the physical splendor and conspicuous wealth of the waterfront backed by Table Mountain, the stories, poems, and "Coon Carnival" celebrations of District Six, and a rich tradition of township jazz.

[*See also* East India Companies, *subentry on* Dutch East India Company.]

## Bibliography

Bickford-Smith, Vivian, Elizabeth van Heyningen, and Nigel Worden. *Cape Town in the Twentieth Century: An Illustrated Social History.* Cape Town, South Africa: David Philip, 1999.

Western, John. *Outcast Cape Town.* Berkeley: University of California Press, 1996.

Worden, Nigel. "Contested Heritage at the Cape Town Waterfront." *International Journal of Heritage Studies* 2 (1996): 59–75.

Worden, Nigel, Elizabeth van Heyningen, and Vivian Bickford-Smith. *Cape Town: The Making of a City.* Hilversum, Netherlands: Verloren; Cape Town, South Africa: David Philip, 1998.

NIGEL WORDEN

**Capstans.** *See* Ship's Equipment.

**Caravel.** *See* Trading Vessels, *subentry on* Medieval Vessels.

**Carbonates.** *See* Offshore Industry.

**Cargo.** *See* Breakbulk Cargoes; Bulk Cargoes; Coal Supply; Ship Materials.

# Caribbean Sea

This entry contains two subentries:

An Overview
Regional Navies

## An Overview

The Caribbean Sea is a warm oceanic basin in the western Atlantic, covering approximately 2.5 million square kilometers (1 million square miles). It is bordered to the north by Cuba, the island of Hispaniola (Haiti and the Dominican Republic), and Puerto Rico; to the east by the islands of the Lesser Antilles, from the Virgin Islands to Trinidad; to the south by the coast of South America; and to the west by Central America. The sea extends from approximately 60 degrees to approximately 90 degrees west longitude, and from 20 degrees to approximately 10 degrees north latitude.

The deepest point in the Caribbean Sea is the Cayman Trench, between Cuba and Jamaica, nearly 8,000 meters (25,000 feet) deep. The shallowest places are shoals located between Jamaica and the Mosquito Coast of Nicaragua and Honduras, within 3.5 meters (11 feet) of the surface. The highest point in the islands of the Caribbean is Pico Duarte in the western Dominican Republic, which is 3,087 meters (10,128 feet) above sea level. Abrupt volcanic peaks characterize the topography of most of the islands of the Caribbean, from the Sierra Maestra in Cuba to the active Soufriere volcano in Guadeloupe.

The Gulf Stream originates in the Caribbean, sending warm water north and east across the Atlantic. The water of the Caribbean Sea is warm, around 24 degrees Celsius (75 degrees Fahrenheit), and is less saline than the open ocean. The water circulates counterclockwise, entering off the coast of Venezuela and exiting through the Yucatán Channel. The passages located between the major islands of the Caribbean archipelago include the Windward Passage between Cuba and Haiti, the Mona Passage between the Dominican Republic and Puerto Rico, and the Anegada Passage separating the Virgin Islands chain from Saint Martin/Maarten. From late summer until late autumn, the region is subject to hurricanes, which frequently destroy major port cities, plantations, and shipping.

### Caribbean Islands and Coasts

The islands of the Caribbean Sea are called the Greater and Lesser Antilles. The largest islands are the four Greater Antilles: Cuba, Jamaica, Hispaniola (Haiti and the Dominican Republic), and Puerto Rico. The Lesser Antilles are divided into the Leeward Islands and the Windward Islands, so named because the easterly trade winds between 10 and 20 degrees north latitude first strike the southernmost and easternmost islands in the chain, the Windward Islands, then the northernmost and westernmost islands, the Leeward Islands.

The Lesser Antilles, from north to south, are Vieques and Culebra off Puerto Rico, the Virgin Islands, Anguilla, Saint Martin/Maarten, Saint Barthélemy (Saint Bart), Saba, Saint Eustasius (Statia), Saint Christopher (Saint Kitts), Nevis, Barbuda, Antigua, Montserrat, Guadeloupe, Marie-Galante and the Saints Islands, Dominica, Martinique, Saint Lucia, Saint Vincent, Grenada and the Grenadines, and a little farther out in the Atlantic to the east, Barbados. Trinidad and Tobago are also considered Caribbean islands, but like the "ABC" islands of Aruba, Bonaire, and Curaçao farther west along the coast of Venezuela, they are geographically an extension of the South American landmass. There are also three islands in the Cayman group near Cuba, as well as the Bay Islands off Honduras, the largest of which is Roatán. The islands of the Caribbean are also known as the West Indies.

### Local Maritime History

New discoveries in nautical archaeology on the west coasts of North and South America have challenged the Clovis theory of terrestrial migration of Asians across the Bering land bridge and south along the gaps in the glacial formations of the late Ice Age. These finds indicate that the earliest human inhabitants of the hemisphere moved by water,

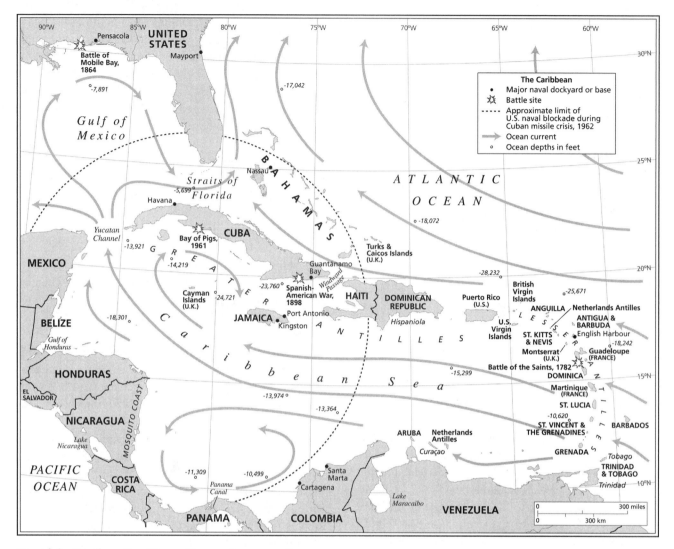

**Map of the Carribean Sea.** MAP BY MAPPING SPECIALISTS LIMITED

rapidly pushing along the coastlines of North and South America to warmer climes. Archaeological evidence from the Caribbean adds to the conclusion that early Americans were ambitious mariners, populating the archipelago from south to north after voyaging in dugout canoes. There are strong links between the extinct culture of the island people living in the Caribbean and the surviving culture of the Yanomamo people of the Orinoco River basin in southern Venezuela, which points to Neolithic maritime ties from the mainland to the Caribbean.

The term "Caribbean" was derived from the name given by the Taino people of Hispaniola to their enemies on other islands to the east, the "Caribs." The Taino described Carib raids to the first Europeans with whom they came into contact in 1492, the Spanish under Christopher Columbus,

claiming that the Carib ate their prisoners. "Carib" became the root of the Spanish word *caníbal* and the English word "cannibal." Upon arrival on his second voyage to the Caribbean, Columbus made landfall at the islands that he named for Saint Ursula and the Eleven Thousand Virgins. Declaring the people living in the Virgin Islands to be "Carib" man-eaters, the Spanish attacked them savagely, setting the precedent for Spanish conquest across the area. Columbus returned to Spain with a cargo of five hundred Indian slaves at the end of this, the second of his four voyages to the Caribbean. On his lesser-known third and fourth voyages, Columbus was shipwrecked on the island of Jamaica, landed on the island that he named Trinidad, explored the Caribbean coast of Central America, Colombia, and Venezuela, and sailed as far as the Orinoco River delta.

There is debate over which ethnic categories are most appropriate for the indigenous population of the Caribbean. The Spanish accepted the distinction between the peaceful and welcoming Arawak people of the northern islands, including the Taino of Cuba and Hispaniola, and the warlike, cannibalizing Carib of the Lesser Antilles. Anthropologists in the twentieth century questioned this taxonomy of the island people, suggesting that the Spanish imposed it because of how they were received by the inhabitants of the various islands that they came to claim, not because of any systematic observation of the people's culture. Across the littoral of the Caribbean Sea, native people were fishing people, gathering shellfish in the intertidal zones, netting fish in the shallows, and snaring and spearing other prey in deeper water from canoes. *Canu* (canoe) is one of the few Taino words, along with *huracán* (hurricane), to enter European languages.

Whether they were Arawak or Carib, the indigenous people of the Caribbean were doomed to virtual extinction by the onslaught of some ninety-three diseases introduced by the Spanish and other European arrivals, the worst of them smallpox, combined with brutal treatment in mines and on sugar plantations. A 1496 census taken by the Spanish on the island of Hispaniola that counted only working-age adults in the possession of the conquistadores, not those who had escaped into the mountains or were too young or too old to be effective laborers, found 1.1 million people. Yet fifty years later, there were only a few thousand native people left in the islands of the Caribbean.

The springboard for Spanish conquest in the Caribbean was the city of Santo Domingo, on the south coast of Hispaniola, founded in 1496 by Columbus's brother Bartholomew. Columbus's son Diego ruled as governor from his palace in Santo Domingo, the Alcázar, which still stands on a bluff above the mouth of the Ozama River. From Santo Domingo, many Spanish expeditions embarked on voyages of conquest across the region, including Alonso de Ojeda to Venezuela (1499), Juan Ponce de León to Puerto Rico (1508), Juan de Esquival to Jamaica (1509), Diego Velázquez to Cuba (1511), and Vasco Núñez de Balboa to Panama (1513). With the conquest of the Aztec and Inca empires on the mainland between 1519 and 1532, Santo Domingo became a backwater of the expanding Spanish New World empire. Many of the domestic species introduced by the Europeans became feral in the mountainous hinterland of the island of Hispaniola, providing a ready supply of food to anyone who could trap or shoot the pigs and cows that roamed free, especially in the western end of the island.

A polyglot population, comprising European and African elements, escapees from the rigors of slavery, colonial restrictions, or naval discipline, subsisted on the wild livestock of Hispaniola. They adopted the technique of preserving meat employed by the Taino, called *barbacoa*, or barbecue, which involved smoking it on a *boucan*. The multinational crowd of *boucaniers*, or buccaneers, traded their barbecue to passing ships off the west coast of Hispaniola, now Haiti, and the nearby island of Tortuga. Soon they began seizing the ships themselves, and became united in their opposition to Spain, which sought to eradicate them from their bases. During the three Anglo-Dutch naval wars of 1652–1674, the maritime powers of Great Britain and the Netherlands competed for control of Tortuga and other strategic points long dominated by buccaneers, pirates, and freebooters (fighters of no nation).

The smaller islands and the wild western portion of Hispaniola, never effectively colonized by the Spanish, offered opportunities for Spain's northern European competitors, England, the Netherlands, and France. The English arrived at Saint Kitts in 1623 and at Barbados in 1627. The Dutch claimed Curaçao, Saint Eustatius, Saba, and Saint Martin/Maarten in the 1630s. The French took Martinique and Guadeloupe in 1635. Other islands were disputed violently for decades, such as Saint Kitts, which changed hands between the British and French repeatedly beginning in 1625, and Saint Martin/Maarten, which has been divided between the French and Dutch since 1648. In the Greater Antilles, Spain held onto Cuba, Puerto Rico, and eastern Hispaniola (Santo Domingo), but it lost control of Jamaica to Cromwell's England in 1655 and relinquished western Hispaniola to France with the Treaty of Ryswick in 1697, in return for the eradication of piracy there. Western Hispaniola became the French colony of Sainte-Domingue. Denmark seized the islands of Saint Thomas and Saint John in the Virgin Islands in 1670, then sold them to the United States in 1917. Sweden purchased Saint Barthélemy from France in 1784 and returned it in 1878.

Under the Spanish colonial mercantile system, the resources derived from Spain's vast New World empire were channeled through the Caribbean Sea annually. The yearly *flota* of galleons brought together precious metals from the mainland, pearls from coastal Colombia, and even silks and spices from the Philippines, transshipped from the Pacific to the Gulf of Mexico via Acapulco and Veracruz. The treasure was gathered at Veracruz, Cartagena on the Caribbean coast of Colombia, and Darién on the Isthmus of Panama, then sent on to Havana on the north coast of Cuba, which has a deep and well-protected harbor near the Gulf Stream. The flotillas that formed every year in Havana ran the gauntlet through the Strait of Florida, past the Bahamas and Saint Augustine on the coast of Florida (founded in 1565), and across the Atlantic to Spain.

Spanish treasure fleets and colonial port cities were the targets of Spain's imperial rivals. Francis Drake, the English admiral, sacked Santo Domingo, Darién, and Cartagena in 1585, and Piet Hein of the Netherlands seized the entire Spanish silver fleet in 1629. The Spanish fought back with attacks on the new northern European plantation colonies and with raids on commerce against all those who infringed on their imperial claims. Still, the Spanish allowed loopholes in their mercantile policy of monopolizing the resources and markets of the New World. They subcontracted their slave trade to other countries, a lucrative privilege called the *asiento*. They also permitted annual trade ships to the British and Dutch that became floating warehouses in port cities across the Caribbean. One of the incidents that resulted from the Spanish coast guard's vigilance against interlopers was the 1739 apprehension of Robert Jenkins, whose ear was severed by the Spanish captain who overhauled him. The War of Jenkins' Ear (1739–1742) resulted from that trade dispute, one of innumerable clashes in the Caribbean arena of empire.

Smuggling to restricted markets in the Spanish Caribbean was an avid pursuit of many different parties for two hundred years. The British, Dutch, and French competed for trade from such metropolitan bases as London, Amsterdam, and La Rochelle, and from such colonial bases as Jamaica, Statia, and Sainte-Domingue. The Dutch West India Company (WIC), founded in 1621, brought the powerful dynamics of joint-stock shareholding and limited free trade to the Caribbean. These factors eroded Spanish control, as did the naval efforts of WIC fleets. The colonists themselves also engaged in smuggling into each other's markets, with the traders of British North America especially active in circumventing Parliament's Navigation Acts that restricted their trade, smuggling goods into and out of Dutch, French, and Spanish islands. Another competing group that the Spanish were unable to control was the Guajira people of Colombia, who were the middlemen for illicit trade from the Caribbean coast all the way to Quito, Ecuador.

Sugarcane was imported from the Canary Islands by Columbus on his second voyage, then cultivated by the Spanish in the Caribbean and by the Portuguese in Brazil. The Dutch brought sugar technology, slaves, capital, and experience to the Caribbean from their occupation of Brazil in the 1630s. Many of the smaller islands were soon planted entirely in sugarcane. Sugar cultivation, with its accompanying slave trade, became the dominant factor in the subsequent development of the Caribbean region. The "sugar frontier" moved across the Caribbean from one island to another, bringing the same social and economic transformations to each place where it became a monoculture. Beginning with Barbados in the 1630s, and continuing through to Cuba and the Dominican Republic in the 1920s, sugar production exerted the same forces on Caribbean culture wherever it came, resulting in a pyramidal racial structure under a small white elite and dependence on outside sources for food supplies and manufactured goods. Under the Navigation Acts, the fishing societies of the British North American colonies, especially Massachusetts, became the primary suppliers of such necessities to the islands, feeding them on salted cod and providing them with wood products such as barrel staves to transport refined sugar from the mills.

With the United States' independence in 1783, the supply of food to the British West Indies was interrupted for a decade, resulting in mass starvation among slaves in Jamaica. Trade resumed under the provisions of Jay's Treaty in 1794, which allowed U.S. vessels of ninety tons or less into the British West Indies. That was the approximate tonnage of the most common Caribbean trading vessels—brigs and schooners about one hundred feet long—so a brisk exchange recommenced between New England and the British sugar islands. The Caribbean sugar trade endured with vigor throughout the nineteenth century and into the twentieth century, then declined in the face of fructose substitutes such as corn syrup. The economies of Cuba and the Dominican Republic continue to rely heavily on sugar production, despite the reduced international market for sugar.

The French Revolution of 1789 ignited a revolution in the French colony of Sainte-Domingue, where nearly half a million slaves worked plantations held by a small minority of white and mixed-race elites. The slaves defeated French armies sent by Napoleon to quell the revolt, invaded the Spanish half of the island, and gained abolition and independence in 1804. The new nation was named Haiti, the Taino word for the area. The Haitian revolution ended the sugar trade from what had been the largest producer in the Caribbean, because the United States and Europe isolated the "Black Republic" and because civil war in Haiti disrupted cane cultivation. The "sugar frontier" shifted to Cuba as a result.

The banana trade also had an important role in Caribbean maritime history. Schooners first brought bananas from Jamaica and Nicaragua to the U.S. markets of Boston and New Orleans in the late nineteenth century. Steam navigation came to the banana trade in the form of the "Great White Fleet" of the United Fruit Company, which pioneered refrigerated storage for the fruit on the northbound trip from such points of production as Cuba, Guatemala, and Colombia. The United Fruit Line also innovated the practice of cruising the scenic Caribbean for paying passengers, who enjoyed fine dining and tourist excursions along the way to and from the banana ports. The cruise industry continues to thrive.

Tourism from the sea attracted visitors from the United States and Europe to the Caribbean, which in turn stimulated steamship lines to offer service from ports such as New York and New Orleans. The Ward Line and the Mallory Line connected New York and Key West to Havana, which became the main tourist destination in the Caribbean. Tourism was also a factor in the political movements that swept the islands after World War II, particularly in Jamaica, where taxi drivers and hotel workers led the efforts to gain independence in 1962, and in Cuba, where resentment of the power of such institutions as yacht clubs fueled the revolution won by Fidel Castro in 1959. That revolution led to a rupture in the old maritime link connecting Cuba and the United States. Since the last departure of the ferryboat *City of Key West* in 1962, there have been few regular seaborne connections between the close neighbors. Three boat lifts of immigrants from Cuba in 1965, 1980, and 1994 have been the largest surges in a constant flow of people across the Strait of Florida by boat.

## Key Ports

Havana, Cuba, is the largest port city in the Caribbean, with a large, well-protected deepwater harbor. The British occupation of the city in 1762 initiated a period of rapid commercial development that was further stimulated by the Bourbon reforms of the 1790s, which opened Spanish colonial ports to increased trade. The Cuban economy shifted from coffee to sugar during the first half of the nineteenth century, spurred by hurricanes in 1844 and 1845 that uprooted coffee plantations, which were replaced by rapid-growing sugarcane. Santiago de Cuba is the largest port on the south coast of Cuba.

Jamaica's most important port was the city of Port Royal, but it was struck by an earthquake in 1692, sinking it into the Caribbean Sea. Kingston replaced it as the principal port and capital of Jamaica.

Cap Haitien on the north coast of Hispaniola was called Cap Français during the period of French colonization, and it was known as the Paris of the Antilles. It was a popular tourist destination because of the Sans Souci palace and the citadel of King Henri Christophe, a soaring fortress on a nearby mountaintop. The AIDS crisis of the late 1970s destroyed the Haitian tourism industry, however, and took Cap Haitien off the route of cruise liners. The port is now heavily silted and sees little traffic. Port-au-Prince, the capital of Haiti, has also fallen on hard times, like the rest of the country. Its remote location within the twin peninsulas of western Haiti impeded the growth of commercial traffic to the port.

The oldest European city in the Americas is Santo Domingo, founded in 1496, now the capital of the Dominican Republic. The shallow Ozama River and the rocky coral coast of the city have hindered development of the port. Ten miles west of the city is the port of Haina, site of the second-largest sugar refinery in the world.

San Juan, Puerto Rico, is a major port with a well-developed infrastructure for container ships and cruise liners, and is one of the largest cities in the Caribbean. Ponce is the major port on the south coast, with a fertile hinterland producing sugar and rum for export.

Bridgetown is the capital and leading entrepôt of Barbados. Like all the major ports in the Lesser Antilles, Bridgetown is located on the lee, or western shore of the island. Its dry-dock facilities and large array of nautical services made it a center for refitting vessels in the sugar trade.

Port-of-Spain in Trinidad grew rapidly during World War II as oil refining on the island gained importance. The steel drums used in the petroleum industry gave rise to the calypso music of the island.

The port of Maracaíbo, Venezuela, is the source of much of the oil refined in Trinidad and in the Dutch "ABC" islands. Lake Maracaíbo is the largest embayment in the Caribbean Sea, a large, shallow expanse dotted with drilling platforms to tap the reserves of petroleum below. At the time of first European contact in 1499, the appearance of native villages built on stilts above the water gave rise to the name of the country, which means "little Venice."

Colón is the Caribbean terminus of the Panama Canal. It was a boomtown during the two periods of canal construction, French and American, which culminated in the permanent opening of the canal in 1916.

## Coastal Fortifications

The Torre del Homenaje guarding the mouth of the Ozama River in Santo Domingo, Dominican Republic, is the oldest coastal fortification in the Caribbean. Completed in 1516, the fort has withstood hurricanes that have devastated the rest of the city, most recently in 1930 and 1999.

El Morro, or Morro Castle, commands the narrow entrance to Havana Harbor. It is built on the high ground west of the harbor, while the fort called La Punta lies across the channel to the east. The cruise liner *Morro Castle* was first famous for its run from New York to Havana, then for its 1933 burning off the coast of New Jersey.

San Juan, Puerto Rico, also has a masonry citadel called El Morro, begun in 1521, that guards the entrance to the harbor. The fort capitulated to U.S. naval forces in 1898, becoming the headquarters of the military occupation of the island.

Brimstone Hill, Saint Kitts, is the largest fortification in the Caribbean. It is a vast complex of works stretching from the ocean to a steep hilltop, built by the British to resist the French, who captured it in 1782.

The walled city of Cartagena, founded in 1533, is one of the oldest and most extensive coastal fortifications in the region. Built to shelter the annual accumulation of wealth from the Spanish Main, the fortress was sacked by Drake in 1585.

In the mid-nineteenth century, the French emperor Napoleon III ordered the construction of Fort Napoleon on strategic Terre-de-Haut Island in the Les Saintes archipelago near Guadeloupe. The fort has been called the "Gibraltar of the Caribbean," despite never being involved in a war.

Panama Canal defenses were a major issue of the diplomacy preceding the period of construction, since the United States insisted on the right to arm and defend the Canal Zone unilaterally. The British yielded that point in 1902, allowing the construction of naval bases at both terminus ports, among other works. The defenses grew during World War II, when the Republic of Panama agreed to new airbases, antiaircraft installations, fortifications enclosing the reservoirs created by the canal, and a submarine base in Balboa, at the Pacific terminus. The canal defenses provided the base for the U.S. invasion of Panama City in 1989, but a decade later, when modern weapons made such closed-in defenses more of a liability than an advantage, the canal and its fortifications were transferred to the control of the Republic of Panama.

## Naval Operations

John Hawkins and Francis Drake were the model Elizabethan "sea dogs," whose constant naval harassment and raids on Spanish colonial ports made them into heroes in England and villains in Spain. The most significant clash in the long naval contest between Great Britain and France was the Battle of the Saintes between Dominica and Guadeloupe in April 1782, when Admiral George Rodney defeated Admiral François Comte de Grasse.

The United States Navy established the West Indies Squadron, based in Key West, to combat piracy in 1810. An explosion aboard USS *Maine* in Havana Harbor on February 15, 1898, led to the U.S. declaration of war against Spain and intervention in Cuba. U.S. Navy battleships destroyed the Spanish Caribbean fleet at the Battle of Santiago on July 3, 1898. After the war of 1898, U.S. naval operations in the Caribbean proliferated, with warships frequently intervening in local disputes. This so-called gunboat diplomacy included amphibious landings at all the major port cities on the island of Hispaniola in 1915–1916, and it led to U.S. Navy and Marine Corps occupations of Haiti (1915–1934) and the Dominican Republic (1916–1924).

The Battle of the Atlantic during World War II saw the most destructive naval operations in Caribbean history, with more than four hundred ships sunk in the region during the first half of 1942. The losses were especially severe in the waters around Trinidad and Curaçao, where oil refining attracted a steady traffic of tankers, and of U-boats to prey on them.

Since 1945, there have been several unofficial invasion attempts reminiscent of the filibusters of the 1850s, which tried to take over Cuba and Nicaragua, among other places. The most famous is the Bay of Pigs invasion of Cuba in April 1961, which brought CIA-trained exiles from the Fidel Castro regime to the south coast of Cuba. Their ships were hit by aircraft fire, and the army of two thousand was pinned down on the beach without air support, all of them being killed or captured.

More recently, the United States conducted successful naval operations against Grenada (1983), Panama (1989), and Haiti (1992).

## Geostrategic Importance

The strategic importance of the Caribbean to the nation-states of early modern Europe lay in potential routes to the Indies. The Treaty of Tordesillas in 1494 divided the New World between Spain and Portugal, at the order of Pope

Alexander VI. The Spanish side of the boundary became the target of Protestant England under Elizabeth I, who covertly sponsored campaigns against the Spanish colonies. "No peace beyond the line" of Tordesillas was the motto of those, like Hawkins and Drake, who attacked the Spanish in the Caribbean.

As a conduit for New World riches and a center of sugar, rum, tobacco, chocolate, and indigo dye production, the Caribbean islands became the most expensive real estate in the world in the late eighteenth century. The wealth of the archipelago greatly enhanced the islands' geostrategic importance, with West Indian islands becoming lucrative war prizes. Realizing that U.S. proximity to the Caribbean was a global advantage, Alexander Hamilton wrote in the *Federalist* (no. 11) that the new country enjoyed a "most commanding position" with regard to this region that was so important to the British and French empires. Hamilton argued for the creation of a U.S. Navy large enough to become the arbiter of geopolitical power in the Caribbean, a force that came into being in 1796.

The Isthmus of Panama became the fulcrum of power in the region with the establishment of a stagecoach line in 1849 and then a railroad linking the oceans in 1855, followed by the Panama Canal in 1914. The geopolitical vision of Admiral Alfred Thayer Mahan, the "sea power thesis" of 1890, dictated the creation of an isthmian canal in order that the U.S. Navy could operate a large single fleet, rather than maintaining separate fleets on the Atlantic and Pacific. The atomic bomb rendered Panama-centered defense planning obsolete, although the large volume of traffic moving through the waterway (nearly 13,500 ships in 2001) continues to make its security an issue of global concern.

## Local Fishing

Fishing has been practiced in the Caribbean since the native people gathered shellfish and netted fish in the shallows and from canoes. Coastal fishermen across the region for generations have used small wooden watercraft, originally under sail and later with auxiliary engines, to handline for such species as tarpon, swordfish, and snapper. The depletion of fish stocks has forced the majority of fishing people to find alternate livelihoods, devastating the economy and culture of towns such as Mariel, Cuba, which had been a fishing community for more than two hundred years.

The practice of whaling is centered on the island of Becquia in the Grenadines, although as late as the 1920s, whaling schooners and brigs from the United States—especially from Provincetown, Massachusetts—made frequent voyages in the Caribbean.

## Regional Vessels

Canoes dug out of large trees were the first boats built in the Caribbean, used by the native people for transportation and fishing. Coasting schooners became the most characteristic regional vessels in the large islands, with Havana becoming a center for shipbuilding. The sugar trade to the North American mainland was handled mainly by brigs built in New England or New York, which were capable of carrying deckloads of livestock in addition to mixed cargoes in their holds. Small, beamy sloops were preferred for interisland commerce among the small islands, vessels of thirty or forty tons, capable of carrying produce and a few animals.

Some unique Caribbean craft are the Becquia whaleboats, which are fashioned like jigsaw puzzles from bits of natural hardwood, and Haitian trading craft built in Cap Haitien, which are pieced together with recycled materials, including patchwork sails stitched from bags and old clothing. A few Cuban fishing boats are also still built in fishing towns like Mariel.

## International Law Issues

The major issues of international law in the Caribbean have been the related issues of smuggling and piracy, leading to many legal disputes and damage claims between nation-states. One of the most famous cases involved Admiral George Rodney, who seized Statia from the Dutch in 1781, in reprisal for Dutch gunrunning to the United States during the American Revolution. Continuing to fly the flag of the Netherlands, Rodney seized incoming trading vessels for weeks, charging them with smuggling, which led to a storm of claims against him at the close of the war. Drug smuggling continues to complicate diplomacy in the Caribbean.

The Monroe Doctrine of 1823 asserted the no-transfer principle for the Caribbean Sea, saying that recolonization of any part of the Americas would be prevented by the United States. Theodore Roosevelt's corollary to the Monroe Doctrine, applied first to the Dominican Republic, gave the United States the role of "international police power" in the region, collecting debts owed by Caribbean nations to European creditors.

Relations with Cuba under Castro have led to many issues of international law as well, including the Bay of Pigs invasion organized by the CIA in April 1961, the trade embargo instituted against Cuba by the United States in January 1962, the naval blockade mounted during the Cuban Missile Crisis in October 1963, and the sabotage of ships and port facilities by the CIA and Cuban exile allies during the 1960s.

[*See also* Atlantic, Battle of the; Cartagena, Colombia; Cruising; Havana; Manila Galleon Trade; Navigation Acts and Laws; Panama Canal; Piracy; *and* Slave Trade.]

## Bibliography

Dunn, Richard S. *Sugar and Slaves: The Rise of the Planter Class in the English West Indies, 1624–1713*. Chapel Hill: University of North Carolina Press, 1972. Details the sugar frontier and plantation society.

Knight, Franklin W. *The Caribbean: The Genesis of a Fragmented Nationalism*. 2d ed. New York: Oxford University Press, 1990. The most sweeping single-volume history of the region available.

Las Casas, Bartolomé de. *A Short Account of the Destruction of the Indies*. Translated by Nigel Griffin. New York: Penguin, 1992. Written in 1542 by a conquistador turned missionary protesting the genocide of indigenous people in the Caribbean.

Langley, Lester D. *Struggle for the American Mediterranean: United States–European Rivalry in the Gulf-Caribbean, 1776–1904*. Athens, Ga.: University of Georgia Press, 1976.

La Pedraja, Rene de. *Latin American Merchant Shipping in the Age of Global Competition*. Westport, Conn.: Greenwood, 1999.

La Pedraja, Rene de. *Oil and Coffee: Latin American Merchant Shipping from the Imperial Era to the 1950s*. Westport, Conn.: Greenwood, 1998. These two authoritative accounts by La Pedraja include data on Cuban, Colombian, and Venezuelan fleets, among others.

Mintz, Sidney. *Caribbean Transformations*. 2d ed. New York: Columbia University Press, 1989. Anthropological focus on Puerto Rico, Haiti, and Jamaica.

Mintz, Sidney. *Sweetness and Power: The Place of Sugar in Modern History*. New York: Viking, 1985.

Rouse, Irving. *The Tainos: Rise and Decline of the People Who Greeted Columbus*. New Haven, Conn.: Yale University Press, 1992.

Sale, Kirkpatrick. *The Conquest of Paradise: Christopher Columbus and the Columbian Legacy*. New York: Plume, 1991. Challenging revision timed for the quincentennial of his first voyage.

Tuchman, Barbara. *The First Salute: A View of the American Revolution*. New York: Ballantine, 1988. This global perspective emphasizes the geopolitical importance of the Caribbean in the late eighteenth century.

Williams, Eric. *From Columbus to Castro: A History of the Caribbean, 1492–1969*. New York: Vintage, 1984. The author was an independence leader and the first president of Trinidad.

Yerxa, Donald. *Admirals and Empire: The United States Navy and the Caribbean, 1898–1945*. Columbia: University of South Carolina Press, 1993. Gives special attention to the Special Service Squadron of the U.S. Navy.

ERIC PAUL ROORDA

# Regional Navies

Since the seventeenth century, the regional growth of naval forces has been strongly influenced both by rivalry and cooperation with the great power navies, including those of Spain, Great Britain, France, Germany, and the United States. The relationship between these empires and the Caribbean colonies, later the independent nation-states, of the region, has often dictated the development of local navies, sometimes promoting them, other times impeding them. No Caribbean navy has ever attained the size and strength necessary to challenge the world-class navies that have loomed so large over the region's history. Even so, on many occasions the force levels have been decisive in the outcome of civil wars and revolutions within Caribbean countries, and of conflicts between them.

## The Role of Naval Power in the Independence of Latin America

The oldest independent republic in the Caribbean region is Haiti, which emerged victorious in 1804 from the bloody, fourteen-year Haitian Revolution against France. Assistance from the U.S. Navy allowed winning general Toussaint-Louverture to consolidate his control by destroying his rival's barges and bombarding his base of operations, the heavily fortified port of Jacmel. Near the crescendo of the war in 1803, the Royal Navy gave crucial help to Jean-Jacques Dessalines, who became the first president of the Republic of Haiti, in capturing the last six French-held ports. At least ten thousand French Navy sailors died in operations during the Haitian Revolution, out of a total death toll of some 350,000 Haitian, French, and British soldiers and civilians. The first Haitian naval vessels were converted merchantmen, mainly from the United States and Great Britain, fighting on both sides of the civil wars that broke out soon after independence. In 1812, the flagship of the small fleet took on a Royal Navy frigate, and had to surrender after losing more than one hundred men. By then, revolutions had also broken out in the mainland colonies of Spain, led by Simon Bolívar. When his first attempts to generate a rebellion failed, Bolívar went into exile in Haiti, out of reach of the Spanish authorities. When he returned to try again in 1816, this time successfully, a squadron of seven Haitian warships accompanied him to his clandestine repatriation.

The Latin American wars for independence began in the Costa Firme, the Caribbean coastal regions of what became Venezuela, birthplace of Bolívar, and Colombia, his adopted home. During the early stages of the conflict, the Spanish Navy and its royalist allies commanded the seas around the Spanish Caribbean colonies from the principal ports of the area: Cartagena, Colombia; Havana, Cuba; Puerto Cabello, Venezuela; and Veracruz, Mexico. Several of the land campaigns of the northern wars centered on capturing these ancient harbors, which were guarded by old and powerful forts, batteries, and city walls. Cartagena was captured by patriot armies, but retaken by a thirty thousand–man army sent on sixty transports from Spain. The patriot squadron was based at Margarita, the largest island on the Venezuelan coast, from 1813 to 1823, except for a period in 1816, when the same Spanish expedition that reoccupied Cartagena destroyed the base. Gaining strength, the patriot navy under Admiral Luis Brión returned to Margarita Island, repulsed a second Spanish attack on it, and began to operate in concert with land forces. Rebel naval forces defeated the Spanish at battles on the Apure River in 1819 and Lake Maracaibo in 1823. With the surrender of Puerto Cabello, the last Spanish bastion, in November 1823, the Caribbean naval war for independence ended.

In addition to playing key roles on both sides of the wars for independence, naval forces subsequently triggered a revival in Caribbean piracy, when certain commerce-raiding privateers could not break the habit of plundering vessels. The labyrinthine archipelagoes of Cuba and Puerto Rico, the last remaining Spanish colonies in the region, were excellent hideouts for royalist raiders, as the Spanish authorities were unable and disinclined to stop their activities, but were quick to object to violations to the sovereignty of their coastal waters. The U.S. Navy established the West India Squadron, based in Key West, Florida, to combat Caribbean piracy.

### The National Navies

The navies of the new Caribbean republics were shaped by several considerations. One common concern was mutual deterrence, especially in the case of Haiti and the Dominican Republic. Another was defense against filibuster expeditions from abroad, invasions by groups of exiles and mercenaries, which threatened Cuba, Central America, and Mexico in particular. National pride also influenced decisions to acquire certain types of naval vessels, such as impressive armed yachts that could double as floating presidential palaces. Internal dangers, such as civil war and revolution, also compelled governments to build up their navies. But in most cases, any attempt to deter aggression by outside powers with large navies proved practically futile. The United States and several European countries exerted naval power in the nineteenth and early twentieth centuries to acquire land, harbors, resources, and outstanding debts from many smaller countries in the Caribbean region, including Mexico, Nicaragua, Colombia, Cuba, Puerto Rico, and Venezuela. No Caribbean national navy has ever been able to provide protection against well-armed "Gunboat Diplomacy."

**Mexico.** The newly independent United States of Mexico hired Admiral David Porter to head its fledgling naval force in 1826, soon after the former commodore of the West India Squadron was court-martialed for violating the sovereignty of Spain. His error had been to pursue royalist pirates into the coastal waters of Puerto Rico, which along with Cuba was all that remained of the once sprawling Spanish New World empire. Both islands served as havens for pirates preying on the shipping of the United States and the new Latin American republics. To combat the threat, the U.S. Navy based an antipiracy force at Key West, Florida, itself recently acquired from Spain. Mexico followed suit, and was permitted to base its small navy at Key West, as well. Mexico was powerless to prevent the U.S. Navy from conducting operations during the war of 1846–1848, as separate U.S. fleets landed troops at Veracruz for the overland campaign to Mexico City and seized the important ports of California. In 1914 the violent adventures of a U.S. Navy liberty party ashore in the oil exporting port of Tampico caused an international incident, which led to the U.S. naval occupation of Veracruz for six months. After the nationalization of the Mexican petroleum industry, the country focused on acquiring a national fleet of tankers. Six of these vessels were sunk by U-boats during World War II.

**Haiti.** The vessels of the Haitian Navy have often proven to be of decisive importance in the internal political struggles that have wracked the country. In one extreme case dating to 1869, the Haitian government purchased the former USS *Pequot* for defense against revolutionaries, renaming it *Terreur*, only to have the warship seized by the rebels themselves. They turned the ship's guns on the national palace, forcing surrender. Another important role for the Haitian Navy has been to repel filibuster invasions, as it did in 1883 and 1888. A third pursuit of the Haitian Navy from 1844 to 1893 was participation in the intra-island conflicts with the neighboring Dominican Republic. Although capable of interdicting mercenaries and waging war with Dominicans, Haitian naval forces were helpless to prevent the U.S. Navy occupation of the country in 1915. By 1920 the Haitian Navy consisted of a single vessel, an aging schooner. The U.S. occupation lasted until 1934, leaving behind a miniscule Haitian Navy, menaced by the growing might of its neighbor, the Dominican Republic.

**Dominican Republic.** The national fleet of the Dominican Republic came into being in 1844, when the nation gained its independence from Haiti. Beginning with five converted merchant vessels, the navy's first mission was to repatriate Juan Pablo Duarte, the leader of the Dominican independence movement, from exile in Curaçao. A few armed schooners prevented a Haitian land attack along the coast shortly thereafter, allowing the Dominican army to withdraw safely, and eventually to end the twenty-two-year Haitian occupation. Five years later, during another war with Haiti, the twelve-ship Dominican fleet defeated the Haitian Navy off the south coast of that country, helping to end an attempted invasion of the Dominican Republic. Independent status lasted only until 1861, when military president Pedro Santana invited Spain to recolonize the nation, partly for protection against another Haitian occupation. Regaining full independence in 1866, the country once again built a national naval force, again mainly for the purpose of deterring Haitian aggression. A half-century of hostilities on the seas ended in 1893, when the presidents of Haiti and the Dominican Republic conducted talks on each other's warships, and concluded a treaty. Like Haiti, the Dominican Republic was unable to resist occupation by the U.S. Navy and Marine Corps, which seized all the major Dominican ports in 1916 with the loss of one ship, cast ashore by a tsunami. The period of U.S. military rule lasted eight years. Afterward, Marine protégé Rafael Leónidas Trujillo Molina seized power and built a powerful navy, mainly with the addition of coastal patrol boats from the United States via the Lend Lease program during World War II, when both modern Dominican merchant ships were sunk by U-boats. The most powerful Dominican naval vessels during the gaudy Trujillo dictatorship doubled as luxury yachts for the dictator.

**Colombia.** Colombia had a much longer Caribbean coastline prior to the loss of the state of Panama, which became independent with the integral support of the U.S. Navy in 1902. The remaining Caribbean coast of Colombia includes several strategic areas. These include the ancient fortified city of Cartagena at the mouth of the Magdalena River; a fertile, banana-producing region served by the port of Santa Marta; and the Guajira Peninsula, an arid region shared with Venezuela that was a center for smuggling during the colonial era. The Colombian littoral continues to be a busy location for smuggling narcotics from zones of production in the interior to markets lying north across the Caribbean Sea. Colombia entered World War II in 1943, its navy losing four vessels during the hostilities. The navy contributed a total of three frigates to the United Nations forces fighting in Korea between 1950 and 1955, as well.

**Panama.** The strategic linchpin of the Caribbean Sea, going back to the days of the Spanish colonial flota system, has been the area of Panama. The Isthmus of Panama became a major concern to the United States with the westward expansion to the Pacific coast that took place in the mid-1840s. The Bidlack Treaty of 1846 signed with Colombia guaranteed access to that narrowest transit across the American continents. The Pacific Mail Steamship Company began stagecoach service between the coasts in 1848, followed by an isthmian railroad in 1855. U.S. naval forces intervened repeatedly on behalf of Colombia to put down Panamanian regional rebellions, until 1903, when President Theodore Roosevelt opted to take control of the failed French canal site and support the creation of the Republic of Panama. A U.S. warship prevented Colombian forces from crossing the isthmus, forcing the troops to return to their transport. The Panama Canal became the preeminent strategic concern of the increasingly more powerful United States immediately upon its final completion in 1916, magnifying the importance of regional navies. One of the largest naval facilities in the region was the U.S. Navy base at Colón. Under the provisions of a treaty signed with the United States in 1977 during the administration of Jimmy Carter, the Republic of Panama took over control of the Canal Zone in 2000.

**Cuba.** Alfred Thayer Mahan wrote in 1887 that Cuba held the key to the entire Caribbean basin. Because of its commanding position on the Windward Passage, Yucatán Channel, and Strait of Florida, the island held the advantage in terms of interdiction in the Gulf of Mexico and choke-point naval warfare. To Mahan, naval war was a study in positions, evaluated for both their military and commercial uses, which led him to focus on Cuba. Furthermore, Cuba's littoral fringe of islands, separated from the mainland and each other by labyrinthine passages, and its numerous harbors, made it a perfect haven for submarines and torpedo boats, much as the Cuban coast had sheltered pirates during the Latin American wars for independence. Cuba did not gain its independence until 1902, but the Cuban Navy made up for lost time by becoming one of the larger navies in the region. But the U.S. Navy retained the most strategic harbor on the whole island, Guantánamo Bay, building the central naval base in the Caribbean region there. The Cuban Navy consisted of two gunboats and twelve patrol boats during World War I, when no enemy submarines materialized. There were six vessels in the fleet, but no anti-submarine capacity, at the time of Pearl Harbor. With the addition of sixteen patrol boats from the United States, the Cuban forces served a great deal of convoy work, but had only a few encounters with German U-boats. Five Cuban merchant vessels were sunk during the Battle of the Atlantic.

When Fidel Castro came to power in 1959, he disbanded the Cuban Navy. But in the wake of the failed Bay of Pigs invasion of April 1961, he established a new navy designed to deter future amphibious attacks. Soviet-built *Komar* warships armed with missiles came into service in 1962, the most powerful weapons possessed by a Caribbean navy heretofore. Also in 1962, the Cold War's bipolar tension nearly broke into open nuclear warfare during the Cuban Missile Crisis. Other Caribbean navies, such as those of Venezuela and the Dominican Republic, contributed their meager naval muscle to the "quarantine" of Cuba, to prevent the entry of more Soviet nuclear arms. Tensions across the Strait of Florida did not dissipate with the end of the naval embargo in December 1962, but witnessed sporadic cat-and-mouse operations between Cuban exile commandos and Cuban naval forces. The steep increase in Cuban naval capacity in the 1980s worried U.S. naval authorities because of Cuba's strategic location on the sea-lanes of the Caribbean. In 1982, the Soviet Union supplied Fidel Castro's regime with an array of advanced naval weaponry, which gave Cuba an ocean "antiship" capability for the first time. The Cuban Navy demonstrated its potency with exercises in 1983 that mobilized the Soviet vessels: two *Polcnocny*-class amphibious landing craft capable of putting a one-thousand-man force onto the beach of a neighboring island; three *Foxtrot*-class diesel submarines; two *Koni*-class frigates designed for warfare against submarines; and two *Styx*-class missile patrol boats armed with *Osa*-class hydrofoil torpedoes. In addition, the large, subsidized Cuban merchant marine and fishing fleets could be employed to lay mines in the busy Caribbean sea-lanes. In October 1986, Cuban naval units attempted unsuccessfully to rescue a Soviet nuclear submarine that caught fire in the Atlantic. With the breakup of the Soviet Union in 1992, the Cuban Navy fell on hard times from the scarcity of replacement parts and the high price of petroleum, which had been subsidized by their erstwhile Cold War ally during the 1980s build-up. For much of the Castro period, one of the Cuban Navy's main duties has been preventing emigration by sea. Sometimes this has meant pursuing and apprehending vessels hijacked in attempts to cross the Strait of Florida to reach the United States.

## Narcotics Trafficking and Security

The international effort to interdict the drug trade has posed a new set of challenges to regional naval forces. Enforcement of narcotics policy places emphasis on coordination between the U.S. Coast Guard and the navies of nations that produce or transship cocaine and marijuana to markets in North America. One manifestation of this is aerostatic surveillance, conducted with helium-filled balloons or stationary blimps in various locations across the region. A much worse realization of the drug wars is the civil conflict in Colombia, which has dragged on since 1959, but which in recent decades has merged with the politics of narcotics production and distribution. The war has taken thousands of lives and costs billions of dollars annually. The problem of security in the Caribbean has greatly increased because of concerns about international terrorism since the attacks on New York City and Washington, D.C., on September 11, 2001. Port security and coastal surveillance are just two prongs of the naval effort to tighten the maritime borders of the Caribbean region.

[*See* also Navies, Great Powers, *subentry on* United States, 1775 to the Present; *and* Panama Canal.]

## Bibliography

De Windt Lavandier, César A. "Dominican Republic." In *Ubi Sumus?: The State of Naval and Maritime History*, edited by John B. Hattendorf. Newport, R.I.: Naval War College Press, 1994.

Griffith, Ivelaw Lloyd, ed. *Caribbean Security in the Age of Terror: Challenge and Change.* Kingston, Jamaica: Randle, 2004.

Scheina, Robert. *Latin America: A Naval History, 1810–1987.* Annapolis, Md.: Naval Institute Press, 1987.

Scheina, Robert. *Latin America's Wars*. Vol. 1: *The Age of the Caudillo, 1791–1899*. Washington, D.C.: Brassey's, 2003.

Yerxa, Donald A. *Admirals and Empire: The United States Navy and the Caribbean, 1898–1945*. Columbia: University of South Carolina Press, 1991.

ERIC PAUL ROORDA

## Caricature and Cartoons

Caricatures and cartoons are pictorial depictions that deliberately exaggerate or distort a subject's distinctive features or peculiarities for comic effect. In addition to overstatement, these pictures also share characteristics of brevity and contemporary insight into a particular social or political issue. In Britain, caricatures were a very popular form of visual entertainment that became conversation pieces in public houses and coffeehouses—wherever people gathered. They were rapidly produced to coincide with contemporary events and were relatively inexpensive to purchase. Caricatures were, in one sense, an art for the masses.

Many caricatures have strong maritime connections, taking as subjects nautical people and events, political figures and situations, and the social aspects of life at sea and ashore. These prints rarely had any regard for ethnicity, class, or gender.

The word "caricature" originated during the early seventeenth century and was first used in relation to drawings done by the renowned Bolognese fresco painter Annibale Carracci (1560–1609). The scholar Lionel Lambourne cites Carracci's understanding that the classical painter and the caricaturist both sought

*Equity or a Sailor's Prayer before Battle.* This caricature by Thomas Tegg (fl. 1880–1840) satirized the rift between officers and men by focusing on the system of distributing prize money to officers on a seniority basis. Here, a sailor who had a reputation for lack of religion, prays that the enemy's gunfire should be distributed in the same manner. THE MARINERS' MUSEUM, NEWPORT NEWS, VA.

***A Party of Pleasure.*** George Cruikshank (1792–1878) published this caricature depicting the dangers of pleasure boating in 1835. THE MARINERS' MUSEUM, NEWPORT NEWS, VA.

the lasting truth beneath the surface of mere outward appearance. Both try to help nature accomplish its plan. The one may strive to visualize the perfect form and to realize it in his work, the other to grasp the deformity, and thus reveal the very essence of a personality. A good caricature, like every work of art is more true to life than reality itself (p. 7).

Another feature common to both maritime paintings and caricatures is that both have a strong narrative element. The intention of the artist is to convey in the image a sense of time and movement. The key to most caricatures is brevity in both image and dialogue so that the point is quickly understood. A more intense observation, however, may also provide far more information about a complex issue or condition. In 1973, for instance, Jeff MacNelly used the image of Captain Ahab hopelessly intertwined with the white whale from Herman Melville's *Moby-Dick* to satirize an economic program that then embroiled President Richard Nixon. (The image can be seen in the collection of the Peabody Essex Museum, Salem, Massachusetts.)

A rich source of humor for many artists was the disparity between the officers and crew of a Royal Navy ship. An unsigned colored etching that eloquently captures this disparity is entitled "EQUITY or a Sailors PRAYER before BATTLE: Anecdote of the Battle of Trafalgar" (published by Thomas Tegg, London, and in the collection of the Mariners'

Museum, Newport News, Virginia). The primary dialogue occurs between an officer and one of the starboard gunners, who is shown kneeling in prayer by his gun. Through the image and in words the artist incisively clarifies the discrepancy aboard nineteenth-century British naval ships, where ship's officers received a much greater portion of the prize money for captured enemy ships than the crew did.

Another abundant source of maritime subject matter involved sailors interacting with land-based society, and, conversely, landsmen going to sea. George Cruikshank (1792–1878), one of the foremost English caricaturists, depicts a humorous scene in a colored etching entitled "JACK JUNK embarking on a CRUIZE" (published by Thomas Tegg, London, and in the collection of the Mariners' Museum). Now ashore, the sailor Jack Junk prepares to take a horse, presumably to the village of Leatherhead shown in the background. The humor derives from Jack's unfamiliarity with the proper way to ride a horse—that is, by facing forward.

Caricaturists also found great humor depicting the follies of landsmen as they put to sea. In one of many similar scenes, this one a colored etching entitled "A Party of Pleasure—Dedicated to the Funny Club" (published by Thomas McLean, London, August 1, 1835, and in the collection of the Mariners' Museum), George Cruikshank depicts a party of well-to-do landsmen aboard a small sailing boat on one of England's rivers. Here Cruikshank relies almost solely on the visual composition rather than on verbal wit to convey meaning. The boat is about to capsize, and there is no question as to the fate that awaits the well-dressed passengers. The calamity of their cruise contrasts with the serenity of other river traffic and a quiet village in the background.

Landlubbers often considered the average seaman to be on the lower rungs of the working class—often taking a moralistic stance with regard to a sailor's lifestyle ashore. An anonymous English colored-etching caricature entitled "JACK in a White Squall amongst Breakers—on the Lee Shore of St. CATHERINES" (published by Thomas Tegg, London, 1811, and in the collection of the Mariners' Museum) portrays a sailor with his hands thrust through his pockets, out of money and unable to pay for his rollicking time in port. While being harangued on either side by women demanding payment for room, sundries, grog, and entertainment, Jack laments his condition: "I am hard up—not a quid left, or shot in the locker—to pay the fiddler—Mi Eyes—what a Squall, how it Whistles trough the Ratlines I must Braill up and Scudd under Bare Poles."

Caricatures and cartoons have often relied on stereotypes for political and propaganda uses. Over time, these stereotypes conveyed universally understood messages. During the Napoleonic Wars, when France and England were mortal enemies, the French Neoclassicist painter Jacques-Louis David (1748–1825) was commissioned to paint grand and regal portraits of Napoleon Bonaparte. Meanwhile, across the Channel, James Gillray (1756–1815), Thomas Rowlandson (1756–1827), and other English caricaturists regularly lampooned Napoleon in the most pejorative manner possible, as "Little Boney" or the "Corsican Ogre." Seen together, the works of David and the English caricaturists have not only intrinsic artistic value but also value as instruments of propaganda. At home, Napoleon's exploits are glorified on large canvases, while in England Cruikshank, among others, vilified him as a vagabond sitting on a chamber pot for a throne—as in "LITTLE BONEY GONE to POT" (1814; see Vogler, p. 5). One value to modern-day viewers of these images is a dramatically diverse perspective into the person and character of Napoleon.

Although caricatures were originally for an audience of meager means, selling for a shilling or less, today they bring a considerably higher price. As an entire body of work, caricatures have been widely accepted and studied as an art subgenre. Many caricaturists, especially in Britain, were quite prolific, creating large numbers of prints that can be studied and interpreted stylistically. Ultimately, these works often give views of people and historic events that other works of art do not express.

[See also Art and Painting.]

## Bibliography

Barker, M. H. *The Old Sailor's Jolly Boat*. London: W. Strange, 1844.

Hillier, Bevis. *Cartoons and Caricatures*. London: Studio Vista, 1970.

Klingender, F. D., ed. *Hogarth and English Caricature*. London: Pilot Press, 1945.

Lambourne, Lionel. *An Introduction to Caricature*. London: Her Majesty's Stationery Office, 1983.

Patten, Robert L., ed. *George Cruikshank: A Revaluation*. Princeton, N.J.: Princeton University Library, 1974.

Robinson, Charles Napier. *The British Tar in Fact and Fiction: The Poetry, Pathos, and Humour of the Sailor's Life*. London: Harper and Brothers, 1909.

Vogler, Richard A. *Graphic Works of George Cruikshank*. New York: Dover, 1979.

N. LYLES FORBES

## Carpenter, William B.

**Carpenter, William B.** (1813–1885), British biologist and chief architect of the *Challenger* expedition (1872–1876). The son of a Unitarian minister, William Benjamin Carpenter was born in Exeter on October 29, 1813, brought up in Bristol, and apprenticed to a local doctor who took him to the West Indies in 1833. After completing his medical training in London and Edinburgh, Carpenter established himself as an influential writer on science and medicine. His publications included *Principles of General and Comparative Physiology* (1839) and *The Microscope and Its Revelations* (1856). In 1844 he became professor of physiology at the Royal Institution and a fellow of the Royal Society. From 1847 he was on the staff of University College, London, as professor of forensic medicine and from 1856 to 1879 as registrar. He continued his literary activities and became involved in a several scientific controversies, including the debate over Charles Darwin's theory of evolution, to which he gave qualified support while regarding such explanations as being revealing of, not replacing, the role of a divine creator.

Carpenter's personal research on the microscopic structure of shells included a study of the foraminifera. From 1855 family holidays were spent sailing (a skill acquired in the West Indies) and dredging on the Scottish island of

Arran. Some interesting discoveries on crinoids led to collaboration with Charles Wyville Thomson, who persuaded Carpenter to join him in a deep-sea dredging proposal to the Admiralty. Their voyage in HMS *Lightning* in 1868, though hampered by weather and an aging vessel, revealed varied fauna at depths previously thought to be devoid of life. Even more conclusive results were obtained during cruises in HMS *Porcupine* in 1869 and 1870.

During these voyages Carpenter was intrigued by the sea-temperature observations made by the naval surveyors. His strength as a scientific writer owed much to his capacity to generalize and synthesize. He quickly interpreted the conditions observed in *Lightning* in the Faeroe-Shetland Channel, as the result of a body of cold, dense Arctic water flowing southward underneath warmer, and therefore lighter, water moving poleward, going on to propose a theory of general oceanic circulation. This was not a new idea, having been discussed by Alexander von Humboldt and others in the early 1800s, but in Britain most writing on ocean currents had followed James Rennell, viewing them as superficial wind-driven phenomena. Carpenter's ideas aroused considerable opposition, particularly from the self-taught physicist James Croll. Searching for evidence to support his views, Carpenter twice sailed to the Mediterranean, in *Porcupine* in 1870 and in HMS *Shearwater*, with Captain George Nares in 1871, to study currents in the Strait of Gibraltar. The hydrographer Sir George Henry Richards was sympathetic to science, and Carpenter used his own influence as vice president of the Royal Society, as well as his extensive contacts in political and intellectual circles, to campaign for the dispatch of a circumnavigation expedition dedicated to the scientific exploration of the sea. Carpenter did not personally take part in the *Challenger* expedition of 1872 to 1876, but it is unlikely that this expedition, which did much to advance the scientific discovery of the oceans, would have taken place without his enthusiasm and perseverance. He was created Companion of the Order of the Bath in 1879 and died in London on November 19, 1885.

[*See also Challenger*; Marine Biology; *and* Thomson, Charles Wyville.]

## Bibliography

Carpenter, William B. *Nature and Man. Essays Scientific and Philosophical*. London: Kegan Paul, Trench & Co., 1888. Reprint. Farnborough, U.K.: Gregg International, 1970. Contains (pp. 3–152) "William Benjamin Carpenter: A Memorial Sketch," by his son J. Estlin Carpenter.

Deacon, Margaret. *Scientists and the Sea, 1650–1900: A Study of Marine Science*. London and New York: Academic Press, 1971. Reprint. Aldershot, U.K.: Ashgate, 1997.

Rozwadowski, Helen M. *Fathoming the Ocean: The Discovery and Exploration of the Deep Sea*. Cambridge, Mass.: Harvard University Press, Belknap Press, 2005.

Thomson, C. Wyville. *The Depths of the Sea. An Account of the General Results of the Dredging Cruises of H.M.SS.* Porcupine *and* Lightning *during the Summers of 1868, 1869, and 1870, under the Scientific Direction of Dr. Carpenter, FRS, J. Gwyn Jeffreys, FRS, and Dr. Wyville Thomson, FRS*. London: Macmillan, 1873.

MARGARET DEACON

**Carrack.** *See* Trading Vessels, *subentry on* Medieval Vessels.

**Cartagena, Colombia** A seaport and naval base on the Caribbean, Cartagena was known historically as Cartagena de Indias to avoid confusion with Cartagena, Spain. It was founded in 1533 by the Spanish conquistador Pedro Heredía on a virtual island that forms, with peninsulas and neighboring islands, a complex inner and outer harbor system. The most secure harbor on what Spaniards called Tierra Firme and the English called the Spanish Main, Cartagena possessed two main entrances, Boca Grande, closest to the city, and Boca Chica; the two entrances have, over time, alternated as the main entrance.

As Spain established regular treasure routes, Cartagena became the principal port for the Tierra Firme fleet, which, ideally, sailed from Spain in August and anchored at Cartagena in early autumn, where it repaired and wintered. With spring, the fleet sailed to Nombre de Dios, and later to Portobelo, malarial anchorages on the coast of Panama, to load the Peruvian treasure brought by pack animals across the isthmus. This fleet then joined the New Spain fleet at Havana for the return voyage to Spain. When Spain created an armada of galleons in the 1580s to escort the treasure fleets, the armada sailed from Spain with the Tierra Firme fleet, which came to be called the *galeones*. Cartagena was also licensed for the slave trade.

French pirates, active before Cartagena's founding, attacked it in 1544 and again in 1560, both times holding it for ransom. John Hawkins and Francis Drake, on a slave trading voyage, threatened Cartagena in 1568. In 1586, with England and Spain at war, Drake assaulted

Cartagena with a large fleet and overwhelmed its two defending galleys, rudimentary fortifications, and outnumbered defenders. The city was sacked, and its inhabitants paid 110,000 ducats (£27,000) in ransom.

Drake's attack hurried planning for Cartagena's effective fortification, which Italian and Spanish engineers oversaw. Stone forts covered the harbor entrances, and walls went up around the town. Though costly, in December 1595 the fortifications prevented another attack by Drake. For the next two centuries Cartagena served as the virtual capital of the Spanish Main, although Santa Fe de Bogotá had become the seat of administration and justice for the region, the kingdom of New Granada.

Behind its forts and walls, Cartagena proved too strong for the buccaneers who infested the Caribbean in the seventeenth century, though raids occurred nearby. But when government-backed English, French, and Dutch forces seized vulnerable Caribbean islands, Cartagena's situation became more dangerous. In 1697 a major French naval expedition, augmented by 650 buccaneers, stormed and plundered Cartagena. Its defenses repaired and further strengthened, Cartagena withstood the English admiral Edward Vernon's siege in 1741.

Cartagena again knew war when in 1811 it declared its independence from Spain. The Spanish general Pablo Morillo recovered it in December 1815 after a four-month siege. After another siege in 1821, Simon Bolívar's army entered Cartagena, which became part of Bolívar's Gran Colombia. This fell apart in the 1830s, and in 1841 Cartagena vainly attempted to secede from the republic of New Granada (Colombia after 1863), dominated by Cartagena's rival Bogotá and the populous highlands. During the civil strife of the nineteenth century, Cartagena languished and began to recover its prosperity only in the twentieth century, becoming a major Caribbean port with a population of close to one million. The impressive remains of its fortifications and the rich colonial architecture of its historic center have won for Cartagena designation as a World Heritage site by UNESCO.

[*See also* Americas, *subentry on* Exploration Voyages, 1500–1616 (South America).]

## Bibliography

Hoffman, Paul E. *The Spanish Crown and the Defense of the Caribbean 1535–1585*. Baton Rouge: Louisiana State University Press, 1980.

Lane, Kris E. *Pillaging the Empire: Piracy in the Americas 1500–1750*. Armonk, N.Y., and London: M. E. Sharpe, 1998.

Segovia Salas, Rodolfo. *Fortifications of Cartagena de Indias*. Translated by Haroldo Calvo Stevenson and Rodrigo Segovia Salas. Bogotá, Colombia: Tercer Mundo Editores, 1982.

PETER PIERSON

# Cartagena, Spain

Cartagena forms one of the great natural harbors of the Mediterranean, with a sheltered inner harbor and a large, deep protected roadstead surrounded by five large hills. Its topography and location have resulted in its use as a naval base throughout history. It was founded in 227 B.C.E. by the Carthaginian general Hasdrubal and was given the name of Cartago Nova. The Romans, under Publius Cornelius. Scipio, conquered the city in 209 B.C.E. and renamed it Colonia Victrix Julia Carthago. The city was sacked by the Vandals in 425 C.E., and it did not regain its stature until it was seized by the Byzantines under Emperor Justinian in 555. The city attained minor status only after the Visigoths expelled the Byzantines in 647. However, following the Muslim conquest of the area in 712, the city became an important trading center. During the Umayyad dynasty, a major naval arsenal was built by Abd al-Rahman I (756–788), which marked the start of the use of the port as a major naval base. The city was destroyed by Fernando II in 1243 and finally was captured by the future Alfonso X of Castile in 1245. Under Castile, the city became an important trading center for both Christian and Muslim shipping. During the wars with the crown of Aragon (1356–1374), Castile used Cartagena as its main naval base.

The city fell into decay after the plagues of the fourteenth century and repeated assaults by Muslim and Turkish pirates. The low point came during the War of Spanish Succession (1702–1713) when the city was captured by the British admiral Sir John Leake in 1706 and then was sacked by Bourbon forces five months later. In 1726 the port saw a resurgence when it was named as the site for the Marine Department of the Mediterranean. The naval arsenal (1751–1754) and the military hospital and barracks quickly followed, as did the first dry dock in the Mediterranean in 1754. The forts of Las Galeras, Los Moros, and La Atalaya were built on the high surrounding hills to guard the anchorage.

In 1873 the city rebelled against the First Spanish Republic and joined the Cantonal revolution. Navy ships joined the revolt and cruised the coast, shelling Almería and threatening Alicante. The ships were declared pirates and eventually were captured by a German frigate. The city fell to government forces in 1874 after a fierce naval battle between rebel and government ships. In 1925 the fortifications protecting the harbor underwent a major overhaul with the

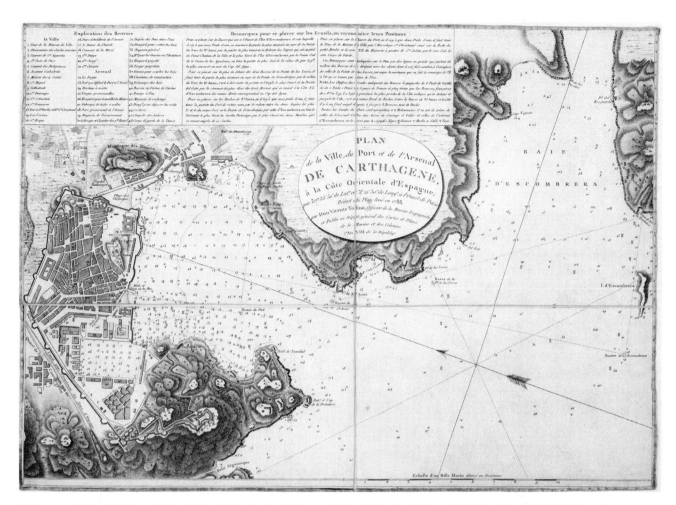

**Cartagena, Spain.** The French Navy's Depôt des Cartes et Plans published this chart in Year VIII of the Republic (1799), based on a survey by the Spanish astronomer, mathematician, and hydrographer Vicente Tofino de San Miguel (1732–1795), who had carried out a survey of the coast of Spain in 1783–1788. © NATIONAL MARITIME MUSEUM, LONDON

placement of Vickers 15-inch and 6-inch naval guns, some of which are still in place. Naval units at Cartagena were involved in the Spanish Civil War (1936–1939) on the side of the Republicans, and the city was the only major port controlled by the Republic. Cartagena was the last city in Spain to fall to General Franco in 1939. Today Cartagena is still the site for the Marine Department of the Mediterranean and one of the four major naval arsenals of Spain.

[*See also* Mediterranean Sea.]

## Bibliography

Agulló Benedí, Carlos. *Historia de Cartagena*. Murcia, Spain: Real Sociedad Económica de Amigos del País y Fundación Universitaria Isidoriana, 1995.

Cerezo Martínez, Ricardo. *Armada española, siglo XX*. Madrid: Poniente, 1983.

Fernández Duro, Cesáreo. *Armada española desde la unión de los reinos de Castilla y de Aragón*. Madrid: Museo Naval, 1972–1973.

Gómez Vizcaina, Aureliana. *Castillos y Fortalezas de Cartagena*. Cartagena, Spain: Liberia Argenta, 1998.

Montojo Montojo, Vicente. *El Siglo de Oro en Cartagena 1480–1640: Evolución económica y social de una ciudad portuaria del Sureste español y su comarca*. Murcia, Spain: Ayuntamiento de Cartagena, Real Academia Alfonso X el Sabio y Universidad de Murcia, 1993.

Soler Cantó, Juan. *Historia de Cartagena: Desde antes de su fundación hasta finales del siglo XX J.C.* Cartagena, Spain: Librería Escarabajal, 1990.

Vernet, Juan, et al. *Al-Andalus y el Mediterráneo*. Cádiz, Spain: Casa de la Cultura, Algeciras (Cádiz) y Museo Provincial de Cádiz, 1995.

LAWRENCE V. MOTT

**Cartels.** *See* Shipping Conferences and Cartels.

# Cartography

This entry contains three subentries:

## An Overview

"Cartography" is defined as the science or practice of projecting a part of the surface of the earth onto a flat plane, such as a piece of paper. The ability to project a three-dimensional globe's curved surface onto a two-dimensional plane—the chart—enabled ships and navies to navigate the oceans of this planet and was essential to Europeans' discovery of and movement across this planet. The history of cartography is a fascinating story of ideas, realized through logical reasoning and hard-won experience, for which many gave their lives through disaster at sea. Over the centuries, the combination of logic and experience has produced increasingly sophisticated methods of projection that have resulted in ever more practical and elegant answers. The maritime equivalent is known as hydrography, or the science of marine surveying, which concentrates on surveying and establishing the position of the seas, the coastline, sea depths, and so forth.

As the imperative for global exploration, and expropriation, gathered apace, so too did the need for charts that were more accurate and, as important, on which could be drawn a navigational course to ascertain the route or course along which to steer a ship to arrive at the appropriate destination. At the same time, the chart enables the navigator to compare progress along a planned voyage, for the wind, tide, and changes in magnetic effect on a ship's compass can all affect the course achieved, and comparison will show what alteration is necessary to get back on track.

But for the seafarer and navigator the chart needs to show the shortest route to take—long-distance voyages, such as across the Atlantic, should follow a "great circle" route, while for short distances this consideration makes negligible difference; but of prime convenience is that a

**Cartography.** This is the oldest surviving nautical chart, called the *"Carte Pisane"* because it was discovered in Pisa in a private collection and purchased for the French national library in 1839. Drawn on sheep or calfskin in Genoa about 1290, it is the first known portolan chart and was made for practical navigation. It is oriented to the north with a detailed drawing of the Mediterranean coastline. The rhumb or loxodromic lines radiate regularly within tangential circumferences, forming 16 compass roses where their points intersect, each with sixteen compass roses and each with 16 rhumb lines, representing the cardinal and ordinal points of the compass separated by angles of 22° 30′. Such a sea chart was dependant on the practical use of a compass and sailing a rhumbline course directly from one destination to another. BIBLIOTHÈQUE NATIONALE DE FRANCE, PARIS

straight line drawn on the chart should be the course that the navigator wants the ship to attain. The type of projection on which the chart is constructed has to be designed to make this possible.

## Development of the Chart

The earliest known map was discovered in the bay of Taranto in Italy in 2003, by the Belgian archaeologist Thierry van Compernolle of Montpelier University, but its existence was kept secret until reported in November 2005. Known as the Soleto Map and displayed in Taranto, it is dated to 500 B.C.E. and is contemporary with Pythagoras. It consists of a small piece of pottery representing the Taranto area of Italy's heel, with zigzag strokes on each side indicating the Ionian and Adriatic seas and is material proof that the ancient Greeks were drawing maps, and perhaps some sort of chart.

**Greek charts.** By the third century B.C.E. in Greece, the known world was being depicted as an oblong based around the Mediterranean, and Dicaearchus (also known as Dicearchus or Dikæarchus) of Messina, Sicily (fl. c. 320 B.C.E.), a student of Aristotle, developed a map of the earth that was on a sphere. It had lines of latitude based correctly on the lines where the noonday sun is at a given angle on a particular day, with a simple north-south and east-west diaphragm centered on Rhodes, the maritime center of their world. Pythagoras had observed the height of the stars to be different at different locations and had surmised that the earth was a globe, but it was a Greek, Eratosthenes of Cyrene (c. 276–c. 194 B.C.E.), the keeper of the Great Library at Alexandria, who demonstrated the earth's circumference. Knowing the distance from Aswan, on the Tropic of Cancer, to Alexandria to be 5,000 stadia, a stadium being 183 meters (200 yards), he saw at the summer solstice that a gnomon casts no shadow but that at Alexandria the sun's shadow gave him an angle subtended from the earth's center of 7°12′ or 1/50th of 360°. He was able to assess the earth's circumference at 252,000 stadia, which, while 4 percent more than today's satellite measurement, was remarkably close. He was then able to draw a map of the known world based on Dicaearchus's with a grid of parallel lines and meridians, again centered on Rhodes.

We know that by 100 C.E. another Greek, Marinus of Tyre, which is about 64 kilometers (40 miles) south of Beirut, was drawing sea maps with equidistant cylindrical projections making a grid of parallelograms (parallels and meridians) centered on Rhodes with proportions of four to five, which gave the Mediterranean an elongated appearance, and he seems to be the first to have done so.

The earth-centered (geocentric) view of the universe is known as the Ptolemaic system, after the Alexandria-based astronomer Claudius Ptolemaeus (today called Ptolemy). He lived from c. 90 C.E. to c. 168 C.E. and wrote about Marinus in his famous work the *Geographia*, which laid down the concept of latitude and longitude as a grid of parallels and curved meridians that later, when his work was rediscovered in Constantinople (Istanbul) around 1400, became the basis for mapping and charting the discoveries of sixteenth-century Europe. He positioned his prime meridian (base line of longitude running from the north pole to the south pole) through the Fortunate Islands, today called the Canary Islands (and charts were being drawn centered on this meridian even into the eighteenth century) but with a straight equator, every 10° up to the farthest known northerly and southerly locations of Thule and Meroë, respectively. Reckoning that the known world was half the globe, he numbered his longitude meridians from 0° to 180°.

Unfortunately he had based his degree of latitude on the circumference of the earth given by Posidonius (c. 135–c. 51 C.E.) of Rhodes—33,336 kilometers (18,000 nautical miles)—instead of on Eratosthenes' much more accurate 46,300 kilometers (25,000 nautical miles), giving a degree of 80 kilometers (50 miles) instead of 97 kilometers (60 miles), with consequent distortion. Fifteenth-century mapmakers and navigators copied this, including Christopher Columbus (1451–1506), who underestimated the distance to Asia from Europe. Perhaps he might not have attempted to reach India if he had known the true distance. Ptolemy's *Almagest*, a great compendium of contemporary Greek astronomical knowledge, drew on the work of Hipparchus (fl. 146–127 B.C.E.), the most important Greek astronomer of his time. Hipparchus had observed the precession of the equinoxes (how the spring and autumn days of equal light and darkness change each year, which is important for accurate astronavigation), and, dividing the world into 360°, put down a system of latitude and longitude to fix geographical positions in relation to the polestar. Perhaps as important was his foundation of trigonometry, essential in the accurate triangulation method of plotting coastlines, explained later, and his proof of the sphericity of the earth. He suggested, too, the idea of time elapse between two points on the earth to measure longitude, although the maritime world had to wait until John Harrison's invention of the chronometer in 1760 for a way of measuring this.

**Chinese charts.** The Chinese had developed sophisticated navigational systems hundreds of years ahead of Europe. Had the Portuguese arrived in eastern waters a hundred years before they did, they would have been dumbfounded at Chinese navigational prowess. But the Chinese had understood astronomy as early as 724 C.E. and were recording altitudes of Canopus, a bright star that shines in the Southern Hemisphere, and the compass is recorded in use by ships in 1090 C.E., at least a hundred years before Europe, and was probably in use much earlier. Chinese compass makers had created a dry needle on a pivot, each end shaped like a fish, with a delicate arrangement that also allowed for variations in dip, the earth's downward magnetic pull that a compass can experience. The zenith of Chinese maritime ability was the series of remarkable voyages of the Chinese navigator Zheng He between 1400 and 1430, but after this Chinese naval power waned as the emperor concentrated on domestic matters. Chinese charts of this period survive, similar in nature to the Europeans' portolans but more schematic, and they trace the routes Zheng He organized. They were printed in the final chapter of the famous treatise on Chinese military and naval technology the *Wu Pei Chih*. They have lines of travel and legends with details of compass bearings to steer, and distances divided by the number of watches (*keng* or *ching*) usually of four hours' duration, while the notes give details of half-tide rocks and shoals with ports and havens, and advisory routes for outward- and inward-bound passages past islands. These were of sufficient accuracy, for example, to lay a course through the Strait of Singapore, which was unknown to the Portuguese for another hundred years.

**Arab charts and navigation.** The Arabs, sailing and trading in the Persian Gulf and Indian Ocean, developed their own style of navigation that differed from the traditions developed in the Mediterranean, although many aspects of their navigation eventually spread to northern European waters. In a detailed treatise on Arabic navigation before the Portuguese sailed into the area and established trading forts, G. R. Tibbetts in 1971 states that the Arabs must have had charts but that none survive. He translates probably the most complete treatise on Arabic seafaring, the *Kitāb al-Fawā' id fī usūl al-bahr wa'l quwā' id* written in 1489–1490 by Ahmād ibn Mājid al-Najdī, who was famously credited by Meccan writers as guiding

the Portuguese under Vasco da Gama to India. Marco Polo (1254–1324), sailing up the west coast of India, tells of good Arabic charts. The earliest surviving Arabic descriptive geographical text of about 850 C.E., the *Kitāb al-Masālik wa'l-mamālik* by Ibn Khurdādhbih, gives an account of Arabic sea trading and the routes to India and the Far East as far as Korea, and the *al-Muhit* (The Encompassing), by the Turkish admiral and writer Sidi Ali Celebi (d. 1562), refers to charts—and the Portuguese refer to Arabs using them.

## Charts in Europe

The portolan is the earliest form of chart that has survived in Europe, and the oldest exemplar—the Carte Pisano, so called because it was found in Pisan—is held in the Bibliothèque Nationale in Paris and dates from about 1275. It was a style of chart developed for a type of seamanship that was applied in the Mediterranean, probably in the 1100s, but the portolan endured for at least five centuries, and the format of its construction spread slowly to northern European maritime countries such as England and Holland. The earliest portolan charts preceded the compass rose and were made on a projection that used the wind rose. Toward the periphery of the chart sixteen more roses were drawn on a circle at maximum radius to fit on the vellum or parchment. This became the design basis for the compass rose, for which the Arab sidereal rose arrangement of thirty-two points of 11.25°, drawn out as rhumb lines (from the Spanish *rumbos* meaning bearings), was favored over the Chinese cosmogonic rose of twelve or twenty-four points. The grid formed by the arrangement of compass roses created a graticule that was used both for creating the chart by placing the coastline and for navigating from it by pricking off a course with a pair of compasses, which, read as a magnetic bearing, was the direction for the ship to steer. The portolan chart developed into an art form with cartographic centers in the maritime states of Venice and Genoa; in northern Italy around Ancona; another in Sicily; and in Spain at Aragon, Palma, Barcelona, Valencia, and in Majorca.

**Spanish and Portuguese charts.** As the Portuguese and Spanish empires grew, the chart developed in style and scope to meet the challenges of exploration and discovery, and to incorporate the latest information for others to follow. Portugal had expanded its knowledge of the west coast of Africa with a series of exploratory southward thrusts, each one sailing further on the basis of the understanding of the previous venture. By 1498, Vasco da Gama had, through the auspice and skills of the Arab navigator Ahmed Ibn Majid (c. 1432–?), rounded the Cape of Good Hope and pioneered the route to India for Portugal. Earlier in 1492, Christopher Columbus, sailing for Spain, had forged a sailing route to the West Indies, laying open the route to America.

Both countries now saw the need for a formal navigational and cartographic bureau that would chart the newfound territories, instruct and examine sailing masters and navigators, issue and update charts, collect trading taxes, and ensure that their information remained secret to the state. Around 1500, Portugal set up the Casa da India (House of India) in Lisbon, and Spain established the Casa de la Contratación (House of Trade) in Seville. Returning Portuguese navigators were reporting the limitations of the plane chart, which represented the earth as flat. In a plane chart the meridians, in converging toward the poles, would distort a course drawn as a straight line across these meridians on a chart at a constant angle such that the actual course achieved over the globe becomes a spiral rhumb line that, if followed to its conclusion, would eventually lead to the pole. The king of Portugal appointed the skilled mathematician Pedro Nunes as his royal cosmographer. Nunes was chiefly known for his translation of Ptolemy's works in 1537 and his treatise on navigation and Portuguese navigational instruments *De arte atque ratione navigandi* (1546), in which he recognized the meridian problem of the plane chart.

**Charting in northern European waters.** In 1497, Giovanni Caboto, a Venetian navigator known in England as John Cabot, sailed with letters patent from Henry VII (r. 1485–1509) of England and, sponsored by a group of Bristol merchants in response to Columbus's discovery of America, sailed to find a northwest passage to the fabled east. He was probably the first to introduce the portolan chart to Bristol, where they still used the rutter. The oldest known English rutter is dated to the early fifteenth century, giving sailing directions to the Strait of Gibraltar, and an early Bristol rutter gives directions on how to return from Spain: "At capfenister go your cours north north est. And ye gesse you ij parties ovir the see and be bound into sebarne [the Severn Estuary] ye must north and by est till ye come into Sowdying [the soundings, or 100 fathom line]."

Mariners in northern waters had traditionally and contemptuously eschewed the "sheepskins" from the Mediterranean, and there was a sharp divide between northern European and Mediterranean styles of navigation. Most English masters and navigators relied on the rutter for many decades to come. Derived from the French word *routier*, in turn taken from the Portuguese *roteiro* (meaning a route or road), the rutter was a pilot book, like a personal notebook, often handed down from father to son, with instructions and sketches or views portraying the chief landmarks visible on passages along the coast. It included depths, the nature of the seabed, and anchorages found en route. The Spanish version was known as a *derrotero*, and the most famous example, although later in the story, is that captured from the Spanish ship *Rosario* by the English buccaneer Captain Bartholomew Sharp in 1681 in the Pacific. The Spanish captain's failure to sink it overboard rendered the Spanish ports of the Pacific coast of South America vulnerable to attack, as the rutter was quickly copied in England by John Thornton (1641–1708), of the so-called Thames School of cartographers.

In the mid-sixteenth century, the parlous state of English cartography was emphasized when no charts or rutters could be found to guide the Royal Fleet to bring Ann of Cleves, the bridal prospect of Henry VIII (r. 1509–1547), safely from Holland to England. The only book of sailing directions printed in English at that time, *The Rutter of the Sea*, was a guide to the English Channel, although it covered voyages to Bordeaux and Andalusia as well. The Dutch pilot book published in 1532 by Jan Seuerszoon as the *Kaert van der Zee* was too parochial. Pierre Garcie, a French sailor, wrote *Le grand routier et pilotage* covering the west coast of France with tides and anchorages, and it was soon translated into English, principally by Copland in 1528. Then in 1541 Richard Proude printed *The New Rutter of the Sea for North Partes*, which were sailing directions for circumnavigating the British Isles; reversing in time, he based it on a manuscript of 1408, although incorporated into Copland's later editions.

Lucas Janszoon Waghenaer, a Dutch sea pilot who had honed his navigational skills from the Zuider Zee to the North Sea and Mediterranean, compiled and published in Leiden in 1584 the first book of charts, called *Spiegel der Zeevaerdt* (The Mariner's Mirror). Comprising a manual of navigation, a pilot book, and a two-volume series of nautical charts covering from Norway to Cádiz, and incorporating the Zuider Zee and the northern coast of Europe, it included the first coverage of the English coasts from The Wash to Cornwall. Influenced by the portolan charts he saw, Waghenaer introduced aspects of charts that are taken for granted today, such as soundings based on a chart datum; symbols for anchorages, buoys, and submerged rocks and reefs; and, innovatively, sketches of coastal approaches that gave the mariner a hint of what lay ahead. His work was euphorically received and translated into French and German editions. Charles Lord Howard (1st Earl of Nottingham, 2d Baron Howard of Effingham; 1536–1624), Lord High Admiral to Queen Elizabeth I (r. 1558–1603), was so impressed with it that he commissioned an English edition. It was translated by Sir Anthony Ashley in London in 1588, the year of the Spanish Armada, with entirely reengraved charts, and published as the *Mariner's Mirrour*. It was in demand for another century and was so popular in England that the name Waghenaer, anglicized to "Waggoner," become the generic term for sea charts of all kinds, supplanting the old term "rutter."

In England two prominent seafarers–Sir Walter Ralegh (1552–1618) and the Earl of Cumberland, George de Clifford (1558–1605), who was captain of the *Bonaventure* during the fight against the Spanish Armada and who fought the Spanish many times in the Caribbean–well understood the need for better navigation. They respectively engaged Thomas Harriot, an Oxford scholar, and Edward Wright, a Fellow of Caius College, Cambridge, to study the problems of navigation. Both young men experienced at first hand the difficulties of navigation with a voyage; Harriot to Virginia in 1585 and Wright to the Azores in 1589. Wright published in 1599 his *Certaine Errors in Navigation Detected and Corrected*, in which he strongly urged seafarers to adopt the Mercator chart projection, published in 1569, which was more accurate in use than was "plane sailing." For example, on a voyage from London to Boston the difference between using the Mercator projection and following a plane sailing course would be almost 966 kilometers (600 miles) because the plane sailing course made good over the ground would tend into a spiral. The Flemish geographer Gerardus Mercator (Gerhard Kremer; 1512–1594) was the first to overcome the problem of projecting a three-dimensional globe onto a two-dimensional surface, constructing his projection of parallels and meridians at right angles. Wright's analogy of a pig's bladder blown up inside a cylinder appealed and slowly took root with English seafarers, but it was at least 1640 before the projection itself became accepted, and then mainly because of French support.

**Rise of Dutch preeminence in maritime cartography.** Mercator's new projection for the first time allowed the mariner and the cartographer to work from the same nautical chart. It was introduced in 1569 to a largely academic world, and it took up to a century before it became universally accepted. But it presaged the ascendancy of cartography centered at Antwerp, and this ascendancy was emphasized by a new map of the world, the *Theatrum Orbis Terrarum* published in 1570 by Abraham Ortelius, who worked closely with Europe's most successful printer, Christophe Plantin; both were friends and colleagues of Mercator. Ortelius dedicated the *Theatrum*, with fifty-three maps covering the world, to the then most powerful monarch, Philip II of Spain (r. 1556–1598). By the end of the sixteenth century the center of cartography had moved to Amsterdam, where mapmakers such as Jodocus Henricus Kramer, Johannes Janssonius, and the Blaeu family improved on Mercator and Ortelius, an ascendancy that lasted for most of the seventeenth century.

**French cartographic supremacy.** In the 1693 the beautifully produced and superior charts of Le Neptune François were published in France by Alexis Hubert Jaillot (c. 1632–1712) and Giovanni Domenico Cassini (Jean-Dominique Cassini; 1625–1712), who started the newly established Observatoire de Paris, where three generations of Cassinis continued his work. Cassini fostered a method of finding longitude by the observation of Jupiter's moons, thus fixing its latitude and longitude. A series of triangulations then fixed the complete coast of France to the prime meridian through Paris, and the French charts of Le Neptune François produced from this survey and incorporating Mercator's projection were far more accurate than any others hitherto. They covered the area from Norway to the Strait of Gibraltar in twenty-nine coastal charts and included depths along suggested coastline routes, ports, sandbanks, and rocks, and they gave France the cartographic edge over the British and the Dutch. The French maintained their lead in this field with the formation in 1720 of their national hydrographic office, the Dépôt des Cartes et Plans de la Marine, preceding the British Hydrographical Office by seventy-five years, with the often ironic situation of the Royal Navy giving battle to the French using French charts. The culmination was achieved with the publication of *Le petit atlas* in 1761 by Jacques-Nicolas Bellin (1703–1772), who ran the Dépôt des Cartes for over fifty years. The atlas covered most of the navigable oceans and coasts in a clear and accurate style in advance of anything else that had been produced up to that time.

**Growing English cartographic proficiency.** During the seventeenth century the English and the Dutch were involved in a series of three maritime wars throughout which the Dutch knew more of the English coastline than the English did. This galled the English, particularly when it was realized that the marine atlas of the London-based cartographer John Seller (1639–1701) was still using old Dutch plates. Consequently in 1681 the English secretary of the navy, Samuel Pepys (1633–1703), ordered the first real survey of British harbors and coasts, to be carried out by Captain Greenvile Collins, with the title Hydrographer to King Charles II (r. 1660–1685).

Starting out from Dover, Collins took command of the yacht *Merlin* to start the survey of the seacoasts of the kingdom with just a measuring chain, lead line, and compass. He measured the coastline with the chain and took bearings of all the headlands; he measured latitude with a quadrant but had no way of measuring longitude. The daunting and expensive undertaking took seven years to complete, and Collins published his results as *Great Britain's Coasting Pilot* in 1693. It comprised forty-eight charts, twenty-seven pages of tide tables, sailing directions, and four pages of coastal views. Collins's achievement should not be underestimated, however. The first edition sold out by 1728 but was reprinted by the London chart sellers Mount and Page, with nineteen further editions until 1792. His incredible body of work finally replaced the old Dutch waggoners on which the British had relied for too long.

**Triangulation.** But the most important development in British surveying came about in the eighteenth century with the work of Murdoch Mackenzie (1712–1797). Toward the mid-1700s the Laird of the Orkneys, James Douglas (14th Earl of Morton; 1702–1768), decided to try to reduce the number of shipwrecks around his isles even though he and the islanders were entitled to a share of any salvage. Following the wreck of the Swedish East India Company vessel *Svecia* in 1740 on an outlying reef, he approached Colin Maclaurin, mathematics professor at Edinburgh University, to see if he knew of anyone who could carry out a survey. Murdoch Mackenzie, a former student and a member of an Orcadian family, came to mind. Mackenzie raised the money needed—he estimated over £638—through subscriptions from foreign East India companies, insurance

companies, and trading houses, approaching institutions that could benefit from such a survey.

Maclaurin knew Jacques Cassini, one of the four generations of Cassinis who ran the Paris Observatory. Cassini was using a triangulation method to check the land coordinates of France, and Mackenzie adapted this system to control his hydrographic survey with a shore-based triangulation network—a maritime surveying breakthrough.

Mackenzie started on the island of Pomona, the main island in the Orkneys. Measuring a base line 4.8 kilometers (3 miles) long on the frozen Loch of Stenness to the north of the island, he took theodolite angles from each end of the various beacons he had set up on the surrounding peaks. With the positions of the triangulation stations laid down, he intersected prominent features along the coast as points from which he could then take the angles of boats anchored by significant rocks or reefs, and so plot the position of these dangers and the coastline. From a boat he then took soundings and fixed these by bearings from an azimuth compass. Finally, he checked the scale of his survey by observing latitude with a quadrant made by John Rowley in 1700 by meridian altitude of the sun on North Ronaldsay and at Kirkwall. He built up a series of five complete charts, had them engraved by Emanuel Bowen in London, and published them in 1750 as a neptune entitled *Orcades*. The Navy Board had merely lent him a chain, plane table, and theodolite, but now, obviously impressed with his work, the board commissioned him to survey the west coast of Britain and the whole coast of Ireland. By the time he retired in 1770, he had completed Ireland and the British coast south to Pembroke. He published a book of his experiences, *Treatise on Maritim Surveying* (1774), in which he described a new method of plotting the position of a ship on a chart by the "resection" method, which used three fixed marks onshore and a "station pointer" to the scale of the chart with the end of each of its three legs positioned on the point and at the angle they had measured. The center of the station pointer is the position of the ship.

The Admiralty appointed Mackenzie's nephew of the same name (Murdoch Mackenzie; 1743–1829)—a lieutenant in the navy who had sailed with John Byron in HMS *Dolphin* in his circumnavigation of 1764–1766—to continue where his uncle had left off, surveying down the Bristol Channel to Land's End and then east to Plymouth. The Thames needed attention in 1775, and the Admiralty ordered Mackenzie, who by then was assisted by his cousin, Graeme Spence, to survey the Thames estuary; their first chart was of the bay at Margate. For this they must have used the resection method Mackenzie had written about and even a form of station pointer, to judge by the abundance of soundings and the clarity of position of sandbanks they managed to include. Spence retired in 1803, writing up his sailing directions as head maritime surveyor to the Admiralty until 1811. In 1806 he had shown Captain Thomas Hurd at the British Hydrographic Office the station pointer that he had invented. Hurd asked for one from the first secretary, William Marsden, which was ordered up from the instrument maker Edward Troughton (1753–1835). This instrument was used throughout the surveying world for the next 130 years, and its impact in allowing a moving vessel to accurately plot resection fixes on board is of similar importance to the later introduction of echo sounders and electronic navigation systems such as Decca and loran.

By the end of the Napoleonic Wars (1803–1815) Britain emerged as the supreme maritime power. With the peace dividend of Pax Britannica the British carried out meticulous surveys during most of the nineteenth century of the majority of the coastlines of the world's continents, with detailed charts of coasts and bays, anchorages, passages, and approaches, chiefly under the lengthy aegis of Rear Admiral Francis Beaufort, the British hydrographer from 1829 to 1855.

## Chart Projections

Peel an apple skin and try to lay it flat, it cannot but split into segments, although it would remain joined around its center, its equator. This is equally true in a representation of our world, since the only true way to represent it is as a globe; but this is hardly feasible for navigation, laying on courses to steer, assessing adherence to that course, making adjustments to get back on track, and perceiving the position relative to coast or continent. Charts that cover a small area (large scale) have, for all practical purposes, no distortion, but in covering a large area (small scale charts), from a few square miles upward, distortions creep in, and different types of projection are needed, depending on purpose. The two main types of chart projections used by navigators in the twenty-first century, discounting electronic forms of chart, including those reliant on the Global Positioning System (GPS), are the Mercator and Gnomonic.

**Charts of historical interest.** There are many hundreds of different projections, each representing a compromise between distortion of area, distance, direction, or shape,

but apart from those of historical interest, we will look only at those that are in common use for charts.

**Stick charts.** Preliterate peoples such as the Micronesians developed their own navigational guide, one that was not laid down on a chart. As the Polynesian people migrated from New Guinea over a period of twenty-five hundred years they spread themselves across islands four thousand miles away and conjecturally must have developed a navigational system using more than an observational knowledge of stars, winds, and currents, one that was recorded and passed down the generations. The Science Museum in London has one of a number of nineteenth-century examples of a stick chart or *Rebbelib* used in the Marshall Islands. These took course direction from the wave patterns created as the Pacific swell changed direction after it came up against the various Macronesian islands, indicated on a palm fiber "grid." It is not known whether this was produced as a result of European chart influence or was typical of those produced far earlier and handed down, but this stick chart covers a north-south distance of over 805 kilometers (500 miles) and is generally accurate.

**Plane charts.** From the late Middle Ages to the sixteenth century, charts were drawn on the assumption that the earth was flat, although all navigators knew well before then that it was not. The errors in longitude that this type of projection induced were explained away as unknown ocean currents. Use of these charts involved little calculation and was called "plane sailing," giving rise to the expression in use today for an easy answer.

**Globes.** The globe is a three-dimensional representation of the earth (terrestrial) and the heavens (celestial), a revolving, free-standing sphere mounted top and bottom at the geographical north and south poles. Although associated with libraries and studies, during the sixteenth century before the invention of logarithms to facilitate astronomic navigation and Mercator's projection, globes were used on board or ashore for navigation. They could be used to find latitude from two altitude readings of the sun or a pair of stars, or to find the rhumb line course and distance between a point of departure and arrival across an ocean or stretch of sea. However, they proved cumbersome for this purpose, and the flat chart soon replaced them.

**Standard Padrón.** The Padrón Real (the Portuguese counterpart was the Padrão Real) was the earliest attempt to create a standard world map or chart. Spain's first pilot mayor, Amerigo Vespucci (1454–1512), was given the task of drawing the first Padrón Real or master chart, which became both the inventory of lands discovered and the guide for drawing future charts and maps. It was first ordered in 1508 by the Spanish equivalent to the Board of Trade, the Casa de la Contratación, and was updated on a continuing basis as returning navigators and masters brought back news of new discoveries and refined understanding of known coasts and continents. During this period Spain was far ahead of other European seafaring nations such as the French, Dutch, and English.

*Curved chart.* A Dutchman, Adriaen Veen, invented the curved chart (in Dutch *gebulte kaart*) in 1594. He was also well known for his globes made with Jodocus Hondius Jr. In an attempt to provide a chart from which a true course could be laid, he took a segment of a globe that was flattened at the bottom and curved at the top, and that could be used with the three-legged compass that he also invented to measure course and distance—all as explained in his *Tractaet vant zee-bouckhouden op de ronde ghebulte pascaert*, published in Amsterdam in 1597. This chart was in use during the late 1590s and early 1600s by Dutch merchantmen voyaging to the East and West Indies.

**Projection and scale.** A certain group of representational solutions, or projections, while never wholly correct, can be acceptable to navigators, since the errors in representation will be negligible, and thus disregarded, in proportion to the amount of the area shown. Thus if the scale is such that any point chosen along a meridian and a parallel is the same (although not totally correct) and the meridian and parallel(s) are at right angles to each other, then very small areas on the chart will have the same shape as corresponding small areas on the earth. This type of projection is known as orthomorphic or conformal—the scale is the same in all directions—and within this there are broadly two categories: those that can be derived from a cone, and those classed as conventional. The conical and zenithal (or azimuthal), and cylindrical projections are of the former type, and among the conventional type are Mercator's cylindrical and Cassini's projections.

*Mercator.* The Mercator projection, still used in the twenty-first century and a tribute therefore to its inventor Gerardus Mercator, a Flemish geographer, was influenced by Ptolemy but was a breakthrough in this quest. The Mercator projection is a cylindrical projection that utilizes parallels running east-west whose distance apart increases toward the poles, with measurements of latitude from 0° at the Equator to 90° at the poles, and equidistant meridians running north-south and divided into 360°, whereby the earth spins conveniently 15° of longitude every hour. This gave rise to the measurement of longitude by comparison between time at the base meridian (Greenwich, England, today, but then at the Canary Islands, the important revictualing stop on the sailing route across the Atlantic) and local time on board ship. It is used for large areas, although the principal advantage is that the meridians and parallels cross each other at right angles, so that a true course to steer can be drawn and measured. Other aspects of the Mercator projection do not have to have the axis through the poles but can be skewed so that the axis is at right angles to the polar axis—known as Transverse Mercator—or along other axes—Oblique Mercator. However, these latter two projections are of no use for navigation.

*Gnomonic.* The shortest sailing distance between the point of departure and arrival (which in sailing terms is the point of last land fix and landfall) is known as great circle sailing. The most obvious great circle is the Equator, and the meridians of longitude passing through the poles are, too, but any course that is sailed along the circumference of the earth that joins these two points will be the shortest distance, and in practical terms a radio signal will travel a great circle route around the world, too. The chart that best portrays this is the Gnomonic chart (from the Latin *gnomon*, meaning an indicator). It is a perspective projection whereby part of a spherical surface is projected onto a plane surface tangential to the sphere's surface. This means that the great circle arcs are projected as straight lines, which the navigator can use to work out course and distance, transferring by means of a succession of latitude and longitude coordinates positions onto a Mercator chart, which will give a series of courses to steer.

As the north-south parallels grow farther apart toward the North and South poles, so the style of chart that works well across the equator and up into the temperate latitudes becomes inaccurate and then dangerous. The distortion this causes toward the poles shows Greenland as the same size as South America, when in reality it is some fifteen times smaller. A different style of projection is necessary for polar navigation, and the Gnomonic chart fulfils that purpose. Hugh Godfray was the first to publish two polar gnomonic charts, one for each of the Northern and Southern Hemispheres, in 1858, although Samuel Sturmey had published a complete explanation of a great circle route from the Lizard to the Bermudas in the *Marinour's Mirror* in 1669.

*Conic.* Conic or conical projections use a cone rather than a cylinder. A simile is that of a dunce's hat placed over a football. The pattern of the globe is projected onto the cone and then is unraveled and spread flat–giving a conic projection. This concept of representation goes back a long way and was used by Ptolemy around 150 C.E.

*Azimuth or zenith projections.* In cartography the zenith is the point in the sky or celestial sphere that is directly overhead from any given point on earth. Its adaptation into common usage is obvious. The azimuth in navigation, too, means the direction or bearing of a celestial body. Both terms come from Arabic; "azimuth" comes from *as sumat* (or sometimes *as-summat*), meaning the way or direction, while "zenith" means the position in the sky directly above the observer. These projections have the chart centered on a particular point–for example, on the North or South Pole–and portray the part of the world as it would seem to an observer directly above that center point, that is, from the zenith.

The best-known azimuthal projection is the orthographic or conformal, used more for perspective views of the earth, moon, or planets. A similar projection is the stereographic projection, which projects the chart from a point on the earth's surface directly opposite the center of projection.

Other important projections have been created that are not cylindrical, conic, or azimuthal. Elliptical projections show the world within an ellipse or flattened oval; for example, Carl B. Mollweide presented his equal area projection in 1805. Another is the Robinson Projection, by Arthur H. Robinson in 1963–a pseudo-cylindrical or orthophanic ("right appearing") projection with concave meridians equally spaced, but with the central meridian selected as convenient to the cartographer. Further refinements are "interrupted projections" whereby the projection is cut along lines of longitude and spread across the page. A set of these is cut into twelve segments called gores and makes for an accurate representation, but one that is impractical for use by navigators.

**Bathymetric chart.** A bathymetric chart shows the underwater contours of the world's seas and oceans. It is like a topographical land map but shows similar information below sea level. Prince Albert I (r. 1889–1922) of Monaco is credited with initiating this form of charting in 1903. Under the auspices of the Intergovernmental Oceanographic Commission (IOC) of the United Nations Educational, Scientific, and Cultural Organization (UNESCO) and the International Hydrographic Organization (IHO), the aim is to provide, as the General Bathymetric Chart of the Oceans (GEBCO), the most authoritative, publicly available bathymetry for the world's oceans and bathymetric charts covering the world. GEBCO has produced separate editions of bathymetric contour paper charts covering the whole world and global ocean floor bathymetry data sets based upon echo-sounding data collected by ships and compiled by experienced geoscientists, used in many scientific laboratories around the world.

**Synoptic chart.** A synoptic chart is essentially a weather map that will show the boundaries of different weather fronts, either cold polar air or warm tropical air, at a particular time and place with centers of high and low pressures and isobars (lines of equal barometric pressure) drawn so that the type of pressure system and time when a weather front will pass can be determined. In theory the wind flows along these isobars at a speed varying inversely with the distance between the isobars, so that the closer the isobars, the greater the wind speed. This theoretical wind is called the geostrophic wind, and a wind scale enables the geostrophic wind to be calculated for any latitude, usually at around two thousand feet, although allowance must be made for the friction of the wind over the earth's surface, and this will vary depending on whether over land or sea.

**Isogonic chart.** The earth has both a north and a south geographical pole (true north or south) and a magnetic north and south pole. The magnetic compass points toward the north magnetic pole, unless it is in an area of strong local magnetic influence that will override the earth's main magnetic field. In 2006 the North Magnetic Pole was in northern Canada at approximate latitude 71° N, longitude 96° W, which is about 2,092 kilometers (1,300 miles) from true north. But it wanders year by year, and the rate of change in variation is noted on a chart.

When a navigator lays off his course on a chart and uses a magnetic compass to steer the ship, he has to allow for the difference between the magnetic compass course and the geographical course measured in degrees from the chart. The angle between a magnetic and a geographic meridian (the lines of longitude) is called "variation." For example, if the variation is shown as 5° W, this means that magnetic north is 5° W of true (geographical) north. A chart that connects the points with the same magnetic variation is called an isogonic chart. The lines of force that lead to the magnetic pole are not straight like the lines that lead to the geographic poles; instead, they weave back and forth according to the varying strengths of the magnetic fields in the earth.

Isogonic or declination charts are plots of equal magnetic declination on a map, yielding its value by visually siting a location and interpolating between isogonic lines. Some isogonic charts include lines of equal annual change in the magnetic declination, or earth's magnetic field (called isoporic lines).

**Electronic Chart Systems (ECS).** Electronic charting has grown in sophistication exponentially into the twenty-first century, and inevitably, in explaining and describing this new technology, acronyms and initials are used in abundance. But the traditional skills of the navigator should still be understood and practiced, since ECS will fail if the power source on board fails. There are two types of electronic charts—vector and raster. Both will display an electronic chart format onto an electronic screen. Raster charts are electronic snapshots of paper charts.

*Vector charts.* Vector charts display a lithographic or paper chart in a point-by-point format, allowing large magnifications without distortion or loss of clarity. Electronic Navigational Charts (ENCs) are official vector charts that conform to strict IHO (International Hydrographic Organization) specifications and can only be issued by or on behalf of a national hydrographic authority. Each IHO member nation is responsible for producing ENCs of its own waters and systematically updating them with all critical safety information. They are the only vector charts that may be used for primary navigation in place of paper charts.

The Electronic Chart Display and Information System (ECDIS) consists of digitized data that records all the relevant chart features such as coastlines, buoys, lights, and so forth. These features and their attributes (such as position, color, and shape) are held in a database structure that allows them to be selectively displayed and queried, creating the potential to manipulate the chart image when displayed on screen. ENCs, because of their vector format, can be programmed to automatically trigger alarms to warn of impending dangers and provide significant benefits in terms of maritime safety, risk management, cost savings, and other operational efficiencies.

*Raster navigational charts (RNCs).* RNCs use raster data to reproduce paper charts in an electronic format. Their familiar paper chart image helps users gain confidence with the use of electronic charts by providing a direct link between display screen and chart table. They consist of thousands of tiny colored dots (pixels), which together make a flat digital image. Every pixel is geographically referenced, enabling accurate real-time (continually updated) display of vessel position when a chart display system is linked to GPS, the global positioning system that allows an electronic instrument (often handheld) to tune into satellite signals. These will give a readout position in latitude and longitude. RNCs can provide automatic links to other onboard systems (for example, warning alarms), but unlike with ENCs, charted features cannot be selectively displayed or queried.

Only an ECS approved by the IHO can legitimately be called an ECDIS and considered by the regulatory authorities to meet the requirements of Safety of Life at Sea (SOLAS).

Two of the major suppliers of electronic charts are the United Kingdom Hydrographic Office and, in the United States, the National Oceanic and Atmospheric Administration (NOAA). The U.K. Hydrographic Office supplies digital charts known as ARCS (Admiralty Raster Chart Service). These digital charts are exact electronic replicas of the Admiralty and Office of Coast Survey (OCS) paper chart series in digital format.

[*See also* Cook, James; Mercator, Gerardus; Oceania, *subentry on* Polynesian and Micronesian Navigation; Ortelius, Abraham; Vikings, *subentry on* Norse Navigation; *and* Wright, Edward.]

## Bibliography

Admiralty, Hydrographic Department. *Admiralty Manual of Hydrographic Surveying.* London: H.M.S.O., 1938. Revised 1948.

Admiralty Charts and Publications. *The Mariner's Handbook*, NP 100 1979. Admiralty Manual of Navigation, vols. 2 and 3. London: Her Majesty's Stationery Office, 1955.

Andrewes, William J. H., ed. *The Quest for Longitude: The Proceedings of the Longitude Symposium, Harvard University, Cambridge, Massachusetts, November 4–6, 1993.* Cambridge, Mass.: Collection of Historical Scientific Instruments, Harvard University, 1998.

Bagrow, Leo. *History of Cartography*. Revised and expanded by R. A. Skelton. Translated by D. L. Paisey. Cambridge, Mass.: Harvard University Press, 1964.

Blake, John. *The Sea Chart: The Illustrated History of Nautical Maps and Navigational Charts*. London: Conway Maritime, 2004.

Blewitt, Mary. *Surveys of the Seas (A Brief History of British Hydrography)*. London: Macgibbon and Kee, 1957.

Bremner, R. W. *Address to the 11th International Symposium for the History of Nautical Science and Hydrography 1990*.

"British Oceanographic Data Centre (BODC)." http://www.bodc. ac.uk.

Campbell, Tony. *The Earliest Printed Maps: 1472–1500*. Berkeley: University of California Press, 1987.

Campbell, Tony. "Portolan Charts from the Late Thirteenth Century to 1500." In *The History of Cartography*, edited by J. B. Harley and David Woodward. Vol. 1, *Cartography in Prehistoric, Ancient, and Medieval Europe and the Mediterranean*. Chicago: University of Chicago Press, 1987.

Cortazzi, Hugh. *Isles of Gold: Antique Maps of Japan*. New York: Weatherhill, 1983.

Courtney, Nicholas. *Gale Force 10: The Life and Legacy of Admiral Sir Francis Beaufort*. London: Headline, 2002.

Crane, Nicholas. *Mercator: The Man Who Mapped the Planet*. London: Weidenfeld and Nicolson, 2002.

Crone, Gerald Roe. *Maps and Their Makers: An Introduction to the History of Cartography*. London: Hutchinson University Library, 1966.

Davids, Carolus Augustinus. *Zeewezen en wetenschap*. Amsterdam/ Dieren, Netherlands: De Bataafsche Leeuw, 1986.

Evans, G. N. D. *Uncommon Obdurate: The Several Public Careers of J. F. W. DesBarres*. Salem, Mass.: Peabody Museum, 1969.

Firstbrook, Peter. *The Voyage of the Matthew: John Cabot and the Discovery of North America*. Toronto: M&S, 1997.

Fisher, Susanna. *The Makers of the Blueback Charts: A History of Imray, Laurie, Norie, & Wilson Ltd*. Saint Ives, U.K.: Imray Laurie Norie and Wilson, 2001.

Hapgood, Charles. *Maps of the Ancient Sea Kings: Evidence of Advanced Civilization in the Ice Age*. Philadelphia: Chilton, 1966.

Harley, J. B., and David Woodward, eds. *The History of Cartography*. Vol 1, *Cartography in Prehistoric, Ancient, and Medieval Europe and the Mediterranean*. Chicago: University of Chicago Press, 1987.

Howse, Derek, and Michael Sanderson. *The Sea Chart: An Historical Survey Based on the Collections in the National Maritime Museum*. Newton Abbot, U.K.: David and Charles, 1973.

Huntingford, G. W. B., trans. and ed. *The Periplus of the Erythraean Sea*. London: Hakluyt Society, 1980.

Kemp, Peter, ed. *The Oxford Companion to Ships and the Sea*. London and New York: Oxford University Press, 1976.

Larsgaard, Mary Lynnette. *Map & Imagery Laboratory*. University of California http://www.library.ucsb.edu/people/larsgaard

Moreland, Carl, and David Bannister. *Antique Maps*. London: Longman, 1983. 2d ed. Oxford: Phaidon Christie's, 1986.

"National Atlas of the United States: Magnetic Field–Secular Variation of the Declination Component for the Epoch 1995.0." http://www.nationalatlas.gov/mld/dsvcntl.html.

"National Oceanic and Atmospheric Administration (NOAA)." http://www.noaa.gov.

Nordenskiöld, Baron Nils Adolf Erik. *Periplus* and *Facsimile Atlas to the Early History of Cartography* (Stockholm, 1889). Reprint. New York: Dover, 1973.

Randier, Jean. *Marine Navigation Instruments*. Translated by John E. Powell. London: Murray, 1980.

Ritchie, G. S. *The Admiralty Chart: British Naval Hydrography in the Nineteenth Century*. London: Hollis and Carter, 1967.

Sider, Sandra, with Anita Andreasian and Mitchell Codding. *Maps, Charts, Globes: Five Centuries of Exploration, a New Edition of E. L. Stevenson's "Portolan charts" and Catalogue of the 1992 Exhibition*. New York: The Hispanic Society of America, 1992.

Snyder, John. *Map Projections: A Working Manual*. Washington, D.C.: Government Printing Office, 1987.

Taylor, E. G. R. *The Haven-Finding Art: A History of Navigation from Odysseus to Captain Cook*. London: Hollis and Carter for the Institute of Navigation, 1971. First published 1956.

Taylor, E. G. R. *Mathematics and the Navigator in the Thirteenth Century*. London: Royal Geographical Society, 1960.

Tibbetts, G. R. *Arab Navigation in the Indian Ocean before the Coming of the Portuguese: Being a Translation of Kitāb al-Fawā'id fī usūl al-bahr wa'l-qawā'id of Ahmād b. Māji al-Najdī*. London: Royal Asiatic Society of Great Britain and Ireland, 1971.

"United Kingdom Hydrographic Office: Electronic Charts FAQ." http://ukho.gov.uk/amd/faqelectronicCharts.asp#1.

Waters, David W. *The Art of Navigation in England in Elizabethan and Early Stuart Time*. 2d ed. Greenwich, U.K.: National Maritime Museum, 1978.

Zandvliet, Kees. *Mapping for Money: Maps, Plans, and Topographic Paintings and Their Role in Dutch Overseas Expansion during the 16th and 17th Centuries*. Amsterdam: Batavian Lion International, 1998.

JOHN BLAKE

# Indigenous Cartography

The term "indigenous cartography" describes cognitively derived and intuitively produced graphical and behavioral representations that facilitate a spatial understanding of things, concepts, conditions, processes, or events in the human world. Formerly derogatorily named "primitive" or, incorrectly, "preliterate" cartography, the category of indigenous cartography embraces the many maps made and understood universally by ordinary people ever since an as yet unestablished stage in the prehistoric cultural development of *Homo sapiens*. Many of these maps were, of course, composite maps: products of shared experiences or tradition or both. Not all such maps, however, were made by peoples indigenous to the areas mapped, and in keeping with the concept of natural language, "natural cartography" would be a better term. The antithesis of natural or indigenous cartography is formal cartography. Rarely acknowledged and often difficult to recognize, many early maps were hybrids—especially those maps of large areas in which locations plotted on mathematically generated graticules were supplemented with indigenous incorporations. The plotted locations were spatially more accurate than the incorporated patterns because the topological geometry of those incorporated patterns did not conserve direction, distance, scale, or shape.

Recently, progress has been made toward systematizing the considerable body of historical and ethnographical knowledge about the indigenous maps of cosmographical, celestial, and terrestrial (including coastal, littoral, and estuarine) worlds. Much less is known about the indigenous maps of the oceans, marginal seas, and islands; this is particularly so for the maritime worlds surrounding Mesoamerica, South America, and Australia. The following is the first ever attempt to systematize what is known.

### Celestial Charts and Cosmographies

Prehistoric rock art contains evidence of maps, some of which are cosmographic, but nothing has been found that convincingly suggests representations of the maritime world, real or supposed. A fourth millennium B.C.E. Egyptian painted dish shows an encircling primeval ocean, as does a Babylonian world map on stone of c. 600 B.C.E. Until the sixteenth century C.E., Mesoamerican cosmographies presented a terrestrial world resting on a primordial sea. From the third century B.C.E. onward, Chinese cosmographies showed small seas separating nine continents, each sea connected to a rectangular enclosing ocean, the outer edge of which met the dome of heaven. Early Brahmanic, Hindu, and Buddhist cosmographies were centered on mountains, around which were radiating continents. These mountains were, in turn, separated and encircled by seas, beyond which was the world's rim. Similar cosmographies were later to be discovered elsewhere, particularly among the native peoples of North America and Arctic Eurasia. One cosmography modeled in 1608 during a three-day performance by Virginia Algonquians con-

sisted of three concentric circles around a fire. The inner circle signified Algonquian country, the middle one North America, and the outer one the edge of the oceanic world. The British Isles were signified by a pile of sticks placed in the ocean. Such cosmographies were sometimes interpreted by Europeans as cartographies. This could be the explanation of "The Sea of China and the Indies" placed immediately west of the Appalachians on John Farrar's "A Mapp of Virginia ..." (1651). The painted tympanum of a Ket (northern Russia) shaman's drum also represented a circular universe, but one of two worlds, the upper of which contained six seas with fish and one without.

Indigenous celestial charts made for use in a maritime context seem to have been rarer than cosmographies. Ming (early seventeenth century C.E.) simple star charts were produced to aid Chinese navigators in the Indian Ocean. Celestial charts were later used in Oceania, but apparently for instructional purposes only. Navigators in the Caroline Islands arranged lumps of coral, coconut leaves, and banana fibers on mats to teach trainees the sidereal compass. In the Gilbert Islands, the beams and rafters of some meetinghouses represented the divisions of the night sky and were used to teach star navigation. In the same islands a special boat incorporating coral fragments was used to teach combined star and ocean-swell navigation.

### Nautical Charts

Indigenous maps only rarely represented sea conditions. The best-known exceptions were the Marshallese *mattang*: stick charts (actually made of the midribs of coconut leaves). These charts were not sailing charts, but rather were used for teaching the abstract principles of swell refraction around a hypothetical island. The *meddo* and *rebbelib,* which may have been postcontact hybrids, were similar in form and function but incorporated actual island groups, albeit topologically.

In the centuries preceding the European age of discovery, ocean navigators almost certainly made and used indigenous nautical charts. Malay seafarers may have made such charts from as early as the first century C.E. in voyaging to regions as far away as southern Africa. The Portuguese certainly made use of Javanese charts in the sixteenth century, one of which represented places as far apart as the Cape of Good Hope, Portugal, the Red Sea, and the Moluccas. In the late thirteenth century, Marco

Polo mentioned nautical charts in connection with Ceylon and the west coast of India. An extant early seventeenth-century Chinese chart of the northwest Indian Ocean is so grossly distorted that the coastlines are almost unrecognizable, but it was practical to the extent that it showed sailing routes, compass courses, and the altitude of the polestar at selected sites. Pīrī Re'īs's 1513 hybrid map of the world may well have incorporated indigenous charts of this kind.

At first contact with Europeans, some oceanic peoples were capable of making charts of extensive island groups. In 1493, King João II of Portugal ordered a Carib that Christopher Columbus had brought back from his first voyage to arrange beans on a table to represent the islands that were supposed to have been discovered. The Carib represented the relative positions of Hispaniola, Cuba, the Bahamas, and several other islands, to which a second Carib added more. In 1769 the Polynesian navigator Tupaia made James Cook a chart of seventy-four Polynesian islands, believed now to spread over an oceanic area larger than the continental United States. In 1910 an Inuit on Chartlon Island drew on the back of a missionary print a remarkably detailed map of the complexly patterned Belcher Islands some 300 miles to the north in Hudson Bay. At that date these islands had been almost forgotten by Euro-Americans.

Most of the evidence for indigenous cartography of maritime areas relates to coastlines, estuaries, littorals, and inshore waters. Many of the maps were made for European explorers and traders, though at earlier dates similar maps were almost certainly made for other expanding maritime people, such as the Arabs and Chinese in the Indian Ocean. Of the extant examples, most are transcripts. Others are known by accounts only. A few of the latter were truly indigenous: for instance, the account of an 1855 event on the Pacific coast of Vancouver Island, in which a group of Indians modeled on a sandy beach a detailed plan of the islands, coves, and beaches in the neighborhood of an Indian settlement they were about to attack. In 1520, Hernán Cortés received from Montezuma II a map of part of the Gulf of Mexico coastline painted on cloth; there is debate about the extent to which this was incorporated in a map printed in Nuremberg in 1624. In 1602, Micmac Indians on an English ship off the coast of southern Maine chalked an outline of the coast to the north as far as Newfoundland—some one thousand miles away. Some maps were of estuaries and short but critical sections of coast. In 1605, Pawtucket or Massachusett Indians inserted on a map supplied by Samuel de Champlain the mouth of the Merrimack River. An estuary bar and perhaps a fog had caused Champlain to miss the mouth when he was sailing down what is now the New Hampshire coast a few days before. In 1619, Delaware Indians, in the course of explaining how to enter the Hudson River, chalked on a chest lid a map of features that were to become known as Manhattan Island, the lower Hudson, the East and Harlem rivers, and Hell Gate. By the middle of the nineteenth century much of the New Zealand coast had been mapped for Europeans by Maori, some of it in surprising detail. During that century, too, much of the Arctic coastline and archipelago off Canada and Alaska were mapped by Inuit and Eskimo for English and American explorers and whalers.

By the late nineteenth century, maps of Arctic coastlines were being made for sale to museum representatives, gold miners, and even tourists. Examples include three-dimensional and bas-relief maps of the fjord coast of southeast Greenland carved in wood by Ammassalik Eskimo and nonindigenous maps of the west coast of Alaska engraved on walrus tusks in large quantities by members of a few Eskimo families. A large Chukchi map on skin, obtained by a whaler crew c. 1870, represents parts of the Chukchi Peninsula coastline as a background to pictographic scenes that include whale, walrus, and seal hunts, whaling schooners, kayaks, and harpooning through the sea ice.

For indigenous maritime peoples, their own maps had multiple significances until well after they were contacted by major expanding powers. Maps that they made for those powers were critical in guiding the expansion and became important components of hybrid maps. Failure of the expanding powers' mapmakers and chart makers to understand indigenous maps—in particular by making the false assumption that the indigenous maps were inferior versions of their own—frequently resulted in incorporations that produced what would later be seen to be grossly distorted spatial representations of the maritime world.

[See also Astronomers and Cosmographers; Nautical Astronomy and Celestial Navigation; and Oceania.]

## Bibliography

Most of the examples in this article, but not the organizing ideas, are drawn from the first four volumes of an ongoing publishing project that will produce the definitive global history of maps, mapmaking, and map use: The History of Cartography, vols. 1, 2.1, 2.2, and 2.3 (Chicago: University of Chicago Press, 1987 and continuing). Each volume is multiauthored, has a detailed index and exhaustive bibliography, is lavishly illustrated, and contains copious citations. The periods, regions, and cultures covered are conveyed in the volume titles: vol. 1, Cartography in Prehistoric,

*Ancient, and Medieval Europe and the Mediterranean,* edited by J. B. Harley and David Woodward (1987); vol. 2, book 1, *Cartography in the Traditional Islamic and South Asian Societies,* edited by J. B. Harley and David Woodward (1992); vol. 2, book 2, *Cartography in the Traditional East and Southeast Asian Societies,* edited by J. B. Harley and David Woodward (1994); and vol. 2, book 3, *Cartography in the Traditional African, American, Arctic, Australian, and Pacific Societies,* edited by David Woodward and G. Malcolm Lewis (1998). See also John Spink and D. Wayne Moodie, *Eskimo Maps from the Canadian Eastern Arctic,* edited by Conrad Heidenreich, Cartographica, no. 5 (Toronto: Gutsell, 1972).

G. MALCOLM LEWIS

# Speculative Cartography

It is difficult for a generation accustomed to the accuracy of today's cartography to appreciate that until the sixteenth century many maps were based on little more than religious dogma, philosophical reasoning, folklore, and legend. The larger the area shown, the more likely such elements were to be dominant, and mapmakers struggled to fit the reports of travelers and voyagers into these broader concepts. Both within and outside Europe, maps tended to be schematic or topological rather than based on astronomical observation. Most examples of early maps that cover wider areas come from Asia; in fact, the earliest surviving printed map is a twelfth-century map of western China. Europe, in comparison, was deficient in mathematical and astronomical knowledge, as well as in navigational instruments such as the magnetic compass. In late medieval Europe, estate maps, route guides, and portolan charts were examples of maps drawn for specific purposes, but for a long time the nearest approach to a general image of the world remained the circular *mappamundi* of Christian cosmology with Jerusalem at its center. The rediscovery in the fifteenth century of the Ptolemaic geography of the second century C.E. led to the production of maps based on a notion of the Indian Ocean enclosed by a continental landmass joined to Asia and Africa. For most European scholars before Christopher Columbus's voyages, this was the nearest representation they had to the perceived shape of the world.

The great surge of seaborne exploration from Europe that began in the fifteenth century resulted in a cartographical revolution. Mapmakers dealing with the reports, journals, and charts reaching them from the oceanic voyages were faced with crucial issues of selection and credibility. For many years maps remained a compromise between traditional cosmology and recent exploration–although during the sixteenth century the world maps of Gerardus Mercator and Abraham Ortelius reflected the discovery of the Americas and the opening of southern sea-routes around Africa and South America, they also included a giant southern continent that in places stretched north of the Tropic of Capricorn to form a landmass that dwarfed the other continents. This represented more than a doffing of the cap to Ptolemy. Considerations of symmetry and balance pointed toward equivalent amounts of land in the southern and northern hemispheres, for, as Mercator wrote, without this the world would tumble to destruction among the stars. Voyages into the southern oceans, although few and far between, strengthened rather than dispelled the illusion of a great southern continent, *Terra Australis Incognita* (or sometimes *Nondum Cognita,* "not yet known"). For masthead lookouts, clouds on the horizon could easily resemble land, and distant islands might be the capes of a continent. In dealing with such sightings the cartographer played an essential role, for an outline on the map, stretching from one defined point to another, seemed to guarantee an actual presence. Examples of this are the "Dieppe maps" of the middle decades of the sixteenth century, which show a subcontinental promontory named "Java la Grande" jutting out of the southern ocean toward the East Indies. The Dieppe cartographers produced maps that hinted at a voyage or voyages of discovery that had charted the east coast of Australia. No firm evidence has been found of any such voyage, and the name "Java la Grande" was to disappear, but the great northern promontory remained on the maps as a ghostly relic of the Dieppe school. Two hundred years later James Cook was alleged to have used his knowledge of one of the Dieppe maps to guide him along the east coast of Australia.

## The Strait of Anian

Equally mysterious in the maps of the northern hemisphere was the appearance in the 1560s of a "Strait of Anian" separating Asia and America. No vessel from Europe had been within thousands of miles of the region (approximately that of modern Bering Strait), but by giving his strait a name–a name, moreover, found in the writing of Marco Polo–the mapmaker Giocomo Gastaldi established the credibility of the strait. Not all cartographers followed him, as there were still those who believed that Asia and America were connected by a land bridge, but the advantages of such a strait to explorers searching for the Northwest or Northeast Passage kept it on the map until the eighteenth century. Because little was known of the vast expanses of the North Pacific, mapmakers had a free hand to speculate and imagine. So, to the east of Japan the huge islands of Yedso,

Company Land, and Da Gama Land, which had been conjured up from the tentative reports of Dutch sea captains, appeared on the maps; the Strait of Anian divided the continents; and, away to the southeast, California was usually shown as an island. All these features promised trade to the merchant and help to the navigator. As mapmaking became an increasingly commercial and competitive business, individual cartographers were aware of the advantages of producing maps that aroused the anticipation of some important discovery. Maps were not simply a factual record; they often speculated about what lay beyond the tracks of the explorers. They had become a form of promotional literature.

In this context national and political considerations could be important, and they may explain why the Strait of Anian moved significantly in location. On some maps made during the seventeenth century, the Strait of Anian moved from its original location near present-day Bering Strait to a site several thousand miles southeast, just north of California. Much of the impetus behind this shift came from French cartographers such as Guillaume Delisle who were plotting the course of French explorers across the North American continent. By the late seventeenth century New France stretched from the Saint Lawrence River and the Great Lakes in the north to the Gulf of Mexico in the south, and expansion to the west—hopefully to the Pacific—had taken the explorers to the Mississippi River and beyond. With no knowledge of the western expanses of the continent or of the mighty barrier of the Rocky Mountains, Delisle and other cartographers were free to speculate. By the end of the seventeenth century a picture of the western half of North America was emerging in which a great river or other waterway ran down to the Pacific, perhaps by way of a "Mer de l'Ouest," a kind of inland Mediterranean Sea. Delisle never showed the Mer de l'Ouest on a printed map for fear that foreigners might discover and exploit it, but his contemporaries and successors were less circumspect. On some maps the Mer de l'Ouest was shown as linked to the Strait of Anian; others had it linked to the Long River described in the fictitious western travels of Baron de Lahontan or to the entrance on the Pacific coast allegedly discovered by Juan de Fuca in 1592.

## The Northwest Passage

In contrast, English cartographers had concentrated on regions farther north, to support the efforts of English seamen to find a Northwest Passage through Hudson Bay or Baffin Bay. In 1578, for example, a map illustrating Martin Frobisher's voyages was published; it showed a strait running just south of the Arctic Circle from Baffin Island along the northern edge of the American continent and into the Pacific by way of the Strait of Anian. After Henry Hudson's voyage of 1610, the search moved to Hudson Bay, whose western shores were often shown almost halfway across a rather attenuated North American continent. A succession of expeditions tried to find the promised strait, but all were turned back by land or ice. Some maps of Hudson Bay continued to depict a wide inlet opening to the west, known reassuringly as Roe's Welcome, or simply the Welcome; others showed a closed coastline, marked Ne Ultra, "no farther." Far away to the west, Russian expeditions under Vitus Bering reached Bering Strait in 1728 and points on the northwest American coastline in 1741, but the relationship of these discoveries to the existence or otherwise of a Northwest Passage remained uncertain.

By the mid-eighteenth century neither the British nor the French had found a way to the Pacific in northern latitudes. It was at this point that the dramatic intervention of two French scholars, Joseph Nicolas Delisle and Philippe Buache, reopened the whole question of the Northwest Passage just when it seemed to be fading. Delisle (the younger brother of the great Guillaume) had served more than twenty years in Russia as adviser to the Bering expeditions, and Buache was one of the foremost geographers of the age. In 1750 they presented to the French Academy of Sciences a memoir and a map in which they linked Bering's discoveries with the supposed voyage in 1640 of a Bartholomew de Fonte. The map showed northwestern America sliced by straits and rivers, where the landfalls of Bering's ships were interspersed with Fonte's discoveries. Farther south, the openings found by Fuca in 1592 and by Martin d'Aguilar in 1603 led into a gigantic Mer de l'Ouest stretching across much of today's western United States and Canada. The memoir and map brought together, in a mixture of the scholarly and the sensational, the individual strands of French speculation about the geography of western North America that had begun with Guillaume Delisle. The thesis split the world of French geographical scholarship, but it remained of considerable influence on the course of North American exploration. James Cook, who reached the northwest coast of America in 1778 in search of a Northwest Passage, was skeptical about the Delisle–Buache system of theoretical geography. Yet Cook himself was deceived by another speculative map, constructed by Jacob von Stählin of the Saint Petersburg Academy of Sciences, which showed Alaska as a giant island along whose eastern shores an ice-free passage might connect with Baffin Bay.

Searches for the straits of Fonte and Fuca continued until the last decade of the eighteenth century, and they created a widening gap between speculative cartographers and practical navigators. One of France's leading mapmakers, Robert Vaugondy, made the case for speculative cartography. He argued that, where precise information was lacking, it was quite legitimate to construct a map that showed the range of possible options for regions not yet properly explored. This type of map would serve as a guide to explorers. Few navigators accepted Vaugondy's attempt to legitimize speculative cartography. The navigators' views were more likely represented by Cook's indignant outburst against Stählin: "what could induce him to publish so erroneous a Map ... that the most illiterate of his illiterate Seafaring men would have been ashamed to put his name to?" There is no doubt that the charting of the difficult northwest coast of America in the later eighteenth century was encouraged by ever more ingenious maps suggesting that the Northwest Passage lay somewhere in that region, and yet this stimulus must be set against the conviction of many of the navigators involved that they had been sent on a wild-goose chase.

## The South Pacific

This same period also saw a new surge of exploration in the south Pacific, stimulated by maps that still showed a great southern continent. The Dutch explorations of the seventeenth century made cartographers rather more cautious as to how they represented the regions southeast of Indonesia. Abel Tasman's voyage of 1642–1643 removed all possibility that the land named New Holland by the Dutch might be part of the southern continent, and it pushed the supposed landmass back at least as far as the stretch of the New Zealand coastline that he had sighted. In general, the Dutch mapmakers showed what had been found rather than what had not been found, but other cartographers were less scrupulous. They explained the Dutch discoveries by insisting that there must be two southern continents: one that resulted from the joining of New Holland, New Guinea, Van Diemen's Land, and possibly Espiritu Santo, and another that stretched away east of New Zealand, perhaps almost as far as Cape Horn. In 1714 Guillaume Delisle produced a map of the Southern Hemisphere based on a polar projection that showed clearly the first of these continents; in 1755 Buache expanded Delisle's Australian outline still farther east, and he added

a second continent. This new continent had New Zealand as its western extremity, but it stretched much farther east than most geographers allowed, because Buache represented the sighting by Bouvet de Lozier in 1739 of the rocky islet of Cap de la Circoncision (Cape Circumcision) in the South Atlantic as part of a great continent. As the modern critic Numa Broc has put it, "We have the impression of seeing a new world recently emerged from the oceans." In England the geographer Alexander Dalrymple argued that the undiscovered southern continent extended through a hundred degrees of longitude, and that it was larger than "the whole civilized part of Asia, from Turkey to the eastern extremity of Japan."

The looming presence of the southern continent dominated the sailing instructions of the British and French Pacific explorers of the 1760s: Samuel Wallis, Philip Carteret, Louis Antoine de Bougainville, and Cook. The tracks of their vessels lopped slices off the supposed continent of Buache and Dalrymple, but it was left to Cook on his second voyage (1772–1775) to put the matter beyond doubt as he crossed and recrossed the Antarctic Circle. At his farthest south, he reached latitude seventy-one degrees south before being stopped by the ice barrier. This was not the fertile land of the speculative geographers but the frozen Antarctic. As Cook wrote in his journal, it was "a final end put to the searching after a Southern Continent, which has at times ingrossed the attention of some of the Maritime Powers for near two Centuries and the Geographers of all ages." Searching for the great southern continent on his first two voyages, and for the Northwest Passage on his third, Cook had found neither, but he had established the framework of the modern map of the Pacific, from New Zealand and the east coast of Australia in the south to the Hawaiian Islands and Bering Strait in the north.

## Legacy

There was still much left to do. The interior of Africa was still largely blank and the polar regions were still little known, but as far as the coastal outlines of the world were concerned further surveys would have more to do with settling detail than with making fundamental discoveries. It was with only a slight degree of exaggeration that one of Cook's officers claimed after the great navigator's death, "The Grand Bounds of the four Quarters of the Globe are known." In this achievement, this accumulation of knowledge, the speculative geographers earned little credit. Their role in stimulating interest in distant regions was ignored in the face of complaints about their uncritical approach, their lack of seagoing experience, and their misdirection of explorers. The navigators of the late eighteenth century—British, French, and Spanish—were agreed in their condemnation of the "closet navigators," the "speculative fabricators of geography." Dr. John Douglas, the editor of the journals of Cook's last two voyages, was representative of those who saw explorers and geographers as natural adversaries: "The fictions of speculative geographers in the Southern hemisphere, have been continents; in the Northern hemisphere, they have been seas." Cook, he concluded triumphantly, had annihilated both fictions. Such strictures underestimated both the importance of promotional geography in securing support for discovery voyages and the difficulties under which cartographers labored as they tried to make sense of the journals and charts brought back by the explorers. It was the common complaint of navigators that they were the victims of the geographers' speculative theories and maps. The geographers might equally retort that they were at the mercy of navigators and their inaccurate observations. Emphasis on disputes between explorers and geographers has obscured their dependence on each other. The relationship might be one of collaboration or antagonism, gratitude or criticism, but it did much to shape the course of exploration in Europe's age of discovery.

[*See also* Anian, Strait of; Buache, Philippe; Mercator, Gerardus; Northwest Passage; Ortelius, Abraham; Terra Australis Incognita; *and* Voyages, Apocryphal.]

### Bibliography

Broc, Numa. *La géographie des philosophes: Géographes et voyageurs français au XVIIIe siècle*. Paris: Ophrys, 1974.

Burden, Philip D. *The Mapping of North America: A List of Printed Maps 1511–1670*. Rickmansworth, U.K.: Raleigh Publications, 1996.

Frost, Alan, and Glyndwr Williams, eds. *Terra Australis to Australia*. Melbourne, Australia: Oxford University Press, 1988. See especially Frost and Williams's "*Terra Australis*: Theory and Speculation" (pp. 1–37), Helen Wallis's "Java la Grande: The Enigma of the Dieppe Maps" (pp. 38–82), and Günter Schilder's "New Holland: The Dutch Discoveries" (pp. 83–116).

Hayes, Derek. *Historical Atlas of the Pacific Northwest*. Seattle, Wash.: Sasquatch Books, 1999.

Lagarde, Lucie. "Le passage du nord-ouest et la Mer de l'Ouest dans la cartographie française du 18e siècle." *Imago Mundi* 41 (1989): 19–43.

Pedley, Mary S. *Bel et Utile: The Work of the Robert de Vaugondy Family of Mapmakers*. Tring, U.K.: Map Collector Publications, 1992.

Shirley, Rodney W. *The Mapping of the World: Early Printed World Maps 1472–1700*. London: New Holland, 1993.

Wagner, Henry Raup. *A Cartography of the Northwest Coast of America to the Year 1800*. Berkeley: University of California Press, 1937.

GLYNDWR WILLIAMS

**Caspian Sea**    Named after the ancient Caspii who lived on its southwestern shores, the Caspian is the world's largest inland body of water. Geographically it is a lake, but it is big and saline, hence the designation "sea." With an area of 386,400 square kilometers (149,200 square miles), the Caspian is one and half times larger than the Persian Gulf and about three-fifths the size of the North Sea. It is 1,200 kilometers (750 miles) long and on average 320 kilometers (200 miles) wide, with a mean water depth of 208 meters (680 feet). Its circumference is about 6,400 kilometers (4,000 miles), with about 1,900 kilometers (1,180 miles) of that in Kazakhstan, 1,600 kilometers (994 miles) in Turkmenistan, 900 kilometers in Iran, 800 kilometers (497 miles) in Azerbaijan, and 1,200 kilometers in the Russian Federation (Daghestan, Kalmukya, and Russia proper). Access to and from the Caspian is effected through Volga–Baltic Sea and Volga–Black Sea canal systems,

**Map of the Caspian Sea.** MAP BY MAPPING SPECIALISTS LIMITED

which are under Russian territorial sovereignty. Azerbaijan is the only Caspian country whose capital, Baku, is on the shore of the sea.

## Physical Features

The Caspian is 27 meters (90 feet) below sea level, but it has been subject to fluctuations that can produce drastic changes in the region. The land reclaimed and cultivated during the sea's recession from the 1930s was inundated in the 1990s, causing economic hardship to many of the ten million people who inhabit the Caspian littoral, six million of them on the Iranian littoral. The once three-islet Ashurada Islands in the southeastern corner of the Caspian were, as of 2005, fused completely with Iran's Miyankala Peninsula.

The sea's water volume of 79,000 cubic kilometers (18,953 cubic miles) is distributed unevenly among its three distinct sectors. The North Caspian, which extends to the 44th parallel, from Chechen Island to Mangyshlaq Peninsula, covers 77,700 square kilometers (30,000 square miles), accounting for 28 percent of the surface area of the sea but only one percent of the total water volume. With an average depth of 5 meters (16 feet), the deepest waters in the North Caspian occur toward the middle and south (20 to 25 meters, or 66 to 82 feet), while the coastal waters in the eastern part are on the average 2.5 meters (8 feet) deep.

Apsheron Peninsula and the underwater geological features that extend to the eastern Caspian constitute the southern limit of the Middle Caspian. This area consists of 53,000 square miles, accounting for 36 percent of the total surface area and 33 percent of the total water volume. It has an average depth of 176 meters (580 feet), and in the central area the depths reach 768 meters (2,500 feet). The South Caspian accounts for 36 percent of the sea's surface area and 66 percent of the total water volume. This area has an average depth of 330 meters (1,080 feet), with the maximum depth of 1,025 meters (3,363 feet) occurring closer to the Iranian coast.

The Middle and South Caspian are prone to earthquakes. The water circulation is affected most by the outflow of the Volga River, which forces the water southward along the western coast, creating a counterclockwise current in the North and Middle Caspian. Off Kazakhstan occurs another counterclockwise current. In the South Caspian, one current flows clockwise from the Apsheron Peninsula to the Aras River, and a second flows counterclockwise along the Iranian coast. The north and south winds can raise storms and waves as high as thirty feet, particularly off the Apsheron Peninsula.

The annual surface rainfall in the Caspian region is 20 centimeters (8 inches). The Volga alone accounts for 85 percent of the annual inflow (230 cubic kilometers [55 cubic miles]) from 150 rivers that empty into the sea. The overall annual evaporation rate is about one meter (40 inches). The average salinity of the sea is 12.8 parts per thousand (ppt), as compared to 37.5 ppt in the Persian Gulf or the Mediterranean Sea and 34 ppt in the North Sea. The lowest salinity is near the mouth of the Volga (1–2 ppt); the salinity in the northeastern part of the sea is 13.2 ppt.

The average air temperature in the summer is 77°F (25°C), with 111°F (43°C) registering on the eastern shores, while the water temperature is about 77°F (25°C), with the southern waters being slightly warmer. In the winter, the northern shores experience average air temperatures of 14°F (–10°C), while temperatures of –4°F (–20°C) are not uncommon. The winter temperature in the southern climes registers as low as 50°F (10°C). The northern Caspian freezes completely in the winter months, often requiring icebreakers for passage. The oil platforms installed in the shallow waters of the northern Caspian, often in waters 3–4 meters (10–13 feet) deep, require special shields to protect them from the ice. Ice floats that break away often drift as far south as the coast of Azerbaijan.

The Caspian's fifty islands, with a total area of 350 square kilometers (140 square miles), are in close proximity to the five noteworthy peninsulas: Agrakhan (Daghestan), Apsheron (Azerbaijan), Cheleken (Turkmenistan), Mangyshlaq (Kazakhstan), and Miyankala (Iran). Among the islands, Kulali is the largest. Situated off the Mangyshlaq Peninsula, this 32-kilometer (20-mile) exposed sandbar is home to a large number of Caspian seal (*Phoca Caspica*). In the northwest, off the Agrakhan Peninsula, are Chechen Island and the Chiterikh Bugorni Islands. In the south, Sara Island is off the Lankaran coast; the Duvani, Nargin, and Bula islands are off Baku; and Suhylan and Suyatu are off the eastern edge of Apsheron Peninsula.

## Hydrocarbon Resources

The Caspian region's oil and natural gas deposits are the third largest in the world, after those of Siberia and the Persian Gulf. Estimates of its reserves range from 30 to 200 billion barrels (bbls) of oil and upward of 200 trillion cubic feet (tcf) of natural gas. The offshore holds an estimated 17–33 bbls of proven oil reserves and potentially up to 200 tcf of natural gas, as compared to the Persian Gulf's 674 bbls of proven oil and 1,700 tcf of gas, or the North Sea's 17 bbls and 156 tcf.

The Kashgan field in the northeast Caspian is arguably the largest offshore oilfield in the world. Located 75 kilometers (47 miles) off Atyrau, Kazakhstan, it extends for some 65 kilometers (40 miles) into the sea and lies under waters that are just 3–4 meters (10–13 feet) deep. The field is estimated to hold potentially 40 billion barrels in place, but only 12–15 billion barrels may be recoverable. From Kashgan westward, there are three other oilfields of note: Kurmangazy, off the Russian-Kazakhstan land boundary, is being developed by Kazakhstan, while Russia is working the Tsentralnoye and Khvalynskaya fields.

The thirty or so offshore oilfields in the South Caspian stretch from Azerbaijan to Turkmenistan. The Gunshenli, Chirag, Azeri, and Kapaz fields are situated more or less in the middle of the sea and are being exploited by Azerbaijan under a regime that was established by the Soviet Union in the 1980s. After demise of the Soviet Union, Turkmenistan disputed Azerbaijan's hold on the fields, especially Kapaz, a part of which lies closer to the Turkmen coast. The dispute between Azerbaijan and Iran over the Araz/Alborz field escalated into open confrontation in July 2001.

The first offshore oil production in the Caspian began in 1945 at Neftkala, off the Apsheron Peninsula. Upon its exhaustion, Gunshenli came on stream and by 1991 accounted for 57 percent of Azerbaijan's total production, while Azerbaijan itself accounted for 70 percent of the Soviet Union's total production. More than any other Caspian country, Azerbaijan relies on its offshore oil production. More than 80 percent of its exploratory work for oil and gas is concentrated in the offshore areas, while two-thirds of its crude and 90 percent of its gas production come from offshore fields.

The Caspian offshore oil production is carried to land terminals either by pipeline or by tankers. Overland pipelines through Russia carry Kazakh and Azeri oil to the Black Sea and Turkmenistan gas to eastern Europe. The pipelines through Georgia and Turkey carry Azeri oil to the Black Sea and Mediterranean Sea, respectively. Planned pipelines will carry oil and gas from the eastern Caspian countries to China, and other pipelines through Iran and Afghanistan/Pakistan will provide an outlet for Kazakh and Turkmen oil and for Turkmen gas. Because of their vulnerability to earthquakes and other risks, the proposed underwater pipelines from Kazakhstan and Turkmenistan across to Baku have raised environmental concerns.

## Biodiversity and Environment

The Caspian has more than 500 plant and 850 animal species, which include some 260 species of land and aquatic birds, 33 species of mammals, and 130 species of fish. Among the fish, most noteworthy is the caviar-producing sturgeon; other fish are carp, herring, kilka, mullet, perch, pike, and sprat. The total annual catch of the five littoral countries is estimated at 400 thousand tons. The Caspian's sturgeon accounts for 70 percent of the world's sturgeon catch and 70 percent of the world's caviar production. Russian vessels from Astrakhan land more than 40 percent of the overall Caspian sturgeon catch.

Because of pollution, overfishing, and blockage to spawning grounds, the life expectancy of the sturgeon, which can live up to 100 years, has been cut to one-quarter of that, while the sturgeon stock has slumped by 90 percent since the 1980s. Still, an export of 58 tons of Iranian caviar in 2005 fetched $25 million in earnings. The price of $2,000 per kilogram ($900 per pound) provides ample incentive for illegal fishing. In an effort to restock, the Caspian countries since the 1990s have been releasing tens of millions of sturgeon fingerlings into the sea each year.

The Caspian seal is the Caspian's only marine mammal. Its annual population is 500,000 (as of 1998), with a total net birth rate of 50,000 against an annual harvest of 40,000 pups. The seal population suffered a severe blow in 1999–2000 when some 16,000 pups died off Azerbaijan and Kazakhstan because of weakened immune systems, arguably caused by oil and chemical pollution.

The transportation of alien aquatic species in ballast water and bilges of ships has increased with international traffic. In 1988 the zebra mollusk native to the Caspian appeared in the American Great Lakes and spread to Mississippi. Conversely, the noxious comb jellyfish (*Mneniopsis leidyi*) has found its way from the eastern seaboard of the United States to the Caspian, where it has no natural predator and competes with the kilka for the plankton. The comb jellyfish is blamed for the decline in the Caspian's kilka, sturgeon, and other fish populations in 1999–2003. In February 2004 the Caspian countries began to combat the jellyfish by releasing into the Caspian the specially bred *Beroe ovata*, another export from the United States, which feeds exclusively on comb jellyfish.

Every year, thousands of tons of petroleum-based pollutants enter the Caspian. Dangerous levels of other contaminants enter the sea from urban, industrial, and agricultural centers located around the sea. Radioactive waste reaches the Caspian from Azerbaijan, Russia, and Kazakhstan. Among the 140 rivers that contribute some level of pollution to the sea, the Volga is by far the biggest offender: in 1995 alone the Volga discharged 150 thousand metric tons of pollutants into the Caspian. In response, the five Caspian countries established in 1995 the Caspian Environment Programme. In 2000 the Cousteau Society declared the Caspian's condition to be critical but not catastrophic.

## Important Ports

Up until the demise of the Soviet Union, the Caspian carried one-half of Soviet Russia's trade with Astrakhan, Makhachkala, Baku, Fort Shevchenko (now Aqtau), and Krasnovodsk (now Turkmenbashy). Soviet timber, machinery, equipment, steel, and cement landed in Bandar Pahlavi (Iran) in exchange for foodstuffs, fresh fruits and vegetables, shoes, detergent, and consumer goods. In the post-Soviet era, in part because of the lure of the region's hydrocarbon deposits and in part because of multinationalization of the Caspian trade, a flurry of development projects ensure the expansion of ports and other facilities. The North-South International Transport Corridor, which stretches from Saint Petersburg in the north to the Persian Gulf, adds urgency to the expansion of port facilities along the western shore of the Caspian.

Three ports—Astrakhan, Oliya, and Makhachkala—handle nearly all of the Russian Federation's maritime trade on the Caspian. Astrakhan has been the most economically significant port on the Caspian littoral. It is located some 100 kilometers (60 miles) inland on the Volga. Fishing, agriculture, oil and petrochemicals, electricity generation, and shipbuilding are among Astrakhan's industries. A railroad system connects it in all directions, including to the Caucasus. In 2000 Russia began developing nearby Oliya into a seaport, complete with oil and cargo terminals. With an overall capacity of 8 million metric tons, the container terminal is designed to handle 270,000 metric tons. A ferry service will eventually link Oliya to all major Caspian ports. Makhachkala, in Daghestan, handles considerable trade with Iranian ports; in 2001 this trade reached 460,000 metric tons.

Baku has been the most important port on the Caspian because of three main factors: oil, deep anchorage, and Russian attention. Oil has been associated with Baku since antiquity. By 1901 it had hundreds of oil refineries, and its oil was shipped by railroad north to Russia. In 1867, Russia relocated its Caspian Flotilla there, and throughout the nineteenth century and until the 1910s the Russian-controlled Baku-based Kavkaz & Mercury Shipping Company monopolized marine transportation, in a navigation season that extended from spring to October.

Anzali (formerly Bandar Pahlavi) is Iran's chief port on the Caspian. Its rise in the nineteenth century was based on Russian trade, with ships from Baku and Astrakhan sailing to the inland emporium at Rasht, despite considerable risk and expense posed by bad weather and shallow approach. Anzali became a commercial and military port under Reza Shah Pahlavi (r. 1925–1941), and the Soviet-Iranian fisheries company had its offices there from 1927 to the 1950s. A naval academy is located at Anzali, which has been the base for Iran's navy since before World War II. More than 400,000 tons of trade passed annually through Bandar Pahlavi before the fall of the Soviet Union. As of 2004, Anzali covered 71.2 square kilometers (27.5 square miles) and was capable of handling oil and other cargo upward of 3 million metric tons; there are plans to increase that capacity to 6 million tons per year. Each of the ten berths has 5.5 meters of water and is capable of accommodating 5,000-ton ships.

Under an international trade practice known as "swap," shipments of Kazakh and Turkmen oil are landed at the Iranian ports of Nowshahr, Neka, and Khazar, and in return, Iran delivers to the international buyer of Kazakh and Turkmen oil the agreed equivalent at Persian Gulf ports. Khazar was established in 1997 and is located 51 kilometers (32 miles) north of Sari; it has 33 loading berths and handles five million metric tons of oil and other cargo, compared to its design capacity of ten million tons. Nowshahr's four cargo and one oil tanker berth handle one million metric tons of cargo and two million metric tons of oil.

Aqtau is Kazakhstan's major port on the Caspian. Formerly known as Fort Shevchenko, and as Aleksandrovsk before that, it was founded in 1846. Aqtau's industries include fishing and sealing, mineral extraction, water desalination, and oil. The port facilities were upgraded in 1999 with the goal of handling annually 7.5 million tons of oil and one million tons of freight, and a new ferry port opened in 2001. Kazakhstan's other important oil port on the Caspian is Atyrau (formerly Gur'ev). Once the region's fish processing center, Atyrau is also home to a part of the Kazakh coastguard and is the site of an expanding military base.

Turkmenbashy is Turkmenistan's principal port. Established in 1869, it was the western terminus of the Trans-Caspian Railroad; a branch line now connects it with Iran. The port was renovated in 2001 to include additional cargo terminals and a ferry port. More than four million tons of cargo were handled by the port in 2001, two-thirds of it oil and oil products. The port accounts for 83 percent of the country's fish catch; its other industries include mineral works, oil refining, food processing, fish canning, and metalworking. The expanding oil trade, particularly in the direction of Iran, has necessitated the development of an oil port at Okarem (Ekerem), which is halfway between Turkmenbashy and Iran. Other ports are Cheleken and Aladja.

## Maritime History

In the eighth century, the Khazars established a capital at Itil at the mouth of the Volga and presided over a commercial empire that stretched as far south as Darband in present-day Daghestan. The ports on the southeastern littoral exported fish and clothing to Itil, and in return the Khazars reexported a variety of goods and slaves from Russian and Bulgarian lands. As maritime trade flourished, plundering of vessels and ports was not far behind. Following a series of earlier raids in the ninth century, the Russian marauders sailed south in 912 and sacked Baku and then Absukun on the southeastern corner of the Caspian. In 965 the Russians from Kiev destroyed Itil and put an end to the Khazar power on the Caspian, their most notable legacy being the name Darya Khazar (Khazar Sea), by which the Iranians refer to the sea to this day.

Following the Mongol invasion in the thirteenth century, the Caspian trade underwent a revival as European merchants in particular sought silk and other products from Persia's Caspian provinces and central Asia. In 1396, however, Timur sacked Astrakhan and the Persian city of Sari, two of the sea's important emporia. In 1428 a Venetian pirate entered the service of the ruler of Darband and accosted the ships sailing out of the Persian province of Astarabad (Gorgan/Golestan). The attempt at thus turning Darband to a commercial port suffered when the decreasing sea level kept away the bigger trading ships.

In 1557, Astrakhan passed under Russian rule, though it was a long time before the port and Russia could project power. The port served a useful transit purpose, however: Russians and English merchants who had received permission to trade across Russia embarked at Astrakhan on passages to the eastern Caspian and to Persian ports. Attacks

on Astrakhan by the Ottoman Turks soon shifted the Persian and English trade to the southern Caspian. In 1613 a shipyard was established at Astrakhan, but Caspian shipping continued to remain in the hands of Muslim traders. In 1646, Baku's trade with Kalmukya, Russia, and central Asian ports consisted of salt, saffron, petroleum, silk, fur, and leather and was carried in a thousand ships. But trade from Baku to the Persian ports suffered at the hands of the Kalmuk and Cossack marauders: in 1636 they sacked Rasht, and in 1667 Stenka Razin's fleet sacked Darband and Rasht and proceeded further east along the Persian littoral and pillaged Farahabad. The 4,000-man Persian fleet that had been assembled for the challenge in 1669 was destroyed in an explosion. Upon returning north in 1670, Stenka Razin sacked Astrakhan, which prompted his arrest and hanging by the Russian government.

In order to prevent the Ottomans from gaining power in the Caspian, Peter the Great in December 1721 ordered the mobilization of a force at Astrakhan for a campaign against the Caucasus and Persia. For the purpose, a new shipyard was established at Astrakhan. When the ice thawed in May 1722, a fleet set sail for a point 112 kilometers (70 miles) north of Darband, carrying supplies for the land forces that were heading south. But Peter was forced to retreat to Astrakhan, and in November the Russian fleet of fourteen ships and two battalions recommenced the Persian campaign and occupied Anzali. In the ensuing treaty signed at Saint Petersburg on September 1, 1723, Peter promised to help the embattled Safavid dynast of Persia to gain his father's throne, and in return the Persian claimant ceded in perpetuity to Russia the cities of Darband and Baku, with all their dependencies the length of the Caspian Sea, as well as the Persian provinces of Gilan, Mazandaran, and Astarabad. The Russian ascendancy in the southern Caspian did not last long past Peter's death in 1725, and by 1735, Nader Shah (r. 1732–1747) succeeded in restoring Persia's former possessions in the Caspian littoral.

Nader Shah understood the value of his Caspian navy. In 1741 he had to rely on private Russian ships to ferry supplies for his campaign against Daghestan. By 1745 two Englishmen, formerly of the Russia Company, entered Nader's service and set up a shipyard near Rasht, surveyed the southern coast of the Caspian, and formed a fleet with the two Russian-built frigates that they had sailed from Kazan years earlier, four smaller ships, and four more ships that were made locally. Displeased with the English involvement, Russia banned all English trade across the Caspian in 1746. A year later, Nader was assassinated, and in 1751 the Russians torched the Persian ships and stores in Rasht-Anzali.

The destruction of Nader's navy relieved the Turkmen marauders of the eastern Caspian, whom Nader tried to check. From the area of present-day Turkmenbashy and Cheleken, Turkmen pirates had been active from the 1550s if not earlier. They plundered as far north as the mouth of the Ural in Russia and as far south and west as the Persian ports in Mazandaran and Gilan.

Under Catherine the Great (r. 1762–1796), Russia ventured again into the southern Caspian. In 1781 an expedition from Astrakhan reached Astarabad, surveyed the bay, and constructed a fort. Agha Mohammad Qajar (d. 1797), the local strongman and future king of Persia, sensed a creeping occupation of his coast and expelled the Russians. Alexander I (r. 1801–1825) fared better against his Persian contemporary Fathali Shah (r. 1797–1834), whom he defeated in a nine-year war. In the Golestan treaty (1813), Persia ceded to Russia its territories on the Caspian littoral from Darband to the Aras River. The treaty recognized Russia's customary right to maintain the only navy on the Caspian, but the commercial vessels of the two countries were accorded equal rights of navigation and cabotage. An identical arrangement was prescribed in the Turkmanchai treaty (1828), which concluded another round of Russo-Persian wars in 1826–1828. But this treaty proclaimed that only Russia could have a navy on the Caspian.

On the eastern shore of the Caspian, the Russian advance south was equally bellicose and was achieved at the expense of the Turkmen. In the 1830s, Turkmen boats raided and pillaged coastal communities with impunity, since the Persian governor of Astarabad had no navy and even less authority on land, while the Russian naval squadron stationed at Sara Island was too distant to help. So when the Persian government requested assistance against the Turkmen, Russia established in 1840 a naval base at Great Ashurada Island at the entrance to Astarabad Bay. The Russian presence subdued the Turkmen's maritime depredations, and the Ashurada Islands remained in Russian control until their turnover to Persia in 1921. As a result of Russian operations in central Asia, Russia and Persia in 1881 formally established their boundary east of the Caspian, beginning at a point on the Hassanqoli Bay south of the mouth of the Atrek River.

Born out of the political turmoil in Persia, in which Britain and Russia took sides, the Russian navy blockaded Anzali in 1909; a few months later, 2,000 troops were ferried from Baku to northern Persia, and by the outbreak of World War I all of northern Persia was under Russian military occupation and its fisheries were placed under Russian wartime administration. What remained of Persian navigation on the Caspian was regulated by the Russian admiralty in order to halt the shipment of contraband and weapons.

By March 1917, the Russian defenses in the Caucasus were crumbling and the British forces in western Persia and Mesopotamia sought to prevent an Ottoman advance. A British force led by Major General L. C. Dunsterville went from Baghdad to Anzali with the intention of sailing to Baku and reaching the Caucasus command center in Tbilisi. The mission was aborted because of anti-British sentiment in Rasht and Anzali and because of rumors of an impending arrival of Soviet troops from Baku. In July 1918, Dunsterville returned to Rasht-Anzali; a contingent of Gurkha cleared the town, while aerial bombardment kept the anti-British Jangali supporters at bay. In Anzali, Commodore T. C. Norris assembled a naval detachment under the British flag, and by August 19 the so-called Dunster force crossed to Baku in support of the anti-Soviet Russian forces. When the Russians retreated north for fear of the advancing Turks, Dunsterville was exposed; he lost 20 percent of his force and retreated to Anzali.

In September 1919, Norris established a base at Krasnovodsk on the Turkmen coast. With four armed merchant ships as well as a Russian fleet, Norris reoccupied Baku in November. Subsequently, the British captured a number of Soviet ships once belonging to Russia's Caspian fleet. In winter 1918–1919, Norris bolstered his position at Baku by arming additional ships and by acquiring motorboats and an air unit. When the ice thawed, a Soviet fleet of thirty ships sailed from Astrakhan to Fort Aleksandrovski. In May, Norris caught up with it and, with the help of air power, sank half the Soviet fleet. Flush with victory, he turned south and razed the site of the former Russian naval station at Great Ashurada. In August 1919 the British government handed over the Norris fleet to the anti-Soviet Russians.

In Baku, the pro-Soviet forces and an alliance of anti-Soviets kept battling it out for control of the town, while an indigenous nationalist movement sought to establish itself in former Russia's Azeri-speaking lands (Azerbaijan) with the help of the Turks. In May 1920 the Soviet army sacked Baku and put an end to Azeri nationalist aspirations. When a besieged anti-Soviet Russian admiral sought safe harbor in Persia's Anzali, the Soviet fleet sailed in hot pursuit and bombarded the port, while Soviet troops poured into Persia. The opportunist Jangali leader Mirza Kucheck Khan declared a Soviet republic of Persia in

Rasht in June 1920 and invited the assistance of the Soviet army in Baku to bolster his position against the central Persian government.

The February 1921 treaty of friendship between Soviet Russia and Persia did little to diminish the previous Russian domination of the Caspian Sea. The Soviets reserved the right to strike preemptively at Persia where the security of the Caspian Sea was at issue, and Persia promised to expel from its naval service any third-country national whose activities were inimical to Soviet interests in the Caspian. The parties further agreed that each should have the right of freedom of navigation under its own flag. Arguably, the treaty opened the door to Persia's acquiring a Caspian navy. After Soviet Russia refused to allow a Persian gunboat to proceed via the Volga to Anzali in 1924, Reza Shah Pahlavi ordered that a navy be assembled from local assets. A 70-ton decrepit ship belonging to a fishing concessionaire was armed with two guns and pressed into service in February 1925. A second boat was acquired from the same concessionaire, and in 1927 the 15-ton vessel began operations as a gunboat.

In 1927, Soviet Russia and Persia entered into a fisheries agreement by which the monopoly of fisheries in the southern Caspian was entrusted to a mixed Soviet-Persian company, which the Soviets dominated. The policing of the fisheries, however, was entrusted to Persia, so in 1928 Persia placed an order with the shipyard in Ancona, Italy, for three 60-ton vessels, each to be armed with 47-millimeter guns and heavy machine guns. Despite the creation of the Convention of Establishment, Commerce, and Navigation (the ECN Convention) in October 1931 between the two countries, the Soviets refused passage to the Persian vessels through the Volga. So, instead, the vessels were shipped in pieces to the Persian Gulf and transported to the Caspian coast, where they were assembled by a team of Italian technicians and were launched in 1933. Meanwhile, to show its hegemony at sea, in April 1933 a Russian squadron appeared off Astarabad and seized a number of Persian fishing boats and their crews.

The 1931 ECN Convention regulated the Soviet-Persian relations in the Caspian. It stated that only vessels belonging to the Soviet Union and Persia could be present anywhere in the entire Caspian Sea. To avoid third-party security risks, each country agreed to employ only its own nationals on board its Caspian vessels. As for fisheries, the convention established a ten-mile belt for exclusive fishing by the nationals of the abutting country. As for shipping, each country's nationals and its commercial and transportation companies were to navigate under their respective national flags. Each country's vessels were to be allowed to engage in cabotage, carrying cargo and passengers between the other country's ports. The convention also provided for the mutual recognition of certificates of capacity and tonnage and application of the international maritime sanitation convention (1929) to their Caspian shipping. The provisions of the 1931 convention were repeated in the 1935 ECN, and were again incorporated in the 1940 Soviet-Iranian treaty of commerce and navigation.

High levels of German and Axis activity in Iran pushed the Soviet and British governments to ignore Iran's declared neutrality. On August 25, 1941, the British occupied southern Iran and the Soviets attacked in the north. A Soviet destroyer along with its squadron of seaplanes arrived off Bandar Pahlavi; the planes, in groups of four, bombed the port and nearby villages. A second day of aerial bombardment resulted in the Iranian surrender, as Soviet land troops now poured into northern Iran. Except for the Shah's yacht, the Soviets seized all of Iran's ships in the Caspian; they were returned in 1946 when the Soviets finally evacuated Iran under pressure from the United States.

## Areas of National Jurisdiction until 1992

In the forty years that preceded the breakup of the Soviet Union there had been no doubt as to the limits of national Soviet and Iranian jurisdiction in the Caspian. In part established by conduct and custom and in part embodied in writing, the Soviet-Iranian maritime boundary was a line that connected the endpoints of the Soviet-Iranian land boundaries on the two sides of the Caspian.

Based on the 1954 Soviet-Iranian frontier agreement and the work of the demarcation commission that was codified in the 1957 Soviet-Iranian frontier agreement, the mouth of the Astara-Chay River served as the terminus of the land boundary on the west of the Caspian, and it was identified with marker 144 on maps. On the east of the Caspian, a point located 2.2 kilometers (1.4 miles) south of the first Soviet fisheries station on Hassanqoli Bay was identified as the spot where the Soviet-Iranian land boundary recommenced, and this was identified by marker 145.

The Astara-Hassanqoli line was consistent with the Soviet government's internal declaration in 1935 and the Iranian government's own assumptions. In the period before the fall of the Soviet Union, the two countries conducted themselves with that line in mind. Both in their bilateral relations, such as naval affairs and aviation, and also in purely domestic pursuits, such as the Soviet exploitation of offshore oil resources, the countries acted as if the line was the limit to their respective areas of national jurisdiction. Fishing, on the other hand, took place irrespective of the line, arguably because two-thirds of Iran's annual catch, especially of sturgeon, ended up in the Soviet Union. Having nationalized its Caspian fisheries in 1953, Iran established in 1963 a northern fisheries company, and by 1970 the company operated a deep-sea fishing fleet consisting of six Soviet-built ships.

In 1969, Iran added another cruiser to its Caspian fleet. This one, a former minesweeper, had been purchased from the United States in 1959 for service in Persian Gulf. On its redeployment to the Caspian, the Soviets permitted its passage through the Volga and hosted it several times when the ship visited Baku on naval visits or docked in Russian ports for repairs. In any event, when in the waters north of Astara, it was boarded by a Soviet pilot and shadowed by the Soviet navy. Other units in the Iranian navy in 1970 included two 65-ton and two 45-ton gunships and several boats and launches.

In 1970, the Soviet Union's ministry of oil and gas demarcated the Caspian into sectors for the purposes of oil exploration and exploitation. In January 1991 the Azerbaijan SSR Council of Ministers and the Soviet Union Ministry of Oil and Gas sanctioned Azerbaijan's activities in offshore fields as far as Kapaz in the middle of the Caspian. There is no evidence to suggest that Iran at any time objected to the conduct of the Soviet Union in the areas north of the Astara-Hassanqoli line.

## Shipping and Shipbuilding

The volume of annual maritime trade in the Caspian was estimated at 67 million metric tons in 2004. About 16 percent of this trade was handled by Iranian ports—exporting asbestos to Germany, tiles to Russia, and fresh fruits to Russia and Turkmenistan, and importing oil products, iron bars, chemical fertilizers, timber, and cement. With the design capacity to handle 50 percent of the Caspian trade, Iranian ships transported only 15 percent of it (in 2003/04, about 10–11 million tons). This asymmetry is explained in part by competition from other state-owned Caspian shipping lines and from foreign-based transportation companies. It is also explained in part by Iran's lack of an oil tanker fleet, since the bulk of the waterborne trade in the Caspian involves oil and oil products.

Khazar Shipping Company (KSCO), a state-owned enterprise that was established in 1992, controls Iran's shipping in the Caspian. Lacking the capacity to meet Iran's shipping needs with its own vessels, KSCO in 2001 hired a Russian transportation company to help with the annual shipment of 600,000 tons of metals, 100,000 tons of oil, and 500,000 tons of transit cargo between Iranian and non-Iranian ports on the Caspian.

To meet its need for oil tankers, Iran has turned inward to the state-owned Sadra Shipbuilding Company. The company's facilities at the Caspian Sea Complex Yard in the suburbs of Neka include a quay 250 meters (820 feet) long with a minimum of 4.5 meters (14.8 feet) of water. In operation since 1989, the yard has built for use on the Caspian multipurpose tugs, supply boats, and stern trawlers, and in January 2004 it launched a 48,000-ton oil tanker dedicated to the Kazakh oil trade. As of 2004 the yard had orders for three 60,000-ton tankers by the Iranian National Oil Company and three 63,000-ton oil tankers by KSCO. Six 60,000-ton oil tankers on order from Russia were scheduled for delivery to KSCO in 2005.

Oil trade is the mainstay of Azerbaijan State Caspian Shipping Company (CSC, or Caspar). In 2001, Caspar tankers delivered 6 million metric tons of oil and oil products from Kazakhstan and Turkmenistan to Baku's terminals for transshipment to the outside world. In the first half of 2004 the company transported 7 million tons of cargo, of which 70 percent was by tankers, 21 percent by ferries, and 9 percent by dry-cargo ships. Of this volume, 6.5 million tons were transported between Caspian ports, 3 million tons of it being oil products. More than 75 percent of Caspar's volume was among the former Soviet Union ports, with 1.4 million to and from Iran.

In 2000 Caspar's fleet consisted of a total of six working vessels, two in ill repair. By October 2004 Caspar's fleet of 367,800 deadweight tons (dwt) had grown to include 72 transport ships (37 oil tankers, 7 ferries, 28 dry cargo ships) and 11 subsidiary ships. The load capacity of its tankers being mostly 4,600 to 12,000 metric tons, Caspar's oil tanker fleet has sought to become economically viable by acquiring larger vessels, with modern loading and unloading technologies. In November 2004 the Russian-built 13,000-dwt tanker *President Heidar Aliev* was launched at Baku, and it is arguably the largest oil tanker of its kind in the Caspian. It measures 149.9 meters (491.8 feet) long, 17.3 meters (56.8 feet) wide, and 10.5 meters high, with a draft (laden with cargo) of 7.4 meters (24.3 feet). Two additional vessels of this class were scheduled for delivery in 2005 and 2006. The State Oil Company of Azerbaijan Republic (SOCAR) has its own fleet of vessels numbering some 300 in 2005, most of which at any given time being engaged in overseas traffic.

The Turkmen Shipping Company has a modest merchant fleet that is engaged primarily in the transportation of passengers and dry cargo to and from Baku and Astrakhan. It employs the vessels of Azerbaijan's Caspar tanker fleet, which in 2003 transported more than four million tons of Turkmen crude. Similarly underdeveloped has been the Kazakh National Maritime Shipping Company. Most of Kazakhstan's oil export, too, is carried in vessels belonging to other Caspian countries, or to international transportation and oil companies operating in Kazakhstan. In 2002 the Kazakh shipping company had on order a 12,000-dwt oil tanker at a shipyard in Finland.

Kazakhstan devotes considerable resources to ensure that the rigs and platforms engaged in exploration and extraction of offshore oil are serviced properly. The cold winters and the relative shallowness of the offshore areas require technological innovations. In September 2000, two Dutch-built icebreaking supply ships were delivered to Kazakhstan to serve the drilling platforms. Named *Arcticaborg* and *Antarcticaborg*, each 675-dtw ship has a maximum draft of 2.9 meters (9.5 feet) and is capable of cutting 0.6-meter (2-foot) ice when going stern first and 1.0-meter (3.3-foot) ice when going bow first. Each is equipped for dry cargo, pulverized goods, and liquid cargo, with twelve cabins on board and twenty berths.

The vessels belonging to the North Caspian Sea Shipping Company (Astrakhan) conduct the Russian shipping in the Caspian. The Volga Shipping Company (Volga Flot at Nizhniy Novgorod) and Volga Don Shipping Company (Rostov-on-Don) also have ties to the Caspian trade. In 2004, Russia announced plans to establish a tanker fleet at Daghestan for the purposes of conducting oil swap with Neka in Iran. The Daghestan shipping line itself was established in 1997, but it operates only a few vessels, one of which is called *Daghestan*.

Russian shipbuilding is an important feature of Caspian shipping. The country has one of the largest shipbuilding capabilities in the world, dwarfing the combined capabilities of the other Caspian countries. There are no fewer than a dozen shipyards in the Volga region alone, among which the plants at Nizhniy Novgorod and Krasny Barrikady have received orders from other Caspian countries.

Russians shipyards also build ships for the international companies doing business in the Caspian. For example, Krasnye Barrikady (Astrakhan) in February 2005 had three tankers under order for a company engaged in transporting oil products from Kazakh and Turkmen

ports to Baku. Each of the tankers is expected to carry 60,000 metric tons of six different types of oil and oil products. This fleet would lessen the current dependency on Azerbaijan's Caspar vessels by the same shipper. In 2004–2005 the Vyborg Shipyard in Saint Petersburg delivered two 12,000-dwt tankers to an international oil company working in Kazakhstan. International companies in the Caspian also meet their individual needs by acquiring vessels from one another. For example, in February 2005 a Scottish marine transportation company acquired from an American construction company in Kazakhstan a total of fifteen vessels, consisting of one supply boat, eight barges, and six utility craft. The acquiring company already had operated thirty-six vessels in Kazakhstan and fourteen in Azerbaijan.

Losses at sea and accidents should be expected from weathered vessels operating in tricky waters susceptible to sudden storms, in a region not known for maintenance. In October 2000, the Azerbaijan oil tanker and ferry *Mercury II*, which was built in Kaliningrad (Russia) in 1998, capsized and sank 80 kilometers (50 miles) off Baku en route from Aqtau with 2,000 metric tons of oil on board. In July 2001, *Vist*, a Russian cargo ship carrying metal and timber from Anzali to Astrakhan, began to take on water near Baku, and were it not for the rescue and towing efforts of Russian vessels in the area and of *Neftgas-8* and *Vikhr-10* belonging to Azerbaijan's oil fleet, the ship would have sunk. The Azerbaijan oil tanker *General Shikhlinski* met its doom in an explosion in Turkmenbashy in July 2002. In February 2004 the Iranian 3,690-dwt dry-cargo ship *Basir* sank twenty miles north of Aqtau.

## Caspian Navies in the Post-Soviet Era

Notwithstanding the declared wishes of the Caspian countries, the Caspian is far from being a demilitarized sea. The development of national navies has continued apace since 1992.

The Russian navy in the Caspian Sea is known as the Caspian Flotilla. It is not exactly a fleet in the manner of Russia's four fleets—Baltic, Northern, Pacific, and Black Sea. The flotilla is a part of Russia's Federal Border Guard Service within the Caucasus Military District. The Flotilla was established in Astrakhan in November 1722, and in 1867 its headquarters was moved to Baku. The Russian naval supremacy in the Caspian continued unabated into the twentieth century. The British presence in these waters near the end of World War I was a brief and curious interlude.

The Flotilla came into its own during World War II when the Caspian assumed a critical role for the defense of Russia and its oilfields in the Caucasus. Almost 88 percent of the 58 million tons of Caspian's waterborne traffic during the war consisted of oil. In 1942 alone a dozen ships ferried oil from Baku to Turkmenistan, and more than a thousand passages were made in that year by Soviet transports and barges. Moreover, the U.S. and British supplies destined for Russia's war effort were transshipped in part from Iran's Caspian ports. To disrupt Russian shipping, Germany laid mines in the northern Caspian near Astrakhan and managed to strike the Russian convoys in the Caspian, more than two hundred times in 1941 alone. To defend against all this, minesweepers were added to the Caspian Flotilla, as were patrol boats of every description and merchant ships that were converted into warships. One of the Russian warships was the *Lenin*, which was built in Saint Petersburg in 1908. Fueled by diesel, it was armed with multiple guns, cannons, and machine guns. It was modernized in the mid-1920s and again just before World War II, during which it defended the Baku-Astrakhan oil route. It was finally scrapped in 1959.

In 1976 the Soviet Union experimented with a prototype wing-in-ground (WIG) craft in the Caspian. Dubbed "monster of the Caspian Sea," it was clocked skimming on a cushion of air over the surface of the water at 550 kilometers/hour (340 miles/hour). A sea vessel capable of transporting 850 people, it failed to actualize even though for an environment like the Caspian it offered operational advantages over aircraft and ships. WIG's speed, cost, and cargo capacity may find a place yet in military planning involving rapid deployment or in civilian transportation.

On the eve of the dissolution of the Soviet Union, the Caspian Flotilla, exclusive of support ships, consisted of two destroyers, twelve frigates, and more than fifty other vessels. Russia offered to divide the fleet equally among itself, Azerbaijan, Kazakhstan, and Turkmenistan. While the last two declined, in 1992 the Azerbaijan coastguard received 25 percent of the fleet's vessels and personnel. On paper at least, Azerbaijan then had fifteen armed boats and warships, and fifty support vessels, of which ten were auxiliary ships. However, these were in less than ideal condition, since Russia had dismantled and removed from them the valuable equipment and armament. By 2000 the Azerbaijan navy consisted of a 2,200-man force with only four or five operational patrol ships.

Following the turnover of the Soviet admiralty installations to Azerbaijan in 1992, Russia moved its naval assets out of Baku and relocated the Caspian Flotilla's headquarters to Zaton near Astrakhan. By 2000, the 3,000-man Russian fleet in the Caspian grew to its largest size, consisting of two frigates, twelve patrol boats, eighteen minesweepers, twenty landing craft, and upward of three hundred other small craft. Among its new acquisitions, in 1997, was the *Don* patrol ship built at the Yaroslavl shipbuilding plant. Nevertheless, the average age of the Russian ships in 1992 was twenty-two years. In an ironic twist, when in January 2001 the Russian fleet staged a demonstration off Baku, one of its warships experienced mechanical difficulties and had to be towed into port and repaired by a crew of mechanics from Baku.

Headquartered at Aqtau, the Kazakh navy was established in August 1996 with a force of 200 men. Its fleet is a specimen of either studied diversification or random acquisition. The nucleus of the Kazakh navy in 1996 had been the five patrol boats from Russia, while two more were being laid down at the Kazakh shipyard in Uralsk. In 1996 the United States promised delivery of seven coastguard cutters, and later in October, Kazakhstan acquired four coastal defense craft from Germany. The two boats from Uralsk, along with a third, were put in service in 1998. By the end of 1998, the Kazakh navy had nine vessels, but by 2000 only five were operational. In July 2001, Turkey donated a patrol boat, and six more motorboats were delivered by Germany.

The 125-man Turkmenistan maritime patrol force was established at Turkmenbashy in 2000, consisting of one Point Jackson–class patrol boat from the United States. In 2001, Turkmenistan purchased twenty Grif (40-ton) and Kalkan-M patrol boats from the Ukraine.

Headquartered at Anzali, with an auxiliary base at Nowshahr, Iran's Caspian force consists of naval units and units belonging to the marine auxiliary of the Revolutionary Guards. In 1994, Iran had sixty combat patrol boats in the Caspian. Because of decades of economic and trade embargo by the United States, Iran learned to improvise in its maritime force deployment. Seagoing recreational motorboats were used in the Persian Gulf in the 1980s, and they now make up a significant part of the Iranian contingent in the Caspian.

The so-called Araz/Alborz Incident between Azerbaijan and Iran in July 2001 proved to be a watershed event in the militarization of the Caspian Sea, even though only months later it was completely overshadowed by the September 11 terrorist attacks in the United States. On July 23, Azerbaijan's exploratory vessels *Geofizik-3* and *Ali Gadzhiev* were in the vicinity of the Araz/Alborz oilfield southeast of Baku and 65 kilometers (40 miles) north of the Astara-Hassanqoli line, which Azerbaijan regarded as Iran's limit in the Caspian. An Iranian military plane buzzed the vessels, and an Iranian warship approached and demanded that the vessels retire five miles from the area. The Azeri vessels left.

For the next week the United States and Russia expressed concern over the proceedings, while Turkey flew several of its jet fighters over Baku as a sign of solidarity with Azerbaijan. What went unnoticed in the rush to criticize Iran's aggressive conduct were three Iranian diplomatic notes to Azerbaijan, dated June 26, 1998, August 18, 1998, and July 21, 2001. In each note Iran stated that activities in the Alborz area by Azerbaijan and its contractors would require Iranian permission, and that irresponsible actions by them would be met with consequences. Azerbaijan did not heed the warnings and plunged ahead regardless, precipitating the stern Iranian response.

The Araz/Alborz Incident highlighted three important aspects of the South Caspian's emerging geopolitics: (1) superiority of the Iranian military over the Azeri and Turkmen forces, (2) volatility of the area because of unresolved offshore claims, and (3) potential for a broader conflict pulling in countries from outside the region. The terrorist attacks on the United States drove home the notion that all the land and offshore oil installations were open and inviting targets to attacks. Russia took stock of its own vulnerability in the region at the hands of Chechen separatists in Chechnya, Daghestan, and Astrakhan.

In April 2002 the Russian president Vladimir Putin inspected the Russian fleet at Astrakhan and underscored the importance of the Russian navy to the security and stability of the Caspian region. At the meeting of the presidents of former Soviet republics in Aqtau in July, Russia proposed a large-scale military exercise for August. Iran offered to join the exercise by sending four warships. When Russia declined Iran's offer, Iran accused Russia of animosity toward it, and Russia agreed to allow Iran to send observers. Turkmenistan, however, boycotted the exercise altogether because it perceived Russia as siding with Azerbaijan over the disputed offshore fields. In August the exercise took place at Kaspisk in Daghestan, with the token participation of Kazakhstan and Azerbaijan: the Kazakh air force contributed an interceptor, and the Azerbaijan navy participated with one combat ship.

The Kaspisk maneuvers were all Russia: President Putin described the multiservice exercises as showcasing Russia's ability to thwart clandestine sea attacks by terrorists, interdict drug smuggling, and conduct search-and-rescue missions in event of disasters. Some 57 combat and supply ships, including amphibious hovercraft, 30 aircraft, and 10,000 servicemen, including 4,000 from the Caspian Flotilla, took part in the maneuvers.

From October 2001 through 2005, the Caspian navies grew apace. Sensing threats from the United States and Israel and wanting to defend its own coastal positions, Iran in 2002 staged in the Caspian a test of missiles launched from cargo ships. By year's end, Iran's 3,000-man Caspian navy counted fifty operational warships and support vessels, a marine corps, a coastguard, and naval aviation units. There were plans in 2002 to double the number of the force and fleet and to consider deploying one of its Russian-built Kilo submarines in the Caspian. While Anzali remains Iran's principal port on the Caspian, Nowshahr, Bandar Turkman, and a few other ports can be militarized at short notice.

The Russian Flotilla's 8,000-man force was distributed in 2004 among several patrol units, minesweepers, radar picket ships, combat and auxiliary craft of various classes, missile and landing hovercraft, and logistics ships. A naval aviation unit is attached to the fleet and has amphibious airplanes and patrol and antisubmarine helicopters. The Flotilla, an adjunct naval aviation unit, a marine brigade, and a hydrographic service together accounted for a force of 20,000 men. Two naval stations on Chechen and Tuleny islands keep watch over merchant shipping in the northern Caspian, and a military airfield has been built in Kaspisk. In April 2004, Russia conducted another naval drill in the Caspian.

By 2002 Turkmenistan had increased its coastguard and navy personnel to 2,000 men. Meanwhile, by the end of 2003 neighboring Kazakhstan had armed its 3,000-man navy with ten coastguard boats, two small hydrographic boats, and three Mi-8 and Mi-2 helicopters. In the same year the United States committed substantial funding for the development of a military base at Atyrau. It was the informed opinion of U.S. Secretary of Defense Donald Rumsfeld that Kazakhstan required assistance in order to protect its oilfields, in whose development U.S. companies were likely to invest nearly $12 billion by 2008. Similarly, in January 2004 the United States initiated a joint military exercise in the Caspian designed to train the Azerbaijan naval fleet to protect its oil platforms.

The size of a fleet is important, but size is not everything. In the event of armed conflict involving the Caspian countries, air power and long-range coastal artillery, missiles and rockets, and ground forces all will contribute to the outcome. Under present conditions and in the foreseeable future, the Russian military, by virtue of its size and capabilities, is unmatched in the Caspian region.

## Seabed Delimitations: 1992–2004

It is often said that the foremost issue confronting the Caspian Sea is the absence of agreement among the littoral countries as to the legal status and delimitation of the seabed. This is an overstatement, as billions of dollars have been committed to the development of offshore oil and gas deposits, while air and water transportation are routine and fishing continues unabated. Risks associated with rival claims over offshore fields—as in the case of Azerbaijan with Iran and Turkmenistan—are a minor consideration as multinational oil companies assess and internalize the risk before making investments. While it is desirable to resolve areas of potential dispute in the South Caspian, it is not an urgent necessity until other offshore or onshore fields that are not in dispute are exhausted.

Nor is the legal status of the Caspian Sea critical. Much has been made of the Caspian being either a sea or a lake, as if one or the other designation would produce an automatic, immediate, and binding division of the water, seabed, and resources of the subsoil. The only agreements capable of such a result were the 1958 Geneva convention on the law of the seas and its successor, the 1982 United Nations convention of the law of the seas. However, neither agreement could apply automatically to the Caspian because the Caspian did not fit the definition of a sea, as it should not, for it is a lake. In 1955, Iranian domestic legislation specifically exempted the Caspian from the jurisdiction of the emerging international agreement on the continental shelf. Neither Iran nor the Soviet Union regarded the Caspian as subject to either the 1958 or the 1982 convention. Nor as an international lake could the Caspian be subject to a division on the basis of a preordained formula. The delimitation of areas of national jurisdiction or sovereignty in the Caspian were, as in the case of other international lakes, a product of imposition or freely negotiated agreement. Prior to 1992, the Astara-Hassanqoli line was all that sufficed for the only two nations bordering the Caspian.

In October 1994 the Russian Federation laid out its position regarding the legal status of the Caspian Sea in a memorandum to the United Nations. The memorandum provided for the exploitation of the Caspian's fisheries and hydrocarbon resources on the basis of concerted action by the littoral countries, refuting the notion of unilateral approaches. Based on the 1921 and 1940 treaties with Iran, Russia took the view that the Caspian was subject to joint usage and that therefore any decision about the future exploitation of its resources must be decided jointly by all the countries bordering its coast. The Russian memorandum went so far as to threaten consequences for any unilateral action in respect to the Caspian Sea.

The emphatic Russian position did little to reverse the actions already taken by Azerbaijan and Turkmenistan. In 1992, Turkmenistan had passed legislation establishing a twelve-mile national zone, akin to a territorial sea. Azerbaijan had gone one better when its 1995 constitution defined the country's territorial sovereignty to include the Caspian Sea (Lake) sector relating to the Azerbaijan Republic. Nevertheless, the joint Russian-Iranian statement of October 1995 reiterated the notion that until rules were worked out for the exploitation of the sea's mineral resources, no coastal state was to undertake actions leading to a division of the Caspian Sea without the agreement of all the other coastal countries.

Naturally, for a country like Russia or Iran that had not as yet discovered oil in the offshore areas adjacent to its coast, a joint exploitation or ownership agreement offered the best theoretical framework to get a piece of the resources that were shown to be in abundance in areas adjacent to Azerbaijan and Kazakhstan. In September 1996, Azerbaijan and Kazakhstan issued a joint statement in which they called for the division of the Caspian Sea into national sectors in accordance with the general principles of international law, conventional and customary, in accordance with judicial decisions, and in accordance with other factors that governed the delimitation of offshore boundaries.

In February 1997, Kazakhstan and Turkmenistan became the first to produce one of the seven bilateral delimitation agreements possible in the Caspian, if the sea were divided under the rules of the U.N. convention on the law of the sea, to which neither country had subscribed. Until such time as the Caspian countries could agree on the status of the sea, the parties stated, their boundary in the Caspian would be a line every point of which was equidistant from the opposite shores—that is, a median line running along the middle of the sea.

In August 1997, Russia invited tenders for exploration of its offshore, a section of which encroached on what Kazakhstan was considering a part of its offshore. Kazakhstan brought the matter to the attention of the United Nations: recognizing the need of the Caspian countries to take practical steps to explore and exploit their offshore resources, the Kazakh statement made it clear that the Russian tender for areas on the Kazakh side of the median line violated its territorial sovereignty. But the statement left the door open to joint exploitation of resources straddling the line.

In February 1998, Russia and Kazakhstan reached an agreement on the delimitation of the offshore on the basis of the median line, as modified here and there to reflect the parties' special understanding. In March, Russia and Azerbaijan announced that they supported the division of the Caspian seabed into five national sectors. In April another Russian-Azerbaijan statement provided for the delimitation of their offshore boundary in reference to the median-line principle.

In July 1998, Russia and Kazakhstan produced a comprehensive set of bilateral undertakings about their future relations. The statement on eternal friendship and alliance made in Moscow on July 6, 1998, contained various military, economic, trade, transportation, and other considerations. The agreement on the delimitation of the seabed of the northern part of the Caspian Sea for the purposes of exercising sovereign rights to the exploitation of its subsoil, also made in Moscow on July 6, 1998, codified the median line as the basis for delimitation of offshore areas, unless the parties agreed to a deviation or adjustment based on impartial considerations. The Russian-Kazakh delimitation agreement applied the principles enshrined in the delimitation provisions of the 1958 and 1982 conventions on the law of the sea. Accordingly, the agreement left unaffected the basic freedoms associated with the high seas: navigation, overflight, fisheries in open areas, and the use of the seabed for laying down cables and pipelines.

With the Russian-Kazakh agreement, Russia's offshore areas in the Caspian were settled. This left Iran as the main remaining proponent of joint exploitation of the sea's resources, even though at times Turkmenistan's ambiguous position had added impetus to the puttering Russian-Iranian position about a condominium (joint ownership) agreement. Two days after the signing of the Russian-Kazakh agreement, the Iranian and Turkmen presidents meeting in Tehran issued a joint statement reaffirming their belief in the condominium approach, but left the door open to the notion that if the Caspian seabed were to be divided into national sectors, then each littoral country should receive an equal share (20 percent) of the seabed.

In December 1998, Iran joined the other Caspian countries in actively seeking exploration of its own offshore area. A few days before the signing of a prospecting agreement with an international oil company, Azerbaijan issued a statement objecting to the proposed activities and rejected Iran's claim to 20 percent of the seabed as inconsistent with Iran's maritime limits delineated by the Astara-Hassanqoli line from the Soviet era. Regardless, in the next year Iran hired the services of a few prospecting companies to look for oil in the areas that were claimed also by Azerbaijan. Born out of the necessity to avert open and armed hostilities in the South Caspian, in August 1999 Azerbaijan and Iran signed a cooperation deal on oil exploitation. Regardless, tensions over the exploration of the Araz/Alborz area degenerated in July 2001 into open confrontation.

In November 2001, Kazakhstan moved to conclude with Azerbaijan the last of its bilateral agreements on the delimitation of the Caspian seabed. This agreement, too, provided primarily for a median line that may be adjusted or modified in part in order to accommodate special circumstances.

Three issues precluded the states of the South Caspian—Azerbaijan, Iran, and Turkmenistan—from concluding bilateral delimitation agreements among themselves. First, in the early days of the post-Soviet era, a ministerial meeting of the Caspian countries in Ashghabat, Turkmenistan, on November 12, 1996, had called for unanimity in defining the legal status of the Caspian Sea. Iran maintained consistently that the several delimitation agreements among the coastal states violated the unanimity principle. Second, overlapping claims by Azerbaijan and Iran as to areas in the southwest Caspian proved difficult to resolve because Azerbaijan believed that the seabed north of the Astara-Hassanqoli line belonged to Azerbaijan's sector of the Caspian, while Iran insisted that it was entitled to a slice of the area north of the line to bring its share up to 20 percent of the seabed. Third, the overlapping claims by Azerbaijan and Turkmenistan as to areas in the middle of the sea proved difficult to resolve because Azerbaijan believed that its rights to the fields were decided in Soviet times, while Turkmenistan believed that Azerbaijan's customary rights should yield to the new emerging order and that the seabed east of the median line should belong to Turkmenistan regardless of Azerbaijan's vested interests.

Any nation's ultimately garnering 20 percent of the Caspian Sea is a matter of principle and politics. Oil, on the other hand, is about money, and as such, proper compensatory schemes may be found to produce mutually agreeable solutions to the standoff in the South Caspian. Compensatory solutions have been discussed at times whereby Turkmenistan would yield a part of its offshore claims in favor of Iran and receive in return from Kazakhstan the difference from Kazakhstan's offshore areas. Azerbaijan rejects any compensatory plan involving what it claims is its sector in the Caspian.

Direct negotiations between Azerbaijan and Turkmenistan in 1999–2001 about the status of the mid-Caspian oilfields bore no fruit. Nor did the good offices of the United States make a difference in the standoff. In March 2003 the situation in the South Caspian developed yet another wrinkle when Iran and Turkmenistan announced an ambiguous plan for each to set up an exclusive national zone off its coast and divide their offshore area on the basis of a line extending northwestward out into the sea from where their land boundaries reached the Caspian. The fields straddling the line would have been subject to joint exploitation. By 2004, however, no concrete agreement had emerged between the two countries.

Amid attempts at bilateral delimitation of the neighborhood's seabed, the Caspian countries have been at work to produce a comprehensive convention on the legal status of the sea. The meeting of the heads of Caspian states in Ashghabat in April 2002, however, failed to produce the much-anticipated agreement. By October 2004 the Caspian countries had agreed fully on eight of the thirty-three articles of the draft convention, with partial understanding on the preamble and eight other provisions.

## Future Trends

The most pressing issue facing the Caspian region is environmental degradation. The Caspian's health is bleak, and given the current rates of pollution the Caspian is likely to meet the same fate as the once moribund Aral Sea. The autocratic regimes that govern the Caspian countries have done little to abate land-based and waterborne pollution. Ironically, in the oil and gas sector, one of the factors that prevents further degradation of the environment in the South Caspian is the international tension that discourages investment in the disputed offshore fields. There is no effective national grassroots movement in any Caspian country to demand the democratization of the planning and decision-making processes that impact the ecology.

The autocratic rule and cults of personality that rule Azerbaijan, Kazakhstan, and Turkmenistan pose a greater danger than any external threat does to the long-term stability of the Caspian region. Foreign domination of oil and gas, and corruption and disparities in wealth offer the makings of internal strife. The Iranian political upheavals in 1951–1953, 1962, and 1979 show how unavoidable clashes are between an elite coddled by foreign interest

and a combination of nationalist and egalitarian yearning for change. And the Russian-Iranian entente in the Caspian will continue to frustrate the efforts by the United States and Turkey to stitch the eastern wing of NATO to Azerbaijan and central Asia.

[*See also* Navies, Great Powers, *subentry on* Russia and Soviet Union, 1700 to the Present; Naval Dockyards and Bases; *and* Oil and Petroleum Products.]

## Bibliography

Amirahmadi, Hooshang, ed. *The Caspian Region at a Crossroad: Challenges of a New Frontier of Energy and Development.* New York: St. Martin's Press, 2000.

Ascher, William, and Natalia Mirovitskaya, eds. *The Caspian Sea: A Quest for Environmental Security.* Dordrecht, Netherlands: Kluwer Academic, 2000. The proceedings of the NATO Advanced Research Workshop on the Caspian Sea, held in Venice, Italy, on March 15–19, 1999.

Caspian Sea Environment. "Caspian Environment Programme." http://www.caspianenvironment.org. An intergovernmental program maintains this Web site, which features the program's various studies and public documents.

Cousteau Society. *The Caspian–Expedition Report on Treasures of the Caspian Sea, October 1998: Summary.* Paris: The Cousteau Society, 2000. Sponsored by the United Nations Educational Scientific and Cultural Organization, this is a groundbreaking review of the Caspian's environmental woes.

Cullen, Robert. "The Rise and Fall of the Caspian Sea." *National Geographic*, May 1999, pp. 2–35.

Dekmejian, R. Hrair, and Hovann H. Simonian. *Troubled Waters: The Geopolitics of the Caspian Region.* London: Tauris, 2001.

De Planhol, Xavier. "Caspian." In *Encyclopædia Iranica*, edited by Ehsan Yarshater. London and Boston: Routledge and Kegan Paul, 1982– .

Kalyuzhnova, Yelena, Amy Myers Jaffe, Dov Lynch, et al., eds. *Energy in the Caspian Region: Present and Future.* New York: Palgrave, 2002.

Mirfendereski, Guive. "Caspian Quartet: Four-Part Essay on the Environmental Demise of the Caspian Sea." http://www.iranian.com/GuiveMirfendereski/2002/May/Caspian/1.html. An easy read on the ecology of the Caspian and the danger posed by earthquakes and shipwrecks.

Mirfendereski, Guive. *A Diplomatic History of the Caspian Sea: Treaties, Diaries, and Other Stories.* New York: Palgrave, 2001. The general history of the Caspian Sea from the 1720s through 2000.

O'Lear, Shannon. "Resources and Conflict in the Caspian Sea." *Geopolitics* 9, no. 1 (Spring 2004): 161–186. Provides an analysis that lacks the usual nationalistic rancor and mercenary advocacy associated with studies about the Caspian.

Shaw, B., T. Paluszkiewicz, S. Thomas, et al. *Environmental Baseline Analysis of the Caspian Sea Region.* Richland, Wash.: Pacific Northwest National Laboratory, 1998. Prepared under contract for the U.S. Department of Energy, this is a very useful and by far the best study of the Caspian environment.

GUIVE MIRFENDERESKI

# Castex, Raoul (1878–1968), French vice admiral and strategic theorist. Admiral Raoul Victor Patrice Castex, born on October 27, 1878, at Saint Omer, the son of an army officer, may be the greatest forgotten writer about strategy of the twentieth century. His eighteen published books and fifty-odd journal articles certainly made him one of the most prolific writers about strategy, and his five-volume *Théories stratégiques* (1929–1935) is a remarkable effort to create universally applicable strategic theory.

The top graduate of the École Navale in 1896, Castex was commissioned into a navy that was split between supporters of a Mahanian battleship fleet designed to contest "command of the sea" and the heirs of the late nineteenth-century Jeune École movement, which argued that torpedo boats and submarines offered a more cost-effective, technologically modern approach to naval strategy than battleships did. As early as 1913, with the publication of *Le grand état-major naval*, Castex took his stand on the Mahanian side, but with an important nuance. A historian himself, Castex approved of Alfred Thayer Mahan's method of deriving lessons from history, but he recast Mahan's conclusions to give them broader utility.

Taken literally, Mahan's insistence on the acquisition of a massive battleship fleet to secure complete "command of the sea" could lead only to despair in countries unsuited to naval predominance. In his magnum opus, *Théories stratégiques*, Castex attempted to make Mahan's ideas useful to countries like France, whose geographical situations militated against a single-minded focus on sea power. For most countries, Castex argued, naval considerations could be only one element of a broader national strategy that he christened *stratégie générale* and that one in English today would call a "grand strategy." Under *stratégie générale* fell military and naval strategy, which were themselves part of a interlocking triad of policy, strategy, and tactics. After *stratégie générale*, Castex's second lasting contribution to strategic theory was the notion of strategic *manoeuvre*, a word best left in the original French to emphasize its complex content. In modern English usage, "maneuver" tends to be combinations of fire and movement; to Castex, strategic *manoeuvre* was a complex scheme of operations allowing a second-rate navy to achieve local superiorities over a superior competitor. It is with the concept of

strategic *manoeuvre* that Castex diverges from Mahan. Castex believed that historical analysis affirmed the importance not only of the fleet but of *manoeuvre* as well, and among the tools of *manoeuvre* were weapons like the submarine, which had no place in Mahan's scheme.

The high point of Castex's naval career was his appointment in 1936 as the first director of France's new College des Hautes Études de la Défence Nationale. Effectively, his job was to teach *stratégie générale* to military officers and civilian administrators chosen to organize France's nation-in-arms. Castex might have had the opportunity to disseminate his idea to an entire generation of French leaders, but the outbreak of World War II halted the work of the college and also halted the director's military career.

In 1937, Castex was one of two potential candidates to become chief of staff of the French navy. He missed the appointment because of his outspoken opinions, his overly academic career path, and the superior political connections of the successful candidate, Admiral Jean Darlan. The enmity between the two men contributed to Castex's involuntary medical discharge from the navy in November 1939.

The concluding ideas of *Théories stratégique* were the theory of "perturbation"—the idea that one European power would always attempt to dominate the Continent—and the idea of an eternal struggle between Asia and the West. Castex argued that sea power had provided the best means of resistance against both expansionist European states and the threat of the East. After World War II, Castex continued to write, warning of the threat from the Soviet "perturbator" and reminding his countrymen of the centrality of naval power in the defense of the West.

Castex's writings have received little attention since his death on January 10, 1968, at Villeneuve de Rivière, but such Castexian ideas as the importance of grand strategy, the role of *manoeuvre* in warfare, and the notion of inexorable conflicts between civilizations are intrinsic to contemporary discourse.

[*See also* Mahan, Alfred Thayer; Strategy; *and* Tactics.]

## Bibliography

Castex, Raoul. *Strategic Theories*. Translated and edited by Eugenia C. Kiesling. Annapolis, Md.: Naval Institute Press, 1994. The only example of Castex's work available in English, this abridged version of the *Théories stratégiques* has an introductory essay and a list of Castex's major publications.

Coutau-Begarie, Hervé. *Castex: Le stratège inconnu*. Paris: Economica, 1985. The only biography of Castex; includes a useful list of the admiral's publications.

Coutau-Begarie, Hervé. *La puissance maritime: Castex and la stratégie navale*. Paris: Fayard, 1985. The most complete exegesis of Castex's thought, emphasizing naval issues rather than grand strategy; includes a comprehensive bibliography.

EUGENIA C. KIESLING

# Chain and Cable. *See* Ship's Equipment.

# *Challenger*, oceanographic research vessel.

Length/beam: 68.9 m x 12.3 m. (226′ x 40.6′). Displacement: 2,306 tons. Hull: Wood. Complement: Approximately 300, plus 6 scientific staff. Built: Woolwich Dockyard, England, 1858. Refitted for scientific work: Sheerness Dockyard, England, 1872.

Originally rated as a twenty-two-gun steam corvette, *Challenger* was selected for duty as a research ship by the British Admiralty in May 1872, and under the supervision of Admiral George Richards, the hydrographer of the navy, and her new commanding officer, Captain George S. Nares, was extensively refitted for a voyage of oceanographic exploration. In preparation for the expedition all but two of the ship's guns were removed in order to accommodate specially fitted laboratories, workrooms, and storage spaces. In addition to the 1,234-horsepower auxiliary-propulsion engine, a small 18-horsepower donkey engine was fitted to assist with deep-sea dredging operations.

The significance of this relatively minor warship is tied directly to her four-year oceanographic expedition conducted between December 1872 and May 1876. While survey and scientific expeditions had been routinely undertaken by the Royal Navy for well over a century, the *Challenger* expedition and the resultant scientific report are credited as the genesis of the science now recognized as oceanography. At the instigation of the prestigious Royal Society, the British Admiralty agreed to fund and equip the project as a logical follow-on to the more modest scientific cruises of HM ships *Lightning*, *Porcupine*, and *Shearwater*. The preliminary results of these earlier scientific voyages pointed up the need for a much more extensive expedition specifically designed to examine all aspects of the biological, chemical, and physical nature of the world's great oceans. This was no small undertaking. While a considerable amount of scientific information had previously been collected, no prior expedition had been undertaken with such an all-encompassing charter or scope of scientific interest.

Captain Nares was a skilled seaman and navigator, who by the time of his appointment to *Challenger* had amassed noteworthy hydrographic and oceanographic experience while commanding officer of *Shearwater*. The expedition's senior scientist was equally well qualified for his duties. Selected by the Royal Society, the noted naturalist C. Wyville Thomson had made a name for himself by participating in the *Lightning* and *Porcupine* expeditions and publishing the scientific findings. Under the expert guidance of Nares and Thomson, nautical survey and scientific equipment was selected and carefully fitted in *Challenger*.

*Challenger*'s voyage of exploration would include a circumnavigation of the globe and encompass all of the world's ocean basins; the scientific results of which were so extensive that they would take over fifteen years to assemble and publish. The work of supervising this massive project fell to John Murray, a subordinate of Thomson's during the voyage, who assumed responsibility after Thomson's death. In due course, fifty large folio volumes were published between 1880 and 1895, accounting for over thirty thousand pages of text and illustrations. Although the voyage results failed to explain fully the nature of ocean circulation, they opened up an entirely new field for the study of deep-sea deposits and established the existence of life in the deep sea and the uniformity of deep-sea fauna. The marine collections of the voyage were deposited at Edinburgh University and the terrestrial collections at the British Museum. *Challenger* was laid up in 1880 and was subsequently sold as a hulk in 1921.

[*See also* Expeditions, Scientific.]

## Bibliography

Deacon, Margaret. *Scientists and the Sea, 1650–1900: A Study of Marine Science*. 2d ed. Aldershot, U.K.: Ashgate, 1997. Provides an accessible synopsis of the expedition and the work of the notable scientists embarked.

Great Britain, Challenger Office, prepared under the superintendence of Sir C. Wyville Thomson, and John Murray, eds. *Report on the Scientific Results of the Voyage of HMS* Challenger *during the years 1873–1876*. 50 vols. London: HMSO, 1880–1895. The first two volumes of the official expedition report provide exceptionally detailed descriptions of every aspect of the ship and the scientific equipment, and a narrative of the four-year voyage. The most thorough account of the ship and expedition available.

Linklater, Eric. *The Voyage of the* Challenger. Garden City, N.Y.: Doubleday, 1972. A popular account of the *Challenger* expedition, with drawings and etchings from the official report.

Rice, A. L. *British Oceanographic Vessels, 1800–1950*. London: Ray Society, 1986. Contains a concise yet thorough description of the ship, the officers and scientific staff, and an especially readable account of the expedition.

ROBERT E. MCCABE

# Chambers, George

**Chambers, George** (1803–1840), British marine painter. Chambers was born in Whitby, Yorkshire, to Mary, the wife of John Chambers, a mariner. The family was poor, and George started work at the age of eight and went to sea two years later, sailing to the Baltic and the Mediterranean. Chambers was very small, and he was often the butt of the crew's cruel jokes. But this led him to turn his attention to painting and decorating, and to making drawings for his shipmates. With his talent as an artist developing, Chambers canceled his indentures at the age of eighteen and became a house painter and decorator in Whitby. In his spare time he practiced drawing, copying from a primer borrowed overnight by a friendly bookshop assistant and returned each morning.

Without formal training, but driven by his determination to succeed as an artist, Chambers moved to London in 1825. There, Christopher Crawford, a publican at Wapping, befriended him, employing Chambers to embellish the premises and helping him to obtain commissions from sea captains for ship's portraits. Wider recognition came in 1827 when the British Institute accepted Chambers's *View of Whitby*. Chambers married that same year, much against Crawford's wishes. Chambers was then engaged to help paint a panorama of London in the Colosseum in Regent's Park, but the enterprise failed and Chambers was left unpaid. He had, however, exhibited at the Royal Academy in 1828 and was able to obtain an increasing number of commissions from influential clients. One of these clients liked a painting that he had seen in a shop window so much that he traced the artist to his lodgings, even though the unscrupulous dealer had painted out Chambers's signature.

After a year as a scenery painter at the Royal Pavilion Theatre in Whitechapel, Chambers attracted the patronage of Lord Mark Kerr, who ordered a series of paintings and otherwise encouraged Chambers, helping him overcome

**Merchantmen and Other Shipping in the English Channel.** George Chambers was the son of a seaman and served as an apprentice at sea before taking up his artistic career. © ANN RONAN PICTURE LIBRARY / HIP / ART RESOURCE, NY

his shyness. In September 1831, Kerr obtained for Chambers an audience of the King and Queen at Windsor, and they each purchased two paintings, one of which recorded the king's recent opening of the new London Bridge. Three of the paintings still remain in the royal collection.

Chambers traveled widely in England, and he particularly enjoyed sketching on the Thames and the Medway. In so doing he displayed real talent as a watercolorist. He first exhibited at the Old Watercolour Society in 1834 and immediately received the accolade of election to full membership. One of the few marine artists working in the medium, Chambers became part of the mainstream of the distinguished British watercolor tradition, bringing to it his deeply felt romantic response to nature without compromising his commitment to nautical fidelity. The large oil painting *The Bombardment of Algiers*, however, which was commissioned by Greenwich Hospital for Naval Pensioners in 1836 and for which he received 200 guineas, is widely regarded as Chambers's greatest achievement.

Two tours in Holland gave Chambers's art a new impetus. But, never strong physically, he found his health in decline. Despite a voyage to Madeira in 1840, Chambers died at his home in Percy Street, London, later in the year. He was survived by his wife, two sons—one of whom followed his father as an artist—and a daughter. Though shy by temperament, Chambers was convivial and relaxed among friends and other artists, and he was particularly generous and helpful to struggling young painters.

[*See also* Artists, *subentry* British; *and* Portraits, *subentry on* Ships.]

### Bibliography

Russett, Alan. *George Chambers, 1803–1840: His Life and Work.* Woodbridge, U.K.: Antique Collectors' Club, 1996.
Watkins, John. *Life and Career of George Chambers.* London, 1841.

ALAN RUSSETT

# Chancellor, John (1925–1984), English marine painter. As a schoolboy, Chancellor won several Royal Drawing Society Medals, but, determined to go to sea, he spent the war years from 1942 as an apprentice officer in the merchant navy.

Despite being sunk twice, Chancellor emerged from the war unscathed but with a far greater knowledge of the sea from the Indian Ocean to the Caribbean. He had also sketched profusely. Although he was unaware of it at the time, Chancellor's apprenticeship as a seaman was also part of his apprenticeship as an artist. It was then that he learned to observe details—of vessels, weather, sky, and sea—and to remember them and above all to understand them.

By 1972 he had owned and skippered *Viper*, a huge sailing barge; spent ten years as yard boatswain and occasional skipper for a company running barges, tugs, and coasters; run his own survey vessel for seven years. In that year Chancellor left the sea to paint full-time, concentrating on two genres: the coasting trade, especially in sailing barges, and representations of particular historical events.

His painting method developed out of his considerable experience at sea and an innate personal requirement for precision and truth. Painstaking research established the state of the wind and weather and consequently that of the sky and sea prevailing at the time of his subject. These were painted in first. He then drew the outline of the ship, inserting all the internal features that could have been seen had the hull been made of glass. Deck beams and frames were marked in with all the accuracy of a naval architect's drawing to ensure that the relationships between the various parts of the ship were correct. Similarly, he drew everything above decks that would have been there, including men working. The drawing completed, the internal structures were erased and areas of the sea or sky that would be covered by hull or sail were scraped smooth so that nothing would show through when the hull was finished. Chancellor then resumed painting, beginning with those parts of the ship farthest away. Inevitably such a practice meant that frequently a feature already painted had to have something else superimposed.

This rather idiosyncratic method was time-consuming and therefore expensive. However, combined with his seaman's knowledge, the method permitted Chancellor to undertake with success extraordinarily difficult subjects without compromising his passion for integrity. A good example is his depiction in a painting called *Sorely Tried* of a very bad moment for HMS *Beagle* in January 1833 when she was sixty miles off Cape Horn.

Because Chancellor died at the early age of fifty-nine, after a productive career of a mere twelve years as an artist, it is difficult to assess his true significance in the world of marine art. Two facts are pertinent, however: his works, though much sought after, rarely come up for sale; and very few artists before or since have attempted subjects that require so complex a mastery of both seamanship and painting skill.

[*See also* Artists, *subentry* British, *and* Painting.]

### Bibliography

Archibald, E. H. H. *Dictionary of Sea Painters of Europe and America.* 3d ed. Woodbridge, U.K.: Antique Collectors' Club, 2002.

Chancellor, John. *The Maritime Paintings of John Chancellor.* Newton Abbott, U.K., and North Pomfret, Vt.: David and Charles, 1984.

ALAN MCGOWAN

## Chanteys. *See* Ballads and Chanteys.

## Chapman, Fredrik Henrik af (1721–1808),

Swedish naval architect and shipbuilder. Chapman was born September 9, 1721, to English parents who had emigrated to Sweden in 1716. His father, Thomas Chapman, was superintendent of the royal dockyard (Nya Varvet) at Göteborg. After his apprenticeship there in 1738–1741, Chapman worked at several other dockyards and studied in Great Britain (1741–1744, 1750, 1756), Holland (1754), and France (1755–1756). Hence he was acquainted with the work of French and the British mathematicians, scientists, and ship designers of his time and the preceding century (including Paul Hoste, William Sutherland, Thomas Simpson, Pierre Boguer, Henri-Louis Duhamel du Monceau, Leonhard Euler, and Mungo Murray).

In 1757 he served as an assistant shipwright in the Swedish navy at Karlskrona, then at Stralsund (1760–1762) and Sveaborg (1762–1764). At Sveaborg he became chief shipbuilder of the inshore fleet, which he completely redesigned. His new fleet contained some fifty ships, both sailing and oared, mainly frigates; it even included amphibious warfare vessels. Chapman returned to Stockholm in 1765, and in 1768 published his most famous work, *Architectura navalis mercatoria*, which consisted of 156 engraved, scaled, 82 × 55 centimeter (32 × 22 inch) plans of ships and boats of all types and sizes and intended for practical purposes, for example, hospital ships and fresh-water carriers. He included tables that gave the ratio of each ship's displacement to its draft (given in Swedish, English, and French units of length). Demand for this expensive collection led in 1775 to an addition to the *Architectura*:

the *Tractat om skepps-byggeriet, tillaka med förklaring och bevis öfver architectura navalis mercatoria.* It presented the theoretical basis of his shipbuilding principles, which combined his thorough scientific knowledge acquired in western Europe with his practical experience in traditional craftsmanship. Because of its importance, the *Tractat* was translated into French (1779), English (1820), Russian (1836), and German (1936). Especially with this, but also with his later works, Chapman aimed to establish a systematic framework for addressing the basic questions of naval architecture, including the ideal proportions for hull dimensions, the ratio of sail area to hull size and the best sail plan, the appropriate positions for center of gravity and the metacenter, the shape of the bow to reduce resistance underwater, the characteristics that make ships work and steer well, and the principles of weight distribution for ordnance and cargo.

In addition to ship design and construction Chapman made great contributions with improvements in shipyard organization, methods, and equipment. His lifelong efforts were highly regarded. He was ennobled in 1772 (becoming "af Chapman") and was a Fellow of the Swedish Royal Academy and a member of the Board of Admiralty. He became superintendent of the main naval dockyard at Karlskrona in 1782, a rear admiral in 1784, and Vice Admiral of the Fleet in 1791. Chapman died at Karlskrona on August 19, 1808.

[*See also* Naval Architecture.]

### Bibliography

Chapman, Fredrik Henrik af. *Architectura navalis mercatoria.* Originally published in 1768. London: Coles, 1971.

Harris, Daniel G. *F. H. Chapman: The First Naval Architect and His Work.* London: Conway Maritime Press, 1989.

ALBRECHT SAUER

## Charlotte Dundas, steamboat (1 funnel, 1 mast).

Length/beam/draft: 17.1 m × 5.5 m × 2.4 m (56′ × 18′ × 8′). Hull: wood. Machinery: horizontal engine, 10 horsepower, sternwheel; 3.5 knots. Designer: William Symington. Built: Alexander Hart, Clyde River, Scotland, 1801.

Built to the design of the Scots engineer William Symington, *Charlotte Dundas* was one of the first operational steamboats in Great Britain. Launched in 1801, her success—and the commercial viability of steam navigation generally—seemed assured when Francis Egerton, Duke of Bridgewater, placed an order for eight similar vessels for use on his extensive network of canals. Symington's prospects died with Egerton in 1803, and steam navigation lay dormant in Britain until the launch of Henry Bell's *Comet* in 1812, five years after Robert Fulton's *North River Steam Boat* entered service in the United States.

Symington had patented and built his first steam engine, for use in a land vehicle, in 1787. The same year he was introduced to Patrick Miller, a self-made banker who had developed an interest in two- and three-hulled vessels propelled by man-powered paddle wheel, and together they produced their first steam-powered boat. In 1788, Symington and Miller built a larger vessel and engine for use on the Forth and Clyde Canal. Although this vessel attained a speed of seven knots, Miller was concerned about the viability of Symington's engine design, and after corresponding with the better-known James Watt, who disparaged Symington's work, Miller abandoned the project.

In 1801, Thomas, Lord Dundas, asked Symington to design a steam tug for the Forth and Clyde Canal, of which he was a governor. Symington got a new patent for an engine that "employed a piston-rod guided by rollers in a straight path, connected by a connecting rod to a crank attached directly to the paddlewheel shaft, thus devising the system of working the paddlewheel shaft"; this type of engine was universally adopted thereafter (*Oxford Dictionary of National Biography*, "Symington"). This engine was mounted in *Charlotte Dundas*, which had one single paddle wheel in the stern and was able to tow two 70-ton barges a distance of 19.5 miles in six hours against a strong headwind. Despite Egerton's enthusiastic endorsement of the project, which would have advanced the adoption of steam navigation in Britain by a decade, officials of the Forth and Clyde Canal abandoned *Charlotte Dundas* after Egerton's death in 1803 for fear that the wash thrown out by such vessels would erode the banks of the canal. Abandoned in a backwater of the canal, *Charlotte Dundas* was finally broken up in 1861.

[*See also* Rivers, Canals, and Inland Waterways.]

### Bibliography

Baker, W. A. *The Engine-Powered Vessel: From Paddle-Wheeler to Nuclear Ship*. New York: Grosset and Dunlap, 1965.

Matthew, H. C. G., and Brian Harrison, eds. *Oxford Dictionary of National Biography*. Oxford: Oxford University Press, 2004.

See the articles on "Egerton, Francis, Duke of Bridgewater," "Miller, Patrick," and "Symington, William."

Paine, Lincoln P. *Ships of the World: An Historical Encyclopedia*. Boston: Houghton Mifflin, 1997.

LINCOLN P. PAINE

# Chartered Companies

This entry contains two subentries:

Iberian World
Northern Europe

---

## Iberian World

Chartered companies in Iberia appeared in 1628 with the establishment of the Portuguese East India Company, following the example of the Dutch East India Company. The Portuguese company was given a monopoly over the trade between Lisbon and the Portuguese empire in the East (Estado da India), and it was required to create a safe route in the Atlantic and Indian oceans against Dutch, English, and French attacks. The Portuguese East India Company only survived five years, and its mission failed, mostly because of general underinvestment, inadequate returns, and a general aversion to modernization.

After the Portuguese gained independence from Spain in 1640, a new project for a commercial company was sponsored by King João IV (r. 1640–1656). In 1649, the Portuguese Company for Trading in Brazil was given the monopoly over the trade between Lisbon and Brazil, especially in the exchanges of wine, olive oil, grain, and codfish. The company was also given the privilege to collect taxes on sugar, tobacco, hides, and cotton exported from Brazil into Portugal. Although this company was created as a reaction to the Dutch occupation of Brazil, the company did not thrive. Contrary to its counterpart for the East Indies, the Portuguese Company for Trading in Brazil had sufficient capital, mainly in the hands of new= Christians (forcefully baptized Jews). Their participation in the company as shareholders had given them royal protection against the confiscations by the Inquisition. The company started to decline when, after the death of King João IV, the protection against the confiscations was withdrawn and private entrepreneurs in Brazil started to organize circuits parallel to those given in monopoly to the company.

After these two seventeenth-century failures, Portugal still tried to organize slave-trading companies that would connect Brazil directly to the west coast of Africa. The General Company for the Trade of Grão-Pará and Maranhão as well as the General Company for the Trade of Pernambuco and Paraíba were far more successful in the eighteenth century than the seventeenth-century companies. However, none of them ever reached the size or importance of their Dutch, English, or French counterparts.

The Portuguese failures of the seventeenth century seem to have been avoided by the Spanish Crown in the eighteenth century. The majority of the Spanish commercial companies were successful and oriented to the American market. The Honduras Company (1714) was the first to be created, but little is known about it. The Spanish Caracas Company (1728) followed. It was created by a group of successful Basque businessmen, whose main goal was to encourage the cultivation and commerce of cocoa, though the company also traded in gold, silver, tobacco, and hides. The company suffered a severe set back with the "free trade" regulations imposed by Charles III (1778). The Company of the Philippines was established in 1733 after careful planning, having as its main goals trade with Africa, India, and the Philippines; the import of spices; the trade of fifty tons of silk; and the transport of up to five hundred thousand *reales* in silver. This last possibility met with strong opposition by the private interests vested in the Philippines and in the other Spanish American colonies, and the Company of the Philippines ended up falling short of its goals. The Company of Buenos Aires, Tucumán, and Paraguay shared the same fate as the Company of the Philippines, failing in its intents because of the fierce opposition by private interest in Lima and Cadiz.

The Royal Trading Company of Havana (1740) and the Royal Trading Company of Barcelona (1755) are examples of good management. The former held a monopoly over the import of cloth, canvas, flour, and slaves, exporting in turn sugar and tobacco, and drawing much of its earnings from contraband. The latter was a mix of preindustrial and commercial enterprise. It held the monopoly of the exports of the Catalan preindustrial output to the Antilles, Central America, Santo Domingo, Puerto Rico, and Margarita, as well as freighting rights in Honduras.

The success of the eighteenth-century Spanish commercial companies can be attributed to two reasons. First, the experience of unsuccessful commercial ventures in Iberia had provided enough experience and management know-how to the newly created companies that they were able to avoid some of the mistakes of the past. Second, the

development of manufactures and preindustrial forms of entrepreneurship provided Spain with an output of novelty products that were directly exported to the broad American colonial market.

[*See also* East India Companies *and* Navies, Great Powers, *subentries on* Portugal, 1500–1808 *and* Spain, 1500–1805.]

## Bibliography

Boxer, Charles R. "Padre António Vieira, S.J. and the Institution of the Brazil Company in 1649." *Hispanic American Historical Review* 29, no. 4 (1949): 474–497.

Carreira, António. "A Companhia de Pernambuco e Paraíba–Alguns Subsídios para o Estudo da sua Acção." *Revista de História Económica e Social* 11 (1983): 55–88.

Carreira, António. *As Companhias Pombalinas de Navegação: Comércio e Tráfico de Escravos entre a Costa Africana e o Nordeste Brasileiro*. Bissau: Centro de Estudos da Guiné Portuguesa, 1969.

Dias, M. N. "Companhias versus Companhias na Competição Colonial." *Revista Portuguesa de História* 16 (1976): 83–104.

Disney, A. R. "The First Portuguese India Company, 1628–1633." *The Economic History Review*, 2d ser., 30, no. 2 (1977): 242–258.

Hussey, Roland D. *The Caracas Company, 1728–1784: A Study in the History of Spanish Monopolistic Trade*. Cambridge, Mass.: Harvard University Press, 1934.

Molina Martínez, M. "Economia." In *América en el Siglo XVIII*, Part 2, *La Ilustración en América*, edited by D. Ramos Pérez and M. L. Díaz-Thechuelo López-Spínola, pp. 223–276. Historia General de España y América, vol. 11. Madrid: Rialp, 1989.

Vicens Vives, Jaime, with the collaboration of Jorge Nadal Oller. *An Economic History of Spain*. Translated by Frances M. López-Morillas. Princeton, N.J.: Princeton University Press, 1969.

Winius, George D. "Two Lusitanian Variations on a Dutch Theme: Portuguese Companies in Times of Crisis, 1628–1662." In *Companies and Trade: Essays on Overseas Trading Companies during the Ancien Régime*, edited by Leonard Blussé and Femme Gaastra, pp. 119–134. Leiden: Leiden University Press, 1981.

CÁTIA ANTUNES

# Northern Europe

The chartered company was a type of maritime business organization to finance exploration, colonization, and foreign trade that developed during the mid-sixteenth century in northern and western Europe in parallel with the overseas expansion of Europe and the development of the nation-state. Typically, a sovereign granted to a company a charter that included the rights of operating a national monopoly to colonize a specific region or to trade in specific commodities. The largest and most powerful chartered companies, the East India companies, operated naval and military forces as well as made laws and treaties with the approval of the national sovereign. In some cases, the state partially subsidized these companies, but the arrangement allowed a state to use private resources for state purposes and to control overseas areas indirectly through this financial mechanism.

There were two types of chartered companies. The older form, called the regulated company, was an association of individual merchants, who traded independently with their own employees and goods under broad company regulations that were designed to benefit all the individual merchants. This arrangement did not involve an accumulation of capital and, therefore, resources were very limited in trying to finance long overseas voyages in large ships requiring heavy armament, large numbers of seafarers, and extensive supplies for chartering factories and colonies in distant lands. In order to meet these needs, the chartered joint stock company was refined and developed from its medieval origins in the late thirteenth and fourteenth centuries to raise sufficient capital for such enterprises, eventually superseding the earlier form of chartered company. Under these arrangements, large amounts of capital could be accumulated, much of which went into permanent investment in overseas infrastructure as well as manpower and ships. Share owners usually received a percentage of the profits that was proportionate to their ownership of shares.

Examples of companies chartered for the purpose of colonization include the Virginia Company of London and the Plymouth Company of London, both originally chartered in 1606 to establish colonies in different areas on the eastern seaboard of North America; the Somers Isles Company, which developed from the London Company for the colonization of Bermuda from 1615; the Massachusetts Bay Company, chartered in 1629 to settle the area near Boston, Massachusetts; the New Sweden Company (Nya Sverige Kompaniet), chartered in 1633 to found the Swedish colony of New Sweden that existed from 1638–1655 in the Delaware River region of North America; the French Company of the American Islands (Compagnie des Îles de l'Amérique), which initially developed Guadeloupe, Martinique, and Saint Christopher (Saint Kitts) between 1631 and c. 1650; and the Brandenburg African Company (Brandenburgisch-Africanische Compagnie), chartered by the elector of Brandenburg to operate two Prussian trading posts in present-day Ghana between 1682 and 1717.

The purpose of the Brandenburg Company's settlements, however, was to engage in the slave trade. Similarly the Swedish Africa Company (Afrikanska Kompaniet or Guineakompaniet) was originally established by Dutch merchants, but later came into Swedish ownership in 1649 to trade in slaves, gold, and ivory until 1658. In 1786, the Swedish king chartered the Swedish West India Company (Svenska Västindiska Kompaniet) to operate the island of Saint-Barthélemy, which was established as a free port. In this case, the Swedish crown owned 10 percent of the shares, but received one fourth of the profits.

In England, the first joint stock company was established in 1551 as the Merchant Adventurers or "Mystery and Company of Merchant Adventurers for the Discovery of Regions, Dominions, Islands, and Places unknown" to finance Richard Chancellor's expedition to the White Sea in his attempt to find a northeast passage to China. Chartered in 1555 as the Muscovy Company, it was granted a monopoly of trade with Russia. In 1579, England chartered the Company of Merchants of the East (known as the Eastland or North Sea Company), a group of established merchants with a monopoly of trade with ports in Scandinavia and the Baltic Sea beyond Russian influence. Two years later, in 1581, a group of merchants successfully petitioned for a charter to trade to Turkey. Initially chartered as the Levant Company (and known as the Turkey Company), it established headquarters at Aleppo, while trading to Smyrna, and Constantinople (Istanbul), and later expanding to the entire Middle East and much of the Mediterranean basin.

In 1660, King Charles II (r. 1660–1685) chartered the Company of Royal Adventurers Trading to Africa, which in 1672 was succeeded by the Royal African Company to trade in slaves on the West African coast. In 1670, Charles II chartered the "Gentlemen Adventurers trading into Hudson's Bay" to seek the northwest passage to Asia, granting them a monopoly over English fur trade in the Hudson Bay watershed region with rights of settlement and government in that area. Although playing a major role in Canadian economic history, its charter was not always respected by other traders in the region, American, British, or French. In 1783–1784, a loosely organized company, the Northwest Company, was established by Scots fur traders, who had taken over the French businesses in Montreal. In 1821, after serious rivalry had developed, the British government intervened and forced a merger with the Hudson's Bay Company.

The charters given to two companies in particular, that which Queen Anne (r. 1702–1714) of Great Britain and Ireland had granted to the South Sea Company in 1711, and that which the French regent, Philippe II (duc d'Orléans), granted to the Compagnie Perpétuelle des Indes in 1717, led to demonstrations of the principal weakness of this financial form.

In 1711, Robert Harley (1661–1724), Britain's chancellor of the exchequer, formed the South Sea Company as a means of financing Britain's participation in the final stages of the War of the Spanish Succession (1701–1714). Investors who had held previously issued government bonds were able to exchange them for stock in the new company, which held a monopoly for trade in the South Seas, including South America. Investor interest was based on the anticipation of high profits to be gained from Spain's concession to Britain of the *asiento* and other advantages during the future Utrecht peace negotiations, but the profits they eventually brought were not realized to the extent imagined beforehand. In 1720 the company was allowed to take over the entire British national debt, exchanging government bonds for company stock. The government agreed to this, expecting substantial profits, but instead wild speculation, fraud, and highly inflated stock values led to widespread financial failures and the "South Sea Bubble" burst in September 1720.

In a similar story in France, John Law of Lauriston (1671–1729), a Scots financier living in France, acquired in 1717 the management of the monopoly on commercial rights originally given in Louisiana to the Companie d'Occident in 1664, and merged them with the French East India Company in 1719 to establish what became known as the Compagnie Perpétuelle des Indes or the Mississippi Company. Subsequently, he became France's controller general of finances and was able to merge the company with the newly established Banque Royale, taking over the national debt, the management of French national revenue, and control of colonial trade. Large numbers of small investors bought company stock in response to exaggerated advertising claims. With speculation, the stocks rose dramatically to highly inflated values. Then the market for these shares suddenly collapsed in the "Mississippi Bubble" of October 1720, ruining many financially.

The chartered company form of investment was largely superseded by the widespread use of limited liability companies, particularly after passage of Britain's Joint-Stock Companies Act of 1844, followed within the next twenty years by similar legislation in France, the United States, and elsewhere.

In the late nineteenth century there was a brief, but largely unsuccessful, return to the use of the older former of chartered monopoly company with the establishment of the British North Borneo Company in 1881, the German New Guinea Company (Deutsche Neuguinea-Kompagnie) in 1884; The German East Africa Company (Deutsch-Ostafrikanische Gesellschaft) in 1885; The Royal Niger Company in 1886; and the British South Africa Company in 1889.

[*See also* Banking and Credit; East India Companies; *and* Shipping Industry, *subentry on* Entrepreneurs and Financiers.]

## Bibliography

Carr, Cecil T., ed. *Select Charters of Trading Companies, A.D. 1530–1707*. Publications of the Selden Society, vol. 28. London: B. Quaritch, 1913.

Carswell, John. *The South Sea Bubble*. London: Cresset, 1960.

Davies, Kenneth Gordon. *The Royal African Company*. London: Longmans, Green, 1957.

Kingsbury, Susan Myra, ed. *The Records of the Virginia Company of London*. Washington, D.C.: Government Printing Office, 1906–1935.

Rich, E. E. *The History of the Hudson's Bay Company, 1670–1870*. Publications of the Hudson's Bay Record Society, vols. 21–22. London : Hudson's Bay Record Society, 1958–1959.

Robert, Rudolph. *Chartered Companies and Their Role in the Development of Overseas Trade*. London: Bell, 1969.

Scott, William Robert. *The Constitution and Finance of English, Scottish, and Irish Joint-stock Companies to 1720*. Cambridge, U.K.: Cambridge University Press, 1910–1912. Reprinted, New York: Peter Smith, 1951.

Sellers, Maud, ed. *The Acts and Ordinances of the Eastland Company*. Camden Society, 3d ser., vol. 11. London: Royal Historical Society, 1906.

Willan, Thomas Stuart. *The Early History of the Russia Company, 1533–1603*. Manchester, U.K.: Manchester University Press, 1956. Reprinted, New York: A. M. Kelley, 1968.

Wood, Alfred Cecil. *A History of the Levant Company*. Oxford: Oxford University Press, 1935.

JOHN B. HATTENDORF

## Chartmakers. *See* Cartography.

## Chatham

A British naval base, Chatham stands on the river Medway, on the north coast of Kent, England. Its foundation is traditionally dated to 1547, when a storehouse was hired at Gillingham. The stretch of the Medway initially known as Gillingham Water swiftly became a major anchorage for royal ships. Wharves were built along it during the reign of Elizabeth I, followed by a mast pond (1570), a large storehouse (1580), and a

**Chatham Dockyard, 1863.** HMS *Achilles*, the first all-iron ship to be built in one of the Royal Navy's dockyards, is under Construction on the left, and HMS *Bombay*, an 84-gun ship-of-the-line built in 1828, is undergoing repairs on the right. © NATIONAL MARITIME MUSEUM, LONDON

ropery (1586). To protect the ships, a new artillery fort was built across the river at Upnor in 1564. The yard expanded downstream from 1618 onward, and a dry dock was built in 1623, a year that also saw the installation of a protective boom across the river. Close both to London and to the battlegrounds in the North Sea, Chatham was particularly well placed during the Anglo-Dutch Wars of the seventeenth century, and was undoubtedly the premier English dockyard during this time. The Buoy of the Nore, where the Medway entered the Thames estuary, also served as the major operational anchorage for the fleet. The 18 kilometers (11 miles) of shallow, winding, tidal river between the Nore and Chatham prompted the construction of a small forward base at Sheerness from 1665; despite its isolated, constricted, and unhealthy location, this survived as a small outport of Chatham until its closure in 1960, after which it was developed into a commercial facility.

The wide, sheltered nature of the Medway made Chatham the obvious place in which to lay up most of the navy's ships that were not in service, or "in ordinary."

It was this function that led to the yard's blackest hour, and one of the most humiliating defeats in British military and naval history. Early in 1667, financial constraints forced King Charles II's government to abandon plans for an active campaign against the Dutch that summer; it was hoped that a combination of flying squadrons and new forts would keep the Dutch at bay until peace was signed. However, the new defenses at Sheerness and along the Medway were incomplete when, on June 7, the Dutch fleet under Michiel Adriaanszoon de Ruyter sailed into the mouth of the Thames. Despite a valiant defense from the guns of Upnor Castle and the other batteries along the river, the Dutch succeeded in breaking the Medway boom on June 12 and burned three of the Royal Navy's largest ships at their moorings. The flagship *Royal Charles* was towed away to the Netherlands, where her sternpiece is still displayed in the Rijksmuseum, Amsterdam.

In later years, Chatham developed into a major center of naval shipbuilding. Throughout the eighteenth century the yard built some of the navy's largest ships, the most famous being Lord Nelson's *Victory*, launched there in 1765.

Chatham made a quick transition to building iron ships in the 1860s, its first, the battleship *Achilles*, being launched in 1863. However, increased sizes—especially after the introduction of Dreadnought battleships early in the twentieth century—meant that Chatham could no longer build the very largest warships, and no battleships were launched there after 1905. The dockyard soon found a new niche as a specialized building yard for submarines, and a total of fifty-seven were built there between 1908 and 1967, the last being the Canadian navy's *Okanagan*.

The switch after 1689 from wars against the Dutch in the North Sea to wars against the French in the Atlantic and the English Channel significantly reduced Chatham's strategic importance, and silting of the Medway was a perennial problem. By 1730 Chatham's workforce was much smaller than that of Portsmouth and the entirely new yard at Plymouth, and Chatham remained a poor third in terms of size and importance for the rest of its life. In 1773 it was decided to use it primarily as a shipbuilding and repair yard, and during the following thirty years, two large new storehouses were built and the ropery was rebuilt. A massive system of defensive fortifications, the "Chatham lines," was built around the dockyard in 1778–1783. The transition to steam power after the Napoleonic Wars somewhat eased Chatham's reputation for difficult navigation but also exposed its inadequacies as a modern naval base. In 1855, therefore, work began on a huge expansion of the yard. A marshy area to the north of the existing facilities, known as Saint Mary's Island, was purchased by the navy, and three large basins and four dry docks were constructed on the reclaimed land. The vast project was eventually completed in 1885, and was supplemented by the construction of a new naval barracks, HMS *Pembroke*, which opened in 1903.

Like all of Britain's dockyards, Chatham worked at full capacity through both world wars. The yard was bombed in September 1917, and again on several occasions during World War II, the worst attack occurring on December 3, 1940. After World War II, the steady decline in the size of the Royal Navy raised serious questions about Chatham's future. The Royal Marine division was disbanded in 1950, the navy's separate Nore Command was abandoned in 1961, and the "dockyard" title disappeared in 1971, when several facilities merged into a redesignated "HM Naval Base." Many of the yard's large buildings were obviously underused, and the basins themselves were increasingly used for subsidiary roles, such as laying up ships in reserve. However, the presence of several marginal constituencies in the Medway area prompted the Labour government of 1964–1970 to give Chatham a new lease on life, and a state-of-the-art facility for refitting nuclear submarines was opened in 1968, apparently securing the base's future. This "reprieve" proved to be short-lived, for the new Conservative government's defense review of 1981 announced that Chatham would close in 1984. Chance dictated that the intervening years saw one of its finest moments: the Argentinian invasion of the Falklands/Malvinas Islands in April 1982 led to a last flurry of activity at the yard, which saw the reactivation of several old ships from reserve to provide cover in home waters for newer vessels that had been deployed to the South Atlantic. Nevertheless, the closure timetable remained inviolable, and on June 21, 1983, the frigate *Hermione* became the last warship to leave the yard. HM Naval Base, Chatham, officially closed on March 31, 1984.

In the years that followed, the Victorian extension of the yard was largely cleared of its naval infrastructure and given over to a mix of residential and commercial buildings, while the basins themselves were turned over to merchant shipping and pleasure craft. The historic southern section of the yard, centered on five eighteenth- and nineteenth-century covered slipways, was preserved as a major heritage site by the Chatham Historic Dockyard Trust. In addition to retaining the major buildings and presenting exhibitions of Chatham's and the navy's history, the old base became the home for a number of preserved warships: by 2006 these were the World War II destroyer *Cavalier*, the Chatham-built submarine *Ocelot*, and the restored Victorian steam sloop *Gannet*. These developments mean that, although the navy itself is long gone, Chatham's long and impressive naval tradition has been preserved and appropriately acknowledged.

[*See also* Naval Dockyards and Bases.]

## Bibliography

Chatham Dockyard Historical Society http://www.dockmus.ik.com/.

Chatham Historic Dockyard Trust http://www.chdt.org.uk/. The Web site of Chatham Historic Dockyard Trust; a useful guide to the yard's history and to the heritage area.

Coad, Jonathan. *Historic Architecture of Chatham Dockyard, 1700–1850.* London: National Maritime Museum, 1982.

Coad, Jonathan. *The Royal Dockyards, 1690–1850: Architecture and Engineering Works of the Sailing Navy.* Aldershot, U.K.: Scolar Press, 1989.

Crawshaw, J. D. *The History of Chatham Dockyard.* Newcastle upon Tyne, U.K.: Isabel Garford, 1999.

Hughes, David T. *Chatham Naval Dockyard and Barracks.* Stroud, U.K.: Tempus, 2004.

MacDougall, Philip. *Chatham Built Warships since 1860.* Liskeard, U.K.: Maritime Books, 1982.

MacDougall, Philip. *Chatham Dockyard in Old Photographs.* Stroud, U.K.: Sutton, 1994.

MacDougall, Philip. *The Chatham Dockyard Story.* Rev. ed. Rainham, U.K.: Meresborough, 1987.

Naval Dockyards Society. http://www.hants.gov.uk/navaldockyard/index.htm/.

J. D. DAVIES

# China

This entry contains two subentries:

Chinese Navigation
Voyages of Exploration

----

## Chinese Navigation

The first European travelers who visited China in the thirteenth century were awed by views of multitudes of boats and ships sailing on rivers and littoral waters, and huddling in busy harbors. This great marine and fluvial shipping activity is explained by China's bulky geography laced with a dense network of rivers and canals, and by a huge population needing enormous quantities of food. In Chinese navigation, marine and fluvial trading were complementary and intimately associated. This association reflected the intricate mingling of the economic and social interests of merchants, tax collectors, smugglers, and pirates. Because smuggling was endemic to Chinese culture, suspicious Chinese authorities set up a control network involving sophisticated regulations and inspections, particularly during the Song dynasty (960–1279). Through the centuries the issue of grain shipping aroused at the imperial court controversies, conflicts, and intrigues about the proper balance of efficiency, advantages, disadvantages, and specific dangers of interior river routes and of inshore coastal shipping.

### The Maritime Expansion of Continental China

Trading between the Muslim sphere and China began in the seventh century, if not earlier. A maritime route, more or less associated with the ancient Perfume Route, starting from Basra (on the Tigris River in Iraq) and from harbors of Arabia along the Persian Gulf, the Red Sea, and the Arabian Sea. The route reached China through Indian, Malayan, and Indonesian waters. Quite possibly some Chinese merchants engaged in overseas trading during the Tang dynasty (618–907) on board purchased or rented Singhalese ships, but because the Chinese lacked local sailing expertise, they were obliged to rely on foreign seamen. What is today called the Maritime Silk Route was a Persian and Arabian monopoly up to the twelfth century. Chinese coastal shipping increased during the tenth century, under the Five Dynasties (907–960), possibly owing to improvements in shipbuilding techniques. Yet an alternative hypothesis may explain Chinese maritime expansion and the development of Quanzhou, the key harbor of the Maritime Silk Route in Fujian Province on the Taiwan Strait. Increasing piracy along Central Asian roads under control of barbarian bandits made ground transportation impossible. Moreover, one merchant vessel could ship 2,000 camels (a unit of measure), and because ships eliminated relays and transfers, they reduced delays and improved profits. In spite of the risks of total loss of goods in cases of misfortune, shipping was profitable on the whole.

In the second half of the thirteenth century, Marco Polo (c. 1254–1324), a Venetian merchant and traveler who

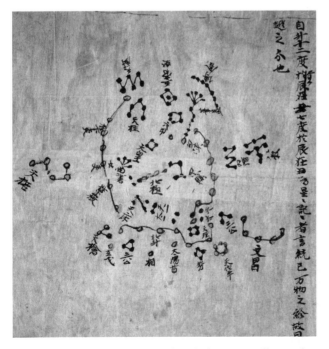

**Chinese Star Navigation.** This chart is from a scroll map that depicts the night sky in the northern hemisphere, based on 12 positions for the planet Jupiter, c. 618–c. 906. BRITISH LIBRARY / HIP / ART RESOURCE, NY

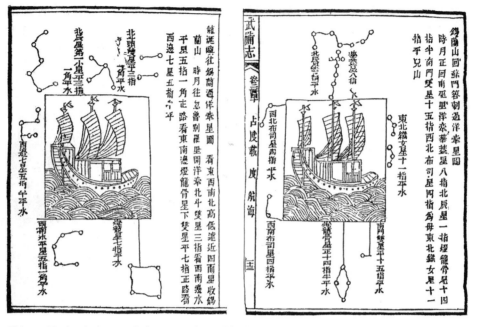

**Chinese Navigation.** Two of Zheng He's four tables for sailing by the stars, by Mao Yuanyi Wubeizhi, 1621. Left, from Sumatra to Sri Lanka; right, from Sri Lanka to Sumatra. COURTESY OF FRANÇOIS BELLEC

spent twenty-four years in China as counselor to Kublai Khan (1215–1294), visited Quanzhou. From the Tang dynasty (618–907), Arabian traders were familiar with this major harbor, which they named "Zaytun." When Portuguese reached China in 1516, they distorted the Arabian place-name into "Cetim" or "Setim," after which they named "satin," the silky Chinese fabric. A shipping office was established there in 1072. It opened one century after the shipping office of Guangzhou (Canton), a harbor active from the Qin dynasty (221–207 B.C.E.). When Marco Polo visited Quanzhou, the harbor was more prosperous than rival Guangzhou. This expansion was part of a Chinese renewal. During the eleventh and twelfth centuries under the Song dynasty (960–1279), the Chinese made impressive advances in mathematics, astronomy, cartography, medicine, the natural sciences, technology, and the arts, including lacquer and porcelain. Simultaneously, business and trade were stimulated by the innovation of paper currency, which appeared in the early eleventh century. The boom in culture and the economy gave rise to a profusion of books and literature, multiplied by xylographic printing, which was invented before 1045.

During the Southern Song dynasty (1127–1279), the wealth of Chinese ports ceased to depend on foreign merchant ships, and China began to develop as a seafaring nation. Marco Polo described the capital of the Southern Song, the modern port city of Hangzhou, as the sumptuous "Quinsay," an Asian Venice. China's relationship with the high sea changed dramatically between the twelfth and thirteenth centuries. Chinese merchant ships ventured on the Indian Ocean in the second half of the twelfth century, after the advent of the Southern Song dynasty (1127). The Indian Ocean appeared in Chinese geography at this time as the Xiyang (Western Ocean). Chinese traders visited Guli (Calicut) on the Malabar Coast of India. The Indian harbor of Cochin was located a hundred of miles south of Calicut. Fishing implements can still be seen there. Huge fisheries, the wide nets of which are balanced with counterweights, are built following a Chinese fishing technique hundreds of years old. Chinese familiarity with the Indian Ocean occurred at the same time as the maritime expansion of Chola, a Tamil kingdom occupying the southeastern part of the Indian Subcontinent along the Bay of Bengal. Quite possibly the Chinese benefited from the Chola's seafaring and navigation expertise on journeys to India.

During the thirteenth century the Asian seafaring trading reversed direction dramatically. The Persian and

Arabian monopoly in the China seas vanished, and junks became common and appreciated in Indian harbors. The Arab traveler and chronicler Abu Abdullah Muhammad Ibn Battuta (1304–1377), who was waiting for the favorable monsoon at Calicut in 1341, declared that the only way to sail for the South China Sea was to embark onboard a Chinese vessel.

## Chinese Ships

Plentiful iconography offers a valuable image of traditional Chinese ships, from common riverboats and coasters to large seagoing junks. Junks came down the ages to the twentieth century without noticeable alterations. A wreck of the Song period (960–1279) was recovered in 1974 from the sludge at Hu Zhu, where Chinese scholars locate the major harbor of old Quanzhou. Mud preserved only the bottom of the hull. Nonetheless, these planks show us a ship about 34 meters (112 feet) long with a loading capacity of 200 tons and a hold divided into 13 watertight bulkheads.

**Junks.** The first European to travel on Chinese waters was probably Giovanni Da Montecorvino (1253–1328), a Franciscan missionary who returned to Khanbaliq (Beijing) in 1293 after a stay in Persia. Half a century later, Ibn Battuta described the Chinese four-decked ships that visited the harbor of Calicut. They could accommodate several dozen merchants, offering them private cabins, lounges, quarters for their servants, sanitation, a bazaar, a barbershop, and a laundry. Built by a simple process, the junk had a hull that was broad and strong, carefully caulked, and divided by watertight bulkheads, which made the ship stiff and safe and determined her shape. The most important shipyards were at Quanzhou and Guangzhou.

Junks had up to seven masts that hoisted tall rectangular sails made of bamboo slats. Designed for catching any breeze above the riverbanks along the Chinese rivers, these sensible sails were also suitable for the open seas. These heavy Chinese sails were efficient only when pushed by fair winds. For this reason, junks sailed slowly, taking advantage of local breezes and tide or river currents.

Iconography of the Song period (960–1279) attests that the Chinese invented the sternpost rudder in the early twelfth century. Xu Jing's *Xuanhe feng shi Gaoli tu jing* (Illustrated Chronicle of an Embassy to Korea) confirmed this invention in 1122. It is probable that this key Chinese invention is earlier by some decades than the European sternpost rudder, which appeared in the Hanseatic (or German) maritime environment.

The efficient aft position of the junk's midship beam (the ship's largest) resulted in a shape with a good heading stability, and even better with retractable aft leeboards. When sailing on running waters, a long-stem oar/rudder increased the ship's maneuverability. However, because she was broad beamed and built without stem or keel, the junk made considerable leeway.

Junks towed or carried up to ten boats, among them one or two heavy sailing barges fitted with oars. Giving the junk full autonomy, these boats were used for loading, unloading, towing, ship-to-shore services, and various sailing and harbor operations. When necessary, oarsmen lined up face to face in two rows to pull a score of long, heavy oars. Soldiers, bowmen, crossbowmen, naphtha throwers, and shield holders dissuaded pirates from bothering these jumbo-size traders.

The junk was rigged with a bewildering combination of retractable leeboards, rudders, and masts. She had bamboo sails, bamboo lattices, and bulwarks for shielding crew and passengers from the spray. She was patched up with numerous makeshift planks. Until large sailing junks disappeared in the mid-twentieth century, this mess gave modern eyes the impression of a strange and hideous building. Yet this apparently badly designed, bungled, and patched-up ship was a sophisticated and safe vessel. Moreover, despite the ship's unattractive appearance to western eyes, the shipyards of Quanzhou were several centuries ahead of European shipyards when early western observers visited China.

**Battleships and treasure ships.** Battleships have been described from the eighth century by Chinese chroniclers, draftsmen, and etchers, and Chinese iconography shows multiple kinds of naval engines of war, and of vessels bristling with towers, armor, spurs, and offensive devices, such as catapults for launching explosives, chemicals, or incendiary substances. While these remarkable ships may have existed, it is impossible to determine that all these military devices were actually built and used at sea. Armored battleships propelled by oars, similar to pre-eighteenth-century Mediterranean galleys, were evidently coastal and summer fighting ships, efficient only on windless bodies of water. In contrast, the human-propelled paddleboats in Chinese iconography could at best be contraptions built for prestige and brief demonstrations.

Chinese ships may have been less seaworthy than the literature suggests. Kublai Khan launched a major military campaign against Japan between 1266 and 1281. In 1274 during operations, a typhoon, the famous *kamikaze* (divine wind), swept over the invading fleet, destroying one-third of it. Other expeditions against Annam (1282–1287), Birmania (Burma, 1283–1284), and Java (1293–1294) were also unsuccessful, despite thousands of ships being built on orders of the khan. According to military tactics of this time, these ships were strictly speaking transport ships rather than fighting ships.

Enormous treasure ships (what we today would call merchantmen), including numerous specialized logistic ships such as troop transports, horse transports, food transports, freshwater tankers, and workshop ships, carried valuable gifts presented or received as tribute during port calls. Yet there is reason to doubt the dimensions of the supernatural ships (*shenzhou*) mentioned by Xu Jing in 1122, and there is greater reason to doubt the dimensions given for Admiral Zheng He's sixty or so nine-masted Indian Ocean treasure ships (*Xiyang boachuan*) of the fifteenth century. The myth of giant Chinese ships arose from enthusiastic descriptions by the first travelers to visit China from the Mediterranean sphere. Odoric of Pordenone (1285–1331), a missionary of Padua, Italy, counted 700 passengers onboard a ship bound for China; Marco Polo said he embarked onboard a junk served by 200 crew members; and Ibn Battuta reported 600 sailors and 400 soldiers on a Chinese ship. These figures were cast in doubt in 1962 when a piece of timber more than 10 meters (33 feet) long was excavated from an ancient shipyard of the Ming dynasty (1368–1644) at Longjiang near Nanjing. Archaeologists identified it as a sternpost rudder. Chinese and western commentators deduced that this artifact belonged to a ship 140 meters (459 feet) long by 50 meters (164 feet) wide, with a displacement of about 1,500 tons.

Though it is possible that a compartmentalized structure inspired by bamboo and cross-planking similar to plywood gave fifteenth-century Chinese ships bending strength, out-of-measure oceangoing traders must be considered a myth. Imperial prestige could justify some hazardous extravagancies for diplomatic purposes, but shipbuilders could not overcome the physical limits set by the laws of hydrodynamics and water resistance (Sleeswyk 1996). New studies of the values of Chinese traditional units of length and hydrodynamic studies and experiments suggest that the length of fifteenth-century Chinese ships was about 60 meters (197 feet).

## Seamanship and Dead Reckoning Navigation

Ancient mariners' navigational accomplishments by dead reckoning were considerable. Sima Qian's chronicle *Shiji* (c. 100 B.C.E., *Records of the Historian*) says that from the reign of King Wei, in the fourth century B.C.E., maritime expeditions set sail several times from the kingdom of Qi (in Shandong Province on the Yellow Sea) in search of the "Three Holy Islands," probably Japan. Maritime relations between China and Japan started during the Han dynasty during the reign of the Guangwu emperor (r. 25–57 C.E.). Diplomatic missions visited the Japanese archipelago during the Three Kingdoms period (220–280). The Japanese empress Jingu Kogo, who reigned from circa 200 to 269, subdued the southern part of Korea. Reaching Japan from China was easy. By sailing along the coast of the Yellow Sea, crossing the Korea Strait, and calling at Tsushima and the Iki Islands, a shipmaster could reduce the different legs to Kyushu to less than 30 miles. This does not mean that navigating the Chinese maritime area was free from difficulties. On the contrary, only extraordinary seamanship could master the dreadfully treacherous waters.

**Coastal navigation.** Chinese coastal itineraries ran over an immense continental shelf that extended out to an imaginary line drawn from Japan to Taiwan and down to Vietnam and Indonesia. Chinese seamanship was based on an oral tradition of navigation rules, which made possible intensive coastal navigation during daylight or clear nights, including short legs on the open sea, weather permitting. Nevertheless, very few written coastal pilot books are known, the earliest dating from the ninth century, during the Tang dynasty (618–907).

Everywhere in the world, early pilots paid attention to the tiniest hydrographical, meteorological, and natural-life signs. Chinese made the best of an exceptionally difficult environment. Onboard coastal vessels the helmsman acted as the pilot, but large traders depended upon one or several specialists in navigation. When sailing inland waters, the pilot was familiar with powerful, opaque, and tumultuous rivers, as well as turbid and shallow coastal waters, sometimes suddenly roused by unforeseeable and furious squalls. Xu Jing called attention to the variable weather over Chinese waters. He could do so because, from the Song period (960–1279), pilots were familiar with the vital art of weather forecasting. *Shufeng xiangsong* (How to Get Fair Winds), a pilot book dated 1403 in the Ming dynasty, explained how to forecast weather from variable aspects of the sky.

The first beacons and buoys were set up during the Tang dynasty (618–907), at private initiatives. They increased in number under the Song (960–1279) and especially under the Yuan (1271–1368) as a response to many catastrophic wrecks of large grain shipments. Archives from the 1310s report that boats fitted out with flags and lanterns were anchored during the harvest period to mark dangers, channels, and fairways.

Tide prediction was one of the oldest of Chinese studies of the sea. This knowledge appeared by 770 in Du Shumeng's *Haichao zhi* (A Survey on Tides). It progressed with Lu Zao's *Haichao fu* (Poems on Tides, 850), and five decades later with such studies as Qiu Guangting's *Haichao lun* (On Tides), Yu Jing's *Haichao tuxu* (An Introduction to Tide Tables), Zheng Junfang's *Chao shuo* (The Theory of Tides), and, in 1206, Yan Su's *Haichao tulun* (Illustrated Discourse on Tides). Tide scales were set up the same year at Ningbo, a historic Chinese harbor on the Bay of Hangzhou some miles south of Shanghai, and in 1056 at Hangzhou. In this area the tidal range is among the widest in not just Asia but also the world.

In his *Pingzhou ketan* (Chronicle of Pingzhou), an irreplaceable document about early Chinese navigation dated 1113, Zhu Yu related memories of his father, a high civil servant in Guangzhou (Canton) around 1090. Zhu Yu said that pilots cast "a line a hundred feet long, fitted with a hook with which they pick up mud from the bottom of the sea. Smelling the odour of the mud, they know where the ship is." A treatise of the Ming dynasty (1368–1644), *Zhinan zhengfa* (How to Determine South), explained how to use a sounding pole or sounding line. Plumbs coated with ox fat or wax were used to pick up samples from the bottom of the sea. The treatise also explained how to estimate speed at sea. The method, similar to that of Europe, consisted in measuring the time it took for a log thrown overboard at the bow to float by the stern. The pilot walked from bow to stern along with the log while reciting a ditty. The ship's speed was roughly deduced from how long it took the ship to sail her own length. This method might have been borrowed from the Portuguese, who were often seen on the China seas from the 1540s.

The speed of a junk was reckoned at about 60 *li* per *geng*, a *geng* being the length of a watch, that is, a tenth of a day or roughly 2.4 hours, and a *li* being equal to 553 meters (1,814 feet) during the Song period. This means that a junk proceeded at a standard speed of 8 knots. But this estimate seems optimistic when compared to speeds calculated from the duration of voyages along identified legs in Chinese sailing directions, whose length we know from modern geography. More realistically, the average speed of a junk was probably 4 or 5 knots, which is consistent with the speeds of the ships of the European East India Companies.

**Sailing by the stars.** According to *Peiwen yunfu*, a twelfth-century encyclopedia, nautical astronomy was practiced as early as the Jin dynasty (265–420). This hypothesis is consistent with the interest in the stars that arose at this time among the people of the sea, the community of seafarers and watermen sailing the rivers and inner coastal waters. Under the influence of Chinese geomancy, seamen interpreted the vault of heaven as a compass of twenty-four points. This enabled them to sail the oceans from any shore reference.

The oldest account of an ocean voyage on the China seas is to be found in Faxian's *Foguo zhi* (Report on the Buddhist Kingdoms). This Buddhist monk sailed to India in 399 and came back from Sri Lanka onboard several ships. From the beginning of the fifth century other monks sailed west to study Buddhism, including Yi Jing, who sailed in 671 to Sanfoqi (Srivijaya), a Buddhist kingdom situated along the Java Sea and Malacca Strait. Yet all the ocean traders sailing the South China Sea were Persian.

The first chronicle attesting to navigation by the stars is Zhu Yu's *Pingzhou ketan*, dated 1113. As mentioned above, Zhu Yu was recounting events that occurred before 1090. He said that numerous traders sailed to and from Arabia, India, and Kunlun country (Sumatra, Java, Borneo, Malaysia and the Moluccas, and the Spice Islands). Zhu Yu said that foreign pilots were watching the stars. He did not mention their ships' nationalities, but they were obviously Persian. Chinese ships finally entered the high seas at the beginning of the twelfth century, when ocean navigation developed under the Southern Song (1127–1279).

The first Chinese pilot navigating by the stars is reported in 1122 in the chronicle *Gaoli tu jing* of our major informer Xu Jing. It seems probable that this science appeared four or five centuries earlier, maybe indistinctly connected with geomancy and the zodiac but not yet translated into a nautical science. Which stars were Chinese pilots watching, and why? During the twelfth century, Ursa Major was far from the earth's axis. The polar distance of the constellation was an average of forty degrees. The Chinese paid particular attention to the part of the sky that they called the Celestial Palace, the residence of the Sovereign of the

Upper Kingdom. The emperor, who was the Sovereign of the Lower Kingdom, sat with his back toward Ursa Major facing south, which was the sacred direction. The Chinese carved up the night sky in groupings different from western constellations. The key constellation for seafarers was Beizhen. It consisted of Polaris and on both sides the closest stars of the Ursa Minor and Cepheus constellations. This long star track crossed the celestial pole in the vicinity of Polaris, at about five degrees from the earth's axis, and turned around it. Like Polaris, Beizhen made the determination of north possible with reasonable accuracy. This determination was easily inverted for south, to accord with imperial protocol.

Framing the Celestial Palace were two long alignments of stars that formed the celestial court. The Western Hedge and the Eastern Hedge turned around two Celestial Pivots, two stars of the Draco constellation: Tianyi (the Celestial Unique) and Taiyi (the Supreme Unique). The hedges flanked the Surrounding Wall as two lines of dignitaries.

At the beginning of the fifteenth century, *Zhinan zhengfa* (How to Determine South) and *Shunfeng xiangsong* (How to Get Fair Winds) gave directions on where the sun, moon, and remarkable stars and planets rose and set. These directions gave sensible references for some of the twenty-four points of the compass. The problem was a little complicated because the trajectories of the sun and moon depend on the seasons. *Zhinan zhengfa* offered good examples of variable astronomical references throughout the year, one example being the following: "During the fourth month, the sun rises at Yin [an azimuth of 60°] and sets at Xu [300°]. The day is ten parts long, and the night is six parts long [out of sixteen parts for the entire day]. The moon rises at Chen [120°] and sets at Shen [240°]."

**The compass.** It is not true that the Chinese invented the mariner's compass. The Chinese discovered far before any other people the bipolarity of the magnet, that is, the natural inclination of a magnetic needle to point in a north–south direction. But because they were concerned with geomancy and not really concerned with overseas travel, they missed an opportunity to take advantage of this phenomenon for navigation. Persians imported the Chinese magnetic needle. This borrowing is attested by the Persian name "kibleh numa" (pointing south), evidently translated from the Chinese, which follows the distinctive imperial tradition of designating south as the global pivot instead of north, as did the Arabs and Europeans. The Persians, who were good seafarers, had the brilliant idea to make the magnetic needle a reference at sea.

The Chinese and Persian maritime magnetic needle was simply set on or in a straw floating on a bowl of water. Muslim pilots introduced the floating needle in the Mediterranean area early in the twelfth century. One century later at Amalfi near Naples (Italy), which was then a leading seafaring city, the needle was fastened to an axis and enclosed in a wooden box. Owing to this improvement, the fragile and unpractical wet magnetic needle was transformed into a trusty dry nautical instrument. It was improved still further when, in the same Mediterranean area, some anonymous seafarer in the early fourteenth century thought of fixing the needle under a cardboard rose. The mariner's compass was born. The mariner's compass then spread back over the Indian Ocean and the South China Sea with Portuguese pioneers and later Dutch traders.

During the whole history of navigation, particularly in the Mediterranean, magnetic heading came after navigation by the stars. When mariners began to use the needle at sea, earth magnetism was ignored. The needle seemed attracted by some supernatural power toward Polaris or any other key star or constellation in the vicinity of the earth's axis. On account of its close relationship with a celestial body, the needle was treated with great respect. As late as 1793, George Stauton, a member of Lord George Macartney's British embassy to the imperial court of China, reported that the compass was honored onboard junks with offerings of meat and fruits. Because motionless stars near the earth's axis were key references of heading, and because the magnetic needle apparently pointed at these stars, it was used as an alternative device when the vault of heaven could not be seen, because of daylight or a cloudy sky.

The oldest legends related to magnetism come from the second millennium B.C.E. One of the most interesting narratives introduces Kuan Zhong, a minister of the seventh-century-B.C.E. kingdom of Qi (on the Shandong Peninsula on the Yellow Sea), from which the first Chinese explorations of Japan embarked. The legend says that Kuan Zhong invented the magnetic needle. The reference is noteworthy in that from antiquity, Shandong was an active seafaring province and also possessed lodestone, a natural magnetic iron oxide.

During the Tang dynasty (618–907), besides the wet magnetic needle, a dry needle appeared, hanging by a hair or a silk thread. It has been suggested that the sensitivity of this kind of magnetic instrument enabled the Chinese to observe early on that the needle was not pointing exactly true north, but deviated slightly eastward for mysterious reasons. This is what we call magnetic declination. First indications of this idea appeared early in the eighth century, and it is clearly attested in the *Shuowen jiezi*, the first Chinese dictionary, compiled by Xu Shen at the beginning of the second century.

The use of a magnetic needle on the China seas is positively mentioned for the first time in Zhu Yu's *Pingzhou ketan*, which relates events that happened prior to 1090. The author's father, who embarked onboard a foreign ship, said that a magnetic needle was used as an alternative instrument for holding the route when stars were hidden. We know that Persians had a monopoly on sea trading in Asian waters at this time, which demonstrates that they first had the idea of using the bipolarity of a magnet for navigating the open seas.

Finally, during the Song period, the erudite Shen Kuo, in *Meng xi bitan* (A Compilation of Idle Writings by the Dreamy Stream), described a dry needle hanging by a silk thread as a common device by 1080. Many sources confirm that the dry needle spread over China during the first third of the twelfth century. Far more remarkable, *Gaoli tu jing*, Xu Jing's 1122 report of an embassy to Korea, states positively that pilots of his ship used a floating needle when the sky was dark. In 1225, Zhao Rugua dramatically emphasized in his *Zhufan zhi* (A Report on Foreign Countries) that seafarers regarded the direction of the ship as a matter of life and death, and so carefully watched the magnetic needle day and night.

As for the spread of the magnetic needle, according to literary sources the magnetic needle was known in Amalfi (Italy) by 1110. This means that it spread from the Muslim sphere nearly simultaneously over the Mediterranean and China. Cautiously, as sources are rare, the following evolutionary process may be proposed. Magnetic navigation spread quickly along the maritime silk route from the Mediterranean to the China seas between the end of the eleventh century and the fourteenth century. This efficient nautical instrument is the result of the Chinese discovery of the bipolarity of the magnet, Persian initiatives in applying this phenomenon to sea navigation, and Mediterranean improvements.

At the beginning of the Yuan dynasty (1276–1368), Zhou Daguan related in 1297 his travels by sea along the shores of Vietnam, down to the South China Sea and the Mekong Delta. He reported the ship's itinerary in a kind of logbook, entering rhombs with such accuracy that it seems probable that the needle was fixed to an axis, as in a Mediterranean boxed compass. The compass was probably transferred from the Mediterranean through the Muslim area back to China. It seems that magnetic navigation became customary during the Yuan, though it may not have been fully generalized. In fact, two credible Italian travelers, Nicolo de Conti in 1440

and Friar Mauro in 1459, reported that Chinese were navigating not by the magnetic needle but by the stars. The stars serve well enough when steady winds such as trade winds or monsoon winds raise even waves. During the day the direction of the swell with regard to the ship's heading offers the pilot a good reference until the following night.

A linguistic development may be interpreted as indicating an improvement of the Chinese magnetic device. "Zhinan zhen" literally means a needle that points south. This was reduced to "zhi nan" (a south pointer) during the sixteenth century. Perhaps this evolution of the vocabulary was made logical by the disappearance of the needle in the mariner's compass, in which the needle was covered by a cardboard rose. Most historians affirm that Dutch traders introduced the mariner's compass on Chinese waters during the seventeenth century. Since the alteration of Chinese maritime vocabulary occurred one century sooner, it seems clear that not the Dutch but the Portuguese, who were the first western seafarers to reach the Celestial Empire in the middle of the sixteenth century, introduced the compass to China.

## Latitude

Chinese pilots could deduce considerable position information from the stars. Before the fifteenth century, Chinese were able to measure latitude at sea by polar stars, and by stars of the austral (or southern) sky when these stars crossed the meridian.

**Latitude by Polaris.** Over the Indian and Chinese maritime area, Polaris and Tianyi (the equivalent Chinese star near the earth's axis) were low on the horizon. Seafarers noticed that their altitudes were visibly proportional with latitude. By paying attention to the position of these stars on their daily small trajectory around the earth's axis, they learned how to measure latitude. Polaris and Tianyi were low enough to be measurable in units of a finger's width.

The Chinese *zhi*, like the Arabian *isba*, was a pragmatic and natural angular unit equal to the width of a horizontal finger at arm's length, roughly equal to 1°36'. A *zhi* was divided into four *jiao*. For a better accuracy, a simple instrument similar to the later western cross-staff was invented in the Muslim sphere in the first half of the sixteenth century, if not earlier. The *kamaal* consisted of several wooden or tortoiseshell tablets tied to a string graduated with knots. At the end of the sixteenth century, Li Xu's *Jiean laoren manbi* (Casual Notes of an Old Man of Jiean) described the *qianxing ban* (plates for the altitude of leading stars), consisting of a dozen ebony plates similar to an obsolete form of the *kamaal*. The altitude of a star was measured by holding the upper and lower edges of the tablet so that they coincide with the horizon and the star. The distance from pilot's eye, measured on the graduated string, could be directly converted into altitude.

**Admiral Zheng He's navigation table.** Between 1405 and 1433, under the Yongle emperor (r. 1403–1424) and incidentally the Xuande emperor (r. 1426–1435) of the Ming dynasty, the Muslim eunuch Zheng He led a series of prestigious westward naval expeditions.

Nautical instructions in force in Zheng He's fleets were the epitome of the Chinese science of navigation during the Ming period. This science has been preserved in a book on the general military arts completed in 1621 by Mao Yuanyi. *Wubei zhi* (On Military Preparations) describes several of Admiral Zheng He's itineraries in a manner similar to European pilot books. Generally speaking, sailing instructions associate headings and distances expressed in numbers of watches (*geng*), roughly 2.4 hours long. Maps inserted in the *Wubei zhi* are of various styles but always symbolic. They were not nautical charts strictly speaking, but memoranda gathering useful information, such as directions by rising and setting stars, latitudes of remarkable points or destinations given in terms of the altitudes of Polaris at these places, and sometimes depths and environmental descriptions.

The linear notions of this document are consistent with a seafaring culture that was not referring to nautical charts, or more precisely, that lacked documents adapted to a graphic determination of the ship's position, as on European waters. While Chinese land charts of this time were accurate and progressive, these nautical "maps" were far from any notion of longitude. As in the ancient Mediterranean tradition, Chinese navigational techniques were based on a long tradition of coastal navigation that relied on the geographical configuration of the Chinese coastline.

More interesting are four tables devoted solely to astronomical navigation. They offer positive proof (at least in some special circumstances) of navigation by star altitude, that is, along a determined parallel. The four astronomical tables (*guoyang qianxing tu*, or chart for crossing the ocean by leading stars) inserted in the *Wubei zhi* covered transits from Sumatra to Sri Lanka and the return, and from Calicut (on the Malabar Coast of India) to Hormuz (at the entrance of the Persian Gulf on Arabia) and the return. Apparently based on different rules, each of them was computed for a specific maritime leg.

A pilot sailing from Sri Lanka to the Strait of Malacca across the Bay of Bengal was asked to pay close attention to the night sky. The table for sailing from Ceylon (Sri Lanka) back to Sumatra directs the attention to the following constellations (Figure 1). To the north of the sky and on the upper part of the table: "The Huagai star at eight fingers above level water. The Beizhen star at one finger above level water." To the south and on the lower part of the table: "The Denglonggu star at fourteen and half fingers above level water. The two Nanmen stars at fifteen fingers above level water." On the lower left side of the table: "To the southwest, the Busi stars at four fingers above level water." On the right side of the table: "To the northeast, the Zhinü star at eleven fingers above the level water." The text specified that the destination was Banda Aceh (Kutaraja), a city of the Kingdom of Acem, which was settled in the northern part of Sumatra and controlled access to the Malacca Strait.

The usual width of a *zhi* given by scholars is 1°37′. This is insufficient to make the table coherent. Adopting 1°8′ as a tentative width, it works much better and the table may be translated like that : "Kochab, (Beta, Ursa Minor) at 14.5° above the water. Polaris (Alpha, Ursa Minor) at 1.8°. Mimosa (Beta, Southern Cross) at 26°. Agena and Rigil al Kentarus (Alpha and Beta, Centaur) at 27°. To the southwest, Pollux (Beta, the Twins) and Procyon (Alpha, Little Dog) at 7.2°. To the northeast, Vega (Alpha, Lyra) at 19.8°."

Detailed calculations confirm that the table made possible eastward navigation by the altitudes of stars, with no chart or instrument other than the pilot's finger, within a latitudinal error of about 100 kilometers (62 miles) on average, which reduced to within some 20 kilometers (12 miles) when referring to Polaris (see Bellec 1994). Because it is difficult to detect the culmination of a star, the signal for starting the measurement process was given by Kochab, one of the guards of Polaris and a star well known by mariners. The process was set off every night when Kochab reached an altitude of eight fingers above level water, as indicated by the table. This key star was the clock of the system, which needed no timekeeper. This gradually changing reference was free of changing ephemeris and independent of local time, which gained one hour from Sri Lanka to Sumatra. It gave the method its ingeniousness.

The error caused by the inaccuracy of the northeast reference could possibly be a safety margin to ensure that the dead-reckoned route did not miss Sumatra. As a matter of fact, the islands of Nicobar and Andaman laid out a dangerous trap between Sumatra and Burma. Yet if the inaccuracy of Zheng He's sidereal rose reached 6°, it was competitive with the best magnetic compass at a time when dramatic errors caused by magnetic declination and iron masses such as anchors and cannons were unknown.

Zheng He's astronomical tables had their limitations. For an astronomical pilot book to be useful, the stars had to be visible at night. The solar day and sidereal day differ by four minutes every day. That is to say, six months after an arbitrary day, the stars that were overhead at midnight are overhead at noon, and thus are invisible. Hence, any astronomical table is useful for travel during a determined period of the year. Different sailing directions, depending on other stars, had to be prepared for different seasons.

Moreover, Zheng He's sailing instructions were set from specific point to specific point. They were not universal, for the vault of heaven changes with latitude. They could not be used for sailing unknown seas, since they required previous observation of heavenly bodies. Therefore, these instructions were not flexible enough to enable discoveries.

## The Long Blackout of Chinese Navigation

For continental-minded, proud Chinese, Zheng He's voyages demonstrated that there were no worthy nations beyond the Western (that is, Indian) Ocean. For lettered counselors at court, the western peoples along the Indian Ocean were worthy only of paying homage and tribute to the emperor.

The Yongle emperor died in 1424, and factions opposed to sea trading assumed power. Their influence had been affirmed a few years earlier, when private trading with foreign countries was forbidden in 1395, and again when private grain transport by sea was forbidden in 1415. As soon as he ascended the throne, the Zhengtong emperor (r. 1436–1449) ordered the building of oceangoing many-masted junks to be punished with death.

When the Portuguese entered the Indian Ocean and the China seas during one of the most brilliant periods of western maritime history, China had turned inward. Huddled inside an interdicted sea and the Great Wall, the Celestial Empire was hibernating, protected from foreign cultural influences. China was neither inquisitive about other peoples nor a conquering nation. Yet the Celestial Empire was powerful, capable, innovative in many technical fields, and, in organization, tolerant, and highly cultured. It missed an opportunity of mastering the Indian and Asian regions before the arrival of Europeans from the early sixteenth century. If China had achieved such an ambition, world history would be dramatically different.

[See also Dead Reckoning; Longitude Finding; Ma Huan; Shipping Companies, *subentry on* Chinese River Trades; Wars, Maritime, *subentry on* China, Korea, and Japan; Yi Sun-sin; *and* Zheng He.]

## Bibliography

Bellec, François. "L'astronomie nautique le long de la route maritime de la soie." In *Les routes de la soie*, edited by UNESCO. Paris: Editions UNESCO, 1994.

Bellec, François. "A Chinese Art of Navigation across the Muslim Waters." In *Maritime Silk Routes Studies*. Fuzhou: China Maritime Silk Routes Studies Centre and Fujian Education Publishing House 1997. In English and Chinese.

Dars, Jacques. *La marine chinoise du Xème au XIVème siècle*. Paris: Economica, 1992.

Hourani, George Fadlo. *Arab Seafaring in the Indian Ocean in Ancient and Early Medieval Times*. Princeton, N.J.: Princeton University Press, 1951.

Lelièvre, Dominique. *Le dragon de lumière*. Paris: France-Empire, 1996.

Li, Shu-hua. "The South-Pointing Carriage and the Mariner's Compass." *Qinghua xuebao* 1 (1956): 63–113.

Lo Jung-Pang. "The Emergence of China as a Sea Power during the Late Sung and Early Yüan Periods." *Far Eastern Quarterly* 14, no. 4 (1955): 489–503.

Ma Huan. *Ying-yai sheng-lan: The Overall Survey of the Ocean's Shores*. Translated by Feng Ch'eng-Chün. Cambridge, U.K.: Hakluyt Society and Cambridge University Press, 1970.

Needham, Joseph. *Science and Civilisation in China*. Vol. 4, part 3, *Civil Engineering and Nautics*. Cambridge, U.K.: Cambridge University Press, 1954–1986.

Pai Tseng-Ho. "On the Ships of Cheng Ho." In *Second Biennial Conference Proceedings*, edited by International Association of Historians of Asia. Taibei, Taiwan: Zhongguo Lishi Xuehui, 1962.

Peng Deqing, ed. *Ships of China*. Beijing: Renmin Jiaotong Chubanshe, 1988.

Saussure, Léopold de. "L'origine de la rose des vents et l'invention de la boussole." In *Instructions nautiques et routiers arabes et portugais des XVe et XVIe siècles*, edited by Gabriel Ferrand. Paris: Paul Geuthner, 1928.

Sleeswyk, André Wegener. "The Liao and the Displacement of Ships in the Ming Navy." *Mariner's Mirror* 82, no. 1 (1996): 3–13.

Swanson, Bruce. *Eighth Voyage of the Dragon*. Annapolis, Md.: Naval Institute Press, 1982.

Waters, David W. "Chinese Junks. The Antung Trader." *Mariner's Mirror* 24, no. 1 (1938): 49–67.

Waters, David W. "Chinese Junks: The Hangchow Bay Trader and Fisher." *Mariner's Mirror* 33, no. 1 (1947): 28–38.

Waters, David W. "Chinese Junks: The Pechili Trader." *Mariner's Mirror* 25, no. 1 (1939): 62–87.

FRANÇOIS BELLEC

# Voyages of Exploration

China is responsible for some remarkable early advances in maritime technology and exploration, yet these advances have had little impact on China's own development later. The story of those advances is one of opportunities lost.

## Environment

Though it was a land-based empire, imperial China (which lasted from 221 B.C.E. to 1911 C.E.) was indeed open to the sea. Its mainland coastline in modern times extends from 20° to 42° N latitude and from 103° to 125° E longitude, like a huge fishhook lying on the western Pacific Rim in the heart of what may be called the "Asian Mediterranean," situated in Southeast Asia.

China is surrounded by the Bohai, Yellow, East China, and South China seas, which link China to the Pacific and Indian oceans. Mainland China has excellent access to these waters, owing to five factors: coastline, topographic features of the coast, climatic patterns, patterns of sea and ocean currents and tides, and inland transportation to the coast. By these criteria, China has some obvious advantages.

In the Qing period (1644–1911), mainland China, including China's territory in the South China Sea region,

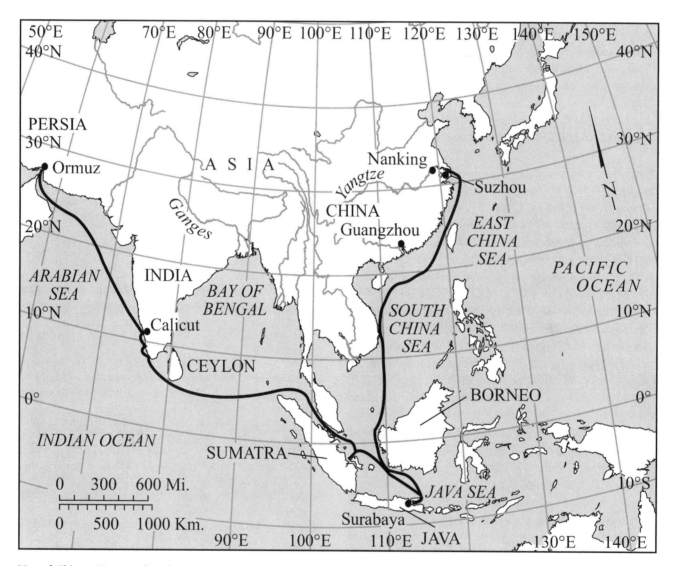

**Map of Chinese Voyage of Exploration.** Route of Zheng He (1371–1433). MAP BY BILL NELSON

had a land border of about 16,000 kilometers (9,900 miles) versus a coastline of more than 18,000 kilometers (11,200 miles), giving it a land-border to coastline ratio of eight to nine. Despite its territorial losses by 1900, contemporary China has one of the longest coastlines in the world, exceeded within the Pacific Rim only by Japan in Asia and by the United States and Canada in North America.

Topographically, the mainland coast has two plains with an elevation of 0 to 200 meters (0 to 656 feet) above sea level. Between these two plains lies a mountainous zone with an elevation of 500 to 1,000 meters (1,640 to 3,280 feet) above sea level. Yet this mountainous area does not handicap sea access, owing to numerous river valleys linking the interior to the coast. In addition, there are two large gulfs (the Bohai Gulf and the Beibu Gulf) and numerous smaller bays and coastal islands, providing shelter from prevailing winds and seas.

The climatic patterns of China's coastal regions (mainly temperature, winds, and sea currents) are favorable for sailing. China's ports are ice-free all year round. The wind pattern in China is dictated by seasonal monsoons coming from the tropics in summer and from the Arctic in winter. In summer the winds blow across China from south to north. In winter they blow in the opposite direction. The monsoons provide China with two advantages for maritime activities: they are highly predictable, and they blow largely along the longitudinal line linking China to the Asian Mediterranean. The entire coast of China is situated between 20° and 42° N latitude, where storms are relatively infrequent. This makes the Yellow, East China, and South China seas very safe for sailing; in Qing times, the annual rate of ships lost in storms in the China seas was only about one percent.

Sea and ocean currents move seasonally in two directions along China's mainland coast: northerly in summer and southerly in winter. This pattern corresponds to the monsoons, and thus it provides Chinese sailors with some extra help in their voyages to South Asia and Southeast Asia and back.

China's inland transportation (roads and waterways) was generally good by premodern standards. Since the third century B.C.E., the empire had an extensive road network in which four out of six arteries led directly to a waterfront. In addition, China has more than two hundred rivers flowing into the sea, with an aggregate navigable length of 160,000 kilometers (99,000 miles). The country also has numerous estuaries; in its eight coastal provinces,

each has an average of about 20 bays and an average of 34.6 river mouths.

Moreover, China's coast is studded with numerous islands (6,536 in all), which in the past provided sailors with shelter from the elements, and thus played a crucial role in the success of private maritime activities under the maritime bans of the Ming and Qing courts.

On the basis of these facts, it can be stated that China has excellent water access, probably among the best of all continental countries. But these favorable conditions alone did not necessarily lead to maritime activities. Throughout Chinese history, sailing was a means for an end, those ends being state politics (including military operations, territorial expansion, administration, diplomacy, exile, rebellion, and resistance against the state), cultural exchange, expeditions, emigration, and trade. These ends were the ones that motivated the Chinese to sail at sea. These ends also explain why and how the state and private sectors were both involved in maritime activities and in the development of maritime technology.

## Navigational Technology and Its Development: Reckoning

The most significant development in Chinese maritime technology of the premodern period was reckoning a ship's position in open waters. Reckoning is a matter of coordinating time and distance in a macrosystem of latitude and longitude with reference points in the cosmic system. There were four key components to reckoning: knowledge of the positions of stars, an accurate calendar system, mapping technology, and measures of time and distance. All these components were developed in China earlier than in most other Eurasian civilizations.

**Knowledge of the positions of stars.** Evidence shows that by the Zhou period (eleventh century B.C.E.–475 B.C.E.) astronomical observation had become a profession, and records had been made on the subject. For example, the positions of Taurus at night were recorded in the *Shang shu* (Book of Ancient History), a Confucian classic written probably during the early Zhou period, as follows: "It shows up from the east at sea level in the sixth month, rises half way up to the zenith in the seventh month, reaches the zenith in the eighth month, declines to the west half way to sea level in the ninth month, drops to sea level in the tenth month" ("Yaodian" [Rules of King Yao]).

Much progress was made in the following Warring States period (475–221 B.C.E.). A recent archaeological discovery in Hubei Province included a chart containing the names of twenty-eight constellations or zones for regular astronomical observations and the positions of 121 stars in the sky, suggesting that by then the Chinese had already grouped celestial bodies and fixed stars (including the sun) and the planets. In Han times (206 B.C.E.–220 C.E.), six treatises on star-guided navigation were written, in a total of 136 volumes. Thus a considerable amount of knowledge was accumulated through the years. In addition, from the Han on, when astronomical observation was an official enterprise, Chinese histories contained a chapter called "Tianwen zhi" (Records of Astronomical Observations), reporting important new discoveries.

Yet official sponsorship did not have a monopoly over astronomy. In the Sui (581–618) and Tang (618–907) periods, popularization of astronomical knowledge was well developed. In a popular work titled *Butian ge* (Ballad of Stars), 1,464 stars and their positions are described.

A closer look at the Chinese achievement reveals a pattern of development from Han to Tang times. Three important quantitative steps were taken. First, around the second century B.C.E., Chinese observers established the relation among the horizontal altitude (*A*) of an object, its declination (*D*), and the geographical latitude of the observer (*L*): $L = 90° + D - A$. Their result was accurate within ±1°9'. Second, between the second and first centuries B.C.E., in a work titled *Zhoubi suan jing* (The Classic for Calculating the Gnomon and Circular Paths of Heaven), the locations of the Big Dipper (Ursa Major) and Polaris in different seasons were calculated. Third, during the Kaiyuan Reign (713–741) of the Tang period, two Chinese astronomers, Tang Yixing and Nangong Yue, undertook nationwide observations, covering latitudes from 51° to 17° N. They reached the conclusion that 1° latitude equals 351 *li* 80 *bu* (a *li* is a Chinese mile; 129.2 kilometers or 80.1 miles). These discoveries established some basic coefficients in relations between cosmic objects and locations on earth.

This general astronomical knowledge laid the cornerstone for reckoning. In the Eastern Jin period (317–420), China had reached the stage of navigation based on astronomic observations; sailors used the sun and other stars as a cosmic reference system to determine ships' locations. This fact was first recorded by Faxian (c. 337–c. 422), a Chinese Buddhist monk who traveled to thirty countries in South Asia and Southeast Asia during his religious pursuit.

By the Tang period (618–907), astronomical navigation had become further quantified and standardized with the invention of the *Tang xiaochi* (Tang handy ruler) and the *liangtianchi* (star-measuring ruler), special devices for navigation based on astronomic observations. These devices, based on the principles of trigonometry, estimated the latitude of a ship's position by measuring the altitude and bearing between the horizon and Polaris or other stars at a given time. In 1974 a star-measuring ruler was discovered in a wreck from the Song period (960–1279) in Quanzhou, providing positive proof of the use of such a technique. In Ming times (1368–1644), not only did this equipment become common, it was used in conjunction with charts. *Zheng He hanghai tu* (The Navigation Chart of Zheng He's Voyages), an embryonic almanac, includes forty measured altitudes in different seasons at chosen locations along the sea routes.

Later the procedure became streamlined and simplified as Chinese nautical astronomers focused on the polestar instead of a cluster of stars. Accordingly, a new device, *qianxingban* (Polaris-aiming plates), was invented. It was recorded in detail later in Chinese literature by Li Xu (1505–1592) as consisting of twelve square plates in diminishing sizes ranging from 24 to 2 centimeters (9.4 to 0.8 inches) long on each side. To measure the altitude of a star, a sailor simply held a plate with his outstretched arm, looked at the sky, and leveled the upper edge of the plate with the polar star, and the lower edge with the horizon. For stars of different altitudes, different plates were used. From the altitude of the star, the latitude of the ship was then calculated. The new device was durable and easy to use, and it provided sailors with a reasonably reliable method for determining a ship's position at sea.

**An accurate calendar system.** China developed a calendar system early on. In the first known calendar, *Xia xiao zheng* (Lesser Annuary of the Xia Dynasty), written during the Shang period (from sixteenth century B.C.E. to eleventh century B.C.E.), the year is divided into twelve months, and relevant phenological tokens (animal signs corresponding with the seasons) are identified. After the Qin period (221–207 B.C.E.), calendar making was centralized by the imperial government, which continuously devoted resources to this field of study. A public good, the imperial calendar gave Chinese sailors an important tool for their operations.

**Mapping technology.** The application of astronomical knowledge, the use of the compass, and sea routes led to the making of navigation charts (*haitu*) during Northern Song times. In 1003 a chart titled *Haiwai zhufan tu* (A Chart of Overseas Countries) was presented to the throne as a treasure, an indication of its value. In 1123 Xu Jing, a Southern Song envoy to Koryo (Korea), produced *Shenzhou suojing daozhou zhanyu erweizhi tu* (Comprehensive Charts of Islands on the Way to Korea). By Yuan times, navigation charts had become readily available. For instance, the government had *Haidao jing* (Classic Charts for Sea Routes) produced and carved on stone tablets so that the public could have easy access to a copy by making rubbings with paper and ink from the inscriptions. By the mid-fifteenth century, Chinese nautical cartography had developed to its peak, with navigation charts covering the South China Sea and the North Indian Ocean, such as "The Navigation Chart of Zheng He's Voyages."

**Measures of time and distance.** By the Tang period, portable water-drip timepieces had been in use on ships, and during the following Song period (960–1279), they became necessities for Chinese sailors. Apart from indigenous Chinese timepieces based on dripping water or sand, which were expensive and bulky because the Chinese had not yet developed glass, the Chinese of this period also used incense (joss sticks) as a cheaper and more portable timepiece with reasonable accuracy. Sometimes candles and oil-burning lamps were also used for keeping time. On wooden ships, the joss stick was also safer than combustion-operated timepieces. Indeed, Chinese sailors used the duration for burning a stick of incense as a unit of time.

These four key components—knowledge of the positions of stars, an accurate calendar system, mapping technology, and measures of time and distance—were only necessary, and not sufficient, conditions for reckoning. To determine a ship's position in the open sea, one needs to know the longitude in coordination with the time and the distance a ship travels. Here three measures of three sets of movements are entwined: the macro-movement of the sun, the macro-movement of earth, and the micro-movement of the vessel itself. The sailor's task is to know the speed and distance traveled by the ship and, with measurements of the first two macro-movements, to locate the ship's micro-

movement on the macro-picture of the sea. This was a huge challenge for the premodern sailor.

By the second half of the sixth century, Chinese sailors developed the *geng* (log) to measure a ship's movements in terms of coordinated times and distances. The first element of the log divided a day (of twenty-four hours) into ten units. The second element measured the ship's speed by calculating the time that it took for a floating wood chip dropped at the bow to reach the stern. This method was particularly suited to large ships, which the Chinese tended to build at that time. The invention of the log marked the beginning of the era of quantitative navigation in Chinese maritime history.

## Navigational Technology and Its Development: Semi-dead Reckoning

Reckoning based on astronomic observations has its limits, however. It can be practiced only when astronomic bodies are visible. During cloudy weather and during much of the daytime, such observations are impossible. A breakthrough occurred with the reinvention of the compass, which ushered in an era of semi-dead reckoning: locating ships in the open seas mainly by measuring traveled distances and compass positions.

There are records of the use of the compass before the Warring States period (475–221 B.C.E.). But it was only some eight centuries later in the Northern and Southern Dynasties period (420–589) that the compass began to be used for navigational purposes. A high point of its use was to establish direct routes from China to Japan across the open sea for some 600 to 700 kilometers (roughly 400 miles). Compasses became common on ships much later still; only in 1119, in Zhu Yu's *Pingzhou ketan* (Pingzhou Table Talk), was the use of the compass on ships explicitly documented as a device for navigating on cloudy days. The main obstacle seems to have been the weight and size of early compasses.

This changed in about the mid-eleventh century. In 1044 the portable compass was first recorded as used to guide army units on maneuvers at night and on cloudy days. Soon the new device became commonly available, and compass making became commonplace. The Song technologist Shen Kuo (Shen Gua), for instance, described four ways of making portable compasses.

About a century later, the compass became indispensable on Chinese ships, as described by Zhao Rukuo (Zhao Rushi), a customs officer in Fujian:

"Sailing to the east from Hainan Island, sailors face sandbars of a thousand *li* and rocks of ten thousand *li*, sky and water merge in one color without end. Oceangoing ships traveling in these waters rely entirely on the compass: sailors watch the device day and night with every caution because a hair-breadth's mistake would cause disaster. It is a matter of life and death" (*Zhufan Zhi* [Records of Foreign Peoples], "Hainandao" [The Hiannan Island]).

The same opinion was shared by Wu Zimu in his *Meng liang lu* (Records of a Dream of Grandeur):

"Once ships enter the open seas, there is no land. It is a dangerous place where monsters live. On windy, rainy and cloudy days, sailing relies on nothing but the compass which is under the charge of the compass operator [*huozhang*]. The compass operator dares not make any mistakes because he is responsible for the lives on the ship."

It is clear that by the end of the thirteenth century at the latest, operating the compass on the ship had become a profession in China.

During the Ming period (1368–1644) and the Qing period (1644–1911), the improved maritime compass was boxed, and the dial had twenty-four divisions of 15° each to make ship positioning more accurate. Meanwhile, the status of compass operators rose steadily. Seagoing ships had compass cabins (*zhenfang*). A compass operator was on duty all the time, day and night. In the fleet of Admiral Zheng He (1371–1433), the compass operator was also the captain of the ship.

Semi-dead reckoning enabled the Chinese to sail across open waters even farther offshore. This created more risks. To confirm and adjust their reckonings, Chinese sailors had to watch for certain types of seaweed, fish, and birds; had to observe the depth, color, and smell of sea water; and had to note the color and smell of sea mud. Nevertheless, it was semi-dead reckoning that allowed Chinese sea exploration to take off. By the twelve century under the Song Dynasty, Chinese long-range ships were almost certainly able to travel to Japan and most places in the Asian Mediterranean in Southeast Asia, including the Philippines, Java, and Malacca of today. Their destinations also extended to the Bay of Bengal and beyond, as shown in Table 1.

TABLE 1. *Expanding Chinese Knowledge of Overseas Places, 1100–1440*

| | No. of New Places | | | | | | |
|---|---|---|---|---|---|---|---|
| | A | B | C | D | E | F | G |
| Southern Song | 42 | 14 | 12 | 0 | 4 | 8 | 80 |
| Yuana | 31 | 21 | 3 | 1 | 2 | 0 | 58 |
| Ming | 6 | 2 | 1 | 2 | 4 | 0 | 15 |
| Total | 79 | 37 | 16 | 3 | 10 | 8 | 153 |

| | No. of New Places | | | | | | |
|---|---|---|---|---|---|---|---|
| | A | B | C | D | E | F | G |
| % of Song in total | 53.2 | 37.8 | 75.0 | 0.0 | 40.0 | 100.0 | 52.3 |
| % of Yuan in total | 39.2 | 56.8 | 18.8 | 33.3 | 20.0 | 0.0 | 37.9 |
| % of Ming in total | 7.6 | 5.4 | 6.2 | 66.7 | 40.0 | 0.0 | 9.8 |

Notes: A: places in Southeast Asia; B: places in South Asia; C: places in the Arabian Sea region; D: places in the Red Sea region; E: places in the East African coastal region; F: places in the Mediterranean region; G: total. a. Incomplete data.

Sources: Southern Song, based on Zhou Qufei's *Lingwai daida* (Knowledge about South China and Beyond) and Zhao Rukuo's *Zhufan zhi* (Records of Foreign Peoples). Yuan, based on Wang Dayuan's *Daoyi zhilüe* (Brief Records of Islands and Their Peoples). Ming, based on Zheng He's voyages (1405–1432).

## Navigational Technology and Its Development: Sea Routes

With the increasing knowledge of and frequent contact with overseas places came sea routes linking China with the outside world. Sea routes were developed in three main phases. First were local short-range routes along China's own coast; then came medium-range routes to East Asia, South Asia, and Southeast Asia; and last were long-range routes to western Asia and East Africa. These phases were coupled with the development of reckoning and semi-dead reckoning.

By the Western Han period (206 B.C.E.–8 C.E.), Chinese ships were recorded to have reached Simhala (now Sri Lanka) at the tip of the Indian subcontinent. In the Eastern Han period (25–220 C.E.), Chinese ships went beyond Sri Lanka to the rest of western Asia. In 97 C.E. Gan Ying, the Chinese envoy to the Roman Empire, went as far as the Persian Gulf and then returned before entering the Roman territory. From Tang times, these sea routes formed the so-called "maritime silk routes" (to distinguish them from the overland *haishang silu*, or "silk roads"), and they were frequently used by Chinese, Indians, and Arabs. This marked a turning point in the Chinese history of maritime trade.

Once semi-dead reckoning was developed, coastal routes were replaced by open sea routes. By Song times (960–1279), Chinese ships were able to cross the open waters of some 2,300 kilometers (1,400 miles) in the Indian Ocean from Malacca to Sri Lanka, avoiding the coastal detour along the Bay of Bengal. They even continued from Sri Lanka to

Qamar in the Arabian Peninsula, covering another 4,000 kilometers (2,500 miles) on the open ocean.

With this progress, the duration of voyages was progressively shortened. In Western Han times (206 B.C.E.–8 C.E.), a trip to the vicinity of Singapore took some 150 days. It took only 40 days in the Song period (960–1279). In Sui (581–618) and Tang times (618–907), it took more than thirty days to travel from Sri Lanka to the Persian Gulf, whereas in Ming times (1368–1644), to cover a similar distance required just twenty-two days. Table 2 shows highlights of this progress.

TABLE 2. *Some Chinese Sea Routes and Sailing Times*

| Sea/Ocean | From[a] | To[a] | Day(s) |
|---|---|---|---|
| **Western Han (206 B.C.E.–8 C.E.)** | | | |
| South China Sea | Guangdong | Singapore | 150 |
| South China Sea | Singapore | Burma | 120 |
| South China Sea | Malacca | Vietnam | 60 |
| Indian Ocean | Burma | South India | 60 |
| Indian Ocean | – | Sri Lanka, | 240 |
| | – | Burma, | |
| | – | Malacca | |
| **Sui-Tang (581–907)** | | | |
| Yellow Sea | China | Japan | – |
| Yellow Sea | Japan | China | – |
| East China Sea | Ningbo | Japan | 3 |
| East China Sea | China | Japan | 14 |
| East China Sea | Japan | Wenzhou | 6 |
| East China Sea | Japan | Ningbo | 4 |
| South China Sea | China | Malacca | – |
| South China Sea | Guangzhou | Sri Lanka | 42 |
| Indian Ocean | Malacca | Bay of Bengal | – |
| Indian Ocean | Bay of Bengal | Sri Lanka | 15 |
| Arabian Sea | Sri Lanka | Persian Gulf | 37 |
| Indian Ocean | China | Persian Gulf | 90 |
| **Song-Yuan (960–1368)** | | | |
| Yellow Sea | China | Korea | 1 |
| Yellow Sea | China | Japan | 7 |
| Yellow Sea | Japan/Korea | China | – |
| East China Sea | China | Japan | 18 |
| East China Sea | Japan | China | 7 |
| South China Sea | South Asia | China | – |
| South China Sea | Quanzhou | Java | 30 |

| Sea/Ocean | From[a] | To[a] | Day(s) |
|---|---|---|---|
| South China Sea | Guangzhou | Banda Aceh[b] | 40 |
| South China Sea | Guangzhou | Sumatra | 40 |
| Indian Ocean | Sumatra | Quilon[c] | 30 |
| Indian Ocean | Quilon | Qamar[d] | 60 |
| **Ming (Zheng He)[e] (1368–1644)** | | | |
| Indian Ocean | Jiangsu | Calicut[c] | – |
| Indian Ocean | – | Calicut | – |
| South China Sea | Jiangsu | Vietnam | 10 |
| Indian Ocean | Vietnam | Calicut | – |
| Arabian Sea | Calicut | Persian Gulf | 10[f] |
| Indian Ocean | Calicut | Zufar | 20 |
| Indian Ocean | Quilon | Muqdisho | 20 |
| South China Sea | Fujian | Vietnam | 10 |
| Indian Ocean | – | Calicut | – |
| Arabian Sea | Calicut | Persian Gulf | 25 |
| Indian Ocean | Calicut | Red Sea | 28 |
| Indian Ocean | – | India | – |
| Indian Ocean | – | India | – |
| Indian Ocean | Somalia | Good Hope (?) | – |
| Indian Ocean | Maldives | Good Hope (?) | – |
| South China Sea | Jiangsu | Sumatra | – |
| Indian Ocean | Sumatra | Calicut | 38 |
| Arabian Sea | Calicut | Persian Gulf | 35 |
| **Qing (1644–1911)** | | | |
| South China Sea | – | Manila | 15 |

Notes: a. If possible, modern names are used to indicate their locations today, which means that the regions only roughly match those in history. b. On the northwest tip of Sumatra, Indonesia. c. On the west coast of India. d. On the south coast of the Arabian Peninsula. e. Partial record, including his detachments. f. The figure is presented as recorded, although it seems incorrect.

Sources: Sun Guangqi, *Zhongguo gudai hanghai shi* (A Nautical History of Premodern China; Beijing: Maritime Press, 1989), pp. 162–165, 294–296, 298, 338, 362, 379, 384–385, 407–408, and 410. Zhang Xun, *Woguo gudai de haishang jiaotong* (Sea Traffic in Premodern China; Beijing: Commercial Press, 1986), p. 43. Gao Weinong, "Tang-Song shiqi Zhongguo Dongnanya zhijian de hanglu zongkao" (A Survey of Sea Routes between China and Southeast Asia in the Tang and Song periods), in *Haijiao shi yanjiu* (Research on the History of Sea Communication) 1 (1987): 33. Zhang Xun, ed., *Zhongguo hanghai keji shi* (A History of Chinese Maritime Technology; Beijing: Maritime Press, 1991), pp. 160, 162–163, and 165–166. L. Carrington Goodrich and Chaoying Fang, eds., *Dictionary of Ming Biography, 1368–1644* (New York and London: Columbia University Press, 1976), pp. 195–198.

## Means of Sailing: Ship Designs

The first seaworthy ships in Chinese history were probably multideckers, a design for the navy. It is documented that during 41–42 C.E. General Ma Yuan commanded a large fleet of multideck warships in his campaign against the Cochin Kingdom (now part of Vietnam). In 399–411 C.E. Sun En and Lu Xun led a rebellion of over 100,000 followers with a fleet of multideckers. The rebels' ships were reported to be too large to enter the Yangzi River, and hence good only for the sea. The multideck design dominated the design of Chinese seagoing ships until the Sui period (581–618).

The twelfth century saw the rise of the Fuzhou-type ship (*fuchuan*), also exclusively for sea voyages. The earliest information on the design can be found in an official record of 1169, after a fleet of forty-two of them (20.5 meters by 4.9 meters, or 67 feet by 16 feet) was built in coastal Ningbo. The main features of the new design were (1) a ballasted keel and bilge keels, together with a low ratio of deck length to beam (2.5:1 to 4.0:1), to improve stability; (2) a V-shaped bottom and the multiple sails (three to twelve), to increase speed; (3) multiple stern rudders, to improve steering; (4) a hull of overlapping clinker planks with multiple holds, to strengthen the ship. These features are evident in three wrecks examined from 1974 to 1979 at Quanzhou, at Ningbo, and on the Korean coast.

During the same period, the *shachuan* ("sand beater," or "shallow-water ship"), another type of seagoing vessel, was also invented. In 1978 a shipwreck (14.6 meters by 4.1 meters by 1.9 meters, or 47.9 feet by 13.5 feet by 6.2 feet, with a minimal displacement of 38 metric tons or 41.8 short tons) was examined in Tianjin. Sunk in 1117, it is the earliest known example of a *shachuan* in Chinese maritime history. This type of ship, commonly known as a junk, has the distinctive features of a keel-less hull with a U-shaped bottom.

The loading capacity of a large multidecker was remarkable: eight hundred troops in a ship, according to records of the Sui period (581–618). A large Fuzhou-type ship was capable of taking a cargo of 1,000 metric tons (1,100 short tons) or 1,000 passengers. Such designs were a crucial for a voyage across the Indian Ocean. Indeed, Fuzhou-type ships formed the backbone of the Ming fleet under Admiral Zheng He during the fifteenth century.

## Sailing Devices and Pilotage

Pilotage is closely related to four areas of technology: reckoning, sea routes, ship propulsion, and ship maneuverability.

The first two of these have been discussed. In the Chinese context, technological development in the latter two areas involved the sail and the rudder, both related to ship design.

Given the prevailing monsoons in the western Pacific and northern Indian oceans, the use of wind power for sailing was a rational choice. This led to the use of sails. The word *fan* (sail) first appeared in authoritative dictionaries in the Eastern Han period (25–220 C.E.)—for example, *Shi ming* (Explanations of Names). The description of the use of sails on ships first appeared also in this period, in a poem titled *Guangcheng qu* (Song of Guangcheng), written in 115 C.E. by Ma Rong: "Link the supply ships and open up the tall sails, cover the cargo, in the cool wind."

The use of sails became increasingly common in the Tang period (618–907), as reflected in numerous poems of the period. For instance, Li Bai (701–762) wrote, "Trees along the Jin River become leafless after the frosts, while the cotton sail fills with the autumn winds." Du Fu (712–770), another well-known poet, referred thus to sails in his "Lüye Shuhuai" (Night Trip Diary): "A soft breeze blows the thin grass on the river bank, while the tall mast guards the ship, the sail lowered for the night." After the Tang, the use of sails was the norm.

Sail design gradually evolved in China. First, the materials used for making sails changed over time. Early sails were made of woven leaves and were not durable. Such a situation lasted until the Five Dynasties period (907–960), when affordable cloth replaced leaves, which eliminated a material constraint on making sails. Second, the shape and structure of sails evolved over time. In the Warring States period (475–221 B.C.E.), a sail was hung like an open fan, probably similarly to the sail on an Arabian dhow. By Song times (960–1279), the sail had become square shaped, with a rigid supporting frame. To facilitate trimming a sail with such a frame, a mechanical Chinese rig was developed. This device spread stresses and cushioned shocks, which made trimming easier. Third, the number of sails mounted on a ship changed. Already during Han times (206 B.C.E.–220 C.E.), multiple sails were mounted on multiple masts to maximize wind propulsion. Some of Zheng He's ships for his fifteenth-century voyages had as many as twelve masts. Fourth, the size of the sail increased. Commercial ships of the Ming period (1368–1644) often had two large sails as tall as 10 *zhang* (24 meters, or 78.7 feet). An enlarged sail indicates improved efficiency. In addition, from Song times (960–1279) masts could be folded onto the deck to prevent damage from storms on the open sea.

In Chinese history, the use of the rudder was first recorded during 179–122 B.C.E. in Liu An's *Huainanzi* (The Duke of Huainan). Archeological findings in the 1950s of two ship models support this claim. By the Five Dynasties period (907–960), the balanced rudder (or axial rudder) had become common on Chinese ships. The new design reduced water resistance to the rudder's surface to achieve higher hydrodynamic efficiency. By the Southern Song period (1127–1279), the fenestrated rudder was invented to reduce water resistance even further. Around the same period, adjustable, multiple rudders were invented. A large Song ship had as many as three rudders with different lengths, designed for different waterways. Also invented were the *pishuiban* (leeboard) and the adjustable *zhongchaban* (fin keel or centerboard).

Technical advancements in Chinese rudder designs and the inventions of the leeboard and the fin keel were undoubtedly related to the improved design of sails. The use of rudder for steering was crucial for jibing and tacking (sailing, in zigzag fashion, into wind), which was the only way to sail across the Indian Ocean against prevailing monsoon winds blowing longitudinally. With this set of equipment, Chinese sailors mastered tacking.

In the extant literature, a systematic description of sail control first appeared during the Three Kingdoms period (220–265) in "Zhou Bu" (Ships) of Wan Zhen's *Nanzhou yiwu zhi* (Exotic Things in the South): "People living near the seas have four sails in line on their ships.... The sails can be set up at an angle to hold the wind from the side. The power from the wind on the quarter is strong enough to push the ship forward." This is unmistakably the technique of sailing with the wind on the quarter.

All these inventions and innovations in Chinese nautical technology were driven by a need to sail faster, farther, and with greater maneuverability. The resulting growth of Chinese sea routes, especially those that crossed the Indian Ocean (from Malacca to Sri Lanka to the Arabian Peninsula) indicates that Chinese technology and piloting skills became adequate for crossing the open seas.

## Impact of the Chinese Maritime Achievement on Asia and Europe

Joseph Needham, a historian of Chinese science and technology, has argued that before European explorers reached Asian waters, there was a process of technological exchange in Asia in which different Asian sailing communities communicated with each other and adopted each others' ideals.

In this process, China more or less maintained a position of technological dominance throughout Asia. Needham's view has been widely accepted.

Gavin Menzies, a naval officer turned maritime historian, has taken this thesis one step further by suggesting that China's medieval maritime technology not only had no match in Asia but also had no rival in the entire world. He hypothesizes that the Ming exploration fleet under Admiral Zheng He went far beyond the Indian Ocean, commonly believed to be the extent of Zheng He's voyages. According to Menzies, the Ming Chinese systematically established some twenty astronomic observatories across both the Indian and Pacific oceans and some twenty maritime stations along the Pacific Rim. The most astonishing claim made by Menzies is that the Ming Chinese were the true discoverers of the Americas ahead of the Europeans.

Although Menzies's revisionist view may yet lead to a rewriting of the maritime history of the world, the main problem with his hypothesis is the lack of solid evidence, especially on Chinese developments. So far the main evidence available is from two travelogues titled *Yingya shenglan* (Tours to Great Sites Overseas) and *Xingcha shenglan* (Voyages on Heavenly Rafts) by Zheng He's two aides, Ma Huan and Fei Xin. Even if one accepts that the evidence was once there but that much of it was ruthlessly destroyed by conservative Confucian officials after Zheng He, as Menzies indicates, it is clear that the alleged great Ming discovery was lost after the 1450s. Thus the purported Ming discovery has left practically no mark on either post-Ming China or the outside world. In the end, it was the European discovery of the New World that changed the course of human history, and thus this is the discovery that really counts.

[*See also* Coastal Navigation; Navigational Instruments; Navigational Manuals; *and* Zheng He.]

## Bibliography

Deng, Gang. *Chinese Maritime Activities and Socio-economic Consequences, c. 2100 B.C.–1900 A.D.* Westport, Conn.: Greenwood, 1997.

Deng, Gang. *Maritime Sector, Institutions, and Sea Power of Premodern China.* Westport, Conn.: Greenwood, 1999.

Menzies, Gavin. *1421, the Year China Discovered the World.* London: Bantam, 2002.

Needham, Joseph. "Civil Engineering." In *Science and Civilisation in China*, vol. 4, pt. 3, edited by Joseph Needham. Cambridge, U.K.: Cambridge University Press, 1971.

Needham, Joseph. "Mathematics and the Sciences of the Heavens and the Earth." In *Science and Civilisation in China*, vol. 3, edited by Joseph Needham. Cambridge, U.K.: Cambridge University Press, 1959.

Needham, Joseph. "Physics and Physical Technology, Part I." In *Science and Civilisation in China*, vol. 4, edited by Joseph Needham. Cambridge, U.K.: Cambridge University Press, 1962.

Needham, Joseph. "Physics and Physical Technology, Part II." In *Science and Civilisation in China*, vol. 4, edited by Joseph Needham. Cambridge: Cambridge University Press, 1965.

KENT GANG DENG

**Chinese Literature**    There is some truth to the popular perception that, throughout history, Chinese societies have not been seagoing. At least this is true of the sedentary agriculturalists in the huge valleys along the Yellow River and the Yangtze, and in the great rice basins such as Sichuan, all places considered cradles of Chinese civilization. It is also true of the Chinese literati, who were not seagoers and were generally unfamiliar with the oceans. However, various of the peoples who have been incorporated into the Sinitic world over the last two thousand years, and particularly those peoples residing along the southeastern coast of what is today China, have been intimately tied to the seas for millennia.

The classical texts of China do not contain a great amount pertaining to the seas, but ancient dictionaries still embrace a range of maritime terms. By at least the eighth century C.E., Chinese texts include descriptions of marine craft, exemplified by the *Taibai yin jing* (太白陰經), a work on military strategy. Some of the earliest textual illustrations of warships are seen in the eleventh-century *Wujing zongyao* (武經總要; A Summary of Military Principles) by Zeng Gongliang (曾公亮). This work served as a template for later naval handbooks and maritime sections in encyclopedias, even into the seventeenth century. *Wubei zhi* (武備志), an account of armaments and military technologies compiled by Mao Yuanyi (毛元儀) and published in 1628, contains illustrations of warships and also a map of Zheng He's voyages as far as Africa in the early fifteenth century. As for maritime nomenclature, the Song author Ren Guang (任廣) included a chapter on terms relating to ships in his *Shuxu zhinan* (書敘指南; Guide to Writing), published in the 1120s. Encyclopedias continued to add to this listing. The eighteenth century saw the publication of *Shi zhou* (釋舟; Explaining Ships) by Hong Liangji (洪亮吉), a seminal text providing detailed explanations of nautical matters and related terminology.

## Seafaring, Trade, and Literature

The production of Chinese maritime literature was intimately linked with successive dynasties' policies on seafaring and maritime trade. During the Southern Song period (1127–1279), the state's enthusiasm for maritime trade encouraged increased interaction with the maritime world and led to a burgeoning of works describing the experiences of mariners. The famous *Pingzhou ketan* (萍洲可谈; Talk of Pingzhou) of 1119, for example, describes various aspects of maritime navigation and trade, and it is the earliest text to mention use of the maritime compass. Another Song period text worthy of note is *Zhufan zhi* (諸蕃志; Descriptions of Foreigners) by Zhao Rugua (趙汝适), available in an English translation by Friedrich Hirth and W. W. Rockhill. It provides us with one of the best accounts of the maritime trading world in East Asia at the beginning of the thirteenth century, giving accounts of Arab traders, the range of commodities traded, and the major markets. *Daoyi zhilüe* (島夷志略; Brief Descriptions of the Islanders) by Wang Dayuan (汪大淵), a similar work from more than a century later, is one of the most detailed premodern Chinese accounts of the overseas lands beyond China. The author spent several decades at sea and abroad and thus personally observed many of the things that he recorded in this work from the 1350s.

The twelfth to fourteenth centuries also saw the emergence of maritime rutters (*routiers*), guides to mariners that included compass directions. A major rutter that has come down to us in manuscript form and that likely dates from the fifteenth century is the anonymous *Shunfeng xiangsong* (順風相送; Smooth Sailing before the Winds). This contains detailed navigational directions for ships sailing from southern China to the various trade ports throughout Southeast Asia. Some of the voyage itineraries have been translated by J. V. G. Mills.

The early fifteenth century saw major maritime missions being dispatched by the Yongle emperor (r. 1403–1424). These were led by several eunuchs, including Zheng He (鄭和; 1371–1433), the most famed. The voyages, which extended from 1405 until the 1430s and reached to many ports throughout Southeast Asia, the Indian Ocean, and the coast of East Africa, were essentially aimed at dominating the region politically and economically, partly to provide legitimacy for the usurping emperor. Major descriptions of these voyages have come down to us in *Yingya shenglan* (瀛涯勝覽; English trans., *Overall Survey of the Ocean's Shores*) by Ma Huan (馬歡) and *Xingcha shenglan* (星槎勝

覽; English trans., *Overall Survey of the Star Raft*) by Fei Xin (費信). These works, both now available in English translation, are invaluable sources on the maritime societies of these regions in the early fifteenth century.

A less-known text, but one also based on these early fifteenth-century voyages, is *Xiyang fanguo zhi* (西洋番國志; Descriptions of Western Countries) by Gong Zhen (鞏珍). These voyages also gave rise to one of the few Chinese works of fiction centered on sea voyages: *Sanbao taijian xia Xiyang ji* (三保太監下西洋記; Account of the Voyages to the Western Ocean by the Sanbao Eunuch, Zheng He), a novel written by Luo Maodeng (羅懋登) and published in 1597. Based on the eunuch-led voyages of almost two hundred years earlier, but also including accounts of all manner of fantastic countries, the novel describes how the mariners, after reaching the countries farthest from China, continued their voyage into hell. There the eunuchs and their military commanders were called to account for the horrific violence that they had inflicted on people during the voyages. Duyvendak and Goode provide useful data on the sources for the novel, and Duyvendak suggests that the novel had didactic purpose: to encourage the Ming court to revive its earlier maritime prowess. The novel remains unusual in Chinese literature for the degree to which it depicts violence by Chinese against foreigners.

In the early seventeenth century, a drama about Zheng He's voyages was written. Dating from about 1615, *Feng tianming Sanbao xia Xiyang* (奉天命三保下西洋; Voyages to the Western Ocean by the Sanbao Eunuch under Imperial Command) showcases the mental sharpness of the Chinese envoys vis-à-vis the foreigners with whom they came into contact during the voyages. The work was intended for performance at elite gatherings.

### Influence of Pirates

The imperial maritime bans from the 1380s until the 1570s greatly restricted unofficial maritime activity and trade and also meant that the subjects of maritime literature were limited to official voyages. However, the *wokou*—literally "Japanese pirates," but actually comprising maritime operators from various backgrounds—and Ming responses to them during the sixteenth century also gave rise to an official literature linked with the sea. The various treatises of the time examined the problems of and presented possible responses to the coastal depredations being suffered along the coast. One of the more famous works in this genre is *Ji-xiao xin-shu* (紀效新書; A New Treatise on Disciplined Services) by Qi Ji-guan (戚繼光; 1528–1587), which addresses a major debate of the day as to whether the pirates should be met on land or water. In this work, Qi urged, inter alia, the establishment of coastal warning systems and meeting the pirates after they had landed.

*Jing-hai ji-lue* (靖海紀略; A Brief Account of the Pacification of the Seas), by Zheng Mao (鄭茂), which examines the attacks by the *wokou* on coastal areas of Zhejing and Jiangsu in the 1550s, as well as military responses, is also well known. But perhaps the most famous work to emerge in response to these maritime marauding activities is the 1561 *Chou-hai tu-bian* (籌海圖編; An Illustrated Account of Maritime Planning) by Zheng Ruo-zeng (鄭若曾). It includes maps as well as other historical and geographical materials relating to coastal defenses from Liaodong in China's north down to Guangdong, and it also includes illustrations of ships and marine armaments.

With the revival of legal private maritime trade in the late sixteenth century, we see the creation of new works relating to the seas. *Dongxiyang kao* (東西洋考; Account of the Eastern and Western Oceans), compiled by Zhang Xie (張燮) in the early seventeenth century, is one of the better-known Chinese works relating to maritime Asia. It contains not only accounts of foreign countries reached by sea from China, but also aspects of maritime culture, maritime routes to various Southeast Asian ports, and the Fujian maritime customs duties for a wide variety of Chinese imports.

With the Manchu/Qing invasion of northern China in the 1640s, numerous groups in the south of China organized themselves in armed opposition. Among the most famous of these groups are the maritime forces of Zheng Chenggong (鄭成功; known in European sources as Koxinga) who operated in the seas between Fujian and Japan. Though these forces were able to drive the Dutch from Taiwan in 1662, they were eventually subdued on that island by Qing marines in the 1680s. The maritime activities of Zheng and his forces are recorded in official Chinese texts, as well as in unofficial histories such as *Taiwan Zheng shi shimo* (臺灣鄭氏始末; A Full Account of the Zhengs of Taiwan) by Shen Yun (沈雲). Given the contemporary importance of Taiwan in Chinese politics since 1949, it is not surprising that Zheng Chenggong has also become the subject of various nationalistic PRC novels and films.

### Increasing Interaction with and Influence of the West

Increasing interaction with western sailors, merchants, missionaries, and travelers from the late sixteenth century changed Chinese perceptions of the seas and of China's place within the maritime world. New information about East Asia led to new ideas about the oceans and their importance, published in such works as Chen Lunjiong's *Haiguo wenjian lu* (Things Seen and Heard in Maritime Lands) of 1730. This remained one of the foremost works on the maritime world up until the 1840s. *Haidao yizhi* (海岛逸志; Jottings from Maritime Islands), published by Wang Dahai (王大海) in 1791, and *Hai lu* (海錄; Account of the Seas), published by Xie Qinggao (謝清高) in 1820, likewise provided much new information on geography, as well as on changing political and economic environments in Southeast Asia and beyond.

It was during this period that another of the few Chinese maritime fictional works was produced. Li Ruzhen (1763–1830), who had failed to pass the Chinese civil-service examination, started writing his *Jing hua yuan* (鏡花緣; Flowers in the Mirror) when he was fifty years old. Set during the Tang dynasty, the novel has a protagonist who is frustrated by the existing political situation and sets sail, arriving in various strange lands where gender roles are reversed and other customs unfamiliar to the Chinese are practiced. The satirical work was obviously directed at Qing government and society, and it has been compared to Jonathan Swift's *Gulliver's Travels* (1726).

The surge in sea trade among China, Southeast Asia, India, and onward to Europe in the second half of the eighteenth century also saw a new age on the southern Chinese coast, with Qing officials facing the most serious maritime threat that they had experienced since the days of Zheng Chenggong. A confederation of pirates, perhaps seventy thousand strong and in some cases supported by the Tây Son polity in Vietnam, threatened fishing ports, coastal traders, and even inland waterways along the south China coast. By 1810, however, following interventions by the Qing and the Portuguese, many of the leaders had surrendered, the confederation had been dismantled, and the crisis was resolved. A seminal work on this suppression is *Jing-hai-fen ji* (靖 海 氛 記; An Account of the Suppression of the Maritime Miasma, 1830) by Yuan Yong-lun (袁 永 綸), which was very swiftly translated into English by C. F. Neumann as *History of the Pirates Who Infested the China Sea from 1807 to 1810*. One of the most prominent of the pirates in this period–Cheung Po-tsai (張 保 仔)–became the stuff of legends in the Cantonese-speaking realm and, during the twentieth century, featured in Cantonese drama and film. The woman pirate leader Cheng I-sao, erstwhile wife of Cheung Po-tsai, also features in Cantonese folklore.

The British navy's exercise of maritime and military strength along the coast of China during the Opium War of 1840–1842 provided the Chinese literati with a new impetus to learn about the seas. The recognition of the importance of sea power led both Chinese and Manchu scholars to attempt to understand more about maritime power and its application. The imperial commissioner Lin Ze-xu, famed for his anti-opium initiatives in Canton in the 1830s, compiled *Si-zhou zhi* (四洲志; An Account of the Four Continents), completed in perhaps 1841, which describes the oceans of the world as well as its major landmasses. Later works by reformers such as Li Hong-zhang (李鸿章) and Zou Zong-tang (左宗棠) advocated the creation of a strong Chinese navy–a story that is well told by John Rawlinson. The seminal work of this reformist genre is *Haiguo tuzhi* (海國圖志; Illustrated Account of Maritime Lands) by Wei Yuan (魏源), completed in 1852. The author, a scholar and statecraft activist, wrote extensively on sea transport and maritime defense, and after the Opium War he compiled this work from European and Chinese sources to analyze western penetration of maritime Asia. Dividing the world into "ocean regions," this account details western maritime commerce and its importance as a factor in what had happened to China.

A range of late nineteenth-century Chinese scholarly texts drew increasingly on western works to introduce the maritime world to the Chinese. Many of these texts were collected into a compendium by Wang Xi-qi (王錫 祺) over the period 1877–1897. Based on Chinese and translated European texts, and published under the title *Xiao-fang-hu-zhai yu-di cong-chao* (Collection of Texts on Geography from the Xiao-fang-hu Studio), this collection introduced to Chinese people the polities, topographies, and societies of all corners of the world. Many of these texts related to Southeast Asia and other maritime realms. Conversely, the huge numbers of "coolie" laborers who sailed from China to Southeast Asia and beyond to work in mines and on plantations during the same period have left, unfortunately, virtually no literature relating to the maritime realm. There are, however, some official texts relating to nongoverment maritime trade during this period, and details of some of these can be found in Jennifer Cushman's *Fields from the Sea*.

The first half of the twentieth century saw, along with a growing number of Chinese in Southeast Asia, an increasing number of works associated with the Asian maritime world, including works by émigré authors such as Yu Dafu (郁達夫), but still remarkably little specifically related to the seas. Since the establishment of the People's

Republic in 1949, there has been the occasional socialist-realist work related to the seas, but because of the negligible role of the navy in the revolution, such works are sparse. It is only in Taiwan that we have seen, following the political changes since the 1980s, the emergence of a recognized maritime literature, a representative work being *Hangkai riji* (航海日記; Journal of a Sea Voyage) by Liang Ch'in-hsia (梁琴霞). This trend derives from Taiwan's being surrounded by seas: its security and livelihood are tied closely to the oceans.

Thus when compared to other traditions, there is a relative lack of a tradition of maritime literature in Chinese society. The agrarian base of the society and the relative unimportance of the sea to the major intellectual centers of China have meant that stories of war, of dynastic change, and of major figures in Chinese history have generally been written without reference to the sea. The works that do exist are generally accounts of shipbuilding, of maritime defense, of outlaws, and of places visited on maritime voyages. Other relevant Chinese works concern the maritime world of Southeast Asia, literature about which is contained in the bibliography compiled by Austin Shu and William Wan. Maritime fiction is thus an almost absent element in the Chinese literary tradition, with the several exceptions noted above and with the further notable exception of Southeast Asian literature written in Chinese, which requires a separate study.

[*See also* China; Literature; Ma Huan; *and* Zheng He.]

## Bibliography

Antony, Robert J. *Like Froth Floating on the Sea: The World of Pirates and Seafarers in Late Imperial South China*. China Research Monograph, no. 56. Berkeley: Institute of East Asian Studies, University of California, Berkeley, 2003.

Chau Ju-kua (Zhao Rugua). *Chau Ju-kua: His Work on the Chinese and Arab Trade in the Twelfth and Thirteenth Centuries*. Translated by Friedrich Hirth and W. W. Rockhill. Saint Petersburg, Russia: Imperial Academy of Sciences, 1911. An English translation of Zhao Rugua's *Zhufan zhi*, a major work on Song China's place in the maritime world, including details of the practices of peoples and the products traded in Southeast Asia, the Indian subcontinent, and the Arab world.

Cushman, Jennifer. *Fields from the Sea: Chinese Junk Trade with Siam during the Late Eighteenth and Early Nineteenth Centuries*. Ithaca, N.Y.: Southeast Asia Program, Cornell University, 1993.

Duyvendak, J. J. L. "Desultory Notes on the Hsi-yang chi." *T'oung Pao* 42 (1954): 1–35. A collection of notes relating to *Sanbao taijian xia Xiyang ji* by a prominent Sinologist, this article investigates some major issues, such as why the author wrote the book.

Fei Hsin (Fei Xin). *Hsing-Cha Sheng-Lan: The Overall Survey of the Star Raft*. Translated by J. V. G. Mills and edited by Roderich Ptak. Wiesbaden, Germany: Harrassowitz, 1996. An annotated translation of one of the key texts on Zheng He's voyages. Contains an excellent bibliography on China's historical links with the East Asian maritime realm.

Goode, Walter. "On the *Sanbao taijian xia Xiyang-ji*." PhD diss., Australian National University, 1976.

Leonard, Jane Kate. *Wei Yuan and China's Rediscovery of the Maritime World*. Cambridge, Mass.: Council on East Asian Studies, Harvard University, 1984. A useful overview of China's perception of the maritime world in the nineteenth century, including aspects of naval power and sea-related statecraft.

Li Ju-chen (Li Ruzhen). *Flowers in the Mirror*. Translated by Lin Tai-yi. Berkeley: University of California Press, 1965. The most widely read translation of Li Ruzhen's early nineteenth-century novel *Jing hua yuan* (鏡花緣).

Ma Huan. *Ma Huan, Ying-yai sheng-lan: "The Overall Survey of the Ocean's Shores" [1433]*. Edited and translated by J. V. G. Mills. Cambridge, U.K.: Cambridge University Press, 1970. Mills translates and annotates the *Yingya shenglan*, Ma Huan's account of the voyages of the Muslim eunuch and admiral Zheng He. Probably the key English work on these voyages.

Mills, J. V. G. "Chinese Navigators in Insulinde about 1500." *Archipel* 18 (1979): 69–93. A useful study of rutters and other navigational texts on the maritime activities of the Chinese in Southeast Asia around 1500.

Murray, Dian H. "Cheng I Sao in Fact and Fiction." In *Bandits at Sea: A Pirates Reader*, edited by C. R. Pennell, pp. 253–282. New York: New York University Press, 2001. Apart from being a lovely account of the famous Chinese woman pirate Cheng I-Sao, this article presents a wide range of the literature, nonfiction and otherwise, relating to aspects of piracy off the Guangdong coast in the nineteenth century.

Murray, Dian H. *Pirates off the South China Coast 1790–1810*. Stanford, Calif.: Stanford University Press, 1987. The best book in English on Chinese piracy. Much original literature is cited or given in translation.

Needham, Joseph, Wang Ling, and Lu Gwei-djen. *Science and Civilisation in China*, vol. 4, *Physics and Physical Technology*, part 3, *Civil Engineering and Nautics*. Cambridge, U.K.: Cambridge University Press, 1971. The best available study of the history of Chinese nautical technology and navigation, and includes aspects of the associated literature.

Netolitsky, Almut. *Das Ling-wai tai-ta von Chou Ch'ü-fei: Eine Landeskunde Südchinas aus dem 12. Jahrhundert*. Wiesbaden, Germany: Franz Steiner, 1977. A German translation of an account of South China in the twelfth century that includes its relations with foreign lands and links to the maritime realm.

Neumann, Charles. F., trans. *History of the Pirates Who Infested the China Sea from 1807 to 1810*. London: Printed for the Oriental Translation Fund, 1831. A translation of Yuan Yong-lun's *Jing-hai-fen ji*, this work provides a detailed account of the maritime figures who were seen as pirates during the early nineteenth century. One of the very few translated texts on Chinese piracy.

Ong Tae Hae (Wang Dahai). *The Chinaman Abroad, or A Desultory Account of the Malayan Archipelago, Particularly of Java.* Translated by W. H. Medhurst. Shanghai: Mission Press, 1849. A useful account of the Southeast Asian maritime realm as seen through the eyes of a Chinese maritime traveler.

Rawlinson, John. *China's Struggle for Naval Development, 1839–1895.* Cambridge, Mass.: Harvard University Press, 1967.

Rockhill, W. W. "Notes on the Relations and Trade of China with the Eastern Archipelago and the Coasts of the Indian Ocean during the Fourteenth Century." *T'oung Pao* 16 (1915): 419–447 and 18 (1917): 61–159, 236–271, 374–392, 435–467, and 604–626. A useful account of the Chinese texts relating to maritime interactions between various Chinese regimes and those of Southeast Asia.

Shu, Austin C. W., and William W. L. Wan. *Twentieth Century Chinese Works on Southeast Asia, a Bibliography.* Honolulu, Hawaii: East-West Center, 1968. A useful guide to Chinese works on Southeast Asia, mainly nonfiction, including references to the Southeast Asian maritime realm.

Wang Gungwu. *The Nanhai Trade: The Early History of Chinese Trade in the South China Sea.* Singapore: Times Academic Press, 1998. First published in 1958 in the *Journal of the Malaysian Branch of the Royal Asiatic Society*, Kuala Lumpur. This is the foremost study of maritime links between successive Chinese governments and those of Southeast Asia up to the tenth century. It includes references to the relevant literature.

GEOFF WADE

# Chroniclers. *See subentries on* Chroniclers of Exploration *under* Dutch Literature, Portuguese Literature, *and* Spanish Literature.

# Clays, Paul-Jean (1817–1900), nautical painter.

The Belgian artist Paul-Jean Clays was born in Brugge (Bruges) on November 20, 1817. From a very young age he was attracted to the sea, rivers, and canals and wanted to become a sailor, but his father sent him to a boarding school in the French port city of Boulogne. His attraction for the sea ultimately overcame his studies, and he became a cabin boy on a coastal cruiser. Upon his return to Bruges, Clays noted down his nautical impressions in the form of drawings. A book of drawings dating back to 1838 bears witness to his dexterity. Clays studied in Paris under Horace Vernet and Theodore Gudin and then settled in Brussels in 1839. That year he presented an impressive series of seascapes at the Brussels show including among others *The Thames* and *Calais Roadstead*. At the Antwerp show in 1840 he presented *Disappearance of the English Three-Master "Douglas" off the Coast of Fecamps*. In 1841

Clays applied for the post of official painter on board a ship of the royal navy. His application was successful, and that same year he set sail on a cutter escorting the huge yacht *Marie-Louise* on her excursions in the North Sea. During this journey he visited England and the Shetland Islands. Clays's seafaring lasted almost eight months and gave birth to a certain number of important works, notably several representations of *Marie-Louise*. Following a journey to Portugal he presented in 1845 *Alfendega in Algarve, Portugal* and *"La Catarina": Portuguese Boat in Distress in Sight of a French Fleet*. In 1848 at the Brussels show he presented *Yarmouth Bay* and *Leith Roadstead near Edinburgh*.

Until 1860 he had always worked with conviction in a Romantic-Realist style that recalled the Dutch seascape painters of the seventeenth century. The 1860s marked a turning point in his art; his seascapes evolved toward a deeper sense of reality, with lighter and freer colors—a more natural composition with less concern for detail. His art is not far removed from the Impressionist style. In 1899, Clays painted two watercolors of an Oostende-Dover steamer for the brand-new postcard industry. He died in Brussels on February 9, 1900.

Clays's works are held in museums and public collections in the Belgian cities of Antwerp, Brugge, Brussels, Ghent, Liège, Nieuwpoort, and Oostende; in England in Sheffield, Leicester, and London; in Germany in Hamburg and Munich; and in New York City.

[*See also* Art; Artists, *subentry* Belgian; *and* Painting.]

## Bibliography

Berko, Patrick, and Viviane Berko. *Seascapes of Belgian Painters Born between 1750 and 1875.* Brussels: Knokke, 1984.

PATRICK BERKO *and* VIVIANE BERKO
*Translated from the Dutch by Selina Baring Maclennan*

# Clipper The clipper was a large, very fast mid-nineteenth-century sailing ship in which cargo capacity and efficiency were sacrificed for speed. The type carried three masts, with square sails on each mast and a large gaffsail on the mizzenmast behind the square sails. In addition there were at least three sails fitted between the bowsprit and the foremast. Staysails filled out the complement in between the masts. The rigs were tall, giving relatively large sail area relative to the size of the ship. Five to six square sails on each of the masts were common. In addition there

***Sea Witch off Cape Horn.*** The American artist Frank Vining Smith (1879–1967) painted this oil on canvas. *Sea Witch* was John W. Griffith's masterpiece of ship design. She was built by Smith and Dimon in New York for the shipping firm of Howland & Aspinwall. During her ten-year career between 1846 and 1856, she held more speed records than any other China packet. THE MARINERS' MUSEUM, NEWPORT NEWS, VA.

were studding sails that could be set on the side of the square sails, increasing area even more. To get the most out of the massive and varied complement of sails, crews were sizable and they spent more time aloft than did crews on other ships of similar size. Clippers had a high ratio of length to breadth and relatively low wetted surface, which decreased the resistance created by friction with the water. There was a sharp stem, the bow raked forward and the masts raked aft. All these features combined to make clippers fast, probably the fastest large cargo sailing ships ever built. They could reach maximum speeds of 20 knots on ocean crossings.

The term "clipper" was in use by the early nineteenth century for relatively fast vessels of various types, including schooners. Sometime after 1815 the term was being used for sharply built small vessels such as schooners used on Chesapeake Bay. The type may have been distinguished by

the sharp rake of the stempost, giving it what was called a clipper bow. *Ann McKim*, built in Baltimore in 1832, was based on the design of pilot boats and so was a variation on an old and established American model. Though said to be the prototype "clipper" ship, she rather fit into a long-term evolution of fast sailing vessels in the period. She was over 46 meters (151 feet) between the posts and was able to make voyages to South America and to China. Designers did not follow *Ann McKim* but rather the design of the packet boat in creating the first true clipper, built in 1845 in New York. The growing trades to the Far East and to California after the gold rush promoted the construction of ships that could make fast passages. A number of records for speed by clippers are held by ships designed by the Boston builder Donald McKay. Starting in 1850, over a period of about eight years he built a series of the type, and while his reputation was for ships that did well in strong winds, his ships were not appreciably different from those of other successful American designers like John Griffiths and William Webb. In the 1850s American production of clippers established a standard that led first to export of examples of the type to Europe and then to imitation in the Netherlands, Sweden, and other seafaring countries but most of all in Britain. The interest in producing the fast ships created something of a shipbuilding boom. But falling freight rates even before the end of the decade meant that builders turned away from producing extreme clippers.

Because of their speed, clippers were suited for long-distance trades in valuable commodities. While they might not be able to manage average speeds greater than about 15 knots, they could make way in almost any weather including very light breezes. That made it possible for them to make fast passages over great distances in record times. As passenger ships they were suited for carrying emigrants from Europe, especially on long voyages such as those to Australia. *Thermopylae* in 1868 on her maiden voyage went from Britain to Melbourne in a record sixty days. The speed records created an atmosphere of competition, with builders and shipowners trying to better past performance. *Cutty Sark*, built in Scotland in 1869, was designed for high speed and with the expectation of beating *Thermopylae*. Both ships were tea clippers destined for use in the tea trade from China to Britain. It was in that trade that the type gained its greatest prominence. The fast ships built for the China trade in New England in the 1840s were progenitors of the clipper ship. In moving tea from China, speed paid, since the first cargoes to reach British ports could yield higher prices. Emerging competition from steam-powered vessels made speed even more critical. Many of the tea clippers in the 1860s were of composite construction, a transitional stage as shipbuilders moved from using wood to exclusively using metal. In 1872 *Cutty Sark* and *Thermopylae* took part in the last great tea race of the clipper ships. *Cutty Sark* lost her rudder in a storm in the Indian Ocean and so finished second. She gradually withdrew from the tea trade after that, as did other clipper ships. The opening of the Suez Canal made trips between Europe and Asia much shorter for steamships. Continued improvements in steam engines meant clippers were forced into trades in wood from the American west coast and wool from Australia. A few of the vessels survived in use into the twentieth century, often sailing from Portuguese ports. In the nineteenth century, the barque was a seagoing four-masted ship with four or five square sails on each of the three masts forward. The

one at the stern carried a gaffsail. It was a rig common on some later clippers. *Cutty Sark*, through a series of coincidences, survived and is preserved at Greenwich, London, as the last remaining example of clippers from the era of their greatest success.

[*See also* Barque; Griffiths, John Willis; *and* McKay, Donald.]

## Bibliography

Chapelle, Howard I. *The Search for Speed under Sail, 1700–1855*. New York: Bonanza, 1967.

Cutler, Carl C. *Greyhounds of the Sea: The Story of the American Clipper Ship*. Originally published 1930. Annapolis, Md.: United States Naval Institute, 1960.

MacGregor, David R. *The Tea Clippers: Their History and Development, 1833–1875*. 2d ed. London: Conway Maritime Press, 1983.

Villiers, Alan. *The Way of a Ship: Being Some Account of the Ultimate Development of the Ocean-Going Square-Rigged Sailing Vessel, and the Manner of Her Handling, Her Voyage-Making, Her Personnel, Her Economics, Her Performance, and Her End*. New York: Scribners, 1970.

RICHARD W. UNGER

# Clouds. *See* Meteorology.

# Coal Supply

This entry contains two subentries:

> Coal Export
> Naval Coaling Stations

---

## Coal Export

In the mid-nineteenth century abundant, easily accessible, and high-quality coal fueled the steam power that transformed Britain into the world's largest industrialized nation. Although 11 million tons of coal was exported by Britain in 1850, economists such as William Stanley Jevons (1835–1882) believed that each country's store of natural resources was finite and warned that, unless coal exports were regulated, there would be insufficient stores for the country's own textile and metallurgical production. Consequently, as Britain increased the export of its mass-produced goods to the colonies, it retained 4.14 tons of coal per head of population for use by domestic industry, compared with 3.13 tons retained per head in America and

1.77 tons in Germany. Britain controlled sea freights by delivering its finished goods at an all-inclusive price and, in return, buying raw materials and basic foodstuffs at the source. This created employment for British shipping companies, which carried 92 percent of colonial trade, two-thirds of which was between the colonies and other countries.

## The Rise of Steam

A turning point came in the 1860s, when demand for steam power rapidly increased in Europe, and British short-sea shipping companies carried an annual average of 10.6 million tons of coal to France, 9 million tons to Germany, and 9.2 million tons to Italy. Including coal supplied as bunkers for steamships engaged in the foreign trade, British coal exports increased fifteenfold. In 1866 Britain operated almost half of the world's maritime capacity, with a fleet of 26,140 sailing vessels of almost 5 million net tons and 2,831 steamships of 876,000 net tons. Its coal-export trade was further enhanced by the opening of the Suez Canal in 1869; the canal shortened steamer routes to the colonies in the East by 4,000 miles. These routes were studded with Britain-supplied coaling stations that briefly boosted the employment of sailing vessels, but the long-term development of sail had ended.

In the 1870s growing demand for steam power by industry in India and the Pacific led to an increase of 7 percent per year in the activity of British tramp steamers. There was also a substantial improvement in the efficiency of steam engines and a fall in shipbuilding costs: for only twice the capital cost of a typical clipper ten years earlier, a 10-knot cargo steamer could carry four times the cargo and cover three times the mileage in a year's work. A 50 percent rise in the price of coal relative to that of other commodities was compensated for in Britain by an equivalent fall in import freight rates subsidized by its large volume of coal exports.

## The Australian Trade

In 1876, when Britain produced 134 million tons of coal compared with Australia's 1.6 million tons, San Francisco imported 89,362 tons from Britain and 88,552 tons from New South Wales. But only two years later Britain's share had fallen to 44,005 tons and New South Wales's had risen to 131,678 tons, despite Britain's reducing its price and the New South Wales price remaining steady. During a worldwide slump in demand for coal and iron in

the 1880s, Britain faced stronger competition from Australia in supplying steam coal to the colonies bordering the Pacific basin. In 1876 New South Wales had shipped 35,273 tons of coal to Hong Kong and 21,778 tons to India, but by 1897 these amounts had risen to 67,181 and 68,883 tons, respectively. The growth in shipments to India occurred despite an increase in the country's annual domestic coal production from an average of less than 1 million tons to almost 4 million tons over the same period.

Sailing ships dominated the Australian coal trade long after they had been supplanted by steamships in other areas; they dominated by exploiting the prevailing winds and currents in the Pacific and by having lower running costs when delayed by port congestion. Since the freight rates offered for coal from New South Wales to California did not cover expenses, vessels carrying general goods from Britain to Australia traditionally found return cargoes to Europe by ballasting to California to load grain or to Chile to load nitrates. What had changed in the 1880s was that a few shipowners, seeking more profitable trading patterns that minimized uneconomic ballast voyages, calculated that it was better to carry cargo at a loss than to ballast. Consequently, they accepted freight rates from New South Wales to America's West Coast that were lower than those paid from Britain. Later, the few were joined by the many when more and more shipowners realized that in one such thirty-thousand-mile circumnavigation with three laden legs, two of which were highly profitable, they could often recoup the entire initial cost of the ship. Shipowners had effectively created a new trade in the Pacific and had shown that the market price for coal had as much to do with freight levels and innovative scheduling as with supply and demand.

## Hazards

There was, however, a high price to pay in terms of ships and lives in the coal export trade. Between 1864 and 1871, of a total of 15,331 wrecks, 7,231 were colliers, and from 1873 to 1901 more than 9,500 seamen died when 1,410 British or colonial coal-laden sailing ships and 251 steamers foundered or went missing. A royal commission in 1876 found that coal-laden ships were more likely to be lost at sea than those carrying cargoes such as bulk grain or timber. Coal was in danger of spontaneously combusting if it was loaded while wet; coal gas could explode in a badly ventilated hold; and a ship could capsize if coal shifted within its unobstructed hold. The average of missing coal-laden ships to all missing vessels was more than forty-two percent, and almost twice as many lives were lost on coal-laden vessels than on ships carrying bulk grain or timber.

### Decline of the British Trade

In 1865 William Jevons predicted that Britain's foreign coal exports would be the alpha and omega of its trade. Almost 80 percent of vessels entered and cleared in British ports in 1870 were British owned, but by 1911, despite a sixfold increase in total tonnage, this had dropped to only 56 percent. At its peak in 1913, Britain shipped 77 million tons of coal—75 percent of the country's exports by weight and 10 percent by value—but this included 21 million tons for bunkering steamers. Although 85 percent of British coal exports went to Europe and the Mediterranean, less than 40 percent was carried in British ships. As Europe, the colonies, and Japan, spurred by national prestige, developed their own merchant fleets, they adopted the commercial practices learned from Britain fifty years earlier: they imported coal "free on board" and exported their raw materials "cost and freight," which favored the employment of their own ships.

[See also Shipping; Trade; and Trade Routes.]

### Bibliography

Hope, Ronald. *A New History of British Shipping*. London: John Murray, 1990.
Howarth, David Armine. *The Story of P & O: The Peninsular and Oriental Steam Navigation Company*. London: Weidenfeld and Nicolson, 1986.
Lubbock, B. "San Francisco Grain Trade." In *The Down Easters: American Deep-Water Sailing Ships, 1869–1929*. Glasgow, Scotland: Brown, Son and Ferguson, 1929.
Lubbock, Basil. "The West Coast." In *The Nitrate Clippers*. Glasgow, Scotland: Brown, Son and Ferguson, 1932.
Palmer, Sarah. *Politics, Shipping and the Repeal of the Navigation Laws*. Manchester, U.K.: Manchester University Press, 1990.

MICHAEL STUART CLARK

# Naval Coaling Stations

The gradual shift to steam as a means of propulsion necessitated the erection of a far more comprehensive logistical infrastructure for both merchant vessels and warships than was required during the sailing era. Creating this infrastructure was relatively straightforward; coaling facilities could, in most cases, be added to existing port facilities, although it should be stressed that until the 1880s sailing ships predominated on most of the world's trade routes, owing to the limitations of steam technology. Coal was therefore most likely to be obtained at major ports that had scheduled, often subsidized, steamship service. Navies could not be similarly selective regarding their scope of operations, and because of engine inefficiency the adoption of steam mandated not only upgrading existing facilities but creating new ones. The operational range of sailing warships was limited by their crews' supply of provisions; that of steamers, by the availability of coal. Owing to the virtual impossibility of coaling at sea, global operations depended on global coaling-station networks, and these required regular resupply and defense, which in turn necessitated coordination and communication.

As of the late 1840s, when France and Britain both began to apply steam to capital ships, only one navy—Britain's—undertook worldwide operations that required such a comprehensive network, and this remained largely the case until the final years of the century. Not surprisingly, therefore, the story of coaling stations and imperial defense policy is largely a British story.

By the late 1850s the British Admiralty was wrestling with the consequences of steam on imperial strategy, although more immediate and local concerns—specifically an ironclad-building race with France—prevented substantive action at that time. The first public airing of the subject came in 1867, when Captain J. C. R. Colomb (1838–1909), Royal Marine Artillery, published the pamphlet "The Protection of Our Commerce and the Distribution of Our War Forces Considered." Like the Admiralty, Colomb understood the centrality of coal to imperial defense, enumerating the places where stockpiles would be required in time of war: Aden, Antigua, Ascension, the Bahamas, Bermuda, Bombay (Mumbai, India), Cape Comerin (India), the Falkland Islands, Fiji, Gibraltar, Halifax (Nova Scotia), Hong Kong, Jamaica, King George Sound (Australia), Malta, Mauritius, Saint Helena, Sierra Leone, Simon's Town (Cape Colony), Singapore, Suez, Sydney, and Trincomalee (Sri Lanka).

The American Civil War (1861–1865), during which Confederate commerce-raiders wrought considerable destruction on the Union merchant fleet, also focused official attention on the imperial dimension. When Alexander Milne (1806–1896), who as junior naval lord in the 1850s had pushed for the establishment of coaling stations, returned to the Admiralty as first naval lord (1866–1868, 1872–1876), the intertwined topics of imperial defense and logistics came to the fore. Milne unequivocally noted in an 1874 memorandum on anti-commerce-raiding measures that "this coal question will, in any future war, be one of the great difficulties which the Admiralty will have to meet" (Milne Papers, National Maritime Museum, MLN144/3 [1]). Of even greater significance, the following year Milne turned the issue of coaling-station defense to the army authorities, maintaining that local defense was the army's responsibility; assigning naval vessels to the task would hinder the service's capacity to provide commerce protection.

The key figure in the subsequent evolution of imperial defense strategy was the officer assigned by the War Office to deal with Milne's initiative, Colonel William Jervois, whose "Memorandum with Reference to the Defenceless Condition of Our Coaling Stations and Naval Establishments Abroad" (January 1875) was the single most important step toward the creation of a comprehensive network of defended coal depots. Jervois took the suggestions of Milne, Colomb, and others, prioritized each location according to the volume of trade that passed it, determined the requisite nature and extent of fortifications for those locations important enough to defend, and calculated the cost—£950,000 overall—of doing so.

This figure was unlikely to win favor with the economy-minded British politicians of the mid-Victorian era, especially since they were enjoying a "peace dividend" owing to France's humiliating defeat by Germany in the Franco-Prussian War of 1870–1871. Only with the prospect of war with Russia in 1877–1878, following Russia's defeat of the Ottoman Empire, was Benjamin Disraeli's government prodded to action, appointing first (1878–1879) the Colonial Office Committee to consider colonial defense and then a Royal Commission chaired by Lord Carnarvon (1879–1882) to study imperial defense globally.

The Royal Commission took most of its cues from Jervois's earlier work, although the number of bases recommended for defense was whittled down. Implementation of those recommendations had to wait until another crisis with Russia erupted—the Penjdeh incident (1885), involving a boundary dispute between Russian and Afghan forces. But by the late 1880s, driven by growing colonial competition, by the emergence of the French Jeune École strategists, who advocated wholesale commerce raiding, and by rising domestic interest in the Royal Navy, the measures advocated by Milne, Colomb, and Jervois were bearing fruit. In the 1890 edition of the *Naval Annual*, Thomas Brassey pointed to continuing weakness at Gibraltar and Hong Kong, but wrote of the arrangements at Malta, Bombay, Karachi, Colombo, Singapore, Saint Helena, Sierra Leone, and the Cape of Good Hope in optimistic terms.

The *Naval Annual* also sheds light on the disparity between British coaling resources and those of would-be rivals. Brassey bluntly observed in the 1888–1889 edition that "we find the resources of our neighbours for the conduct of naval operations in distant waters slender indeed in comparison with those which we command" (p. 231). France, still Britain's only significant naval competitor, had a numerically substantial coaling network, comprising Algeria, the Comoros (between Madagascar and Africa), the Congo, Corsica, Gabon, Guiana, Madagascar, Martinique, New Caledonia, Obock (Djibouti), Pondicherry (India), Réunion (Indian Ocean), Saint-Pierre (Newfoundland), Saigon, Senegal, Tahiti, Tonkin, Tunis, and Western Guinea. The Afro-centricity of this network, however, was unmistakable.

Moreover, French resources overseas were often significantly inferior to their British counterparts. The Continental naval commentator E. Weyl lamented the inferiority of the French naval arsenal at Saigon to the British facility at Hong Kong, finishing with the unequivocal observation, "For any power not possessing the numerous stations at the disposal of England the difficulty of coaling in many parts of the globe would be almost insuperable" (quoted in Brassey's *Naval Annual*, 1887–1888, p. 148). Admiral Sir John Fisher's boast that "five strategic keys lock up the world"—referring to Singapore, the Cape of Good Hope, Alexandria, Gibraltar, and Dover, all of which belonged to Britain—was, if anything, an understatement; the coal that fueled George Dewey's U.S. Navy squadron en route to Manila Bay in April 1898 was purchased from the British at Hong Kong.

[*See also* Communications, Naval; Corbett, Julian; Fisher, John; Naval Administration; Naval Dockyards and Bases; Naval Logistics, *subentry* After 1850; Ports; Strategy; *and* Wars, Maritime, *subentries on* Nineteenth-Century Wars *and* World Wars.]

## Bibliography

Brassey, Thomas, et al. *The Naval Annual*. Portsmouth, U.K.: J. Griffin, 1886–. For contemporary treatment, the best published source available, although Brassey's Anglocentrism ensures that foreign developments get short shrift.

Lambert, Andrew. "The Shield of Empire, 1815–1895." In *The Oxford Illustrated History of the Royal Navy*, edited by J. R. Hill and Bryan Ranft, pp. 161–199. Oxford: Oxford University Press, 1995. A succinct overview of British naval policy generally during the Pax Britannica. Trade defense and coaling stations are integrated into this treatment.

Marder, Arthur J. *The Anatomy of British Sea Power: A History of British Naval Policy in the Pre-Dreadnought Era, 1880–1905*. New York: Knopf, 1940. Still the best work on the subject, although some of Marder's conclusions warrant revision.

Milne, Alexander. *The Milne Papers*. National Maritime Museum, Greenwich, U.K. The best primary-source collection for British naval administration in general and for the navy's imperial defense policy during 1866–1876 in particular.

Milne, Alexander. *The Milne Papers: The Papers of Admiral of the Fleet Sir Alexander Milne, Bt., K.C.B. (1806–1896)*. Edited by John Beeler. Aldershot, U.K., and Burlington, Vt.: Ashgate, 2004. An important collection of primary documents that details the evolution of steam-era imperial defense thought at the British Admiralty during the 1850s.

Ropp, Theodore. *The Development of a Modern Navy: French Naval Policy 1871–1904*. Edited by Stephen S. Roberts. Annapolis, Md.: Naval Institute Press, 1987. Deals in passing with the topic of coaling stations, especially on pp. 263–267, and provides a map contrasting French and British coaling stations in the 1890s on pp. 264–265.

Schurman, Donald M. *Imperial Defence 1868–1887*. Edited by John Beeler. London: Frank Cass, 2000. The authoritative work on the evolution of British imperial defense strategy, based on coaling stations.

JOHN F. BEELER

# Coastal Navigation

This entry contains two subentries:

An Overview
Aids

## An Overview

Coastal navigation may be defined as the guiding of a ship from one place to another without losing sight of land for more than some hours. It has been practiced for millennia—perhaps since 3500 B.C.E.—by traders for whom access to their markets was easier by sea than by land. The requirements of coastal navigation include knowing the position and direction of the ship's travel, the dangers to be avoided, the depth of the water, the nature of the seabed, the time and direction of the tidal stream, and information about havens, and having a basic meteorological forecast. The methods of acquiring all this information fall into two groups: direct and indirect. Direct methods of navigation, although of ancient origin, are still pertinent today, and indirect methods are the results of centuries of evolution of nautical science.

### Direct Methods of Navigation

Direct methods of navigation rely on the senses and include using position and direction, landmarks and seamarks, times and tide, and speed and distance.

**Position and direction.** A Sanskrit manuscript manual of navigation of 434 C.E. describes coastal pilotage as relying on the senses: sight, sound, smell, and touch. At sea, the sight of clouds over distant hills, the sound of waves breaking on shore, the smell of land, and the feel of a warm breeze can all give some indication of the direction of land. Cliffs, hills, the profile of the land, the color of the sea, and the depth and nature of the seabed can, with local knowledge, fix a ship's position. To establish the direction of travel, a mariner can use the sun by day and Polaris (in the Northern Hemisphere) or Canopus (in the Southern Hemisphere) by night. Wildlife may also be used to indicate direction: nonpelagic seabirds, such as gulls, return to land at night, and other birds can be seen migrating along known routes. Farther out to sea, flocks of seabirds may be seen feeding on fish attracted to plankton brought to the surface by currents meeting the continental shelf. In the Mediterranean, early navigators used the wind for navigation: the feel of the wind (warm or cold, dry or humid) defined its direction. The winds' courses, consequently, were named on a wind rose after the direction from which the winds blew.

Having established a cardinal point, a mariner could extrapolate left or right to obtain his required course by holding his hand at arm's length. The width of a fist subtends an angle of about 10° at the eye, and with thumb and fingers abducted, the angle is slightly less than 20°—not an accurate bearing, but better than nothing.

**Landmarks and seamarks.** In addition to natural features, man-made constructions are used as landmarks, some because they happen to be in prominent positions, others because they were constructed specifically as aids to navigation. As early as 629 B.C.E., the Huaisheng Temple on the River Zhujiang in China, and in the third century B.C.E. the Pharos at Alexandria in Egypt, were built as navigational marks. In the first and second centuries C.E., the Romans constructed many towers for defense and for navigation on the shores around their empire. By the eleventh century the city of Bremen (in Germany) had marked the passage up the Weser, and the city of Brugge (in Belgium) had buoyed the two approaches from the River Schelde to the town of Sluys. The buoys appear to have been moored barrels—in 1288, off Warnemünde, they were recorded as *signum quod tunna dicitur* (a mark defined by a barrel)—that were perhaps removable in winter or at the approach of enemy ships. As a permanent warning of the Scharhörn reef at the entrance to the Elbe, a wood and stone tower known as the Nige Wark, now Neuwerk, was built on the reef in 1310.

Fifteenth-century European sailing directions (also known as "rutters" or "pilot books") listed many church steeples, castles, natural features, and even prominent trees as landmarks and suggested pairs of marks that could be aligned in transit to give a leading line into a haven or between shallows. For example, the approach to Dieppe is described in the Middle Low German *Seebuch* thus: "unde brengen de kerke ende de ghalge over eyn unde setten uppe x vadem" (and bring the church and the gallows into transit and anchor in ten fathoms).

The cost of building and maintaining structures and fire beacons as aids to navigation was generally borne by a tax on passing ships, levied by the local port town. From 1280 the town of Brielle in the Netherlands maintained two fire towers at the mouth of the Maas River with money raised by such a tax, and similarly, in the fifteenth century, levies were used to maintain the buoyage and lights off Copenhagen and through The Sound (Øresund). Although there was some earlier marking of sandbanks on the east coast of England, the Thames was not marked in any way until the end of the sixteenth century, partly because of fear of enemy intrusion and partly because of intransigence by local pilots safeguarding their work. The central organization and maintenance of buoyage and lights began in various places in Europe in the seventeenth century and is now generally the responsibility of the governments of maritime nations.

**Tides and time.** Tide, time, and the moon are interrelated, a fact that is the basis of all tidal calculations. Before reliable seagoing timepieces were available, mariners relied on stars to tell the time, using, in the Northern Hemisphere, the "pointers" of Ursa Major—Dubhe and Marak—or the "guards" of Ursa Minor—$\beta$ and $\gamma$—as the hands of an astral analog clock. The moon may also be used for timekeeping, but more important, it was for many centuries used as the reference for tidal times. To simplify an extremely complex phenomenon, during each fourteen-day period the range of the heights between high and low tide increases and decreases. When the moon is new or full, the range is at its maximum, and there is a "high (and low) water spring" tide (HWS and LWS) at approximately the same time every two weeks at each location. The mean of that time has been called variously "tide hour" and "high water, full and change" (HWF&C); it is now a theoretically calculated time known as the "Establishment," or "lunar-tidal interval."

Before clocks were available at sea, the time of HWS was stated as the compass bearing of the full moon; thus "moon bearing south" indicated HWS at midday (or midnight).

The moon "retards" by about 1° of a 32° compass rose for each day of the lunar cycle, which corresponds to approximately 45 minutes. With this information, a mariner could find the time of high water at any location on any day by adding forty-five minutes to the time of HWS for each day of the "age" of the moon. On the fifth day of lunation, therefore, high water is 5 times 45 minutes, or 3 hours 45 minutes after the time of HWS; at a location with HWS occurring at a lunar bearing of southwest (at 15.00), high water on the fifth day would be approximately west by north (at 18.45).

For a coastal seafarer, the speed and direction of the tidal stream is important; he can find himself opposed by a current faster than the speed of his ship, or he can be carried forward by the stream faster than he anticipated. Until the nineteenth century, there was no method of recording stream speeds, but the vital times of reversal of tidal streams around the coasts were listed in the rutters as lunar bearings. These reversals do not necessarily occur at the same time as high water and low water ashore; this common phenomenon is referred to in the English rutters as "one tide under another." Tidal times, ranges, and stream directions are now found in tables, published annually, for all primary and secondary ports.

**Speed and distance.** The distance traveled by a ship is the product of her speed multiplied by her time on passage. Seafarers can estimate the speed of the ship by timing an object in the sea passing down her side from bow to stern; the seafarers count seconds with their pulses or by saying "one-and, two-and, three-and …" Knowing the ship's length, the seafarers can convert this time to speed through the water, although because of currents, this speed is not necessarily the speed over the seabed. Time on passage, required to calculate the distance run, may be of several hours or days duration. It can be estimated by observation of the sun or of the astral clock at the beginning and end of the journey. Shorter periods of elapsed time required for intricate inshore navigation can be measured by the recitation of a Paternoster and an Ave Maria, which takes a minute, or of a Miserere, which takes three minutes.

Visible distances at sea could be estimated by eye; thus the units of distance included "as far as a man can jump" (about 2–3 meters [6.5–9.8 feet]), a ship's length (20–40 meters [65.6–131.2 feet]), a bow shot (about 100 meters [328 feet]), a mile, and a "kenning" (about 17 nautical miles). The kenning, or *veuë* in French, was probably the maximum distance at which a man at the top of a 50-meter mast could discern the coast.

## Indirect Methods of Navigation

Indirect navigational methods, ranging from simple optical and mechanical aids to sophisticated electronic and satellite-based systems, now allow accurate estimates of a ship's position, course, and speed. Rudimentary navigational aids, reputedly used by Norse seafarers, include the sun compass and a light-polarizing crystal. The sun compass consisted of a disk of wood with a central pin—in effect, a sundial. If north and the pin's shadow were marked peripherally at the beginning of a voyage, theoretically the disk could be used to relocate north and find again the initial latitude—provided that there had been no great lapse of time. Because a clear crystal of calcite (calcium carbonate) can polarize diffused light, it has been suggested that the "sunstone" mentioned in the Norse sagas was a piece of Iceland spar. This, held up to an overcast sky, should reveal the position of the sun, but much depends on the density of the cloud and the quality of the crystal. The use of both devices remains unproved.

**Depth.** Ever since man put to sea, a pole, or a weight on the end of a line, has been used to measure depth. With a lump of wax or tallow pressed into a hollow at the bottom of the weight, a sample of the seabed could be brought to the surface. With local knowledge or information from sailing directions, the depth and nature of the seabed could indicate the ship's position or assess the conditions for anchoring. For example, the early English rutter's "opyn of the saym in lx fadim ther is sondi wose and blak fischey stonys amonge" (off the Île de Seine in 60 fathoms there are black fish-shaped stones among sandy mud) gives an accurate positional fix with a direction from land, a depth, and a description of the seabed. For coastal work, a 3.3- or 6.6-kilogram (7- or 14-pound) piece of lead was used with a line of 25 or 30 fathoms. The line would be knotted and flagged with pieces of cloth or leather originally an arm's span apart—hence the word "fathom" from the Old English *fæðm*, an embrace—and later standardized to 1.85 meters (6 feet). In the twentieth century, sonar devices were introduced that measure the time taken for a sound signal to travel from the ship to the seabed and back, and that convert the time to a distance.

**Elapsed time and speed.** For the indirect measurement of elapsed time, sandglasses, first recorded at sea in the thirteenth century, were used. The Chinese sandglass appears to have recorded two and a half hours—the duration of a helmsman's watch; in northern waters, a half-hour glass was used to count the passing hours. From the mid-fifteenth century, half-minute or quarter-minute glasses, together with a ship's log, were used to make a more accurate assessment of the ship's speed. The log, a block of wood attached to a line knotted at regular intervals, was thrown over the stern of the vessel at each watch. The distance between knots—six or seven fathoms—was related to what was thought to be the length of a nautical mile and to the duration of the test. The number of knots pulled overboard while the sandglass emptied gave an immediate measure of the ship's speed in knots (nautical miles per hour). In the mid-nineteenth century, the patent log was introduced. This consisted of a rotator dragged astern by a nontwisting line that was transmitting its revolutions to a dial on the taffrail of the ship, thus recording the distance run. In the twentieth century various types of "bottom logs"—devices fixed to the ship's hull below the waterline—were introduced; these depended on a rotator, a "pitot tube," or a pair of electrodes, all activated by and recording the current flowing past.

Global Positioning System (GPS) navigational systems are now in general use; these record continuously the ship's speed, course, and distance run and display the required course to, and estimated time of arrival at, a waypoint or destination.

**Magnetic compasses.** The earliest magnetic compasses were "lodestones," pieces of magnetite ore (ferric oxide) suspended by threads. Although in ideal conditions these pointed north, they were largely useless on a heaving ship. The discovery that iron could be magnetized by stroking it with magnetite led—perhaps in the eleventh century in China and in the late twelfth century in the Mediterranean—to north-seeking needles being floated with a straw in a bowl of water or oil. In the early fourteenth century, probably in Italy, the needle was attached to a card (the "rose") marked with cardinal and half-cardinal points and balanced on a pin. As the mounting improved and as shelter was provided by a binnacle, an increasing number of points could be usefully marked on the rose until, as mentioned by Geoffrey Chaucer in *A Treatise on the Astrolabe* (c. 1390), roses with thirty-two points (each of 11.25°) were in use at sea.

In coastal navigation the magnetic compass can also be used for taking bearings on landmarks or seamarks; two such bearings on objects in known positions, preferably more than 45° apart, allow the navigator to fix the ship's position on a chart. Although many directional bearings are given in fifteenth-century sailing directions, there are few cross bearings to fix a position, possibly because a sight had not yet been fitted to the top of a ship's compass (a "pelorus" or "azimuth ring"), or because of the absence of charts. A rare example in the *Seebuch* reads "dar licht ene rudse aff twe mylen in de zee de het idensteyn unde licht suden unde norden van rammeshovet unde van der haven pleymuden licht se suthsutwest" (there lies a rock in the sea, two miles off, called Eddystone, and it lies south and north of Rame Head and south-southwest of Plymouth harbor), which, while establishing the position of the rock, indicates that positional cross-bearings were possible.

Magnetic variation is the (varying) angle between compass bearings of the magnetic and geographic poles. Although recognized in China in the eleventh century, variation was not appreciated in the West until, in the mid-fifteenth century, it was observed by Portuguese seafarers off the African coast. Attempts to correct the compass card for this error failed over long passages because of the considerable change in variation, but for the short distances involved in coastal navigation, and without charts orientated to true north, variation would have been regarded as a constant error. Since the nineteenth century, variation has been plotted around the world and is shown, with its annual change, on all sea charts. Magnetic deviation, which is caused by iron on the ship, has—again, since the nineteenth century—been corrected by the accurate placing of pieces of iron and magnets around the compass. In the twentieth century, gyroscopic compasses completely free from magnetic errors were introduced, and the GPS systems now in use record a ship's course as a true bearing.

**Latitude and longitude.** A ship's terrestrial position in terms of its spherical coordinates—that is, its latitude and longitude—may be found only with the aid of instruments. Latitude, determined by measuring the angle between the horizon and an astral body, appears to have been a component of Chinese navigation several centuries before Portuguese seafarers began to use it in the third quarter of the fifteenth century. A variety of instruments, such as the sixteenth century's backstave, quadrant, and astrolabe—all of which were superseded by the eighteenth-century sextant—have been used to determine the "meridional altitude" of the sun by day or of Polaris or Canobus by night. An accurate measurement of longitude, again by sextant, was not possible at sea until John Harrison's invention of a reliable timepiece in the eighteenth century. For coastal navigation, neither latitude nor longitude is of vital importance because land is rarely out of sight for long, and dead reckoning will normally give an acceptable position. Today a GPS navigational system may be used to confirm a calculated position.

**Radio-wave instruments.** During the twentieth century, instruments making use of radio waves were introduced to improve coastal navigation. To fix a ship's position, the earliest instruments consisted of a receiver with a direction-finding antenna with which a bearing to a shore-based transmitter could be obtained; if two transmitters were in range, a positional fix was possible. Later, ships were fitted with receivers that picked up and made phase comparisons of continuous-wave radio signals transmitted by a network of shore stations. These "hyperbolic" systems, one type of which is known as Decca, can give the ship's position extremely accurately but are now becoming obsolete, giving way to the more reliable and accurate GPS navigational systems.

To find by radio waves the distance and direction from a ship to an object, a beam of radio pulses is transmitted from a rotating antenna on the ship, and any "echoes" are displayed on the navigator's cathode-ray screen; this system is called radar, *radio detecting and ranging*. As the antenna rotates, it scans the horizon to a distance governed by the power of transmission, and the display screen presents a 360° two-dimensional view of the ship's surroundings as far as that horizon.

**Sailing directions and charts.** The first western sailing directions were the Greek *periploi* and *limenes*; *periploi* gave passage information, and *limenes* gave port information. These led to the mid-thirteenth-century Italian *portolano* (atlas), which in turn was the inspiration for the fourteenth- and fifteenth-century manuscript rutters in Portuguese, Spanish, German, Dutch, English, and French. The use of both sailing directions and charts implies literacy, and it must be assumed that, when most shipmasters were illiterate, the necessary information for their next voyage was read to them by colleagues or port officials. In the East, the sailing directions for Zhu Di's 1421 Chinese fleet have survived in the *Wu pei chi* documents, but it is probable that there had been earlier, now unknown, pilots.

The earliest-known printed pilot is in French and was compiled by Pierre Garcie, and this was followed in 1520 by his *Le grant routier de la mer*, the first rutter illustrated with profiles of the coast. All sailing directions divide coastal areas into sections, but the information may be set out in narrative or in thematic form; information in narrative form reads as if on passage, while information in thematic form has courses, depths, tides, and so on collated for each geographical section. It is possible that sketch maps of ports and havens were used in conjunction with sailing directions, but none has survived. Today, pilot books are much more comprehensive and list every detail of harbors, lights, buoys, passages, tides, hazards, and radio communications that a shipmaster can possibly require.

The early history of charting is largely unknown. Eskimo carvings on ivory of a coastline have been found, Indonesian seafarers used charts of woven vegetation, and Greek seafarers possibly had simple charts to support their *periploi* and *limenes*. The earliest surviving western chart is the Pisan, of about 1300, but its compiler almost certainly used information from earlier charts. With the introduction of the compass and an increasing amount of data coming to the cartographers, the quality of charts quickly improved, and by 1375 the *Catalan Atlas* provided usable charts for long passages.

Most sailing directions and charts are today published by official hydrographic institutes, directly or indirectly under governmental control, but specialist editions are prepared and issued commercially for specific interests such as exploration companies and the wreck-diving and yachting fraternities.

**Pilots.** Pilots are frequently taken on board ships entering or leaving estuaries and harbors. In some situations the presence of a pilot is obligatory, while in others it is at the shipmaster's discretion. There are many references in medieval sailing directions to the use of pilots around Europe; for example, at the mouth of the River Guadalquivir, the *Seebuch* states, "unde men mach setten uppe vj vadem unde dan sol len rechte vort de loetsmans an bort komen" (and one must anchor in six fathoms and by law a pilot shall come on board). The thirteenth-century *Code d'oleron* specifies the split of costs between the merchant shippers (for local pilotage) and the ship (for deep-sea pilotage). The code also specifies the sanctions against pilots involved in accidents; loss of life or of a ship incurred the death penalty. Today, officially qualified pilots, whose use is frequently obligatory, are controlled by the national authorities of all maritime nations.

[*See also* Ancient Navigation; China, *subentry on* Chinese Navigation; Law, *subentry on* Pilots and Pilotage; Logs and Ship's Journals; Nautical Astronomy and Celestial Navigation; Navigational Instruments; *and* Vikings, *subentry on* Norse Navigation.]

### Bibliography

China MSA. "Aids to Navigation." http://www.aton.gov.cn/ HBEng/module/eng-atonchina-history.aspx?style=030000.

Needham, Joseph. *Science and Civilisation in China*. Cambridge, U.K.: Cambridge University Press, 1954.

Rose, Susan. "Mathematics and the Art of Navigation: The Advance of Scientific Seamanship in Elizabethan England." *Transactions of the Royal Historical Society*, 6th ser., 14 (2004): 175–184.

Sauer, Albrecht. *Das "Seebuch": Das älteste erhaltene Seehandbuch und die spätmittelalterliche Navigation in Nordwesteuropa*. Hamburg, Germany: Kabel, 1996.

Schnall, Uwe. *Navigation der Wikinger: Nautische Probleme der Wikingerzeit im Spiegel der schriftlichen Quellen*. Oldenburg, Germany: Stalling, 1975.

Taylor, E. G. R. *The Haven-Finding Art*. London: Hollis and Carter, 1956.

Ward, Robin M. "The Earliest Known Sailing Directions in English: Transcription and Analysis." *Deutsches Schiffahrtsarchiv* 27 (2004): 49–92.

Waters, David W. *The Art of Navigation in England in Elizabethan and Early Stuart Times*. London: Hollis and Carter, 1958.

Waters, David W. *The Rutters of the Sea*. New Haven, Conn.: Yale University Press, 1967.

ROBIN WARD

# Aids

The lighthouse is one of the oldest and most recognizable man-made coastal aids for mariners. The first lighthouse structure in recorded history was the Pharos of Alexandria, one of the seven wonders of the ancient world. The Egyptians began the structure about 300 B.C.E. and finished it about 280 B.C.E. It reportedly served for at least ten centuries.

The Romans had several lighthouses at such locations as Messina, Ostria, and Ravenna. For many centuries after the fall of Rome, there is very little recorded about lighthouses. By around 1100 C.E., trade began to flow more easily between nations, and shipping again needed aids to navigation. The Italians led the way in lighthouse use. Venice had a lighted structure by about 1312 and Pisa by 1326. Other maritime nations soon followed.

By 1590, more lighthouses appeared in Europe and a few in India and Japan. The lighthouse at the entrance to the River Gironde on the French Biscay coast dates from 1612 and was still in operation in 2001. (There is some evidence there have been warnings for navigation at this location back to at least 800.) During the period 1600–1700, England led all other countries in number of lighthouses, from one to fourteen, all on the east and south coasts. By 1861, the first worldwide listing of lighthouses appeared and by 1874 the list revealed over 2,500 entries in over thirty countries.

The use of lighthouses in the United States began slowly and crudely. Some of the early lights in the New England colonies were simply lighted baskets hanging from a pole atop a hill. The lights of the individual colonies were usually funded and built by the colonies and therefore tended to be near important ports of trade and not necessarily close to hazards to navigation.

Before the colonies broke with England, there were at least eleven permanent lighthouse structures in what is now the United States. The year the first permanent lighthouse structure was built in the United States is not definitely known, but most historians of U.S. lighthouses feel that Little Brewster Island, in Boston Harbor, is the first lighthouse in North America. Merchants had petitioned for a light structure in 1713, and the light was first displayed in 1716. The new United States realized the national value of lighthouses. The ninth law passed by the new government dealt with aids to navigation. On August 7, 1789, the national government assumed the responsibility for all aids to navigation and took over all existing lighthouses as well as those under construction.

From 1789 until 1852 lighthouses in the United States grew sporadically under bad management. In 1852, Congress created a nine-member U.S. Lighthouse Board. While there were problems with the management of the lights, there was growth. In 1822, for example, there were seventy lighthouses in the United States. By 1852, there were 331 lighthouses and 42 lightships. The U.S. Lighthouse Board marked the beginning of a period of amazing growth and stability for the lights in the United States. One of the most important things that the board accomplished was the publication of the annual *Light List*. The publication recorded all the aids to navigation in the United States, describing their locations and characteristics. With this publication, a navigator could quickly identify an aid to navigation and thus have an idea of his position. The board also established a system of correcting the list, known as the "Notices to Mariners," which let navigators know of changes and additions between the publications of the *Light List*. The Lighthouse Board was in effect until 1909, when Congress created the Bureau of Lighthouses. During the tenure of the Lighthouse Board, the number of lighthouses and aids to navigation increased dramatically. In the 1850s, for example, there were 297 major lighthouses in the United States. By 1910 this had increased to 1,397. In 1939, President Franklin D. Roosevelt merged the U.S. Lighthouse Service into the U.S. Coast Guard, which is now responsible for all federal aids to navigation.

The first commissioner of lighthouses was George R. Putnam. Putnam was born in Davenport, Iowa, on May 24, 1865, and led an adventurous life. He began by studying law, but then he decided that he would enter engineering, and he graduated from Rose Polytechnic Institute in Indiana. He joined the Coast and Geodetic Survey and for the next twenty years was involved in mapmaking. Until the turn of the twentieth century, most of Putnam's assignments were to polar or sub-polar regions in Alaska and Greenland. In 1900 he was assigned to the Philippines. His last assignment for the Coast and Geodetic Survey was in Washington, D.C.: he was appointed the first commissioner of lighthouses on July 1, 1910. Putnam had good relations with the U.S. Congress. He was also a very good writer, authoring an excellent book on the U.S. Lighthouse Service. Putnam held his position until his retirement in 1935, and he died on July 2, 1953.

## Features of Lighthouses

Lighthouse locations dictate the size of a light structure. Lights that are in low areas will be tall, while those on high rocky ground will be short. Light structures are also used as day markers by navigators. Toward this end, some light towers are painted in special patterns to help identify them. For example, the Elbow Reef Lighthouse, in the Bahamas, has horizontal red and white stripes.

One way in which navigators may distinguish one lighthouse from another is through the characteristics of its light. A light may be fixed (steady) or occulating (flashing), and it may be red or white. Because of the technology of the times, the early lighthouses were usually fixed white lights. The French first perfected a means of rotating either the light and the reflectors or the lenses. The device consisted of a simple clockwork motor, which worked like the weights on a large cabinet clock, with the descending weight activating the rotational movement. The first lighthouse to use a flashing light characteristic was at Carlsten lighthouse in Sweden in 1781. When the Fresnel lenses came into operation in the United States, the large, heavy lenses rested on wheels or ball bearings in a track at the base of the lens. Several times a night, a keeper would have to wind the clockwork mechanism to raise the weight to the top of the tower in order to keep the lens moving. To create a colored light, colored panels were inserted into the lens, or the lamp had solid color.

A constant theme in the history of lighthouses is the search for the best type of light for use in the aid to navigation. Until the twentieth century, the basic ingredient of light illumination was a flame. The first aids were open fires fueled by wood and built on hills. When towers began to be used, the flame was transported to atop the tower. Coal eventually replaced wood. In Europe, some lights began to use candles, which was not as messy as coal and was easier to use. Candles could also be enclosed by lanterns to provide a steady light. The candles, however, did not give off as bright a light. Despite this, candles continued to be used into the nineteenth century.

The next step in improving the lights was the introduction of lamps. Some of the early lamps used solid, circular wicks, and others used flat wicks. The light in the English Eddystone light in 1759, for example, used a flat wick. The lamps, however, gave off a smoke that coated the glass of the interior of the lantern, thus dimming the light. One counter to this was the introduction of the spider lamp, which consisted of a pan of oil with four wicks protruding from it. The spider lamp was first used in the United States at the Boston light around 1790. Even though the lamps were considered unsatisfactory, because they gave off acrid fumes that burned the eyes and nostrils of keepers and therefore limited the time that he could remain in the lantern room, they were used in the United States until 1812.

Considered the first major revolution in lighting lighthouses, in 1781 the Swiss scientist Ami Argand (1750–1803) invented a lamp that had a hollow circular wick. Oxygen passed along the inside and outside of the wick, thus allowing the flame to burn brightly and intensely, as well as without smoke. English lighthouses began using the Argand lamps in 1789 and fitted them with 18- to 20-inch reflectors. Experiments with reflectors in Europe since at least the seventeenth century led, by the end of the eighteenth century, to the parabolic reflector, with the flame of the lamp at the center of the reflector. The Argand lamp with parabolic reflector served for many years in lighthouses, but it took some time before the Argand lamp with parabolic reflector was accepted for use in U.S. lighthouses. Captain Winslow Lewis (1790–1850), an unemployed ship captain, persuaded the federal government to adopt his Argand lamp with parabolic reflector in U.S. lighthouses in 1810, and it became the standard for U.S. lighthouses.

It was a French road engineer, however, who made the greatest change in lighting lighthouses. Augustin Jean Fresnel was born in Broglie in 1788. His life was plagued with poor health. At first his teachers thought him slow, but when he entered secondary school he exhibited a remarkable ability in mathematics. Fresnel entered the École Polytechnique. Napoleon wanted the best students trained to be officers, while the rest were regulated to civil servants and engineers used for building roads and canals.

With his poor health, Fresnel was assigned to finish his technical training at the school of bridges and highways. In his spare moments of supervising road crews, Fresnel began to think of light. His invention of the lens that bears his name revolutionized lights. In 1821, Fresnel's lenses were installed in the lighthouses of France. The French lighthouses became so superior, the lenses were soon in all the lighthouses of Europe. Fresnel died on Bastille Day 1827, largely ignored by his countrymen.

Once the Fresnel lens was in operation, there was no need for further work on developing the lens. With the acceptance of the Fresnel lens, the lighthouses of the United States were divided into six orders, according to the type of lens in the light. The large first- and second-order lenses were for important coastal lights, and the other orders were for bays, harbors, and rivers. Efforts could now turn to better illuminants for the light.

The illuminants for the light ran a gauntlet of wood, coal, and oil. For many years, sperm whale oil was the principal oil in the lamps. This became too expensive and a variety of experiments were conducted, including lard oil and oil made from wild cabbage seeds. In the United States, kerosene began service in 1864. Incandescent oil vapor became the next step in lights. This marked the last step in the use of flame for lighthouse illumination.

The first use of electricity in lighthouses was at Dungeness Lighthouse on the coast of England in 1862, but the experiment was abandoned. In the United States, electricity for lighthouse purposes began with an arc light in the Statue of Liberty in New York City harbor in 1886. During the 1920s and 1930s, the Bureau of Lighthouses converted most lighthouses in the United States to electricity. In 1968, the U.S. Coast Guard introduced its Lighthouse Automation and Modernization Project (LAMP) to speed up the process of automating the lighthouses. By 1995, only Boston Light Station, the oldest light in the United States, remained under the supervision of a U.S. Coast Guard crew.

## Lightships

In areas where the technology of the time could not construct light structures, special vessels, called lightships, were stationed. Most histories of aids to navigation give the eighteenth century as the beginning of lightships. There are, however, some indications that the pre-Christian Romans used lightships when they placed fire baskets in galleys to act as an aid to mariners and to let pirates know that a warship stood nearby. The first lightship in Great Britain came about when a single-masted ship, *Nore*, took up station at the Nore sandbank in the Thames estuary in 1731. *Nore* had two ship's lanterns hoisted high on the mast and spaced twelve feet apart from the cross arm.

Lightship development in the United States lagged behind that of England and Europe. The first use of a lightship, then called a "lightboat," in the United States was at Willoughby Spit in Virginia in 1820. The lightship could not stand an exposed position (outside the protection of land), so the service moved it to Craney Island, near Norfolk, Virginia. By 1821 there were four "inside" lightships, vessels located within the shores of the United States in Chesapeake Bay. The first "outside" lightship in the United States was established in 1823 at Sandy Hook, New Jersey. The name was changed to the Ambrose Channel Lightship on December 1, 1908.

The number of lightships in the United States rose and fell. In 1837, for example, there were twenty-six, by 1852 there were forty-two, but then in 1889 there were twenty-four and in 1917, fifty-three. By 1842 the lightships of the United States tended to be from 40 to 230 tons burden, built of wood, rigged for sail, and with no machinery-driven propulsion. If driven off station during a storm, the lightship had to sail to port and await better weather before attempting to regain its station.

Up to 1852, the lightships carried one or two lanterns, with either a compass or a common lamp with ten to twelve wicks extending from it. The lightship at Brandywine Shoal, Delaware, had two oil lamps, each with twelve cylindrical wicks. For a fog signal, the lightship at Diamond Shoals, North Carolina, carried a six-pound cannon for firing in foggy weather.

In 1880 the French began experiments to find hulls that would remain stable in heavy weather. The British took these data and incorporated them into their design for a ninety-foot iron ship with three watertight compartments belowdeck. In 1882, the United States had its first iron lightship built and sent to New Jersey. In 1891, the first three lightships with machinery propulsion came into service in the United States and were sent to the Great Lakes. Most of the United States' lightships were stationed on the East Coast, with the first vessel for the West Coast established in 1892 near the mouth of the Columbia River, which divides the states of Washington and Oregon.

There were two great dangers for crews in duty aboard lightships. One is weather. In England, for example, during a severe gale in January 1953, the lightship at Spurn Head broke loose from its moorings and drifted twelve miles before being rescued. The second danger is from collision. Many lightships in Europe suffered collisions. In 1912,

the Belgian West Hinder lightship, while under tow into harbor, received a fatal blow with a string of pontoon barges and capsized, drowning the crew of ten. On May 15, 1934, for instance, the passenger liner SS *Olympic* struck and sank lightship *No. 34* off Nantucket Shoals, Massachusetts, causing the deaths of seven of the eleven-man crew. The service recorded at least 150 collisions involving lightships, and as technology improved, the U.S. Coast Guard sought ways of replacing the costly lightships. On November 1, 1961, an offshore light tower was established at Buzzard's Bay, Massachusetts. The structure was based upon offshore drilling platforms used in the Gulf of Mexico. This marked the beginning of the end for lightships.

In water too deep for offshore light structures, large navigational buoys now take station, such as at Owers Station off the south coast of England. The end of lightships in the United States officially came on March 29, 1985, when the last lightship departed station. The global positioning system (GPS) and lighthouse automation have also done away with the manning of offshore light structures and large navigational buoys (LNBs).

## Fog Signals

Fog signals could be very important to mariners entering a harbor. Most people associate fog signals with lighthouses, but in the United States most fog signals at light stations were north of Chesapeake Bay, while there were very few south of there. George R. Putnam, the commissioner of the Bureau of Lighthouses, once reported that the light station at Seguin Island, Maine, logged 2,734 hours of fog in one year—that is, in one out of every three hours, fog shrouded the station.

The first fog signal in what is now the United States, a cannon, went into service in 1719 at Boston. This was not an unusual method of signaling in the murk: England still tested cannons as fog-signaling devices as late as the 1860s. By 1857, the U.S. Lighthouse Board hired a retired army sergeant to fire the first fog signal on the West Coast at Point Bonita, on the opposite side of San Francisco's Golden Gate. The use of cannon for fog signaling stopped shortly thereafter. In the 1880s in Scotland and Ireland gas guns became fog signals. The guns used an explosive mixture of acetylene gas and air ignited by a spark.

Bell boats helped warn mariners trying to enter San Francisco's foggy harbor. Bell boats were in use in Delaware Bay in 1885. The boats were thirty feet long and twelve feet wide, and they were turtle-backed. Suspended under deck scaffolds, the bells weighed half a ton. The boat's motion caused four clappers to strike the bell. The boats were without crews and were held in place by heavy moorings. By 1887 bell boats were no longer in use.

In the 1820s, fog bells came into use at many lighthouses in New England. The bells at first were struck by hand. Around the 1860s, the U.S. Lighthouse Board installed devices that rang the bells mechanically. At Bell Rock off the coast of Scotland, the fog bell is operated by wind power. Italy also experimented with wind powered bells. The main problem with this method was that foggy days are days of calm winds. The lighthouse board found a clockwork mechanism, using a falling weight as a source of power, to be the most practicable. The early devices, however, were unreliable. By the 1920s, an electrically operated bell was in service, as was a device that automatically struck the bell in thick weather. The device, operated by a hydroscope, used human hair to measure moisture. When the moisture in the air approached 100 percent, the hydroscope would trip a switch, which turned on the electrical current to power the bell.

All maritime nations experimented with several sound devices designed to warn the mariner in low visibility. Locomotive whistles were tested, but the sound was diffused too quickly. Compressed air for a signal was first used at the Beavertail Lighthouse, on the south end of Conanicut Island at the entrance of Narragansett Bay, Rhode Island, in 1851. The air compressor was operated by a horse, or it could be pumped up by hand. Experiments with steam-powered whistles began in 1855. The first light stations regularly equipped with steam whistles were West Quoddy Head and Cape Elizabeth, both in Maine, in 1869. The signals used a ten-inch locomotive or ship whistle. A siren with a large cast-iron trumpet was first installed at the Sandy Hook, New Jersey, East Beacon in 1868.

By the 1870s the siren trumpet, bell, and whistle were the accepted fog signals in the United States, with the bell used in such inland waters as Chesapeake Bay. By 1900 there were 377 fog signals in the United States, exclusive of those on buoys. Both electricity and the diesel engine began to power fog signals after the turn of the twentieth century. Also around the turn of the century, a Canadian company developed the diaphone signal in three models: single tone, two tone, and chime. The U.S. Lighthouse Service was so impressed with this when it was introduced in the United States in 1914 that the service acquired the rights to manufacture the equipment in the United States.

After World War II, the U.S. Coast Guard began to phase out many of the older devices, replacing them with new electronic horns. The International Association of Lighthouse Authorities declared that fog signals were no longer necessary for the needs of navigation, so only a few diaphragms and the new electronic pure-tone signals remain.

## Buoyage

Just as important as lighthouses, lightships, and fog signals to aiding mariners in arriving safely is the buoy. Buoys mark hazards and channels, and the size, shape, and color scheme of the buoys impart important information to the mariner. The first use of buoys in northern Europe was in the early fifteenth century in the Vlie, which empties into the Zuider Zee. These early aids to navigation guided ships into Amsterdam and Kampen. In sixteenth-century Sweden, the Pilot Service Organization maintained markers onshore and on shoals. It is not clear whether the shoal-water markers were buoys or structures, but at least some buoys were used. Some markers were hollow wooden casks bound with iron bands and moored with a chain and large stone. At the time, apparently, the symbol for an aid to navigation was either a broom or something in the shape of a broom.

In the United States, several buoys marked the entrance to Delaware Bay as early as 1767. There is also evidence of four buoys being transferred from Massachusetts and three from Pennsylvania to the new federal government in 1789. The buoys were either small barrels or bundles of wood bound with rope or iron bands. The first wood spar buoys (long telephone-pole-shaped devices) began to see service in the United States in 1820 and were weighted at one end to make them stand upright in the water. Wood remained the primary material for buoys until the middle of the nineteenth century, when boiler iron came into use. New iron buoys were compartmented to make sinking difficult. The first bell buoy came into use in 1855. Waves activated the bell clappers. By 1855 at least 1,034 buoys guarded U.S. waterways. Twenty-one years later, in 1876, the first whistle buoy was on station, and five years later a buoy lighted by a combination of oil and gas went into service.

Testing of electric buoys in the United States began between 1888 and 1903, with power from a cable running underwater to a group of wooden-spar buoys. Batteries later replaced this unsuccessful venture. By 1900 the number of buoys in the United States had risen to 4,842. The first metal tall-type nun (conical shaped) and can (flat topped) buoys came into use the same year. Buoys powered by acetylene gas came into use in U.S. waters ten years later. By the time that the U.S. Lighthouse Service became a part of the U.S. Coast Guard in 1939, there were 16,000 buoys in U.S. waters.

Buoys remain on station because of chains attached to a bridle using shackles and swivels. Originally the device used as an anchor was a large stone. This was replaced with regular ship's mushroom anchors. The device now used, called a sinker, is a large concrete block. Buoys must be pulled annually to check the chain and to give the buoy an overhaul. In areas of freezing, the buoys must be removed each year before freeze-up and then reset in the spring.

Buoys come not only in various shapes, but also in different color schemes that help navigators. The United States now uses a buoyage system that conforms to that of the International Association of Lighthouse Authorities (IALA) and is designated as "System B–the Combined Cardinal and Lateral System (red to starboard)." Under this system, green buoys mark the port (left) side of a channel when entering from seaward, or a hazard that must be passed by keeping the buoy on the left side. Red buoys mark the starboard (right) side of a channel when entering from seaward, or a hazard that must be passed by keeping the buoy to seaward. Red-and-green horizontally banded buoys mark junctions in a channel, or hazards that may be passed on either side. If the top band is green, then the preferred channel is with the buoy to the boat's left, and if the top band is red, then the buoy is to the boat's right. Red-and-white vertically banded buoys, called "sea buoys," are safe water marks and are used to mark offshore approach points, or are used as fairway or midchannel markers. The establishment of a color scheme came from England in the middle of the nineteenth century.

Canada has basically the same system as the United States. Northwestern Europe–England and France, west to Ireland, north to Norway and Sweden, east to Poland and Russia–uses a buoyage system known as "System A–the Combined Cardinal and Lateral System (red to port)."

Buoys are also numbered to indicate which side of the channel they mark and to help the navigator find the buoy's charted location. In the United States, numerals increase from seaward and are kept in sequence, with even numbers on the right side of the channel and odd on the left. Lighted buoys in the United States have red lights to starboard and green to port.

The U.S. Coast Guard also maintains aids to navigation along the Atlantic and Gulf of Mexico Intracoastal Waterways (ICW). The coloring, numbering, and lighting of buoys are the same as in the lateral system of buoyage–in this case, if a vessel is bound north to south along the

Atlantic and south to north and east to west along the Gulf coast. For example, a ship bound from New Jersey to Florida will have red buoys on the starboard side. To indicate that the aids are a part of the intracoastal waterway, they have a distinctive yellow marking. All aids along the intracoastal waterway with a red buoy to starboard have a yellow triangle, and those to port have a yellow square.

## Ranges

Not a part of the buoyage system, but an important feature of aids to navigation, are ranges; these are used to determine the centerline of a channel. A range consists of two fixed aids to navigation positioned with respect to each other so that when seen in line they indicate that the navigator's ship may be in safe waters. The ship only "may" be safe because if it is too close or too far away from a specific distance of the front marker, it could be in danger. Ranges are either unlighted or lighted.

## Electronic Aids

World War II hastened the development of electronics to help piloting. LORAN (long-range aids to navigation) began when electronics engineers of the U.S. Coast Guard and U.S. Navy began developing theories that would eventually lead to a chain of LORAN stations. The theory is based upon the speed of light and radio waves, both traveling at about 299,800 kilometers (186,000 miles) per second. A controlling station, the "master," transmits a pulsed signal that is radiated in all directions. The signal travels in a straight line until received by the secondary, the "slave," station. At the same time, the signal is intercepted by any ship equipped with a LORAN receiver in the area. The receiver converts the signal to a visual display on an oscilloscope. The slave station also receives the master signal, waits a certain amount of time, and then transmits its own signal.

The slave signal is received by the receiver on a ship, where it appears as a second trace on the oscilloscope. The receiver on the ship is arranged so that the master signal is on top of the oscilloscope and the slave is on the bottom and slightly to the right. The navigator then rotates knobs on the LORAN receiver until the slave signal is directly below the master signal, and the knobs eventually cause the superimposing of the two signals. This completed, the navigator records a number from the direct-reading counter on the set. This number indicates how many microseconds pass between the time a master signal reaches the receiver and the time a slave signal triggered by that master signal arrives at the set. With this number the navigator refers to a specially printed LORAN chart of the general area in which the ship is operating. The chart is overprinted with numerous lines, each of which represents a LORAN time difference. The lines are labeled in microseconds. By matching the reading with the lines on the chart, the navigator determines that the position is somewhere along one of the lines. Because the lines usually extend for long distances, a single line with no other information is almost useless. By taking readings on two or more master-slave stations, however, the navigator can determine the position with accuracy.

A navigator can usually obtain a fix within two or three minutes. Weather usually does not affect LORAN, which is usable at daytime ranges of up to 750 nautical miles and at night almost double that distance. The system described is known as LORAN A. The U.S. Coast Guard also developed a "C" system with accuracy to within a quarter of a mile and ranges above three thousand nautical miles. There are some deficiencies within the LORAN system. These deal with the nature of radio waves, which are along the earth's surface and via the sky. A skywave takes longer to reach the set and can introduce a margin of error.

The LORAN wave also travels over land and water, two different mediums. LORAN assumes the speed of a radio wave to be constant, when in reality the speed is altered when a wave passes over land. LORAN also does not cover all areas. Work started on the LORAN chain of stations in 1942, with the first stations set up by the U.S. Navy; these were eventually taken over by the U.S. Coast Guard. The North Atlantic chain came into operation in midwinter of 1942, and the Aleutian chain began in the same year. The service eventually spread throughout the Pacific and the world.

## VTS

Electronics has also allowed those on shore to assist the master of a ship to navigate the approaches to busy harbors. The British pioneered the use of shore-based radar and very high frequency (VHF) communication to assist vessels entering port, now known as vessel traffic systems (VTS). The first major use of the system was for the port of Liverpool in 1948. The first U.S. port to use the system was Long Beach, California, in 1949. By 1964 the ports of Hamburg and Rotterdam had fully operational systems consisting of a series of shore-based radar and a VHF communications network. The results were successful. In Rotterdam, for example, collisions in the approach to the harbor were reduced fourfold, in spite of an increase in the volume of shipping. Canada's establishment of a control system on the Saint Lawrence Seaway in 1968 also proved very successful. By 1972, collisions were, on average, four a year, with no loss of life or ship sunk. This is a marked contrast from twelve serious collisions a year during the four-year period prior to the inception of the system. The VTS is now used worldwide.

## GPS

One of the greatest improvements in navigation through electronics is the use of satellites and the global positioning system (GPS). A navigator has only to press a button to receive a readout of the position without the tuning of LORAN. The position is accurate to within feet. The rapid and accurate positioning of GPS had caused the U.S. Coast Guard to consider phasing out LORAN, but recent information that it is possible to tamper with the GPS signal has caused this decision to be reconsidered.

[*See also* Global Positioning System; Nautical Astronomy and Celestial Navigation; Navigational Instruments; *and* Navigational Manuals.]

## Bibliography

Adamson, Hans Christian. *Keepers of the Lights*. New York: Greenberg, 1955. Lively account of U.S. lighthouses and keepers.

Bathurst, Bella. *The Lighthouse Stevensons: The Extraordinary Story of the Building of the Scottish Lighthouses by the Ancestors of Robert Louis Stevenson*. London: HarperCollins, 1999.

Boutry, Georges A. *Augustin Fresnel: His Time, Life, and Work, 1788–1827*. London: John Murray, 1949. One of the few works in English on Fresnel.

Cairo, Robert F. "Notes on Early Lightship Development." *U.S. Coast Guard Engineer's Digest* 188 (July–September 1975): 3–14.

Carlson, Victor. *Maritime Telegraph Systems: Buoys, Beacons, Tidal Signals, Etc.* Stockholm, 1890.

Cipra, David L. *Lighthouses, Lightships, and the Gulf of Mexico*. Alexandria, Va.: Cypress Communications, 1997. A very good study of the lighthouses and lightships of one region in the United States.

Clifford, Mary Louise, and J. Candace Clifford. *Women Who Kept the Lights: An Illustrated History of Female Lighthouse Keepers*. Williamsburg, Va.: Cypress Communications, 1993. Very good study of the role of women in the U.S. Lighthouse Service.

Duxbury, Ken. *Coastal Navigation*. London: Luscombe, 1976.

Edwards, E. Price. *Our Seamarks: A Plain Account of the Lighthouses, Buoys, and Signals Maintained on Our Coasts, With Illustrations*. London: Longmans, Green, 1884.

El-Rabbany, Ahmed. *Introduction to GPS: The Global Positioning System*. Boston and London: Artech House, 2002.

Flint, Willard. *Lightships of the United States Government: Reference Notes*. Washington, D.C.: U.S. Coast Guard, 1989. The best source for information on U.S. lightships.

Holland, Francis Ross., Jr. *America's Lighthouses: Their Illustrated History since 1716*. Brattleboro, Vt.: Stephen Green Press, 1972. One of the standard works on the history of the U.S. Lighthouse Service.

Jerrome, Edward George. *Lighthouses, Lightships and Buoys*. Oxford: Blackwell, 1966.

Marshall, Amy. *A History of Buoys and Tenders*. Washington, D.C.: U.S. Coast Guard, 1996. The best short work on the subject.

Noble, Dennis L. *Lighthouses and Keepers: The U.S. Lighthouse Service and Its Legacy*. Annapolis, Md.: Naval Institute Press, 1997. Covers lighthouses, lightships, fog signals, buoy tenders, buoys, and electronic aids.

Putnam, George R. *Sentinel of the Coasts: The Log of a Lighthouse Engineer*. New York: Norton, 1937. A lively book that is a standard on the U.S. Lighthouse Service.

Schram, John. *Advanced Coastal Navigation*. Melbourne: Schram, 1983.

Strobridge, Truman R. *Chronology of Aids to Navigation and the Old Lighthouse Service, 1716–1939*. Washington, D.C.: Government Printing Office, 1974. An invaluable reference aide to the key dates in the history of aids to navigation in the United States.

Toghill, Jeff. *Coastal Navigation for Beginners*. Rev. ed. London: Ward Lock, 1980.

Updike, Richard W. "Winslow Lewis and the Lighthouses." *American Neptune* 28, no. 1 (January 1968): 31–48. Detailed account of the importance of Winslow Lewis to the development of U.S. lighthouses.

Westrop, Jane M. *Dynamic Positioning by GPS*. Nottingham, U.K.: University of Nottingham Press, 1990.

Wheeler, Wayne. "The History of Fog Signals, Part 1." *Keeper's Log* (Summer 1990): 20–23. Detailed account of fog signals.

Wheeler, Wayne. "The History of Fog Signals, Part 2." *Keeper's Log* (Fall 1990): 8–15.

Willoughby, Malcolm F. *The U.S. Coast Guard in World War II*. Annapolis, Md.: Naval Institute Press, 1957. Chapter 11, "The Story of Loran," gives a detailed account of the beginnings of LORAN.

DENNIS L. NOBLE

**Coast Defense** From the earliest time that ships were capable of transporting fighting men and matériel across the oceans, mankind has devised ways of protecting coastal settlements. Throughout the two and a half millennia of recorded history, to the twentieth century, two-dimensional land and sea warfare has attended the struggle between forces to attain military or naval superiority. For centuries these contests were the sole preserve of emperors, kings, or feudal overlords, responding to threats from the sea, whether in the form of small-scale raids or a large-scale invasion attempt, defined by contemporary military experience.

Following the introduction of effective gunpowder artillery and the increased destructive power of the warship from the end of the fifteenth century, distinct phases in the growth of coast-defense measures can be identified on a national and later transnational scale, as newly formed departments of state with dedicated military engineering and ordnance establishments responded to the changing circumstances. This change was slow during the era of the wooden sailing ship and the muzzle-loading, smoothbore gun firing solid shot. However, the pace rapidly gathered momentum through the technological advances and industrialization of the second half of the nineteenth century.

## Early History of Coastal Defense

One of the earliest recorded examples of effective coast defense occurred in the First Punic War (264–241 B.C.E.) when the Romans repelled the assault of Carthaginian ships with land-based mangonels. During the Second Punic War's siege of Syracuse (214–212 B.C.E.) a Roman army under Marcellus constructed a floating platform for a siege machine with which to batter the city walls. In response, Archimedes, the mathematician, devised a stone-throwing onager that destroyed the platform at great range before it could be brought into service. In Julius Caesar's first landing in Britain in 55 B.C.E., his ships were deliberately driven onto the beach to provide stable platforms from which to discharge the shipboard catapults. The Romans, having later organized their own fleet, the *Classis Britannica*, established protected bases on the south and east coasts of England with the construction of stone forts, the largest—with twenty stone towers—being Portchester. These forts were strengthened after 300 C.E. and incorporated in the defenses of the "Saxon Shore" on both sides of the English Channel. Their solid corner towers probably hosted stone-throwing catapults such as the onager, with its high trajectory for smashing through ships' decks.

The English King Alfred also developed a system of fortified coastal towns, or *burhs*. These offered refuge for an entire community in the face of raids or landings from the sea. The founding of Portsmouth as a harbor large enough to contain the fleets assembled for the Crusades heralded the concept of the port as a defended base from which to conduct national defense. After the loss of Normandy in 1204, the outlying Channel Islands of Jersey and Guernsey, retained by the English crown, were fortified as royal strongholds that could be supplied by sea. In the Hundred Years War (1337–1453) against France, French, Castilian, and Portuguese galleys ravaged the coastline, sacking Portsmouth in 1337, followed by devastating raids on Southampton, Plymouth, and Bristol. The very real danger of attack from the sea induced Edward III to take the war to the enemy, and the defeat of the French fleet at the Battle of Middelburg in 1339 was significant for its clear demonstration of the projection of naval power and the first shipboard use of the new gunpowder artillery by an English vessel. The conditions had now been created for the opening of the contest between the warship and land-based artillery.

In the French assault on Plymouth in 1403, the entrance to Sutton Harbour was barred by a heavy chain used as a boom defense. In the same attack, cannon fire was brought to bear on the approaching ships from hastily prepared positions on the Hoe. At this early date guns were of primitive construction with a slow rate of fire, unreliable and difficult to aim, being mounted on fixed wooden beds. The first Master of the Ordnance was created by Henry V in 1414. Later, Edward IV, benefiting from advances in gunfounding techniques on the Continent, brought Flemish craftsmen to the Tower of London to establish the Royal Armouries. The earliest coast-defense works, common throughout Europe, were open "bulwarks"—earthen breastworks with stone or wooden gun platforms. Existing masonry fortifications could be converted for artillery by the insertion of gunports in their vertical walls, but in 1481 the first English, purpose-built coastal artillery fort was erected at Dartmouth Castle. A second fort was built opposite it, at Kingswear.

The succeeding Tudor dynasty, faced with an ever-growing threat from the Continental maritime powers of France and Spain, recorded the first specific parliamentary act for temporary coast defenses in 1512. But Henry VIII's break with Rome in 1538 signaled a program of coastal defense on a previously unmatched scale. The entire coast of England and Wales was divided into districts, and the new, permanent works were centrally funded as part of a national defense policy. The distinctive, compact "Devyce" forts were essentially tiered, circular gun chambers mounting the heaviest artillery to fire on opposing ships and designed to be self-defensible. By 1545 the country's coast defenses had been placed on a secure footing, with trained garrison forces and a reorganized beacon early-warning system. In the history of military architecture, however, "Harry's Walls" are considered transitional works. The blockhouse built at Sharpenode on the Isle of Wight in 1547 was the first English coastal fort to feature triangular bastions for flank defense by artillery of the landward face. Perhaps more important, this was where the Royal Navy was created, with a permanent fleet of purpose-designed warships and an efficient administration to support it.

The Mediterranean coasts of Italy and the island of Malta had already witnessed the appearance of coastal towers as a form of linear defense, manned by small numbers of men and used as lookout posts with one or two guns mounted on the roof. These towers were usually square, but occasionally round, with thick, battered walls defended via machicolations—a distinctive design that was to find intermittent favor in modified form in many parts of the world. Galleys remained in use in this theater until the early eighteenth century, and such towers were capable of opposing the limited forward-firing, centerline artillery carried on these ships.

## Maritime Powers and Fortification

As the European maritime powers of Spain, Portugal, France, the Netherlands, and England competed to extend their influence in the pursuit of overseas possessions and foreign trade during the sixteenth and seventeenth centuries, they took with them their techniques of fortification. The principles of the Italian trace were widely adopted with low, broad-faced bastions capable of mounting a greater number of heavier smoothbore, muzzle-loading guns on the new wheeled carriages. Coastal forts were built by the Portuguese at Mombasa in West Africa and at Macao in distant China, by the Dutch in the East Indies, and by the Spanish in South America and on the Florida coast. Permanent works were sited on salient headlands and offshore islands, and it was now generally accepted that masonry forts, providing stable platforms for heavy guns that delivered concentrated artillery fire, were superior to tall-masted wooden sailing ships, which were unstable and subject to wind and tides. Ships were maneuverable and might outflank a shore position, but their hulls, masts, and rigging were susceptible to damage if they closed with well-serviced shore batteries, especially those capable of firing red-hot shot. The belief in the superiority of forts over ships would persist throughout the smoothbore era, but a determined commander might still run in under the guns of a fort or battery and put them out of action with accurate short-range fire.

In 1588, with the English fleet in a strong position providing the traditional first line of defense, the Spanish

Armada was defeated at sea. But almost a century later, in June 1667, with the Dutch fleet in temporary command, the Thames and Medway were threatened with serious incursions. The unfinished fort at Sheerness was closely engaged by three Dutch ships-of-the-line and evacuated after nine of its guns were destroyed. In the following month Harwich was the target of a Dutch fleet when eight warships were detached to bombard the newly constructed Landguard Fort. At this same time, in his desire to challenge the supremacy of the English fleet with a new warship-building program, the French king Louis XIV ordered Rochefort to be developed as a secure naval base and arsenal, with a ring of coast-defense works to protect the Aix Roads and Charente estuary. Semicircular batteries, secured by tower redoubts at Fort Louvois and Fort Lupin, were constructed to designs by the celebrated French engineer Sébastien Le Prestre de Vauban. In addition to fortifying the naval bases at Dunkerque and Le Havre, he completed the reconstruction of the defenses at La Rochelle, as well as improvements to the principal island fortresses of Château d'Oléron and Saint-Martin-de-Ré. The latter successfully withstood a naval bombardment and assault by a combined Anglo-Dutch force in 1696.

A significant event in the contest between ship and shore technologies was the introduction of the bomb vessel by the French at the bombardment of Algiers in 1682. The advantages of a small boat carrying a heavy mortar or howitzer in shallow coastal waters, capable of bombarding shore establishments and warships at anchor with explosive shells, were quickly appreciated by the English. Their first bomb vessels were engaged in attacks on Saint-Malo in 1693 and at Le Havre the following year. Ship-rigged, unlike the French bomb ketches, they were manned by artillerymen who served the mortars supplied by the Board of Ordnance. In 1707 the naval phase of the plan to capture Toulon by an Anglo-Dutch force succeeded in first destroying coastal batteries, which allowed the bomb vessels to close the harbor and sink two French ships of the line. This type of vessel would be developed later as a powerful means of engaging coast defenses.

In response to French support for the American colonists in their War of Independence and the perceived threat to the Channel Islands, Jersey's governor, General Henry Seymour Conway, implemented a chain of twenty-three coastal towers in 1778 said to have been inspired some twenty years earlier by a scheme for the defense of towns by Comte Hermann Maurice de Saxe. The three-story round, loopholed towers, with Coehoorn mortars on the roof, were a relatively inexpensive but effective first line of defense of an exposed shoreline and, where advantageous, featured a concentric gun battery. Another fifteen towers were constructed on the neighboring island of Guernsey, predating the later Martello towers raised between 1805 and 1812 against the Napoleonic threat of landings on the south and east coasts of England. These were true gun towers with lower, more robust stone walls, inspired by the action at Mortella Point on Corsica in 1794. Similar towers were constructed before the end of the Napoleonic Wars by the British around Dublin Bay in Ireland, Scotland, the Channel Islands, Canada, Sicily, and the Adriatic, and later still in Bermuda, Mauritius, and South Africa.

The French Revolutionary and Napoleonic Wars witnessed the widespread adoption of the short-barreled carronade and the unpredictable but highly incendiary Congreve rocket, first used in the bombardment of Boulogne in 1806. In the bombardment of Copenhagen the following year by Admiral James Gambier's fleet, rockets were again used as a supplement to naval gunfire, contributing to the destruction of the Danish coastal batteries and the capture of the entire fleet of sixty-four warships. In France fear of British naval attack, particularly of amphibious assault in the form perfected in the 1750s using flat-bottomed landing boats and effective cooperation between military and naval forces, led to the development in 1811 of the *tours modèles* as artillery redoubts, square on plan with two floors in three types for sixty, thirty, or eighteen men. The three patterns of *corps de garde défensifs* of 1846 were similarly intended as detached gun towers or as redoubts for larger batteries.

During the same period, under the threat of war with England, the United States began to consider the defense of its Atlantic coastline. The early First System works such as Fort McHenry at Baltimore and Fort Mifflin at Philadelphia were based on the pentagonal designs of French engineers. The works of the Second System, however, began to take on a distinctive appearance with the creation of the Corps of Engineers in 1802 and were, in the majority of cases, successful in resisting British attacks on these defended harbors in the War of 1812. From 1817, the Third System witnessed the full embodiment of the principles of the French engineer Marc René Montalembert in his "perpendicular fortification" first proposed in 1776, mounting a greater number of guns in casemates for additional protection. These guns could, by sheer weight of fire, overwhelm an attacking warship. Among these massive, multitiered polygonal works built as part of a systematic peacetime program was Fort Adams, at Newport, Rhode Island, which mounted a remarkable 468 guns manned by a garrison of twenty-four hundred men. But during the American Civil War, Fort Sumter, South Carolina, and Fort Pulaski, Georgia, underwent devastating bombardment from the new heavy rifled guns and ironclad monitors, leading to the eventual abandonment of large masonry forts.

Lord Palmerston's order for the Royal Navy to bombard the port of Acre, the last foothold of Egyptian rule in Syria in 1840, was an earlier convincing demonstration of the effectiveness of concentrated naval gunfire against exposed masonry defenses. The development of the steam, screw warship and the growth of Cherbourg as a fortified arsenal and naval base on the Channel coast posed a serious threat to Britain's principal naval bases at Portsmouth and Plymouth. As part of the Admiralty's offensive strategy designed to neutralize Cherbourg, new harbors at Portland and Alderney were commenced in the late 1840s. The forts built for their defense were to be rendered obsolete within a decade by the introduction of rifled artillery and the first ironclad steam warships, during which the experiences of the Crimean War (1854–1856) again threatened the balance between ship and shore technologies. The attack on the Baltic fortress of Bomarsund revealed the disadvantage of the semicircular casemated work, where no more than six guns could be brought to bear on a single warship. In the Black Sea operations of 1854, however, the French and British fleets combined to bombard the casemated coastal forts at Sevastopol as a diversion from the main, land-based assault and suffered severe damage to a number of their ships from accurate defensive fire. In the Baltic campaign of 1855, after the Kronstadt defenses had been reconnoitered, the Russian island fortress of Sweaborg was chosen to demonstrate the long-range flotilla attack planned for Cherbourg. Thorough preparations preceded this spectacularly successful bombardment lasting two days and one night in the shallow coastal waters, culminating in the total destruction of the arsenal. At the bombardment of Kinburn later in the year, where three French steam-powered floating batteries, mortar vessels, steam gunboats, and rockets were again used, the Black Sea fortress surrendered after a prolonged engagement. Although the floating batteries had to be towed into position, their resistance to counter-battery fire presaged the appearance of the ironclad warship, which would again pass the advantage to naval attack.

In the immediate aftermath of the Russian War, Anglo-French naval rivalry was renewed with the growth of the French steam fleet and the continued threat to British dockyards. The Royal Commission of 1859 recommended the construction of new defenses for Plymouth, Portsmouth, and the Isle of Wight, including four armored sea forts at Spithead, Milford Haven in Wales, and the Thames and Medway estuaries. Low-profile polygonal fortifications featuring open barbette gun positions behind broad earthen ramparts, multistory caponiers for flanking fire within the deep ditches, and defensible redoubts in the gorge were the order of the day. This plan form would be adopted for many of the new coast defenses throughout the British Empire, owing largely to the work of Colonel William F. D. Jervois, secretary to the 1859 commission, who directed attention to colonial security issues and the provision of fixed coastal defenses for overseas coaling stations and bases as far apart as Canada, Australia, and South Africa. These works were modified over succeeding decades to accommodate the new heavy rifled muzzle-loading guns that grew to 17.72-inch caliber and one hundred tons in weight. Two of the guns were emplaced in Malta and Gibraltar. The application of more efficient breech-loading ordnance, soon to be given the additional protection of armored turrets, was regularly reviewed by successive Royal Artillery and Engineer Works Committees. Continental ordnance manufacturers, such as Krupp in Germany, Schneider in France, and Skoda in Bohemia, vied with Armstrong and Vickers in England to provide the armament and armor plate for the burgeoning international coast-defense market.

The bombardment of Alexandria in 1881 established the importance of dispersion and concealment in minimizing the effectiveness of naval gunfire on coast defenses, as advocated by G. S. Clarke in his book *Fortification*. Higher muzzle velocities, greater penetrative power, and increased ranges of breech-loading guns enabled shore batteries to be sited at greater intervals and the number of guns in each battery to be reduced. For the same reasons it became necessary to advance the line of defense to keep the opposing warships out of range of their objective. There was much discussion on the relative merits of barbette mountings and casemated positions, and following trials in the British service a system of disappearing mounts was adopted for a short period. In considering the design of the new coast batteries, the service of the guns and the protection of the battery personnel were of primary importance. Two-gun batteries in open barbette emplacements, fought simultaneously in one grouping with the widest arcs of unobstructed fire (not possible in a four-gun battery), was the most efficient arrangement. Reinforced concrete with earth cover came to be universally accepted as surpassing masonry as a form of protection.

## Advent of Long-Range Guns

The 9.2-inch breech-loading gun was adopted as the standard British long-range weapon to oppose battleships or heavy cruisers, and the 6-inch breech-loading gun would be for use against light cruisers at shorter ranges. These guns were to be mounted in emplacements designed for better concealment, with improved fire control first achieved in the 1880s by the depression rangefinder. The later Watkin position finder enabled the bearing and range of the moving target to be predicted and communicated to the guns by means of electrically operated dials. For additional protection of open harbors and estuaries, mines and torpedoes were to be used together with floating booms. Submarine mines, introduced in 1873, were developed in two forms and electrically fired; observation mines were laid on the seabed and activated by use of the position finder, and buoyant contact mines were discharged on impact. The Brennan torpedo, introduced around 1890, was wire-controlled from an engine room on shore but was installed in only a few of the major home and overseas bases.

A new threat to port installations and night attack on shipping in harbors was posed by the appearance of the torpedo boat, beginning in the late 1880s. Experiments carried out by the British led to the adoption of the powerful defense electric light (DEL), with a dispersed, fixed, or concentrated roving beam that could illuminate a channel or examination anchorage. To combat the lightly armed fast torpedo boat, the 12-pounder quick-firing (QF) gun, using fixed ammunition with a smokeless powder, was mounted near the waterline in conjunction with the DELs. The new class of torpedo-boat destroyer, which by 1900 displaced 550 tons and was capable of twenty-seven knots, in turn became an additional threat to harbor defenses and was later opposed by the more powerful 4.7-inch QF gun. The automatic sight automatically laid the gun for elevation on the observed target, contributing to an increased rate of fire at short range on a rapidly moving warship. These new techniques, complemented by advances in the science of ballistics and mathematics, required the artillery officer and gunner to be trained to a higher standard of efficiency. The British School of Gunnery at Shoeburyness was matched by the founding of similar establishments in other countries. On this basis the coast defenses of British-defended ports at home and abroad were reequipped during the first five years of the twentieth century.

## Twentieth-Century Developments

European, Asiatic, and American powers, including those with strong naval forces, now embarked on programs of serious coastal defense, supplemented for a short period by dedicated coast-defense ships. Germany placed greater emphasis on heavy-caliber, long-range batteries such as those on Heligoland and its principal North Sea and Baltic ports. Italy, too, emplaced heavy batteries around its naval bases at Genoa, La Spezia, and Taranto, with 280-millimeter coastal howitzers in armored cupolas manufactured by Gruson. Austria-Hungary established similar works at the harbors of Trieste and Pola. In Spain, the Atlantic bases at Ferrol and Cartagena on the Mediterranean coast were given new heavy coastal batteries after the Spanish-American War of 1898. France embarked on a program of rationalization in battery layout and armament, and introduced unique *batteries de rupture* at Brest and Cherbourg, comprising twin 320-millimeter guns in fixed, waterline casemates aimed at penetrating the heavy side armor of passing warships. In the United States, the recommendations of the Endicott Board of 1886, also spurred on by the Spanish-American War as well as the Taft Board of 1905, led to greater emphasis on concrete emplacements with underground magazines, heavier armament in the form of seacoast mortars, and the disappearing gun of 10-inch caliber, which depressed on recoil below a high parapet, enabling the crew to reload in safety. America's acquisition of overseas territories led to new coastal defenses in the Panama Canal zone, Hawaii, Cuba, and the Philippines, where the "concrete battleship" of Fort Drum in the entrance to Manila Bay mounted two twin 14-inch armored gun turrets.

## World War I

World War I saw the testing of new ideas under battle conditions. The words of Sir Howard Douglas, written in 1860 in *A Treatise on Naval Gunnery*, proved to be prophetic: "no substantial demolition of the defences . . . can be effected unless the damages inflicted by the attacks of the ships can be followed up and completed." Two groups of coastal batteries were emplaced by the Germans on the occupied Belgian coast around Oostende and Zeebrugge, which were important submarine bases. These defenses were expanded to protect the right flank of the German forces entrenched in Flanders, mostly in four-gun batteries in open concrete emplacements some distance from the shoreline, using forward battery command posts with stereoscopic rangefinders for indirect fire. For the first time antiaircraft guns were employed to combat aerial bombing and reconnaissance. From 1915, until their evacuation in October 1918, these batteries successfully repulsed repeated naval attacks by monitors and counterbombardments from the land front.

Immediately after the Turkish declaration of war in November 1914, a combined force of English and French battleships appeared to have successfully destroyed the forts at the entrance to the Dardanelles. In reality this action served only to attract German support for strengthening the defenses. The early bombardment by the combined fleet of battleships in February 1915, as a precursor to the abortive Dardanelles campaign, indicated that attacking units would have to anchor for direct shooting to score effective hits on the guns. When the bombardment resumed, HMS *Queen Elizabeth* attacked at long range using spotter aircraft as the first line of ships entered the straits. Two battleships were repeatedly hit by shore batteries and withdrew damaged, and three of the four ships in the second line were sunk by mines or Turkish gunfire. The complete failure of this attack highlighted the futility of capital ships operating in confined waters against well-serviced shore batteries.

## World War II

In the interwar period many countries modernized their coast defenses, particularly Russia, France, Italy, and Spain. In Germany, following Adolf Hitler's rise to power, the Heligoland fortress was completely rebuilt after demolition by the interallied mission. The United States began by mounting large guns on open, high-angle, barbette carriages, soon to be replaced by 12-inch and 16-inch guns in well-camouflaged standard two-gun concrete casemated batteries. Britain embarked on major coast-defense installations at Hong Kong and Singapore, where the 15-inch and 9.2-inch batteries failed to provide an effective deterrent as the Japanese overran the base in February 1942. At home, between June 1940 and January 1941 when imminent German invasion threatened, the British defenses were bolstered by the rapid construction of numerous 6-inch- and 4-inch-caliber emergency batteries in light concrete gunhouses, with distinctive director towers and searchlight positions. The first radar sets for gun-laying were installed in February 1941, as part of an accelerated program for more 9.2-inch counterbombardment batteries and 6-inch close-defense batteries. Two 14-inch guns, formerly used by the navy and christened "Winnie" and "Pooh," were emplaced on permanent turntable mountings near Dover to take on the heavy German cross-Channel batteries in the Pas de Calais.

Battery Lindemann (three 40.6-centimeter guns), Todt (four 38-centimeter guns), and Grosser Kurfürst (four 28-centimeter guns) had been built to protect the naval flanks of Hitler's projected invasion of Britain. With the indefinite postponement of "Operation Sealion," the opening of the assault on Russia in June 1941, and America's entry into the war in December of that year, the decision was made to fortify the entire Atlantic coastline of occupied western Europe. The principal defense concentrations, including heavy antiaircraft batteries, would lie around the major ports, particularly those on the Biscay coast from which the U-boat offensive was to be conducted. Based on standard designs in reinforced concrete, the German fortress engineers developed an entirely new series of bunkers for coast defense constructed by the Organization Todt and derived from the earlier West Wall examples. The design of the artillery casemates and the layout of the heaviest batteries drew on the experience of World War I, but their overall operational efficiency was severely hampered by confusion in the command structure and the bewildering array of emplaced booty artillery from the arsenals of occupied Europe. The best-equipped batteries were those of the German navy that mounted modern artillery, fire-control equipment, and radar. Intensive construction of field defense works and beach obstacles in early 1944 failed to fill the gaps in the permanent defenses of the Atlantic Wall. Delays in construction were exacerbated by progressively aggressive aerial bombardment of the defenses and lines of communication as the Allied invasion drew nearer. The ill-fated raid on Dieppe in 1942 convinced the German command that the invasion would involve an assault on a major port, while the Allied landings at Salerno in 1943 provided the test for a large-scale amphibious assault on the open coast. With overwhelming aerial superiority and naval gunfire support, the Normandy landings of June 1944 succeeded in smashing through one of the relatively weak German coastal sectors but not without serious losses where determined artillery and infantry strongpoints remained intact. In other locations along the Atlantic Wall, duels between heavy naval units and shore batteries frequently favored the defender, and the density of the defenses around the so-called fortress areas ensured that they remained in German hands until the end of the war in Europe. In the Pacific, where the fighting continued, American forces remorselessly subdued the coastal defenses of the Japanese-held island chains with the same overwhelming firepower.

## After World War II

At the end of World War II coast defense went into rapid decline, with guns and equipment placed under "care and preservation" in many countries. In the United States most of the ordnance was quickly scrapped before the Coast Artillery Corps and the last harbor-defense commands were discontinued in 1950. A similar path was followed in Britain, where coast artillery was finally abolished in 1956. Elsewhere, countries that were unable to compete with the superpowers but remained under threat from neighboring states retained and upgraded their coast defenses. Both Sweden and Finland maintain many of their prewar sites, installing lighter automatic, rapid-firing ordnance in low-profile armored turrets with underground command, communications, and accommodation bunkers. Mobile, radar-guided antiship missile batteries provide a valuable addition to the coast-defense armory employed in many countries, including China. Russia's heavy coastal batteries survived in an active state until the late 1980s, although they were probably not combat-ready as claimed; these included the triple 305-millimeter turreted batteries at Sevastopol and Vladivostok. As the American landings at Inchon in 1950 and those against Iraqi-occupied Kuwait in 1990 demonstrated, even in the missile age hardened coast defenses can still influence the planning and outcome of amphibious assaults.

The rapid scientific progress in missiles and weapons delivery systems and the continuing growth of air power have eliminated the need for large-scale fixed coastal defenses in countries able to take advantage of the new technology. These advances should not distract us from the strategic, political, economic, and social context in which coastal fortifications developed, for their effectiveness cannot always be determined as the consequence of successful military or naval action. History demonstrates that technological superiority is rarely decisive and often short-lived, and that the wider dissemination of technical knowledge often leads to its practical application in distinctive ways. The risk and scale of anticipated attack have always determined the nature and form of coast defense, ranging from the concentration of limited mobile forces in the threatened area to the protection of an entire coastline with a line of fixed defenses. Coast defense can thus be considered complementary to, and a measure of, the naval strength of a country. In most instances these defenses acted simply as a deterrent and were never tested in battle. Those that were assaulted were closely examined to determine where they had succeeded or failed in the constant struggle for supremacy between warships and land-based artillery.

[*See also* Navies, Great Powers, *and* Wars, Maritime.]

## Bibliography

Clarke, Sir George Sydenham. *Fortification: Its Past Achievements, Recent Developments, and Future Progress.* 2d ed. London: John Murray, 1907. Reprint, Liphook, U.K.: Beaufort, 1989.

Clements, W. H. *Towers of Strength: The Story of the Martello Towers.* Barnsley, U.K.: Leo Cooper, 1999.

Hogg, Ian V. *Coast Defences of England and Wales, 1856–1956.* Newton Abbot, U.K.: David and Charles, 1974.

Hore, Peter, ed. *Seapower Ashore: 200 Years of Royal Navy Operations on Land.* London: Chatham, 2001.

Hughes, Quentin. *Military Architecture: The Art of Defence from Earliest Times to the Atlantic Wall.* 2d ed., revised and expanded. Liphook, U.K.: Beaufort, 1991.

Kauffmann, J. E., and Robert M. Jurga. *Fortress Europe: European Fortifications of World War II.* Conshohocken, Pa.: Combined Publishing, 1999.

Kauffmann, J. E., and H. W. Kauffmann. *Fortress America: The Forts that Defended America, 1600 to the Present.* Cambridge, Mass.: Da Capo Press, 2004.

Lewis, Emanuel Raymond. *Seacoast Fortifications of the United States: An Introductory History.* Washington, D.C.: Smithsonian Institution Press, 1970. Reprint, Annapolis, Md.: Naval Institute Press, 1993.

Longmate, Norman. *Defending the Island: From Caesar to the Armada.* London: Hutchinson, 1989.

Longmate, Norman. *Island Fortress: The Defence of Great Britain, 1603–1945.* London: Hutchinson, 1991.

Maurice-Jones, Kenneth Wynn. *The History of Coast Artillery in the British Army.* London: Royal Artillery Institution, 1959. Reprint, Uckfield: Naval and Military Press, 2005.

Mehl, Hans. *Naval Guns: 500 Years of Ship and Coastal Artillery.* Translated by Keith Thomas. Annapolis, Md.: Naval Institute Press, 2002.

Osborne, Mike. *Defending Britain: Twentieth-Century Military Structures in the Landscape.* Stroud, U.K.: Tempus Publishing, 2004.

Parker, Geoffrey. *The Military Revolution: Military Innovation and the Rise of the West, 1500–1800.* 2d ed. Cambridge, U.K.: Cambridge University Press, 1996.

Rolf, Rudi. *Der Atlantikwall: Die Bauten der deutschen Küstenbefestigungen, 1940–1945.* Osnabrück, Germany: Biblio, 1998.

Rolf, Rudi. *A Dictionary on Modern Fortification: An Illustrated Lexicon on European Fortification in the Period 1800–1945.* Middelburg, The Netherlands: PRAK, 2004.

Saunders, Andrew D. *Fortress Britain: Artillery Fortification in the British Isles and Ireland.* Liphook, U.K.: Beaufort, 1989.

COLIN PARTRIDGE

# Cochrane, Thomas (1775–1860), the beau ideal
of the romantic naval hero and the prototype of the fictional
naval hero for authors from Frederick Marryat to Patrick
O'Brian. Cochrane was born on December 14, 1775, in
Lanarkshire, Scotland, the eldest son of an impoverished Scottish nobleman. Joining the Royal Navy under the patronage of
his uncle, Alexander Cochrane, he became a brilliant seaman
and a master of the unconventional in warfare. Once given
an independent command, he terrorized the enemies of his
country and alienated its senior figures with equal facility. His
capture of the far larger Spanish frigate *El Gamo* from the tiny
brig *Speedy* in 1801 made Cochrane famous, but the exploit
also alienated Earl St. Vincent, the most powerful man in
the navy, putting Cochrane's career on hold for several years.
Returned to the front line in 1804, Cochrane made a fortune
in prize, entered Parliament as an advanced radical in 1807,
and then conducted a master class in amphibious harassment
on the Spanish coast, feats recorded by midshipman Marryat.
In Parliament Cochrane attacked corruption in naval administration, prize courts, and politics.

In 1809 Cochrane led a remarkable attack on a French
fleet trapped in the Aix Roads, using rockets and explosions
vessels, although the admiral, James Gambier, refused to
exploit the opportunity. Cochrane's public condemnation
of Gambier caused the establishment to close ranks, ending
his sea service for some years. He developed a plan to use
poison gas, which was considered feasible but unethical and
dangerous in the wrong hands. Implicated in a stock market
fraud in early 1814, he was disgraced, removed from the
navy, and stripped of his honors. Undaunted, he signed up to
fight for South American liberation. After leaving England in
1818, he rose to new heights of popular fame, the cause and
his heroism meeting the mood of the age and the interest of
the London financiers who funded the infant South American republics. Boarding the Spanish frigate *Esmerelda* at
Valparaíso, Chile, in November 1820 cemented his place in
the pantheon of naval greats. After falling out with the local
leadership over strategy and money, however, Cochrane
seized the war chest, paid his squadron and himself, and in
1823 decamped to Brazil to serve in the war with Portugal.
Again disgusted at not being paid for his services, he sailed
to England in 1825 and resigned.

Cochrane had arrived in time to serve in the Greek
War of Independence, helping his old radical colleagues
collect and spend a small fortune in the cause. He
ordered two frigates and six steam warships, and delayed
his departure until some of them were ready. This left the
work of the war to his Greek colleagues, notably Andreas
Vokos Miaoulis. After Cochrane's arrival in March 1827,
his planned fire-ship attack on the Egyptian fleet at Alexandria failed and he achieved little before October, when
the battle of Navarino effectively ended the war. Marryat's
novels were already translating him from angry radical
into national hero. In 1832 Cochrane was restored to the
Navy List, his political allies now being in government.
His only command was in the West Indies, in 1848–
1851. In the Crimean War (1853–1856) he was briefly
considered for command in the Baltic; when the siege
of Sevastopol stalled, his poison gas plan was revived,
although it was not employed. His last years were devoted
to writing his memoirs, complaining about monies allegedly still owed by various governments, and becoming a
national icon. He died in London on October 31, 1860,
and was buried at Westminster Abbey, an unusual fate
for a radical scourge of the establishment. As a master of
coastal warfare and special operations, Cochrane will be
of interest as long as naval history is studied or sea fiction
is written.

[*See also* Marryat, Frederick; Miaoulis, Andreas Vokos; *and*
O'Brian, Patrick.]

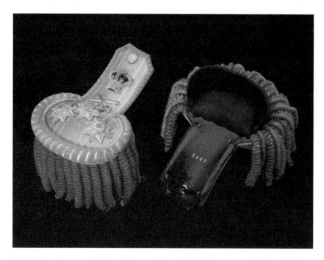

**Lord Cochrane's Epaulettes.** Lord Cochrane purchased these
1846-pattern epaulettes for his naval uniform in 1848, when
he took up his final appointment as Commander-in-Chief of
the North American and West Indies Station. The epaulettes
feature a crown worked in velvet, metal, and silk thread above a
crossed sword and baton in base metal over three stars that have
been worked in silver thread, purl, and spangles. © NATIONAL
MARITIME MUSEUM, LONDON

## Bibliography

Grimble, Ian. *The Sea Wolf.* London: Blond and Briggs,
1978.

Lambert, Andrew D. Entry on Cochrane in *The Oxford Dictionary of National Biography*, vol. 12. London: Oxford University Press, 2004.

ANDREW LAMBERT

# Cockerell, Christopher   (1910–1999), English inventor.

Sir Christopher Sydney Cockerell, C.B.E., R.D.I., was born in Cambridge on June 4, 1910, and died June 1, 1999. His father, Sir Sydney, was a curator of the Fitzwilliam Museum. Cockerell was educated at the Gresham School, in Holt, Norfolk, then Petershouse in Cambridge, studying engineering before starting wartime work inventing for the Marconi Company from 1935 until 1950, when he took over a boatyard with his wife Elinor (also known as Margaret).

An accomplished engineer as well as a prolific inventor, Cockerell's most outstanding contribution was the hovercraft—sometimes called air-cushioned vehicle, ground-effect machine, or surface-effect ship—although he saw his work developing radar and wave power as equally important. He patented the hovercraft idea in 1955, but it was four years before the first man-carrying prototype, *SRN1*, flew. Built by Saunders Roe, the flying-boat specialists on the Isle of Wight, the four-ton craft resembled a flying saucer. It crossed the English Channel in July 1959, on the fiftieth anniversary of the French aviator Louis Blériot's first aircraft crossing of the Channel, with Cockerell as human ballast on the bow. With a 0.30-meter (1-foot) hover height generated by a jet engine, the craft could fly over land and water, and with the invention of the flexible skirt around the craft, hover height was gradually increased to 1.8 meters (6 feet), making rougher weather and tougher terrains manageable for this experimental machine.

Within four years the world's first commercial hovercraft, service began from Rhyl, Wales, to Wallasey, Merseyside, England, across the Bristol Channel. This was soon followed by another across The Solent with *SRN2*, a twenty-seven-seat passenger craft with four jet engines. By 1966 a regular scheduled cross-channel service was started, which for over thirty-two years used the giant *SRN4* hovercraft. *SRN4* could carry 426 people and 61 cars at up to 70 knots.

From the start, Cockerell knew his invention had military potential, and it was kept on the secret list against his will for several years. Britain became the first military to use hovercraft extensively in service, with trials all over the world. Today the U.S. Navy is the single biggest user of amphibious hovercraft, which were used in both Gulf wars, especially the hundred-ton landing craft air cushion (LCAC), which can carry a battle tank, many troops, and several four-ton vehicles. The advantage of the hovercraft is that it can land troops high and dry on the beach and can carry loads at high speed to 70 percent of the world's beaches. The craft also have mine countermeasure roles and are more resilient to mines than are conventional vessels.

Today hovercraft are used mostly by coast guards and paramilitary services to rescue people, patrol shallows, and police less accessible areas. They are used in Canada, the Middle East, and Scandinavia in largest numbers, where their ability to traverse marsh and to cross and even break ice is useful. The longest-running hovercraft service is still on The Solent, now in its fifth decade. The only notable change is the use of diesel engines rather than the noisier and expensive gas turbines and welded structures and composite materials rather than riveted aircraft hulls.

One of Cockerell's other ideas was the sidewall hovercraft, which used rigid sides rather than full skirts to contain the lift air. These craft were not amphibious but could run with cheaper underwater propulsion. Diesels from the start, they ran successfully in Russia and the Far East. Cockerell's dream of seeing a nuclear-powered hovercraft was never realized, but the potential is still there. Today hovercraft have found a niche role and are an established form of specialist transport being built worldwide. Many of the patents have now expired, enabling a free-for-all opportunity, a situation that would have pleased Cockerell.

[*See also* Lifesaving from Shore-based Stations.]

## Bibliography

Wheeler, Raymond L. "Sir Christopher Sydney Cockerell." *Royal Society of London* 47 (2001): 67–89.

WARWICK JACOBS

# Cog   Also known in various languages as a *Kogge, koga, kagh,* and *cocha,* a cog was a type of ship used in trade in northern Europe from the eleventh through the fifteenth centuries. In the eleventh and twelfth centuries the cog's prototype—the flat-bottom ships used in the Rhine estuary—began to be built with high sides. This adaptation enabled them to sail to the Frisian Islands and then on open sea. Cogs appeared in the Baltic Sea in the thirteenth century. They were used by the Hanseatic League in the fourteenth century and soon became the most common ships there, carrying between ten and sixty tons of cargo.

Archaeological evidence of ships identified as cogs (from Brugge, Belgium; Bremen, Germany; Vejby, Denmark; Skanör, Sweden; Nijkerk, Netherlands; and other sites) has established the most common features of construction: a hull with a beam keel and a bottom made of flush-laid planking (the carvel planking technique of construction). The stems viewed from the side were straight and slanted. They were assembled from the shorter arm of a knee (the second arm joined the keel) and the inner stems. The outer stems were fixed to the inner one when the planking was complete. The side planks were overlapped in the clinker way, joined with nails bent from the inside. Watertightness was achieved by forcing moss into grooves, which were then covered by wooden laths secured by iron clasps. The vertical stiffeners consisted of floors, ribs, and crossbeams, often with the heads running through the planking above the waterline. The ratio of width to length of a cog's hull was about one to three. Beginning in the thirteenth century the hull was covered with a steady deck and castles (platforms) surrounded by blanks. Aft superstructures and a crow's nest were added in the fourteenth century.

A cog had one mast and a square-rigged sail and was steered with a rudder that initially was mounted on the starboard side of the ship but from around the 1240s was hung on the sternpost. Its fastest speed was about five knots. The flat bottom enabled these vessels to sail into the shallow ports of the south Baltic Sea and even to sail against river currents. Beginning in the late fourteenth century, after the implementation in many Hanseatic League ports of the law of store—the trade monopoly given to local tradesmen—cogs were surpassed in popularity by other kinds of ships, mainly hulks and carracks.

[*See also* Baltic Sea *and* Trading Vessels, *subentry on* Medieval Vessels.]

### Bibliography

Crumlin-Pedersen, Ole. "Danish Cog Finds." In *The Archaeology of Medieval Ships and Harbours in Northern Europe*, edited by Seán McGrail, pp. 17–34. BAR International Series 66. Oxford: B.A.R., 1979.

Ellmers, Detlev. "The Cog as Cargo Carrier." In *Cogs, Caravels, and Galleons: The Sailing Ship, 1000–1650*, edited by Robert Gardiner, pp. 29–46. London: Conway Maritime Press, 1994.

Greenhill, Basil. *The Archaeology of Boats and Ships*. London: Conway Maritime Press, 1995.

Hoffmann, Gabriele, and Uwe Schnall. *Die Kogge: Sternstunde der deutschen Schiffsarchäologie*. Altenburg, Germany, 2003.

Lahn, W. *Die Kogge von Bremen*. Bremen, Germany: E. Kabel, 1992.

McGrail, Seán. *Boats of the World: From the Stone Age to Medieval Times*. Oxford and New York: Oxford University Press, 2001.

JERZY LITWIN

## Coins, Medals, and Seals

The custom of depicting ships on coins dates from the sixth century B.C.E. and is nearly as old as coinage itself. The Greeks, Phoenicians, and Romans, seafaring peoples in the Mediterranean whose power and wealth heavily depended on shipping, chose this subject for their coins. Ships symbolized the importance of shipping for warfare and commerce. The Romans commemorated important victories on land and at sea with special issues of coins, which put on display the power of the empire in general. Roman coins circulated throughout the empire and were thus an effective means of propaganda.

At the end of the first century C.E., the Roman Empire had grown from a military power to an economic power, and the Roman emperors did not fail to stress their role in the increase of the prosperity of the empire. On coins, the theme of maritime warfare was replaced by representations of merchant shipping and newly developed Mediterranean harbors. Presumably, the representations of ships on coins derived from depictions on a more monumental scale. In this way, coins, however small, provide a fairly reliable source of information on the development of shipbuilding and rigging from 500 B.C.E. onward. For instance, the influence of Greek ship types on Roman shipbuilding can be clearly derived from various coins from this period.

During the early Middle Ages, coins and city seals reflected the maritime activities of European nations engaged in seaborne commerce. Many overseas merchant routes were used to maintain contacts among countries in the Baltic, the regions along the North Sea coast, France, Spain, and the Mediterranean. Coins from the ninth century with depictions of ships have been found from Viking settlements like Haithabu (Hedeby) on the Danish-German border, the Hansa city of Dorestad in the Netherlands, and the Anglo-Saxon region. Different types of ships, such as hulks, cogs, and knarrs, are known through coins and, in the late Middle Ages, were also depicted on the seals of harbor cities like La Rochelle in France, Lübeck in Germany, and Hastings and Sandwich in England. The seals of New Shoreham (Hulcesmouth), England, from 1295, and of Elblag (Elbing) from 1367 and Gdansk (Danzig) from 1200 and 1400 (both in former West Prussia, now part of

**Medal Commemorating the Sinking of *Lusitania*.** Designed by Karl Goetz (1875–1950), this medal was struck in Munich in August 1915. This highly controversial medal gave the wrong date for the sinking, using 5 May instead of the correct date of 7 May. The British government exploited this by using it as evidence of premeditation. In this context, copies of the medal were circulated widely in Britain. The Germans later reissued the medal with the correct date. © NATIONAL MARITIME MUSEUM, LONDON

Poland) provide important evidence on ship design and rigging from their periods and serve as an important source of knowledge of the development of shipbuilding.

From the sixteenth century on, coinage for the most part lost its role of commemorating important historical events in favor of the medal. During the reign of the Russian tsar Peter the Great (r. 1682–1725), a series of medals were issued to immortalize Russian expansion politics in the Baltic region. The most famous series of medals was issued by the French kings Louis XIV (r. 1643–1715) and Louis XV (r. 1715–1774). This so-called *Histoire métallique*, which consisted of several hundred medals, was dedicated to victories on land and at sea, thus glorifying their reigns. The obverse generally showed the portrait of the ruler, the reverse a scene from the battle. Cartography also was a source of inspiration for historical medals, showing maps or bird's-eye views of the battleground. Exactitude was not required; motifs like ships engaged in battle were combined from different sources, such as contemporary engravings or drawings, which were used time and again. The whole—motifs and symbolism, an inscription in Latin and an exergue with the date of the event—is strongly reminiscent of ancient coins. Inscriptions in native languages did not appear until the second half of the nineteenth century.

Medals struck on maritime-historical occasions, such as a naval battle, were used either as a token of reward for the naval officers who had participated in the battle or as a token of remembrance in general that could be purchased by collectors.

Historical medals with naval subjects were also produced retrospectively. The United States Mint issued a series of medals clearly patterned after the *Histoire métallique* in France, the difference being that portraits of naval officers who had played an important role in U.S. history adorn the obverse, instead of monarchs. The French-inspired style used in historical medals in both Europe and the United States contrasted sharply with the medals of the twentieth-century German medalist Karl Goetz (1875–1950), whose (in-)famous medal on the sinking of the Cunard luxury liner *Lusitania* (1915) clearly stated its propagandistic intentions and displayed a coarse sarcasm on medals hitherto veiled by an elegant symbolic approach. Rather than a rupture in style and tradition, however, Goetz's medals proved to be an exception, inspired by German expressionism and the carnage of World War I.

From the early nineteenth century onward, in addition to awards for individual gallantry, navies began to develop a series of medals awarded to both officers and men for service in specific battle actions and campaigns, for long service, and for various skills, such as shooting pistols and rifles. Nearly every navy in the world developed some form of these medals, with a relatively large number appearing during the twentieth century in the Soviet and the United States navies. In addition, other maritime services and related organizations also awarded medals, such as those given to naval officers by Lloyds of London and those presented for saving lives at sea. All of these medals used varying types of distinctive maritime and naval symbolism, along with emblems specifically tied to the events and achievements involved. In the twentieth century, paper money, providing more space for depictions of scenes and symbols than coins and medals do, regained some lost ground as a means of propaganda. Like the Greeks and Romans before them, rising economic powers like China and Singapore in particular displayed their power by depicting ships, trains, airplanes, and harbors on their banknotes.

In the United States, maritime themes on coins were largely confined to the half-dollar coins issued to commemorate special maritime-historical events, such as the tricentennial of the arrival of the Pilgrims (1920). In the twentieth century, shipping lost its predominant role as a theme on European currency. Norway, not being a member of the European Union, proved to be an exception. When each member country of the European Union

had the right to choose its own obverse on the Euro, the new common currency introduced in 2002, shipping proved to be a national symbol of minor importance. Only Greece adhered to a maritime tradition by depicting ships on the smaller denominations of 1, 2, and 5 Eurocents, which respectively show an ancient trireme galley, a three-masted corvette from the Greek War of Liberation (1821–1829), and a twentieth-century VLCC (very large crude-oil carrier). On its ten-cent coin, the dime, Canada since 1937 has had an image of *Bluenose*, a Grand Banks fishing schooner from Nova Scotia built in 1921. In 2005 the United Kingdom issued two £5 crown coins to commemorate the bicentenary of the Battle of Trafalgar, one showing Admiral Horatio Lord Nelson on the reverse, the other showing an image of HMS *Victory*.

## Coins on Ships

The gold eight-Escudos piece from Ecuador (1838–1841), nailed to the mainmast of the Nantucket-based whaling vessel *Pequod* by captain Ahab in chapter 36 of Herman Melville's famous novel *Moby-Dick* (1851), is perhaps the best-known example of a coin on board of a ship.

Yet the custom of placing coins aboard ships is much older. On sailing vessels, tradition had it that a coin should be placed in the footing of the mast, its value reflecting the wealth of the ship's commissioner. In the case of iron ships, a coin was placed in the rudder gudgeons of the keel. As the coin had to have been minted in the same year as the ship was built, these coins provide a valuable source of information for dating wrecks in which such coins are found. An example of such dating is a wreck, found in the Thames in England in 1962, that proved to be from the second century C.E. Even in the twenty-first century, this tradition is still followed in the Mediterranean for wooden-built boats.

Another category of coins on ships comprises coinage minted specially for use on board of shipping companies' ships. Passengers of liner ships or cruise vessels could exchange their currency for tokens, which could be used to buy drinks and goods during their journey on board of the ship. These tokens were decorated with the name of the ship or the mark of the shipping company and the denomination of the coin.

[*See also* Shipwrecks.]

## Bibliography

Baxter, Barbara A. *The Beaux-Arts Medal in America*. New York: American Numismatic Society, 1988

Ben-Eli, Ari L., ed. *Ships and Parts of Ships on Ancient Coins.* Haifa, Israel: National Maritime Museum Foundation, 1975.

Cox, Barry, ed. *Lifeboat Gallantry: The Complete Record of Royal National Lifeboat Institution Gallantry Medals and How They Were Won.* London: Spink, 1998.

Dorling, H. Taprell, Francis K. Mason, and George Philip. *Ribbons and Medals: The World's Military and Civil Awards.* London: George Philip, 1974.

Douglas-Morris, Kenneth. *The Naval Long Service Medals, 1830–1990.* London: the author, 1991.

Gawler, Jim. *Lloyd's Medals 1836–1989: A History of Medals Awarded by the Corporation of Lloyds.* Toronto: Hart, 1989.

Failor, Kenneth M., and Eleonora Hayden. *Medals of the United States Mint Issued for Public Sale.* Rev. ed. Washington, D.C.: U.S. Government Printing Office, 1972.

Frederiks, J. W. *De Meesters der Plaquette Penningen.* 's-Gravenhage, Netherlands: Nederlandsch Genootschap voor Munt- en Penningkunde, 1943.

Hill, David. "An East Anglian Penny of about 830 A.D." *Mariner's Mirror* 80 (1994): 326–327.

Iversen, J. *Medaillen auf die Thaten Peter des Grossen.* St. Petersburg, Russia: Buchdruckerei von Wilhelm Pratz, 1872.

Jacquiot, Joseph. "La place des médailles, des médaillons, des camées et des intailles, dans l'art et l'histoire de 1715 à 1774." In *Louis XV: Un moment de perfection de l'art français,* compiled by Musée de la Monnaie, pp. 521–546. Paris: Hotel de la Monnaie, 1974.

Kienast, Günther W. *The Medals of Karl Goetz.* Cleveland, Ohio: Artus Co., 1967. Supplement, Lincoln, Nebr., 1986.

Mountbatten, Louis Alexander. *British Naval Medals: Commemorative Medals, Naval Rewards, War Medals, Naval Tokens, Portrait Medallions, Life-Saving Medals, Engraved Pieces, Etc.* London: John Murray, 1919.

Mountbatten, Louis Alexander. *Naval Medals: Commemorative Medals, Naval Rewards, War Medals, Naval Tokens, Etc., of Foreign Countries.* London: John Murray, 1921–1928.

National Maritime Museum. Research Guide U2: Maritime Medals. http://www.nmm.ac.uk/server/show/conWebDoc.615.

Riccardi, Edoardo. "Coins in Wrecks." *Mariner's Mirror* 79 (1993): 202–205.

Scarlett, R. J., comp. *Under Hazardous Circumstances: A Register of Awards of Lloyd's War Medal for Bravery at Sea 1939–1945.* Dallington, U.K.: Naval and Military Press, 1992.

U.S. Navy Service and Campaign Medals. http://www.history.navy.mil/medals/.

Vermeule, Cornelius C. *Numismatic Art in America: Aesthetics of the United States Coinage.* Cambridge, Mass.: Harvard University Press, 1971.

Werlich, Robert. *Orders and Decorations of All Nations.* Washington, D.C.: Quaker Press, 1965.

PIETER JAN KLAPWIJK

# Colbert, Jean-Baptiste (1619–1683), secretary of state for the navy and colonies of France. Born at Reims on August 29, 1619, Jean-Baptiste Colbert was the son of a draper. At the age of twenty-one in 1640,

probably through the influence of an uncle who married the sister of the war minister François-Michel le Tellier, Colbert became commissaire ordinaire des guerres at the war office. In 1651–1652, during the Fronde, Colbert served as an intermediary between le Tellier, the exiled cardinal Jules Mazarin, and King Louis XIV (r. 1643–1715). During this period, Colbert wrote a defense of Mazarin, earning his trust and an invitation to manage the cardinal's personal finances after he returned to power. After Mazarin's death in 1661, Colbert orchestrated the political downfall and arrest of the then superintendent of finance, Nicolas Fouquet, who was charged with, among other things, the corrupt administration of naval affairs. Replacing Fouquet on the royal council, Colbert was formally named secretary of state for the navy and colonies by Louis XIV in 1669, and his responsibilities also grew to include royal finances and economic affairs, along with industry, buildings, and culture. Famous for his efforts to rationalize and codify French law and for engineering an "economic miracle," his reform program was always based on his mercantile plans to build the battle fleet along with the French merchant marine. Primarily as a challenge to Dutch commercial supremacy, Colbert introduced protectionist tariffs and founded trading companies: two, for the East and the West Indies, in 1664; a company "of the North" in 1669; and one for the Levant in 1670. Further colonization of New France, or Canada, was encouraged, as was the French presence in Louisiana. This complemented stations founded in Senegal and French activity in the Caribbean, especially on Saint Domingue.

Recent evidence of Colbert's rampant nepotism has tarnished his reputation for selfless, accountable, and bureaucratic government, but he nevertheless brought his gift of organization to the navy. Two famous ordinances, one of 1681 and the other of 1689 by his eldest son and his successor as secretary for the navy, Jean-Baptiste Antoine Colbert, marquis de Seignelay (1651–1690), created a naval hierarchy and regulated maritime affairs, which they oversaw with a series of naval intendants. These were powerful agents acting as direct representatives of the royal will in each of the main ports: Brest, Rochefort, and Toulon. Here, along with modern fortifications, arsenals were built, for much of Colbert's effort was spent on improving the supply of materials along with the conditions and pay of French sailors. He founded hospitals at Rochefort and Toulon and a naval college at Bordeaux and provided financial support for the wounded and the widowed. Like others in his position, however, Colbert could not overcome the perennial shortage of seafarers in France. He introduced the system of "maritime classes" whereby all eligible men were registered and required to serve on board the king's ships in every third year. This was a difficult scheme to administer, and it became impossible with the increasing demands of war at sea.

By the time of Colbert's death on September 6, 1683, the navy had 220 ships, though his legacy continued under Seignelay. In the following years, France successfully faced the combined naval forces of Europe. On November 3, 1690, just months after the famous victory over the Anglo-Dutch fleet at Beachy Head, Seignelay died and with him the political and administrative will with which the "two Colberts" briefly endowed France with the strongest battle fleet in Europe.

[*See also* Navies, Great Powers, *subentry on* France, 1660 to the Present.]

## Bibliography

Ames, Glenn J. *Colbert, Mercantilism, and the French Quest for Asian Trade*. De Kalb: Northern Illinois University Press, 1996. A good modern study.

Asher, Eugène L. *The Resistance to the Maritime Classes: The Survival of Feudalism in France*. Berkeley: University of California Press, 1960. An influential study of the administrative context.

Cole, Charles Woolsey. *Colbert and a Century of French Mercantilism*. Hamden, Conn.: Archon, 1964. A classic study of French mercantilism.

Dessert, Daniel. *Fouquet*. Paris: Fayard, 1987. This study of a rival reconsiders Colbert's role.

La Roncière, Charles de. *Histoire de la marine française*. Vol. 5. Paris: Plon, 1920.

Meyer, Jean. *Colbert*. Paris: Hachette, 1981.

Murat, Inès, *Colbert*. Paris: Fayard, 1980.

ALAN JAMES

# Collaboration. See Agents and Managers; Shipping Conferences and Cartels.

# Collier. See Trading Vessels, *subentry on* Early Modern Vessels.

# Colombo The Arabs were, in the fifteenth century, the first to use the open roadstead of Colombo on the west coast of Sri Lanka (called Ceylon until 1972), the strategically located island in the Indian Ocean, as a center of commerce. The Arabs were followed by the Portuguese and the Dutch, who ruled the coastal belt of Sri Lanka from 1505 to 1656 and from 1656 to 1796, respectively, and made it a popular emporium in the East. But it was the British who, having succeeded the Dutch in the coastal belt in 1796 and made Sri Lanka a crown colony in 1815, transformed the open, dangerous roadstead into one of the leading international ports in the region. The spread of plantation agriculture, accompanied by the development of the railroad network with Colombo as the maritime terminus, made Colombo Port assume the gateway function for the whole island.

In the 1860s, when the need arose to develop the two ports of Colombo and Galle on the same coast to accommodate larger-capacity steamers, economic factors weighed heavily in favor of concentrating investments and all port functions in one port: Colombo. Since cargo handled at Colombo was generally break bulk and carried mostly in vessels that visited the port for a short stay to use it as a port of call, the uppermost consideration in the transformation of the open roadstead to a safe harbor was expeditious dispatch. Hence the timesaving strategy of midstream berthing, which, with the use of the lighterage system of cargo handling then in use, enabled operations to be carried out from both sides of the vessel. Following the construction of three breakwaters—South-West, North-East, and the Island—under the first Colombo Port development program launched in 1875–1912, Colombo became one of the world's largest artificial harbors, covering one square mile and capable of berthing forty-three vessels at a time. By 1912 it was also well equipped with warehouses, transit sheds, coaling depots and jetties, and a dry dock.

The concentration of all port functions at Colombo Port was followed by further development in the city. Colombo, as Sri Lanka's capital city, already had an administrative complex, the national legislature, the national museum, and various cultural institutes. After the development of the port, other important establishments appeared as well, including leading commercial and industrial institutions, transport agencies, tourist hotels, and leading schools and institutes of higher education. Major sanitary problems were effectively solved, and the twin openings flanking the island breakwater, which permitted easy egress and ingress of water, made the port area free of pollution. Colombo thus earned a reputation as a healthy port in a healthy city. The employment of a casual immigrant labor force helped the port achieve a high level of efficiency, which gave Colombo a reputation as the greatest port in the East for quick dispatch of vessels. All these advantages, together with the island's locational advantage in the Indian Ocean, made Colombo such an attraction for vessels passing through the Suez Canal that it held sway as the Clapham Junction of the East for shipping. Indeed, in 1910, by handling a shipping tonnage of 14,170,780 compared with 1,272,498 for cargo, Colombo ranked as the seventh greatest port in the world and the third in the British Empire.

During the 1920s Colombo's position as a port of call was threatened by the use of fuel oil for engine propulsion, because oil enabled vessels to cover long distances without the need to refuel. During World War I (1914–1918) 36 percent of shipping tonnage using Colombo Port was for bunkering services, but by 1934–1938 this was reduced to 12 percent. However, the post–World War II recovery of world trade and the Korean boom of the early 1950s brought unexpected prosperity to the port and revived the port's shipping-services sector. Enjoying a sound financial position, Colombo also saw, in 1950–1956, the execution of the First Post-Independence Port Development Programme. It provided Colombo with three deepwater quays—Queen Elizabeth, Prince Vijaya, and Delft—supplemented with adequate warehouse and transit floor area, as well as an oil dock.

However, because of serious industrial unrest created by the strongly unionized permanent dock labor force that had gradually replaced the casual labor force, international shipping started to avoid Colombo. Total ship arrivals declined from 2,525 in 1958 to 1,579 in 1974. Inevitably, port development activities slowed, until 1966, when construction of a container berth was begun. Progress was slow because of lack of funds, and the berth was not completed until 1980. In 1979 the Sri Lanka Ports Authority (SLPA), an autonomous body, was set up to manage the country's ports. The SLPA, by developing a cordial relationship with port employees, not only made Colombo Port free of industrial unrest but also helped improve port efficiency. With Japan's involvement in funding, planning, and providing technical assistance, a program of container-infrastructure development began in 1980. The Jaye Container Terminals I, II, III, and IV, which were inaugurated in 1982, 1984, 1995, and 1996, respectively, were the major accomplishments of that program. In addition to equipping these terminals with mechanical appliances, the SLPA by itself also undertook two major projects: the construction of the Unity Container Terminal and the development of the Port Computerisation Programme, both of which were completed in 1995. To prevent port congestion, the SLPA and some major port users began setting up inland container depots outside the city of Colombo, and by 1995 thirteen of them were in use.

In 1984 Colombo handled 142,811 teus (twenty equivalent units) and was ahead of Mumbai (Bombay) in container throughput; thereafter, with rapid progress, Colombo reached the million mark in 1995 and 1.9 million in 2003. The fast rate of growth of container traffic at Colombo was attributable largely to the use of the port as a transshipment hub for feeder services, to the extent that in 1997 transshipment containers constituted 73 percent of the teus handled, compared with 6.9 percent in 1979. The success of the transshipment trade helped make the SLPA the most profitable of Sri Lanka's top hundred companies. Thus, after ups and downs, Colombo Port has become once again a valuable asset to Sri Lanka.

[*See also* Indian Ocean *and* Ports.]

## Bibliography

Boxer, C. R. *The Dutch Seaborne Empire, 1600–1800*. London: Hutchinson, 1965.

Broeze, Frank, Peter Reeves, and K. McPherson. "Imperial Ports and the Modern World Economy: The Case of the Indian Ocean." In *Journal of Transport History*, 3d ser., vol. 7, no. 2 (September 1986): 1–20.

Dharmasena, K. *The Port of Colombo, 1860–1939*. Colombo, Sri Lanka: Ministry of Higher Education, 1980.

Dharmasena, K. *The Port of Colombo, 1940–2000*. Colombo, Sri Lanka: JICA, 2003.

K. Dharmasena

**Columbus, Christopher** (c. 1451–1506), navigator who is best known for his 1492 voyage westward from Europe to America. The best evidence about his origins suggests that he was born in or near Genoa, the son of an artisan and tavernkeeper who held minor political posts from time to time. After a rudimentary elementary education, Columbus began serving on merchant voyages to the eastern and western Mediterranean. Over time he became familiar with many aspects of maritime trade and command at sea.

In the mid-1470s he took up residence in Lisbon, then the center of exploration into the ocean now known at the Atlantic. While based in Portugal, Columbus participated in voyages down the African coast at least as far as Guinea and southwestward to the Canary Islands and Madeira. Toward the north he may have sailed as far as Ireland and Iceland, and he certainly gathered information about conditions in the northwestern seas. Columbus also managed to insert himself into court circles in Lisbon and married into the Perestrello clan, a family of Genoese

**Christopher Columbus.** As far as is known, Columbus never had his portrait painted during his lifetime. Nevertheless, there are numerous images of him with a wide range of facial types. This portrait, called the Cevasco portrait in honor of the donor, has been attributed to Ridolfo di Ghirlandaio (1483–1561) and is exhibited in Columbus's birthplace of Genoa, Italy. ERICH LESSING / ART RESOURCE, NY / MUSEO NAVALE DI PEGLI, GENOA

extraction that had been ennobled for service to the Portuguese crown. His wife's late father had been governor of the island of Porto Santo near Madeira. Columbus spent several years there as well, increasing his knowledge of the western ocean. He also read broadly about geography and travel, and he certainly knew the famous story of Marco Polo's travels to China and Japan two centuries earlier.

By the early 1480s Columbus had developed a theory that mariners could reach Asia by sailing west, rather than continuing down the African coast searching for an eastward opening toward Asia, as Portuguese mariners were doing. He presented his theory to the king of Portugal but failed to gain royal support. It is not clear why, but there are two strong possibilities: experts at the Portuguese court may have known that Columbus had greatly underestimated the size of the western ocean, and the Portuguese may have been afraid to violate their 1479 treaty with Castile that reserved exploration west of the Canary Islands to Castile.

Rebuffed, Columbus left Portugal in 1485 and presented his scheme to Queen Isabella of Castile and her husband King Ferdinand of Aragon. The possibilities for trade and for spreading the knowledge of Christianity to Asia strongly appealed to the monarchs, but they postponed judgment, distracted by their continuing war against the Muslim kingdom of Granada. Nonetheless, they began paying Columbus a stipend while their advisers considered his scheme. Despite their doubts, the monarchs finally authorized a voyage in 1492, providing one-eighth of the financial backing and two of the three ships he needed—the caravels *Niña* (estimated at 55 *toneladas*) and *Pinta* (estimated at 75 *toneladas*). With the aid of his contacts in southwestern Spain, Columbus raised the rest of the funds, recruited crewmen, and leased a merchant vessel (*nao*) of about 105 *toneladas* for his flagship, which is known to history as *Santa María*. A *tonelada* equaled about 1.42 cubic meters (50.15 cubic feet), indicating carrying capacity, and was slightly smaller than the old French sea ton (*tonneau de mer*) of Bordeaux (1.44 cubic meters [50.85 cubic feet]). The combined crews of all three ships numbered some ninety-seven men and boys.

The small fleet left southwestern Spain on August 3, 1492, heading for the Canary Islands, and it departed from the Canaries on September 8. After a relatively uneventful voyage the fleet made landfall on October 12 somewhere in the Bahama Islands, which Columbus assumed to be near the Asian mainland. He sailed on to the islands later known as Cuba and Hispaniola and made contact with local inhabitants along the way. Communicating largely through gestures and exchanges of food and gifts, Columbus persuaded himself that many of the local peoples were apt for work, trade, and conversion to Christianity. He also noted their weaponry and the intermittent warfare in the region, particularly between the fierce Caribs and other groups that feared them. After reconnoitering the area for gold, trade goods, and other opportunities for profit, Columbus and the crew of *Niña* returned to Spain early in 1493, taking with them seven of the local inhabitants. He left thirty-nine men behind on Hispaniola for lack of space, since *Santa María* had been wrecked on Christmas Eve, 1492, and the commander of *Pinta*, Martín Alonso Pinzón, had gone off exploring on his own. All thirty-nine left on Hispaniola were dead in a matter of months, killed in skirmishes with the local inhabitants.

Columbus had proven that land lay just a few weeks away in the western ocean, a revelation that made him famous throughout Europe in a very short time. The Spanish crown sponsored him on three more western voyages (1493–1496, 1498–1500, and 1502–1504), during which he reconnoitered many additional islands, the coastline of central America, and much of the northern coastline of South America, always in search of the Asian mainland. It took years and dozens of other voyages for Europeans to recognize that the lands Columbus discovered were not part of Asia, but were instead a new world unknown to ancient and medieval geography.

Isabella and Ferdinand entrusted Columbus with administering Spanish colonies on his second and third voyages, only to take that authority away when he proved to be an ineffective administrator who often defied royal orders. He nonetheless retained many financial privileges from the crown and died a wealthy man in Valladolid, Spain, in 1506.

Columbus's erroneous belief that Asia and Europe were separated by a relatively small western ocean inspired him to undertake one of the most important voyages in world history. He would not have been able to carry out that voyage without an arrogant faith in himself that was responsible for his greatest triumphs and his worst humiliations. Although historiography of the late twentieth century often blamed Columbus for the deleterious effects of Europe's global exploration and colonization, his deserved fame rests on the intellectual audacity of his scheme and on the unquestioned importance of his voyages for subsequent world history.

[*See also* Americas, *subentry on* Exploration Voyages, 1492–1509, *and* Navigators.]

### Bibliography

*The Book of Privileges Issued to Christopher Columbus by King Fernando and Queen Isabel, 1492–1502.* Edited and translated by Helen Nader, with Luciano Formisano. Berkeley: University of California Press, 1996.

*The Diario of Christopher Columbus's First Voyage to America, 1492–1493, Abstracted by Fray Bartolomé de las Casas.* Translated by Oliver Dunn and James E. Kelley Jr. Norman: University of Oklahoma Press, 1989.

Fernández-Armesto, Felipe. *Columbus.* Oxford and New York: Oxford University Press, 1991.

Flint, Valerie I. J. *The Imaginative Landscape of Christopher Columbus.* Princeton, N.J.: Princeton University Press, 1992.

Herbert, John R., ed. *1492: An Ongoing Voyage.* Washington, D.C.: Library of Congress, 1992.

*The "Libro de las profecías" of Christopher Columbus.* Translated by Delno C. West and August Kling. Gainsville: University of Florida Press, 1991.

Phillips, William D., Jr., and Carla Rahn Phillips. *The Worlds of Christopher Columbus.* Cambridge, U.K., and New York: Cambridge University Press, 1992.

Summerhill, Stephen J., and John Alexander Williams. *Sinking Columbus: Contested History, Cultural Politics, and Mythmaking during the Quincentenary.* Gainsville: University Press of Florida, 2000.

*Testimonies from the Columbian Lawsuits.* Edited and translated by William D. Phillips Jr., with Mark D. Johnston and Anne Marie Wolf. Turnhout, Belgium: Brepols, 2000.

CARLA RAHN PHILLIPS

# Communications, Commercial. *See* Mail Services; Telecomunications; Telegraphy.

# Communications, Naval
Naval communications operate at two levels: the ability to exchange information between ships acting together tactically, initially within visual range, although latterly more widely, and the ability to control operations at a distance from a central point, called strategic communications. Today these two strands have merged, as net-centric warfare and satellite systems enable ships to communicate globally in real time.

### Ship-to-Ship Systems

In ancient galley warfare, communication between ships used burnished shields, colored flags, and trumpets. Medieval sailing warships were less sophisticated; though naval combat remained little more than a close-quarters melee with hand weapons, the value of signals for a senior officer was limited to the timing of initial attack. During the 1588 Spanish Armada campaign, English commanders supplemented daily command briefings by literally "speaking" to other ships, delivering orders verbally. The pace of warfare was slow, and the English ships were highly maneuverable.

The development of linear tactics based on sustained artillery broadsides in the mid-seventeenth century sparked the development of more sophisticated flag signal systems, which allowed the admiral, usually operating from the center of the line, to direct the entire fleet. For 150 years flag signals were developed to convey tactical instructions, but they were not a true communication system. They did not permit the exchange of ideas, nor the exposition of orders that had not been settled beforehand. The signal code of the British officer Home Riggs Popham (1762–1820), adopted in 1805, enabled officers to exchange signals in conversational form. Admiral Horatio Lord Nelson used Popham's code to send a morale-boosting personal message to his entire fleet. This was the first occasion when an admiral was able to speak to every man under his command. Having flown "England expects that every man will do his duty," he did not try to micromanage the battle.

Throughout the nineteenth century, flag signaling was improved and complemented by masthead semaphore telegraphs and the flashing-light system pioneered by Phillip Colomb (1831–1899) for tactical control at night. This enabled admirals to direct their fleets in detail, rather than rely on Nelsonic initiative and sound doctrine. Wireless radio added a new level of communication, for over-the-horizon signals. It was no coincidence that the Royal Navy captain Henry Jackson (1855–1929) made a major contribution to the technical breakthrough of Guglielmo Marconi (1874–1937). In 1914, John Jellicoe used flag, light, and radio signals to control a massive armada of dreadnoughts, cruisers, and destroyers. Intellectually this was the very reverse of Nelson's approach; Jellicoe's use of improved communications avoided the need to develop sophisticated dispersed tactics.

Having enhanced their ability to communicate, navies began to worry about the security of their messages. In both world wars German encryption systems were "broken," with serious tactical, operational, and strategic consequences. The consequences of Allied access to U-boat "Ultra" traffic were particularly serious because the submarines relied on central direction by shore-based wireless for target information, while simply using wireless betrayed the location of U-boats to Allied forces through high-frequency direction finding (HF/DF).

The introduction of computerized communications network systems after World War II enabled squadrons to share information effectively without human intervention; these were pioneered by the United States' 1962 Naval Tactical Data System (NTDS). Modern network centric warfare enables ships to combine sensors and weapons systems, and to share tasks with air and ground forces, turning a fleet into a single fighting organism.

## Strategic Communications

As the naval historian Julian Corbett stressed, naval warfare is primarily a question of controlling communications. Men have communicated by sea for three thousand years, but strategic communications rarely rate a line. Typically Thucydides (d. c. 401 B.C.E.) mentions the subject only when recording the remarkable performance of an Athenian messenger galley.

Sea communication was generally faster than comparable land systems before the railway. This gave naval powers significant advantages, especially when wars were fought at very long distances from the metropole. By the seventeenth century, major navies used specialist dispatch boats to carry messages to fleets on station, and this system was developed down to the emergence of radio. In addition, information was moved by government-controlled vessels. Britain instituted the Post Office Packet system, operating from Falmouth, to move vital intelligence around the world, through a chain of regular connections. To keep costs down, the packets also carried private and commercial information. British success in moving and using intelligence on a strategic level provided a major advantage in the long cycle of wars with France, 1688–1815. To increase the speed of transmission between ship and shore, Britain and France in the Napoleonic era built networks of shutter or semaphore telegraphs covering hundreds of miles. The British system linked London with Chatham, Portsmouth, and Plymouth.

The development of steamships offered the prospect of timetabled strategic communications. By 1830 the Royal Navy was providing a monthly service connecting Falmouth with Corfu, via Lisbon, Gibraltar, and Malta. However, Britain could not afford to set up such regular steam links with its chain of global possessions. Instead, the government privatized the carriage of mail, including official messages in 1837, using mail contracts with private shipping companies. Companies like Cunard provided shipping capacity on specified routes at stipulated intervals in return for annual subsidies. Communications dominance gave Britain a massive advantage over its competitors.

The Submarine Telegraph Cable, pioneered in Britain, added a new dimension to strategic communications. The first undersea cable was laid between Britain and France in 1851. In the Crimean War (1853–1856) a combination of land and underwater cables linked London, Paris, and the Crimean port of Balaklava shortly after the Anglo-French invasion. Operations could be directed from the metropole.

The first transatlantic cable was laid in 1858, and the route was conquered in 1866. By the early 1870s cables linked Britain with Australia. The rapid development of the cable network transformed British strategy. Submarine cables gave Britain security for vital messages. Britain used the new system to transform imperial strategy from one involving the spread of significant forces across the globe to one in which London could direct forces from the major fleets to any point on the globe with remarkable speed.

This strategy worked because the communications nodes were also the sites of major coal stocks and of the dry docks essential to maintain steamships. The British could afford this unique global network because almost all the cables, dry docks, and coal stocks were operated at a profit by British commercial interests. Small subsidies secured priority use of these facilities in wartime, while the private sector acquired naval protection. Britain dominated the manufacture, laying, and ownership of submarine telegraph systems down to 1914, as a by-product of a unique global empire of trade, commerce, and communication.

At the outbreak of war in 1914, Britain cut German cables and dominated secure communications for the rest of the war. German attempts to use neutral cables resulted in the betrayal of the infamous Zimmerman Telegram that helped to bring the United States into the war.

Wireless helped fleet commanders, especially at night or in fog, but it was immediately seized upon by shore-based authorities, who used it to take control of events at sea. In 1910, Admiral Sir Arthur Wilson, the first sea lord, directed fleet exercises from Whitehall by wireless. This facilitated the global strategic direction of operations from a central headquarters. In 1914–1918 the Admiralty exercised strategic control over the Grand Fleet by wireless, leaving the commander in chief with tactical control, as well as some operational freedom. At the same time, wireless control from the center exacerbated the age-old danger that the enemy might understand signals and thereby gain a vital advantage.

Wireless offered Germany an alternative to the cable before 1914, when Berlin could communicate with the Pacific via central Africa. The British attacked this network at the outbreak of war, crippling the German attempt to wage a truly global war. With cable and wireless communications cut, the Germans were unable to warn their admiral in the South Pacific, Graf Maximilian von Spee, that the British had dispatched an overwhelming force to intercept him. The British victory at the Falkland Islands in December 1914 was a triumph for strategic communications.

In World War II cable communications remained highly important, the Axis being significantly disadvantaged by the lack of secure links between Berlin and Tokyo. Wireless gained greater prominence because of the speed at which major campaigns moved and because of the distances involved. This was especially noticeable in the Pacific. Here the U.S. Navy broke into Japanese wireless codes, providing major strategic, operational, and tactical benefits at the Battle of Midway in June 1942.

The space-age post-1945 communications technology expanded exponentially as computer processing speeds rose. American satellite communications systems were developed to support the Polaris Submarine-Launched Ballistic Missile (SLBM) system, and Global Positioning System (GPS) offered advanced navigation for military purposes, including cruiser missile operations. Below the surface, ultralow-frequency radio signals are used for shore links with submerged SLBMs. Communications dominance still delivers massive advantages to navies, but the major threats of the twenty-first century are asymmetric and require different approaches.

[*See also* Navies, Great Powers; Strategy; Tactics; Telecommunications; Telegraphy; *and* Wars, Maritime.]

### Bibliography

Friedman, Norman. *Seapower and Space: From the Dawn of the Missile Age to Net-centric Warfare*. London: Chatham, 2000.

Gordon, Andrew. *The Rules of the Game: Jutland and British Naval Command*. London: Murray, 1996.

Headrick, Daniel. *The Invisible Weapon: Telecommunications and International Politics, 1851–1945*. New York: Oxford University Press, 1991.

Tunstall, Brian. *Naval Warfare in the Age of Sail: The Evolution of Fighting Tactics 1680–1815*. Edited by Nicholas Tracy. London: Conway Maritime Press, 1990.

ANDREW LAMBERT

# Communities

This entry contains six subentries:

## An Overview

Throughout the world a variety of communities have been involved in maritime activities since ancient times. Such communities have been sustained by numerous occupations associated with the sea: fishing and harvesting other marine resources, salt making, sailing, trade, shipbuilding, and piracy. Some maritime communities have focused on a very limited range of activities, such as fishing, but other maritime communities contain a variety of sea-bound occupations ranging from fishing through sailing and shipbuilding to trade.

## Early Settlements

The earliest maritime communities comprised fisherfolk and collectors of tidal and riverine marine resources: shellfish, birds' eggs, turtles, ambergris, crocodiles, salt, and migrating species of fish such as salmon. Such settlements were among the earliest of all human settlements. In the Persian Gulf, in Southeast Asia, and along the Pacific coast of South America, there is ample evidence that fishing predated agriculture as an incentive for a collective human activity giving rise to the first permanent human settlements. Some of these sites indicate an almost total reliance on the harvest of the sea, but others provide evidence of farming and/or hunting and gathering. Such a mixture of harvests provided a basic but almost indestructible existence. Around the Mediterranean, on the Atlantic seaboard of Europe, in the Caribbean, on the North Sea and Baltic littorals, along the coast of East Africa from the Horn to the Mozambique Channel, through South and Southeast Asia, to Australasia, and across the Pacific from the Philippines to Polynesia and coastal North and South America—in all these places fishing, farming, hunting, and gathering evolved as a secure way of life that balances the returns of the land with the harvest of the sea.

Although most fisherfolk developed some relationship with the land, some formed predominantly maritime communities, in contrast to the wandering lifestyle of the land-based hunter-gatherer. Such communities have all but vanished, but small groups of sea gypsies, such as the Moken of the Andaman Sea in the Bay of Bengal and the Orang Laut of maritime Southeast Asia, have survived.

The only other maritime communities that appear so sea-bound are pirate communities. From the ancient sea peoples of the Mediterranean 4,000 years ago, to the Barbary corsairs of North Africa 200 years ago, to the present-day motorized gangs of the South China Sea and the Strait of Melaka (east of Malaysia), pirates have preyed on shipping. While some communities, particularly in the Caribbean and the Atlantic, were little more than ephemeral bands of bandits, many—most notably the Vikings of the eighth to eleventh centuries, the Arab "pirates" of the Persian Gulf in the eighteenth and nineteenth centuries, and some modern pirate groups—were, or are, from established coastal communities that combine opportunistic piracy with farming, seafaring, shipbuilding, and trade as a means of survival.

With the development of water-borne trade and communication, there was increasing occupational specialization in maritime communities. Fishermen were the first sailors, and their settlements were the nodal points for the first trading voyages and for the evolution of shipping technology as it changed to meet new needs and challenges. From their harvest of the sea, fishermen also contributed items for trade, such as cured and salted fish, salt, pearls, shells, seaweed, coral, ambergris, and turtle shells. Occupational specialization in maritime communities transformed fishermen into sailors, harvesting specialists, merchants, and shipbuilders. In some maritime communities there emerged a new hierarchy based on control of larger trading vessels and particular resources. As sailing craft grew larger and more capital-intensive, the fisherman and sailor became the servants of the merchant and shipowner, although small family-owned fishing craft survived into modern times.

## Linking Communities

Until modern times these more complex maritime communities were fragmented from one another. Each community was largely self-sufficient and sustained by its fisherfolk, sailors, craftsmen, merchants, and shipowners. Each community was a self-contained hierarchy with minimal horizontal contact between similar groups across a number of communities. Merchants were the exception: from the ancient Coromandel Coast of southeast India to the Baltic and the merchant cities of the North Sea in medieval Europe, there is evidence of associations and guilds of maritime merchants cutting across community boundaries and linking merchants from particular maritime regions.

Many maritime communities were linked to resource-rich hinterlands, and their prosperity came from marketing marine resources and trading commodities. The Baltic Hansa communities from the medieval period shipped and traded the fish, timber, and ores of Scandinavia and amber, timber, furs, and grain from Poland and lands to the east. East-coast English communities flourished on the wool and herring trades. From the beginning of the present era, maritime communities of Gujarat, in west India, exported the textiles and grain of the Indo-Gangetic basin, and were linked by caravan into central India, central Asia, and the transcontinental Silk Route. Before the coming of the Europeans in the sixteenth century, northern Javanese maritime communities prospered on the export of Java's rice and the redistribution of cotton textiles from South Asia and spices from the archipelago.

Occasionally, particularly as long-distance maritime trade expanded, a community would evolve into an exchange center or entrepôt without any significant links to the hinterland. In the Persian Gulf 5,000 years ago, Bahrain and Kuwait performed this function. Both flourished as fishing, pearling, and trading communities having marginal attachment to their hinterlands but extensive links with other regions that they serviced with their intermediate geographic position. Later and elsewhere in Asia the same function was performed by seaside market places on either side of the Isthmus of Kra, by Melaka, and later by Singapore and Hong Kong. In the Mediterranean similar maritime communities evolved ranging from ancient Cyprus, which functioned as an entrepôt between the Aegean and the eastern Mediterranean (although Cyprus added copper into its trade mix), to Venice and Genoa, which grew wealthy as western Europe's entrepôts for trade with the Muslim-controlled Levant at the eastern end of the Mediterranean and with the Black Sea.

## Marine Resources

For all this variety, the essential lure of the sea was fish. The availability of fish determined the number of fishermen and sailors, and the development of maritime communities. Where fish were scarce, maritime communities were restricted by the natural limits on the catch. The resource-rich eastern Mediterranean Sea eclipsed the relatively poorer western Mediterranean, resulting in a concentration of maritime communities west of Sicily until barely 400 years ago. The North Sea and Baltic eclipsed the Atlantic until the cod fisheries of Newfoundland were opened up at approximately the same time. The southern stretches of the Indian and Pacific oceans, while rich in fish, could not be exploited until modern fishing and shipping technology were available from the twentieth century. In both these oceans, maritime communities were concentrated north of the Equator, with the exception of scattered ancient fishing and trading communities along the coast of East Africa and the fishing and agricultural economies of the Pacific islands, from the Philippines and New Guinea to Polynesia and New Zealand.

Where marine resources were plentiful and were matched by resource-rich hinterlands, a concentration of fishermen, sailors, and potential export cargoes led to the development of particular maritime regions. Rivers and caravans linked such regions to inland markets and commodities, and the resulting communities developed extensive maritime commercial networks for transporting people and goods to contiguous maritime regions. At least 2,000 years ago the Persian Gulf, Gujarat, the Malabar and Coromandel coasts, Orissa, and Bengal formed distinctive maritime regions in the Indian Ocean, as did the eastern Mediterranean and to an extent the South China Sea. Within these regions were clusters of maritime communities of varying size and prosperity, and often with a limited life span subject to the vagaries of river flows, sea levels, and the political and economic stability of their hinterlands. By the beginning of the common era the entire Mediterranean was a distinctive maritime region, reflecting the growth of the Roman Empire. And by the medieval period in Europe, the Red Sea, the Baltic, the Black Sea, the North Sea, and East Africa had evolved as distinctive maritime regions on the basis of a critical mix of marine, agricultural, and resource wealth. As with their more ancient counterparts elsewhere in the Indian Ocean and South China Sea, the fortunes of these regions were subject to geographic and human forces over which they had minimal control. Consequently, the life and fortunes of individual communities ranged from short and brutal to long and glorious—from communities marked today only by archaeological remains to coastal cities such as Alexandria, London, and Bharuch (India), whose histories stretch back 2,000 years.

## Development of Diasporas

While the prosperity of coastal communities was anchored in their access to maritime and terrestrial resources, until the coming of steam their long-term rhythms were dictated by the pattern and regularity of wind systems. In the Indian Ocean, the annual monsoons determined sailing times, the duration of voyaging, and routes. Other oceans and seas had less spectacular wind systems, but all such systems were seasonal. This natural seasonality not only shaped traveling and fishing schedules but also encouraged the development of diasporas of merchants and sailors. The need to collect cargoes and refit vessels prompted many maritime communities of foreign sailors, traders, and shipowners to form around the Mediterranean and in Asian waters by the beginning of the common era. In succeeding centuries similar diasporas spread around the Indian Ocean and South China Sea, and in the wake of the overseas expansion of western Europe that began five centuries ago, new diasporas grew in Africa, the Americas, Asia, and the Pacific.

The development of diasporas was enriching culturally and economically. The expansion of Hinduism and

Buddhism into Southeast Asia, which began at least 2,000 years ago, was intimately associated with the growth of maritime trade and the development of complex maritime communities in parts of Southeast Asia, through which the civilizations of South Asia influenced local societies. One thousand years ago Islam began spreading in a similar manner out of the Middle East: along shipping routes through maritime communities along the coast of East Africa and in the Comoros and Madagascar. At roughly the same time Islam also spread eastward along the ancient maritime routes linking South and Southeast Asia and took root in maritime communities stretching from such ports as Aceh and Melaka astride the Strait of Melaka to the spice-rich islands of eastern Indonesia.

Maritime communities were the nodal points where different cultures came into contact and were also the filters through which new cultures permeated into the hinterlands. As Michael Pearson has argued with respect to the Indian Ocean, these "littoral societies" linking land and sea were the meeting points for a range of peoples, cultures, and ideas. In the Mediterranean similar societies existed in ancient Crete, Greece, and the Levant, and later in the maritime culture of Venice. In the Black Sea, littoral communities provided meeting points between the peoples of Eurasia and those of Greece and Rome. In the Baltic, merchants, warriors and Christian missionaries from Hansa communities were vital agents in the diffusion of German culture and Roman Catholicism. And later European coastal settlements in Asia, Africa, the Americas, and Australasia were the bridgeheads for the diffusion of European culture, technology, and political and military power.

In time the growing internal complexity of maritime communities and the expansion of their external linkages gave rise to particular lifestyles. Not only were such communities frequently more cosmopolitan than land-based communities; they also contained specialized groups—such as fishermen, sailors, shipowners, and merchants—whose intimate linkage to the sea and its seasons created distinctive subcultures. These subcultures had sea-oriented religious beliefs and practices (ranging from Hindu deities in the Indian Ocean region to particular Christian and Muslim saints in the Mediterranean, Indian Ocean, and Atlantic); group organizations (such as merchant guilds in the Baltic, the Mediterranean, the Indian Ocean, and China); music; food; and a range of social practices.

The overseas expansion of Europe that began with the Portuguese and Spanish did not immediately change the life of existing maritime communities across much of Asia and Africa but rather simply added a new element to preexisting maritime communities from Tangiers on the Moroccan coast to Melaka on the east coast of Malaysia. In the Americas, southern Africa, the Mascarenes and Australasia, in contrast, they created new maritime communities. The Mascarenes were uninhabited prior to European and African slave settlement in the eighteenth century, and although there are hints of maritime trade networks in the Caribbean dating as far back as the Mayan civilization more than 1,500 years ago, and along the coasts of southeast Africa and northwest Australia predating European settlement in these areas, most significant maritime communities in the Americas, South Africa, Australia and New Zealand developed from European settlements in maritime landscapes previously devoid of large indigenous maritime communities, and where European settlement marginalized preexisting indigenous maritime activity.

### Ports and Harbors

Europeans brought a new urban facility to traditional maritime communities outside Europe: the port. The port as we understand it today, a constructed harbor with permanent docking and storage facilities, was the creation of classical Mediterranean communities, beginning with Mycenaean and Phoenician maritime communities, although traces of such structures are found in ancient sites in Mesopotamia and the Indus valley. Outside Europe there were great cities with recognizably permanent ports before Europeans sailed the Atlantic, Indian, and Pacific oceans—Surat (India), Kilwa (East Africa), Melaka (Malaysia), and Guangzhou (China)—but they were the exception rather than the rule. For the most part, maritime communities were defined not by a particular port but by a variety of points (e.g., beach and inlet market places, tidal harbors) at which cargoes were exchanged or fishermen gathered. Some were seasonal or ephemeral and were subject to changing ecological conditions, hinterland politics, the depletion of terrestrial and marine resources, and the vagaries of market demand. But some were more substantial, with links to fishing, agriculture, and resource-rich hinterlands.

The particular demands of the European merchant—all-weather trading, administration, and military bases—led to the rapid growth of a new maritime facility: the constructed permanent harbor with all its ancillary features. Mombasa, Aden, Karachi, Mumbai (Bombay), Chennai (Madras), Kolkata (Calcutta), Yangon (Rangoon), Melaka, Singapore, Jakarta, Fremantle, Sydney, Hong Kong, New York, Boston, Charleston, New Orleans, Dakar, Shanghai,

Buenos Aires—all ports of the modern world—are products of European expansion and not a natural evolution of maritime communities, although some grew out of preexisting settlements. The growth of these ports over several centuries had a profound impact on maritime communities. They encouraged spatial concentration of maritime activity, with the result that there was an increasing concentration of activities such as shipbuilding, trade, and the recruitment of sailors in a relatively small number of ports. Only communities with a specific maritime function, such as fishing and whaling, continued to flourish around the world, from Scotland and New England in the Atlantic to southern India and Western Australia in the Indian Ocean. The newer behemoths slowly reduced smaller multifunction coastal communities in importance, and increasingly the sailor became a member of a distinctive community divorced from fishing communities. In maritime regions such as the Mediterranean, the North Sea, and the Atlantic seaboard of Europe, the growth of such major ports as Marseilles, Alexandria, Genoa, Bordeaux, Southampton, London, Liverpool, Manchester, Amsterdam, and Hamburg led to the decline of lesser ports as maritime activities became concentrated in a smaller number of centers—a process aided by the growth of railway and canal systems. The story was repeated throughout Asia, Africa, and the Americas, and the coming of steam accelerated the process.

## The Influence of Technological Developments

The introduction of steam navigation in the nineteenth century was a major point of disjunction in the life of maritime communities. Navigation was now all-weather, as opposed to fair-weather, the locally owned sailing craft was increasingly replaced by vessels owned by European shipping companies, and the skilled manpower needed by the new vessels could no longer be provided by the traditional groups within maritime communities. Up-country recruitment of manpower not only reinforced the distinctiveness of sailor communities in ports but also broke the ancient connection between fishermen and sailors, reducing many coastal communities to a marginal existence as fisherfolk. Yet the process of the diffusion of steam was relatively slow. The steam vessel ousted the sailing vessel from many routes, but sail still survived. Greek island communities maintained profitable fleets of sailing vessels until the early twentieth century, and in Asian waters (and among remote fishing communities elsewhere), Arab and Asian craft still occasionally combine both technologies, servicing niche cargo markets and the fishing industry.

Steam navigation and the emergence of the modern port radically changed life for many maritime communities. Most were increasingly marginalized as new labor demands, the spread of railways and modern roads, the development of modern navigational aids, and the absolute decline in the number of points where land and ocean interacted worked to reduce the maritime functions of ancient maritime communities. Some survived because of particular functions (e.g., fishing, whaling, pearling, or the handling of a specific commodity such as timber, grain, or minerals), but most were increasingly divorced from the sea, and unless they could find a niche within, or associated with, the new ports, they vanished as distinctive communities.

The functions of the old maritime communities were taken over by new communities located in the new ports that emerged in the last two hundred years. These new communities were the centers of maritime life—the places where ships were constructed and naval bases were located, where new land-based communications systems were focused, where merchants and sailors gathered, and where international trade was conducted. Some ancient maritime communities did find a niche in the new order. In Kuwait, for example, local shipowners adapted rapidly to new market demands and survived on the small pickings of the Persian Gulf and Arabian Sea carrying trade, as did Omanis with respect to the East African trade. Similar niches enabled the Paravas of south India, the Maldivians in the Indian Ocean, and various maritime communities across Southeast Asia to survive into the modern world, but increasingly their maritime world has shrunk, and their role as the interface between different cultures has been subsumed by the growth of the modern port and by changing maritime and communications technology. While traditional fishing communities have survived in many parts of the world, their prospects have been blighted by the rise of large-scale capital-intensive fishing, fish farming, and the globalization of the industry that now threatens the existence of many smaller, capital-poor coastal fishing communities.

While the development of steam navigation had a profound effect upon the life of maritime communities and restricted maritime life essentially to the compass of a relatively small number of large modern ports, it was the container revolution, beginning in the 1960s and 1970s, that revolutionized the life of ports and essentially divorced them from the communities in which they were embedded.

Containerization greatly reduced the demand for port labor, decimating the distinctive social and political communities of wharf laborers that developed in the modern port in the last two centuries. The new very large vessels constructed for the container trade not only required new specialized dock facilities but also have much smaller labor requirements. This factor has precipitated a dramatic decline in the number of sailors and in the power of maritime trade unions. This development, in tandem with the changing patterns of recruitment based on costs rather than on traditional calling, has all but eliminated the sailor from many port communities. More often than not, the port city of the early twenty-first century is either a coastal city with an attached port that is serviced by sailors from other countries and that has only indirect impact on the social and economic life of the community, or is a discrete industrial facility specifically constructed to handle containers and often physically quite separate from any coastal urban setting. Of a similar nature are an increasing number of ports developed to handle one export commodity, such as the oil ports in the Persian Gulf and West Africa and the iron ore ports of Western Australia.

Steam navigation and the container evolution have fundamentally altered the life of maritime communities. Coastal communities survive clustered around fishing ports, cruise-liner facilities, ship-construction yards, naval bases, yachting marinas, maritime museums, and seaside resorts, but increasingly the sea has declined as a major source of employment and inspiration and as a highway linking different maritime communities and cultures.

[*See also* Communities, Maritime; Fishing, *subentry on* Economic History; Ports; *and* Trade.]

## Bibliography

Banga, Indu, ed. *Ports and Their Hinterlands in India 1700–1950.* New Delhi: Manohar Publications, 1992.

Basu, Dilip K., ed. *The Rise and Growth of the Colonial Port City in Asia.* Lanham, Md.: University Press of America, 1985.

Braudel, Fernand. *The Mediterranean and the Mediterranean World in the Age of Philip II.* 2 vols. New York: Harper and Row, 1972–1973.

Broeze, Frank. *The Globalisation of the Oceans: Containerisation from the 1950s to the Present.* St. John's, Newfoundland: International Maritime Economic History Association, 2002.

Broeze, Frank, Peter Reeves, and Kenneth McPherson. "Imperial Ports and the Modern World Economy: The Case of the Indian Ocean." *Journal of Transport History,* 3rd series, 7 (1986): 1–20.

Broeze, Frank, ed. *Brides of the Sea: Port Cities of Asia from the 16th–20th Centuries.* Sydney, Australia: NSW University Press, 1989.

Broeze, Frank, ed. *Gateways of Asia: Port Cities of Asia in the 13th–20th Centuries.* London: Kegan Paul International, 1997.

Chaudhuri, K. N. *Asia before Europe.* Cambridge, U.K.: Cambridge University Press, 1990.

Chaudhuri, K. N. *Trade and Civilisation in the Indian Ocean.* Cambridge, U.K.: Cambridge University Press, 1985.

Curtin, Philip D. *Cross-Cultural Trade in World History.* Cambridge, U.K.: Cambridge University Press, 1984.

Hoyle, B. S., and D. A. Pinder, eds. *European Port Cities in Transition.* New York: Halstead Press, 1992.

Kathirithamby-Wells, J., and John Villiers, eds. *The Southeast Asian Port and Polity: Rise and Demise.* Singapore: Singapore University Press, 1990.

Knight, Franklin W., and Peggy K. Liss, eds. *Atlantic Port Cities: Economy, Culture, and Society in the Atlantic World, 1650–1850.* Knoxville: University of Tennessee Press, 1991.

McPherson, Kenneth. *The Indian Ocean: A History of People and the Sea.* New Delhi, India: Oxford University Press, 1993.

Murphey, Rhoads. "Traditionalism and Colonialism: Changing Urban Roles in Asia." *Journal of Asian Studies* 29 (1969): 67–84.

Pearson, Michael N. "Littoral Society: The Case of the Coast." *Great Circle* 7, no. 1 (1985): 1–8.

Ray, Himanshu Prabha. *The Archaeology of Seafaring in Ancient South Asia.* Cambridge, U.K.: Cambridge University Press, 2003.

Smith, M. Estellie. *Those Who Live from the Sea: A Study in Maritime Anthropology.* St. Paul, Minn.: West Publishing Co., 1977.

Westerdahl, Christer. "The Maritime Cultural Landscape." *International Journal of Nautical Archaeology* 21, no. 1 (1992): 5–14.

Yueng, Yue-man, and Xu-wei Hu, eds. *China's Coastal Cities: Catalysts for Modernization.* Honolulu: University of Hawaii Press, 1992.

KENNETH MCPHERSON

# Arab Communities

At least five thousand years ago inhabitants of the Persian Gulf region were engaged in local and long-distance trade. From Bahrain to the coast of the modern United Arab Emirates (UAE) and Oman, archaeological sites—most frequently on islands—provide evidence of early fishing settlements that evolved into centers of prehistoric Arab trade and navigation. The largest of these ancient settlements was Dilmun on the island of Bahrain: the source of the biblical tales of Eden and Noah and the Great Flood. Dilmun and lesser ports were vital links on long, coast-hugging maritime trade routes connecting the civilizations of Mesopotamia and the Indus valley via Oman, the Makran coast, and the Indus delta. The Arabian shore of the gulf with its flat hinterland, shallow waters, and fertile offshore islands stood in sharp contrast to the arid rugged mountain shore on the Iranian side of the gulf with few natural harbors and even fewer offshore islands suitable for human habitation.

Gulf ports involved in this early trade were revictualing ports and added in cargoes such as copper ingots, stone, dates, onions, and pearls. Some were linked by caravan routes to inland centers on the Arabian Peninsula and, in time, to the eastern Mediterranean.

## Development and Prosperity

The evolution of these Arab port communities was paralleled by the development of complex maritime skills leading to the formation of particular coastal and island-based Arab communities whose livelihood depended on their roles as sailors, fishermen, pearl divers, shipbuilders, and merchants. Within these littoral communities, occupational lines were not rigid, and given the seasonal nature of sea travel before the coming of the steam engine, many inhabitants changed their occupations according to the seasons.

The early prosperity and success of these communities can be in part measured by the rapid evolution of Arab maritime technology and navigational skills. The ubiquitous Arab dhow, in all its variations, was at least two thousand years ago probably the preeminent shipping type across the Arabian Sea, particularly after Arab sailors had fathomed the intricacies of the monsoon wind systems that enabled them to sail directly across the Arabian Sea to the western coast of India, Sri Lanka, and the Maldives, and to the middle reaches of the East African coast.

The development of these precocious skills was given impetus by the growth of large empires across the central lands of the Middle East from Anatolia and the Mediterranean to the Indus valley. But this development, and the prosperity of the gulf communities, was cyclically disrupted by the waxing and waning of land-bound civilizations and markets across the Middle East and the Mediterranean. The disruption of the Mesopotamian and Indus civilizations three to four thousand years ago was followed by a millennium of obscurity and decline for the gulf communities. But the rise of the frankincense and myrrh trade, and the emergence of first imperial Persia and then Alexander III (Alexander the Great, 356–323 B.C.E.) and his Greek and Roman successors in the first millennium B.C.E., ushered in a new age of prosperity for gulf communities. This resurgent wealth was based on the trade in ivory, gold, silk, pepper, spices, timber, porcelain, aromatic gums, and foodstuffs from Africa and south and east Asia, to which gulf communities also added cargoes of dates, pearls, and dried fish.

The middleman role of gulf Arab communities in this great East–West trade continued without serious break into the thirteenth century C.E. Both the successor state to Rome (Byzantium) and imperial Persia continued to use the gulf as a conduit to the cargoes of the East, although Byzantium did attempt to lessen this dependence by moving to divert it through the Red Sea. However, the primacy of the gulf as the main route to the Indian Ocean was confirmed in the seventh century C.E. with the rise of Islam and the creation of an Islamic empire centered on Baghdad that incorporated much of Byzantium and all of Persia.

The gulf maritime communities readily converted to Islam and were ideally located to benefit from the rise of a huge empire centered on Mesopotamia and Iran. For the next five hundred years they pushed the boundaries of Arab maritime knowledge as far east as southern China and to the southwest along the coast of East Africa as far as Madagascar. In the process they developed a near monopoly of the East African trade in gold, ivory, slaves, timber, and metals and proved formidable rivals for south Asian sailors and traders eastward across the Bay of Bengal in the search for silk, porcelain, pepper, spices, tin, and jungle products.

This lucrative trade was not, however, exclusively in the hands of gulf Arabs. Persians from the opposite shore of the gulf were also prominent in the trade until at least the thirteenth century when the Mongol invasions of Iran and Mesopotamia fatally undermined Persian maritime enterprise and led to an overall decline in the gulf trade. But before this catastrophe the measure of gulf Arab and Persian influence can be gauged by the growth of Arab and Persian diasporas throughout the western Indian Ocean from the Comoros to the Maldives. Along the coast of East Africa, southern India, and the Maldives during these centuries, Arab and Persian merchants from the gulf intermarried with locals. This led to the foundation of prosperous Muslim trading cities along the coast of East Africa and the development of the Afro-Asian Swahili culture and language, the seeding of substantial Muslim communities along the Malabar and Coromandel coasts of southern India, and the conversion of the inhabitants of the Maldives from Buddhism.

In these processes it is not always possible to distinguish the separate roles of Arab and Persian or of people from the Red Sea versus people from the gulf, but what is evident is that members of various Arab communities in the gulf were major players in this vast diaspora of Muslims. Minor players in this gulf diaspora were non-Muslims such as Jews (from the early centuries of the present era) and later Armenians.

## Economic Decline

The Mongol destruction of the medieval Islamic empire and the imperial capital at Baghdad adversely affected the gulf Arabs. Mesopotamia entered a long period of decline, and the center of Arab Muslim wealth and power shifted west to the sultanate of Egypt. This in turn led to the triumph of the Red Sea route over that of the gulf, but from the late fifteenth century two new powers emerged in the Middle East—the Ottoman Turks and the Safavids in Iran—whose creation of two huge land-based empires somewhat revived the fortunes of the gulf Arab maritime communities.

However, the benefits of this land-based revival have to be set against the adverse impact on Muslim maritime trade from the early 1500s by the arrival of the aggressive Christian Portuguese in the Indian Ocean. Driven by a mixture of religious and mercantile motives, the Portuguese launched a violent campaign to eliminate Muslims from maritime trade. To do this they attempted to seal off the gulf from international trade. For a while they held the island port of Hormuz off the Persian coast at the mouth of the gulf, but with a maritime empire strung out from Mozambique to Macao, they overstretched themselves and were eventually driven from the gulf.

Encouraged by these successes, gulf Arab forces, led by Yemen, drove the Portuguese from their base at Fort Jesus in Mombasa on the coast of East Africa and from Lamu and Zanzibar farther to the south. In the process the Yemenis established a mini-empire stretching from the gulf to Zanzibar and grew wealthy from the export of slaves and ivory and the development of clove plantations.

This revival of gulf Arab fortunes obscures a harsher reality. Yemenis were the main beneficiaries of this development, while other gulf Arabs were less lucky. Overall from the sixteenth and seventeenth centuries the gulf trade declined. The decline was not precipitous, but as European political and economic power increased across the Indian Ocean, there was a growing diversion of cargoes around the Cape of Good Hope. This factor—combined with a rapid increase in more cost-efficient European shipping tonnage along many routes previously sailed by gulf shipowners, a steady fall in Middle Eastern demand, and the lack of interest of most European trading nations in the markets of the area—turned the gulf into an economic backwater. Some Arab communities in the gulf continued to survive

on maritime trade and pearling, and by the eighteenth century several districts in eastern Arabia, lower Iraq (Basra), Kuwait, Bahrain, and southwest Iran (Arabistan) formed a regional market dependent on a niche trade with India and the pearling industry.

Despite this overall decline in the fortunes of gulf Arab communities, trade was still sufficiently profitable to encourage a migration of inland Arabian pastoral tribes to the gulf coast. During the eighteenth century various tribes established bases at Kuwait, Bahrain, and Qatar, from where they became seafarers, pearlers, and fishermen with considerable fleets of merchant vessels. But increasing European commercial interest in the gulf from the latter half of the nineteenth century limited the field of operations for gulf mercantile communities, whose fortunes received a further blow in 1862 when the opening of the Suez Canal confirmed the primacy of the Red Sea route as the main shipping route between the Mediterranean and the Indian Ocean.

## Geopolitical Importance

Although the gulf had become an economic backwater by the early nineteenth century, it was of growing geopolitical importance. While the port of Basra at the head of the gulf was firmly controlled by the Ottomans, the Arabian shore of the gulf was a political no-man's-land divided among various tribes who contested for control of port marketplaces. The increasingly powerful forces of the fundamentalist Islamic Wahabi movement frequently attacked their political and economic rivals as they spread from inland towns to the more prosperous coastal settlements. Eastern Arabia lay beyond the control of the Ottoman Turks despite their attempts to garrison parts of it, and it remained a cockpit of ephemeral tribal and sectarian rivalries for control of particular ports and trading areas.

For British India the gulf was part of its turbulent frontier alongside Afghanistan. The threat of a Napoleonic invasion via the gulf prompted the British to begin to assert their interest in the area. To a fear of the French was added a concern for the security of British Indian trade with the gulf in the face of Wahabi incursions and local resistance to foreign mercantile intrusion. Although fears of French ambitions dissipated after 1815, they were replaced by growing British concerns about Russian expansion into Central Asia, Afghanistan, and Iran; by a revival of Ottoman ambitions in Eastern Arabia; and, by the end of the century, by German plans for a rail link between Basra, Baghdad, and beyond.

In response to real and perceived threats to their interests, the British moved to organize the gulf to defend these interests. An informal British empire or sphere of influence in the gulf was developed, and a number of gulf Arab maritime communities were declared protected states, in effect demarcating the area as under British influence and preventing any other power from moving into the political vacuum of the gulf. Thus Kuwait, Bahrain, Qatar, and a collection of sultanates on the Trucial Coast (the modern UAE) emerged during the nineteenth century as independent states under the umbrella of British protection. Following World War I, mainland Arabia passed under Wahabi control and emerged as the state of Saudi Arabia.

But, for all its geopolitical importance to the British, the gulf remained an economic backwater until the end of World War II. Oil had been discovered in the area in the early twentieth century, but it was not until the 1950s that the independent gulf states and Saudi Arabia began to realize the full potential of this new source of wealth. By the end of the twentieth century, oil had transformed the economic life of all the states in the gulf. Traditional, maritime occupations were largely replaced by massive capitalist development in banking, oil refining, industrial development, service industries, tourism, shipping, and communications (note the number of gulf-based international airlines). In addition, following the withdrawal of British protection in the 1960s, the Arab gulf states established the Gulf Cooperation Council to promote their interests, and later the microstates of the Trucial Coast joined to form the United Arab Emirates.

[*See also* Kuwait; Oil and Petroleum Products; *and* Pearl Fishing and Farming.]

## Bibliography

Abu-Hakima, Ahmad Mustafa. *History of Eastern Arabia, 1750–1800: The Rise and Development of Bahrain and Kuwait.* Beirut, Lebanon: Khayats, 1965.

Al-Tajir, Mahdi Abdalla. *Bahrain 1920–1945: Britain, the Shaikh, and the Administration.* London: Croom Helm, 1987.

Crawford, Harriet. "Mesopotamia and the Gulf: The History of a Relationship." *Iraq* 67, no. 2 (Autumn 2005): 41–46.

Fattah, Hala. *The Politics of Regional Trade in Iraq, Arabia, and the Gulf, 1745–1900.* Albany: State University of New York Press, 1997.

Hawley, Donald. *The Trucial States.* London: Allen and Unwin, 1970.

Kelly, J. B. *Britain and the Persian Gulf, 1795–1880.* Oxford: Clarendon, 1968.

Peck, Malcolm C. *The United Arab Emirates: A Venture in Unity.* Boulder, Colo.: Westview; London: Croom Helm, 1986.

Philby, H. St. J. B.. *Saudi Arabia.* London: Benn, 1955.

Rice, Michael. *The Archaeology of the Arabian Gulf: c. 5000–323 B.C.* London and New York: Routledge, 1994.

Troeller, Gary. *The Birth of Saudi Arabia: Britain and the Rise of the House of Sa'ud.* London: Cass, 1976.

Wilson, Arnold Talbot. *The Persian Gulf: An Historical Sketch from the Earliest Times to the Beginning of the Twentieth Century.* Oxford: Clarendon Press, 1928.

KENNETH MCPHERSON

# China

China, half surrounded by seas, possesses not only agriculture, but also maritime culture, dating back some eight thousand years. From primitive times, ancestors of the Chinese have set foot on the winding coastlines that extend nearly thirty thousand miles. In particular, the Yiren and Haiyi ethnic groups established kingdoms along the coastal regions of China before the Qin dynasty, among them the kingdoms of Yan and Qi in the northern coastal areas, the kingdoms of Wu and Yue in the eastern coastal areas, and the kingdom of Baiyue in the southern coastal areas. Most of these kingdoms prospered through fishing, salt production, maritime transportation, and trade. After Ying Zheng, the first emperor of the Qin dynasty (221–206 B.C.E.), unified China, these coastal peoples further developed their maritime culture under the administration of the central government.

Moreover, maritime communities and their culture directly and indirectly influenced and promoted the development of inland agricultural civilization in various political, economic, and cultural aspects. In fact, Chinese culture and civilization was an amalgamation of the inland culture and civilization and maritime culture and civilization. It was the Chinese maritime communities that ventured out on the seas, made expeditions to remote areas during the Qin and Han dynasties, opened up the maritime Silk Route (linking China with Southeast Asia, India, and the Near East), traded with other countries, and promoted interactions between maritime culture and the inland culture. This interaction gave rise to China's rich, advanced culture. In particular, it sped up exploration of the maritime Silk Route, stimulated an open-door policy from the peak of the Han dynasty (206 B.C.E.–220 C.E.), led to a system of Sino-foreign relations and a tribute system, and extended China's cultural influence throughout the Chinese cultural sphere, especially from the Tang dynasty (618–907).

Maritime communities, the main creative force of Chinese maritime culture and civilization, were mainly composed of numerous fishing villages, ports, and city communities in the extensive coastal regions, on the many islands, and along bays, and their populations consisted of fishermen, salt producers, boatmen, wharf workers, and maritime merchants.

## Location of China's Early Maritime Communities and Their Cultures

So long ago as the Paleolithic Age, people developed various maritime lifestyles along the Chinese coastal areas. The discovery of large numbers of seashells from food and ornaments are proof of seaside lifestyles of those early maritime communities. Information about Neolithic maritime cultures is far more abundant. There are numerous shell-mound sites in the coastal regions—such as the Dongxing shell-mound site in Guangxi Province, the Sanya Luobidong site in Hainan Province, and the abundant mounds and seashell sites in the Zhujing Delta—all of which contained great numbers of mussels, seashells, and fishing nets, demonstrating that these people were living off the sea.

In the coastal regions of Taiwan, Fujian, and Zhejiang and on the Zhoushan Islands in the East China Sea, large numbers of shell mounds dating back to the Neolithic Age have been discovered. The Fuguodun shell-mound site, the Keqiutou shell-mound site, and the Tanshishan site, all in Fujian Province, speak of maritime transportation between Fujian and the Ryukyu Islands in prehistoric times. The Neolithic remains on the Zhoushan Islands point to maritime life there. In Zhejiang Province, the remains of coastal buildings at the Yuyao site and the fishing tools and canoe oars discovered at the Hemudu site even more obviously present us with evidence of a distinct maritime culture in prehistoric times. From the extensive shell-mound sites along the Yellow Sea and the Bohai Sea, and from the Dongyi and Haidai archaeological sites in the Jiangsu coastal regions and the Shandong and Liaodong peninsulas, we can see how people in prehistoric maritime communities chose their residences and relied on maritime resources.

From the twenty-first century B.C.E. to the establishment of the Qin Empire in the early third century B.C.E.—the period of the Xia, Shang, and Zhou dynasties—various maritime communities evolved along the Chinese coast. During the Xia period (twenty-first century–seventeenth century B.C.E.) and the Shang Period (sixteenth century–eleventh century B.C.E.), people in the northern coastal areas possessed considerable navigational skills, sufficient for carrying out large-scale explorations and applications of maritime resources and

transporting sea products to inland areas, some of which became tribute to the central monarchies. Already at this time, some maritime communities were worshiping sea gods, an aspect of maritime culture that became ever richer and more extensive. During the time of the Western and Eastern Zhou period (eleventh century–475 B.C.E.), especially during the Spring and Autumn period (722–481 B.C.E.) and the Warring States period (475–221 B.C.E.), maritime culture continued to develop. The most powerful kingdoms—such as Yan and Qi in the northern coastal regions around the Bohai Sea, Wu and Yue in the eastern coastal regions along the East China Sea, and Baiyue along the South China Sea—gradually became prosperous from fishing, salt production, and convenient maritime transportation to other parts of China and foreign countries. At that time, the arts of shipbuilding and navigation improved, and kingdoms began to develop as maritime powers.

## Main Maritime Communities in Chinese History

After the foundation of the Qin dynasty in 221 B.C.E., China mainly experienced a unified, centralized imperial government that lasted more than two thousand years. Chinese maritime communities—whether residing in coastal areas, on islands, in seaports, even in boats and ships on the seas—always played an important role in Chinese cultural development. The following are six main kinds of Chinese maritime communities that played a significant role in the development of Chinese culture.

**Maritime communities of fishermen and islanders.** China's coastline extends about 18,000 kilometers (11,200 miles; longer during the Han and Tang periods, since the country was larger during those times), and there are approximately 6,500 islands in Chinese coastal waters. Thanks to ample offshore fishing resources, there are many fine fishing grounds along the coasts, such as the Bohai, Zhoushan, and Shensi fishing grounds. These fisheries support millions of fishermen and islanders. Apart from big islands like Taiwan and Hainan and peninsulas like Shandong and Liaodong, the small islands, such as the Zhoushan, Miaodao, and Changshan islands, support mainly fishermen. These people have developed a unique lifestyle, including their dress, food, housing, transportation, taboos, and religious beliefs. They worship gods of the sea, gods of fish, gods of boats, and a god of fishing nets, and they have built countless holy temples to their gods, including Longwangye (the Sea Dragon King), Pusa Niangniang (the goddess of mercy), and Mazu or Tianhou (the goddess of boats and ships). In fishing festivals every year, coastal fishermen and islanders gather for worshiping the gods, enjoying folk-theater performances, and trading goods.

**Maritime communities of salt-field workers.** From ancient times China had an advanced salt industry. For thousands of years, the government organized salt-field communities in many Chinese coastal areas. Workers in the salt fields boiled seawater or evaporated it in the sun to produce salt. Such communities accounted for a considerable proportion of the coastal population. For example, even after the sharp decrease in population from the end of the Jin period (1115–1234) to the beginning of the Yuan period (1279–1368), there were still almost 52,000 Zaohu families (families engaged in salt production) in the salt fields in northern China, about five percent of the total population in that region. In 1264–1268, in just Zhejiang, there were more than thirty-four salt fields and 17,000 Zaohu families, for a total population of 100,000 or so. In 1343, Hejian salt field, Hebei Province, alone supported about 5,774 Zaohu families, or a total population of approximately 30,000. In 1462, during the Ming dynasty, there were about 24,453 Zaohu families (at least 100,000 people) in just Dongguang County (including present-day Dongguang City, Shenzheng City, and Hong Kong) in Guangdong Province. These communities were unique in their lifestyle, social customs, and worship of the god of salt.

**Port maritime communities.** Imperial China had many ports. Situated mostly around estuaries and bays were thousands of small-size wharves, hundreds of medium-size ports, and dozens of large major ports. Famous major ports of traditional times include Guangzhou Port (Canton, originally Fanyu Port) and Xuwen Port along the coast of the South China Sea; Fuzhou Port (originally Dongye Port), Quanzhou Port (originally Citong Port), and Ningbo Port (originally Mingzhou Port) along the coast of the East China Sea; Yangzhou Port along the coast of the Yellow Sea; Langya Port, Mizhou Port, and Dengzhou Port along Shandong Peninsula coast of the Yellow Sea; and Tianjin Port and Jieshi Port (later named Qinhuangdao Port) around the Bohai Sea. The development of these ports brought prosperity to their cities and regions and, through transportation on rivers and canals, also improved the material and spiritual life of inland areas, including the court. Ports and the maritime Silk Route linked China to Southeast Asia, India, and the Near East.

The port cities that opened after the Opium War (1839–1842)—ports such as Hong Kong, Shanghai, Qingdao, and Dalian—rapidly became China's most important international ports and metropolises. In many of these port cities, foreign sojourner residents have always been an important component of the population. For example, in Guangzhou Port in the Tang and Song dynasties and in Quanzhou Port in the Song and Yuan dynasties, the number of foreign sojourner residents (seaman, merchants, and monks from Arabia, Persia, India, and Southeast Asia) totaled about 100,000. These foreigners, called foreign guests (*fanke*), lived in residential districts for foreigners (*fanfang*). In the northern coastal areas, foreigners came mainly from the Korean Peninsula. After the Opium War and before the foundation of the People's Republic of China, special areas for foreigners were forcibly opened up and even whole ports and cities in China's coastal regions were designated as foreign concessions. Thus, one after another, foreign communities formed in China's port cities during that period.

**Communities of maritime merchants.** For thousands of years merchants have contributed to the development of Chinese society and culture. They transported and traded products not only within China but also with foreign countries. It was maritime merchants who created and promoted the maritime Silk Route linking China first with Southeast Asia and later with India and the Near East. Over the millennia the merchants formed many maritime trade communities, the biggest and most influential one being the Fujian Trade Society. From the Tang period (618–907), and especially in the Ming (1368–1644) and Qing (1644–1911) periods, merchants of the Fujian Trade Society have left their mark on coastal ports, river ports, and canal docks. Their domestic trade consisted mainly of official and private agricultural products, minerals, and handicrafts, while their overseas business consisted of traditional Chinese goods such as silk, porcelain, tea, and spices. To safeguard their maritime journeys to ports in China and abroad, maritime traders of the Fujian Trade Society worshiped the goddess Mazu, or Tianhou (the title that many emperors conferred on this deity). They also built temples to Mazu wherever they traveled. Such temples served not only as places of ritual but also as provincial guildhalls where the traders could gather.

Zheng He (1371–1433), the famous diplomat-navigator of the Ming court, led seven maritime journeys to what people then called the West Sea. Over a period of twenty-eight years (1405–1433), his fleets, with crews and passengers totaling more than 28,000 people, reached Southeast Asia, India, West Asia, and even some parts of Europe, where they sought friendly ties with foreign countries and traded exquisite Chinese curios, farm products, and handicrafts. At this time China's maritime technology and seafaring were more advanced than the West's. Following Zheng He's death, successive emperors abandoned such voyages and turned on a centuries-long path of isolation. Such great navigations owed their success to the existence of large-scale maritime trade communities, including maritime unions and sailors.

**Maritime communities of pirates.** Pirates, usually called sea thieves (*haizei*) in traditional China, consisted of three main types. One was the armed forces who attacked and looted merchant fleets and coastal towns, such as the Wokou (referring to the armed sea robbers in the early Ming period, composed mainly of Japanese pirates and later including Chinese pirates). These pirates long harassed the nearby seas and coastal areas of China, mainly in the Ming period (1368–1644), and caused great damage and much threat to the defense of those coastal areas. They thus influenced the Ming emperors' maritime policies and even the course of China's development.

Another type of pirate group was made up of civilians from coastal areas who rebelled against the government, including the great maritime uprising at the end of the Eastern Jin period (317–420) led by Sun En and Lu Xun, considered among the first Chinese pirates. There were many similar rebellions throughout history. Finally, there were smugglers during the maritime-prohibition period in the Ming and Qing (1644–1911) periods. Based mostly in the southeast coastal areas of China, the pirates consisted mainly of bands from Guangdong, Fujian, Jiangsu, and Zhejiang. Some of their leaders became notorious, among them Wang Zhi, Xu Hai, Wu Ping, Lin Feng, and Zheng Zhilong. These pirate communities helped promote illicit foreign trade. Their maritime activities and smuggling facilitated Chinese immigration, mainly from the coastal regions, and led to the establishment of "Chinatowns" in almost every corner of the world.

**Danmin maritime communities.** The Danmin are people who live on the sea and rivers mainly in Guangdong, Guangxi, and Fujian provinces in south and southeast China. Historical records about them appear from the Wei (220–256), Jin (266–316), and Northern (386–581) and Southern (420–589) periods, when they were called Jiaoren, Youtingzi, Baishuilang, and later Danmin. They lived on boats and had no fixed abodes, never married

inland people, and lived off fishing and pearl gathering. As early as the Jin period, there were more than 50,000 Danmin households, making for a population total of about 700,000. They originated mainly from the Baiyue ethnic group in the southeast coastal areas of China, and some of them belonged to the Kejia ethnic group, a group whose ancestors moved to the south from the northern interior areas of China because of war and social instability in earlier periods. With the modernization of the Chinese economy, the number of Danmin has been decreasing, and their distinctive features have also been diluted.

## Modern Chinese Maritime Communities

With the modernization of the Chinese economy, especially since the 1980s, Chinese maritime communities have developed in two directions. One trend is to develop modern shipping, shipbuilding, coastal industries, and maritime trade both at home and abroad. Such development occurs mainly in the major modern port cities, such as Hong Kong, Shenzhen, Guangzhou, Shanghai, Qingdao, Tianjin, and Dalian. Many of these cities are now some of the world's largest ports. In these port cities one can notice the internationalization of the population, economy, and culture.

Another trend in Chinese maritime communities is the transition to modern fishing–that is, deep-sea and offshore fishing. Inshore fishing resources have been seriously affected by pollution and overfishing, and offshore fish cultivation has also taken its toll on the fisherman's livelihood. Fishing communities have also been affected by the modern industrialization and urbanization of most coastal cities. As a result, traditional modes of fishing have fallen by the wayside, and Chinese fishermen and islanders have been forced to change their lifestyles. Yet they have limited capacity to take up deep-sea fishing. Fortunately, the Chinese central government and local governments of coastal provinces are aware of these problems and are working to improve the livelihood of fishing communities.

[*See also* Aquaculture, Social History of; Fishing; *and* Shipping Companies, *subentry on* Chinese River Trades.]

## Bibliography

Deng, Gang. *Chinese Maritime Activities and Socioeconomic Development, c. 2100 B.C.–1900 A.D.* Westport, Conn.: Greenwood Press, 1997.
Levathes, Louise E. *When China Ruled the Sea: The Treasure Fleet of the Dragon Throne, 1405–1433.* New York: Simon and Schuster, 1994.

Pulleyblank, Edwin G. "The Chinese and Their Neighbors in Pre-historic and Early Historic Times." In *The Origins of Chinese Civilization*, edited by David N. Keightley. Berkeley and Los Angeles: University of California Press, 1983.

Qu Jinliang. *Haiyang wenhua yu shehui* (Maritime Culture and Maritime Societies). Qingdao, China: Haiyang Daxue Chubanshe, 2003.

Schafer, Edward H. *The Golden Peaches of Samarkand*. Berkeley: University of California Press, 1963.

Sun Guangqi. *Zhongguo gudai hanghai shi* (A History of Chinese Traditional Maritime Transportation). Beijing, China: Haiyang Chubanshe, 1989.

Wang Rongguo. *Haiyang shenling: Zhongguo haishen xinyang yu shehui jingji* (The Sea Gods and Spirits: Chinese Maritime Beliefs and Socioeconomic Life). Nanchang, China: Jiangxi Gaoxiao Chubanshe, 2003.

Xu Xiaowang. *Mazu de zimin* (The Descendents of the Goddess Mazu). Shanghai, China: Xuelin Chubanshe, 1999.

Ye Dabing, ed. *The Selected Papers on Maritime Folklore of Chinese Islanders*. Wenzhou, China: Wenzhou Folklore Society, 1989.

Zheng Guangnan. *Zhongguo haidao shi* (A History of Chinese Pirates). Shanghai, China: Huadong Ligong Daxue Chubanshe, 1998.

QU JINLIANG

# Oceania

Barry Cunliffe, in his book *Facing the Ocean* (2001), has called islands in-between spaces, "neither entirely of the land nor of the sea" (p. 31). But in Oceania, in the heart of the Pacific, islands are the only land. Indigenous Oceanians traditionally viewed the sea between them not as a barrier but as a network of sailing routes that linked inhabited landfalls. Tongan scholar Epeli Hau`ofa calls his region "a sea of islands," emphasizing this web of interconnections rather than what appears to continental observers as insignificant dots scattered across the world's largest ocean. Both authors recognize that islands need the sea, for marine resources and foreland ties. Unlike the Mediterranean Sea or the Indian Ocean, which have been cross-crossed by trade and power struggles for millennia, the Pacific, which covers one-third of the globe, was long divided by sheer size into segmented maritime zones. The Asian segment was the most active historically, and island southeast Asia provided an ancient gateway to Oceania, a realm of twenty-five thousand islands in the autonomous center of the Pacific.

## Early Migrations and Navigation

Pacific island geography is conventionally divided into three subregions with Greek-derived labels: in the southwest, Melanesia (islands of "dark-skinned" inhabitants); in the northwest, Micronesia (mostly small atolls); and in the east, Polynesia ("many islands"), roughly demarcated by the triangle of Hawai'i, Easter Island (Rapanui), and New Zealand (Aotearoa). The ancestors of the Melanesians began to travel from southeast Asia into Oceania during the last ice age, perhaps fifty thousand years ago, when the sea level was as much as three hundred feet lower than it is today. Hunting and gathering migrants could thus walk much of the way, but they needed nautical skills in parts of eastern Indonesia, where the continental shelves did not provide ancient land bridges, and, even more importantly, beyond New Guinea. By thirty thousand years ago, when sea levels were beginning to rise, Melanesians inhabited more than 150 sites across a wide area of islands and coasts in "near" Oceania, leading archaeologist Patrick Kirch to call their dispersal "the earliest purposive voyaging in the history of humankind" (p. 67).

The Bismarck and Solomon islands east of New Guinea were a "voyaging corridor," where early round-trip raft or canoe journeys not only populated intervisible islands but also established ongoing exchange networks for such items as obsidian, which was used for toolmaking, and prestige handicrafts. Skilled boatbuilders and navigators competed with agriculturalists, priests, warriors, and traders in a dynamic world where leadership was generally earned, not a birthright. By nine thousand years ago, the inhabitants of the interior of New Guinea irrigated root crops, such as taro and yams, raised pigs and chickens, and traded with coastal peoples for shell valuables and religious artifacts. Meanwhile, the Siassi of New Britain exchanged products from their own small island for what their neighbors had, sailing from coast to coast and bartering one item for another until they had what they needed, such as sacrificial pigs for ceremonies. Langalanga used strings of shells as currency, and Motuans developed a pidgin language for communication. In the Trobriands, sailors followed the "kula ring" circuit, exchanging shell necklaces for armbands to build partnerships for peaceful trade among linguistically diverse peoples.

The second major wave of voyagers into Oceania came after the ice-age glaciers had melted, in the second millennium B.C.E. They spoke Austronesian ("southern islander") languages that originated among the coastal peoples of China and aboriginal Taiwan and today cover all of Oceania except for some Papuan speakers in Melanesia. One branch of Austronesians sailed west to Madagascar, while another went the opposite way to Easter Island, making this language family the most widely dispersed before 1500 C.E. Its able mariners began voyaging eastward from

**A Native House in Oceania.** This photograph was taken on the island of Yap in October 1971. Dr. James P. McVey, NOAA Sea Grant Program

southeast Asia in 1600 B.C.E., reaching the limits of Polynesia between 300 and 800 C.E. They navigated by celestial bodies, winds, and currents in outriggered or double-hulled sailing canoes, bringing along a cultural kit of horticulture, domestic animals, and fishing methods. Archaeologists have traced the southern stream of these migrants using a style of decorated pottery called Lapita, whose oldest sites near New Guinea date to about thirty-five hundred years ago and whose most recent sites in Samoa and Tonga date to a half millennium or more later (Kirch, pp. 94–95).

The ancestors of Micronesians formed the northern branch of this eastward migration, arriving in their western archipelagoes as early as thirty-six hundred years ago. An atoll is a ring of coral sand left around a lagoon after a volcano has subsided into the sea, and the narrow freshwater lens of an atoll does not support much vegetation apart from coconut palms. Because such ecosystems are so fragile, atoll dwellers had to rely on marine resources and network with other islands, so they kept their canoe-building and navigation skills longer than elsewhere in Oceania. Yet many volcanic islands in Micronesia are not small at all, such as Yap, which had a social caste system and far-flung tributary networks. From Palau, voyagers brought large coral disks that Yapese used as money, while the *sawei* system linked Yap with more than a dozen atolls

to the east, whose annual fleets exchanged their resources for high island products and also support in times of natural disaster, such as tidal waves or typhoons. On Guam, tenant farmers in the interior were ruled chiefly by clans on the coast, who built impressive houses on stone pillars. On another large island, Pohnpei, invaders in 1100 C.E. built ninety-two artificial islets off the southeast shore and erected a stone capital called Nan Madol, whose priests ruled Pohnpei for five hundred years.

Polynesia, the largest of the three subregions, required voyages across open sea of up to two thousand miles. Oral traditions speak of famous fishermen who voyaged for months far out to sea and found uninhabited islands, then returned home to bring their families. In other cases, new arrivals on inhabited islands had to earn acceptance by serving the host societies. In Hawai'i the population rose after first settlement in about 500 C.E. and competitive warfare increased, so chiefs organized *ahupua'a*, or land-use slices from the mountains to the sea that allowed inhabitants access to every ecosystem. People built artificial fish ponds along the shore and elaborate terraces for irrigated taro patches. The colder climate of New Zealand forced the first Maori to adapt their tropical cultural kit after their arrival in 800 C.E. Taro did not succeed but *kumara* (sweet potato) did, and people learned to create winter clothing and shelter. As clans descended from legendary canoe voyagers spread out over the land, they buried the umbilical cords of the newborn, rooting their identity in the new soil. Easter Island is famous for its huge clan ancestor statues, but apparently cutting down trees for farming and for moving the statues into place caused an ecological crisis and civil war that led rival groups to topple many of the statues by about 1500 C.E.

Voyaging continued in much of Polynesia for many centuries. From Ra`iatea in the Society Islands, the Arioi missionaries spread the worship of `Oro, traveling in flower-decorated fleets that brought theatrical entertainment and fertility feasts to distant coves. Samoa, Tonga, and Fiji regularly exchanged prestige goods, such as Samoan fine mats and elaborate tattooing, Tongan bark cloth and whale teeth, and Fijian canoe wood and red bird feathers. Chiefly families from the three archipelagoes intermarried to form political alliances, and junior lineages of the Tongan monarchy sent out voyagers to establish themselves on islands such as Niue, Tuvalu, Wallis (Uvea), and Futuna. They created tribute relations with Tongatapu, where the annual procession of the yam festival passed through a huge coral arch into the royal compound. Samoa and Tonga regarded their divine monarchs as offspring of the sea god Tangaloa. In fact, Pacific islanders believed that the physical world emerged from powerful spiritual forces that spawned the heavens, realms of the dead, islands, and the sea. Hawai'ians, for example, say that a sky father and earth mother gave birth to their islands, and that the life-giving taro plant was an older sibling of the first human, suggesting a genealogical relationship with the land.

Outside scholars once debated whether Oceanians simply drifted on the currents to new islands or engaged in deliberate voyages of discovery. In 1947 Thor Heyerdahl built the *Kon Tiki*, a replica of a Peruvian balsa sailing raft, and rode the prevailing current to the Tuamotu atolls east of Tahiti. His daring experiment proved that such a voyage was possible, and might explain the basis for Inca legends about sailing to the west and back. Most scholars rejected Heyerdahl's claims that the ancestors of the Polynesians came from America, because linguistic and archaeological evidence points to southeast Asia as the ancient homeland of Pacific voyagers. Yet the sweet potato was domesticated in South America, and both its cultivation and its Quechua Indian name *kumar* were adopted by Polynesians before European contact. Moreover, new DNA studies suggest that Polynesians carry not only Melanesian but also distinctively Native American genotypes, implying interaction with the Americas. Clear evidence is lacking, but

contact may have occurred between eastern Polynesians in the Marquesas-Societies area and Native Americans of Ecuador; scholars disagree about who contacted whom.

In 1976, supporters of Oceanian navigation skills built *Hokule`a*, a replica of a double-hulled Polynesian voyaging canoe, and sailed it from Hawai'i to Tahiti, a distance of more than two thousand miles, without using modern instruments. The navigator, a Micronesian named Mau Piailug, used the sun, stars, winds, and currents to find his way, sailing at an angle to the prevailing easterlies. Since that epic reenactment, *Hokule`a* has voyaged from Hawai'i to New Zealand and Easter Island and back, and Oceanians have built other replicas to celebrate their ancient seafaring heritage. Traditionally Oceanians claimed the sea as territory. In matrilineal Micronesia it was the realm of male sailors, who built canoe houses on the shore, while women owned the land and reefs. Melanesians gave use rights to portions of lagoons or reefs to certain families, who might also be restricted to specific fish species and fishing techniques. Hawai'ians divided the sea into many different belts extending outward from the land, from the beach to the reef shallows to the deep ocean beyond the reef, and also had many terms for the moods of the sea and the tides. Indigenous Pacific navigators knew not only pathfinding skills but also special religious rituals to safeguard the journey, and ongoing interactions linked the region.

## European Exploration and Interaction

In 1521 Ferdinand Magellan survived stormy Cape Horn and, in relief, misnamed the Pacific. Not only was his expedition the first to cross that ocean, but it did so without seeing any inhabited island until it reached Guam. The first encounter with native people turned tragic, because the Spaniards were starving and ill, and curious Chamorros came out to the ships and explored them eagerly until the Europeans lost patience and starting shooting to defend their property. Magellan called Guam the Island of Thieves and sailed on to the Philippines, where he died in another encounter ashore. By the late sixteenth century Spanish treasure galleons began to link Manila and Mexico with the first annual transpacific voyages. Expeditions from Spanish Peru had more tragic encounters in the Marquesas and parts of Melanesia while searching for ancient King Solomon's gold—hence the name Solomon Islands. Other European countries sent privateers to intercept the Spanish galleons over the next two hundred years, just as they did in the Atlantic, but maritime contact with indigenous peoples remained fleeting. In the early 1700s, for example, Alexander Selkirk spent four years alone in the Juan Fernandez islands off Chile and became the basis for Robinson Crusoe. An exception was Guam, which the Spanish colonized from 1668 on as a port of call on the galleon route; they nearly depopulated the Marianas archipelago through conquest and epidemic diseases.

Early European exploration of the Pacific was limited by the huge distances and the need for regular supplies of fresh water and food. In 1763, however, peace between England and France generated a new era of scientific exploration by naval expeditions. By 1767 the British had found Tahiti, which became a crucial provisioning port. After initial violence, Tahitian chiefs such as the Pomare family welcomed explorers and traders with food and women, thus generating the touristic myth of paradise in the South Seas. The British also founded a convict colony in Australia in 1788, which established regular commerce with indigenous peoples across the region. Ships buying Tahitian pork to feed the convicts soon found sandalwood in the Marquesas and Fiji, and fur traders circulating between northwest America and China also found sandalwood in Hawai'i. Europeans and Americans sold island bêche-de-mer (sea slug) and tortoiseshell to China, and some foreign sailors left their vessels to become beachcombers who served as cultural brokers between ship and shore. In the late 1700s whaling and seal-hunting began in the waters around Australia and New Zealand and spread to the Japan grounds by the 1820s. New England whalers made annual circuits around the region, wintering along the Line (equator) and trading for provisions with islanders, whom they often recruited as crew. By the 1860s the American Civil War caused a boom in cotton plantations in Australia and Fiji, and after the war planters shifted to sugar, copra, and coffee. The search for local labor led to a strategy of removing Oceanians from their home islands to work in Fiji, Samoa, and Queensland, where they would be at the mercy of their employers until their contracts expired. European and American missionaries also landed on the islands, and they often criticized abuses in the labor trade. Unwelcome microbes also disembarked and soon decimated epidemiologically vulnerable native populations, as they did in the Americas.

## Colonization and Decolonization

In the early phase of interaction with the world economy, some chiefs became more powerful and acquired Western-style schooners and whaleboats. But a frontier of debts spread across Oceania, accompanied by threats from foreign gunboats by the 1840s. Planters and traders, for example, fueled civil wars in Samoa by trading guns for land, and in 1893 they overthrew the Hawaiian monarchy. Settlers alienated indigenous lands in Australia, New Zealand, and New Caledonia, and Asian indentured laborers eventually outnumbered the native people in Fiji and Hawai'i. Islanders provided labor on ships, on plantations, in guano-collecting gangs on central Pacific atolls, and in pearl diving and bêche-de-mer gathering. Perhaps 150,000 "kanakas" left their homelands to work, and whole archipelagoes were annexed as recruiting zones (e.g., Vanuatu, Solomon Islands). Some left voluntarily on contract, but others were "blackbirded" (kidnapped); many never came back, but those who did, or who landed on strange islands after leaving their ships, acted as intermediaries between island leaders and outsiders. The colonization of Oceania intensified by the mid-nineteenth century, when steamship routes began to criss-cross the Pacific. Britain acquired a dozen colonies, and France, Germany, the United States, and Chile (Easter Island) joined the worldwide scramble for "unclaimed" real estate. The Spanish-American War of 1898 led to U.S. annexation of the Philippines, Guam, and Hawai'i, and in 1899 the United States and Germany partitioned Samoa.

Two world wars and a Cold War would bring new maritime tensions to Oceania. In World War I, the German navy could not prevent the seizure of its colonies by Japan (Micronesia), Australia (New Guinea), and New Zealand (western Samoa) as League of Nations mandates. But these transfers caused minimal disruption among indigenous peoples, apart from having to learn new colonial languages. World War II, however, was fought over a wide area in the western Pacific, and islanders were caught in naval and amphibious battle zones. Many died from bombing raids and dislocation, while others fought alongside their allies of the moment. Oceanians also gained new material tastes, such as for canned fish and meats, new political and religious ideas, and better wages at military bases. But United Nations–backed postwar decolonization was complicated by the strategic competition of the Cold War. Many islanders, for example, suffered from exposure to nuclear testing in the Marshall Islands by the United States, in Australia by the British, and in the Tuamotus by France. In addition, self-government in Micronesia was limited by U.S. ambitions to deny the area to the Soviet bloc, and the ANZUS defense treaty among Australia, New Zealand, and the United States effectively circumscribed indigenous sovereignty movements. In 1985 self-governing island countries in the Pacific Forum signed the

South Pacific Nuclear-Free Zone treaty, but it does not ban visits by nuclear-powered and armed vessels, and Britain, France, and the United States did not sign until 1996.

In the 1980s, when the U.N. Law of the Sea allocated two-hundred-mile Exclusive Economic Zones to maritime countries, the tiny dots of Oceania suddenly loomed larger in importance. The Pacific Forum negotiates as a bloc with foreign fishing companies, and it operates its own shipping line, which is a blessing for out-of-the-way islands. The atoll nations of Kiribati and Tuvalu opened maritime training centers to send young sailors abroad on foreign vessels. Ironically, global warming trends threaten the future existence of such countries because of gradual sea-level rise. Talk of a Pacific Century usually emphasizes the dynamic export economies of east Asia and the rise in transpacific trade, rather than Oceania, which is often portrayed as overpopulated and resource-poor. But the inner Pacific remains a "sea of islands" with many links. Not only do outside countries invest in and provide development assistance for Oceania, but new streams of outmigration for education and employment, in Hau`ofa's view, simply extend its opportunistic voyaging frontiers to industrial countries on the anglophone Pacific rim. Contemporary voyagers send or carry remittances of money and gifts to their families back home, and receive from them handicrafts and foods, including coolers of fish—now most often by air.

[*See also* Magellan, Ferdinand, *and* Oceania.]

## Bibliography

Beaglehole, J. C. *The Exploration of the Pacific.* 3d ed. Stanford, Calif.: Stanford University Press, 1966. Based on primary sources, the standard work on early European explorers.

Buck, Peter. *Vikings of the Pacific.* Chicago: University of Chicago Press, 1959. Originally published in 1938, its wealth of oral traditions on seafaring are still useful.

Chappell, David. *Double Ghosts: Oceanian Voyagers on Euroamerican Ships.* Armonk, New York: M. E. Sharpe, 1997. Examines real-life "Queequegs" from 1522 to 1887.

Denoon, Donald, et al. *The Cambridge History of the Pacific Islanders.* Cambridge, U.K., and New York: Cambridge University Press, 1997. The most recent and comprehensive historical overview.

Firth, Stewart. *Nuclear Playground.* Honolulu: University of Hawai'i Press, 1987. Shows well the American, French, and British nuclear testing legacy in the region.

Hau`ofa, Epeli. "Our Sea of Islands." *The Contemporary Pacific* 6, no. 1 (1994): 148–161. A much-discussed indigenous attempt to offer a more holistic vision of the region.

Howe, K. R. *Where the Waves Fall: A New South Sea Islands History from First Settlement to Colonial Rule.* Honolulu: University of Hawai'i Press, 1984. A very useful overview, except of Micronesia, to the late nineteenth century.

Hviding, Edvard. *Guardians of Marovo Lagoon: Practice, Place, and Politics in Maritime Melanesia.* Honolulu: University of Hawai'i Press, 1996. A rare study of the relationship between Melanesians and the sea, put in contemporary context.

Irwin, Geoffrey. *The Prehistoric Exploration and Colonisation of the Pacific.* Cambridge, U.K., and New York: Cambridge University Press, 1992. A scholarly study of seafaring and navigation.

Kirch, Patrick Vinton. *On the Road of the Winds: An Archaeological History of the Pacific Islands before European Contact.* Berkeley: University of California Press, 2000. The most up-to-date and reliable synthesis of the complex prehistory of the region.

Oliver, Douglas L. *Oceania.* 2 vols. Honolulu: University of Hawai'i Press, 1989. An anthropological overview, with an excellent chapter on exchange systems.

Steinberg, Philip E. *The Social Construction of the Ocean.* Cambridge, U.K., and New York: Cambridge University Press, 2001. Portrays Oceania as one of three types of maritime hegemony.

DAVID CHAPPELL

# Seafarers Ashore

A seaman's life ashore was characterized in large measure by two types of experience—that available in his home port and that available in his ports of call. Admittedly many seafarers—especially single, long-serving ones in the nineteenth century—had no home; others claimed a residence far from those major ports where the dangers ashore could be as great as those afloat. The seamen who worked out of the smaller hunting and coasting ports usually were better integrated into the fabric of local society than those in complex ports in the age of sail where business, concentrated in the oceangoing trades, attracted men of many nationalities, including footloose adventurers uninterested, at least in their younger years, in conventional, settled family life. The rhythms of the hunting, coasting, and deep-sea trading communities and the seafarers who came ashore in them have been the subject of nineteenth- and twentieth-century novels, sea shanties dating from as early as the age of European discovery, reminiscences of both career and casual sailors, and scholarly publications in the fields of social, labor, gender, and maritime history.

## Hunting Communities

Seafarers' families have been best studied in hunting communities, especially those involved in fishing and whaling. The economic activity of the men at sea created work and

**Seafarers Ashore.** *Sailor and Girl,* watercolor by Otto Dix (1891–1969), illustrates a couple in a brothel. The original is in the Otto Dix Foundation, Vaduz, Liechtenstein. ERICH LESSING / ART RESOURCE, NY / © 2007 ARTISTS RIGHTS SOCIETY (ARS), NEW YORK / VG BILD-KUNST, BONN

women in the fisheries as net menders, line knitters, sellers, refurbishers of seamen's outfits, and managers during their husbands' absences at sea. In whaling ports in colonial America, wives undertook significant business responsibilities because of their husbands' expeditions to the whaling grounds, which could be several years in duration. J. Hector St. John de Crèvecoeur (*Letters from an American Farmer,* 1782; reprint, New York: Penguin Classics, 1981, p. 157) observed that in Nantucket in the 1760s whalers' "wives in their absence are necessarily obliged to transact business, to settle accounts, and, in short, to rule and provide for their families…. The men at their return, weary with the fatigues of the sea … cheerfully give their consent to every transaction that has happened during their absence, and all is joy and peace." By the mid-nineteenth century, captains of whaling vessels in the tightly knit society of American whaling ports expected, not always successfully, the managing shipowners to look out for their wives and families during their long absences. One reason was the irregularity of advance payments out of the anticipated share (or lay) to dependents while the breadwinner was at sea, even in the case of the older, reliable career whalemen who most needed support for their families. For women, in the period when whaling was at its height, the Victorian notion of separate spheres, which assigned them to a dependent, domestic role, was largely rhetorical in circumstances where they continued to be the family's financial managers, frequent supporters, and, through their handiwork and housekeeping, the reproducers of their husbands' labor.

## Coasting Communities

The second category of port, which engaged in coastal trades, produced seafarers who often combined seafaring with other employment and therefore remained well integrated in their local communities. In the nineteenth century many were married men whose absences from home were short enough—one or two months—to enable them to maintain a reasonable semblance of family life. The crews of coasting vessels were often small—as were the vessels—and if not kith and kin, the sailors were well known to each other. When young Benjamin Doane coasted as cook and foremast hand on the trading schooner *Two Sons* in western Nova Scotia in 1839, he boarded between voyages in the south-shore port of Barrington, at the home of either the captain or the captain's business partner, the mate (*Following the Sea,* Halifax: Nimbus Publishing/ Nova Scotia Museum, 1987). Since year-round specialization was not economically feasible, such seafarers also

added responsibilities for their families, especially their wives. In many fishing ports families processed the fish brought home by the husbands, sons, and fathers. The women in the Newfoundland fishing communities of Carbonear and Harbour Grace constituted the shore crew, and in the fishing season they unloaded the fish as the vessels arrived, working late into the night to make marketable fish, a procedure that consisted of splitting the cod, salting it, and placing it on the flakes—wooden stages—to dry. When the fish were dry, they stacked them for transport to the fish merchants. By the nineteenth century, payment by the fish merchant was through the truck system, which tended to perpetuate the indebtedness of fishing families. This was a family economy, not a wage economy: the mercantile hierarchy could discipline family members to perform effectively in this grueling trade without the fear of wage-law jurisdiction. Fishing communities elsewhere—in the North Sea in the early twentieth century, for example—provide other indications of the complementary employment of shore

tended to perform the dockside functions of loading and unloading their vessels, although sailors also did this work in many complex ports before the organization of dockers' unions. In the off seasons sailors left the sea and pursued other employment in farming, timbering, fishing, and the like. Seasonality in the age of sail also meant that in shipbuilding ports they joined the construction crews during periods when sea voyages were too risky. Seafaring men in European and North American ports often owned shares in the vessels, and some could, as a result of successful service and family connections, look forward to making the transition from forecastle to cabin. Coasting took on a different flavor for the indigenous people of West Africa, where Kru seamen were often discharged from British vessels along the coast, far from home. Undaunted, they took their pay in goods, which they proceeded to trade in the villages they visited as they returned by canoe to their place of residence. They, too, engaged in supplementary employment. Coasting seafarers were truly "jacks of all trades."

## "Sailortown": Deep-Sea Trading Communities

By far the most significant maritime communities in terms of the number of seafarers going ashore and the range of services available were international ports of call, where the majority of seamen were transients, not residents. Complex, deep-sea ports could be found in every state and territory that developed a merchant seafaring tradition. During the ages of sail and steam—from the voyages of discovery to World War II—each urbanizing port produced a "sailortown," known to nineteenth-century British seafarers as "Fiddler's Green" (paradise)—replacing the less organized "beach"—to cater to every need and desire of the seafarer. First coined by author Cicely Fox Smith in the 1920s with respect to London, the term "sailortown" was adopted by later popularizers of seafaring life, most notably old salt and shantyman Stan Hugill (*Sailortown*, London: Routledge and Kegan Paul; New York: Dutton, 1967), and entered the academic lexicon in the 1970s when historians, anthropologists, sociologists, and folklorists began to explore the social history of port life.

Many of the descriptions of sailortown have come down to us through folklore, both in story and song. In his lurid but also nostalgic account, Hugill portrayed amiable, fun-loving "Sailor John" as subject to excessive but also dangerous gratification, which meant that he was frequently drugged, robbed, beaten, diseased, or murdered in the dives and haunts of the world's ports. Although Jack's vulnerability and gullibility graphically emerge from the

Hugill interpretation, it is really the seaman's sense of adventure and stereotypical masculinity that the reader is expected to appreciate. The women workers of the ports who supplied the sexual partners and prurient entertainment for Jack are described dismissively as whores, harlots, hags, harpies, harridans, tarts, soiled wares, courtesans, nymphets, morons, and so on. Only those women who supplemented their boardinghouse keeping with "crimping" (employment brokering for sailors) merited Hugill's admiration.

As for individual ports, whether north, south, east, or west, in Hugill's largely Victorian-era tour of the world's ocean communities, all sailortowns shared many similar features relating to location near the waterfront, provision of services, and questionable practices. By the second half of the nineteenth century Liverpool's sailortown was described as a hotbed of sailor kidnapping for unsolicited voyages, known as "shanghaiing," where its most famous boardinghouse master and crimp, Paddy West, was rumored to have shanghaiied his own son. In Henry Mayhew's London of the 1850s the major sailortown activity was focused on the Ratcliffe Highway in the parishes of Saint George, Wapping, and Shadwell. Here could be found the usual contrasts of sailortown life such as a sailors' home, established as a refuge as early as 1835, cheek by jowl with the far more popular sailors' dance halls, which specialized in child prostitution. Antwerp was highly prized for its tailor shops, a service that reminds us of the importance of Jack's time ashore for the purposes of securing his sea outfit. Genoa's prostitutes liked to pose in the cemetery for photographs with their sailormen, a quirk that captures the occasional individuality of a port's culture.

Across the Atlantic, the crimps of New York were adept at deception in the shipping of unsuspecting men and specialized in making deals with incoming masters to facilitate the turnover of crews. Ashore men had to be careful to avoid being doped and robbed in the taverns or brothels. In Boston's sailortown, one of the most successful counterweights to the crimps was Father E. P. Taylor, a Methodist preacher and former sailor himself, whose seamen's bethel (God's house) was frequently attacked, a sure sign that his mission was a threat to customary practices. In New Orleans, some sailors aspired to the delights of the sporting houses of Storyville, which were beyond the financial reach of most of their mates. The crimping fraternities were also engaged in a lively sailor trade on the West Coast where the gold rushes produced the initial shortages. The highest "blood money" a captain ever paid for a crewman was alleged to be in Vancouver. Farther south San Francisco's

"Barbary Coast," noted for its excesses, was the sailortown par excellence. Legend has it that Shanghai Brown, a Norwegian crimp in San Francisco, shipped his dead father as a drunk seaman in order to avoid paying the cost of his funeral.

Further afield, sailors enjoyed pornography in Buenos Aires, bowling alleys in Honolulu, punks (homosexuals) in Melbourne, and massage parlors in Shanghai. In trades that encouraged discharge abroad because of the lack of return cargoes, ex-sailors sometimes entered the local workforce. In Calcutta (Kolkata), for example, it was not unusual for sailors on vessels engaged in the case-oil trade to become coolie drivers or policemen.

## Opportunity and Danger

In one way or another most ports featured in Hugill's account suggest a combination of opportunity and danger for visiting seamen. Some of the opportunities related to family. Not all sailors were rakes or had a girl in every port. Seafaring contributed to family formation for hard-pressed minority groups such as African American seamen in the first half of the nineteenth century. Some were able to earn enough to support wives and children, a rare occurrence for free blacks in antebellum America. In British ports dockside daughters began to marry seamen of color, a form of immigration for British colonial subjects. Their offspring contributed to the creation of the interracial population of the major ports of the United Kingdom. As knowledgeable local women, the white, black, or interracial wives of colonial seamen were in a better position than their newly arrived husbands to organize their life ashore.

Some of the dangerous characteristics of sailortown persisted into the age of steam. A seaman's essay included in a collection compiled by longtime Marine Society president Ronald Hope provides an apt illustration (*The Seaman's World: Merchant Seamen's Reminiscences*, London: Harrap, in association with The Marine Society, 1982). J. N. Dickinson of the SS *Marbelton* went ashore during carnival time in 1930s Buenos Aires. When he was returning to his vessel along a dark, deserted road after enjoying his pints of beer and the festive music, he fell in with two other sailors, a Maltese and a Swede, who proceeded to attack and rob him. The assailants were arrested shortly thereafter and, to his consternation, so was the victim. All three were charged with drunkenness, fighting, and disturbing the peace, and were imprisoned. Fortunately for the Englishman, who had no luck convincing the police that he should be allowed an interpreter, the Spanish-speaking Maltese sailor, who had a wife and children in Cardiff, decided to befriend him and return some of his property. After two days and a session at stable cleaning with other weekend drunks, the two were released and enjoyed breakfast together in recognition of "the brotherhood of the sea," leaving behind the beachcombing Swede, a man with a local criminal record, to serve a jail sentence.

While it might be unwise to generalize about the nature of port life around the globe and across the centuries, some common characteristics of seafarers' port experiences can be identified within specific historical contexts. Scholars of the eighteenth century have concentrated on the impact of British naval impressment on the development of both work and politics in port society of the Atlantic world. On land, seafarers often led or joined popular protests in the streets and thereby demonstrated examples of preindustrial workers' solidarity against repressive or unjust state policies. The widespread recruitment for service at sea of nonwhites unleashed a series of tensions that resulted in the nineteenth century in the passage of laws in the slave states of the United States to prevent free and foreign black seamen from going ashore and mingling with enslaved or free African Americans. If they did disembark, they were likely to spend their shore leave in jail. In another part of the British world at the end of the eighteenth century, vessels in Asia bound for the Atlantic started to recruit Indian seamen, known as lascars, whose sojourns in London came to symbolize the inequities and discrimination colonial seamen of color experienced on foreign shores.

## Reception Ashore

By the mid-nineteenth century, the responses of port society to the transient seafarer focused on his consumption patterns, his heathenism, his welfare, and his labor market potential. All these elements are central to an understanding of sailortown. Sailors' tastes ashore were not unlike those of the present-day tourist. They ranged across the whole spectrum of personal services: accommodation, food and drink, clothing and souvenirs (often including tattoos in the sailor's case), and leisure activities. For sailors who did not live on board ship while in port, lodging could be found in specialized sailors' boardinghouses often run by former sailors or sailors' wives. In New York in 1846 only one hundred of the twenty-two hundred African American seamen who sailed out of that port lived with their families; the rest were transient. Of these, four hundred boarded in a temperance home for black sailors (the Coloured Sailors' Boarding House), one hundred stayed in the notorious Five Points district, and sixteen hundred stayed in sixteen other nontemperance boardinghouses for black sailors. Boardinghouse keepers like Liverpool's Paddy West, whose influence over sailors, particularly in circumstances where they were also employment agents, was excessive, were dubbed boarding "masters." If the sailor was a stranger to the port, he was often dependent on his boardinghouse master for advice on where to buy goods and services if they were not directly available in the house itself. Even sailors who lived in the forecastle during port calls were released from their shipboard duties from time to time. In the mid-nineteenth century, the transient casual sailor, especially if he was young or dissolute, was unlikely to spend his shore leave (known as liberty in the American service) or bouts of unemployment in refined pursuits. His concerns were far more basic and reflected the urges that he felt when he was released from the prisonlike environment of the forecastle or later, with respect to the "black gang" on steamers, from the hellish dungeon of the stokehold.

As was the case with most working-class men in the western tradition, the tavern was a major attraction not only for imbibing alcohol, which was seldom available at sea, but also as a source of news and information about home, shipping opportunities, and local customs. There the seafarer made new friends and found sexual partners. Prostitution was a sine qua non of communities that catered to visiting male workers. As in military ports, there is evidence that some women resorted to a form of serial monogamy—faithfulness to one sailor for the duration of his visit—rather than having the multiple partners common among the more commercialized sex workers. Since occasional prostitution was a form of economic survival for poor women everywhere, it seems likely that it was a resort of sailors' young wives, left for long periods on their own without the support of their husbands' wages, as well as sailors' widows, two groups identified by William W. Sanger in his 1858 study of prostitution in New York, *The History of Prostitution*. Evidence from British seaports pertaining to the operation of the Contagious Diseases Acts (1864–1886), which were designed to control venereal diseases by mandating regular medical examinations of prostitutes, revealed that women identified as sailors' prostitutes could be either seafarers' port "wives," that is, women who were their exclusive wives only while they were in port, or their legal wives who resorted to casual prostitution in their absence in order to make ends meet.

## Seamen's Missions and Homes

Within every seafaring population there were both family and nonfamily men who had no interest in dissipation. For them, as well as the sailor boys they hoped to rescue from the clutches of the "land sharks," nineteenth-century reformers provided alternatives to the usual dens of sailortown. The origins of the "alternative" facilities in the British Empire, the United States, and Scandinavia can be traced to a number of early nineteenth-century influences including an evangelical awakening in the Royal Navy and the city mission movement, both of which promoted Bible distribution, educational reform, and philanthropic interests. Zealous evangelicals identified sailors among the helpless and heathen and established bethels on either ship or shore to cater to seafarers. As the seafaring trades opened up contacts with aboriginal people in the Pacific, some port missionaries assumed the role of moral guardians of the natives, including the men who went to sea, and placed themselves between visiting seafarers engaged in whaling and the obliging people of islands like Hawai'i.

Missions were numerous and widespread and ranged from the Bristol Channel Seamen's Mission, begun in the 1830s, to the Finnish Seamen's Mission, which had a presence in both Britain and the United States by the 1890s. By the late nineteenth century many specifically religious missions had been replaced by institutes and clubs that combined other services for sailors with spiritual care and created a nonthreatening environment. The sponsors were in some cases voluntary organizations like seamen's friend societies and in other cases specific individuals. Two of the best-known organizations with branches worldwide were the British and Foreign Sailors' Society, the antecedents of which date from 1819, and the Missions to Seamen established in 1856. Although in many countries individual independent facilities existed side by side with the multiport branches of countrywide and international organizations, each American-sponsored facility was totally independent in nature, at least until World War II.

Sailors' or seamen's homes and "rests" appeared in many ports, often as a project of a subscription society for the betterment of sailors, but in other cases as a result of mission origins, middle-class women's moral reform, business concerns, ethnic opportunism, or racial discrimination. They provided visiting sailors with clean accommodation at a moderate rate. They might also include a reading room, an indication that the caliber of seafarer included literate men interested in respectable pursuits. With the rise of the temperance movement in western society, eating houses as well as boardinghouses with a temperance focus appeared in the area of the docks. Not only did these services for seamen represent a contrasting culture to the traditional rough and tumble dockside experiences, but increasingly, in circumstances where seafaring itself was professionalizing and diversifying, they met a growing demand for more orderly facilities by men (and women) attracted to seafaring as a career in the more predictable packet vessels and liner trades. For example, the Sailors' Institute in Montreal, established in the 1860s, offered three kinds of programs: moral, recreational, and utilitarian. The first consisted of religious services, temperance meetings, and elevating reading materials. Recreational facilities varied over time and included newspapers and magazines, games, concerts and other entertainments, festivals, and, after World War I, sports and dances. In terms of basic personal services, the institute offered letter-writing opportunities and a post office, a savings bank as well as a bureau de change, baths, food and nonalcoholic drinks, some boarding facilities, and, when times were tough, relief in the form of free food, lodging, and job counseling. At the same time, the proprieties of class and gender were strictly maintained. The 1907 annual report indicates that officers and petty officers did not lounge with deckhands and firemen, and that stewardesses were cosily cloistered in their own room.

## Segregation

Racially segregated seamen's homes, like the ones in New York, reflected cultural preferences as well as discriminatory practices. Throughout the workforces of the maritime world, beginning with lascars, international crews used to nonwestern traditions sought facilities ashore that enabled them to practice their religious observances, dietary preferences, and other ethnic customs. In the largest ports, the polyglot nature of crews encouraged ethnic boardinghouses and eating places of both the charitable and commercial variety. The British government promoted segregated housing such as the Strangers' Home for Asiatic Seamen in Limehouse, London, but the shipping companies preferred substandard housing for their workers. P & O maintained an old hulk at Royal Albert Dock for its workers; Elder Dempster opened a spartan hostel in Liverpool's Upper Stanhope Street for its West African seamen. Antiforeign elements in Britain interpreted the presence of facilities for "coloreds" in a port like Cardiff as an inducement to non-British seamen whose presence in large numbers was blamed for depressing all seamen's wages.

## Services for Seamen

Beyond both the rough and respectable services of sailortown were the institutions that provided welfare for sailors and their families. The most impressive facilities for family members were orphanages for seamen's children and schools for seafarers' sons, both naval and merchant, which appeared in London during the age of sail. Benevolent citizens in Britain were particularly moved by the plight of shipwrecked seamen and established refuges for them in the nineteenth century. In addition, seamen's hospitals, which in North American ports were sometimes combined with space for immigrants, gave sailors a chance to recover from accidents and disease. Finnish seamen in London, for example, were treated, along with other categories of seamen, in the Dreadnought Seamen's Hospital in Greenwich. Sick seamen who found themselves in Saint John, New Brunswick, had access to the Kent Marine Hospital, which accommodated residents and nonresidents, black and white, English speakers and non-English speakers. In the absence of such facilities, poorhouses and workhouses accepted disabled seamen. Where there were no institutions, poor-law jurisdictions like those in eighteenth-century New England colonies determined the residence of settlement and sent the injured sailor or his destitute family home to be cared for by the overseers of the poor. In these circumstances the community paid; where there were hospitals for seafarers, services were free to sailors, and, if not run by a charity, the cost was usually recovered from the shipmaster or through taxes on shipping to which sailors indirectly contributed. In Canada, for example, a tonnage duty supported the Sick and Disabled Seamen's Fund administered under the aegis of the federal Department of Marine. In ports of the tropics where European and North American sailors died in very large numbers from contagious fevers, the solution to the health problem took the form of local recruitment. Men native to the tropics gradually took over the crewing of vessels trading in areas particularly sickly for northerners.

Penniless sailors often ended up in jail, the alternative welfare institution of most North American cities. Large ports established refuges for men who had left the sea service such as the Home for Aged Mariners in Liverpool. By the end of the nineteenth century, sailors down on their luck like crewmen who lived in the holds of tramp steamers and cattlemen on the North Atlantic run found relief in Salvation Army refuges that provided cheap accommodation and short-term labor. In interwar Britain, especially during the height of the Depression, the fear that colored "alien" seafarers might cause disorder as a result of the competition for jobs resulted in deportation of those without local family connections.

## Desertion

Desertion, the seafarers' activity that attracted the greatest state attention, occurred in most major ports although not always for the same reasons. It could be a positive or negative initiative by the sailor depending on whether it was the pull of the port or the push from his vessel that acted as the motivation. On the positive side, desertion could provide the seafarer with a new shipping engagement at a better rate of wages. For men on vessels that began their voyage in Britain in the mid-nineteenth century, articles were signed providing for a monthly wage, at least one month of which was paid in advance to enable the sailor to outfit himself for the voyage. If he sailed to North America he might have no wages to lose by deserting and might even be in debt to his vessel. The attraction was the considerably higher wages in a new engagement in ports on the eastern seaboard or the Saint Lawrence River. British colonial seamen on Asiatic articles often changed ship in Britain in order to secure work at a better wage rate. Asiatic articles, dating from 1834, provided a lower rate of wages than the standard ones and, officially, discharge in the colonial home port only. The chances for alternative employment on shore or new interpersonal relationships also promoted desertion in intermediate ports. On the negative side, intolerable conditions aboard ship such as mistreatment by officers, prompted men to leave when the opportunity arose. The dreadful working conditions some seamen encountered in early twentieth-century tramp steamers provided another reason for desertion. Increasingly in the twentieth century it was the experience of poor economic or political conditions at home that caused seamen from developing nations to escape a vessel in a foreign port when it was slated to return them to their place of origin.

Most official policies at the height of the shipping era in western society were aimed at eliminating desertion. Until late in the nineteenth century the British continued to subscribe to the notion that commercial seafaring acted as the nursery for naval seamen and must therefore be regulated, although the repeal of the Navigation Acts (1849–1854) opened the merchant service to a greater proportion of non-British seamen. It was pressure from commercial shipping interests that finally forced the government in the 1850s to establish mercantile marine offices to oversee the engagement and discharge of sailors. British shipowners did not receive much cooperation in North America, where fluidity in the sailor labor market was often in the best interests of locally owned or operated vessels. Moreover, most captains on both sides of the Atlantic were reluctant to charge their deserters if the court proceedings meant costly delays in sailing schedules. If a deserter went to jail, chances are he would be released to join his departing vessel, but in cases where he was apprehended after his vessel had already sailed, he could find himself in the local jail for a lengthy term. The police, the magistrates, and the jailors were therefore kept busy with cases relating to sailors' misbehavior as well as those arising out of their legitimate labor grievances. Many urban governments established water police forces to discourage both desertion and dockside crime, but, like other port officials, the law enforcers were open to bribery.

## Crimping

Of necessity desertion was closely connected to crimping. Crimps took advantage of labor shortages to entice seamen to leave one vessel to ship on another, or they deliberately created a shortage by manipulating the sailor labor market to their own advantage. A hiding place for the deserter and a new engagement depended on the services of the free enterprise agent or crimp as middleman. Even the legitimately discharged seafarer did not escape the crimp who, in his role as a broker, took him in and encouraged him to spend his accumulated as well as his forthcoming wages until they were exhausted, a result that was expedited by the levy of exorbitant interest charges. With the boarding master's assistance, a feckless sailor could end up in a new berth with little or nothing to show for either the previous or current engagement. In the second half of the nineteenth century government shipping masters found they had little protection against the crimps since the crimps could combine to drive up the going wage rate and were known to intimidate sailors to sign crimp-initiated articles in full view of the shipping officer. The boarding master/crimp was indeed one of the most adaptable businessmen of sailortown. When an obstacle was placed in the way of his trade, he always found a way around the problem. In ports on both sides of the Atlantic, crimps formed associations to promote their interests. They resisted the abolition of the advance note in both the British and American merchant marines in the 1880s. Indeed their business and the economic welfare of sailortown itself depended on the maintenance of a method for collecting the debts incurred by visiting seafarers. The Cardiff Boarding Masters' Guarantee

Association substituted its own "demand" note with the cooperation of the port's shipping industry and thereby helped to encourage Parliament to restore the advance note. For their part, land sharks in the United States transferred the cost of the supply system to the ship's master, who was forced to pay a bonus for each of his crewmen, and he in turn deducted the amount from the wages of the newly shipped sailors.

Remarkable stories of crimps abound. One of the more colorful on the western side of the Atlantic was Jim Ward. A famine-era Irish immigrant to the port of Quebec in the mid-nineteenth century, Ward had a career that included experience as sailor, crimp's runner, tavern keeper, and boardinghouse keeper, a common combination of activities for crimps everywhere. As Quebec's most notorious Rue Champlain crimp he employed intimidation in his dealings with visiting shipmasters and brutality in his sailor-stealing tactics. Quebec was a high-demand port in the mid-nineteenth century because of an export-oriented shipbuilding and timber industry that annually created a sailor shortage at the beginning of the spring navigation season in the Saint Lawrence River. By the time that the Canadian government had passed legislation in 1873 to curb desertion, the shipbuilding industry was in decline and Ward was exploring other options. In fact, like many of his fellow citizens, Ward was only a summer resident of Quebec. In the winter he migrated south to conduct business in the timber and cotton ports of the United States. As a stevedore in Savannah, Georgia, he acquired a sterling reputation that was suitably marked during his funeral in 1891 by the waterfront workers downing their tools and the visiting vessels flying their flags at half-mast. Indeed the conventional view of crimps can be misleading because it has come down to us either from official sources in which their activities were seen as a drain on the profits of shipping or popular sources in which only the extreme swashbuckling, criminal elements have been featured. In most cases, however, crimps proved to be useful agents for visiting seamen who had few personal resources with which to improve elements of their employment. As often as not the relationship between the crimp and the sailor, who were usually cut from the same cloth, was characterized as much by camaraderie as conflict, by business as exploitation. A variation on the crimp-based style of employment agent for seamen obtained in nonwestern ports where sailors' engagements tended to be in the hands of land-based headmen or, in the case of the serangs in India, foremen who not only did the hiring but also sailed with their seafaring gangs.

## Changes in the Modern Era

In the twentieth century, maritime communities provided more protections and services for seamen ashore, although with change there was also continuity, which was usually pro-employer and often racist. A combination of legislation and collective bargaining put crimps out of business in most countries. Notable legislation was the American Seamen's Act of 1915, which gave the articled seafarer an opportunity to leave his vessel in ports of call without deserting. In the British, American, and Canadian merchant marines, unionization of seamen rendered maritime communities a site for divisiveness based on rivalries and discrimination based on race. Moreover, the long-standing social services for seamen ashore, such as missions and homes, were interpreted by unions to be agencies of social control. In Britain during the post–World War I economic slump, seamen (and unemployed seamen) from various British colonies and areas of influence like the Middle East, Africa, and the Caribbean were subjected to the exclusionary provisions of wartime alien legislation. Codification of this policy in 1925 as the Coloured Alien Seamen Order required all nonwhite seamen in port to prove their British nationality, something that was not easy, or to register as aliens. As a result, seamen of color who were British subjects were exposed to police harassment in British seaports. The landward discrimination against British colonial seamen lasted until World War II. For many seamen, however, the greater speed of travel brought new benefits. Except for those affected by Depression-era unemployment, seafarers by the 1920s and 1930s, whatever their ethnicity, found that the quicker voyages and greater opportunities for return to a home base, combined with steady jobs, enabled them to enjoy a more stable family life. More seamen married once their workplace became powered by engines, and more took advantage of the pay system of allotment, which had existed for dependents also in the nineteenth century, whereby the family could receive a portion of the wages in the breadwinner's absence at sea.

Merchant seamen ashore were treated with considerably more respect and consideration by their countries during wartime. During World War II, the United Seamen's Service of the United States established port facilities for merchant seamen both at home and abroad to provide rest and recovery, social service, accommodation, a drink of beer, and social and cultural activities in a club environment. Other countries also rallied to the needs of merchant seamen during wartime; for example, the exiled Dutch, Belgian, and Norwegian governments maintained facilities for their seamen in the major convoy port of Halifax. In Britain after World War II, services for seamen in the British welfare state, including first- or second-generation "colonial" seamen domiciled in Britain, were coordinated by the Merchant Navy Welfare Board, which worked with the century-old missions, as well as with some newer organizations like the Roman Catholic Apostleship of the Sea.

By the late twentieth century the sailortowns of the major maritime communities of the age of sail had been converted to tourist attractions designed to liberate visitors brought by multistory cruise ships from their money. In contrast, the duration of the shore leave of seafarers employed on luxury and container vessels now proved too short to make a comparable impact on local economies.

[*See also* Fishing; Religion, *subentry on* Missions to Seafarers; Tattooing; *and* Whaling.]

## Bibliography

Balachandran, G. "Recruitment and Control of Indian Seamen: Calcutta, 1880–1935." *International Journal of Maritime History* 9, no.1 (June 1997): 1–18. Explores the tensions in the sailor labor market between traditional (serang) and modern (union) employment practices in which British shipping companies preferred the former and Indian seamen the latter.

Bolster, W. Jeffrey. *Black Jacks: African American Seamen in the Age of Sail*. Cambridge, Mass.: Harvard University Press, 1997. A study of black seafaring labor—slave and free—in antebellum America, including the prominence of black seamen in maritime communities.

Cadigan, Sean T. *Hope and Deception in Conception Bay: Merchant-Settler Relations in Newfoundland, 1785–1855*. Toronto: University of Toronto Press, 1995. Examines the transition from hired to family labor in Newfoundland fishing communities and the role of the truck system.

Chappell, David. "Kru and Kanaka: Participation by African and Pacific Island Sailors in Euroamerican Maritime Frontiers." *International Journal of Maritime History* 6, no. 2 (December 1994): 83–114. Compares and contrasts the experience of two colonial sources of seafaring labor and the impact of their voyaging on their settlement patterns.

Daunton, Martin. "Jack Ashore: Seamen in Cardiff before 1914." *The Welsh History Review/ Cylchgrawn Hanes Cymru* 9, no. 2 (1978): 176–203. Examines the problems inherent in the establishment of the National Amalgamated Union of Sailors and Firemen (later National Seamen's and Firemen's Union) in Cardiff's sailortown

Dixon, Conrad. "Lascars: the Forgotten Seamen." In *Working Men Who Got Wet*, edited by Rosemary Ommer and Gerald Panting, pp. 265–281. Saint John's: Maritime History Group, Memorial University of Newfoundland, 1980. A brief overview of the employment of lascar seamen by the East India Company and later the steamship lines trading to India.

Dixon, Conrad. "The Rise and Fall of the Crimp, 1840–1914." In *British Shipping and Seamen, 1630-1960: Some Studies*, edited by Stephen Fisher, pp. 49–67. Exeter, U.K.: University of Exeter Papers in Economic History, 1984. An analysis of the operations of crimps in four types of setting during their nineteenth-century heyday.

Fingard, Judith. "Evangelical Social Work in Canada: Salvationists and Sailors' Friends, 1890–1920." In *Social Welfare, 1850–1950: Australia, Argentina, and Canada Compared*, edited by D. C. M. Platt, 25–44. London: Macmillan, 1989. Explores philanthropic services for merchant seamen in Montreal and Saint John.

Fingard, Judith. *Jack in Port: Sailortowns of Eastern Canada*. Toronto: University of Toronto Press, 1982. A discussion of the seaman's port life in Quebec, Saint John, and Halifax during the nineteenth century.

Fury, Cheryl A. "Elizabethan Seamen: Their Lives Ashore." *International Journal of Maritime History* 10, no. 1 (June 1998): 1–40. Examines the landward subculture of Elizabethan sailors, both married and unmarried.

Hinkkanen, Merja-Liisa. "When the AB Was Able-Bodied No Longer: Accidents and Illnesses among Finnish Sailors in British Ports, 1882–1902." *International Journal of Maritime History* 8, no. 1 (June 1996): 87–104. The health problems of Finnish sailors in British ports suggests that seafaring was a high-risk occupation with respect to accidents.

Hohman, Elmo Paul. *Seamen Ashore: A Study of the United Seamen's Service and of Merchant Seamen in Port*. New Haven, Conn.: Yale University Press, 1952. A study of the landward aspects of the American merchant marine, particularly in the 1940s, and the work of the United Seamen's Service during and after the World War II.

Howell, Colin, and Richard J. Twomey, eds. *Jack Tar in History: Essays in the History of Maritime Life and Labour*. Fredericton, New Brunswick: Acadiensis Press, 1991. A collection of essays on seafarers, by a number of historians, that are useful for brief insights into the eighteenth-century maritime world and gender issues.

Kennerley, Alston. "British Government Intervention in Seamen's Welfare, 1938–1948." *International Journal of Maritime History* 7, no. 2 (December 1995): 75–113. An examination of seamen's welfare within wider welfare developments of the mid-twentieth century and the role of the Merchant Navy Welfare Board.

Kennerley, Alston. "British Seamen's Missions in the Nineteenth Century." In *The North Sea: Twelve Essays on Social History of Maritime Labour*, edited by Lewis R. Fischer, Harald Hamre, Poul Holm, and Jaap R. Bruijn, pp. 79–97. Stavanger, Norway: Stavanger Maritime Museum/The Association of North Sea Societies: 1992. An overview of the first hundred years of the seamen's mission movement in Britain.

Kverndal, Roald. *Seamen's Missions, Their Origin and Early Growth: A Contribution to the History of the Church Maritime*. Pasadena, Calif.: William Carey Library, 1986. An exhaustive study of British and American seamen's missions before the mid-nineteenth century.

Norling, Lisa. *Captain Ahab Had a Wife: New England Women and the Whalefishery, 1720–1870*. Chapel Hill: University of

North Carolina Press, 2000. An examination of women's role in the New England whale fishery.

Press, Jon. "Philanthropy and the British Shipping Industry, 1815–1860." *International Journal of Maritime History* 1, no. 1 (June 1989): 107–127. Examines charities established for seamen and their families in Great Britain in the first half of the nineteenth century.

Tabili, Laura. *"We Ask for British Justice": Workers and Racial Difference in Late Imperial Britain.* Ithaca, N.Y.: Cornell University Press, 1994. An analysis of the employment and settlement of men of color in Britain in the first half of the twentieth century in which seamen and racism figure prominently.

Van der Veen, Annemiek. "Independent Willy-Nilly: Fisherwomen on the Dutch North Sea Coast, 1890–1940." In *The North Sea: Twelve Essays on Social History of Maritime Labour*, edited by Lewis R. Fischer, Harald Hamre, Poul Holm, and Jaap R. Bruijn, pp. 181–196. Stavanger, Norway: Stavanger Maritime Museum/The Association of North Sea Societies: 1992. A description of the lives of the fisherwomen in three fishing communities on the Dutch North Sea coast.

Walkowitz, Judith R. *Prostitution and Victorian Society: Women, Class, and the State.* Cambridge, U.K., and New York: Cambridge University Press, 1980. A study of the British Contagious Diseases Acts and their female opponents in which one of the ports featured is Southampton.

JUDITH FINGARD

## Seafarers' Wives and Children

The impact of seafaring on community life is a subject that has rarely been considered by maritime historians. When they started the *International Journal of Maritime History* in 1989, however, the editors called for maritime studies to focus more on social and economic subjects, and in the following two decades historians did start paying attention to family life and to women's roles in seafaring communities.

Historians' traditional lack of interest in seafarers' families is related to the assumption that sailors were unattached young men who preferred to have no obligations whatsoever. The notion that seamen commonly remained unmarried was based on the idea that the salary of most seamen—of sailors especially—was too low to maintain a household with wife and children. Furthermore, the ideal of male breadwinning supposedly dictated labor and household divisions between husbands and wives until the beginning of the twentieth century. While husbands were held responsible for the family's basic income, women's financial contribution was thought to be marginal and of minor importance. According to this line of reasoning, young men did not start a family until they were able financially to support a family. From early modern times to the first decades of the twentieth century, these views were indeed widely shared and spread by ecclesiastical authorities, government officials, and trade boards. However, historians more recently have come to the understanding that while the division of male breadwinners and female additional earnings may have been the ideal way of living until the beginning of the twentieth century, it certainly was not universal in maritime communities anywhere. Recent investigations have shown that from early modern times to the present, sailors throughout the world did marry and start families, despite their insufficient earnings. Furthermore, various studies on seamen's families have revealed that—whether the study concerned sixteenth-century fishing communities in Portugal, overseas trading towns in seventeenth-century Holland, whale-fishery towns in eighteenth-century America, or seafaring ports in nineteenth- and twentieth-century Britain—seamen's wives enjoyed, because of the frequent absence of their husbands, a greater sense of independence than most other women did.

How women actually maintained their families ashore varied a great deal, depending on their age, their marital status, their access to resources, their legal competencies, local practices, and whether they lived in rural or urban settings. Port towns long had the reputation of existing on the edge of civilization, and seafarers and their wives were often associated with immoral and illegal behavior. Indeed, in seventeenth-century Dutch port towns, the wives of seamen sometimes made a living by working as prostitutes, but most women provided their families with an income from other occupations and earnings.

In any port town from early modern times to the twentieth century, seamen's wives typically earned money from occupations that were related to the seafaring industry: trading in local merchandise, taking in young sailors as boarders, doing piecework for the shipping industry. In sixteenth-century Portugal, women were prominent not only at local maritime markets, but also in the financing of fishing voyages and in merchandising fish cargoes. During the absence of their husbands, seamen's wives often enjoyed opportunities to obtain legal competencies that other married women or unmarried women could not have. Such legal competencies allowed seamen's wives to contract loans, to engage in various financial transactions, and to have access to inheritances. Seventeenth-century Dutch wives of sailors of the East India Company were engaged in all kinds of financial and legal transactions; wives of whalers in nineteenth-century America were likewise familiar with settling debts, buying and selling property, paying taxes, and obtaining insurance during their husband's voyages. Seamen's wives also had typical female occupations, such as spinning, sewing, retailing, or being in domestic service. To make ends meet, women married to seamen often made use of their greater opportunities to have access to credit. With the promise of future earnings from their husbands or fathers, seamen's relatives could obtain loans from moneylenders and goods from tradesmen and shopkeepers, or they could receive credit from landlords.

Since seafaring towns depended largely on the women in their communities—there was typically a surplus of women—widespread mutual support was the norm. Town councilmen, church leaders, and other officials felt responsible for the well-being of poor seamen and their families. When other resources had failed, seamen's families could opt for poor relief or for other help from local authorities, until they were able to gain sufficient earnings again. This seems to have been the norm in all seafaring communities from early modern times to the present. In seventeenth-century Holland, town leaders, civil courts, church councils, and trading companies were all involved in maintaining seamen's families. By making sure that seafaring families survived financially, such institutions served their own interests as well; urban communities benefited from families who were able to provide for themselves. On the other hand, by making use of public services, seamen's families were often subject to discipline and control by town councilmen, church leaders, and sometimes trading companies. In eighteenth-century Rhode Island, for instance, town councils solved the family's poverty by contracting out older children as servants to craftsmen, while in Britain in the nineteenth and twentieth centuries the Board of Trade put considerable pressure on seafarers to conform to a breadwinning norm. Seamen's families may have been more independent than the average family in early modern and modern urban communities, but they were subject to greater pressure and social control as well.

[*See also* Shipboard Life, *subentry on* Women aboard Ship, *and* Wages and Salaries.]

### Bibliography

Abreu-Ferreira, Darlene. "Fishmongers and Shipowners: Women in Maritime Communities of Early Modern Portugal." *Sixteenth Century Journal* 31, no. 1 (2000): 7–23.

Burton, Valerie. "Household and Labour Market Interactions in the Late Nineteenth Century British Shipping Industry: Breadwinning and Seafaring Families." In *The Microeconomic Analysis of the Household and the Labour Market, 1880–1939,* edited by Timothy W. Guinnane and Paul Johnson, pp. 99–109. Seville, Spain: Universidad de Sevilla, 1998.

Creighton, Margaret S., and Lisa Norling. *Iron Men, Wooden Women: Gender and Seafaring in the Atlantic World, 1700–1920.* Baltimore: John Hopkins University Press, 1996.

Fury, Cheryl. "Elizabethan Seamen: Their Lives Ashore." *International Journal of Maritime History* 10, no. 1 (1998): 1–40.

Heijden, Manon van der, and Paul van de Laar. *Rotterdammers en de VOC: Handelscompagnie, stad en burgers.* Amsterdam: Bert Bakker, 2002.

Howell, Colin, and Richard J. Twomey, eds. *Jack Tar in History: Essays in the History of Maritime Life and Labour.* Fredericton, New Brunswick: Acadiensis Press, 1991.

Norling, Lisa. *Captain Ahab Had a Wife: New England Women and the Whalefishery, 1720–1870.* Chapel Hill: University of North Carolina Press, 2000.

MANON VAN DER HEIJDEN

**Conferences.** *See* Shipping Conferences and Cartels.

**Conrad, Joseph** (1857–1924), British writer. Józef Teodor Konrad Korzeniowski was born in Berdichev in the Ukraine, a part of Poland then under Russian control, on December 3, 1857, and died in Bishopsbourne, Kent, on August 3, 1924. Joseph Conrad, as his name was Anglicized, became a major writer in Britain during the early decades of the twentieth century and the most accomplished and influential writer of sea fiction in the English language. Biographers often treat his life in three distinct phases: childhood and youth in Poland (1857–1874), seafaring first in France and then in the British Merchant Service (1874–1894), and finally as a writer ashore in southeastern England for the remainder of his life (1894–1924). His experience growing up in occupied Poland, followed by sailing out of Marseilles and then as foremost hand, mate, and captain in the British Merchant Service, provided an extraordinary store of material for his career as a writer of short stories and novels through thirty years. His father, Apollo Korzeniowski, a writer and translator, and his mother Ewa (née Bobrowska) were members of the landowning class, which sought autonomy for Poland. Apollo moved his wife and only child to Warsaw in 1861, where his home became a center of clandestine activity to throw off the yoke of Russian rule. He was arrested that fall and imprisoned in the Warsaw Citadel, tried the following spring and sentenced to exile in Vologda with his wife and son, then four years old. During an exile in various places that lasted for seven years, Ewa died and Joseph

**Joseph Conrad.** Walter Tittle (1883–1966) painted this oil on canvas portrait. SNARK / ART RESOURCE, NY / NATIONAL PORTRAIT GALLERY, LONDON

had many health difficulties before Apollo was allowed to return to Kraków, where he died and was acclaimed a Polish patriot. Young Conrad, then eleven years old, was looked after by his father's friends until his maternal uncle, Tadeusz Bobrowski, became his guardian and source of family support.

While growing up with a literary father in exile, Conrad's formal education was spotty, but he listened to his father recite Polish Romantic poetry and he read widely in Polish and French translations of literature, including the sea fiction of the English novelist Frederick Marryat (1792–1848) and of the American novelist James Fenimore Cooper (1789–1851), and the *Toilers of the Sea* by the French novelist Victor Hugo (1802–1885), one of his father's translations. So it is not surprising that at the age of fourteen, with both parents dead and stuck in a troubled country, Conrad told his relatives that he wished to go to sea. They tried to dissuade him for several years but finally made arrangements with family friends in Marseilles when it became apparent that he could be conscripted into the Russian army. When Conrad had just turned seventeen, his sea life began as a passenger on board *Mont-Blanc* sailing for Saint-Pierre, Martinique. After several more voyages to the West Indies as apprentice on *Mont-Blanc* and steward on *Saint-Antoine*, Conrad, now just nineteen, apparently began to sow his wild oats in Marseilles. Illness kept him from sailing on the next voyage of *Saint-Antoine*, and he was kept from further voyages as an alien subject to Russian military service without a permit from the consul. Unemployed and racking up considerable debts, young Conrad lost all the money he had invested in questionable voyages to the Spanish coast, blew the remainder of his allowance at Monte Carlo in an attempt to recover, and then attempted suicide. Rescued once more by his uncle Bobrowski, he made firm plans to join the British Merchant Service.

Conrad's sixteen-year career in that service began with a voyage from Marseilles to the Sea of Azov as a paying apprentice on board the steamer *Mavis*, which brought him to England in 1878. He served on fifteen other ships under the Red Ensign of the British merchant fleet, signing on in the full range from ordinary seaman to third and second mate, chief mate, and captain as his sea career progressed. He passed the second mate's examination at age twenty-two, the first mate's at twenty-seven, and the master's a month before his twenty-ninth birthday, a typical sequence for ambitious young seaman. He had also become a naturalized British subject earlier that year and considered himself a "British master mariner beyond a doubt," which would remain a source of pride throughout his life. In contrast to the West Indian voyages of his French years, most of the time he sailed eastward to ports in India, Bangkok, Singapore, the Dutch East Indies, and especially Australia. Among his ships, some voyages are writ large in his later fiction, especially on *Palestine*, renamed *Judea* in "Youth," on *Narcissus*, also with the voyage track essentially unchanged in *The Nigger of the "Narcissus,"* and *Otago*, his sole command and the ship at the core of the action in "The Secret Sharer," "A Smile of Fortune," and *The Shadow-Line*. In assessing Conrad's sailing career, Zdzislaw Najder, a respected Conrad biographer, concludes that "it climbs between 1874 and 1889" until the 1890 expedition to the Congo breaks both his health and his morale, "leading to a steady and rapid decline. After three years the captain is back to being only second mate, and it is on a ship (the *Adowa*) going nowhere" (Najder, p. 160). Circumstances, including the continuing decline of opportunities as sailing ships lost their trades to steamships, would qualify that judgment. And there was a brief and wonderful coda for Conrad as the chief mate of the renowned wool clipper *Torrens* for two round trips to Australia in 1892–1894, a fitting end to his sailing years.

The fiction that grew from his sea career and provided the most detailed portrait of life in the British Merchant Service during the last three decades of the nineteenth century is complex, compelling, and sometimes difficult to interpret. Sea experience generates more than a third of his fiction, a dozen stories and novels, as well as many essays and *The Mirror of the Sea* (1906), an elegiac tribute to the dying world of commercial sailing ships.

Seafarers and ships also enter many of his "land" novels, providing narrators, frames, and sometimes crucial events. Captain Lingard initiates the action and serves as a force behind the scenes in Conrad's first two novels, *Almayer's Folly* (1895) and *An Outcast of the Islands* (1896). In the complicated tapestry of *Nostromo* (1904), Captain Mitchell provides a surface view of events, and the voyage of a lighter filled with silver serves as the hinge of action. Marlow, the retired seaman who narrates many of the early voyage tales, returns as narrator of *Chance* (1913), again telling the tale to former seafarers; the novel begins with reminiscences of a mate's examination, includes the mate Powell and Captain Anthony as principal characters, and reaches its denouement on board ship. In *Victory* (1915), the protagonist Axel Heyst frequently visits Captain Davidson, who narrates part of the story. Dominic Cervoni, an idealized strong and simple seaman, plays an important role in *The Arrow of Gold* (1919), a semiautobiographical novel. Captain Lingard returns as the central character in *The Rescue* (1920), a novel begun twenty-four years earlier. *The Rover* (1923) is built around Jean Peyrol, an old pirate and wandering seafarer who returns to France and dies helping the French fleet escape Horatio Nelson's blockade of Toulon during the Napoleonic Wars (1799–1815). In such ways are many of the "land" novels informed by seamen ashore and the perspective of their values.

## The Voyage Tales

The voyage fiction is more rigorously committed to life on board ships, though some narratives have significant land entanglements. Many of these tales came early in Conrad's new career as a writer living ashore but still remembering his sea years in vivid detail. Others came later, often reflecting an imaginative return to his experiences as captain of the Australian barque *Otago* in 1888–1889, his sole command. Most of them are long short stories or novellas in length, sizes that suited his focus on action at sea. The first published was *The Nigger of the "Narcissus"* (1897), a brilliant fictional evocation of the voyage he took as second mate of the *Narcissus* from Bombay to Dunkerque in 1884. In this powerful novella, Conrad, with the abandon of new writers not yet chary of conserving their sources for future work, draws into the tale characters from other voyages. Yet the major figures—Captain Allistoun; the old seaman Singleton; Donkin, the rabble-rouser from London slums; and James Wait, the West Indian Negro who dies on the voyage—all belong to the real voyage, as does Conrad himself, represented in the story as a junior mate. Throughout, it is a study in varieties of egoism and the tensions they create in the enclosed community of a ship. Captain Allistoun risks his ship in the gale by "hard driving" (carrying too much sail too long) with the hope of making a fast passage that would be mentioned in nautical papers; Donkin can preserve himself only by leading dissension in the crew; Wait's malingering and obsession with his coming death gradually corrupt the crew, whose pity for him is essentially displaced self-pity. Only the necessity of working together to save the ship thrown on her beam ends in the storm dulls these competing egoisms temporarily, and they cannot be laid to rest until Wait dies. When Wait says that he belongs to the ship *Narcissus* he sets the dominant theme of the story, and although that was the real name of the ship that Conrad sailed on he could not have been unaware of its symbolic appropriateness to the unfolding story.

Next comes "Youth" (1898), a long autobiographical story based on Conrad's experience as mate of the barque *Palestine* from 1881 to 1883. A decrepit old ship loaded with mishandled coal, she spends more time in port for repairs than at sea, but after several false tries she finally heads out for Bangkok. The voyage is doomed from the start, and it represents the fate of many ships lost at sea in the closing decades of the nineteenth century as penurious owners sought to squeeze profits out of a dying trade. In it we meet Marlow for the first time, a retrospective older narrator looking back both wistfully and ironically at his own youth, a "romance of illusions" in the final words of the story. When the coal inevitably catches fire through spontaneous combustion and the ship burns to the waterline and sinks, young Marlow's heart leaps at the thought of his first command, a lifeboat headed for a nearby shore where he gets his first vision of the exotic lands in the Far East. The disillusioned older men listening to Marlow nod their heads, fully understanding the double perspective of the tale.

A year later Marlow resurfaces to tell a far blacker tale, recounting Conrad's debilitating experience with

Belgian colonialism in the jungles of the Congo in 1890. In "Heart of Darkness" (1899), Conrad's most famous and frequently studied story, Marlow's control of irony dominates the entire narration, undercutting any European ideas of progress; as the rhetoric of the exploiters becomes meaningless sound in the depths of the jungle, so does the idea of civilization itself crumble. Technically a land story, this dark tale has the structure of a voyage, with the outer frame beginning and ending in voyages between Belgium and the Congo and the inner frame a voyage up and down the river, partly overland and partly afloat. Marlow is there to command a steamboat that he finds wrecked, and disintegration and ruin become the controlling image of everything he sees. Like Kurtz at the inner station, the man of enlightened words who has descended into pure, nonverbal savagery before he dies, Marlow emerges from this voyage infected with despair.

Next comes *Lord Jim* (1900), where Marlow's role as narrator becomes even more complex. Working with the same impulse that generated "Youth," Conrad imagines what a young man who goes to sea with a head full of the adventures in light sea literature might do when faced with a real crisis. Jim expects that he would behave heroically and cannot comprehend what he in fact did: jump from the bridge of a steamship he thought was sinking and thereby abandon the multitude of passengers, pilgrims on the way to Mecca, to their fate. The same imagination that had led him into a seagoing career envisions the havoc that will result when the overcrowded ship sinks, and Jim becomes the precursor of many Conradian seamen cursed with lively imaginations that will disable their capacity to act. To be sure, Jim is surrounded by corrupt and venal officers of *Patna*, who pressure him to join them in leaving the ship, but the self-image that he had nurtured is irremediably shattered by his impulsive act. When the ship is found afloat and a court of inquiry follows, Marlow meets Jim and begins to piece together his story, fascinated by the flaw or "soft spot" in an otherwise able young man, one that undermines his own faith in the seamanlike order of the maritime world. This is the first of Conrad's runaway novellas that grew into full-blown novels, partly because of the unanswered question, What then? So after the court of inquiry, Marlow puts the disgraced Jim in touch with Stein, a rich merchant and trader who eventually sends Jim to Patusan. There, in the much longer second part of the novel, Jim does succeed in performing many heroic feats to quell intrigues among the competing native peoples and even willingly walks into a heroic death to make amends for his principal mistake, yet in the end this romantic world

becomes just as illusory as the sea adventures that he first dreamt of.

Conrad next offers *Typhoon* (1902), a magnificent storm novella to match the central gale scene in *The Nigger of the "Narcissus."* Here the story of the typhoon that besets the steamship *Nan-Shan* is told in the third person but includes three perspectives: those of the stolid Captain MacWhirr, a man with limited vision; of the young mate Jukes, again a figure loaded with imagination; and of the engineer Solomon Rout, whose name suggests his judgment. As in *Lord Jim*, the ship takes on human cargo, a hold full of coolies returning home with their savings after seven years of work abroad. As signs of an approaching typhoon appear in the South China Sea, MacWhirr consults a book on avoiding major storms, required knowledge in Board of Trade examinations for captains, and concludes that it is all hypotheses and suppositions. He decides against changing course to avoid the typhoon, wondering how he could justify the additional coal bill to the owner; Jukes, on the other hand, battens down the hatches and prepares the ship for the beating it will soon take. As *Nan-Shan* heads straight into the typhoon, images of its savage assault on the ship are matched by chaos in the hold below, where all the coolies' chests have broken open, spilling out their dollars, while the coolies are swarming up a ladder to break through the hatch that separates them from the external fury of the typhoon. This scene immobilizes Jukes at the height of the storm, while an oblivious MacWhirr sticks to the bridge, refusing to acknowledge the chaos engulfing his ship, and a busy Rout keeps stopping and starting the propeller shaft to prevent cavitation as the bow plunges and the stern rises into the air in immense seas. When the ship enters the calm eye of the typhoon, the story essentially stops: we do not see *Nan-Shan* entering the most dangerous quadrant in the second half of the storm. A coda shows us a battered ship entering port in the sunshine, with some order restored. The narrating voice celebrates MacWhirr's unthinking endurance, but details in the text also highlight his mistakes.

Another steamship novella follows, "The End of the Tether" (1902), in which land entanglements destroy the integrity of an otherwise faithful captain. Wanting to leave a legacy to his impoverished daughter after the bank holding his savings has failed, Captain Whalley, a sailing ship man, lends what money he has left to Massey, a greedy shipowner, to help maintain a decrepit *Sofala* with the understanding that he will remain her captain for three years as a condition of repayment. In this corrupt version of the sea world, Whalley himself hangs on to his command to preserve his investment as he is going blind, no longer fit to command. The denouement is built on ironic layers of deception when Massey places iron bars near the compass, which Whalley cannot see, to run the ship on a reef and collect the insurance. With these shore concerns, all involving money, any semblance of order in the sea world dissolves, and the denouement is a shouting match between owner and the captain as the ship sinks. The last tale in this first era of Conrad's sea fiction, "Falk" (1903), explores a theme of "Heart of Darkness" in a new setting. It portrays a Dutch East Indies harbor world of petty malice, centered in Schomberg's hotel ashore, and bourgeois primness on board the German ship *Diana*, with Captain Hermann, his wife, four children, and a silent niece constructed with "regal lavishness" living on board. In this world the disruptive, more elemental force is Falk, who runs the only tug in town and wants to marry Hermann's statuesque daughter. Suspecting the narrator's competing interest, Falk at first refuses to tow his ship but later enlists him as an intermediary in his quest. With direct honesty, Falk insists that a dark episode in his past—killing and eating the only shipmate left alive on a stranded steamer to survive—be revealed to his future bride. Thus the story injects strong primitive desire into a world that pretends not to recognize it, recalling the last section of "Heart of Darkness" in which Marlow brings his story back to those who cannot understand it.

Conrad's second cluster of voyage tales, published between 1910 and 1912 with a final treatment in 1917, relate directly or tangentially to his sole permanent command as captain of *Otago* for fourteen months in 1888 and 1889. The first is one of his most powerful short stories, "The Secret Sharer" (1910), with some veiled autobiographical details drawn from the unusual circumstances surrounding his assumption of command. In it a young, insecure narrator stands the first night anchor watch, traditionally a duty of mates, to become acquainted with his new ship and discovers an exhausted naked swimmer hanging on to a ladder over the side. As the swimmer comes on board and is clothed in the captain's sleeping suit, the captain hears his story and begins to identify with him, a peer in age, training, and status in the British Merchant Service. Leggatt's story retells with variations one of the most notorious incidents during an 1880 voyage of the famous *Cutty Sark* (here named *Sephora*): when a rebellious seaman refused to help set a foresail to save the ship "during the maddening howling of that endless gale," Leggatt grabbed him by the throat just as a huge sea came aboard and was still holding on to the dead man's neck when the deck cleared.

Relieved of duty as chief mate and confined to his cabin, he escapes overboard and swims to avoid prosecution for murder. By the time *Sephora's* captain comes on board looking for his escaped mate, the narrator is committed to hiding Leggatt in his cabin, and the tension of maintaining that secrecy from his mates and crew becomes increasingly intolerable. On the pretense of looking for a land wind, the captain risks his first command by heading inshore to let Leggatt swim to freedom, where only a successful tack of a ship whose handling he does not yet know prevents running ashore. In the tense denouement, that difficult maneuver for a square-rigged ship (technically making sternboard while tacking) depends on knowing when to reverse the helm, which the young captain accomplishes by watching the white hat that he had given Leggatt to cover his head.

The two other stories of the same era focus on the land entanglements of young captains, both commercial and romantic. "A Smile of Fortune" (1911) draws on and transforms some of Conrad's own experience on the island of Mauritius in 1886. The narrating captain is wary of being taken in and manipulated by Jacobus, the older ship chandler, as he waits for scarce bags for a cargo of sugar. In fact, he does fall prey to Jacobus's schemes, both to sell him an unwanted cargo of potatoes and to foist off his petulant illegitimate daughter in marriage. But, as the title indicates, the young captain escapes both entanglements by selling the potatoes at a profit and sailing away. In contrast, "Freya of the Seven Isles" (1912), a long tale of a love triangle gone wrong, is based on a yarn told of the young captain of *Costa Rica* in conflict with the commander of a Dutch gunboat in the East Indies. In the story, Jasper Allen is planning to elope on his brig *Bonito* with Freya, who has rejected Heemskirk. In the melodramatic ending Heemskirk tows the brig onto a reef, where it is pillaged, Jasper goes mad, and Freya dies of pneumonia. The more interesting part of the story lies in its earlier pages, where Jasper, who identifies his beautiful brig with Freya, courts her by performing risky maneuvers with seamanlike precision.

Conrad's final use of his *Otago* experience occurs in *The Shadow-Line* (1917), a novella closely based on the events surrounding his assumption of command and first voyage from Bangkok to Singapore in 1888. As in earlier tales that closely follow the contours of his own voyages—*The Nigger of the "Narcissus"* and "Youth," for example—a sense of authenticity emanates from every page. In this "calm piece," as Conrad called it, conditions emerged that wrecked many sailing ship voyages just as surely as storms, including disease and the malaise of knowing that nothing could be done. The malfeasance of the previous captain, who like many in that isolated position had lost his balance, is largely invented but not unrealistic, and the mate Burns's obsession with his ghost represents the prevalence of superstition on sailing ships. The young captain, like many other seamen in Conrad's stories, has enough callow egoism to remain unresponsive to those who help him. Yet, like the young captain of "The Secret Sharer," he has proven himself by the end of the story, in this case by enduring the stress of calm and disease and by bringing his ship safely through a storm short-handed. Thus in *The Shadow-Line*, a title that images coming to maturity, Conrad has returned to the source and method of his most powerful voyage tales, transforming and deepening his own experience at sea.

## Interpreting Conrad's Sea World

Many of Conrad's readers today have no direct experience at sea beyond a ferry or a cruise ship, and even among those who have sailed only a lucky few have climbed aloft to work on the yards of a square-rigger. What happens to the aesthetic of rendering so eloquently expressed in the preface to *The Nigger of the "Narcissus"* for the rest of Conrad's readers? Will they indeed "by the power of the written word" alone be able to "hear," "feel," and "before all, see" what is happening on the decks of *Narcissus, Judea,* or the unnamed ships of "The Secret Sharer" and *The Shadow-Line*? At the end of the nineteenth century in the opening paragraph of "Youth," Conrad does not worry about his readers' context: "This could have occurred nowhere but in England, where men and sea interpenetrate, so to speak—the sea entering into the life of most men." But by 1915, in the author's note to *Within the Tides*, he is aware of increasing distance between his readers and knowledge of a very specialized sea world: "The problem was to make unfamiliar things credible." One early answer was a bit of a dodge: plant seafarers inside the voyage tales as listeners who could mediate between the narrator and readers. Since these listeners remain silent much of the time in "Youth," they do not magically re-create the missing context of professional seamanship. The trouble is, they are not telling us how to make sense of the absurd events that have occurred during *Judea's* voyage, only nodding assent to the abstract theme of lost youth. Looked at from this angle, the familiar frames of "Youth" and "Heart of Darkness" are a bit like buffers in a computer: they have information you might need, if only you could get at it. And using Marlow as a

seafarer narrator does not fully solve the problem either, because he is actively involved in the stories he tells and often expresses strong attitudes toward their events. This narrative device, in spite of its many structural benefits, has again failed to accomplish the end of providing a missing context that is somehow independent of the narrator's convictions and judgments.

The problem is not inconsiderable for a writer whose vision is always filled with overlapping ironies. To see them you must know something in the context of the sea world that highlights otherwise innocuous details and gives them special importance in developing the narrative, assessing the action (or lack of it) by characters, and complicating or disconfirming judgments of moral value offered by narrating voices. Those voices, whether authorial or located within variously placed narrators, are dominant in the voyage fiction from *The Nigger of the "Narcissus"* through *The Shadow-Line*. They also resonate through *The Mirror of the Sea* (1906) and many other sea essays that Conrad wrote throughout his life, suggesting that they play a role in his perception of the sea world that goes beyond the narrative strategies of the voyage tales. In this volume and other maritime essays, he developed an elaborate sea creed, a full-blown moral system drawing on and expanding the practices and traditions of the British Merchant Service. This creed first took shape in his fiction, where it appears in the voices of various narrators or in the voice of an omniscient author. In analogies throughout his sea essays, Conrad expands the practical skill of seamanship into an aesthetic of truth in art and an ethic linking work on board ship with honesty, duty, honor, fidelity, and a religious sense of vocation. In the fiction that world is characterized through frequent dichotomies between the corrupt land and the pure sea, supported by lots of black and white imagery. Above all else the essays and narrative voices of the stories insist on the simplicity of the sea world, where competence and fidelity to duty can sustain moral values.

Yet discrepancies between the ideal value attributed to the discipline of seamanship and the acts of flawed seamen, who are by no means immune from blunders or irresponsibility, suggest discontinuity rather than concordance between Conrad's celebration of seamanship and his use of it in the voyage fiction. As we listen to the narrating voices in many of the stories, homilies on seamanship evoke its ideal value and power, yet they also obscure the fact that bad seamanship is as prevalent as good. The gallery of Conrad's fictional seafarers exhibits a mixed lot—shirkers and malingerers as well as those who are steadfast, the inept as well as the competent, slaves of habit and routine as well as those with foresight, captains who take unnecessary risks as well as those who exercise due caution. Nearly every one of Conrad's fictional voyages contains either a mistake in seamanship or an abnegation of responsibility on the part of a seaman. Like the officers and men of the British Merchant Service, they represent the full spectrum on scales of competence and incompetence, imagination and obtuseness, fidelity and infidelity, moral rigor and slackness—all in varying degrees and combinations. It is easy to identify those at the bottom ends of those scales—the disreputable officers of *Patna*, the mad former captain in *The Shadow-Line*, Massey in "The End of the Tether," malingerers like Donkin and Wait—as well as a few less developed, "flat" characters near the top like Singleton and the French Lieutenant in *Lord Jim*. But the vast majority cannot be so easily categorized—like Captain Archbold, who loses his nerve under the duress of an extended gale; Jim, who is betrayed by an overactive imagination; or Leggatt, victim of his own moment of violence. Even harder to place are those otherwise competent captains who betray their trust or risk their ships for other values—Whalley continuing to navigate while his blindness grows, the young master of "The Secret Sharer" standing into the reefs around Koh-ring to release Leggatt, McWhirr smashing into the typhoon instead of dodging it for the sake of the owner's coal bill, Allistoun refusing to cut the masts and right his ship. Of course these infidelities and mistakes in seamanship provide the dramatic substance of their stories, but they also represent a fairly grim reality in seafaring life. Throughout the period that Conrad sailed in the British Merchant Service, there were many complaints about the declining competence of its men and officers. In the long-voyage sailing ship trades, especially, where profits were growing meager and ships were less well maintained and often overloaded, procuring good seamen became more and more difficult. In 1872, British consuls complained about the "dram drinking" and recklessness of officers, and the "Report of the Royal Commission on the Saving of Life at Sea" of 1887 blamed the increase of strandings and collisions on "the neglect by the master or officers of the most ordinary rules and precautions of seamanship" (Foulke, pp. 111–112). Such facts qualify the "one of us" motif that echoes through *Lord Jim*, and they undercut any simplistic faith in the traditions of the British Merchant Service as a rule of life.

When the action of a story or novel involves men working a ship at sea, both character and plot often hinge on instrumental uses of seamanship. The problem for readers unfamiliar with ships and sailing is knowing what captains, mates, and foc'sle hands ought to do in a particular situation. The storm scene at the center of *The Nigger of the "Narcissus"* illustrates the kinds of irony that evolve from discrepancies between what is said by a narrating voice and what is seen or heard on board ship. Its meaning is far more complicated than the pronouncements of an overriding narrative voice, which excuses and even celebrates the captain's error in seamanship. Clues that undercut such pronouncements are clearly there, for those who know how to read them, but they are submerged in a rhetoric of praise for the unflinching captain and in images that show him holding the ship up from final disaster by sheer force of will. When the overpowered ship has been knocked on her beam ends, the call to "cut" enough of the masts away to right her is anticipated by the boatswain, who crawls toward the "big axe kept ready for just such an emergency," a sensible precaution for surviving the crisis and completing the voyage successfully. An anonymous member of the crew voices this directly: "If the blamed sticks had been cut out of her she would be running along on her bottom now like any decent ship, an' giv' us all a chance." In testimony before the Committee on the Manning of Merchant Ships in 1894, just two years before Conrad began writing the story, he was aware of the dangers of "hard driving" that could lead to a knockdown (Bojarski, p. 22). And in a masterstroke of narrative strategy, the crew's repeated calls for the proper action are echoed by the despicable Donkin, whose yells of "cut! cut!" opposed by the captain's "no! no!" are finally silenced by a blow from a crew member who cannot stand the doubt. In terms of seamanship Donkin is right, Captain Allistoun is wrong. This is a trick that Conrad plays on readers a number of times, letting unreliable or too imaginative characters utter maritime truths. One thinks immediately of Mr. Burns, the nervous mate in "The Secret Sharer," or Jukes, who senses the full chaos in *Typhoon*.

The sea world that Conrad lived in and knew is just as full of anomalies and ironies as the shore life he wrote about later in *Nostromo*, *The Secret Agent*, and *Under Western Eyes*. But it is probably less accessible to modern readers because they have more trouble discerning the double vision that includes both what is seen in stark reality and what is superimposed on it an idealized vision of heroic or at least steadfast fidelity. Perhaps the British Merchant Service represented an island of solidity amid waves of metaphysical doubt. Like his Victorian predecessors, Alfred, Lord Tennyson (1809–1892) and Matthew Arnold (1822–1888), Conrad looked for some assurance of moral order in a world that seemed to contain none, ranging from the anarchy of the East Indies to the black hole in the middle of Africa where Marlow finds some consolation in the practical instructions of a tattered seamanship manual. The voyage tales are a vortex that sucks in both the pessimism of Arthur Schopenhauer (1788–1860) and the need for belief of Guy de Maupassant (1850–1893), while Conrad, like Gustave Flaubert (1821–1880), swirls around the perimeter dissecting illusions, one by one. He also identifies with *Don Quixote*, repeatedly, and that is perhaps the best model for understanding the bifurcation between voice and vision throughout Conrad's voyage tales: Sancho Panza is always there with the grubby details. Like a descendant of the good Don, Conrad could speak of fidelity and human solidarity in the British Merchant Service with rhetorical flourishes, but like Sancho, he was unable to shut his eyes and pretend that it was always so. No matter how much he wanted to believe that his sea world was governed by moral order, he never quashed the evidence against such a hypothesis.

[*See also* English Literature *and* Literature.]

# Bibliography

## Primary Works

Conrad, Joseph. *Collected Edition of the Works of Joseph Conrad.* 21 vols. London: Dent, 1946–1955. Reprinted from the Uniform Edition of 1923–1928, without the dramas. This is the most accessible collected edition, but many stories and novels are also available in a variety of paperback editions. Among them Norton Critical Editions are especially useful because they contain sources, backgrounds, reviews, and criticism.

Karl, Frederick R., and Laurence Davies, eds. *The Collected Letters of Joseph Conrad.* 8 vols. Cambridge, U.K., and New York: Cambridge University Press, 1983– . Karl, a biographer of Conrad, and Davies have collaborated on this definitive edition of Conrad's letters. Altogether the volumes include more than thirty-five hundred letters in English, French (original and translated), and Polish (translated), both professional and personal.

Reid, S. W., executive ed. *Cambridge Edition of Joseph Conrad.* Cambridge, U.K.: Cambridge University Press, 1990– . A new scholarly edition of Conrad's works, with full textual and bibliographic apparatus, as well as introductions to establish the context for each volume. Volumes in print include *The Secret Agent*, edited by Bruce Harkness and S.W. Reid wuth the assistance of Nancy Birk, 1990; *Almayer's Folly*, edited by Floyd Eugene Eddleman and David Leon Higdon, 1994; and *Notes on Life and Letters*, edited by J.H. Stape, with the assistance of Andrew Busza, 2004. Two more volumes are scheduled for publication in 2007, *A Personal Record*, edited by J.H. Stape and Zdzislaw Najder, and *'Twixt Land and Sea*, edited by Jacques Berthud, Laura Davis, and S.W. Reid.

## Secondary Works

Bojarski, Edmund. "Conrad at the Crossroads: From Navigator to Novelist with New Biographical Mysteries." *The Texas Quarterly* (Winter 1968): 22.

Carabine, Keith, ed. *Joseph Conrad: Critical Assessments.* 4 vols. Robertsbridge, U.K.: Helm Information, 1992. An Extensive Survey of Conrad criticism edited by one of England's most active and prolific Conrad scholars.

Daleski, H. M. *Joseph Conrad: The Way of Dispossession.* London: Faber and Faber, 1977. Explores the way in which Conrad's fear of losing "full possession of myself" plays out in his sea fiction and land tales.

Foulke, Robert D. "Life in the Dying World of Sail, 1870–1910." *The Journal of British Studies* 3, no. 1 (1963): 105–136. Reprinted in *Literature and Lore of the Sea*, edited by Patricia Ann Carlson, pp. 72–115. Amsterdam: Rodopi, 1986. Covers conditions in the British Merchant Service during Conrad's years at sea.

Foulke, Robert D. "Voyages of Endurance: *The Nigger of the 'Narcissus.'*" In *The Sea Voyage Narrative*, pp. 137–158 New York: Twayne, 1997.

Gordan, John Dozier. *Joseph Conrad: The Making of a Novelist.* Cambridge, Mass.: Harvard University Press, 1940. Reprint. New York: Russell and Russell, 1963. A pioneering study of Conrad's first years as a writer, from 1894 to 1900; focusing on *Almayer's Folly*, *The Nigger of the "Narcissus,"* and *Lord Jim*, Gordan explores both the sources and the development of texts as Conrad taught himself his craft.

Graver, Lawrence. *Conrad's Short Fiction.* Berkeley and Los Angeles: University of California Press, 1969. Analyzes Conrad's use of the "long short story" form, in which much of Conrad's voyage fiction is cast.

Guérard, Albert. *Conrad the Novelist.* Cambridge, Mass.: Harvard University Press, 1958. A seminal and influential study combining close textual study and archetypal analysis, especially as applied to *The Nigger of the "Narcissus," Lord Jim*, and some of the shorter sea fiction.

Hawthorn, Jeremy. *Joseph Conrad: Narrative Technique and Ideological Commitment.* London: Arnold, 1992.

Johnson, Bruce. *Conrad's Models of Mind.* Minneapolis: University of Minnesota Press, 1971.

Karl, Frederick R. *Joseph Conrad, the Three Lives: A Biography.* London: Faber and Faber, 1979. A lifelong student of Conrad, Karl produces a massive and detailed biography focused on the relationships among Conrad's three lives as Pole, sailor, and writer.

Knowles, Owen. *An Annotated Critical Bibliography of Joseph Conrad.* New York: St. Martin's, 1992. Adds two more decades of prolific writing about Conrad to previous bibliographies.

Knowles, Owen. *A Conrad Chronology.* Houndmills, U.K.: Macmillan, 1989. This slim but very useful reference volume covers the major events in Conrad's life by year from 1857 to 1893 through his early life and sea career, then month by month with specific days noted from 1894 until his death in 1924. Appendices include a select who's who and a brief description of key locations.

Lothe, Jakob. *Conrad's Narrative Method.* Oxford: Clarendon Press, 1989.

Najder, Zdzislaw. *Joseph Conrad: A Chronicle*. Cambridge, U.K.: Cambridge University Press, 1983. A biography written between 1957 and 1977 by Poland's most eminent Conrad scholar, supplemented for the English edition in 1983. Clearly written and authoritative.

Sherry, Norman. *Conrad's Eastern World*. London: Cambridge University Press, 1966. A meticulous tracing of sources for *Lord Jim*, "*The End of the Tether*," *The Shadow-Line*, and "*The Secret Sharer*," as well as the eastern land fiction, with many related documents in appendices.

Teets, Bruce E., and Helmut E. Gerber. *Joseph Conrad: An Annotated Bibliography of Writings about Him*. DeKalb: Northern Illinois University Press, 1971. A massive annotated bibliography of writing about Conrad from 1895 to 1966, including 1,977 entries ranging from reviews and dissertations to articles and books.

Villiers, Peter. *Joseph Conrad: Master Mariner*. Dobbs Ferry, N.Y.: Sheridan House, 2006. Noted voyager and sea writer Alan Villiers left this book unfinished when he died, and now his son Peter has completed it for publication. It deals with the sea context of Conrad's own voyages, including the ships, crews, weather, sea conditions, and difficulties encountered.

Watt, Ian. *Conrad in the Nineteenth Century*. London: Chatto and Windus, 1980. A major study of Conrad's early fiction, combining biography, history, and interpretation. Includes long chapters on *The Nigger of the "Narcissus*," "Heart of Darkness," and *Lord Jim*.

ROBERT D. FOULKE

# Consolato del Mare. *See* Law, *subentry on* Classical and Medieval Law.

# Constable, John (1776–1837), English painter.
Born on June 11, 1776, at East Bergholt, Suffolk, John Constable was the fourth of six children born to Golding Constable (1739–1816) and his wife, Ann Watts (1748–1815). Golding Constable was a corn and coal merchant as well as a gentleman farmer who had inherited substantial property, including a watermill on the river Stour on the boundary between Essex and Suffolk. Initially sent to boarding schools, John Constable received his principal education at Dedham Grammar School, where his early artistic leanings were encouraged. From the age of sixteen he began training to work in the family businesses, but at age nineteen he met and was encouraged to pursue art by Sir George Howland Beaumont (1753–1827), a well-known painter who had local connections. When Constable's younger brother was able to replace him in business, Constable contacted Joseph Farrington (1747–1821), a member of the Royal Academy, who opened the way for Constable to study painting in London between 1799 and 1809. During this period and during his visits home, Constable developed his commitment to outdoor landscape painting, the genre in which he earned fame and which sustains his posthumous reputation.

Constable fervently believed that landscape painting was the superior genre. Despite his disdain for marine painting and his thought that scenes of ships and boats were hackneyed subjects incapable of beautiful sentiment, he nevertheless produced important work that very successfully captured the maritime atmosphere, particularly in his oil sketches and watercolors of beach scenes.

In April 1803, at the age of twenty-six, Constable spent a month on board the East Indiaman HEICS *Coutts*. This period included a short passage from London to Deal. In these weeks Constable made about 130 oil sketches of shipping, apparently consciously emulating the style of Willem van de Velde the Younger (1633–1707), some of whose work he had seen. Among the vessels that Constable sketched was HMS *Victory*, just as she was being refitted at Chatham in preparation for Vice Admiral Lord Nelson to break his flag in her the following month in preparation for taking command in the Mediterranean. Three years later, Constable used these sketches for his only attempt to depict a sea battle, *His Majesty's Ship "Victory" in the Battle of Trafalgar between Two French Ships of the Line*. While painting this watercolor, Constable consulted a Suffolk seaman who had been at the battle.

On several occasions, Constable spent his holiday on the coast. In 1816 he and his wife stayed with a friend in Osmington, Dorset, overlooking Weymouth Bay. Here he painted several versions of *Weymouth Bay* (National Gallery, London) and probably his study of waves, *Rough Sea* (Paul Mellon Collection, U.S.). These watercolor paintings were the antecedents of marine-related paintings that he did on other visits to the shore, first in nearby Essex (*Harwich Light House*, c. 1820; Tate Gallery) and Norfolk (*Yarmouth Pier*, 1822; Denver Art Museum).

Between 1824 and 1828, Constable completed other works, several of which included local vessels, on a series of holidays spent at Brighton. They included *Brighton Beach with Colliers* and *Hove Beach with Fishing Boats* (Victoria and Albert Museum, London). Constable completed only one large oil canvas from these various seaside visits: *The Marine Parade and Chain Pier* (1827; Tate Collection, London).

An important group of Constable's major oil paintings are those that depict the landscape in which he was raised around Dedham and near his father's mill at Flatford, an area that has come to be known as "Constable country."

***Beach with Rough Sea and Fishing Boats.*** Constable painted this scene at Hove Beach near Brighton, England, in 1824. SCALA / ART RESOURCE, NY / VICTORIA AND ALBERT MUSEUM, LONDON

Among these works there are several that depict aspects of inland navigation as part of the landscape. Chief among them are *Boatbuilding near Flatford Mill* (1814–1815; Victoria and Albert Museum, London); *View on the Stour near Flatford Mill* (1822; Huntington Art Gallery, San Marino, California), which illustrates barges preparing to enter Flatford Mill lock; and another view, *A Boat Passing a Lock* (1826; Royal Academy, London).

Constable died at his home, 35 Charlotte Street, Fitzroy Square, London, on April 1, 1837, and was buried in Saint John's churchyard in Hampstead.

[*See also* Art; Artists, *subentry* British; *and* Painting.]

## Bibliography

Beckett, R. B., ed. *John Constable's Correspondence.* 6 vols. Ipswich, U.K.: Publications of the Suffolk Record Society, vols. 4, 6, 8, and 10–12, 1962–1968.

Cordingly, David. *Marine Painting in England, 1700–1900.* New York: Clarkson Potter, 1973.

Parris, L., C. Shields, and L. Fleming-Williams, eds. *John Constable: Further Documents and Correspondence.* London: Tate Gallery and the Suffolk Record Society, vol. 18, 1975.

JOHN B. HATTENDORF

## Constantinople. *See* Istanbul.

**Constanța** The biggest port on the shores of the Black Sea, Constanța is located in southeast Romania, at 44°10′ N and 28°09′ E; it lies in a gulf that is dominated by a small cliff in the north and by the Carasu Valley in south. This harbored town, the most important in the Dobruja historical territory between the Danube and the Black Sea, is the capital of Constanța County (*judeţul*). At Constanța, the Danube–Black Sea Canal connects the Danube with the Black Sea, providing a cheaper and shorter waterway transport toward central Europe and the North Sea, via the Rhine-Main Canal.

The oldest part of the city is situated on a peninsula where the Neolithic culture of Hamangia was present and where Greek settlers founded the ancient city-state (*polis*) of Tomis. In the first century B.C.E. the Romans took over the region known in Imperial Rome as Scythia Minor, and in the fourth century C.E. the city was reconstructed by the emperor Constantine the Great (r. 306–337), from whom the city took its new name. After the invasions of the Goths, Huns, Avars, and Gepidae, the settlement declined; a village (*custendge*) is mentioned during the Ottoman administration. After the Russian-Romanian-Ottoman War (the Romanian war of independence, 1877–1878)—during which Dobruja became a province of the Romanian independent state—Constanţa was enlarged and developed as a modern industrial and trading town. A factor in this social development was the construction in 1895 of a bridge over the Danube, one of the longest in the world at that time, and the construction of a new modern port; both of these achievements are connected with the name of the prodigious engineer Anghel Saligny.

In the twentieth century the harbor became an important point on maritime maps: the silos, the terminal of pipelines, the docks, the dams, the lighthouse, the piers, the oil-drilling systems, the maritime station for passengers and trade, the shipyards, the companies (NAVROM and others), the cruises, the traffic. The port played a role in the two world wars (in 1918 the Allies liberated it from the occupation of the Central Powers), the Cold War, the revolutionary mutation from the watershed years 1989–1990, the transition, and many aspects of globalization.

Historic monuments in Constanţa include an ancient urban district, dating from the seventh century B.C.E.; a Roman edifice with a mosaic, dating from the reign of Constantine the Great—the surface area of the edifice is 2,000 square meters (21,528 square feet)—a Roman wall (*valum romanum*); and the aqueducts; a Genovese lighthouse; the Orthodox Cathedral of Saint Peter and Saint Paul (the Archbishopric of Tomis, located in the ancient urban district); a Muslim mosque (the new building was erected before World War I); a casino designed by the architect D. Renard and built in 1910; and a national historical and archaeological museum, with exhibits of treasure, located in the former town hall. Constanţa is also the site of many important museums, such as the Romanian Maritime Museum, and institutes of scientific research and culture.

Important statues include those of Ovid (Publius Ovidius Naso, c. 43 B.C.E –17 C.E.), exiled Roman poet; Mihai Eminescu (1850–1889), national poet inspired by the Black Sea; Anghel Saligny (1854–1925), architect and engineer, and the builder of the Danube Bridge and con-

structor of the Constanţa modern port; and Vasile Pârvan, an eminent archaeologist.

In the early twenty-first century, Constanţa has about 310,471 inhabitants and includes the biggest sea resort of Romania—Mamaia—with one of the best beaches in Europe (located 6 kilometers [3.7 miles] north of Constanţa). Together with the new Constanţa South Port (including the oil terminal), Constanţa is the biggest Romanian shipyard and the sixth European port with direct access to the Pan-European Corridor VII, having a new container terminal on Pier II South, as well as Ro-Ro and ferryboat terminals suitable for the development of short-sea shipping serving the Black Sea and the Danube riparian countries. The new status of Port of Constanţa is as a "port with customs facilities," with future expansion planned. Constanţa is also the coordinating tourist center of the Romanian coastal resorts, with Mihail Kogă lniceanu International Airport located in the vicinity.

[*See also* Ports.]

Miron Florea

## Containerization. *See* Unit Loads.

## Container Ship

"Containerization" refers to the stowing of freight in metal containers of uniform size and shape for transportation. Once stowed in containers, all kinds of oddly shaped boxes and bags, machines, and even liquids (for example, fuel oil) can be handled as a single unit. In 1965 the International Organization for Standardization (ISO) accepted standard container sizes—ten, twenty, thirty, and forty feet in length—although different-size containers are still used today.

Two methods are available for loading and unloading containers. Roll-on, roll-off (Ro-Ro) was popular during World War II, but eventually lift-on, lift-off proved to be much more efficient. Lower costs resulting from reductions in the number of crew members and from mechanized cargo handling, together with economies of scale, explain the success of the container ship. A container ship can be turned around in less than thirty-six hours and spends as little as 20 percent of its time in a port, which contributed greatly to solving the problem of port congestion in the 1950s and 1960s. The ability to transport large boxes on trains, trucks, and inland ships, eliminating the need to unload specific cargo, is known as "intermodalism" and is another major feature of containerization. Containers also reduce pilferage and damage to goods in ports.

The first generation of container ships in the 1950s could carry a few hundred containers of twenty-feet equivalent units (TEUs), and the second generation could carry 1,500 of them. A typical third-generation vessel was *Liverpool Bay* (1971) with a capacity of 2661 TEUs. These ships were still able to pass through the Panama Canal. "Post-Panamax" ships—ships that have at least one dimension too large to allow the ship to pass through the Panama Canal—increased to well over 3500 TEUs (for example, *Nedlloyd Asia*, built in 1991). In 2006 Maersk Sealand alone operated twenty-one vessels able to carry at least 6000 TEUs.

The container as we have come to know it is largely the brainchild of Malcolm McLean (1914–2001), a former North Carolina trucker. In 1955 he sold his trucking company and bought Waterman Steamship Company and its subsidiary Pan Atlantic Tanker Company. The parent company was renamed Sea-Land Service, Inc., in 1960. On April 26, 1956, McLean introduced the first scheduled container service between Port Elizabeth, New Jersey, and Houston, Texas, with the converted Pan Atlantic T2 tanker *Ideal X*, carrying fifty-eight containers on deck. On the West Coast, the Matson Navigation Company used a converted C3-type cargo vessel, *Hawaiian Merchant*, to carry containers between San Francisco and Honolulu from August 1958 on. The company soon set up a research department that designed the first cellular or full container ship, *Hawaiian Citizen* (1960). Matson removed the cranes from his ships, relying instead on container terminals with large shore-based gantry cranes. The Australian company Associated Steamships ordered the first newly built cellular container ships in 1963. However, McLean is usually credited with initiating the container revolution. In April 1966, *Fairland* set sail for Europe on its first transatlantic service between Port Elizabeth and Rotterdam. Other companies soon followed the example set by Sea-Land—companies such as Atlantic Container Lines, Moore-McCormack, and United States Lines. High operating costs and relatively low profits forced a concentration of container shipping lines in the 1990s (for example, P&O Nedlloyd, Maersk Sealand, and Nippon Yusen Kaisha).

[*See also* Shipping Companies *and* Shipping Revolution.]

## Bibliography

Broeze, Frank. *The Globalisation of the Oceans: Containerisation from the 1950s to the Present*. Saint John's, Newfoundland: International Maritime Economic History Association, 2002.

Gardiner, Robert, ed. *The Shipping Revolution: The Modern Merchant Ship*. London: Conway Maritime Press, 1992.

Gibson, Andrew, and Arthur Donovan. *The Abandoned Ocean: A History of United States Maritime Policy*. Columbia: University of South Carolina Press, 2000.

Graham, M. G., and D. O. Hughes. *Containerisation in the Eighties*. London and New York: Lloyd's of London Press, 1985.

FERRY DE GOEY

**Convoy** The origins of convoy are almost lost in antiquity. On land the grouping of any entity for self-protection seems virtually biological and springs from the benefits of clustering. Herds of animals threatened by predators will join together, partly in order that the greater organism—the group—will survive and partly in order to confuse the enemy. At sea, certain animals behave in the same way, as did man-made entities. The large fleets of the classical era were so arranged as to provide self-protection. Later the *flotas* of the Spanish overseas empire were put together to provide a defense against English raiders. The main principle of the convoy as practiced in the modern world had two elements. First, grouping as described above, and second, the placing of protective forces otherwise known as escorts in the vicinity of the group. The escorts were put in the position of greatest danger to the protected forces, when they were just about to be attacked. This had a number of sequential benefits. The attackers might be deterred by the mere presence of the protecting force. If not, then having to take account of the protectors might at least distract the attackers, or the attackers might even turn their attention to fighting the protecting ships instead of the protected prizes. Finally, the presence of the protective escorts made a counterattack possible.

During the period of the French Revolution and the Napoleonic Wars (1792–1815) convoy was extensively practiced by the various coalitions against the French, especially by the British. Convoy's success was also related to the attitude of the burgeoning London insurance market, which imposed punitive rates on those shipowners who chose to operate their ships outside the system. However, the century's undoubted innovation for all ships was the rise and spread of steam propulsion, and convoy was no longer practiced. It is not possible to be sure exactly why this was the case, although the ensuing general peace, which lasted close to a hundred years, undoubtedly played a part, if only psychologically.

### World War I

What this lack of convoy use meant in reality was that when World War I began in 1914, convoy was in no nation's mind, nor were any of the nations familiar with the realities of the technique. At the outset this was not thought to be important because, from the viewpoint of the Allies, blockade would deal with the difficulties of surface raiders. The Germans in particular did deploy some blockades, especially in distant waters, but the scale of their effort posed no large-scale threat to shipping. When a large-scale threat to shipping occurred, it came from a somewhat unexpected quarter: the relatively new innovation of the submarine. Prior to the war the submarine had not been considered a particular problem because it was thought that international law had constrained the submarine to such an extent that it could not operate effectively against merchant shipping. What changed everything was the series of German campaigns of unrestricted submarine warfare, in which submarines sank merchant ships, often without significant warning. This was relatively easy for the submarines to do, since ships were sailing independently and on relatively predictable routes. Further, a submarine could surface, sink its target with gunfire, and submerge again long before any surface forces might be on the scene.

There were two fundamental problems to solve: the protection of shipping and dealing with a submerged submarine. For the best part of two and a half years, protection of shipping was not properly addressed for a number of reasons. There was a marked offensive mindset present in the British Admiralty and this manifested itself in what might be called "hunting tactics." Under these tactics, groups of destroyers would sweep the seas looking for submarines. Unfortunately, any half-competent submarine would submerge long before it was sighted by a destroyer. The problem was complicated by faulty statistics that suggested that the scale of the convoy escort problem lay beyond realistic solution.

In the end a significant step toward solving the problem came from a slightly unusual direction: the French coal trade. A consequence, not immediately obvious, of Italy entering the conflict by going to war with Austria-Hungary was that Britain had to supply France with considerable quantities of coal. The coal was moved across the English Channel from ports such as Falmouth in the west and Dover in the east. However, these independent sailings were much disrupted by submarines, often as much by their mere presence keeping colliers in harbor as by actual sinkings. Help was at hand at the end of 1916, when the French suggested grouping ships together—otherwise known as a convoy system—and escorting them with trawlers and drifters. This was done with great success, and there was subsequently very little coal shipping lost to submarines.

More important, the flow of coal was maintained without impediment. The Admiralty side of this operation was run by a young commander, Reginald Henderson, who considered that the convoy system could be applied to ocean shipping. By undocumented means this view was transmitted to the cabinet secretary, Maurice Hankey, and a trial scheme of convoy began from Gibraltar to the United Kingdom in May 1917. This was an instant success and was extended to virtually all ocean shipping, largely nullifying the submarine problem. Dealing with submerged submarines was a huge scientific and technical challenge, but one that seemed to be well on the way to being solved by the end of the war in 1918 by means of active sonar and depth charges.

## World War II

World War II, however, saw a revival in submarine warfare, and the submerged submarine's vulnerability to underwater detection was largely nullified by the tactic of carrying out surface attacks by night. The British, at least, were quick to return to convoys, and this, coupled with initial German problems in having to reach Atlantic battlegrounds via roundabout northern routes, limited U-boats' the effectiveness considerably.

The German invasion of France in 1940 gave the submarine arm easy access to the Atlantic via French bases, giving the submarines a boost in their campaign against merchant shipping. Nevertheless, a convoy could well be difficult to find in the broad Atlantic, and although its protection could vary greatly in quality, submarines might yet be fought off. The British began their system of keeping escort groups together, maximizing their effect.

The entry of the United States into the war in 1940 removed an important constraint from the U-boats, and a number of them moved to the east coast of the United States, where, because of an initial reluctance to adopt the convoy system, targets were easy both to find and to sink. After some months, however, convoy was adopted by degrees, extending down the U.S. east coast, then into the Gulf of Mexico, and then into the Caribbean. This not only reduced losses but also meant that the submarines had to again choose the mid-Atlantic for their continued offensive.

From mid-1942 to mid-1943 the war against convoys was on an immense scale and was bitterly fought. At times there were more than one hundred submarines at sea, but even this number could not target every single convoy. A combination of technical factors, growing Allied strength and skill, and good intelligence—including, among many other elements, the ability to decode German signal traffic, known as Ultra—led to the defeat of the U-boats by May 1943. After that Allied convoys went on their way, more or less unmolested, and were a key factor in the western strategy on land against the Axis forces.

In the Pacific, the Japanese initially showed a lack of interest in convoy and other prudent anti-submarine warfare (ASW) measures. As a result, the most successful submarine campaign against shipping was fought by the Americans against the Japanese, resulting in the near-total loss of the Japanese merchant marine and Japan's consequent inability to sustain the offensive, leading to its ultimate defeat.

### Postwar Period

In the postwar years, interest in convoy has been variable, not least because there has not been any large-scale hot maritime war. In the 1980s there was considerable interest within the North Atlantic Treaty Organization (NATO) in what was called the defended lane concept, in which area search assets such as towed-array frigates and nuclear submarines would operate in boxes on either side of a lane in which merchant shipping could transit, probably not in convoy. This was never tried in war.

On the other hand, there have been instances where merchant ships have been escorted by warships for the merchant ships' protection. Notably, this occurred in the Persian Gulf during the Iran-Iraq War of 1980–1988, especially during the so-called Tanker War in the latter part of that conflict. Although this was rarely referred to as convoy, that is what it was.

Although convoy attracts little apparent interest now, it is possible that changes in world circumstances such as a substantial rise in the use of violence at sea—anywhere from piracy to terrorism to total war—may yet render convoy a salient maritime topic.

[*See also* Anti-Submarine Warfare; Atlantic, Battle of the; Shipping; *subentry on* State-owned Shipping; Submarine; Warships, *subentry on* Modern Warships; *and* Wars, Maritime, *subentries on* World Wars *and* Wars after 1945.]

### Bibliography

Barley, Freddie, and David Waters. *The Defeat of the Enemy Attack on Shipping: A Study of Policy and Operations.* 2 vols. London: Historical Section, Admiralty, 1957. Reprint. Burlington, Vt.: Ashgate, 1997; London: Navy Records Society, 1998.

Bijl, A. *De Nederlandse convooidienst: De maritieme bescherming van koopvaardij en zeevisserij tegen piraten en oorlogsgevaar in het verleden.* The Hague, Netherlands: Nijhoff, 1951.

Crowhurst, Patrick. *The Defence of British Trade, 1689–1815.* Folkestone, U.K.: Dawson, 1977.

Gannon, Michael. *Black May.* New York: Harper Collins, 1998.

Gardner, W. J. R. *Decoding History: The Battle of the Atlantic and Ultra.* Annapolis, Md.: Naval Institute Press, 1999.

Hague, Arnold. *The Allied Convoy System, 1939–1945: Its Organization, Defence, and Operation.* Annapolis, Md.: Naval Institute Press, 2000.

Milner, Marc. *North Atlantic Run: The Royal Canadian Navy and the Battle for the Convoys.* Annapolis, Md.: Naval Institute Press, 1985.

Morison, Samuel Eliot. *The Atlantic Battle Won, May 1943–May 1945.* History of United States Naval Operations in World War II, vol. 10. Boston: Little, Brown, 1956.

Morison, Samuel Eliot. *The Battle of the Atlantic, September 1939–May 1943.* History of United States Naval Operations in World War II, vol. 1. Boston: Little, Brown, 1947.

Rohwer, Jürgen. *The Critical Convoy Battles of March 1943: The Battle for HX.229/SC122.* Annapolis, Md.: Naval Institute Press, 1977.

Roskill, S. W. *The War at Sea, 1939–1945.* 3 vols. in 4. London: Her Majesty's Stationery Office, 1954–1961.

Seth, Ronald. *The Fiercest Battle: The Story of North Atlantic Convoy ONS 5, 22nd April–7th May 1943.* London: Hutchinson, 1961.

Syrett, David. *The Defeat of the German U-boats: The Battle of the Atlantic.* Columbia: University of South Carolina Press, 1994.

W. J. R. GARDNER

# Cook, James

**Cook, James** (1728–1779), English explorer and navigator. James Cook was born on October 27, 1728, in the village of Marsden, Yorkshire, where his father was a day laborer. He served an apprenticeship in the North Sea coal trade, during which he began to learn navigation, mathematics, and astronomical observation. He joined the Royal Navy in 1755, serving mostly in North America during the Seven Years' War, when he continued his self-education and distinguished himself by his diligent and accurate charting of the Saint Lawrence River, and later of the coasts of Nova Scotia and Newfoundland, and by the observation of an eclipse of the sun. These qualifications led to his being offered the command of *Endeavour*, the ship chosen to undertake the Royal Society's project of observing the 1769 transit of Venus across the face of the sun from the newly discovered island of Tahiti in the middle of the Pacific Ocean—to which purpose the Admiralty added that of another search for the purported Southern Continent.

**Captain James Cook.** Commissioned from the artist Sir Nathaniel Dance (1735–1811) by Sir Joseph Banks for his personal collection, Cook posed for this portrait "for a few hours before dinner" on May 25, 1776, just before Cook left on his third voyage. © NATIONAL MARITIME MUSEUM, LONDON

## First and Second Voyages

Cook sailed from Plymouth on August 26, 1768. His route took him past Cape Horn to Tahiti, then south to New Zealand, whose two main islands he charted, then west to the previously unknown eastern coast of Australis, which he also charted and where he nearly lost *Endeavour* in "the most dangerous navigation that perhaps ever Ship was in." After taking possession of the east coast of "New South Wales," he turned west into Torres Strait. He lost almost a third of his crew to illness at Batavia, on the homeward leg, before reaching England again in July 1771.

The first circumnavigation was notable for Cook's extensive charting and for the collections made by the scientists who sailed with him, but the large task that it did not accomplish was the discovery of *Terra Australis Incognita*. This became the fundamental purpose of Cook's second circumnavigation. Accompanied by Tobias Furneaux in *Adventure*, Cook sailed in *Resolution* in July

1772. After calling at the Cape of Good Hope, he crossed the southern Indian Ocean. In January 1773 he became the first navigator to cross the Antarctic Circle. Reaching New Zealand on March 25, he paused at Dusky Sound. He had sailed 117 days and 16,000 kilometers (nearly 10,000 miles) without sight of land. Because of the regimen that he insisted on, his crew was in good health.

Cook refreshed the ships in Queen Charlotte Sound, and then he searched that area of the southern Pacific where he had not sailed on his previous voyage. In mid-July, having found no land, he turned north, reaching Tahiti on August 15. Cook sailed again in September and spent the next fourteen months crisscrossing the southern Pacific Ocean, during which he passed the Antarctic Circle twice more, and visiting most of the major island groups, including the Marquesas Islands, sighted by Mendaña, and the New Hebrides, sighted by Quirós.

Cook began his return from New Zealand in November 1774, reaching the western entrance of the Strait of Magellan in mid-December, Cape Town in March, and anchoring at Spithead on July 30. He had been away three years and eighteen days, had sailed more than 110,000 kilometers (over 68,000 miles), and had lost only four of his crew. He had shown that there was no Terra Australis, unless it lay about the pole, where "no man will ever venture."

On his return, the Admiralty promoted Cook to post-captain, and appointed him to the fourth such position on the establishment of Greenwich Hospital, a very considerable honor as well as a comfortable sinecure for someone without wealth or social or political power, and of comparatively junior rank. The Royal Society elected him a fellow and awarded him its Copley Medal. Over the autumn and winter months Cook prepared the narrative of his second voyage for publication, and he mingled with London's high and literary society. However, when it became clear that the Admiralty intended to mount a third voyage of Pacific exploration, this time in search of the Northwest Passage, Cook found himself unable to accept his quiet retirement.

## Third Voyage, Death, and Legacy

Cook sailed in *Resolution* in July 1776 and was joined at Cape Town by Charles Clerke in *Discovery*. The two ships then called at New Zealand and the Cook, Tongan, and Society Islands. In January 1778, crossing the North Pacific, Cook discovered the Hawai'ian Islands. From March to October he charted the northwestern American coast and its adjacent islands. He reached Alaska, called

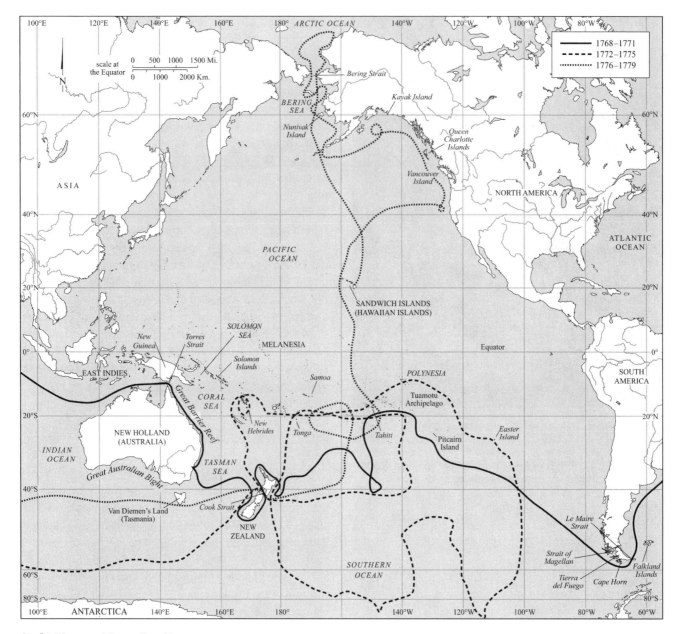

**Cook's Voyages.** MAP BY BILL NELSON

at the Aleutian Islands, passed through the Bering Strait into the Arctic Ocean, and sighted the eastern coast of Asia. He then decided to return to winter at the Hawai'ian Islands, which he reached at the end of November 1778.

After Cook's death at Kealakekua Bay, Hawai'i, on February 14, 1779, in a violent confrontation with the Hawai'ians, his officers continued the voyage, examining the northern coast of Asia before going to Macau. The ships reached England in early October 1780, having been away more than four years.

There is a singularity to Cook himself, and a quality to his voyages, that set both him and them apart. No one before him stayed at sea longer or maintained an expedition at such a distance from home ports. His diligence in charting and observing was matched only by those junior officers whom he trained so rigorously. On the first voyage, he made consistent use of Nevil Maskelyne's lunar tables, thus demonstrating that it was possible to calculate longitude at sea much more accurately than had previously been the case (even if this involved tedious hours of mathematics). On the second, he used John Harrison and Larcum Kendall's chronometer successfully, thus showing the much greater convenience of this method. Though he did not himself understand properly what actually combated scurvy, by his general regimen he showed how this age-old scourge of sailors might be fought. And, in advance of his age, he had a developed sense of the relativity of cultural values, which distinguished his dealings with the peoples of the Pacific.

In awarding him the Copley Medal, the Royal Society's president, Lord Morton, said of Cook that he had "fixed the bounds of the habitable earth, as well as those of the navigable ocean, in the southern hemisphere." This was true, but misses something of Cook's singularity. Georg Forster, one of his companions on his second voyage, conveyed this better when he wrote in 1787:

> His mind, which knew no idleness, was constantly reflecting on means of relieving the hardships of his people's harsh way of life and in so doing to lengthen the duration of the voyage, to expand the scope of his discoveries and to enrich our knowledge ... by means of new observations on nature, on human as well as on animal vegetable and inanimate bodies.... No one knew the value of a fleeting moment better and no one used it so scrupulously as he. In the same period of time no one has ever extended the bounds of our knowledge to such a degree.

[See also Endeavour; Northwest Passage; Pacific Ocean, subentry on Exploration Voyages in the Eighteenth Century; and Terra Australis Incognita.]

## Bibliography

J. C. Beaglehole, The Life of Captain James Cook (London: Hakluyt Society, 1974), incorporates the results of a lifetime of scholarship and remains the most detailed biography. Glyndwr Williams, "Seamen and Philosophers in the South Seas in the Age of Captain Cook," Mariner's Mirror 65 (1979): 3–22, and Alan Frost, The Voyage of the "Endeavour" (Sydney, Australia: Allen and Unwin, 1998), offer additional insights into Cook's thinking and personality. Michael Hoare, " 'Cook the Discoverer': An Essay by Georg Forster, 1787," Records of the Australian Academy of Science 1, no. 4 (1969): pp. 7–16, makes available Forster's views. Two recent books are Anne Salmond, The Trial of the Cannibal Dog: Captain Cook in the South Seas (London: Allen Lane, 2003), and Nicholas Thomas, Discoveries: The Voyages of Captain Cook (London: Allen Lane, 2003).

ALAN FROST

# Cooke, E. W. (1811–1880), English marine artist.
Trained in his father's studio, where drawings by some of the chief artists of the day, including J. M. W Turner, passed through for engraving, Edward William Cooke had the Port of London—with massed international shipping—almost on his doorstep, providing subjects of absorbing interest for a youngster with an obsessional desire to show how things were constructed and how they worked. Fine draftsmanship and attention to detail, fostered by the engraver's art, resulted in his production in 1829 (at age seventeen) of Fifty Plates of Shipping and Craft, enlarged in 1831 to Sixty Five Plates of Shipping and Craft, a volume of small etched plates that is still justly celebrated for its detailed record of build and rig among everyday boats and vessels of many types. There had been similar collections before, but Cooke's standard showed a new seriousness, as much nautical archaeology as marine art. He was aware of rapid changes occurring among the vehicles of seaborne commerce. Steam had arrived, the age of the photographer was dawning, and Cooke by 1840 had established himself as an exacting marine recorder, visiting France, the Netherlands, and Italy during the first half of the century. Working craft in their environment interested him profoundly, more than current movements in art, and he became known for this uncompromising attention to structure and a determination to illustrate the rig of even the smallest craft. Aiming to join the art establishment, with election to the Royal Academy as the pinnacle of his profession (achieved in 1864), he exhibited many paintings from 1834, in London and in the provinces. He became known as "Van Kook" from his devoted depiction of Netherlands fishing and trading boats and, after 1851, increasingly for his views of the lagoons and islands around Venice, with their variety of characteristic craft, which Cooke painted from his adapted gondola. Specialization, a characteristic of Victorian painters, led to the Royal Academy and a picture-buying public relying on E. W. Cooke to provide decorative portraits of exotic craft in an authentic setting, portraits that today are recognized as possessing archaeological significance. The Mediterranean coasts of Spain and North Africa as well as the Nile River yielded models of working sailing craft that were added to his repertoire. Geological features as well as atmospheric or meteorological phenomena were a special study and delight, so that experts in many fields applauded his work.

Autumnal Venetian sunsets, of which the vastly influential art historian and critic John Ruskin wrote in glowing terms, featured largely in Cooke's art, as did the unmistakable crepuscular glories of the Nile fringed with palms and ruins of antiquity. In his 1936 book Sail and Power, the yacht sailor and designer Uffa Fox wrote of Cooke as "the marine artist to whom seamen owe most," pointing out the mass of relevant historical information on the rig of sailing craft to be extracted from Cooke's drawings and sketches.

***Dutch Pincks at Scheveningen.*** E. W. Cooke painted this oil on canvas in 1860. HIP / Art Resource, NY / Guildhall Art Gallery, London

The American Nathanael Herreshoff was also an admirer. An habitual sketcher, classifying and filing the smallest details in a systematic range of boxes in his studio, Cooke covered every subject he encountered. His sketchbooks did not survive. At his posthumous studio sale, held by Christie's in London in May 1880, thousands of pages from this vast reference collection, mirroring an industrious half century, were dispersed among dealers and connoisseurs, and these drawings continue to circulate. He published two volumes: *Leaves from My Sketch-books* in 1875 and 1876, lithographic reproductions of pencil studies supported by informatively entertaining text. A diary that he kept from 1829 until the end of 1879 provided a valuable itinerary, the basis of a study of his life and works, including a catalogue raisonné.

[*See also* Art; Artists; *and* Herreshoff, Nathanael.]

## Bibliography

Cooke, E. W. *Sailing Vessels in Authentic Early-Nineteenth-Century Illustrations*. New York: Dover, 1989.

Cooke, E. W. *Shipping and Craft*. London: Masthead, 1970. Facsimile edition with commentary by Roger Finch.

Munday, John. *E. W. Cooke RA, FRS, FSA, FLS, FZS, FGS, 1811–1880: A Man of His Time*. Woodbridge, Suffolk, U.K.: Antique Collectors' Club, 1996.

JOHN MUNDAY

# Cooper, James Fenimore (1789–1851),

American writer. Born in Burlington, New Jersey, on September 15, 1789, James Fenimore Cooper was the son of Elizabeth Fenimore, from a New Jersey Quaker family, and William Cooper, a Federalist congressman and the founder of Cooperstown, New York. Although he is known today as a novelist of the American wilderness, Cooper's reputation in his lifetime rested in large measure on his invention and development of the sea novel. He was the first significant writer to adopt seamen as the principal characters of his novels, to employ the ship as their major setting, and to focus their central action on the struggle for existence in an oceanic world.

## Sea Novels of the Early and Middle Periods

Encouraged by Lord Byron's infusion of maritime life with the spirit of Romanticism in such poems as "The Corsair" and "The Island" and by Walter Scott's incorporation of terrain and storm as meaningful elements in fiction, Cooper published his first novel of the sea, *The Pilot*, in 1824. Set in the era of the American Revolution, the work is notable for the moody Byronism of its central character, a thinly disguised version of John Paul Jones, and for its introduction of the common seaman as hero in the figure of the boatswain Long Tom Coffin. Cooper's next two sea novels, *The Red Rover* (1827) and *The Water-Witch* (1830), focus on the figures of a gentlemanly pirate and a dashing smuggler, rather awkwardly joining the devices of Shakespearean romance to a masterly treatment of seamanship in the eighteenth century. After Cooper's return in 1834 from seven years' residence in Europe, his sea novels took a decidedly new turn. The first, *Homeward Bound* (1838), abandoned the heroics of its predecessors for comic realism, focusing on the interactions of the passengers on board a transatlantic packet ship.

With *Mercedes of Castile* (1840), *The Two Admirals* (1842), and *The Wing-and-Wing* (1842), Cooper returned to the materials of the maritime past, but this time with a serious concern for the relation of his characters to the large social and political events that enclose them—Christopher Columbus's first voyage of discovery, the struggle between England and France in the War of the Austrian Succession, and Admiral Horatio Lord Nelson's occupation of Naples during the Napoleonic Wars, respectively. In these three novels the aura of fantasy that invests Cooper's first three sea romances is gone, replaced by a sober attention to character and scene. The ocean is no longer the arena of freedom, offering an escape from the oppressions and responsibilities of shore society, but rather is the testing ground of common human experience, where universal meanings and values appear more starkly and truly than they do amid the complexities and conventions of life on land.

### Late Novels

Cooper's last three sea novels—*Afloat and Ashore* (1844), *Jack Tier* (1846–1848), and *The Sea Lions* (1849)—are at once his least familiar and his most interesting. In these books the note of dark realism that Richard Henry Dana Jr. had sounded in his autobiographical *Two Years before the Mast* (1840) is voiced again and again. The glamorous outlaws and naval heroes of the past that populate the earlier books give way to working seamen, striving to make a living amid the actualities of the writer's own century. Despite this general similarity in their materials, however, the three novels differ sharply from one another in their design, for they represent the most daring of Cooper's experiments in the imaginative uses of maritime experience. Thus *Afloat and Ashore*—a sprawling double novel whose second part is sometimes titled *Miles Wallingford* after the central character of the work—is, uniquely among Cooper's sea novels, narrated in the first person; Miles himself recounts his first voyage before the mast, his slow rise to command and ownership of a merchant vessel, and

the wreck and bankruptcy that end his nautical career. Set at the turn of the nineteenth century, the early action of the novel mirrors the events of Cooper's own first experience at sea and then expands into a sweeping representation of American maritime activity in the period, ranging from the crowded Thames to the remote islands of the Indian and Pacific oceans.

The balanced realism of *Afloat and Ashore* is pushed in the direction of the grotesque in *Jack Tier*. Here the writer turns the formulas of his early sea romances inside out: the dashing outlaw becomes the slovenly and treacherous Captain Spike, while the beautiful girl who adopts masculine clothes in order to follow her renegade lover to sea is transformed into Jack Tier, a dumpy, tobacco-chewing middle-aged woman, who is brutally sacrificed

**James Fenimore Cooper.** EMMET COLLECTION, MIRIAM AND IRA D. WALLACH DIVISION OF ART, PRINTS AND PHOTOGRAPHS, THE NEW YORK PUBLIC LIBRARY, ASTOR, LENOX AND TILDEN FOUNDATIONS

by Spike. Set in the 1840s, the world of the novel is a bitter and diminished one, as if the once pristine age of sail were contaminated by an ugly and unscrupulous modernity. In *The Sea Lions*, the penultimate novel of his career, Cooper shifts the scene to the 1820s as he adopts still another approach to his maritime materials. Ostensibly a somber depiction of the Antarctic seal fishery, the novel soon gathers the resonance of symbolic narrative as Roswell Gardiner, the self-assured and shallow young sealer who is Cooper's protagonist, experiences a spiritual regeneration during the long ordeal of wintering in the far south, while his rival and double, the ruthless Jason Daggett, suffers a lingering death. Abandoning his youthful pride of reason, Gardiner at last returns in a jury-rigged schooner, a craft appropriately "cut down and reduced."

Although Cooper's achievement as a writer of the sea rests chiefly on these ten novels, maritime elements figure importantly in several of his other works of fiction. He first sketched a Yankee sealing captain in the amusing character of Noah Poke in the otherwise unsuccessful comic fable *The Monikins* (1835). In *The Pathfinder* (1840), Cooper united the two great genres of his fiction—the sea novel and the wilderness tale—by setting the story on Lake Ontario and its forested shores in the era of the French and Indian War and by bringing the woodsman hero of the Leatherstocking Tales and his Indian companion into juxtaposition with a young lake sailor and a dogmatic old blue-water seaman. The curious but powerful book *The Crater* (1847) begins as an absorbing narrative of South Sea voyaging and island survival before it becomes a savage allegorical denunciation of contemporary American society.

## Cooper's Life and Nonfiction

That the sea plays a significant if various role in more than a third of Cooper's fiction reflects his lifelong interest in maritime and naval affairs. As a boy of sixteen he had run away from his Cooperstown home to go to sea, eventually finding a berth as an ordinary seaman in the merchantman *Stirling*, bound for England and the Mediterranean. That voyage before the mast, in late 1806 and 1807, subjected the young Cooper not only to all the usual miseries of a green hand but also to the dangers of the conflict between Britain and Napoleonic France that was then raging throughout the maritime world. Nothing daunted, on his return to the United States he enlisted as a midshipman in the navy, at a time when war with Great Britain seemed imminent. After a brief period of duty in New York Harbor on board the bomb ketch *Vesuvius* in early 1808, Cooper was sent that summer to the shores of Lake Ontario to join a party overseeing the construction of a naval vessel. In the fall of 1809 he returned to New York City and joined the sloop-of-war *Wasp*. But sea duty never came, and, bored by the inaction and now intent on marriage, he left the navy in May 1810.

Despite the brevity of Cooper's service, it provided him with friends and associations that kept him in close touch with naval affairs for the remainder of his life. The chief product of that interest was his *History of the Navy of the United States of America* (1839), a project to which he devoted years of research. The work was for decades the standard treatment of its subject and still retains something of the value of a primary source, for its author knew and interviewed many of the principal actors in the events that it chronicles. Much the same can be said of his later and less formal *Lives of Distinguished American Naval Officers* (1846). Cooper's concern for naval matters embroiled him in bitter controversies, notably his defense of the accuracy of his *History of the Navy* in a long pamphlet, *The Battle of Lake Erie* (1843), that answered the criticisms of the partisans of Oliver Hazard Perry, who claimed that Cooper had slighted the role played by their hero in the battle and magnified that of his second in command, Jesse Duncan Elliot. Among the Perry partisans was the writer and naval officer Alexander Slidell Mackenzie, who—at the very moment that the controversy was at its height and while commanding the U.S. brig *Somers*—executed at sea and on his own authority three supposed mutineers, one of them the midshipman son of the secretary of war. Despite the rashness and stupidity of such an act in peacetime, Mackenzie was acquitted by a court-martial. Cooper, initially sympathetic to Mackenzie, followed the trial with an interest that soon turned to outrage at the blatant injustice of its conduct. When the official proceedings of the court were published in 1844, appended to the document was Cooper's judicious but devastating "Elaborate Review" of the affair. But not all of Cooper's nonfictional writings on maritime matters concern naval notables. The most appealing of the others is the simple and poignant *Ned Myers* (1843), his redaction of the life story of a battered old seaman who as a boy had been his companion on the voyage of *Stirling*.

For all the range and authority of these historical and biographical works, Cooper's importance as a maritime writer of international reputation and influence resides chiefly in his sea fiction. Over the quarter of a century that separates *The Pilot* from *The Sea Lions*, his novels provided the examples and created the audience for Frederick Marryat in England, Eugène Sue in France, and Herman Melville in the United States, as well as for the armada of lesser writers who have followed his example, in his own century and since. It was left to the greatest of his heirs, Joseph Conrad, to identify the essence of Cooper's legacy: "in [Cooper's] sea tales," Conrad wrote in his *Notes on Life and Lett*ers (1921), "the sea inter-penetrates with life; it is in a subtle way a factor in the problem of existence." Cooper died in Cooperstown on September 14, 1851.

[*See also* American Literature; Fiction; *and* Literature.]

### Bibliography

**Primary Works**

Many of Cooper's writings can be found only in unedited nineteenth-century editions. The so-called Darley Edition published in thirty-two volumes in New York between 1859 and 1861 by W. A. Townsend and Company is generally considered the standard edition of the novels and is in the collections of nearly all major libraries. The following list identifies relevant works that are available in modern editions having reliable texts and useful introductions and annotation.

*Afloat and Ashore; or, The Adventures of Miles Wallingford*. Edited by Thomas Philbrick and Marianne Philbrick. 2 vols. New York: AMS Press, 2004.

*The Crater; or, Vulcan's Peak*. Edited by Thomas Philbrick. Cambridge, Mass.: Harvard University Press, 1962.

*Ned Myers; or, A Life before the Mast*. Edited by William S. Dudley. Annapolis, Md.: Naval Institute Press, 1989.

*The Pilot: A Tale of the Sea*. Edited by Kay Seymour House. Albany: State University of New York Press, 1986. Also available in *James Fenimore Cooper: Sea Tales*, edited by Kay Seymour House and Thomas Philbrick. New York: Library of America, 1991.

*The Red Rover: A Tale*. Edited by Thomas Philbrick and Marianne Philbrick. Albany: State University of New York Press, 1991. Also available in *James Fenimore Cooper: Sea Tales*, edited by Kay Seymour House and Thomas Philbrick. New York: Library of America, 1991.

*The Two Admirals: A Tale*. Edited by Donald A. Ringe, James A. Sappenfield, and E. N. Feltskog. Albany: State University of New York Press, 1990.

*The Wing-and-Wing; or, Le Feu-Follet: A Tale*. Edited by Thomas Philbrick. New York: Henry Holt, 1998.

**Secondary Works**

Beard, James Franklin, ed. *The Letters and Journals of James Fenimore Cooper*. 6 vols. Cambridge, Mass.: Harvard University Press, 1960–1968.

Philbrick, Thomas. *James Fenimore Cooper and the Development of American Sea Fiction*. Cambridge, Mass.: Harvard University Press, 1961.

Ringe, Donald A. *James Fenimore Cooper*. New York: Twayne, 1962. The most comprehensive and balanced critical survey of Cooper's writings.

Taylor, Alan. "James Fenimore Cooper Goes to Sea: Two Unpublished Letters by a Family Friend." *Studies in the American Renaissance* (1993): 43–54. The only significant advance on Beard's treatment of the circumstances surrounding the young Cooper's voyage before the mast.

THOMAS L. PHILBRICK

# Copenhagen, Bombardment of

The British capture of the Danish fleet at Copenhagen in 1807 must be accounted one of the most successful combined operations in the history of warfare—swift, ruthless, a nearly faultless case study of how land and sea forces can be brought together at the decisive place in overwhelming strength. It is also a prime example of the principle of preemptive war in action.

### Background

In June 1807 Denmark was an isolated outpost of neutrality in the Baltic region, where Napoleon was at war with a coalition made up of Britain, Prussia, Russia, and Sweden. The Swedes still held out in their province of Swedish Pomerania, but the remainder of northern Germany was under Napoleon's control, and the main theater of war lay in eastern Poland.

At the time, the European provinces of the Danish state included not only the kingdom of Denmark proper but also Norway to the north and the duchies of Schleswig and Holstein to the south. Denmark was a power of the second rank, but her navy, which included about twenty ships-of-the-line, was potentially a significant factor in northern Europe. Since the resumption of hostilities between Britain and France in 1803, the Danish navy had lain unrigged at the main naval base in the harbor of Copenhagen, a token of Denmark's neutral and pacific intentions. Britain had derived considerable benefit from Danish neutrality as some ports in western Jutland served as a semiclandestine conduit for British trade with the continent, and relations between the two countries were cordial until late 1806. After that, British fears that the French might move into Holstein and that the Danes would be too timid to resist had soured the atmosphere, as had Danish protests at the British Orders in Council of January 1807 and the increasingly frequent

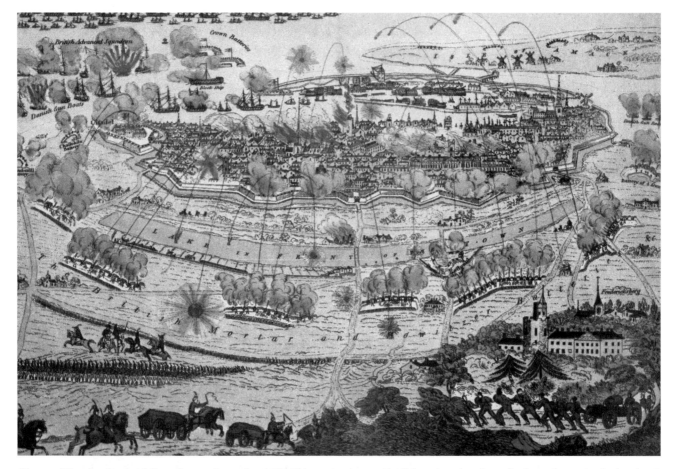

***Siege and Bombardment of Copenhagen, September 1807.*** This contemporary English watercolor shows both sea forces in the bombardment. THE GRANGER COLLECTION, NEW YORK

detention of Danish merchant vessels by British warships on the high seas.

However, the British attack on Denmark was prompted not by this deterioration in Anglo-Danish relations but by the reversal of Russian foreign policy after Napoleon inflicted a severe defeat on the Russian army at Friedland on June 14, 1807. The battle of Friedland led to the celebrated meeting between Napoleon and Alexander I on a raft at Tilsit on June 25 and the signature on July 7 of a secret treaty of alliance between Russia and France.

In the first weeks of July, the British government received a flow of ever more alarming reports from Tilsit about the new turn in Russian policy, along with others that the French were preparing to march into Holstein. There was also an entirely erroneous report that the Danes were starting to rig their fleet for sea, a measure that could only be directed against Britain. If the Danish navy became both operational and hostile, it could be used to obstruct Britain's

vital trade with the Baltic countries and might even come to form part of an invasion fleet directed toward the British Isles—or so British ministers would subsequently claim.

The British government was right to be worried about Denmark. The secret treaty of alliance concluded at Tilsit on July 7 stipulated that France and Russia would compel Denmark, along with several other smaller states, to close its ports to British shipping and declare war on Britain. British ministers never learned the precise terms of the treaty, but they were undoubtedly correct in believing that the spirit of the Tilsit alliance was profoundly inimical to Britain and that Danish neutrality was beyond salvation. Whether the Danes would have yielded to French and Russian demands or opted to side with Britain can never be known—the British government decided to strike against Copenhagen and confronted the Danes with an ultimatum before Franco-Russian pressure could be applied.

The overriding British aim was to gain possession of the Danish fleet so that it could not be turned against Britain. In one respect, an assault on Copenhagen was more difficult than it had been in 1801, when the British navy had been able to threaten the city with bombardment from the sea after Horatio Nelson's victory at the battle of Copenhagen. Since then the Danes had constructed a battery off the eastern shore of the city that made it impossible for naval forces alone to attack Copenhagen. A combined operation involving troops would therefore be required, but the distribution of British and Danish land forces was favorable for a British expedition to Zealand. On July 8, a force of 8,000 to 9,000 British troops under the command of Lieutenant General Lord William Schaw Cathcart had arrived off Pomerania to assist the Swedes. They could easily be withdrawn and sent to Zealand, and there were also substantial forces available in England for the operation. Above all, since 1805 the bulk of the Danish field army had been stationed in southern Jutland, and Zealand was consequently denuded of regular Danish troops. Given the overwhelming naval power that Britain could bring to bear, the Danes were caught in a trap from which they could not escape.

## The Battle

Once the decision to mount the operation had been made, the British moved swiftly to secure their objectives. A special envoy was sent to demand the surrender of the Danish fleet into British hands for the duration of the war, but no one expected that his mission would be successful and both troops and warships were on their way toward Denmark before he left England. On July 19 orders were sent to Cathcart instructing him to withdraw from Pomerania and unite his forces in The Sound with 16,000 troops that were being sent from Britain. A week later, on July 26, Admiral James Gambier sailed for The Sound from Yarmouth with sixteen ships-of-the-line and numerous smaller vessels. By the time it became clear in mid-August that the diplomatic negotiations with the Danes for the peaceful surrender of the fleet had failed, there were enough British troops in The Sound for a landing on Zealand. On August 16 the greater part of the British force disembarked unopposed at Vedbæk, nineteen kilometers (twelve miles) north of Copenhagen. By the following day, the whole of the western part of Copenhagen on the island of Zealand was invested by British troops.

This unopposed landing reflected not only the strategic surprise that had been achieved but also the absence of the Danish field army in Jutland. In August 1807 there were only about 7,500 Danish regulars on Zealand, and even though they were augmented by the island's peasant militia and auxiliary forces raised from among the inhabitants of Copenhagen, the defenders of the city numbered only between 13,000 and 14,000 men against a British force that eventually reached 26,000 troops—all of them regulars.

The Danish army in Jutland was a potential threat to the success of the British operation, and here British naval power played a central role. Gambier had been instructed to detach a squadron to guard the Store Strait and prevent the shipment of any Danish troops from Jutland and Fyn to Zealand and its adjacent, smaller islands. Between August 2 and 9, this squadron, under Commodore Richard Goodwin Keats, worked its way south through the Store Strait. By August 9 Keats had taken up a position off the island of Møn with his ships-of-the-line after distributing his smaller warships along the way to police the Store Strait. Zealand and its adjacent islands had been isolated from the rest of the Danish state. This was absolutely decisive to the success of the British operation at Copenhagen.

It only remained to reap the fruits of the overwhelming military preponderance that had been achieved on Zealand. That is not quite how it seemed to the men on the spot, however. The British forces were able to advance within 730 meters (2,400 yards) of Copenhagen's defensive works and to drive back without difficulty a sortie of the defenders, but Cathcart, who had been given overall command of the land forces, was surprised by the strength of the ramparts, which were protected by deep flooded ditches. The Danish gunboats at Copenhagen also proved an irritant. They operated in shallow waters where the larger British warships could not get at them, and they carried artillery with a longer range than that of the gun brigs and bomb vessels that Gambier sent against them. Above all, Cathcart was worried about the risk that, if the capture of the Danish fleet were delayed, the coming of bad weather and dark nights would drive the British squadron in the Store Strait from its stations and enable the Danes to send fresh troops to Zealand.

A regular, protracted siege was therefore not an appealing option, but there was another way: a bombardment of Copenhagen directed not at military targets but at the city as a whole. As one of Cathcart's subordinate officers, Lieutenant Colonel George Murray, put it, the object of resorting to this "harsh measure" would be to obtain the surrender of the Danish fleet "by the sufferings of the inhabitants themselves" and by obliging "all persons of whatever description, to undergo the same hardships and dangers." This was the road that Cathcart chose to follow. If terror bombardment proved ineffective, he intended to try to storm the ramparts of Copenhagen and take the city by coup de main.

In the end, that was not necessary. The bombardment began at 7:30 on the evening of September 2 and continued through the night, for twelve hours. It was resumed over the two following nights. William Congreve's incendiary rockets, employed in a major military operation for the first time, contributed significantly to both the terror and the devastation. It is estimated that about one-third of the buildings in the city were destroyed or damaged.

On September 5 the Danish commander in Copenhagen concluded that he had no option but surrender, and the articles of capitulation were signed on September 7. Under their terms, the Danish fleet was handed over to the British, who were given possession of the dockyard and arsenal of Copenhagen for a period of six weeks to prepare the Danish vessels for removal to Britain.

### The Aftermath

The British had achieved total victory over the Danes, and they would benefit from that victory for the remainder of the Napoleonic Wars. Once the British forces evacuated Zealand on October 20, 1807, and set sail for England with the Danish fleet as a trophy, Britain found itself at war with Denmark, but it was a Denmark whose teeth had been drawn. The Danes lacked the resources to build new ships-of-the-line, and the gunboats and privateers that they sent against the great British convoys entering and leaving the Baltic through the Store Strait or The Sound between 1808 and 1813 were unable to inflict major damage on Britain's Baltic trade or its naval dominance of the Baltic.

[*See also* Baltic Sea; Intelligence; Naval Dockyards and Bases; Navies, Great Powers; Ports; Strategy; Technology and Weapons; *and* Wars, Maritime, *subentry on* Anglo-French Wars.]

### Bibliography

Fortescue, J. W. *A History of the British Army.* Vol. 6: 1807–1809. London: Macmillan, 1910. Offers a tolerably coherent and accurate description of British land operations on Zealand in 1807. Delightfully supercilious in tone.

Munch-Petersen, Thomas. "Lord Cathcart, Sir Arthur Wellesley and the British Capture of Copenhagen in 1807." In *Wellington Studies 11*, edited by C. M. Woolgar, pp 104–122. Southampton, U.K.: Hartley Institute, 1999. Supplements and supersedes the account of operations in Fortescue (above) and served as the main source for this encyclopedia entry.

Munch-Petersen, Thomas. "The Secret Intelligence from Tilsit: New Light on the Events Surrounding the British Bombardment of Copenhagen in 1807." *Historisk Tidsskrift* 102, pt. 1 (2002): 55–96. In Danish. Provides new evidence on the celebrated "secret intelligence from Tilsit."

Munch-Petersen, Thomas. *Defying Napoleon. How Britain Bombarded Copenhagen and Seized the Danish Fleet in 1807.* Forthcoming.

Ryan, A. N. "The Causes of the British Attack upon Copenhagen in 1807." *English Historical Review* 68 (January 1953): 37–55. Discusses the growth of Anglo-Danish tensions during the run-up to the attack.

Ryan, A. N. "The Defence of British Trade with the Baltic, 1808–1813." *English Historical Review* 74, no. 292 (July 1959): 443–466. A superlative description of the Baltic convoys and the duel between the British Baltic fleet and enemy gunboats and privateers.

Ryan, A. N. "Documents Relating to the Copenhagen Operation, 1807." In *The Naval Miscellany*, edited by N. A. M. Rodger, volume 5, pp. 297–329. Publications of the Navy Records Society, vol. 125. London: Printed for the Navy Records Society, 1984. A very useful collection of some of the key documents.

Ryan, A. N. "The Navy at Copenhagen in 1807." *The Mariner's Mirror* 39 (1953): 201–210. A succinct account of the naval operations.

Trulsson, Sven G. *British and Swedish Policies and Strategies in the Baltic after the Peace of Tilsit in 1807: A Study of Decision-Making.* Lund, Sweden: Gleerup, 1976. Includes a discussion of the motives behind the attack.

THOMAS MUNCH-PETERSEN

# Coral Reefs. *See* Marine Biology.

# Corbett, Julian (1854–1922), British naval analyst and historian. Julian Stafford Corbett was born in Surrey, England, on November 12, 1854, the son of a successful London property developer. He graduated from Cambridge with a first-class law degree, qualified, and practiced briefly. However, family wealth allowed him to indulge a passion for travel, visiting the United States, India, and much of Europe. After a trio of minor historical novels, he produced brief lives of George Monck (1889) and Sir Francis Drake (1890). Through this work he came into contact with John Knox Laughton. He joined the Navy Records Society in 1893, to which he contributed as editor and administrator. Under Laughton's guidance he developed into a fine archival historian, producing his first major book, *Drake and the Tudor Navy*, and the Records Society volume, *The Spanish War*, both in 1898. In *The*

*Successors of Drake* (1900), he began to develop the strategic and tactical themes that dominated the rest of his working life.

After 1903, Corbett lectured to the newly established Naval War Course and to the Army Staff College at Camberley. While his lectures were historically based, their purpose became increasingly didactic. Influenced by Colonel George Sydenham Clarke, a leading defense commentator and secretary of the Committee of Imperial Defence, these lectures were published as *England in the Mediterranean* (1904), a strategic overview with contemporary relevance. This book moved the level of naval strategic analysis beyond that of his American contemporary Alfred Thayer Mahan, a process that continued when Corbett came into contact with the theoretical ideas of the Prussian military philosopher Carl von Clausewitz. From these ideas he developed the framework for his analytical work. The first lecture series to benefit from this new understanding was published as *England in the Seven Years' War* (1907), using the higher direction of the conflict as a case study in "British strategy" for a contemporary audience. To this end he was prepared to alter the historical record in search of a clear analytical structure. Similar concerns underpinned his historical masterpiece, *The Campaign of Trafalgar* (1910). During this period Corbett worked with Admiral Sir John Fisher, providing historical insight and a few carefully crafted articles in leading journals supporting the admiral's reforms, working with Herbert Richmond, one of Fisher's junior naval assistants. The War Course strategy lectures developed into *Some Principles of Maritime Strategy* (1911), a historically based argument for a maritime as opposed to a Continental strategy, which became the key text in the development of limited war theory and is still the foundation of British strategy.

After completing the confidential history *Maritime Operations of the Russo-Japanese War 1904–05* (1914) for the Committee of Imperial Defence, Corbett began work on the core strategic narrative of the new European war, which was embedded in the *History of the Great War: Naval Operations*. Knighted in 1917, he completed three volumes, which covered the period down to the end of the 1916 battle of Jutland, before his untimely death in Sussex on September 21, 1922. Controversies concerning Winston Churchill's period as first lord of the admiralty, the Dardanelles offensive of 1915–1916, and the battle of Jutland may have contributed to his ill health.

Corbett remains the outstanding naval strategic thinker, reflecting his legal training, detailed historical work, recognition of the needs of the present, and sophisticated intellectual grasp.

[*See also* Fisher, John; Laughton, John Knox; *and* Mahan, Alfred Thayer.]

## Bibliography

Corbett, Julian. *Some Principles of Maritime Strategy*. Edited by Eric Grove. Annapolis, Md.: Naval Institute Press 1988.

Hattendorf, John B., and James Goldrick, eds. *Mahan Is Not Enough: The Proceedings of a Conference on the Works of Sir Julian Corbett and Admiral Sir Herbert Richmond*. Newport R.I.: Naval War College Press, 1993.

Schurman, Donald M. *Sir Julian Stafford Corbett: 1854–1922*. London: Royal Historical Society, 1981.

ANDREW LAMBERT

## Cordage. *See* Ship's Equipment.

## Coriolis Force. *See* Earth Sciences.

## Corvette. *See* Warships, *subentry on* Early Modern Warships.

## Couppel, Marin-Marie Durand

(1901–1987), French navigator and marine painter. Marin-Marie Paul Durand-Couppel de Saint-Front, better known as Marin-Marie, was born on December 10, 1901, in Fougerolles, Normandy, to a Nonconformist family. His father was a lawyer (as was his grandfather) who preferred to live as a gentleman farmer and who was, above all, an enthusiastic yachtsman. Marin-Marie inherited from his father an interest in the arts, knowledge of seamanship, and a love of the sea. As a boy, he discovered the sea and sailed at Chausey, a tiny French archipelago near the British Channel Islands and the family's summer residence. Marin-Marie's mother, who was a talented draftswoman and aquarellist, initiated Marin-Marie into painting.

Having spent two pleasant years at a British Catholic school, Marin-Marie completed his studies at Rennes, Brittany. In accordance with family tradition, he studied law and attended the art school in his spare time.

Together with other unknown painters, Marin-Marie first exhibited his paintings in Paris in 1923 and 1924.

Among the painters whom he exhibited with, Maurice Utrillo (1883–1955) and the Japanese-born Tsuguharu Foujita (1886–1968) later became world famous. Called up for military service in 1925, Marin-Marie embarked as volunteer stoker on board the mixed three-master *Pourquoi-Pas?* (Why Not?), bound for Greenland. This private ship flew the flag of the Yacht Club de France in polar waters. She was under command of her owner, the Arctic scientist Jean Charcot (1867–1936), who was nicknamed the "Polar Gentleman" by Sir Ernest Shackleton, the British explorer of Antarctica. Marin-Marie spent two successful years on board *Pourquoi-Pas?* Quickly promoted to the rank of master of the captain's longboat, he had many opportunities to sketch and paint the ship's activities off Iceland and in the Scoresby Sound in Greenland. Once discharged from military service, Marin-Marie entered fully into his career as a painter. In 1927, he exhibited at the Salon of the Société Nationale des Beaux-Arts de la Mer (National Society of Marine Fine Arts) and organized his first one-man show in Paris. His exhibition was titled Sailing Ships No Longer to Be Seen, and all of his watercolors and gouaches were purchased within a few days. Subsequent exhibitions of his work were also successful.

Marin-Marie took any opportunity to sail the English Channel in his small cutter, *Rose-Marine*, or as the skipper of yachts competing in ocean races. He was a longtime friend of Alain Gerbault (1893–1941), who achieved the first French solo circumnavigation in *Firecrest* in 1923–1929. In the early 1930s, Marin-Marie planned an exhibition in the United States and decided to sail to New York City. In 1933, he achieved the second solo sailing across the Atlantic Ocean in his 11-meter (36-foot) cutter *Winibelle II*. Because of the economic depression in the United States, the exhibition at the Kennedy Gallery on Fifth Avenue was a failure, and Marin-Marie was forced to sell his boat. Three years later, after demonstrating that a 60-horsepower diesel boat could cross the Atlantic, Marin-Marie shipped his 12-meter (40-foot) motorboat, *Arielle*, built specially for him near Paris, to the United States. He departed from New York in 1936 and completed—for the fist time—a most hazardous eighteen-day solo voyage across the Atlantic. The Cruising Club of America awarded Marin-Marie the prestigious Blue Water Medal for that year.

In 1932, Marin-Marie played an unexpected role in the design of the legendary French transatlantic liner *Normandie*. Asked to paint an artist's view of the ship under construction at Saint-Nazaire, Marin-Marie suggested modifying drastically the stereotyped drawing of the three funnels, giving the liner an innovative silhouette. In 1935, he was appointed official painter to the French navy. Marin-Marie died on June 11, 1987, at Saint-Hilaire du Harcouët, Manche.

While most of the modern French marine artists were painting seascapes from the shore, in the Impressionist tradition, Marin-Marie was rare among French marine painters for being also an experienced seaman who could represent ships at sea realistically. Using gouache to be as quick as possible, he had the opportunity of painting from nature the last sailing cod-fishing bankers and the last tall ships at work. He could express from memory every aspect of the high seas under changing skies. For this reason, Marin-Marie occupies a leading place in the French maritime heritage as an artist who witnessed marine sights and activities that disappeared during his lifetime.

[*See also* Art; Artists; Painting; *and* Yachting and Pleasure Sailing.]

### Bibliography

Baron, Cristina. *Marin-Marie*. Exhibition catalog. Paris: Musée de la Marine and Editions Ouest-France, 1989.

FRANÇOIS BELLEC

# Courts

This entry contains four subentries:

An Overview
Ad Hoc Arbitrations
International Court of Justice
Permanent Court of International Justice

---

## An Overview

Over the centuries, many different courts and tribunals have contributed to the development of the law of the sea by establishing and clarifying its principles and by resolving disputes over the interpretation and application of maritime conventions. The major influence has been that of standing international courts, such as the International Court of Justice and the International Tribunal for the Law of the Sea. Decisions of ad hoc international courts and tribunals, as well as judgments by national judicial bodies applying international law, have also made significant contributions to this development.

## Judicial Decisions and Other Sources of the Law of the Sea

Apart from judicial decisions, the sources of international maritime law are threefold. First, several multilateral treaties, most notably the United Nations Convention on the Law of the Sea (hereinafter "the LOS Convention"), set out broad legal principles; in addition, many international conventions lay down technical standards on matters such as ship construction and crewing, the safety of navigation, and the prevention of marine pollution. A second source is the general practice of states accepted as law, and a third source is the general principles of law. In the early twenty-first century, conventions represent the main source of international maritime law. They exert the primary influence upon the legislative and administrative practice of states, as well as upon the standard-setting work of intergovernmental organizations. Increasingly, therefore, judicial decisions represent no more than a secondary or indirect source of the law of the sea.

Nonetheless, judicial decisions are still capable of influencing the development of the law in more than one way. Previous decisions are often cited in argument, and in that way they influence the thinking of other judges. Thus, although international courts are not bound by their own previous decisions or by those of other courts, judicial decisions may become precedents in the sense that they are given due weight in deciding later cases on similar topics. Courts seek to maintain consistency in disposing of their cases. A decision may also become a precedent for other decision makers, such as legislators and administrators. Second, some provisions in conventions are cast in very general terms—such as the aim "to achieve an equitable solution" in article 83 of the LOS Convention concerning the delimitation of the continental shelf; courts and tribunals have given content to that rather imprecise test in deciding actual boundary cases, with the result that the law is based partly upon the broad principle in the convention and partly upon judicial precedents that applied it in actual situations. Third, disputes have arisen from facts or situations that were not wholly foreseen in formulating conventions: here courts have been able to apply the stated intentions of the negotiating states and general principles of law in order to avoid a legal vacuum. In these ways, several decisions have exerted considerable influence upon the development of particular areas of the law.

## Principal International Courts and Tribunals Applying the Law of the Sea

Among the various international courts and tribunals, the International Court of Justice has exerted the principal influence upon the development of the law of the sea. Whereas its predecessor, the Permanent Court of International Justice, was concerned only rarely with maritime issues, such issues have regularly come before the present court. It has made decisions upon several important issues, including rights of passage through straits used for international navigation, the drawing of straight baselines for measuring the breadth of the territorial sea, international fisheries, the delimitation of maritime boundaries between neighboring states, whether adjacent or opposite, and the legal concept of the continental shelf. The International Tribunal for the Law of the Sea has contributed to the development of the modern law in a variety of ways, especially by clarifying the scope of the duty of states to cooperate over the preservation and protection of the marine environment, by its decisions on the flagging of ships and the prompt release of arrested vessels and their crews, and by its decision on the degree of force that may be used by law-enforcement officers in effecting the arrest of a ship at sea. Starting with the *Alabama* arbitration in 1871, ad hoc courts and tribunals have also contributed to the development of the law on issues such as the flagging of vessels, international fisheries, powers of arrest, and maritime boundaries between neighboring states.

National courts normally apply not international law but rather the law of the particular state concerned. There have been instances, however, where national courts have applied international law, either directly or as part of the national legal order, and created precedents that at the time were not reflected in international conventions or in the general practice of states. For example, in the early part of the nineteenth century, several important decisions were given by Sir William Scott, sitting as a judge in England, concerning the breadth of the territorial sea. Precedents have also been set by the Privy Council in London (for example, on piracy and on the status of vessels without a flag), by the U.S. Supreme Court (for example, on Alaskan baselines and on the status of foreign crews in U.S. ports), by the Conseil d'État in France (for example, on the position of foreign ships in French ports), and by many other national courts.

## Impact of Judicial Decisions upon the Parties and upon Third Parties

The parties to a case are bound in their mutual relations by the decision(s) on the merits of the issues before the court. They are obliged to respect the judgment and to make any necessary changes to their positions and legislation. Even a decision on an interlocutory issue, such as an order prescribing provisional measures pending a decision on the merits, can have wider effects. An interim order may encourage further negotiations, as in the case before the International Court of Justice concerning passage through the Great Belt (Finland versus Denmark) and the case before the International Tribunal for the Law of the Sea concerning land reclamation in Johore Strait (Malaysia versus Singapore). In both instances, the ensuing negotiations were successful, resulting in the withdrawal of the merits from adjudication.

In some instances, decisions have had a major impact upon third parties generally, and especially upon coastal states. Following the International Court of Justice's decision in 1953 that Norway's baselines for measuring the breadth of the territorial sea were not contrary to international law, many other states proceeded to draw baselines in a similar manner around parts of their own coasts. Some key phrases in the judgment were included in the LOS Convention, thereby codifying them. As a result, the decision is still influencing indirectly the practice of states. Similarly, the term "natural prolongation" of the coastal state in article 76 of the LOS Convention, which concerns the outer limit of the continental shelf, can be traced back to the decision of the International Court of Justice in the North Sea *Continental Shelf* cases (Denmark and the Netherlands versus Germany).

At the same time, it should be kept in mind that a rule first established in a judicial decision can be reversed by a new international convention. An example of such international law reform is provided by the only maritime decision given by the Permanent Court of International Justice, namely the *Lotus* case (France versus Turkey). The court's decision, to the effect that Turkey could prosecute an officer of a French vessel that collided with a Turkish vessel on the high seas, was a source of concern to the shipping industry, and the rule was changed by international agreements. Today, the institution of penal or disciplinary proceedings in respect of collisions beyond the territorial sea is confined to the flag state and the state of nationality of the accused person, to the exclusion of the victim state.

## Limitations upon the Influence of Courts

Courts do not choose the cases coming before them, and they can act only to the extent to which jurisdiction has been conferred upon them by the parties. For example, some interesting legal issues were raised by the *Fisheries Jurisdiction* case (Canada versus Spain) concerning Spanish fishing vessels operating near the Canadian

200-mile limit, but the International Court of Justice was unable to determine these issues since it found after due consideration that it did not have jurisdiction over the dispute. Even where jurisdiction clearly exists, a court faced with a controversial issue that is currently under negotiation at a diplomatic conference cannot lay down the law before the legislator has laid it down (Fisheries Jurisdiction case, U.K. versus Iceland, 1974). In practice, a court's decision may well not settle the dispute between the parties, because often there are political, social, and economic aspects in addition to the strictly legal issues. Courts are usually unable to supervise the implementation of their judgments, although they may be called upon to consider requests for interpretation or revision where new facts have come to light. After judgment day, the parties will often have to hold bilateral talks about the implementation of the decision and in order to settle the wider dispute. The eventual settlement may well take account of both the judgment and some quite separate political elements, even where the judgment has prescribed a specific course of action for the parties. Despite all these limitations, judicial decisions have exerted considerable influence upon the development of the law of the sea at different times, especially in clarifying areas of the law that have not been the subject of codification or standard setting by means of an international convention.

[*See also* Law; Law of the Sea; Scott, William; *and* United Nations Conferences on the Law of the Sea.]

## Bibliography

Adede, A. O. *The System for Settlement of Disputes under the United Nations Convention on the Law of the Sea*. Dordrecht, Netherlands, and Boston: Nijhoff, 1987.

Caminos, H., and V. Marotta-Rangel. "Sources of the Law of the Sea." In *A Handbook of the New Law of the Sea*, edited by Rene-Jean Dupuy and Daniel Vignes, vol. 1, chap. 2. Dordrecht, Netherlands: Nijhoff, 1991.

Collier, John G., and Vaughan Lowe. *The Settlement of Disputes in International Law: Institutions and Procedures*. Oxford: Oxford University Press, 1999.

"The International Court of Justice." http://www.icj-cij.org.

"The International Tribunal for the Law of the Sea." http://www.itlos.org and http://www.tidm.org.

Jennings, Robert. "The Differences between Conducting a Case in the ICJ and in an ad hoc Arbitration Tribunal—An Inside View." In *Liber amicorum Judge Shigeru Oda*, edited by Nisuke Ando, Edward McWhinney, and Rüdiger Wolfrum, pp. 893–909. The Hague, Netherlands, London, and New York: Kluwer Law International 2002.

Jennings, Robert, and Arthur Watts, eds. *Oppenheim's International Law*. 9th ed. Harlow, U.K.: Longman, 1992.

Klein, Natalie. *Dispute Settlement in the UN Convention on the Law of the Sea*. Cambridge, U.K.: Cambridge University Press, 2005.

Lauterpacht, Sir Elihu, and C. J. Greenwood. *International Law Reports*. 125 vols. Cambridge, U.K.: Cambridge University Press, 2004.

Merrills, J. G. *International Dispute Settlement*. 3d ed. Cambridge, U.K.: Cambridge University Press, 1998.

"Oceans and Law of the Sea." http://www.un.org/Depts/los/index.htm. The Division for Oceans Affairs and Law of the Sea of the Secretariat of the United Nations coordinates information about the work of courts and tribunals of all kinds, as well as organizations within the U.N. system, regarding the law of the sea.

DAVID H. ANDERSON

# Ad Hoc Arbitrations

States have long had recourse to arbitration for the determination in accordance with international law of their maritime and other disputes. An early example was the General Treaty on Friendship, Commerce, and Navigation of 1794 between the United Kingdom and the United States, known as the "Jay Treaty" after the U.S. secretary of state. The treaty set up three mixed commissions to resolve outstanding issues, including shipping disputes. A later example was the Alabama Arbitration under the Washington treaty of 1871, which arose from the sailing of *Alabama* from England to help the Confederate cause during the American Civil War. The tribunal was composed of nationals of the two parties—the United Kingdom and the United States—plus nationals of Italy, Switzerland, and Brazil. The applicable legal principles were stated in an annex to the treaty. In several ways this arbitration, which resulted in the award of compensation in 1872, served as a model for later arbitrations, as well as for the constitution of the Permanent Court of Arbitration by the Hague conventions of 1899 and 1907.

The existence since 1922 of standing courts and tribunals has not meant that recourse to ad hoc arbitration has ceased. Such arbitrations are held pursuant to some form of international agreement according to which the parties appoint the arbitrator(s) and the registrar, determine the question for decision, and prescribe the procedural rules governing matters such as the number, order, and publication of the written and oral pleadings. The parties are under the obligations to meet the costs of arbitration and comply with the award. In some cases an ad hoc arbitration is conducted within a framework, such as those provided by the Permanent Court of Arbitration and, more recently, Annex VII to the Convention on the Law of the Sea of 1982.

Ad hoc arbitrations have contributed to several parts of maritime law, including that pertaining to the flagging of ships, the regulation of international fisheries, the policing of ships at sea, and maritime delimitation.

## Cases Concerning the Flagging of Ships

In the case of *Muscat Dhows* (1905) an ad hoc tribunal established under the auspices of the Permanent Court of Arbitration had to consider the question of the grant of the flag to ships. France had authorized some subjects of the sultan of Muscat to fly the French flag on their dhows, and the question for decision was whether the United Kingdom was obliged to treat these dhows as French for the purposes of a treaty between France and the United Kingdom. The court held that, generally speaking, it was for each state to determine who were its nationals and which ships were entitled to fly its flag. In the case of *Montijo*, an arbitration between Colombia and the United States in 1875, it was held that the flag flown by a ship was prima facie evidence of its nationality. These findings have now been included in the Convention on the Law of the Sea as article 91, together with the additional conditions that there should be a genuine link between the ship and its flag state and that the flag state must effectively supervise all ships flying its flag.

## Cases Concerning Fisheries and the Taking of Other Living Resources

The *Bering Sea Fur Seals* arbitrations of 1895 and 1902 arose from two similar attempts, the first by the United States to control sealing by Canadian vessels and the second by Russia to regulate catches by U.S. vessels. The aim in each instance was to conserve the seal stocks both on the high seas of the Bering Sea and in the adjacent U.S. or Russian territorial waters. Objections to the arrests were based on the argument that seals were available on the high seas to catchers from all nations. In both case arbitrations the tribunal held that unilateral conservation measures could not be imposed by a coastal state on foreign vessels on the high seas, however worthy the aim of conservation. In the Canada–United States case the tribunal also exercised a power conferred on it by the parties to draw up regulations for U.S. and Canadian vessels alike. However, the regulations proved to be ineffective in practice when the vessels concerned changed their flags to those of third states. The disputes were settled by an agreement concluded in 1911 by all the states involved. These cases show that unilateral measures can apply on the high seas only to vessels flying the flag of the state concerned and not to foreign vessels. Conservation measures for the living resources of the high seas are effective only if an international agreement is concluded that attracts the support of all the participants in the activity, whether fishing or sealing. The law on this point is now contained in articles 116 to 120 of the Convention on the Law of the Sea.

## Cases Concerning the Policing of Ships at Sea

The law relating to the use of force by patrol vessels when making arrests at sea was developed in the cases of *I'm Alone* (1935), arising from the enforcement of Prohibition in the United States, and *Red Crusader* (1962), a Scottish fishing vessel boarded off the Faeroe Islands. In these cases international commissions concluded that, although under international law reasonable and necessary force could be used in order to effect an arrest at sea, the degree of force used in the particular circumstances had been excessive. Human life should not be endangered without good reason. These findings were cited with approval by the International Tribunal for the Law of the Sea in its judgment in the *M/V Saiga (No. 2)* case in 1999. This is a rare example of a part of maritime law that is based not on conventions but on the decisions of tribunals.

## Cases Concerning Maritime Delimitation

The *North Atlantic Coast Fisheries* arbitration, decided in 1910 under the auspices of the Permanent Court of Arbitration, concerned the question of the true meaning of a reference to "bays" in a fisheries treaty between the United Kingdom and the United States. The issue was whether the treaty applied to all Canadian bays or only those that measured six miles or less in width at the mouth. The tribunal decided that the term applied to every bay on the coast in question. The tribunal held that the width of an indentation was less important than its depth and that the three-mile belt of territorial waters was to be measured from a notional line across the mouth. The decision influenced, initially, the work of the conference convened by the League of Nations in 1930 to consider the law of territorial waters and, much later, the terms of article 10 of the Convention on the Law of the Sea, which permits a twenty-four-mile closing line to be drawn across the natural entrance points of deep bays.

The first arbitration on maritime boundaries was the *Grisbadarna* case of 1909, between Norway and Sweden. The issue concerned their territorial sea boundary in a stretch of water just south of the Oslo Fjord strewn with islands and banks. The conduct of the case was noteworthy for its speed and efficiency and for the fact that the three arbitrators visited the scene of the dispute. The tribunal decided to employ the method of drawing a line perpendicular to the general direction to the coast rather than drawing a median line equidistant from the nearest points on the respective coasts (the method most often used today). The decision is best known for the dictum that a state of affairs of long standing should be changed as little as possible. This dictum was applied so as to avoid dividing a fishing bank used by Swedish vessels by slightly adjusting the perpendicular, in much the same way that modern tribunals adjust initial equidistant lines in order to achieve an equitable result.

The arbitration of 1977 between France and the United Kingdom concerning the delimitation of the continental shelf in the English Channel has influenced later decisions, as well as the practice of states in negotiating boundaries. The ad hoc Court of Arbitration, established by treaty, was charged with drawing the boundaries in three disputed areas. In the court's decision, applying both conventional and customary law, the Channel Islands were confined to a maritime enclave of no more than twelve nautical miles because they lay not only on the French side of the Channel but also in the arms of the Breton and Norman coasts. The primary boundary was held to be a line equidistant between the nearest points on the English and French coasts in the English Channel. However, in the western approaches to the Channel, the Scilly Isles were accorded only half effect in drawing this line because, being diminutive and a good distance off the mainland, they would otherwise have deflected disproportionately the course of the westernmost stretch of the boundary out into the North Atlantic.

In the law on the delimitation of the continental shelf, this decision has been cited as a precedent for treating small islands on their merits, according them enclaves or half effect or full effect as appropriate to achieve an equitable result. More important, perhaps, the decision adopted the method of drawing a provisional line equidistant between the respective coastal base points, assessing its fairness to the two parties, and making any appropriate adjustments to achieve an equitable result. This is now the aim specified in articles 74 and 83 of the Convention on the Law of the Sea, and the court's practical method is widely used by international courts and tribunals. The Court of Arbitration succeeded in unifying customary and conventional law in a manner that is still proving to be helpful worldwide. In particular, its decision influenced, in different ways, two later ad hoc arbitrations: those between Guinea and Guinea-Bissau off West Africa (1985) and between Canada and France (in respect of Saint Pierre and Miquelon) in the Gulf of Saint Lawrence (1992).

In the maritime boundary arbitration between Eritrea and Yemen, lying on opposite sides of the Red Sea, the method was again followed of drawing a provisional equidistant line between the two mainlands (ignoring small islands on both sides) and then adjusting this line to achieve equitable results by discounting certain small features. The tribunal's awards of 1998 and 1999 specified that the traditional artisanal fishing regime was not to be disturbed by the establishment of the maritime boundary, applying the Islamic legal concepts of the region in addition to general international law. This decision was successful in both composing the different interests of the parties and strengthening some existing trends in international law, thereby neatly illustrating the value of ad hoc arbitration.

In 2006 the first decision on the merits of a dispute by an ad hoc tribunal sitting under Annex VII to the United Nations Convention on the Law of the Sea established the maritime boundary between Barbados and Trinidad and Tobago. The boundary is equidistant from the respective coasts, subject to an adjustment at the eastern end that takes account of the longer eastern frontage of Trinidad and its existing maritime boundary with Venezuela. The tribunal also found that the parties were under a duty to agree on conservation measures for flying-fish stocks, including some Barbadian access to the fishery in Trinidadian waters.

[*See also* Fishing; Flags; Law; *and* Law of the Sea.]

## Bibliography

Churchill, R. R., and A. V. Lowe. *The Law of the Sea.* 3d ed. Manchester, U.K.: Manchester University Press, 1999.

Collier, John G., and A. Vaughan Lowe. *The Settlement of Disputes in International Law.* Oxford: Oxford University Press, 1999.

Jennings, Sir Robert. "The Differences between Conducting a Case in the ICJ and in an Ad Hoc Arbitration Tribunal: An Inside View." In *Liber Amicorum Judge Shigeru Oda,* edited by Nisuke Ando, Edward McWhinney, and Rüdiger Wolfrum, pp. 893–909. The Hague, London, and New York: Kluwer Law International, 2002.

Merrills, J. G. *International Dispute Settlement.* 3d ed. Cambridge, U.K.: Cambridge University Press, 1998.

O'Connell, D. P. *The International Law of the Sea.* Edited by I. A. Shearer. 2 vols. Oxford: Clarendon Press, 1984.

Schwarzenberger, Georg. *International Law as Applied by International Courts and Tribunals.* 3d ed. Vol. 1. London: Stevens and Sons, 1957.

Simpson, J. L., and Hazel Fox. *International Arbitration.* London: Stevens and Sons, 1959.

DAVID H. ANDERSON

# International Court of Justice

This entry first describes the International Court of Justice (ICJ) by stating its nature, membership, and competences, and then discusses the role that the court has played so far in the development of the law of the sea.

## Nature, Membership, and Competences of the Court

The International Court of Justice was established in 1946 as part of the settlement of World War II. There was a large element of continuity with the former Permanent Court of International Justice, which was founded in 1922 after World War I. The Statute of the International Court of Justice is based heavily upon the statute of the former court, the main changes being to make the new court part of the system of the United Nations instead of part of the defunct League of Nations. The two statutes have several virtually identical provisions, and even the numbering of the articles is the same. The most important change was that the International Court of Justice was designated as "the principal judicial organ of the United Nations," and its statute was made an integral part of the United Nations Charter. Indeed, chapter 14 (articles 92–96) of the charter is about the court's place in the system.

The continuity of the two courts was physical as well as juridical. The archives of the Permanent Court of International Justice survived the war intact in the Peace Palace at The Hague in the Netherlands, and the International Court of Justice was established in the same building. The decisions of the two courts have always been published in official *Reports,* and the judges have been respectful of earlier decisions. Decisions of the former court, as well as decisions of the present court, are regularly cited as persuasive precedents both by counsel pleading in the court and by the court in the reasoning of its decisions.

In the ICJ there are fifteen "members of the court" (judges). They are normally elected for nine years and may be eligible for reelection. Candidates are nominated by the-oretically neutral, expert bodies in each member country of the United Nations. The Security Council and the General Assembly vote independently on a usually large list of candidates. A successful candidate must get an absolute majority in both places. The voting continues until the necessary number of persons are thus elected. From the beginning of the court, the nine-year terms have been staggered in batches of five, so that at each routine election there are five members of the court to be elected, or in some cases reelected. To know what really happens, one needs to be able to read between the lines of the rules laid down in the Statute, which may also be true for other United Nations courts and tribunals, such as the International Tribunal on the Law of the Sea.

Article 2 of the court's Statute provides that judges are to be "elected regardless of their nationality." It would be difficult to do this strictly while at the same time observing article 9, which provides that at "every election, the electors shall bear in mind not only that the persons to be elected should individually possess the qualifications required, but also that in the body as a whole the representation of the main forms of civilization and of the principal legal systems of the world should be secured."

The establishment of the ICJ in 1946 was followed by a process of decolonization and the steady emerging of many newly independent sovereign states, which became members of the United Nations. It was understandably felt by many of these new states that the court was subject too much to western and European influence. This led to the creation of understandings about the geographical distribution of judges and led to influence exercised by unofficial but powerful regional groups, which predetermine much United Nations business. There is also an understanding that each of the five permanent members of the Security Council (China, France, Russia, the United Kingdom, and the United States) always have a judge on the court. Despite all these constraints, the ICJ has in recent decades managed to be broadly representative of the international community as a whole and has certainly had its share of able judges.

The normal jurisdiction of the ICJ "comprises all cases which the parties refer to it and all matters specially provided for in the Charter of the United Nations or in treaties or conventions in force" (article 36.1). This is its so-called contentious jurisdiction over disputes between parties, culminating in "judgments," which are binding upon all parties. This is different from its "advisory jurisdiction," in which the court may give an advisory opinion on any

legal question asked of it by certain qualified organizations. These opinions, though not binding, amount to an authoritative recommendation. There have been no ICJ advisory opinions directly concerning maritime matters.

Only states can be parties before the court (article 34 of the Statute). The court's contentious jurisdiction over disputes between states is confined to disputes where both parties consent in some way to submit the case to the ICJ (article 94.1 of the United Nations Charter). Consent might have been given in a previous agreement, such as a treaty or convention with a jurisdiction clause (a chronological list of the many such agreements can be found in every ICJ yearbook). For the law of the sea, the most general of these conventions is part 15 of the 1982 Convention on the Law of the Sea.

There may also be "compulsory jurisdiction" because the respondent party has made a declaration under the "optional clause" (so called because its original form was an optional protocol) of article 36.2 of the Statute. But a large proportion of the contentious-jurisdiction cases coming before the court are the result of a special agreement made between the parties for the purpose of the case. Whether strictly necessary or not, making a special agreement on the jurisdiction of the court in respect of a defined dispute or kind of dispute often has great value, not only because it clarifies the task of the court, but also because negotiating a special agreement can temper feelings between the parties and so better equip them for the profitable use of the discipline of a court hearing.

Most cases, whether for a judgment or for an opinion, are heard and decided by the full court, that is, all fifteen members. Sometimes when an ad hoc judge is nominated by a party that does not have a national judge on the court, the full court will then comprise sixteen or even seventeen judges. Instead of the full court, another possibility is for the appointment of Chambers of the Court (articles 26–29 of the Statute). The court has made chambers more attractive by allowing the parties virtually to choose the members of it. While other considerations may guide parties to choose between the full court and a chamber, one factor may be the nature of the confidential deliberation phase of reaching a decision. There is a big difference between a deliberation of the full court, which necessarily consists largely of a series of speeches called for in the order in which intentions to speak come to the notice of the president, and the deliberation in a chamber commonly of five judges, where true cross-discussion and argument is possible. And yet the full court is usually the choice of the parties, for then there is no need for possible delays and discussions about the membership of a chamber. Also, the full court's decision, because of its broader representative character, may be thought to carry more weight, even although article 29 of the Statute provides that "a judgment given by any of the chambers provided for in Articles 26 and 29 shall be considered as rendered by the Court."

The procedures of the court or chamber are laid down by the Statute of the Court and by the Rules of Court, which the court itself devises. The faithful application of these procedures is part and parcel of the settlement of disputes by the court. The essence of these procedures is adversarial confrontation. The parties first confront each other, confidentially, in the phase of exchanging written pleadings and making submissions to the court, and then in public oral proceedings before the court in the Great Hall of Justice in the Peace Palace at The Hague. It is this due process of public confrontation that the parties seek and expect when they take a case to the ICJ.

Obviously, this manner of proceeding puts great responsibility and power into the hands of the counselors hired by the parties. There is now, informally and unofficially, the beginnings of an international bar, for it is the constant experience of the judges that among the lead counsels of cases emanating from all over the world appear the same familiar names on one side or the other. This is no doubt in part because the Statute of the Court recognizes only French and English as the languages of the court, so the choice may be somewhat limited.

After the conclusion of these somewhat theatrical performances, when the case has been formally handed over to the judges for a decision, the question arises as to what the judges should aim for in their deliberations. They can find themselves in somewhat of a dilemma: Do they act as umpires assessing the performances of the rival teams of counsel deciding "who won," or do they boldly seek to do justice between the two parties? For in any case worth taking to so high a tribunal, there are choices that have to be made. The dilemma sometimes surfaces when the court decides a case on a ground not argued by counsel on either side. Then articles appear in legal journals complaining that a court should never decide on a basis not properly argued and sifted through in the forensic arguments of the parties. To this the judges may justly reply that they ought not to be prevented from doing their own research, and that to call the parties back into court for further argument, though it does sometimes happen, is expensive in terms of both time and money.

The trial procedures—due process—are carefully crafted to be an efficacious method of settling disputes. They still have something of the color of joustings from the age of chivalry. In following the strict rules of procedure, the need always to hear the opposing point of view—what the French call the process of contradiction—makes up a compelling ritual. After properly going through the process, it is very difficult then for a party to the dispute not to accept the result. It is not easy to find any judgment of the ICJ that has not been implemented, whether openly or covertly, whether immediately or later on.

The court does not merely dispose of the dispute or disputes involved in a case. It follows the tradition of common-law courts in setting out, often at some length, the reasoning that has led it to its decision. Inevitably, these precedents (decisions and reasons) are later consulted both by parties and their counsel and by the court itself. There cannot, of course, be any system of binding precedent. Nevertheless, previous decisions tend to be followed.

## The Court's Role in the Development of the Law of the Sea

What effect, then, have ICJ decisions had on particular aspects of the law of the sea? One must say "particular aspects," because the extent of the court's influence on shaping the law depends on what disputes have been brought to it for decisions. At the beginning of the twenty-first century, when the court has become busy with a long waiting list of cases, it is able to use lines of cases to better elaborate rules of law. In looking at some of the cases concerning disputes over the law of the sea, it will not be possible to do more than sketch the decisions, but these sketches should give an impression of the place of the court in maritime international law.

One of the most influential cases was the first one that came before the new court: the *Corfu Channel* case between Albania and the United Kingdom. On October 22, 1946, two British destroyers, when proceeding through the Corfu Channel in the territorial waters of Albania, struck mines that both caused considerable damage to the vessels and led to loss of life (45 crew members lost their lives, and 42 were wounded). On November 12–13, the British navy itself then swept the channel clear of mines. The dispute over these happenings went first to the Security Council of the United Nations, which recommended that the parties refer the matter to the court. Eventually the parties reached the Special Agreement of March 25, 1948.

There were two questions for the court: first, whether Albania was responsible for the mine explosions, and second, whether the United Kingdom had violated international law by passing through Albanian territorial waters and then again by sweeping the channel mines in November. The questions on Albanian responsibility for laying the mines concerned law and fact. The factual issue was whether the Albanian coast guard should have seen the laying of the mines and warned international shipping bodies of the danger, since Albania itself did not have the resources to lay the mines. The matters of fact were settled by appointing a commission of neutral naval officers to inspect the sites and answer eight precise questions asked by the court. The legal issue was whether, in international law, foreign warships enjoy a right of innocent passage through a territorial strait commonly used for passage between two parts of the high seas.

On the crucial legal matter of innocent passage, the court decided that warships do enjoy this right in this kind of territorial strait, and the decision was later adopted as law in article 16.4 of the 1958 Geneva Convention on the Territorial Sea and the Contiguous Zone. The decision was later adopted in articles 37 and 38 of the 1982 Convention on the Law of the Sea. The judgment also decided that Albania was responsible for the explosions, since the mines could not have been laid without its knowledge, in which case there was a duty to warn shipping. The court found that Albania should therefore pay compensation for the damage and loss of life (some compensation was paid about four decades later). It also decided, however, that the sweeping operation by the British navy could not be justified as the exercise of a right of innocent passage, but this declaration by the court granted Albania merely appropriate satisfaction.

The importance of fisheries as a resource and the rule that fisheries in territorial waters (normally a breadth of 3 miles, or 4.8 kilometers, from the coast) were a coastal-state monopoly quickly raised questions about the proper locations of territorial sea baselines and limits. By far the most important case was the second one to come before the ICJ: the *Fisheries* case between the United Kingdom as claimant and Norway as respondent (ICJ *Report* 1951, p. 116). The dispute was about how the law applied to the somewhat unusual west coast of Norway: some 1,500 kilometers (about 932 miles) of mountainous coast, much broken by fjords and bays and having, at a very considerable distance from the mainland coast, a *skaergaard*, or rock and islet rampart. This structure made it difficult to find any clear line between coast and sea. In 1935 the Norwegian government had decreed that all the extensive waters on the coastal side of a system of straight lines joining points on the *skaergaard* were national waters and that the breadth of the territorial sea was measured from the straight lines around the *skaergaard*. Norway claimed a 4-mile (6.4-kilometer) territorial sea, and this was not disputed by the United Kingdom. The resulting extensive claim to exclusive fishery was a legal novelty, and the question for the court was whether or not the claim was in accord with international law. The court decided by 10 votes to 2 that the method employed for delimiting the Norwegian fisheries zone was not contrary to international law, and by 8 votes to 4 that the lines fixed in application of this method were not contrary to international law. The decision was later adopted in article 7 ("Straight Baselines") of the 1982 Convention on the Law of the Sea.

It seems that the court had persuaded itself that the west coast of Norway was geographically very rare, if not unique. Ironically, the west coast of Scotland was similar, and the United Kingdom later applied the court's decision to that coast. The judgment also later inspired the very extensive claims of archipelagic states.

The great majority of law of the sea cases that found their way to the ICJ were about boundaries, including limits of national jurisdiction at sea. These disputes were technologically driven. The then-novel possibilities of exploiting oil and gas by drilling in the seabed led to national-jurisdiction claims over the continental shelf, the area of seabed and subsoil adjacent to the coast but outside territorial waters, a seaward prolongation of the landmass off many coasts. But how far was the continental shelf lawfully to extend? And where should the seafloor boundary be between opposite or adjoining coasts? Many such cases went to the court, usually when negotiations for an agreement had failed, and when some decision was needed because exploration had shown promise and drillers wanted certainty about where they were permitted to drill.

The mother of such cases was the ICJ decision in the *North Sea Continental Shelf* cases, involving the continental shelf off the coasts of Denmark, Germany, and the Netherlands (ICJ *Report* 1969, p. 3). The parties had attempted to reach a negotiated settlement, but progress was halted by a disagreement over a legal question: the 1958 Convention on the Continental Shelf provided in article 6 that between opposite or adjacent states, where they fail to agree on the boundary between them, and unless a different boundary is justified by special circumstances, the boundary "shall be determined by the application of the principle of equidistance from the nearest points of the baselines from which the breadth of the territorial sea is measured." The problem was that the Netherlands and Denmark were parties to that convention and opined that the equidistance method was applicable, but Germany was not a party and claimed that applying that principle would be unfair to Germany. Thus a crucial point was whether that method as stated in the convention was also a rule of customary law and so binding upon a nonparty. This was the question put to the court: "What rules and principles of international law are applicable in the delimitation as between the Parties?"

The court favored Germany by 11 votes to 6 in an elaborately argued judgment. There was, said the court, no single method of delimitation that all the parties in the case were obliged to use. Accordingly the delimitation should be made by agreement "in accordance with equitable principles, and taking account of all the relevant circumstances." The court had also gone so far as to show in a diagram what it regarded as the boundaries that the exercise would produce. The parties seized upon the answer given to the actual questions they had posed—whether the equidistance method was or was not binding—and were then able to resume negotiations, which happily resulted in agreed boundaries, though somewhat different from the ones indicated by the court.

The tension between equidistance and equitable principles (though semantically meaning much the same thing) was later one of the chief areas of contention in the Third United Nations Conference on the Law of the Sea, where the larger maritime powers on the whole favored equidistance and the third world went for equitable principles. The result, embodied in article 83 of the 1982 Convention on the Law of the Sea, is a masterpiece of ambiguity but on the whole might be said to favor equity.

At the next stage the court faced a new kind of claim to the seas in 1972: the Icelandic claim of an exclusive fisheries claim extending to a distance of 50 miles (80 kilometers) offshore. This was opposed in cases brought to the court by Germany and by the United Kingdom. This case was not easy for the court because this part of the law of the sea was beginning to change. In the 1982 Convention on the Law of the Sea, the Icelandic claim was in effect validated in the form of the new notion of the "exclusive economic zone." Iceland decided not to appear before the court, and this it was entitled to do (article 53 of the Statute of the Court). The court contented itself by deciding that the 50-mile claim, for various reasons, could not be opposed by either of the two claimants (ICJ *Report* 1972, p. 12, and 1973, pp. 3 and 302).

In the *Aegean Sea Continental Shelf* case, the continental-shelf question emerged again in a politically delicate dispute between Greece and Turkey over their respective claims to the continental shelf. The court decided that it did not have jurisdiction in the case (ICJ *Report* 1974, p. 3; 1976, p. 3; and 1978, p. 3).

In a case between Libya and Tunisia, however, the court was able to determine an equitable continental-shelf boundary. This case illustrated an ancillary problem, for Italy strongly argued to be allowed to intervene in the case. Permission was not granted, but in the final judgment the court was careful not to involve itself in the parts of the boundary where Italian interests clearly were possibly involved (ICJ *Report* 1981, p. 3, and 1982, p. 18), so much so that the question arose as to whether Italy had done better by losing the case for intervention than if it had won.

It was then becoming clear that to deal with the continental-shelf boundary and the water-column boundary separately could lead to problems, for the most elementary questions of convenience and enforcement demanded that the location of these boundaries be identical. This very issue was raised in the important *Gulf of Maine* case between Canada and the United States. By agreement of the parties, this case was sent not to the full court but to a Chamber of the Court, the membership of which was virtually chosen by the parties. In this area of sea, which contained probably the most important fishing banks in the world, the parties were agreed that they wanted the chamber to fix a single boundary. In a decade of strenuous negotiations, the parties had agreed on draft treaties that fixed a boundary acceptable to both teams. This treaty, however, needed ratification by the president and the Senate of the United States, and senators started introducing amendments. These obviously were not acceptable to Canada. So both governments agreed that the only way out was to go to the ICJ, where a settlement could be reached that was binding upon both parties.

In a long judgment (ICJ *Report* 1984, p. 246), the chamber did fix the boundary. The judgment was unusual in that the parties had demanded a single boundary for both the shelf and the water column. The chamber was much preoccupied with what was then a novel task. Each of these two kinds of boundaries had hitherto developed separately and was determined by its own proper combination of factors or criteria. Therefore, concluded the chamber, it was necessary to find a combination of criteria "which does not give preferential treatment to one of these two objects to the detriment of the other, and at the same time is such as to be equally suitable to the division of either of them" (ICJ *Report* 1984, p. 327). The demand for a single maritime boundary was certain to become a permanent feature of disputes.

Several of the cases that followed were also mixed disputes involving both land boundaries and maritime boundaries. Where there was a disputed land boundary ending at the coasts of adjacent states, it was necessary to decide the location of the land boundary to know where the maritime international boundary can begin.

A dispute between El Salvador and Honduras was about an internal land boundary and also the boundaries within the waters of the Bay of Fonseca. This bay is a celebrated example of a "historic bay," that is, one whose interior waters are, for historic reasons, entirely national even though the breadth of the bay's entrance line is longer than is normally permitted for such a bay. This was submitted to a Chamber of the Court by a special agreement of 1986. Nicaragua, which also had a coast on the bay, requested permission to intervene, and this was granted by the chamber (ICJ *Report* 1990, p. 92). Nicaragua, in the terms of its request, agreed to accept the chamber's decision, which, by article 27, is in any event "considered as rendered by the Court." This complicated series of disputes was decided in a long and detailed judgment (ICJ *Report* 1992, p. 351).

Several maritime delimitation matters followed. In a case between Denmark and Norway, *Concerning Maritime Delimitation in the Area between Greenland and Jan Mayen* (ICJ *Report* 1993, p. 38), a disputed maritime boundary for a large area of the North Atlantic was settled by the court. The complicated case *Qatar v. Bahrain* also settled a long-standing dispute about maritime boundaries and the ownership of certain islands in "the Gulf."

A major maritime- and land-boundary decision was handed down in the case of *Cameroon v. Nigeria, Equatorial Guinea Intervening* (Merrills). The case was important not only in settling the dispute but also because the court was determined to make a usable pattern of the varied notions of equidistance, equity, and special circumstances. In that process the court dealt with the tension between customary law and article 83 of the 1982 Convention on the Law of the Sea and made the law more predictable.

Thus the ICJ not only has dealt with many disputes but also has played a major part in the elaboration of the law of the sea. The reader should not take away the impression that the maritime cases have been only about the delimitation of boundaries, although that has been far and away the most important work. For example, there was a case brought by Finland against Denmark about rights of passage through the Great Belt (ICJ *Report* 1991, p. 12). Denmark was constructing between Zealand and Funen a new bridge that, though high enough over the water for most shipping to pass freely, would create difficulties for tall oil rigs built in Finland that, for export, needed to pass through the Great Belt, the main seaway out of the Baltic. The ventilation of the disagreements in the court hearings enabled the parties, under the court's encouragement, to renew negotiations and reach a compromise agreement (ways were found to make it practicable for the superstructure of the rigs to be dismantled during passage).

There was also a hotly contested case between Spain and Canada about Canadian legislation designed for fisheries conservation and management, under which it had boarded a Spanish ship on the high seas (ICJ *Report* 1998, p. 432). The decision of the court was that it had no jurisdiction over the matter, since this matter was squarely within an anticipated reservation made by Canada on accepting the court's jurisdiction under article 36.2 of the Statute of the Court (the so-called optional clause).

[*See also* Law, *subentries on* Twentieth-Century Law through 1945 *and* Private Maritime Law; Law of the Sea; *and* United Nations Conferences on the Law of the Sea.]

## Bibliography

Attard, David Joseph. *The Exclusive Economic Zone in International Law*. Oxford: Clarendon Press, 1987.

Charney, Jonathan I., and Lewis M. Alexander, eds. *International Maritime Boundaries*. 5 vols. Dordrecht, Netherlands: Nijhoff, 1993–2005. See volume 5, edited by David A. Colson and Robert W. Smith.

Churchill, R. R., and A. V. Lowe. *The Law of the Sea*. 3d ed. Manchester, U.K.: Manchester University Press, 1999.

Francalanci, Giampiero, Daniela Romanò, and Tullio Scovazzi, eds. *Atlas of the Straight Baselines*. 2d ed. Milan, Italy: Giuffrè, 1989.

Francalanci, Giampiero, and Tullio Scovazzi. *Lines in the Sea*. Dordrecht, Netherlands: Kluwer, 1994.

International Court of Justice. *Reports of Judgments, Advisory Opinions, and Orders*. The Hague, Netherlands: International Court of Justice, published annually.

Merrills, J. G. "Land and Maritime Boundary between Cameroon and Nigeria (*Cameroon v. Nigeria, Equatorial Guinea Intervening*), Merits, Judgment of 10 October 2002." *International and Comparative Law Quarterly* 52, no. 3 (2003): 788–797.

O'Connell, D. P. *The Influence of Law on Sea Power*. Manchester, U.K.: Manchester University Press, 1975.

Rosenne, Shabtai. *The World Court: What It Is and How It Works*. 5th ed. Dordrecht, Netherlands: Nijhoff, 1995.

Shaw, Malcolm N. "The Law of the Sea." In *International Law*, 5th ed. Cambridge, U.K.: Cambridge University Press, 2003.

Soons, Alfred H. A. *Marine Scientific Research and the Law of the Sea*. Dordrecht, Netherlands: Kluwer, 1982.

Weil, Prosper. *The Law of Maritime Delimitation: Reflections*. Cambridge, U.K.: Grotius Publications, 1989.

ROBERT JENNINGS

# Permanent Court of International Justice

The Covenant of the League of Nations first called upon its member states to settle disputes by peaceful means, such as arbitration or judicial settlement. So that states would have a body to which they could turn if such means failed, it charged the Council of the League with drawing up "plans for the establishment of a Permanent Court of International Justice," competent to determine disputes of an international character and to give advisory opinions. Early in 1920 the council formed a Committee of Jurists, composed of thirteen leading experts from different countries, to draft the court's statute. They reviewed a plan drawn up in 1907 for a Permanent Court of Arbitral Justice, the Statute of the Central American Court of Justice, and several plans prepared by governments and experts. Two controversial issues were the method of electing judges (resolved by requiring absolute majorities in both the Assembly and the Council of the League), and the question of whether the Court's jurisdiction should be compulsory over all parties to the statute (as the committee recommended) or should instead depend on the consent of the parties in each instance (as the major powers contended). The committee's draft statute, with amendments, was approved in December 1920 and opened for signature in a protocol whereby signatory states accepted, subject to ratification, the terms of the statute. The issue of compulsory jurisdiction was compromised: compulsory jurisdiction could be accepted by a signatory state by making a declaration under an optional clause to the protocol. The protocol entered into force in September 1921, after a majority of the members of the league had ratified it. In total, 50 states accepted the statute, including many European and Latin American states, and over half also accepted the optional clause, so compulsory jurisdiction applied among them. The United States signed but did not ratify the protocol, despite efforts to adjust its terms to meet various conditions proposed by the U.S. Senate.

The initial eleven judges (and four deputy judges) were elected in September 1921 for nine-year terms. A party to a case without a national on the court was entitled to nominate a judge ad hoc. Between 1923 and 1939, the court decided 21 contentious cases and gave 26 advisory opinions, many arising from the post–World War I settlement. The court ceased to function when the Hague was occupied by Germany in 1940. The judges having all resigned in January 1946, the court was dissolved by resolution of the Assembly of the League on April 18, 1946, the day of the inauguration of the International Court of Justice.

The Permanent Court of International Justice decided two cases that touched partly upon maritime law, and both decisions had some lasting relevance. The first arose from the refusal of the German authorities to permit S.S. *Wimbledon*, a British vessel chartered to a French company, to enter the Kiel Canal because it was carrying munitions to a Polish naval base in March 1921, when Germany was neutral in regard to a war between Poland and Russia. France and Great Britain objected to this refusal of passage on the grounds that article 380 of the Versailles Peace Treaty provided that the canal should be open to merchant vessels of all nations at peace with Germany on equal terms. The case was referred to the court by France, Great Britain, Italy, and Japan, and Poland was permitted to intervene as a party to the treaty. The court held, by a majority, that the refusal was wrong and contrary to the treaty. In considering the question of what conduct was incompatible with neutrality, the court stated, "When an artificial waterway connecting two open seas has been permanently dedicated to the use of the whole world, such waterway is assimilated to natural straits in the sense that even the passage of a belligerent man-of-war does not compromise the neutrality of the sovereign State under whose jurisdiction the waters in question lie." Compensation was awarded to France for the prejudice sustained by the vessel and its charterers.

The second case was that of S.S. *Lotus*, a French mail-ship that collided in August 1926 with a Turkish steamer in the Aegean Sea at a point beyond territorial waters. The steamer sank, and eight Turkish nationals drowned. When *Lotus* reached Istanbul, one of its officers was prosecuted, together with the Turkish captain of the sunken steamer, and both were convicted and imprisoned. Turkey's Penal Code provided that a foreigner who offended abroad against Turks and was then arrested in Turkey could be punished under the code. France objected to the prosecution of the officer, advancing two arguments: first, a state does not have jurisdiction over offenses committed by foreigners abroad solely by reason of the nationality of the victim; second, international law recognizes the exclusive jurisdiction of the flag state as regards everything occurring on board a ship on the high seas, including acts and omissions leading to collisions. Faced with this dispute, Turkey and France agreed to submit the question to the Permanent Court of International Justice. The court held, by the president's deciding vote (the votes being equally divided 6 to 6), that Turkey had not acted contrary to the principles of international law. In rejecting the first French argument, the court found that the offense on board *Lotus* had produced effects on board the steamer, which the court assimilated to Turkish territory. As regards the second argument, the court, while accepting that a vessel on the high seas was subject only to the authority of the flag state, held that it did not follow that another state could never exercise territorial jurisdiction over acts occurring on board a foreign ship on the high seas. The court again assimilated a ship on the high seas to the territory of the flag state. Several judges delivered powerful dissenting opinions: that by the British Judge Robert Finlay, for instance, characterized this assimilation as "a new and startling application of a metaphor," since a ship is a movable chattel, not a place. The decision caused serious disquiet in international maritime circles. A diplomatic conference in 1952 disagreed with its conclusions as regards collisions and adopted a convention that confined jurisdiction over officers following a collision to either the flag state or the state of which the accused was a national. This provision, repeated in the United Nations Convention on the Law of the Sea, is now generally accepted.

[*See also* Flags; Law, *subentry on* Twentieth-Century Law through 1945; Law of the Sea; Straits, *subentry on* Laws Governing Straits; *and* United Nations Conferences on the Law of the Sea.]

## Bibliography

Fachiri, Alexander P. *The Permanent Court of International Justice: Its Constitution, Procedure, and Work.* 2d ed. London: Oxford University Press, 1932.

Hudson, Manley O. *The Permanent Court of International Justice, 1920–1942: A Treatise.* New York: Macmillan, 1943.

International Court of Justice. http://www.icj-cij.org. This Web site now carries decisions of the Permanent Court of International Justice.

Lindsey, Edward. *The International Court.* New York: Crowell, 1931.

Lloyd, Lorna. *Peace through Law: Britain and the International Court in the 1920s.* Woodbridge, U.K.: Royal Historical Society; Rochester, N.Y.: Boydell Press, 1997.

Rosenne, Shabtai. *The Law and Practice of the International Court, 1920–2004.* 4th ed. Leiden, Netherlands, and Boston: Martinus Nijhoff.

Schenk, B., Graf von Stauffenberg, ed. *Statut et règlement de la Cour Permanente de Justice Internationale: Eléments d'interprétation.* Berlin: C. Heymann, 1934.

Schlochauer, Hans-Jurgen. "Permanent Court of International Justice." In *Encyclopedia of Public International Law*, vol. 3, edited by Rudolf Bernhardt. Amsterdam: Elsevier, 1997.

Spiermann, Ole. "Who Attempts Too Much Does Nothing Well: The 1920 Advisory Committee of Jurists and the Statute of the Permanent Court of International Justice." In *The British Yearbook of International Law 2002*, vol. 73, pp. 187–260. Oxford: Clarendon Press, 2003.

DAVID H. ANDERSON

## Cousteau, Jacques-Yves

**Cousteau, Jacques-Yves** (1910–1997), naval officer, oceanographer, filmmaker, and environmentalist. Jacques Cousteau was the most effective popularizer of oceanography in the twentieth century. Born on June 11, 1910, at Saint-André de Cubzac, France, near Bordeaux, he was the son of Daniel (a lawyer) and Elizabeth Cousteau. He developed a love for natural bodies of water in 1920, swimming and diving at a summer camp in Vermont. At twenty he entered the French naval academy at Brest, where, already an experienced amateur filmmaker, he recorded his international training cruises with a camera he had had since he was thirteen. After graduation he was assigned duty as an artillery instructor in the French navy and stationed at a base in Toulon. There he began a daily routine of swimming and diving and with friends began experimenting with watertight goggles and a portable underwater breathing device, an apparatus that supplies oxygen to divers, which he later patented and made commercially available in 1946 as the Aqua-lung. He also developed a waterproof case for his camera, which permitted him to record his experiments. During World War II Cousteau worked with the Underground, spying on the Italian occupation forces, for which he was named Chevalier de la Légion d'Honneur in 1946. He retired from the French navy in 1956 with the rank of commander and, in 1957, became the director of Monaco's Oceanographic Museum, a position he held until 1988.

To further his marine research, a patron leased Cousteau a retired 400-ton navy minesweeper for one franc a year. In this vessel, which he converted to a laboratory and named *Calypso*, he explored oceans, lakes, and rivers and produced both films and books drawn from his ongoing log. In 1952 in the Red Sea he took the first color film shot at a depth of 46 meters (150 feet). Off the coast of Marseille he discovered the hull of an ancient Greek freighter sunk in mud 40 meters (130 feet) deep. A more commercial use of his underwater explorations was an offshore oil survey made by divers using his Aqua-lung. In the 1960s he began the creation of three submarine laboratories on the continental shelf, the first manned undersea colonies. The third, called Conshelf III, housed six researchers 101 meters (330 feet) underwater for three weeks in 1965. His book *The Silent World* (1953) sold 5 million copies in 22 languages, and his full-length documentary films, including *The World of Silence* (1956) and *World without Sun* (1965), were international successes and won three Academy Awards. His many television films garnered a total of seventeen Emmys. The scientific community was not unanimous in its support for his popular presentation, however; critics accused him of focusing more on showmanship than on scientific research and manipulating his material by including studio shots in footage purporting to be natural. He admitted to reenacting underwater scenes and staging dramatic confrontations.

In his latter years, Cousteau's interest in underwater exploration never flagged, but he grew increasingly concerned with such social issues as marine conservation and world peace. In 1973 he created the nonprofit Cousteau Society, for the protection of ocean life, and he became widely known as an environmentalist and social activist. Widely honored, he received the United Nations International Environment Prize in 1977, was elected to the Académie Française in 1989, and was awarded the U.S. Medal of Freedom in 1985. He died in Paris on June 25, 1997, and was buried at his birthplace. An extraordinarily charismatic figure, he had a profound influence on the public's understanding of the seas and their relation to human life.

[*See also* Marine Biology.]

### Bibliography

Dugan, James. *Man under the Sea.* New York: Harper, 1956.
Iverson, Genie. *Jacques Cousteau.* New York, Putnam, 1976.
Madsen, Axel. *Cousteau: An Unauthorized Biography.* New York: Beaufort, 1986.
Munson, Richard. *Cousteau: The Captain and His World.* New York: Morrow, 1989.

DENNIS WEPMAN

**Cranes.** *See* Shipyard Equipment.

**Crimps.** *See* Recruitment.

**Crossing the Line** "Crossing the Line" did not always signify crossing the Equator. In the late Middle

**Crossing the Line Ceremony.** This photograph was taken on board the Union Castle Steamship Company's S.S. *Windsor Castle*, c. 1960. © NATIONAL MARITIME MUSEUM, LONDON

Ages, in the very early days of the coasting trade, a sailors' baptism was always held on ships that crossed the border between two shipping districts. Known cases where sailors' baptisms were held in European seafaring are, among others: Cape Kullen, flatly visible before sailing into the Sound, before the passage into the Baltic; the Northern Cape on the course to Arkhangel'sk (Russia); Pointe du Raz, situated on the farthest point of Brittany, before the ships made their way to the ports of the French Atlantic coast and the Bay of Biscay; and the Berlengas, a group of islands off the Portuguese coast, for ships passing the Strait of Gibraltar. Sailors' baptisms near the Berlengas Islands became customary toward the end of the sixteenth century on the Dutch vessels bound for East India. The Equator was passed without fanfare from the crew.

On French ships, however, sailors' baptisms on the Equator took place in 1529 and in 1557. In the second half of the seventeenth century, the initiation ritual near the Equator also occurred on Dutch, Portuguese, and English ships. The oldest evidence of sailors' baptisms on the Equator on board Spanish, Danish, Swedish, and German ships dates from the first half of the eighteenth century. At the end of that century, the custom was also adopted on board American ships.

The sailors' baptism occurred in the seventeenth century and in the first decades of the eighteenth century as follows. The experienced sailors got the newcomers on deck, where the old hands jumped around in disguise, playing kettle drums. In most cases, the candidates for baptism encountered a mock judge before the great mast, before whom they had to stand at attention. In order to show his respect, the sailor who was to be baptized sometimes had to endure the judge's foot on his neck, or kiss the foot. All of this created feelings of humiliation, alienation, and detachment in the candidate. The break with his social past and his admission into the ship's community was ultimately symbolized by the actual sailors' baptism. The candidates were hoisted up to the end of the yard and plunged into the water below the deepest point of the keel three times.

Halfway through the eighteenth century, the practice began of having some playing the role of Neptune, who would pretend to visit ships as they passed the Equator. In this role playing, Neptune generally took over the role of the mock judge. With the advent of Neptune, ducking from the yard disappeared as well. Its place was taken by the shaving ceremony, in which the experienced sailors smeared the naked or very scantily dressed newcomer with oil, tar, or other filth and laid him on a plank above a barrel of seawater or sewage. Then he was shaved with a piece of wood or another rough object. When the dirt was largely removed by the shaving, the plank was pulled out from under the candidate and he was submerged in the barrel of seawater or wastewater. Those who found the whole ritual offensive could buy their way out of the baptism. They thereby contributed to the feast that concluded the sailors' baptism.

Rituals like the sailors' baptism facilitated the socialization and acculturation of newcomers on board. During the baptism, the candidate was made aware of his individuality and his isolation so that he realized he was dependent on the others and could not survive without them. He was then supposed to accept his membership in the ship's community and eat, laugh, and drink heartily with the other sailors during the feast. In this manner, camaraderie based on mutual protection and friendship was established.

However, the sailors' baptism did not always foster solidarity among the ship's community. Sometimes, tensions were discharged and social roles were temporarily reversed. The social structure itself could be dissolved temporarily. In this case, an "authority of riot" took over the ship, in which the "most respected" on board were "lawless and witless." Therefore, officers usually steered clear of the festive ritual, in order to maintain their authority. Already in the seventeenth century, attempts were made to discourage the practice as hazing.

Similar ceremonies and mock fraternal initiations were in use in the late twentieth and early twenty-first centuries for the Order of the Blue Nose for sailors who have crossed the Arctic Circle; the Order of the Red Nose for sailors who have crossed the Antarctic Circle, the Order of the Golden Dragon for sailors who have crossed the International Date Line; the Order of the Ditch for sailors who have passed through the Panama Canal; the Safari to Suez for sailors who have passed through the Suez Canal; the Royal Diamond Shellback for sailors who cross the Equator at the Prime Meridian off the coast of West Africa; the Realm of the Czars for sailors who crossed into the Black Sea; and the Order of Magellan for sailors who circumnavigated the globe.

[See also Shipboard Life.]

### Bibliography

Henningsen, Henning. *Crossing the Equator: Sailors' Baptism and Other Initiation Rites.* Copenhagen: Munksgaard, 1961.

Ketting, Herman. *Leven, werk, en rebellie aan boord van Oost-Indiëvaarders 1595–1650.* Amsterdam: Aksant, 2002.

Rediker, Marcus. *Between the Devil and the Deep Blue Sea: Merchant Seamen, Pirates, and the Anglo-American Maritime World, 1700–1750.* Cambridge, U.K.: Cambridge University Press, 1993.

HERMAN KETTING
*Translated from the Dutch by Alexa Nieschlag*

**Cruiser**  In the early nineteenth century, the word "cruiser" referred to a role—to a warship on independent duty, detached from the main fleet to search for the enemy—rather than to a specific ship type. Initially all these ships were fast sailing-ships with guns on the broadside. During the 1830s a number of paddle frigates were built with a small number of very heavy guns, but from 1850 these were superseded by wooden, screw frigates. The American Civil War (1861–1865) turned thoughts to commerce raiding, and a number of very long and fast frigates were built, such as USS *Wamapanoag*. These ships were too long for wooden construction, but unarmored iron ships were not favored because of the brittle characteristics of iron.

Gradually the "protected cruiser" evolved, with a thick deck close to the waterline and closely subdivided 'tween decks above. The invention of improved armor enabled the bigger ships to be fitted with an armor belt that was resistant to cruiser-mounted guns. A ship of this type was very big and cost as much as a battleship. Other types of cruisers also developed and were termed "armored cruiser," "light cruiser," and "heavy cruiser."

By the outbreak of World War I, major navies had both battle cruisers with battleship-caliber guns for the fighting role and also light cruisers of 4,000–5,000 tons with guns of 4-inch to 6-inch caliber. During the war, the light cruiser grew in size and had a uniform armament of guns of about 6-inch caliber.

The Washington Naval Limitation Treaty of 1922 defined a cruiser as less than 10,000 tons with guns of 8 inches or less. Most navies built such ships in considerable numbers, but it was not possible to reconcile numerous 8-inch guns, high speed, and armor within these limits; most ships therefore sacrificed armor. During the 1930s there was a trend to build big cruisers with up to fifteen 6-inch guns, while other navies built much smaller ships in order to get the numbers required within the overall tonnage limit.

During World War II, the cruiser lost its scouting role to aircraft; its new role was to protect carriers from attack by aircraft and surface ships. In postwar years this role was extended, with large ships carrying the big, early guided missiles. The term "cruiser" is now interchangeable with large destroyer.

[*See also* Aircraft Carrier; Battleship; Warships, *subentry on* Modern Warships; *and* Wars, Maritime, *subentry on* World Wars.]

### Bibliography

Brown, David K. *The Grand Fleet: Warship Design and Development, 1906–1922.* London: Chatham, 1999.

Brown, David K. *Nelson to Vanguard: Warship Design and Development, 1923–1945.* London: Chatham, 2000.

Brown, David K. *Warrior to Dreadnought: Warship Development, 1860–1905.* London: Chatham, 1997.

Brown, David K., and George Moore. *Rebuilding the Royal Navy: Warship Design since 1945.* London: Chatham, 2003.

Brown, David K., ed. *The Design and Construction of British Warships 1939–1945.* Vol. 1, *Major Surface Vessels.* London: Conway Maritime Press, 1995.

Lacroix, Eric, and Linton Wells. *Japanese Cruisers of the Pacific War.* Annapolis, Md.: U.S. Naval Institute Press, 1997.

Raven, Alan, and John Roberts. *British Cruisers of World War Two.* London: Arms and Armour Press, 1980.

DAVID K. BROWN

# Cruising

The passenger-cruising industry employed over 200,000 persons in 2004, providing vacations at sea for upward of 10 million passengers annually. Several hundred engine-powered oceangoing passenger ships were in operation, from the 1,471-ton *Nantucket Clipper* (launched 1984) of the Clipper Cruise Line, which can carry 102 passengers, to the 150,000-ton *Queen Mary 2* (launched 2004) of the Cunard Line, which has a capacity for more than 2,000 passengers. There are a number of other large cruise liners with accommodation for more than 3,500 passengers each. The most luxurious of these vessels are less a means of transport than a destination in themselves, with the ports of call being secondary in the minds of many passengers.

### Origins

As early as 1844 the Peninsular and Oriental Steam Navigation Company (P&O) advertised a "special Mediterranean tour," which apparently was designed to serve as an alternative, or supplement, to the traditional grand tour of Europe. Passenger cruising in the United States dates to 1867, when Samuel Langhorne Clemens (Mark Twain) and a group of friends made arrangements to take the paddle-wheel steamer *Quaker City* to the Mediterranean Sea in order to tour the sites of antiquity.

The English tourism agent Thomas Cook promoted the first "round the world" trip in 1872, in which a variety of steamship lines, special land tours, and excursions were featured. Jules Verne's *Around the World in Eighty Days* stimulated the public imagination for such adventure when it was published in London in 1876. Lord Thomas and Lady Annie Brassey had their private yacht *Sunbeam* fitted out for cruising and went around the world in the height of luxury in 1876–1877. In 1878 Lady Brassey's book, *A Voyage in the "Sunbeam," Our Home on the Ocean for Eleven Months*, became a best seller.

The lure of faraway places took further hold in 1877, when former president Ulysses S. Grant and a large party sailed on the American Steamship Company's *Ohio* from Philadelphia to Liverpool on the first leg of a trip around the world. Grant returned to the United States on board the Pacific Mail liner *City of Tokio*, which sailed from Tokyo to San Francisco, in 1878. Grant's adventures were described in an 1879 work titled *Tour Around the World*, which was widely read in the United States.

Various authors sought to record their experiences in the form of travelogues. Among these was Alexander Clark, a Methodist minister, whose *Summer Rambles in*

**Cruising.** Sunbathing on board S.S. *Uganda*, c. 1967–1982. The British India Steamship Navigation Company built *Uganda* in 1952 for its East African service. In 1967, Howaldtswerke AG in
Hamburg, Germany, refitted the ship for use as an educational cruise ship. Her original 300 passenger cabins were turned into 43 dormitories with bunks, 14 classrooms, a 400-seat assembly area,
a library, and two swimming pools to accommodate 920 students. Based in the Mediterranean, her
student passengers arrived by chartered aircraft © NATIONAL MARITIME MUSEUM, LONDON

*Europe* (1879) described the transatlantic crossings as
"pleasurable" experiences, covered European tours from
1876 to 1878, and captured the imagination of the reading
public. Among the transatlantic steamship lines, beginning around 1880 the Inman Line and the Red Star Line
produced annual descriptions of their service, ships, and
tours.

The Inter-Oceanic Steam Yachting Company bought the
P&O liner *Ceylon* in 1881, and sent her out on the first
commercial "round the world cruise." Her passengers were
made to feel that while on board *Ceylon* they enjoyed all the
comforts of home and could avoid the discomforts of less-
refined areas and ports of the world. The voyage of *Ceylon*

covered some 58,000 kilometers (36,000 miles) over a ten-
month period. She left Southampton on October 16, 1881,
and completed her circumnavigation on August 22, 1882.

P&O picked up the idea in 1889, when *Chimborazo*
was sent on a Mediterranean cruise; the financial returns
were satisfactory enough to warrant repetition. By the mid-
1890s the French Line was marketing tours to North Africa
and the Middle East. North German Lloyd and Hamburg-
American Lines were producing comprehensive annual
books featuring their ships to Europe, overland railroad
service, and Continental tours. Actual cruises, or round-
trip transatlantic crossings featuring brief stays in Europe,
were described in some of these publications.

In areas of the world holding special claim to scenery of unique beauty, such as the Norwegian fjords, local steamship lines enhanced their summer schedules and the comforts afforded by their regular vessels in order to offer seasonal "cruises." Originating in the 1870s, these summer cruising experiences remain popular in the region today.

In 1898 the American Steamship Company (American Line) specifically outfitted *Ohio* to take a "solar eclipse cruise" to Scandinavian waters. In 1899 the American Line sent *Paris*, one of its larger vessels and a former blue-ribbon liner, on an extended cruise to the Caribbean. The cruise was limited to four hundred elite passengers and visited some of the principal islands and ports of the Spanish-American War fought the previous year. The 10,800-ton *Paris* and its passengers and crew frequently overwhelmed Caribbean port facilities, but the locals welcomed the influx of wealthy, gullible tourists. War-related excursions led by "expert tour guides" sprang up overnight, and "genuine military souvenirs" in the form of rusty machetes proliferated.

## Growing Popularity of Cruising

After 1900 the American Line offered immigrants to the United States the opportunity to book inexpensive round-trip third class (steerage) tickets in order to visit friends and family in the Old Country. This helped to fill vacant berths in the eastbound steerage cabins. Steamship companies operating liner services on the North Atlantic experienced slowdowns during the winter months, when passenger numbers dipped and cargo became scarce after the delivery of seasonal goods intended for the holiday markets. Frequently, crews were dismissed and vessels laid up for several months until trading and travel conditions improved. Looking for some means of beneficially employing a ship during the winter, Albert Ballin, the presiding genius of the Hamburg-American Line (HAPAG), in 1891 modified the liner *Augusta Victoria* (launched in 1884) for a winter Mediterranean cruise. The two principal German steamship lines, Hamburg-American and North German Lloyd, subsequently made similar adaptations. The financial results proved so rewarding that Ballin in 1906 commissioned a cruising yacht, *Oceana*. She proved to be so successful that in 1910 *Deutschland*, which had lost a great deal of money in regular service, was converted into a large cruise liner and renamed *Victoria Luise*. Her luxurious cabins and public rooms remained the same, but her new engines were much slower (and cheaper to run), and her hull was painted white to make her more suitable for tropical climes.

Thereafter, in the period before and after World War I, a portion of many passenger fleets was sent cruising in order to try and meet expenses during slack seasons. The Caribbean, and particularly Cuba, became a favored destination for American travelers. Never was this more true than in the period after World War I when the institution of Prohibition caused many American travelers to head for Havana on the vessels of the Ward Line. After the advent of the Great Depression in 1929, the Cunard Line painted its huge record-breaker *Mauretania* (1907) white, hoping that it would make money as a cruise ship. The results were uncertain, and many ships built for the North Atlantic found their careers suddenly shortened as they were withdrawn from service and scrapped. On the other hand, the outbreak of World War II found the Holland-America Line with a brand-new superliner, *Nieuw Amsterdam*, and nowhere to operate her except in Caribbean waters, since the North Atlantic was regarded as too dangerous for so valuable a vessel. When the Netherlands was attacked by Nazi Germany, however, every unit of the Dutch Merchant Marine became part of the Allied war effort.

After World War II the need to move large numbers of displaced persons, war brides, and immigrants absorbed all available shipping for several years. Creative management looked ahead to more normal peacetime conditions and when the Cunard Line had the opportunity to order an intermediate-size vessel it built the 35,000-ton *Caronia*, designed as a dual-purpose ship and launched in 1949. *Caronia* could serve as a giant yacht to carry the wealthy on cruises all over the world and, when required, could make a transatlantic crossing. In many ways she was the ideal passenger liner, capable of earning her way by either cruising or in regular liner service.

The introduction of jet airplanes in the mid-1950s caused a revolution in the commercial passenger-liner industry. Airplanes could make the trip to Europe in six hours, as opposed to four and a half days over sometimes rough seas for an ocean crossing. The year 1956 marked the first time that more passengers traveled to Europe by air than by sea, and the total number of individuals booking passage on ships for a transatlantic crossing was cut in half almost overnight.

Some managers of commercial shipping acknowledged the changing industry in their orders for new ships. Holland-America, for instance, immediately began to design and commission only multipurpose passenger liners like *Statendam* and *Rotterdam*, launched in 1957 and 1959, respectively, which could serve as North Atlantic liners in the summer months and as cruising vessels in the winter season.

Other steamship lines, such as Canadian-Pacific, Le Compagnie Générale Transatlantique (French Line), and the Italian Line, persisted in designing and ordering traditional single-purpose passenger liners for their North Atlantic services, and they were driven into extinction by the middle of the 1970s.

## Modern Cruise Industry

The travel revolution of the period 1955–1975 made cruising fundamental to survival for companies wishing to operate passenger liners. This radical rethinking of purpose also produced a revolution in design and led to the creation of the modern cruise ship and cruise industry. The Home Lines showed the way with the magnificent *Oceanic* (launched 1965), designed solely for cruising year-round; it became a fabulous moneymaker. All others learned to follow suit or perished. Initially, for many companies, this meant refitting older ships originally built for other markets. Among the new priorities for successful cruise ships were outdoor swimming pools, round-the-clock entertainment and dining, and air-conditioning capable of dealing with the warmest tropical climates. The position of "cruise director" on any vessel became vital to the success of the business. If first-run Hollywood movies were fundamental to a cruise ship's entertainment program in the 1960s, professional cabaret programs with first-class singers and dancers became mandatory by the mid-1970s, and glitzy casino operations by the 1980s.

The attractions of the cruising destinations now compete with the cruise ship and its extensive onboard amenities. These ships appeal to individuals seeking an all-expenses-paid vacation, in which they can travel from port to port without having to change their accommodation. Cruise passengers have many travel itineraries to choose from, including Alaska, the Caribbean, the South Pacific, the Mediterranean, Scandinavia, and Atlantic Canada. Cruise ships range in size from enormous superliners accommodating thousands to elegant small ships carrying one hundred or two hundred passengers and traveling on waterways inaccessible to larger vessels.

According to the industry group Cruise Lines International Association (CLIA), the number of passengers taking cruises has grown by about 10 percent each year and in 2003 passed the 10 million mark. The bulk of these passengers originated in North America, where the passenger totals for the first half of 2004 were 4.3 million, while passengers originating from other places numbered almost 700,000. The total number of passengers was over 5 million in the first half of 2004, representing a 10 percent increase. Within the cruise industry, itineraries of one to five days accounted for 31.2 percent of the market. Cruises of six to eight days represented 55.8 percent of the total, while longer cruises of nine to seventeen days made up 12.6 percent of the market, and much longer cruises, such as world cruises, accounted for only 0.4 percent of all passengers.

A significant factor in the cruise industry since the 1980s has been consolidation, as companies sought to benefit from economies of scale and increase profitability. Carnival Cruise Lines grew from humble origins in 1972 to become the largest cruise liner conglomerate in the world. In 2004 Carnival announced an order for no fewer than five new vessels totaling over 500,000 tons at a cost of over $2.5 billion. Another giant cruise ship conglomerate is Royal Caribbean International (RCI), whose five Voyager class ships total over 139,000 tons each, and whose 2006 entry *Freedom of the Seas* weighed in at over 158,000 tons. An order made in 2006 for RCI will exceed 225,000 tons and have accommodations for 5,400 passengers. Meanwhile Carnival has also announced its "Pinnacle Project" with the Italian shipyard Fincantieri to build ships in excess of 180,000 tons. In the twenty-first century, as long as passenger liner cruises are seen as safe, comfortable vacations, the expansion of the cruise industry should continue.

[*See also* Caribbean Sea, *subentry* An Overview, *and Queen Mary* and *Queen Elizabeth*.]

## Bibliography

Bonsor, N. R. P. *North Atlantic Seaway: An Illustrated History of the Passenger Services Linking the Old World with the New*. Rev. ed. 5 vols. Jersey, U.K.: Brookside Publications, 1975–1980.

Cudahy, Brian J. *The Cruise Ship Phenomenon in North America*. Centreville, Md.: Cornell Maritime Press, 2001.

*International Journal of Maritime History*. International Maritime Economic History Association. Saint Johns, Newfoundland: Maritime Studies Research Unit, 1989–.

Kendall, Lane C., and James J. Buckley. *The Business of Shipping*. 7th ed. Centreville, Md.: Cornell Maritime Press, 2001.

Kludas, Arnold. *Great Passenger Ships of the World*. Translated by Charles Hodges. 5 vols. Cambridge, U.K.: Stephens, 1975–1977.

Maginnis, Arthur J. *The Atlantic Ferry, Its Ships, Men, and Working*. London: Whittaker, 1892.

*Steamboat Bill*. Journal of the Steamship Historical Society of America. West Barrington, R.I.: The Society, 1958–.

*Travel Weekly*. The National Newspaper of the Travel Industry. New York: Ziff-Davis, 1984–.

Williams, David M. "The Extent of Transport Services' Integration: SS *Ceylon* and the First 'Round the World' Cruise, 1881–1882." *International Journal of Maritime History* 15, no. 2 (December 2003): 135–157.

WILLIAM H. FLAYHART III

# Cruising Literature

This entry contains four subentries:

An Overview
Blue Water Passages in Small Sailboats
Tall Ships
Yacht Racing

---

## An Overview

Like any pastime that people care about passionately, yachting has a long history of exceptional writing. The best books combine adventure, vigorous narrative writing, strong personalities, a degree of introspection, keen observation of nature, and technical advice.

Until the mid-nineteenth century, most writing about yachts was fragmentary. The English historian Roger North, in his *Autobiography* (c. 1698), described himself as being "extremely fond of being master of any thing that would sail" and identified two strands of sailing. One is technology: sailing, he said, was "another of my mathematical entertainments." The other is escape. North waxed poetic about one cruise: "For the day proved cool, the gale brisk, air clear, and no inconvenience to molest us, nor wants to trouble our thoughts, neither business to importune, nor formalities to tease us, so that we came nearer to a perfection of life there, then I was ever sensible of otherwise."

### From Passengers to Seamen

Cruising writing evolved quickly in the mid-nineteenth century from travelogues written by passengers to detailed narratives written by active sailors. The first writer to focus on yachting as yachting was Mrs. Nicholas Matthew Condy, whose *Reminiscences of a Yachting Cruise* (1852) provided a sardonic account of a cruise along the Devon coast in a yacht of the Royal Yacht Squadron. Yet the author was a landlubber, not a sailor. When the wind came up, Mrs. Condy writes that "flap went the mainsail, creak went the boom," and she resigned herself to dining "in a most decidedly uncomfortable manner."

The first real sailing book about a long cruise is *Letters from High Latitudes* (1857), the Marquis of Dufferin's lively account of a 9,600-kilometer (6,000-mile) voyage to the Arctic and back in his schooner *Foam*, during which he passed closer to the North Pole than any other ship. He kept the reader on edge right from the opening sentence: "Our start has not been prosperous." At that time, other yachtsmen were making cruises in smaller yachts and writing about them in yachting magazines and books. The best of these writer-sailors was R. T. McMullen, who described many of his voyages around the British Isles in *Down Channel* (first edition 1869). There he laid out the two kinds of yachting. One, which he rejected, was disengaged "yachting proper." The other was the new and more demanding "yacht sailing."

Other pioneers of "yacht sailing" were John MacGregor, who wrote wildly popular books about his kayak and yacht cruises, including *The Voyage Alone in the Yawl "Rob Roy"* (first edition 1867), and E. E. Middleton, who in *The Cruise of the "Kate"* (1870) described a single-handed voyage around England. When Sir Thomas Brassey (the publisher of *Brassey's Navy Annual*), his wife, Annie, and their children cruised around the world in the 170-foot auxiliary schooner *Sunbeam*, Annie wrote *In the Trades, the Tropics, and the Roaring Forties* (1885) and three other books about their trials and joys, books that became essential volumes in Victorian libraries.

These writers did not just tell of the risks of sea life. They delighted in it, and this delight became a theme of cruising writing. "The harder the struggle, the more persistent the effort," wrote Thomas Brassey. McMullen referred to his own "hard sailing habits" and compared a life of pains and joys on board a small yacht at sea to "successfully gathering roses off thorns." A recurring theme was that amateur sailors can make their way successfully without the assistance of professional seamen. Out of this tradition came Erskine Childers's thriller *The Riddle of the Sands* (1903), the best work of fiction about yachting and perhaps the only spy story whose solution lies in a tide table. Although the plot was fictitious, the setting and the seamanship were based on Childers's own sailing experiences.

### Professional Writers

Most of this writing was done as an avocation, but as yachting developed into a trade, a number of capable writers who sailed were able to make a living at boating magazines. Among the best of these were Maurice Griffiths in England and, in America, Thomas Fleming Day and Alfred F. Loomis.

The editor of *Yachting Monthly* for many years, as well as a yacht designer, Griffiths turned out charming, gently instructive yarns of cruising in the Thames estuary that were collected in books such as *The Magic of the Swatchways* (1932). Day, the editor of *The Rudder* magazine from 1890 to 1917, was less subtle. He employed his pen as a sledgehammer against the old notion that the sea is to be feared and is a place solely for professional seamen. He founded the first ocean race for amateur sailors in normal size boats, the Bermuda race, and wrote two books about his own ocean crossings in strikingly small yachts. One crossing was in a 26-foot sailboat and is described in *Across the Atlantic in "Sea Bird"* (1911), the other was in a small powerboat and is described in *The Voyage of the "Detroit"* (1912). Alf Loomis's style was closer to Griffiths's. Writing for several magazines before settling down as a columnist for *Yachting*, he was one of the first Americans not only to cruise extensively in small boats in remote waters but also to come home and tell others about it in books that featured a wry style, including *Fair Winds in the Far Baltic* (1928) and *Hotspur's Cruise in the Aegean* (1931).

## Ocean Cruising

The great unknown for yachtsmen was the deep sea. Among the first amateur sailors of small boats to cross an ocean and report on the experience was E. F. Knight, an English lawyer turned adventurer turned war correspondent who wrote about a voyage to South America in *The Cruise of the "Falcon"* (1888). Knight later returned to South America on a search for treasure whose only fruit was another exciting book, *The Cruise of the "Alerte"* (1890).

The most widely known of all cruising books is Joshua Slocum's *Sailing Alone around the World* (1900), about the first single-handed circumnavigation. Born in Nova Scotia and naturalized as a U.S. citizen, Slocum was a sea captain who had been tossed ashore by the collapse of the American maritime trade. He headed out from Fairhaven, Massachusetts, in 1895 in a boxy, old, 36-foot fishing sloop, *Spray*, and when he returned three years later, he was eager to write a book. Already the author of two small volumes about previous adventures at sea, he had mastered a clean, humorous, modern, conversational writing style. While his ostensible subject was the world and how to sail

around it, his deeper interest often lay with his own solitary self; *Sailing Alone* has been favorably compared with Henry David Thoreau's *Walden* (1854) as a reflection on solitude.

The influence of Slocum's book cannot be overestimated. In print continuously since 1900, *Sailing Alone* has inspired any number of other men and women to follow in the author's tracks. The first was an outrageous character of whom little is known for sure except that he was a professional seaman, went by the name of John C. Voss, and (inspired as much by Slocum's book sales as by his seamanship) in 1901 sailed out into the Pacific in a dugout canoe with a journalist as crew and reporter. Voss wrote about this stunt colorfully in *The Venturesome Voyages of Captain Voss* (1913). The American outdoors writer Jack London, in *Cruise of the "Snark"* (1911), energetically— but, in the end, sadly—told a far less triumphant story of a *Spray*-inspired ocean voyage.

London's and Slocum's stories stimulated a star French tennis player, former World War I ace, and successful businessman, Alain Gerbault, to go to sea. Even though he knew almost nothing of sailing and his boat was unsuitable for the trip, Gerbault became the third single-handed sailor and the first non-American to make a circumnavigation, after Slocum and Harry Pidgeon. In *Fight of the "Firequest"* (1926) and *In Quest of the Sun* (1929), Gerbault told of his six-year circumnavigation in the romantic and sometimes mystical spirit of a man who had turned his back on land. His personal slogan was "Je deviens un marin et seulement un marin" (I become a sailor and only a sailor). Three years after completing his great voyage, Gerbault sailed alone to Indonesia, where he died in 1941, still a relatively young man.

## Post–World War II Cruising

Gerbault's escapist spirit was echoed later by another French loner, Bernard Moitessier, whose *Cape Horn: The Logical Route* (1969; also titled *The First Voyage of the "Joshua"*) tells of a dangerous trip around Cape Horn in a boat named for the great Slocum himself.

Other postwar sailor-writers, however, were not so much fleeing land as looking for keen adventure offshore. The best of them were three sailor-writers: William Albert Robinson, Bill Tilman, and Miles Smeeton. In 1952, William Albert Robinson, an American émigré to Tahiti who had already done a single-handed circumnavigation, sailed out into the Southern Ocean in search of "the ultimate storm." He found it and described it in *To the Great*

*Southern Sea* (1956). Unsurpassed in yachting writing are Robinson's descriptions of the storm, of "white phosphorescent avalanches that I felt towering over my head astern but did not see until they burst down on us and swept by on either side."

Another of these postwar writers was H. W. "Bill" Tilman. In *"Mischief" in Greenland* (1964) and other books, he described rough-and-ready voyages in an ancient Bristol pilot boat with a crew of college boys. His purpose was not to find storms during the voyages but to go mountaineering, making what he called "geriatric climbs," at his destinations.

Exciting though Tilman's books are, they lack personality. For that as well as raw action, there is nothing better than the former British army officer Miles Smeeton's books about cruising with his wife, Beryl, in the ketch *Tzu Hang*. The best is *Once Is Enough* (1959), about two near-fatal accidents near Cape Horn and the leadership of the remarkable Beryl in the recoveries. A theme in these books is a continuing debate about the responsibility that voyagers carry relative to their neighbors in other ships. Because they wished to be completely independent and did not want to put rescuers at risk, the Smeetons refused to carry even a ship-to-ship radio.

Women were not well represented in cruising stories before Beryl Smeeton. An able female cruising writer is Lin Pardey, who, with her husband, Larry, produced a series of warmly encouraging books starting with *Cruising in "Seraffyn"* (1976). If a running theme of the Pardeys' books (like others) is that cruising need not be uncomfortable, another gifted writer who sailed as part of a family team, Hal Roth, provided a decidedly different conclusion in *Two against Cape Horn* (1978), an astonishing account of a shipwreck at the cape.

Since 1975 the focus of cruising writing has shifted inward, moving the spotlight from the cruise and boat to the meaning of the experience for the sailor-writer within the setting of his or her life. Most sailor-writers had raised a barrier between land and sea, but in recent years a few gifted writers turned cruising books into personal nautical travelogues into the soul. Among them were Alvah Simon's *North to the Night* (1998), set in a boat during an extended period of being frozen-in by ice, and Jonathan Raban's *Passage to Juneau: A Sea and Its Meanings* (1999), in which a single-handed voyage north from Seattle stirred up a number of reflections. In Willy de Roos's *North-West Passage* (1980), ruminations arose during an epic voyage as de Roos became the first yachtsman to pass through the ice-clogged Northwest Passage. Like many other first-rate

sailor-writers, including McMullen, Slocum, and Smeeton, de Roos was unafraid to admit that he was afraid: "A man who undertakes a dangerous course of action must begin by accepting the prospect of living with anxiety," he wrote. "It is a bad policy to avoid the feeling of anxiety by mentally minimizing the danger. It is better to remain conscious of the risk and to accept the fact that one is afraid."

## Manuals

If any one thing can ease that anxiety, it is knowledge, which is why it is no surprise that as cruising began to spread, technical manuals on seamanship, yacht design, and yacht construction appeared and quickly composed an important part of yachting literature.

The first book on yacht design, P. R. Marett's *Yachts and Yacht Building* (1856), was closely followed by the first manual on yacht seamanship for amateurs, *Yarns for Green Hands* (first edition 1860; later titled *The Yacht Sailor: A Treatise on Practical Seamanship, Cruising, and Racing*). The author was William Cooper, writing under the pen name "Vanderdecken." Cooper's immediate successor as yachting's technical authority was Dixon Kemp, who wrote the thick *Manual of Yacht and Boat Sailing* (first edition 1878). Over succeeding decades, many other seamanship manuals were published. The most influential for cruising yachtsmen was *Yacht Cruising* (first edition 1910), by Claud Worth, an English medical doctor and cruising sailor whose instruction followed the case method of reproducing or summarizing the logs of his own cruises, freely admitting mistakes, and then commenting on them. Later writers on cruising seamanship included the world voyager and graceful writer Eric C. Hiscock, author of several wonderful cruise narratives as well as *Cruising under Sail* (first edition 1950). As recent manuals have been packed with more and more detailed information, literary quality has suffered, although that does not always detract from their practicality.

A genre exclusive to yachting with its own literary tradition is known in Britain as the "yachtsman's guide" or "cruising handbook" and in the United States as the "cruising guide." Part pilot book, part tourist guide, part personal narrative, these books and pamphlets— often quirky if not eccentric in their preferences—offer advice on harbors, facilities, and pilotage specifically for yachtsmen. An early example was *Our Silver Streak; or, the Yachtsman's Guide from Harwich to Scilly* (1892), by Sir Arthur Underhill, founder of the Royal Cruising

Club. In America, the standard was set by Robert F. Duncan in *A Cruising Guide to the New England Coast* (first published 1936). Duncan's book is now in its twelfth edition, written in part by the original author's grandson, an indication of the strength of tradition in cruising literature.

[*See also* American Literature; English Literature; London, Jack; Slocum, Joshua; *and* Yachting and Pleasure Sailing.]

## Bibliography

Anderson, J. R. L. *The Ulysses Factor: The Exploring Instinct in Man*. New York: Harcourt Brace Jovanovich, 1970.

Raban, Jonathan, ed. *The Oxford Book of the Sea*. Oxford: Oxford University Press, 1992.

Rousmaniere, John. *After the Storm: True Stories of Disaster and Recovery at Sea*. New York: International Marine/McGraw-Hill, 2002.

Rousmaniere, John. "The Rediscovery of the Sea." *Sea History*, no. 115 (Summer 2006): 26–29.

Rousmaniere, John, ed. *Desirable and Undesirable Characteristics of Offshore Yachts*. New York: Norton, 1987.

Spurr, Daniel. *Heart of Glass: Fiberglass Boats and the Men Who Made Them*. Camden, Maine: International Marine, 2000.

Toy, Ernest W., Jr. *Adventurers Afloat: A Nautical Bibliography*. 2 vols. Metuchen, N.J.: Scarecrow Press, 1988.

JOHN ROUSMANIERE

## Blue Water Passages in Small Sailboats

The pleasure-cruising literature associated with small sailing vessels, defined here as those less than 40 feet on deck, evolved from travelogues such as John MacGregor's account of crossing the English Channel in his tiny canoe yawl *Rob Roy*, described in *The Voyage Alone in the Yawl "Rob Roy"* (London: Rupert Hart-Davis, 1954; first published in 1867). Such travelogues were quite popular in the late nineteenth century, yet they were merely precursors of so-called "blue water" literature. The earliest small-boat Atlantic crossings were motivated by a desire for fame and fortune. Such crossings demonstrated that tiny sailing vessels could be seaworthy in the most literal sense. This struck a responsive chord with the public, setting the stage for Alfred Johnson's 1876 single-handed 59-day crossing in his 20-foot decked-over dory, *Centennial*, from Gloucester, Massachusetts, to Abercastle, Wales. A competition to be the smallest ever to cross ensued, a competition resulting in an ongoing exploration of both psychological and technological limits. Bernard Gilboy made a six-month nonstop

**Brigantine *Yankee*.** Moored at Manchester Marine, Manchester-by-the-Sea, Massachusetts, where her owner, Irving Johnson (1905–1991), replaced her engine about 1953. BURRAGE LARCOM WOODBERRY

transpacific passage in the 19-foot *Pacific* in 1882–1883. John Barr Tompkins has edited and annotated Gilboy's log as *A Voyage of Pleasure* (Cambridge, Md.: Cornell Maritime Press, 1956). An excellent biography of Howard Blackburn, who lost all his fingers to frostbite while trying to survive in a dory, and who subsequently completed two transatlantic passages in small gaff-rigged sloops, is *Lone Voyager*, by Joseph E. Garland (Boston: Little, Brown, 1963).

Solo voyages in microcruisers enthrall the public even today. One of the more significant books is the English sailor Ann Davison's *My Ship Is So Small* (New York: Sloan, 1956), an account of her 1952–1953 transatlantic voyage and Caribbean cruise in the 23-foot sloop *Felicity Ann*, significant for revealing the extreme mood swings encountered by single-handers. Another significant book is the English-born Canadian John Guzzwell's *Trekka round the World* (London: Adlard Coles, 1963; often republished), an account of building and circumnavigating from 1955 to 1959 in his 20-foot 10-inch strip-planked yawl, which held the record for the smallest circumnavigator until 1974. Guzzwell's superb seamanship and competence shine through his prose, making the book a valuable teaching tool. There is the famous Japanese circumnavigator Kenichi Horie's *Koduku* (translated by Takuichi Ito; Rutland, Vt.: Charles E. Tuttle, 1964), an account of his 8,530-kilometer

(5,300-mile) transpacific passage from Japan to California in 1962 in the 19-foot hard-chine sloop *Mermaid*. Yet another significant book is Robert Manry's *Tinkerbelle* (New York: Harper and Row, 1966), in which a middle-aged copyeditor from Cleveland, Ohio, crosses the Atlantic from Falmouth, Massachusetts, to Falmouth, England, in 1965 in his 13-foot 6-inch sloop; the story became an inspiration to others who felt imprisoned by their daily routine. The commercial airline pilot Hugo Vihlen failed to achieve his ambitions as an astronaut; he consoled himself by claiming the record for the smallest sailboat to cross the Atlantic. This he first did in 1968 in the 6-foot *April Fool*, making an 85-day passage from Casablanca to just off the coast of Florida; to reclaim the record, he made, in 1993, a 105-day passage in the 5-foot 4-inch *Father's Day* from Saint John's, Newfoundland, to Falmouth, England. Both vessels were designed to be maximally short but capacious. Vihlen's two books—*April Fool* (Chicago: Follett, 1971) and *The Stormy Voyage of Father's Day* (with Joanne Kimberlin; Saint Paul, Minn.: Marlor Press, 1997)—reveal what is needed to achieve the seemingly impossible.

The distinction of being the first person to make a single-handed circumnavigation belongs to Nova Scotia–born Joshua Slocum (1844–1909?), a professional sea captain who built the 36-foot 9-inch sloop *Spray* from the remains of an old oyster sloop. It is fortunate that he had literary ambitions, and indeed the book about his circumnavigation, *Sailing Alone around the World* (New York: Century, 1900), was not his first. He hoped to profit from his unique voyage, and his wry Yankee humor and nautical adventures have made his book the classic circumnavigation account—it is still widely read and remains in print. Slocum completed a technical circumnavigation on May 8, 1898, when *Spray* crossed her outbound track of October 2, 1895. *Spray* was beamy at 14 feet 2 inches, and she was shallow drafted at 4 feet 2 inches. She weathered Cape Horn gales but did not round the horn. Slocum sailed through the Strait of Magellan, having a difficult time because of the violent and erratic weather. The merits of *Spray*, which was converted to a yawl for easier handling by one person, have been debated. Replicas of *Spray* have circumnavigated, one of which, *Pandora*, was the first small yacht to round Cape Horn. She did overturn, however, as have many small vessels during a Cape Horn passage.

John Claus Voss's *The Venturesome Voyages of Captain Voss*, originally published in 1913, is another classic in the Slocum tradition; it remains in print within International Marine's six-volume series *The Sailor's Classics*, edited by Jonathan Raban. Voss (1858–1922), like Slocum, was a professional sea captain at the end of the age of commercially viable large sailing vessels. Voss hoped to benefit from Slocum's popularity but believed his written account would be profitable only if his vessel were smaller and unique. Accordingly, he decked over a large Indian dugout canoe and stepped three small gaff-sail masts. Counting the figurehead, *Tilikum* was 38 feet long overall, 5-feet 6-inches wide, and drew 2 feet when completely loaded. Voss sailed from Victoria, British Columbia, to London (1901–1904). Although Voss never crossed his outbound track, he rounded Africa and survived many gales by streaming a sea anchor, a cone-shaped canvas bag, from the bow. In addition to sea anchor specifications and technical advice, Voss's book includes an account of surviving a typhoon in the 25-foot 8-inch yawl *Sea Queen*.

Others benefited from the popularity of the *Spray*; many persons wrote books, some becoming classics that are currently in print or readily available. Harry Pidgeon, from Iowa, built the hard-chine 34-foot yawl *Islander*, an enlarged Sea Bird type. Pidgeon circumnavigated twice, first from 1921 to 1925, a voyage that is described in *Around the World Single-Handed* (New York: Appleton, 1933). Pidgeon was the second person to circumnavigate alone. Perhaps the most famous classic in translation is the Argentine rancher Vito Dumas's *Alone through the Roaring Forties*, translated by Captain Raymond Johnes (New York: de Graff, 1960). Dumas circumnavigated from June 1942 to July 1943 in *Legh II*, a 31-foot 6-inch double-ended ketch, rounding the great capes and making only three landfalls, thereby opening new nautical horizons in the brutal southern oceans. Single-handed racers such as Robin Knox-Johnston and Bernard Moitessier followed Dumas's example, beginning a tradition that has spawned today's technologically superb global racing vessels, seaworthy cruisers, and the sea literature of organized racing.

Cruising literature is better represented by books in which a multitude of landfalls are described. From an ethnological perspective, the more interesting accounts predate commercial jet aircraft and large charter-boat fleets. French sailors, in particular, have immersed themselves in the local cultures encountered with each new landfall. Alain Gerbault has written two classics, *The Fight of the "Firecrest"* (New York: Appleton, 1926) and *In Quest of the Sun* (London: Hodder and Stoughton, 1929), which were reprinted as a dual edition, *"Firecrest" Round the World* (New York: David McKay, 1981). *Firecrest* was a 39-foot pilot cutter with an 8-foot 6-inch beam. Gerbault battled tired sails and rigging while crossing the Atlantic, and he repaired his vessel with local help after she lost her ballast keel on a reef north of Fiji.

Another cruising classic is the Bermudan-born Richard Maury's *The Saga of Cimba* (1939), which was recently reissued in *The Sailor's Classics* with an introduction by the editor, Jonathan Raban (Camden, Maine: International Marine, 2001). In November 1933, Maury and crew set off for the South Seas in a 35-foot Nova Scotia schooner they had modified for cruising. Storms, rollovers, and island cultures are encountered, but the book is superb literature, not merely a tale of adventure or a travelogue.

Some sailors, such as the British couple Eric and Susan Hiscock, have both multiple circumnavigations and multiple books to their credit, books that have educated several generations of voyagers. The Hiscocks were consummate cruisers, not record seekers, and sailed without rollovers or dismastings. *Around the World in "Wanderer III"* (London: Oxford University Press, 1956 and 1975) presents a paradigm of a successful cruising couple's voyage in a 30-foot sloop.

The Hiscocks inspired other couples such as (American) Lin and (Canadian) Larry Pardey, whose books are familiar to all cruising sailors. Lin's clear, candid, and effective prose style captures life ashore and aboard the 24-foot *Seraffyn*, an engineless Marconi-rigged pilot cutter. More recently, the Pardeys rounded Cape Horn in the 29-foot engineless *Taleisin*. *Seraffyn's European Adventure* (New York: Norton, 1979; Arcata, Calif.: Pardey Books, 1998) reveals both the pleasurable and unattractive aspects of cruising life.

Cape Horn beckons to cruisers who are normally content to explore distant places and diverse cultures. The Americans Hal and Margaret Roth have written many books on cruising. *Two against Cape Horn* (New York: Norton, 1978) is an inspiring account of a cruising couple facing arduous conditions. Much has been written about rounding the Horn. A classic cruising account of a failed attempt (recently reissued in *The Sailor's Classics*) is the English-born Canadian Miles Smeeton's *Once Is Enough* (New York: de Graff, 1959). Miles Smeeton, his wife, Beryl, and John Guzzwell were sailing the 46-foot ketch *Tzu Hang* 1,450 kilometers (900 miles) west of Magellan Strait when she was pitchpoled, dismasted, and damaged. Despite the damage and Beryl's injuries, *Tzu Hang* was sailed 1,350 miles under jury rig to Coronel, Chile. The Smeetons finally rounded the Horn on their third attempt.

A sailboat race has been defined as two sailboats going in the same direction. It was in this spirit that the *Observer*'s Single-handed Transatlantic Race (OSTAR) was initiated in 1960. The participants were serious sailors who used the race as an incentive to sail across the Atlantic. There were few rules and little formal organization compared to races today. The accomplishments of today's global racers stagger the imagination, but racing today bears no resemblance to cruising, nor to the early days of the OSTAR or the original 1968 Golden Globe nonstop single-handed race around the world. Many of the participants of the 1960 OSTAR and the first Golden Globe represent a who's who in sailing: David Lewis, Francis Chichester, Colonel H. G. Hasler, Valentine Howells, and Jean Lacombe in the OSTAR, with vessels ranging from Lacombe's 21-foot *Cap Horn* to Chichester's winning 39-foot *Gipsy Moth III*. Hasler, inventor of windvane steering, had fitted *Jester* with a Chinese-style junk rig. The 1968 Golden Globe contained an odd assortment of inexpensive and ill-suited vessels compared to those of global racers in the early twenty-first century. The slow and heavy double-ended cruising ketches—similar to Dumas's *Legh II*—sailed by Robin Knox-Johnston and Bernard Moitessier survived the southern latitudes with little damage, Moitessier's steel *Joshua* being the most durable. The Golden Globe produced two classic accounts: *A World of My Own* (London: Cassell, 1969), by the winner, Robin Knox-Johnston, and *The Long Way*, written by Bernard Moitessier and translated by William Rodarmor (Dobbs Ferry, N.Y.: Sheridan House, 1995; first published in 1973). Moitessier might have won: instead he sailed on to Tahiti rather than face crowds. Peter Nichols, a critically acclaimed author and sailor, has produced a penetrating analysis of the 1968 Golden Globe, *A Voyage for Madmen* (New York: Harper Collins, 2001), revealing the significant psychological and technological factors.

Francis Chichester and David Lewis achieved fame more from their solitary exploits than from participation in organized races. Chichester's books include *"Gipsy Moth" Circles the World* (New York: Coward-McCann, 1967) and *The Romantic Challenge* (New York: Coward-McCann and Geoghegan, 1971); these books derive from self-imposed goals. David Lewis is perhaps best remembered for his attempt to circumnavigate Antarctica, an attempt he describes in *Ice Bird* (New York: Norton, 1976). Lewis, a prolific author, studied the psychological aspects of the OSTAR. His work to record and replicate the ancient methods of Polynesian navigation is of significant value.

Inspired by the ancient Polynesians, James Wharram has designed catamarans for the backyard builder with global ambitions. Arthur Piver's trimarans also have demonstrated what homebuilt multihulls can accomplish.

Multihull vessels now routinely cruise the oceans, most being high-tech production boats evolved from the earlier pioneering efforts in plywood.

Blue water cruisers now sail to frozen regions to encounter untamed nature. A precedent was set by a mountaineer, Major H. W. Tilman, who sailed his 45-foot pilot cutter *Mischief* to high latitudes when others sought the tropics. *"Mischief" in Patagonia* (New York: Cambridge University Press, 1957) is the first of Tilman's *Mischief* books. (*Mischief* and Miles Smeeton's *Tzu Hang* are over 40 feet, but they merit inclusion here nonetheless.)

Other recent cruising accounts of icebound seas deserve mention. Tim and Pauline Carr's *Antarctic Oasis: Under the Spell of South Georgia* (New York: Norton, 1998) describes sailing a small and ancient wooden gaff-rig cutter in polar regions; impressive sail handling and seamanship are displayed. Some sailors have chosen to spend the winter aboard a vessel frozen in ice: there is both Alvah Simon's *North to the Night: A Spiritual Odyssey in the Arctic* (Camden, Maine: International Marine, 1998) and also Deborah and Rolf Bjelke's *Time on Ice: A Winter Voyage to the Antarctic* (Camden, Maine: International Marine, 1998).

The sea has not changed, but in the twenty-first century an electronic umbilical cord links sailors with land. Comprehensive bibliographies of books on blue water voyaging appear in the works listed below.

[*See also* Cruising; Slocum, Joshua; *and* Yachting and Pleasure Sailing.]

## Bibliography

Borden, Charles A. *Sea Quest: Global Blue-Water Adventuring in Small Craft*. Philadelphia: Macrae Smith, 1967.

Clarke, Derrick H. *Blue Water Dream*. New York: David McKay, 1981.

Coote, John O., ed. *The Norton Book of the Sea*. New York: Norton, 1989.

Doherty, John Stephen. *The Boats They Sailed In*. New York: Norton, 1985.

Gidmark, Jill B., ed. *Encyclopedia of American Literature of the Sea and Great Lakes*. Westport, Conn.: Greenwood Press, 2001.

Henderson, Richard, ed. *Singlehanded Sailing: The Experiences and Techniques of the Lone Voyagers*. 2d ed. Camden, Maine: International Marine, 1988.

Henry, Pat. *By the Grace of the Sea: A Woman's Solo Odyssey around the World*. Camden, Maine: International Marine, 2003.

Holm, Don. *The Circumnavigators*. Englewood Cliffs, N.J.: Prentice-Hall, 1974.

Lundy, Derek. *Godforsaken Sea*. New York: Anchor Books, 2000.

Wilts, Heide. *Auf der Route der Albatrosse*. Bielefeld, Germany: Delius, Klasing, 1996.

LEE F. WERTH

# Tall Ships

The term "tall ship" likely owes its currency to John Masefield's popular 1902 poem "Sea Fever" and to the International Tall Ships Race begun by the Sail Training Association of Britain in 1956. Although it is a nautically imprecise term, it is probably best understood as connoting any large, ocean-going, traditionally rigged sailing vessel, with or without auxiliary power, in which sail is, or may be, the primary mode of propulsion.

## Nineteenth Century

The idea of deliberately undertaking a lengthy sea voyage in such a vessel for a purpose other than the necessity of getting to a destination is one that probably would have seemed absurd prior to the nineteenth century. After 1815, however, the wealth and leisure brought by the Industrial Revolution, the expansion of empires (and hence Western civilization) into the far reaches of the world's oceans, the steady development of steam propulsion, and the century of relative peace that followed the end of the Napoleonic Wars made it possible for pleasure cruising to be undertaken in relative safety and comfort. Published accounts of noteworthy voyages—often in the form of journals or letters sent home from ports visited—soon took their place in the travel literature of the day.

*The Story of George Crowninshield's Yacht "Cleopatra's Barge" on a Voyage of Pleasure to the Western Islands and the Mediterranean, 1816–1817* describes one of the earliest examples of this type of cruise, although the account remained unpublished until 1913. The owner, a prominent merchant and shipowner of Salem, Massachusetts, personally supervised the construction and fitting out of his 192-ton brigantine, often referred to as the first American yacht, in which he sailed across the Atlantic and into the Mediterranean in great style.

British accounts dominate most of the rest of the nineteenth century, and several achieved wide popularity as travel literature, going through many editions. Two deserve special note. In the summer of 1856 Lord Dufferin (Frederick Temple Hamilton-Temple-Blackwood, 1st Marquis of Dufferin and Ava; later a prominent diplomat and governor general of both Canada and India) sailed in his schooner-yacht *Foam* from Oban in Scotland to Iceland, Jan Mayen Island, and Spitzbergen. His highly entertaining *Letters from High Latitudes* (1857) is remarkable for its accounts of sailing in the ice and its descriptions of the arctic scenery, as well as for its lively observations of crew members and passengers.

Two decades later Lord Thomas Brassey (1836–1918), a lawyer, noted yachtsman, naval reformer, and then member of Parliament for Hastings, commissioned the building of his 531-ton, steam-auxiliary, three-masted barquentine *Sunbeam*, and in subsequent years made several lengthy voyages with his family. Accounts of these voyages were published by Lady Anne Brassey, the most popular being *A Voyage in the "Sunbeam," Our Home on the Ocean for Eleven Months* (1878). The Brasseys sailed west around the world via Rio de Janeiro, through the Strait of Magellan to Valparaíso, thence across the Pacific via Tahiti and Hawai'i to Japan, China, and Singapore, and finally homeward via Ceylon, Aden, and the newly opened Suez Canal. A striking aspect of this and other accounts of the period is the luxury in which the Brasseys traveled and the extent to which they were, to a remarkable degree, on a tour of the British Empire.

American accounts began making their way into print toward the end of the century and, like their British counterparts, frequently took the form of the journals and letters of passengers and guests aboard the luxurious yachts of wealthy and socially prominent owners, with the emphasis more often on the places visited rather than on the seafaring aspects. The various vessels owned by the railroad tycoon and yachtsman Arthur Curtiss James figure prominently, especially the schooner *Coronet*, which he owned during the last decade of the nineteenth century. *Coronet Memories* (1899), a compilation of journals of various guests aboard during the period 1893–1899, includes a superb account, by James's friend George B. Spaulding, of the schooner's return passage from San Francisco to New York by way of Cape Horn following her support of the Amherst Eclipse Expedition to Japan in 1896.

That year also saw the posthumous publication of Robert Louis Stevenson's *In the South Seas*, and although the maritime dimension of this collection of letters and tales is relatively small, the occasional brief passages on sailing among the Marquesas Islands and Tuamotu Archipelago by one of the best and best-loved writers of his era, aboard his chartered schooner-yacht *Casco*, are among the most evocative of the many descriptions of a region of the world that would figure prominently in later cruising literature.

## Twentieth Century

World War I and its aftermath kept would-be voyagers ashore for a number of years, just as its 1939–1945 sequel was to do two decades later. Nevertheless, the opening of the Panama Canal to navigation in 1914 was to make cruising to the islands of the South Seas considerably easier for Atlantic-based adventurers, both European and American, so that when tall ships cruising (largely by Americans) slowly began to resume in the 1920s, much of it was to places like the Galápagos Islands and the islands under French mandate. The aim was still to cruise in comfort, but also to visit places presumably unspoiled by civilization. Few of the accounts that resulted during this period are of great interest, and in any event the collapse of the world's economy in 1929 all but put an end to cruising in the luxurious style of the nineteenth century.

One interesting circumnavigation, undertaken in 1928 in the 76-foot converted fishing schooner *Chance* by a group of young Yale University graduates, set a pattern that would become prevalent during the Great Depression. The voyage resulted in two books: Edward Dodd's *Great Dipper to Southern Cross* (1930), the account of the first half of the westward voyage from New London, Connecticut, to Sydney, Australia; and Alexander Brown's *Horizon's Rim* (1935), the second half from Sydney to New Bedford, Massachusetts. The participants shared expenses and employed only enough paid crew to provide skills they lacked.

In the late 1920s and 1930s, as it became obvious that the era of the big cargo-carrying, oceangoing square-riggers was nearing an end, several adventurers and writers who were to shape the future of what became known as sail training undertook voyages in these vessels and wrote about their experiences. These books, *Falmouth for Orders* (1929), by the Australian journalist Alan Villiers, *Round the Horn in a Square Rigger* (1932) by the American Irving Johnson, *The Last Grain Race* (1956) by the British travel writer Eric Newby, and Frank Baines's *In Deep* (1959), provide a superb picture of life aboard a Cape Horner in the waning days of commercial sail. Two of these authors went on to acquire vessels of their own in order to recruit expense-sharing young people on ocean voyages in which the paying volunteers were the crew, with only a handful of professional seafarers (including the authors). This was an idea that had first been proven by the American Warwick M. Tompkins, who acquired the North Sea pilot schooner *Wander Bird* in 1929 and had already taken some three hundred young people on thirteen North Atlantic voyages by the time he achieved his ambition of rounding Cape Horn from east to west, a voyage that he recounts in *Fifty South to Fifty South* (1938).

Johnson, who had sailed with Tompkins as mate, acquired a North Sea pilot schooner himself in 1933, christened her *Yankee* (the first of three), and embarked on the first of a series of eighteen-month, westward circumnavigations with young people as crew, recounted (largely by his wife Electa, who was a full partner in the enterprise) in *Westward Bound in the Schooner* Yankee (1936). Each of the subsequent voyages also resulted in a published account. Almost simultaneously, Villiers acquired the 212-ton iron full-rigged ship *Georg Stage*, built in Denmark in 1882 as a school ship, rechristened her *Joseph Conrad* in honor of the famed seafaring novelist, and recruited volunteer crew for an eastward circumnavigation of nearly two years from New York—a voyage vividly told in *The Cruise of the* Conrad (1937).

The British author Adrian Seligman's *Voyage of the* Cap Pilar (1939) tells a similar story. After failing to pass his exams at Cambridge, the author had sailed for several years in the big steel barques of Finnish shipowner Gustaf Erikson. He and his new wife acquired a laid-up French barquentine formerly used in the cod fishery, fitted her out, recruited a volunteer crew to share costs, and sailed eastward around the world from London, arriving home (like Newby in the barque *Moshulu*) just at the outbreak of war in Europe. At nearly the same moment, the American historian Samuel Eliot Morison launched a voyage to verify the navigational aspects of Columbus's route to the New World in the schooner-yacht *Capitana*, elegantly recounted in Morison's "Letters of the Harvard Columbus Expedition," published in *By Land and By Sea: Essays and Addresses* (1953).

The Johnsons resumed their voyages after the war, but made their last circumnavigation in 1953–1955. By then, air travel had made once-exotic islands more accessible, civilization was more hurried, and deep water cruising was more likely to be done in smaller yachts than in tall ships. Nevertheless some noteworthy accounts appeared in the second half of the twentieth century. Villiers's *Give Me a Ship to Sail* (1959) provides a fascinating record of the construction in England and sailing to America of the *Mayflower* replica. The American wildlife photographer Herbert Smith's *Dreams of Natural Places* (1981) is a beautifully illustrated account of his building a new schooner, *Appledore*, and sailing her westward around the world from Portsmouth, New Hampshire, with his family and a paying crew. Harvey Oxenhorn's *Tuning the Rig* (1990) recounts his experience as a trainee aboard the barquentine *Regina Maris* on a humpback whale research expedition to Greenland, and George Moffett's *Aboard an American Classic* (2002) records the transatlantic voyage of the schooner *Brilliant* in a tall ships race from Halifax, Nova Scotia, to Amsterdam in 2000.

Although the day of leisurely tall ship cruising as it was known in the nineteenth and early twentieth centuries is clearly past, the last two books noted may well be indicators of how the desire for adventure, and the need to write about the experience, will endure. Both of these works spring from what may be loosely called the sail training movement, which had its origins in the pioneering work of Tompkins, Villiers, and Johnson in the 1930s, and began to blossom in the 1960s with the advent of Tall Ships Races in Europe under the guidance of the U.K.-based Sail Training Association. As a result of the popularity of these events with young people, an enduring public fascination around the globe with tall ships and the age of sail, and the growth of the adventure travel industry, the number of tall ships around the world grew remarkably in the last decades of the twentieth century, and that trend seems destined to continue.

While in general cruises aboard sail training vessels or sailing cruise ships tend to be brief and thus unlikely to produce serious literary results, at least one excellent account of an around-the-world voyage aboard the barque *Picton Castle*—a North Sea trawler converted in the late 1990s for the purpose of world voyaging in very much the style pioneered by the Johnsons—had appeared by 2004. *Fair Wind and Plenty of It: A Modern-Day Tall Ship Adventure* (2004) by Rigel Crockett, a young Canadian who sailed as an able seaman during *Picton Castle*'s first voyage, 1997–1999, is a rousing tale of personal discovery and growth in what can only be described as a deliberately atavistic profession, and provides a good indicator that the genre of tall ships cruising literature will survive for a long time to come.

[*See also* Training Ships *and* Yachting and Pleasure Sailing.]

## Bibliography

Brassey, Annie Allnut. *A Voyage in the "Sunbeam": Our Home on the Ocean for Eleven Months*. London: Longmans, Green, 1878.

Hamilton, John. *Sail Training: The Message of the Tall Ships*. Wellingborough, U.K.: Stephens, 1988. The author was for many years the race director of the U.K.-based Sail Training

Association. A comprehensive and sympathetic portrait of the modern sail training movement.

Johnson, Irving. *Westward Bound in the Schooner "Yankee": By Captain and Mrs. Irving Johnson, with Drawings by Roland Wentzel.* New York: Norton, 1936.

Oxenhorn, Harvey. *Tuning the Rig: A Journey to the Arctic.* New York: Harper and Row, 1990.

Parrott, Daniel S. *Tall Ships Down: The Last Voyages of the* Pamir, Albatross, Marques, Pride of Baltimore, *and* Maria Asumpta. Camden, Maine: International Marine/McGraw-Hill, 2003. The author, an experienced sail training captain, examines the factors that led to the loss at sea of the ships named, and along the way provides a thorough and balanced picture of the evolution of sail training in the late twentieth century.

Toy, Ernest W., Jr. *Adventurers Afloat: A Nautical Bibliography.* Metuchen, N.J.: Scarecrow, 1988. A comprehensive, four-volume, usefully annotated bibliography of literature about voyages in every conceivable type of craft.

Villiers, Alan. *Cruise of the* Conrad: *A Journal of a Voyage round the World, Undertaken and Carried Out in the Ship* Joseph Conrad, *212 Tons, in the Years 1934, 1935, and 1936 by way of Good Hope, the East Indies, the South Seas, and Cape Horn.* London: Hodder and Stoughton Limited, 1937.

Villiers, Alan. *The Way of a Ship: Being Some Account of the Ultimate Development of the Ocean-Going Square-Rigged Sailing Vessel, and the Manner of Her Handling, Her Voyage-Making, Her Personnel, Her Economics, Her Performance, and Her End.* New York: Scribners, 1970. A thoroughly researched and comprehensive work that does justice to its subtitle.

DAVID V. V. WOOD

# Yacht Racing

Often overlooked as a genre, writing about yacht racing has, over the years, provided exciting stories of sailors and vessels driving hard at sea, as well as valuable technical analysis of the developments that created the distinctive art and science of yacht design.

## From 1866 to 1936

As yacht racing became a distinctive sport and the number of yacht clubs grew, many British and American newspapers had yachting columnists who wrote at length about races and technical matters. The first yachting periodical was the British *Hunt's Yachting Magazine* (founded 1852), while the first American magazine to treat yachting seriously was *Forest and Stream* (founded 1873), whose yachting editor, William P. Stephens, a leading authority, went on to write one of the great books about the sport, *Traditions and Memories of American Yachting* (1945). *The Rudder* (founded 1890), edited and largely written by the curmudgeonly Thomas Fleming Day, was the first

important American yachting magazine. While none of those three pioneering magazines is published today, their formula of blending news, inspiration, and instruction is alive in yachting periodicals. Yachting journalism then was not objective journalism. Writers considered it a duty to take sides in bitter controversies about the America's Cup races and about the relative merits of narrow British cutters and beamy American sloops.

In terms of book publishing, yacht racing lagged many years behind yacht cruising. Dixon Kemp touched on racing technology in his well-known *Manual of Yacht and Boat Sailing* (1878), but it was not until 1884 that the first book about yacht racing was published, *American Yachts: Their Clubs and Races*, with magnificent illustrations by Frederick S. Cozzens. Its tone was set by a quote from the author, J. D. J. Kelley: "To get the marrow out of yachting requires leisure, patience, and money." This luxurious book was a good indication of the third of these things.

The point of view of the racing sailor was first presented in the autobiography of Samuel Samuels, a professional captain whose hard driving earned him the nickname "Bully." His title, *From Forecastle to Cabin* (1887), neatly summarizes his theme, which is one of great ambitions realized. In December 1866, Samuels sailed in the first yacht ocean race as captain of the winner, the 108-foot schooner *Henrietta*, which he called "the little plaything." The stakes of $60,000 were held by Leonard Jerome, Winston Churchill's maternal grandfather, who sailed in *Henrietta*. On the ninth day out, a southwest gale overtook *Henrietta*, and in the wild sea the ship's carpenter went berserk—even Bully Samuels felt obliged to heave-to. On another boat, a wave swept six sailors out of the cockpit to their deaths.

That accident cast a pall over the sport for almost forty years, with only the occasional match race across an ocean. The first big ocean race finally came in 1905, when eleven yachts averaging 163 feet in length raced from New York to Lizard Head, England, for the Emperor's Cup, which had been put up by Kaiser Wilhelm II of Germany. The winner, the 184-foot three-masted schooner *Atlantic*, set a record of 12 days, 4 hours that was not broken until 2005. *Atlantic*'s professional skipper, Charlie Barr, the most successful racing captain of his day, drove *Atlantic* hard. When a gale blew in and left the decks awash, her rightfully nervous owner, Wilson Marshall, reportedly urged Barr to heave-to, only to be lectured, "You hired me to win this race and that is what I intend to do." The Emperor's Cup race inspired the first book about an ocean race to be written by participants. *The Cruise of the* Fleur-de-Lys *in the Ocean Race*

(1905) was written by Lewis Atterbury Stimson, a prominent surgeon and the yacht's owner. He took a strong role in managing the yacht, assisted by his daughter Candace, a capable sailor in her own right. A recent account of this important and colorful race is Scott Cookman's *Atlantic: The Last Great Race of Princes* (2002).

A year after the Emperor's Cup race, in 1906, the first ocean races to Bermuda and Hawai'i were sailed. The Bermuda Race, founded by Thomas Fleming Day, is especially notable because it introduced the revolutionary idea that all-amateur crews in boats no longer than forty feet on deck could race in the ocean. The Bermuda Race inspired the British to start racing around Fastnet Rock, off Ireland, in 1925. The Fastnet in turn inspired the Australians to create the Sydney-Hobart Race twenty years later. Since then not a year has passed without a major ocean race of 965 kilometers (600 miles) or more. The sea was now a playground. Yacht measurement rules were honed to encourage seaworthy, weatherly boats that could stand up to an offshore gale and claw off a lee shore. An international community of competitive owners and talented yacht designers developed a breed of good boats for offshore racing as well as cruising. Meanwhile, boats were strengthened by construction using materials that started with wood and, after World War II, evolved to fiberglass, aluminum, and eventually carbon fibre and other high-tech composite.

The rise of ocean racing from a job for professionals like Bully Samuels in huge schooners to an avocation for amateur sailors in normal sloops and yawls was chronicled by Alfred F. Loomis in one of the best of all histories of yachting, *Ocean Racing: The Great Blue-Water Yacht Races, 1866–1935* (1936). Loomis went so far as to track down and name every boat and sailor that had participated in an ocean race—in all, more than 200 boats and 1,650 men and women, with a total of only ten fatalities.

### From 1936 to 1960

As ocean racing resumed and matured after World War II, writing about it split in several directions. A few gifted writer-sailors share their delight in the pleasures and paradoxes of sailing aggressively in the ocean aboard good boats with collegial crews. Three of the best books by such writers are, ostensibly, accounts of racing in hard weather in the North Atlantic. Erroll Bruce's *When the Crew Matter Most: An Ocean Racing Story* (1961) is about what it takes to win a long-distance race. William Snaith's *Across the Western Ocean* (1966) is a playful, philosophical essay on life at sea in a racing boat.

The third of these books is Carleton Mitchell's *Passage East* (1953). Mitchell was a gifted writer, photographer, and (not least) sailor; he set a record that has never been approached when his small yawl *Finisterre* won three straight Newport-Bermuda Races in 1956–1960. He nicely summarized "the somewhat fantastic nature of ocean racing" this way: "Here we are, nine men, driving a fragile complex of wood, metal, and cloth through driving rain and building sea, a thousand miles from the nearest harbor; no one to see or admire or applaud; no one to help if our temerity ends in disaster…. In us all there is a devotion to the somewhat formal and unspoken ideal of simply keeping the boat going at her maximum speed, a dedication that carries us beyond considerations of personal comfort and even safety." Mariners had been pushing that hard for centuries; now they were doing it not for pay or to win wars, but for trophies and the satisfaction of it.

A different subgenre of writing about racing concerns technology, without which no boat could sail. After World War II, a few first-rate manuals provided sailors with advice and education. For many years the best and most influential writing was by English writer-sailors. The yacht designer John Illingworth, in *Offshore* (1949), described advanced yacht technology. K. Adlard Coles's *Heavy Weather Sailing* (1967) became the standard manual on storm tactics and strategy. Racing sailors' insatiable demand for better technology has produced a number of rewarding books on sailing theory, beginning with Manfred Curry's *Yacht Racing: The Aerodynamics of Sails and Racing Tactics* (1927) and leading to *Sailing: Theory and Practice* (1964) and other sophisticated books on aerodynamics and yacht design by the Polish scientist Czeslaw A. Marchaj. One important step in the evolution of yacht design was the use of scale models to test a boat's performance in a towing tank. The leading yacht designer of the 1930–1975 period, Olin J. Stephens II, described this research in his autobiography *All This and Sailing, Too* (1999). There Stephens also addressed the long, contentious history of yacht measurement, which was laid out in greater detail by Peter Johnson in *Yacht Rating* (1997).

### From 1960 to the Present

Ocean racing became increasingly varied and risky, and more writing was done about it. The first single-handed transatlantic race, in 1960, stimulated great interest among sailors and nonsailors alike, all of whom were intrigued by the challenges presented by solitude and the sea—challenges that were first described by Joshua Slocum in his cruising classic, *Sailing Alone around the World* (1900). Francis Chichester's intense, quarrelsome "Gipsy Moth" *Circles the World* (1967), about Chichester's one-stop cruising circumnavigation at the age of sixty-five, was an international best-seller. Single-handed races around the world added whole new elements of danger. The Golden Globe 1968 nonstop solo race around the world, sponsored by the London *Times*, led to three deaths, two by suicide. The best commentary on this irresponsible event is *The Strange Voyage of Donald Crowhurst* (1970), Nicholas Tomalin and Ron Hall's shocking story of an entrant who tried to win by fraudulent means, only to throw himself overboard before he reached the finish line.

Subsequent disastrous races have stimulated their own books. The two most deadly storms to sweep through a racing fleet since the gale in the 1866 race were, first, in the 1979 Fastnet race, with 15 deaths, and, later, in the 1998 Sydney-Hobart race off Australia, with six deaths. Each deadly race was described in several books, including John Rousmaniere's *Fastnet, Force 10* (1980) and Rob Mundle's *Fatal Storm* (1999). Around-the-world races by single-handed as well as crewed boats have their own inherent risks and drama that have inspired many books, including Pete Goss's account of an astounding rescue at sea in *Close to the Wind* (1999) and writer Derek Lundy's story of a solo around-the-world race (and the close community it fosters among its competitors), *Godforsaken Sea* (1998).

All this time, top-level yacht racing was becoming ever more technical and professional. This transition was described by Gary Jobson and Martin Luray in *World Class Sailing* (1987), while the technological developments are laid out in Michael Levitt's history of the world's pre-eminent sailmaker, *The North Sails Story* (rev. ed. 2007), and in the autobiography of the sailmaker, designer, and builder Ted Hood, *Through Hand and Eye* (2006, written with Michael Levitt). As the boats became more complicated, competition became more intense. Races were televised, many boats were commercially sponsored, and the sport was reopened to professional sailors, who had long been barred from steering during races.

After seven decades years as an amateur sport, yacht racing (at least a part of it) was again a business. There was little time available for leisure and reflection. Much writing became more packaged and less profound. Carefully crafted, personal reflections often gave way to spontaneous e-mails and telephone calls from mid-ocean (even mid-gale) to satisfy sponsors' demands for constant publicity as large keel and multihull boats careered around the Southern Ocean at unprecedented speeds.

An exception to this new trend is the young English ocean sailor Ellen MacArthur's sailing memoir *Taking on the World* (2003). There she presents an intimate view both of the demands of racing these sometimes dangerous vessels and of the complex motivations that push sailors to race in them for weeks on end. This young woman, who set a new around-the-world singlehanded record early in 2005, first took up the sport because she was entranced by Arthur Ransome's *Swallows and Amazons* series of children's sailing books.

## The America's Cup

The first book written about yacht racing was about the America's Cup. Hamilton Morton's *The America's Cup: A Nautical Poem* was just that—a quirky 123-page epic poem about the races in the 1871 cup match off New York. That demonstrates the passion that the America's Cup has inspired since the yacht *America* won (and gave its name to) the race in 1851. Not surprisingly, then, some of the best and most beautiful books about yachting are about racing for the cup. One, the history of the cup's first fifty years and eleven matches, is Winfield M. Thompson and Thomas W. Lawson's *The Lawson History of the America's Cup* (1902; reprint 1986), which set a standard that has rarely if ever been matched except in a few books, like François Chevalier and Jacques Taglang's *America's Cup Yacht Designs, 1851–1986* (1987).

While the America's Cup has earned a reputation for controversy, if not notoriety, it also was the setting for fine books written by three winning skippers. The title of Robert N. Bavier Jr.'s *A View from the Cockpit* (1966) reflects the intimacy of his story of winning the 1964 cup match. In *Comeback: My Race for the America's Cup* (1987), four-time cup winner (and twice loser) Dennis Conner takes the reader through the exquisite agony of high-pressure racing for one of the world's premier trophies.

Two of the best first-person books about the cup were written by Harold S. Vanderbilt, the skipper and part-owner of the boats that won the three matches sailed in J-Class sloops in the 1930s. Vanderbilt's first book, "Enterprise": *The Story of the Defense of the America's Cup in 1930* (1931), concerns the campaign in the boat *Enterprise*. Vanderbilt's *On the Wind's Highway* (1939) is his story of his wins in *Rainbow* and *Ranger* in 1934 and 1937. These two books are superb examples of the blend of drama and technical interest that makes for the best writing about yachting. In the first and second matches, Vanderbilt had relatively slow, underdog boats that he gradually improved until they won. He then made sure that his last boat, *Ranger*, was unbeatable. A legendary technological marvel, she had an average victory margin of more than 1.6 kilometers.

A gifted, creative man (he invented the game of contract bridge), Vanderbilt had a profound knowledge of racing tactics and rules. To this day, an important tactic for starting a sailboat race is called "the Vanderbilt start." He also understood yachting technology far better than most other yachtsmen. But what makes Vanderbilt's two books gems of yachting literature is their understanding about people. Vanderbilt is responsible for one of the most memorable and graceful lines written by one competitor about another. In 1930, his opponent was Sir Thomas Lipton, the colorful tea merchant who had been trying without success to win the America's Cup for more than thirty years. As *Enterprise* finished the last race, Vanderbilt, his feelings deeply mixed, went below and in the log wrote these words of sympathy for the old man: "Our hour of triumph, our hour of victory, is all but at hand, but it is so tempered with sadness that it is almost hollow." Such a touch raises a book about competition and technology to the level of literature.

### Small Boats

While racing in small boats does not share the glamour of the America's Cup and Bermuda Race, it is no less exciting or technically fascinating, and it has a tradition of good writing.

When the English boat designer and builder Uffa Fox created the first sailboat that could plane—or skip across the water—in 1927, he made sailing truly athletic and spawned a vast number of small, inexpensive, fast boats. His story is told in June Dixon's *Uffa Fox: A Personal Biography* (1978) and in Daniel B. MacNaughton's short biography of Fox in *The Encyclopedia of Yacht Designers* (2006), an excellent source on boat designers. There are a few classic books about small-boat racing. Robin Steavenson's *When Dinghies Delight* (1955) and *Marks to Starboard* (1958) concern dinghies on English rivers and estuaries. Stuart H. Walker, a U.S. racing sailor (and like Steavenson a medical doctor), wrote or edited a number of books about dinghies and small keel boats, including *Performance Advances in Small Boat Racing* (1969) and *Advanced Racing Tactics* (1976). Charles Stanley Ogilvy, a professor of mathematics, wrote several lovely books, among them *Win More Sailboat Races* (1976). The prosaic titles of these books belie their descriptive power and their understanding of the men and women caught up in this quirky sport.

Since the decline in nautical book publishing began during the 1990s, most writing about yacht racing is once again in magazines, most notably in the American *Sailing World* and *Speed & Smarts* and in the British *Seahorse*.

[*See also* American Literature; America's Cup; English Literature; *and* Yachting and Pleasure Sailing.]

### Bibliography

Conner, Dennis, and Michael Levitt. *The America's Cup: The History of Sailing's Greatest Competition in the Twentieth Century*. New York: St. Martin's Press, 1998.

Dear, Ian. *Fastnet: The Story of a Great Ocean Race*. London: Batsford, 1981.

Holm, Ed. *Yachting's Golden Age: 1880–1905*. New York: Knopf, 1999.

Jobson, Gary. *Fighting Finish: The Volvo Ocean Race: Round the World 2001–2002*. Norwich, Vt.: Nomad Press, 2002.

Johnson, Peter. *The RYA Book of World Sailing Records*. London: Adlard Coles Nautical, 2002.

Rousmaniere, John. *A Berth to Bermuda: One Hundred Years of the World's Classic Ocean Race*. Mystic, Conn.: Mystic Seaport/Cruising Club of America, 2006.

Rousmaniere, John. *In a Class by Herself: The Yawl "Bolero" and the Passion for Craftsmanship*. Mystic, Conn.: Mystic Seaport, 2006.

Rousmaniere, John, ed. *Desirable and Undesirable Characteristics of Offshore Yachts*. New York: Norton, 1987.

Spurr, Daniel. *Heart of Glass: Fiberglass Boats and the Men Who Made Them*. Camden, Maine: International Marine, 2000.

Toy, Ernest W., Jr. *Adventurers Afloat: A Nautical Bibliography*. 2 vols. Metuchen, N.J.: Scarecrow Press, 1988.

JOHN ROUSMANIERE

# Cuniberti, Vittorio

**Cuniberti, Vittorio** (1854–1913), officer of the Italian Naval Engineer Corps. Vittorio Emilio Cuniberti was born on June 7, 1854, in Turin, where in 1877 he completed his studies in civil engineering. The following year he entered the Regia Marina (the Italian Royal Navy), and in 1880 he received a second degree, in naval engineering and mechanics.

In 1890, Cuniberti collaborated with Benedetto Brin, the general inspector of the Naval Engineer Corps, to formulate a better underwater defense for battleships. He became famous in 1893 after publishing a three-part article in the Italian review *Rivista marittima* that promoted the use in ship's boilers of naphtha instead of coal. The German emperor Wilhelm II invited Cuniberti to advise in the conversion of some of the German navy's ships to naphtha.

In 1898, Cuniberti became a member of the Italian navy's committee for fleet construction. He planned the four battleships of the Regina Elena class, designed to support the activities in the Mediterranean of the Triple Alliance, of which Italy had been a member since 1882. He also analyzed the use of submarines and their engines. His design for a monocaliber battleship, armed with twelve 305-millimeter (12-inch) guns, was judged by the navy to be too financially ambitious. He was, however, allowed to publish an article about the project. His article on the design in the British naval review *Jane's Fighting Ships* in 1903 presented the theories that led to the construction of the famous HMS *Dreadnought* in 1904. After other prestigious assignments, Cuniberti was authorized to participate in the international contest organized by the Russian navy for the expansion of their fleet. His entry heavily influenced the construction of the four battleships of the Gangut class.

Cuniberti was promoted to major general in 1910. Two years later he wrote another article for *Jane's Fighting Ships* that aroused much interest. It affirmed that future battleships would have guns with a caliber of 406 millimeters (16 inches) and armor up to 450 millimeters (17.7 inches) and would reach speeds of 25 knots. In 1913 the position of inspector general of the Naval Engineer Corps became vacant. Cuniberti believed that this position was due him, but Edgardo Ferrati, a younger and less well-known officer, was selected. Cuniberti, offended by this choice, resigned. He died in Rome soon after, on December 19, 1913, having attained great international fame for his studies of and work with battleships and submarines, for his vast culture, and for his detailed technical knowledge.

[*See also* Battleship; *Dreadnought*; Naval Architecture *and* Navies, Great Powers, *subentry on* Italy, 1500–1945.]

## Bibliography

Breemer, Jan S. "Where Are the Submarines?" *U.S. Naval Institute Proceedings* 119, no. 1 (January 1993): 37–42.

Brown, David K. *Warrior to Dreadnought: Warship Development, 1860–1905*. London: Chatham, 1997.

Cuniberti, Vittorio Emilio. "The Battleship of the Future: *Invulnerable*." In *Jane's Fighting Ships*, edited by Fred T. Jane, pp. 544–546. London: Sampson Low, Marston, 1912.

Cuniberti, Vittorio Emilio. "An Ideal Battleship for the British Fleet." In *Jane's Fighting Ships*, edited by Fred T. Jane, pp. 407–409. London: Sampson Low, Marston, 1903.

Gardiner, Robert. *Steam, Steel, and Shellfire: The Steam Warship, 1815–1905*. London: Conway Maritime Press, 1992.

MARCO GEMIGNANI

# Cunningham, Andrew

**Cunningham, Andrew** (1883–1963), British Admiral of the Fleet. Andrew Browne Cunningham (Viscount Cunningham of Hyndhope) was born on January 7, 1883, in Dublin to a Scottish family and entered HMS *Britannia* in 1897, passing out as a midshipman in 1898 (tenth in a class of sixty-five). He served in destroyers for over thirty years, commanding a torpedo boat in 1904 and from 1908 to 1918 commanding the destroyer *Scorpion*. An instinctive seaman, he emerged as one of the rising stars of the Royal Navy, gained unparalleled knowledge of the Mediterranean (in which he spent more than a third of his career), and helped evolve destroyer tactics. The Dardanelles campaign (1915–1916) demonstrated his superb ship-handling skills and the destroyer's versatility. After exciting service in the Dover Patrol (1918), he served as a flotilla commander in the 1920s and was appointed as rear admiral (destroyers) in the Mediterranean Fleet (January 1, 1934), subsequently acting as second in command of the fleet before brief service (1938–1939) as deputy chief of the naval staff. As commander in chief, Mediterranean Fleet (June 1939), he commanded the only offensive force in the Middle East. Italian battleships were attacked by Fleet Air Arm Swordfish in Taranto (November 11, 1940), sinking one and crippling two, establishing a moral ascendancy and confirming aircraft as a major maritime influence. Cunningham defended Greece and Crete (March–May 1941), which cost him many ships, put his men in fear of air attack, and reduced him to a defensive posture, though he had triumphed at the battle of Matapan (March 28 and 29, 1941), sinking three Italian heavy cruisers and two destroyers and damaging a battleship. Cunningham capitalized on his opportunities, issuing crisp and decisive orders; using Ultra intelligence, radar, naval aircraft, and night fighting skillfully; and taking bold options. His battered fleet had to fight hard to keep Malta going through its "second siege" (December 1941–August 1942). He was sent to Washington as head of the British Admiralty delegation (June–October 1942), mainly to extract cooperation from Admiral Ernest King, but he was the American choice as naval commander of the Mediterranean landings (November 1942–September 1943). Appointed as Admiral of the Fleet in January 1943, he was the obvious successor to the dying Dudley Pound as first sea lord in October 1943. He disliked being a desk admiral, though he had much experience; the confidence of the Royal Navy, the British public, and the Americans; a strong sense of duty; and a shrewd adaptability. He presided over the Normandy landings (June 6, 1944), saw off a recrudescent U-boat threat (January–May 1945), and established a British Pacific Fleet against the opposition of Winston Churchill and Ernest King. Created a viscount in January 1946, he was uncomfortable directing peacetime naval reductions and, after suffering a heart attack, retired in June 1946, having given a new focus to the Royal Marines and the Fleet Air Arm. He wrote a readable autobiography and continued to speak on naval matters until his sudden death in London on June 12, 1963.

[*See also* King, Ernest.]

## Bibliography

Cunningham, Andrew Browne. *A Sailor's Odyssey: The Autobiography of Admiral of the Fleet, Viscount Cunningham of Hyndhope*. New York: Hutchinson, 1951.

Simpson, Michael. *A Life of Admiral of the Fleet Andrew Cunningham: A Twentieth-Century Naval Leader*. London: Frank Cass, 2004.

Simpson, Michael, ed. *The Cunningham Papers*. Vols. 1–2. Aldershot, U.K.: Ashgate/Navy Records Society, 1999–2006.

Winton, John. *Cunningham*. London: John Murray, 1998.

MICHAEL SIMPSON

## *Curaçao*, paddle steamship.

Length/beam/draft: 39.22 m × 8.07 m × 4.96 m (130.6′ × 26.1′ × 16.6′). Tonnage: 438 gross registered tons. Hull: wood. Complement: 42. Armament: 2 × 12-pounder carronade. Machinery: two steam engines, 100 horsepower; 8 knots. Built: J. H. and J. Dake, Dover, England, 1825.

On October 24, 1826, the American and Colonial Steam Navigation Company of London sold for £11,500 its brand-new paddle steamship *Calpe* to the Dutch Royal Navy, which renamed it *Curaçao*. Built in 1825 by J. H. and J. Dake at Dover, *Curaçao* had two engines of fifty horsepower each (built at Henry Maudslay's factory in London) and was rigged as a three-masted fore-and-aft schooner.

*Curaçao* started a steam packet service for the Dutch overseas possessions of Suriname (from the port at Paramaribo) and the island of Curaçao. Her commander, Lieutenant J. W. Moll (1792–1849), had been familiar with steam propulsion for two years. The ship's first voyage began from the Netherlands, at the naval base at Hellevoetsluis, near Rotterdam, on April 26, 1827, with a crew of forty-two men, two engineers from Liège, Belgium, and six firemen. Passengers and mail were on board as well. *Curaçao* became the first steamship to operate between Europe and South America and the first to cross the Atlantic Ocean in both directions using steam engines most of the time. Homeward-bound from Curaçao from July 6 to August 4, 1827, the ship was under power for twenty-two consecutive days because of unfavorable winds. On her second trip, in 1828, the engines ran for thirteen consecutive days during the first two weeks.

After three trips to the Americas, the last in 1829, *Curaçao* stayed in Dutch waters and the North Sea until 1839 because of the separation of Belgium from the Netherlands in 1830 and the uncertainties before a final agreement was reached. Then she was stationed in Suriname for two periods, from 1840 to 1842 and from 1844 to 1846. In 1843 she transported the body of King William I from Hamburg to Rotterdam. *Curaçao* was withdrawn from service in 1846. Her engines, which were still in good condition, were installed in a new vessel and the hull was sold for scrap in 1850.

## Bibliography

Bruijn, J. R., H. J. den Heijer, and H. Stapelkamp. *Julius Constantijn Rijk (1787–1854): Zeeman en Minister*. Amsterdam: De Bataafsche Leeuw, 1991.

Van Nouhuys, J. W., ed. *De eerste Nederlandsche transatlantische stoomvaart in 1827 van Zr Ms Stoompakket Curaçao*. Werken uitgegeven door de Linschoten-Vereeniging, vols. 29 and 53. The Hague: Martinus Nijhoff, 1927 and 1951.

JAAP R. BRUIJN

## Curran, Joe

(1906–1981), seaman and maritime labor leader. Joseph Edwin Curran was born in New York City on March 1, 1906. In 1922 he entered the American merchant marine, and in 1933 he joined the Maritime Workers Industrial Union, a radical group sponsored by the Communist Party. After the union disbanded in early 1935 Curran entered the International Seamen's Union, which was sponsored by the American Federation of Labor (AFL). Later that year he sailed aboard SS *California*. On March 1, 1936, SS *California* docked in San Pedro, California, and the next morning Curran demanded that the company that owned the ship increase wages or face a strike. The company refused and Curran called a sit-down strike that continued until March 5.

When the ship docked in New York City, the owner fired Curran and sixty-four crew members and blacklisted them from the company. Curran and the other blacklisted seamen then called an impromptu strike. Known as the "36 Spring Strike," it lasted nine weeks but failed to achieve any results. The East Coast seamen again went on strike in October 1936. The "Fall Strike," one of the bloodiest in American history, claimed twenty-eight lives and lasted eighty-six days. The strike thoroughly discredited the International Seamen's Union and catapulted Curran to the head of the East Coast maritime labor movement.

The rank and file founded a new seamen's union on May 5, 1937, the National Maritime Union (NMU); it elected Curran president and joined the Congress of Industrial Organizations (CIO). In 1939 the NMU called an ill-fated tanker strike against the Standard Oil Company and several other major liquid bulk carriers. This disastrous strike almost destroyed the union.

When the United States entered World War II the NMU issued a no-strike pledge that it meticulously fulfilled. Shortly after the war Curran became the first major American labor leader to purge Communists from the union. Between 1945 and 1948 Curran and the Communists battled for control of the union. The conflict climaxed in 1948 when delegates at the union's national convention reelected Curran and voted to remove all Communists from the union.

In 1941 the CIO national convention elected Curran vice president, a position he held until that organization consolidated with the AFL in 1955. Curran, who helped

**Cutter Yacht *Santanita*, c. 1893.** *Santanita* had the longest waterline length of any sailing cutter: 28.5 meters (93 feet 6 inches). She displaced 130 tons, had a mainsail of 464.5 square meters (5,000 square feet), a 28-meter (92-foot) long boom, and reached 17 knots, the fastest recorded speed of any gaff-rigged racing cutter. © NATIONAL MARITIME MUSEUM, LONDON

organize the AFL-CIO, served as one of its vice presidents from 1955 until he retired in 1973. He served on the AFL-CIO Executive Council, cochaired the Labor-Management Committee, and founded and served as the first chairman of the AFL-CIO Maritime Committee.

Curran's greatest contribution to the American labor movement was his enlightened racial policy. In 1937 the National Maritime Union included in its first constitution an article that opened membership to everyone, regardless of race, creed, color, or sex. Curran strongly backed Hugh Mulzac's appointment as the first African American to command an American merchant vessel. A letter that Curran wrote in 1942 to President Franklin Roosevelt, condemning the government's racially motivated maritime hiring practices, led Roosevelt to issue a presidential order desegregating the merchant marine. Curran's fight for racial equality in the merchant marine climaxed in 1944 when he signed American organized labor's first national contract guaranteeing no discrimination on the basis of race, creed, or color. Curran retired in 1973 and died on August 14, 1981.

[*See also* Unions.]

## Bibliography

Bernstein, Irving. *Turbulent Years: A History of the American Worker, 1933–1941.* Boston: Houghton Mifflin, 1970.

Goldberg, Joseph P. *The Maritime Story: A Study in Labor-Management Relations.* Cambridge, Mass.: Harvard University Press, 1958.

Willett, Donald. "Joe Curran and the National Maritime Union, 1936–1945." PhD diss., Texas A&M University, 1985.

DONALD WILLETT

**Custom.** *See* Law, *subentry on* Classical and Medieval Law.

**Cutter**   In the eighteenth century, the term "cutter" denoted a relatively fast vessel, auxiliary to war fleets, for carrying stores and passengers. From about 1740, British and U.S. customs services employed revenue cutters to patrol inshore waters against smuggling. They were typically small single-masted vessels with a bowsprit carrying a

**Cutter Drill.** Francis Benjamin Johnston (1864–1952) took this photograph of U.S. Naval Academy midshipmen rowing a cutter out into Chesapeake Bay, c. 1902. This type of oared naval sailing cutter was a descendant of the type of cutter that originated in Deal, England, in the early eighteenth century. LIBRARY OF CONGRESS, PRINTS AND PHOTOGRAPHS DIVISION

mainsail, foresail, jib, and gaff-topsail; cutter brigs, however, had square sails.

In England a type of clinker-built boat was introduced in the first quarter of the eighteenth century and used as a ship's boat in the Royal Navy. It ranged in size from sixteen to thirty-four feet in length and carried six, eight, ten, or twelve oars. Sometimes called a Deal cutter after its origin at Deal, Kent, the type also could carry one or two masts and was later adapted for mechanical propulsion.

In the nineteenth century, "cutter" was a generic term for a small, swift boat usually under ten tons, rigged as simply as possible with a pole mast, bowsprit, boom, and gaff. The word came to denote many small vessels, especially fishing boats, and also sailing yachts, first in Britain and later elsewhere. In the 1860s, British North Sea fishing smacks operating in fleets passed their catches to a cutter, which then sailed to port. Later, steam vessels in this trade were also known as steam cutters.

The word passed into common usage in other languages around the North Sea and came to denote specific vessels, such as the Danish fishing cutter, but later the word became less distinctive. In the Netherlands, twentieth-century cutter design originally showed strong Danish influence, but by 1930 all Dutch cutters were fishing with the side, or pair, trawl. Modern Dutch statistics count all beam trawlers and other inshore fishing craft regardless of length as cutters, in accordance with the practice of fishermen. In a loose application, Trinity House traditionally applies the term to its pilot vessels and tenders, while the U.S. Coast Guard uses the designation for its ships, recalling the revenue cutters from which that service originated.

[*See also* Seiner.}

## Bibliography

May, W. E. *The Boats of Men-of-War*. Rev. ed. Annapolis, Md.: Naval Institute Press, 1999.

POUL HOLM

# D

## Dahl, Johan C. C.

**Dahl, Johan C. C.** (1788–1857), Norwegian and German painter. Born on February 24, 1788, in Bergen, Norway, as the son of a mariner, Johan Christian Clausen Dahl was trained as a decorator. From 1811 to 1818 he was a student at the then famous Copenhagen Academy. In the summer of 1818 he traveled to Dresden, where his twenty-year-long friendship with the painter Caspar David Friedrich (1774–1840) began. The young artist spent 1820 and 1821 in Italy. In Naples he created numerous oil studies of nature. His preferred subjects were the moving sea, waves breaking on the beach, and the Mediterranean sky. In Italy Dahl's painting style matured into a free, almost proto-impressionist approach, with parallels only in the landscape painting of his English contemporaries John Constable (1776–1837) and J. M. W. Turner (1775–1851).

In the summer of 1821 Dahl returned to Germany and became the leading landscape painter in Dresden next to Friedrich. In 1823 he moved into Friedrich's house, which deepened the friendship between the two very different artists. Their landscape paintings are comparable only in their occasionally having congruent subjects, without having intellectual similarities. In Dresden, aside from large-format landscape compositions, Dahl created numerous small oil studies, in which he sought to record atmospheric phenomena and fleeting constellations of the sky. Cloud studies he viewed as an independent subject reflecting life itself and, in the depiction of light and air, its constant changes. The Romanticists' predilection for the transient and their longing for vast and unlimited space finds a place here, even though Dahl's freehanded style of painting points far beyond the Romantic era.

Dahl visited Norway again in 1826 and traveled there in 1834, 1844, and 1850 as well. In spite of his almost constant absence, his life-long connection to his homeland is apparent in the subjects of his portraits of nature. A preference for dramatic vistas, such as cragged coastlines with tempestuous seas, scenes of shipwrecks and wrecks in the surf, foaming waterfalls under storm clouds, accentuates the realistic conception of his art. He placed himself within his national tradition by incorporating both peasant figures and historical monuments and by deeply expressing rough Nordic nature in its solitary grandeur.

Dahl died on October 13, 1857, in his adopted hometown of Dresden, Germany. The museums of Bergen (Billedgalleri) and Oslo (Nasjonalgalleriet) have the most extensive holdings of his paintings and drawings; his written estate is conserved by the library of the University of Oslo.

[*See also* Art, *and* Artists, *subentry* Danish.]

### Bibliography

Bang, Marie Lødrup. *Johan Christian Dahl, 1788–1857: Life and Works*. 3 vols. Oslo, Norway: Universitetsforlaget, 1987.
Guratzsch, Herwig. *Wogen-Wolken-Wehmut: Johan Christian Dahl 1788–1857*. Schleswig, Germany: Stiftung Schleswig-Holsteinische Landesmuseen Schloß Gottorf; Munich, Germany: Haus der Kunst, 2002.

KARL-HEINZ MEHNERT

## Dalrymple, Alexander

**Dalrymple, Alexander** (1737–1808), Scottish hydrographer. Alexander Dalrymple was born on July 24, 1737, at Newhailes, near Edinburgh, a younger son of Sir James Dalrymple, second baronet (1692–1751). He joined the East India Company and was appointed a writer at Madras on November 1, 1752, rising to sub-secretary by 1759. Dalrymple made three voyages between 1759 and 1764 to the Philippines, Borneo, and Sulu, "to discover a new route to China through the Molucca Islands and New Guinea," eventually leaving Madras in 1763 to return to London to promote a trading settlement at Balambangan.

In London in 1765 Dalrymple continued research into the "counterpoise" theory of a great southern continent, publishing *An Historical Collection of the Several Voyages and Discoveries in the South Pacific Ocean* in 1769–1771. After summarizing his work in 1767 in *An Account of the Discoveries Made in the South Pacifick Ocean Previous to 1764*, he became the Royal Society's candidate to lead

**Alexander Dalrymple.** A pencil drawing by George Dance the Younger (1741–1825), dated 1794. NATIONAL LIBRARY OF AUSTRALIA

and to publish charts and nautical instructions for the East Indies navigation, a lifelong responsibility. He advocated chronometer log-keeping with tables for wind and weather, deriving from John Smeaton's calibration of windmill sails the wind scale he later transmitted to Francis Beaufort. Dalrymple's scheme of charts of the Indian Ocean was hampered by the lack of reliable longitude data, but between 1779 and 1794 he published almost six hundred plans, charts, views, and sailing directions for the East Indies as his *General Collection of Nautical Publications*.

A close friend of Sir Joseph Banks in the Royal Society club, Dalrymple worked with Philip Stephens, Evan Nepean, James Rennell, and William Marsden in providing topographical information for Vancouver's voyage to the North Pacific, for the Colonial Office in the Nootka Sound controversy of 1790, for Charles Cathcart's embassy to China in 1788, and for ports of refuge in South America for the southern whale fishery. Dalrymple also corresponded with Charles-Pierre Claret de Fleurieu, at the Depot de la Marine in Paris. He used his relationship with Samuel Wegg of the Hudson's Bay Company to argue a case to unite the Hudson's Bay and East India companies' operations in shipping furs from Northwest America to China, although this eventually came to nothing.

Dalrymple was appointed hydrographer also to the Admiralty on August 13, 1795, ostensibly to organize an unwieldy collection of charts and plans, but primarily to give official status to his geographical advice. He spent five years, with Aaron Arrowsmith and John Walker as assistants, sorting and evaluating charts, and in 1800 hired engravers and obtained a rolling-press. Without authority to commission surveys, he could engrave charts only from materials supplied by officers, manuscripts in the hydrographical office, and foreign printed charts. Proof impressions from over 150 such plates are known, including the surveys of Murdoch Mackenzie and Graeme Spence for the south coast of England from the Thames to the Lizard, but there was no budget to publish charts formally. Dalrymple continued to issue charts and plans for the East India Company after 1795, and in 1804 reprinted for the Admiralty sets of his company charts and nautical directions as the *Collection of Nautical Memoirs and Journals*.

Dalrymple took into the Admiralty in 1795 the charts and journals of the voyage of Joseph Antoine Bruni d'Entrecasteaux, brought to Saint Helena by Elisabeth-Paul Edouard, chevalier de Rossel, when the expedition broke up in Batavia. He encouraged James Horsburgh, who later succeeded him as hydrographer to the East India Company, to publish charts and sailing directions from his voyages between

the transit of Venus expedition. After a misunderstanding between the Royal Society and the Admiralty in April 1768 over the command of the chosen ship, *Endeavour*, Dalrymple declined to take second place, and James Cook was subsequently appointed both commander and Royal Society observer. Dalrymple was nonetheless elected a fellow of the Royal Society in 1771, with Benjamin Franklin and Nevil Maskelyne among his supporters.

He corresponded with the French hydrographer Jean Baptiste Nicolas Denis d'Après de Mannevillette through the 1770s, and between 1769 and 1775 published charts and navigational memoirs from his 1760s voyages and a series of *Plans of Ports in the East Indies*.

Dalrymple returned to Madras in 1776, establishing with an Arnold chronometer the value of longitude observations at sea for recommending best tracks at different seasons, and for constructing accurate charts. In London in April 1779 he was retained by the company at £500 a year to examine the ships' journals in East India House

India and China, and in 1805 he provided Beaufort with a set of his East India Company charts and sailing directions.

The controversy that led to Dalrymple's dismissal and death in 1808 arose from changes in the Admiralty's expectations for the hydrographership, and from his own intransigence. Cautiously declining to evaluate "the compleat set of all Charts published in England" he had assembled in 1807 because he was unfamiliar with the coasts they covered, he suggested a committee of naval officers to advise on charts for fleet use, and Sir Home Riggs Popham, E. H. Columbine, and Thomas Hurd duly began work in November 1807. The issue chosen to ease Dalrymple into retirement was that of the copies he had made of the charts of d'Entrecasteaux's voyage. Treating these as confidential, Dalrymple repeatedly refused to supply them to the chart committee, and was dismissed by the Board of Admiralty on May 28, 1808. He died three weeks later on June 19 at the age of seventy-one, probably of a heart attack. The hydrographic office was immediately reconstituted, also as a chart supply office, under Thomas Hurd as his successor.

Dalrymple's library of voyages and travels, atlases, charts, maps, and nautical papers was bequeathed to the Admiralty, and formed the core of the Admiralty library and of the hydrographic office collections. Almost four hundred of his copper plates, declined by the East India Company, were bought by the Admiralty as scrap metal, and many were reissued by Hurd as Admiralty charts.

[*See also* Beaufort, Francis; Cook, James; *and* East India Companies, *subentry on* English East India Company.]

### Bibliography

Cook, A. S. "Alexander Dalrymple (1737–1808), Hydrographer to the East India Company and to the Admiralty, as Publisher." Ph.D. diss., University of Saint Andrews, 1992.

Fry, H. T. *Alexander Dalrymple (1737–1808) and the Expansion of British Trade.* London: Royal Commonwealth Society by Frank Cass & Co., 1970.

Gould, R. T. "A History of the Hydrographic Department of the Admiralty." UK Hydrographic Office archives. Taunton, UK, c. 1925.

"Memoirs of Alexander Dalrymple." *European Magazine and London Review* 42 (1802), 323–328, *321–327, 421–424.

ANDREW S. COOK

# Dampier, William (1650–1715), English

buccaneer, naturalist, explorer, and author. William Dampier, born the second son of a tenant farmer in East Coker, Somerset, received a good education, including a grounding in Latin and arithmetic. He completed service in the Royal Navy during the third Anglo-Dutch War (1672–1674) and several short-lived engagements in merchantmen before joining the buccaneers. In April 1680 he participated in the attempted assault on Panama. After failing to secure the city, the buccaneers hijacked vessels in the bay and burst loose into the Pacific, scouring the coast for prizes. In April 1681 Dampier abandoned the expedition to return overland to the Atlantic. After a period spent among French and English adventurers raiding Costa Rica, he sailed to Virginia in July 1682.

In August 1683 Dampier entered the Pacific a second time, visiting the Galápagos before heading westward across the ocean in *Cygnet*. He arrived in Guam on May 20, 1686, after a voyage of over 9,600 kilometers (6,000 miles) on short rations. He cruised in the North China Seas before threading through the Philippines and Dutch East Indies toward Timor. On January 5, 1688, *Cygnet* anchored on the west coast of New Holland (Australia), where she remained for at least a month. Dampier remained

**Captain William Dampier.** An engraving published by Charles Sherwin in the 1780s after the oil on canvas portrait painted in 1697 by Thomas Murray (1663–1735). NATIONAL PORTRAIT GALLERY, LONDON

uncertain whether Australia formed part of *Terra Australis Incognita*. *Cygnet* proceeded to the Nicobar Islands in the Indian Ocean, where Dampier left her. He spent the next eighteen months exploring Melaka, Tonkin, Madras, and Sumatra before returning to England on September 16, 1691. On arrival he completed the first English circumnavigation since Thomas Cavendish in 1588. He had been away thirteen years.

In August 1693 Dampier shipped aboard *Dove*, one of four ships intending to undertake a trading voyage to the Caribbean. He spent a protracted period with this flotilla in La Coruña, during which time mutiny broke out on board one of the ships. He may have spent some of this time preparing materials that would eventually form the basis of *A New Voyage Round the World*, published in 1697. In 1699 he was given command of HMS *Roebuck* with a commission to undertake a voyage of discovery into the Pacific. This was one of the first voyages mounted by the Royal Navy with the express purpose of gathering scientific information. *Roebuck* arrived on Australia's northwest coast in August 1699. Dampier conducted a careful survey of the area of coastline he named Shark Bay. Afterward he departed in the direction of New Guinea hoping to locate the eastern coast of the mysterious Southern Continent.

*Roebuck*'s worm-ridden condition curtailed her deployment. She sank in February 1701 at Ascension Island, and her crew transferred into East India vessels for the voyage home. In September Dampier was court-martialed for the loss of *Roebuck* and tried again in June 1702 for assault on a subordinate officer. The voyage had been a mixed affair, but it was an opportunity to assemble materials for a new publication, *A Voyage to New Holland*, which appeared in two volumes (1703 and 1709).

In September 1703 Dampier sailed to the Pacific for the fourth time. He was commodore of a privateering expedition. He commanded *St. George*. His consort, *Cinque-Ports*, carried the Scottish sailor Alexander Selkirk as master, or mate. The outward leg was mostly spent raiding coastal towns and looting small prizes. The vessels eventually parted company. Dampier bungled an ambush on the Manila Galleon (Spanish vessels that sailed between the Philippines and Mexico) in September 1704 while *Cinque-Ports* sailed for the Strait of Magellan, delivering Selkirk ashore at Juan Fernández, where he insisted on landing. Selkirk's opinion that *Cinque-Ports* was unseaworthy was confirmed when she sank shortly thereafter. Dampier arrived in England in 1707 after a

period of imprisonment in Batavia on suspicion of piracy. He was further embarrassed by subordinates who charged him publicly with malfeasance.

In 1708 Dampier sailed as pilot of another privateering expedition into the Pacific. Two ships, under the command of Woodes Rogers, *Duke* and *Duchess* were to pursue the Manila Galleon, a prize that had evaded Dampier for three decades. After rounding Cape Horn in January 1709 both vessels put in at Juan Fernández, where Selkirk was recovered after four years' isolation. By December both vessels were poised on the coast of southern California. On December 21, Rogers took the smaller of two vessels making the run from Manila to Acapulco. On Christmas Day he fought an unsuccessful action with the larger vessel before stretching away westward for the long voyage home. In October 1711 Dampier stepped ashore for the last time and retired to the parish of Saint Stephen's, Coleman Street, London, where he died in 1715.

Dampier's printed writings were produced with considerable assistance from senior figures in the Royal Society, and they influenced the development of natural philosophy and navigation over a period of two centuries. *A New Voyage Round the World* helped shape early scientific protocols with its presentation of exhaustive empirical data. The German naturalist Alexander von Humboldt (1769–1859) and the English naturalist Charles Darwin (1809–1882) both acknowledged their admiration for the volume. A supplement published in 1699 included "A Discourse of Winds," commended by James Cook (1728–1779), Richard Howe (1726–1799), and Horatio Nelson (1758–1805). It was used in the compilation of *Admiralty Sailing Directions* well into the twentieth century.

*A Voyage to New Holland* excited Britain's expansionist aspirations. Dampier's encomium on the mercantile potential of New Britain drove forward exploration of *Terra Australis Incognita* in defiance of rational considerations. In April 1770 when James Cook and Joseph Banks strained for their first glimpse of Aborigines on Australia's southeast coast, they had Dampier's book to hand.

*New Voyage* had profound implications for literature, precipitating the phenomenal popularity of voyages and travels in the early eighteenth century. It was rightly considered the first of its kind, a model of good practice for the flood of authentic voyage narratives that followed it.

[See also Pacific Ocean, *subentry on* Exploration Voyages, 1520–1700; *and* Voyage and Travel Accounts.]

## Bibliography

### Primary Works

Dampier, William. *Captain Dampier's Vindication of a Voyage to the South-Seas, in the Ship St George*. London, 1707.

Dampier, William. *A New Voyage Round the World*. Edited by Sir Albert Gray, with a new introduction by Percy G. Adams. New York: Dover, 1968.

Dampier, William. *A Voyage to New Holland, &c. in the Year 1699*. Edited by James Spenser. Gloucester, U.K.: Alan Sutton, 1981.

Esquemeling, John. *The Buccaneers of America*. Edited and introduced by Henry Powell. London: Swan Sonnenschein, 1893.

### Secondary Works

Deacon, Margaret. *Scientists and the Sea, 1650–1900 : A Study of Marine Science*. Aldershot, U.K., and Brookfield, Vt.: Ashgate, 1997.

Edwards, Philip. *The Story of the Voyage: Sea Narratives in Eighteenth-Century England*. Cambridge, U.K., and New York: Cambridge University Press, 1994.

Preston, Diana, and Michael Preston. *A Pirate of Exquisite Mind: Explorer, Naturalist, and Buccaneer: The Life of William Dampier*. New York: Walker, 2004.

Williams, Glyndwr. *The Great South Sea: English Voyages and Encounters, 1570–1750*. New Haven, Conn.: Yale University Press, 1997.

Williams, Glyndwr, and Alan Frost, eds. *Terra Australis to Australia*. Melbourne, Australia: Oxford University Press in association with the Australian Academy of the Humanities, 1988.

JAMES KELLY

# Dana, Richard Henry, Jr. (1815–1882),

American sailor, author, and lawyer. A sixth-generation descendant of a prominent Boston family, Richard Henry Dana Jr. gained literary fame as the author of *Two Years before the Mast* (1840), an autobiographical account of life aboard a merchant vessel. Born in Cambridge, Massachusetts, on August 1, 1815, Dana was the son of the poet and journalist Richard Henry Dana Sr. and was raised in an atmosphere of rarified intellectual discussion and declining family fortune.

## Two Years

After his sophomore year at Harvard, Dana suffered an attack of measles that weakened his eyesight and left him unable to read. To strengthen himself, Dana chose to go to sea, deliberately spurning the opportunity to travel as a passenger in favor of working as a merchant sailor. He left Boston on August 14, 1834, sailing for California on board the hide-carrier brig *Pilgrim*, and returned September 22, 1836, on board the ship *Alert*. As even the names of the vessels imply, Dana's two years constituted a symbolic education and remained a touchstone of memory throughout a law career marked by modest success and frustrated ambition.

Dana's accounts of his outbound and return voyages, along with his descriptions of the boredom and backbreaking work of collecting hides on the California coast, had a first-person authenticity that resonated with a reading public curious about the far West and "the common man." America's nautical literature had previously been dominated by James Fenimore Cooper (1789–1851), whose Romantic sea novels were focused on historical themes and dark, Byronic heroes. Dana, by contrast, promised to deliver a "voice from the forecastle," and his muscular style served as a lasting corrective to Cooper, who himself eventually imitated Dana. *Two Years* was praised by Ralph Waldo Emerson (1803–1882), William Cullen Bryant (1794–1878), and Edgar Allan Poe (1809–1849) for its gritty, documentary portrayal of a sailor's life. Herman Melville (1819–1891) so admired the work that he called Dana a "sea-brother" and engaged him in correspondence as he was writing *Redburn* (1849), *White-Jacket* (1850), and *Moby-Dick* (1851). Dana's plainspoken perspective was widely copied by both fiction and nonfiction writers to present the factual realities of life at sea.

While nineteenth-century appreciations of *Two Years* turned on the honesty of its narrative voice, more recent studies focus on its rich ambiguities and ambivalences. Dana was a well-heeled Bostonian more than he was a common sailor, and his overeager apprenticeship both disguises and reveals that he would never be "one of them"—that is, would never be a sailor for life, with a sailor's enduring hardships and limited prospects. Dana's shipboard experience was, in this way, almost literally a "junior year abroad," after which he returned to Harvard and graduated with his original class. The tension between his landed gentility and sea-bred toughness is everywhere on display in *Two Years*, and indeed there are moments when Dana feels trapped by the sailor identity that he so earnestly cultivated. When he realizes, for example, that *Pilgrim* will stay in California longer than anticipated, Dana uses his connections to change vessels and come home earlier than the rest of his shipmates. The fact that he records this negotiation, as well as the reaction it arouses among the men, is itself a sign of his willingness to confront the difficult questions of allegiance and identity. Perhaps the most compelling scene in the book comes when Dana witnesses the flogging of a fellow sailor and vows silently to himself that, should he return home safely to Boston, he will do everything he can to redress the abuses of sailors at sea.

## Legal Practice

Dana kept his promise, at least initially, when he returned to Boston and, in his law practice, represented sailors against the interests of captains and owners. In fact, he wrote *Two Years before the Mast* while in law school, partly in the hope of establishing a maritime clientele. It was published in 1840, and became an immediate success with an eastern readership responsive to frontier stories and sympathetic to the sufferings of sailors. Dana's book contract with Harper's, negotiated by his father and William Cullen Bryant, gave him $250 and twenty-five copies of the text. He turned down the option of receiving a percentage of the book's sales, an unfortunate choice given its enormous popularity. In 1841, Dana published a nautical manual, *The Seaman's Friend: A Treatise on Practical Seamanship*, which explains in layman's terms the details of a ship's rigging and movement, the customs and usages of the merchant service, and the duties of masters and seafarers.

While the arc of Dana's subsequent career moved away from the sea and into politics, in the public mind he always remained the author of *Two Years before the Mast*. Significantly, his adult professional life exhibited its own tensions between safety and risk. While Dana's religious, cultural, and political instincts were conservative, and while he was staunchly antiabolitionist, he nonetheless defended the rights of fugitive slaves in a number of landmark cases in Boston in the 1850s. For his efforts he was at one point knocked unconscious by a street thug and boycotted by supporters of slavery. Active in the Free Soil movement and an important figure in the Massachusetts Constitutional Convention of 1853, Dana was a tireless worker with an incisive legal mind, but he was never rewarded with appropriate power or position. He ran for public office in 1868 and lost overwhelmingly; he was plagued for more than a decade by a plagiarism accusation that proved to be without merit; in 1876 he was nominated by President Ulysses S. Grant to become ambassador to England, a post he very much desired, but his candidacy was unsuccessful. Surrendering to what he saw as a pattern of failure, he and his wife eventually retired to Rome, where Dana died on January 6, 1882.

In his later years Dana was given to melancholy, and saw the irony that his "boy's book" would outlast his other achievements. Following periods of stress and overwork, Dana often took enforced vacations; these intervals of rest and physical exercise brought back the memory of his two-

year "parenthesis," as he called it. In 1869, Dana included a "Twenty Four Years After" chapter to *Two Years* after he revisited California, and this chapter along with his short book *To Cuba and Back* (1859) verify that he retained his eye for arresting maritime images throughout his life.

[*See also* American Literature; Autobiographies, Journals, and Diaries; *and* Literature, *subentries on* An Overview *and* Voyage Narratives.]

## Bibliography

### Primary Works

Dana, Richard Henry, Jr. *The Seaman's Friend* (1841). Toronto: Dover, 1997.

Dana, Richard Henry, Jr. *To Cuba and Back* (1859). Edited by C. Harvey Gardiner. Carbondale: Southern Illinois University Press, 1966.

Dana, Richard Henry, Jr. *Two Years before the Mast* (1840). Edited by Thomas Philbrick. New York: Penguin, 1981. In the best current edition of Dana's book available, Philbrick follows the original version of *Two Years* as it was first published. Philbrick's suggestive introduction analyzes Dana's text both as an initiation narrative and as a narrative of captivity.

### Secondary Works

Adams, Charles Francis. *Richard Henry Dana: A Biography*. 2 vols. Rev. ed. Boston: Houghton Mifflin, 1891. The first biography of Dana, written by a sympathetic contemporary.

Conrad, Bryce. "Richard Henry Dana, Jr., and *Two Years before the Mast*: Strategies for Objectifying the Subjective Self." *Criticism: A Quarterly for Literature and the Arts* 29, no. 3 (Summer 1987): 291–311. Examines the relationship between the "I" and "eye" in *Two Years*.

Egan, Hugh. " 'One of Them': The Voyage of Style in Dana's *Two Years before the Mast*." *American Transcendental Quarterly* 2, no. 3 (September 1988): 177–190. Discusses Dana's book as literary art.

Gale, Robert. *Richard Henry Dana, Jr.* New York: Twayne, 1969.

Lawrence, D. H. "Dana's *Two Years before the Mast*." In *Studies in Classic American Literature*. New York: Thomas Seltzer, 1923. Lawrence's provocative account places Dana in an idealistic strain of American literature; Lawrence is particularly illuminating in his analysis of the flogging scene.

Lucid, Robert Francis. "The Influence of *Two Years before the Mast* on Herman Melville." *American Literature* 31 (November 1959): 243–256.

Philbrick, Thomas. *James Fenimore Cooper and the Development of American Sea Fiction*. Cambridge, Mass.: Harvard University Press, 1961. Discusses the lasting influence of Dana on James Fenimore Cooper and other writers of sea fiction.

Shapiro, Samuel. *Richard Henry Dana, Jr.: 1815–1882*. East Lansing: Michigan State University Press, 1961.

HUGH EGAN

**Dance.** *See* Dance and Drama.

**Dance and Drama** For as long as human beings have plied the waters of the world, their stories have been reenacted in song, dance, and drama. Theatrical entertainment celebrating the exploits of famous sailors and commemorating important voyages or naval engagements has, for thousands of years, held great fascination for shoreside audiences. Only recently has drama been considered distinct from music and dance, making it difficult to distinguish separate categories of maritime theater. The most useful distinction for this entry is the distinction between nautical dance and drama performed by professional actors ashore, and the dance and drama practiced by the sailors themselves at sea and in seaside taverns and theaters.

### Shipboard Dance and Drama

The earliest types of shipboard theater took the form of various ceremonies and rituals. The best known of these is the "crossing the line" ceremony. The Greek poet Callimachus (c. 270 B.C.E.) described a seamen's good luck ritual, performed when calling at the island of Delos, which involved dancing around a "horned altar" and biting the trunk of a sacred olive tree. Ritual dances were also common among ancient Polynesian seafarers. One of the most spectacular of these is the *tuki waka* of the Maori of New Zealand (1000–1200 C.E.). This chant coordinated as many as a hundred paddlers in a single massive war canoe, and it was accompanied by intricately synchronized gestures with the paddles: churning the water, waving the paddles in the air, striking the paddles against the canoes' hulls—creating a thunderous sound to intimidate enemies.

Shipboard dancing appears to have been an established tradition aboard European ships by at least the seventeenth century. For example, when the British privateer Woodes Rogers visited Guam in March 1710, the indigenous people entertained his men with dancing, and he invited local dignitaries to his ship, where they were entertained by the sailors' dancing. These sorts of interactions occurred throughout the period of European exploration and colonialism. Stories from the journals of James Cook, Louis-Antoine de Bougainville, George Vancouver, and many others show that dance was an important form of cultural exchange, but it was not used only for entertainment and diplomacy. The infamous Captain William Bligh hired an Irish fiddler named Michael Byrne to provide music aboard HMS *Bounty*, insisting that his men dance

**Dance and Drama.** Navel cadets learning the hornpipe on board the cadet training ship HMS *Arethusa* in 1929. MARY EVANS PICTURE LIBRARY, LONDON

for exercise. This policy became widely accepted, and in 1808, Dr. Edward Cutbush, a U.S. Navy surgeon, wrote a book recommending dance for the health of all sailors, and, notably, advocated the hiring of African American fiddlers because of their presumed repertoire of popular dance tunes.

The dance form most closely associated with European sailors is the hornpipe. Originating with shepherds in Wales, Scotland, and England, the hornpipe is first mentioned in literature of the late fifteenth century. By the eighteenth century the hornpipe was popularly known as a sailors' dance, primarily because of its association with a specific hornpipe tune called the "College" or "Sailors' Hornpipe," based on a song called "Jack's the Lad." The hornpipe popularized by sailors was a solo dance that became a highly individualized expression in which each dancer tried to outdo the others with his own particular virtuosic steps. Many cultures adapted the sailors' dance into their own traditions. Captain James Cook's men danced when they first landed at Tahiti in 1769; they found upon their return several years later that the Tahitians had created their own elaborate hornpipe variants.

In the early nineteenth century, dances like the waltz, the schottische, and particularly the polka came into vogue among seamen. While sailors were always to be found dancing with local women in the music and dance halls of port towns, these couples' dances were also practiced at sea. Whaling ships in the nineteenth century had a tradition known as the "gam," in which whaling crews met at sea to socialize, and dancing of this sort was a common feature at these occasions. Gams provided a much-needed break from the monotony of the typical whaling voyage, and were an opportunity for generating camaraderie among the diverse crew. Not only were hornpipes and polkas danced during gams, but whalers also witnessed the Spanish fandango, Maori *haka*, Hawaiian hula, and a wide variety of Portuguese, African American, and many other national and ethnic dance traditions.

Besides music and dance, theatrical entertainment was also found at sea, although there are far fewer written accounts. Sailors occasionally rigged up a stage on deck, usually at the break of the poop or quarterdeck, where they could replicate the sorts of entertainments found in shoreside theaters and music halls. These shows were quite varied, usually incorporating music and dance, dramatic readings or recitations, blackface routines or other ethnic humor, and scenes from Shakespeare or other popular playwrights. In rare cases, seamen of a literary disposition wrote their own plays. For example, the journal of George Gould, carpenter on the Nantucket whaler *Columbia*

(1841), includes a detailed script for a reenactment of a whale hunt, complete with stage directions. Reenactments like this also found a place on mainland stages in the form of whaling panoramas, which often included an authentic whaleboat and a group of men to act out the action as the panorama displayed vivid scenes from a typical voyage.

Most of what is known of seamen's theatrical activities comes not from accounts of voyages, but from the playbills advertising their performances at shoreside theaters. Naval, merchant, and whaling crews often formed troupes of variety players, frequently specializing in the routines of blackface minstrelsy. These troupes became popular attractions ashore, especially in port towns far from America and Europe, like Canton, Sydney, or Manila. For instance, in 1858 an amateur troupe from the British warship HMS *Vixen* performed at Honolulu's Royal Hawaiian Theatre, presenting the comedy *Charles II*, comic and sentimental songs, a hornpipe, a set of blackface songs, and the popular farce *Budget of Blunders*. Variety shows like this did not disappear in the twentieth century. Amateur music making, theater, and dance are still a part of life aboard twenty-first-century military and merchant ships. These entertainments have remained important expressions of the diversity and talent of the world's seamen.

## Nautical Dance and Drama Ashore

Many of the themes of modern maritime drama were developed by Greek playwrights in the fifth century B.C.E. Naval battles were depicted by Aeschylus in plays like *The Persians* (472 B.C.E.), about the Battle of Salamis. The tragedian Euripides focused on the dilemmas and choices faced by famous seafarers like Odysseus in *The Cyclops* (408 B.C.E.) and Jason in *Medea* (431 B.C.E.). In his famous play *The Trojan Women* (415 B.C.E.), Euripides depicts the deities Athena and Poseidon cursing the Achaean navy for the ruthlessness with which it plundered the city of Troy. These themes, centering on the heroic yet problematic lives of sailors, have wound their way through nautical drama for millennia.

The great seafaring cultures of Polynesia also had numerous genres of elaborately choreographed dance dramas, such as the hula of Hawaii and the *hiva* of many other parts of Polynesia. These performances combined music, dance, pantomime, drama, and humor to tell stories of heroes and gods, often depicting journeys across vast stretches of the Pacific in voyaging canoes. When Pacific islanders began regularly sailing on European and American ships in the eighteenth and nineteenth centuries, they continued the tradition of depicting their voyages with mimetic dance and narrative chant.

Evidence of maritime dance and drama on the European stage before the seventeenth century is scanty, but a few notable morality plays, such as Sebastian Brandt's *Narrenschiff* (1494) and Alexander Barclay's *Ship of Fools* (1509), used maritime themes. The sailor as a distinctive character type began to emerge in the late 1500s; for example, Shakespeare's charming ruffian Petruchio, from *Taming of the Shrew* (1594), is said to be a prototypical theatrical sailor. Several maritime plays appeared on the British stage in the early seventeenth century, most notably Thomas Heywood's *Fortune by Land and Sea* (1607) and *The Travels of Three English Brothers* (1607) by John Day, William Rowley, and George Wilkins. Most historians, however, point to Shakespeare's *The Tempest* (1611) as the first significant play of this genre. Like the Greek tales of Odysseus, *The Tempest* explores the dilemmas faced by sailors lost in a strange land, transporting its audience to an exotic locale filled with mysterious inhabitants possessing magical powers.

As the nautical genre developed on European stages, playwrights made use of sailors' slang and jargon, even borrowing sailors' songs and ballads in the name of authenticity, while stage technicians created ever more realistic and spectacular storm and battle effects. These elements flourished during the colonial era of the mid- to late eighteenth century in an explosion of nautical pantomimes and melodramas that fed the European and American publics' interest in exploration and naval conquest. Late eighteenth-century nautical pantomimes moved away from the genre's origins in the magical comic characters of French commedia dell'arte, utilizing a new style called *ballet d'action*, based more on historical and literary themes. The shipwreck melodrama in the tradition of *The Tempest* remained very popular, represented by such popular pantomimes as the 1781 adaptation of Daniel Defoe's classic novel *Robinson Crusoe* (1719). The pantomime version of Robinson Crusoe was subtitled *Harlequin Friday*, indicating that the indigenous people of foreign lands continued to be portrayed onstage as magical and mysterious.

Other pantomimes recounted the stories of famous explorers. For example, Richard Sheridan's *Pizzaro in Peru; or, The Death of Rollo* (1799) contrasted the beauty and innocence of the New World with the corruption and violence of the Old World. Similarly, Jean François Arnould-Mussot's *La mort du Capitaine Cook* (1788), later brought to London as *The Death of Captain Cook* (1789), depicted Hawaiian islanders as unspoiled by the concerns of modernity; yet when Cook brings them objects symbolizing civilization, he finds tragically that they are susceptible to sins like envy and murder. Pantomimes based on the lives of explorers, however, were primarily vehicles for elaborate spectacles of scenery, costume, and dance. An important example was John O'Keefe's *Omai; or, A Trip around the World* (1785), which told the story of a Tahitian named Omai who had come to London in 1774 and who acted as interpreter and cultural ambassador for Cook. The pantomime's climax was a procession of dancers representing the different cultures encountered by Cook, dressed in costumes based on the drawings of Cook's artists William Hodges and John Webber. The score for *Omai*, composed by William Shield, combined theatrical music with sailors' songs, and also attempted to mimic the music of Pacific Islanders, even calling for the use of wood blocks and nose flutes. This set the trend for many of the subsequent exploration melodramas, which frequently were advertised as featuring the authentic dances and customs of the indigenous people encountered by European explorers.

During this era, plays, operas, and pantomimes depicting naval engagements were also very common in Great Britain, as the British navy reached the peak of its global power. These plays celebrated the lives of Britain's great heroes, like Horatio Nelson, while establishing the common British "tar" as a representation of all that was noble and good in the British character. Of course naval battles also made for exciting stories and provided vehicles for patriotic songs and sentiments. Some theaters went to great lengths to stage mock naval battles, most notably London's Sadler's Wells Theatre, which installed a gigantic water tank on stage in which scale model ships could engage one another. Plays of this genre include Sheridan's *The Glorious First of June* (1794), William Pearce's *The Death of Captain Faulknor* (1795), and Thomas Dibdin's *The Mouth of the Nile* (1798) and *The Hermione* (1800). A notable feature of naval plays was the sailors' hornpipe, which moved easily from the deck of the ship to the theatrical stage and was also frequently performed as an entr'acte. Many professional dancers became specialists in the form. For example, T. P. Cooke, who starred as William in the nautical melodrama *Black Eyed Susan*, claimed to have combined twenty-four variants of the hornpipe, collected in port towns around Britain, to create his signature routine.

In the nineteenth century, nautical melodramas became dominated by supernatural themes and a dark, almost macabre, sensibility. One of the most prolific playwrights of this period was the British dramatist Edward Fitzball, whose surreal, supernatural sea plays always featured pyrotechnic effects and bloody story lines. Among his most popular nautical melodramas were *The Floating Beacon* (1824), *The Pilot* (1825), *The Flying Dutchman* (1827), and *The Red Rover* (1829). The peak of the nautical melodrama could be said to have been Douglas Jerrold's *Black Eyed*

*Susan* (1829), which was based on a popular ballad by John Gay. The play, with its extensive use of sailors' slang, inspired many imitations and burlesques, and remained popular well into the 1860s.

In the twentieth century, nautical drama moved from stage to screen, and the theatrical genre became far less common. There are a few important works, however, like Eugene O'Neill's one-act sea plays, first published in 1919. These early works are significant for their characteristic atmosphere of tension and for their depiction of seafaring life at the turn of the twentieth century. They are best represented by the character study *The Moon of the Caribbees* and the intense whaling drama *Ile*. World War II inspired a number of plays for the American stage based on life in the U.S. Navy. In 1944 the choreographer Jerome Robbins teamed with the composer Leonard Bernstein to create a ballet titled *Fancy Free*, which told the story of two young sailors on shore leave in New York. The ballet was such a critical and popular success that it was adapted, with book and lyrics by Betty Comden and Adolph Green, into the classic musical comedy *On the Town* (1944). Other musicals with naval themes followed, like Rodgers and Hammerstein's *South Pacific* (1949), but the most effective theatrical depiction of naval life in that period was *Mister Roberts* (1948). Adapted from a novel by Thomas Heggen, the play uses a standard plot of nautical drama: a tyrannical captain is confronted by a good-hearted and noble officer. Its mix of comedy and drama, its snappy and realistic dialogue, and its skilled cast led by Henry Fonda garnered the Tony Award for Best Play in 1948, assuring a Broadway run of six years.

Playwrights, choreographers, and composers have also turned back to the nineteenth century for maritime-themed productions. During the bicentennial year 1976, Steven Sondheim produced a remarkable musical play titled *Pacific Overtures*, which, in part, told the story of Commodore Perry's expedition to Japan in 1853, attempting to convey the Japanese perspective on the encounter. The use of Japanese instrumentation and dance elements combining western ballet and Japanese Kabuki made *Pacific Overtures* a somewhat unusual Broadway production. However, when compared with eighteenth- and nineteenth-century productions like *Omai* or *The Death of Captain Cook*, this multicultural mix of pantomime, ballet, music, and drama seems a logical continuation of a centuries-old tradition of nautical theater.

[*See also* English Literature; Literature; Music; *and* Shipboard Life.]

## Bibliography

Clifton, Larry. *The Terrible Fitzball: The Melodramatist of the Macabre*. Bowling Green, Ohio: Bowling Green State University Popular Press, 1993. A well-researched account of this little-known playwright who created many popular nautical melodramas and whose use of fantastical special effects was proto-cinematic.

Cutbush, Edward. *Observations on the Means of Preserving the Health of Soldiers and Sailors*. Philadelphia: Thomas Dobson, Fry and Kammerer, 1808. Written by a surgeon in the U.S. Navy, this book helped to establish the common policy that dancing was important as exercise for maintaining the health and well-being of sailors.

Freeman, Terence M. *Dramatic Representations of British Soldiers and Sailors on the London Stage, 1660–1800*. Studies in British History, vol. 36. Lampeter, U.K.: Edwin Mellen Press, 1995. Freeman's book takes up the work begun by Watson and brings the research and analysis up to date. This is truly the definitive work on the character of the sailor, particularly the British tar, as depicted on the London stage during the eighteenth century.

Glenn, George D. "Nautical 'Docudrama' in the Age of the Kembles." In *When They Weren't Doing Shakespeare: Essays on Nineteenth Century British and American Theatre*, edited by Judith L. Fisher and Stephen Watt, pp. 137–151. Athens, Ga.: University of Georgia Press, 1989. This essay discusses the social context and style of British naval dramas during the late eighteenth and early nineteenth centuries.

Hays, Michael, and Anastasia Nikolopoulou, eds. *Melodrama: Cultural Emergence of a Genre*. New York: St. Martin's Press, 1996. This edited volume on the history and sociopolitics of melodrama includes two excellent essays on nautical plays of the eighteenth and nineteenth centuries, "The Ideological Tack of Nautical Melodrama" by Jeffrey Cox and "He Never Should Bow Down to a Domineering Frown: Class Tensions and Nautical Melodrama" by Marvin Carlson.

Lawler, Lillian B. "The Dance of the Ancient Mariners." *Transactions and Proceedings of the American Philological Association* 75 (1944): 20–33. An interesting description of the "mariners' dance" performed on the island of Delos in the third century B.C.E.

McLean, Mervyn. *Weavers of Song: Polynesian Music and Dance*. Auckland, New Zealand: Auckland University Press, 1999. An encyclopedic work covering the indigenous performance traditions of every island group in the Polynesian culture complex, from Hawaii to New Zealand to Easter Island.

Miller, Pamela A. *And the Whale Is Ours: Creative Writing of American Whalemen*. Boston: David R. Godine, 1979. This fascinating collection of whalers' writings includes a one-act play depicting a whale hunt, dating to 1841, from the journal of George Gould, carpenter on the Nantucket whaler *Columbia*.

O'Neill, Eugene. *Seven Plays of the Sea*. New York: Vintage Books, 1972. This is an edition of O'Neill's seven one-act sea plays. These early works show the master playwright honing his craft, using the memorable characters he met during his youthful years as a merchant seaman. The seven plays, first published in 1919, are *The Moon of the Caribbees, Bound East for Cardiff, The Long Voyage Home, In the Zone, Ile, Where the Cross Is Made,* and *The Rope.*

Parr, Anthony, ed. *Three Renaissance Travel Plays.* The Revels Plays Companion Library. Manchester, U.K., and New York: Manchester University Press, 1995. A collection of three important British nautical melodramas from the early seventeenth century: *The Travels of Three English Brothers* by John Day, William Rowley, and George Wilkins (1607); *The Sea Voyage* by John Fletcher (1622); and *The Antipodes* by Richard Brome (1638). The book also includes a lengthy and detailed introduction.

Watson, Harold Francis. *The Sailor in English Fiction and Drama, 1550–1800.* New York: Columbia University Press, 1931. A seminal work on the topic of maritime themes in English literature and drama. Although much of the focus is on literature, the sections covering theater are full of interesting details and commentary.

JAMES REVELL CARR

## Danish Literature. *See* Scandinavian Literature.

## Danish Sound Dues

The Sound (Øresund), a narrow passage between the towns of Elsinore on the island of Sjælland, Denmark, and Helsingborg in Scania, Sweden, enabled Denmark to hold the keys to the Baltic for many centuries. From 1429 onward, benefiting from control of both banks of the strait, King Erik VII of Pomerania imposed a toll on all ships entering or leaving the Baltic and using Danish territorial waters, making them stop near the Kronborg fort (near Elsinore) to pay the toll. This, in theory, was to rid The Sound of pirates and to maintain lighthouses. The measure provoked very strong opposition from the Hanseatic towns, but the king, who needed new funds, succeeded in enforcing his decision. The customs office kept a close watch over The Sound, and the artillery of the Danish forts and the ships carrying out surveillance kept watch to stop all illegal movement. The collection of this toll, the most important source of income for the Danish king, continued for more than four centuries. In 1857, following a suggestion made by the United States, the toll was abolished in return for compensation of almost 67 million crowns.

The tax on passing through The Sound changed as time passed. The simple toll, initially one rosenoble, was progressively increased depending upon a ship's tonnage. Then in the course of the fifteenth and sixteenth centuries, a variety of duties on goods—especially wine, salt, and copper—were added. In the seventeenth century, as

**Danish Sound Dues.** *A Dutch Ship entering the Sound near Kronborg Castle, Denmark, 1614* by Hendrik Cornelisz. Vroom (1566–1640). Kronborg Castle, located near Helsingør (Elsinor) at the northern end of the island of Zealand and at the narrowest point of The Sound (Øresund), was the key controlling point for payment of the dues. The Sound is only 4 kilometers (2.5 miles) wide here. The eastern shore was Danish until 1658 and has since been part of Sweden. BILDARCHIV PREUSSISCHER KULTURBESITZ / ART RESOURCE, NY/STAATLICHE MUSEEN ZU BERLIN, BERLIN

Dutch traffic in the Baltic increased and Sweden's political power asserted itself, the Netherlands and Sweden found it hard to accept the Sound tax and entered into conflict with Denmark. Denmark had to give in to its adversaries, and following the treaty of Kristianopel (1645), the graded toll was abolished and replaced by a tax hitting different goods more or less heavily. Danish cargoes were exempted from the toll, as were those of certain other privileged towns and those of Sweden, depending on the political situation of the time. After the Great Northern War (1700–1721), only goods belonging to Danish subjects escaped the tax.

If illegal passage was difficult and dangerous, the concealment of goods may be considered widespread, at least until 1618, the year that the ships were obliged to call in. The captains declared a much larger volume of lightly taxed goods in place of highly taxed ones (rye in place of wheat, for example), concealing in their cargo the highest taxed products (brandy) or, in the case of goods difficult to check (wood), failing to mention a part of their cargo. Discharging goods in Hamburg and transporting them to the Baltic along the German rivers via Lübeck was also a solution commonly used to avoid The Sound.

The Sound toll registers make up an exceptionally valuable historical source for knowledge of shipping in northern Europe. The first register dates back to the year 1497. There are large gaps in the first half of the sixteenth century, but the gaps are much more limited up to the seventeenth century, and the source is complete for the eighteenth century.

[*See also* Baltic Sea; North Sea, *subentry on* An Overview; *and* Straits.]

### Bibliography

Hill, Charles E. *The Danish Sound Dues and the Command of the Baltic: A Study of International Relations.* Durham, N.C.: Duke University Press, 1926.

Johansen, Hans Christian. *Shipping and Trade between the Baltic Area and Western Europe 1784–1795.* Odense University Studies in History and Social Sciences, vol. 82. Odense: Odense University Press, 1983.

Knoppers, Jake V. Th. "A Comparison of the Sound Accounts and the Amsterdam Galjootsgeldregisters." *Scandinavian Economic History Review* 24, no. 2 (1976): 93–113.

PIERRICK POURCHASSE

# Danzig. *See* Gdánsk.

# Dardanelles and Bosphorus. *See* Straits, *subentry on* An Overview.

# Davis, John (c. 1550–1605), polar explorer. John Davis may have been born at Sandbridge, Devon, in about 1550; his father was a yeoman on the estate of Stoke Gabriel. Together with his elder brother Edward, John often explored the Dart estuary nearby. Along the way, they quite likely met up with Humphrey and Adrian Gilbert and the Gilberts' half brother Walter Ralegh. This group of west country men produced some remarkable feats as explorers.

After his initial education, of which nothing is known, Davis went to sea at an early age, and by the age of twenty-eight he was already an accomplished captain. From 1579 until 1585 he was back home again, and in 1582 he married Faith Fulford. By this time the search for the Northwest Passage had been firmly pressed on his mind by his friend Humphrey Gilbert—on whose voyages Davis probably had taken part—who died on the way home from a voyage to Newfoundland in 1583. Early in 1583 a series of meetings took place with, among others, Secretary of State Francis Walsingham. The subject of polar exploration as a new route to the Indies was of particular interest to the English in their growing struggle against the Spanish and Portuguese empires since the second half of the sixteenth century.

Davis made three successive voyages from 1585 to 1587 into the polar regions, each time during the summer months. On his first voyage he found his way blocked by ice at 66° N, then sailed around Greenland and investigated its west coast, reaching Cumberland Gulf. The second voyage reached only 60° N and was mainly used to investigate the inlets and islands of the east coast of Canada. This voyage was further marred by troublesome encounters with the local Inuit and incidents among his own crew as well, with stormy weather along the way. On his third voyage, Davis pressed northward through Davis Strait into Baffin Bay and reached the limit of the ice pack at 72° N, where high winds forced him to retire southward. Davis's three voyages are in many ways outstanding, charting waters where no Europeans had gone before and each time returning safely. Although these voyages ultimately proved unsuccessful, some place-names still endure.

Davis, after probably taking part in the Armada campaign, next tried his hand at privateering from 1589 to 1590 with some success, but it was his navigational skills that truly marked him out among his contemporaries. He joined as rear admiral the voyage of Thomas Cavendish in

1591–1593 to China and Japan via Cape Horn but with disastrous results, causing a mutiny on board his ship for which he was later arrested. Back home he began developing a variant of the backstaff (the Davis, or English, quadrant), which enabled navigators to measure the height of the sun more precisely. Davis's innovative suggestion was to use the cross-staff facing away from the sun so that the user had to slide the instrument's transom until its shadow coincided with a vane at the end of the graduated staff.

In addition, he described a method to correct for the error in observation created by ocular parallax. Davis also published two books: *The Seaman's Secrets* (1594) and *The Worlde's Hydrographical Description* (1595), an appeal for further exploration of the Northwest Passage, in which he never lost his interest. With *The Seaman's Secrets*, Davis became the first Englishman to publish a practical treatise on navigation. Based on practical knowledge from his northern voyages and the Cavendish voyage, it provides an important document on the state of English navigational understanding at the time of its publication, showing the gaps between theory and practice. It deals with plane sailing, celestial navigation, the use of the backstaff (later called the Davis quadrant), the compass, great circle navigation, navigation in high altitudes, and other matters.

By this time, Davis had amassed a small fortune, though his personal life proved more troublesome because of his estranged wife. After a voyage as master of Ralegh's ship to the Azores in 1596–1597, he joined several expeditions to the East Indies, first as pilot for the Dutch in 1598–1600 on the voyage of Cornelis de Hssoutman, and then twice for the newly established British East India Company. It was here, off Borneo, in the ship *Tiger* that Davis was killed by Japanese pirates on December 29 or 30, 1605. Davis was not one of the great Elizabethan privateering men, but was foremost among the early explorers.

[*See also* Navigational Instruments; Navigational Manuals; Navigators; Northwest Passage; Privateering; *and* Ralegh, Walter.]

### Bibliography

Cooper, E. R. "The Davis Backstaff or English Quadrant." *Mariner's Mirror* 30 (1944): 59–64.

Hicks, Michael. "John Davis." In *Oxford Dictionary of National Biography*, vol. 15, edited by H. C. G. Matthew and Brian Harrison, pp. 447–450. Oxford: Oxford University Press, 2004.

Hitchcock, R. F. "Cavendish's Last Voyage: The Charges against Davis." *Mariner's Mirror* 80 (1994): 259–269.

Hitchcock, R. F. "Cavendish's Last Voyage: Purposes Revealed and Concealed." *Mariner's Mirror* 87 (2001): 5–14.

Markham, Albert Hastings, ed. *The Voyages and Works of John Davis, the Navigator*. Hakluyt Society, 1st ser., vol. 59. London: Hakluyt Society, 1880.

Mörzer Bruyns, W. F. J. *The Cross-staff: History and Development of a Navigational Instrument*. Zutphen, Netherlands: Walburg Pers, 1994.

Waters, David. *The Art of Navigation in England in Elizabethan and Early Stuart Times: The Earl Mountbatten of Burma*. New Haven: Conn.: Yale University Press, 1958.

OTTO VAN DER MEIJ

**Dawson, Montague** (1895–1973), maritime painter. Contrary to the popular myth that he was born at sea, Montague Dawson was born in Chiswick, West London, in 1895, the son of an engineer, inventor, and expert Thames yachtsman, and the grandson of Henry Dawson, a successful landscape painter. Montague Dawson's own artistic talent was evident from childhood, and he had a lifelong fascination for the sea and ships, together with a seaman's practicality.

In 1910, Dawson was employed by a commercial art studio, where he learned and developed the art of illustration. During World War I he served as a naval officer, mostly on trawlers and minesweepers, and managed to continue his artistic career by becoming a contributor to *The Sphere*, a magazine that used his illustrations to record the war at sea. During shore leave, Dawson visited Charles Napier Hemy, RA, a well-known marine painter who influenced Dawson greatly.

By the 1930s, Dawson had established himself as a leading marine artist, and during World War II he illustrated not only for *The Sphere*, but also for the Admiralty, this time working from photographs taken during battles and from other top-secret reference materials brought to his home by Admiralty officials. These materials, combined with eyewitness accounts, were the source for Dawson's dramatic battle scenes. He also visited such places as the Vickers shipyard in Barrow-in-Furness to sketch vessels in dry dock or under construction. These visits laid the foundation of his international reputation for absolute accuracy.

As with many men at the top of their profession, Dawson was single-minded. Rising at 5.30 A.M., he worked through the day, sometimes until the early hours of the next morning, breaking only for meals. He was always a perfectionist and would scrape off days of painstaking work, including depictions of intricate rigging, without hesitation if he was not satisfied. Working seven days a week, Dawson took two or three weeks to complete a painting, and the end of each masterpiece often found him mentally and physically exhausted.

Inevitably, a time came when the extraordinary and worldwide demand for Dawson's work far outstripped his restrained rate of production. Eventually his health began to fail, and although he preferred to stand while working, he was now forced to sit. This did not, however, affect his creativity, and in his later paintings the subtlety and variety of the sea color combined with the masterly vigor of the waves is breathtaking. Dawson's loose technique for the painting of the sea contrasted with his meticulous and sensitive treatment of the ships, a combination that proved to be an irresistible.

Speaking of his work, Dawson had this to say: "People want a ship as a point of focus and interest. But, I only look on the ship as part of the whole composition. I like to get a broad sky effect as well. I am after atmosphere in the elements. To get the painting to live is the most difficult part. You have to respect your subject, be almost frightened by it. There's nothing like the boil and the swell of rough sea." In speaking of his direct experience, both of being at sea and of painting in his studio, Dawson has surely inspired many marine artists. His example of expressing sea and sky in all their moods, and the precise detail he brought to his vessels—whether battleships, clippers, or racing yachts—has provided other marine painters with a challenge that would ensure that only the most dedicated artists succeed.

[*See also* Artists, *subentry* British, *and* Painting.]

## Bibliography

Ranson, Ron. *The Maritime Paintings of Montague Dawson.* Newton Abbot, U.K.: David and Charles, 2004.

RON RANSON

**Dazzle Painting**    A method of camouflage that was designed to elude detection by German submarines, "dazzle painting" was first used on British ships during World War I. From the beginning of the war, the German Navy had mainly deployed its submarine force and kept the Hochseeflotte (high sea fleet) in the harbors. By February 1915, Germany had accomplished a complete blockade of England

*A Convoy of the First World War, c. 1918.* This oil painting by Herbert Barnard John Everett (1876–1945) illustrates the interplay of color, light, and sea reflection that made dazzle painting an effective way to impede visual identification and optical range finding. © NATIONAL MARITIME MUSEUM, LONDON

(a move comparable to the British blockade of the German North Sea ports), seriously threatening supply lines from the United States and transit to the European mainland. Allied losses became dramatic, up to 60 ships per week. Between 1914 and 1918, 4,837 merchant ships were sunk.

The British Admiralty feverishly searched for a means of defense. From the summer of 1915 so-called Q-ships, freight ships or fishing vessels with cannons placed behind camouflage screens, were equipped to lure German submarines. As soon as a submarine surfaced to begin an attack with its onboard artillery, it would receive a full blast from the Q-ship's concealed cannons. Until August 1917, 180 Q-ships were in use, eliminating a total of 11 submarines. A more effective remedy was to travel in convoy, with submarine fighters providing protection. The Germans replied with so-called "wolf packs," teams of submarines attacking simultaneously at night from various sides.

Traveling in convoy was only possible on the great Atlantic routes. Individual vessels continued to be vulnerable, and the need for defense remained great. Ideas and proposals abounded, ranging from the extremely naïve to the highly ingenious. The solution was, remarkably, often sought in painting the ships. Most such proposals were made by artists, though some were initiated by scientists. The most successful of these camouflage methods was dazzle painting.

Early in 1917, the traditional sea painter Norman Wilkinson had the idea of painting ships with color patterns in such a way that their detection in "periscope distance" would become more difficult. By obscuring the shape of the ship, the camouflage would confuse the enemy as to the course, distance, and speed of the vessel, thus reducing the chance of a successful attack. Wilkinson's proposal was adopted by the British Admiralty, and the freighter *Industry* was the first test of the "dazzle" design. When the outcome of that experiment was too long in coming, Wilkinson turned to the Controller General of Merchant Shipping, who responded with enthusiasm. In June 1917, Wilkinson was commissioned to set up an organization for the design and execution of dazzle painting for the first fifty transport vessels. This Dazzle Section was housed in the prestigious Burlington House, the home of the Royal Academy of Arts in London; until the end of the war, numerous designs were created and tested there. The system was mainly developed empirically, with little theoretical underpinning. If a design was deemed good, it was painted on "color charts," the silhouette drawing of the vessel type in question, and was sent to the Dazzle Officers in the British commercial shipping ports. These

Dazzle Officers, many of them professional artists, supervised the execution of the painting. By the end of June 1918, a total of 2,367 ships had been painted, 195 of them warships and 60 of non-British nationality.

The dazzle painting technique was adopted by the French, Russian, Italian, and Belgian navies. The Japanese government was at the point of implementing a similar system when the war ended. In the United States, following the declaration of war on April 6, 1917, a Camouflage Section was established within the navy. Although there were many proposals in the United States regarding methods of camouflage painting, the British dazzle painting method was chosen. The U.S. Camouflage Section developed 495 different camouflage designs, 302 of which were meant for commercial ships. On March 1, 1918, there were a total of 1,256 U.S. ships with dazzle painting, mainly vessels that operated in the war zone.

The actual effectiveness of dazzle painting was difficult to determine, even for the Committee on Dazzle Painting (established by the British Admiralty). After a lengthy examination that included consultation with many naval experts, on June 31, 1918, the committee came to the conclusion that "no convincing arguments have been found in support of this form of camouflage. At the same time, statistics suggest that it does not have a negative effect either, and when one considers the indisputable boost for self-confidence and morale of the officers and crews that this painting gives rise to … one must recommend carrying on with the Dazzle system."

Dazzle painting was an exceptional phenomenon, particularly for the similarity that its designs bear to the imagery of the avant-garde art movements that preceded World War I: Futurism, Cubism, and the English Vorticism. These movements were characterized by their fragmentary depiction of reality and a preference in subject matter for the world of machines and velocity. Ironically, the method that adopted these modern motifs was realized by a very traditional sea painter.

[*See also* Wilkinson, Norman.]

## Bibliography

Bittinger, Charles, et al. "Report on Naval Camouflage." Camouflage Training School, New York. This report can be found in the National Archives in Washington, D.C.

Gayer, Albert. *Die deutschen U-Boote in ihrer Kriegsführung, 1914–1918.* Berlin: E. S. Mittler, 1920–1921.

Gibson, R. H., and M. Prendergast. *The German Submarine War.* New York: R. R. Smith, 1931.

"Instructions to Dazzle Officers." Confidential Admiralty Interim Order no. 3753/17.

"Report of the Committee on Dazzle Painting." London, July 31, 1918.

Roskam, Albert. *Dazzle Painting: Kunst als camouflage, camouflage als kunst.* Rotterdam: Stichting Kunstprojecten en Uitgeverij Van Spijk, 1987.

Scheer, Admiral Reinhard. *Deutschlands Hochseeflotte im Weltkrieg: Persönliche Erinnerungen.* Berlin: Scherl, 1920.

Wilkinson, N. *A Brush with Life.* London: Seeley, 1969.

Williams, David L. *Naval Camouflage: A Complete Visual Reference, 1914–1945.* Annapolis, Md.: Naval Institute Press, 2001.

ALBERT ROSKAM

# Dead Reckoning

Dead reckoning is the method of navigation by which a ship's position is estimated, using the knowledge of the position at departure, the steered courses, and the distances made good since departure. Before latitude and longitude could be determined at sea by other means, dead reckoning was the only way to find the position at sea when a ship was beyond the sight of land.

## History

The basis of the art of navigation is experience handed down by seafarers from generation to generation. It includes the knowledge of prevailing winds, winds caused by seasonal changes, sea and tidal currents, water depths, and the estimated sailing time between various ports. When Persian and Arabian navigators sailed across the Indian Ocean and, roughly from the eighth century C.E., toward China, they used for orientation a wind rose that was based on the rising and setting of sixteen recognized stars. Latitude was roughly found from the altitude of the sun and the polestar. In the ninth century, in some parts of the Indian Ocean, shore-sighting pigeons were used on Persian ships, to set course to the nearest land. The lodestone, which when rubbed along an iron needle magnetizes the needle so that it points toward the north, was not used by Arab and Persian navigators before the end of the eleventh century.

Early mariners in the Mediterranean navigated in much the same way as Arab seafarers, but they had the advantage of sailing in an enclosed sea where land was never far off. They, too, estimated their position with the use of phenomena observed around them, like the rising, culmination, and setting of the sun, and the direction and force of prevailing winds. At night zenith stars were indicators for their position relative to the northern and southern shores of the Mediterranean, while the altitude of the polestar and of the sun at noon provided an indication of latitude. Knowledge of longitude was based on sailing times between the eastern and western shores of the Mediterranean. Before the introduction of the magnetic compass, navigators steered a course by memorizing the place on the horizon of certain rising or setting stars. The magnetic compass was probably introduced on ships in the Mediterranean by crusaders during the thirteenth century.

In the early Middle Ages, Norsemen and Irish monks started to cross the North Atlantic Ocean toward Iceland. Because of the long Arctic summer, stars were of less use to navigation here than in southern latitudes. To estimate position relative to the track to Iceland, the Shetland and the Faeroe islands were used as stepping-stones. Navigators also observed migrating birds, which showed them in what direction land lay, and there is mention of Norsemen using ravens taken on board for this purpose. Seafarers found that a concentration of clouds over the horizon indicated a distant landmass. The compass came into use in the north of Europe shortly after it was introduced in the Mediterranean.

Sailors from islands in the South Seas traditionally crossed large stretches of ocean in search of food and trade, and they learned to practice dead reckoning with great precision. Their navigational skills were handed down from generation to generation without much western influence until the English and French explorers arrived in the eighteenth century. Because the tradition was continued in the Pacific much longer than elsewhere, more is known about the complex and often sophisticated techniques and methods used by early navigators in this region.

Different techniques were developed and used by navigators from the various island groups. Pacific islanders used a wind compass, which gave the directions of islands based on the character of the wind (for instance, moist, dry, hard, or gentle). The star compass was defined by the directions in which a number of bright stars were seen. When sailing north of the equator, the polestar was used for an indication of latitude, and the constellation of the Southern Cross was used to set courses in the Southern Hemisphere. During their training, Pacific islanders memorized zenith stars for a number of islands. These are stars with a declination equal to the latitude of the island in question and which pass overhead there, from east to west. The islanders also memorized the bearings from one island to another. When dead reckoning on long sailing tracks, the islanders combined their knowledge of zenith stars and the bearings of reference islands (*etaks*) that they passed, and whether these were below the horizon. To aid in determining their position, South Sea navigators observed birds, cloud formations, and ocean swells. In the Pacific, swells travel over great distances, and reflections and deflections caused by intervening islands create anomalies in the pattern. These anomalies can be recognized by experienced islanders at a great distance and used for orientation. In some island groups stick charts were developed. These consisted of a pattern of sticks tied together with small shells attached to them. The sticks indicated sea currents, and the shells represented islands.

Dead reckoning as it is defined today is the method of finding a ship's latitude and longitude with the knowledge of courses and distances made good from the last position. This has been practiced since the beginning of the maritime expansion of the Portuguese and Spanish navigators in the fifteenth century. Following techniques developed by astronomers, Iberian seamen learned how to calculate their latitude accurately by observing the altitude of the polestar at night and the sun's altitude at culmination, using the mariner's astrolabe and the cross-staff. The more complex problem of finding longitude at sea was not solved until the eighteenth century, when the method of lunar distances and later the chronometer became available.

Besides finding longitude through the estimation of courses and distances made good, navigators sometimes used the variation of the magnetic compass for that purpose. Variation is the angle between the directions of the magnetic and the geographic poles. Depending on the place on the earth, it can be east, west, or zero. As the position of the magnetic pole migrates over time, the variation increases or decreases. Acknowledging the apparent relation between longitude and variation, the sixteenth-century Dutch scholars Petrus Plancius and Simon Stevin designed methods of converting variation into longitude. For this to be successful in practice, however, these methods require a vast amount of data on the magnetic variation, which at the time of Plancius and Stevin was not available. Toward the end of the seventeenth century the English astronomer Edmond Halley, commanding HMS *Paramore* (or *Paramour*), gathered data on the variation and augmented this with data drawn from old ship's logs. The result was laid down on special variation charts. Ships of the Dutch East India Company, when crossing the equator in the Atlantic Ocean in the eighteenth century, were instructed to estimate their longitude by comparing the observed magnetic variation with the value provided in their printed sailing instructions. They were required to cross the line where

the area of calms is at its narrowest, which, depending on the season, can be in the middle or the west of the ocean. The same technique was used to estimate longitude when sailing across the Indian Ocean toward the Australian coast. The islands of Saint Paul and Amsterdam are situated approximately halfway along the route, and the local variation was known. Even without sighting the islands the mariners would know their halfway position by observing the variation.

When longitude could be found accurately at sea—by the method of lunar distances and by chronometers—in the second half of the eighteenth century, it became possible to calculate a fix several times a day. Because the opportunity to obtain a fix could be missed, seamen continued to navigate by dead reckoning and to plot their estimated position on the sea chart. A cloudy sky prevents the taking of celestial observations, and such weather can last for days. In such cases dead reckoning was the only means of knowing a ship's position, however uncertain. This remained the case until radio navigation was introduced at the beginning of the twentieth century, first through radio direction finding (RDF) and later through radar and hyperbolic radio systems. With these aids, within certain limitations, a position line or a fix could be obtained. It was not until the introduction of navigation by satellites of the Global Positioning System (GPS) in the late twentieth century that a fix was available continuously.

So long as the factors that a navigator uses for calculations in dead reckoning are uncertain, the resulting position is not entirely reliable. Errors introduced by uncertain factors such as current and leeway accumulate, and if a fix to eliminate these is not obtained, the error in the estimated position can become considerable and lead to a dangerous situation. One of the best-known disasters caused by the limitations of dead reckoning was the loss of three large ships of the Royal Navy on the Isles of Scilly at the extreme southwest of England in 1707. The ships had sailed from the Strait of Gibraltar for the English Channel, but because of bad weather they had unknowingly drifted westward. This error in dead reckoning cost the lives of almost two thousand seamen and led to the founding of the Board of Longitude.

### Practice

Course and speed are the two most important factors in dead reckoning. There are various methods of registering courses and speeds, and the practice of dead reckoning can be done by construction and by calculation.

**The course.** A ship's course is the angle between the meridian and the direction in which a ship sails. It is reckoned from the geographic north and is expressed in degrees from 0 to 360 or in one of the thirty-two compass points, which equal 11° 15′. The course to steer is determined on the sea chart with the help of the drawn rhumb lines. A rhumb line is a line on a chart and the track of a ship that follows a single compass bearing, preserving the same angle with all meridians crossed in succession. Using a ruler and the rhumb lines and compass roses drawn on the chart, the navigator determines the course that must be steered to reach the destination. The course is shown on the chart as a straight line drawn between the ports of departure and destination. If the course crosses navigational obstructions such as shallows, reefs, or sandbanks, it will be necessary to divert and to steer two or more subsequent courses. Before the advent of steam propulsion, if the direction of the wind was unfavorable, it could also be necessary to tack (that is, to sail on various alternating courses at angles to the wind), because a sailing ship cannot sail directly into the wind.

The course is steered by using a ship's magnetic compass. The value of the magnetic variation must be added to or subtracted from the true course found on the chart to determine the compass course to be steered. Since the variation is not constant, it should be checked often during a voyage and applied to the course. A second magnetic anomaly to be dealt with is deviation, the compass error that is caused by the effect of ship's metal on the compass. Deviation became a more complex issue when, in the nineteenth century, ships were increasingly being built with iron and steel.

Leeway is another factor to be taken into account. This is the angle between the compass course and the course made good, caused by the wind pushing the ship sideways. The correction is called drift and should be applied to the course in order to avoid diversion. Leeway can be determined by observing the angle between the keel of the ship and the ship's wake, and it can be measured by, for example, towing a floating line astern.

Finally, the influence of sea currents can set a ship off her course. Unlike leeway, current set cannot easily be detected, and before sea currents were charted and were registered in sailing directions and tide manuals, knowledge of currents was based on the personal experience of seafarers handed down through generations.

**The speed of a ship.** In order to know the distance made good, a navigator must know the speed of the ship. Until the sixteenth century this could be only estimated, and the

estimating was done on the basis of a seaman's personal experience, sometimes with the aid of a sandglass. By knowing his ship and the sailing conditions on his regular route, including sea and tidal currents, a navigator could estimate the ship's speed fairly accurately. Aids to measure the speed, called logs, became available in the early sixteenth century. To find the distance made good, the hourly or two-hourly logged speeds were added up during a watch, to give the total distance made good during that watch.

A successful log was first described by William Bourne in his *A Regiment for the Sea* (1574). It consisted of a reel with a knotted line and a shaped piece of wood at the end and was used with a sandglass. It must have been in use before Bourne, because a log reel was found in the wreck of the royal yacht *Mary Rose* of 1545. The second method was the Dutchman's log, which became available at the end of the sixteenth century. Toward the end of the eighteenth century mechanical logs were designed that enabled a more accurate measurement. These were improved during the nineteenth century and are known under the general name patent log. Patent logs were used until the 1980s, when they were definitely superseded by electrical logs. With these, navigators could read their ship's speed and the cumulative mileage continuously from displays in the wheelhouse.

Although the accuracy of logs increased considerably, until the patent log was invented the logged speed was a mere snapshot. The slightest change in the wind between observations meant that the ship went faster or slower than the log had shown. All logs have in common that they give the speed of the ship through the water and do not account for current set. A head-on current or a current from astern decreases or increases the ship's speed with speed of the current. To know the speed of the ship relative to the sea bottom, it is necessary to account for current set. In the late twentieth century, ultrasonic logs were developed, which measured the speed relative to the sea bottom. GPS also determines positions relative to the sea bottom, and the knowledge of time and distance between two positions provides the true distance and speed made good.

The length of a mile is generally based on the length of a degree of latitude, which in turn is derived from the knowledge of the circumference of the earth. The inability to measure the circumference accurately led to errors and to miles of various lengths. Until the Renaissance the sea mile, also called the "league," was based on the value calculated by Ptolemy. As the western maritime expansion commenced in the fourteenth century, seafaring countries established their own sea measurement. Popular were the

English, in which there were twenty leagues of three miles to a degree of latitude, the Spanish, which had seventeen and a half leagues to a degree, and the Dutch or German, with fifteen leagues to a degree. In 1615 the Dutch astronomer and mathematician Willebrord Snel recalculated the length of a degree as 352,347 feet. This led to the adoption in England and Holland of the new length of the sea mile, and led to the adjustment in knotting of log lines from forty-two to forty-seven feet between knots. Until the nineteenth century, sea charts often had scales for several sea miles, so the charts could be used by navigators from other countries. The modern sea mile, or nautical mile, has been in use since the nineteenth century and equals one minute of latitude, of which there are sixty to a degree. This means that the modern sea mile equals just over 1,852 meters; the length of a league has been set at three nautical miles. The term "knot," meaning "nautical mile per hour," was derived from the knotted log line.

**Instruments for recording course and speed.** Devices were developed to record the sailed courses and the ship's speed so that they could afterward be used to find the estimated position. The traverse board was a circular wooden plank on which rhumb lines were marked by a series of equidistant holes representing the hourly or two-hourly periods during which a ship sailed on a particular course. A number of pegs were fixed by strings to the center of the board, and they were stuck in the holes corresponding with the sailed course. A second set of holes and pegs on the board was used to record the hourly or two-hourly logged speed of the ship. At the end of the watch the navigator would read the information from the traverse board, transfer it onto the sea chart, and find his dead-reckoned position.

Another way to record courses and distances run was with a watch slate. This was a rectangular slate on which a number of columns were drawn and recordings made with chalk or a slate pencil. The navigator filled in the true and compass courses, the logged speeds, the direction and force of the wind, the compass variation, and other particulars relevant to navigation. As with the traverse board, the information was processed at the end of each watch and was drawn on the chart.

**Dead reckoning by construction.** The most basic way to plot an estimated position was as follows. The distance made good in miles, found with the log, was taken from the scale of the chart with a pair of dividers. One leg of the dividers was placed on the previous position, the other

leg scratched over the course line drawn in the chart. The intersection of the course line and the scratch indicated the position by dead reckoning. This could be combined with the true latitude found from the sun at noon or from the altitude taken of a culminating star in twilight, which was drawn as an east-west line in the chart. There were also various kinds of scientific instruments to find the position without arithmetic. The first was the Gunter scale, a mathematical rule invented by the Englishman Edmund Gunter in 1620. It remained in use at sea well into the nineteenth century, especially on British and North American ships. The Gunter scale was followed in 1627 by the plane scale invented by John Aspley. This instrument became equally popular among navigators. The plane scale was adapted by the Dutch and became known as a *pleinschaal*, and it was used into the nineteenth century. A third device, the *sinical* or nautical quadrant, was invented in the second half of the seventeenth century and became especially popular among mariners in southern Europe. The attained latitude could be found through construction, using the known sailed courses and distances made good.

Methods of finding the estimated position with mathematical instruments were popular because they avoided the use of arithmetic and consequently reduced the risk of making errors. Because of their relative crudeness, these instruments were less accurate than a calculation. As the professional requirements for navigators became stricter during the nineteenth century, the use of instruments for dead reckoning was discouraged in favor of calculations. The result was that said instruments disappeared from ships altogether.

**Dead reckoning by calculation.** Until the sixteenth century the dead-reckoned position was found by a combination of the latitude and the knowledge of the speed and steered courses. The manner in which a seaman could work with these factors depended on his knowledge of mathematics. In the first half of the sixteenth century, methods became available for seamen to calculate their estimated position with the known latitude at departure, the recorded courses, and the distance made good. The Portuguese mathematician Pedro Nunes provided tables with which the change in longitude could be found for each change in degree of latitude. It was necessary to know how many miles and in which compass direction the ship had sailed along a rhumb line. However, these tables were not practical because they did not account for the decreasing distance between meridians as the latitude increases. This problem was solved at the end of the century by the Englishman Edward Wright, who calculated tables of increasing latitude and laid these down in his "tables of rhums." Like Nunes's tables, these were for courses other than north, south, east, and west. The Dutch scholar Simon Stevin, in his booklet *De zeylstreken* of 1608, studied the rhumb and renamed it a *kromstreek*. This was later translated by Snel into Latin as *"loxodrome,"* the name that is still in use in the twenty-first century for a line on earth that preserves the same angle with meridians. The loxodrome gets closer and closer to the pole, but never reaches it.

The next step in the process of perfecting the tables was set by Claes Jansz Lastman, a teacher in the art of navigation in Amsterdam. In 1621, Lastman published a navigational manual that included his tables to "raise or lay a degree" on charts on the Mercator projection. Some ten years later logarithms, which had been invented by the Scottish mathematician John Napier in 1614, were adapted for navigation by the Englishman Henry Briggs and were published in tables by the Dutchman Adriaan Vlacq in 1633. In his 1621 publication, Lastman also explained how to calculate the position with the use of trigonometry, and for this purpose he provided sine, tangent, and secant tables. This method was once again improved when the Rotterdam surveyor Ezechiël de Decker in 1631 announced how to perform trigonometric calculations using logarithms. In principle the method of calculating the estimated position is still in use. Although GPS enables navigators to find fixes continuously, it is still good seamanship to check positions against dead reckoning.

[*See also* Global Positioning System; Inertial Navigation; Longitude, Institutes of; Nautical Astronomy and Celestial Navigation; Navigational Instruments; Sailings; *and biographical entries on figures mentioned in this article.*]

## Bibliography

Cotter, Charles H. *A History of Nautical Astronomy.* London: Hollis and Carter, 1968.

Davids, C. A. *Zeewezen en wetenschap: De wetenschap en de ontwikkeling van de navigatietechniek in Nederland tussen 1585 en 1815.* Amsterdam and Dieren, Netherlands: De Bataafsche Leeuw, 1985.

Hewson, J. B. *A History of the Practice of Navigation.* 2d ed. Glasgow: Brown, Son and Ferguson, 1963.

Hourani, George F. *Arab Seafaring in the Indian Ocean in Ancient and Early Medieval Times.* Rev. ed. Princeton, N.J.: Princeton University Press, 1995.

Howse, Derek. *Greenwich Time and the Longitude.* London: Philip Wilson, 1997.

Jonkers, A. R. T. *North by Northwest: Seafaring, Science, and the Earth's Magnetic Field.* Göttingen, Germany: Cuvillier Verlag, 2000.

Lewis, David. *We, the Navigators: The Ancient Art of Landfinding in the Pacific.* Canberra: Australian National University Press, 1972.

Schnall, Uwe. *Navigation der Wikinger: Nautische Probleme der Wikingerzeit im Spiegel der schriftlichen Quellen.* Oldenburg, Germany, and Hamburg, Germany: Stalling, 1975.

Taylor, E. G. R. *The Haven-Finding Art: A History of Navigation from Odysseus to Captain Cook.* 2d ed. London: Hollis and Carter, 1958.

Taylor, E. G. R., and M. W. Richey. *The Geometrical Seaman: A Book of Early Nautical Instruments.* London: Hollis and Carter, 1962.

Waters, David W. *The Art of Navigation in England in Elizabethan and Early Stuart Times.* London: Hollis and Carter, 1958.

WILLEM F. J. MÖRZER BRUYNS

**Declaration of London, 1909.** *See* Law, *subentry on* Law of Naval Warfare.

**Declaration of Paris, 1856.** *See* Law, *subentry on* Law of Naval Warfare.

**Dee, John** (1527–1609), British scientist, magician, and advisor on maritime affairs. Dee was one of Tudor England's most learned men and one of England's earliest and boldest advocates of a British Empire—a term he has been credited with coining.

In 1548, shortly after becoming one of the foundation fellows of Trinity College, Cambridge (where he was under-reader in Greek), Dee traveled to Louvain and Paris, where he studied with and lectured to the foremost Continental cosmographers. By Elizabeth's coronation in 1558, Dee was busy creating his period's largest library and establishing his household as an academy on the fringes of the university, the city, and the court. From this base in Mortlake, situated on the river Thames and near the royal palace at Richmond, Dee served as a scholarly advisor until the 1580s, when he turned increasingly to angel magic and alchemy, partly under the patronage of Emperor Rudolf II in Prague. Before his death in 1609 Dee was forced to move from Mortlake to Manchester, leading to a series of increasingly bitter complaints that the government had failed to compensate him for his service and failed to put his advice into action.

In a series of maps and treatises from the 1550s to the 1590s, Dee developed an expansionist program that he called "this British discovery and recovery enterprise." Supporting both the discovery of new lands (particularly in the polar regions left unexplored by the Spanish and Portuguese) and the recovery of territories that once arguably belonged to the British Crown (thanks largely to the legendary exploits of King Arthur, Prince Madoc, and Saint Brendan), Dee gradually claimed for his queen and countrymen a vast imperial dominion covering most of the seas and much of the land in the Northern Hemisphere. The cornerstone of this ambitious program was a four-volume work that Dee called *The British Monarchy*. Volume 1 survives as *General and Rare Memorials Pertaining to the Perfect Art of Navigation* (1577), an argument for the establishment of a small naval force. The second volume was titled *The British Complement of the Perfect Art of Navigation*: this text does not survive but would have consisted mostly of "Queen Elizabeth Her Tables Gubernautic" (a collection of tables of longitudes and latitudes for the polar regions, where magnetic variation made navigation notoriously difficult). All that is known of the third volume is that it was burned by Dee. The fourth and final volume was to be called "Of Famous and Rich Discoveries," and the manuscript that survives of that text (in a damaged state) is a straightforward collection of materials on geography and navigation, particularly concerning the search for passages to the northeast and northwest.

Dee also outlined his world picture in a series of maps (some of which adopt a polar projection), and in two additional manuscript treatises, compiled at the request of Queen Elizabeth and her ministers. In 1577 and 1578, Dee produced a series of position papers on Elizabeth's title to foreign lands. These survive in a copy made in 1593 with the umbrella title "Brytanici Imperii Limites" (On the Limits of the British Empire). This collection was used by Lord Burghley in his deliberations on England's relations with competing maritime powers, and a few years later, in 1597, Dee was again called on to spell out his arguments in a brief summary titled "Thalattokratia Brettaniki" (The British Sea-Sovereignty).

While Dee's texts reached few readers, and while the government proved reluctant to pursue his plans, Dee made a tangible (and not simply imaginative or ideological) contribution to English maritime history. He was responsible, first, for creating the most complete and up-to-date collection of classical and Continental knowledge on the science of navigation and the history of empire. His library contained not only a special section for "historical books pertaining to navigation" but a collection of scien-

tific instruments. Second, he used this knowledge to advise the Elizabethan trading companies and train their seamen: from the 1550s to the 1580s he provided scholarly support to the ventures of the Muscovy and Cathay companies and the voyages of Hugh Willoughby, Richard Chancellor, Humphrey and Adrian Gilbert, Martin Frobisher, Arthur Pet, Charles Jackman, and John Davis.

[*See also* Davis, John, *and* Frobisher, Martin.]

## Bibliography

Dee, John. *The Limits of the British Empire*. Edited by Ken MacMillan and Jennifer Abeles. Westport, Conn.: Praeger, 2004.

Sherman, William H. *John Dee: The Politics of Reading and Writing in the English Renaissance*. Amherst: University of Massachusetts Press, 1995.

Taylor, Eva Germaine Rimington. *Tudor Geography, 1485–1583*. London: Methuen, 1930.

WILLIAM H. SHERMAN

**Defoe, Daniel** (1660–1731), British author, projector of schemes, journalist, and spy. Defoe, perhaps the most prolific author writing in English in his time, acutely observed the beginnings of Britain's greatness as an overseas power. During his lifetime Britain developed the most capable navy in the world. The nation's security and prosperity rested predominantly on its fortunes at sea, and naval prowess became synonymous with British identity.

Maritime expansion on this scale precipitated a new class of literature, the voyage narrative. William Dampier's quasi-scientific journal of circumnavigation, *A New Voyage round the World* (1697), is generally considered the first of its kind. Based on mariners' journals, voyage narratives combined acute firsthand reports of unfamiliar regions of the world with tales of adventure. With careful editing the journal's raw materials were transformed into a finished product that was both educational and pleasurable. If, in the process, fictive elements were introduced, this only enhanced the voyage narrative's appeal. The overwhelming success of Dampier's narrative proved that this cocktail was irresistible to an emerging popular readership endowed with the education, leisure, and disposable income to indulge its newly formed tastes.

Acceptance of an increasingly secular epistemology in mid-seventeenth-century England produced the climate in which voyage narratives could thrive. In developing the ideas of Francis Bacon, John Locke, and René Descartes, the Royal Society promoted the new sciences, extending the humanist project of placing man, not God, at the center of the cosmos. This drive ensured the enthusiastic reception of voyage narratives as documents of empirically gathered information concerning the most remote spaces on earth. By the time Defoe became redundant as a government propagandist, around 1718, travel literature peaked as the most sought-after form of polite literature after religious writing. Voyages became so popular that the supply of authentic narratives dried up, inducing a number of enterprising authors to infiltrate the market with counterfeits. Defoe was one such writer.

## The Voyage Narratives

Defoe's great voyage narratives—*Robinson Crusoe* (1719), *Captain Singleton* (1720), and *New Voyage round the World* (1724), all published anonymously—bear no relation to the actual sea miles covered by their author. In 1680 Defoe may have made a voyage to Oporto with the aim of touring parts of Europe, and in late August 1692 he sailed from Cornwall to London before a making a foolhardy dash across the channel as a smuggler. Otherwise, his only experience of salt water was speculative. He was part owner of *Desire*, the first vessel lost to enemy action during the War of the Spanish Succession; he dabbled with a company that operated a diving bell off *Lizard*; and he made disastrous investments in marine insurance. Defoe's impulse to write sea stories toward the end of his life arose because they became highly fashionable at exactly the time that he became redundant as a political writer. To a projector and theorist like Defoe, the voyage narrative beckoned as an irresistible literary gamble.

*Robinson Crusoe* went on sale on April 23, 1719. The novel, with its dazzling account of island life, commences with a series of voyages that establish Crusoe's extraordinarily diverse naval career. After disobeying his father by running off to sea, he sails variously as a passenger, supernumerary, private trader, ship's officer under instruction, slaver, slave, sentry, fisherman, pirate, supercargo, and interloper. Apart from service in the Royal Navy and passage as a stowaway, he runs through almost the entire range of possible seagoing experience. In short, Crusoe is cast as an archetypal mariner, and his "original sin" transcends his act of filial disobedience to signify the collective guilt shared among the tribe of Zebulun.

Defoe radicalizes the voyage narrative. Crusoe's shipwreck is providential, a signal instance of divine displeasure at man's sustained disobedience. His subsequent moral and spiritual regeneration, over the next twenty-eight years, constitutes a meticulously detailed allegory. Defoe's projection of assertive economic individualism leading to conversion and subsequent zealous piety hijacks the genre to extend a distinctively Puritan epistemology to a numberless congregation of readers. Overwriting the voyage narrative with a discourse that attenuated the form's stylized empiricism was a creative masterstroke. At the same time, the duality of *Robinson Crusoe*—its combination of maritime adventure and religious allegory—mapped precisely the expectations of the two most important literary consumer groups. Defoe published a sequel, *The Farther Adventures of Robinson Crusoe*, just four months later.

*Captain Singleton* charts the career of its eponymous hero, a pirate, in a way that develops *Robinson Crusoe*'s winning formula. Defoe introduces a Quaker, William Walters, whose steady Puritan influence brings about Singleton's repentance after a life of spectacular criminality. Upon these sure foundations Defoe erects two monumental geographic discoveries, one in each half of the novel. First, Singleton traverses the unexplored regions of the African interior. Second, he sails south along the uncharted eastern coast of Australia, describing what he sees. In the process Defoe achieves a breathtaking degree of topographical accuracy. He correctly indicates Lake Victoria as the source of the Nile, almost 150 years before the fact was established, and he dismisses the existence of *Terra Australis Incognita* half a century before James Cook sailed on a reciprocal course along the same littoral to achieve the same end. Defoe simply trained his mind's eye on the last two significant blanks on the world's maps and inscribed them, certain that he would be dead before any contradictory evidence might come to light.

*A New Voyage round the World* is a problematic novel slanted toward a readership of merchants and projectors. It was probably written as a response, matured over many years, to the inception of South Sea Company in 1711. Robert Harley conceived the company as a means of relieving the treasury of a floating national debt, amounting to nearly ten million pounds. Profits were to be derived from commercial enterprise in the Pacific, and sole trading rights in Spanish America were granted, but the company collapsed amid scandal in 1720. Defoe has often been blamed as the originator of the scheme, whereas he was in fact deeply skeptical of it. In 1711 he proposed an alternative plan to Harley's, involving the establishment of a British colony in modern Chile and Argentina. This scheme seems to inform the novel.

Published less than six months after Harley's death, *A New Voyage round the World* was to be Defoe's last novel. It is a *roman à thèse* designed to enlist the sympathy of its readers for a serious scheme of colonization and commerce. This time Defoe used the voyage narrative as economic propaganda, refining mercantilist ideology (by which national power is protected through the exploitation of a large labor force, with profits contained within national boundaries) with new ideas concerning free trade (by which artificial restrictions on the level or composition of trade are lifted). The result is a desultory affair, a dull narrative of circumnavigation in an easterly direction by anonymous multinational traders with all eyes peeled for potential markets. It lacks Defoe's customary insights into human nature, and his stale treatment of familiar themes is evidence of his failure to reinvent his colonial project successfully in fiction. The plan was simply too ambitious to be contained within a single voyage.

## Defoe as Historian

Defoe's voyage narratives form a special subgenre within the canon of his writings. They complement other narratives about military adventurers and urban delinquents, highlighting the author's grasp of important cultural issues and their potential potency in the literary marketplace. He almost certainly drew widely on contemporary published sources, and his earlier career as a journalist no doubt had an incalculable effect in alerting him to materials that might be exploited. Tradition has it that Crusoe is a reflection of Alexander Selkirk (1676–1721), circumnavigator, whose contrarious nature manifested itself at an early age in his determination to go to sea against his father's wishes. Selkirk spent four years alone on the island of Juan Fernández until he was recovered on February 2, 1709, when two Bristol privateers, *Duke* and *Duchess* (with William Dampier on board *Duke*), touched at the islands. Although there are points of similarity between Defoe's novel and Richard Steele's published account of Selkirk's isolation (*The Englishman*, December 1–3, 1713), the same is true of many other potential sources. Available evidence will admit only that Defoe was probably familiar with a fraction of the innumerable voyage narratives depicting shipwreck that were available and that his novel is probably informed by some of these.

Defoe's seascapes afford an elastic membrane containing a complex exploration of the political, economic, and social implications of Britain's projection of power at sea. *Robinson Crusoe* cast a voyage narrative into the most significant early example of imaginative prose fiction in the whole of English literature. It influenced the shape of the novel at a crucial stage in its early development, and it generated a new literary subgenre, the robinsonade. If Defoe went on to write the voyages that constitute Charles Johnson's *General History of the Most Notorious Pyrates* (1724 and 1728), as some scholars maintain, he deserves further recognition as the greatest contemporary historian of piracy in the golden age.

[*See also* English Literature *and* Literature, *subentry on* Voyage Narratives.]

## Bibliography

Backscheider, Paula. *Daniel Defoe: His Life*. Baltimore and London: Johns Hopkins University Press, 1989.

Defoe, Daniel. *Captain Singleton*. Edited by Shiv K. Kumar. London: Oxford University Press, 1969.

Defoe, Daniel. *A New Voyage round the World*. Edited by George A. Aitken. London: Dent, 1895.

Defoe, Daniel. *Robinson Crusoe*. Edited by Tom Keymer. Oxford: Oxford University Press, 2005.

Defoe, Daniel. *Serious Reflections during the Life and Surprising Adventures of Robinson Crusoe*. London, 1720.

Edwards, Philip. *The Story of the Voyage*. Cambridge, U.K.: Cambridge University Press, 1994.

Fishman, Burton J. "Defoe, Herman Moll, and the Geography of South America." *Huntingdon Library Quarterly* 36, no. 3 (1973): 227–238.

Foulke, Robert. *The Sea Voyage Narrative*. London: Prentice Hall, 1997.

Jack, Jane H. "A New Voyage round the World: Defoe's Roman à Thèse." *Huntingdon Library Quarterly* 24, no. 4 (1961): 323–336.

Johnson, Charles. *A General History of the Pyrates*. Edited by Manuel Schonhorn. London: Dover, 1999.

McKeon, Michael. *The Origins of the English Novel: 1600–1740*. Baltimore: Johns Hopkins University Press, 1988.

Starr, George A. *Defoe and Spiritual Autobiography*. Princeton, N.J.: Princeton University Press, 1965.

Williams, Glyndwr. *The Great South Sea: English Voyages and Encounters, 1570–1750*. New Haven, Conn.: Yale University Press, 1997.

JAMES KELLY

**Degaussing.** *See* Magnetism, *subentry on* Ship's Magnetism.

**Desertion.** *See* Discipline and Punishment, *subentry on* An Overview.

**Destroyer.** *See* Warships, *subentry on* Modern Warships.

**Dhow.** *See* Islamic World Vessels.

**Diaries.** *See* Autobiographies, Journals, and Diaries.

**Diet.** *See* Health and Health Care.

# Discipline and Punishment

This entry contains three subentries:

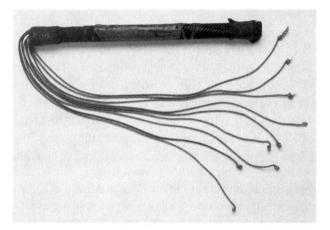

**Cat O' Nine Tails.** The name for this instrument of naval punishment, perhaps deriving from the wounds it inflicts, which are similar to cat scratches, was first recorded in English in 1694. It is similar to instruments used in other countries, such as the Dutch *zevenstaart*. © NATIONAL MARITIME MUSEUM, LONDON

## An Overview

General William T. Sherman once remarked that "an army is a collection of armed men obliged to obey one man." In essence, the same has always been true of ships at sea. Be it a merchantman peacefully plodding from one port of call to another or a man-of-war actively seeking an engagement with the enemy, the hazards of the sea require that the crew of a ship be ready at any time to carry out the orders of their captain and his designated officers. The annals of maritime history are replete with stories of ships and squadrons that were saved from disaster by well-disciplined ship's companies responding promptly to orders. Likewise, many shipwrecks and defeats can be ascribed to breakdowns in discipline and dereliction of duty. Although maritime technology has changed and advanced through the ages, the need for effective command and control at sea never changes, and this has resulted in a body of law and tradition that has evolved from earliest times through today.

### Ancient Codes and Practices

Maritime trade and commerce had its earliest beginnings along the rivers of Egypt and Mesopotamia and the shores of the eastern Mediterranean. The oldest known law code, the *Code of Hammurabi* (eighteenth century

B.C.E.), not only detailed how contracts for the carriage of goods by ships should be drawn up and administered, but also specified punishments for captains who deliberately sank their vessels to collect the insurance. The first legal code specifically dealing with maritime affairs was the *Lex Rhodia*, which dates from around 480 B.C.E. This code was dedicated primarily to regulating contracts and other matters pertaining to cargo handling, but it did contain provisions for punishing sailors for fighting among themselves. It also specified that merchants, captains, or officers who gravely injured or killed sailors by punching or kicking them—presumably while enforcing discipline—should be fined or even put to death. This punishment of officers highlights a problem that persists on board merchant vessels even today. The captain and his officers are the sole enforcers of discipline at sea; they rely mainly on their own physical prowess and moral authority, but if their methods exceed certain limits, they can find themselves in trouble when the ship reaches port. For instance, the famous American naval officer John Paul Jones found his career as a merchant ship captain cut short in 1773 when a powerful blow that he gave to a common sailor led to the sailor's death and to Jones's own flight from arrest and trial.

Normally, however, naval discipline has focused on controlling the crew rather than on the officers. The crew of a naval vessel not only must be orderly enough to cope with the normal perils of the sea, but also must be steady enough to sail their ship into battle and risk their lives in unhesitating obedience to their officers' commands. The existence of navies goes back to at least 1200 B.C.E., when the Egyptians built a fleet to patrol the eastern shore of the Mediterranean. Full-fledged naval battles were fought throughout the period among the Egyptians, Phoenicians, Persians, Greeks, and eventually the Romans. These were battles between fleets of oared galleys, some manned by slaves chained to their sweeps and some manned by free citizens serving their polis. No official naval code of discipline is known to exist until the Romans built an extensive navy during the Punic Wars (264–202 B.C.E.) and adopted the law of the Roman legions, the *Magistri Militum*, to govern it. This code, which took as its basic rationale the premise that "the sailors should fear their own officers more than they fear the enemy," became the basis for the Articles of War that governed all European-pattern navies until well after the end of World War II.

The Articles of War differed substantially from the maritime codes that governed merchant ships. The captain of a naval vessel had a much more elaborate personnel structure to administer, with layers of subordinate commissioned officers, warrant officers, petty officers, and ratings arranged in a rigid hierarchy. For minor offenses, the captain could hold court at sea and prescribe his own punishments, most of which were traditional and customary. For major offenses, many of which carried the possibility of a death sentence, the captain could fall back on an elaborate system of justice involving courts of inquiry, court-martial boards, judge advocates, defense counsel, rules of evidence, sworn testimony, cross-examination, and review by higher authority. Unlike the merchant captain who was subject to shoreside criminal and admiralty courts, the naval captain was answerable only within the service, and it was universally assumed that men serving in the navy had given up the legal rights and protections that civilians, including merchant mariners, usually enjoyed. The navies of the Roman Empire could not be sustained into the Middle Ages, so written evidence regarding discipline at sea is sparse until the age of exploration and the modern era. Presumably the Vikings, Anglo-Saxons, Normans, Saracens, Chinese, Venetians, and other ancient and medieval seafaring nations enforced discipline on board their ships, but little is known on the subject until voyages are chronicled. Columbus's journal and the accounts of his voyages make clear that he was obliged to rely mainly on the force of his personality and the occasional unsheathing of his sword to control his flagship's crew, and that he never fully mastered the other captains in his fleet.

## More Modern Naval Codes and Practices

After 1500, the gradual evolution of modern national navies begins, and with it the tradition of severe disciplinary practices aimed at the common seamen. Officers, on the other hand, were treated with increasing lenience and delicacy, as was thought to befit their status as "gentlemen." The primary punishments for minor offenses—flogging with a cat-o'-nine-tails, confinement in irons, a bread-and-water diet, and running the gauntlet—and also the punishments for serious offenses—keelhauling or flogging to death—were obviously inherited from Roman times. The advent of sailing ships added hanging from the yardarm and being shot out of a cannon to the list of drastic punishments, and sometimes new methods were devised. In the seventeenth-century Dutch navy, for example, one penalty for striking a superior officer was for the miscreant to be hung in a basket from the bowsprit with a bottle of beer, a loaf of bread, and a knife. When he had endured his limit of hunger, thirst, and discomfort, he was expected to use the knife to cut away the rope holding the basket and consign himself to the sea. Continental navies like the French and Spanish fleets were known for the harshest discipline and indeed used some revolting punishments. The British fleet had Articles of War, first promulgated in 1661 and periodically revised, that were just as harsh, but they were somewhat tempered by an informal social contract that existed between free common Englishmen and their gentleman superiors. It was generally understood that the crews had certain traditional prerogatives and indulgences, and that if the officers respected these, then the bulk of the men would do their duty without the need for much compulsion. In fact, ambitious common sailors could attach themselves to a promising officer's retinue, following him from command to command and exchanging service and loyalty for advancement. Because of their status as gentlemen, officers above warrant rank could not be physically chastised. Their only punishments consisted of being relieved of duty, confined to their quarters, put on watch and watch, relieved of command, suspended from duty, or dismissed from the service. The execution of Admiral John Byng for losing a battle off Minorca in 1756 was a glaring exception.

The one naval crime that all officers lived in fear of was, of course, mutiny. The wresting of command of a ship or fleet from the hands of its lawfully appointed officers by all or part of the crew was relatively rare before the age of the French Revolution; when mutiny did happen, it was often the result of overzealous discipline that crossed the line between harshness and sadism. Such was the case of Captain Hugh Pigot of the British frigate *Hermione* in 1797: Pigot's excesses drove his crew to murder him and some of his officers and even to deliver their ship to the Spanish, with whom Britain was at war at the time. With the advent of the French Revolution, virtually the entire officer corps of France's navy was put off their ships, and sailors from the lower decks were placed in command with a mandate to apply the principles of liberty, fraternity, and equality to the governance of the fleet. The results of this experiment were chaotic ships, botched campaigns, and consistent defeats in battle. Eventually, under Napoleon, traditional officers and orthodox discipline were restored, but the damage could never be entirely repaired. At about the same time, the British endured mass uprisings at their fleet anchorages at Spithead and the Nore. While there was some slight contact between the mutineers and French revolutionaries, the real cause of these uprisings was the British Parliament's neglect to pay the men their wages and the influx of many pressed men into the service. With a slight improvement in wages and conditions, the mutinous squadrons were returned to duty—although a few ringleaders paid the ultimate price for their revolt.

When navies entered the era of steam and steel, the nature of service at sea changed. Boilers and engines, power-operated turret guns, electrical and hydraulic auxiliaries, and radio and other technologies demanded highly skilled and relatively well-educated sailors, but the attitudes and disciplinary practices of the officers were slow to make the transition. Although flogging and other Roman-derived forms of punishment were generally phased out by the mid-nineteenth century, most navies still followed the well-worn paths of harshness and punitive treatment and preserved the extreme social gap between the officers and the ratings. The result was that navies performed well enough in peacetime, but when war came and conditions became more stressful, whole fleets became unstable. The Russian navy experienced extensive mutinies in 1905 and again in 1917. The German and Austro-Hungarian fleets revolted on the cusp of their national defeat in 1918. The crews of French warships sent to patrol in Russian waters in 1919 staged work stoppages, and in 1931 the British Home Fleet was temporarily crippled by a seaman's strike over a 10 percent pay cut.

World War II brought about a tremendous if temporary expansion of the navies of the United States, Britain, and Canada. Literally millions of young people who had been socialized in democratic societies came face to face with the arcane strictures of the Articles of War, often applied in an arbitrary and illogical manner by hastily trained reserve officers. The memories and impressions of naval service that these wartime sailors carried back into civilian life soon led the British navy to democratize its practices, while the United States Navy scrapped the ancient Articles of War in favor of a newly formulated Uniform Code of Military Justice that brought military jurisprudence more into line with civilian practice and established a body of legal professionals, the Judge Advocate General's Corps, to regularize the administration of military law. Since 1950, all the navies of the NATO powers and many others have revamped their attitudes toward naval discipline to encourage reenlistment, advancement and promotion, the acquisition and improvement of technical skills, and service pride. These are essential for personnel who must operate the highly complex mechanisms that are modern warships. One recent social experiment, the integration of women into warship's crews, has led to some new disciplinary issues. These include fraternization, sudden unavailability of key personnel because of pregnancy or child-care issues, romantic rivalries on shipboard, and even excessive water consumption. Contemporary navies also have to address crimes that their personnel commit off-station and against civilians. The old-fashioned shore patrols of yesteryear have been largely replaced by professional military policemen and detectives working for the Naval Criminal Investigative Service.

## Modern Changes in Practices on Board Merchant Ships

There has also been an evolution regarding disciplinary methods on board merchant ships. During the nineteenth century, sailing merchantmen reached their zenith with the introduction of the fast packets and clipper ships. The demand for speed under sail led to larger ships with tall, heavily sparred rigs. To sail these vessels and make them pay, merchant seamen had to be driven as mercilessly as the ships themselves, and this gave rise to "hell ships" captained by ruthless masters backed up by as many as four "buckoo" mates. Prime seamen became scarce as slowly rising standards of living ashore and factory employment lured the better men away from the seafaring life. The large crews necessary to handle the new ships had to be filled out with waterfront toughs, men crimped and shanghaied from bars and brothels, and social misfits. The life of a merchant seaman afloat had never been easy, as Richard Henry Dana's *Two Years before the Mast* (1840) testifies, but now the work was much harder, treatment was more severe, and green or ham-handed sailors were taught their craft with the help of fists, boots, and belaying pins.

The advent of steam-driven merchant ships did little to improve things at first. Sailing ships, with their low operating costs, forced steamship operators with higher overheads to economize by cutting crew-related expenses. Food was poor, living quarters were cramped and rudimentary, and wages were held to very low levels. Sailing-ship operators replied by building ever larger vessels, switching from wood to iron construction, replacing hemp rigging with steel wire, and replacing wooden masts and yards with tubular-steel top hampers. Crew size was cut so drastically that a huge wooden Yankee downeaster or a British four-masted steel bark often set sail with a mere twenty men to serve as foremast hands. The captain now had only two mates to enforce his will, both mates chosen as much for their handiness with their fists as for their knowledge of celestial navigation. The resulting brutality led to very few mutinies, but it did cause many men to jump ship, leaving before their shipping articles had been fulfilled and thus forfeiting their pay. In extreme cases, where men had died from beatings or been permanently maimed, newspaper publicity or lawsuits might lead to the arrest and imprisonment of an overzealous mate. Oddly enough, captains were seldom held responsible in such cases.

## Changed Practices with Unions and World War II

The long twilight of sailing ships and the large-scale conversion to steam navigation in the late nineteenth and early twentieth centuries coincided with the rise of the labor movement. One of the pioneers of maritime unionism was Andrew Furuseth, founder of the Sailor's Union of the Pacific (SUP). Soon after its inception, this organization began to publish a newsletter called *The Red Record* to expose and publicize instances of criminal brutality on ships plying the Cape Horn route and discharging crews at West Coast ports. Furuseth's exposés highlighted particularly notorious ships, like the barks *Reaper* and *Harvester*, and eventually resulted in the imprisonment of mates like "Bully" Hansen, who had boasted that he killed a man

on every voyage. The union men were themselves a pretty tough lot. As membership grew, they sought to monopolize the crewing of ships, often fighting pitched battles with scab crews hired by owners who hated the very idea of unionization. To make matters worse, rival unions sprang up, most notably the Maritime Federation of the Pacific (MFP) and the National Maritime Union (NMU).

The SUP was essentially anarchist in its philosophy, and by the 1930s it was affiliated with the American Federation of Labor. The MFP and the NMU were radically socialist in their politics and closely aligned with the Congress of Industrial Organizations. As the last of the sailing ships disappeared from the waterfront, the two groups of unions fought it out with each other over whose members would man the threadbare steamers of the Depression era. Militant seamen waved union rulebooks under the noses of angry mates and skippers. So-called sea lawyers and performers staged quickie strikes that were supported by equally militant longshoremen. In 1934 and again in 1937 the MFP succeeded in crippling the entire San Francisco waterfront in labor actions that almost took on the character of civic insurrections. Under the leadership of the SUP's Harry Bridges and the NMU's Joe Curran, centuries of maritime tradition were aggressively challenged and largely undone.

World War II forced an uneasy compromise among the contending forces. The unions wanted desperately to preserve their hard-won gains, and the government needed a drastically expanded and totally reliable merchant marine to carry the weapons of war. In return for union-scale wages and union-dictated living and working conditions, the unions agreed to a no-strike pledge and took responsibility for removing recalcitrant seamen and other performers, in effect becoming the ultimate enforcers of discipline. Because ships in wartime sailed under navy orders, any merchant seaman who failed to report for duty or jumped ship was subject to a military tribunal and imprisonment.

During the course of the war, all the Allied merchant marines expanded drastically, almost fivefold in the case of the United States, but when the war was over there began a long, slow decline. Unionized merchant ships required not only higher pay but much-improved food, better sleeping arrangements, and the payment of overtime wages for any work done outside of normal watch standing. American ship owners either quit the business altogether or set up new corporations under flags of convenience. After a certain time lag, the steamship companies of the European maritime nations followed suit. Most of the ships that have plied the high seas since the 1990s have become effectively internationalized. Owners taking refuge behind a bewildering array of multinational corporations and charter parties have become difficult to identify. The manning of a single ship might involve deck officers from one country, engineer officers from another, and common seamen from yet a third nation. Many seamen are from poor countries and sail under yearlong contracts. Their craft has decayed to the point where it requires little more than watch keeping, line handling, lifeboat drill, and an endless round of chipping and painting rust. What happens on board these multinational and multiethnic ships in terms of discipline and abusiveness is largely a mystery, save for rare occasions when there is a murder or when some pattern of severe mistreatment causes desperate sailors to seek shoreside intervention by smuggling a message ashore or by escaping the ship and seeking asylum.

As things stand now, naval discipline continues to modernize and become more humane and liberalized. Navy sailors who have undergone extensive technical training and acquired valuable expertise are treated more like valuable members of a team, and the best among them are actively encouraged to upgrade to officer status. Merchant seamen have proved much more difficult to emancipate. The labor movement helped for a time until the ship owners found a way to leave the unions behind, restoring once again the conditions that prevailed under the old *Lex Rhodia*.

[*See also* Courts; Law; Naval Administration; Shipping, *subentry on* State-owned Shipping; *and* Unions.]

## Bibliography

Byrne, Edward M. *Military Law*. Annapolis, Md.: Naval Institute Press, 1970.
Dugan, James. *The Great Mutiny*. New York: Putnam, 1965.
Generous, William T. *Swords and Scales: The Development of the Uniform Code of Military Justice*. Port Washington, N.Y.: Kennikat, 1973.
Haws, Duncan, and Alex A. Hurst. *The Maritime History of the World*. 2 vols. Brighton, U.K.: Teredo Books, 1985.
Hill, J. R., ed. *The Oxford Illustrated History of the Royal Navy*. New York: Oxford University Press, 1995.
Horn, Daniel. *The German Naval Mutinies of World War I*. New Brunswick, N.J.: Rutgers University Press, 1969.
Kemp, Peter, ed. *The Oxford Companion to Ships and the Sea*. Oxford: Oxford University Press, 1976.
Newell, Gordon. *Sea Rogues Gallery*. Seattle, Wash.: Superior Publishing, 1971.
Rodger, N. A. M. *The Wooden World: An Anatomy of the Georgian Navy*. London: Collins, 1986.
Valle, James E. *Rocks and Shoals: Order and Discipline in the Old Navy, 1800–1861*. Annapolis, Md.: Naval Institute Press, 1980.

JAMES E. VALLE

## Galley Discipline and Punishment

In the history of the Mediterranean world during the early modern period, particularly in France, the Italian states, Malta, the North African states, Spain, and Turkey, the oarsmen of galleys have conjured associations with religious intolerance, cruelty, oppression, arbitrary arrests, and all the worst aspects of forced labor afloat. In the late seventeenth and early eighteenth centuries, French Protestants and their supporters widely publicized the notorious cruelty associated with religious and social injustice when thousands of Protestants were condemned to the galleys for religious reasons. In the eighteenth century, galleys seemed, in some quarters, to symbolize reactionary thinking. By the mid-nineteenth century, the notoriety of galley punishment had been romanticized, and Victor Hugo (1802–1885) perpetuated this image through his character Jean Valjean in the novel *Les Misérables* (1862). This has been further perpetuated through modern film interpretations.

All galleys were labor-intensive vessels. When fully manned, each vessel typically required from 350 to 500 men for propulsion. Those that employed these vessels had to search widely and intensively for sufficient manpower. While the religious aspects were widely known, it was less well known that galleys were also manned by captured Muslim slaves as well as by a wide range of criminals. While the experiences within France are most widely known, domestic courts in the southern German states, Austria, and Switzerland sentenced offenders to service in the Papal navy as well as in war galleys of Venice, Genoa, and Naples from the middle of the sixteenth century through the mid-eighteenth century. Even before sentencing to the galleys became an option in French law in 1676, it was already an option in use in French judicial practice to commute a death sentence to a life term as a galley oarsman. People convicted of desertion from the army as well as those convicted for theft, blasphemy, sacrilege, perjury, begging, vagabondage, falsehood in giving oaths, and unspecified reasons were sent to man galley oars.

The galley did play a role in the history of the Counter-Reformation, and Protestants were exceptionally harshly treated in galleys, but historians have shown that conditions changed over time and that there were different circumstances and treatment for different types of oarsmen. In France and elsewhere in Europe, the use of galleys for penal detention was dramatically reformed between 1700 and 1748. By the 1770s and 1780s further improvements for correctional and rehabilitative purposes were introduced. By the end of the ancien régime in France, the galleys were a remarkable, but little appreciated, example of an exceptional penal system that was ahead of its time and contrasted with that ashore, where conditions were extremely harsh and prisons even required prisoners to pay, or to find someone one to pay, for their food. By this era, states were interested in preserving the health, physical well-being, and even the spiritual welfare of those condemned to provide the motive power of these warships, and they provided an abundance of food and clothing for them. In nearly every respect, galley punishment was an exception in the history of European criminal punishment.

[*See also* Galley; Propulsion, *subentry on* Hand Power; *and* Shipboard Life.]

## Bibliography

Bamford, Paul W. *Fighting Ships and Prisons: The Mediterranean Galleys of France in the Age of Louis XIV*. Minneapolis: University of Minnesota Press, 1973.

Mallet, Michael Edward, ed. *The Florentine Galleys in the Fifteenth Century: With the Diary of Luca di Maso degli Albizzi, Captain of the Galleys, 1429–1430*. Oxford: Clarendon Press, 1967.

Monga, Luigi, trans. and ed. *The Journal of Aurelio Scetti: A Florentine Galley Slave at Lepanto (1565–1577)*. Medieval and Renaissance Texts and Studies, vol. 266. Tempe: Arizona Center for Medieval and Renaissance Studies, 2004.

Schlosser, Hans. "Der Mensch als Ware: Die Galleerenstrafe in Süddeutschland als Reaktion auf Presirevolution und Großmachtpolitik (16.–18. Jahrhundert)." In *Aktuelle Probleme der Marktwitshaft in gesamt- und einzelwirtshaftlicher Sicht: Festgabe zum 65. Geburtstag von Louis Perridon*, edited by Reinhard Blum and Manfred Steiner, pp. 87–114. Berlin: Duncker and Humblot, 1984.

Schlosser, Hans. "Die infamierende Strafe der Galeere." In *Festshrift für Hans Thieme zu seinem 80. Geburtstag*, edited by Karl Kroeschell, pp. 253–263. Sigmaringen, Germany: Jan Thorbecke, 1986.

Schlosser, Hans. "Die Strafe der Galeere als poena arbitraria in der mediterranen Strafpraxis." *Zeitschrift für neue Rechtsgeschichte* 19, nos. 1–2 (1988): 18–37.

Schlosser, Hans. "Die Strafe der Galeere als Verdachtstrafe." In *Nit anders denn liebs und guets: Peterhauser Kolloquium aus Anlaß des achtzigsten Geburtstags von Karl S. Bader*, edited by Clausdieter Schott and Caludio Soliva, pp. 133–141. Sigmaringen, Germany: Jan Throbecke, 1986.

JOHN B. HATTENDORF

# Naval Discipline and Punishment

The essentially risky business of seafaring required that a ship should be operated in an efficient and orderly manner, and this in turn dictated from the earliest times a disciplined approach and a hierarchical crew structure. In vessels whose principal function was war or warlike activity, this requirement was reinforced by a need for effective deployment of force in action and thus, often, by a need for the well-drilled and directed use of violence.

Such discipline was common in the naval forces of ancient Greece and Rome. The oared propulsion of war vessels, with its premium on precise and strong physical movement that did not interfere with similar activity adjacent to it, made an additional demand for order and cohesion. Enforcement in galleys crewed by freemen had to be a mixture of incentive, cajolery, and punishment of transgressors; in oared vessels propelled by slaves, the sanction of physical punishment was proportionately far greater.

When sail became the principal motive force, the need for skill in handling a ship was enhanced, while the need for physical effort, though still important, was proportionately diminished. In consequence, a spread of expertise in managing steering, ropes, and sails was required, and there developed a more complex hierarchy involving subordinate officers and key skilled enlisted men. In addition, the handling of armament, now including firearms from musketry to great guns, required new and complex drills, again involving middle managers and specialists. These activities—the working of the ship and its conduct in battle—for some time remained under separate commands, but by the sixteenth century, experience in armed vessels (which most ships were, even if they engaged in trading) showed that a unified structure under a single officer (called the captain) was necessary for the safe and effective discharge of a ship's functions.

As national navies became established in the sixteenth and seventeenth centuries, a corpus of discipline developed by custom in each service, but there were wide variations among ships and among nations. In England, the first codification of rules was made in the Articles of War of 1652, with a revised version issued under the crown in 1661. Yet these codes did not seek to regulate every aspect of good order in the king's ships or to prescribe specific punishments for each breach; they were directed mainly at the conduct of officers and confined provisions concerning the ship's company to generalities that captains and officers could interpret as they saw fit. Even when the Articles of War were revised in 1749, ninety years later, the same approach applied; the main effect of the revision was to discourage captains and officers from holding back in action, as had occurred at the Battle of Toulon in 1744. The death penalty became mandatory under several such articles, and it was under one of these that Admiral John Byng was shot in 1757 after losing the Battle of Minorca.

Action against the enemy apart, offenses in warships fell into two categories: civil crimes and misdemeanors (theft, murder, and fighting among equals), and professional misconduct (insubordination, striking superior officers, negligence, and absence from duty). Spanning the two, and often responsible for other offenses, was drunkenness. Because a ship was often far from land and any civil authority, jurisdiction over both kinds of offenses rested in the first instance with the captain. He had wide powers to punish summarily, but he could also refer the more serious alleged offenses to a court-martial if there were sufficient ships in company to form a court.

In the seventeenth and eighteenth centuries, by far the most common sentence on naval enlisted men was flogging with a lash. It has been calculated that over 85 percent of convicted miscreants were punished in this way. The procedure was well established by custom: a day after sentence, which gave all concerned some time for reflection, the man was bound to a grating and then, in the presence of all officers and ship's company, with the marine contingent standing guard, was subjected to the prescribed number of lashes, delivered by a boatswain's mate (or a succession of them if the sentence was heavy) on his bared back with a cat-o'-nine-tails. On completion, he would be taken below and put under medical supervision.

Flogging in this way was a brutal punishment, but it lasted only a short while, and the main aftermath was physical. There is much evidence that it was accepted as a fact of naval life and was generally taken as just. Moreover, the alternatives were limited: deprivation of liberty was difficult to manage within the confines of a ship, deprivation of pay had no immediacy when payments were few and far between, and the more bizarre punishments, such as running the gauntlet, were appropriate only to certain offenses, such as theft.

For very serious offenses, more condign punishments than flogging at the gangway were available. Death, normally by hanging at the yardarm, was reserved for murder and sodomy (both very rare), mutiny, and some cases of desertion. Flogging round the fleet, where the miscreant was taken in a boat and subjected to a certain number of lashes alongside each ship, was viewed by courts-martial, which alone had authority to order it, as an alternative to the death penalty. Convicted officers could face a wider variety of punishments, all meted out by court-martial: dismissal from the ship or service, reduction in rank, loss of seniority, and mulcts (or penalties) of pay. Officers' offenses also covered a wider range, including embezzlement, various kinds of professional negligence, and in some cases cruel treatment of their ships' companies. Yet this did not deter some captains from inhuman treatment of their men; well known is the extreme case on board *Hermione*, where Captain *Hugh Pigot* and several officers were murdered by an enraged crew (1795).

In the navies of other European countries and the United States, up to 1815 discipline and punishment varied in detail but not in essence. France had the additional sanction of service in the galleys for more serious offenses, the Dutch were said to engage in keelhauling, and the Russians made use of the knout (a whip), but the principles of short, sharp, summary punishment held for all fleets. Indeed, little change was observable up to the middle of the nineteenth century, although with more ordered training and conditions of service, including more regular pay and leave, there was relaxation of the harsher elements of discipline and punishment.

In the second half of the nineteenth century there occurred a much higher degree of codification. In Britain, the Naval Discipline Acts of 1860–1866, with the closely adjacent Queen's Regulations and Admiralty Instructions, laid down in detail the duties and responsibilities of all naval personnel, the offenses created by neglect or infraction of those obligations, and in many cases the maximum punishments for them. The Royal Navy suspended flogging in peacetime in 1871 and altogether in 1879.

Other navies similarly clarified their disciplinary codes in this period. They were helped by a long period free of major naval wars yet full of minor conflicts, many of a colonial nature, that gave opportunities for action and prestige at home. The generally good image of navies meant that discipline was relatively easy to preserve, though drink continued to generate a certain amount of disorder. Mulcts of pay and leave became more important sanctions.

Yet national characteristics continued to have a powerful bearing. In the young Imperial Japanese Navy, the most powerful motivator was often fear of shame at having done something wrong. The Imperial German Navy was rigidly hidebound by social ranks and a professional pecking order. The Tsarist navy was notable for its backward attitude to discipline, and this resulted in a strongly revolutionary attitude first seen in 1905 but extending through to 1921. The Soviet navy thereafter featured political commissars in ships, though command was vested in the captain. Prestige did much to motivate discipline in the U.S. Navy. This prestige was engendered by the strategic theories of Admiral Alfred Thayer Mahan and the navy's successful war against Spain in 1898; its sailors in the Great White Fleet (1908) were regarded as ambassadors for their country.

During World War I, discipline in all fleets was tested by the rigors of long vigils in northern waters and by convoy and submarine campaigns. Mutiny and unrest in the German High Seas Fleet in 1917–1918 was a contributing cause of Germany's eventual collapse. Even though there was a great influx of conscripts during World War II, particularly into the Royal and U.S. navies, there was no less a disciplined approach than in previous conflicts, but it was more realistic and less rigid, and in practice it was more effective.

The second half of the twentieth century saw increasing freedom of both conduct and expression, notably in western countries, and naval discipline reacted as might have been expected. In many cases financial penalties replaced more physical ones, though deprivation of liberty remained a sanction. The presence of women in many warships brought some new problems, nearly all satisfactorily solved after initial difficulties.

A conclusion reached by most historians is that naval discipline and punishment have throughout the ages corresponded closely with the laws, manners, and customs of the time on shore. Where they did not, naval efficiency suffered.

[*See also* Mahan, Alfred Thayer; Mutiny; *and* Shipboard Life.]

### Bibliography

Byrn, John D., Jr. *Crime and Punishment in the Royal Navy*. Aldershot, U.K.: Scolar Press, 1989.

Davies, J. D. *Gentlemen and Tarpaulins: The Officers and Men of the Restoration Navy*. Oxford: Clarendon Press, 1991.

Herwig, Holger H. *"Luxury Fleet": The Imperial German Navy, 1888–1918*. London: Allen and Unwin, 1980.

Howarth, Stephen. *Morning Glory: A History of the Imperial Japanese Navy*. London: Hamish Hamilton, 1983.

Lavery, B., ed. *Shipboard Life and Organization 1731–1815*. Aldershot, U.K.: Ashgate for the Navy Records Society, 1998.

Morris, James M. *History of the US Navy*. London: Hamlyn, 1984.

Pacini, Eugene. *La marine*. Luxembourg: Collections Mémoires, 1996.

Pope, Dudley. *Life in Nelson's Navy*. London: Chatham, 1997.

Rodger, N. A. M. *Articles of War: The Statutes Which Governed Our Fighting Navies, 1661, 1749, and 1886*. Havant, U.K.: Kenneth Mason, 1982.

Rodger, N. A. M. *The Wooden World: An Anatomy of the Georgian Navy*. London: Collins, 1986.

Ropp, Theodore. *The Development of a Modern Navy: French Naval Policy, 1871–1904*. Shrewsbury, U.K.: Tri-Service Press, 1987.

Saunders, Malcolm George, ed. *The Soviet Navy*. London: Weidenfeld and Nicholson, 1958.

Wells, John. *The Royal Navy: An Illustrated Social History, 1870–1982*. Stroud, U.K.: Alan Sutton with the Royal Naval Museum, 1994.

J. RICHARD HILL

# Docks and Slips

In the time of wooden shipbuilding, vessels were built on the waterfront on suitable terrain and were launched after completion of the hull. The slipway, an inclined surface leading to the waterway, was usually reinforced with discarded timber, thus providing a solid floor. An exception was the Dutch East India Company yard in Amsterdam, where a purpose-built beech floor, complete with pile-foundation, was uncovered in the 1990s.

The keel was laid on a series of wooden blocks, and the hull was supported by posts. Wax or fat or another slick material was applied to the keel before launching, although for ships to get stuck on the slipway was not uncommon. In the Dutch Republic the practice of building ships with their bows facing the waterfront prevailed, whereas in England and France ships were launched stern first. Wherever there was insufficient space for launching forward or backward, ships were launched sideways—a practice still in use in the twenty-first century. In the eighteenth century, naval vessels in France were launched in a cradle, a sliding structure between the keel and the slipway surface, which supported the hull during launching. With the advent of steam power and the growing need of combining ship maintenance and construction, marine railways found increasing use in the nineteenth century.

### Evolution of Dry Docks

In the era of the wooden sailing ship the need for floating docks for performing ship maintenance was limited. Smaller vessels were shored up on the beach; larger ones were careened with the use of hulks or tackles ashore. However, careening was a cumbersome operation, and the forces exerted on hull and rigging could lead to structural damage. An alternative was offered by the dry dock. Initially these took the form of tidal docks, followed by graving docks (which were emptied by pumps), marine

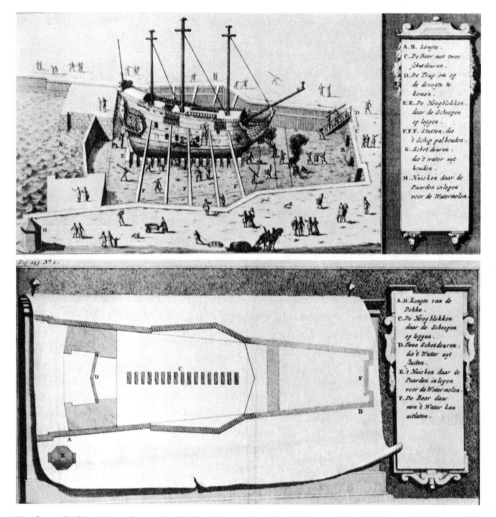

**Docks and Slips.** An early graving dock with wooden sheet-piling and double doors, Vlissingen, the Netherlands. COURTESY OF SJOERD HENGST

railways (which utilized a rolling carriage), and finally floating dry docks, which could be submerged under a vessel and then raised.

Lifting ships afloat was first practiced for a reason other than maintenance. In the Dutch Republic, silting of the Zuider Zee led to the use of so-called ship's camels to lift the bigger ships over the shallows of Pampus into Amsterdam. These lifters, invented by Meeuwis Meindertszoon Bakker around 1690, consisted of two close-fitting forms placed at either side of the ship, joined with tackles underneath the keel and then pumped dry. Their shape ensured maximum support and stability to the ship, which would be lifted only a couple of feet. Dutch craftsmen introduced the use of ship's camels in areas with similar shallow-water obstacles, like Italy (Venice) and Russia (Saint Petersburg). The Italian

engineer Marco Coronelli (1650–1718) made the first reported design of composite or sectional ship's camels.

Although the major seagoing powers recognized the necessity of dry docks for the maintenance of their navies, such structures were expensive to build. To minimize costs, in some parts of Europe hulks were beached and weighted with ballast, and then the stern was cut off and doors fit in its place to create a graving dock. An English shipmaster is said to have made a floating dry dock at Kronstadt during the reign of Peter the Great by gutting a hulk and fitting a watertight gate in its stern, and his example was followed in Britain, where numerous ships were converted into floating docks for use on the Thames. From the 1820s these were no longer tolerated because they encroached the river, but the practice has persisted in other regions.

The first design of a purpose-built floating dry dock is a French model of circa 1774, representing a sectional floating dry dock of interlocked caissons. The watertight caissons were to be emptied with hand pumps, similar to the Dutch camels. There is no report of the design ever having been carried out. Despite many patents for floating dry docks in Great Britain, France, and the United States after 1808, most engineers of the time favored marine railways. The Canada floating dock, built by John Farrington in Montreal in 1826, was the first successfully exploited floating dry dock. It had no watertight compartments and relied on the floatability of wood and on the tide. With the end gate open it would float below water level, allowing a ship afloat to enter. If the ship's draft was too great, the dock was ballasted, a ballast scow being part of the dock's equipment. The dock was then floated to its bed at high tide, where it emptied at low tide, was pumped dry, and the gate was closed and caulked. It was put into operation in 1827 in Quebec, where other docks soon followed. Solidly built, these structures lasted for decades. The earlier ones were of the box type, which enclosed the ship in its entirety. Later ones (after 1870) were of the platform type, which could accommodate ships of greater length than the dock itself.

Although news of the Quebec docks soon spread, no floating docks are reported in Europe before the 1843 wooden docks by J. D. Diets in Amsterdam, who improved and enlarged a design by the American John S. Gilbert. Diets built three steam-powered commercial docks in Amsterdam and built an even larger dock for Le Havre, which he copied again for the Dutch navy in East India, where conditions for constructing graving docks, which required excavation, were unfavorable.

The need for docks increased both with the advent of iron, because increased ship size made careening more complicated, and with the advent of steam, because paddle wheelers were almost impossible to careen, while the screw propeller required regular maintenance. For greater capacity—and to avoid shipworm in the many floating docks intended for the tropics—iron floating docks were made from the 1860s onward. In 1862, Randolph, Elder & Co. in Glasgow built an iron dock for the French navy establishment in Saigon and one for the Dutch firm Cores de Vries in Batavia (Jakarta); the latter dock sank

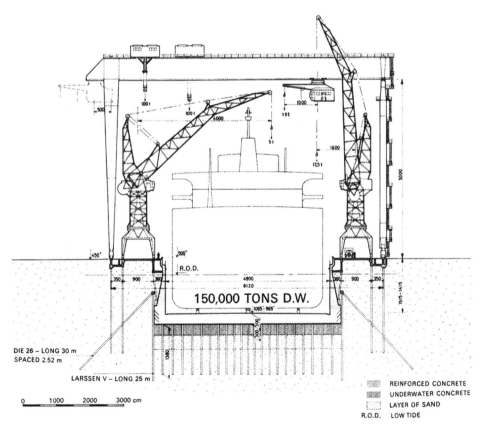

Cross section of a graving dry dock, Wilton Fijenoord. Courtesy of Sjoerd. Hengst

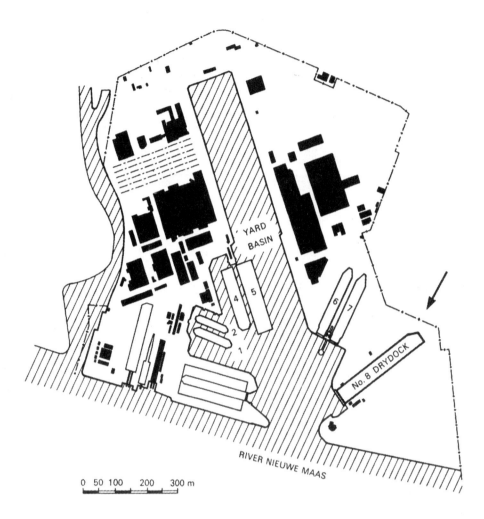

**Graving Drydock.** Location of a graving dock in a typical modern yard. This drawing of the Wilton Fijenoord Shipyard in 1971 illustrates a yard that built new ships and repaired ships. COURTESY OF SJOERD HENGST

on arrival in 1863. The first iron docks of the Dutch navy (1864 and 1876), built in Amsterdam by the Koninklijke Fabriek voor Stoom en andere Werktuigen, were also destined for Batavia. The London firm Rennie & Sons built an iron dock for the Spanish navy establishment at Cartagena, Colombia. At the 1862 World's Fair in London, several designs were shown, in addition to other systems such as hydraulic lifts.

## Graving Docks

The first dry docks completely constructed in masonry with gates date from the seventeenth century; according to J. P. Merino, the first was built between 1669 and 1671 in Rochefort, France. Operationally, the greatest problems appear to have been leaking of the doors,

manual pumping (aided by horses), and mud entering the docks when they were flooded. A notable development in graving docks was the two-section dock, the first of which was built in Rochefort between 1683 and 1700. Two graving docks were placed end to end and were separated by doors, and the entrance from the River Charente was equipped with a floatable ship door (*bateau porte*) in wood. The ship door was replaced between 1725 and 1734 by double doors because the problem of leaking had not been resolved. The identical double-section design with a floatable ship door was used for the construction of two graving docks in the Netherlands in the beginning of the nineteenth century. These three docks were still in use at the turn of the twenty-first century. The sides of the docks had platforms at different levels, while the shape of the docks followed the lines of the ships, and the platforms could serve as working areas when the ship was being repaired, cleaned, or painted. Double-section docks were later used for shipbuilding. One of the first double-section docks was built by the Chantiers de l'Atlantique as part of the assembly area of the yard.

Graving docks gradually increased in size, and the cross section of the dock became rectangular, with vertical walls and a flat floor. With the advent of oceangoing tanker vessels, graving docks became an alternative to floating docks for ship repair and as a final assembly site for new ships, floating docks being unable to accommodate the expanding very large crude carrier (VLCC) and ultra-large crude carrier (ULCC) fleets. These ships, which generally featured flat bottoms, were docked on parallel rows of blocks, which followed the shape of the hull. In some repair yards (such as Verolme Botlek in Rotterdam), a dry dock originally designed for the building of tankers of up to one million tons deadweight featured an internal partition, flexibly positioned, which made it possible to dock ships or large platforms for the offshore industry at one end for extended periods and to use the second part for short-term repair work.

Developments in European shipyards were aimed at reducing the assembly period by maximizing space and minimizing the number of modules compared with the traditional system, whereby only one ship could be handled on a slipway or in a dock. With the tandem system, two ships are built at the same time. The part of the ship containing the engine room is built for one vessel while the forward part of a second ship is assembled and joined with a previously built engine-room section. A variation on the tandem system was the "ship and a half system" of Austin & Pickersgill, in which two aft ends with engine rooms were built simultaneously side by side, together with one fore end, with the intention of building as much as possible under cover. The twin dock system, whereby two ships were built side by side, was used at the Wilton-Fijenoord shipyard in Schiedam, Netherlands, and was later applied by the Pallion Yard in Great Britain in a completely covered dock. Japanese shipyards (such as the Koyagi works of Mitsubishi Heavy Industries and the Chita yard of Ishikawajima-Harima Heavy Industries) applied similar systems on a larger scale, using heavyweight gantry cranes and covering block assembly areas and docks.

**Dedicated Containership on a Slipway.** Verolme Botlek, 1973. Courtesy of Sjoerd Hengst

**Side Launching.** 1946. Courtesy of Royal Schelde

The extrusion system was developed at the Arendal shipyard in Norway. In a relatively small covered part of a dock, a cross section of the hull was completed and pushed out of the assembly area. As soon as a following section was ready, the ship was pushed out farther. This procedure was repeated until the ship was complete. This system, which was also used in Great Britain by Cammell Laird on a slipway, did not significantly shorten the assembly period but increased productivity because the work was done under cover.

## Slipways

The launching of ships on a slipway has always been an event; it is also time-consuming and labor-intensive and has therefore become a less common practice. During the construction of a ship on a slipway, the ship's bottom is supported by keel blocks. The tops of these blocks are aligned in an appropriate angle and are at an average height above the slipway of approximately 1.5 meters to provide workers suitable access to the hull. With the declivity of the slipway being around one in twenty, the declivity of the launching way may vary between 1 in 16 and 1 in 25 in order to avoid excessive pressure on the end of the slipway and consequently on the ship's bottom because of tipping of the vessel during launching, or at the bow of the vessel at

the last stage of the launching, when bow pressures may become very high. This means that the calculations for the exact slope must be made before the assembly of the ship on the slipway. Sliding ways are usually straight or sometimes with camber. Cranes and scaffolding are completely different.

Before launching, the assembled weight of a ship on the berth is transferred from the keel blocks to the launching way, which consists of a standing way and a cradle on which the ship moves. A suitable lubricant between the two parts is needed to overcome any initial friction. Before the weight is transferred, the centerline blocks are removed step by step, and the fixed ground-way(s) are installed with the sliding cradle in subsequent sections and aligned and wedged. The weight is gradually transferred to the launching way through the removal of keel blocks, which is done quickly so as to prevent the cradle from sinking into the standing way. The cradle is released from the standing way by mechanical, hydraulic, or electromechanical means. In the event that the vessel does not move immediately, hydraulic rams put pressure on the head of the cradle to start the movement. In lieu of the traditional launching on a greased standing way, carriages on rails can also be used for smaller-size vessels.

Another method is the so-called side-launching of ships, which is used when space is lacking to launch longitudinally. This method continues to be used in the northern Netherlands, where most shipyards are located alongside canals.

[See also Naval Dockyards and Bases; Repair of Ships; Shipbuilding, Commercial; and Shipyards.]

## Bibliography

The information on docks and slips comes mainly from archival sources, travel reports from naval engineers, and articles in contemporary naval and technical periodicals and manuals.

Barry, Patrick. *Dockyard Economy and Naval Power*. London: Sampson Low, 1863. Reprint. Boston: Elibron Classics, 2001.

Corlett, Ewan. *The Iron Ship: The History and Significance of Brunel's "Great Britain."* New York: Arco, 1975.

Dietz, Brian. "Dikes, Dockheads, and Gates: English Docks and Sea Power in the Sixteenth and Seventeenth Centuries." *Mariner's Mirror* 88, no.2 (May 2002): 144–152.

Jarvis, Adrian. *Port and Harbour Engineering*. Brookfield, Vt.: Ashgate Variorum, 1998.

Marcil, Eileen Reid. *The Charley-man: A History of Wooden Shipbuilding at Quebec 1763–1893*. Kingston, Ontario: Quarry Press, 1995.

SJOERD HENGST *and* ALAN A. LEMMERS

# Dönitz, Karl (1891–1980), German grand admiral.

Karl Dönitz was born on September 16, 1891, in Grünau, near Berlin. In April 1910 he joined the Imperial Navy, where he ranked among the highest in his training class; he was promoted to ensign on September 27, 1913. During World War I Dönitz served as a signal officer until September 1916 on the light cruiser *Breslau*, in the Mediterranean and the Black Sea. Later he became commander of submarines in the Mediterranean. During a convoy attack in 1918 his submarine (UB-68) was lost and Dönitz was taken prisoner of war by the British. In the navy of the Weimar Republic and the Third Reich he served on torpedo boats and as a staff officer before taking command of the training cruiser *Emden* in 1934. From 1935 on, he was in charge of the development of the new submarine fleet. Drawing on his World War I experience, he developed the tactic of attacking convoys with groups of submarines by night. In his 1939 book *Die U-Bootswaffe* (The Submarine Fleet) he described the advantages of surface attacks by night.

It is merely a legend that as early as 1938–1939 Dönitz had a submarine-based strategy that rivaled Admiral Erich Raeder's concept. Only after the outbreak of World War II did he demand rapid reinforcement of the submarine fleet, with the goal of having three hundred operable boats, one hundred of which were intended to operate in the North Atlantic at all times.

Promoted to rear admiral in October 1939, Dönitz commanded the submarines with great tactical skill. He maintained close contact with commanders and crews, who were impressed with his open and direct leadership style and placed great trust in him. In a realistic assessment Dönitz concluded in November 1941 that only submarines "could help to achieve a positive outcome for this war." He described his views of the submarine in war in a diary entry for April 15, 1942:

> The enemy merchant navies are a collective factor. It is therefore immaterial where any one ship is sunk, for it must ultimately be replaced by new construction.

> What counts in the long run is the preponderance of sinkings over new construction. Shipbuilding and arms production are centred in the United States, while England is the European outpost and sally port (*U-Boat War in the Atlantic, 1939–1945*. Vol II, page 15).

In other words, if over a long period of time more ships could be sunk than the enemy could replace by building new ones, the British economy and defensive powers would weaken and finally collapse.

Dönitz criticized the dissipation of the navy's resources in early January 1942: "We are in a tight spot, which shows very clearly again that everything, every single resource, should be put into the submarines—since the fiction that we are still a naval power with an armed surface fleet collapses as soon as the war makes but the least demand of us in this regard."

The harsh reality of the war at sea led Dönitz to give orders that might be classified as war crimes. When a German submarine was attacked by an American airplane during attempts to rescue survivors of the sunk British troop transporter *Laconia* in September 1942, he ordered all submarine commanders to stop trying to save crew members of ships that had been sunk, because saving them contradicted "the most primitive demand of warfare, which is to destroy enemy ships and crews." Instead, they should consider that the enemy "does not think about women and children when bombing German cities." The prosecution at the 1946 Nuremberg trial interpreted this so-called "Laconia order" as an instruction to destroy survivors of shipwrecks, in violation of international law. However, the Nuremberg court also held that it had not been proven beyond doubt that "Dönitz intentionally ordered the killing of shipwreck survivors."

After he took over the supreme command of the navy with his promotion to grand admiral, Dönitz's goal from

**Grossadmiral Karl Dönitz.** Grand Admiral Dönitz congratulates U-boat sailors in May 1942, while he was commanding the German submarine force. LIBRARY OF CONGRESS, PRINTS AND PHOTOGRAPHS DIVISION

January 1943 on was to change Adolf Hitler's mind about the course of the war. In his opinion resources should be shifted from the army and air force to the navy. To achieve this he aimed to prove the importance of warfare at sea. In spite of his awareness of their slim chances of success and survival, Dönitz sacrificed numerous submarines and their crews to convince Hitler of the unbroken aggressive spirit of his forces.

In Dönitz the navy had a charismatic leader with a strong connection to Hitler and Nazi ideology, a fact that he demonstrated forcefully in both public and private. After the attempt on Hitler's life on July 20, 1944, Dönitz called the conspirators "paid accessories" of the enemy and tried to impress on his most senior flag officers that the armed forces would fail entirely if they did not cleave fanatically to the man "to whom they have sworn loyalty."

Only Hitler's death ended the demonic hold he had over Dönitz. Named by Hitler as his successor, Dönitz changed "from an almost blind instrument of a criminal to a responsible soldier of the traditional Prussian school" (Salewski 1975), demonstrating a sense of reality and responsibility by ending the war and, in its last days, having many people evacuated across the Baltic Sea to the west. For this last achievement the navy was given much public credit.

On October 1, 1946, Dönitz was found guilty by the International Military Tribunal in Nuremberg of crimes against peace and of war crimes. After serving his ten-year prison sentence, he lived as a recluse in Aumühle, near Hamburg, until his death on December 24, 1980. The substantial consideration he gave to his actions between 1935 and 1945 is reflected in his memoirs and other publications. Although he had lost two sons in the war, he did not show any regret for what he had achieved with his power of command. Incorrigible in his obstinacy, he refused to come to terms with his own past.

[*See also* Anti-Submarine Warfare; Arctic Convoys; Atlantic, Battle of the; Aviation, *subentry on* Naval Aviation; Convoy; Naval Administration; Naval Logistics; Navies, Great Powers; Ports; Strategy; Tactics; Underwater Weapons; *and* Wars, Maritime, *subentry on* World Wars.]

### Bibliography

Bird, Keith W. "Karl Dönitz: Der 'unbesiegte' Admiral." In *Die Militärelite des Dritten Reiches*, edited by Ronald Smelser and Enrico Syring, pp. 129–152. Frankfurt am Main, Berlin: Ullstein, 1997.

Dönitz, Karl. *Die U-Bootswaffe*. Berlin: Mittler, 1939.

Dönitz, Karl. *Mein wechselvolles Leben*. Göttingen, Germany: Musterschmidt, 1968.

Dönitz, Karl. *Memoirs: Ten Years and Twenty Days*. Annapolis, Md.: Naval Institute Press, 1990.

*Fuehrer Conferences on Naval Affairs 1939–1945*. Annapolis, Md.: Naval Institute Press, 1990.

Howarth, Stephen, and Derek Law, eds. *The Battle of the Atlantic 1939–1945: The 50th Anniversary International Naval Conference*. Annapolis, Md.: Naval Institute Press, 1994.

Kraus, Herbert. "Karl Dönitz und das Ende des "Dritten Reiches." In *Deutsche Marinen im Wandel: Vom Symbol nationaler Einheit zum Instrument internationaler Sicherheit*, edited by Werner Rahn, pp. 525–545. Munich: Oldenbourg, 2005.

Ministry of Defence (Navy). *U-Boat War in the Atlantic, 1939–1945*. London: Her Majesty's Stationery Office, 1989.

Mulligan, Timothy P. *Neither Sharks nor Wolves: The Men of Nazi Germany's U-Boat Arm, 1939–1945*. Annapolis, Md.: Naval Institute Press, 1999.

Padfield, Peter. *Dönitz: The Last Führer; Portrait of a Nazi War Leader*. London: Gollancz, 1984.

Salewski, Michael. *Die deutsche Seekriegsleitung 1935–1945*. Vol. 2: *1942–1945*. Munich: Bernard and Graefe, 1975.

Salewski, Michael. "The Submarine War: A Historical Essay." In *U-Boat War*, edited by L.-G. Buchheim. New York: Bantam, 1979.

Thomas, Charles S. *The German Navy in the Nazi Era*. Annapolis, Md.: Naval Institute Press, 1990.

WERNER RAHN

# Dorestad

The port of Dorestad was a major port of the Carolingian Empire during the eighth century. Stretching for almost three kilometers along the bank of the Kromme Rijn, close to the meeting point of the rivers Rhine and Lek, the town was the main customs post of the empire, with its own mint and extensive trading connections throughout northern and western Europe.

Archaeological investigations in the 1970s, which uncovered more than thirty hectares of housing and wharves, suggest that Dorestad was a town of considerable size for its day. The town appears to have had an outer layer of agricultural settlement, but it owed its growth and prosperity to trade. Evidence of the importance of trade is suggested by the fact that, as the river moved eastward, the wharves of the port were extended, reaching a length of up to two hundred meters by the middle of the ninth century. Remains of barrels used to line wells indicate a lively trade in Rhenish wine; millstones from the quarries of Niedermendig near Koblenz found their way through Dorestad to destinations in northern Germany, Denmark, and England.

Explicit mention in a letter from King Offa of Mercia to the emperor Charlemagne around 796 of woolen cloaks made in England and exported to the empire hints at the existence already in the Anglo-Saxon period of a textile trade across the North Sea, in all likelihood between ports such as Gipeswic (Ipswich) and Dorestad.

Dorestad's prosperity did not long survive Charlemagne. Viking raids, including a particularly destructive one in 834, the continuous silting of the Kromme Rijn channel, and disorder following the emperor's death contributed to the town's ruin; it was completely destroyed in 864. Less than a century later, Dorestad was referred to in a charter as "villa quondam Dorstet, nunc autem Uuik nominata" (the former town of Dorestad, now called Wijk). The modern village of Wijk bij Duurstede lies on the site of this onetime flourishing trading center and port.

[*See also* Ports *and* Trade]

## Bibliography

Clarke, Helen, and Björn Ambrosiani. *Towns in the Viking Age*. Rev. ed. Leicester, U.K.: Leicester University Press, 1995.

Hodges, Richard. *Dark Age Economics: The Origins of Towns and Trade, AD 600–1000*. 2d ed. London: Duckworth, 1989.

Verwers, W. J. H. "Dorestad: A Carolingian Town?" In *The Rebirth of Towns in the West, AD 700–1050*, edited by Richard Hodges and Brian Hobley, pp. 52–56. London: Council for British Archaeology, 1988.

DAVID KIRBY

# Doria, Andrea

(1466–1560), Genoese admiral of galleys. Andrea Doria was born in Oneglia (which currently constitutes a part of Imperia, a town southwest of Genoa) on November 30, 1466, to a family of ancient nobility, but not of wealth.

In 1484 Doria went to Rome and served as a guard of Pope Innocent VIII (r. 1484–1492). In this period, observing the internal struggles both in Genoa and Rome among various families wishing to rise to power, he was inclined to consider his own personal wealth, fortune, and power, which he practiced in an authoritarian way, as supreme.

He then served the armies of some lords in the Italian peninsula, and in 1512 he built the first two galleys of his own personal fleet. In the following years he served the Republic of Genoa, using these ships to fight first the French fleet and later Muslim pirates, obtaining in 1519 the first major victory against them in the Tyrrhenian Sea.

Subsequently Doria used his galleys to serve Francis I (r. 1515–1547), king of France, but in 1525 the Holy Roman

***Andrea Doria as Neptune.*** Agnolo Bronzino (1503–1572) painted this portrait about 1534 for Paolo Giolo's gallery of illustrious men. SCALA / ART RESOURCE, NY/PINACOTECA DI BRERA, MILAN

emperor Charles V (r. 1519–1556) began contacting him, wishing to hire him, and finally succeeded in 1528, when Doria's personal fleet had grown to twelve galleys.

In the following years Doria, who became lord of Genoa and lieutenant of Charles V, operated in the Mediterranean to restrain Muslim expansionism and to defend the parts of the Italian coasts under imperial power from attacks by Khair ad Din, known as Barbarossa.

Barbarossa often operated with French ships; first he installed himself in Algiers, then in 1534 he conquered Tunis. In 1535 Charles V organized an amphibious operation to drive Barbarossa from Tunis, submitting the fleet to Doria, and the enterprise was successful.

After other naval battles, in 1538 the famous battle of Prevesa took place between Barbarossa's fleet and a Christian fleet. Doria's galleys took part, but did not get too

involved, so while the Christians suffered a bloody defeat, Doria's twenty-eight ships suffered hardly any damage.

In 1541 Charles V decided to attack Algiers and assigned the command of the ships to Doria. The landing of the Christian troops in Africa was successful, but a terrible storm hit the fleet while it was anchored at Cape Matifoux, and only the sailing ability of Doria enabled him to save part of the fleet and Charles V himself.

In 1552 Doria fought with his galleys against Siman Pasha in the southern Tyrrhenian. In 1553 and in 1554 he sustained the garrisons that defended Corsica from a local rebellion supported by the French and the Turks. In 1556 Charles V abdicated, after which Doria served under the command of his son, King Philip II of Spain (r. 1556–1598); during the same year Doria transported reinforcements to Naples, threatened by the French troops.

Doria, by now ninety, avoided embarking, and he submitted the command of his personal fleet to his nephew Gian Andrea Doria, who was present at the disastrous battle of Djerba on March 2, 1560. Disappointed by this defeat, Doria died in Genoa on November 25, 1560.

[*See also* Barbarossa; Medieval Navies, *subentry on* Italian States; *and* Navies, Great Powers, *subentry on* Italy, 1500–1945.]

## Bibliography

Balard, Michel. "Genoese Naval Forces in the Mediterranean during the Fifteenth and Sixteenth Centuries." In *War at Sea in the Middle Ages and Renaissance*, edited by John B. Hattendorf and Richard W. Unger, pp. 137–149. Woodbridge, U.K.: Boydell and Brewer, 2003.

Braudel, Fernand. *The Mediterranean and the Mediterranean World in the Age of Philip II*. Translated by Siân Reynolds. Berkeley: University of California Press, 1995. Although the first edition of this work was published soon after the end of World War II, it has often been revised. This book is useful for understanding the context in which Andrea Doria lived.

Perria, Antonio. *Andrea Doria il corsaro: La casata e le gesta del più grande ammiraglio genovese del sedicesimo secolo*. Milan: SugarCo, 1982. This book is one of the most recent and complete biographies of Doria.

Vargas Hidalgo, Rafael, ed. *Guerra y diplomacia en el Mediterráneo: Correspondencia inédita de Felipe II con Andrea Doria y Juan Andrea Doria; Ilustrada con cartas de Carlos V, Don Juan de Austria, Juana de Austria, Andrea Doria, Juan Andrea Doria, virreyes, generales, embajadores y espías*. Madrid: Ediciones Polifemos, 2002. Correspondence between Philip II (son of Charles V), Andrea Doria, and his nephew Gian Andrea Doria, who inherited his fleet.

Zazzu, Guido Nathan. *Andrea Doria nell'età d'oro di Genova*. Genoa: De Ferrari, 1996. Focuses on activities carried out by

Andrea Doria while administrating Genoa during the sixteenth century.

MARCO GEMIGNANI

## Douwes, Cornelis (1712–1773), Dutch nautical scientist.

Born in Terschelling, the son of a skipper who sailed regularly to Bremen on a merchant vessel, as a young man Douwes studied navigation and probably went to sea as a mate. Around 1731 he became a teacher in the art of navigation, mathematics, and artillery in Amsterdam. In 1747, Douwes applied for the position of teacher of artillery at the Amsterdam admiralty, offering also to teach navigation, trigonometry, astronomy, and the use of navigational instruments. His proposition resulted in the founding of the Algemeen Zeemans-Collegie in Amsterdam. At this nautical school, which was jointly financed by the admiralty, the Dutch East India Company, the Society of Suriname, and the city of Amsterdam, lieutenants, mates and masters, and Amsterdam orphans were trained by Douwes free of charge. In 1749 he was also appointed the official mathematician of the admiralty and examiner of the lieutenants. That year, the admiralty appointed a nautical instrument maker to supply Douwes's pupils with navigational instruments. In 1752, Douwes became a member of the newly founded Hollandsche Maatschappij der Wetenschappen (Royal Holland Society of Sciences and Humanities).

Douwes developed a method of finding latitude with "double altitudes," which he described in a manuscript in 1749. The principle was not new, but Douwes's method was the first to be of practical use to seamen. It was published in 1754, but the necessary tables did not appear in print until 1761. In the meantime, Dutch and British seamen practiced the method at sea, using copied manuscript tables. It was first published in England in 1759, whereupon the Board of Longitude awarded Douwes *fifty pounds*. In later years the method was also published in France, Germany, Spain, and America, and was used at sea. It remained popular well into the nineteenth century, the last Dutch edition of the tables appearing in 1858. In his own country Douwes was an active promoter of the English inventor John Hadley's octant. Douwes published a user's manual in 1747 and also wrote a manual for a newly invented azimuth compass. After Douwes's death in 1773 the Algemeen Zeemans-Collegie was continued by his brother-in-law Sierd Geerds, who as teacher at the college was assisted by Douwes's son, *Bernardus Johannes*, as adjunct mathematician at the admiralty in Amsterdam.

[*See also* Education and Training; Nautical Astronomy and Celestial Navigation; *and* Navigational Instruments.]

### Bibliography
Cotter, Charles H. *A History of Nautical Astronomy.* London: Hollis and Carter, 1968.

Crone, Ernst. *Cornelis Douwes, 1712–1773: Zijn leven en zijn werk.* Haarlem, Netherlands: H. D. Tjeenk Willink & Zoon, 1941.

WILLEM F. J. MÖRZER BRUYNS

## Dover

Dover's sheltered position on the coast of Kent in southeastern England and its proximity to Continental Europe are the basis of its role in maritime history. The 1992 discovery of a Bronze Age boat, which later went on exhibit at the Dover Museum, demonstrated that Dover had been involved in cross-channel trade for at least 3,500 years. The Romans made Dover their main British port, building a harbor there, as well as two lighthouses. Dover later became one of the Cinque Ports, which, beginning in the twelfth century, received commercial privileges in return for providing manpower and ferry services for the crown.

In 1606 a royal charter created the Dover Harbour Board, which administered the port's revenues and was responsible for its maintenance and development. Dover has since remained a trust port, with board members appointed mainly by the British government, and has enjoyed significant freedom from shareholder interests. The fluctuating attention of the naval authorities led to the building of Admiralty Pier between 1847 and 1875 and eventually to the completion of the outer harbor in 1909, creating a square mile of enclosed water within which the modern port has flourished. Cross-channel steamers regularly used the pier beginning in the 1850s, and rival railway companies ran connecting trains beginning in the 1860s.

Dover had a prominent role in both world wars, becoming in 1914 the site of the first enemy bomb to fall on Britain and then in 1940 the recipient of most of the soldiers escaping from Dunkerque. The cross-channel trade was further developed by the Southern Railway between the wars, with ferries employed for, among other things, the luxury London–Paris Golden Arrow service. Notable innovations included the first dedicated car ferry, introduced by Townsend in 1928, and the Southern's Night Ferry in 1937, which allowed railway sleeping cars to cross by ship.

After 1945 tourism rapidly increased the passenger trade, to more than 2 million by 1959—more than double that of 1939—and to more than 9 million by the end of the 1970s. Car traffic grew spectacularly, to 1 million a year by 1976, assisted by the introduction of "drive-on" stern-loading ships in the early 1950s and of "drive-through" or "roll on, roll off" (Ro-Ro) ferries by the mid-1960s. Larger ferries by the 1980s allowed Ro-Ro car traffic on two continuous decks, with simultaneous loading and unloading. Dover also became a major freight-handling port in these decades, aided by the increasing focus of Britain's external trade on Continental Europe. By the 1990s, Dover was one of the busiest ports in the country in terms of value (around £50 billion a year by 2000), and was in the top ten in terms of bulk (more than 19 million metric tons).

In 2000, Dover was the largest passenger ferry port in northern Europe and was the major cross-channel port in the United Kingdom, with 43 percent of the market and more than 16 million passengers. It was also Britain's largest Ro-Ro port, handling approximately 1.7 million trucks. This growth was facilitated by the ever-expanding facilities provided by the Harbour Board, which by 2000 included eight Ro-Ro passenger berths, three major freight berths, two cruise-liner terminals, and a hoverport.

[*See also* Passenger Trades *and* Ports, *subentry on* Characteristics of Cities.]

### Bibliography

Crompton, Gerald. "Transport." In *Kent in the Twentieth Century*, edited by Nigel Yates, pp. 117–152. Woodbridge, U.K.: Boydell, 2001.

Hasenson, Alec. *The History of Dover Harbour*. London: Aurum, 1980.

Hendy, John. *Ferry Port Dover: The Development of Cross-Channel Vehicle Ferries, Their Services, and Allied Infrastructure.* Staplehurst, U.K.: Ferry Publications, 1998.

Ove Arup and Partners. *Port of Dover*. Kent, U.K.: Kent County Council, 2001.

GERALD CROMPTON

# Downs, Battle of the

The Battle of the Downs, which took place on October 21, 1639, between the Spanish and Dutch navies, is important because of the use of line tactics and fireships, the role of neutral England, and the changes in the international statuses of Spain and the Dutch Republic. During the Thirty Years' War (1618–1648), Spain pursued a wide-ranging maritime policy. In this, the central figure was the count-duke of Olivares, the principal minister and favorite of King Philip IV from 1622 to 1643. The armada of Flanders, mainly built up from 1619 onward, not only escorted convoys with troops and bullion from Spain to the southern Netherlands, but also undertook offensive actions against economic targets, mainly the Dutch mercantile and fishing fleets. It was most active during the 1630s, as were the Dunkerque privateers. The transport of troops by sea had become of vital importance, since the so-called overland route from Genoa to Germany and the southern Netherlands had been disrupted. In September 1639, a great armada of forty-seven Spanish, Portuguese, Neapolitan, and Flemish warships escorting thirty vessels carrying troops, including English and Hanseatic ones, sailed from La Coruña in northern Spain to bring 23,000 men—two-thirds of whom were Spanish and Italian soldiers—plus an amount of silver and gold, to Dunkerque. The destruction of the Dutch navy in the English Channel and the North Sea was a second goal, and if possible, also the destruction of the Atlantic navy of France, an enemy of Spain since 1635. Don Antonio de Oquendo was in command.

The Dutch navy had only recently been better organized under the inspiring new leadership of Lieutenant Admiral Maarten Harpertszoon Tromp; for instance, discipline among the captains had returned. In the summer of 1639 the navy's problem was what to give priority to: blockade of Dunkerque, convoy service, or concentration of forces for meeting the so-called Second Armada head on. No definite choice was made, and on September 15 only a major part of the fleet met the Spaniards in the English Channel off Beachy Head. Tromp had only eighteen ships. The next day the first battle took place. The Spaniards, under the command of Don Antonio de Oquendo, had the advantage of the wind. Tromp ordered his ships in line formation, and close behind one another the Dutch ships cut repeatedly the front of the far more numerous enemy, using their heavier broadsides to considerable effect. The belligerents, however, were blown by the northwest wind to the French coast. The Dutch on the leeside only narrowly escaped from being trapped. The fleets had lost one ship each.

The second battle started at 1:00 A.M. on September 18. The Dutch had been reinforced with twelve ships of the Dunkerque blockading squadron. This time they attacked from the weather side and again in line formation. The Spaniards were completely surprised by the night attack. By 3:00 P.M., the Dutch had used up their ammunition, and they disengaged. Oquendo could not reach Dunkerque and had to seek shelter in the Downs, where he was soon blockaded by the Dutch.

The Downs, the roads between North- and South-Foreland or between Ramsgate and Deal/Dover, and partly protected by the Goodwin Sands, were in English territorial waters. Thus the Spanish navy was anchoring in neutral waters, officially open to only seven or eight foreign warships at a time. England was then profiting greatly from its neutrality in the Dutch-Spanish conflict after a treaty with Madrid in 1630. Dover, in particular, had become a great entrepôt, strategically placed to allow Spanish cargoes to be transshipped into English carriers and to be brought by them to Dunkerque. This was, of course, a thorn in the Dutch flesh, but accepted. An English squadron, under the command of Sir John Pennington, was present at the Downs to uphold English neutral rights and to keep the belligerents separated. In practice, the English commander was not neutral, and—against his word to Tromp—he let fourteen lighter Spanish vessels, with 4,000 soldiers on board, secretly slip away to Dunkerque. Already by September 21, the Dutch government had given Tromp permission to make an attack at the Downs and to disregard English objections.

For five weeks a strange spectacle unfolded. The Spaniards were locked up, not daring to leave the Downs, the Dutch acted as guardians, and the English tried desperately to maintain their sovereignty in their own waters. Tromp offered to provide Oquendo with masts and ammunition, goods that the Spaniard had claimed to be badly in need of before being able to depart. Dutch men-of-war intercepted English merchant vessels on their way to the southern Netherlands, smuggling Spanish soldiers. The spectacle became a tourist attraction for visitors on the shore and in small boats. In the Dutch Republic, bets were made on the final outcome.

The Dutch naval authorities did their utmost to reinforce Tromp's fleet. Many merchantmen were hired and transformed into warships, as was still common practice. Eleven were prepared as fireships. Finally, the Dutch fleet counted ninety-five men-of-war, almost all of them smaller than the Spanish ships, but mostly of better sailing quality. Only Tromp's flagship *Aemilia* could match in tonnage and guns Oquendo's flagship *Santiago*. Tromp could choose the day of attack; he chose October 21—it was the third battle since September 16. The northwest wind was favorable for Tromp. His force had been split up into five squadrons, and one would observe the reaction of Pennington, who would remain passive. The fight itself is hard to describe in detail. The Downs offered possibilities only for a melee, not for the use of standoff gunfire. The Spaniards were immediately in disorder, surprised as they were by the moment of the attack and in

fear of the Dutch fireships. More than twenty vessels ran ashore and were immobilized. Some of the rest escaped into open water, some reached Dunkerque, others ran aground, and many fell into Dutch hands. Late in the afternoon, Oquendo's energetic behavior could only at the last moment persuade his crew to resume fighting before his own flagship would have been captured by Tromp's flagship—and so Oquendo's flagship escaped in the darkness. The most spectacular fight was around the largest Portuguese ship, *Santa Teresa*—more than 1,200 tons and called "Goliath" by Dutch sailors—which was finally burned by a fireship. At 7:00 P.M., Pennington and his men saw a great flash like lightning over Foreland, which was the gunpowder magazine that blew up when the fire reached it. Only one Dutch ship was lost, also set on fire by a Dutch fireship when she lay entangled in the bowsprit of an opponent.

The Dutch losses were negligible, the Spanish losses very heavy. Two-thirds of the warships were lost, fourteen of them captured by the Dutch. Seven thousand men were killed or taken prisoner. As a result of the Battle of the Downs, Spain lost its recently acquired reputation as a new and important naval power. But the more practical outcome of the sending of the Second Armada was not so bleak. The bullion had reached its destination, as had at least one-third of the troops, and the English later returned eight of the ships stranded on the Foreland coast. The international effect on Spain, however, was disastrous. Spain disappeared as a naval power from the English Channel and the North Sea. Peace with the Dutch Republic on Spanish terms was beyond any possibility. Moreover, Spain's status was further weakened by the outbreak of rebellion in Portugal and Catalonia in 1640.

In the Dutch Republic, the overall morale soared after the victory over the Spaniards. The Dutch navy had firmly established its position as the leading naval power in Europe, and Tromp was its uncontested leader. An unexpected effect of the victory was the exhaustion of the admiralties' finances by the enormous effort to keep a large fleet at sea so late in the autumn season and to reinforce it quickly on such an unusual scale. Smaller squadrons in 1640 were the result, and the Dunkerque privateers again operated almost unhindered.

[*See also* Amsterdam; Blockade; Convoy; Navies, Great Powers *subentries on* Spain, 1500–1805 *and* Dutch Republic, 1577–1714; Tromp, Maarten Harpertszoon; *and* Wars, Maritime, *subentries on* Anglo-Dutch Wars *and* Anglo-Spanish Wars.]

## Bibliography

Boer, M. G. de. *Tromp en de Armada van 1639*. Amsterdam: Noord-Hollandsche Uitgevers Maatschappij, 1941.

Boxer, Charles R., ed. and trans. *The Journal of Maarten Harpertszoon Tromp, Anno 1639*. Cambridge, U.K.: Cambridge University Press, 1930.

Bruijn, Jaap R. *The Dutch Navy of the Seventeenth and Eighteenth Centuries*. Columbia: University of South Carolina Press, 1993.

Goodman, David. *Spanish Naval Power, 1589–1665: Reconstruction and Defeat*. Cambridge, U.K.: Cambridge University Press, 1997.

Israel, Jonathan I. *The Dutch Republic and the Hispanic World 1606–1661*. Oxford: Clarendon Press, 1982.

Kepler, J. S. *The Exchange of Christendom: The International Entrepôt at Dover 1622–1641*. Leicester, U.K.: Leicester University Press, 1976.

Prud'homme van Reine, Ronald B. *Schittering en schandaal: Biografie van Maerten en Cornelis Tromp*. Amsterdam: Arbeiderspers, 2001.

Stradling, R. A. *The Armada of Flanders: Spanish Maritime Policy and European War, 1568–1668*. Cambridge, U.K.: Cambridge University Press, 1992.

JAAP R. BRUIJN

**Dragger.** *See* Fishing Vessels.

**Drake, Francis** (1540–1595), English seaman and circumnavigator. Drake was born in Tavistock, in Devon, England, probably in February or March 1540. He was the son of Edmund Drake, a shearer turned priest. The name of his mother is not known with certainty, and although Drake's father may have entered into a form of marriage with her, clerical marriage was illegal at the time, making Francis illegitimate. After a series of criminal misadventures, Edmund Drake left Tavistock, probably in 1543, and ten years later he was serving as a curate at Upchurch, in Kent. He seems to have played no part in bringing up his son—which was probably just as well. Francis was placed at an early age into the household of William Hawkins of Plymouth, to whom Edmund was related. Francis was thus a cousin to John Hawkins, who was about seven years his senior.

Very little is known about Drake's upbringing, but he must have received some schooling, because in later life he was both literate and numerate. Principally, however, he was trained to the sea and sailed as an apprentice mariner on several of Hawkins's ships. In 1558, at the age of eighteen, he was bursar of an unnamed trader in the Bay of Biscay. Since William Hawkins was both a merchant and an opportunist pirate, it is likely that Drake learned

**Sir Francis Drake.** This 1591 portrait is painted in the style of Marcus Gheehaerts the Younger (1561–1635). © NATIONAL MARITIME MUSEUM, LONDON

both businesses simultaneously. At some point after 1559, when Edmund Drake had returned to Upchurch after a discreet withdrawal during the reign of the Catholic queen Mary Tudor, he is alleged to have placed Francis on one of the small traders plying between the Medway River and the Dutch coast. In due course, so the story runs, Francis inherited the boat, but it may already have belonged to one of the Hawkins, for whom Drake was working it. Whatever the truth of the matter, Drake seems to have completed his training out of the Medway rather than Plymouth.

By about 1560 he had enough money to invest in trade goods and go as a seaman on one of the Hawkins's voyages to Guinea. He seems to have gone on several of these voyages between 1562 and 1567, although in a fairly humble capacity, and he is seldom mentioned by name. In so doing, he completed his training in trading, slaving, and piracy. Edmund Drake died in 1567, and later that year Drake was given what seems to have been his first command—that of *Judith* in John Hawkins's slaving/trading voyage to West Africa and the Indies. When Hawkins's small fleet was caught by the Spaniards at San Juan de Ulúa in September 1568, *Judith* and *Minion* escaped. *Minion*, Hawkins's ship, was seriously overmanned and underprovisioned, but (according to Hawkins) *Judith* sailed home without offering him any relief. The truth was probably less simple, but relations between the two men deteriorated thereafter. Over the following years Drake made a number of voyages to the Caribbean of a frankly piratical nature, exploiting the weaknesses in Spanish colonial defenses. Not all of his raids succeeded, but he made a fearsome reputation as El Draque—the dragon. It was during these years that Drake's characteristics as a leader developed. In battle he was an inspiring commander and, tactically, a brilliant opportunist. As a strategist he was second rate, and unable to control a large situation when the opportunity arose. He enjoyed excellent relations with his seamen, but he was frequently at odds with the gentlemen volunteers who accompanied a number of his voyages. These men generally lacked discipline, and Drake was tactless and heavy handed in his approach, and intolerant of all criticism of his leadership, however justified. By this time he was a militant Protestant, who carried a copy of the *Acts and Monuments* in his cabin and inflicted readings on his unfortunate Spanish prisoners. At the same time, he became rich, indulged in legitimate merchandise, and became a substantial citizen of Plymouth. In 1569 he married Mary Newman and set up a home base in the town. By 1577 he was a recognized seafighter and sailor, and a favorite at court—not least because of the large profits he brought home. Consequently, when a major voyage was being contemplated, and investors from the city and the court attracted (including Queen Elizabeth I), Drake was an obvious man to put in charge. The original intention probably did not extend much beyond annoying the Spanish king Philip II and bringing back some plunder, but it turned into an epic three-year circumnavigation, which not only established Drake's reputation as a great navigator but signaled England's capacity to execute a global strategy. When he brought his last surviving ship home in 1580, Elizabeth knighted him and accepted the lion's share of his profit. Although the voyage was marred by the execution of Thomas Doughty, a gentleman who carried his independence too far, it brought Drake great riches and great glory.

These were the years of Drake's greatest reputation, and when the showdown with Spain finally came in 1585, Drake was chosen to lead a punitive raid to the Indies, this time as an official act of war. For the first time he was a privateer rather than a pirate. In 1587 he carried out what was probably his most successful military operation, when he raided Cádiz and destroyed most of the supplies being prepared for the Spanish Armada against England. When the Armada came in 1588, Drake was a vice admiral against it, and although he acquitted himself creditably, he was not at his best in big operations, and was accused of endangering the fleet by disobeying orders. The following year, however, his career was virtually ended when his joint command with Sir John Norris of an expedition to put Dom Antonio on the Portuguese throne ended in chaos and fiasco. The reason lay in the joint-stock nature of the enterprise, and its confused priorities, but both Drake and Norris were legitimately accused of disobeying the queen's instructions and were disgraced. Norris eventually recovered favor, but Drake never did. He was allowed one last fling at the Caribbean in 1595, along with Sir John Hawkins, but the expedition failed and both commanders died at sea.

Drake's first wife died in 1582, and in the same year he married Elizabeth Sydenham. He retained his Plymouth base, was mayor of the town, and acquired a country estate and a coat of arms. In spite of the cloud over his later career, he died a rich and highly respected man.

[*See also* Buccaneers and Buccaneering; Hawkins, John; Navies, Great Powers, *subentry on* British Isles, 1500 to the Present; Naval Administration; Privateering; Strategy; Tactics; Technology and Weapons, *subentry on* 1300–1850; *and* Wars, Maritime, *subentry on* Anglo-Spanish Wars.]

### Bibliography

Corbett, Julian S. *Drake and the Tudor Navy*; with a History of the Rise of England as a Maritime Power. 2 vols. London and New York: Longmans, Green, 1898. Reprint. Two vols. in one. Aldershot, Hants, U.K.: Temple Smith; Brookfield, Vt.: Gower, 1988.

Kelsey, Harry. *Sir Francis Drake: The Queen's Pirate*. New Haven, Conn.: Yale University Press, 1998.

Thompson, G. M. *Sir Francis Drake*. New York: Morrow, 1972.

Wernham, R. B. *The Expedition of Sir John Norris and Sir Francis Drake to Spain and Portugal, 1589*. Aldershot, Hants, U.K.: Temple Smith for the Navy Records Society; Brookfield, Vt.: Gower, 1988.

Wilson, Derek. *The World Encompassed: Francis Drake and His Great Voyage*. New York: Harper and Row, 1977.

DAVID LOADES

# Drama, English and American

English sea drama goes back at least to fourteenth-century productions of the Noah story, staged with some realism by sea-related guilds. In the York shipwrights' "Building of the Ark," for instance, God tells Noah to select only tall trees, cut their ends square (not slanted), and use board-and-batten construction with nails and glue. In the Wakefield "Noah and the Ark" Noah sounds the water's depth while his wife takes the tiller.

## Sixteenth to Nineteenth Centuries

From the sixteenth through the eighteenth centuries, English sea plays may be classified as realistic or satiric (the critic Harold Watson used this division in his survey of plays about sailors). Realism tends toward believable characters and action at sea or on islands. In the opening storm of William Shakespeare's *The Tempest* (1611), the seamanship of an earthy boatswain trumps the empty political authority of a duke and a king. After the shipwreck all suffer a sea-change and are reunited on a mysterious island—a formula plot derived from Greek romance. *The Sea Voyage* (1622), by John Fletcher and Philip Massinger, *The Prisoners* (1640), by John Killigrew, and *The Successful Pyrate* (1713) by Charles Johnson (probably Daniel Defoe) are realistic in this sense. However, satire in sea plays tends toward caricatured sailors and action on land, as in Thomas Middleton's *The Phoenix* (1603) and Ben Jonson's *The Staple of News* (1625). After the Restoration unrealistic caricatures predominate. For example, Captain Manly in William Wycherley's *The Plain Dealer* (1676) is a blunt, fire-breathing swaggerer who responds to most situations afloat and ashore with an oath and a kick. Near the end of the eighteenth century mediocre propaganda plays with stirring naval themes—such as George Colman's *The Jealous Wife* (1761) and Frederick Pilon's *Fair American* (1785)—held the stage.

The nineteenth century, heralded by the model of George Brewer's British comic opera *Banian Day* (1796), enhanced cant with stirring music. American theater, heavily influenced by British tradition, was almost all saber-rattling nationalism. The title of American playwright William Dunlap's 1812 play says it all: *Yankee Chronology; or, Huzza for the Constitution! A Musical Interlude, in One Act: To Which Are Added, the Patriotic Songs of the Freedom of the Seas, and Yankee Tars*. James Ellison's *American Captive* (1812) similarly offers jingoism—spiced with nautical jargon—as America's marines attack the shores of Tripoli. The nineteenth century also favored stage adaptations. At least two of James Fenimore Cooper's novels were made into plays by British writers: Edward Fitzball adapted *The Pilot* (novel, 1824, play, 1826); Samuel Chapman adapted *The Red Rover* (novel, 1827, play, 1828). Douglas Jerrold's

*Black-Eyed Susan* (1829) anticipates Gilbert and Sullivan in its melodramatic satire on the British Navy.

In the latter part of the century James A. Herne, an American playwright, captured the sea's melodrama in four nautically accurate plays: *Hearts of Oak* (1879), *Drifting Apart: or, Mary, the Fisherman's Child* (1888), *Shore Acres* (1892), and *Sag Harbor* (1899). In England the most notable sea plays of the period were comic operas by William S. Gilbert and Arthur S. Sullivan. *H.M.S. Pinafore* (1878) and *The Pirates of Penzance* (1879) satirize romantic conventions: naval heroism and misunderstood pirates.

## Twentieth Century

Sea drama came into its own with twentieth-century naturalism. *Riders to the Sea* (1904), by John Millington Synge, makes us feel poetic fatalism as an Irish mother mourns the last of her six drowned sons. Joseph Conrad turned his short story "To-morrow" (1902) into the play "One Day More" (1905): a woman cannot escape her demanding blind father with a flirtatious but feckless sailor. At the same time, J. M. Barrie used island settings for fantasies: in *The Admirable Crichton* (1902) a desert-island shipwreck allows a capable butler to rise temporarily above his social class; in *Peter Pan* (1904) a magic island fosters unending childhood.

Eugene O'Neill, the first American playwright to win the Nobel Prize for Literature and four-time Pulitzer Prize winner, stands alone for the quality and intensity of his sea plays. From 1916 to 1918 he produced four stark one-act plays about mystery within the ordinary lives of merchant sailors aboard a British tramp steamer: "Bound East for Cardiff" (1916), "In the Zone" (1917), "The Long Voyage Home" (1917), and "The Moon of the Caribbees" (1918). The four were combined into the play *S.S. Glencairn* (1924) and later adapted as the movie *The Long Voyage Home* (1941). His full-length plays are similarly haunted. In *The Hairy Ape* (1922) a ship's fireman loses his sense of belonging and eventually his life; in *Anna Christie* (1922) a woman seems to rediscover love but is abandoned by her father and her lover—both sailors.

Much twentieth-century sea drama makes pointed use of seaside settings. *The Outside* (1917), a one-act play by Susan Glaspell, contrasts the safe harbor of Provincetown (where she and O'Neill worked) with the destructive sea. Paul Green envisions the sea ambivalently as lifeblood and threat in historical sagas about Roanoke Island in *The Lost Colony* (1937) and the Jamestown settlement in *The Founders* (1957). In Edward J. Moore's *The Sea Horse* (1974) a sailor and a barmaid quarrel about the competing attractions of living at sea or on land. Beach settings encourage characters to reexamine life's meanings: in Edward Albee's surrealistic *Seascape* (1975), a weary suburban couple meet two evolving humanoid lizards on the beach; in Tina Howe's *Coastal Disturbances* (1986) the sea's rhythm evokes comic recollections; in Terrence McNally's *Lips Together, Teeth Apart* (1991) revelations are more painful than comic. Two notable American musicals explore the isolation of islands: in John Weidman's *Pacific Overtures* (1976), lyrics by Stephen Sondheim, Japan suffers the forced opening by Westerners in 1853; in Lynn Ahrens's *Once on This Island* (1990) mythic lovers confront hurricanes and caste restrictions in the French West Indies.

Some twentieth-century plays use shipboard settings to isolate people and intensify experience. In Elmer Rice's *Between Two Worlds* (1934) passengers on an ocean liner experience the effects of both capitalism and communism. *The Grand Tour* (1951) examines a doomed shipboard romance. Two plays dramatize wartime life on board American navy minesweepers: *Mister Roberts* (1948), by Thomas Heggen (based on his 1946 novel; made into a 1955 movie), focuses on comic squabbles; Herman Wouk's *The Caine Mutiny Court-Martial* (1953, play; based on his 1951 novel *The Caine Mutiny*) determines whether a mutiny occurred. Other major dramatizations of books deserve mention. The dangers faced by convoying ships during World War II can be seen from the British point of view in *The Cruel Sea*, a 1953 movie directed by Charles Frend, based on Nicholas Monsarrat's 1951 novel. John Huston adapted *Moby-Dick* in his 1956 movie. *Billy Budd* became a 1951 Broadway play by Louis Osborne Coxe and Robert Chapman, a 1951 opera with music by Benjamin Britten and book and lyrics by E. M. Forster, and a 1962 movie directed by Peter Ustinov.

The last quarter of the twentieth century saw a spate of distinguished sea plays. *Lakeboat* (1970, revised 1980) by David Mamet focuses on the lives of those who do mind-numbing work on board an iron-ore vessel on the Great Lakes. Steven Dietz's *Ten November* (1987) examines the inexplicable sinking in 1975 of *Edmund Fitzgerald* in Lake Superior: vignettes of shipboard routine are punctuated by the songs (music and lyrics by Eric Peltoniemi) of the three sisters of fate. John Guare's Nantucket Cycle—*Gardenia* (1982), *Lydie Breeze* (1982), *Women and Water* (1984), and a promised fourth play, "Bullfinch's Mythology"—examines the American Dream of generations of characters, stemming from a mutiny-murder on board a whaler through the founding and dissolution of a utopian community on Nantucket Island.

[*See also* Fiction, *subentry on* Sea Fiction, *and* Literature.]

## Bibliography

Gidmark, Jill B., ed. *Encyclopedia of American Literature of the Sea and Great Lakes*. Westport, Conn.: Greenwood Press, 2001. Alphabetical listing of brief articles (some with bibliographies) on authors, works, and relevant topics (e.g., drama of the sea). Includes a useful literary/historical timeline.

Hochman, Stanley, ed. *McGraw-Hill Encyclopedia of World Drama: An International Reference Work in 5 Volumes*. 2d ed. New York: McGraw-Hill, 1984. Individual entries on authors and comprehensive surveys of the history of American and English drama.

Lewis, Charles Lee. *Books of the Sea: An Introduction to Nautical Literature*. Annapolis, Md.: U.S. Naval Institute, 1943. Chapters on English and American sea plays, with convenient reading lists, by author.

McElroy, Davis D., and Lucille A. McElroy, eds. British Drama League. *Four Centuries of Sea Plays, 1550–1950: A Representative List of Theatrical Productions Involving Sailors, Ships, and the Sea*. London: British Drama League, 1960. Typewritten sixty-five-page booklet includes some fifteen hundred plays, arranged alphabetically by author and indexed by year. Keywords (e.g., pirates, ships, songs) identify sea-related elements for each play.

Raban, Jonathan, ed. *The Oxford Book of the Sea*. Oxford, Oxford University Press, 1992. American and British prose and poetry (many in excerpts), organized chronologically. Introduction offers a thoughtful discussion of themes.

Springer, Haskell, ed. *America and the Sea: A Literary History*. Athens: University of Georgia Press, 1995. A scholarly compendium of long essays about genres and topics; with a fifty-six-page unannotated bibliography. Includes some references to plays.

Watson, Harold Francis. *The Sailor in English Fiction and Drama, 1550–1800*. New York: Columbia University Press, 1931. Classifies sailor-dramatizations as either realistic (the *Tempest* school of Shakespeare) or caricatured (the "comedy of humours" school of Ben Jonson).

STEPHEN CURLEY

## *Dreadnought,* battleship.

Length/beam/draft: 160.3 m × 25 m × 8.8 m (526′ × 82′ × 29′). Tonnage: 21,845 displacement. Hull: steel. Complement: 657–773. Armament: 5 × 6″ (5 × 2), 18 × 12-pounder, 2 × 9-pounder; 5 × 18″ torpedo tubes. Designer: Sir Philip Watts. Built: Portsmouth Dockyard, England, 1906.

HMS *Dreadnought*, 1907. By permission of the Trustees of the Imperial War Museum, London, Q 38705

HMS *Dreadnought* was laid down on October 2, 1905, where she was launched on February 10, 1906, and placed in commission in December 1906. *Dreadnought* represented a quantum leap in all-around performance, instantly rendering existing battleships obsolescent and becoming the generic term for the "all-big-gun" battleship. With improved fire control and range-finding equipment, *Dreadnought* had twice the firepower of her precursors and twice the effective range. This was a response to the rapid increase in the range of the torpedo, which rendered impossible the old battle tactics of fighting at one to two miles. Her turbine engines were the first to be used in a battleship. She made twenty-one knots, three knots faster than her solid, staid predecessors. Although little bigger than those earlier ships, *Dreadnought* was carefully designed to make an architectural statement: stripped down, loaded with guns, and fast. An instant design icon, she became the symbol of British power in the Edwardian age.

The new ship was masterminded by Admiral Sir John Fisher, first sea lord from 1904 to 1910. Fisher assembled the best and brightest technical minds in the Royal Navy and British industry for the project. But *Dreadnought* was more than just another fighting ship. The cost of the Royal Navy had been rising steadily since the 1890s, and Britain was struggling to match the spending of its rivals. Appointed to reduce costs without sacrificing strength, *Dreadnought* was a critical part of the answer. Fisher thought that by raising the stakes he would force most rival navies to stop building battleships.

For maximum political impact, and to test her novel systems, the ship was built in record time. Although battleships usually required two or three years, *Dreadnought* was built in twelve months. She met every expectation, giving the Royal Navy a massive lead in new technologies, while paralyzing every other navy. While other navies were working out what to do, Britain built ten dreadnoughts. Most simply gave up; only Germany and the United States built dreadnought fleets before 1914. The German challenge was derailed by the new ship. Not only did *Dreadnought* force a massive increase in the cost of its new ships, but it forced Germany to reconstruct the Kiel Canal, the strategic waterway that allowed German ships to move between the Baltic and the North seas. By the time the canal was ready, Germany had lost the naval arms race begun by *Dreadnought*. Fisher summed up his life's work with the motto: "Fear God and Dread Nought."

By 1914 the latest "super-Dreadnoughts" were twice as big and twice as powerful as *Dreadnought*. She served through World War I, ironically missing Jutland, the one great dreadnought event, but she sank the German submarine U-29 on March 18, 1915, with her bow. No other battleship ever sank a submarine. Placed in reserve at Rosyth in 1919, *Dreadnought*, by now quite obsolete, was sold for scrap in 1922 and broken up at Inverness, Scotland, in 1923.

[*See also* Battleship; Warships, *subentry on* Modern Warships; *and* Wars, Maritime, *subentry on* World Wars.]

## Bibliography

Brown, David K. *Warrior to Dreadnought: Warship Development, 1860–1905*. London: Chatham, 1997.

Mackay, Ruddock F. *Fisher of Kilverstone*. Oxford: Clarendon Press, 1973.

Roberts, John. *The Battleship Dreadnought*. London: Conway Maritime Press, 2001.

Sumida, Jon Tetsuro. *In Defence of Naval Supremacy*. London: Unwin, 1989.

ANDREW LAMBERT

**Dredger**    Of old, dredging was a business mainly of the Dutch, who in the sixteenth and seventeenth centuries invented the first tools to remove silt from the bottom of harbors and waterways. This practice was necessary since many merchantmen could not pass sandbanks that blockaded the main ports of Amsterdam and Rotterdam. Floatable dredgers were used from the mid-eighteenth cen-

tury. Initially they were based on man- or horsepower, but around 1850 bucket dredgers with steam propulsion were invented. The vessels had a vertical or slanting ladder on which buckets were transported up and down. The rotation of the buckets caused them to continually fill with spoil. The buckets were emptied in the cargo space (hopper) of the dredger.

Today there are two kinds of self-propelled dredgers: those that work according to the old principle of shoveling sand (such as bucket dredgers or grab dredgers) and those with a suction pipe (hopper dredgers, reclamation dredgers, or cutter dredgers). Around 1880 cutter dredgers were first used in the United States. While some types of dredgers are especially suited to sand, cutter dredgers can handle heavy soil and even rocks by cutting the materials before extraction. Some dredgers store spoil in their own hoppers; others use barges or pipelines to transport the spoil to shore. Dredgers in operation are moored with cables and anchors, or by spuds (iron piles) in the bottom.

An alternative to conventional dredging is water injection dredging (WID), in which large quantities of water under low pressure are injected in silt. The silt rises in a cloud that can be driven in a specific direction. The silt resettles on the bottom, so WID can be used with polluted sediment. It is considered to mimic natural processes and is also a cost-effective form of dredging.

[*See also* Working Vessels.]

## Bibliography

Herbich, John B. *Coastal and Deep Ocean Dredging*. Houston, Tex.: Gulf, 1975.

Roorda, A., and J. J. Vertregt. *Floating Dredges: A Treatise on the Construction and Design of Floating Dredges, Engine Power, Internal Arrangement, Pumping Arrangement, etc.* Haarlem, Netherlands: H. Stam, 1963.

Vandersmissen, Hans. *Ophogen en uitdiepen: Tien eeuwen Nederlands baggerbedrijf*. The Hague, Netherlands: Smits, 1986. Concerns the history of the Dutch dredging industry over ten centuries.

J. E. KORTEWEG

**Dubai**    Dubai, which is located at a creek on the northeastern coast of Arabia, was settled in 1833 by about eight hundred members of the Bani Yas tribe, who used the location as a base for pearling and trade. Overshadowed by Abu Dhabi and Sharjah, Dubai remained a minor port throughout the nineteenth century. A major turning point in the port's history occurred in 1902, when Persia asserted its sovereignty over the dependency of Lingeh on the southeastern coast of Persia, imposing high customs and harbor dues there. The ruler of Dubai, Sheikh Maktoum bin-Hashar, took advantage of this opportunity by making Dubai a free port: it soon attracted trade from Lingeh and began to establish itself as the entrepôt of the eastern Persian Gulf. By 1904 the British India Steam Navigation Company had included Dubai on its Bombay (Mumbai)–Basra service. At the outbreak of World War I the port had a multicultural population—mainly Arabs, Indians, and Persians—of about ten thousand.

Pearling was the mainstay of the port's trade, but it collapsed in the 1930s because of competition from cultivated Japanese pearls. This setback, together with the impact of the 1930s depression, war, and political instability, led to economic stagnation. Following Britain's 1968 announcement of its intention to withdraw from the Persian Gulf region, seven emirates combined in 1971 to form the United Arab Emirates, a move that enhanced political stability and economic progress in the region. Under the enlightened leadership of Sheikh Rashid bin-Sa'id, an absolute monarch who gained power in 1958 and ruled until his death in 1990, Dubai was transformed from a small dhow port city into a dynamic globalized port city. A key driver of the growth was the discovery of oil in the mid-1960s and the start of oil exports in 1969. Also during the 1960s, a lucrative entrepôt trade developed in consumer goods for the region: imports increased from £3 million in 1958 to £42 million in 1967 to £200 million by the mid-1970s.

Although Dubai creek was adequate for the port's traditional dhow traffic, it could not cope with large, deep-draft vessels, so the rapid expansion of trade led to pressure to increase the port's capacity. A modern harbor, Port Rashid, was opened in 1972, and container-handling facilities were added in 1976. Jebel Ali, the world's largest man-made port, is located about 35 kilometers (22 miles) southwest of Dubai and has 74 berths, and a 10,000 hectare free-trade zone was opened in 1979. By 2004 Dubai was the world's tenth-largest container port, handling 6,400 twenty-foot equivalent units (TEUs), and the Jebel Ali free-trade zone contained more than 3,880 companies from more than 100 countries. In 2004 the Dubai Port Authority (DPA) won the title of best port in the Middle East for the tenth year in a row. The DPA has invested in offshore terminal operations, and by 2005 it was the world's sixth-largest global port operator.

As oil reserves have declined, Dubai's economy has increasingly depended on business, transport, and tourism.

In the 1980s, with assistance from Emirates Airlines, Dubai developed sea–air transshipment of high-value electrical goods from East Asia to Europe. The airport has become the region's main hub, with more than 18 million passengers in 2003. Dubai has a reputation of being a vibrant, tolerant, and cosmopolitan city, a "Hong Kong of the Middle East." The progress of the port city is a reflection of the drive and entrepreneurship of successive generations of its rulers, merchants, and shipowners.

[See also Ports.]

## Bibliography

Broeze, F. "Dubai: From Creek to Global Port City." In *Harbours and Havens: Essays in Port History in Honour of Gordon Jackson*, edited by Lewis R. Fischer and Adrian Jarvis, pp. 159–190. Saint Johns, Newfoundland: International Maritime Economic History Association, 1999. An excellent survey of Dubai's history.
Melamid, Alexander. "Dubai City." *Geographical Review* 79, no. 3 (July 1989): 345–347. A useful overview of the city's history.
MALCOLM T. TULL

## Dubrovnik

**Dubrovnik**    The Croatian city of Dubrovnik, with a population of about thirty thousand, lies at 42°40′ N, 18°05′ E. From ancient times to the twentieth century, Dubrovnik (also known as Ragusa) was an important east Adriatic merchant port and trade junction for Balkan, Mediterranean, and European emporia. Its long and tempestuous naval history is evident in the remains of the city port dating from the first century B.C.E. and in remnants of arsenals built in 784. The port, whose current appearance dates back to the fifteenth and sixteenth centuries, was designed by Pasko Milicevic. The city and port are protected by imposing walls 1,940 meters (1.2 miles) long, with twenty-seven fortresses and bastions that witnessed centuries of hard-fought freedom.

Dubrovnik was initially a self-governed city-state and was a sovereign republic from 1358 to 1808, when it was subjugated by Napoleon. It had its own legislature, which passed the Statute in 1272 and its supplements: regulations on freeboard (1341), quarantine and lazaret (1377), abolishment of the slave trade (1416), the naval code (1535), and the naval insurance code (1562). The city had numerous consulates and business subsidiaries throughout the world. The sixteenth century was the golden age of Dubrovnik's economic power, its merchant and warships being comparable to those of Venice. Its shipbuilders were world-famous, constructing transoceanic sailboats that reached India and the New World—indeed, the city's dominance in shipping is indicated in the English language by the word "argosy," which derives from "Ragusa." After the loss of independence in 1815, Dubrovnik became part of the Austro-Hungarian Empire, and the current deep port in Gruž Bay was built three kilometers (less than two miles) west of the original port to accommodate larger steamboats.

Dubrovnik in the twenty-first century is important only as a port of call for tourist cruise liners. In 2004, 504 moorings and 457,334 passengers were recorded. It is also the headquarters of Atlantska Plovidba, Croatia's largest bulk-carrier company. The city's important institutions include the Historical Institute at Hrvatska Akademija Znanosti i Umjetnosti (the Croatian Academy of Sciences and Arts), the University of Dubrovnik, the Inter-University Centre, the Scientific Library, the Maritime School (established in 1852), the Maritime Museum, the State Archives, and the summer festival.

Among Dubrovnik's numerous renowned citizens have been Nikola Sagroevic, who studied sea tides; Beno Kotruljevic, who wrote books about trade; the mathematician, physicist, and astronomer Ruder Boškovic; and Petar and Andrija Ohmucevic, who served as admirals in the Spanish navy.

[*See also* Ports.]

### Bibliography

Foretic, Vinko. *Povijest Dubrovnika do 1808.* 2 vols. Zagreb, Croatia: Nakladni Zavod Matice Hrvatske, 1980.

Harris, Robin. *Dubrovnik: A History.* London: Saqi, 2003.

Luetic, Josip. *Pomorci i jedrenjaci Republike Dubrovacke.* Zagreb, Croatia: Nakladni Zavod Matica Hrvatske, 1984.

Mitic, Ilija. *Dubrovacka država u medunarodnoj zajednici (od 1358 do 1815).* 2d ed. Zagreb, Croatia: Nakladni Zavod Matica Hrvatske, 2004.

Nicetic, Antun. *Povijest dubrovacke luke.* Dubrovnik, Croatia: Hrvatska Akademija Znanosti i Umjetnosti u Zagrebu, 1996.

ANTUN NICETIC

# Duguay-Trouin, René (1673–1736), French corsair and naval officer. René Duguay-Trouin was one of the most successful of France's corsair captains during the War of the English Succession (War of the League of Augsberg, 1688–1697) and the War of the Spanish Succession (1701–1714). Born in Saint-Malo on June 10, 1673, into a family of wealthy shipowners, Duguay-Trouin

was just eighteen years of age when he first commanded a privateer, the 14-gun *Dancyan.* Two years later, in 1693, he was appointed captain of *Hercule,* a royal vessel of 28 guns set forth specifically to damage enemy commerce, a feat achieved through the capture of two valuable English West Indiamen. Duguay-Trouin was rewarded not only with a share in the proceeds of such seizures, but also with the command of more potent vessels and, as his prize-taking record improved, with honors bestowed by Louis XIV. Appointed *capitaine de frégate légère* in 1697 and *capitaine de vaisseau* in 1705, Trouin was ennobled as sieur du Guay in June 1709, by which time he had captured twenty enemy warships and three hundred merchantmen. His most brilliant campaign occurred in 1711, however, when he led a force of seventeen ships and 5,486 men in a successful amphibious attack on Rio de Janeiro.

Duguay-Trouin's commerce-raiding career was underpinned by a conjunction of private and state resources. From Saint-Malo—a port with long-held interests in the Newfoundland fisheries and a growing stake in the long-distance trades to South America and the East Indies—he received the financial support of a mercantile consortium organized by his eldest brother, Luc. From the state—which in 1694–1697 and in 1704–1712 invested in corsairs rather than in its battlefleet—he received patronage and material support, notably vessels, armaments, and manpower. In essence, therefore, René Duguay-Trouin was the archetypal exponent of *guerre de course,* a strategy that generated large prize hauls and personal wealth for some investors but that failed to deliver victory in the sea war to France. He died in Paris in 1736.

[*See also* French Literature]

### Bibliography

Bromley, John S. *Corsairs and Navies, 1660–1760.* London: Hambledon Press, 1987.

Le Nepvou de Carfort, H. É. *Histoire de du Guay Trouin.* Paris: Plon-Nourrit, 1922.

DAVID J. STARKEY

# Duhamel du Monceau, Henri Louis
(1700–1782), French botanist, agronomist, and naval administrator. Henri Louis Duhamel du Monceau, inspector general of the French navy and head of the French navy's school for engineer constructors, was born in Paris in July

1700, into the prosperous family of Alexandre Duhamel de Denainvilliers and Anne Trottier. His elder brother inherited the Denainvilliers estate, and later in life Henri Louis bought the Monceau estate. He never married.

Duhamel du Monceau initially studied law in Paris, but he wanted to become a botanist and worked with the Jussieu family, which oversaw the royal garden. In 1727 he developed a treatment for a disease of the saffron plant, bringing him to the attention of the Académie Royale des Sciences of Paris and the minister of the navy, Jean-Frédéric Philippe Phélypeaux, Count of Maurepas. Maurepas employed Duhamel du Monceau on an unofficial basis to solve problems for the navy. Duhamel du Monceau made his most important contribution in 1737, when he and the naturalist Georges-Louis Leclerc, Count of Buffon, prepared a report on the strength of various woods. In 1739, Maurepas appointed Buffon intendant of the royal garden but selected the disappointed Duhamel du Monceau as the first inspector general of the navy, a position that he held until his death.

In this role, Duhamel du Monceau was continually visiting ports and dockyards to identify and disseminate the best methods of carrying out tasks, including the organization of naval hospitals, rope making (the topic of his *Traité de la fabrique de manoeuvres pour les vaisseaux*, published in 1747), sail making, and preservation of ship's timbers. He continued his research in forestry, botany, fisheries, and agronomy as an integral part of this work, eventually compiling an eight-volume study of trees and timber, *Traité complet des bois et des forêts* (1755–1768). All this work was aimed at stretching the limited naval budget by maintaining and using more efficiently the fleet and its crews.

But Duhamel du Monceau also saw the need to improve naval construction, and in 1741 he established the first professional school for naval engineers and architects, at his house in Paris. The school was eventually moved to the Louvre palace and became known as the École de la Marine. In 1752, Duhamel du Monceau wrote the first textbook of naval architecture, *Elémens de l'architecture navale*, which combined the theoretical and practical aspects of shipbuilding. Although the theory was based principally on Pierre Bouguer's *Traité du navire* (1746), the mathematics was rendered in a systematic format that students could use by rote. *Elémens de l'architecture navale* was translated into several languages and served as the principal textbook of naval architecture throughout Europe for almost a century.

In 1765, Duhamel's school and textbook became the centerpieces of the École des Ingénieurs-Constructeurs de Vaisseaux Royaux, created under a sweeping reform carried out by the minister of the navy, Etienne-François, Duke of Choiseul. Under this system, naval constructors were required to undergo extensive schooling in ship theory, as well as a practical apprenticeship at the beginning of their careers. This became the model for the new wave of professional corps of constructors and schools of naval architecture that arose throughout Europe and the Americas during the 1800s.

After suffering a stroke, Duhamel du Monceau died in Paris on August 13, 1782.

[*See also* Bouguer, Pierre; Education and Training; *and* Naval Architecture.]

## Bibliography

Allard, Michel. *Henri-Louis Duhamel du Monceau et le ministère de la marine*. Montreal: Leméac, 1970.

Ferreiro, Larrie D. *Ships and Science: The Birth of Naval Architecture in the Scientific Revolution, 1600–1800*. Cambridge, Mass.: MIT Press, 2007.

Villiers, Patrick. "De la lutte contre la maladie du safran à la direction de l'inspection générale de la construction navale, une alliance inattendue: Duhamel de Monceau et Maurepas." Presented at the Eighth Anglo-French Naval Historian's Conference, "The Rational and the Irrational: Science and the French and British Navies, 1700–1850," National Maritime Museum, Greenwich, U.K., April 30–May 3, 2001.

LARRIE D. FERREIRO

# Dupuy de Lôme, Stanislas-Charles-Henri-Laurent

(1816–1885), French naval architect and politician. Stanislas-Charles-Henri-Laurent Dupuy de Lôme, considered by both historians and his contemporaries to be the greatest naval architect of the nineteenth century, created the first armored steam warship, *Gloire*, and in the process helped transform France into a leading naval power. Born on October 15, 1816, into a naval family in Ploëmeur near Lorient, he studied under the great engineer Frédéric Reech at the École Polytechnique from 1835 to 1837. In 1842 the junior naval architect was sent on an important mission to Britain to investigate the construction of iron ships and steamships. Dupuy de Lôme spent nine months at many shipyards, particularly at the Birkenhead yard of Laird, Son, & Co., and he maintained close communication with John Laird throughout his career. On his return to France, Dupuy de Lôme wrote an influential report, *Mémoire sur la construction des bâtiments en fer*, that bolstered the case for iron ships.

His first major steam warship, the 90-gun screw frigate *Napoléon* (launched 1850), was considered a great success and soon found service in the Crimean War (1853–1856). That war also saw the introduction of armored floating batteries. Subsequently, Dupuy de Lôme (by now *directeur du materiel*, equivalent to the chief constructor) sought to combine iron and steam, and in 1859 he launched the ironclad *Gloire*, the first of four warships to unite the modern elements of steam engines, screw propulsion, and iron armor. In fact, French industry was not able to produce enough iron to build all four ships entirely in metal, so *Gloire*'s hull was wooden; but the next ship, *Couronne* (1861), was all iron. The French navy was immediately at the forefront of naval innovation, but only for a short time. In 1860 the British navy launched HMS *Warrior*, which was larger, faster, and more heavily armored, and carried more guns. However, Dupuy de Lôme was by now building warships (like *Solférino*) with ram bows, which many considered to be the preferred naval weapon.

Dupuy de Lôme turned his attention to other areas as well. In 1863 he reluctantly permitted the construction of the submarine *Plongeur* under Charles Brun, but he used its lessons twenty years later in *Gymnote*, the first successful submarine (actually completed by Gustave Zédé). In 1869, Dupuy de Lôme retired from the navy to direct the construction of passenger and merchant ships—including the first train ferries—at several commercial shipyards. In 1870 he found himself amid the siege of Paris during the Franco-Prussian War; to help break the siege, Dupuy de Lôme developed a dirigible airship, which was not used because it became ready only a few days before the capitulation of the French army. Already decorated with the Légion d'Honneur in 1845 and made a member of the Académie des Sciences since 1866, Dupuy de Lôme was elected to several political offices, becoming senator for Morbihan in 1877. Dupuy de Lôme died in Paris on February 1, 1885.

[*See also Gloire*; Naval Architecture; Ship and Boatbuilders; Ship Construction; Shipbuilding Materials; *and* Warships, *subentry on* Modern Warships.]

## Bibliography

Battesti, Michèle. *La marine de Napoléon III: Une politique navale*. Paris: Service Historique de la Marine, 1997.
Institut d'Histoire des Conflits Contemporains and Service Historique de la Marine, ed. *Marine et technique au XIXe siècle: Actes du colloque international, Paris, École Militaire … 10–12 juin 1987*. Paris: Service Historique de la Marine, 1988.
Service Propagande Édition et Information. *Bi-centenaire du génie maritime, 1765–1965*. Paris: Service Propagande Édition et Information, 1965.

LARRIE D. FERREIRO

# Dutch Literature

This entry contains two subentries:

An Overview
Chroniclers of Exploration

## An Overview

Although the Netherlands is a preeminently maritime country, sea literature never played a major role in literary trends. However, the sea plays a more or less important part in many novels, poems, and plays for both adults and children. This can be seen in the major contributions of Dutch writers to maritime literature from the seventeenth to the twentieth century, including works of poetry and plays, socially engaged literature, great maritime novels, travel stories, biographies, and youth literature and comics.

### Poetry and Plays

Nowadays only the lyrical poetry by Joost van den Vondel (1587–1679) is still read, but in the seventeenth century he was considered a great and versatile writer. In his poems, but also in his celebrated plays, Vondel often paid attention to maritime aspects of the golden age of the Dutch Republic. For instance, in the play *Gijsbrecht van Aemstel* (1637), in which the hero of the same name (and in him, symbolically, the town of Amsterdam) is overthrown, Dutch (maritime) history plays an important part. In the poem *Het lof der Zeevaert* (Hymn of Navigation, 1623) Vondel presents a proud and masterly survey of the maritime history of his country. In 478 verses he pleads for peaceable trade, which in his view (and in the eyes of many Dutch commoners of the golden age) was preferable to aggressive war.

At the end of the nineteenth century Daniël François Scheurleer (1855–1927), a banker and an expert in the history of music, performed an important job by collecting all sorts of songs and ballads from former eras. In his tripartite study *Van varen en van vechten: Verzen van tijdgenooten op onze zeehelden en zeeslagen, lof- en schimpdichten, matrozenliederen* (From Sailing and Fighting, 1914) ancient Dutch maritime songs, verses, and rhymes were brought together. Through these popular verses the interested reader gains a clear view of the way the man in the street saw the navy and the important naval battles of the seventeenth, eighteenth, and nineteenth centuries.

It was only in the twentieth century that a Dutch poet dealt mainly with maritime themes. Jan Jacob Slauerhoff (1898–1936) studied medicine and published his first collection of poetry, *Archipel* (Archipelago), in 1923. His models were such French Symbolist poets as Charles Baudelaire (1821–1867) and Arthur Rimbaud (1854–1891). Between 1923 and 1929 Slauerhoff served as a ship's surgeon and from 1932 to 1935 he again sailed far from home. He traveled to China, Japan, Dutch East India (Indonesia), South Africa, and throughout South America. Slauerhoff had a delicate constitution and for a short time maintained a medical practice in Tangier, so as to benefit from the North African climate. His collection of poetry *Soleares* (1933) became widely known, as did the novels *Het verboden rijk* (Forbidden Empire, 1932) and *Het leven op aarde* (Life on Earth, 1934). Slauerhoff was a romantic, and his poetry is characterized by discontent with the society in which he lived, combined with an intense anticipation of passion. In his poetry Slauerhoff passionately expresses his desires and the impossibility of finding his own place on earth except in his poems. These romantic feelings are placed against the background of foreign civilizations, particularly Chinese culture. Shortly after his thirty-eighth birthday and after the publication of his final collection of poetry, *Een eerlijk zeemansgraf* (An Honest Watery Grave, 1936), Slauerhoff died from malaria in combination with neglected tuberculosis.

## Socially Engaged Literature

Beginning in the nineteenth century, social questions played a an important role in literature. Herman Heijermans (1864–1924) began as a drama critic and columnist for a newspaper and soon began to write plays himself, dealing with social questions such as the gruesome circumstances of miners. His well-known play *Op hoop van zegen: Spel van de zee in vier bedrijven* (The Good Hope, 1900) is about Dutch fishermen who were sent to sea in perilous wrecks. The fisherwoman Kniertje is one of the most famous figures in Dutch literature. Heijermans wrote in a realistic style but sometimes fell into sentimentality. He also was active in the socialist movement. Heijermans was one of the few Dutch playwrights who gained international fame.

Another well-known, socially conscious novel of the mid-twentieth century is Jan de Hartog's *Hollands Glorie: roman van de zeesleepvaart* (Holland's Glory, 1940), concerning abuses in the world of deep-sea-towage.

## Great Maritime Novels

Not all authors who wrote maritime books were seen as great literary writers. Anthony van Kampen (1911–1991), for example, traveled the world with great interest in maritime matters and in far regions. He wrote novels about New Guinea, the region of the Amazon, and Greenland. The sea serves as a leitmotif throughout his works. His most famous books about the sea are novels like *Ketelbinkie* (1946), about a cabin boy who at last becomes a captain. In 1946 Kampen founded the magazine *De Blauwe Wimpel* (The Blue Ribbon), covering navigation and shipbuilding in the Low Countries. Kampen's books are considered as popular literature rather than literary works.

The same is true of works by Jan de Hartog (1914–2002). In the Netherlands de Hartog's novels are seen as boyish adventure books, not as literature of high standing. De Hartog gained recognition as a literary writer only when he emigrated in the 1960s to the United States, where he wrote many more maritime novels.

The more highly esteemed Arthur François Émile van Schendel (1874–1946) was not a typical maritime author, but the sea plays an important role in one of his books. Van Schendel wrote symbolic, neoromantic literature with a timeless adventurousness. His was the imagination of an absolutely free existence, full of loneliness, melancholy, and longing for happiness. His great breakthrough came with *Het fregatschip Johanna Maria* (1930; English trans., *The Johanna Maria*, 1935). In this symbolic novel Van Schendel describes the fate of Dutch commoners, who were swayed by the philosophical-religious questions of determination or free will, destiny or chance, human sin or grace of God. In *Het fregatschip Johanna Maria*, as the captain and the sailmaker argue over which of them loves the ship more, Van Schendel subtly outlines the historical development of navigation. Van Schendel was an English teacher and lived after 1921 in Florence, Italy.

Traditionally the colony of the Dutch East Indies (Indonesia) formed an important theme in Dutch literature. Many great novelists who wrote about the colonial period also paid attention to maritime themes. From the seventeenth century onward travel stories were published that had been written by voyagers to the Far East. In the nineteenth and twentieth centuries more and more novels about the overseas island kingdom were written. Van Schendel, for example, wrote *Jan Compagnie* (John Company, 1932) about the Dutch East India Company, and the work of the internationally known Louis Marie Anne Couperus (1863–1923) also has maritime aspects.

## Travel Stories

The strong rise of the Dutch publishing industry around 1600 coincided with the period in which the Dutch ventured on long voyages of discovery. One of the first and most important authors of travel books was Jan Huyghen van Linschoten (1563–1611). This Dutch geographer worked as a tax collector or bookkeeper for the archbishop of Goa, and in this capacity he collected information on India and the Far East. After his return to the Dutch Republic he published his experiences in his *Itinerario, Voyage, ofte Schipvaert naer Oost ofte Portugaels Indien* (1596). This book was published in English as *Iohn Huighen van Linschoten: His Discours of Voyages into ye Easte and West Indies; Devided into Foure Bookes* (1598). The first part describes Portuguese India, the second part is devoted to the ocean routes to India and China, and the third part deals with the west coast of Africa and the east coast of America. His book stimulated Dutch attempts to seek an ocean route to India for themselves and was of great importance for the history of Dutch exploration. The *Itinerario* was also translated into French, German, and Latin.

Another famous Dutch travel account was written by Gerrit de Veer, son of an Amsterdam notary. He accompanied Willem Barents (c. 1550–1597) on his second and third expeditions to the north and he based his *Waerachtighe Beschryvinghe Van drie seylagien, ter werelt noyt soo vreemt ghehoort* (1598) on these experiences. Veer added a report on the first expedition, based on notes kept by Barents. Veer's story soon was translated into German, English, French, Latin, and Italian, and is known to this day as an example of the experiences of a group of people in distress. The English translation was published under the title *The True and Perfect Description of Three Voyages, so Strange and Woonderfull, that the Like Hath Never Been Heard of Before: Done and Performed Three Yeares, One after the Other, by the Ships of Holland and Zeland, on the North Sides of Norway, Muscouia, and Tartaria, towards the Kingdomes of Cathaia & China* (1605).

Accounts of ships in heavy storms and of shipping disasters were very popular. One voyager, the Hoorn skipper Willem IJsbrandtsz. Bontekoe (1587–after 1646) became well known

when his *Iournael ofte Gedenckwaerdige beschrijvinghe vande Oost-Indische Reyse van Willem IJsbrantsz. Bontekoe van Hoorn* (1646) was published. When it appeared, the book immediately became immensely popular among the Dutch people, for Bontekoe vividly describes the disastrous voyage of 1618–1619 to the Dutch East Indies in which his ship exploded and the crew had to save themselves in small open boats. Eventually only 56 of the 206 crew members managed to reach Batavia. Johan Fabricius wrote the very popular youth novel *De scheepsjongens van Bontekoe* (Java ho!: The Adventures of Four Boys Amid Fire, Storm, and Shipwreck, 1924), which was reprinted several times.

Dutch travel stories about the East Indies from the first half of the nineteenth century remain understudied, but hundreds of worthwhile itineraries were published. One of the most interesting travel books from this period was written by the versatile naval officer Quirijn Maurits Rudolph ver Huell (1787–1860). In the years 1816–1819 he traveled on board *Admiraal Evertsen*, a Dutch ship-of-the-line, to the Dutch East Indies. Huell captured the images of this new world in words and pictures. Years later he published in two parts his book *Herinneringen van eene reis naar de Oost-Indiën* (Recollections of a Voyage to the East Indies, 1835–1836) and produced some hundred watercolors.

Many Dutch travel accounts from the seventeenth, eighteenth, and nineteenth centuries are published in the series *Werken uitgegeven door de Linschoten-Vereeniging*. The Linschoten-Vereeniging was founded in 1908 following the example of the British Hakluyt Society. Every annotated travel account contains the original text and an explanation of the circumstances that gave rise to the voyage. By 2006 more than one hundred editions had been published.

## Biographies

As the accounts of famous and perilous voyages and their travelers were published, so were biographies of Dutch naval heroes. One of these was Geeraert Brandt's *Het leven en bedrijf van den heere Michiel de Ruiter* (The Life and Times of Michiel de Ruiter, 1687). Michiel Adriaanszoon de Ruyter, the most famous Dutch admiral and naval hero, died in 1667. Although in biographies the lives of naval heroes are often exaggerated, Brandt's biography gives a just impression of Ruyter's personality and significance for seventeenth-century Dutch seapower. Brandt's biography was reprinted many times in the eighteenth, nineteenth, and twentieth centuries. It appeared also in the form of anthologies, interlaced with numerous anecdotes that made it attractive to children.

Other Dutch naval heroes, like Pieter Pieterszoon Hein (1577–1629), Maarten Harpertszoon Tromp (1598–1653), and his son Cornelis Tromp (1629–1691) were never the subject of a proper and comprehensive contemporary biography until the twentieth century.

Naval heroes received more attention during the nineteenth century. In 1844 the poet J. P. Heye (1809–1876) wrote the text for the famous *Een triomfantelijk lied van de Zilvervloot* (A Triumphant Song of the Zilvervloot), set to music by J. J. Viotta (1814–1859). This song, still sung at sporting events and other public occasions, made Heye's name immortal.

### Youth Literature and Comics

In considerations of popular literature, children's books and comics ought to have a place as well. There were three popular Dutch comics with a maritime theme. The first, *De avonturen van Kapitein Rob* (The Adventures of Captain Rob), was created by the illustrator Pieter Joseph Kuhn (1910–1966) with texts by the journalist Evert Werkman (1915–1988). Although not all the adventures take place at sea, this comic has a maritime character. It first appeared shortly after World War II, so it is not surprising that the leading figure's name is *De Vrijheid* (Freedom). Between 1945 and 1966 seventy-two stories were published as a daily comic in the newspaper *Het Parool*. The seventy-third story was left unfinished on Kuhn's sudden death. Afterward the stories were reprinted in separate book editions and paperbacks. The second example of a Dutch maritime comic is *Eric de Noorman* (Eric the Viking) by Hans G. Kresse (1921–1992). The third comic was created by Marten Toonder (1912–2005). Toonder is well known for his comics on Heer Olivier B. Bommel and Tom Poes (Sir Oliver B. Bommel and Tom Puss), in which "Kapitein Wal Rus" (Captain Walrus) performs. But Toonder's most important maritime creation was *Kappie*, which perhaps was created after the example of his father, who was a merchant marine officer. Toonder is remembered for his contribution to the Dutch language of many colorful sayings and expressions.

Johannes Hendrik Been (1859–1930) was a teacher and from 1895 the town archivist of Brielle, where Maarten Harpertszoon Tromp was born. He wrote a great number of boys' books, of which some became classics. For example *Maerten Harpertsz. Tromp: Een zeemanszoon uit de 17de eeuw* (Maerten Harpertsz. Tromp: A Seaman's Son from the Seventeenth Century, 1896) and *Paddeltje: De scheepsjongen van Michiel de Ruyter* (Paddeltje: The Cabin Boy of Michiel de Ruyter, 1908).

[*See also* Hartog, Jan de, *and* Literature.]

### Bibliography

Campenhout, Frans van. *Leven en werk van Jan de Hartog.* Antwerp: De Nederlanden, 1987.

Goedkoop, Hans. *Geluk: Het leven van Herman Heijermans.* Amsterdam and Antwerp: Arbeiderspers, 1996.

Hazeu, Wim. *Slauerhoff: Een biografie.* Amsterdam and Antwerp: Arbeiderspers, 1995.

Kousemaker, Evelien, and Kees Kousemaker. *Wordt vervolgd: Stripleksikon der Lage Landen.* Utrecht: Het Spectrum, 1979.

Parr, Charles McKew. *Jan van Linschoten: The Dutch Marco Polo.* New York: Crowell, 1964.

Ritman, Lex. *Kapitein Robs stormachtige leven.* The Hague: Panda, 1995.

Roeper, V. D. and G. J. D. Wildeman. *Reizen op papier: Journalen en reisverslagen van Nederlandse ontdekkingsreizigers, kooplieden en avonturiers.* Amsterdam: Vereeniging Nederlandsch Historisch Scheepvaartmuseum and Nederlands Scheepvaartmuseum; Zutphen: Walburg Pers, 1996.

Salverda, Murk, ed. *Hollands glorie: Het water als thema in de Nederlandse literatuur tussen 1900 en 1960.* The Hague: Letterkundig Museum, 1988.

Tiele, P. A. *Mémoire bibliographique sur les journaux des navigateurs néerlandais: Réimprimés dans les collections de De Bry et de Hulsius et dans les collections hollandaises du XVIIe siècle, et sur les anciennes éditions hollandaises des journaux de navigateurs étrangers; la plupart en la possession de Frederik Muller a Amsterdam.* Amsterdam: Frederik Muller, 1867. Reprinted Amsterdam: N. Israel, 1960 and 1969.

Verhoeven, Garrelt Verhoeven, and Piet Verkruijsse. *Journael ofte Gedenckwaerdige beschrijvinghe vande Oost-Indische Reyse van Willem Ysbrantsz. Bontekoe van Hoorn: descriptieve bibliografie 1646–1996.* Zutphen: Walburg Pers, 1996.

RON J. M. W. BRAND *and* JOKE E. KORTEWEG

# Chroniclers of Exploration

From the 1590s onward, ships from the Netherlands swarmed out over all the world's oceans. Even before then the Dutch had sailed on Spanish and Portuguese vessels to America and Asia. The most important Dutch traveler was Jan Huyghen van Linschoten, who went to India in 1583 as the secretary to the newly appointed bishop to Goa, the capital of the Portugese Empire in Asia. During this stay he collected a large number of documents on the Portuguese in Asia. After his return to the Netherlands he compiled a voluminous book in four parts on the Portuguese presence, trade, shipping, and the peoples of Asia, including information on the geography and produce of different regions. Most of this material had not previously been published. Details on the West African coast and the West Indies were also included. In addition, the book contained the first Portuguese sailing directions from Europe to Asia in print in any language and an account of Linschoten's own travels.

Linschoten's *Itinerario, Voyagie ofte Schipvaert* (Amsterdam, 1595–1596) was truly encyclopedic and illustrated with thirty-six large engravings and seven maps. The book was translated into French, German, Latin, and English. It served as a reference work for the Dutch and the English during the first decades of the seventeenth century and is a good example of later trends in Dutch travel literature. The accounts of th e first Dutch voyages were published soon after their termination; they were richly illustrated with maps and charts.

Beginning in 1595 Dutch ships regularly sailed to Asia; a number of expeditions were sent to the Pacific coast of South America and across the ocean toward Southeast Asia and Japan. These early Dutch voyages created much interest in the Netherlands and elsewhere. Most of the accounts were published and were translated into the major European languages, but after a number of years interest in travel literature declined somewhat in the Netherlands.

In 1645 a Amsterdam publisher, Jan Jansz (better known as Johannes Janssonius), published a large collection of accounts of Dutch voyages. The compiler was probably influenced by earlier similar collections of travel narratives by Richard Hakluyt and Samuel Purchas in England and Theodor de Bry and Levinus Hulsius in Germany. The *Begin ende Voortgangh Vande Vereenigde Nederlandtsche Geoctroyeerde Oost-Indsiche Compagne* (Beginning and Progress of the Dutch United Charted East India Company; Amsterdam, 1645) includes all the Dutch East India Company's major voyages, with the first voyage to the East Indies in 1595–1597, the polar voyages under Willem Barents in 1594–1597, the circumnavigation of Van Noort in 1598–1600, the discovery of Cape Horn in 1616, and many more. In all, thirty travel accounts were republished in this book, in addition to some shorter texts that appeared for the first time. The name of the compiler, Isaac Commelin, does not appear in the book but is known from other sources. The collection also gave a new impetus to others to publish older and some new travel accounts as well. In the Netherlands two publishers, Hartgers (1648) and Saeghman (c. 1663), even copied the success of *Begin*

*ende Voortgangh*—as the two volumes are usually referred to—in versions for the lower end of the book market.

Commelin's work was much used and cited in later centuries and established a canon of early Dutch travel accounts. It was adapted and translated into English by John Harris in his *Navigantium atque itinerantium bibliotheca, or A Compleat Collection of Voyages and Travels* in 1705 and into French by René-Auguste-Constantin de Renneville in 1702–1707 as *Recueil des voyages qui ont servi à l'établissement et aux progrès de la compagnie des Indes Orientales, formées dans les Provinces Unies des Païs-bas.*

Besides compiling earlier accounts of separate travel narratives, other writers mainly collected material on a specific region. Nicolaas Witsen (1641–1717), the son of a rich merchant, accompanied a diplomatic mission to Moscow in 1664–1665 and acquired a lifelong interest in the Russian Empire. Witsen kept in correspondence with leading Russian families during his distinguished career, in which he became burgomaster of the city of Amsterdam and one of the directors of the Dutch East India Company. With an extensive network of connections he was able to assemble a vast collection of curiosities, books, and manuscripts. In 1692 he had a "pre-publication" version printed of *Noorden Oost Tartarije*, followed in 1715 by an expanded edition for the general public. This book provides in just over a thousand pages a wealth of information on Russia, Siberia, and the entire eastern Pacific south of Japan. He made use of a great number of travel accounts, both in print and in manuscript, a number of which have been lost. Although Witsen's book contains important sources, it suffers from rather erratic composition, making it difficult to use. In 1854 the Hakluyt Society published one of its travel accounts, and other parts have been translated.

Another important author was François Valentijn (1666–1727), a minister with the Dutch East Company for many years in what is now Indonesia. During this stay he collected information, with the help of a friends and correspondents, about many aspects of the history and life of the Dutch in Asia. In 1724–1726 his *Oud en Nieuw Oost-Indien* was published in five volumes (often bound in six to eight large folio volumes) with about fifty-five hundred pages. This book contains detailed information on the peoples and their costumes in present Indonesia and the other Dutch settlements of the Dutch East India Company in South Africa, India, Ceylon (Sri Lanka), and elsewhere. It is the most comprehensive single publication on the history and conflicts of the Dutch East India Company, with many maps, charts, and views of the Dutch settlements. The book remained the principal single work, especially on Southeast Asia, well into the nineteenth century, and the sections on Ceylon and South Africa have been published in English.

[*See also* Literature, *subentry on* Voyage Narratives; *and* Voyage and Travel Accounts.]

## Bibliography

Nearly all the important early Dutch accounts of voyages have been published in a scholarly edition in their original language in the series Werken uitgegeven door de Linschoten-Vereeniging (Works Issued by the Linschoten Society), including the travels of Linschoten, Witsen, and many of the original accounts in Commelin's 1645 collection. A complete bibliography is available at http://www.linschoten-vereeniging.nl. Linschoten's *Itinenario* was published by the Hakluyt Society in English (1885) There is no modern scholarly edition of Valentijn in the original Dutch. The parts of Valentijn on Sri Lanka (1975) and South Africa (1971–1973) are available in English editions. Parts of Witsen's work (a voyage into Tartary ) were made available by the Hakluyt Society in an English edition (1854), but most of his work still awaits a scholarly edition.

Arasaratnam, Sinnappah, trans. and ed. *François Valentijn's Description of Ceylon*. London: Hakluyt Society, 1978.

Beekman, E. M. *Troubled Pleasures. Dutch Colonial Literature from the East Indies, 1600–1950*. Oxford: Clarendon Press, 1996. See especially the chapter on Valentijn.

Boxer, C. R. "Isaac Commelin's 'Begin ende Voortgangh' " In his *Dutch Merchants and Mariners in Asia 1602–1795*. London: Variorum Reprints, 1988.

Burnell, Arthur Cooke, and P. A. Tiele. *Voyage of John Huyghen van Linschoten to the East Indies from the Old English Translation of 1598*. London: Hakluyt Society, 1885. Reprint, New Delhi: Asian Educational Services, 1988.

Earl of Ellesmere, trans. and ed. *History of the Two Tartar Conquerors of China, Including the Two Journeys into Tartary of Father Ferdinand Verbiest in the Suite of the Emperor Kang-hi: From the French of Père Pierre Joseph d'Orléans, of the Company of Jesus. To Which Is Added Father Pereira's Journey into Tartary in the Suite of the Same Emperor, From the Dutch of Nicholaas Witsen*. London: Hakluyt Society, 1854. Reprint, New York: B. Franklin, 1971.

Gelder, Roelof van, Jan Parmentier, and Vibeke Roeper. *Souffrir pour parvenir: De wereld van Jan Huygen van Linschoten*. Haarlem, Netherlands: Arcadia, 1998. Includes a bibliography of works by Linschoten.

Habiboe, R. R. F. *Tot verheffing van mijne natie: Het leven en werk van François Valentijn (1666–1727)*. Franeker, Netherlands: Van Wijnen, 2004.

Lach, Donald F., and Edwin J. Van Kley. *Asia in the Making of Europe*. Vol. 3: *A Century of Advance*. Chicago: University of Chicago Press, 1993.

Parr, Charles MacKew. *Jan Huygen van Linschoten: The Dutch Marco Polo*. New York: Crowell, 1964.

Peters, Marion. "From the Study of Nicolaes Witsen (1641–1717): His Life with Books and Manuscripts." In *Lias. Sources and Documents Relating to the Early Modern History of Ideas* 21, no. 1 (1994): 1–47.

Serton, P., R. Raven-Hart, and W. J. de Kock, eds. *Description of the Cape of Good Hope with the Matters Concerning It, Amsterdam 1726*. 2 vols. Cape Town, South Africa: Van Riebeeck Society, 1971–1973.

Valentijn, François. *Oud en Nieuw Oost-Indien, vervattende Een Naaukeurige en Uitvoerige Verhandelinge van Nederlands Mogentheyd In die Gewesten, benevens Eene wydluftige Beschryvinge der Moluccos, Amboina, Banda, Timor, en Solor, Java, etc.* 8 vols. Franeker, Netherlands: Van Wijnen, 2003–2004. A facsimile of the 1724–1726 edition.

DIEDERICK WILDEMAN

# E

**Earth Sciences** Modern studies of the nature and development of Earth's main characteristics are collectively known as the earth sciences. These are commonly divided into three principal components: atmospheric, hydrologic, and geologic investigations. Pertaining to the skies are meteorology (physics of the weather), climatology (general weather patterns in relation to geography, latitude, and circulation), and astrogeology (rocks from other celestial bodies and their associated features on Earth, such as tektites and meteorite-impact craters). Surface water in solid and liquid state is the main object of interest in glaciology (ice caps and glaciers), hydrology (water on and in the ground), and oceanography (oceanic circulation, tides, waves, chemistry, depth, and marine biology). As far as the solid earth is concerned, one can distinguish geodesy (size and shape of the planet), geomorphology (landforms), volcanology (volcanoes), paleontology (fossil record), stratigraphy (sedimentary deposition), geochronology (isotopic rock dating), mineralogy (minerals), petrology (rocks), geochemistry (chemistry of rocks), and structural geology (geometrical relationships of geological features). In addition, the physics of Earth (density, magnetic and electric fields, thermal properties, internal structure, and dynamics), in particular regarding the inaccessible deep interior, are analyzed by geophysics, by means of mathematics and indirect measurements (gravimetry, seismology, geomagnetism, and studies of heat transport and electric fields). Alternatively, a different division separates the above disciplines into those concerned with: (1) Earth's surface and atmosphere; (2) physico-chemical aspects of rocks; (3) extraterrestrial rocks; (4) landforms; (5) geologic history; and (6) applied earth sciences (location and exploration of fossil fuels, building foundations, erosion, and hazards from natural disasters).

To some extent, these boundaries are artificial; in order to observe, classify, and explain the presence and development of particular features, earth scientists may have to draw upon a number of the aforementioned specializations in parallel. The shape of a continental coastline may, for instance, have been affected not just by the current erosion and deposition due to winds, rivers, currents, and tides, but by its formation history, the types and chemistry of rock involved, the oceanic plate subducting beneath it, the glaciers that covered it during a former ice age, and the latitude and orientation of the continent millions or billions of years ago. Earth sciences thus tend to require both a multidisciplinary approach and a broad spatial and temporal range.

In the present context of maritime history, a more practical classification is adhered to, identifying the few sciences that have deeply and directly affected navigation in past and present, those numerous sciences with little or no bearing at all on shipping, and the intermediary category concerned with those aspects of Earth that bear some (perhaps unexpected) relevance to ships at sea. The first group contains meteorology, oceanography, and geomagnetism, each of which is treated in a separate entry. The second group mainly involves the study of rocks in one form or another, and is disregarded here. The third group is treated below, focusing in turn upon the maritime implications of Earth's shape, density, rotation, and its inner composition and dynamics.

## Geodetic Explorations

On a clear day in harbor, one can observe that departing ships appear to sink slowly behind the horizon; the topsails of tall ships still remain visible while the hull is already out of sight. The underlying concept of a spherical earth can be traced back to antiquity, attributed to Greek philosophers Pythagoras (fl. sixth century B.C.E.), Parmenides (c. 515–445 B.C.E.), Aristotle (384–322 B.C.E.), and Hipparchus (c. 190–c. 120 B.C.E.). Nevertheless, the honorary title "father of geodesy" is usually bestowed upon Eratosthenes of Cyrene (c. 276–194 B.C.E.), geographer, philosopher, and director of the Alexandria library. By combining the latitudinal physical distance between Syene (Aswan) and Alexandria with their angular difference of simultaneous noonday shadows, he was the first to obtain a reliable estimate of Earth's circumference, accurate to about

15 percent. Classical and Arabian geographers promulgated this insight during the next millennium. Even at the height of the European Middle Ages, flat-Earth dissidents remained a small minority; holders of this belief had all but disappeared by the early fifteenth century. Among European supporters of the spherical hypothesis were Bede (eighth century), and Roger Bacon, Albertus Magnus, and Vincent of Beauvais (all thirteenth century).

A new technique to measure the size of the earth was conceived by the Danish astronomer Tycho Brahe at the end of the sixteenth century, following theoretical foundations laid down in 1533 by Dutch polymath Gemma Frisius, who proposed trigonometric surveying for creating a comprehensive network of regional maps. Applied to the entire planet, it was developed into a science by the Dutch mathematician Willebrord Snel (1580–1626). In Snel's *Eratosthenes Batavus* (1617), geodetic surveying by triangulation yielded a figure only 3.4 percent too small. The triangulation method is still used today, consisting of a baseline of known size and latitude, and a chain of connecting triangles between landmarks. Given the measured angles and spherical trigonometry, the lengths of all sides and the network's coordinates could be worked out, eventually producing the physical distance of one latitudinal degree, which when multiplied by 360 gave the earth's circumference. The result profoundly affected Dutch cartography, which divided a degree of meridian arc into fifteen "German" miles, hitherto assumed to be 5,355 meters (17,570 feet) each, but following Snel adjusted to 7,158 meters (23,485 feet).

The accuracy of triangulation was, of course, limited by the capacity of the sighting instruments. In 1669–1671 the French astronomer Jean Picard employed the latest telescopes, and derived a planetary radius equivalent to 6,372 kilometers (modern average: 6,371.2 kilometers [3,958.9 miles]). His network consisted of thirteen triangles, extending 1.2 degrees northward from Paris. The determination of the length of a meridian degree had been the first great task assigned by King Louis XIV (r. 1643–1715) to the young Parisian Académie Royale des Sciences, founded in 1666 by Louis's minister Jean-Baptiste Colbert (1619–1683). As part of the French effort to accurately map their country, knowledge of Picard's findings was spread from 1678 in the *Connoissance des Temps*, the first French state-sponsored nautical almanac, issued by the Académie. French geodetic inquiries would peak during the next century, due in part to their relation to the longitude problem and the effects of gravitation (see below).

## Planetary Density and Gravitational Force

Among a multitude of tables of celestial and geographical positions, the literate mariner would also find a pendulum clock instruction in the French nautical almanac. Taking a timekeeper on board ship was one of the suggestions to solve the longitude problem: a chronometer set to the time on a prime meridian could be compared en route with local time; each four minutes' difference would equal one degree of easting or westing. Already formulated in theory by several scholars in the sixteenth century, it was still found wanting in practical capacity throughout the seventeenth and much of the eighteenth centuries. Dutch polymath Christiaan Huygens (1629–1695) spent over thirty years on the construction of a seaworthy chronometer, based on a pendulum design. His first prototype was tested at sea by captain Robert Holmes in 1663–1664, with encouraging but inconclusive results. Through his membership of the French Académie, the inventor was able to send two of his clocks along with the astronomer Jean Richer nine years thereafter. Although both instruments regrettably stopped working during the Atlantic crossing to Cayenne, French Guiana, Richer did bring back worrying news regarding the inexplicable inconstancy of his own seconds-pendulum. This simple device (3 feet and 8.6 lignes long; 1 ligne = 2.3 millimeters) beat seconds in perfect time at Paris (lat. 48°50′ N), but had to be shortened by 1.25 lignes (2.8 millimeters [.1 inch]) at Cayenne (lat. 4°55′ N) to keep the same pace. If its lengthened period of oscillation was ignored, the pendulum lost about two and a half minutes per day near the equator.

Ten years later (1682), another French expedition headed by the academics Jean Varin, Jean des Hayes, and Guillaume de Glos confirmed the effect, having to shorten their seconds-pendulum by two lignes (4.5 millimeters [.18 inch]) at Île de Goree (just off Cape Verde, at 14°40′ N), and slightly more in the West Indies. That same year, Huygens received formal approval to have both his clocks and a seconds-pendulum tested on a Dutch East Indiaman. Four years later, the navigators Thomas Helder and Johannes de Graaf received explicit instructions for mounting, regulating, and maintaining the devices, prior to departing in the *Alcmaer* for the Cape of Good Hope. Upon the ship's return in 1687, the logbooks showed that the clocks had performed poorly during heavy seas, and according to the chronometer longitudes, the ship had sailed right through Scotland and Ireland. In his 1688 report for the Dutch East India Company, Huygens identified Earth's rotation as the one and only cause; the resulting centrifugal force diminished the weight of bodies by a factor dependent on latitude. This meant that a pendulum would be about a third of a percent lighter on the equator than at the poles, and consequently maintain a longer period with decreasing latitude. When adding this variable compensation, the ship's tracks showed a reasonable correspondence with the ordinary dead-reckoned position.

Huygens was not the only one studying this problem. Across the Channel, the natural philosopher Isaac Newton (1642–1727) had discussed the issue at length in his monumental *Philosophiae Naturalis Principia Mathematica* (1687), using both Richer's and Varin's observations, and including astronomer Edmond Halley's pendulum experiments on Saint Helena (1676–1678) in the South Atlantic Ocean. Unlike Huygens, Newton did not stop at the centrifugal force acting on the pendulum, but postulated that the planet itself was affected by it as well, producing a flattening at the poles and an equatorial bulge. The philosopher thus posited that Earth was not a sphere but an oblate spheroid, estimating the equatorial semi-axis to be 1/230 longer than the polar semi-axis (the true value is about 1/298, amounting to a difference between polar and equatorial radius of about 21 kilometers [13 miles]). Given Newton's law of universal gravitation, the pull on the pendulum from the center of Earth would lessen with the square of the distance, and that distance was greater at the equator than at the poles. Consequently, the instrument suffered a combined effect of rotation and Earth's ellipticity. In addition, the latter implied that the length of a meridian degree also varied with latitude, invalidating Picard's earlier global value for near-equatorial and near-polar regions.

The confusion was aggravated after a new triangulation survey in France by astronomers G. D. and J. Cassini, eventually published in 1720. Father and son had extended Picard's arc north to Dunkerque and south to Barcelona, and reached the remarkable conclusion that a latitudinal degree was shorter north of Paris and longer to the south, which would imply that Earth was a prolate spheroid (that is, elongated at the poles and flattened at the equator). The French Academy decided to settle the controversy by sending out two expeditions, to repeat the measurements further apart. One went to Lapland (Torne River near the Arctic Circle, 1736–1737), under Pierre-Louis Moreau de Maupertuis (with Alexis-Claude Clairault, Charles Étienne Louis Camus, and Pierre-Charles Lemonnier), the other to Peru (1735–1743) under Charles-Marie

de la Condamine and Pierre Bouguer. Not only did the joint findings convincingly confirm Newton's oblate ellipsoid shape (flattening: 1/216.8), Bouguer also discovered that the gravitational attraction of nearby mountains could deflect the pendulum, but much less than expected if the mass of the Andes had merely been added to the crust. Instead, Bouguer postulated a "sinking" of the crust to maintain hydrostatic equilibrium in his 1749 *Théorie de la figure de la Terre*; the term *isostasy* would eventually be coined in 1899, by the geologist Clarence Edward Dutton (1841–1912).

In Britain, the astronomer royal Nevil Maskelyne (1732–1811) performed the same experiment in 1774–1776 to weigh the whole Earth, given the known mass of the pendulum bob, and measuring its deflection from the mountain Schiehallion in Scotland. In 1798 Henry Cavendish (1731–1810) improved the initial estimate with the aid of two leaden balls and a torsion balance, and found a mean density of 5.45 g/cm3 (about twice as dense as granite). Earlier assumptions of huge cavities in Earth's deep interior subsequently began to give way to concepts in which density increased with depth.

Around the same time (1792–1799), French engineers Jean Delambre and Pierre Méchain remeasured the latitudinal arc between Dunkerque and Barcelona more accurately (flattening: 1/311.5) to support the new length unit of the meter, defined as one ten-millionth of the meridian arc through Paris, from equator to pole. The original idea of a decimal length measure based upon the earth can be traced back to Lyon vicar Gabriel Mouton in 1670. The French government provisionally approved the resulting metric system in 1791, formally adopted it (alongside the medieval system) by 1795, finally granting it a monopoly from 1840. Its spread across the globe was initially advanced by the French Revolution and Napoleonic military conquests, later more peacefully through the international Metric Convention of 1875.

In nineteenth-century gravity research, pendulum experiments were increasingly performed on exploration voyages in high latitudes in the northern and southern hemisphere. The former army officer Edward Sabine, chiefly known for his work on geomagnetism, contributed with measurements during the 1819 wintering on Baffin Island during John Ross's search for the Northwest Passage in the *Hecla* and *Griper*, and again in 1822 in the *Pheasant*, gravity surveying along the African and American coasts, and in the *Griper* to Greenland and Spitsbergen. Sabine derived an ellipticity of 1/289, which led to further improvements in world charting. In 1828 pendulum observations were obtained as far south as the southern Shetland Islands during the *Chanticleer* expedition (1828–1831).

Meanwhile, British physicist Henry Kater had developed the reversible physical pendulum in 1818, which made absolute measurements of the gravitational constant possible for the first time. The instrument gradually supplanted the ordinary pendulum, and remained a trusted tool until the 1940s. For land surveys the torsion balance was increasingly used in the early decades of the twentieth century, followed by the spring balance gravimeter from the 1930s. The impetus largely came from the oil industry, which sponsored gravimetric technology because of its potential to locate underground salt domes, in which oil deposits tend to accumulate. In 1952 the French physicist Charles Volet developed a free-fall vacuum chamber to measure absolute gravitation; laser interferometry has improved precision on land even further.

Accurate measurements at sea long remained more difficult to obtain. Although the Dutch Vening Meinesz pendulum apparatus was successfully operated on submarines from 1923, disturbances at the surface (wind, waves, ship movements) remained problematic until the 1950s. Spring-type gravimeters for shipboard use were independently developed by Anton Graf (first tested at sea in 1956) and L. J. B. LaCoste (at sea from 1958). At the time, oceanic gravimetry was also revolutionized by simultaneous recording of bathymetry, gravity, and geomagnetic measurements, introduced during the International Geophysical Year (1957–1958). The technical problems of gravimetry in airplanes were finally overcome in 1959.

The Soviet *Sputnik I* satellite, launched in 1957, inaugurated the space age for gravimetry. The forces, perturbing any low-altitude satellite's orbit as predicted from the earth's central attraction alone, have to be continuously tracked and compensated for, producing a detailed gravity map. Ten years of such observations went into the global Geodetic Reference System, adopted by the International Union of Geodesy and Geophysics in 1967. In addition, since the American *Seasat* series from 1978, satellites have used radar altimetry to repeatedly measure the height of the ocean surface everywhere. When multiple readings are averaged for each sampled point (in order to lose the effects of winds, waves, and tides), a precision of a few centimeters can be reached.

Combining these data, scientists have been able to model the so-called geoid, the physical equipotential surface of gravity, corresponding to mean sea level. Because it reflects the true mass distribution within the earth, it undulates irregularly within about a hundred meters (330 feet) above and below the theoretical international reference ellipsoid. Cartographic surveys, based on astronomical methods, spirit level, and local horizon, therefore have to take these anomalies into account, lest serious errors occur. The closer it is studied, the more the earth's shape is found to defy the simple notion of a perfect sphere.

## Tides and Earth Rotation

Earth's mass is by no means the only source of gravitational attraction experienced at the surface; the moon and sun especially produce a notable effect as well. Oceanic tides will immediately come to the mariner's mind, ruled by a complex interplay of lunar and other astronomical cycles, generating two tidal bulges that incessantly circle the globe. Less well known is that tides equally extend to the atmosphere and to the body of the earth. Due to Earth's elasticity, the tidal pull is able to deform the solid surface to a limited extent. The observed marine tide consequently only reaches about seven-tenths of its predicted displacement; this is because the seafloor underneath (and any tidal marker embedded in it) is elevated too. However, as the planet completes its daily spin under the moon, this partly anelastic bodily Earth tide suffers from a twelve-minute (2.9 degrees) tidal lag relative to the waters' more immediate response. Consequently, the moon exerts a stronger force on the nearest tidal bulge than on the far one, producing a torque in the opposite sense to Earth's rotation. This tidal friction thus acts as a brake, slowly lengthening the day (of 86,400 seconds) by about 2.3 milliseconds per century.

Conjunctions between Earth, Moon, and Sun not only cause regular spring tides, but occasionally produce solar or lunar eclipses for specific regions. Given current knowledge of celestial mechanics, it is a simple exercise to compute the exact time and place where past occultations would have been visible. Historical records of these awesome events (mainly from European, Arabian, Chinese, and Babylonian sources) stretch the past twenty-five hundred years or so, and show an ever widening discrepancy in time with the predicted decreasing spin rate based on tidal friction alone. The actual increase in the length of the day (1.8 milliseconds per century) indicates another long-term component at work, accelerating the globe's rotation by about 0.5 milliseconds per century. Once again the shape of Earth is to blame; postglacial rebound (ground uplift after removal of glacial loads from the last ice age in high latitudes) continually reduces Earth's oblateness, like a pirouetting skater pulling in her arms. Smaller fluctuations in rotation are due to exchange of angular momentum between mantle and core, and mantle torques by atmospheric winds and ocean currents.

Earth rotation and global circulation patterns are more directly linked by the Coriolis force (also known as the Coriolis acceleration). It was named after the French mathematician Gaspard-Gustave de Coriolis (1792–1843), who first discussed it in 1835. It is a force invented to keep Newton's laws of motion valid for an observer in a rotating reference frame such as the earth. It acts only on bodies in motion, and changes their direction (not their speed), increasing in effect from equator to each geographical pole. When viewed at the surface along the direction of intended motion, the Coriolis force appears to deflect movement to the right in the northern hemisphere, and to the left in the southern, due to the object's conserved angular momentum from the earth's spin while changing latitude. Parallels of latitude (small circles) increase in circumference from pole to equator; when changing latitude, an object will carry with it Earth's spin velocity from its latitude of departure, which will be different elsewhere.

The Coriolis force exerts a significant influence on the general circulation patterns; for instance, on the shape of atmospheric pressure gradients, gyres of air and oceanic currents, the phenomenon of "hooked" trade winds across the equator (where the Coriolis force changes direction), and the subtropical jet stream. In addition, it affects the level bubble in instruments carried on ships and planes, and even a vessel's course (most noticeable in ballistic-missile trajectories).

A separate effect concerns the change in centrifugal force, the vertical component of the Coriolis force. An object moving east is traveling around the rotation axis at a greater speed than Earth's surface (larger centrifugal force), whereas an object "going west" at moderate speeds actually just turns east more slowly than the planet (smaller centrifugal force). Consequently, the former direction results in weight loss relative to measurement at rest, the latter in weight gain. The Hungarian physicist Lóránt Eötvös (1848–1919) realized that gravimetric readings while moving east or west had to be compensated dynamically; even at moderate speeds the disturbance would otherwise totally drown any crustal signal of interest.

## Earth's Composition and Dynamics

The main reason to perform extensive geophysical surveys is that about 97 percent of Earth's volume is inaccessible to us. From ancient times, this mysterious underworld has often been associated with heat and violence, fueled by the frightening spectacles of erupting volcanoes and earthquakes. Hot sulfurous gases were thought to circulate through a vast network of subterranean caverns, driven by an infernal furnace at the center. Contrastingly, from the late seventeenth century, various geomagnetic hypotheses explained the changing magnetic field by considering a distinct magnetic nucleus rotating inside the crust, separated by a fluid or gaseous medium. The Oxford physicist Servington Savery was the first to propound the influence of core topography on the magnetic field, remarking in 1732 that anomalies might be due in part to "surface irregularities of the internal Magnet." Furthermore, the concept of an extremely hot, molten core inside a solid crust received wider recognition through the *Protogaea* (written 1691–1693, published posthumously 1749) by the natural philosopher Gottfried Wilhelm Leibniz (1646–1716) and *Histoire naturelle des minéraux* by the naturalist Georges-Louis Leclerc, Comte de Buffon (1707–1788). In a different work from 1778, the latter author assumed that Earth had come into being as a molten body separated from the sun by cometary impact, slowly cooling to its present temperature in about seventy-five thousand years. Nineteenth-century mathematicians deemed Earth's former fully liquid state responsible for its observed ellipticity and a smooth increase of density with depth. In 1887, George Howard Darwin (1845–1912, son of Charles) concluded from tidal observations that the concept of a fluid interior was untenable; other geologists thought that the cooling process caused the globe to contract, with mountain ranges making up the residual crustal slack, like a wrinkled prune.

Only since the advent of seismology in the early twentieth century has the interior started to reveal its secrets. In 1906 Richard Dixon Oldham discovered the core; its radius (ca. 3,485 kilometers [2,166 miles]) was correctly delineated seven years later by Beno Gutenberg. In 1926 Harold Jeffreys concluded from bodily Earth tides that the core could be liquid; ten years later, Inge Lehmann showed the existence of the inner core, proved to be solid by A. M. Dziewonski and F. Gilbert in 1971. From the 1950s, the liquid outer core was considered the seat of the geomagnetic field, its convection (moving at fifteen to thirty kilometers [9.3 to 18.6 miles] per year) maintaining a fluid dynamo. A much slower convection process (centimeters per year) is believed at work in the mantle, which over geological time behaves as a liquid too. The thermal energy driving these motions mostly stems from the time of formation, the decay of radioactive isotopes, and the slow solidification of the liquid outer core onto the solid inner core.

The crust and the top of the mantle together make up the lithosphere, consisting of an interlocking mosaic of rigid plates. Although continental plates are much thicker (35–70 kilometers [21.7–43.5 miles]) than oceanic ones (7–8 kilometers [4.3–5 miles]), they are so much lighter that they float higher in the mantle than the parts that make up the ocean floor. Pushed and pulled along by mantle convection underneath, they slide and scrape past each other at "conservative" boundaries, causing fracture zones and earthquakes. At midocean ridges the hot upwelling mantle continually forms new crust, pushed outward to both sides. This rifting process is called seafloor spreading, generating shallow earthquakes and fault lines. Where plates converge, the heavier (oceanic) one will subduct under the lighter (continental) one, producing a deep trench and a plane of compression at an angle of thirty to sixty degrees to the surface, where many deep earthquakes occur. Partial melting then spawns a chain of volcanoes parallel to the plate boundary further inland. The concept of plate tectonics arose in the late nineteenth century, but was only confirmed with ocean bottom evidence in the early 1960s.

Finally, isolated mantle "hot spots" away from plate edges can produce a string of volcanoes (sea mounts or island arcs) while the plate moves over it. Oceanic islands associated with such mantle plumes include Ascension, the Azores, Bermuda, the Canaries, the Cape Verdes, the Carolines, the Comoros, the Galápagos, Hawaii, Madeira, Réunion, Saint Helena, Samoa, Trinidad, and Tristan da Cunha. Although seafarers have little to fear from undersea volcanic eruptions, submarine earthquakes have a far greater destructive potential. Not only can they cause massive underwater landslides on the continental slope (turbidites), they are also responsible for the tsunami, a very long-period surface wave traveling extremely fast, initially low but piling up to great heights in shallows, before wrecking entire coastal regions. Past and present evidence of such disasters remind us that Earth has always been a very dynamic environment; the earth sciences greatly help to understand the forces that continue to shape it.

[*See also* Cartography; Magnetism, *subentry on* Geomagnetism; *and* Meteorology.]

## Bibliography

Bennett, Jim A. *The Divided Circle: A History of Instruments for Astronomy, Navigation, and Surveying*. Oxford: Phaidon, Christie's, 1987.

Bolt, Bruce A. *Inside the Earth: Evidence from Earthquakes*. San Francisco: Freeman, 1982. Lucid introduction to seismology's contribution to the earth sciences.

Brown, Geoff, Chris Hawkesworth, and Chris Wilson, eds. *Understanding the Earth: A New Synthesis*. Cambridge, U.K., and New York: Cambridge University Press, 1992. Introductory overview, with hardly any mathematics.

Brush, Stephen G., and Helmut E. Landsberg, with Martin Collins. *The History of Geophysics and Meteorology: An Annotated Bibliography*. Vol. 7 of *Bibliographies of the History of Science and Technology*. New York: Garland, 1985.

Burke, John G., ed. *The Uses of Science in the Age of Newton*. Berkeley: University of California Press, 1983. Discusses seventeenth-century determinations of the length of a degree.

Davies, Geoffrey F. *Dynamic Earth: Plates, Plumes, and Mantle Convection*. Cambridge, U.K., and New York: Cambridge University Press, 1999. Introductory-level discussion of plate tectonics and mantle dynamics.

Fowler, C. Mary R. *The Solid Earth: An Introduction to Global Geophysics*. 2d ed. Cambridge, U.K., and New York: Cambridge University Press, 2004. Broad, accessible overview with a minimum of mathematics.

Good, Gregory A., ed. *Sciences of the Earth: An Encyclopedia of Events, People, and Phenomena*. New York: Garland, 1998. Historical treatment; period overviews, concepts regarding the inner earth.

Hancock, Paul L., and Brian J. Skinner, eds. *The Oxford Companion to the Earth*. Oxford and New York: Oxford University Press, 2000. Accessible explanations of numerous individual topics.

Lowrie, William. *Fundamentals of Geophysics*. Cambridge, U.K., and New York: Cambridge University Press, 1997. Many earth sciences topics covered with clear and elaborate diagrams.

Marcorini, Edgardo, ed. *The History of Science and Technology: A Narrative Chronology*. 2 vols. New York: Facts on File, 1988. Geodesy, pendulum clocks, eighteenth-century concepts regarding the inner earth.

McCormmach, Russell, Lewis Pyenson, and Roy Steven Turner, eds. *Historical Studies in the Physical Sciences*. Baltimore: Johns Hopkins University Press, 1979.

Press, Frank, and Raymond Siever. *Understanding Earth*. 3d ed. New York: Freeman, 2001. Aimed at undergraduate students, with many clear illustrations.

Schliesser, Eric, and George E. Smith. "Huygens's 1688 Report to the Directors of the Dutch East India Company: On the Measurement of Longitude at Sea and Its Implications for the Non-Uniformity of Gravity." *De Zeventiende Eeuw* 12, no. 1 (1996): 198–214. Huygens, Newton, pendulums, centrifugal force, and ellipticity.

Sears, Mary, and Daniel Merriman, eds. *Oceanography: The Past*. New York: Springer-Verlag, 1980. Plate tectonics, oceanic drilling.

Stephenson, F. Richard. *Historical Eclipses and Earth's Rotation*. Cambridge, U.K., and New York: Cambridge University Press, 1997. Book-length treatment of changes in the length of day.

Taylor, Eva Germaine Rimington. *The Mathematical Practitioners of Tudor and Stuart England 1485–1714*. Cambridge, U.K.: Cambridge University Press, 1954. Details seventeenth-century struggles to determine the figure of the earth.

Taylor, Eva Germaine Rimington. *The Mathematical Practitioners of Hanoverian England 1714–1840*. Cambridge, U.K.: Cambridge University Press, 1966. Details eighteenth-century struggles to determine the figure of the earth.

Worzel, Lamar J., and J. C. Harrison. "Gravity at Sea." In *The Sea: Ideas and Observations on Progress in the Study of the Seas*, vol. 3, edited by M. N. Hill. New York: Wiley, 1963. Discusses early-twentieth-century gravimetry.

A. R. T. JONKERS

# East India Companies

This entry contains four subentries:

An Overview
Dutch East India Company
English East India Company
French East India Company

## An Overview

East India companies were the main channel through which trade passed between Europe and Asia from the seventeenth until the early nineteenth century. From the later eighteenth century, the British company was also to become an imperial power, ruling millions of Asian subjects.

### Trading with Asia

Europe had traded with Asia through the Middle East for many centuries before the age of the East India companies. European demand for Asian commodities was the stimulus for this trade. The opening up of an all-sea route between Europe and Asia, following the first voyage round the Cape of Good Hope to India by the Portuguese Vasco da Gama in 1498, increased the volume of trade and brought some of it directly to Atlantic Europe. It did not, however, alter its fundamental pattern: the exchange of high-value Asian commodities, such as pepper and spices, silk and cotton cloth, or porcelain, for bullion shipped from Europe.

Those Portuguese who went to Asia in the sixteenth century were officially the servants of a royal enterprise, sailing in the king of Portugal's ships, establishing trading posts under the king's authority and obtaining goods to be sold on his behalf in Europe. By contrast, the East India companies of the seventeenth century were great corporations of private merchants, but conditions in Asia meant that they operated in ways that were similar to those pioneered by the Portuguese.

Trade with Asia had certain distinctive features. Commercial opportunities were abundant. Asian artisans and cultivators were highly skilled. Asian merchants were as rich and as sophisticated in their trading methods as any contemporary Europeans. Asian rulers were generally favorable to the extension of foreign trade. Profit margins could be spectacular, but the costs were very high, as were the risks. The length of the voyage, at least six months round the Cape, meant that the biggest and most expensive merchant ships, later to be called East Indiamen by the British, had to be used. A large capital outlay was required for the goods and bullion to be taken to Asia, on which a return could not be expected for at least two years. Money usually had to be advanced to obtain commodities in the following year. To supervise the supply of goods and get the best prices, it was necessary to maintain European agents on a permanent basis in Asia. This could be done by seeking trading rights in existing ports from Asian rulers or by gaining control of enclaves by treaty or by force.

Highly expensive operations for which it was necessary to spread the risks meant that successful Asian trade in the early modern period was likely to be beyond the scope of individual European merchants. By the end of the sixteenth century it was proving to be beyond the scope even of the Portuguese monarchy. In the early seventeenth century, however, combinations of Dutch and English merchants were to engage in it successfully.

### Dutch Dominance in the Seventeenth Century

The Portuguese had tried to ensure that the great bulk of the most valuable commodities going from Asia to Europe, that is, pepper and the rarer spices, was carried to Lisbon in their ships. In the first half of the sixteenth century they had enjoyed some success. By the end of the century, however, the routes through the Middle East had revived and the Portuguese, now united with the Spanish monarchy, were coming under attack from their Protestant northern European enemies, the Dutch and the English.

The Dutch were at first by far the most formidable enemies. Dutch voyages to Asia began in the 1590s. By 1601 fourteen different Dutch concerns were trying to trade with Asia. To eliminate damaging competition between them, the Dutch government brought about the creation of a single United Netherlands Chartered East India Company with an exclusive monopoly of Dutch trade to Asia in 1602. This was what was known as a joint stock operation, that is, one in which, instead of individual merchants trading on their own account, shareholders pooled their resources under the management of directors, who organized the trade and paid out dividends to investors in a permanent capital. In the Dutch case, a huge capital was raised, the equivalent of £14 million in English currency. From the outset the company was given great powers and became something of a state within the Dutch state. In Asia it could raise armed forces, conduct diplomacy, and wage war. It was intended to be an instrument of war as well as of commercial competition against Spain and Portugal.

The English East India Company was at first a much more modest concern. In 1600 a group of merchants obtained a charter giving them exclusive rights to trade to Asia. A joint stock structure was set up of shareholders subscribing funds to be managed by elected directors. The first venture was the dispatch of four ships to Asia in 1601 for which £68,000 was subscribed. All the early English operations were on a smaller scale and much less lavishly funded than those of the Dutch. A permanent stock was not established until 1657.

Within twenty years, the Dutch and the English had achieved what the Portuguese had never been able to do: pepper and spices from the 1620s came to Europe almost exclusively via the Cape in their ships rather than overland through the Middle East. The Dutch were dominant in the first half of the seventeenth century and plied a highly profitable trade. They established themselves at key points in the Indonesian archipelago, especially in the main pepper ports on the north coast of Java, where they developed their new capital at Batavia (modern Jakarta), and in the small Molucca islands, source of the rare spices. There they increasingly applied coercion to the island rulers, compelling them to deliver their crops to the Dutch, and forcibly excluding Asian and European competitors, including the English. Policies of destroying the spice crops surplus to the Dutch requirements and decimating the population of some of the islands were carried to new heights by Jan Pieterszoon Coen, governor general of the company's Asian operations in 1617–1623 and 1627–1629. The spice and pepper trades were supported by profits made from an elaborate system of inter-Asian trade. The Dutch shipped commodities like Indian cotton cloth to be sold in Indonesia or copper from Japan, where after 1639 they were the only Europeans permitted commercial access, for sale in India.

In the later seventeenth century the balance began to shift more toward the English. The still very powerful Dutch company spent more and more of its resources in enforcing its attempts to control the pepper and spices, for which the demand in Europe was reaching its ceiling. It spent heavily on war to conquer territory in Java and to eliminate the trading city of Makasar in Sulawesi. By the end of the century the company's finances were going into deficit. The English by contrast developed new trades by importing Indian cotton cloth, for which European demand soared from the 1670s, with only limited overheads in the form of settlements tolerated by Indian rulers.

## British Dominance in the Eighteenth Century

The British company's trading operations, largely based on its Indian settlements at Chennai (Madras), Kolkata (Calcutta), and Mumbai (Bombay) and on the export of cotton cloth and silk, grew apace in the first half of the eighteenth century. By mid-century the company was also developing a lucrative trade with China, supplying British consumers with tea for which they were showing an insatiable demand. The company was sending twenty or thirty large ships a year to Asia and had a turnover of up to £2 million on its sales. It was a major power in British commercial and financial life, closely linked to the British government.

The Dutch company still traded on a huge scale. It diversified its activities away from an exclusive reliance on pepper and spices. The Dutch competed with the British in exporting Indian textiles and developed a profitable trade in coffee from Java. Much of its inter-Asian trade passed, however, to the British. The British company permitted private ships, owned by individuals resident in India, to trade anywhere in Asian waters. These ships were much more competitive than the Dutch company's own vessels. Continuing heavy expenses and a failure to make profits in Asia meant that the Dutch company operated at a deficit throughout the eighteenth century.

In the early eighteenth century, the French East India Company, founded in 1664, became a considerable force in Asian trade. By the 1730s and 1740s the volume of its largely Indian trade posed a serious challenge to the British. Other European countries sponsored generally short-lived East India companies, such as the Ostend Company, based in the Austrian Netherlands (1715–1732), a Swedish (1731–1807) and a Prussian (1754–1765) company and the Danish one (established 1616; reorganized 1732, rechartered 1772–1807), which alone established itself on a lasting basis with settlements in India. Common to all these ventures was a reliance on Dutch and British personnel, expertise, and money. They were in a real sense parasites on the two great companies.

## Empire and the Failure of the Companies

Force had been an integral part of the European presence in Asia since the arrival of the Portuguese. Gunned European ships had been used to disrupt Asian competition at sea. On small islands, or on Sri Lanka or Java, as the Dutch had shown, control could be asserted over areas where key products were produced. War against the great mainland empires, the Moguls in India or the Chinese, was quite another matter, but with the disintegration of the Mogul system and the increase in European military resources in the mid-eighteenth century, intervention in India became a possibility.

Rivalry between Britain and France was the impetus for the building up of European forces in India. The French and British companies, reinforced by royal warships and soldiers, became proxies for their respective states in their worldwide wars. In order to defeat their European enemies, both sides enlisted Indian allies, who were to provide them above all with the financial resources with which to wage war, a process that began on the southeast coast. Alliance passed quickly into subordination, as the victorious British took direct control of the resources that they needed. They turned their allies in the south into satellites, while assuming what amounted to outright authority over the very rich province of Bengal after 1757, when they deposed a ruler who had attacked their settlement in Calcutta (Kolkata). Territorial empire, once firmly rooted in Bengal and in the eastern half of the Indian peninsula, spread at an uneven speed but inexorably across the rest of India in the first half of the nineteenth century.

Empire gave the British company huge resources from the taxation that it levied from the millions of people placed under its rule. This enabled it to maintain great armies, predominantly of Indian soldiers, called "sepoys." British military power on this scale made a French revival impossible and eclipsed the Dutch. Crippled by its debts, the Dutch company was at the mercy of British attacks when the Republic sided with Britain's enemies in European wars. In 1799 the insolvent company was formally dissolved.

The British company by contrast went from strength to strength. Its role, however, underwent a great transformation from commerce to government. The company's trade withered in the early nineteenth century. It came under attack for failing to meet the needs of an industrializing society. There was strong pressure for private merchants and private shipping to be given increased access to Asia, both to boost exports of Indian raw materials for British industry and to develop India as a market for British manufactures. The company lost its Indian monopoly in 1813 and stopped trading altogether after 1833, when China was opened to private trade.

By then its transformation into a military and administrative body was complete. The servants of the East India Company no longer bought calicoes, but they assessed and collected the taxation of huge areas, took responsibility for maintaining law and order, and acted as judges in a hierarchy of courts. This great transformation was at first an unwelcome development to contemporaries who regarded the entrusting of political power to merchants as against all principles of good governance. For the British state to take on such responsibility in place of the company seemed, however, to eighteenth-century opinion to raise even greater dangers. The state must mean either the king or the politicians. For the supposed wealth of India to be entrusted to either of them was thought to threaten the subversion of the constitution. The alternative of leaving the governing of India to the East India Company, subject to a degree of state supervision, seemed to be the safest course. In time, the company's servants appeared to develop a considerable aptitude for government, which was to ensure the survival of their regime until the catastrophe of the great Indian revolt of 1857. Only then did the last and the greatest of the East India companies cease to have any effective existence.

[*See also* East Indiaman.]

## Bibliography

Bassett, David K. "Early English Trade and Settlement in Asia 1602–1690." In *Britain and the Netherlands in Europe and Asia*, edited by J. S. Bromley and E. H. Kossman, pp. 89–103. London: Macmillan, 1968. A useful outline of English activities.

Boxer, C. R. *The Dutch Seaborne Empire, 1600–1800.* London: Hutchinson, 1965. Puts the Dutch company into the context of Dutch overseas expansion in general.

Blussé, Leonard, and Femme Gaastra, eds. *Companies and Trade: Essays on Overseas Trading Companies during the Ancien Régime.* Leiden, Netherlands: Leiden University Press, 1981. Essays on all the companies.

Bruijn, Jaap R., and Femme S. Gaastra, eds. *Ships, Sailors, and Spices: East India Companies and Their Shipping in the 16th, 17th, and 18th Centuries.* Amsterdam: NEHA, 1993.

Chaudhuri, K. N. *The English East India Company: The Study of an Early Joint-Stock Company, 1600–1640*. London: Frank Cass, 1965. Describes the early years of the English company.

Chaudhuri, K. N. *Trade and Civilisation in the Indian Ocean: An Economic History from the Rise of Islam to 1750*. Cambridge, U.K., and New York: Cambridge University Press, 1985. A highly stimulating overview of the role of trade in Asian history.

Chaudhuri, K. N. *The Trading World of Asia and the English East India Company, 1660–1760*. Cambridge, U.K.: Cambridge University Press, 1978. Magisterial account of trading conditions in Asia.

Das Gupta, Ashin, and M. N. Pearson, eds. *India and the Indian Ocean 1500–1800*. Calcutta: Oxford University Press, 1987. The essays are primarily written from the point of view of Asian rather than company history. A valuable corrective to Eurocentric treatments.

Furber, Holden. *Rival Empires of Trade in the Orient, 1600 to 1800*. Minneapolis: University of Minnesota Press, 1976. Valuable survey.

Glamman, Kristof. *Dutch Asiatic Trade, 1620–1740*. Copenhagen: Danish Science Press, 1958. The starting point for modern treatments of the Dutch.

Lawson, Philip. *The East India Company: A History*. London and New York: Longman, 1993. Accessible survey of the British company.

Meilink-Roelofsz, M. A. P. *Asian Trade and European Influence in the Indonesian Archipelago between 1500 and about 1630*. The Hague: Nijhoff, 1962. Puts the Dutch and the Portuguese into their Asian context.

Steensgaard, Niels. *Carracks, Caravans and Companies: The Structural Crisis in the European-Asian Trade in the Early 17th Century*. Copenhagen: Studentlitteratur, 1973. Challenging assessment of the impact of the companies in the seventeenth century.

Sutherland, L. S. *The East India Company in Eighteenth-Century Politics*. Oxford: Oxford University Press, 1952. Definitive treatment of the role of the Company in Britain.

PETER. J. MARSHALL

# Dutch East India Company

The Dutch East India Company (Vereenigde Oostindische Compagnie or VOC) was for a long time the most successful of all the chartered companies of the seventeenth and eighteenth centuries. The company was founded in 1602 and grew to be the largest enterprise in the world. Within three decades it replaced the Portuguese as the dominant commercial power in the European-Asian trade. The success of the VOC can be illustrated by impressive figures of shipping and trade and the numbers of servants in the service of the company. In the eighteenth century

the VOC gradually lost its lead over its competitors. The outbreak of the Fourth Anglo-Dutch War in 1780 plunged the company into an acute financial crisis from which it could not recover. The VOC could be rescued from bankruptcy only by the state and was finally dissolved at the end of 1799.

## The Charter of 1602

The VOC was founded on March 20, 1602, when the States-General issued a charter, or Octrooi, in which its rights and obligations as well as its internal organization were described. The company was an amalgamation of six smaller companies that had sent ships to Asia since 1594. These smaller companies became "chambers" in the newly formed united company. The formulation of these articles was the result of a political compromise—with the intention to persuade the merchants from Zeeland to participate in one united company—rather than of the wish to design a management system best suited for intercontinental trade. The charter provided also a legal basis for the VOC in Asia. The company was given the right to enter into treaties with Asian powers on behalf of the States-General, to build fortifications, and to muster soldiers and to administrate its possessions. Moreover, the charter gave the new company a monopoly for the Dutch trade to Asia; in this way the government rewarded the directors (*bewindhebbers*) for their willingness to unify their pre-companies. At the same time the state could defend granting the monopoly by providing the possibility for every citizen to invest as much as he wished in the company. This became an important innovation: the share capital, amounting to nearly 6.5 million guilders, became a permanent share capital, providing the directors with the financial means to invest in ships, forts, and factories in Asia.

## Expansion in the Seventeenth Century

The first fleets equipped by the VOC were really fleets of war, and the aggression was in the first instance directed against the Portuguese, not against Asian states. However, the company changed its policy when it became clear that these military means could be used more effectively for strengthening its position in the market. The critical financial situation around 1610 induced the directors to formulate a number of objectives. First, the VOC should follow the Portuguese example and establish in Asia a center

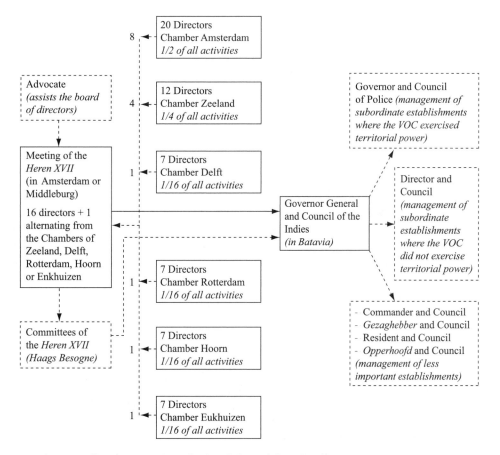

**Dutch East India Company.** Organizational chart of the VOC. COURTESY OF FEMME S. GAASTRA

of trade, administration, and government, a rendezvous. That place should be the seat of a governor-general and council, who should form the "High Government" over the company's factories in Asia. Second, a monopoly in the fine spices—at this stage nutmeg, mace, and cloves—should be established by conquering the production areas of these spices and exclude the competitors. Finally, the VOC should take advantage of the existing commercial trade relations in Asia and try to penetrate into the intra-Asian trade.

The directors appointed a governor-general in 1609, but it took ten years before a rendezvous could be established. In 1619 Batavia (present-day Jakarta), strategically positioned near Strait Sunda, was founded after defeating Javanese and English forces. Then the VOC directed its attention to the monopoly of the fine spices. The conquest of the Banda Islands in 1622 gave the VOC a monopoly in nutmeg and mace. The concentration of the culture of

cloves on Ambon and the expulsion of all possible competitors ("smugglers," as the VOC would call them) from ports in the vicinity, such as Macassar, was completed in 1664. Finally the Dutch were able to drive the Portuguese from Ceylon in 1665 and thus gain the monopoly in cinnamon. The possession of Ceylon, moreover, strengthened the position of the Dutch East India Company in the Indian Ocean. The grip of the VOC on the trade and shipping in Asia was further enhanced by the conquest of Malacca in 1642.

In the meantime the company succeeded in establishing an Asian network of shipping and trade. It was Jan Pietersz Coen, the energetic but ruthless governor-general (1618 to 1623 and again from 1627 to 1629), who had urged the directors in Europe time and again to send enough money and ships to make the necessary investments in creating such a network. The ideal situation, by which this trade should give such profits that the export of precious metal to buy the Asian products for Europe was no longer necessary, was never reached. But between 1640 and 1680, the company's trade in Asia proved extremely profitable and gave the VOC an enormous advantage over its European competitors. The fundament of this trade network was the triangle of Japan (where the VOC was the only European trade partner and from where silver and copper was exported to India), India (from where textiles were carried to the Indonesian archipelago), and Java and the Moluccas as producers of pepper and spices. But the network was much more complex and included, for instance, China or Taiwan, which could deliver gold for India and silk for Japan. In this way the VOC gained a unique position: it could escape from the dictate—bullion for goods—of the European-Asian trade. For a long time the Dutch could send out moderate amounts of silver and gold to Asia for their rich return cargos, relying on profits made in the Asian trade.

## Changes after c. 1680

The intra-Asian trade met a number of problems after the 1680s. Silver exports from Japan were already forbidden in 1668, but gold proved to be a lucrative alternative. However, soon other restrictions in the Japan trade decreased the once-important profits made there. After 1700 the trade of the VOC in Persia and Surat was hurt by the internal troubles. At the same time the expenses in Asia were rising. The company could compensate the losses in Asia with a growing trade between Europe and Asia. Reasons for this growth were the rising demand for new Asian products in Europe: Indian textiles, coffee, and tea.

The VOC more than doubled its European-Asian trade after 1700, and that was, considering the strong competition, an impressive achievement. The performance in the tea trade with Canton was not as bad as is sometimes suggested: the Dutch company succeeded in achieving second place, behind the English company. The increase in the demand for textiles or tea and coffee was not at the expense of the consumption of spices. The volume of the trade in spices and pepper stayed on the same level, and these products remained important and profitable trade items until the very end of the existence of the Dutch company. The introduction of coffee on Java after 1700 gave the island a new position in the trade system of the VOC. Coffee became an important product in the yearly shipments to the Netherlands.

TABLE 1. *The number of ships and those on board going to and returning from Asia, 1602–1795*

|  | OUTWARD BOUND | | HOMEWARD BOUND | |
| --- | --- | --- | --- | --- |
| YEARS | THOSE ON BOARD | NO. OF SHIPS | THOSE ON BOARD | NO. OF SHIPS |
| 1602–1610 | 8,500 | 76 |  | 44 |
| 1610–1620 | 19,000 | 117 | 14,500 | 50 |
| 1620–1630 | 23,700 | 141 |  | 71 |
| 1630–1640 | 28,900 | 157 | 10,000 | 75 |
| 1640–1650 | 33,100 | 165 | 11,900 | 93 |
| 1650–1660 | 40,200 | 205 | 13,000 | 103 |
| 1660–1670 | 40,900 | 238 | 14,400 | 127 |
| 1670–1680 | 42,700 | 232 | 15,900 | 133 |
| 1680–1690 | 37,800 | 204 | 16,400 | 141 |
| 1690–1700 | 43,000 | 235 | 18,300 | 156 |
| 1700–1710 | 49,600 | 281 | 22,400 | 193 |
| 1710–1720 | 59,900 | 310 | 26,500 | 245 |
| 1720–1730 | 71,700 | 382 | 34,300 | 319 |
| 1730–1740 | 74,300 | 375 | 34,600 | 311 |
| 1740–1750 | 73,100 | 314 | 23,900 | 234 |
| 1750–1760 | 80,500 | 290 | 28,000 | 244 |
| 1760–1770 | 85,500 | 292 | 27,700 | 233 |
| 1770–1780 | 75,500 | 290 | 28,400 | 244 |
| 1780–1790 | 61,900 | 298 | 17,700 | 227 |
| 1790–1795 | 22,900 | 119 | 9,900 | 113 |

Other data confirm the growth of the Dutch-Asiatic trade after 1700: the VOC fitted out more ships, sent out more men, and shipped much more bullion to Asia than before. Growing volumes of trade are, of course, not necessarily a sign of lucrative trade or of a healthy financial situation. Indeed, there was reason for the directors to be worried about the developments. Their growing investments in the trade yielded relatively lower returns. In the decade 1660–1670 the Dutch chambers of the VOC had to invest 80 million guilders to realize a net profit of 12 million guilders (the sales being 92.3 million). In 1770–1780 they had to invest 198 million guilders to earn 13 million.

TABLE 2. *The equipage, the invoice value of the imports and the value of the sales of the Asian products of the VOC, 1640–1795 (in guilders)*

| PERIOD | EQUIPAGE | IMPORTS | SALES |
| --- | --- | --- | --- |
| 1640–1650 | 42,700,000 | 25,600,000 | 78,400,000 |
| 1650–1660 | 71,100,000 | 26,800,000 | 84,200,000 |
| 1660–1670 | 80,400,000 | 31,400,000 | 92,300,000 |
| 1670–1680 | 77,000,000 | 33,700,000 | 91,300,000 |
| 1680–1690 | 87,600,000 | 45,300,000 | 103,400,000 |
| 1690–1700 | 106,900,000 | 44,200,000 | 127,200,000 |

TABLE 2. *(Cont.)*

| PERIOD | EQUIPAGE | IMPORTS | SALES |
|--------|----------|---------|-------|
| 1700–1710 | 122,600,000 | 55,100,000 | 139,500,000 |
| 1710–1720 | 135,200,000 | 65,000,000 | 163,700,000 |
| 1720–1730 | 172,900,000 | 87,200,000 | 185,600,000 |
| 1730–1740 | 159,000,000 | 68,900,000 | 167,000,000 |
| 1740–1750 | 148,700,000 | 72,300,000 | 159,700,000 |
| 1750–1760 | 184,900,000 | 88,200,000 | 188,000,000 |
| 1760–1770 | 198,900,000 | 89,800,000 | 213,600,000 |
| 1770–1780 | 186,500,000 | 78,100,000 | 199,600,000 |
| 1780–1790 | 212,300,000 | 55,600,000 | 145,900,000 |
| 1790–1795 | 86,700,000 | 19,700,000 | 61,200,000 |

THE TERM *EQUIPAGE* COVERS ALL EXPENSES: for building and fitting out the ships, for the goods and treasure for Asia, for salaries paid out in the Netherlands, for interest payments, and so forth.

The focus on the intra-Asian trade provided the VOC with a great variety of products for Asian markets, even after the setbacks in the eighteenth century. Pepper and tin could be sold in China, silks in Japan, spices and copper in India, and cotton textiles in the Indonesian archipelago. When the company had to export more precious metals for its trade, it was never hampered by state regulations. This may explain why the Dutch did not try to develop Asian markets for the products of an industrializing economy to nearly the extent that England did. There were, however, protests from the cities of Haarlem (the silk industry) and Leiden (drapers) to the massive imports by the VOC of Indian textiles. The company could not totally ignore these protests and guaranteed the Leiden drapers the purchase of a certain amount of high-quality cloth, mainly for export to China.

## Decline and Collapse

The decline and final collapse of the VOC has set pens in motion since the eighteenth century. A great number of factors seem to have been responsible: poor management at home, an inadequate bookkeeping system, serious corruption on the part of the servants of the VOC in Asia, growing costs of the overseas administration, and inadequate financing with short-term loans, making the company vulnerable in times of crisis. Shifts in the trading patterns in Asia and in the European-Asian trade may in the end have worked more to the disadvantage than to the advantage of the company. Finally, the high death-rate in Batavia, caused by malaria, undermined the military

power of the company and caused considerable financial losses as well.

The Fourth Anglo-Dutch War (1780–1784) might well have been the final blow for the company, which suffered considerable losses of ships and products. Moreover, investors at home lost confidence in the company, which could now borrow money only with support of the government. Moreover, the VOC was no longer able to defend its factories overseas and had to ask for naval support. In 1784 Dutch naval ships arrived for the first time in Asian waters. However, this naval support was limited, and when the Netherlands was invaded by revolutionary French forces, and the Dutch Republic was replaced by a French satellite state in 1794, most of the VOC factories were conquered by the British.

[*See also* Amsterdam, *subentry on* Commercial Port; Banking and Credit, *subentry* Early; Blaeu, Willem Janszoon; East Indiaman; Navies, Great Powers, *subentry on* Dutch Republic, 1577–1714; *and* Shipping, *subentry on* Netherlands.]

### Bibliography

Bruijn, J. R., F. S. Gaastra, and I. Schöffer. *Dutch-Asiatic Shipping in the 17th and 18th Centuries*. Rijks Geschiedkundige Publicatiën nos. 165, 166, 167. The Hague: Nijhoff, 1979–1987.

Gaastra, Femme S. *The Dutch East India Company. Expansion and Decline*. Zutphen, The Netherlands: Walburg Pers, 2003.

Glamann, Kristof. *Dutch-Asiatic Trade 1620–1740*. Copenhagen and The Hague: Danish Science Press, 1958, 1980.

Jacobs, Els M. *Koopman in Azië. De handel van de Verenigde Oost-Indische Compagnie tijdens de 18e eeuw*. Zutphen, The Netherlands: Walburg Pers, 2000. An English edition of this work is in preparation.

Korte, J. P. de *The Annual Accounting in the Dutch East India Company*. Translated by L. F. van Lookeren Campagne-de Korte. Amsterdam: Uitgeverij Aksant, 2000.

Roelofsz, M. A. P., R. Raben, and H. Spijkerman, eds. *De Archieven van de Verenigde Oostindische Compagnie/The Archives of the Dutch East India Company (1602–1795)*. The Hague: Sdu Uitgeverij Koninginnegracht, 1992.

FEMME S. GAASTRA

## English East India Company

The formation in 1600 of the Company of Merchants of London trading to the East Indies was the culmination of a century's efforts by the English to obtain the luxuries of the East directly by sea. Elizabeth I's charter granted

**English East India Company.** Thomas Hosmer Shepherd (1792–1864) painted this view, engraved by Joseph Constantine Stadler (fl. 1780–1812) and published by Rudolph Ackermann (1764–1834) in June 1817. © NATIONAL MARITIME MUSEUM, LONDON

the company an exclusive trade between England and the lands beyond the Cape of Good Hope and the Strait of Magellan. Permission was given to export silver, an unpopular but necessary condition as there was little demand for European goods in Asia. Each voyage, later a group of voyages, was organized as a separate joint stock, the only way to attract sufficient capital to build large, high quality, defensible ships and purchase a costly return cargo.

The objective was to obtain spices from the Spice Islands, the Moluccas. The company's ships successfully withstood Portuguese attempts to exclude them from the trade of western India, and a trading base was established at Surat. Gujarati cottons were purchased to exchange for the more valuable spices, but the Dutch eventually excluded the company from the spice trade, causing decline and an end to its shipbuilding activities.

Oliver Cromwell's charter of 1657 revived the company. A modern permanent joint stock facilitated investment was used to establish numerous bases, all subordinated to presidencies at Surat and Madras (Chennai). The company successfully marketed Indian textiles in Europe, exploiting the "India craze" in clothing and soft furnishings and generating huge profits. Wealthy merchants, many at the

heart of the company, were attracted to providing ships for this luxury trade. The company's dependence enabled the owners to secure a ship's employment throughout its life and its replacement to ensure the continued employment of an experienced commander.

Those excluded from this rich trade formed a rival company, the two merging in 1709 to form the United Company of Merchants of England trading to the East Indies. The charter granted by Parliament renewed previous privileges in return for the loan of the company's total stock to the state. Half a century of steady growth followed. China tea, first imported direct from Canton in 1700, overtook Indian textiles by mid-century as the major import from the East despite the extremely high customs duties that encouraged widespread smuggling. Annual fleets of up to twenty ships traded from the Red Sea to Canton from the presidencies of Bombay (Mumbai), Madras (Chennai), and Calcutta (Kolkata), securing the company's position as a pillar of the financial establishment.

An early by-law provided for the hiring of ships by fair and open competition, but a combination of wealthy owners soon reestablished the customs of the "hereditary bottom" and the "perpetuity of command." Supported by the builders and suppliers, the principal owners secured consistently high freights, exploiting the company's and the nation's dependence on their services as carriers of troops and military and naval stores.

The acquisition of the revenues of Bengal in the years following Robert Clive's victory at Plassey in 1757 completely changed the nature of the company: the trader became sovereign. The revenues were henceforth to finance the exports and meet the costs of administration and defense. The expected surplus, to be shared with government, never materialized. Continued expansion of the company's territories drove up administrative and military costs forcing the company repeatedly to appeal to the government for financial support, which was always forthcoming since such an important financial institution could not be allowed to collapse. Government intervention in the company's management was inevitable. By Pitt's India Act of 1784 government assumed control of the political and diplomatic aspects of governing the Indian territories, leaving commercial decisions and administration to the company.

At the same time the government acceded to the company's wishes by virtually removing the duties on tea, eliminating smuggling. Immediately the volume of tea imported doubled and continued to rise, necessitating the creation of a special fleet of large ships to fetch the tea direct from Canton. Finding the silver to buy the tea dominated the company's planning. Part was obtained by increasing exports of base metals and woolen cloth, a requirement of successive charters, though they always sold at a loss. The major part was acquired by channeling the accumulated savings of company servants in India into purchasing Gujarati raw cotton and Bengal opium, carried to China by private traders. The silver earned was deposited in the company's treasury at Canton in return for bills of exchange drawn on London, enabling the company's employees to bring their fortunes home. The huge profits from the sale of China tea in London roughly equaled the company's debts in India.

In the final decades of the eighteenth century the company and the high cost of freight exacted by the shipowning monopolists were blamed for the depressed state of trade between England and India. As the time for the renewal of the charter approached in 1793 the northern manufacturers and the shipowners of India and the outports campaigned to open up the Indian trade. The extent to which British money illegally financed Indian cargoes carried to Europe in American ships alarmed government. London's position as the chief port of entry for Asian produce had to be preserved. But on the renewal of the charter in 1793 government required the company only to make available to the private trade a portion of tonnage in its ships to and from India. In 1796 the cost of freight fell when the company's directors successfully reintroduced free and open competition in the provision of the company's ships, now totaling thirty to forty ships annually.

The India trade was thrown open to all on the renewal of the charter in 1813 but the company retained its privilege as sole importer of China tea until the charter renewal of 1833 when opinion no longer tolerated monopoly and the company withdrew from trade altogether. Its role as government's administrator of its Indian empire continued until 1858 when, in the aftermath of the uprising, the crown assumed full responsibility. The company was disbanded in 1874.

[*See also* East Indiaman; Indian Ocean, *subentry on* An Overview; Kolkata; *and* Mumbai.]

## Bibliography

Bowen, H. V. "400 Years of the East India Company." *History Today* 50 (July 2000): 47–53.

Bowen, H. V., Margarette Lincoln, and Nigel Rigby, eds. *The Worlds of the East India Company*. Suffolk, U.K.: Boydell Press, 2002.

Bulley, Anne. *The Bombay Country Ships, 1790–1833*. Richmond, Surrey, U.K.: Curzon, 2000.

Chaudhuri, K. N. *The Trading World of Asia and the English East India Company 1660–1760*. Cambridge, U.K., and New York: Cambridge University Press, 1978.

Furber, Holden. *John Company at Work*. Cambridge, Mass.: Harvard University Press, 1948.

Keay, John. *The Honourable Company: A History of the English East India Company*. London: HarperCollins, 1991.

Lawson, Philip. *The East India Company: A History*. Harlow: Longman Group UK Ltd, 1993.

Parkinson, C. Northcote. *Trade in the Eastern Seas, 1793–1813*. Cambridge, U.K.: Cambridge University Press, 1937.

Philips, C. H. *The East India Company, 1784–1834*. Manchester, U.K.: University Press, 1961.

Sutton, Jean. *Lords of the East: The East India Company and Its Ships (1600–1874)*. London: Conway, 2000.

JEAN SUTTON

## French East India Company

The great Compagnie perpétuelle des Indes (1719–1769), successor to the feebly run and undercapitalized Compagnie française des Indes orientales (1664–1719), was a royal chartered company that enjoyed a distinguished if relatively brief existence, and owed much of its success—but also its ultimate dissolution—to dependence upon the French crown.

Founded in an amalgamation between a series of small French-owned Asiatic, Oriental, African, and American trading companies as part of John Law's calamitous financial strategy for reforming the crown's finances in 1719–1720, the new corporation survived the collapse of Law's system, emerging as a government-controlled operation dependent essentially on private investment for its operating capital. Tax privileges intermittently awarded by the crown to the company sustained investor confidence by guaranteeing annual dividends, and state support in other forms enabled the company to function effectively as a mercantile force in Europe and Asia. Endowed with all the former companies' trading possessions and *points d'appui* (supply stations) in Asia, Africa, and the Americas, together with a range of new facilities and privileges, the corporation developed far more powerful commercial, military, and naval capabilities than its predecessors. With its center of operations at Pondicherry close to Madras on the Carnatic coast, and with *comptoirs* (trading posts) at Chandernagore, Karikal, and Machilipatnam, the company relied heavily for its commercial functioning, its defense, and its ability to wage war on the support of a substantial fleet of Lorient-built, armed East Indiamen whose chief base of operations in the Indian Ocean was the fortified harbor at Île de France (Mauritius), off Madagascar.

Abandoning all but its oriental components at the start of the 1730s, the company latterly derived its trading profits from trade with India and China. Its liquidity at home was sustained by new share issues, loans from the crown, lotteries, and tax revenues. In the East, the company raised loans at different times from missionaries, from its own servants, and from Indian investors. Its credit was also sustained by high volumes of annual sales. These ran at about 10 million livres a year prior to 1730, and at an average of 21 million over the next decade, reaching a peak of 26 million livres in 1751–1752. The company sold few French goods in the East, relying on bullion obtained from Cadiz for four-fifths of its purchases from Asiatic markets. Turnover and profits were impressive. A report of 1743, covering trading over the previous two decades, estimated that a total of 136,104,522 livres had been spent on oriental purchases that were subsequently sold for approximately double this amount, showing a gross profit of 65 million livres. By the 1740s the French company's commercial

performance compared favorably with that of the English East India Company.

As a dependency of the crown, the company also enjoyed a number of privileges that affected its maritime operations. Lorient, in Brittany, was consigned to the company for its exclusive use as a port, where it administered its domestic affairs, auctioned its imports, built many of its own ships, and trained its own naval officers. The company enjoyed the special privilege of conscripting sailors from among royal naval reserves, and as a result suffered few manning problems. Cooperation with the navy, "La Royale," was close, and the state readily supplied officers and ships for the defense of company interests. But the relationship did not always work to company advantage. La Royale was a weak institution in the first half of the eighteenth century and, thinly stretched over both hemispheres, had the right to commandeer company vessels in time of war to the detriment of the company's trade. When the navy itself was required to defend company possessions, it charged 100,000 livres apiece for the use of royal vessels in the middle years of the century, and often declined to comply with the requirements of the company's chiefs in India. This was all the more ironic in that the greater proportion of most royal squadrons assigned to the defense of the company during the Anglo-French conflicts of 1744–1748 and 1757–1763 consisted of the company's own East Indiamen. For instance, Bertrand-François Mahé de La Bourdonnais's fleet prior to the blockade of Madras in 1746 consisted of one royal ship and seven merchantmen; and that of Admiral Comte d'Aché on the Coromandel coast in 1758 was composed of one royal ship and nine East Indiamen.

The company's fleet stood up well to comparison with that of "La Royale." It kept up with developments in Dutch and British naval design, and was usually well maintained. In 1723 it consisted of seventy-six vessels of over one hundred tons, all of which were armed against piracy, and for defense in time of war. Seventeen of these vessels were pierced for over forty cannon, ten could deploy thirty to forty cannon, and a further twenty-one ships carried from sixteen to thirty cannon. Full armament greatly reduced commercial carrying capacity, so peacetime armament tended to be light. An East Indiaman was generally expected to last only six voyages before becoming unserviceable, and ships were not routinely replaced. Storm damage, piracy, war, and varying availability of substitutes affected fleet size, which fluctuated considerably. The War of the Austrian Succession drastically whittled down the fleet, and by 1748 it consisted of only twenty-six vessels, though by the mid-1750s there were sixty-two vessels in service. For the long haul trades with China and India, ships of 450 to 600 tons were exclusively used, and there were approximately eight round-trip sailings a year. The company trained its naval officers to a level of proficiency as high as that of "La Royale," but maintained strict distinction in rank between long-haul and short-haul officers. It was not impossible for officers to transfer from the company navy to royal naval service, though this usually involved loss of rank. However, when the company's wartime losses and heavy involvement in the royal debt crisis destroyed its credit and led to its collapse in 1767–1769, its naval officers were absorbed without difficulty, and without loss of rank, into "La Royale."

[*See also* East Indiaman.]

### Bibliography

Dalgleish, Wilbert Harold. *The Company of the Indies in the Days of Dupleix*. Easton, Pa.: Chemical Publishing Company, 1933. A rare publication, but still one of the most extensive and best accounts in English of the organization and operation of the company.

Haudrère, Philippe. *La Compagnie française des Indes au XVIIIe siècle (1715–1795)*. Paris: Editions Librairie de l'Inde, 1989.

Haudrère, Philippe. "The French East India Company and Its Trade in the Eighteenth Century. In *Merchants, Companies and Trade: Europe and Asia in the Early Modern Era*, edited by Sushil Chaudhuri and Michel Morineau, pp. 202–211. London and New York: Cambridge University Press, 1999.

Mézin, Louis, and Pierre Deleur, eds. *Mahé de La Bourdonnais: La Compagnie des Indes dans l'Océan Indien*. Cahiers de la Compagnie des Indes, no. 4. Port-Louis: Musée de la Compagnie des Indes et la Société des Amis du Musée, 1999. A collection of articles on La Bourdonnais's commercial, administrative, and fighting activities, and especially useful on his role in fortifying the Île de France in the Indian Ocean as a naval base.

Vigié, Marc. *Dupleix*. Paris: Fayard, 1993. Well-researched recent biography of the most significant figure in the company's history, offering insights into the way the company worked.

PATRICK TUCK

## East Indiaman

In the sixteenth century when the Portuguese began regular voyages from Europe to the East Indies, they used caravels and *naus*, big carracks that were among the largest wooden ships ever built. These were called East Indiamen but were similar to contemporary European three-masted ships. It was not until around 1600 that shipbuilders in Europe turned their attention to creating a vessel designed especially for voyages to the Far East. The founding of the English East India Company in 1600 and its Dutch counterpart in 1602 led to a dramatic increase in the volume of goods shipped between Asia and Europe around the Cape of Good Hope. The companies took an interest in having purpose-built ships, and their trading success gave them the capital to afford a specialized type. The Dutch chose to build their East Indiamen—or *retourschepen* as they were called, to indicate the expectation that they would come back—in company-owned shipyards. Some other European East India companies did that as well but more often the enterprises arranged to have their ships built under contract by private firms.

The East Indiaman had a typical full-rig with square sails on the fore- and mainmasts and a lateen sail on the mizzen. There was also a square sail slung under the bowsprit and over time, as on warships, a gaffsail replaced the lateen mizzen. Because of the length of the voyages such ships undertook and the fact that they were a fighting arm of the companies in Asia, they were more heavily armed than other cargo ships. Often they were hard to distinguish from small men-of-war. They were bluff-bowed with broader, flatter bottoms and more angular bilges than warships to gain greater carrying capacity but at a sacrifice of speed. The armament of East Indiamen rose to as much as fifty or more guns in the eighteenth century, though smaller numbers were the norm. While in the 1680s the English East India Company built or chartered vessels of from nine hundred to thirteen hundred tons, such large East Indiamen were exceptional. In the eighteenth century a smaller size, around six hundred tons, was found optimal. Although a number of Dutch East Indiamen were large ships, eleven hundred to twelve hundred tons, they generally became shorter, falling from a maximum length of fifty-two meters (171 feet) in the seventeenth century to forty-five meters (148 feet) in the eighteenth. The bottom of the hull was often double-planked to give greater strength and durability. To move the extra weight of hull and guns, the East Indiaman took on more canvas, rigging three and even four sails one above the other on the fore- and mainmasts and one or two square sails above the triangular sail on the mizzenmast. The stern was built up as on warships, creating cabins for the officers and distinguished passengers, though over time Dutch East Indiamen tended to lose their high sterns.

The end of the European East India Companies in the closing years of the eighteenth and early nineteenth

***Harbor of Dragor.*** C. Wilhelm Eckersberg painted this oil on canvas in 1826. RÉUNION DES MUSÉES NATIONAUX / ART RESOURCE, NY

centuries did not put an end to the construction of East Indiamen. Already in the 1780s size began to increase and by 1793 an English East Indiaman reached twelve hundred tons. The type, perhaps larger than ever and carrying even more canvas, was a prestige vessel and dominated seaborne trade to Asia until supplanted by the clipper in the mid-nineteenth century.

[*See also* East India Companies *and* Trading Vessels, *subentry on* Early Modern Vessels.]

## Bibliography

French, Christopher. "Merchant Shipping of the British Empire." In *The Heyday of Sail: The Merchant Sailing Ship 1650–1830*, edited by Robert Gardiner, pp. 10–32. London: Conway Maritime Press, 1995.

Harris, Daniel G. *F. H. Chapman: The First Naval Architect and His Work.* London: Conway Maritime Press, 1989.

Hoving, A. J. "Seagoing Ships of the Netherlands." In *The Heyday of Sail: The Merchant Sailing Ship 1650–1830*, edited by Robert Gardiner, pp. 34–54. London: Conway Maritime Press, 1995.

MacGregor, David R. *Merchant Sailing Ships 1775–1815: Their Design and Construction.* Watford, U.K.: Model and Allied Publications, 1980.

Marsden, Peter. *The Wreck of the Amsterdam.* London: Hutchinson, 1974.

RICHARD W. UNGER

## Eckersberg, C. Wilhelm (1783–1853),

Danish painter and professor. Since the middle of the nineteenth century, Christoffer Wilhelm Eckersberg has been regarded as the true father of Danish painting. Born in Blakrog, Als, Denmark, on January 2, 1783, he was educated as a painter of motifs from history. He was appointed professor at the Danish Academy of Fine Arts in 1818 and worked with dedication in this capacity until his death. Eckersberg had a significant impact on his many pupils, and the so-called Copenhagen School of which he is representative is regarded as the golden age in Danish art history.

Eckersberg grew up in a small costal town in the south of Jutland and was trained as a house painter before moving to Copenhagen to attend the academy, where he advanced very quickly. In 1809 he won the Great Gold Medal and a scholarship to study abroad for six years. While in Paris during 1809–1813, Eckersberg was a pupil of Jacques-Louis David in 1811. In Paris he learned the importance of studying nature closely and made further progress in theory. Painting from live models and using local colors and bright lighting were important qualities in his work. Eckersberg made several figure paintings based on themes from ancient history. In Rome in 1813–1816 he produced a great number of charming informal Roman townscapes that were true to nature, stringently proportioned, and in delicate cool colors, works that were later much appreciated by his pupils as examples of his skill and true genius.

Upon his return to Copenhagen in 1816, Eckersberg became a member of the Academy of Fine Arts and a professor of painting and was eventually entrusted with official tasks of producing paintings of history for the royal palace of Christiansborg. Simultaneously he had private commissions for portraits, altarpieces, and landscapes, enjoying success in each area. Eckersberg lived a happy family life in his academy apartment at the Charlottenborg Palace in the heart of Copenhagen. A few steps away are the quays of the Copenhagen harbor, from which vantage Eckersberg had a direct view of the Royal Naval dockyard, where the new men-of-war were being built. A short walk away he could observe the roads and the Øresund, the strait between Denmark and Sweden. Eckersberg's diaries tell of a committed teacher educating numerous academy students and private pupils as well, several from abroad. From the 1820s he took them on excursions into the countryside or cruising, training his students to observe nature and establishing the Danish tradition of painting outdoors.

Ever since childhood Eckersberg had taken an interest in different types of ships, the frigate being his favorite. From 1821 he painted more than 125 marine motifs, always based on direct studies, a few of them telling a story or depicting an episode. Ships with all details in rigging were always the key motif, while the sea, clouds, and sky, however impressive, were secondary. To ensure the correct drawing, he took advice from shipbuilders and naval officers. In the 1820s he often emphasized the moods, and in the 1830s his main interests were perspective and the movement of waves. Eckersberg's masterly works from the 1840s represent the culmination of his great experience as a painter.

Eckersberg's paintings appear to be simple and straightforward renderings of nature. However, a closer study reveals how consciously they are constructed in accordance with perspective and classical proportioning. Like other artists before him, Eckersberg had a keen interest in physics, making a series of meteorological observations

and studies of clouds. His predilection for perspective led him to publish two theory books on the subject, in 1833 and in 1841. Critics dispute whether his paintings, which are so true to nature, should be interpreted as representing Neoplatonic idealism. Nevertheless, his insistence on direct and repeated observations, his candor and diligence, and the choice of simple motifs made an enormous impact on his pupils and on the development of a tradition in Danish art—a tradition based on classicism and naturalism.

[*See also* Art; Artists, *subentry* Danish; Painting; *and* Portraits, *subentry on* Ships.]

## Bibliography

Bramsen, Henrik. *Danish Marine Painting*. Copenhagen, Denmark: Burmeister and Wain, 1962.

Fischer, Erik. *C. W. Eckersberg, His Mind and Times*. Hellerup, Denmark: Edition Bløndal, 1993.

Jørnæs, Bjarne. "Eckersberg, C. W." In *Weilbachs Kunstnerleksikon*, edited by Sys Hartmann, vol. 2. 9 vols. Copenhagen, Denmark: Munksgaard Rosinante, 1994.

Møller, Dorthe Falcon. "Skibe i søen." In *C. W. Eckersberg*, edited by Lise Funder and Claus Hagedorn-Olsen, pp. 67–74. Aarhus, Denmark: Aarhus Kunstmuseum, 1983.

Winkel, Niels. *Naturstudiet i Eckersbergs marinemaleri*. Copenhagen, Denmark: Skolen for Kunstpædagogik, Kunstakademiet, 1976.

Winkel, Niels. "Perspective et coloris." In *C. W. Eckersberg*. Paris: Maison du Danemark, 1984.

ELISABETH FABRITIUS

# Economic History
The vast majority of humans inhabit the landmasses that currently occupy 30 percent of the earth's surface. Yet their relationship with the other 70 percent of the earth's surface—which is covered by oceans, seas, lakes, and river systems—is, and always has been, highly significant. This relationship is one of interaction, of mutual dependence, between human societies and the marine environment.

On the one hand, the physical properties of the oceans and seas have a critical bearing on the terrestrial environment, which, in turn, influences the development of human societies. Whereas the oceans absorb carbon dioxide and release oxygen, moderating the world's climate and replenishing its atmosphere, and thereby making human existence possible, their encroachment through sea-level change, erosion, or sudden inundation jeopardizes the lives and livelihoods of coastal dwellers. Moreover, the abundance,

**Economic History.** The foreign business district of Yokohama in a triptych by Hiroshige Utagawa (c. 1842–1894). This shows an active maritime business area with the port in the background. LIBRARY OF CONGRESS, PRINTS AND PHOTOGRAPHS DIVISION

spatial distribution, and diversity of mammals, fish, salt, oil, aggregates, and other marine resources are among the factors that shape the long-term pattern of anthropogenic development.

On the other hand, human societies actively use the sea and its resources. Such exploitative activity assumes many different forms in various temporal and spatial contexts. The exploitative activity is—and has been since time immemorial—generally stimulated by economic forces and conditioned by human technological capabilities in relation to the physical properties of the marine environment. In essence, people mainly use the sea to sustain or enrich themselves, objectives that are attained through the assembly and application of an array of human, financial, and material resources.

In pursuing these economic goals, human societies interact in multifarious ways with the marine environment. Arguably, the most important of these interactions relates to transport and communications; more specifically, to the use of the surface of the sea, together with the land-water interface, as a means of conveyance for food, raw materials, fuel, manufactured goods, people, and information. In this respect, human societies have sought to transform a dangerous, hostile environment that separates landmasses into a facility that connects the continents, islands, and mainlands where people live.

Creating a seaway out of a saltwater barrier has had a pervasive and profound influence on human history. It has enabled regions to specialize in the production of goods that are transported comparatively cheaply, and often in bulk, to markets across inland seas, along the coast, or over the oceans. The carriage of garum and wine within the Roman *mare nostrum*, the shipment of coal, fish, and grain "down east" from New England to the Gulf of Mexico, and the conveyance of West Indian sugar, East Indian spices, and Australasian meat and wool to northwest Europe are among countless examples of how seaborne commerce has facilitated the division of labor and the exploitation of comparative advantages on intraregional, interregional, and transcontinental scales. This applies also to the free and forced movement of people—together with their customs, beliefs, and identities—because ocean passages served to populate areas of labor scarcity, while easing demographic pressures in departed lands, long before the advent of air transport. Using the sea's surface as a means of transport therefore underpinned the emergence of increasingly complex cultural, religious, and racial melting

pots in the so-called new worlds of the Americas, Africa, and Australasia.

As an integral feature of economic activity, seaborne trade tends to fluctuate in line with levels of production and consumption in the economies in which it is rooted. At the broadest scale, seaborne commerce reflects the extent, character, and prosperity of the international economy. In the period from 1870 to 1914, for instance, the growing intensity and spread of industrialization within Europe and North America, as well as the incorporation of primary producing regions in South America, Africa, and Australasia into the industrial market, precipitated a dramatic increase in the volume and value of world trade. Conversely, during the 1920s and 1930s, the prolonged depression experienced by the major industrial economies of the North Atlantic region was reflected in the stagnation of global commerce.

Such ebbs and flows are also evident at national and local levels, as the case of Britain in the nineteenth and early twentieth centuries illustrates. Here, the configuration of the economy, with its reliance on imports of food and raw materials and exports of coal and manufactured goods—notably textiles, machinery, iron, and steel—dictated that the nation was a leading contributor to, and beneficiary of, the prolonged expansion of international seaborne commerce in the 1870–1914 period. In the period from 1919 to 1938, however, British trade contracted appreciably as the erstwhile strengths of an export-led economy became sources of weakness in a much-altered economic context. At the local level, moreover, the thriving coal-export regions of the late nineteenth century—northeast England and southern Wales—experienced falling traffic levels in the interwar era, and then experienced absolute, terminal contraction when oil supplanted coal as the world's chief energy source in the second half of the twentieth century.

## Shipping Revolutions

The provision and deployment of vessels to carry goods and people over seas gives rise to a range of commercial activities that are often significant features of the economies and societies in which they are located. The ship lies at the heart of this sea-transport provision. Although countless types of vessel have been used to carry cargoes since the medieval era, three periods of comparatively intense change in vessel technology can be discerned. The first of these climacterics, which are sometimes called "shipping revolutions," occurred in the fifteenth century, when improvements in navigational knowledge, hull construction, and rigging and the addition of a third mast gave Europeans the ability to cross the Atlantic. Innumerable incremental technological developments took place over the next four centuries, but the wooden-hulled, three-masted, fully rigged sailing ship that conveyed Columbus to the New World in 1492 remained in principle the vehicle that carried European goods, culture, and people across the globe until the second half of the nineteenth century.

Then a second shipping revolution took place. This involved the gradual replacement of wood by iron, and then steel, as the principal material in the construction of hulls, and the transition from wind power to mechanical propulsion through the successive development of simple, compound, and triple-expansion marine engines. Such innovations combined to enhance considerably the efficiency and safety of shipping, which greatly reduced the costs of sea transport and facilitated the integration of South America, Africa, Asia, and Australasia into the international market economy, which had hitherto focused on the North Atlantic basin.

Gradual improvements in the propulsion, navigational equipment, and capacity of ships ensued until the 1960s, when merchant shipping entered another period of revolutionary change. This transition entailed more than just an increase in the efficiency and operational range of vessels. Though there was a great increase in the size of many types of ship, and though new forms of specialized cargo vessels—liquid gas and chemical tankers, container ships, bulkers—were introduced, the modern shipping revolution also impacted on the location, configuration, and functioning of ports. Central to this transformation was the packing of cargo into standard units—pallets, road and rail trucks, containers—that were lifted directly onto, or driven straight into, the vessel. Such "unitization" greatly expedited the flow of cargo from land transport to sea transport by eliminating the need to "break bulk"—that is, unitization eliminated the time-consuming (and expensive) need to unload a multiplicity of man-sized cargo units from road or rail vehicles, store them in a warehouse, and then remove them to the ship's hold. But unitization required gantry cranes rather than stevedores, deepwater termini instead of city-center docks, and space to landward for marshaling standard cargo units as opposed to storing an array of assorted cargo types. In essence, unitization entailed the substitution of capital for labor and the relocation of port activity. As a consequence, by the

mid-1980s cargoes were being conveyed in fewer, much larger, and more specialized vessels, and their movements between land and sea were now much swifter and conducted mainly in estuarial ports linked to hinterlands by trunk roads and railways.

## Operation

The operation of cargo-carrying vessels is a business that has long since been conducted along capitalistic lines, the ship belonging to investors who pay for the labor of seafarers. Such capital assets are usually set forth to generate income, either by facilitating the profitable exchange of goods or through the imposition of charges, or "freights," for the hire of hold space to consignees of cargoes. As Basil Greenhill points out in *The Advent of Steam: The Merchant Ship before 1900*, "a merchant ship, it cannot be overemphasized, is built for one purpose only: to make money, to produce, like any other piece of machinery, a reasonable return on capital invested" (p. 8). This economic objective has generally driven technological change. It has also had political ramifications, for states have generally perceived shipping as a stimulant of wealth, employment, and income in their domestic economies, as well as a source of vessels and labor that can be recruited to serve the nation in times of emergency.

The interplay of market forces and government policies—which often serves to confuse business competition with international rivalry—has largely conditioned the character and distribution of merchant shipping over time and space. In some instances this has resulted in a "passive" interest in the provision of tonnage, with nations or regions engaging heavily in seaborne trade without investing in merchant shipping. Examples of such passivity are legion. In some instances, such as the transport of goods and people from conquered or dependent territories, this was an involuntary response. In other instances it reflected a rational appraisal of the relative costs of shipping commodities by home-owned vessels as against foreign vessels. In 2000, for example, Australia possessed a merchant fleet of fifty-five vessels and a seafaring workforce of fewer than 2,200 men. Yet in the same year, more than 500 million metric tons of cargo moved into or out of Australia's seaports, an aggregate that accounted for 99 percent of the nation's imports and 96 percent of its exports. A similar, if less pronounced, situation has prevailed in many areas of the North Atlantic region since the 1970s, with shipowners in Britain, the Netherlands, Germany, and other nations with long-established shipping traditions deciding to dispose of their vessels rather than compete against cheaper foreign operators, even with regard to the carriage of goods to or from home ports.

Other places have actively endeavored to develop their interests in the business of shipping. This positive approach to tonnage provision has generally occurred by dint of the initiative of private shipowners, the interventionist policies of the state, or a combination of both. It has yielded several forms of shipping enterprise conducted in a variety of frameworks. Over the centuries, for instance, vessels owned and manned in one country have shipped goods produced and consumed in other countries. Such carrying business reflects to some extent the inability or unwillingness of so-called passive areas to ship their own goods. The role of the Dutch in supplying Portuguese and Spanish American settlements is a case in point, for these outposts were starved of provisions because of the inadequacy of Iberian shipping. Neutral powers, notably the Dutch Republic, Denmark, Russia, Sweden, and the United States, provided a similar service to belligerents whose shipping capacity was impaired during the Anglo-French conflicts of 1739–1815.

In other contexts, the greater efficiency of their operations has enabled carriers to gain major shares in other nations' import and export trades. The Dutch were notable in this respect during the late sixteenth and the seventeenth centuries. Favored by their location at the commercial crossroads of the Baltic, southern Europe, Germany, and the British Isles, the shipping interests of the emergent United Provinces expanded rapidly after the revolt against Spanish rule in 1568. By the 1620s, Dutch shipowners had cornered the market in Europe's carrying trades and therefore deployed the lion's share of Europe's merchant tonnage. Likewise, in the twentieth century, a number of nations provided carrying services, with Greece leading the way by virtue of the purchase of cheap, American-built Liberty ships in the aftermath of World War II and the implementation of astute deployment strategies, especially in the oil tanker market.

The ability to carry other nations' cargoes requires that access to that market be feasible and financially worthwhile. Over the centuries, however, states have intervened in the market to foster the shipping interests of their citizens. During the late fifteenth and the sixteenth centuries, for example, the Portuguese and Spaniards capitalized on their pioneering adoption of the three-masted ship by establishing colonies in the Americas. One of the principal objectives of these imperial frameworks was to reserve the carriage of goods within American waters, and

between the colonial periphery and the metropolitan core, to vessels belonging to the mother country. This was to be accomplished by the enactment of laws, to be applied by force, which not only prohibited non-Iberians from engaging in such trade, but also categorized their transgression as piracy, a crime punishable by death. Violence and diplomatic tension might ensue when interloping ventures were resisted by imperial forces, as John Hawkins, Francis Drake, and their crews discovered at San Juan de Ulloa in 1563. Indeed, it was not until 1670, long after other European powers had established secure footholds in the Caribbean, that Spain revoked its right to indict interlopers for piracy, bringing to a close a long period in which there had been "no peace beyond the line"—the "line" having been drawn in 1494 under the terms of the Treaty of Tordesillas, which divided the world between Portuguese and Spanish territories along the fairly arbitrary line 46°37′ W longitude.

## Chartered Companies and Protective Legislation

Monopoly trading rights were asserted by two other mechanisms in the early modern era. First, European states granted charters to companies of merchants formed specifically to trade with particular parts of the world. In England, the late sixteenth and early seventeenth centuries witnessed the award of exclusive commercial privileges to bodies such as the Levant, Muscovy, Hudson's Bay, and African companies in state-sponsored endeavors to develop, respectively, the Mediterranean, Russian, Canadian, and slave trades. Other countries established chartered companies with similar objectives, the French West India Company, Denmark's Kongelige Grønlandske Handel (Royal Greenland Trading Company), and the Swedish East India Company being typical of the genre. However, the largest and most effective of these institutions were the English East India Company (EIC), formed in London in 1600, and its Dutch counterpart, the Vereenigde Oostindische Compagnie (VOC), established in 1602. With the VOC focusing on the Spice Islands (Indonesia) and the EIC focusing on the Indian Subcontinent and later China, these firms grew to exercise great economic and political power in their respective spheres of influence; their vessels, which were the largest merchant ships afloat, possessed a significant military as well as commercial capability in the waters of the East Indies. The VOC and the EIC were well organized, wealthy, and politically influential at home, and thus it was only in the late eighteenth century that the monopoly rights of the VOC were formally eroded, and it was later still, in 1813, that the EIC's privileges were partly undermined.

Protective legislation was the second mechanism used by states to shape the contours of overseas trade and shipping. In many respects this was a response to the hegemony established by the Dutch in the European and transatlantic carrying trades in the 1580–1620 period. Resentful of the extent to which their imports and exports were delivered in vessels that generated income and employment for the United Provinces, European maritime states intervened in the shipping markets by enacting so-called Navigation Laws designed to reduce dependence on Dutch tonnage and foster the growth of their domestic sea-transport industries. Enshrined in legislation and policed by navies and coast guards, this mercantilist strategy was implemented independently by various European powers, most notably England (Britain after 1707), France, Sweden, and Denmark. The strategy was designed to reserve a nation's colonial and coasting trades for its own merchant fleets, and to channel such commerce through its own ports where customs duties could be levied. This strategy was deployed most effectively by Britain. Although the Navigation Laws passed by Parliament from 1650 onward led to tension, and ultimately to revolution, in the North American colonies, they served to foster Britain's colonial trades and shipping interests. Indeed, by the 1690s the British merchant fleet had eclipsed its Dutch counterpart in terms of tonnage registered–a lead that widened as the eighteenth century progressed.

## The Growth and Contraction of British Shipping

In essence, this mercantilist system combined elements of the rigid, centralized, restrictive framework that marked the Iberian imperialism of an earlier epoch with the preferential duties and discriminatory freights imposed after World War I to ensure that a nation's cargoes were conveyed in home-flagged vessels. Initially questioned by Adam Smith's *Wealth of Nations* (1777), the system was gradually dismantled during the first half of the nineteenth century as the "free trade" movement gathered momentum in Britain, its liberalizing influence fueling the "free navigation" sentiments that culminated in the abolition of the Navigation Laws in 1850–a course of action pursued over the ensuing twenty years by the other maritime states of the North Atlantic region.

During this period, most of the technical developments in hull construction and vessel propulsion that constituted

the second shipping revolution took place, and they were adopted most effectively in Britain. As a consequence, from the 1860s until the outbreak of World War I, metal-hulled, steam-driven British vessels were a vital component of the world's shipping provision. Carrying coal and manufactured goods to all regions of the globe, and carrying food, raw materials, and manufactures back to feed the people and factories of the first industrial nation, the British merchant fleet accounted for 60 percent of the world's tonnage in 1913. In that year, this fleet carried 53 percent of the United Kingdom's considerable foreign trade, 80 percent of British intra-imperial trade, and 25 percent of the world's carrying trade. Such deployment figures indicate where Britain's advantages lay in this era; though shipping operated in a relatively free market, which benefited the most efficient carrier, a rapidly expanding domestic economy and a far-flung, growing terrestrial empire connected by sea served to stimulate demand for British tonnage to unprecedented levels.

As with the Dutch in the seventeenth century, this golden age was just a passing phase, and Britain's shipping interests experienced relative and then absolute contraction after 1918. State policies partly explain this demise. World War I significantly weakened Britain's position, with more than 2.5 million net tons lost to enemy action and still more requisitioned by the state. British shipowners therefore lost market share to emerging shipping nations such as Japan, Greece, Norway, and–most important in the short term–the United States. This set the pattern for the next fifty years, with Britain's persistent relative decline given added impetus by the tariff barriers and discriminatory cargo measures established to protect the growing business of emergent shippers from British competition, and the decline was compounded by the tonnage and market losses of World War II.

Market forces also worked to undermine Britain's pre-1914 preeminence, as demand for the products of the hitherto buoyant export industries–coal, iron and steel, textiles, engineering goods–remained depressed throughout the interwar period, while the economic "miracles" enjoyed in the post-1950 era by Japan, Germany, Southeast Asia, and China further impaired Britain's export performance. Accordingly, Britain's share of global tonnage fell from roughly 60 percent to 16 percent between 1913 and 1960, with Japan becoming in 1966 the premier shipowning nation, in terms of tonnage registered–some 270 years after the British had assumed that rank. By 1990 the proportion of the world's fleet flying the red ensign had diminished to just over 1 percent, while the Greek fleet, at 80.1 million deadweight tons (dwt), was the world's largest, ahead of Japan (72.8 million dwt), the United States (59.8 million dwt), and Norway (45.5 million dwt).

## Characteristics of Modern Shipping

Such figures are approximations based on the vessels owned by individuals and companies domiciled—rather than tonnage registered—in these nations. This reflects the changes that have occurred in the institutional fabric of the global shipping provision since the early twentieth century. In a highly competitive market, shipowners have felt increasingly constrained by the measures applied to their industry by nation-states concerned with improving safety standards, regulating labor recruitment, and protecting the marine environment. Such controls generally run counter to the interests of vessel operators seeking to reduce costs to maintain profitability, a conflict of interest that has encouraged those engaged in international shipping ventures to try to circumvent the constraints of national administrative regimes.

This strategy was evident in the early twentieth century. In 1917, for instance, a number of American shipping companies transferred their vessel registrations to Panama to avoid paying high wartime rates of taxation, a device that was used after the war when cruise operators responded to the prohibition of alcohol sales aboard vessels that were classed as American property and therefore governed by U.S. laws. Such cost-cutting policies were deployed much more vigorously in the final third of the twentieth century, as shipowners reacted to the profound technological and structural innovations of the modern shipping revolution, and to the steep fall in demand for tonnage following the oil crises of 1973 and 1975.

In the volatile market of the 1960s and 1970s, cost reduction was the means to survival. Increasingly, this entailed unitization and the deployment of modern specialized vessels, many of which were registered in "flag of convenience" countries such as Liberia and Panama, where comparatively lax regulations regarding ship safety offered significant savings. Flagging-out also relieved shipowners of the obligation to recruit highly trained, comparatively expensive seafarers from their own countries. This delivered major reductions in labor costs and taxes, as well as precipitating the displacement of western European and North American seafarers by workers from low-wage countries in Southeast Asia, Africa, and eastern Europe. As a result, shipping became more of a global business than an aggregation of competing national shipping industries, with capital and labor moving almost as freely across national terrestrial boundaries as they do over the sea.

**Shipbuilding.** While the work of vessels and seafarers takes place largely at sea, the business of shipping stimulates much activity on land. Shipbuilding, for instance, is closely related to shipping in that most of the products of shipyards are designed to meet the needs of shipowners. Until the mid-nineteenth century, in all maritime districts, this generally entailed the construction of wooden sailing vessels for sale in local or regional markets. Although there were some exceptions—such as the production of vessels in British North America that were dispatched across the Atlantic for disposal in the British market—the majority of shipping centers were provided with new tonnage built to order, or sometimes as a speculation, on slipways in the immediate vicinity. Timber was either available locally or could be imported comparatively easily by sea, while the labor of shipwrights and their apprentices rarely imposed a constraint on production, which was normally conducted on a comparatively small, labor-intensive scale. This pattern began to change with the increasing deployment of iron-hulled vessels powered by steam from the 1820s.

The location and scale of the modern shipbuilding industry, which was largely distinct from its wooden counterpart, were influenced strongly by the desirability of cheap access to the key raw materials and manufactured components—coal, iron (or steel from the 1880s), boilers, and marine engines. In Britain, where iron and steel shipbuilding developed rapidly in the second half of the nineteenth century—to the extent that more than four-fifths of world tonnage was launched from British yards in the early 1890s—these locational factors determined that the industry should become concentrated in northeastern England and Clydeside in west Scotland. With the scale of production growing in tandem with the increase in average vessel size, and with the growth in products built for burgeoning national and international markets, shipbuilding was one of Britain's largest and most vibrant industries in the twenty-five years before 1913. As other countries entered the industry, notably during and after World War I, British shipbuilding followed a similar path to that traveled by British shipping—that is, a long period of relative decline leading to sharp, absolute contraction in the 1970s as more efficient producers, chiefly Japan and South Korea, dominated the market.

**Seaports.** The business of shipping is also intimately connected with many facets of the operation of commercial seaports. It is in these coastal, riverside, or estuarial sites that the cargoes carried by sea are loaded and discharged, a process that entails the storage, stowage, and shipment of goods, generally in conjunction with various modes of land carriage. Inputs of human labor and mechanical equipment are required to undertake these tasks, the balance between the two depending on the technological capability of any given era. In general, human effort was very much in the preponderance until the 1960s, when most of the world's major ports began to shed labor and enhance their capital equipment to cater for unitized forms of cargo. With space to landward required for the collection and transshipment of containers, and with storage areas required for oil, gas, and other bulk products, port facilities located near the hearts of great port cities were largely abandoned in favor of deepwater estuarial sites remote, both physically and socially, from centers of population.

At the same time, many of the ancillary activities generated by shipping and port activity vanished from these districts. In former times, mundane, if critical, administrative matters relating to the recruitment and payment of labor, assembly of cargoes, negotiations with consignees, payment of bureaucratic fees, and drawing up of accounts were invariably undertaken in ports, whether on the kitchen table of the humble owner-skipper, in the merchant's countinghouse, or in the opulent offices of the shipping line's headquarters. From such hubs emanated the various spokes that supported the shipping industry—the agents, brokers, lawyers, chandlers, victuallers, and merchants whose specialist services and expertise supplied shipowners with advice to inform their decisions.

**Financial services.** At the same time, activities beyond the shipowner's immediate network developed to smooth the flows of seaborne trade and shipping provision. Financial services were vital in this respect, since the movement of goods in the holds of comparatively expensive vessels sailing across a hostile environment to foreign countries entails high physical risks and uncertain financial returns. It is therefore no coincidence that banks, marine insurers, commodity exchanges, and other financial institutions have developed in port cities.

Indeed, there is a strong positive correlation evident in the locational pattern of trading centers and finance houses; accordingly, the long-term sequential shift in the focus of seaborne commerce from the Mediterranean to the Iberian peninsula, northwest Europe, North America, and the Pacific Rim has been mirrored in the development of financial institutions in Italian city-states, Seville, Antwerp, Amsterdam, London, New York, Hong Kong, and Shanghai over the last five hundred years. In each case the invisible earnings generated by this business were highly significant, with cities such as Amsterdam, London, and New York continuing to profit from their burgeoning financial interests long after their direct involvement in seaborne trade and shipping had waned. Accordingly, over the long term, as an integral component of global business activity the use of the sea for purposes of transport and communication has followed the same developmental course pursued by the world's economy.

[*See also* Banking and Credit; Chartered Companies; East India Companies; Fishing, *subentry on* Economic History; Offshore Industry, *subentry on* Economic History; Pearl Fishing and Farming, *subentry on* Economic History; Ports; Proprietorial Partnerships; Shipping; Shipping Companies; Shipping Finance, 1950 to the Present; Shipping Industry; Shipping Revolution; *and* Trade.]

## Bibliography

Davis, Ralph. *The Rise of the English Shipping Industry in the Seventeenth and Eighteenth Centuries.* London: Macmillan, 1962.

Gardiner, Robert, and Philip Bosscher, eds. *The Heyday of Sail: The Merchant Sailing Ship, 1650–1830.* London: Conway Maritime Press, 1995.

Gardiner, Robert, and Alastair Couper, eds. *The Shipping Revolution: The Modern Merchant Ship.* London: Conway Maritime Press, 1992.

Gardiner, Robert, and Basil Greenhill, eds. *The Advent of Steam: The Merchant Steamship before 1900.* London: Conway Maritime Press, 1993.

Harlaftis, Gelina, and David J. Starkey, eds. *Global Markets: The Internationalization of the Sea Transport Industries since 1850.* Saint John's, Newfoundland: International Maritime Economic History Association, 1998.

DAVID J. STARKEY

# Education and Training

This entry contains two subentries:

Naval Training
Nautical Certification

**Naval Education and Training.** A mathematics class at the U.S. Naval Academy in about 1902. Library of Congress, Prints and Photographs Division

## Naval Training

The origins of formal naval education and training date from the last quarter of the seventeenth century and were coincidental with the first notions of organizing naval personnel on a permanent basis and in substantive grades. The datum point for the training process in the Royal Navy lies with the establishment of the first examination for promotion to lieutenant, which was introduced by Samuel Pepys, secretary of the Admiralty, in December 1677. The test required candidates to have served a minimum of three years at sea and to demonstrate a competence in navigation and seamanship. Only when these subjects were mastered and a certificate of sobriety, diligence, and obedience was produced could the young officer aspire to promotion and higher command. Several commentators have identified the lieutenant's examination as a vital measure in improving competence within the officer corps, and the procedure does, certainly at the start, seem to have been a sizable career hurdle. Pepys certainly thought so, and by the end of March 1678 he was noting not only that standards had improved but also that the number of officers was now more carefully regulated and controlled.

The prospect of having to appear before an examination board seems to have stimulated some unofficial instruction on board ships and also, more commonly, in a number of private mathematical schools situated along the riverbank in London. Aspirant naval officers would attend prior to proceeding to sea or between voyages, as the future Admiral Robert Fairfax did at Wapping in 1680. The tutors were often former ship's masters, river pilots, or surveyors, and many published textbooks and plans of learning specifically designed for young officers. Among the writers were Peter Perkins, a former schoolteacher who produced *The Seaman's Tutor* in 1682, and Mathew Norwood, whose *Systems of Navigation* was described as "more familiar, easy and practical than hitherto done." Perhaps the best known was the former ship's master Samuel Sturmy, whose *Mariner's Magazine*, first published in 1679, ran to four editions.

Though shoreside instruction was clearly of value, it could not totally convey the practical difficulties of navigating afloat. This situation was identified by the serving officer Edward Harrison, who bemoaned the lack of training for naval officers and in particular regretted that mathematics teachers seldom went to sea. The result, he claimed, was that "most of the scholars when they come to sea are half to begin again." This brought a response from the Admiralty, which in April 1702 authorized payment of £20, to be added to a midshipman's pay and given to anyone willing to undertake the duties of ship's schoolmaster. The task was limited but specific—to instruct young gentlemen "not only in the theory but the practical part of Navigation" and also "to instruct the Youth in the art of Seamanship." Vacancies were to be created in ships of the third, fourth, and fifth rate, and captains were warned to accept only those who could show that they were of "sober background and conversation."

Thus began the naval schoolmaster system in the Royal Navy. It lasted throughout the eighteenth century and beyond, although doubts were frequently expressed about the value of the work and about the caliber of the men who carried it out. The schoolmaster, despite presumably some educational pedigree of his own, remained a humble member of the crew, poorly paid and living in the lower deck of the ship, a space that doubled as his classroom. It must have been difficult, uncomfortable, and unrewarding work—particularly in comparison to his counterpart ashore—and estimates of the number and the quality of the men prepared to undertake the task vary considerably. Certainly the schoolmaster does not figure prominently in contemporary portraits of life afloat, at least until the last years of the eighteenth century. Admiralty records, however, confirm that more than a thousand warrants to teach aboard warships were issued from 1712 to 1824, and a number of men recorded careers of twenty-five and thirty years in a succession of ships. Some of these men were clearly disaffected, even dangerous, like William Mears, schoolmaster of HMS *Pegasus*, who in 1786 attempted to kill the future King William IV, then a captain. Nevertheless, there were others who gave lengthy and devoted service—one of the best known was Pascoe Thomas, who accompanied Admiral George Anson on his four-year circumnavigation of the world in HMS *Centurion* and who wrote a substantial diary of the epic voyage.

For the British, who placed great value on practical skills, the schoolmaster-at-sea system, albeit uneven and inefficient, must have seemed the natural solution to the training problem. It allowed the young officer to pursue theory and practice simultaneously and permitted him to jostle in the throng of humanity aboard ship and learn skills alongside the seamen he would eventually lead. It also provided exposure to hardship and danger, a process seen as essential to the character and leadership qualities of an officer and gentleman. Yet not all navies had arrived at the same conclusion. At about the time that British youngsters of twelve years or younger were being packed off to sea, the French were establishing naval colleges ashore. As early as 1670 schools were opened at Toulon and Rochefort that accommodated several hundred students, and a third college was established later at Brest. The Spanish adopted a similar system at the start of the eighteenth century, and about 1750 Dutch junior officers were obliged to take courses ashore and to pass formal examinations before being promoted. A dedicated nautical college was established for officers of both the merchant and military navy in Amsterdam in 1785.

## Naval Academy and the Britannia System

Many in England were content with the notion that the quarterdeck should also serve as the classroom, but European naval educational initiatives did not go wholly unnoticed. In 1733 the Admiralty opened a naval academy within the walls of Portsmouth dockyard. It had up to forty scholars, who followed a syllabus—similar to their French counterparts—that included arithmetic, geometry, trigonometry, navigation, fortification, and gunnery. Though the teaching was of a high standard and the facilities were generally well appointed, the institution was never popular and seldom ran to capacity. The academy was reorganized in 1773 and again between 1806 and 1808 when it was renamed the Royal Naval College. From this point student numbers were more buoyant, but the college still saw only a fraction of the overall officer entry; it was closed, ostensibly as an economy measure, in April 1837.

For the next twenty years all young officers joining the Royal Navy proceeded directly to operational warships, devoid of any formal induction and without any systematic training other than that provided by the dwindling number of naval schoolmasters, who by this time were termed "naval instructors." This so-called pitchfork system commanded some support within the officer corps, but by the early 1850s even the most entrenched advocates recognized that it was not producing either the number or the quality of young officers capable of passing the lieutenant's examination. One estimate suggested that in the decade up to 1855 more than one-third of youngsters were failing to progress beyond the rank of midshipman. Thus in 1857, following the successful introduction of induction schemes for junior seamen and in particular the campaigning efforts of Captain Robert Harris, Royal Navy, the first dedicated officer training ship was established in Portsmouth harbor. Two years later HMS *Britannia*, an old wooden-walled battleship, was recommissioned, and the so-called *Britannia* system, destined to train all junior seamen officers in the Royal Navy for the reminder of the nineteenth century, was initiated.

The decision to conduct training in an old ship rather than in a purpose-built college was based partly on financial stringency and partly on the premise that *Britannia* represented a compromise between those who favored training solely at sea and those who preferred a dedicated institution ashore. Though it was always intended to operate as a school—its cadets did not officially join the service until they passed out—the syllabus concentrated on mathematics and seamanship to the virtual exclusion of all other subjects. Even this narrow curriculum failed to produce satisfactory results, for the students seem to have been too young to cope with the mass of material on offer.

Life aboard *Britannia* may not have been mentally stimulating, but it was undoubtedly physically demanding, and the Spartan conditions, harsh discipline, and routine that accounted for virtually every minute of the day made the term "Dartmouth trained" synonymous with Victorian notions of hardiness, self-sufficiency, and "esprit de corps." The British were both content with their system and happy to subject it to scrutiny and review. Between 1870 and 1886 at least five Admiralty committees examined the subject of officer education and, while acknowledging that academic training in foreign navies was more accomplished, felt that their own system with its emphasis on character and leadership was preferable. Hence the harbor training ship endured until 1905, and almost all British senior naval officers of the first half of the twentieth century—including John Jellicoe, David Beatty, Andrew Cunningham, and Bertram Ramsay—were products of the *Britannia* system.

Not surprisingly, other navies saw the training and education process somewhat differently, and by the mid-nineteenth century the Germans, the Russians, and the Dutch were conducting initial officer training ashore in purpose-built colleges. The Italian navy also favored training ashore in converted schools in Naples and Genoa, and the French employed a combination of ship and shore, with their original colleges combined at Brest in 1827. The United States, which had originally experimented with the schoolmaster-at-sea concept, founded a small naval asylum at Philadelphia in 1838, and seven years later it founded a naval academy on the banks of the Severn River at Annapolis. The onset of the Civil War (1861–1865) led to temporary removal to Newport,

Rhode Island. By the late 1870s, inspired by the leadership of Commodore C. P. Rodgers, the naval academy was teaching not only traditional courses in mathematics and science but also history, languages, and law. Several commentators have noted that by this stage, the academy, though not awarding degrees, was assuming the characteristics of a bona fide educational institution, with a broad recruitment profile and growing intercollegiate and international contacts. In 1878 the U.S. government dispatched academy professor J. R. Soley to Europe to report on foreign systems of naval education and to make recommendations as to how the American system might be improved. He seems to have been unimpressed, particularly by the British, noting in his report that "the high scientific and professional attainments of many English naval officers are not in consequence, but in spite, of their early education."

## U.S. System of Naval Training

Among the characteristics in education and training that identified the U.S. Navy as significantly different from its European counterparts was its treatment of naval engineers. Throughout the 1870s the U.S. Naval Academy had run separate courses for what were termed cadet-engineers and cadet-midshipmen, but after congressional intervention in 1882 the distinction was abolished and a common curriculum was introduced. In 1899 the Naval Personnel Act amalgamated the two groups, and midshipmen were expected to master both specialist engineering skills and the general knowledge required by the seaman officer. The academy's four-year course set out to do just this.

In Britain, entirely different schools had been maintained for engineers and seaman officers, but following the American example, Admiral Sir John Fisher, as second sea lord, attempted to introduce combined training at the new Royal Naval College, Dartmouth, opened in 1905. The so-called Selbourne scheme undertaken at Dartmouth and its associated preparatory school, the Royal Naval College, Osborne, had some initial success, and the syllabus—which combined mathematics, science, and practical engineering instruction—was probably unique in British contemporary secondary education. Nevertheless, resentment toward the notion of common training, particularly from within the executive branch, remained strong, and segregation returned in 1925, setting the organizational pattern in the Royal Navy that exists to the present day.

Though the development of naval education saw some progress in the first half of the twentieth century, the formal training regimes of the principal navies seem to have been characterized by routine rather than by innovation. The curriculum at the U.S. Naval Academy, despite degree accreditation in 1931, remained closely prescribed and relatively unchanged until after World War II. The Dartmouth program, praised initially for its pioneering approach, soon settled into a smooth-running machine that admitted few new ideas. In Japan the naval college founded with British help in 1870 was inculcating habits of discipline and conformity through a sixteen-hour working day and an arduous physical regime that had changed little since the previous century. Old training habits apparently died hard. Indeed, the most significant innovation of the period came from outside the principal institutions, with the 1925 U.S. congressional decision to establish a Naval Reserve Officer Training Corps (NROTC) in selected civilian universities. This measure allowed students to follow courses in naval subjects coincidentally with their other studies and thus gain both a degree and a commission in the Naval Reserve. From humble beginnings in just six colleges, the NROTC expanded more than tenfold and eventually overtook the Naval Academy as the principal source of young officers for the U.S. Navy.

The success of the NROTC program and the requirement to man an expanded postwar fleet led the United States to examine a series of officer training and education options in the years following World War II. The possibility of a second naval academy was briefly considered, as was a plan to dispense completely with single-service education in favor of a civilian university program. However, the 1950 report of the Service Academy Board endorsed the system of individual service institutions, combined with a substantial NROTC, and this declaration of faith helped both to stimulate reform and to promote a more liberal and diversified academic program at Annapolis. The appointment of a civilian dean in 1963 and an increase in the numbers of civilian faculty extended the process, although a parallel drive toward more practical training for midshipmen has also been in evidence.

## Naval Education Reforms

The British postwar experience was somewhat different. Faced with a declining fleet, limitations on manpower, and a heavily pressurized defense budget, officer training saw little basic change, and for some years after World War II Dartmouth remained a fee-paying institution with thirteen-year-old entrants. Fundamental reform was, when it arrived in the 1960s, the product of external factors derived

from two distinct sources. The first was the increasing popularity of what is generally termed the systems approach to training. Pioneered in the U.S. Army, this approach employed a training regime tightly controlled by the functions of analysis, design, development implementation, and evaluation. The Royal Navy, long in favor of vocational approaches to training, embraced the concept enthusiastically and undertook an extensive overhaul of its methods, leading to a series of shorter, more practically orientated courses. The second force for change was the rapid expansion in British higher education and the requirement to attract a substantial graduate entry into the service. A series of new induction schemes was devised and the armed forces briefly considered founding their own degree-awarding institution—a proposal that eventually foundered on economic grounds in 1968. From this point the Royal Navy gradually abdicated the role of academic instruction to the civilian universities and thus opted to take an increasing number of older, graduate entrants into its ranks.

The origins of higher education for naval officers, at least as the concept is understood in the twenty-first century, are somewhat later and probably lie in the years following the closure of the Royal Naval College in 1837. While the British habit of recruiting officers at a particularly early age and educating them in a predominantly practical environment produced first-rate seamen, it did little to equip them for the later stages of a career. This was recognized in 1839 when the Admiralty directed that the institution should reopen to provide additional means of scientific education for officers of the fleet. Its students were experienced officers from the executive branch either following academic courses prior to gunnery training or undertaking voluntary study—captains, commanders, and lieutenants were allowed to spend up to twelve months in each rank following any aspect of college teaching. Standards were high, and the small staff included significant figures in the navy's industrial revolution, including the corrosion expert W. D. Hay and the pioneering engineer Thomas Brown. Brown's arrival at the college in 1841 coincided with the purchase of the instructional tender *Bee*, the first screw-driven vessel to be ordered by the Admiralty and the first to undertake a detailed trials program. Yet despite some innovative work, the college always remained at the periphery of mainstream naval activity. The bulk of its students were military officers whose aspirations were to overall command rather than the management or operation of machinery. Few of the college's courses were mandatory, and the college only ever saw a fraction of the overall officer corps for any sustained period. By the late

1860s the college was underfunded and was a target for criticism in the periodical and service press.

The issue of advanced study was addressed by the first committee to examine the higher education of naval officers, under the leadership of Rear Admiral Charles Shadwell. Their report, published in July 1870, argued that while the academic element of a number of foreign systems of naval education might preclude the need for further training, within the British system some form of advanced study at a later career point was vital. The committee's principal recommendation was that a new college should be established with an expanded teaching staff and a student body ranging in rank from sublieutenant to captain that would pursue courses in "those branches of scientific investigation of most interest to the Navy." The new institution, situated in the spectacular buildings of the former Greenwich Hospital, opened on February 1, 1873, and thus became the Royal Navy's first, properly constituted, onshore training establishment. The Royal Naval College expanded rapidly, and within four years it had a teaching staff of thirty-one and a student population of several hundred, including British serving officers and civilians and officers from the navies of China, Japan, and Denmark.

It is evident that while Greenwich offered an expanded view of the purposes and place of higher education in an officer's career, certainly compared to its Portsmouth predecessor, it nevertheless remained a conservative and narrowly oriented establishment. The curriculum was almost exclusively technical in nature, and although it included some limited language study and specimen lectures in international law, these subjects were invariably presented as practical skills to be mastered, rather than objects of genuine academic endeavor. Thus despite the presence of some gifted teachers, particularly John Knox Laughton, who campaigned tirelessly for the inclusion of naval history in the syllabus, the initial progress soon faltered. In 1877 the first external inspector's report noted that unless the status of the teaching staff could be raised and a broader field of study encompassing history, strategy and tactics, and political geography was imposed, then the progress of the Royal Naval College as an institution of genuine higher education would be impeded. The warning went unheeded, and by the early 1880s, with the Admiralty still unwilling to make study at the college a compulsory career component, student numbers began to fall, teaching staff members were made redundant, and—far from becoming a naval university or embryonic staff college—Greenwich gradually assumed the status of an advanced technical school.

Though the British notion that successful warfare was merely a matter of superior practical skill may have stifled institutional progress, there were a number of officers and civilians keen to encourage higher study of naval matters and to argue that modern naval warfare was a complex undertaking. J. K. Laughton, compulsorily retired from Greenwich in 1885, moved to Kings College, London, where he pursued the development of disciplined naval history as the basis for future strategic and tactical doctrine. Captain Sir John Colomb and Vice Admiral Philip Colomb, writers and activists, were influential in encouraging the study of history as a means of defining principles of naval warfare. Admirals Sir Cyprian Bridge and Sir Reginald Custance lectured and taught and were unstinting in their efforts against a naval "materiel" school that derided the past and placed faith solely in the acquisition of new weapons and equipment. Later the writer and lecturer Sir Julian Corbett, who taught at Greenwich, was prominent in this area, and his book *Some Principles of Maritime Strategy* (1911) sought to establish tenets governing the conduct of war at sea. Though there is little evidence that all these efforts had any effect on general naval policy, they bore some fruit with the establishment of a senior officers' war course at Greenwich in 1900. It failed to prosper, however, and within five years had transferred to Portsmouth dockyard to become a tactical school more concerned with practical matters than with broader thinking.

In the United States the case for reform in the higher education of naval officers was being energetically advanced by Captain (later Rear Admiral) Stephen B. Luce. The outstanding figure in the field of training and development in the U.S. Navy, Luce had twice served on the staff of the U.S. Naval Academy and had commanded training vessels and the apprentices training squadron. In the late 1870s his energies turned to higher education, and he began a campaign to establish a school where "the science of war, naval tactics, military and naval history, international law, military and naval law" might be taught. Luce visited Great Britain, where he met and corresponded with J. K. Laughton, and Luce exploited his professional contacts at home, particularly with Brigadier Emory Upton, who had examined army organization in Europe and was a keen advocate of training for high command.

In 1884, largely through Luce's efforts, the Naval War College was established in Newport, Rhode Island, and the following year the first students joined an institution designed to be "a place of original research on all questions relating to war and the prevention of war." Luce, as a commodore, was appointed president of the college, and he gathered around himself an outstanding staff that included the international law professor James R. Soley, the naval historian Captain Alfred T. Mahan, the war-gaming expert William McCarty Little, and the army lieutenant Tasker Bliss. There was still much opposition to the concept of the academic study of war, and in its early days the college—situated in a former poorhouse—was underfunded and taught few students. It was probably the appointment of Mahan that guaranteed the survival of the institution, for the publication in 1890 of his book *The Influence of Sea Power on History* made the author internationally famous. Mahan's theories had a significant impact on both the established and the emerging navies of the world, and although expansion and rivalry were already well under way by the time that the book appeared, Mahan's arguments served as an important template and justification.

Despite the influence of a number of outstanding individuals—Mahan at Newport, Corbett at Greenwich, Gabriel Darrieus of the École Supérieure de Marine in France, and Curt von Maltzahn, professor of strategy at the German Naval Academy—the provision of higher education for officers of the world's navies made somewhat desultory progress, and it was only in the wake of World War I that some reform was evident. Again this movement seems to have been associated with personalities generally acknowledged as talented but wayward.

In Great Britain the principal proponent was the sailor and scholar Sir Herbert Richmond, who, despite arousing much prejudice and opposition, was eventually appointed admiral-president at Greenwich. Richmond believed that many of the shortcomings of the Royal Navy in World War I were derived from a failure to develop a coherent system of higher education for its senior officers. His appointment allowed him to return the war course to the college, where it ran alongside a newly established one-year staff course, and by the early 1920s Greenwich was teaching a complete cross section of officer-students. Richmond also made an important contribution to the establishment of the Imperial Defence College (1926), an institution designed to foster international understanding and promote discussion of higher defense issues; it continues today as the Royal College of Defence Studies. In France, the École de Guerre Maritime was also under talented leadership, in the shape of Admiral Raoul Castex, author of a five-volume study of maritime strategy that aroused considerable interest, particularly among aspiring naval powers. In the United States, the Naval War College continued to expand and develop, particularly under the presidencies of rear admirals William S. Sims (1919–1922) and William V. Pratt (1925–1927),

and the institution became increasingly focused on war planning and the potential of a Japanese naval threat.

The decade leading to World War II demonstrated that some navies were clearly more comfortable than others with the relationship between the theory and practice of warfare and the requirement for detailed staff training. France, Germany, and Russia, perhaps because of their status as secondary naval powers and the requirement to argue a strong naval case, seem to have placed considerable emphasis on theoretical study, although how far this emphasis informed national policy is difficult to quantify.

Others were more pragmatic in their approach. Many individual American naval officers were uncomfortable with the academic study of warfare, but the U.S. Navy maintained its leadership in the movement to place training within the context of a complete career, and most wartime seagoing flag officers were products, willingly or not, of the war college system. In Britain, where the notion of warfare as a purely practical pursuit lingered, theoretical study was often viewed not only skeptically, but also with a hostility that did not necessarily disqualify promotion to the highest rank.

## The Modern Period

The postwar years saw a general increase in the provision of higher education and training for naval officers, much of it prompted by the challenges of new technology. As the world's navies entered the nuclear age, it seemed that the persuasive arguments of the matériel school were returning to the classrooms and lecture halls and that "training" rather than "education" was to predominate. This process was given impetus in the 1960s with the introduction of systems approaches to training that had been tried in officer induction and seemed to hold out the prospect of shorter courses with more measurable outcomes. Much faith, particularly in the Royal Navy, was placed in "programmed" and "distance" learning techniques, and a new school of education and training technology was established in 1969 to oversee this activity.

Yet not everyone was convinced by promises of a shorter, cheaper, better educational regime or by the argument that methods appropriate to basic training might be used successfully at a higher level. In the United States, attempts were made to deal more fundamentally with the problem of the intellectual development of career officers, and in particular how to return the Naval War College to a position of leadership and new thinking. Under the presidency of Vice Admiral Stansfield Turner (1972–1974), a former Rhodes scholar at Oxford, wide-ranging reforms were introduced that encouraged students to read and write more extensively, placed emphasis on assessment, and injected new rigor in the curriculum.

The Turner reforms were adopted in varying degrees by the other American service colleges, and the curricular approach that set out to develop analytical and problem-solving skills—particularly applicable to modern joint operations—was widely emulated. In 1990, the college was first accredited to grant its graduates a master's degree in strategic studies and international security affairs. In 1998 the British further advanced the process by closing their individual staff colleges, including Greenwich, and replacing them with a single, purpose-built Joint Service Command and Staff College. This decision effectively brought to a close the era of higher education as a single service concept in the Royal Navy.

It will be clear that the world's major navies have often been uncomfortable with the competing claims of training and education and in particular with how infinite forms of thinking might be formally combined with the achievement of closely defined objectives. It is also clear that this central question has prompted a wide range of answers, and a survey suggests that even where there is agreement about the ends to be attained, considerable variation is evident in the methods adopted to achieve them. It is thus still relatively rare to find identical training routines among the principal navies of the world, and initial officer training may vary in length from twelve months to four years according to national preference.

Nevertheless, at aspirant level what is sometimes termed the "Athens v. Sparta" debate—whether professional expertise is best derived from conditioning and practical application or from the fashioning of the intellect—appears to be enduring and widely shared. It is also apparent that, regardless of the navy concerned, much contemporary training and education practice tends to retain the distinguishing characteristics of its formative period. How long this will endure in the face of shorter careers, broader recruitment profiles, and what some see as an increasing disparity between the values of military life and of civilian life is harder to predict.

At a higher level, much recent attention has been directed to the training and education required to operate at the most senior rank, and attendance at staff-college is now invariably seen as a vital component for career officers, regardless of nationality. There has also been a common drive to find civilian accreditation, particularly the awarding of university degrees, to consolidate the process of professional education. Perhaps above all the trend toward joint and combined operations and the requirement for navies to operate increasingly within a coalition environment has prompted a move away from single service orientation, not only at an operational level, but also in its associated training and educational activity.

[See also Navies, Great Powers, subentries on British Isles, 1500 to the Present; and United States, 1775 to the Present; and Training Ships.]

## Bibliography

Dickinson, H. W. "*Britannia* at Portsmouth and Portland." *Mariner's Mirror* 84, no. 4 (November 1998): 375–384.

Dickinson, H. W. *Educating the Navy: Eighteenth and Nineteenth Century Education for Officers of the Royal Navy*. Abingdon, U.K.: Taylor and Francis, 2007.

Dickinson, H. W. "The Origins and Foundation of the Royal Naval College, Greenwich." *Historical Research* 72, no. 177 (February 1999): 92–111.

Dickinson, H. W. "The Portsmouth Naval Academy 1733–1806." *Mariner's Mirror* 89, no. 1 (February 2003): 17–30

Hattendorf, John B., B. Mitchell Simpson III, and John R. Wadleigh. *Sailors and Scholars: The Centennial History of the Naval War College*. Newport, R.I.: Naval War College Press, 1984.

Karsten, Peter. *The Naval Aristocracy: The Golden Age of Annapolis and the Emergence of Modern American Navalism*. New York: Free Press, 1972.

Lambert, Andrew. *The Foundations of Naval History: John Knox Laughton, the Royal Navy, and the Historical Profession*. London: Chatham, 1998.

Lewis, Michael. *The Navy in Transition, 1814–1864: A Social History*. London: Hodder and Stoughton, 1965.

Lewis, Michael. *A Social History of the Navy, 1793–1815*. London: Allen and Unwin, 1960.

Pack, S. W. C. *Britannia at Dartmouth*. London: Redman, 1967.

Rodger, N. A. M. "Training and Education: A Naval Dilemma over Three Centuries." *Hudson Papers* 1 (January 2001): 1–34.

Shurman, D. M. *The Education of a Navy: The Development of British Naval Strategic Thought, 1867–1914*. London: Cassell, 1965.

Sullivan, F. B. "The Naval Schoolmaster during the Eighteenth Century and the Early Nineteenth Century." *Mariner's Mirror* 62, no 4. (November1976): 311–326.

Sweetman, Jack. *The U.S. Naval Academy: An Illustrated History*. 2d ed., revised by Thomas J. Cutler. Annapolis, Md.: Naval Institute Press, 1995.

Taylor, E. G. R. *The Mathematical Practitioners of Hanoverian England, 1714–1840*. Cambridge, U.K.: Cambridge University Press, 1966.

Van Crefeld, Martin. *The Training of Officers: From Military Professionalism to Irrelevance*. New York: Free Press, 1990.

H. W. DICKINSON

**Nautical Certification.** The training ship HMS *Worcester* was the second ship of this name that served the Thames Nautical College. This 86-gun ship-of-the-line, originally laid down in 1833 but not launched until 1860, served at anchor at Greenhithe from 1877 to 1939. © NATIONAL MARITIME MUSEUM, LONDON

# Nautical Certification

In most seafaring cultures, nautical training and qualification are closely linked to the nautical hierarchy, essential for securing a clear chain of command and immediate reaction in case of emergency. The captain is the head of this hierarchy, and is the master. Initially, the term "captain" applied only to commanders of warships. Only by courtesy is the master of a merchant vessel known as "captain." Even today, "master" is the legal term for the commander of a British merchant ship, and "master" will therefore be used in this article.

Such a nautical hierarchy has existed for hundreds of years, not only on board European ships, but also on non-European ships, such as those of the fifteenth-century Chinese. In medieval Arab shipping, a nautical hierarchy existed with a master at the top, who was also responsible for navigating the ship. The key qualification for promotion in Arab shipping was knowledge of navigation, and the necessary skills were imparted within family networks.

The same was true for Polynesian seafarers, although there is some evidence of some kind of navigation schools on certain islands.

The correlation between qualification and status within the nautical hierarchy can also be observed in maritime terminology in most European languages. The head of the nautical hierarchy was called *kybernetes* in Greek, *gubernator* in Latin, *sturmann* in medieval German, and *pilote* in French. But this head did not necessarily also govern the ship. For a long time, property or social status was crucial for achieving command; only in the early modern period did professional qualification become decisive.

For a long time, the training of fishermen was separate from that of seamen, and to some extent it still is today. Usually fishermen learned their trade aboard the vessels of their fathers or relatives, the information about fishing grounds being passed from generation to generation but concealed from outsiders. Only at the turn of the twentieth century, with the emergence of industrialized high-sea fishing and increased governmental control over licensing and nautical education, did the training of fishermen become more formalized, similar to that of seamen.

## Ancient Times

Although we have only fragmentary information about early shipping in the Mediterranean, there must have been some kind of professional training, since merchant shipping as well as the emerging navies needed skillful seamen. Given what practice was in later periods, one can assume that, in general, seafarers learned their profession during the everyday management of the ship.

Likewise, not much is known about the career patterns of the ancient seamen. At least it can be assumed that the commanding officers of the Egyptian expeditions during the third and second millennia B.C.E. were chosen by the pharaoh from the nobility, not from the ranks of professional seamen. From the turn of the first millennium B.C.E., the Phoenicians—skilled navigators originating from what is now Lebanon—established coastal and deepwater routes for both trade and voyages of discovery, not only in the Mediterranean but also in the Atlantic Ocean. The Phoenician sailors were freemen, whereas later, in Greek and Roman merchant shipping, the crews often consisted entirely of slaves. Certainly a firm knowledge of seamanship and navigation skills was required for promotion to master. Since the Greeks already had sailing directions, which were called *periploi* and the usage of which required reading skills, reading can also be understood as a necessary professional requirement.

On Greek warships, the supreme command was held by the *trierarch*, who in general was a military officer, while the *kybernetes* or navigator was a professional seaman. The main task of the *kybernetes* as head of the nautical hierarchy was the management of the ship. His equivalent in the Roman navy was the *gubernator*. Since the effective handling of an oar-propelled warship required extensive training, the oarsmen generally were not slaves, but rather they were comparatively well-paid specialists who also had some chance of professional promotion.

As early as the fourth century B.C.E. the navy of Rhodes had developed a differentiated nautical hierarchy of professional seamen, the officers in many cases having risen from oarsman to the higher ranks. Likewise in the Roman navy, as in the Roman army, men could rise from the lower ranks to the top ranks, the division into a military and a nautical hierarchy being abolished to a certain degree. In most cases the men were recruited from provinces, such as Phoenicia, Greece, or Egypt, and had to sign up for a fixed twenty-six-year period of service. They could rise to *magister navis* (captain) or even to *navarchus* (commodore), but the higher ranks, equivalent to modern admirals, were reserved for members of the Roman aristocracy.

## Middle Ages

After the decline of the Roman Empire, highly developed merchant shipping collapsed in the Mediterranean, and permanent maritime fighting forces almost disappeared until their reemergence in the early modern period. Since only few medieval states—most notably the Byzantine Empire, Arab-ruled Egypt and Syria, the Republic of Venice, the Knights of the Order of Saint John, and the Ottoman Empire—were able to maintain a regular navy, a fighting fleet was usually improvised by converting merchant vessels into warships. New trade systems were also established in the Middle Ages, as in the Mediterranean by Italian merchant republics like Venice or Genoa or in northern Europe by the Hanseatic League, a mercantile confederation of German towns; these new systems led to an increase of merchant shipping.

For most of the Middle Ages, different hierarchies existed on board ships, with merchants or military men holding command, while a parallel nautical hierarchy managed the ship. Thus the captains or *patrono* of Venetian galleys always had a navigation specialist aboard, called the *omo di conseio* on private ships and the *armiraio* on the flagship. On board early Hanseatic merchant vessels, the overall command was held by the *schipher*, commonly a merchant, who was the owner of the ship and its cargo but did not exert the nautical control. This was the task of the *sturmann* or navigator, who usually was a professional seaman. This division of responsibilities had its roots in the Viking period. While the command of a Viking warship generally was held by a chieftain or jarl, there was a chance for experienced seamen to rise to the position of *stýrimadr*, responsible for navigating the ship.

Only in the twelfth century did the position of master and shipowner separate, since merchants now managed their businesses from their hometowns. Although part ownership was still a requirement for assuming command of a merchant vessel, most masters now were seamen who were capable of taking the nautical control themselves. From the fourteenth century, a more complex nautical hierarchy developed, the status on board now being dependent on the degree of professional competence. Professional training usually took place in a rather incidental way during the ordinary working of the ship. Since every seaman had to start at the bottom and advance gradually through the ranks within the nautical hierarchy, a career pattern based on nautical expertise developed. Taking into account the sailing-direction manuals, like the fifteenth-century German *Seebuch*, it seems that reading skills might also have been necessary for a nautical career. Although the social division between the master and his crew deepened, each seaman still had a chance to become mate or even master, provided that he had acquired the necessary professional qualifications.

## Sixteenth to Twentieth Centuries

The expeditions of the Portuguese and Spaniards in the fifteenth and sixteenth centuries had a great effect on the evolution of navigation and nautical training. Although the famous nautical academy in Sagres, Portugal, allegedly founded by Prince Henry the Navigator (1394–1460), never existed, the first indications of vocational training and of mechanisms to ascertain the qualification of navigators can be determined in fifteenth-century Portugal. In 1484, King John II of Portugal convened a group of mathematicians, the "Junta de Matematica," that elaborated the *Regimento do astrolabio et do quadrante*, a navigation manual that laid the foundations of modern astronomical navigation. From at least the beginning of the sixteenth century, this scientific achievement was supplemented by systematic nautical vocational training.

At this time, in Portugal as well as in Spain, the professional training of navigators was subject to strict governmental control, since nautical information was treated as a state secret. For this reason, instruction in navigation was provided only by a limited number of institutions, and was thus restricted to a small nautical elite. In Portugal at the beginning of the sixteenth century, the pilots assigned for the journey to India were educated at the Aula de Matematica, while the Casa da India, founded in 1503 as the governmental board for the control of the Indian trade, was concerned with the general oversight of the navigators' professional competence. In a similar way, the Spaniards in 1503 established the Casa de Contratación in Seville. Although mainly an institution for the governmental control of the American trade, the Casa de Contratación also supervised the competence of pilots. In 1508, the position of *piloto mayor* (chief pilot) was created at the Casa de Contratación for instructing and examining the pilots destined for the Americas. The first holder of this position was the famous Florentine navigator Amerigo Vespucci

(1451–1512). Every pilot assigned to the American trade had to attend this institution for one year. After passing a professional examination, the pilots received a certificate of qualification, the *carta de examinación et aprobación*. Further, in 1523 the position of cosmographer was created, and in 1552 a professorship of cosmography and navigation was created, which marked the beginnings of a nautical academy in Seville. Thanks to the combination of practical experience and theoretical knowledge, an entirely new approach to nautical education was established in these recently founded Portuguese and Spanish navigation schools.

One characteristic of early modern European shipping was the fusion of the different hierarchies on board into just one hierarchy, a hierarchy dominated by nautical qualification. In the sixteenth century, responsibilities on board Portuguese ships were still strictly separated. While the captain or *capitão-mor* was responsible for the defense of the ship and held the overall command, the pilot was responsible only for navigation. Similarly, on Spanish ships sailing to America, the command was divided between the captain or *capitan de mar*, who was responsible for the navigation, and the military commander or *capitan de guerra*.

Later, the different nautical and nonnautical tasks amalgamated. Now the commander of a warship was not only a fighter but also a seaman, while the master of a merchant vessel now had to perform economic tasks as well. Likewise, nautical education became increasingly formalized, leading to a more professional training for officers in the navy as well as in the merchant service, although the common seamen's instruction in practical seamanship still followed the traditional pattern of on-the-job training.

At the same time, as a consequence of the emergence of state navies, employment at sea separated into two specialized branches: naval and merchant. Since the profession of naval officer in most countries was reserved to the upper classes, men from the lower classes were generally excluded from receiving a naval officer's commission. Thus while it remained usual for common seamen to switch between service on board warships and service on board merchant vessels, switching between merchant shipping and the navy was less common among the officers. There were, however, exceptions. For instance, during the eighteenth and early nineteenth centuries, Danish naval officers sometimes served as mates or masters on merchant ships. For this purpose they were granted leave of absence from the navy for a maximum of three years. Similar to this, from the eighteenth century up to 1830, it was not unusual for unemployed Dutch naval officers to take command of ships of the Verenigde Oostindische Compagnie (VOC), the Dutch East India Company. However, in Denmark as in the Netherlands, merchant service in most cases was only a temporary assignment, since in either country only few officers actually left the navy for service on merchant ships. On the other hand, merchant mates and masters sometimes also served as naval officers. For example, Danish trading companies often arranged for royal commissions for their masters. Likewise, Danish merchant mates and masters served as naval officers during the Anglo-Danish war of 1807 to 1813. Similarly in Great Britain, mates and masters from the merchant service were appointed as so-called sailing masters at the rank of warrant officers in the Royal Navy, but only rarely did they rise to the rank of commissioned officer.

Moreover, since the constitution of the naval forces was part of the process of early modern state building, the navies were under governmental control from the beginning, while governmental influence on merchant shipping in most countries was extended only by degrees over the centuries. Considering the unequal conditions in both services and for reasons of clarity, professional training and career patterns in naval and merchant services are here analyzed separately, although developments in merchant shipping and in navies occurred simultaneously and with a certain amount of interaction.

## Navies

Until the middle of the seventeenth century, most European navies had a clear division between the nautical and the military hierarchies. As in ancient and medieval times, the commanders of warships were in most cases military men whose main task was to fight with the ship, while a subordinated nautical hierarchy had nautical control.

Only in the sixteenth century did the early modern states begin to build up permanent navies, which were not turned into professional fighting forces before the seventeenth century. Likewise a new, professional officer corps began to emerge. While professional ascent remained open for all in merchant shipping, social barriers emerged in most navies when the profession of sea officer became a respectable career for the sons of noble and middle-class families, thus banning men from the lower classes from rising to commissioned officer.

In particular, the French navy suffered from social conflicts within the officers' corps. Under King Louis XIV

(r. 1643–1715) a professional navy was created. The king's minister, Jean-Baptiste Colbert, established a school at Dieppe in 1665 under Père Denis as *maître d'hydrographie*, and a naval college was operating in Saint-Malo by 1669. The first training cruise for instruction took place in 1670. In the 1660s, the works of a Jesuit from Chambéry, Père Claude François Milliet de Châles, became standard texts, and a centralized educational system began to develop. In 1681, at the initiative of the Duke of Luynes, a short-lived academy was established at Indret, Baase-Loire, for future naval officers. In the same year, naval vessels were outfitted at Rochefort, Brest, and Toulon as school ships for the education of officers. In 1686 the academy at Indret was closed, and from that time until 1786, the three newly reorganized companies of Gardes de la Marine at Brest, Rochfort, and Toulon formed the focus for naval officer education. Under Jesuit direction, a body of scholars gathered in the naval schools to educate future French officers to highly advanced scientific levels in mathematics, navigation, ballistics, hydrography, and ship construction, as well as in dance, drawing, calligraphy, pilotage, history, tactics, and the art of fortification. The emphasis, however, lay on theoretical education, while practical training was largely neglected.

To secure a body of seamen for the French navy, the "Inscription maritime" was introduced, obliging the coastal population to compulsory naval service. The officers of the "grand corps" were generally recruited from the nobility, while there were also officers taken in from the merchant navy, who, because of their blue uniforms, were known as *officiers bleus* and rarely rose above the rank of pilot, the French equivalent to "sailing master." Frequent social clashes between the two classes of officers disrupted the effectiveness of the navy. After severe defeat in the Seven Years' War (1756–1763), the officers' training was changed to emphasize practical sea training; the efficiency of this training was shown during the American War of Independence. During the French Revolution, the royalist officers' corps was replaced by officers promoted from the lower ranks or recruited from the merchant service. But revolutionary fervor did not make up for professional training, and thus the new officer corps never achieved the excellence of the old royal French navy, although under Napoleon the officers' training was reformed with some success. After 1815, the French navy was reorganized, emigrants who had not been to sea for the previous twenty-five years being reinstated. Thus, like the Royal Navy, the French navy suffered from an overaged officers' corps in the first half of the nineteenth century.

In some respects the development of the Dutch navy took a different course from that of other European navies. Because of the federal structure of the Dutch Republic, the Dutch navy consisted of five admiralties, each of them competent for the commissioning of their own naval officers. Although nautical competence was, at least from the middle of the seventeenth century, indispensable for a career as a naval officer, for a long time no systematical professional training for future officers existed in the Dutch navy. Only by the late 1740s, much later than in most other navies, did all five Dutch admiralties require examinations of nautical competence as a precondition for further promotion. For the recruitment of seamen, the Dutch navy, like the merchant service, relied mainly on the maritime labor market, while the officers from the late sixteenth to the late eighteenth centuries were recruited from the higher social classes with only few exceptions, like the famous admiral Maarten Harpertszoon Tromp (1597–1653), who had risen through the ranks.

Some social barriers between officers and men existed in the British Royal Navy, although they could be overcome by patronage. In the eighteenth century, British naval officers were mostly recruited from the nobility and the middle classes. There was no entrance examination, and every commander of a ship of war had the right to accept boys as midshipmen, who generally started their careers at an age of ten to fifteen. From 1677, all midshipmen in the Royal Navy had to pass an oral examination on seamanship and navigation before promotion to lieutenant, thus securing a minimum professional standard. For a successful career, an officer could not rely on professional training alone; he was also dependent on the protection and interest of senior officers. This, however, applied only to promotion up to the rank of post captain, since admirals were promoted exclusively from the top of the captains' list according to seniority.

Professional seamen in the Royal Navy could rise to the rank of warrant officer. Instead of holding a royal commission, warrant officers were examined and appointed by the Navy Board. Among these warrant officers ranked the carpenter, the sailmaker, and the gunner, as well as the surgeon and the chaplain. With the exception of the surgeon and the chaplain, the professional training of warrant officers was in general identical to the training of seamen for the merchant service, which was the main source of seamen for the Royal Navy—either by free enlistment during peacetime or by impressment during war. Merchant seamen were considered superior to those trained by the navy, because naval seamen were specialized only in certain tasks as a result of the division of labor prevalent in the navy, while merchant seamen were trained in many tasks.

The highest position held by a warrant officer in the Royal Navy was the "sailing master," or simply "master," who was responsible for the nautical control of the ship. Often masters were recruited from the merchant service and had to pass an examination administered by Trinity House, London, prior to their appointment. A master had about the same status and pay as a lieutenant and was generally accepted among the commissioned wardroom officers. The reason for appointing masters was the claim that many commissioned officers neglected and forgot the little navigation that they had learned in order to pass their examination. Despite the increasing professionalism of naval officers, the master disappeared only in the 1880s, his duties being taken by the staff commander or by a navigating lieutenant. Only then was the amalgamation of the military and nautical hierarchies complete. In the nineteenth century, social barriers between officers and seamen in the Royal Navy increased, and the ascent from the lower decks to the rank of commissioned officer became virtually impossible until the twentieth century. The conditions for admission as midshipman were still minimal, and the officer's training in general equaled that of the eighteenth century.

In contrast, in the Dutch navy the professional training of naval officers had been reformed thoroughly since the middle of the eighteenth century, with the admiralties of Amsterdam and Rotterdam in the lead. Thus in 1748 a public navigation school for the professional education of future naval and merchant officers had been established in Amsterdam, and from 1749 onward, all naval officer candidates from Amsterdam had to pass a test of competence. This process of professionalization in the Dutch naval officers' corps showed remarkable success and was continued after the centralization of Dutch naval administration at the end of the eighteenth century. Then in 1803 a naval academy was established on board the frigate *Eurydice*, and in 1829 the attendance at this academy became mandatory for all cadets. The boys entered service at thirteen to sixteen years old and were trained as officers in a four-year curriculum. When the joint education of naval and army officers at the officers' school in Breda after 1850 proved unsatisfactory, the training of naval officers was transferred to Den Helder in 1854. In 1857 the Koninklijk Instituut voor de Marine was established in Willemsoord, and future Dutch naval officers continue to be trained there today.

In 1830, the French navy also established a naval academy for the training of future officers. At first, this academy was afloat; only in the 1930s was it transferred to a land base near Brest. In 1897, the École des Hautes Études Navales was established in Paris as a center of higher military education, in reaction to the conflict on maritime strategy between the *jeune école* and the *école historique*. Today the school is known as the Centre d'Enseignement Supérieur de la Marine (CESM).

When the U.S. Navy was founded in 1794, the training of the officers' corps was centered on practical shipboard experience under the guidance of a schoolmaster, modeled after the example of the Royal Navy. The establishment of the U.S. Naval School at Annapolis, Maryland, in 1845 was a consequence of the USS *Somers* incident in 1842, when a midshipman was executed for mutiny. In 1850 the Naval School was transformed into the United States Naval Academy. The cadets were trained in sciences, languages, navigation, and engineering. Changes in education and training have reflected the evolution of technology; thus since 1933, U.S. Naval Academy midshipmen graduate with a bachelor of science degree. Today, the professional training of American naval officers consists, besides the military component, of courses in engineering, sciences, humanities, and social sciences, but since the 1920s, many officers have also been acquired directly from civilian universities for short-term commissions, with a growing percentage remaining in service for full careers.

Although a naval academy for the Royal Navy was established at Portsmouth as early as 1737, it never had a major impact on the service at large. British naval officers' training was reformed only in the 1850s. At that point, disputing whether the future officers should receive a broader education ashore or practical training on board ship, the Admiralty settled on a compromise and in 1859 established HMS *Britannia* as a static training ship. In 1863 the vessel was moored at Dartmouth, Devon, thus establishing the tradition of Dartmouth Royal Naval College. The minimum age for admission was fixed at thirteen, and only in 1946 was it raised to sixteen. Pre-sea training on board *Britannia* took one year. The curriculum consisted of navigation, mathematics, languages, and seamanship. Following an examination, the boys went to sea as midshipmen. After five years and another examination, they were promoted to sublieutenant. Only at this point, as with promotion to an equivalent rank in other navies—for example, the German Leutnant zur See—did they receive their commission, thus establishing their status as naval officers.

From 1873, sublieutenants attended the Naval College in Greenwich, their subsequent promotion to lieutenant being dependent on their achievements. Further promotion to commander and captain depended not only on merit but also on patronage by senior officers and by the chosen specialization. While officers who belonged to the "executive" branch—that is, the nonspecialized sea officers (the so-called "salt-horses") or those specialized in, for example, gunnery or navigation—could hope for a commanding post and eventually for promotion to admiral, these career prospects were blocked for engineering officers.

In 1837, engineers appeared for the first time on board ships of the Royal Navy. Only in 1847 did they receive the status of commissioned officers in the Royal Navy, but they were still ranked inferior to the sea officers. Since engineers usually were of humbler origins, sea officers refused to accept them as social equals. Only in 1903 did the engineers cease to be a civil branch, but it was as late as 1925 that special rank insignia for engineers were introduced. Likewise, in the German navy, the engineers had to fight well into the 1890s for equality in status with the sea officers. In the U.S. Navy, engineers had been commissioned officers from the beginning—albeit in a separate officers' corps. In 1890, after a bitter struggle for supremacy between the two corps, sea officers (called "line officers") and engineers were finally amalgamated into a single "line officer" corps with the unusual feature of sharing their training and education as well as their sea assignments.

As in most other navies, engineers in the Royal Navy were trained and educated apart from the sea officers. In the 1870s, a hulk was established as a training facility for engineers, and in 1880 the location was changed to the newly founded Royal Naval Engineering College in Keynham. From 1888 on, the training of engineers took six years of theoretical and practical education, by turns aboard, ashore, and in the shipyards.

Under the Fisher-Selbourne Scheme of 1903, a not entirely successful attempt was made to create a uniformed officers' corps and to abolish career restrictions for certain branches. Now all future officers underwent the same training and all had to pass the same examination for lieutenant, although only in the 1980s was all initial officer training concentrated at Dartmouth. From 1903 to 1923, cadets served one year at the junior college at the Royal Naval College, Osborne—a wing of Osborne House, Queen Victoria's former summer residence on the Isle of Wight—before they changed to a two-year training course in Dartmouth. After a six-month sea preparation course on board a training vessel, the men were distributed on the ships of the fleet as midshipmen. After examination and promotion to sublieutenant, the officers chose their specialization. Only 5 percent of them took up a career as engineer, since engineering was still considered to be socially inferior. By the mid-1950s again the necessity for a structural change in officers' training emerged. The entry age was raised to eighteen years and the training at naval college was extended to a seven-term course, including two terms of sea training. Also, a route from the ranks to commissioned officer was opened, and the opportunities for all officers to gain university degrees were expanded. Thus a uniformed officers' corps was established in the Royal Navy, with all branches wearing identical insignia and enjoying the same career opportunities. In 1971 the officers' specializations were also abolished.

Like the officers' education, recruitment and training of the ranks in the Royal Navy was reformed in the 1850s, when a serious shortage of seamen led to the introduction of time contracts. Likewise, the professional training was improved, the career patterns for the ranks of petty and warrant officer were reformed, and an old-age pension scheme for naval seamen was established. All these reforms helped to make the navy a more attractive employer and to provide it with a core of long-serving, professionally trained seamen. Until then, the navy in peace had relied on the regular maritime labor market, competing with the merchant service. After World War II, the increasing discrepancy between wages in the navy and wages ashore led to serious recruitment problems, especially among the qualified personnel essential for modern naval warfare. In 1990, women became part of the crew of combatant ships, but only in 1994 were they fully absorbed into the Royal Navy.

The reformed education scheme of the Royal Navy proved an attractive model for foreign, European, and non-European navies. Thus when the Japanese in the second half of the nineteenth century created a modern, European-style navy, they followed the British model in naval organization and training.

Another naval latecomer was Germany, who only at the turn of the twentieth century entered the circle of the major sea powers. The profession of naval officer enjoyed an enormous prestige in the militarist German society. Aspirants for a career as a commissioned officer in the Kaiserliche Marine (Imperial Navy) required a secondary school diploma (Abitur) and had to pass an admission examination held every year at the end of March; Germans who were Jewish or who were members of the working class were practically excluded because of social bias. The working class was excluded simply by the requirement of extensive parental financial support. For those who were accepted as officer candidates, service began on April 1. After a four-week basic military training course, the cadets went on a one-year cruise on board a training ship. After their return, they were promoted to *Fähnrich zur See* (midshipman) and attended a one-year course at one of the naval officers' schools. In 1910, all sea officers' training was concentrated at the newly established Marine-Schule (naval academy) at Flensburg-Mürwik. The curriculum consisted of fifteen subjects, including sports, language, mathematics, electricity, ship construction, military tactics, fortification, navigation, seamanship, gunnery, and engineering, but it entirely left out training the skills of leadership—a mistake that was felt bitterly at the end of World War I, when widespread naval mutinies initiated the military and political collapse of Germany. After passing the officer's exam, promotion to *Leutnant zur See* (lieutenant) followed after a total of at least forty-two months. But these officers received inadequate payment, thus being dependent on their parents' financial support until their promotion to *Oberleutnant zur See* (first lieutenant). Staff officer posts and flag rank had to attend additional courses of instruction, as well as instruction for specializations in torpedoes, gunnery, and marine engineering. Promotion depended entirely on an officer's position on the rank list, although in certain cases accelerated advancement by merit or through the emperor's patronage was possible. An officer was forced to leave the service when he had been passed over twice.

As in the Royal Navy, engineering officers were trained and educated separately in the German Imperial Navy. Aspirants for an engineer officer's career had to prove a certain degree of formal education as well as thirty months of experience on a shipyard. Following basic military training, the future engineers went on board ship, after which they attended a technical school. After a four-year period as engineer aspirant, another one-year course followed, ending with qualification as a marine engineer.

For the ranks, the German Imperial Navy relied heavily on drafted seamen. The petty officers were recruited from seamen who had signed time contracts, some of them eventually making the navy their career. For the ranks and petty officers, promotion was slow, which caused much frustration. Only after eighteen to twenty years of service could they hope for promotion to warrant officer.

After World War I, the Reichsmarine altered naval training, when, beginning in 1921, engineers were given the same rank as sea officers. At that point, candidates for the naval engineer's career participated in the same training-ship education as their sea officer colleagues. During Adolf

Hitler's regime, the pressure to produce officers quickly forced the Marine Schule to shorten its courses, first to nine and then to only seven months, with an increasing emphasis on practical service over long-term education in electricity, languages, and mathematics.

When the Bundesmarine, the navy of the NATO-aligned Federal Republic of Germany, was founded in 1956, the old militarist traditions in German naval officers' training were abolished. The cadets were no longer educated as part of a military elite, but as citizens in a democratic state. Navigation and seamanship still dominated the curriculum, only now leadership also was part of the professional training of future officers. In 1957 or 1958, it became possible to rise by merit from the noncommissioned officer rank to commissioned officer. From 1956 to 1969, cadet instruction was largely unchanged, but in 1969 the officers' training was reformed. At this point, *Fachoffiziere*–commissioned officers who had risen through the ranks with all rights and privileges, but who were not eligible for promotion above the rank of lieutenant-commander–were given additional promotion possibilities. Also, in the 1970s, academic education became an integral part of the training of German naval officers. In 1957, the Führungsakademie der Bundeswehr (German Armed Forces Command and Staff College) was established at Bad Ems, but soon moved to Hamburg. The Stabsakademie der Bundeswehr (Bundeswehr Staff College) merged with it in 1973, the new institution then serving as the highest level of professional military education for naval officers.

The rank and file of the German navy consists of conscripts and volunteers with short time contracts. The petty and warrant officers consist of time-contract volunteers and of professional soldiers. Because of the increasing significance of high technology for modern naval warfare, the German navy tries to attract qualified personnel with a professional qualification scheme and career opportunities.

## Merchant Shipping

In the early modern period there was little difference, if any at all, in the early stages of the professional training of ordinary seamen and of officers for the merchant service. A maritime career usually started at an age of twelve to fifteen years. But while boys in Continental Europe learned their profession rather incidentally during the everyday management of the ship, in Britain an additional method of nautical education existed, similar to that of craft guilds. To be an apprentice, one entered into an agreement to serve a master for a certain period while being trained as a seaman. This form of training usually had better results than the Continental method, although apprentices often were accepted only to serve as cheap laborers.

With increasing ability and experience, a seaman could, within a few years, rise from boy to ordinary seaman and eventually to able seaman, each promotion involving an increase of pay and professional status. Promotion to the higher ranks required further qualifications. By the middle of the eighteenth century a mate or master needed to be able to read and write, and a master also needed some commercial knowledge, because of the decline of the supercargo; masters of merchant ships were often also entrusted with mercantile tasks. In the second half of the nineteenth century, however, masters' commercial responsibility began to decline again as the introduction of the telegraph increased shipowners' control over their ships' affairs. Thus today masters are again mere ship drivers and carriers of cargo.

A maritime profession somewhat separated from merchant shipping was whaling. Although there were few professional and personal relations between whaling and merchant shipping, the career patterns were almost identical, both in European whaling in Greenland waters from the seventeenth to the nineteenth centuries and in British and American whaling in the Pacific Ocean during the nineteenth century. As in the merchant service, the ascent was gradual from rank to rank, and patronage and interest were similarly known. On the other hand, the hierarchy aboard whaling ships was much more finely spun than on merchant vessels. Besides the usual posts–boatswain, mate, master–there were additional posts aboard whalers, such as harpooner or boat steerer. The discipline aboard whalers was in many cases even harsher than on merchant ships, especially on board American whalers in the nineteenth century.

However, a nautical career, be it in merchant shipping or in whaling, depended not upon qualification alone, since patronage by masters and owners was helpful. In addition, being promoted to master demanded leadership ability, along with sobriety and a good reputation. With promotion to master was connected not only a professional but also a social rise in status, since a new master was now part of a managerial class. Above all, a sufficient knowledge of the art of navigation was necessary for promotion to mate or master. This navigation training tended not to be part of general shipboard nautical training.

Besides the foundation of modern scientific navigation, the Portuguese and Spanish expeditions in the fifteenth and sixteenth centuries had also resulted in the emergence of an entirely new form of nautical vocational training, merging practical experience with theoretical knowledge. From the Iberian Peninsula this new form of professional training spread throughout Europe. Most notably, the Italian navigator Sebastian Cabot (c. 1476–1557), who was one of the successors of Vespucci in the office of *piloto mayor* in Seville, contributed to the distribution of the new knowledge of navigation in northern Europe when he entered English service in 1551. In 1574 the first nautical handbook was published in English. Only a few years later, in 1597, Gresham College, which still exists, was founded in London as a public institution for the instruction of applied sciences, such as mathematics, astronomy, and navigation.

Nevertheless, the common way of obtaining navigation skills in the early modern period was studying with a private navigation teacher—many retired shipmasters offered instruction—or in a private school. Navigation training was combined with making charts and nautical instruments. By 1580, private navigation teachers had established themselves in the Netherlands. Soon this approach to navigational qualification became customary throughout Europe, particularly in the Netherlands, Denmark, Germany, England, and Scotland. This form of vocational training was accessible to every seafarer who had some elementary education, and the costs were comparatively low. When attending a single course, the topic usually took only a few months to learn, although many seamen had no choice but to split their instruction into a number of successive courses between voyages, thus extending their period of training.

The syllabus at such schools included basics such as arithmetic, including logarithms, geometry, and trigonometry, as well as the use of charts (plane charts and Mercator's projection), navigation instruments (including compass, log, and quadrant), celestial navigation, and the ship's journal. Sometimes instruction might be restricted to working with nautical charts and plotting a course, and often it was limited to learning a set of simple rules by heart, not focusing on a real comprehension of the problems of navigation. Teachers regularly made use of so-called "Schat-Kamer" books, manuals on navigation that presented examples of the most common navigation tasks and their solutions. One of the earliest of these books was by Claes Hendricksz. Gietermaker, *'t Vergulde licht der zeevaert ofte konst der stuurlieden* (1660), but the term "Schat-Kamer book" comes from a later Dutch manual, *Schat-Kamer ofte Konst der Stuer-Lieden* (1702), by Klaas

de Vries. In England, similar manuals existed for seamen, and some remained in print for more than a century, such as Richard Norwood's *The Seaman's Practice*, first published in 1637 and still being advertised for sale in 1776. Others were Nathaniel Colson's *The Mariner's New Kalendar*, in print from 1676 through 1785, and Thomas Haselden's *Seaman's Daily Assistant*, in print from 1745 through 1803. Many teachers produced their own manuals, however, and often pressed them on their students. There were no examinations or licensing. Although limited in method and substance, this traditional form of navigation training for a long time proved sufficient for the nautical qualification of mates and masters.

Besides this form of plain vocational training, navigational education at an academic level had also existed since the seventeenth century. For instance, in Britain navigation was taught at an academic level not only at Gresham College but also at the Royal Mathematical School at Christ's Hospital, founded in 1673 in London. And in the Netherlands, navigation was taught from 1711 at the Athenaeum Illustre, a predecessor of the University of Amsterdam.

To raise the general level of navigation skills and education among merchant mariners, public navigation teachers or schools were established in many European countries, either by private initiatives or by governments. As early as 1619 a public navigation teacher had been appointed in Copenhagen to instruct both sailing masters and selected seamen in Danish royal service free of charge, and in 1675 a navigation school was established in the house of the shipmaster's guild in Copenhagen.

In the Netherlands, this approach was promoted especially by the VOC, the Dutch East India Company. As early as 1619, the Kamer Amsterdam, one of the six regional chambers of the VOC, appointed an official examiner, and by the middle of the seventeenth century, all mates applying for a position aboard an East Indiaman within the domain of the Amsterdam chamber of the VOC had to pass a professional examination. By 1730 another four chambers had followed, and from 1751 all applicants for a post of master or mate in the VOC had to pass such an examination. Between 1743 and 1755 the VOC also maintained a nautical institution, the Academie de Marine in Batavia (now Jakarta), on the island of Java. In 1748 the VOC, the Admiralty, and the city of Amsterdam established the first public navigation school for the professional education of future officers for the navy, the VOC, and the merchant service, the curriculum ending with a compulsory examination. From 1749 onward, all candidates applying in Amsterdam for officers' posts in the navy or in the VOC had to pass such an examination. This example was not followed in other Dutch towns, with the exception of Rotterdam. However, several charitable nautical institutions were established, notably the Kweekschool voor de Zeevaart in Amsterdam, founded in 1785 as a school for boys who aspired to the position of officer in the merchant service.

In contrast, navigation training in the British merchant service was provided on an almost entirely private basis. In the eighteenth century, the English East India Company carried apprentices, known as midshipmen, and also examined its mates in seamanship and navigation. By the late eighteenth century, a network of private and charitable nautical institutions had emerged, with a number of excellent navigation schools, such as Neale's Mathematical School, established in 1715 in London, Charlton's Mathematical School in Whitby, and the Hull Trinity House Navigation School, established in 1787.

In France, seamen often started their careers as apprentices at an age of about twelve years and reached the rank of able seaman at the age of seventeen. Since the beginning of the seventeenth century, navigation teachers and schools were present in the major French ports. Colbert created chairs of hydrogaphy at Nantes in 1671 and at Rennes in 1673. The famous nautical school at Le Croisic was founded in 1691 by Jean Bouguer, a professor of hydrography and the father of the famous French mathematician Pierre Bouguer (1698–1758). Usually the young sailors attended these schools between voyages. According to the Ordonnance de la Marine of 1681, all seamen applying for a position as merchant master had to produce a certificate of passing a test of competence in navigation before an expert board, validated by a court of admiralty. In order to take this examination, a seaman had to be at least twenty-five years old, have at least five years of nautical experience, and have two terms of service of three months' length in the French navy. Basic school learning seems not to have been a prerequisite, since only in 1786 did the ability to read and write become necessary.

During the eighteenth century in Germany, a number of public navigation schools were established. The first one was founded in 1749 in Hamburg by the Admiralität, Hamburg's maritime authority. In 1783 the Hamburg Patriotische Gesellschaft (Patriotic Society) established a second school, but it closed in 1797. In 1798, a public navigation school was founded in Bremen, followed by one in Lübeck in 1808 and others in various German and northern European towns. Because of the decline of merchant shipping that resulted from the war between Great Britain and France, most navigation schools on the European Continent were closed during the Napoleonic Wars and reopened only after 1814; the Bremen school reopened as late as 1825.

By reason of significant improvements in scientific navigation during the second half of the eighteenth century, the traditional methods of vocational navigation training were proving increasingly insufficient by the end of the century. Since the use of new instruments like the sextant, as well as the new techniques of finding latitude, required a high degree of expertise, instruction by simply memorizing a given set of rules had to be replaced by instruction aiming at a real understanding by the learner. For this reason, too, basic school learning–reading, writing, and arithmetic–now became required for a career in merchant navigation.

At first these new methods of scientific navigation reached only a small nautical elite. In most countries the navies took the lead in the propagation of this knowledge, while the merchant service was in general more reluctant to adopt the new techniques, since in many cases—for example, coastal shipping—the traditional methods of navigation were still sufficient. Yet the worldwide expansion of merchant navigation made the advancement of the professional qualification of mates and masters a necessity. Thus in several European countries by the end of the eighteenth century, many public navigation schools had taken up instruction in the newly developed methods of scientific navigation.

In many cases these institutions were not an instant success, because of the skepticism of many seamen and shipowners concerning the value of this new method of nautical training. But in the nineteenth century the inadequate level of nautical qualification of many mates and masters was revealed. One remedy lay in the introduction of compulsory professional examinations. After he successfully passed, the examinee was issued a certificate as proof of qualification.

Prior to the nineteenth century, nautical examinations had been compulsory in few countries—notably, Spain or France after the issue of the Ordonnance de la Marine in 1681. Beginning in 1707, all mates and masters from Copenhagen were obliged to pass an examination. This obligation was not extended to the remainder of the Danish state until the middle of the nineteenth century, although the Danish government tried to increase the number of voluntary examinees by granting privileges, such as remission or even exemption from compulsory naval service.

When government influence on merchant navigation was gradually extended during the nineteenth century, mandatory professional examinations were introduced in many other European countries. This reform of navigation training did not, however, succeed without dispute, because the increased degree of public control over merchant navigation was often despised by masters and owners as undue interference into commercial affairs. Moreover, although compulsory examination could ensure a minimum standard of qualification, it did not help to raise the degree of professional expertise in general, since many aspirants learned only enough to pass the exam.

In most German states, examinations were introduced during the first decades of the nineteenth century, one of the last states being Hanover in 1845. When in 1827 Lübeck introduced compulsory examinations, examinees had to be twenty-one years old and able to prove four years of sea service. Only in 1870 was a uniform code of examination issued for the German states, which after the German unification in 1871 became part of the central government's oversight.

Likewise in the Netherlands mandatory examinations for mates and masters were introduced during the second half of the nineteenth century, albeit at first only for certain sectors of merchant shipping. The remarkable recovery of the Dutch shipping industry after 1815, however, gave a fresh impetus to nautical professionalization. In 1823 the Dutch government appointed public navigation teachers in several Dutch ports, teachers who offered free tuition to all seamen. Additionally, examinations were held that were compulsory for mates in naval services but optional for mates in merchant services. Regarding merchant shipping, however, the scheme proved to be almost a complete failure. More successful was the establishment of nautical schools by local or provincial authorities or by private organizations that prepared seamen to pass tests of competence before local examination boards. In 1851 the Dutch government approved this development by leaving the matter of nautical examination to the local authorities, subsequently abolishing the state-founded navigation teachers in 1856. Nevertheless, the trend toward higher professional standards in navigation was further promoted by the so-called *zeemanscolleges*, nautical associations of mates and masters, as well as by the introduction of tests of competence—made compulsory in 1868—for mates in the service of the Nederlandsche Handel Maatschappij, a government-supported trade company founded in 1824 as successor to the previously dissolved VOC.

After 1860, Dutch shipping went into a lengthy crisis and also was drastically reorganized because of technological changes. This crisis was accompanied by a considerable reduction of the number of local nautical schools, and private teachers became almost extinct. Only now did the Dutch government renew its engagement. In 1877 the local examination committees were replaced by a governmental board of examination. Although these examinations were still optional, many shipping companies preferred to hire certified officers—for example, graduates of the Kweekschool—even before the introduction of compulsory examinations for mates in 1904.

In Great Britain, examinations became mandatory following the Mercantile Marine Act of 1850, although the English maritime authority, Trinity House, had held voluntary navigation examinations since 1845. At first only mates and masters of foreign-going ships were obliged to hold certificates of competency issued by the Board of Trade, after a professional examination. The requirements for admission to that examination were sea experience in a deck capacity—for example, as apprentice or able seaman—minimum age, and a testimony of good conduct and sobriety. At the same time, many new navigation schools were founded to provide additional training facilities. In 1854 compulsory examination was extended to passenger ships in the home trade, though the home trade in general was not brought within regulations before 1980. From 1862, engineer officers on foreign-going ships also had to be licensed.

As a result of the invention of steam propulsion, a new class of seafarers emerged in the nineteenth century. The new technology opened new occupational opportunities for nonseafarers, like artisans or former industrial workers. Nevertheless, there was a strong prejudice against them among traditional seamen; a social separation between deck and engine-room personnel existed well into the twentieth century.

Trimmers, shifting the coal from the bunkers to the furnace, were the bottom of the engine-room hierarchy. If they had the skills necessary for the maintenance of the furnaces, they could be promoted to stoker or fireman by the chief engineer. Just as in a deck position, to rise to the higher ranks a professional education was required. In general, the training and examination of the engineers followed the same patterns that the training and examination of deck officers did. Thus the future engineer had, for qualification, to attend a technical school and had to pass examinations, though in Britain an apprenticeship in an engineering workshop ashore was a prerequisite. Their good technical qualifications made marine engineers also attractive to the industry ashore. The constant drain ashore of qualified marine engineers became a big problem in many countries.

As soon as 1858 special examinations for mates on steam vessels had been introduced in several Dutch ports and at some nautical schools; for example, at the Kweekschool voor de Zeefart, courses on steam propulsion were added to the curriculum after 1860. In 1886 special examinations in steam navigation were introduced for mates in the Netherlands, although the examinations' contents were much the same as those for mates in sail navigation.

In Germany the vocational training of ship's engineers was left at first to the discretion of the shipowners. But by 1880 an increasing number of accidents caused by professional incompetence led to the introduction of compulsory examinations for marine mechanics. Likewise, the first institutions for the education of marine mechanics were established in the 1880s. For admission, students had to prove a technical apprenticeship aboard a seagoing ship as well as a certain period of sea service. After attending school they had to pass a test of competence before an independent examination board; the test consisted of, among other things, assessments in English, engineering, and mathematics. Additionally, three different grades of qualification of *Seemaschinist* (sea machinist) for coastal, medium-distance, and long-distance voyages were established. The senior mechanics in Germany later received title *Ingenieur* (engineer), and connected with this title came a rise in social status. Thus in 1909, besides the older ranks of *Seemaschinist*, the new top grade of *Schiffsingenieur* (ship's engineer) was established, a qualification required mainly for service on large cargo and passenger vessels.

For a long time, professional training in European merchant shipping had been based on tradition and experience, though the training became more and more formalized. After a successful examination, a certificate or license was issued by governmental institutions; the certificate allowed the examinee to apply for a certain defined post on board, such as second or chief mate or master. The development in the nineteenth century of a system of nautical education and obligatory examinations thus could be adequately described as a process of an increasing of professionalism in European merchant shipping—a process that eventually became a worldwide model for the professional training in the merchant service.

At first, in most countries, only the examination was the exclusive domain of government control. The examinees could decide, considering the nautical knowledge that they needed, whether to study at a public navigation school or with a private teacher, or not to attend any school at all. However, because of the increased complexity of the curriculum, a sufficient school education became a precondition for nautical training during the nineteenth century. The government's control was later also extended to the curriculum, which led many European countries to abolish private navigation schools in favor of state-run nautical training institutions.

Likewise, the old forms of recruitment, based mostly on personal relations and patronage, were superseded by abstract qualifications that were provided by both examination and certification by governmental authorities. Thus in many European countries, public registers of seamen, their qualifications, and their conduct were introduced. This certainly was useful for masters and shipowners, since it made the task of finding a reliable and well-qualified crew much easier. It also opened new career opportunities for seamen, since they now could offer a public and therefore reliable proof of qualification while in search of employment.

By the end of the nineteenth century this kind of proof of professional competence had been introduced in all major maritime nations, with qualifications and requirements varying in detail from country to country. For instance, in Great Britain only masters, mates, and engineers going abroad needed a license, while in Germany in 1900 a minor grade qualification of *Steuermann/Kapitän auf kleiner Fahrt* (mate/master on medium-distance voyages) was added below the major qualification of *Steuermann/Kapitän auf großer Fahrt* (mate/master on long-distance voyages), with equivalent qualification grades for engineers. In 1905 another qualification for masters on coastal ships was added.

Also by the end of the nineteenth century, either by attending a nautical academy or by serving an apprenticeship as a cadet, another way for qualifying as an officer in the merchant service (beside the traditional rise through the ranks) had been established. This cadet system was especially preferred in Britain, although "promotion through the rank" existed parallel well into the 1950s. Most shipping companies now carried two to four apprentices on board as officer trainees, who did not form part of the regular crew. After a four-year apprenticeship, they qualified for the examination for mate. Apprentices who had attended training at a training institution ashore were granted remission of sea time of between three and twelve months from the four years of apprenticeship. After the *Titanic* disaster in 1912 and the human losses of World War I, pre-sea training for future seamen was intensified.

By the 1950s, pre-sea training for officer apprentices was well established in Britain, although a good number still went to sea unprepared.

Unlike other European countries, there were no nautical schools run by the state in Britain. Before the 1920s, however, there was a wide variety of private and charitable institutions, the latter often aided by public grants. In the twenty-first century most nautical schools in Britain are run within the local further-education system. During the 1960s a number of additional shore courses were introduced that made ascent to the rank of officer less easy for the man taking the traditional route through the ranks. Regardless of many changes in recent times that have made British nautical education rather difficult to survey, nautical training in Britain now complies with the current standards of the international maritime training convention, the 1995 amendments to the 1978 International Convention on Standards of Training, Certification, and Watchkeeping for Seafarers (STCW; the amended version is called STCW 95).

In the United States, the government also became concerned with the training of officers for the merchant service, but—as was typical of the American government's federal structure—education was primarily the responsibility of the individual states. In 1862, Congress passed the first Morrill Act to provide grants in the form of federal lands to each state for the establishment of public institutions to promote higher education. In 1874, an act of Congress extended this idea to nautical education by obliging the U.S. Navy to place ships at the disposal of local nautical schools for merchant marine cadet training. The first of these ships was USS *Saint Mary's*, which was placed in New York harbor for the use of the newly established New York Nautical School. In 1929 this institution was renamed the New York State Merchant Marine Academy, where deck officers as well as engineers were trained. Applicants had to be between seventeen and twenty-one years of age. Besides the theoretical teaching ashore, for training the young men were educated on board a sailing vessel, which, owing to the technological change, was replaced by a motor-propelled vessel in 1930. Other important nautical schools in the United States are the Massachusetts State Nautical School, established in 1891, the California Nautical School, established in 1929, the Maine Maritime Academy, established in 1942, the Texas Maritime Academy, established in 1962, and the Great Lakes Maritime Academy, established in 1969. Most of these institutions had been incorporated into the university system by the early twenty-first century.

The U.S. Merchant Marine Act of 1891 obliged all U.S. Mail contractors to put cadets on board every mail ship, their number depending on the size of the ship. In Denmark a similar merchant officer trainee scheme was established after World War II because of the shortage of qualified personnel, but it turned out to be not very successful. Up until 1934, the U.S. government allowed the individual American states to manage nautical education with the assistance of the loan of a naval vessel for ship training. In 1934 a disastrous fire occurred on board the passenger ship *Morro Castle*, and 134 people were killed. The tragedy led the U.S. Congress to establish an efficient and standardized system of maritime training. Congress passed the Merchant Marine Act of 1936, and consequently, two years later, the U.S. Merchant Marine Cadet Corps came into being. The first training was given at temporary facilities until the academy's permanent site in Kings Point, New York, was established in 1943.

All in all, the cadet model was the exception. Until the middle of the twentieth century, even in Britain and the United States, most mates and masters qualified themselves without ever having attended a nautical academy or ever having served as an officer trainee. In Denmark, for example, seamen until the 1920s could qualify themselves as mates or masters in the home trade by visiting the nautical school for fifteen months and passing the subsequent examination. After attending an additional course of six months they could qualify for master. Thus a seaman who had started his career at age fifteen could pass for master at only twenty-three. The education for marine engineers was organized along much the same lines. In Denmark, future marine engineers had to attend a technical school, with previous training as artisan necessary for admission. After successfully passing the examination and serving some time at sea as an engineer's assistant, engineers could by means of a further examination qualify themselves as chief engineer.

In Germany, practical experience and theoretical knowledge was combined in the training of mates and masters. Ever since the reform of nautical training in 1926, a three-semester course and a subsequent examination was necessary for qualification as mate, provided that one had initial professional training as able seaman. After two years of sea service as fourth and third mate, and an additional one-semester course with subsequent examination, a seaman could pass for master, although only 60 percent of the graduates of the mate's course later qualified as master. The professional training of engineers was organized in a manner similar to that of nautical officers.

After World War II, nautical education in Germany was begun again only in 1948. From the founding of the Federal Republic of Germany, the nautical schools as well as the examinations came under the control of the coastal federal states (*Bundesländer*), supervised by the central government, which also issued the certifications. In 1964 nautical education was reformed. To pass the examination for mate or assistant engineer, a four-semester course at a nautical school was necessary, as well as an additional qualification after two years of sea service to pass for master or chief engineer.

Since the 1960s there has been an international trend toward an increased academic education for officers in the merchant service. For instance, in Portugal the master's certificate is combined with a bachelor's degree, while in Poland the master's certificate is combined even with a master's degree. Likewise in Britain, academic courses for nautical qualifications have been invented, but only a few cadets choose this route for qualification as mate or master. In Germany, nautical academic education is situated within the universities of applied sciences and consists of a six-semester course, including two semesters of practical sea training. Nevertheless, in Germany the usual nautical career also followed the traditional pattern of professional training as able seaman and of subsequent visit to a nautical school or university of applied sciences. Both career paths were followed by almost equal numbers.

Until the second half of the twentieth century in many European countries, not only general sea service but a certain period of service on board sailing vessels was required for admission to nautical schools. Because of the decline of merchant sail shipping, sail training vessels were introduced in many countries as an alternative, supported either by private initiatives or by the state. In Britain, this practice had ended as early as 1914, while in Germany sail training in the merchant service ended only after the training ship *Pamir* sank in a heavy gale in 1957. At the same time, obligatory sea time in sailing vessels was abolished in Denmark. In only some states—for instance, the former Soviet Union, and now Russia—was the tradition of sail training in the merchant service preserved until recent times.

## Current Developments in Merchant Shipping

Until the end of the twentieth century, each country issued its own regulations concerning the examination and qualification of merchant officers and engineers. This nonuniform and confusing situation was aggravated during the process of decolonization, although nautical vocational training in many of the new states was modeled on their respective former colonial powers. However, because of the increasing technological complexity in merchant navigation from the 1960s onward, the urge for an international regulation of the minimum qualification standards of officers and engineers emerged. Thus in 1978 the International Maritime Organisation (IMO), the United Nations agency concerned with the safety of shipping, adopted the International Convention on Standards on Training, Certification, and Watchkeeping (STCW 78), which aimed at the establishment of international minimum qualification standards in merchant shipping. Five years later, in 1983, the IMO established the World Maritime University in Malmö, Sweden, to provide graduate-level education and applied research for the maritime industries. By 2006, the university had graduated 1,800 advanced students.

For several reasons the STCW 78 convention was not a full success and had to be revised in 1995, not least because the international shipping industry again had been the subject of considerable changes on a global scale. Because of the ever-accelerating technological progress in the late twentieth and early twenty-first centuries, requirements as well as training and career prospects for officers in merchant shipping had changed fundamentally since 1978. While navigation has become easier thanks to modern satellite devices, new types of cargo, containers, and the effects of modern communications on sea trade induced new professional demands. At the same time, to save costs in the highly competitive international shipping trade, the number of crew members has been reduced to a minimum. Many European shipowners have transferred their vessels to flags of convenience, replacing seamen and officers from western Europe with seamen from eastern Europe, Asia, and China, who are much cheaper because of their substantially lower wages and reduced social security costs. On German merchant ships in the early twenty-first century, up to 90 percent of the crew's complement is from foreign countries; sometimes the master is the only German national on board. Thus the profession of seaman has increasingly lost its attractiveness in western Europe, and many nautical schools have been closed. The level of qualifications of seamen from non-Western countries, however, differs widely. While some foreign seamen are poorly trained, others are very well qualified. Seamen from eastern Europe and the Philippines, for instance, have an especially good reputation.

The 1995 revised International Convention on Standards of Training, Certification, and Watchkeeping for

Seafarers (STCW 95) is the renewed attempt to introduce internationally minimum standards for the training and qualification of seamen. One aim of STCW 95 is to establish better professional training for seamen and mariners from underdeveloped countries. Some of these countries had, however, some problems with adjusting their maritime training facilities to the standards codified in STCW 95. A good example is the Philippines—a country with, in fact, a long tradition in nautical vocational training. As early as 1820, the Spanish colonial authorities under the name of Escuela Nautica de Manila founded what is now the national Philippine Merchant Marine Academy. Although Philippine seafarers have the largest share in the global maritime labor market, in 2001 only thirty-five nautical schools of more than one hundred throughout the Philippines complied fully with the STCW 95 requirements. The Philippine government made efforts to better the situation. Thus in 2005 approximately one hundred maritime schools and training centers in the Philippines conform with the standards codified in STCW 95. Nevertheless, substandard schools are still generating underqualified graduates. A quite interesting project is the Norwegian Training Center in Manila. This private institution was founded to ensure vocational training in compliance with STCW 95 and to prepare its students for service in the Norwegian merchant fleet, the biggest employer of Philippine seamen worldwide.

The pressure to meet the standards of STCW 95 is also felt in the Pacific region. Because the income of seafarers plays an important role in the economy of several Pacific Island countries, training in compliance with STCW 95 became very important, since job losses would have severe effects on these countries. Thus a number of Pacific Island countries, among them Fiji, made great efforts to establish a regional maritime education program in 2000; the program was supported financially by the British Department for International Development. The program aimed at providing upgraded training for seafarers in the Pacific Islands in order to meet the standards required under the STCW 95 convention. The program also maintains close linkages with Australian and New Zealand maritime authorities.

In the early twenty-first century more than two hundred institutions in more than eighty countries train in accordance with the STCW 95 standards, supervised by international experts. Countries recognized as giving full effect to the requirements established in the convention are registered on the so-called White List by the IMO.

The introduction of STCW 95 also had effects on nautical education in western European countries. For instance, before the adoption in 1998 of the STCW 95 regulations in Germany, a three-year course at a university of applied science was necessary to become licensed as master in the international trade on vessels of any size, while a certificate from a nautical school qualified one only for commanding ships of less than 8,000 gross registered tons—the traditional division of certification for masters and engineers in long-distance voyage, medium-distance voyage, and home trade having been abolished in 1992. After the adoption of STCW 95, German certifications were adjusted to international standards. This adoption was, however, not undisputed in the German maritime community, since it was feared that the high standards of German nautical training might be downgraded. Today—provided that one has a previous professional training of three years as *Schiffsmechaniker* (ship's mechanic, or able seaman)—two years at a nautical school prepare one for examination as master. After a certain period of sea service as mate, the applicant is entitled to command ships of any size in any trade. Still, the universities of applied sciences educate on a high academic level, while the new approach marks a return to a more practical form of nautical training.

Future prospects for European seamen are contradictory. While seamen are facing enormous problems caused by global wage competition, professional prospects for well-trained officers and masters still seem to be good, especially if seamen have acquired additional nautical and economic qualifications.

[*See also* Ancient Navies; Naval Administration; Navies, Great Powers; Shipboard Life; Shipboard Organization; Shipping, *subentry on* State-owned Shipping; Training Ships; Whaling; *and biographical entries on figures mentioned in this article*.]

## Bibliography

Acerra, Martine, with Jean Meyer. *L'empire des mers: Des galions aux clippers.* Fribourg, Switzerland: Office du Livre, 1990. Survey of the major European navies, especially the British and the French, from the seventeenth to early nineteenth centuries.

Anthiaume, Albert. *L'abbé Guillaume Denys, de Dieppe, 1624–1689: Premier professeur royal d'hydrographie en France.* Paris: E. Dumont Fils, 1927.

Asaert, G., with M. Bosscher, J. R. Bruijn, and W. J. van Hoboken, eds. *Maritieme Geschiedenis der Nederlanden.* 4 vols. Bussum, Netherlands: De Boer Maritiem, 1977. A comprehensive survey of Dutch maritime history, covering social as well as economic and technological aspects of naval and merchant navigation.

Bösche, Klaus, et al., eds. *Dampfer, Diesel, und Turbinen die Welt der Schiffsingenieure*. Hamburg, Germany: Convent, 2005. A comprehensive history of the profession of ship's engineers in Germany.

Bruijn, Jaap R. *The Dutch Navy of the Seventeenth and Eighteenth Centuries*. 2d ed. Columbia: University of South Carolina Press, 1993.

Casson, Lionel. *The Ancient Mariners: Seafarers and Sea Fighters of the Mediterranean in Ancient Times*. 2d ed. Princeton, N.J.: Princeton University Press, 1991. The principal authority on ancient Mediterranean seafaring; covers both merchant and naval shipping.

Davids, Karel. "Het navigatieonderwijs aan personeel van de VOC." In *De VOC in de kaart gekeken: Cartografie en navigatie van de Verenigde Oostindische Compagnie 1602–1799*, edited by Patrick van Mil. The Hague: SDU, 1988.

Davids, Karel. "Technological Change and the Professionalism of Masters and Mates in the Dutch Mercantile Marine, 1815–1914." In *Proceedings of the International Colloquium "Industrial Revolutions and the Sea," Brussels, 28–31 March 1989*, edited by Christian Konickx. Collectanea Maritima 5. Brussels: Koninklijke Academie voor Wetenschappen, Letteren en Schone Kunsten van België, 1990.

Deggim, Christina. *Hafenleben in Mittelalter und Früher Neuzeit: Seehandel und Arbeitsregelungen in Hamburg und Kopenhagen vom 13. bis zum 17. Jahrhundert*. Hamburg, Germany: Convent, 2005.

Dollinger, Philippe. *Die Hanse*. 4th ed. Stuttgart, Germany: Kröner, 1989. Classic survey of Hanseatic history.

Earle, Peter. *Sailors: English Merchant Seamen 1650–1775*. London: Methuen, 1998. Excellent study of the social history of English merchant shipping, very close to the sources.

Ellis, Richard. *Men and Whales*. New York: Knopf, 1991.

Feldbæk, Ole, et al., eds. *Dansk Søfarts Historie*. 7 vols. Copenhagen: Gyldendal, 1997–2001.

Healey, James C. *Foc'sle and Glory-Hole: A Study of the Merchant Seaman and His Occupation*. New York: Greenwood Press, 1936. Fine study on the professional training in British and American merchant shipping in the first half of the twentieth century.

Hill, J. R. ed. *The Oxford Illustrated History of the Royal Navy*. Oxford and New York: Oxford University Press, 1995.

Hillmann, Jörg, with Reinhard Scheiblich. *"Das Rote Schloss am Meer": Die Marineschule Mürwik seit ihrer Gründung*. Hamburg, Germany: Convent, 2002. Excellent survey on the professional training of German naval officers from the imperial navy to recent times.

Kennerley, Alston. "Merchant Marine Education in Liverpool and the Nautical College of 1892." *International Journal of Maritime History* 5, no. 2 (1993): 103–134. Very informative study of the history of professional education in the British merchant marine.

Kennerley, Alston. "Nationally-Recognised Qualifications for British Merchant Navy Officers, 1856–1966." *International Journal of Maritime History* 13, no. 1 (2001): 115–135.

Le Bouëdec, Gérard. *Activités maritimes et sociétés littorales de l'Europe atlantique 1690–1790*. Ivry-Sur-Seine, France: Armand Colin, 1997. Provides information on nautical vocational training in France.

Marcus, Christof, with Dieter W. F. Schoppmeyer. *200 Jahre Seefahrtsschule Bremen*. Bremen, Germany: Hauschild, 1999. Examination of two hundred years of professional nautical training at the Bremen navigation school.

Matthei, Dieter, Jörg Duppler, and Karl-Heinz Kuse, eds. *Marineschule Mürwik*. Herford, Germany: Verlag E. S. Mittler, 1985, 1989.

Mehl, Lothar. "Die Anfänge des Navigationsunterrichts unter besonderer Berücksichtigung der deutschen Verhältnisse." *Paedagogica Historica* 8 (1968): 372–441. Good survey on the development of nautical professional education in Europe, with an emphasis on German navigation training.

Rahn, Werner. "Die Ausbildung an der Marineschule Mürwik 1910 bis 1980." In *Die Deutsche Marine: Historisches Selbstverständnis und Standortbestimmung*, edited by Günter Luther, pp. 143–170. Herford, Germany: Deutsche Marine Institut, 1983.

Randles, William Graham Lister. *Geography, Cartography, and Nautical Science in the Renaissance: The Impact of the Great Discoveries*. Aldershot, U.K., and Burlington, Vt.: Ashgate/Variorum, 2000.

Sandman, Alison Deborah. "Cosmographers vs. Pilots: Navigation, Cosmography, and the State in Early Modern Spain." PhD diss., University of Wisconsin, Madison, 2001.

Scharnow, Ulrich. "STCW-Übereinkommen 1995 und das Berufsbild des deutschen Nautikers." *Schriftenreihe des Schiffahrtsinstitutes Warnemünde an der Hochschule Wismar* 1 (1998).

Schmidt, Rüdiger. "Die Professionalisierung der nautischen Fachbildung: Die Seefahrtschule in Bremen 1799–1869." In *Seefahrt an deutschen Küsten im Wandel 1815–1914*, edited by Jürgen Brockstedt, pp. 11–138. Neumünster, Germany: Wachholtz, 1993. Research paper on the process of increasing professionalism in German merchant shipping during the nineteenth century, using the example of the Bremen navigation school.

Speelman, Jennifer Lyn. "Nautical Schools and the Development of United States Maritime Professionals, 1874–1941." PhD diss., Temple University, 2001.

Vergé-Franceschi, Michel. *La marine française au XVIIIe siècle: Guerres, administration, exploration*. Paris: Sedes, 1998. Part 3, chapter 2, provides an overview of the development of naval education from the seventeenth century.

Vergé-Franceschi, Michel, ed. *Marine et éducation sous l'ancien régime*. Paris: Éditions du CNRS, 1991.

Vicente, María Encarnación Rodrígue. "Die Wirtschaft in Spanisch-Amerika zur Kolonialzeit." In *Gold und Macht, Spanien in der Neuen Welt*, edited by Magdalena Huber-Ruppel and Ludwig Scharl, pp. 137–161. Vienna: Kremayr and Schierau, 1986. Short survey on the economic history of Spanish trade with its American colonies, emphasizing the role of the Casa de Contratación.

Wells, John. *The Royal Navy: An Illustrated Social History 1870–1982*. 2d ed. Phoenix Mill, U.K., and Dover, N.H.: Sutton, 2000.

Witt, Jann M. " 'During the Voyage Every Captain Is Monarch of the Ship': The Merchant Captain from the Seventeenth to the Nineteenth Century." *International Journal of Maritime History* 13, no. 2 (2001): 165–194. Annotated English abstract of *Master Next God?*

Witt, Jann M. *Master Next God? Der nordeuropäische Handelsschiffskapitän vom 17. bis zum 19. Jahrhundert.* Hamburg: Convent, 2001. Dissertation on the legal definition, social role, and professional training of merchant masters in northern Europe from the seventeenth to the nineteenth centuries. Includes English and French conclusions.

JANN M. WITT

# Elder, John

**Elder, John** (1824–1869), British engineer and pioneer of steam compound machinery. In his short life, John Elder revolutionized steam engine design and manufacture. This was one of the factors that enabled the River Clyde in Scotland to become the undisputed center of world shipbuilding some years later. Elder attended the High School of Glasgow, and the civil engineering department of Glasgow University, and served a five-year apprenticeship under Robert Napier (the father of Clyde shipbuilding). After spending time as a pattern maker, and a draftsman, he returned to Napier's aged twenty-five as chief draftsman. In private life he had wide interests; he was an accomplished organist and an active church member.

Three years later he and Charles Randolph set up Randolph Elder and Co. and a great adventure began. They carried out advanced design work on steam engines and ship propulsors and within a year, their first of fourteen or fifteen patents had been established.

Most dealt with steam compound engines, where two stages of steam expansion enabled significant savings in fuel consumption. This was no amateur affair, but fundamental research demonstrating knowledge of entropy and the new field of thermodynamics. Their first ship was SS *Brandon* for the Limerick Steamships, which in 1854 achieved a 30 percent reduction in coal usage. With planned publicity and with patent rights secured, Randolph and Elder were an immediate success story. They extended their product range by buying a small shipyard in Govan in 1858 and then in 1864, moving to the famous Fairfield Shipyard still in operation (in 1874 renamed John Elder and Co.).

In 1869, the output of the yard was over 25,000 tons, among the best in Britain and twice as much as any Scottish rival. The yard earned a good name for fair dealing and thoughtful industrial relations; Elder instituted an accident fund (then a novel idea) and gave an amount equal to the workforce of four thousand. In the same year Elder died suddenly, an event regarded in west Scotland as close to a national disaster.

Mrs. Isabella Elder took up the reigns and ran the shipyard successfully for nearly a year while putting in place new directors and a manager. She used her wealth for social and educational needs, including at Glasgow University, the founding of Queen Margaret College for women undergraduates, and the establishment of the world's first chair of naval architecture, at the University of Glasgow, named after her late husband, now the joint Department of Naval Architecture and Marine Engineering of the Universities of Glasgow and Strathclyde.

## Bibliography

*Historical and Descriptive Account of the Works of the Fairfield S & E Co Ltd, Glasgow.* Glasgow, 1898.

MacQuorn Rankine, W. J. "Sketch of the Life of John Elder." *Transactions of the Institution of Engineers and Shipbuilders in Scotland (Glasgow)* 15 (1871–1872).

McAlpine, C. Joan. *The Lady of Claremont House: Isabella Elder, Pioneer and Philanthropist.* Argyll Publishing, Glendaruel, Argyll, 1997.

Walker, Fred M. *Song of the Clyde: A History of Clyde Shipbuilding.* 3d ed. Edinburgh: Birlinn, 2001.

FRED M. WALKER

# Elwertowski, H. J.

**Elwertowski, H. J.** (1912–1973), British scientist. H. J. (Henryk Jerzy) Elwertowski was the leader of the team that designed and developed the first British version of the Ships Inertial Navigation System (SINS). Born in Dabrowa Gornicza, Poland, on May 18, 1912, and educated at Warsaw University, he worked on the design of antiaircraft fire control equipment before enlisting in the artillery. When, in 1939, Poland was overrun by the Germans, he crossed into Hungary and was briefly interned before escaping and making his way, via Yugoslavia and Italy, to France. There he joined the Polish Forces in exile but, before Paris fell, moved on again and, traveling via Spain, Portugal, and Gibraltar, eventually reached England early in 1942.

Elwertowski joined the scientific staff of the Admiralty Research Laboratory (ARL) at Teddington, later to become the Admiralty Gunnery Establishment (AGE), where he was responsible for the design and production of a novel tracker and predictor for army light antiaircraft guns. (It was there that in 1946 he married Betty Stilgoe, who worked for the British scientist Sir Edward Appleton.) Promotion followed swiftly and when AGE moved to its new headquarters at Portland in 1954, Elwertowski became head of the Stabilisation Group, initiating a new generation of precision gyroscopic stable references required for modern naval weapon systems.

In 1959 he was appointed chief scientist at the Admiralty Compass Observatory (ACO) at Slough, specifically to take charge of the development of a British SINS for the new nuclear submarine program that was already well advanced. The tight time-scale led to a severely telescoped development program, but under his leadership SINS progressed from a blank sheet of paper to a working "breadboard" model in the remarkably short time of two years. Seagoing "experimental" models (using valves) were followed in 1966 by a fully engineered version (UK SINS Mk 1) exploiting the rapid advances in transistor technology.

Initially the very high precision gyroscopes pioneered by Dr. Charles Stark Draper at MIT, and essential for the operation of SINS, could only be obtained from the United States, but arrangements were soon made for one marine type to be manufactured under license in the United Kingdom. Elwertowski also initiated a highly successful program of hydrodynamic gas-bearing research at ACO, and it was the incorporation of this technique into the British-made SINS gyros that enormously increased their accuracy and endurance. This work became the subject of a highly successful two-way information exchange with the United States.

In 1962, when the United Kingdom decided to adopt the Polaris nuclear deterrent, Elwertowski was a member of the Navigation Mission to the United States, which recommended important changes to the system then in use by the U.S. Navy. The ACO proposed and developed a much simpler method for checking the vital azimuth accuracy in harbor, known as the Heading Transfer Test (HTT). This led to a more compact configuration, saving several million dollars per submarine.

Under his guidance the scientific staff of the ACO more than doubled and its responsibilities were widened to include radio navigation aids for the Royal Navy and all weapon stabilization. In addition he took a lead in a number of fields (for example, Ring Laser research) where at the time there appeared to be little significant industrial capability.

Although UK SINS Mk 1 performed well at sea, it was an analog system that could provide only a limited polar navigational capability. (Nevertheless, with ACO support, HMS *Dreadnought* did make a successful sortie to the North Pole in 1971.) However, in response to the Royal Navy's need for a full transpolar capability, Elwertowski initiated a bold redesign, using digital techniques, which led to the excellent UK SINS Mk 2. Sadly, after a year as head of the ACO, he died in 1973 and did not see its completion.

[*See also* Inertial Navigation.]

### Bibliography

Fanning, Antony E. *"Steady as She Goes." A History of the Compass Department of the Admiralty.* London: HMSO, 1986. P. 309 and chap. 12.

A. E. FANNING

## *Emden*, *Dresden*-class light cruiser.

Length/beam/draft: 117.9 m × 13.5 m × 5.5 m (386′ × 44′ × 18′). Tonnage: 3,664 displacement. Hull: steel. Power: Machine 2-shaft 3-cylinder VTE, 12 Navy boilers. 13,500 indicated horsepower = 23.5 knots. Armor: Deck 20–30mm, CT 100 mm, gunshields 50 mm. Armament: 10 × 10.5 cm; SKL/40, 8-5.2; SKL/55 QF; 2 × 4.5 cm TT sub beam. Complement: 361. Built: Danzig Navy Yard, launched May 26, 1908, commissioned July 10, 1909.

Probably the best-known vessel in the Imperial Navy, the light cruiser *Emden* was the last one with a piston steam engine. Put into service in 1909, she sailed to East Asia the following year and was stationed there for the next four years to safeguard German interests in China and in the Pacific. One day before the outbreak of the war with Russia, *Emden,* under the command of Fregattenkapitän Karl von Müller, an exceptionally able officer, left Tsingtao for a short sortie against Russian traffic, captured a steamer a day later, and returned to base for a few hours. Then he left Tsingtao, together with the auxiliary cruiser *Prinz Eitel Friedrich*. Both ships joined Admiral von Spee's force on August 12, 1914. Only two days later *Emden* was dispatched to the Indian Ocean and captured or sank twenty-three merchantmen in a cruise that lasted until November 9. She shelled oil installations in Madras and entered Penang harbor in a surprise attack, sinking the Russian cruiser *Zhemchug* and the French destroyer *Mousquet*. She obstructed Allied trade, disrupted shipping schedules, which alarmed the Bengal Chamber of Commerce, slowed the transport of vital war supplies, delayed the departure of troop ships, and harmed the reputation of the colonial powers.

*Emden* finally succumbed to her pursuers and to the lack of military supply bases. When a landing party tried to cut the telegraph cables at the station at Cocos Keeling Island, the superior Australian light cruiser HMAS *Sydney* surprised *Emden* and battered her in a running fight for more than an hour. Captain von Müller steered his beaten cruiser ashore on Keeling Island to save the survivors. The ship was a wreck and burnt out. *Emden*'s casualties included 134 dead and 65 wounded; 182 survivors were rescued by HMAS *Sydney*. The landing party, under the command of the first officer Kapitänleutnant von Mücke, escaped in the requisitioned schooner *Ayesha* to the Dutch East Indies. After transferring to the steamer *Choising* and after sinking the sailing vessel, the landing party eventually arrived to a hero's welcome in Constantinople in June 1915 after a seven-month odyssey that included a march through the Arabian Desert.

Captain Karl von Müller and 181 men of the crew were held in captivity on Malta. Since he behaved with the utmost correctness in warfare and took the greatest possible care to avoid casualties, the British held him in high regard and he is considered one of the great seamen of the age. *Emden*'s success as a surface raider was helped by luck. By the end of the year most of the German surface raiders were either destroyed or neutralized. In 1920–1921 the Prussian and the German governments allowed surviving crew members to add the cruiser's name to their surnames.

[*See also* Wars, Maritime, *subentry on* World Wars.]

### Bibliography

Hoyt, Edwin P. *The Last Cruise of the "Emden."* London: Andre Deutsch, 1967. Kemp, Peter, ed. *The Oxford Companion to Ships and the Sea.* London: Oxford University Press, 1976.

Lochner, R. N. *The Last Gentleman-of-War: The Raider Exploits of the Cruiser "Emden."* Annapolis, Md.: Naval Institute Press, 1994.

Raeder, Erich, *Der Kreuzerkrieg in den ausländischen Gewässern.* 2 vols. Berlin: Mittler, 1922–1923.

Vat, Daniel van der. *Gentlemen of War: The Amazing Story of Captain Karl von Müller and the S.M.S. "Emden."* New York: Morrow, 1984.

Walter, John *The Kaiser's Pirates: German Surface Raiders in World War One.* Annapolis, Md.: Naval Institute Press, 1994.

LARS U. SCHOLL

---

***Endeavour,*** Captain James Cook's ship on his first Pacific voyage (1768–1771).

Length/beam: 32.3 m × 8.9 m (106′ × 29.25′). Tonnage: 368. Hull: wood. Complement: 100. Built: Fishburn's, Whitby, England, by early 1768.

*Endeavour* was not the usual neat naval sloop or frigate of previous discovery voyages, but a cat-built (bluff-bowed) Whitby collier. She was chosen for her strength, shallow draft, and storage capacity. Originally named *Earl of Pembroke*, she was purchased by the Admiralty in March 1768 and renamed *Endeavour*. For her Pacific voyage, alterations were made that included the addition of a lower deck and an extra skin of planking to protect against shipworm. On board were a hundred men—crew, marines, and supernumeraries. These last included the astronomer Charles Green, the naturalists Joseph Banks and Daniel Solander, and the artists Alexander Buchan and Sydney Parkinson. Their presence on board was a reminder that in origin the voyage was a scientific enterprise whose main objective was to observe the transit of Venus at Tahiti in the Society Islands. The additional instructions given to Cook before he sailed turned the voyage into a more ambitious enterprise, for he was also to search for the rumored great southern continent, *Terra Australis Incognita*.

*Endeavour* sailed from Plymouth on August 26, 1768, and reached the Society Islands in April 1768, after rounding Cape Horn. Cook sailed south from the Society Islands in August 1769. He reached latitude 40° South without sighting land and turned west to New Zealand, whose coasts he charted in a little more than six months by means of a superb running survey. He then headed for that other region of mystery, the eastern parts of New Holland. He sailed north along the previously unknown east coast of present-day Australia and through Torres Strait, whose existence had theretofore been uncertain. With only one ship, and without the loss of a single man from scurvy, Cook had put five thousand miles of coastline on the maps. For the return journey, *Endeavour* departed from Batavia on December 26, 1770. Five months after rounding the Cape of Good Hope, she reached England on July 13, 1771.

*Endeavour* had served her purpose magnificently—not least during the crisis point of the voyage, which came in June 1770 when she not only survived a holing on the Great Barrier Reef but also could be careened for repairs at the nearby Endeavour River thanks to her flat bottom. Although Cook's ship was to change for his future voyages, the type of ship was not. *Resolution* of his second and third voyages was of the same build and came from the same Whitby shipyard as *Endeavour*, "whose good qualities," Cook wrote, "enabled me to remain so much longer in the South Sea than any one had been able to do before."

[*See also* Cook, James; Expeditions, Scientific; *and* Terra Australis Incognita.]

## Bibliography

Beaglehole, J. C., ed. *The "Endeavour" Journal of Joseph Banks 1768–1771*. 2 vols. Sydney: Angus and Robertson for the Trustees of the Public Library of New South Wales, 1962.

Beaglehole, J. C., ed. *The Journals of Captain James Cook on His Voyages of Discovery*. Vol. 1: *The Voyage of the "Endeavour," 1768–1771*. Cambridge, U.K.: Cambridge University Press for the Hakluyt Society, 1955.

Parkin, Ray. *H.M. Bark "Endeavour": Her Place in Australian History, with an Account of Her Construction, Crew, and Equipment and a Narrative of Her Voyage on the East Coast of New Holland in the Year 1770*. Melbourne, Australia: Miegunyah Press, 1997.

Williams, Glyndwr. "The *Endeavour* Voyage: A Coincidence of Motives." In *Science and Exploration in the Pacific: European Voyages to the Southern Oceans in the Eighteenth Century*, edited by Margarette Lincoln, pp. 3–18. Woodbridge, U.K.: Boydell Press, 1998.

GLYNDWR WILLIAMS

**Endurance,** barquentine that was one of the two vessels of Sir Ernest Shackleton's Imperial Trans-Antarctic Expedition of 1914–1917.

Length/beam: 44 m × 7.5 m (144′ × 25′). Tonnage: 350 gross registered tons. Hull: wood. Complement: 28. Built: Framnaes shipyard, Sandefjord, Norway, 1912.

Launched on December 17, 1912, *Endurance* was originally called SY *Polaris* and was built for ice navigation at the Framnaes shipyard, Sandefjord, Norway, on the orders of the Polaris Society (Société Polaris), a limited company whose subscribers included J. B. Charcot, Otto Nordenskjöld, and Lars Christensen. Designed by Aanderud Larsen in cooperation with Adrien de Gerlache de Gomery, the Belgian polar explorer, she measured 144 feet overall, with a 25-foot beam. There was accommodation for ten passengers who were to make tourist cruises to Spitsbergen, Greenland, and elsewhere in the Arctic. Weighing about 350 tons, SY *Polaris* was a three-masted barquentine with auxiliary coal-fired triple expansion engines and electric light. Tourist cruises never took place, however, and *Polaris* was bought by the British Antarctic explorer Sir Ernest Shackleton for £13,000 on March 25, 1914. Renamed *Endurance* after Shackleton's family motto, "By endurance we conquer," the barquentine sailed to the West India Dock, London, commanded by de Gerlache.

The main aim of the Imperial Trans-Antarctic Expedition was to make the first crossing of the Antarctic continent by dog sledge from Weddell Sea to Ross Sea, much of the journey over unknown territory. *Endurance* departed from the Thames on August 1, 1914, just before the outbreak of World War I (1914–1918). The vessel arrived in South Georgia on October 26, 1914, where a month was spent in preparation for the voyage south, which began on December 5. Ice conditions in the little-known Weddell Sea proved difficult, and *Endurance* was beset on January 19, 1915, in latitude 76°34′ S, longitude 31°30′ W. She drifted to 77° S but then was carried northward, still firmly gripped by the sea ice. She was never released. Wrecked by the relentless pressure of the floes, she had to be abandoned and eventually sank on November 21, 1915, watched by Shackleton and his men from what he called Ocean Camp, where dogs, tents, boats, and salvaged stores had been assembled.

The northerly drift of the ice eventually transported the party to open water north of the Antarctic Peninsula, where three ship's boats were launched. These were *James Caird* (now preserved at Dulwich College, southeast London), *Stancomb-Wills*, and *Dudley Docker*, named after subscribers to the expedition. On April 15, 1916, the party reached Elephant Island, where twenty-two men remained for several months under the leadership of Frank Wild. Shackleton and five others, including the captain of *Endurance*, F. A. Worsley, as navigator, departed in *James Caird* across some of the stormiest seas in the world for South Georgia. After making a remarkable first crossing of the island, Shackleton was able to make contact with the outside world—a world at war—from the whaling station at Grytviken. The Admiralty had already convened a relief committee. *Discovery* was refitted at Devonport Dockyard and sailed south, towed by two armed trawlers. However, Shackleton himself organized the rescue of the party on Elephant Island, using the Chilean naval vessel *Yelcho*, captained by Luis Pardo; on August 30, 1916, they found the party "All safe; all well." According to a report in the *Times* (London) of July 28, 1914, *Endurance* was insured for £15,000, but it is not known whether this was ever paid.

[*See also* Antarctica and the Southern Ocean.]

## Bibliography

Huntford, Roland. *Shackleton*. London: Hodder and Stoughton, 1985.

Lansing, Alfred. *Endurance: Shackleton's Incredible Voyage.* New York: McGraw Hill, 1959. Reprinted several times.

Savours, Ann. *The Voyages of the "Discovery": The Illustrated History of Scott's Ship.* London: Virgin, 1992.

Schelfhout, Charles Emmanuel. *Les Gerlache: Trois générations d'explorateurs polaires.* Aix-en-Provence, France: Editions de la Dyle, 1996.

Shackleton, Sir Ernest. *South: The Story of Shackleton's Last Expedition 1914–1917.* London: Heinemann, 1919. Reprinted several times.

ANN SAVOURS

# English Literature

British sea literature includes every work of imaginative, dramatic, aesthetic, or symbolic quality within the wider range of British writing relating to the sea, whether imagination re-creates fact or convinces us through fiction. These works extend from the beginnings of English to the present, through every genre from short lyric poems to multivolume histories. At their height—as in Ariel's lyric "Full fathom five" from William Shakespeare's *The Tempest* (1611), Jim's leap overboard in Joseph Conrad's *Lord Jim* (1900), and the barque *Judea* burning on a calm sea at the climax of his short story

**English Literature.** Daniel Defoe. © NATIONAL MARITIME MUSEUM, LONDON

"Youth" (1902)—works in this area of British literature match the greatest in any other. They are distinct both from literary writing not centered on the sea (although exploiting marine imagery, vocabulary, or incident) and from writing on marine subjects with no literary characteristics. By this test *The Seafarer* (from the Exeter Book, late tenth century) is the earliest work of English sea literature, while *Lord Jim* (1900), British in its imperialistic worldview and highly literary in its worries about perception and expression, may not be a sea novel. Arguably, what Jim incurs in his desertion of the crippled *Patna* is central to a sea story—itself part of a complex work of tragic fiction. In any such work, one dominant literary genre can incorporate others—which remain recognizable—as parts of a larger design. Alternatively, Jim's qualities as a sailor confined to the land by his disgrace, and Marlow the narrator with his seafarer's "take" on human behavior, might be judged to inform the whole book. In contrast, although Lord Byron's *Don Juan* (1819–1824) is not classifiable as sea literature, canto 2 of that work might be. Despite the British perspective typified by an unsolicited ad for Mann's marine pumps (verse 29), its account of storm and cannibalistic ordeal impressed all Europe—although John Keats (1795–1821) on his own death-voyage denounced its "gloat[ing] and jeer[ing]." Moreover, it ends in a "sea, sand and sex" romance. Episodes lacking such clear boundaries, such as the King James Bible's versions of Jonah and the Whale or Paul's shipwreck (Acts 27), form a penumbra or matrix for sea literature itself.

Sometimes, bringing literary expectations to a text—as we do to a novel—we may be struck by a sense of historical significance. At other times, intent on a history, unsuspected literary qualities might impress us, as with the English geographer Richard Hakluyt (c. 1552–1616). And British sea literature will usually seem quite distinctive in both its literariness and its historical value. Consider all those areas where it most strongly reflects the national or local culture, which sustains it and to which it contributes: its concentration on the sea environment, its representation of those who live on the sea or by the sea, and its distinctive positioning of the observer-narrator. But it need not entail seafaring. Iris Murdoch's *The Sea, The Sea* (1978), suffused with the sea's nearness, life-giving, death-dealing, and symbolic richness, belongs to sea literature—although it features swimming and sea monsters, not ships or sailors. Any use of the sea might spark creativity, from duels under sail to today's surfing and kayaking.

Moreover, the absence or inadequacy of works from certain periods may in itself be significant. Why was the great age of British sea power so patchily represented at the time, not really radically questioned before Herman Melville's *Billy Budd* (1924), and waiting for its first fully adequate treatment in Patrick O'Brian's prose epic? But sea literature has contributed throughout to the creation of a British national identity transcending all local or regional ones. Some works seek to redefine values through critical reevaluation of the past and its current image, as in Barry Unsworth's *Losing Nelson* (1999), and some to preserve or commemorate what is threatened. History is also involved in the loneliness of extreme experience at sea, incommunicable to others. From *The Seafarer*'s estranged view of men ashore "well-seen at wine-round" to the Scottish "Caller Herring" with its scorn of Edinburgh socialites "screw[ing] their faces" at fish so perilously caught, this voice always reflects what it is isolated from. Thus what is most distinctively "literary" and pleasurable about British sea literature points us beyond it to the majestic realities it seeks to confront—both natural and historical.

## Seafaring and Sea-Keeping

In this overview at least, British sea literature begins with the English language and in England. True to *The Seafarer*'s sense of the sea's strangeness, and the yearning it arouses, the Middle Ages often represent the human spiritual journey as a sea voyage. Like the monk's coracle in the *Voyage of St. Brendan* (ninth–tenth centuries) whose construction and maintenance are described in detail despite its otherworldly destination, the church as ship of faith reflects the techniques of medieval shipbuilding. In John Lydgate's fifteenth-century English translation of Guillaume de Deguileville's *Pilgrimage of Life* (c. 1330–1358), the "frets," or strakes strengthening the hull, represent God's commandments. So too with the use of ships. In John Skelton's satire *The Bowge of Court* (c. 1498), the ship of fools inspired by the floating asylums of Flanders becomes a seagoing vessel. Skelton's dreamer joins the merchants boarding the ship off Harwich to negotiate for the cargo (while taking passage to the next port). The crowded poop represents the folly of a scholar seeking favor among the backstabbing parasites at court. Cleverness itself is overtaxed, as in Psalm 107, in which storm-tossed sailors are brought to "their wits' end."

An earlier, more literalistic text is *The Libelle of Englyshe Polycye*, written around 1436 and later printed in Hakluyt's *The Principall Navigations, Voiages, and Discoveries of the English Nation* (1589). Combining didactic poetry, satire, and persuasive epistle, it addresses councilors acting

for Henry VI in his minority, echoing the opinion of the Merchant in *The Canterbury Tales* by Geoffrey Chaucer (c.1342–1400), who "wolde the see were kept for any thing / Bitwixe Middelburgh and Orewelle"–ports vital to English trade. The *Libelle* broods over the Channel and North Sea, with glances toward Bristol and the Atlantic. Although its use of a new word, "policy," reflects its practical purpose, it has pronounced literary value.

The principal appeal of this text, however, is reflected in Hakluyt's claim that "more matter and substance could in no wise be comprised in so little a roome." This implies a need for discernment, and a pleasure in exercising it, not only here but in all his texts. He compares the antiquated style of the *Libelle* to a Russian palace: outwardly plain, concealing gilded magnificence. Similarly, his readers should enjoy looking deeper, beyond the curiosity, excitement, or horror of his narratives, to the colonialist, strategic, and mercantilist substance of his argument.

Hakluyt helped to establish one icon of English seapower: the plucky, handy, potent, and compact Elizabethan warship–seen again in Thomas Nashe's *Pierce Penilesse* (1592), in which Spain's "Armadoes, that like a high wood overshadowed the shrubs of our low ships, fled from the breath of our cannons, as vapours before the sun." This is echoed in the prose account of *Revenge*'s last fight by Sir Walter Ralegh (1552–1618), which surpasses the fanciful soufflé of Gervase Markham's tragic-epic treatment (1595), as it does the Victorian jiqngoism of the "ballad of the Fleet" by Alfred, Lord Tennyson (1809–1892), also based on it.

In the meantime, Elizabethan popular ballads, such as Thomas Deloney's on the Armada, ensured that the English sailor's image would match his ship. Through music and song, ideas of his courage and enterprise would contribute to England's self-definition as a seagoing nation–and later to Britain's. In formal contrast, the poems "The Storm" and "The Calm" by John Donne (1572–1631) convey the perspective of a highly literate landsman–a volunteer with the Earl of Essex's forces–on extreme experience at sea. Both simplicity and sophistication help to build the tradition.

In seventeenth-century Britain, among the interplay of spiritual aspirations and millennial hopes, nascent science, growing materialism, and colonialist expansion, a whole range of written genres–accounts of discoveries or of shipwrecks, ballads, reflective essays such as those on cannibals by the French essayist Michel de Montaigne (1533–1592), manuals of seamanship such as those of John Smith (c. 1580–1631)–is reflected in works now enjoying high cultural status, such as *The Tempest*. These in their turn influence writing more directly centered on the sea or more dependent on its imagery. Shakespeare's play begins with a burst of nautical language as the boatswain struggles to save the king's ship. Its apparent loss reflects William Strachey's *True Reportory* of a Bermudan shipwreck (written in 1610 as a record of providential survival, and read by Shakespeare before publication). What happens similarly on his imaginary island—survival, mutiny, wise governance averting disaster—has recently been read as a dramatic exploration of colonization in its impact on indigenous people, personified by Caliban. But for his part, Shakespeare plainly intended to affirm Prospero's civilizing influence, and the more markedly protestant poetry of the midcentury took this further. One outcome of the English Revolution was a consolidation of sea-power under Oliver Cromwell (1599–1658), as celebrated in Andrew Marvell's *The First Anniversary* (1655). This poem is not about the protector's navy, but its invincibility reveals his significance. The baroque presentation of his ships ("That through the center shoot their thundering side / And sink the earth that doth at anchor ride") is linked to that regal symbol, the sun—repositioned and reenergized. The sun of Cromwell's virtue outpaces and outshines its celestial counterpart, as it does hereditary rulers. Naval hegemony bespeaks God's own restored authority. However, millenarian hopes remain tentative: "If these the times, then this must be the man."

Taken together, the sea-related writing of this period has a complexity of attitude and implied audience that adds greatly to its literary interest, and to its fertility in the minds of later readers. Popular verse continues to celebrate the war-winning and wealth-generating prowess of sailors as well as their attractiveness. Ballads such as "The Jovial Marriner" (c. 1677) are aimed at communities linked to the sea, as Restoration London was in its business and in the voluntary naval service of its boldest courtiers; it is not surprising to find Charles Sackville, Earl of Dorset using this form in his "Song Written at Sea" (1665), priced at sixpence.

Ironically, the true literary inheritor of this is not himself British. The American writer Herman Melville (1819–1891) repeatedly recalls Marvell, and his replacement of Cromwell's sun with a yellow Man-in-the-Moon "to light up th[e] rather gloomy looking subject" of the primordial naval victory of the American naval officer John Paul Jones (1747–1792), like a music hall footlight, attests (as does the sailor's ballad concluding *Billy Budd*) the bearing of both popular and elite culture on sea warfare—and the inability of both to resolve the difference between civilization and barbarism.

## British Sea-Power and the Modes of Writing

Another superb ballad, "The Death of Admiral Benbow" (1702), marks a new century, but sea literature was to share in the evolution of a more explorative prose form. The general cultural consciousness of seafaring probably explains how Daniel Defoe (1660–1731) could broaden his fictional range to include the piratical hero, as with Robinson Crusoe inciting belief through accumulation of detail. With its nautical terminology *Captain Singleton* (1720) provokes our effort to understand. Knowledge is the key, poising Singleton's informed intelligence, however fictional its basis (as in his trans-African journey), against his immorality. This softens our disapproval of "Captain Bob," much as the sheer technical competence of his Portuguese gunner, cutler, and carpenter overcomes his ethnic prejudice against them.

Where Defoe represents the informal discipline of a pirate vessel, resolving issues through debate, Tobias Smollett's own sea experience is reflected in *The Adventures of Roderick Random* (1748), with its picture of naval tyranny. This moves from a comic blend of reportage and caricature to an ironic satire on incompetent leadership in the 1739–1742 War of Jenkins' Ear. Threading through the episodic story, with its seemingly random events and reversals of fortune, is a figure whose legacy extends over three centuries, Tom Bowling. He unifies the book through his influence on the hero's fate, leading to Roderick's final voyage and romance-like reunion with his father. Appropriately, Bowling evades closure in the happy ending, by going back to sea. Despite Smollett's shocking acceptance of his slaving voyages as a way to wealth, his ebullience, kindness, and self-belief—seen in his constant use of nautical jargon, bequeathed to his successors—are still attractive. He shows up the cruel or inadequate officers who thwart the hero and his work—and the best interests of the new, unitary British state and "nation." Tom, like Roderick and Smollett himself, is a "North Briton" and his salty phrases must be spoken in a Scots accent. In marked contrast to the brutal Irishman and effete Englishman who, in turn, command *Thunder*, it is the lowly Scots and Welsh who give force to it.

Despite the novel's vital role, British sea literature is also much enriched by the verse of the eighteenth century and Romantic period. A pungent blend of ideology (or jingoism), realism, and symbolism associates newly forged nationhood with world hegemony at sea—something to be worked with, or worked against, later. It is seen in the lyric of "Rule Britannia" (by another Scot, James Thomson), in the two great lyrics of pathos and terror of William Cowper (1731–1800), "The Loss of the Royal George" and "The Castaway," and in William Falconer's *The Shipwreck* (1762) as he engages the reader with a crew's heroic efforts to avert disaster. Popular verse remains important, whether it expresses the grievances of seafarers, as in the songs of the "Nore Mutiny" (1797), or their cheerful subordination, as in the officially sponsored entertainments of the English dramatist Charles Dibdin (1745–1814), or mourns for Horatio Nelson. Dibdin's "Tom Bowling"—now rhyming "Bowling" with "howling," Cockney-style—fuses Smollett's nautical metaphor with "manliest beauty," propelling the handsome sailor into his varied subsequent history. Although his physique reflects work aloft, his incarnations will include both foremast hands and officers (noting that Melville's Jack Chase appears as both).

But profounder psychological and spiritual qualities are seen in the English poet George Crabbe's verse tale, *Peter Grimes* (1810), and the "lyrical ballad" of Samuel Taylor Coleridge, *Rime of the Ancient Mariner*, first published in 1798. One derives from close personal observation of a Suffolk fishing community, the other from an intense reimagining of things seen by other men, such as the English navigator John Davis (c. 1550–1605) and the English mariner James Cook (1728–1779), in remoter places (as demonstrated by John Livingston Lowes in his *Road to Xanadu*, 1927). Crabbe's readers will be troubled as much by the community's confused response to Grimes as by his behavior, while Coleridge's mariner draws us inexorably into his outcast state. Both poems play on the old superstitious link between becalmed ships or boats and human wrongdoing. This accesses our own fears, and Coleridge heightens our empathy with his acute blend of the specific, the nonspecific, and the bizarre in a ship with no apparent command structure to alienate us, and no skills beyond steering—and shooting. We stand among the enormous company of two hundred men as they superfluously "work the ropes," oddly positioned "knee to knee." The horrors and wonders over the side, the illuminated "steersman's face" added (after Coleridge's own voyage to Malta) in the revision of 1817, and the hypnotic rhythm ("Alone, alone, all, all alone") inevitably capture us. In contrast, Byron can be vividly precise, as in his prose sketch of an Aegean storm, and the "gallant frigate tight" of *Childe Harold*, canto 2, with its "lone chieftain, who majestic stalks / Silent and feared by all"—or sumptuously lyrical, as in his apostrophe to the "deep and dark blue ocean" ending that poem. As for the poet Percy Bysshe Shelley (1792–1822), his own death, as recounted with intense personal feeling by Mary Woll-stonecraft Shelley (1797–1851) in her "Note on the Poems of 1822," is a marine tragedy far more affecting than the Gothic horror of his "A Vision of the Sea," and more inspirational—as witnessed by John Rousmaniere's recent *After the Storm* (2002). But the pleasure of yachting, which bred confidence in Captain Roberts's unstable design, still lights up Shelley's poetic fragment "The Boat on the Serchio." His misplaced trust in past naval expertise parallels Byron's respect for the service whose political masters they both despised. Faulty construction, as suggested by the Channel 4 (U.K.) program *Wreck Detectives* (March 20, 2003), also explains the loss of the poet William Wordsworth's brother John, who was in command of *Earl of Abergavenny* when it sank in 1805. This now conditions the heroic stoicism of Wordsworth's *Elegiac Stanzas*, with their contrast of calm and storm, childlike serenity and manly fortitude, enduring mind (the castle), and failing body (the ship).

After Trafalgar, the naval novel pioneered by Smollett changed, like the navy itself, in response to political change. *Persuasion* (1817) may not be a naval novel, but it stems from Jane Austen's love for her naval brothers Francis and Charles, celebrating their energy, enterprise, and respect for each other's individual gifts and interests. In contrast, the comedy of Frederick Marryat (1792–1848) reflects clinically on the efficiency and social role of "the service," in a conservative and evangelical response to the shockwaves from France and perhaps to the Byronic posturing and moral anarchy of Edward Trelawny's *Adventures of a Younger Son* (1831), whose renegade hero recalls Defoe's "Captain Bob." Marryat's *Mr. Midshipman Easy* (1836) assails the French egalitarianism taught to Jack at home. It is abolitionist in its portrayal of a black character, and insists that a chaplain can also be a seafarer. A newly stressed link between "officer" and "gentleman" implies an unacceptable risk in promotions from the lower deck.

Edward Howard's *Rattlin the Reefer* (1836), named after one of Smollett's sailors, reacts against the books he helped Marryat to produce. His hero's career begins in no happy home and ends with no happy marriage, and he acknowledges the grief endemic to naval life. The loss overboard of Gubbins, the "volunteer" felon, through unfeeling discipline, casual cruelty from companions, and the icy downdraft of a sail, is said to foreshadow Melville.

## Conrad and Kipling: Surrendering Sail, Celebrating Steam

Inevitably, following his own earlier career, Conrad, the greatest sea writer claimed by Britain, focuses on the merchant service, smaller crews giving greater scope to the study of relationships and group dynamics. Every major motif and character type in sea literature comes under scrutiny. Conrad's inquiry into the individual and collective strengths and weaknesses of seafarers both reacts against previous writing and draws on the "yarns" of those who "followed the sea." His characters–agents of imperial expansion–inhabit a world already transformed by European power.

*The Nigger of the "Narcissus"* (1897) presents extreme experience at sea–and the difficulty of describing it. Conrad pits his own realism against the campaigning accounts of hardship at sea that had, he believed, harmed those they sought to protect, whether through writing (American sailor and lawyer Richard Henry Dana [1815–1882]) or legislation (reformer Samuel Plimsoll [1824–1898]). His narrator knows what is said further aft but lives, unidentified, in the forecastle, opposing his close-up view of Singleton as the exemplar of seamanship to his portrayals of sentimentality, shirking, or malice. This is Conrad's nearest approach to a working-class perspective, that is, to a prospective clouding of the real priorities. Singleton incarnates all that is separate, and mute, in the true sailor's qualities and experience. His enigmatic words "Ships are all right; it's the men in them" imply that speech is superfluous: men either will not learn or do not need to be told. His laborious reading affords him no contact with reality, and from the shore's perspective–inconsistently illiterate–he is merely a "disgusting old brute." On land, like *Narcissus* herself, he "cease[s] to live." Conrad's words achieve his preface's project "to make you see" somebody wordless and invisible without their mediation.

Steam power's impact on communications, international and personal, is felt in Conrad's *Typhoon* (1903). Stolid Captain McWhirr and his well-found ship symbolize each other. He respects only the measurable, from flags and cabin locks to coal bills, ignoring the sea's immeasurableness. When he is finally faced with this, his confession of weakness and fear goes unnoticed in one of his tedious letters to his wife, who treats him as a machine for income generation. There are two gifted letter writers on board, Solomon Rout (whose feeling for his engines in the seaway saves the ship) and Jukes, the mate. For Rout, McWhirr's restoration of order after the storm is impossible to convey to his readers at home, and Jukes still does not fully appreciate (as McWhirr did) that fairness, however mechanistic, surpassed force as a way of maintaining stability among "a cargo of chinamen." The habit of exploitation, wherever practiced, clouds both perception and communication.

In contrast to McWhirr, the hero of *Lord Jim* (1900) is overimaginative. Through Marlow, Conrad examines the allure of a boyish adventurous spirit, stirred by "a course of light holiday literature" in which reality is never detached from dream. Preoccupied with his own feelings, Jim slips from scorn of his abject fellow officers into fascination, despite his clear duty to *Patna*'s Muslim passengers. Much later, he honors the letter of duty rather than its substance and, again, deserts a group of indigenous people–this despite the extraordinary achievement and wish fulfillment of becoming their "Lord," his white-clad figure recalling the historical James Brooke (raja of Sarawak, 1803–1868), glimmering in the darkness as Marlow sails away. He unites the handsome sailor (fortunate in love) with the god-like colonial administrator as tested to destruction in *Heart of Darkness* (1902).

In "The Secret Sharer" (1910) Conrad further probes the relationship of image, substance, perceiver, and perceived. The story of a homicidal mate abetted by a captain–drawn from an unhappy phase in *Cutty Sark*'s career–exposes the relationship among personal obligation, self-knowledge, and professional duty. The untried skipper finds his own latent waywardness mirrored in Leggatt, his "double," who comes to him out of the sea as if from the subconscious and returns to it just in time to avert the loss of his authority–while Leggatt, like Jim, retreats into the anonymous world of the "other," without the law.

Transformation and self-recognition are also themes handled in the sea writing of Rudyard Kipling (1865–1936). Like Frank Bullen's *The Cruise of the "Cachalot"* (1898), which he admired, Kipling's *Captains Courageous* (1897) treats the American fisheries from a British perspective– and, according to a later letter, portrays America's "grubby ideals." This may reflect Kipling's disillusionment following his debacle in Vermont, but it is supported by the book's incidents and imagery, despite its sympathetic portrayal of New Englanders. Harvey Cheyne Jr., the rich kid cured by work and democratic discipline on *We're Here*, learns the horror of unfeeling violence when another schooner is run down by a liner and when–as if in a folktale–a murderer's corpse, buried at sea, returns to reclaim the knife just gleefully acquired by Harvey. But Harvey's new zest for work exposes him to his father's brutal business efficiency, and he looks forward to "getting his knife into" Dan Troop, the son of his rescuer, now in his employ. This is Kipling's perspective on the epoch of the robber barons.

As for Britain, the verse monologues "McAndrew's Hymn" and "The *Mary Gloster*" poise their protagonists between contempt for the snobbery of Victorian society and pride in the recognition they have won from it—surpassed by their delight in their own technological mastery. McAndrew's engines re-create in Calvinist terms the medieval ship of faith, while Anthony Gloster's intended ship funeral, reuniting him with his wife buried far away at sea, recalls *The Seafarer*. The fourteener couplets—in effect, ironed-out ballad stanzas—reflect the lateral and vertical divisions in British culture, the insular empire facing the world empire.

## The Twentieth Century: Exposé, Epic, Elegy

With its seven-line stanzas, John Masefield's *Dauber* (1913) points back beyond Conrad's *Narcissus* to Shakespeare's narrative poem *The Rape of Lucrece* (1594) and the verse romances of Chaucer. It uses a form connoting both love and the elemental powers behind it to explore the passion for beauty. This lures a farm boy to sea, to be rejected as "a female ripe to faint" before suffering the brute reality of sea, weather, ship, and toiling men, which he had so longed to paint. The death of "Dauber," near the end, could be read as Masefield's symbolic sidelining of his own problem of communication. But although being hardened by Cape Horn into a real sailor invites his hero to confine himself to that role, his dying words, "It will go on," affirm the need to continue sharing experience.

Meanwhile, Conrad was still active and the Anglo-German naval arms race in progress. Virginia Woolf's *The Voyage Out* (1915) heightens the characteristic estrangement previously experienced by female passengers in the shipboard ambience—whether imagined by men, as in Sir George Dallas's *The India Guide* (1785), or reported by women, as in Mary Crompton's good-humored journal of her honeymoon voyage in *Great Britain* (written in 1866). Woolf used a transatlantic voyage to liken the male-dominated government and industry of Britain to the ship's machinery and to express her revulsion at the Royal Navy's "sinister gray vessels, low in the water and bald as bone." Ironically, her broader sense of the interplay of gender and historical role through a single ongoing figure, seen in her *Orlando* (1928), was later to be adapted for his own purposes by Nicholas Monsarrat in *The Master Mariner: Running Proud* (1979).

Writing from the passenger's perspective, whether the genre is cruise journal, novel, or poem, continued intermittently to the end of the century. Malcolm Lowry's *Through the Panama* (1961) is a novella in the form of a cruise journal written by a fictional character planning to use his notes for a novel. Reflecting the epoch of Marshall Plan aid with an American-built ship under French command, its layered text exploits the Coleridgian marginal gloss to expose the interplay of earlier histories and voyage narratives within the writer's imagination. This broadens the familiar theme of the alienation of sea and land, and is seen especially in the transit of the Canal—seagoing ships deep within the land are as strange to it as the land is to the people on their decks. The frame narrator, a Swede, recounts what is historically significant to Lowry as a Scot, that is, Scotland's attempt three centuries earlier to colonize the isthmus and control its trade. Evelyn Waugh's *The Ordeal of Gilbert Pinfold* (1957) is at once realistic in its shipboard setting and its transient community of passengers and surreally reflective of the voyage—or ordeal—of an individual soul. Besides echoing the anxieties of the early Cold War period, Pinfold's hallucinations truthfully project his fear and loathing of postwar British society, from which his conservative culture and his Catholicism isolate him. They would be impossible without Waugh's wartime familiarity with public-address systems, telegraphy, and the daily routines and discipline of the merchant marine. Finally, Andrew Motion's journal "Sailing to Italy" (1997) exploits the residual possibility of reaching that destination in that way, to try to re-create the physical conditions and sensations vying with illness during Keats's journey to Italy in 1820. The strangeness of the sea beckoning the small twentieth-century ship's company out of sight of England figures Keats's voyage of death and Motion's struggle to establish imaginative touch. A work of sea literature is created inevitably in the attempt to achieve that purpose, paralleling Motion's own high-cultural task as the British laureate with his skipper's other role as a preserver and performer of sea songs.

Twentieth-century writing on the navy was similarly divided between retrospection and current realities. The collected stories of Captain L. A. Ritchie (formerly L. A. da Costa Ricci), as published in *The "Bartimeus" Omnibus* (1933), present the service before, during, and after World War I as a microcosm of British society, at once preserving class divisions and working across them. From "A Galley's Day," conveying the excitement of racing under sail in ships' boats—ending as the petty officer helmsman accepts his pint from the wardroom but keeps the full story for his messmates—to the dark tale of a former master-at-arms turned sexually abusive landlord, Ritchie follows the navy through the prolonged crisis of war. He reflects the naval ethos at a period when its political and strategic importance, human and material resources, problematic technical development, and prestige were all at a peak.

As imaginative re-creations of World War II at sea, Monsarrat's *The Cruel Sea* (1951) and C. S. Forester's *The Ship* (1943) are surpassed only by Lothar-Günther Buchheim's *Das Boot* (1973; *The Boat*, 1974). Monsarrat follows a smaller ship's company that is diverse socially and psychologically but held together by a strong partnership of captain and first lieutenant through a long-drawn-out conflict, while Forester concentrates on one decisive action in the Mediterranean, featuring a single cruiser. *The Ship*'s representation of teamwork matched to technology turns propaganda into literature, although the pivoting of everything on the firing and impact of a single shell seems unconvincing. He excels "Bartimeus" in his treatment of the navy as microcosm, including a working-class poet in his ship's company and making him credible—more so for the rapture with which the youth finds a Keatsian beauty in destruction.

The real sea poetry of this conflict is little known but often of high quality. It includes songs, as collected by Cyril Tawney (e.g., the "Twenty-Third Flotilla Song," to the tune of "Lili Marlene"), the dramatic or reflective lyrics of Charles Causley, Norman Hampson, and others, and Alan Ross's long poem "J.W.51B: A Convoy" (1975). This war's verse and its visual art often reflect each other—as the abstracted shapes of Ross's poem "Destroyers in the Arctic" recall the geometrical patterning of gun-flashes in Eric Ravilious's painting "HMS *Ark Royal* in Action."

Meanwhile the subliminal support afforded to Forester's wartime readers (including British prime minister Winston Churchill himself) by his first three Horatio Hornblower novels, would have arisen from their seemingly escapist representation of an earlier, more consistently successful phase of British sea power. Horatio's technical skills, courage, improvisation, and powers of leadership probably reflected Churchill's own aspirations. On resumption of the saga, issues destined for fuller treatment by Patrick O'Brian, from power-bloc politics to the complexities of professional and social advancement, were progressively introduced.

But William Golding's studies of spiritual isolation and power relations at sea probe the idea of Britishness far more profoundly. In *Pincher Martin* (1956), the tenacious ego of Golding's drowned villain-hero constructs its own residual rock from fragments of memory and survival training. His stock naval nickname, "Pincher," suits the satanic selfishness that clings to an illusionary body, stranded on a real rock. Martin—failed actor, false friend, rapist, and, latterly, slapdash officer and would-be murderer—personifies the "low, dishonest" 1930s depicted by the poet W. H. Auden

(1907–1973). All this depends absolutely on the marine setting. In contrast, the trilogy beginning with *Rites of Passage* (1980) lacks the earlier book's sustained intensity but deploys a richer range of resources. Golding shows the corruption, cruelty, and arbitrary power to which naval discipline was prone. He crosses the complexities of the land-based class system with those of his dilapidated ship, with its labyrinthine complications of authority, status, and influence. This heralds 1980s Britain, with its failing industries, frenetic networking, and ruthless individualism. The cult of pop-star celebrity is also brought ironically to mind by the Reverend James Colley's disastrous and uncomprehending admiration for the corrupt and cynical handsome sailor Billy Rogers.

Patrick O'Brian's epic spirit is far more celebratory, with its positive interactions between conventional opposites—England and Ireland, Britain and France, Catholic and Protestant, science and religion, naval force and diplomatic craft, musical skill and seamanlike adaptability, masculinity and femininity, sea and land—besides such intensely realized encounters as Stephen Maturin's with the orangutans in *The Thirteen Gun Salute* (1989) and Jack Aubrey's with the vengeful Dutch sixty-four-gun ship in *Desolation Island* (1978).

Whatever is destined to feature in the equivalent of this overview, a hundred years from now, will perhaps have grown from the new attitudes and approaches evidenced in recent writing, such as Julian Stockwin's lower-deck perspective on the Napoleonic naval novel in *Kydd* (2001) and Ellen MacArthur's neopagan relation to the sea, revealed in her *Taking on the World* (2002)—or it might confirm the possibility raised by Douglas Dunn in *The Donkey's Ears* (2000) of reviving the long poem as a way of linking the mental and emotional states of those at sea to a society on land: how might Russia's doomed voyage to Tsushima foreshadow the miscalculation and mayhem of twentieth-century power politics and mechanized war? Both sea stories and factual narratives should gain much from the further prominence of women sailors, whether sailing solo or in company, over the years ahead.

[*See also* Conrad, Joseph; Fiction; Kipling, Rudyard; Literature; *and* O'Brian, Patrick.]

## Bibliography

### Primary Works

Coote, John, ed. *The Faber Book of the Sea: An Anthology*. London: Faber, 1989. A carefully balanced, thematically organized collection covering the contrasted moods and aspects of life at sea and on shore, compiled by a former naval officer. See also the companion volume edited by Coote, *The Faber Book of Tales of the Sea: An Anthology* (London: Faber, 1991).

Firth, C. H., ed. *Naval Songs and Ballads*. London: Publications of the Navy Records Society, 1908. Although available only in major reference libraries, this is a full and varied collection, including, for example, a mildly satirical ballad by Captain Marryat.

Murray, Glen, ed. *Scottish Sea Stories*. Edinburgh: Polygon, 1996.

Palmer, Roy, ed. *The Oxford Book of Sea Songs*. Oxford and New York: Oxford University Press, 1986. An invaluable means of access to the tradition of popular verse relating to the sea, and to its music.

Tawney, Cyril, comp. *Grey Funnel Lines: Traditional Song and Verse of the Royal Navy, 1900–1970*. London: Routledge, 1987. As the title indicates, this brings the oral tradition of the British navy a good way into the second half of the twentieth century.

### Secondary Works

Auden, W. H. *The Enchafèd Flood; or, The Romantic Iconography of the Sea*. London: Faber and Faber, 1951.

Carlson, Patricia A., ed. *Literature and Lore of the Sea*. Costerus, New Series, vol. 52. Amsterdam: Rodopi; Atlantic Highlands, N.J.: Distributed in the United States by Humanities Press, 1986. Although its reference is mainly American, its general critical principles and treatment of "lore" are of equal relevance to British sea literature.

Lowes, John Livingston. *The Road to Xanadu: A Study in the Ways of the Imagination*. Boston: Houghton Mifflin, 1927. A classic critical and scholarly study of the Romantic imagination, in marine mode.

Neill, Anna. *British Discovery Literature and the Rise of Global Commerce*. Houndmills, Basingstoke, U.K., and New York: Palgrave, 2002.

Peck, John. *Maritime Fiction: Sailors and the Sea in British and American Novels, 1719–1917*. New York: Palgrave Macmillan, 2001.

Sherry, Norman. *Conrad's Eastern World*. Cambridge, U.K.: Cambridge University Press, 1966. Like Sherry's subsequent *Conrad's Western World* (Cambridge, U.K.: Cambridge University Press, 1971), this shows how to link the seagoing experience of sea writers—and their broader knowledge of society and politics at any given period—to their literary production.

ROBERT COCKCROFT

## Ensor, James

**Ensor, James** (1860–1949), Belgian artist. Ensor was born on 13 April 1860 in Oostende, Belgium, on the North Sea, and died there in 1949. His father, of British origins, owned a shop where one could find the thousand wonders of the sea: shells, small boats, and the like. Ensor received his first lessons in drawing at age thirteen, and at fifteen he painted his first small works on card and wood.

They are mostly seascapes, scenes of dunes and landscapes of the lowland region known as the Polders. Two years later he settled in Brussels, where he studied at the Academy of Fine Arts. He returned to Oostende, where he set up his studio and built his career, leaving his hometown only for short visits to Paris, London, and the Netherlands. In addition to painting in oils, he was a watercolor artist, etcher, and engraver. In the early 1880s Ensor participated in avant-garde exhibitions and was cofounder of the XX Club and of the Contemporary Art Society.

Ensor holds an important place in the Belgian school and wielded considerable influence over an entire generation of artists. Many writers, art critics, painters, and eminent personalities visited his studio; Jean Cassou, the former curator of the Museum of Modern Art in Paris, remarked that "a visit to James Ensor in his ethereal house, abounding with seashells and the rhythm of the sea," was one of his "most marvellous memories." Ensor's art testifies to his lifelong contact with the ocean. His works include *Seascape* (1880), *Afternoon in Oostende* (1881), and *The Port of Oostende* (1890), all in the Antwerp Museum of Fine Art, and *Christ Calming the Storm*, in the Oostende Museum of Fine Art.

[*See also* Art; Artists, *subentry* Belgian; *and* Painting.]

### Bibliography

Berko, Patrick, and Viviane Berko. *Seascapes of Belgian Painters Born between 1750 and 1875*. Brussels: Knokke, 1984.

PATRICK BERKO and VIVIANE BERKO
*Translated by Selina Baring Maclennan*

## Ericsson, John

**Ericsson, John** (1803–1889), Swedish-born American inventor and mechanical engineer. Ericsson was born at Långbanshyttan, Värmland, Sweden, on July 31, 1803, the son of Olof Ericsson, a mine supervisor. He and his brother Nils Ericson (1802–1870) received a military upbringing and became officers in the Swedish Army Engineer Corps. John Ericsson constructed a hot-air engine that was designed to be fueled with wood. In 1826, he left the army and moved to England, where he demonstrated his invention; but because coal was the main fuel used in England, the invention did not become popular. In 1829, Ericsson participated in a locomotive competition sponsored by the Liverpool and Manchester Railway and held near Rainhill. For the competition, Ericsson developed a steam locomotive called *Novelty*, which raced and lost against George Stephenson's *Rocket*.

Steamboats were moved by ship wheels, which were both vulnerable elements aboard warships and took room away from artillery. Ericsson initially developed a system of contra-rotating propellers, which consisted of two propellers of opposite pitch, placed one behind the other. A hollow shaft carried the forward propeller, and the shaft for the other propeller revolved inside it. Ericsson demonstrated the workings of this propeller before Admiralty authorities on the Thames with a boat 45 feet long. Technically, the test launch was successful. However, the Admiralty was not interested in the invention because of the bad quality of the steering, and they rejected it in 1837. The Admiralty preferred the screw propeller, invented at the same time by the Englishman Sir Francis Pettitt Smith (1808–1874). Meanwhile, Ericsson's experiments had caught the attention of the American consul in Liverpool, Captain R. F. Stockton (1795–1866). Thanks to Stockton's intervention, Ericsson built a larger ship, named *R. F. Stockton*, still using contra-rotating propellers, and the boat was launched in 1838. Experimental journeys went well, especially after one of the two propellers was removed. In 1839, the *R. F. Stockton* departed for America, followed by Ericsson. Once he had arrived, his first project was to build a prototype for a new class of ships, USS *Princeton*, with screw propulsion. At that time, better insights into the principles of thermodynamics were known, and following these principles, Ericsson built a hot-air engine with four cylinders, each measuring 4.27 meters (14 feet) in diameter, for the so-called caloric ship *Ericsson*. However, the ship, with its water displacement of 2,200 tons, did not reach the speed that had been aimed for, and the gigantic hot-air engine was replaced by a steam engine. Ericsson had more success with his smaller hot-air engines, thousands of which were sold.

In 1861, Ericsson constructed the armored ship *Monitor*, which featured a revolving turret. His concept led to a revolution in maritime warfare. After this success, Ericsson continued working on new inventions until his death in New York on March 8, 1889.

Despite a controversy about his being the true inventor of the revolving turret, Ericsson achieved great fame with the design of USS *Monitor*. After his death, his body was transported to Sweden on the American cruiser USS *Baltimore*, and he was buried at Filipstad, Värmland. He made the writing of his biography difficult by burning all his seventy-five notebooks and two wagonloads of drawings three years before his death. Only a few of his drawings are extant. However, a significant collection of manuscripts are preserved at the Library of Congress and at the American Swedish Historical Museum, in Philadelphia.

[*See also* Warships, *subentry on* Modern Warships.]

## Bibliography

Bryant, Lynwood. "The Role of Thermodynamics in the Evolution of Heat Engines." *Technology and Culture* 14 (April 1973): 153–165.

Church, William Conant. *The Life of John Ericsson*. 2 vols. New York: Scribners, 1890.

Corlett, Ewan. *The Iron Ship: The Story of Brunel's SS "Great Britain."* Rev. ed. London: Conway Maritime Press, 1990.

Lamm, Michael. "The Big Engine That Couldn't." *American Heritage of Invention and Technology* 8, no. 3 (Winter 1993): 40–47.

White, Ruth Morris. *Yankee from Sweden: The Dream and the Reality in the Days of John Ericsson*. New York: Holt, 1960.

JAN M. DIRKZWAGER
*Translated from the Dutch by Alexa Nieschlag*

**Ermak.** *See* Yermak.

# Eschels, Jacob

**Eschels, Jacob** (1757–1842), sea captain and author. Jens Jacob Eschels authored one of the earliest surviving authentic autobiographies of a German sea captain, a work of remarkable literary value, and one of the most important sources for German maritime history in the second half of the eighteenth century. Eschels was born on December 12, 1757, on the northern Frisian island Föhr, a place well known as the home of many sailors of the Dutch and German merchant and whaling fleets. He was the son of a poor family, his father having served before the mast with the Dutch East India Company (VOC). In 1769, when he was eleven years old, Eschels became a cabin boy on an Amsterdam whaler, which was wrecked in the Arctic, but he returned home safely. Each of the following years saw him on a different whaler. In the winters at home and eager for knowledge, the young man thoroughly studied pilotage and navigation.

In 1778 he decided to sign up on merchant ships in the future and sail European waters. In 1781 Eschels eventually crossed the Atlantic Ocean bound for the West Indies. In Grenada he took the chance to change to a Hamburg-based ship to be an *Unter-Steuermann* (second mate). The following year in Hamburg, he joined the barque *Henricus de Vierde* as first mate, which he commanded in her homebound voyage as captain since her former captain had died of disease in Haiti. He commanded this ship on numerous voyages from Arkhangel'sk to the Mediterranean and—from 1788 on—to Charleston and various other North American ports until 1798. Eschels then stayed ashore due to the disastrous conditions for the German sea trade during the coalition wars between France and Great Britain. He became a manufacturer of tobacco products, a merchant, a shipowner, and a surveyor for shipping affairs in the then Danish Altona, adjacent to Hamburg. He wrote his voluminous autobiography before 1832, initially only for his family (with an addendum in 1833). Two years later in 1835 his autobiography was published. Eschels died on June 7, 1842, in Altona, Schleswig-Holstein, leaving behind his third wife and six children.

[*See also* German Literature.]

### Bibliography

Eschels, J. J. *Lebensbeschreibung eines alten Seemannes*. 1835. Rev. ed., edited by A. Sauer. Hamburg: Kabel Verlag, 2006.

ALBRECHT SAUER

**Evertsen Family**  The Evertsen family is unique in naval history. Nineteen of its members over a period of one hundred years were naval officers, including five admirals, all serving the admiralty of Zeeland, in the Dutch Republic. No fewer than five Evertsens were present in the North Sea battle of Lowestoft in 1665. In Dutch naval history the only comparable family is the Van Wassenaers, who produced ten naval officers (five admirals) over a period of three hundred years.

The port city of Vlissingen (Flushing) was the Evertsens' birthplace. The first generations did not reach the ranks of flag officers for various reasons, such as an early death at sea for Jan Evertsen (1570–1617), whose widow, Mayken Jans, prepared her five sons for a naval career. During most of the Eighty Years' War, also known as the Dutch Revolt, Zeeland was a frontier province. This meant that there were several inland naval engagements—such as Sluis in 1603 and Slaak in 1631—often crucial but less spectacular than the outright sea battles later in the century.

The first generations of Evertsen men married the daughters of colleagues; later they married into the city's oligarchy. Cornelis Evertsen de Jongste (1642–1706) became a confidant of the stadtholder William of Orange (later King William III of England). The Evertsens' financial position depended largely on their naval income, in particular from the lawful profits made on the provisioning of their ships and their monthly wages as flag officers. Cornelis and his younger brother Geleyn (1655–1721) both owned a mansion on the island of Walcheren. Together with the De Moor and Banckert families, the Evertsens are inseparable from the naval history of Zeeland. Only Michiel De Ruyter, also from Vlissingen, is better known.

Like the four other admiralties in the Dutch Republic, the admiralty of Zeeland had its own corps of officers and flag officers. The father and grandfather of Johan Evertsen (1600–1666) had both become captains, and in 1664 Johan was the first Evertsen to reach the highest position of lieutenant admiral, having become vice admiral in 1636. Johan Evertsen took part in the Battle of the Downs in 1639, commanded during the first Anglo-Dutch War (1652–1654), commanded in Danish waters in 1659, and was killed in the Two Days' Battle (1666) during the second Anglo-Dutch War (1665–1667). The career of his brother Cornelis (1610–1666) followed almost the same course. He became vice admiral in 1664 and was promoted to lieutenant admiral in 1665. He was killed in the Four Days' Battle (1666). Cornelis had better interpersonal skills than Johan had, and he felt more familiar with the new battle strategy for ships of the line. Johan had been formed in the days of boarding and single-ship fights against Dunkerque privateers; he was also regularly involved in conflicts with naval administrators and colleagues in Holland.

From boyhood, Cornelis Evertsen de Jonge (1628–1679) trod in the footsteps of his father, Johan. He became vice admiral in 1666, and he took part in the Medway raid in 1667, in the four battles of the third Anglo-Dutch War (1672–1674), and in expeditions to the West Indies (1674), the Baltic (1676), and the Mediterranean (1678). He did not become lieutenant admiral, because Adriaen Banckert (c. 1620–1684) held this position from 1666 and survived him.

Cornelis Evertsen de Jongste, son of Cornelis, had the most varied career. As with all Evertsens, he went to sea very young. He commanded the Zeeland squadron in the conquest of New Netherlands in 1673, was sent on a secret mission to London in 1678, and was promoted to vice admiral in 1679 and lieutenant admiral after Banckert's death. He secretly prepared the Dutch fleet for the Glorious Revolution of 1688, and commanded the fleet in 1689–1690, including for the Battle of Beachy Head in 1690. He was the first Zeeland officer to command the

Dutch fleet, but he was soon replaced by a colleague from Holland. Geleyn Evertsen, vice admiral in 1695 and lieutenant admiral in 1707, commanded squadrons in the Nine Years' War (1689–1697) and at the start of the War of the Spanish Succession (1702–1713). His only great battle was La Hogue in 1692 and the bombardment of Copenhagen in 1700. The decline of Zeeland's naval forces and rankling animosities with England and Holland kept Geleyn ashore from 1704.

[See also Beachy Head, Battle of; Downs, Battle of the; Four Days' Battle; Navies, Great Powers, subentry on Dutch Republic, 1577–1714; Ruyter, Michiel de; Tromp, Maarten Harpertszoon; and Wars, Maritime, subentry on Anglo-Dutch Wars.]

## Bibliography

Roos, Doeke. Twee eeuwen varen en vechten 1550–1750: Het admiralengeslacht Evertsen. Vlissingen, Netherlands, 2003.
Shomette, Donald G., and Robert D. Haslach. Raid on America: The Dutch Naval Campaign of 1672–1674. Columbia: University of South Carolina Press, 1988.
Warnsinck, Johan Carel Marinus. De vloot van den koning-stadhouder, 1689–1690. Amsterdam: Noord-Hollandsche Uitgeversmaatschappij, 1934.
Warnsinck, Johan Carel Marinus. Drie zeventiende-eeuwsche admiraals: Piet Heyn, Witte de With, Jan Evertsen. Amsterdam: P. N. Van Kampen, 1943.

JAAP R. BRUIJN

**Exhibitions**    Exhibitions of maritime history subjects originated with didactic displays for private audiences of specific government officials or private interest groups. Exhibits of ship models such as those in the Winter Mansion of Peter I (r. 1682–1725) at Saint Petersburg, first established in 1709, and another at the Louvre Palace, Paris, in 1748, were intended to explicate principles of naval architecture to students and government ministers. Similarly, the National Gallery of Naval Art, established in 1823 in the Painted Hall of Greenwich Hospital, London, exhibited paintings and artifacts to extol achievements in defense of the realm for an audience of naval veterans.

## Technology and Culture

Several nineteenth-century world expositions in London, Paris, Philadelphia, Vienna, and elsewhere included exhibits of western and nonwestern watercraft, presenting current achievements in technology and traditional culture simultaneously. Fairs with maritime themes, such as the Naval Exhibition held at Chelsea in 1891, the World's Columbian Exposition held at Chicago in 1893, and several international fisheries exhibitions held around Europe and America, included extensive exhibits of maritime history, as well as of contemporary and historical marine art, as a platform to trumpet the progress of modern technology. Museums began interpreting maritime history for the general public in the later nineteenth century. An exhibit in 1889 at the Peabody Academy of Science in Salem, Massachusetts (now the Peabody Essex Museum), documented American merchant voyages of fifty to a hundred years earlier, probably in response to the passing of the era of sail.

Exhibitions of a single category of object have reflected cultural, geographical, or technological orientations to subject matter, either in the context of discovery, such as the nonwestern watercraft models commissioned by Admiral Pâris from the Louvre model-making studio during the 1880s, or as a presentation of soon-to-be-lost traditional technology, as in the Maze collection of Chinese Junk Models in the Science Museum of London, exhibited in the 1930s. Synoptic histories of world watercraft, from ancient times to the present, are periodically undertaken, such as at the Commercial Museum in Philadelphia during the 1960s and at the Musée Naval in Monaco today; but regional and national histories, such as the overview of Dutch naval architecture at the opening of the Nederlandsch Historisch Scheepvaart Museum, Amsterdam, in 1922, have been far more common.

Exhibits developed by science museums interpret maritime objects from a technical orientation, frequently employing the collection of a single institution or individual to outline broad themes of industrial and cultural history. At the Science Museum in London, marine construction was a major element of the engineering collections that were established in 1864. The collections included the Admiralty collections that were transferred from Somerset House, commercial collections from several sources, and, from 1874, scientific and navigating instruments. Navigation was treated as a minor component of the history of scientific inquiry at the opening of the Museum of the History of Science in Florence, Italy, in 1929, but it was treated with far greater emphasis at the Exposition Internationale de la Technique de L'eau at Liège, Belgium, in 1939.

Other exhibits have utilized private collections to examine themes in the history of technology, either for specialized or for broad-based audiences. The Massachusetts Institute of Technology exhibited the marine print collection of the ship designer Arthur H. Clark in 1924 for an audience of naval architects and students, while the

Peabody Museum of Salem displayed the Allan Forbes collection of whaling prints in 1919 as a general exhibit of industrial history.

## Maps, Books, Photography

Archives and libraries have interpreted maritime history through books, manuscripts, and maps often drawn from a single collection. An early prototype was an exhibit of books on navigation held at the John Carter Brown Library in Providence, Rhode Island, in the 1930s. Other major exhibits include naval records at the Public Record Office, Kew, United Kingdom, in 1950; the Henry C. Taylor collection pertaining to navigation and navigators at Yale University in 1971; and Maps of the Columbian Encounter at the Golda Meir Library, Milwaukee, Wisconsin, in 1990.

In recent years, some exhibits have examined specific facets of the collection of one institution, particularly those with large portions of their holdings in storage, as a strategic move to highlight the depth of a collection for a brief period, rather than exhibit only a small selection from many object categories. Several have been designed both for the host museum and as traveling shows, such as the photography exhibit Capturing Poseidon: Photographic Encounters with the Sea held in Salem in 1998 and in Sydney, Australia, in 1999. Others are organized specifically as loan shows, such as The Boundless Deep ... : The European Conquest of the Oceans, 1450 to 1840, made up of collections from the John Carter Brown Library and exhibited at the Newport Art Museum in Rhode Island in 2003. The deepest private collections have supported multiple shows, such as the wide-ranging collection of Peter Tamm, which has been the basis of many exhibits in Germany, including Schiffe aus Knochen und Elfenbein, Altonaer in 1976, Seefahrt und Geschichte in 1986, Aqua Triumphalis in 1991, and Schiffahrt und Kunst aus den USA in 1993.

Exhibits that commemorate the anniversaries of significant dates are ever-popular in art and history museums. The spate of exhibits held on the Columbian quincentenary, most notably Circa 1492 at the National Gallery of Art in Washington, D.C., embraced a date with broad public recognition. In 1976 the Altonaer Museum of Hamburg, Germany, commemorated American independence with Amerikansche Schiffsbilder, a loan exhibition of marine art from United States museums. Anniversary exhibits of famous vessels are often timed with the vessel's launch date, such as the 1916 exhibit in Salem, Massachusetts, in celebration of the first deepwater luxury yacht in the country, launched in Salem one hundred years before. Exhibits commemorating the achievements of an individual are regularly timed near a birth or death date.

## Art

Museums have long exhibited art to illustrate and interpret history. For instance, in 1883 there was a call to create a museum (never realized) devoted specifically to the paintings of the marine artist François Roux as illustrations of the French merchant marine. Authenticity in illustrating vessels, harbors, and events is the measure of quality for the works displayed in such exhibits. Some exhibits have hung paintings in chronological order by launch date of the ships depicted, while others present only works produced during the time that the ships were afloat, emphasizing the veracity of firsthand experience. There were many exhibitions of the Macpherson collection of maritime prints around the time of its purchase to become the basis of the United Kingdom's new National Maritime Museum in 1928. One exhibition organized the collection into separate exhibits of naval and shipping subjects, while another was advertised as pictorial adjuncts to naval and maritime history. Another major marine art exhibit of the time, at the Burlington Fine Arts Club in London, differentiated between art created to fulfill the needs of sailors, such as builder's models and instruments, and works inspired by the sea, such as paintings and commemorative silver. During the 1930s and 1940s, many exhibits outlined historical events and the representation of them in art simultaneously, while exhibits of marine artists emphasized the subject matter in which they specialized. Examples include Hull Shipping Pictures at the Hull Museum in 1932; À la Gloire de la Marine à Voiles at the Musée de l'Orangerie in 1935; Ship Portraits by the Roux family of Marseilles at the Penobscot Marine Museum in Searsport, Maine, in 1939; and American Steamships 1807 to 1946, held in 1946 at the Mariners' Museum in Virginia.

Art museums have approached maritime works from the opposing perspective. More concerned with art than with history, these exhibits have been organized around principles of connoisseurship and artistic expression. Important marine art exhibits have included Five Centuries of Marine Painting, at the Detroit Institute of Art in 1942; The Coast and the Sea: A Survey of American Marine Painting, at the Brooklyn Museum in 1948; the enormous and wide-ranging Trois Millénaires d'Art et Marine, at the Petit Palais in 1965, featuring art from Europe, America, and Asia, including academic and popular arts and antiquities; Seascape and the American Imagination, at the Whitney Museum in New York City in 1975; The Art of the Van de Veldes, at the National Maritime Museum in London in 1982; Mirror of Empire: Dutch Marine Art of the Seventeenth Century, at the Minneapolis Museum of Art in 1990; and Manet and the Sea, at the Art Institute of Chicago in 2003.

Several modern exhibitions of considerable conceptual breadth have used a maritime story line to explore multiple cultural themes. Some of the most ambitious and innovative exhibits of recent times include The Oceanliner: Speed, Style, Symbol, at the Smithsonian Cooper-Hewitt Museum in 1980; Magnificent Voyagers: The U.S. Exploring Expedition, 1838–1842, at the Smithsonian Natural History Museum in 1985; Portugal-Brazil: The Age of Atlantic Discoveries, at the New York Public Library in 1990; The Maritime Holy Land: Mediterranean Civilization in Ancient Israel, in Genoa in 1992; Life of a Sailor, at Philadelphia's Independence Seaport Museum in 1999; Carlos V: La Naútica y la Navegación, at the Museo Pontevedra, Spain, in 2000; and longer-term installations like Voyages, which opened at Mystic Seaport, Connecticut, in 2000.

The legacy of museum exhibits exists in their printed catalogs, whether they are made up simply of entries and descriptions of objects, or include interpretive text as well. By necessity, this essay emphasizes those exhibits for which catalogs were produced. A selection of important maritime history exhibit catalogs follows.

[*See also* Art *and* Museums.]

## Bibliography

All references are catalogs to exhibits mentioned in the text. Most are out of print, but some are still available from the host museum shops. Many of the rare and out-of-print sources are available from online book dealers and specialized maritime libraries.

*À la gloire de la marine à voiles.* Paris: Musée de l'Orangerie, 1935.

*American Steamships 1807 to 1946 in Paintings, Models, and Related Material.* Newport News, Virginia: The Mariners' Museum, 1946.

*Amerikanische Schiffsbilder.* Hamburg, Germany: Altonaer Museum, 1976.

*Aqua Triumphalis: Maritime Kostbarkeiten aus der Sammlung Peter Tamm.* Herford, Germany: Koehler, 1991.

*Catalogue–Art Department: The International Maritime Exhibition.* Boston: Mills, Knight, 1889.

*Catalogue of a Loan Exhibition of Ship Portraits by the Roux Family of Marseilles.* Searsport, Maine: Penobscot Marine Museum, 1939.

*Catalogue of a Loan Exhibit of Paintings and Prints from the Macpherson Collection.* London: Guildhall Art Gallery, 1928.

*Catalogue of an Exhibition of Marine Art.* London: Burlington Fine Arts Club, 1929.

*Catalogue of an Exhibition of Naval Records at the Public Record Office.* London: Public Record Office, 1950.

*Catalogue of the Collections in the Science Museum, South Kensington: Water Transport.* 5 vols. in 4. London: H. M. Stationery Office, 1924.

*The Clark Collection of Marine Prints.* Cambridge, Mass.: Technology Press, 1924.

*The Coast and the Sea: A Survey of American Marine Painting.* New York: Brooklyn Museum, 1948.

Cordingly, David. *The Art of the Van de Veldes.* London: National Maritime Museum, 1982.

Ducros, Jean, ed. *Trois millénaires d'art et marine.* Paris: Marine Nationale et Ville de Paris, 1965.

Finamore, Daniel. *Capturing Poseidon: Photographic Encounters with the Sea.* Salem, Mass.: Peabody Essex Museum, 1998.

*Five Centuries of Marine Painting.* Detroit, Mich.: Detroit Institute of Art, 1942.

German, Andrew. *Voyages: Stories of America and the Sea.* Mystic, Conn.: Mystic Seaport Museum, 2000.

Guedes, Max Justo, and Gerald Lombardi, eds. *Portugal-Brazil: The Age of Atlantic Discoveries.* Lisbon, Portugal: Bertrand Editora; Milan: Ricci; New York: Brazilian Cultural Foundation, 1990.

Harley, J. B., assisted by Ellen Hanlon and Mark Warhus. *Maps and the Columbian Encounter: An Interpretive Guide to the Travelling Exhibition.* Milwaukee: Golda Meir Library, University of Wisconsin Press, 1990.

Hattendorf, John B. *"The Boundless Deep … ": The European Conquest of the Oceans, 1450 to 1840; Catalogue of an Exhibition of Rare Books, Maps, Charts, Prints, and Manuscripts Relating to Maritime History from the John Carter Brown Library.* Providence, R.I.: John Carter Brown Library, 2003.

*Historique de la construction navale et de la navigation.* Liège, Belgium: Exposition Internationale de la Technique de L'eau, 1939.

*Illustrated Catalogue of the "Maze Collection" of Chinese Junk Models in the Science Museum, London, 1938.* London: Science Museum, 1939.

Kababian, John S., comp. *The Henry C. Taylor Collection.* New Haven, Conn.: Yale University Library, 1971.

Kashtan, Nadav. *The Maritime Holy Land: Mediterranean Civilizations in Ancient Israel from the Bronze Age to the Crusades.* Genoa, 1992. Catalog for the exhibition Colombo 500.

Keyes, George S. *Mirror of Empire: Dutch Marine Art of the Seventeenth Century.* Minneapolis, Minn.: Minneapolis Institute of Arts; Cambridge, U.K., and New York: Cambridge University Press, 1990.

Levenson, Jay A., ed. *Circa 1492: Art in the Age of Exploration.* Washington, D.C.: National Gallery of Art; New Haven, Conn.: Yale University Press, 1991.

Locker, Edward Hawke. *The Naval Gallery of Greenwich Hospital.* London: Harding and Lepard, 1831.

*The Macpherson Collection: An Impression—The Sea Story of the English-Speaking Race*. London, 1927.

*The Macpherson Collection: Naval Section*. London: The Grieves and Arlington Galleries, 1924.

*The Macpherson Collection: Shipping Section*. London: Whitechapel Art Gallery, 1924.

*Musée Naval, Monaco: Catalogue d'Exposition*. Monte Carlo, Monaco: Musée Naval, 2003.

Museum of the History of Science, Florence, Italy. The history of the science museum in Florence is described on the museum's Web site, http://www.imss.fi.it/museo/index.html.

*One Hundredth Anniversary of the Building of "Cleopatra's Barge," 1816–1916: Catalog of the Commemorative Exhibition*. Salem, Mass.: Peabody Museum, 1916.

*Platen-album*. Amsterdam: Nederlandsch Historisch Scheepvaart Museum, 1922.

*Schiffahrt und Kunst aus den USA*. Hamburg, Germany: Schiffahrts-Verlag Hansa, 1993.

*Schiffe aus Knochen und Elfenbein: Sammlung Peter Tamm und anderer Besitz*. Hamburg, Germany: Altonaer Museum, 1976.

*Seefahrt und Geschichte*. Herford, Germany: E. S. Mittler and Sohn, 1986.

Sheppard, Thomas. *Hull Shipping Pictures*. Hull, U.K.: Hull Museum of Fisheries and Shipping, 1932.

Spector, Henry, ed. *The Ship Model Collection of the Commercial Museum, Reviewed in Relation to Maritime History*. Philadelphia: Commercial Museum, 1964.

Stein, Roger Breed. *Seascape and the American Imagination*. New York: Potter, 1975.

Viola, Herman J., and Carolyn Margolis, eds., with the assistance of Jan S. Danis and Sharon D. Galperin. *Magnificent Voyagers: The U.S. Exploring Expedition, 1838–1842*. Washington, D.C.: Smithsonian Institution Press, 1985.

Wilson-Bareau, Juliet, and David Degener. *Manet and the Sea*. Chicago: Art Institute of Chicago; Philadelphia: Philadelphia Museum of Art; Amsterdam: Van Gogh Museum; New Haven, Conn.: Yale University Press, 2003.

Wroth, Lawrence. *Some American Contributions to the Art of Navigation, 1519–1802*. Providence, R.I.: John Carter Brown Library, 1947.

Wroth, Lawrence. *The Way of the Ship: An Essay on the Literature of Navigational Science*. 2d ed. Mansfield Center, Conn.: Martino Publishing, 2001. Originally published in 1937.

DANIEL FINAMORE

**Expeditions, Scientific** Although the science of the oceans—what we now call oceanography—is generally reckoned to have had its origin as a separate discipline in the three-and-a-half-year scientific circumnavigation in HMS *Challenger* from 1872 to 1876, many less extensive oceanographic observations and collections had been made during voyages in the previous two centuries, albeit generally as subsidiary activities to the voyages' main objectives. Furthermore, as early as the 1690s the Royal Navy pro-vided the astronomer and mathematician Edmond Halley (1656–1742) with a purpose-built ship, the tiny 64-foot *Paramore* (or *Paramour*), to undertake voyages in the Atlantic Ocean entirely devoted to scientific observation. *Paramore* was therefore probably the first vessel built anywhere in the world that was specifically meant for scientific purposes.

Like other scholars of his day, Halley was interested in many natural phenomena. One of these was terrestrial magnetism, and the objective of *Paramore*'s first two cruises, from October 1698 to July 1699 and from September 1699 to September 1700, was to measure magnetic variation throughout the Atlantic Ocean, an objective supported by the Admiralty because of its importance in navigation. The resulting chart, showing the magnetic variation using isolines—that is, lines joining points of equal value—was the first printed example of this simple but extremely useful technique that has been employed widely ever since.

Halley's third cruise, from June to October 1701, was devoted to a study of the tides in the English Channel. In this case, the chart he produced showed the tidal range at each of the many stations occupied by *Paramore* and also enabled the navigator to calculate when the tidal currents change direction.

During the first half of the eighteenth century, little oceanographic work was undertaken during major voyages, though Peter Forsskål (1732–1763), the naturalist on a Danish expedition to Arabia Felix in *Grønland* in 1761, made extensive biological collections and numerous measurements of surface salinity. He also tried to compare the salinity at depth with that at the surface, but with little success because of the inadequacy of his equipment. Similarly, the French astronomer Jean Chappe d'Auteroche (1728–1769) measured seawater specific gravity and subsurface temperatures during a voyage to Mexico in 1768. Such oceanographic observations, albeit still rather limited by the enthusiasm, or lack of it, of the ships' officers, became more or less routine on French voyages of exploration in the late eighteenth and early nineteenth centuries.

In Britain, serious marine scientific studies began with the voyages of James Cook (1728–1779) in the 1760s and 1770s. The principal objective of Cook's first voyage in *Endeavour* from 1768 to 1771 was to observe the transit of Venus across the face of the sun from the recently discovered Tahiti. These astronomical observations were completed successfully, and Cook went on to make excellent surveys of New Zealand and the west coast of Australia, while major botanical and zoological collections were made by other members of the voyage, notably Joseph Banks (1744–1820) and his accompanying specialists.

**Scientific Expedition.** *Walking on the Pack* by John Edward Davis (fl. 1832–1842). Davis depicted men of Sir James Clark Ross's expedition in 1842 with HMS *Erebus* and HMS *Terror* in the background. Scott Polar Research Institute, Cambridge, UK / The Bridgeman Art Library

However, little oceanographic work was undertaken during the voyage other than a few tidal observations, including observation of the diurnal variation in the tides, which became apparent when the ship went aground on a reef off the east coast of Australia. More attention was paid to the collection of marine data during Cook's second (1772–1775) and ill-fated third (1776–1780) voyages, particularly salinities and water temperatures both at the surface and, in some cases, in the deeper layers. The main objective of these voyages was geographical exploration, particularly the search for a possible southern continent or Terra Incognita, but they also demonstrated the accuracy and navigational value of John Harrison's recently developed chronometers.

In 1773, during a voyage in search of a practicable sea route to the North Pole, Captain Constantine Phipps (later Lord Mulgrave) made a number of deep-sea soundings and subsurface temperature measurements from HMS *Racehorse* and *Carcass*. The temperature measurements, using a self-registering thermometer invented by Lord Charles Cavendish (1703–1783) in 1757, were not very successful, but one of the soundings, at a depth of 683 fathoms near Spitsbergen, corresponds closely to modern soundings in the same area and remained the deepest reliable sounding until well into the nineteenth century.

The long period of almost continuous hostility between France and Britain from 1793 to 1815 did not entirely put a stop to exploratory voyages by the two nations, for both navies sent out major expeditions to Australia in the early years of the nineteenth century, each guaranteeing the other immunity from hostile military or naval interference. And both countries' expeditions were fairly disastrous.

The French expedition from 1800 to 1804, in the vessels *Géographe* and *Naturaliste* under the command of Nicolas Baudin (1754–1803), suffered from terrible personality clashes, particularly between the commander and the scientists led by the naturalist François Péron (1775–1810), and also had many deaths, including that of Baudin himself. The British expedition, in HMS *Investigator* under the command of Matthew Flinders (1774–1814), was almost equally unfortunate, but for different reasons. Having left England in July 1801, Flinders first surveyed the southern coast of Australia before calling at Port Jackson (present-day Sydney), where he met up with the French expedition, the two countries being at that time temporarily at peace. Flinders then circumnavigated the island continent in a counterclockwise direction, confirming that it was a single landmass and not, as had been thought possible, dissected by a north-south waterway. But by the time *Investigator* returned to Port Jackson she was in a terrible state and quite unfit to continue with the expedition. Flinders decided to leave his scientists in Australia to continue their collections and observations, but to return to England himself to obtain a replacement vessel. On the way, the tiny 29-ton vessel in which he tried to sail home was in such bad condition when she was crossing the Indian Ocean that Flinders called in at the French possession of Île de France, now Mauritius, for repairs. Unknown to Flinders, France and Britain were again at war, and the local French governor simply threw him into prison as a suspected spy. Despite diplomatic protests, both British and French, Flinders's incarceration lasted six and a half years, and he finally arrived back in England only in October 1810. In the meantime, the stranded *Investigator* scientists had managed to get the ship patched up, and she eventually limped home to Liverpool in October 1805.

Both the British and the French expeditions had made valuable geographic discoveries and obtained extensive botanical and zoological collections. But their oceanographic work was limited. Péron consistently measured the sea surface temperature four times a day throughout the voyage, but his attempts to measure subsurface temperatures by collecting samples in an insulated container were restricted to just a couple of occasions, partly because of limitations of his technology and partly because of the lack of support, and even the positive opposition, of the commanding officer Baudin. Flinders was much more supportive of such observations and, like Péron, tried to make regular surface and subsurface temperature measurements, but these observations ceased only a few weeks into the expedition when all the supplied thermometers had been broken.

The end of hostilities in 1815 left both navies with numerous ships and officers underemployed. In Britain this situation contributed to the long series of naval expeditions to polar regions during the nineteenth century, initially to the Arctic in search of the Northwest Passage, but also later to the Antarctic.

The first Arctic voyage, in *Isabella* and *Alexander* in 1818 under the command of John Ross (1777–1856), was probably the most productive from an oceanographic point of view. In addition to seeking a passage between the Atlantic and Pacific through northern Canada, Ross was to undertake an extensive scientific program, including observations on magnetism, meteorology, tides, currents, and soundings, and the collection of biological, mineralogical, and seabed samples. He was also to measure subsurface water temperatures wherever possible, and for this purpose he was provided with self-registering thermometers of the type invented by the instrument maker James Six (1731–1793) in the 1790s. A considerable body of data and samples was obtained, including subsurface temperatures apparently as low as 25.5°F and soundings that brought up seabed-dwelling animals from depths of almost 2,000 meters (6,560 feet)—that is, much deeper than the previous record soundings. Although there is now some doubt about the veracity of these results, they should have dispelled two influential and erroneous theories that held sway through much of the nineteenth century. The first of these was the so-called "azoic theory," later developed by Edward Forbes (1815–1854), according to which the deep ocean, beyond a depth of a few hundred meters, was completely devoid of life. The second, the "4°C theory," held that seawater, like freshwater, has its maximum density at about 4°C (about 39°F), so that water at this temperature would be found to occupy the whole of the deep-ocean basins. In the event, the expedition results never received the attention they deserved, mainly because of a controversy about whether Lancaster Sound was blocked to the west by a mountain range, as Ross maintained, or was open (as indeed it is), as was claimed by several of the more junior officers.

Subsequent British Arctic expeditions in the second quarter of the nineteenth century, including those in search of the ill-fated expedition in HMS *Erebus* and *Terror* under the command of Sir John Franklin (1786–1847) from 1845 to 1848, made major geographical advances, but in general their oceanographic contributions were not particularly significant.

Meanwhile, however, important oceanographic observations were being made by other nations. James Six's self-registering thermometers, for instance, were used extensively during the Russian circumnavigations during 1802–1806 under A. J. Krusenstern (1770–1846), and the later ones under Otto von Kotzebue (1787–1846) in 1815–1818 and 1823–1826. In fact, the temperature and specific-gravity measurements made by the physicist Emil Lenz (1804–1865) during Kotzebue's second voyage were the most extensive and reliable made in this period and, like Ross's results, proved that the density of seawater continued to increase with decreasing temperature well below 4°C. However, despite this information being specifically pointed out to the British Admiralty by the German scientist Alexander von Humboldt (1769–1859), the 4°C theory continued to hold sway. Furthermore, it was still not widely realized that thermometers lowered into the sea to measure subsurface temperatures needed to be protected from the effects of water pressure that would otherwise cause them to register erroneously high readings. Thus when James Clark Ross (1800–1862), nephew of John Ross, was given command of HMS *Erebus* and *Terror* for a major Antarctic expedition from 1839–1843, he was supplied with unprotected thermometers and, as a consequence, obtained misleading results.

Although the main objectives of James Clark Ross's expedition were to measure the earth's magnetic field in the Southern Hemisphere and to locate the South Magnetic Pole, Ross was also expected to undertake an extensive program of scientific work, including the collection of subsurface temperature data and carrying out deep-sea soundings. He made many series of temperature measurements during the expedition, down to depths of about 2,000 meters (6,560 feet), but because he was using unprotected thermometers he never recorded temperatures lower than 4°C, whereas many of them should have been considerably lower than this. Despite having participated in his uncle's 1818 voyage and having witnessed much lower temperatures being encountered, Ross believed his own results supported the 4°C theory. Furthermore, as an extension of this idea, he identified what he called a "circle of mean temperature" at about 56° S where, he believed, the water temperature was at a uniform 4°C throughout the water column. This mistake contributed to the persistence of the azoic theory for a further quarter of a century, while another *Erebus* and *Terror* mistake took sixty years to correct.

In the 1840s, the standard method for sounding–that is, measuring the depth of the sea beneath a ship–was the centuries-old technique of lowering a heavy weight on the end of a rope and recording the length of rope paid out when the weight reached the seafloor. This technique was quite adequate down to depths of a thousand or even two thousand meters (3,280 to 6,560 feet), but in deeper water it became increasingly less reliable because of many factors, but principally because of the difficulty of determining exactly when the weight reached the bottom and ensuring that the sounding line had not been carried sideways by water currents. During the *Erebus* and *Terror* expedition, Ross made a number of very deep soundings, including one in the Weddell Sea in which he paid out some 7,300 meters (23,950 feet) of rope, apparently without reaching the bottom. The true depth in this area, less than 5,000 meters (16,400 feet), was established during the Scottish National Antarctic Expedition in *Scotia* between 1902 and 1904.

Improvements in the techniques for obtaining deep-sea sounding were stimulated in the middle decades of the nineteenth century by the needs of the emerging technology of submarine telegraphy. These improvements centered on the use of thin line (and eventually wire) and on the development of techniques for releasing the weights once they had reached the bottom, enabling the thin line to retrieve a sample of the seafloor sediment. Both aspects were pioneered by the U.S. Navy, and particularly by Matthew Fontaine Maury (1806–1873), director of the National Observatory in Washington, and a series of voyages by U.S. and Royal Naval vessels used the new techniques to undertake depth surveys of the north Atlantic during the 1850s and 1860s. During this same period there was increasing interest in the possibility of finding animal life in the deep oceans.

In 1841–1842 the Manx-born biologist and geologist Edward Forbes served as naturalist on board HMS *Beacon*, which was employed on surveying duties in the Mediterranean. Forbes was able to make a number of dredge hauls down to a depth of some 420 meters (1,380 feet), particularly in the Aegean, and he noted a significant decrease in the amount of animal life collected with increasing depth. Based on these results he formulated the azoic theory according to which the deep ocean, beyond a depth of 500–600 meters (1,640–1,970 feet), would be found to be entirely lifeless. Despite a number of counterindications, including the presence of encrusting animals living on a submarine telegraph cable that was retrieved for repair in 1860 from a depth of more than 2,000 (6,560 feet) meters in the Mediterranean, the azoic theory was still widely adhered to in the mid-1860s. However, two British scientists, Charles Wyville Thomson (1830–1882), professor of natural history at Queens University, Belfast, and W. B. Carpenter (1813–1885), a physiologist at the University of London, were convinced that the theory was incorrect and persuaded the British Admiralty to enable them to test their ideas and to undertake other oceanographic work, including subsurface temperature measurements using pressure-protected thermometers. In 1868 they were provided with a small paddle steamer, HMS *Lightning*, to undertake a short cruise to the north and west of Scotland, and in 1869 and 1870 they used a somewhat larger steamer, HMS *Porcupine*, for a series of cruises around the British Isles and into the Mediterranean. The results were dramatic, including the collection of abundant animal life from depths in excess of 4,000 meters (1,312 feet) and the demonstration that subsurface temperatures could be considerably lower than 0°C—thus disproving both the azoic and the 4°C theories. Accordingly, the Admiralty provided the much larger steam-assisted screw corvette HMS *Challenger* for the scientific circumnavigation that is still generally considered to be the most important voyage in the history of oceanography.

*Challenger* sailed from Portsmouth in December 1872 under the command of Captain George Strong Nares (1831–1915) and with a scientific team headed by Wyville Thomson. By the time she returned to England in May 1876, she had covered almost 69,000 nautical miles across all the major oceans except the Indian and had occupied 362 official stations, that is, localities subjected to a full scientific program including sounding the depth and collecting a sediment sample, obtaining subsurface water samples and temperature measurements, and taking biological samples in midwater and on the seafloor.

The results were written up by an international galaxy of scientists and published in fifty large volumes, initially under the editorship of Wyville Thomson and subsequently under that of John Murray (1841–1914), one of the junior naturalists on the expedition. The final volume of the reports appeared 1895, and these publications, along with the vast biological and mineralogical collections made during the expedition—collections still housed mainly in the Natural History Museum in London—are considered to be essentially the foundation of modern oceanography and are still widely consulted.

In 1874, at the same time as the *Challenger* expedition, USS *Tuscarora* conducted an extensive sounding survey across the northern Pacific and made many subsurface temperature measurements. Following the success of the *Challenger* expedition, many other nations dispatched vessels on voyages devoted to ocean science, though the voyages were rarely as extensive as that of *Challenger* either in duration or in geographical area covered. Before the

end of the nineteenth century these included the French ships *Travailleur* and *Talisman* in the North Atlantic in the 1880s; the Italian ships *Washington* in the Mediterranean in 1885 and *Vettor Pisani* on a circumnavigation; and the German vessels *National*, which investigated the plankton of the North Atlantic in 1889 under Victor Hensen (1835–1924), the father of quantitative biology, and *Valdivia* in the Atlantic, Indian, and Antarctic oceans in 1898 and 1899 under the scientific leadership of the deep-sea ecologist Carl Chun (1852–1914). This period also saw the beginning of the extensive series of scientific cruises in the Mediterranean, North Atlantic, and Arctic oceans by Prince Albert I of Monaco (1848–1922) in his yachts *Hirondelle*, *Princesse Alice*, *Princesse Alice II*, and *Hirondelle II*, cruises conducted almost every year between 1885 and the outbreak of World War I.

The first half of the twentieth century saw an enormous growth in interest in marine science and in the development of relevant technology, partly stimulated by military concerns during the two world wars. Marine laboratories and major oceanographic research programs, sometimes with a specifically commercial orientation, were established in several countries, including Britain, France, Germany, the Scandinavian countries, and the United States. Scientific cruises during this period tended to emulate the *Challenger* and other late nineteenth-century expeditions in covering large ocean areas and usually all oceanographic disciplines, from biology through physics and chemistry to geology. Typical examples from this period are the British Discovery Investigations of the 1920s and 1930s, during which a series of cruises were mounted to study the oceanography of the Southern Ocean; each cruise lasted many months. The program was named for the sail-assisted steam barque, built originally for the National Antarctic Expedition from 1901 to 1904 under the command of Captain R. F. Scott (1868–1912) and used in the investigations until it was replaced by an all-steam vessel, *Discovery II*, in 1929. This period came to an end shortly after World War II with the circumnavigation of the Danish naval vessel *Galathea* from 1950 to 1952, probably the last voyage of such a length and geographical scope to be devoted to the serious study of all aspects of oceanography. Since that time, apart from a major international program in the 1960s to study the Indian Ocean, oceanographic cruises have tended to be shorter, usually lasting no more than a few weeks, to be increasingly specialized and technological, and to be concentrated on a relatively small area of ocean. So the cruise of *Galathea* may be taken as marking the end of what might be considered the heroic age of marine science, beginning with Halley and *Paramore* at the end of the seventeenth century and reaching its zenith with *Challenger* in the 1870s.

[*See also* Antarctica and the Southern Ocean; *Challenger*; Halley, Edmond.]

## Bibliography

Deacon, Margaret. *Scientists and the Sea 1650–1900: A Study of Marine Science.* London and New York: Academic Press, 1971.

Deacon, Margaret, Tony Rice, and Colin Summerhayes, eds. *Understanding the Oceans: A Century of Ocean Exploration.* London and New York: UCL Press, 2001.

Kunzig, Robert. *Mapping the Deep: The Extraordinary Story of Ocean Science.* London: Sort of Books, 2000.

Linklater, E. *The Voyage of the* Challenger. London: John Murray, 1972.

McConnell, Anita. *No Sea Too Deep: The History of Oceanographic Instruments.* Bristol, U.K.: Adam Hilger, 1982.

Murray, John, and Johan Hjort. *The Depths of the Ocean.* London: Macmillan, 1912.

Rice, Anthony L. *British Oceanographic Vessels, 1800–1950.* London: The Ray Society, 1986.

Rice, Anthony L. *Voyages of Discovery: Three Centuries of Natural History Exploration.* London: The Natural History Museum and Scriptum Editions, 2000.

Ritchie, G. S. *The Admiralty Chart: British Naval Hydrography in the Nineteenth Century.* Edinburgh, U.K.: The Pentland Press, 1995. First published in 1967 by Hollis and Carter, London.

Schlee, Susan. *A History of Oceanography: The Edge of an Unfamiliar World.* London: Robert Hale, 1975.

Thomson, C. W. *The Depths of the Sea.* London: Macmillan, 1873.

TONY (A. L.) RICE

**Exploration by Vasco da Gama.** The pillar erected in 1498 by Vasco da Gama at Malindi, where the Galana River enters the Indian Ocean on the southeast coast of present-day Kenya. This is where Da Gama contracted with the Muslim navigator Ibn Majid to employ his knowledge of the monsoon winds and to sail eastward from Africa to reach Calicut (Kozhikode) in India. WERNER FORMAN / ART RESOURCE, NY

## Exploration to 1500

Educated Europeans in the late Middle Ages knew quite a bit about the universe they lived in, even before the voyages of Christopher Columbus. They knew perfectly well that the earth was a sphere, but many details were unknown or mistaken. Their knowledge was the product of several centuries of practical experience, coupled with new and newly discovered treatises in academic geography.

Academic knowledge expanded with the early-fifteenth-century translation of two recovered works by the Hellenistic natural philosopher Ptolemy (Claudius Ptolemaeus): the *Almagest*, on astronomy, and the *Geography*, which provided a convenient framework for depicting the globe in a graphic form. Ptolemy divided the earth into 360 degrees, which became the basis for subsequent European maps. He had two fundamental misconceptions, however. First, he believed that Africa and Asia were joined by lands connecting their southern tips, making the Indian Ocean a landlocked sea, inaccessible to ships sailing from Europe around Africa. Fortunately for those contemplating such a voyage, Enea Silvio de' Piccolomini (1405–1464), who became Pope Pius II, rejected the idea that the Indian Ocean was an enclosed sea, and he argued this in his own work summarizing much of Ptolemy's *Geography*. Ptolemy's other error was his conception of the earth's size; he imagined it to be about one-fifth smaller than it is. In the same period the cardinal Pierre d'Ailly published a geography called *Imago Mundi* (1410), for which he relied on geographical treatises by classical writers and Muslim scholars. D'Ailly's conclusions included fundamental errors, for example, that Asia covered much more of the globe from east to west than it actually does and that the oceans cover much less of the globe than they do.

These fifteenth-century geographical ideas found physical expression in Martin Behaim's globe of 1492, which presented a view of the world that was almost identical to the concept that Columbus had formed. The Americas are totally absent from Behaim's globe, Japan is located far from the mainland of Asia, and the ocean between Europe and the East is amply strewn with islands. Whether Columbus and Behaim had close contact with each other is unknown, although both men had lived in Lisbon and had gained access to the Portuguese court, where courtiers and experts regularly discussed the latest geographical discoveries. Behaim's depiction of the world and Columbus's concept of it both grew out of the academic geography available at the end of the fifteenth century.

Despite the advances, Europe still had limited information about the world's other major civilizations. Contacts with the Muslims had taught Europeans something about the interior of Africa, including the fact that gold was obtained there. During the early fifteenth century, Portuguese voyages down the western shore of Africa added more direct practical knowledge. The Europeans had no knowledge of the civilizations in the Americas, despite the Scandinavian voyages that had reached North America around the year 1000. By the late fifteenth century the Greenland colony was abandoned and Scandinavians were going no farther west than Iceland. Memory of their earlier voyages had never entered the mainstream of European thought. Implausible as it may seem, European scholars and merchants in the fifteenth century probably knew more about distant Asia than about any other part of the world outside Europe.

### The Spice Trade

The spice trade provided one of the most important motivations for European expansion. During the Crusades (1095–1291) western Europeans wrested control of Christian holy places from the Muslims and established the Kingdom of Jerusalem, with its related principalities, along the eastern shore of the Mediterranean. Long-lasting commercial developments arose by which western European merchants began to take the economic initiative in the eastern Mediterranean from the Muslims and to maintain it thereafter. Crusaders first developed a taste and demand for exotic spices, which improved the palatability of food in the thousands of years before advanced preservation

techniques developed. The European elite adopted the crusaders' appreciation for Asian spices and consumed increasing amounts during the late medieval centuries. Muslim traders acquired spices in India and the South Asian islands, and then they took them across the Indian Ocean to the Persian Gulf and the Red Sea. In ports of the eastern Mediterranean, particularly Alexandria, European merchants bought spices from Muslims to resell in Europe, where they commanded high prices. Even if the buyers of Oriental spices and other luxury goods formed only a tiny part of the total European population, their purchasing power helped to keep the entire structure of long-distance trade functioning. Because of the profits to be made from the spice trade, many other Europeans were eager to participate in it, but the Italians and their Muslim trading partners held an effective monopoly through their control of the eastern Mediterranean.

### Asia

By the fourteenth century many Europeans knew where spices came from. Indeed, many European missionaries and merchants had traveled to Asia—some as far as China—and reported on what they had seen. Most reached Asia by overland caravan routes through central Asia. Those routes were open to travelers in the thirteenth and fourteenth centuries because of what has been called the Pax Mongolica, a period when Mongol rulers held sway from North China to the Black Sea and guaranteed safety along the trade routes.

Mongol ascendancy began when Genghis Khan secured the unity of the Mongols and related tribes in 1206. The Mongols were fierce mounted warriors who relied on their powerful horses for mobility. They had powerful bows, well-made steel arms and armor, and mastery of the siege tactics necessary to capture fortified towns. All their military skills were put to good use in the rapid conquests of North China, Persia, and Russia. When Genghis Khan died in 1227, Mongol authority stretched from East Asia to eastern Europe. The Mongols were a distant threat and not yet the enemies of Europe; in contrast, the Muslims were close by and had been enemies for centuries. Consequently, popes and later kings thought that the Mongols might prove useful against the Muslims at a time when the crusader states faced increased Muslim pressure.

Pope Innocent IV sent Giovanni da Pian del Carpini as his envoy to the Mongol khan in 1245, the year after Jerusalem fell to the Muslims. The papal ambassador went by land from Kiev to the Mongol capital of Karakorum and was present at the coronation of Güyük Khan. Carpini gave the khan the pope's letter, which called on the khan to join an alliance against the Muslims and to recognize papal supremacy. Not surprisingly, the khan did not recognize papal supremacy and nothing came of the military alliance. Still, Europe learned more about Asia, thanks to Carpini's written account of his journey, which found its way into the world history of Vincent of Beauvais, court historian to Louis IX of France. King Louis sought to strengthen contacts with the Mongols by sending two more western ambassadors: Andrew of Longjumeau in 1248 and William of Rubruck in 1253–1255. Their accounts, too, have survived. Taken together, the Christian missions to the Mongols prepared the way for the Christian merchants who soon followed.

In the later Middle Ages many Italian merchants were willing to try new ventures in the search for economic gain. One of the best-known episodes began in 1269 when Marco Polo left for China. Polo stayed for eighteen years in China, where he served as a bureaucrat in the court of the Mongol khan, Kublai. While Marco Polo resided at the Mongol court, John of Monte Corvino arrived in Beijing and later became its first archbishop, presiding over a large archdiocese but few Christians. Marco Polo provided one of the most accurate accounts of China and the East that Europeans had at their disposal, although many readers thought the tale more fanciful than real. Accounts by other travelers also appeared and spread through Europe, some of them genuine and others woven from legend rather than from practical experience. In 1340, drawing on information from Marco Polo and others, Francesco Balducci Pegolotti wrote a commercial guide to the spices and other products of Asia. He even provided a generally accurate indication of where those products originated.

Unfortunately for the Europeans, political conditions in the Middle East made following up on this knowledge impossible. After the collapse of the Mongol Empire, new and aggressive Muslim empires gained importance from the Mediterranean to India. They would not allow Europeans free passage along the routes they controlled. Consequently, some Europeans contemplated a bold alternative that had been discussed for centuries: to bypass the Muslims altogether by finding a sea route to India, in order to purchase the spices directly at their sources.

The Vivaldi brothers from Genoa made an early voyage out into the Atlantic to seek the sea route to Asia. In 1291 their small fleet sailed through the Strait of Gibraltar with the avowed aim of reaching India by circumnavigating Africa. They never returned, and they left no traces of their fate except for some equivocal signs on the African coast opposite the Canary Islands. The hope of finding a sea passage to India remained alive to inspire the Portuguese and the Spaniards as they added new areas of Africa and the Atlantic to European knowledge in the fifteenth century.

## Africa

The failed Vivaldi voyage exemplified the growing southern European interest in Africa and the Atlantic. In the late Middle Ages, Genoese, Catalans, and other Christian merchants of the Mediterranean established a series of trading posts in the ports of North Africa from Egypt to Morocco. Through agreements with the local Muslim rulers, these merchants were able to maintain residences, offices, and warehouses, usually in segregated neighborhoods. There they bought the products of North Africa and, in the eastern Mediterranean, Asian goods as well. In the western Mediterranean, they were especially taken with the goods of West Africa brought across the Sahara Desert by Muslim caravan traders.

Prominent among the West African products were slaves and gold. Muslim merchants tapped into sources south of the Sahara in three major mining areas: Bambuk, Buré, and Akan. Muslim caravan traders acquired gold in sub-Saharan Africa and took it northward across the desert to North African ports, where European merchants, especially Italians and Spaniards, acquired it through trade, but often on unfavorable terms. Although the Muslims maintained a monopoly on the Saharan caravan routes, Europeans knew enough about Africa to be aware that Africans had rich kingdoms in the lands to the south of the Sahara.

By the fifteenth century one of the primary Portuguese motivations for exploring the African coast was to intersect the gold trade. The city of Ceuta, on the Moroccan coast opposite Gibraltar, was closely linked with the trans-Saharan caravan trade, which was one factor in the Portuguese decision to conquer the city in 1415. Thereafter the Moroccans diverted most of the trade away from Ceuta, although the city remained an important outpost for the Portuguese. Pseudoknowledge of Africa coexisted with reality in the minds of Europeans. They were aware of the real kings of Africa but also believed in a legendary king called Prester John, supposedly a powerful Christian monarch whose lands lay beyond the area under Muslim control. The curious legend of Prester John encouraged the Portuguese to think that he could become an ally in the struggle against Islam. The Portuguese eventually found Christian Ethiopia, but its ruler lacked the resources to launch any sort of crusade against Islam.

There were also much more ordinary motives for Portuguese expansion into Africa. Beginning in the 1440s Portuguese mariners brought back slaves from Atlantic Africa to Europe, supplementing the Muslim-controlled Saharan slave trade. Portuguese merchants bought wheat in North Africa, particularly in Morocco, to supplement production at home and to trade for other goods in West Africa. In addition, both the Portuguese and the Castilians had well-established fishing fleets that provided fish for home consumption as well as for exports. They saw the Atlantic waters off Africa as suitable places to extend their fishing grounds. Like sugar plantations and the slave trade, the expanded fishing grounds and grain trade developed as part of a generalized search for profitable opportunities in Africa and elsewhere.

At some point, as the Portuguese explored and traded southward along the African coast, they began a seriously search for a sea route to Asia. The cosmography of the day held that the world's landmasses were closely linked to one another, surrounded by vast oceans that covered the rest of the globe. To reach Asia by the most efficient sea route required a voyage around Africa, which was held to be much smaller than it really is. Luckily for the Portuguese, the African coastal trade and the products of the Atlantic island economies were profitable enough to finance continuing efforts to find a way around the vast continent.

Bartolomeu Dias finally reached the southern tip of Africa in 1488, which the Portuguese king appropriately dubbed the Cape of Good Hope. The hope came true when Vasco da Gama took a Portuguese fleet to India in 1497 and returned to tell the tale, revealing in the process extensive geographical knowledge about the southeast coast of Africa, the Indian Ocean, and India itself. The search for India also motivated Columbus and the monarchs of Spain who eventually backed his enterprise, and Columbus began his first voyage in the years between Dias's discovery of the Cape of Good Hope and Da Gama's voyage to India. The difference was that Columbus proposed a westward approach to Asia, which experienced mariners considered more dangerous and less promising.

The conditions for successful European exploration had been developing over the late Middle Ages. When Columbus set out in 1492 to explore the ocean as far west as Asia, he built his enterprise on a foundation of experience, knowledge, and speculation that had been accumulating in Europe for centuries.

[*See also* Behaim, Martin; Columbus, Christopher; Gama, Vasco da; Medieval Navies, *subentries* on Christian Mediterranean, Islamic World, Italian States, Portugal, *and* Spain; *and* Ptolemy.]

## Bibliography

Abu-Lughod, Janet L. *Before European Hegemony: The World System, A.D. 1250–1350*. Oxford: Oxford University Press, 1989.

Bentley, Jerry H. *Old World Encounters: Cross-Cultural Contacts and Exchanges in Pre-Modern Times*. Oxford: Oxford University Press, 1993.

Brotton, Jerry. *The Renaissance Bazaar: From the Silk Road to Michelangelo*. New York: Oxford University Press, 2002.

Fernández-Armesto, Felipe. *Before Columbus: Exploration and Colonization from the Mediterranean to the Atlantic, 1229–1492*. Philadelphia: University of Pennsylvania Press, 1987.

Friedman, John Block, and Kristen Mossler Figg, eds. *Trade, Travel, and Exploration in the Middle Ages: An Encyclopedia*. New York: Garland, 2000.

Jackson, Peter, and David Morgan, eds. *The Mission of Friar William of Rubruck*. London: Hakluyt Society, 1990.

Jones, Gwyn. *The Norse Atlantic Saga: Being the Norse Voyages of Discovery and Settlement to Iceland, Greenland, and North America*. New ed. Oxford: Oxford University Press, 1986.

Larner, John. *Marco Polo and the Discovery of the World*. New Haven, Conn.: Yale University Press, 1999.

Lewis, Archibald R. *Nomads and Crusaders, A.D. 1000–1368*. Bloomington: Indiana University Press, 1988.

Morgan, David. *The Mongols*. Oxford: Basil Blackwell, 1986.

Muldoon, James, ed. *The Expansion of Europe: The First Phase*. Philadelphia: University of Pennsylvania Press, 1977.

Phillips, J. R. S. *The Medieval Expansion of Europe*. 2d ed. Oxford: Clarendon Press, 1998.

Phillips, William D., Jr., and Carla Rahn Phillips. *The Worlds of Christopher Columbus*. Cambridge, U.K.: Cambridge University Press, 1992.

WILLIAM D. PHILLIPS

# Ex Voto

**Ex Voto** From an abbreviation of the Latin phrase *ex voto suscepto*, meaning "from the vow made," *ex voto* refers to a votive offering made in gratitude or devotion. The practice of offering votive objects—vowed to Christ, the Virgin Mary, or the saints—in expectation of, or in thanks for, divine aid dates from the early years of Christianity. Votives can range from humble objects to resplendent works by professional artists. The most common votives or tokens were made of wax, bone, wood, inexpensive metals, silver, tin, copper, bronze, or gold. They often were made in shapes that symbolized the miracle that was being sought or for which gratitude was being offered; ex votos of this type might be shaped like body parts, people, animals, houses, or boats.

The ex voto painting had its origins in Italy in the fifteenth century. The first ex voto paintings were created as an expression of piety and thanksgiving by the affluent. Later, from the seventeenth century, the practice spread across the

**Italian Ex Voto.** This is one of more than 6,000 ex votos dating from the nineteenth century onward that are preserved in the cloister of the 1656 Italian baroque–style Benedictine Sanctuaire de Notre-Dame-de-Laghet at La Trinité, one of the major places of pilgrimage on the coast of Provence and northwestern Italy. This ex voto records the loss of the brig *Nuovo Sucorso,* Captain Francesco Raffo, about five miles off the coast of Sicily on September 18, 1854. The bottom line has a typical inscription: V.F.G.A. (Votum Fecit Gratiam Accepit: vow made, grace received) with the names of the donors. SNARK / ART RESOURCE, NY

social classes. At least since the sixteenth century, there was a steady increase in the number of pilgrimage churches and donations of ex voto paintings, partly because of a belief in the manifestation of miracles and appearances of the Virgin Mary. This tradition increased in popularity throughout the nineteenth century and the first decades of the twentieth.

Ex voto paintings in the maritime countries have naturally reflected a maritime theme. The tradition expanded around the Mediterranean basin and on the Atlantic coast; it was brought to the New World, where it flourished in South and Central America. As in the case of all ex voto paintings, the ones donated by mariners were put on display by the donors themselves; maritime ex votos were placed in the sanctuaries consecrated to the Virgin Mary, Saint Nicholas, Saint Peter, and Saint Andrew—the saints who were considered the protectors of seamen and fishermen.

An ex voto painting was not necessarily donated by the recipient of divine aid. A family member or a close friend might make a vow on behalf of the mariner to ensure his safe return, though such cases are rare. There are instances in which copies of the same incident are found in different churches; these works usually involve two or more persons separately caught in the same perilous situation at sea. More often, the same ship appears in different ex votos that depict various incidents in which the captain or one or more crew members were saved from dangerous situations at sea by the intercession of the saints.

The majority of maritime votive paintings were donated by local fishermen, sailors, and sometimes soldiers employed on the ships (captains and crew members) to churches in the places where they lived and sometimes to pilgrimage churches. In only a few cases were ex votos brought to a church near the place of the event for which thanks were being given. In many churches, especially in pilgrimage churches, so many ex votos and other votive objects were offered to the Virgin Mary or to the saints over the centuries that the church, the sacristy, and the rooms at the side of the church were insufficient to contain them. Often a new building was constructed to house votive offerings. Fortunately, some sanctuaries still maintain archives that record the offerings of ex votos.

The huge collections of maritime ex votos were in small churches, which could be seen from the open sea, often situated near the ports, on the islands, high rocks or hills, or near lighthouses. These sanctuaries were filled with maritime ex voto paintings, donated as a thanksgiving for an answered prayer, or as a reaction to a miracle received at sea; rarely were they donated as a request for a safe return, although before going to sea, seamen and fishermen often went to the churches to make their vows and to pray for protection.

The Virgin Mary appears in ex voto offerings as Our Lady of Health, Our Lady of the Holy Rosary, Our Lady of Sorrows, Our Lady of the Light, Our Lady of the Apparition, or Our Lady of Consolation. Less frequent are devotions directed to other saints, such as Saint Nicholas, Saint Joseph, or Saint Catherine, and these often appear in the company of the Madonna. Only a few ex voto paintings carry the image of Jesus Christ, crowned with thorns, carrying the cross, crucified, or risen with the cross in hand.

Paintings were commissioned by individuals or purchased, often from untrained folk artists who used dramatic poses, chiaroscuro, and realistic portrayals to convey a religious message. These were naïve, simple paintings with a visual directness, expressiveness, and dynamism. The patrons and the artists were not interested in the conventions of academic art. They sought to produce an image that stimulated devotion. Marine ex voto paintings were painted in a limited range of colors, using reds, blues, dark yellow, and dark green. The soot of church candles, along with general aging, has made the pictures appear darker; the thin layers of the pigment and the varnish have in many cases worn away. It may be assumed that the ex votos look darker today than they did when originally painted.

The painting of ex votos was considered a profession in itself. In some countries around the Mediterranean the ex voto painter was called *madonnaro* because of the customary consecration of ex votos to the Madonna. If not highly competent, these painters nevertheless showed sufficient talent to reproduce the ideas of their clients. Professional *madonnari* signed their paintings with their initials, so it is possible to trace their work. Professional painters of ex votos were usually self-taught members of painters' workshops, working in towns and ports from Venice to Dubrovnik, Kotor, Ancona, Genoa, Naples, Palermo, Marseille, Barcelona, La Rochelle, Lisbon, and Malta.

The painters followed similar techniques in coastal towns around the Mediterranean and elsewhere. Each sizable town had one or two accomplished painters of maritime ex votos; some of them were able to create remarkable ship's portraits or to employ a bird's-eye view. Some very detailed ex voto paintings are rare examples of a high-quality, significant marine art.

In other cases, a poor fisherman or seaman could not afford a professional painter, so the donor himself painted the ex voto. Such paintings are primitive but nevertheless impressive, depicting a range of human tragedy including burning ships, seamen swimming from a sinking boat, and other dramatic events.

The oldest votive paintings were executed on panels. Later examples were painted on canvas. Wood was also used for this purpose, although wood is very susceptible to humidity and cracks easily. Watercolor or gouache on paper was widely used after 1800 and was protected with glass. This medium is most adapted for fine depictions of rigging. The best ship portraits are mostly those done on paper. Cardboard was used very rarely, as was sackcloth; such materials, which allow no delicate finishing, reveal the dire financial conditions of the donor.

The paintings are small and are often rectangular in form; the average size of ex voto paintings is 30 by 40 centimeters (12 by 16 inches), 30 by 50 centimeters (12 by 20 inches), or 50 by 70 centimeters (20 by 28 inches); some are 60 by 80 centimeters (24 by 30 inches), and there are exceptions of 150 by 200 centimeters (60 by 80 inches) and larger. The frames vary, depending on the financial resources of the donors.

## Iconography

Maritime ex voto paintings are characterized by a typical iconography, which includes three or four characteristic motifs in each painting. The first and main element is the depicted miraculous event causing the survival of the donor. The deep trust of the sailors in the intervention of the saints in time of need is clearly attested. The works depict a variety of disasters, tragedies, and dramatic circumstances, from storms to hurricanes, from enemy attacks to sea battles, from material damages to the boat to injured and dead members of the crew. A special thematic group shows attacks by pirates on sailing boats transporting expensive cargo. The background of the narrative often depicts landmarks that are of extreme importance; they can help identify the locality of the disaster, showing coastal towns, fortifications, mountains, seaports, islands, or the configuration of the landscape. Details like flags or architectural elements may also provide important historical information.

The narrative scene usually occupies more than one-half or three-quarters of the pictorial space. An inscription, or legend, which states the donor's prayer to the Virgin or the saints and gives thanks for the miracle, usually occupies the lower part of the painting. The inscription often includes the names of the persons who were involved in the event at sea, the date when the event occurred, its location, and the name of the person who is giving thanks for the miracle. The writings are in Latin or in broken Italian, French, Spanish, English, Maltese, or other languages. The syntax, spelling, and abbreviations reveal the donor's and painter's knowledge of written language. Many ex votos of the generally illiterate public contain the inscriptions "V.F.G.R." (*voto fecit gratia ricevuta*) or "V.F.G.A." (*votum fecit gratiam accepit*), meaning "vow made" or "grace received," or simply "E. V." (*ex voto*), meaning "in fulfillment of a vow." Sometimes the inscriptions are not original to the work; oil and watercolor transcriptions are noticed on many ex votos. Sometimes the writing is missing because it was attached to the picture on the front side (written on a piece of paper) or written on the back, where it has faded away due to adverse conditions.

The third iconographical element of an ex voto maritime painting is the presentation of the intercessory figure, usually the Virgin Mary or one of the saints to whom the prayer was given. This motif is usually placed in the right or left upper corner of the painting. The artists depicted the Virgin or saints in traditional poses using conventional iconography. There was not a great deal of difference among the various artists in their composition. Similarity was very typical.

The Virgin Mary is sometimes painted simply, standing or sitting, alone or with the child, dressed in white or red and blue, with a veil on her head, sometimes crowned or with stars or rays around her head. Sometimes this is just a depiction of her head; in some works she is depicted in a similar manner to that of her image on the main altar in the church. Cases in which the motif of the saints is larger indicate a miracle that happened at sea.

The fourth iconographical element of the painting is the donor praying for mercy. Many times, mostly on small ex votos, this element is missing. When the donor is depicted, his place is usually in the left or right lower corner of the painting, kneeling in prayer.

Containing two, three, and sometimes four characteristic iconographic motifs, mariners' ex votos constitute a firsthand source of documentary information on the life and work of sailors and fishermen as well as historical events at sea. Depictions of the large vessels and small boats that were in use for many centuries and elements in different scenes of misfortune are often the only contemporary images that survived until the present. The seamen's ex votos are rich in fantasy, drama, and visual dynamism. Along with the modest written sources, these illustrations are a precious source of information on naval history, fishing, habit and customs in general (use of equipment, tools, clothing, etc.).

## Historical Importance and Interpretation

The inscriptions of ex voto paintings provide a wealth of historical information about seafarers. The written information often records names and locations, identifies boats, including their equipment and sails, as well as travel routes and the cargo that was being transported. Many inscriptions provide a date for incidents such as shipwrecks, pirate attacks, and battles. The pictures are therefore of great documentary value. The historical study of votive paintings can trace the evolution of ship construction; in each region, specific types of ships are consistently present in ex voto paintings. The paintings also reveal sail arrangements on various types of vessels and the use of sails in a storm. Some provide a list of names of captain and crew.

In terms of artistic value, some paintings are rare examples of high-quality, detailed ship portraits by significant marine artists. Others, more naïve, are nevertheless authentic examples of popular craftsmanship and reliable evidence of the religious devotion of seafaring people. Technically they are sometimes inaccurately executed; the humbler examples are not necessarily faithful representations of the conventional characteristics of the ships they portray. However, they employ a dynamic and direct visual language and constitute a unique testimony to a singular cultural phenomenon.

Only a relatively small number of ex votos have been preserved, although many small churches had a large number of them in times past. Unfortunately not all authentic elements of the inventories have been preserved in these smaller churches around the Mediterranean and along the coastlines of the Atlantic Ocean. Some of the churches are in ruins. Malta has maintained a great quality and quantity of its original collection, and some Italian, Croatian, Spanish, and French collections have been preserved as well. In pilgrimage churches, on the other hand, the ex voto collections are still enormous and are in good shape. All maritime museums and some town or local coastal museums along the Mediterranean have significant collections of maritime ex votos. Many exhibitions have been organized in Europe, the United States, Mexico, and Canada.

[*See also* Motifs; Museums; Religion, *subentry on* Seafarers' Religion; *and* Spanish Literature, *subentry on* An Overview.]

## Bibliography

Amich Bert, Julián. *Mascarones de proa y exvotos marineros*. Barcelona, Spain, and Buenos Aires, Argentina: Argos, 1949.

Borg, Isabelle. *The Maritime Ex-Voto: A Culture of Thanksgiving in Malta*. Malta: Insight Heritage Books, 2005.

Boullet, François, and Colette Boullet. *Ex-voto marins*. Paris: Éditions Maritimes et d'Outre-mer, 1978.

Braun, Thomas. *Ex-voto*. Brussels, Belgium: Vromant, 1932.

Butler, Samuel. *Ex voto*. London: Jonathan Cape, 1928.

Cousin, Bernard. "L'ex-voto: Document d'histoire, expression d'une société." *Archives des Sciences Sociales des Religions* 48, no. 1 (1979): 107–124.

Cuschieri, Andrew, and Joseph Muscat. "Maritime Votive Paintings in Maltese Churches." *Melita Historica* 10, no. 2 (1989): 121–144.

Giffords, Gloria Fraser. *Mexican Folk Retablos: Masterpieces on Tin*. Tucson: University of Arizona Press, 1974.

Kriss-Rettenbeck, Lenz. *Ex voto: Zeichen, Bild, und Abbild im christlichen Votivbrauchtum*. Zurich, Switzerland: Atlantis, 1972.

Mayes, Frances. *Ex voto*. Barrington, R.I.: Lost Roads Publishers, 1995.

Micieli, Nicola. *Ex voto per il millennio*. Milan, Italy: Il Grandevetro/Jaca Book, 2000.

Morisset, Jean-Paul. *Quebec Ex-Voto Paintings*. Ottawa: National Gallery of Canada, 1977.

Muscat, Joseph. "Maritime Ex-Voto Paintings." *Treasures of Malta* 4, no. 3 (Summer 1998).

Port of History Museum, Philadelphia. *Mariners' Votive Offerings in the Montenero Sanctuary (Ex voto marinari del Santuario di Montenero)*. Pisa, Italy: Arti Grafiche Pacini, 1984.

Roque, Alfredo Vilchis, and Pierre Schwartz. *Infinitas Gracias: Contemporary Mexican Votive Painting*. Translated by Elizabeth Bell. San Francisco: Seuil Chronicle, 2004.

Simonetti, Farida. *Ex voto marinari del Santuario di Nostra Signora del Boschetto di Camogli*. Genoa, Italy: Tormena, 1992.

Toschi, Paolo. *Bibliografia degli ex-voto italiani*. Florence, Italy: Olschki, 1970.

Tripputi, Anna Maria. *Bibliografia degli ex voto*. Bari, Italy: Melagrinò, 1995.

Vinkovic, Vanja, ed. *Gospa Trsatska Kraljica Jadrana stoljeca vijere u Marijin Trsat*. Rijeka, Croatia: Gorin, 1996.

Žitko, Duška. *Ex voto: Votivne podobe pomorcev*. Knjižnica Annales 2. Koper, Slovenia, 1992.

DUŠKA ŽITKO